# Building a Green Future Through Essential Decision-Making Competencies

Jarmila Duháček Šebestová
*Silesian University in Opava, Czech Republic*

Cristina Raluca Gh. Popescu
*University of Bucharest, Romania & The Bucharest University of Economic Studies, Romania*

IGI Global
Scientific Publishing
Publishing Tomorrow's Research Today

Vice President of Editorial Melissa Wagner
Director of Acquisitions Mikaela Felty
Director of Book Development Jocelynn Hessler
Production Manager Mike Brehm
Cover Design Phillip Shickler

Published in the United States of America by
IGI Global Scientific Publishing
701 East Chocolate Avenue
Hershey, PA, 17033, USA
Tel: 717-533-8845
Fax: 717-533-7115
Website: https://www.igi-global.com E-mail: cust@igi-global.com



Library of Congress Cataloging-in-Publication Data

Names: Šebestová, Jarmila, 1977- editor. | Popescu, Cristina Raluca Gh., 1983- editor.
Title: Building a green future through essential decision-making competencies / [edited by] Jarmila Duháček Šebestová, Cristina Raluca Gh. Popescu.
Description: Hershey, PA : IGI Global Scientific Publishing, [2025] | Includes bibliographical references and index. | Summary: "Competencies in general represent a set of knowledge, skills, abilities, attitudes, and values that enable personal development. Entrepreneurs use their competencies to have a successful business and could profit from them in particular areas such as decision making or in area of strategic planning. It is useful to open the discussion about SDG, ESG influence on decision making process within green competencies portfolio. There is reason to collect recent knowledge, containing AI influence in decision-making process to open the discussion within wider audiences"-- Provided by publisher.
Identifiers: LCCN 2025004053 (print) | LCCN 2025004054 (ebook) | ISBN 9798337301891 (hardcover) | ISBN 9798337301907 (paperback) | ISBN 9798337301914 (ebook)
Subjects: LCSH: Social responsibility of business. | Sustainable development. | Entrepreneurship--Moral and ethical aspects. | Entrepreneurship--Environmental aspects. | Decision making,
Classification: LCC HD60 .B845 2026 (print) | LCC HD60 (ebook) | DDC 658.4/08--dc23/eng/20250403
LC record available at https://lccn.loc.gov/2025004053
LC ebook record available at https://lccn.loc.gov/2025004054

British Cataloguing in Publication Data
A Cataloguing in Publication record for this book is available from the British Library.

# Editorial Advisory Board

# Table of Contents

# Detailed Table of Contents



EntreComp is a comprehensive model developed by the European Commission to help all interested individuals to understand and develop necessary entrepreneurial skills. This approach defines entrepreneurship as a key competence for lifelong learning and is designed to be used across various educational, professional, and social contexts. Using this model, each person could develop itself in area of creating new business activity. The framework is logically structured into three main competence areas, which are connected into one integrated system from idea creation to idea implementation.



The rise of urbanization drives the demand for intelligent traffic monitoring systems, integrating computer vision, machine learning, and real-time data processing for smart urban infrastructure. By leveraging sensors, MEMS (Microelectromechanical systems), and wireless communication networks, modern traffic systems are capable of dynamically adapting to varying traffic conditions, optimizing traffic flow, and improving overall road safety. The intelligent traffic monitoring system (ITMS) integrates vehicle detection, real-time traffic data analysis, and adaptive control mechanisms to minimize congestion and reduce emissions. Here, it explores the use of machine learning algorithms to predict traffic patterns and pedestrian behavior, contributing to a more sustainable and efficient urban mobility network. These advancements offer scalable, cost-effective solutions for cities aiming to reduce traffic bottlenecks and enhance public safety, ultimately supporting the vision of smart and sustainable urban environments.

Reducing greenhouse gas emissions and adapting to impacts of climate change are pivotal in developing solutions to secure a greener and fairer future. Building and scaling ideas to support climate tech solutions crucially help society adapt to climate change. Funding cutting-edge ideas and initiatives, while engineering commercially-viable solutions, fosters tailored support in creating sustainable solutions to climate crisis. This research tackles climate and sustainability crisis, addresses studies' outcomes that more people ought to become engineers to provide solutions to climate crisis, and sheds a new light on general believe that a constant supply of electricity without burning fossil fuels is a must for present and future generations. A major accent is placed on circular economy principles, with powerful targets: recycling and reusing metals and plastics as well as recovering and using energy from industrial processes that would otherwise be sadly wasted. Harnessing creativity, innovation, and engineering is paramount for an inclusive economy and sustainable society.



This paper focuses on the effects of Green HRM system on employees working in Education sector. Green HRM System lay down guidelines and procedures for integrating and retaining teaching staff and other employees so that the institutions can fulfill the goals and objectives for which they have been established. Due to the emergence of many ecological challenges in the education sector in the last few decades, green human resource management has created like a new idea that has been adopted by many Education sector today. To increase employee awareness, today many Education sector around the world combine traditional corporate social responsibility initiatives with green HR policies. Green HRM System help employees become aware of their duties and many education sector have developed green initiatives to support students and employees in charge of protecting the environment, however, Green HRM system and policies are completely impossible to implement.



This chapter looks at green competencies in the management of sustainable business by an entrepreneur. This work aims at putting forward a conceptual framework of a structure for teaching entrepreneurial education with sustainability integrated into the curriculum. Innovation priorities include a sustainable decision-making approach for the circular economy, green innovation, and incorporating sustainable developmental and enterprise goals into entrepreneur training. Implications and examples from practices and original research findings are presented to inform the choices of educators, policymakers and those who venture into the world of private enterprise.



The flourishing significance of sustainability in entrepreneurship has led to the requirement for a thorough model that incorporates critical capabilities crucial for making strategic decisions associated with environmental, social, and economic objectives. This chapter develops a model for sustainable entrepreneurship competencies, emphasizing seven core areas: systems thinking, foresight thinking, normative behavior, diversity, interpersonal skills, responsible actions, and strategic management. These competencies enable entrepreneurs to make decisions that balance profitability with sustainability, encouraging long-term business success while addressing global issues. This chapter determines how sustainable competencies drive innovation and evolution in green business practices by investigating real-world case studies and exploring decision-making processes.



In the rapidly changing global scenario repleted with escalated levels of pollution, greenhouse effects and global warming, we are currently transitioning through one of the most difficult phases of human civilization. Under these grave circumstances, there is a pressing need for the successful implementation of green economic growth for all the nations of the world regardless of their demographical locations. This research work is aimed at two objectives: first, the conceptualization of IsoEnvironmental Pressure (IEP) Curve – which is my new contribution to the existing literature of Green Economy and Sustainable Development (SD) based on the works of Victor and Sers (2019), and second, formulation of Grand Index of Green Growth and Sustainability (GIGGS) for the time period of 10 years (2012 – 2021) for 5 sample countries in order to analyze the factors that are responsible to influence the green growth and sustainable development of a country from a normative point of view.



This research explores a complex lawsuit between Chevron Corporation and the Huaorani community of Lago Agrio, an indigenous group affected by oil pollution in the Ecuadorian Amazon. It focuses on the consequences of this pollution from legal, ethical, and socio-environmental perspectives within the oil fields operated by the international company. The issue has sparked heated debates and litigation both

One of the major concerns of the present-day business environment is to create environmentally friendly business enterprises for sustainable business practices. This paper aims to scan the business environment of Bangladesh to find out the environmentally friendly business operations. This paper considers the secondary method of collecting the necessary information. It found that several business organizations adopted green manufacturing practices in Bangladesh. This paper presents environmentally friendly manufacturing practices of ready-made garments, electronics, and construction and proposes a green manufacturing operations framework. It found that green manufacturing practices ensure emission control and improve workplace conditions and employees' well-being.



Talent management is a key element of sustainable HRM, crucial for long-term organizational success. In the Visegrád Four (V4) region—Czech Republic, Slovakia, Poland, and Hungary—talent management remains underutilized, often overshadowed by short-term HR functions. This study explores its role in fostering economic, social, and environmental sustainability. Findings highlight low investment in training, challenges in talent retention, and a lack of structured development programs. Organizations risk higher turnover, reduced innovation, and weaker resilience. Integrating talent management with sustainability goals can enhance workforce stability, diversity, and green HRM practices. Recommendations include increasing awareness, investing in training, leveraging data-driven HR strategies, and fostering cross-sector collaboration. Strengthening talent management in the V4 region is essential for competitive, sustainable growth in a dynamic global market.



Current global society is marked by aggressive competition and an abundance of information with dramatically different levels of relevancy. The lack of the publication of relevant information undermines the sustainability commitment of all and destroys sustainable entrepreneurship. Building a green future is a common endeavor which is feasible only if proper information is shared, i.e. decision-making competencies rely on relevant, reliable, readable and freely accessible information about sustainability. The EU policies and law have been heralding this idea and led to the taxonomy and standardization of information for and about sustainable entrepreneurship. This chapter explores their roots and current setting by comparatively and critically mapping the pertinent EU norms, visualizing them via tables and analyzing what, how, why and where is taxonomized and standardized and by providing an assessment glossing. The pathway towards relevant information for sustainable entrepreneurship is not smooth and easy, it is rather a dynamically advancing crusade upon which the EU has embarked.

**Chapter 14**



This study analyzes the integration of sustainability principles and circular economy concepts into the higher management education curriculum at a specific university (Newton University). The aim is to assess students' awareness, knowledge, and readiness to apply these principles in future managerial roles. A quantitative questionnaire was administered to 115 final-year management students. Findings reveal that although 56% of respondents were aware of the term "circular economy," only 10% could accurately define it. Moreover, while all students recognized "sustainability," 70% were unable to provide an accurate definition within the environmental and social context of business. Nearly 90% consider these topics essential for their future practice. These results underscore the need for deeper curricular integration and innovative pedagogical approaches to enhance practical readiness for sustainable management.

**Chapter 15**



Entrepreneurial skills have evolved significantly since initiatives like the "Green Paper on Entrepreneurship" (EU Commission, 2003) and the "Small Business Act" (European Commission, 2008), which emphasized knowledge, competencies, and sustainability. Entrepreneurs today prioritize long-term sustainability over short-term profits (Elkington, 2018), leveraging frameworks like the Sustainable Development Goals (SDGs) and Environmental, Social, and Governance (ESG) standards to integrate ethical practices with financial performance.Despite these obstacles, ESG and SDG frameworks present opportunities for innovation through systems thinking, foresight, and interdisciplinary collaboration (Senge, 1990). By adopting "green thinking," entrepreneurs mitigate external threats, foster innovation, and drive sustainability. This chapter explores the role of networking, strategic thinking, and ethics in sustainable practices, offering insights into aligning business strategies with global sustainability goals for long-term success.

**Chapter 16**



This chapter examines key factors influencing brownfield regeneration in the Czech Republic within regional development. The aim is to identify and evaluate determinants of successful revitalization by developing a systematic framework for assessing redevelopment potential. Using factor analysis and comparative methods, the study analyzes economic, environmental, and social factors based on CzechInvest (2024) data. Key determinants include land ownership, prior land use, contamination levels, and investment potential. The findings show that clear ownership, economic incentives, and infrastructure investments enhance regeneration, while regulatory complexity and remediation costs hinder it. The study contributes to data-driven policy recommendations to optimize land-use planning and investment incentives for sustainable brownfield redevelopment.



The chapter identifies and discusses various challenges affecting adoption with the emergence of green decision-making into sustainable development. The study finds major barriers in traditional practice ICT, finance, resistance to change, and lack of digital skills especially in SMEs. This research highlights the potential role of emerging technologies, such as artificial intelligence (AI), Internet of Things (IoT), and blockchain, in improving sustainable decisions based on systematic reviewing 277 articles and textual analysis with IRaMuTeQ. This research indicates that overcoming such challenges and ensuring a resilient transition would call for an integrated strategy comprising financial incentives, training, and sound regulatory frameworks. The study encourages the development of a culture of sustainability and technological innovation to maintain values through time.



This chapter addresses the role of ESG-oriented leadership in startups, exploring whether integrating ESG principles contributes to long-term success or come with additional challenges. While sustainability has become a strategic imperative for businesses worldwide, its adoption among startups remains complex mostly because of financial constraints. Despite this, emerging trends suggest that investors are gradually recognizing ESG as a competitive advantage. While entrepreneurship is becoming more challenging due to financial and market uncertainties, an increasing number of early-stage entrepreneurs prioritize their social and environmental impact over pure profitability. Yet, the lack of standardized ESG metrics continues to be a significant barrier, creating an "acronym soup". While the financial benefits of ESG leadership in startups may not be immediately apparent, the long-term advantages such as stronger talent retention and investor interest make sustainability a strategic asset rather than a cost.



This chapter presents lessons from the SDG Labs project, a transnational initiative fostering green skills by integrating social economy entities and higher education. Through socially driven green Labs, the project explored innovative educational methods, including Living Labs, simulation-based learning, and participatory co-creation. Findings highlight gaps between theoretical environmental knowledge

# Foreword

The IGI Global book on *Building a Green Future Through Essential Decision-Making Competencies*, edited by Associate Professor PhD. Jarmila Duháček Šebestová (Silesian University in Opava, Opava, Czechia) and Professor PhD. Habil Cristina Raluca Gh. Popescu (University of Bucharest and The Bucharest University of Economic Studies, Bucharest, Romania), has a wide target audience, as follows: firstly, the academics represent the primary audience for the market, given the fact that researchers have become more and more avid to debate and learn about this topic, while displaying their willingness to build and develop their competences needed for the green transition; secondly, the students and university libraries represent another powerful audience for the market, having to take into account that sustainable success implicates mastering skills for a greener future; and, thirdly, the business communities, entrepreneurs, and policymakers, among others, are the ones that participate through their actions at the process of building a sustainable future, having as starting points the GreenComp conceptual reference model, critical thinking, leadership, environmental literacy, cultural competence, and data analysis for a greener and sustainable future (European Commission, 2025).

These days, green skills training has become an essential tool in meeting the industry's demands for a green workforce, especially when thinking about the fact that the whole world strives towards net zero goals, which have turned out to be an overwhelming priority to education providers and businesses alike. What is more, the development of green skills has become a priority, since people have to be prepared for the growing number of green jobs which will offer unlimited opportunities to move towards a more sustainable economy. Furthermore, developing green skills involves investing a lot time as well as resources in supporting the transition to building a green future through essential decision-making competencies and the educators and employers are becoming more and more dedicated to the green roles (Organization for Economic Co-operation and Development (OECD), 2023).

Besides all the aforementioned ideas, collaboration can successfully develop green skills, taking into account that a sustainable future requires the necessary skills and the knowledge that will ensure its optimum development. In addition, there is the need for education and training excellence in green creativity and innovation all around the world, so that the data on the environmental impact of the individuals, communities, and organizations will be collected, ultimately, so that informed decisions will be taken for the benefit of a resource-efficient and sustainable society (United Nations Children's Fund (UNICEF), 2024).

In the end, it needs to be highlighted that this current book successfully provides practical guidance for youth, students, communities, researchers, international development partners, policymakers, entrepreneurs, organizational leaders, and not only, on the one hand, in offering a better understanding of the Sustainable Development Goals and, on the other hand, in accessing green skills opportunities. In continuation, the book emphasizes the need for tailored solutions in terms of building green skills and, in the same time, sheds a new light on the immense potential provided by context-specific solutions that green skilling programs, green job opportunities, and green sectors have to offer at present and in the future.

**Franklin Roberto Quishpi Choto** PhD in the City, Territory and Sustainable Planning program from the Rovira I Virgili University, line of research: Territorial and Urban Dynamics, sociodemographic transformations. Master in Regional Development and Territorial Planning, Pontificia Universidad Católica del Ecuador, Specialist in Leadership, Climate Change and Cities FLACSO, Economist from the National University of Chimborazo, studies urban adaptations and rural-urban relations. Currently responsible for the Amazonian headquarters of the State University of Milagro and post-graduate professor at the Technical University of Quevedo, UNEMI and University of Guayaquil.
**Mario Rivas Alemán** Professor at the Technical University of Manabí (Ecuador). Expert in local development processes with an emphasis on participation for the defense and promotion of human rights, linked to NGOs and public institutions. Teaching in virtual environments on aspects of legislation applied to information, higher education, human rights and professional ethics. Member of the Euro-Mediterranean Observatory of Public Space and Democracy -URJC- (Spain).

**Franklin Roberto Quishpi Choto**
*Rovira I Virgili University, Spain, Milagro State University, Ecuador*

**Mario Rivas Alemán**
*Universidad Técnica de Manabí, Ecuador*

## REFERENCES

European Commission. (2025). GreenComp Conceptual Reference Model. Available on-line at https://joint-research-centre.ec.europa.eu/greencomp-european-sustainability-competence-framework/greencomp-conceptual-reference-model_en. Accessed on the 1st of February 2025.

Organization for Economic Co-operation and Development (OECD). (2023). Assessing and Anticipating Skills for the Green Transition. Unlocking Talent for a Sustainable Future. Report. Available on-line at https://www.oecd.org/en/publications/assessing-and-anticipating-skills-for-the-green-transition_28fa0bb5-en.html. Accessed on the 1st of February 2025.

United Nations Children's Fund (UNICEF). (2024). *Skills for a Green Transition: Solutions for Youth on the Move*. United Nations Plaza.

# Foreword

What does building a sustainable future mean in this day and age? Which are some essential competences and skills that specialists need these days in order to be able to advocate for social justice or for environmental sustainability? Can individuals and communities globally work harmoniously with nature? Are young people today prioritizing the development of sustainability skills? Are communities equipped in becoming partners in developing solutions to economic, environmental, and social challenges?

These are just a few questions answered, at length, with numerous solutions and cases studies provided as guidance, in the IGI Global book on *Building a Green Future Through Essential Decision-Making Competencies*, edited by Associate Professor PhD. Jarmila Duháček Šebestová (Silesian University in Opava, Opava, Czechia) and Professor PhD. Habil Cristina Raluca Gh. Popescu (University of Bucharest and The Bucharest University of Economic Studies, Bucharest, Romania).

In these days context, there are numerous ways to build a sustainable future, having in mind the vital Global Goals as well as the pivotal Partnerships for these Global Goals. However, they all have in common the utmost necessity to master those essential skills for a sustainable future (European Commission, 2025a). Hence, some of these critical skills that should be acknowledged are: first of all, environmental literacy skills, due to its power to shed a new light on the human-environment connections; second of all, critical thinking and problem-solving skills, due to the fact that addressing issues effectively in today's modern world represents a must; third of all, collaboration and communication skills, due to the power of information, knowledge and ideas which need to be shared and closely analyzed for a better and secure future for all; and, fourth of all, data analysis skills and action-oriented mindset, taking into account that examining and interpreting data offers valuable insights regarding certain issues and, in like manner, enables the process of making evidence-based and informed decisions (European Commission, 2025b).

What is more, current international reports provided by reputed organizations have successfully shown that global qualitative and quantitative analysis ought to be encountered, at all times, at the very core of the complex process of enhancing the skills of individuals, precisely due to the importance of the transition to the environmental sustainability which should rely on specific data and highly accurate facts (International Labor Organization, 2025). Furthermore, greening the global economy, while closing the green skills gap, may be done only when considering the steps capable to leverage building the quality infrastructure for a sustainable workforce (International Training Centre of the ILO, 2024).

Hence, the quality professionals' worldwide need to thoroughly reconsider their role played in helping individuals, communities, governments, policymakers, and organizations in navigating the global shift towards green jobs. Nevertheless, today's realities have shown that the creation of these highly anticipated green jobs depends on the availability of people's relevant skills and training. So, in this given context, the IGI Global book on *Building a Green Future Through Essential Decision-Making Competencies*, sheds a new light, among many others, on: the manner in which green jobs are defined; the environmental preservation and restoration ought to be done in an optimum manner; and, the global green skills gap needs to be addressed in terms of creating high quality infrastructure and fostering well equipped environmental management systems.

In the end, although individuals, communities, and organizations may continue to encounter environmental aspects they cannot control or cannot influence, at a first glance, by focusing on the green skills as well as on the implementation of the environmental management systems they will be able to reach the precious goal of enhancing environmental performance, ultimately fulfilling the environmental obligations.

**Seda Yıldırım** has a PhD degree in marketing. She currently works at Tekirdag Namık Kemal University in Turkey. She studies sustainable development, 2030 sustainable development goals, sustainable consumption patterns, higher education, consumption patterns, environmental quality, and food security. She has many publications including book chapters, proceedings, and articles (in journals indexed with WOS and SCOPUS). She won the Emerald literati award - Outstanding Paper Award 2022. #LiteratiAwards https://www.webofscience.com/wos/author/record/R-8595-2019. ORCID:https://orcid.org/0000-0003-4367-6652

**Seda Yıldırım**
*Tekirdag Namik Kemal University, Turkey*

## REFERENCES

European Commission. (2025a). Green Transition. Available on-line at https://reform-support.ec.europa.eu/what-we-do/green-transition_en. Accessed on the 1st of January 2025.

European Commission. (2025b). Our Projects. Available on-line at https://reform-support.ec.europa.eu/our-projects_en. Accessed on the 1st of January 2025.

International Labor Organization. (2025). Skills for a Greener Future: A Global View. Available on-line at https://www.ilo.org/publications/skills-greener-future-global-view. Accessed on the 1st of January 2025.

International Training Centre of the ILO. (2024). Skills for a Greener Future. Available on-line at https://www.itcilo.org/courses/skills-greener-future. Accessed on the 1st of January 2025.

# Preface

In an era marked by environmental degradation, climate change, and socio-economic disparities, the urgency for sustainable decision-making has never been greater. As we work towards building a greener and more equitable future, it is essential that we equip individuals and organizations with the competencies necessary for responsible and informed decision-making. *Building a Green Future Through Essential Decision-Making Competencies* is a timely compilation of research that highlights the critical role these competencies play in fostering sustainability across a variety of sectors, from business to education and urban infrastructure.

This edited volume brings together a diverse group of scholars and experts who examine the essential competencies required to drive sustainable development and innovation. The chapters explore frameworks, models, and real-world applications that can help shape a more sustainable future for both individuals and organizations. Drawing from a range of disciplines, including entrepreneurship, human resource management, and environmental sciences, the contributions offer valuable insights into how decision-making processes can be aligned with sustainability goals.

## CHAPTER OVERVIEW

### Chapter 1: Basic Competency Frameworks within Sustainable Business Models

Authors: Jarmila Duháček Šebestová & Cristina Raluca Gh. Popescu

This chapter introduces the *EntreComp* framework, developed by the European Commission, to guide individuals in developing entrepreneurial competencies essential for creating sustainable business models. It highlights the connection between lifelong learning, entrepreneurship, and sustainability, offering a structured approach to cultivating skills necessary for environmental and social responsibility in business.

### Chapter 2: Advancements in Intelligent Traffic Monitoring System Design for Smart Urban Infrastructure

Authors: Arun Chakravarthy R. et al.

This chapter explores how intelligent traffic monitoring systems (ITMS) that integrate machine learning, sensors, and real-time data can optimize traffic flow and reduce environmental impacts. The authors illustrate how these advancements can contribute to more sustainable urban mobility by enhancing road safety and reducing congestion and emissions.

### Chapter 3: Green Future Ideas and Scalable Technologies Essential for Innovators, Scientists, Researchers, and Engineers: Cutting-Edge Initiatives and Commercially-Viable Solutions for a Fairer Future

Authors: Cristina Raluca Gh. Popescu & Rahul Verma

Focusing on the role of innovation in combating climate change, this chapter emphasizes the importance of scalable climate-tech solutions. The authors explore how funding cutting-edge ideas and engineering commercially viable technologies can help adapt to and mitigate the effects of climate change, with a strong focus on principles of the circular economy.

### Chapter 4: Building a Green Future Through Essential Decision-Making Competencies in Green HRM

Author: Deepa Sharma

This chapter examines how Green Human Resource Management (HRM) systems can shape the sustainability culture within educational institutions. By focusing on integrating eco-friendly policies and raising environmental awareness among employees, the author emphasizes the importance of Green HRM in fostering a sustainable organizational culture.

### Chapter 5: Building Green Competencies in Entrepreneurial Education

Authors: Hemlata Parmar & Utsav Murari

In this chapter, the authors propose a framework for integrating sustainability into entrepreneurial education. They emphasize the importance of teaching students how to incorporate sustainable decision-making practices into their entrepreneurial ventures, thereby aligning business models with environmental and social sustainability goals.

### Chapter 6: Developing a Model for Sustainable Entrepreneurship Competencies

Author: Muhammad Usman Tariq

This chapter presents a comprehensive model for developing sustainable entrepreneurship competencies, focusing on strategic decision-making for balancing profitability with environmental and social responsibility. The author highlights the critical competencies required for entrepreneurs to navigate sustainability challenges and promote green business practices.

### Chapter 7: Formulation of Grand Index of Green Growth and Sustainability (GIGGS): A Cross-Country Empirical Study

Author: Debasish Roy

This chapter introduces the Grand Index of Green Growth and Sustainability (GIGGS), a framework for assessing green growth and sustainable development across different countries. By analyzing key environmental and economic indicators, the author presents a conceptual tool for tracking and promoting sustainable practices worldwide.

## Chapter 8: The Violation of Human Rights by Chevron-Texaco Oil Company in the Ecuadorian Amazon: The Lago Agrio Case

Authors: Arturo Luque González, Geomayra Castro Cedeño, Maira Pinargote Mendoza & Cristina Raluca Gh. Popescu

This chapter investigates the environmental and human rights violations caused by the Chevron-Texaco oil operations in the Ecuadorian Amazon. The authors examine the socio-economic, environmental, and legal ramifications of corporate negligence, shedding light on the broader consequences of industrial pollution on indigenous communities.

## Chapter 9: Rights of Nature in Ecuador

Authors: Arturo Luque González, Dolores Alexandra Bravo Bravo, Ligia Nevárez Vera & Cristina Raluca Gh. Popescu

This chapter explores Ecuador's pioneering legal recognition of nature as a subject of rights. The authors analyze the constitutional provisions that protect nature and discuss the implications for environmental justice and sustainability within the broader legal framework of the country.

## Chapter 10: The Organizational Economics of Knowledge Management

Authors: José Vargas-Hernandez, Francisco Javier González, Teresea Salazar-Echeagaray & Omar Vargas-González

This chapter examines how organizational economics can complement knowledge management strategies in promoting sustainable business practices. The authors argue that integrating these two fields can help organizations balance economic performance with sustainable and ethical decision-making.

## Chapter 11: Green Manufacturing Practices for Sustainable Development: Selected Scenarios of Bangladesh

Author: SSM Huda

This chapter explores the adoption of green manufacturing practices in Bangladesh, focusing on the ready-made garments, electronics, and construction industries. The author proposes a framework for green manufacturing operations, emphasizing the benefits of reducing emissions and improving workplace conditions for both environmental and employee well-being.

## Chapter 12: Talent Management as a Pillar of Sustainable HRM in the V4 Region

Authors: Helena Marková & Sampras Femi Robert

This chapter focuses on the importance of talent management within the Visegrád Four (V4) region in promoting sustainability. The authors argue that integrating talent management with sustainable HRM practices can help organizations achieve long-term resilience and contribute to green human resource management goals.

### Chapter 13: Taxonomy and Standardization of Information for and About Sustainable Entrepreneurship in the EU

Author: Radka MacGregor Pelikánová

This chapter examines the European Union's efforts to standardize information related to sustainable entrepreneurship. By analyzing EU policies and legal frameworks, the author explores how standardized, accessible information is essential for informed decision-making in sustainability practices.

### Chapter 14: Building Competencies for Sustainability Decision-Making Among Management Students

Authors: Renata Paksiova, Petra Pribilova & Roman Brauner

This chapter presents a study on the integration of sustainability and circular economy principles into the curriculum for management students. The authors assess students' awareness and understanding of these concepts, highlighting the need for more in-depth education on sustainable decision-making practices.

### Chapter 15: Challenges and Innovations in Applying SDG and ESG Frameworks

Authors: Akshat Jain & Deeksha Ganguly

Entrepreneurial skills have evolved significantly since initiatives like the *Green Paper on Entrepreneurship* (EU Commission, 2003) and the *Small Business Act* (European Commission, 2008), which emphasized knowledge, competencies, and sustainability. Entrepreneurs today prioritize long-term sustainability over short-term profits (Elkington, 2018), leveraging frameworks like the Sustainable Development Goals (SDGs) and Environmental, Social, and Governance (ESG) standards to integrate ethical practices with financial performance. Despite these obstacles, ESG and SDG frameworks present opportunities for innovation through systems thinking, foresight, and interdisciplinary collaboration (Senge, 1990). By adopting "green thinking," entrepreneurs mitigate external threats, foster innovation, and drive sustainability. This chapter explores the role of networking, strategic thinking, and ethics in sustainable practices, offering insights into aligning business strategies with global sustainability goals for long-term success.

### Chapter 16: Analysis of Factors Influencing Brownfield Redevelopment in the Context of Regional Development

Authors: Jaroslav Škrabal & Martin Vybiral

This chapter examines key factors influencing brownfield regeneration in the Czech Republic within regional development. The aim is to identify and evaluate determinants of successful revitalization by developing a systematic framework for assessing redevelopment potential. Using factor analysis and comparative methods, the study analyzes economic, environmental, and social factors based on CzechInvest (2024) data. Key determinants include land ownership, prior land use, contamination levels, and investment potential. The findings show that clear ownership, economic incentives, and infrastructure investments enhance regeneration, while regulatory complexity and remediation costs hinder it. The study contributes to data-driven policy recommendations to optimize land-use planning and investment incentives for sustainable brownfield redevelopment.

## Chapter 17: Green Decision-Making Competencies in Sustainable Development: A Systematic Review

Authors: Mouhcine Rhouiri, Mehdi Bensouda & Mohamed-Habiboullah Meyabe

The chapter identifies and discusses various challenges affecting adoption with the emergence of green decision-making into sustainable development. The study finds major barriers in traditional practice ICT, finance, resistance to change, and lack of digital skills, especially in SMEs. This research highlights the potential role of emerging technologies, such as artificial intelligence (AI), Internet of Things (IoT), and blockchain, in improving sustainable decisions based on systematic reviewing 277 articles and textual analysis with IRaMuTeQ. This research indicates that overcoming such challenges and ensuring a resilient transition would call for an integrated strategy comprising financial incentives, training, and sound regulatory frameworks. The study encourages the development of a culture of sustainability and technological innovation to maintain values through time.

## Chapter 18: Does ESG-Oriented Leadership Pay Off in Startups? A Theoretical Perspective

Authors: Burak Özdogan & Deniz Dirik

This chapter addresses the role of ESG-oriented leadership in startups, exploring whether integrating ESG principles contributes to long-term success or comes with additional challenges. While sustainability has become a strategic imperative for businesses worldwide, its adoption among startups remains complex mostly because of financial constraints. Despite this, emerging trends suggest that investors are gradually recognizing ESG as a competitive advantage. While entrepreneurship is becoming more challenging due to financial and market uncertainties, an increasing number of early-stage entrepreneurs prioritize their social and environmental impact over pure profitability. Yet, the lack of standardized ESG metrics continues to be a significant barrier, creating an "acronym soup." While the financial benefits of ESG leadership in startups may not be immediately apparent, the long-term advantages, such as stronger talent retention and investor interest, make sustainability a strategic asset rather than a cost.

## Chapter 19: From Theory to Practice: Developing Green Skills Through Social Economy and Higher Education

Authors: Amanda Da Matta, Mihaela Vancea, Lukas Valek & Olga Valkova Tarasova

This chapter presents lessons from the SDG Labs project, a transnational initiative fostering green skills by integrating social economy entities and higher education. Through socially driven green Labs, the project explored innovative educational methods, including Living Labs, simulation-based learning, and participatory co-creation. Findings highlight gaps between theoretical environmental knowledge and practical sustainability skills. While social economy entities grasp basic concepts like the circular economy, advanced green competencies—such as environmental impact assessment—are less integrated. Effective interventions involve hands-on learning through green business simulations and multi-stakeholder collaboration. Institutional barriers, including limited policy support and regulatory challenges, often hinder scaling sustainable projects. Addressing these requires strengthening institutional frameworks and enhancing environmental literacy. The project underscores the need to align education with social economy demands, setting a benchmark for knowledge-driven green economies.

## Chapter 20: Sustainable Decision-Making for SME Resilience: The Role of Governance and Leadership in Ghana

Authors: Isaac Nketsiah & Thea Van der Westhuizen

Small and medium enterprises (SMEs) are vital to Ghana's economy, contributing 70% of GDP and providing key employment. However, business volatility, intensified by crises like COVID-19, exposes SMEs to significant risks. Sustainable decision-making through governance and leadership is crucial for resilience. This chapter explores governance frameworks and leadership practices that enhance SME resilience, focusing on sustainability-driven decision-making. A systematic literature review synthesizes research on governance structures, leadership strategies, and environmental uncertainties. Findings highlight the importance of board diversity, risk management, transformational leadership, and stakeholder engagement in strengthening resilience. The chapter offers recommendations for policymakers, business leaders, and researchers to develop sustainable governance and leadership frameworks for SMEs in an increasingly uncertain, environmentally conscious global economy.

## CONCLUSION

Together, these chapters provide a comprehensive exploration of the competencies necessary to make informed, responsible decisions that promote sustainability across various sectors. They offer readers valuable frameworks, case studies, and insights to equip individuals, organizations, and policymakers with the tools needed to navigate the complex challenges of building a sustainable future. Whether you are a student, educator, entrepreneur, or policymaker, this book serves as both a guide and a call to action for developing the decision-making competencies that will shape a greener and more equitable world for future generations.

# Acknowledgement

Professor Dr. Cristina Raluca Gh. Popescu would like to offer the deepest gratitude to distinguished Professor PhD. Fahri Özsungur, from Mersin University, the Department of Social Work, Turkey, for the inestimable contribution to the success of the book. The constructive feedbacks as well as the infusion of ideas and thoughts provided were crucial for the success of the current book project.

In addition, Professor Dr. Cristina Raluca Gh. Popescu wants to express the heartfelt gratitude to Professor Dr. Divya Chowdhry, Dean, the Jagran Institute of Management, Kanpur, India and Professor Dr. Harvinder Kaur, Campus Director, the Delhi Skill and Entrepreneurship University, India. The positive thoughts as well as the creative ideas were pivotal to the success of the project, while the importance of critical thinking in times in which green innovation and green technologies are vital to the society was thoroughly praised and acknowledged.

Likewise, Professor Dr. Cristina Raluca Gh. Popescu would like to show the greatest appreciation to a dear friend and wonderful international research colleague, Lecturer Dr. Rahul R. Verma, from the University of Delhi, India. These days, working together to accomplish great goals is paramount, which makes interdisciplinary and international research and development on sustainability and sustainable development projects paramount. Additionally, knowledge, innovation, and education have come to support in an unprecedented manner the way in which research and development activities are performed, hence, excellence in research is vital in supporting the balance between individuals' and communities' needs, and the environments' health and well-being.

In the spirit of wonderful collaboration relationships that lead to great ideas, creative thinking, hard work, vital knowledge, and a life-long learning path, Professor Dr. Cristina Raluca Gh. Popescu is extremely grateful for the opportunity to have collaborated once again together with Professor Dr. Arturo Luque Gonzales, from the Technical University of Manabí, Portoviejo, Ecuador and the Euro-Mediterranean Observatory on Public Policies and Democratic Quality, Rey Juan Carlos University, Spain. The impressive experience as well as the immense dedication to the current research project has demonstrated, once more, that doing things with care and putting positive ideas into practice makes a great difference for the success of scientific works.

Besides these, Professor Dr. Cristina Raluca Gh. Popescu is highly thankful to Professor Dr. Seda H. Bostancı, from the Tekirdağ Namık Kemal University, Turkey, for the collaborative spirit as well as the constructive and positive friendship displayed during so many years. These days, there are just a few occasions in which one may take the time to discover new ways of expressing creative ideas and thoughts due to the rapid rhythm in which everything is moving and evolving, and Professor Dr. Seda H. Bostancı has shown great dedication as well as tremendous desire to work towards facilitating knowledge and constructive projects that have come to support sustainability and sustainable development.

Having in mind the importance of circular economy and, in particular, the links between sustainability, sustainable development, and the principles of the circular economy, Professor Dr. Cristina Raluca Gh. Popescu wants to emphasize the dedication shown by Professor Dr. Seda Yıldırım, from Tekirdağ Namık Kemal Üniversitesi, Turkey, through her research and constructive feedbacks towards promoting sustainable practices in all fields. By acknowledging, through the ideas and thoughts promoted by the professor that integrating circular economy principles in all industries, all these industries will, ultimately, reduce waste and enhance resource efficiency, the transformation is impressive and inspiring: the waste will be transformed into valuable resources, while productivity will increase, and urban resilience will boost.

# Chapter 1
# Basic Competency Frameworks Within Sustainable Business Model

**Jarmila Duháček Šebestová**
https://orcid.org/0000-0002-7493-0759
*School of Business Administration in Karviná, Silesian University in Opava, Czech Republic*

**Cristina Raluca Gh. Popescu**
https://orcid.org/0000-0002-5876-0550
*University of Bucharest, Romania & The Bucharest University of Economic Studies, Romania*

## ABSTRACT

*EntreComp is a comprehensive model developed by the European Commission to help all interested individuals to understand and develop necessary entrepreneurial skills. This approach defines entrepreneurship as a key competence for lifelong learning and is designed to be used across various educational, professional, and social contexts. Using this model, each person could develop itself in area of creating new business activity. The framework is logically structured into three main competence areas, which are connected into one integrated system from idea creation to idea implementation.*

## INTRODUCTION

In this day and age, specialists worldwide strongly believe there is an overwhelming need to focus on key concepts, such as, for example, sustainability, sustainable development, sustainable business environment, and sustainable business models (Aldosemani *et al.*, 2025). Hence, numerous debates and controversies have come to light in the last years and, interestingly, almost all of them, somehow, tend to revolve around the pivotal question (Popescu & Popescu, 2025): How can a sustainable business model be created? On the one hand, this major question had as immediate result the general belief that a sustainable business model will have as main focus ensuring the benefits of the consumers, mainly centering on doing that without bringing any harm to the planet and to the future generations to come and, on the other hand, this powerful question had as immediate effect the companies' desire to show

DOI: 10.4018/979-8-3373-0189-1.ch001

support to the environment, using a green-friendly approach, in order to foster long-term success and resilience (Wang *et al.*, 2022).

Although it may seem new, the idea of focusing on the health of individuals and communities as well as on the well-being of the environment and the planet has somehow guided mankind from the very beginning, but, unfortunately, there seemed to be always far more pressing aspects that led businesses decisions and businesses processes, at a general level (Popescu, 2021; Todino *et al.*, 2023). The crucial ideas, such as, profit and profitability, efficiency, efficacy, and effectiveness, performance and excellence, business process management targeting impressive market quotas, cost reduction and the maximization of resources potential for the benefit of the companies, have one way or another managed to be among the main choices and the pivotal targets that the companies' leaders and managers tended to address first throughout their objectives and goals, which led, over the last decades, to them paying less and less attention to the environment and to the individuals as human beings that require protection, attention, specific care, great respect, and responsible actions (Popescu, & Verma, 2025; Soler *et al.*, 2021).

Going even further with this current analysis, there is a lot to be stated regarding the connections that may be encountered and that should, ultimately, be encountered between sustainability, responsibility, social responsibility, corporate social responsibility, and sustainable business models (Rondon, 2021; Smith, 2019). Although, at a first glance, all these terms may look like concepts that ought to be brought in today's conversations related to successful business strategies simply in order to please the audiences and comply with these days' rules and regulations, there is far more than meets the eye when addressing the importance and the outcomes derived from addressing, in the right and ethical manner, the relationship between corporate social responsibility and sustainable business models (Peraza & Furumura, 2022). In this matter, first of all, companies are encouraged to position themselves as leaders in sustainability, which would be something that these entities could do by focusing, on the one hand, on their concrete actions towards the environment and, on the other hand, on their commitment to promote responsible resource use – without having to cut costs and without needing to alter the quality of their products so that they would ultimately end up by delivering low value products and services to their consumers and will become models that their employees will not want to follow on the long-run (Olesika *et al.*, 2021; Phan *et al.*, 2021). Additionally, second of all, companies are inspired to make a positive contribution in the world, by being constantly motivated to create lasting value both to the consumers and to the employees – hence, always or almost always generating positive thoughts and vibrations coming from all around, which would position them, little by little, among the major players on the marketplace (Ngai, 2021). Nevertheless, third of all, companies of all sizes and having all types of activities are supported to focus on sustainability and address the main pillars of sustainability, even though, some of the first assumptions would be that large corporations would be the ones more suitable to adopt sustainable strategies and create sustainable business models – in particular, probably due to their financial power and their already accumulated valuable experience on the marketplace (Leger *et. al.*, 2019). In other words, all the entities activating on the marketplace are called to adapt their specific practices to the new sustainable business models patterns and requirements and, moreover, are expected to break new grounds and become bolder and inquisitive in order to ensure their survival and success in tremendously challenging times (Lee, 2020).

## THEORETICAL BACKGROUND

Having said all that, specialists are extremely attracted these days to additional key concepts, such as, entrepreneurship, entrepreneurial skills, frameworks due to be used by entrepreneurs to enhance their sustainable development strategies within the companies, and environmental sustainability education for entrepreneurs, while addressing the key solutions of building the skills needed for the innovative entrepreneurship, the lifelong learning processes and strategies, and the active engagement in addressing environmental challenges (Khan & Vuopala, 2019). In this particular case, those entrepreneurs keen on sustainability practices and sustainable development business strategies take into account the fact that sustainability refers to those processes that take place in organizations and that are done at the optimum level at which the resources are preserved and, also, the balance between long-term environmental health and individuals' and communities' well-being is acknowledged and ensured (David *et al.*, 2022). All in all, in this matter the discussion goes into the direction of green business practices, which ought to build and steered in the direction of sustainable development, having as main aim the companies' ability to meet the current needs of these days' generations without compromising the future generations' ability to meet their own needs and without bringing any harm to the people and to the nature (Asrin, 2021). This great principle of sustainable development needs to always align with the companies' green business practices, hence making sure that the businesses development strategies will be creative, innovative, robust, resilient, and powerful drivers to the companies' long-term responsibly achieved success (Berggren & Worth, 2023).

Unfortunately, history has shown on far too numerous occasions, that there is a very big difference between the initially chosen objectives and goals, and the business paths and business strategies will ultimately decide to go. There are various explanations for all these major discrepancies in initially declared statements and the ultimately obtained outcomes, but, essentially, one of the recurring problems that could be brought to the attention is the most common one of all, namely the companies' desire to make profit at any cost, without considering the repercussions, without being able to show any decency and any respect to the individuals, the communities, and the environment, and, without even being able to recognize that, in far too many situations, the harm done was not even worth the risks and the troubles taken (Borja *et al.*, 2010). Additionally, although there will always be some explanations provided by the companies' managers and leaders for this type of behavior, there is no real justification for cases like this especially since all those activities and actions that are intended to the individuals, the communities, and the environment may be irreversible, since the results could be so dramatic that no one and nothing will ever be capable to help and to support those individuals, communities, and environment to reach the initial state, the one before all the disasters generated (Heller-Schuh *et al.*, 2011).

The next step would be to think, under these complex circumstances, about those powerful multinational corporations that have the tendency, far too often, to hide behind elaborate international trade treaties and international commercial laws that somehow have managed to act in their favor, by somehow encouraging and propelling controversies, misleading the public opinion that all these companies act in the best interest of communities by, for example, providing jobs, helping emergent economies to develop at a faster pace, and supporting the environment, and so on. Nevertheless, all these assumptions and all these ideas ought to be taken with a grain of salt, since there seems to be a price for everything and, additionally, each coin normally ought to have two sides and both sides ought to be closely turned and analyzed in order to be able to have in front of the eyes all or almost all the implications possible. While taking into consideration the ample process of job creation initiated by these multinational companies, other facets of their activities ought to be analyzed, namely: first of all, what salaries to these companies offer (Chenchouni *et al.*, 2022); second of all, are the salaries that these companies offers fair, while compared to similar jobs in other regions, countries, and so on; third of all, do these companies create the right balance between the employees personal development and professional development; fourth of all, do these companies show respect towards their workers and the environment, do they act responsibly; and, fourth of all, are these companies committed to displaying in what manner their activities affect individuals and communities lives and, also, the natural habitats and ecosystems. In addition, while taking into account the aspects that characterize the help that these companies are supposed to provide to governments and emergent economies to develop at a faster pace, while supporting the environment, there are major elements to consider as well: first of all, how powerful are the lobbing actions of these big corporations and which are the implications of these lobbing actions (Bubevski, 2025); which are the true interests served through these lobbing actions, who is behind those actions, and will these actions result in the companies' opportunity not to comply to the laws and regulations anymore (Assyne, 2022).

All in all, these days' specialists have drawn great attention to the fact that individuals tend to make the wrong assumption that the companies are always acting in the best interest of the people and the environment, they test their products very responsibly, and they always act with great caution when it comes to addressing health and well-being matters (Armacanqui *et al.*, 2024); the reality has shown, on far too many instances, that the rhythm in which the companies create and innovate today does not offer them the chance to thoroughly research their newly brought to light products and services, the tests being usually made on a small number of subjects and may prove to be less relevant than the ones made in the past decades (AlHashmi *et al.*, 2021). Under these circumstances, it is only normal to discover that, in some situations, the use of certain products and services, for only a few days, by a very small number of individuals that were part of the group on which the tests were performed, is not really capable in offering concrete data on how safe the ingredients are to the health of the people and to the environment (Frolovičeva, 2023). Besides these, there are other cases in which it has been demonstrated that the companies were well aware for decades that their products were dangerous and that they were gravely affecting both human lives and the environment, yet choosing to hide these aspects from the general public in order to protect themselves, their reputation, hence continuing to prosper with the price of human lives and by harming the natural habitats, the biodiversity, and the ecosystems (Faller, 2024; Hardy Bednar & Godkin, 2009).

While considering the aspects surrounding the concept of sustainability it seems that the idea of power has profound implications and tremendous influence in the companies' abilities and capacities to make the right choices when being confronted with choosing between people's health, environmental balance, business ethics, reputation, corporate social responsibility, and sustainable business behaviors and models (Neal & Neal, 2019). Making the right choice in the case of companies is not always easy and that is precisely why the countries' governments ought to have rigorous laws intended to protect the population and the environment (Molina *et al.*, 2020; Bahl, 2021). The need to be the best there is on the marketplace and the desire to obtain the competitive advantage on the marketplace may be, in some cases and for some companies, the arguments that are powerful enough to make them forget that sustainability is the key to survival and the aim to support the planet and its inhabitants (Martzog *et al.*, 2021). When having to make a choice, there will most certainly be cases in which sustainable development would not be a priority anymore for those companies, since their immediate goal might revolve around profitability at any cost (Cartelli, 2012; Cleveland & Hinojosa, 2019).

There are so many aspects that could be brought to the attention when addressing the individual competences and the opportunities offered by researchers and specialists to facilitate the understanding of these individual competences in the general framework that addresses the case of the SDGs. Nevertheless, the authors of this original and powerful book chapter strongly believe that the European Union Competence Framework is of great essence in today's context, especially when addressing the case of long life learning programs and the vital need to include environmental sustainability in all areas of our lives – both the personal side of our lives and the professional side of our lives (Vuorikari *et al.*, 2022; Carretero Gomez *et al.*, 2017). In this given context, offering a better and a more in-depth understanding the European Union Competence Framework becomes crucial, the accent being on the following important aspects: firstly, the EntreComp, Greencomp and Lifecomp and Digicomp are of vital important these days; secondly, the development of key competences according to European Union frameworks means, ultimately, having to consider EntreComp for entrepreneurial skills; and, thirdly, the links are crucial, as follows, namely, LifeComp for personal, social, and educational competences and GreenComp for environmental sustainability, with a major focus on Digital Competence Framework for Educators (DigCompEdu) (Bacigalupo *et al.*, 2016; Carretero Gomez *et al.*, 2017; Sala *et al.*, 2020; Bianchi *et al.*, 2022; Sala & Herrero Ramila, 2022).

When having to make the right choices in terms of building the optimum set of competences and skills in the entrepreneurial domain, specialists have reached a very valuable agreement, namely the fact that there is always the stringent need to have a structured approach to building the skills needed for innovative entrepreneurship, for lifelong learning and, in like manner, for encouraging the active engagement in addressing environmental challenges (Bianchi *et al.*, 2022; Tsionis, 2015). To begin with, it is very important to know that in a European Commission recently published report highly suggestively entitled "GreenComp. The European sustainability competence framework" the accent is placed on three major ideas, as follows: (a) first of all, the necessity to rely on science and on valuable scientific studies in order to create those policies that would have the real power to support the links that have existed from the very beginning between the people and the environment, hence learning to focus on "science for policy", which is crucial these days (Eklund *et al.*, 2023; Boguslawski *et al.*, 2017); (b) second of all, the necessity to address the changes that took place in nature in the last decades and which have determined specialists to wonder whether or not the individuals, the communities, and the society as a whole are truly working towards the benefits of humanity and the planet or against nature and the environment, hence learning to focus on "environment and climate change", which are pivotal these days (Scalabrino, 2022).; and (c) third of all, the necessity to address the importance and the role of long life learning, research, and education in terms of building trust, fostering innovation, harboring creativity, and supporting the willingness to do good in the society rather than address with ought properly and responsibly thinking about the limitations of resources and the sustainability principles, hence learning to focus on "innovation and growth", which are major interests these days not only for individuals and communities, but also for the companies' leaders and managers, the government, the politicians, and the country leaders (Bianchi *et al.*, 2022).

Having said all that, it ought to be taken into consideration that the European Union's countries are extremely dedicated to the SDGs, especially due to the actions taken through the European Green Deal – which is regarded, on the one hand, as the main catalyst intended "to promote learning on environmental sustainability" and, on the other hand, as a valuable source capable to create "a European sustainability competence framework" (Bianchi *et al.*, 2022; Caena & Redecker, 2019). There are numerous aspects that could be highlighted when addressing the significant and truly wonderful role of GreenComp and among all these aspects the following ones are those which require great care and major reflection not only on the short-term, but also on the medium-term and on the long-term, namely: (a) to start with, GreenComp sheds a new light on "a set of sustainability competences" which are intended to become very important for the European Unions' education programs as well as a source of inspiration for other nations interested in fostering sustainability and sustainable development for the benefit of humanity and the environment (Bianchi *et al.*, 2022; Punie & Redecker, 2017); (b) additionally, GreenComp is intended to support knowledge in all its forms as long as those forms are aligned with the SDGs in the way that it helps learners to enhance their "skills and attitudes that promote ways to think, plan and act with empathy, responsibility, and care for our planet and for public health" (Bianchi *et al.*, 2022; Punie & Redecker, 2017); and (c) besides all these, GreenComp is considered an extremely powerful and reliable "framework for learning for environmental sustainability", given the fact that it represents a framework developed on several consultations with reputed experts and dedicated stakeholders that have dedicated their works to support the very essence of suitability and sustainable development (Bianchi *et al.*, 2022). It needs to be acknowledged that GreenComp is based on four major "interrelated competence areas" which are "embodying sustainability values", "embracing complexity in sustainability", "envisioning sustainable futures", and "acting for sustainability" (Bianchi *et al.*, 2022). Likewise, it needs to be emphasized that, on the one hand, each area that is part of GreenComp "comprises three competences that are interlinked and equally important" and, on the other hand, "GreenComp is designed to be a non-prescriptive reference for learning schemes fostering sustainability as a competence" (Bianchi *et al.*, 2022; Punie & Redecker, 2017).

## DEVELOPMENT OF KEY COMPETENCES ACCORDING TO EU FRAMEWORKS

### Entrepreneurship Competence Framework (EntreComp)

EntreComp is a comprehensive model developed by the European Commission to help all interested individuals to understand and develop necessary entrepreneurial skills. This approach defines entrepreneurship as a key competence for lifelong learning and is designed to be used across various educational, professional, and social contexts. Using this model, each person could develop itself in area of creating new business activity (Bacigalupo et al., 2016). The framework is logically structured into three main competence areas, which are connected into one integrated system from idea creation to idea implementation (see Table 1).

*Table 1. A structure of Entrepreneurship Competence framework*

| Competence Area | Skills | Example of use |
|---|---|---|
| Ideas and Opportunities | Spotting Opportunities | Be able to identify and use opportunities to create business value. |
| | Creativity | Creative approach to solve problems and generate unseen solutions. |
| | Vision | Be able to plan the future and setting goals. |
| | Valuing Ideas | Be able to think about the value of ideas and sharing them. |
| | Ethical and Sustainable Thinking | All decisions have to be based on ethical principles and sustainability. |

continued on following page

*Table 1. Continued*

| Competence Area | Skills | Example of use |
|---|---|---|
| Resources | Self-Awareness and Self-Efficacy | Understanding own strengths and weaknesses. Be able to evaluate them and plan improvement. |
| | Motivation and Perseverance | Staying motivated and resilient within changing environment. |
| | Mobilizing Resources | Gathering and managing resources effectively, be able to think about resource limits. |
| | Financial and Economic Literacy | Understanding financial and economic concepts to create financial plans or evaluate return rates. |
| | Mobilizing Others | Inspiring and involving others to support the idea, which was created |
| Into Action | Taking the Initiative | Being proactive and taking the lead in idea implementation. |
| | Planning and Management | Planning, organizing, and managing projects as part of idea implementation |
| | Coping with Uncertainty, Ambiguity, and Risk | Ability to handle uncertainty and risks within changing conditions. |
| | Working with Others | Collaborating and networking with others as competitive advantage. |
| | Learning through Experience | Learning from experiences and reflecting on them to reduce failure in action. |

Source: McCallum et al., 2018

These competences are designed to be adaptable and applicable to various contexts, from education and training to professional and personal development as well (Joensuu-Salo et al., 2022). EntreComp skills development have to be seen as a combination of self-awareness, practical experience, and targeted learning within one concept. The use of this competency model brings many challenges, especially within competency level evaluation (López-Núñez et al., 2022). According to the previous structure, the individual competencies of the model can be assessed in several ways, such as (a) *self-assessment and reflection*, when self-evaluation is based on current skill levels included within the framework and an individual sets measurable goals for improvement; (b) *education and training*, which includes life long learning courses focused on entrepreneurship, creativity, financial literacy, and project management skills development; (c) practical experience and collaboration due to participation within projects, mentors and experience within entrepreneurial community; (Eimler & Straßmann, 2023).

These competencies can also be actively developed with the help of digital competences (DigiComp), which in the entrepreneurial mindset can develop the areas of analysis, risk attitudes and planning the implementation of the created idea (Hammoda, 2022).

## Digital Competence Framework (DigComp)

DigComp is a valuable tool for individuals, educators, and policymakers to enhance digital literacy and competence across various contexts, especially presented as DigComp 2.1 and DigComp 2.2 (Vuorikari et al., 2022, Danailova, 2024). DigComp is generally mentioned as an initiative by the European Commission to help individuals develop and assess their digital skills. It provides a common understanding of digital competence and it is structured around five key areas, as summarized below (Table 2, Carretero Gomez et al., 2017).

*Table 2. A structure of Digital Competence framework*

| Competence Area | Skills | Example of use |
|---|---|---|
| Information and Data Literacy | Articulating Information Needs | Identifying what information is needed, ability to make information requirement |
| | Locating and Retrieving | Finding and accessing digital data, information, and relevant content |
| | Evaluating | Assessing the relevance and credibility of sources, awareness against fake news |
| | Managing | Organizing and storing digital data and content to be available and sorted |
| Communication and Collaboration | Interacting | Communicating and collaborating through digital technologies using different tools and networks |
| | Sharing | Sharing information and content by topic or with selected groups. |
| | Engaging in Citizenship | Participating in society through digital means, using them to share information. |
| | Managing Digital Identity | Managing digital presence and reputation, securing identity. |
| Digital Content Creation | Developing Content | Creating and editing digital content. |
| | Integrating and Re-elaborating | Combining and modifying existing content within ethical context |
| | Copyright and Licenses | Understanding and applying copyright and licenses to do not violate someone´s rights |
| | Programming | Giving instructions to a computer system, coding information |
| Safety | Protecting Devices | Ensuring the security of devices and data to prevent data theft and misuse. |
| | Protecting Personal Data | Safeguarding personal information and privacy |
| | Health and Well-being | Understanding the impact of digital technologies on health, e-health apps use |
| | Environmental Impact | Being aware of the environmental effects of digital technologies |
| Problem Solving | Identifying Needs and Problems | Recognizing digital needs and issues within chosen situation |
| | Solving Technical Problems | Troubleshooting and resolving technical issues with apps or programmes actively used |
| | Creatively Using Technology | Innovating and improving processes with digital tools, seeking for new ideas |
| | Staying Up-to-date | Keeping up with digital trends and advancements to be able to innovate |

**Source:** own elaboration based on Carretero Gomez et al., 2017.

These skills are advantageous for development because they have 8 levels defined for evaluation, which makes it possible to measure the progress of each student or entrepreneur, unlike EntreComp, where evaluation takes place, for example, through 360-degree feedback. Mattar et al. (2022) evaluated different possibilities to measure DigComp level for individuals, when the most frequent were self-report measures and performance assessments, open-ended questionnaires, interviews, and observations or direct knowledge questions. All mentioned instruments gave opportunity to quantitatively or qualitatively measure the progress in DigComp development. DigComp is becoming a part of everyday life due to the progressive digitalization of processes, so it is necessary to connect it with the LifeComp concept.

## Life Competence Framework (LifeComp)

LifeComp is a conceptual framework, meaning it is non-prescriptive and can be adapted to various educational and professional contexts. It is designed to help individuals thrive in a rapidly changing world by fostering personal fulfillment, social inclusion, and lifelong learning. It was also presented as an initiative by the European Commission in 2018 (Sala et al., 2020). It aims to provide a shared understanding of these competences and is structured around three main areas, such as personal, social and learning areas (Table 3, Stahl, 2021).

*Table 3. A structure of Life Competence framework*

| Competence Area | Skills | Example of use |
|---|---|---|
| Personal | Self-Regulation | Managing emotions, thoughts, and behaviors effectively |
| | Flexibility | Adapting to change and being open to new ideas |
| | Well-being | Maintaining physical and mental health |
| Social | Empathy | Understanding and sharing the feelings of others |
| | Communication | Effectively conveying and receiving messages |
| | Collaboration | Working well with others to achieve common goals |
| Learning to Learn | Growth Mindset | Believing in the ability to grow and improve through effort |
| | Critical Thinking | Analyzing and evaluating information to make informed decisions |
| | Managing Learning | Planning, monitoring, and reflecting on learning process |

Source: own elaboration based on Stahl, 2021.

According to Garavaglia et al. (2021) is necessary to incorporate DigComp and LifeComp to unify values and promote lifelong learning process or to develop educational framework. In a line with Cacciamani & Fujita (2023) the integration of both competency frameworks leads to knowledge-oriented society. Knowledge based models are closely connected with LifeComp values, especially in area of lifelong learning process. Development of those skills could help individuals to be connected with tasks, modern trends and innovation using. (Tan et al., 2021). When the environment is changing, the most important is to support green and sustainable approach within business or business education, which is connected with European Sustainability Competence Framework (GreenComp).

## European Sustainability Competence Framework (GreenComp)

GreenComp aims to equip individuals with the knowledge, skills, and attitudes needed to live, work, and act in a sustainable manner. It is applicable across various educational, professional, and social contexts, making it a versatile tool for promoting sustainability. It provides a common understanding of what sustainability as a competence entails and is designed to support education and training for lifelong learning, promoted by European Commission within four areas (Table 4, Bianchi et al., 2022).

*Table 4. European Sustainability Competence Framework*

| Competence Area | Skills | Example of use |
|---|---|---|
| Embodying Sustainability Values | Valuing Sustainability | Recognizing the importance of sustainability and integrating it into daily life. |
| | Supporting Fairness | Promoting equity and justice in sustainability efforts |
| | Promoting Nature | Valuing and protecting natural ecosystems. |
| Embracing Complexity in Sustainability | Systems Thinking | Understanding the interconnectedness of social, economic, and environmental systems. |
| | Critical Thinking | Analyzing and evaluating sustainability issues from multiple perspectives |
| | Problem-Solving | Developing innovative solutions to sustainability challenges. |
| Envisioning Sustainable Futures | Futures Literacy | Imagining and planning for sustainable futures |
| | Strategic Action | Setting goals and taking actions that contribute to sustainability. |
| | Adaptability | Being flexible and responsive to changing sustainability contexts |
| Acting for Sustainability | Agency | Taking initiative and responsibility for sustainability actions |
| | Collaboration | Working with others to achieve sustainability goals. |
| | Influence | Advocating for and promoting sustainable practices |

Source: own elaboration based on QUEST, 2022

Mertens et al. (2025) mentioned, that GreenComp have to be evaluated and included into school curricula to support learning and action processes.

When the all competency frameworks were shortly presented, it is significant to mention, that all concepts were based on European Commission works. The question is, which competency frameworks could be used as an alternative to European concepts? The Table 5 below presents a suggestion for comparative concepts within competency frameworks outside the EU that align with the goals of GreenComp, LifeComp, DigiComp, and EntreComp.

*Table 5. A comparison of European and non-European concepts*

| Model | Alternatives | Main purpose | Source |
|---|---|---|---|
| EntreComp (Entrepreneurship Competence Framework) | OECD's Entrepreneurship360 | This initiative supports entrepreneurship education and training across different countries. | OECD, 2024 |
| | Entrepreneurial Learning Initiative | Focus on fostering entrepreneurial skills and mindset. | ELI, 2007 |
| DigiComp (Digital Competence Framework): | ISTE Standards | The International Society for Technology in Education (ISTE) provides standards for the use of technology in education, applicable globally. | ISTE, 2024 |
| | UNESCO's ICT Competency Framework for Teachers | This framework guides teachers in integrating ICT into their teaching practices. | UNESCO, 2018 |
| LifeComp (Personal, Social, and Learning to Learn Competence Framework) | OECD's Social and Emotional Skills Framework | This framework focuses on the development of social and emotional skills in students worldwide. | Steponavičius et al., 2023 |

continued on following page

*Table 5. Continued*

| Model | Alternatives | Main purpose | Source |
|---|---|---|---|
| | CASEL's SEL Framework | The Collaborative for Academic, Social, and Emotional Learning (CASEL) provides a widely recognized framework for social and emotional learning. | CASEL, 2020 |
| GreenComp (Green Competence Framework) | UNESCO's Education for Sustainable Development (ESD) | This framework promotes sustainable development through education and is used globally. | UNESCO, 2024 |
| | The Earth Charter | An international declaration of fundamental values and principles for building a just, sustainable, and peaceful global society. | Earth Charter, 2000 |

Source: own elaboration

These frameworks share similar goals and principles, aiming to equip individuals with the necessary skills and competencies for personal development, digital literacy, sustainability, and entrepreneurship as previous model, so it is possible to create an integrated model of sustainable skills based on previous concepts.

## UNIFIED COMPETENCE MODEL WITHIN SUSTAINABLE CONTEXT

Integrating EntreComp, LifeComp, DigComp, and GreenComp into a unified model can create a comprehensive framework for developing essential competences for personal, professional, and societal growth. By adopting systems thinking, we can develop more effective, resilient, and sustainable solutions to the complex challenges we face nowadays. We can create a comprehensive framework that equips individuals with the competences needed to thrive in a complex, interconnected world (Seiber, 2018). By this model creation we could benefit from (a) Holistic Understanding of competencies; (b) Comprehensive Solutions; (c) Long-Term Perspective; (d) Innovation and Adaptationand (e) Collaboration and Stakeholder Engagement (Whitebell, 2022).

When EntreComp is seen as general background, other sets of competencies develop main model. It could be presented in several ways as competence tree (figure 1) or learning process diagram (Figure 2).

*Figure 1. Competence tree*

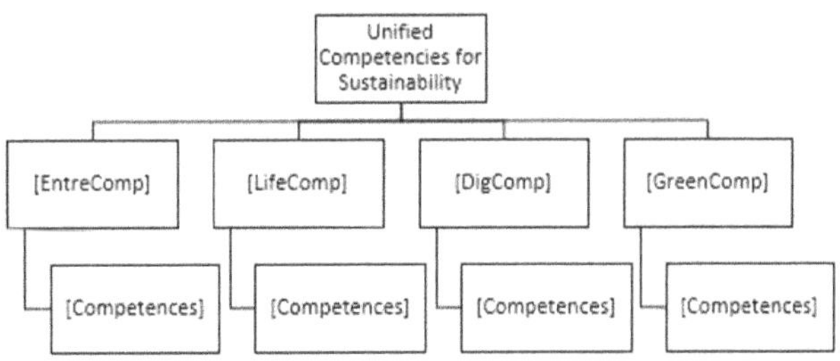


*Source: Own Elaboration*

Integrating EntreComp, LifeComp, DigComp, and GreenComp into a unified competence model significantly contributes to sustainable development by fostering a comprehensive set of skills and attitudes that promote economic, social, and environmental sustainability.

*Figure 2. Learning process diagram*

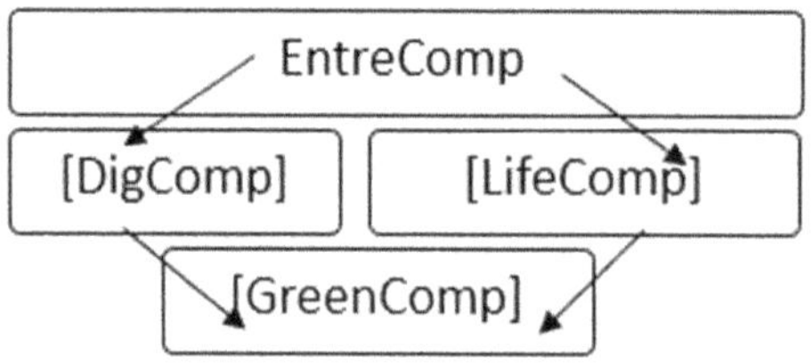


*Source: Own Elaboration*

Presenting the unified competence model graphically can help in visualizing the interconnections as could be seen in Tables 1 to 4. Suggested model covers four main areas, which have similar roots from each competency model. (see Table 6)

*Table 6. An Integrative model*

| Area | Model | Comment | Key metrics |
|---|---|---|---|
| Personal Development and Well-being | LifeComp | Focuses on self-regulation, flexibility, well-being, empathy, communication, collaboration, growth mindset, critical thinking, and managing learning | *Self-Regulation*: Number of stress management workshops attended.<br>*Flexibility*: Percentage of employees adapting to new roles or tasks.<br>*Well-being*: Employee satisfaction scores from wellness surveys |
| | GreenComp | Emphasizes valuing sustainability, supporting fairness, promoting nature, and maintaining well-being | |
| Digital Literacy and Innovation | DigComp | Covers information and data literacy, communication and collaboration, digital content creation, safety, and problem-solving | *Information and Data Literacy*: Accuracy and relevance of information retrieved for projects.<br>*Digital Content Creation*: Number of digital content pieces created and shared.<br>*Problem-Solving*: Time taken to resolve technical/non technical issues. |
| | EntreComp | Encourages creativity, vision, valuing ideas, and mobilizing resources, which are essential for digital innovation. | |
| Entrepreneurial and Strategic Action | EntreComp | Focuses on spotting opportunities, taking initiative, planning and management, coping with uncertainty, and learning through experience. | *Spotting Opportunities*: Number of new business ideas proposed.<br>*Planning and Management*: Percentage of projects completed on time and within budget.<br>*Learning through Experience*: Number of lessons learned documented after project completion. |
| | LifeComp | Supports strategic action through critical thinking, adaptability, and collaboration. | |

continued on following page

*Table 6. Continued*

| Area | Model | Comment | Key metrics |
|---|---|---|---|
| Sustainability and Ethical Thinking | GreenComp | Promotes systems thinking, critical thinking, problem-solving, futures literacy, strategic action, adaptability, agency, collaboration, and influence. | *Systems Thinking*: Number of sustainability initiatives implemented. *Strategic Action*: Reduction in carbon footprint or waste produced. *Collaboration*: Number of cross-departmental sustainability projects. |
| | EntreComp | Integrates ethical and sustainable thinking into entrepreneurial activities | |

Source: Own Elaboration

Organizations can effectively implement and benefit from a unified competence model that integrates EntreComp, LifeComp, DigComp, and GreenComp. For an integrated model combining GreenComp, LifeComp, DigiComp, and EntreCompit is possible to use a combination of followed methods, summarized within Table 7.

*Table 7. KPI and model assessment*

| Competency Area | Core competency | Assessment Method | KPI Example |
|---|---|---|---|
| GreenComp | Sustainability Awareness | Self-Assessment, Project-Based | Reduction in carbon footprint by 10% |
| LifeComp | Social Skills | 360-Degree Feedback, Behavioral Interviews | Employee satisfaction score of 80%+ |
| DigiComp | Digital Literacy | Skills Tests, Simulations | 90% of employees certified in basic ICT skills |
| EntreComp | Innovation | Project-Based Assessments, Managerial Assessment | 5 new product ideas per quarter |

Source: Own Elaboration

These integrating frameworks creates a robust and versatile competence model that equips individuals with the skills and attitudes needed to drive sustainable development across various domains such as:

**Holistic Skill Development** (Entrecomp/LifeComp/DigComp/GreenComp). This cause understanding how different components of a system interact and influence each other. Combining these frameworks provides a holistic approach to competence development, addressing personal growth, digital literacy, entrepreneurial skills, and sustainability. Especially EntreComp encourages entrepreneurial thinking, innovation, and the creation of value in a sustainable manner. It promotes ethical and sustainable decision-making, which is crucial for developing sustainable business practices. With the combination with LifeComp, which develop personal and social competences, such as empathy, collaboration, and critical thinking. These skills are essential for fostering inclusive and equitable societies, which are key components of sustainable development. On the other hand, DigComp develops digital literacy and problem-solving skills, enabling individuals to leverage technology for sustainable solutions. Digital competences are vital for addressing modern sustainability challenges, such as smart cities and digital governance. Finally, GreenComp with its focus on sustainability competences, including systems thinking, strategic action, and promoting nature. These competences empower individuals to act responsibly and advocate for sustainable practices in all areas of life.

**Promoting Innovation and Ethical Practices** (EntreComp/GreenComp). They both encourage the development of innovative solutions that are both economically viable and environmentally sustainable. This integration ensures that entrepreneurial activities contribute positively to sustainability goals.

**Enhancing Resilience and Adaptability** (LifeComp and DigComp) These frameworks help individuals develop resilience and adaptability. Skills such as flexibility, self-regulation, and digital problem-solving enable individuals to navigate and thrive in a rapidly changing world.

**Fostering Collaboration and Social Inclusion** (LifeComp and GreenComp). Emphasize the importance of collaboration, empathy, and social inclusion. These competences are essential for building inclusive communities that work together towards common sustainability goals.

**Supporting Lifelong Learning and Continuous Improvement with Sustainable Development Goals (SDGs).** (Entrecomp/LifeComp/DigComp/GreenComp). The integration promotes a culture of lifelong learning, where individuals continuously develop and refine their competences. This ongoing development is crucial for adapting to new sustainability challenges and opportunities. The unified model directly supports several SDGs, such as quality education (SDG 4), decent work and economic growth (SDG 8), reduced inequalities (SDG 10), sustainable cities and communities (SDG 11), and climate action (SDG 13).

By integrating these measurement methods and decision-making skills, organizations can effectively track and enhance their sustainability impact, contributing to a more sustainable future.

## IMPLEMENTATION AND FURTHER STEPS

The implementation of integrated skills set could help to Education, Training and professional development, because of an existence of unified model, which could be suitable for curricula and training programs to provide a well-rounded education. In a line with that, the integrated model could be helpful because it is adaptable, innovative, and sustainability-minded. Finally, is suitable for community initiatives and policy-making to promote inclusive, sustainable, and digitally literate societies.

## DISCUSSION AND CONCLUSION

Although some specialists might believe, initially, that building a green future through essential decision-making competencies might be a requirement that ought to be addressed only to specific regions or specific countries, it needs to be closely considered that all regions and all countries around the Globe have the obligation to be part of this complex process (Eberz *et al.*, 2023). First of all, the success of the competences needed for the green transition may be encountered in the manner in which individuals, communities, organizations, and governments will create those connections between the green transition and the Sustainable Development Goals (Lee *et al.*, 1994; Tasioulas *et al.*, 2025). Second of all, for this green transition, one of the major requirements is to discover those people that are willing to adapt to the new challenges, are willing to take action, and, ultimately, will not be afraid to enlarge their skill sets and competences, fulfilling their tasks with courage and dedication (Finkelstein *et al.*, 2025). Third of all, there are numerous competences needed for the green transition: some of them apply to individuals and their families; others require far more impressive efforts as well as financial support, which will lead to offering more power to communities and the leaders of these communities, but will also mean that a lot will be expected in return (Yildirim & Bostanci, 2022); in addition, these competences should be supported by strong management decisions, so that they will be enabled as expected, in a timely manner and, also, their success rate will be measurable (Özsungur, 2021); in continuation, country representatives and leaders play a vital role in this case, since sustainable success means creating the right skills for the green transition, promoting these skills, finding solutions to implement these skills and, benefiting from the implementation of these skills for many, many years to come (Xin *et al.*, 2025). It is essential these days for everyone to master the skills for a green future in order to be able to support sustainable success (Feng *et al.*, 2025). In this matter, among the major skills could be encountered the following ones, without, however, limiting them to the following elements: to begin with, a greener future includes environmental awareness, since the focus ought to be, in this case, on responsibility, social responsibility, and corporate social responsibility (Yildirim, 2022); also, a greener future refers to resource management and innovation fostering, for example, the GreenComp conceptual reference model with the twelve competences organized in the four main areas, especially since gaining green skills requires ambition, dedication, perseverance, training, and, most importantly, love for nature and the environment, in general (Hu & Wang, 2025).

Having highlighted all these, the future of work in the green transition is of great essence: the workers are expected to be equipped with the right skills; the global job market is expected to experience far-reaching challenges and be built on stronger links between education and solid assessments of the skills needed for the green transition (Swim *et al.*, 2011); the accent ought to be placed on interdisciplinary, since creating connections and relationships between different fields will draw on attitudes, knowledge, and values that will facilitate greening the future of the planet as well as foster environmentally sustainable complex decision-making processes (OECD, 2024a); and, collaboration will be also a valuable source of developing green skills, since collaboration could be part of the principles on which some projects are built at an international level or the way in which some individuals and communities would like to work together in the benefit of their children and their businesses (Chen *et al.*, 2025). What is more, resource-efficient and sustainable society may have at its core "green life skills" for a sustainable future but, also, it might need solid data on which to base the future decisions in order to ensure the success of the decisions taken. Furthermore, in this matter, that is exactly the reason why building a sustainable future relies on essential green skills for individuals and organizations, focusing on: collecting, analyzing, and interpreting data in order to be able to establish which the green competences are needed at one moment; discovering the environmental impact of informed decisions, having as basis knowledge and well-equipped learners with green competences; revising the curricula to address emerging priorities in education is a must these days, especially in the context in which these skills for a just transition to a green future are needed; addressing the effectiveness of programs and policies in this matter is, also, highly expected, especially when the accent falls on transferable skills that are used in many occupations (Bayliss *et al.*, 2025).

In this day and age, the skills for a green transition address, additionally, the highly sensible case of migration and, in particular, the youth on the move. Hence, these situations could explore the manner in which green skills and sustainability could drive business growth, creativity, innovation, knowledge, and long-term success while being supported by teamwork, leadership, risk management, design, and communication (Lin *et al.*, 2025). Nevertheless, by learning new skills and improving the capacity to detect potentially successful opportunities is not necessarily something expected only from the youth, since green skills should not only apply and address to young people, they should take into account all individuals and, additionally, they all should develop a stronger entrepreneurial movement that would resonate with everyone and that should lead to shaping a more equitable, inclusive, and sustainable future (Sulaiman, 2025).

When thinking about the green mobility revolution, one might have in mind the way in which sustainable travelling could have an effect on students becoming more responsible and resilient, while others might come to the conclusion that curiosity, well-designed and comprehensive thoughts, and critical thinking skills will be enhanced as a result of such complex experiences (Fuady *et al.*, 2025).

Besides all the aforementioned ideas, new elements should also be considered, as follows: identifying and exploring green competences for individuals – particularly the ones employed, will ultimately have the power to enable these people to perform at their places of work while displaying an ecological behavior and making use of their green competences required at the places of work; moreover, productivity and employment growth could be increased by simply improving the individuals the skills for green jobs, hence motivating people to become more and more aware of their behavior and their impact on everything they do on a day-to-day basis; furthermore, by making use of digital guides on sustainable career choices, green industries could begin to thrive (Özsungur, 2024; Liu *et al.*, 2025).

In the end, these green competences may not only apply at the places of work, they could very well be extremely useful in other circumstances, such as, for example, when willing to use the land more sustainably, when creating new habitats for wildlife, when plating more trees, and when supporting the development of native species (Kuo *et al.*, 2025; Miles-Novelo & Anderson, 2023). Another vital example could be encountered in the case of countries' green buildings strategy, which could start from identifying a crucial set of green competences and skills due to be used as reference and which could end up by building new green home or investing in energy efficiency programs and projects (Özsungur, 2025a; Özsungur, 2025b; Bostancı & Yıldırım, 2021). Additionally, the aspects mentioned in the lines above could be supported by reducing energy usage or by energy bills, which could be the result of individuals and communities accessing the green skills programs that will make them more aware of the importance of their actions and decisions, going far more than their work, hence, moving into their homes and other pivotal areas of their lives (Bostancı & Yıldırım, 2022; Kumpiw *et al.*, 2025).

There are several studies that have come to support these findings, which can only lead to the conclusion that there is a growing need for dedicated and skilled individuals able to seek green jobs, but, in the same time, focus on greening the lives that are currently lived as well as the communities that expect support and understanding in this matter (OECD, 2024b; OECD, 2025).

All in all, the question why there is the need for digital skills for a green future might surprise by the number of answers that could generate when asked. The exact same case would be when wondering, for instance, what will the purpose of green industrial skills for a sustainable future. The number of answers as well as the diversity of ideas when analyzing these questions would most likely be enormous. Moving even more closely to the connections that could be made between the skills for a green future and the relationships with the green economy, the following aspects ought to be brought to light: the digital skills for a green future are expected to make the world cleaner, greener, and more sustainable; these digital skills for a green future are extremely powerful for the green economy, so they are vital in supporting the emerging green sectors, while offering the opportunity to the individuals and to the businesses to skill and reskill depending on the circumstances; and, also, social and green enterprises can make a very powerful impact on the future, ensuring a green future based on making the right environmental and career decisions.

## Conflicts of Interest

All authors declare that they have no conflicts of interest.

## ACKNOWLEDGMENT

This research received no specific grant from any funding agency in the public, commercial, or not-for-profit sectors. Author Contributions: Conceptualization, Jarmila Duháček Šebestová (J.D.S.) and C.R.G.P. (Cristina Raluca Gh. Popescu); methodology, J.D.S. and C.R.G.P.; software, J.D.S. and C.R.G.P.; validation, J.D.S. and C.R.G.P.; formal analysis, J.D.S. and C.R.G.P.; investigation, J.D.S. and C.R.G.P.; resources, J.D.S. and C.R.G.P.; data curation, J.D.S. and C.R.G.P.; writing—original draft preparation, J.D.S. and C.R.G.P.; writing—review and editing, J.D.S. and C.R.G.P.; visualization, J.D.S. and C.R.G.P.; supervision, J.D.S. and C.R.G.P.; project administration, J.D.S. and C.R.G.P.; funding acquisition, J.D.S. and C.R.G.P. All authors have equally contributed to the manuscript. All authors have read and agreed to the published version of the manuscript.

## REFERENCES

Aldosemani, T., Lytras, M. D., & Ordóñez de Pablos, P. (Eds.). (2025). *Innovative Educational Frameworks for Future Skills and Competencies*. IGI Global., DOI: 10.4018/979-8-3693-7555-6

AlHashmi, M. H., Khan, M. M., & Ajmal, M. M. (2021). Implementing Sustainable Procurement Strategy in the Oil and Gas Sector: Analytic Hierarchy Process Approach. [IJSSMET]. *International Journal of Service Science, Management, Engineering, and Technology*, *12*(2), 59–77. DOI: 10.4018/IJSSMET.2021030104

Armacanqui, J. S., Nash, S. S., Eyzaguirre Gormendia, L., & Moghanloo, R. (Eds.). (2024). *Sustainability Applied to Unconventional Oil and Gas Field Exploration and Development*. IGI Global., DOI: 10.4018/979-8-3693-0740-3

Asrin, F., Saide, S., & Ratna, S. (2021). Data to Knowledge-Based Transformation: The Association Rules With Rapid Miner Approach and Predictive Analysis in Evergreen IT-Business Routines of PT Chevron Pacific Indonesia. [IJSKD]. *International Journal of Sociotechnology and Knowledge Development*, *13*(4), 141–152. DOI: 10.4018/IJSKD.2021100109

Assyne, N. (2022). Towards a Security Competence of Software Developers: A Literature Review. In I. Management Association (Ed.), *Research Anthology on Agile Software, Software Development, and Testing* (pp. 2050-2064). IGI Global Scientific Publishing. DOI: 10.4018/978-1-6684-3702-5.ch098

Bacigalupo M, Kampylis P, Punie Y and Van Den Brande L. (2016) EntreComp: The Entrepreneurship Competence Framework. EUR 27939 EN. Luxembourg (Luxembourg): Publications Office of the European Union. JRC101581.

Bahl, A. S. (2021). Topical Use of Plant Extract-Based Oil Blend in Relieving the Symptoms of Primary Dysmenorrhea: An Independent Clinical Study. [IJHSTM]. *International Journal of Health Systems and Translational Medicine*, *1*(1), 47–61. DOI: 10.4018/IJHSTM.2021010102

Bayliss, C., Ouelhadj, D., Dadashzadeh, N., & Fletcher, G. (2025). Mobility-as-a-Service Personalised Multi-Modal Multi-Objective Journey Planning with Machine-Learning-Guided Shortest-Path Algorithms. *Applied Sciences (Basel, Switzerland)*, *15*(4), 2052. DOI: 10.3390/app15042052

Berggren, E., & Worth, A. (2023). Towards a future regulatory framework for chemicals in the European Union – Chemicals 2.0, REGULATORY TOXICOLOGY AND PHARMACOLOGY, ISSN 0273-2300, 142, p. 105431, JRC132966.

Bianchi, G., Pisiotis, U., & Cabrera Giraldez, M. GreenComp The European sustainability competence framework, Punie, Y. and Bacigalupo, M. editor(s). (2022). EUR 30955 EN, Publications Office of the European Union, Luxembourg, ISBN 978-92-76-46485-3, , JRC128040.DOI: 10.2760/13286

Boguslawski, R., Van Gansen, K., Valayer, C., Borzacchiello, M., & Pignatelli, F. (2017). European Union Location Framework Blueprint, EUR 28931 EN, Publications Office of the European Union, Luxembourg, ISBN 978-92-79-77060-9 (online),978-92-79-86359-2 (ePub), (online), (ePub), JRC108216. DOI: 10.2760/975822

Borja A, Elliott M, Carstensensen J, Heiskanen A, Van De Bund W. (2010). Marine Management - Towards an Integrated Implementation of the European Marine Strategy Framework and the Water Framework Directives. MARINE POLLUTION BULLETIN 60 (12). p. 2175-2186. JRC60639.

Bostancı, S. H., & Yıldırım, S. (2021). Sustainable Communities vs. Climate Refugees: Two Opposite Results of Climate Change. In Popescu, C. (Ed.), *Handbook of Research on Novel Practices and Current Successes in Achieving the Sustainable Development Goals* (pp. 298–319). IGI Global Scientific Publishing., DOI: 10.4018/978-1-7998-8426-2.ch015

Bostancı, S. H., & Yıldırım, S. (2022). The Role of Municipalities in Achieving Water Security: The Case of Turkey. In Castanho, R. (Ed.), *Handbook of Research on Sustainable Development Goals, Climate Change, and Digitalization* (pp. 268–286). IGI Global Scientific Publishing., DOI: 10.4018/978-1-7998-8482-8.ch017

Bubevski, V. (2025). *Oil and Gas Risk Assessment and Management: Emerging Research and Opportunities*. IGI Global., DOI: 10.4018/979-8-3373-0959-0

Cacciamani, S., & Fujita, N. (2023). Promoting Life Competences in the Knowledge Society: The Contribution of Knowledge Building Model for Educational Systems. [S]. *Interaction Design & Architecture*, (57), 27–46. DOI: 10.55612/s-5002-057-002

Caena, F., & Redecker, C. (2019). Aligning teacher competence frameworks to 21st century challenges: The case for the European Digital Competence Framework for Educators (DIGCOMPEDU), EUROPEAN JOURNAL OF EDUCATION, ISSN 0141-8211, 54 (3), p. 356-369, JRC117352.

Carretero Gomez, S., Vuorikari, R., & Punie, Y. (2017). DigComp 2.1: The Digital Competence Framework for Citizens with eight proficiency levels and examples of use, EUR 28558 EN, Publications Office of the European Union, Luxembourg. ISBN 978-92-79-68006-9 (pdf),978-92-79-68005-2 (print),978-92-79-74173-9 (ePub), (online), (print), (ePub), JRC106281.DOI: 10.2760/38842

Cartelli, A. (Ed.). (2012). *Current Trends and Future Practices for Digital Literacy and Competence*. IGI Global., DOI: 10.4018/978-1-4666-0903-7

CASEL. (2020). CASEL'S SEL Framework. https://casel.org/casel-sel-framework-11-2020/

Chen, Y., Zhang, J., Wang, F., Zhang, J., Wu, W., & Li, H. (2025). Study on Carbon Emission Reduction Strategy of CCUS Technology in Natural Gas Supply Chain Considering Government Subsidies. *Processes (Basel, Switzerland)*, *13*(2), 550. DOI: 10.3390/pr13020550

Chenchouni, L., Kheder, M. K., & Chenchouni, H. (2022). When the Blessed Resource "Oil" Curses: Environmental Degradation Related to Oil Exploration Fueling Socio-Political Conflicts. [IJSESD]. *International Journal of Social Ecology and Sustainable Development*, *13*(1), 1–17. DOI: 10.4018/IJSESD.292076

Cleveland, S., & Hinojosa, C. (2019). Complexity Framework for the Project Management Curriculum. [IJITPM]. *International Journal of Information Technology Project Management*, *10*(1), 34–54. DOI: 10.4018/IJITPM.2019010103

Danailova, I. (2024). The implementation of DigComp (European Digital Skills Framework) for digital competence assessment and evaluation. *Nauchni trudove*, (1), 87-125.

David, K. G., Wu, Y., & Pei, C. (2022). Openness to Innovation as a Driver of Knowledge Integration in High-Tech SMEs: The Roles of Social Capital and Network Competence. [IJKM]. *International Journal of Knowledge Management*, *18*(1), 1–21. DOI: 10.4018/IJKM.291102

Earth Charter. (2000). The Earth Charter. https://earthcharter.org/read-the-earth-charter/preamble/

Eberz, S., Lang, S., Breitenmoser, P., & Niebert, K. (2023). Taking the Lead into Sustainability: Decision Makers' Competencies for a Greener Future. *Sustainability (Basel)*, *15*(6), 4986. DOI: 10.3390/su15064986

Eimler, S. C., & Straßmann, C. (2023). Future Proof: Hackathons as Occasions to Experience Entrepreneurial Thinking. *Progress in Entrepreneurship Education and Training: New Methods, Tools, and Lessons Learned from Practice*, 417-429.

Eklund, L. G., Sibilia, A., Salvi, A., Antofie, T., Rodomonti, D., Salari, S., Poljansek, K., Marzi, S., Gyenes, Z., & Corban, C. (2023). Towards a European wide vulnerability framework. *Publications Office of the European Union, Luxembourg, JRC118850*. Advance online publication. DOI: 10.2760/353889

ELI. (2007). Entrepreneurial Learning Initiative. https://elimindset.com/about/history/

Faller, R. J. (2024). From Working Groups on Facebook to Online Shopping by WhatsApp: Mobilizations From Communication to Development. [IJDLDC]. *International Journal of Digital Literacy and Digital Competence*, *15*(1), 1–17. DOI: 10.4018/IJDLDC.359338

Feng, Y., Feng, Y., & Liu, Z. (2025). Normative Influences on Carbon Offset Behavior: Insights from Organic Farming Practices. *Sustainability (Basel)*, *17*(4), 1638. DOI: 10.3390/su17041638

Finkelstein, A., Budd, M. A., Gray, B. E., Mirsky, J., Tirosh, A., & Polak, R. (2025). Personalized Culinary Medicine: Qualitative Analyses of Perceptions from Participants in Action and Contemplation Stages of Change Through a One-Year Bi-Center Randomized Controlled Trial. *Nutrients*, *17*(4), 704. DOI: 10.3390/nu17040704 PMID: 40005034

Frolovičeva, V. (2023). Multidimensionality of Digital Research in Educational Science. [IJDLDC]. *International Journal of Digital Literacy and Digital Competence*, *14*(1), 1–17. DOI: 10.4018/IJDLDC.335853

Fuady, M., Buraida, , Kevin, M. A., Farrel, M. R., & Triaputri, A. (1632). Buraida, Kevin, M. A., Farrel, M. R., & Triaputri, A. (2025). Enhancing Urban Resilience: Opportunities and Challenges in Adapting to Natural Disasters in Indonesian Cities. *Sustainability (Basel)*, *17*(4), 1632. Advance online publication. DOI: 10.3390/su17041632

Garavaglia, A., Petti, L., & Triacca, S. (2021, October). Integration of LifeComp and DigComp 2.2 as a Theoretical Framework for Media Education. In *ATEE Spring Conference* (pp. 59-70). Cham: Springer International Publishing.

Hammoda, B. (2022). Mapping Digital Technologies Used in Entrepreneurship Education against the Competences They Develop Using Entrecomp Framework as a Reference: A Systematic Literature Review. *INTED2022 Proceedings*, 5489-5498.

Hardy Bednar, D., & Godkin, L. (2009). An Exploratory, Longitudinal Study of Factors Influencing Development of a Networked Company. [IRMJ]. *Information Resources Management Journal*, *22*(3), 59–72. DOI: 10.4018/irmj.2009070104

Heller-Schuh B, Barber M, Henriques L, Paier M, Pontikakis D, Scherngell T, Veltri G, Weber M. (2011). Analysis of Networks in European Framework Programmes (1984-2006). EUR 24759 EN. Luxembourg (Luxembourg): Publications Office of the European Union. JRC63467.

Hu, Z., & Wang, S. (2025). Multi-Scenario Simulation of Ecosystem Service Value in Beijing's Green Belts Based on PLUS Model. *Land (Basel)*, *14*(2), 408. DOI: 10.3390/land14020408

ISTE. (2024). ISTE Standards. https://cms-live-media.iste.org/ISTE*STANDARDS*2024.pdf

Joensuu-Salo, S., Viljamaa, A., & Varamäki, E. (2022). Testing the EntreComp framework and its relation to start-up behaviour in seven European countries. *Journal of Small Business and Enterprise Development*, *29*(6), 920–939. DOI: 10.1108/JSBED-04-2021-0156

Khan, F., & Vuopala, E. (2019). Digital Competence Assessment Across Generations: A Finnish Sample Using the Digcomp Framework. [IJDLDC]. *International Journal of Digital Literacy and Digital Competence*, *10*(2), 15–28. DOI: 10.4018/IJDLDC.2019040102

Kumpiw, W., Damrongsak, D., Jaitiang, T., Wongsapai, W., Sangkakorn, K., Daroon, S., Khiaolek, K., Srichai, P., Auttarat, S., Krajangchom, S., & Chinachan, T. (2025). Performance Tracking of Sustainable Tourism Goal (STG) Criteria for Achieving Thailand's Greenhouse Gas Mitigation Targets in the Service Sector: A Case Study of Large Thai Hotels. *Sustainability (Basel)*, *17*(4), 1635. DOI: 10.3390/su17041635

Kuo, C.-C., Lin, G.-F., Farooqui, A., Huang, S.-H., & Tseng, S.-F. (2025). Development of a Next-Generation Cooling Channel Technology with High Cooling Efficiency by Roughing Cooling Channels Using a Combination of Laser Machining and Embossing Techniques. *Micromachines*, *16*(2), 225. DOI: 10.3390/mi16020225 PMID: 40047667

Lee, H., Oliveira Martins, J., & van der Mensbrugghe, D. (1994). "The OECD Green Model: An Updated Overview", *OECD Development Centre Working Papers*, No. 97, OECD Publishing, Paris, https://doi.org/DOI: 10.1787/18151949

Lee, S. (2020). Pedagogical Foci of Teaching Cantonese as a Second Language: From Linguistic Competence to Pragmatic Use. [IJCDLM]. *International Journal of Curriculum Development and Learning Measurement*, *1*(1), 1–10. DOI: 10.4018/IJCDLM.2020010101

Leger, M., Valverde, R., & Gagnon, S. (2019). An Innovative Framework to Integrate CIO Competencies Within the Business Technology Management Body of Knowledge. [IJOCI]. *International Journal of Organizational and Collective Intelligence*, *9*(3), 1–18. DOI: 10.4018/IJOCI.2019070101

Lin, S., Zhu, H., Liu, J., Li, F., & Zheng, C. (2025). Why Do Tourists Visit the Food Market? A Host–Guest Sharing Model Based on the Theory of Self-Regulation. *Land (Basel)*, *14*(2), 407. DOI: 10.3390/land14020407

Liu, Y., Zhang, M., Zhao, Y., Wei, J., Zhou, S., & Shi, X. (2025). Effect of Environmental Factors on Grassland Biodiversity and Biomass in the Zhangye Region. *Agronomy (Basel)*, *15*(2), 476. DOI: 10.3390/agronomy15020476

López-Núñez, M. I., Rubio-Valdehita, S., Armuña, C., & Pérez-Urria, E. (2022). EntreComp questionnaire: A self-assessment tool for entrepreneurship competencies. *Sustainability (Basel)*, *14*(5), 2983. DOI: 10.3390/su14052983

Martzog, P., Hoyer, S., & Kuttner, S. (2021). Student Teachers' Uncertainty Competence and Its Measurement. [IJTEPD]. *International Journal of Teacher Education and Professional Development*, *4*(2), 50–65. DOI: 10.4018/IJTEPD.2021070104

Mattar, J., Ramos, D. K., & Lucas, M. R. (2022). DigComp-based digital competence assessment tools: Literature review and instrument analysis. *Education and Information Technologies*, *27*(8), 10843–10867. DOI: 10.1007/s10639-022-11034-3

McCallum, E., Weicht, R., McMullan, L., & Price, A. (2018). EntreComp into Action: get inspired, make it happen (M. Bacigalupo & W. O'Keeffe Eds.), EUR 29105 EN, Publications Office of the European Union, Luxembourg. , JRC109128DOI: 10.2760/574864

Mertens, A., Eppinga, M. B., Arens, P., de Scisciolo, T., John, N., Sultan, S., Buys, N., & Mijts, E. N. (2025). The GreenComp Evaluation Roadmap: a roadmap for in-depth holistic evaluation of the integration of the GreenComp framework in higher-education curricula. International Journal of Sustainability in Higher Education, Vol. ahead-of-print No. ahead-of-print. DOI: 10.1108/IJSHE-02-2024-0119

Miles-Novelo, A., & Anderson, C. A. (2023). Avoiding a grim future: The climate crisis and its effects on human aggression and violence. *Advances in Environmental and Engineering Research, vol. 4*, issue 2. https://www.mendeley.com/catalogue/b2614e57-4a7c-310a-bae1-2a894491697f/ OR Link.

Molina, G. J., Onyejizu, E. F., Morrison, J. L., & Soloiu, V. (2020). Surface Effects on Engine Materials of Mineral Oil Dilution With Methyl Esters and Biodiesels. [IJSEIMS]. *International Journal of Surface Engineering and Interdisciplinary Materials Science*, *8*(2), 1–18. DOI: 10.4018/IJSEIMS.2020070101

Neal, J., & Neal, B. L. (2019). *Workforce Education at Oil and Gas Companies in the Permian Basin: Emerging Research and Opportunities*. IGI Global., DOI: 10.4018/978-1-5225-8464-3

Ngai, P. B. (2021). Discourse Analysis for Intercultural Competence Development. [IJBIDE]. *International Journal of Bias, Identity and Diversities in Education*, *6*(1), 17–30. DOI: 10.4018/IJBIDE.2021010102

OECD. (2024). Entrepreneurship 360. https://www.oecd.org/en/about/programmes/skills-for-smes-and-entrepreneurs/entrepreneurship-360.html

OECD. (2024a). Training Supply for the Green and AI Transitions: Equipping Workers with the Right Skills, Getting Skills Right, OECD Publishing, Paris, https://doi.org/DOI: 10.1787/7600d16d-en

OECD. (2024b). Policies for a plastic pollution-free future by 2040. Green Talks LIVE. Retrieved online from https://www.oecd.org/en/events/2024/10/policy-scenarios-for-eliminating-plastic-pollution-by-2040.html. Accessed on the 16th of February 2025.

OECD. (2025). *Empowered Citizens, Informed Consumers and Skilled Workers: Designing Education and Skills Policies for a Sustainable Future*. OECD Publishing., DOI: 10.1787/311cdbeb-

Olesika, A., Lama, G., & Rubene, Z. (2021). Conceptualization of Digital Competence: Perspectives From Higher Education. [IJSEUS]. *International Journal of Smart Education and Urban Society*, *12*(2), 46–59. DOI: 10.4018/IJSEUS.2021040105

Olszewski, S. (2024). *Reaching Professional Competence*. IGI Global., DOI: 10.4018/978-1-6684-8607-8.ch004

Özsungur, F. (Ed.). (2021). *Handbook of Research on Policies, Protocols, and Practices for Social Work in the Digital World*. IGI Global., DOI: 10.4018/978-1-7998-7772-1

Özsungur, F. (Ed.). (2024). *Empowering Entrepreneurial Mindsets With AI*. IGI Global., DOI: 10.4018/979-8-3693-7658-4

Özsungur, F. (Ed.). (2025a). *Navigating Organizational Behavior in the Digital Age With AI*. IGI Global., DOI: 10.4018/979-8-3693-8442-8

Özsungur, F. (Ed.). (2025b). *Nexus of AI, Climatology, and Urbanism for Smart Cities*. IGI Global., DOI: 10.4018/979-8-3693-5918-1

Peraza, A. V., & Furumura, Y. (2022). Project-Based Learning to Develop Intercultural Communicative Competence in Virtual Exchange Contexts. [IJCALLT]. *International Journal of Computer-Assisted Language Learning and Teaching*, *12*(3), 1–17. DOI: 10.4018/IJCALLT.307059

Phan, T. C., Le, P. A., Phan, T. M., Hoang, L. P., Le, H. T., Ngo, T. T., Nguyen, D. T., & Van Tran, H. (2021). Identifying and Applying the Information Technology Competence Framework in an Online Teaching Environment. In Dhir, H. (Ed.), *Handbook of Research on Barriers for Teaching 21st-Century Competencies and the Impact of Digitalization* (pp. 356–382). IGI Global Scientific Publishing., DOI: 10.4018/978-1-7998-6967-2.ch019

Popescu, C. R. G. (2021). Measuring Progress Towards the Sustainable Development Goals: Creativity, Intellectual Capital, and Innovation. In Popescu, C. (Ed.), *Handbook of Research on Novel Practices and Current Successes in Achieving the Sustainable Development Goals* (pp. 125–136). IGI Global Scientific Publishing., DOI: 10.4018/978-1-7998-8426-2.ch006

Popescu, C. R. G., & Popescu, G. N. (2025). The Power of Data Analysis in Transforming Businesses Performance: Improved Decision-Making, Real-World Applications, and the Sustainable Development Goals. In Popescu, C. (Ed.), *Building Inclusive Global Knowledge Societies for Sustainable Development* (pp. 169–208). IGI Global Scientific Publishing., DOI: 10.4018/979-8-3693-6298-3.ch008

Popescu, C. R. G., & Verma, R. R. (2025). Evolving Towards Topics on Sustainable Development Goals: Research and Innovation Projects in Education for Inclusive Global Knowledge Societies. In Popescu, C. (Ed.), *Building Inclusive Global Knowledge Societies for Sustainable Development* (pp. 43–64). IGI Global Scientific Publishing., DOI: 10.4018/979-8-3693-6298-3.ch003

Punie, Y., & Redecker, C. (Eds.). (s). (2017). European Framework for the Digital Competence of Educators: DigCompEdu, EUR 28775 EN, Publications Office of the European Union, Luxembourg. ISBN 978-92-79-73718-3 (print),978-92-79-73494-6 (pdf), (print), (online), JRC107466.DOI: 10.2760/178382

Rondon, B. (2021). Experimental Characterization of Admittance Meter With Crude Oil Emulsions. [IJECME]. *International Journal of Electronics, Communications, and Measurement Engineering*, *10*(2), 51–59. DOI: 10.4018/IJECME.2021070104

Sala, A., & Herrero Ramila, C. (2022). LifeComp into Action: Teaching life skills in the classroom and beyond, EUR 31141 EN, Publications Office of the European Union, Luxembourg, ISBN 978-92-76-54524-8, , JRC130003.DOI: 10.2760/22023

Sala, A., Punie, Y., Garkov, V., & Cabrera Giraldez, M. (2020). LifeComp: The European Framework for Personal, Social and Learning to Learn Key Competence, EUR 30246 EN, Publications Office of the European Union, Luxembourg, ISBN 978-92-76-19417-0, , JRC120911.DOI: 10.2760/922681

Scalabrino, C. (2022). European sustainability competence framework background document, Publications Office of the European Union, Luxembourg. ISBN 978-92-76-57357-9, , JRC130849.DOI: 10.2760/378627

Seiber, M. (2018). Systems Thinking and How It Can Help Build a Sustainable World: A Beginning Conversation. https://thesolutionsjournal.com/systems-thinking-can-help-build-sustainable-world-beginning-conversation/

Smith, E. C. (2019). Developing Cultural Competence: Challenges and Best Practices in Higher Education. [IJMSE]. *International Journal of Marketing and Sales Education*, *2*(2), 1–17. DOI: 10.4018/IJMSE.2019070101

Soler, K. M., Baltasar, L. B., Díaz, C. K., & González, M. L. (2021). Happiness: An Approach to Labor Competence. In R. Perez-Uribe, D. Ocampo-Guzman, N. Moreno-Monsalve, & W. Fajardo-Moreno (Eds.), *Handbook of Research on Management Techniques and Sustainability Strategies for Handling Disruptive Situations in Corporate Settings* (pp. 342-354). IGI Global Scientific Publishing. DOI: 10.4018/978-1-7998-8185-8.ch016

Stahl, D. (2021). LifeComp: Competences for life and learning in times of transition. https://epale.ec.europa.eu/en/blog/lifecomp-competences-life-and-learning-times-transition

Steponavičius, M., Gress-Wright, C., & Linzarini, A. (2023). Social and emotional skills: Latest evidence on teachability and impact on life outcomes. OECD Education Working Papers, No. 304, OECD Publishing, Paris. DOI: 10.1787/19939019

Sulaiman, M. A. B. A. (2025). Green Product Innovation as a Mediator Between Green Market Orientation and Sustainable Performance of SMEs. *Sustainability (Basel), 17*(4), 1628. DOI: 10.3390/su17041628

Swim, J. K., Stern, P. C., Doherty, T. J., Clayton, S., Reser, J. P., Weber, E. U., Gifford, R., & Howard, G. S. (2011). Psychology's contributions to understanding and addressing global climate change. *The American Psychologist*, *66*(4), 241–250. DOI: 10.1037/a0023220 PMID: 21553950

Tan, S. C., Chan, C., Bielaczyc, K., Ma, L., Scardamalia, M., & Bereiter, C. (2021). Knowledge building: Aligning education with needs for knowledge creation in the digital age. *Educational Technology Research and Development*, *69*(4), 2243–2266. DOI: 10.1007/s11423-020-09914-x

Tasioulas, S., Watson, J., Kasampalis, D. S., & Tsouvaltzis, P. (2025). Integration of Color Analysis, Firmness Testing, and visNIR Spectroscopy for Comprehensive Tomato Quality Assessment and Shelf-Life Prediction. *Agronomy (Basel), 15*(2), 478. DOI: 10.3390/agronomy15020478

Todino, M. D., Campitiello, L., & Di Tore, S. (2023). Simplexity to Improve Human-Machine Interaction in 3D Virtual Reality. [IJDLDC]. *International Journal of Digital Literacy and Digital Competence*, *14*(1), 1–8. DOI: 10.4018/IJDLDC.330423

Tsionis G. (2015). European building inventory framework. EUR 27603. Luxembourg (Luxembourg): Publications Office of the European Union. JRC98981.

UNESCO. (2018). UNESCO's ICT Competency Framework for Teachers. https://www.unesco.org/en/digital-competencies-skills/ict-cft

UNESCO. (2024). UNESCO's Education for Sustainable Development (ESD). https://www.unesco.org/en/sustainable-development/education

Vuorikari, R., Kluzer, S., & Punie, Y. (2022). DigComp 2.2: The Digital Competence Framework for Citizens - With new examples of knowledge, skills and attitudes, EUR 31006 EN, Publications Office of the European Union, Luxembourg. ISBN 978-92-76-48883-5, , JRC128415.DOI: 10.2760/490274

Wang, X., Quirke, M., & McGuckin, C. (2022). The Importance of Social Competence for 21st Century Citizens: The Use of Mixed Reality for Social Competence Learning in Mainstream Education. In Correia, A., & Viegas, V. (Eds.), *Methodologies and Use Cases on Extended Reality for Training and Education* (pp. 242–268). IGI Global Scientific Publishing., DOI: 10.4018/978-1-6684-3398-0.ch010

Whitebell. (2022). Sustainability is all about systems-thinking—here's why. https://www.rit.edu/sustainabilityinstitute/blog/sustainability-all-about-systems-thinking-heres-why

Xin, X., Li, P., Tang, L., & Xu, A. (2025). Entrepreneurship and Education: An Analysis of the Impact of Compulsory Education Policies in Counties in China. *Sustainability (Basel), 17*(4), 1639. DOI: 10.3390/su17041639

Yildirim, S. (2022). The Consumer Role for Sustainable Development: How Consumers Contribute Sustainable Development Goals. In I. Management Association (Ed.), *Research Anthology on Measuring and Achieving Sustainable Development Goals* (pp. 872-888). IGI Global Scientific Publishing. https://doi.org/DOI: 10.4018/978-1-6684-3885-5.ch047

Yildirim, S., & Bostanci, S. H. (2022). Digital Transformation in Public Services: A Review of Turkey During the COVID-19 Pandemic. In Marchisio, E. (Ed.), *Handbook of Research on Applying Emerging Technologies Across Multiple Disciplines* (pp. 30–54). IGI Global Scientific Publishing., DOI: 10.4018/978-1-7998-8476-7.ch003

# Chapter 2
# Advancements in Intelligent Traffic Monitoring System Design for Smart Urban Infrastructure

**R. Arun Chakravarthy**
https://orcid.org/0000-0002-3505-2447
*KGiSL Institute of Technology, India*

**C. Sureshkumar**
https://orcid.org/0000-0003-4287-2096
*KGiSL Institute of Technology, India*

**M. Arun**
https://orcid.org/0009-0009-4512-609X
*KGiSL Instiute of Technology, India*

**R. S. Ranjani Shree**
https://orcid.org/0009-0001-7092-5856
*KGiSL Institute of Technology, India*

## ABSTRACT

*The rise of urbanization drives the demand for intelligent traffic monitoring systems, integrating computer vision, machine learning, and real-time data processing for smart urban infrastructure. By leveraging sensors, MEMS (Microelectromechanical systems), and wireless communication networks, modern traffic systems are capable of dynamically adapting to varying traffic conditions, optimizing traffic flow, and improving overall road safety. The intelligent traffic monitoring system (ITMS) integrates vehicle detection, real-time traffic data analysis, and adaptive control mechanisms to minimize congestion and reduce emissions. Here, it explores the use of machine learning algorithms to predict traffic patterns and pedestrian behavior, contributing to a more sustainable and efficient urban mobility network. These advancements offer scalable, cost-effective solutions for cities aiming to reduce traffic bottlenecks and enhance public safety, ultimately supporting the vision of smart and sustainable urban environments.*

DOI: 10.4018/979-8-3373-0189-1.ch002

## 1. INTRODUCTION

An overview of the latest advancements in traffic monitoring systems, with a focus on the key features of traffic classification is given in this chapter. It discusses various vehicle distribution systems, research topics, technical challenges, and the hardware/software design and implementation experiences associated with these systems. Additionally, the article delves into system performance evaluation and highlights pertinent open questions and future research directions. The aim is to provide academia, industry professionals, and government agencies with valuable insights for selecting appropriate technologies to enhance traffic management operations. Presently, there is a global surge in vehicular traffic, leading many nations to grapple with traffic issues, including frequent accidents involving emergency vehicles and other traffic. This study aims to devise an intelligent traffic signal control system capable of dynamically adjusting to evolving traffic patterns. Its objectives are to alleviate congestion and minimize wait times for all road users. The envisioned system integrates sophisticated sensor technology, machine learning algorithms, and real-time data analysis to achieve these goals. The integration of these elements allows traffic signal systems to collect and process information from the surrounding environment and make informed signal timing decisions. Machine learning algorithms predict traffic patterns and optimize signal cycles accordingly, leading to efficient traffic management. The survey outlines the specifics of each vehicle classification system. These systems are generally categorized into three classes based on their deployment location: roadway-based, on-road, and off-road systems. Further categorization of vehicle classification systems is based on sensor types and the utilization of sensor data for classification purposes.

Roadway-based vehicle classification systems employ sensors either on or beneath the road surface. Various sensor types are utilized in on-road vehicle classification systems, including piezoelectric sensors, magnetometers, vibration sensors, and loop detectors. These sensors extract diverse information from vehicle data, such as vehicle length, axle count, and distinct signal or waveform characteristics, effectively capturing the vehicle's physical attributes and movement patterns. However, a major drawback of this approach is the significant installation and maintenance costs, as the road must be cut to install sensors beneath the surface. Congestion on road networks manifests in lower speeds, extended travel times, and increased traffic switching. A common scenario is the physical use of roads by vehicles, where traffic congestion arises as vehicles interact, slowing down traffic flow. Extreme congestion occurs as road capacity, or the capacity at junctions along the road approaches its limit. When vehicles come to a complete halt for a prolonged period, it is termed a traffic jam.

They focus on implementing an efficient and adaptable traffic management system for two-lane roundabouts. Given the high incidence of traffic accidents at intersections, this approach to road traffic control offers greater convenience and effectiveness. An effective traffic management system is essential for this purpose. Automatic steering and traffic monitoring play crucial roles in this endeavor. Another approach involves the use of electronic sensors, as discussed by Chandrasekhar et al., which can detect vehicles and generate signals Additionally, the system has adaptive features to accommodate emergency vehicles, pedestrians, and non-motorized transportation. In particular, the cost of building additional facilities to ensure the safety of construction workers and maintain traffic flow during construction would be prohibitive. The goal is to create a comprehensive and responsive traffic signal system that not only prioritizes safety but also increases the overall efficiency of urban transportation networks. Possible problems caused by traffic congestion are:

1) Heavy traffic congestion,
2) Need to wait even when there is no traffic,
3) Emergency vehicles stuck in traffic, and
4) Lack of traffic information for users.

*Figure 1. Block diagram of an intelligent traffic control system using PLC*

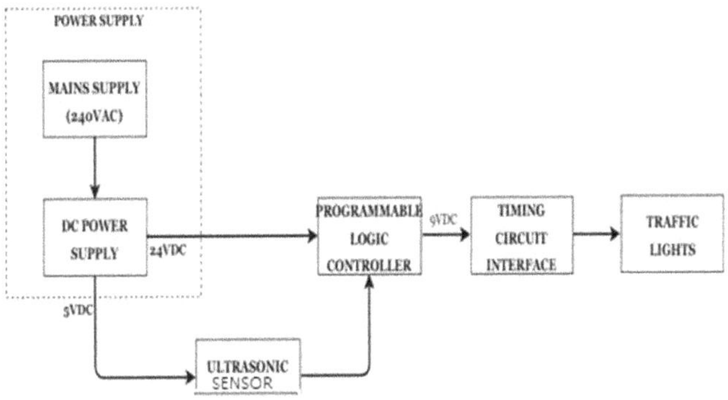


Additionally, many articles concentrate solely on traditional traffic monitoring methods like loop detectors. Interestingly, the majority of research endeavors prioritize vision-based vehicle classification techniques, overlooking various other emerging solutions in this field. Although several studies provide comprehensive overviews of vehicle classification systems employing different sensor types, they tend to focus narrowly on specific systems, such as UAVs. This study explores the implementation of an efficient and adaptable road traffic control system at a two-lane roundabout. Given the high frequency of traffic accidents at intersections, this approach offers a practical and convenient means of regulating road traffic.

This research contributes to the ongoing efforts to create intelligent transportation systems, providing a foundation for developing advanced traffic signal control mechanisms. The implementation of such systems has the potential to significantly improve the overall functionality of intersections, contributing to a smarter and more sustainable urban infrastructure.

## 2. LITERATURE SURVEY

Numerous studies have explored traffic monitoring systems with a particular focus on vehicle classification. Although the Federal Highway Administration (FHWA) provides general guidelines for the selection of such systems, these primarily emphasize established industrial solutions, often overlooking ongoing research challenges and the potential of emerging technologies. For instance, the FHWA guidelines are not tailored to address advanced adaptive solutions or hybrid models that could enhance efficiency and accuracy in diverse traffic scenarios. This creates a gap in the literature, emphasizing the need for innovative approaches that integrate real-time data processing and smart control mechanisms.

In one such study, Kouvelas et al. utilized the Webster method to derive fixed traffic signal controls for isolated junctions, applying it to real-time operations. Simulation results from this approach demonstrated its effectiveness, particularly under saturated traffic conditions. Building on this foundational research, the current project leverages advanced hardware to implement a dynamic traffic control system. Key components include the Allen Bradley MicroLogix 1000 PLC as the central controller, decade counter 4017 and 555 timers for timing interfaces, and LEDs for output display. These devices collectively facilitate the implementation of a cost-effective and adaptable traffic management solution capable of addressing both routine and peak traffic conditions.

*Figure 2. System architecture*

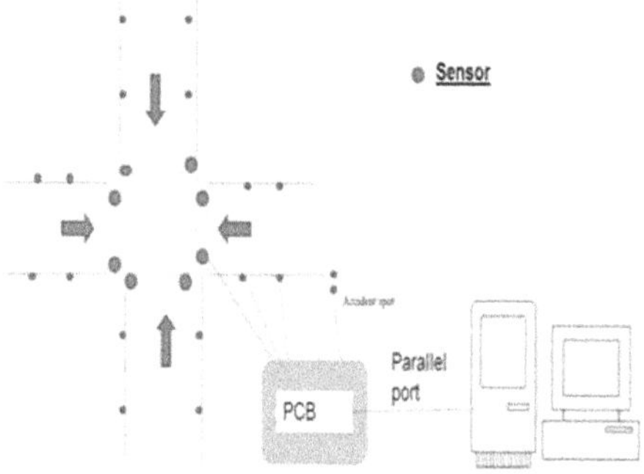


This method eliminates the need for a pre-specified fixed traffic signal plan, offering a more flexible and accurate approach to managing traffic flow. By dynamically adapting to real-time traffic conditions, this system overcomes the limitations of conventional fixed-signal methodologies, which often fail to address sudden fluctuations in traffic density. The ability to respond to actual traffic patterns not only improves operational efficiency but also minimizes delays, making it a promising solution for modern urban traffic management. This adaptive approach leverages advanced algorithms and sensor technologies to provide a robust framework for efficient traffic control.

## Vehicle Classification Systems:

Vehicle classification systems are essential for intelligent traffic management, allowing for the identification and categorization of vehicles based on their size, type, and behavior. These systems can be divided into three main categories: roadway-based, on-road, and off-road systems, each utilizing different sensor technologies and deployment strategies.

**Roadway-based Systems:** These systems use embedded sensors, such as piezoelectric sensors, inductive loop detectors, and magnetometers, to gather detailed information about vehicles, including axle count, length, and speed. Notable studies, such as those by Khan et al. (2022), have shown high accuracy in vehicle classification through sensor fusion techniques, but they also point out challenges like high installation costs and the disruptions caused during deployment.

**On-road Systems:** This category includes mobile sensors and cameras mounted on vehicles or roadside infrastructure. Recent advancements in computer vision, as highlighted by Zhang et al. (2021), utilize deep learning for real-time vehicle detection and classification, significantly enhancing performance across various lighting and weather conditions.

**Off-road Systems:** These systems employ unmanned aerial vehicles (UAVs) and satellite imagery to gather large-scale traffic data. For instance, Kocer et al. (2020) investigated the use of UAVs for traffic monitoring, stressing the importance of robust algorithms to manage occlusion and varying altitudes.

### Traffic Congestion Management

Traffic congestion remains a critical issue for intelligent transportation systems (ITS). Numerous methodologies have been proposed to tackle congestion, including signal optimization, adaptive control mechanisms, and vehicle management strategies.

The problem is that inductive-loop technology does not impact human traffic, which is one of the important factors for enhancing vehicle presence verification in case of default, as well as counting. However, such systems engaged in high installation and maintenance costs, as typical in studies of urban traffic solutions (Patterson et al., 2021).

A video-based surveillance system has been driving high attention these days, using aid in analyzing traffic for the real-time basis, while identifying video through the working principle of computer vision. As a part of this, the modern approach has given birth to a bit of investment with a goal to separate vehicles and start training a selection of deep learning algorithms like CNN in the interest of increasing accuracy of recognizing a vehicle under very low light or other adverse weather conditions (Mitra et al., 2019).

New variables and initial research have found that LiDAR and thermal image sensor systems could provide very precise information about vehicle dimensions and speed without being affected by lighting environments. Particularly, LiDAR technology could provide unique 3D data about traffic flow (Smith et al. 2022).

### Machine Learning and Artificial Intelligence in Traffic Control

The revolution in Traffic Monitoring Systems by Machine Learning (ML) and Artificial Intelligence (AI):

AI-enabled super sharp systems set adaptive traffic control to the task of analyzing real-data, optimizing the timing of signals. Organizations like Chen et al. (2020) saw for instance reinforcement techniques produce good results in the dynamic traffic management of intersections.

## 3. METHODOLOGY

### 3.1. Hardware Module

The hardware consists of a USB-based web camera and a general-purpose PC as the central unit for diverse image processing tasks. The experimental setup comprises toy vehicles and light-emitting diodes (LEDs) serving as a prototype for a real-world traffic light control system. LEDs symbolize the traffic signal system, with drivers employed as resistors to regulate the voltage flow to the LEDs.

### 3.2. Software Module

For the simulation and testing of each module, MATLAB is employed. Additionally, open-source Arduino software is utilized to write and upload code to the board, as well as to control the LED lights.

**Methodologies:** The sensor sends the current traffic information to the microcontroller and the microcontroller analyzes the sensor & its way. The microcontroller decides the traffic level of each road. Then the Microcontroller decides on glowing signals and then the system stores the traffic information. They include Video Surveillance, Data Fusion, Machine Learning and AI, Traffic Simulation, Communication and Connectivity, Predictive Analytics, Crowdsourcing and Mobile Apps.

### 3.3. Camera

One of the most commonly utilized sensors in roadway-based vehicle classification systems is the camera. Cameras offer abundant information for vehicle classification, including visual features and the geometry of passing vehicles. Unlike in-road-based systems, which necessitate multiple sensors to cover various lanes (requiring at least one sensor per lane), a single camera is capable of classifying vehicles across multiple lanes (see Fig. 5).

*Figure 3. A camera-based traffic monitoring system*

### 3.4. Image Acquisition

Typically, an image is regarded as a two-dimensional function, denoted as f(x, y), where x and y represent plane coordinates. The intensity or grey level of the image at any given point is referred to as its amplitude. To create a digital image, it's essential to convert the continuous x and y values into finite discrete values. The input image depicted in Figure 4 provides a perspective of four crossroads.

*Figure 4. Perspective of four crossroads*

### 3.5 RGB to GRAY Conversion

Color perception in humans is facilitated by cones, sensory cells sensitive to specific wavelengths. These cones, sensitive to green, red, and blue light, collectively contribute to the perception of color in RGB images. However, to process such images, they often require conversion to grayscale.

### 3.6 Image Filtering and Filling

Median filtering, a nonlinear operation, proves more effective than convolution when the aim is to both reduce noise and preserve edges. The function medfilt2(A, [m n]) conducts median filtering of matrix A in two dimensions. Each output pixel retains the median value in the m by n neighborhood surrounding the corresponding pixel in the input image. medfilt2 pads the image with zeros along the edges, potentially distorting the median values near edges within [m n]/2. To perform median filtering using a default 3-by-3 neighborhood, use B = medfilt2(A). If A is an indexed image, B = medfilt2(A, 'indexed', ...) processes it accordingly, padding with zeros for uint8 or with ones for double. Furthermore, the padding behavior can be controlled with padopt, where 'zeros' (default), 'symmetric', or 'indexed' options are available. If 'symmetric', A is symmetrically extended at the boundaries, while 'indexed' pads with ones for double and zeros otherwise.

### 3.7. Edge Detection

Edge detection serves as a fundamental tool in machine vision and computer applications, especially for revealing and extracting image features. Common edge detection methods include the Sobel, Prewitt, Boolean, Marr-Hildreth, and Canny techniques. In this study, opt for the Canny edge detection method due to its high accuracy. Table 1 provides a comparative summary of various edge detection techniques, showcasing their respective accuracy levels in detecting images.

## 3.8. Design Methodology

Designing an intelligent traffic management system involves several key steps, starting from understanding the problem to developing algorithms, selecting hardware and software components, integrating them into a cohesive system, and evaluating overall performance. The design methodology outlined below highlights these crucial phases in creating an intelligent traffic system tailored for urban environments.

### 3.8.1. Problem Definition and Requirements Analysis

The initial step in designing any intelligent system is to grasp the problem and gather comprehensive requirements. In the case of a traffic management system, the main objective is typically to optimize traffic flow, minimize congestion, enhance safety, and give priority to specific vehicles, such as emergency or public transport vehicles, while ensuring the efficient use of existing infrastructure.

Key Requirements:

**Real-Time Traffic Monitoring:** The system should continuously monitor traffic conditions using sensors, cameras, and various data acquisition methods.

**Traffic Signal Control:** Signals need to be adjusted dynamically based on traffic load to minimize wait times for both vehicles and pedestrians.

**Emergency Vehicle Priority:** The system must be capable of detecting emergency vehicles and prioritizing their movement through intersections.

**Integration with Existing Infrastructure:** The new system should seamlessly integrate with the current traffic infrastructure, ensuring it is scalable and adaptable.

**Security and Privacy:** Data collection and transmission must be secure to guard against hacking and to protect privacy, particularly concerning vehicle and driver information.

### 3.8.2 System Design Objectives

The next step is to define the objectives of the system. These objectives serve as the foundation for the system's design, ensuring that every component contributes to achieving these goals.

Objectives for the Intelligent Traffic Management System:

**Optimization of Traffic Flow:** Aim to reduce traffic congestion by adjusting traffic signals in real-time according to vehicle density.

**Enhanced Emergency Response:** Give priority to emergency vehicles in traffic to facilitate quicker response times.

**Scalability and Flexibility:** The system should be designed to scale with increasing urban populations and be adaptable to different urban settings.

**Cost Efficiency:** The system needs to provide a cost-effective solution for cities by utilizing affordable sensors, cameras, and controllers.

**User-Friendly Interface:** The system should be straightforward for traffic operators to monitor and manage, featuring intuitive graphical displays.

### 3.8.3. Hardware Selection

Choosing the right hardware is essential for optimal system performance. The hardware components generally consist of sensors, cameras, controllers, and communication devices.

Sensors and Cameras:

Traffic Sensors: Various types of sensors, including inductive loop sensors, ultrasonic sensors, infrared sensors, and cameras, are employed to collect data on vehicle presence, speed, and flow. These sensors are strategically positioned at critical points like intersections, highways, and pedestrian crossings.

**Cameras for Vehicle Detection:** High-resolution cameras equipped with image processing algorithms are utilized for detecting and classifying vehicles. They can also identify different vehicle types and assess traffic congestion levels.

**Environmental Sensors:** Weather sensors and other environmental sensors provide valuable context for analyzing traffic flow, as conditions like heavy rain can significantly affect traffic patterns.

Controllers:

**Programmable Logic Controllers (PLCs)**: PLCs manage traffic signals and work in conjunction with sensors and cameras. They implement pre-defined logic to adjust traffic lights in real time based on incoming sensor data.

**Microcontrollers and Embedded Systems: These** devices can efficiently process and control local traffic signals, minimizing reliance on centralized systems.

Communication Infrastructure:

**Data Transmission Networks:** A reliable and robust communication network is crucial for transmitting real-time sensor data to central control systems. This may involve technologies such as Wi-Fi, Ethernet, or 5G networks.

**Cloud Integration:** Utilizing a cloud-based system allows for data storage, real-time processing, and analytics, offering scalability and remote monitoring capabilities.

## 3.9 Software Implementation

The admin plays an important role in setting the time to a particular signal, so the rights of the admin must be preserved. It can be done with the help of authentication which means by providing a username and password. So password must be a combination of alphabets and numbers with a minimum of 6 characters. In case of the absence of an admin, a person other than the admin cannot modify the process of assigning time-slot to signal without permission of the admin.

*Figure 5. User registration*

*Figure 6. User login*

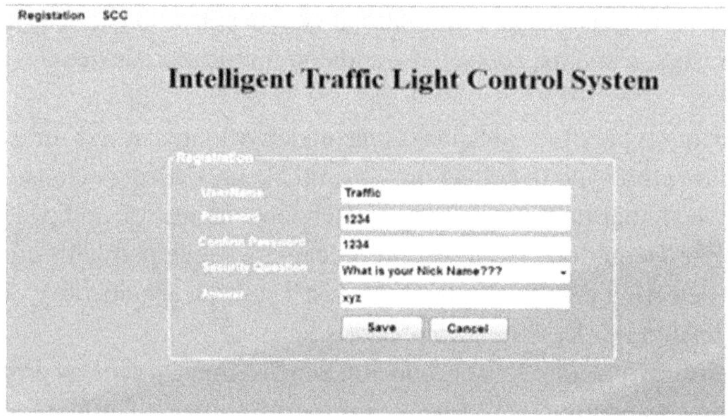


*Figure 7. Intelligent traffic controller system*

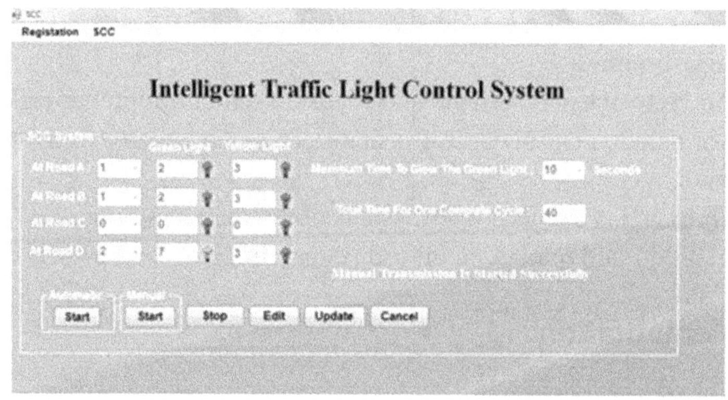


## 3.9.1 Software Design

The software serves as the brain of the intelligent traffic management system. It processes data from sensors and cameras, makes decisions based on established algorithms, and sends commands to the traffic lights.

### 3.9.2 Software Components

Traffic Signal Control Software: This is the main application that manages traffic light cycles. It employs algorithms to modify signal timings based on traffic flow, the needs of emergency vehicles, and other relevant factors.

**Data Processing Software:** This component handles the real-time data gathered from sensors and cameras. It includes algorithms for vehicle detection, traffic flow analysis, and vehicle classification (such as differentiating between private cars, buses, and emergency vehicles).

**Machine Learning Algorithms:** These algorithms analyze historical and real-time traffic data to predict traffic loads and recommend optimal signal timings. They can also enhance emergency vehicle detection, adapting more effectively to changing traffic conditions.

**User Interface (UI):** The UI enables traffic operators to monitor current traffic conditions, manually adjust signal timings when needed, and access reports generated by the system. It also allows operators to respond to emergencies in real time.

Key Algorithms:

Vehicle Detection: Image processing techniques (like Canny edge detection and Hough transforms) are utilized to identify vehicles and assess their speed. Sensor data further supports these observations.

**Traffic Flow Analysis:** Algorithms that measure vehicle density and flow at intersections help the system adjust signal timings to maximize throughput.

**Emergency Vehicle Prioritization:** A classification algorithm identifies emergency vehicles and modifies traffic signals to facilitate their passage with minimal delay.

### 3.9.3 System Integration

Once the hardware is selected and the software is developed, the next step is to integrate the system components. This process ensures that sensors, cameras, controllers, and software work together seamlessly.

Key Integration Considerations:

**Communication between Sensors and PLCs**: It's essential for sensors to transmit data to PLCs, which then adjust traffic light patterns according to established rules.

**Real-time Data Processing:** Integrating real-time data from sensors and cameras into the software system is vital for making informed decisions. This requires the development of APIs to facilitate communication among different software modules.

**Centralized vs. Decentralized Control:** In a centralized system, all data is processed at a main control station. Conversely, in a decentralized system, local traffic control units make decisions based on nearby data, while periodically sending updates to the central system.

### 3.9.4 System Testing

Testing is crucial to confirm that the system operates as intended in real-world scenarios. This phase includes evaluating hardware, software, and communication components.

Types of Testing:

**Unit Testing:** Each component of the system, like sensors and algorithms, is tested individually to verify they function correctly on their own.

**Integration Testing:** The interactions between various components, such as sensors sending data to PLCs, are tested to ensure smooth communication.

**System Testing:** The entire system is assessed to replicate real traffic situations and confirm that the software adjusts traffic signals appropriately.

**Performance Testing:** The system is analyzed for its response time, scalability, and capacity to manage high traffic volumes in various settings.

**Stress Testing:** The system is evaluated under extreme conditions (e.g., heavy traffic or environmental disruptions) to ensure it remains stable and reliable.

### 3.9.5. Security and Privacy Considerations

Given that traffic management systems often handle sensitive information, protecting data security and privacy is critical. This involves defending against cyber threats and adhering to privacy regulations.

Security Measures:

**Encryption:** Data sent from sensors, cameras, and controllers should be encrypted to avoid interception.

**Access Control:** The system must implement strict access control measures, ensuring that only authorized personnel can change traffic signal timings or access sensitive information.

**Data Anonymization:** Personal data, such as vehicle identification, should be anonymized to safeguard privacy.

**Firewall and Intrusion Detection:** Establishing firewalls and intrusion detection systems to defend against hacking attempts.

### 3.9.6. Deployment and Maintenance

After the system has been designed, tested, and validated, it is ready for deployment in the urban environment. This phase involves installing the necessary hardware, setting up communication networks, and confirming that the software operates correctly.

Deployment Steps:

**Hardware Installation:** This includes placing sensors, cameras, traffic signal controllers, and communication infrastructure at crucial traffic intersections.

**Software Deployment:** The traffic control software is installed on both central and local servers, ensuring it integrates well with the existing infrastructure.

**System Calibration:** The system's settings, such as sensor sensitivity and traffic light timing, are adjusted to align with local traffic patterns.

**Pilot Testing:** The system is tested in a limited area to assess its effectiveness before proceeding with full-scale deployment.

## 3.10 Technical Specifications of Sensors

The sensors used in the intelligent traffic monitoring system are very much crucial for making the data collected accurate and reliable. These are the technical specifications for generally used sensors for the system:

Camera Sensors

**Resolution:** Full HD, with a capture of 1920x1080 pixels, can capture fine details pertaining to the vehicles and surroundings.

**Frame Rate:** A frame rate of about 30-60 fps is necessary for smooth real-time data capture.

**Field of View (FOV):** A wide angle of 90-120 degrees is excellent so that multiple lanes can be viewed simultaneously with the help of the lenses.

**Low Light Capability:** Equipped with IR filters or night vision, 24-hour, seven-day operation can be carried out around the clock.

Ultrasonic Sensors

**Range:** Approximately 20 to 400 cm, along with an accuracy of ±1 cm.

**Frequency:** It typically operates at 40 kHz for distance measurement.

**Use Case:** It detects vehicle presence and measures distances at intersections.

Piezoelectric Sensors

**Sensitivity:** It is 0.1 pC/N, which implies it is sensitive enough for precise axle and measuring vehicle weights.

**Durability:** Very strong mechanical stress-resistant in the road.

Radar Sensors

**Frequency Range:** 24 GHz to 77 GHz is used in detecting moving objects.

**Range:** Up to 200 meters with high precision.

**Use Case:** Measures vehicle speed and detects emergency vehicles.

Algorithms for Emergency Vehicle Detection

Incident emergency vehicle detection at actual time involves the use of some of advancements from the advanced signal processing and machine learning aspects of it as well. These are few of the methods through which it is done:

Acoustic Detection Algorithm:

Microphone arrays are used, listening for siren frequencies for siren detection. Different types of frequency patterns of the siren can isolate them. The aperture is around 500-2000 Hz using fast Fourier transform (FFT).

Image Recognition Algorithm:

Convolutional Neural Networks (CNNs) are applied to the process of assessing emergency vehicles. Test-driven procedures are considered reflector lights or vehicle writing (e.g., "AMBULANCE").

Real-time object detection frameworks such as YOLO (You Only Look Once) are employed.

## 4. PERFORMANCE AND EVALUATION

The development of a prototype for real-time image processing aimed at automating traffic signal systems, incorporating density estimation and the detection of emergency vehicles like ambulances, has been completed. This new method offers several advantages, including the elimination of sensors or RFID tags, which alleviates the burden on traffic sergeants. Regarding the sequence of traffic lights, a modern traffic light control system typically entails four directional states for users, as depicted in Figures 8(a) to 8(d).

*Figure 8. Turning lane for East-South and West-North direction*

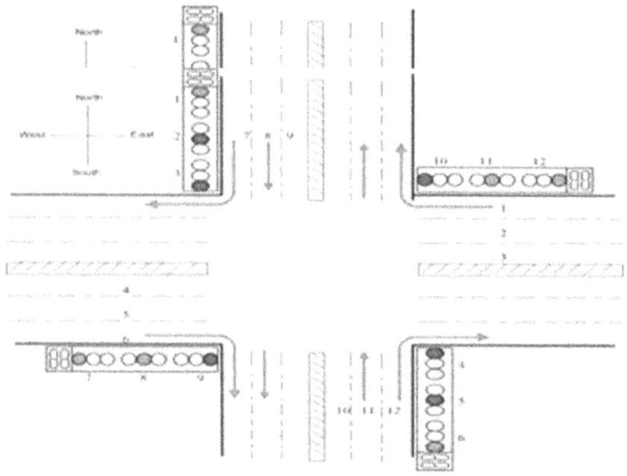

*Figure 9. Straight lane for North-South and South-North direction*

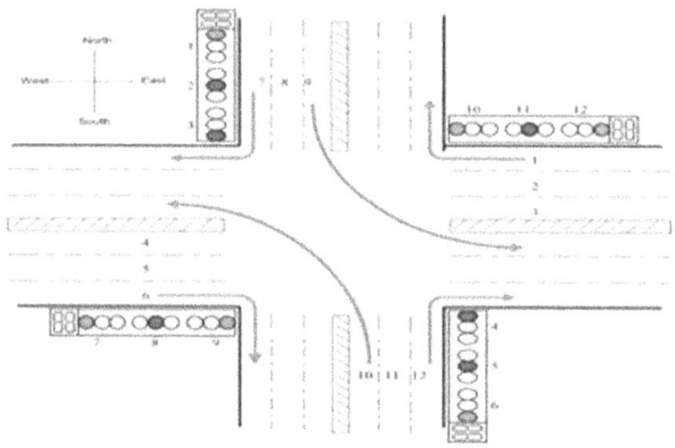

*Figure 10. Turning lane for South-West and North- East direction*

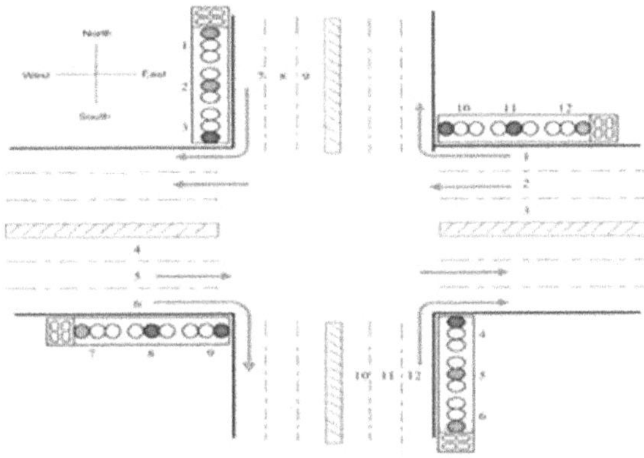

*Figure 11. Straight Lane for East-West and West-East direction*

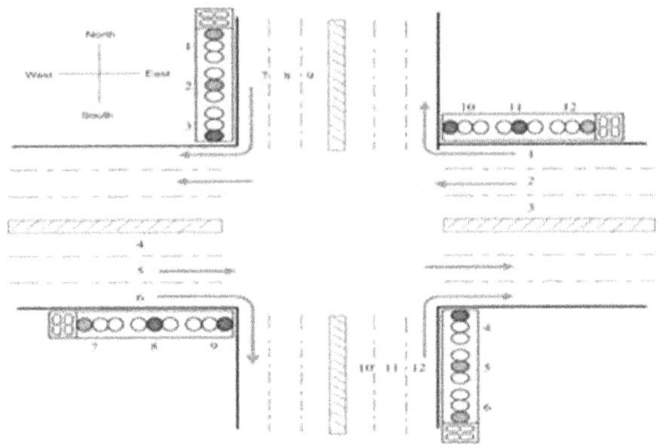

*Figure 12. Table of sequence of modern traffic light*

| Direction | East-West Direction | | | | | | | | | North-South Direction | | | | | | | | | Lane Direction |
|---|---|---|---|---|---|---|---|---|---|---|---|---|---|---|---|---|---|---|---|
| TL No: | 1 | | | 2 | | | 3 | | | 7 | | | 8 | | | 9 | | | |
| Color | R | Y | G | R | Y | G | R | Y | G | R | Y | G | R | Y | G | R | Y | G | |
| State1 | 0 | 0 | 1 | 1 | 0 | 0 | 0 | 0 | 1 | 0 | 0 | 1 | 1 | 0 | 0 | 1 | 0 | 0 | turning lane for ( E-S & W-N) direction |
| State2 | 0 | 0 | 1 | 1 | 0 | 0 | 0 | 1 | 0 | 0 | 0 | 1 | 1 | 0 | 0 | 1 | 0 | 0 | |
| State3 | 0 | 0 | 1 | 0 | 0 | 1 | 1 | 0 | 0 | 0 | 0 | 1 | 1 | 0 | 0 | 1 | 0 | 0 | straight lane for E-W & W-E) direction |
| State4 | 0 | 0 | 1 | 0 | 1 | 0 | 1 | 0 | 0 | 0 | 0 | 1 | 1 | 0 | 0 | 1 | 0 | 0 | |
| State5 | 0 | 0 | 1 | 1 | 0 | 0 | 1 | 0 | 0 | 0 | 0 | 1 | 1 | 0 | 0 | 0 | 0 | 1 | turning lane for (S-W & N-E) direction |
| State6 | 0 | 0 | 1 | 1 | 0 | 0 | 1 | 0 | 0 | 0 | 0 | 1 | 1 | 0 | 0 | 0 | 1 | 0 | |
| State7 | 0 | 0 | 1 | 1 | 0 | 0 | 1 | 0 | 0 | 0 | 0 | 1 | 0 | 0 | 1 | 1 | 0 | 0 | Straight lane for( N-S & S-N) direction |
| State8 | 0 | 0 | 1 | 1 | 0 | 0 | 1 | 0 | 0 | 0 | 0 | 1 | 0 | 1 | 0 | 1 | 0 | 0 | |

Upon energizing the device, the states of sensors and their corresponding input ports are utilized to update the output ports on the PLC, in accordance with the logic program stored in the microprocessor's memory. Subsequently, the system initiates its default traffic operation, alternating based on predetermined timing. This cycle persists until any sensor detects a high state, at which point the traffic lights on the corresponding road track with the activated sensor switch to green and remain so until the preset duration elapses. Meanwhile, the lights on other road tracks remain inactive, eventually reverting to their normal state.

## Steps to handle the system:

- Log into the System.
- Select the control type.
- If Automatic mode is selected, proceed to step 4; otherwise, go to step 8.
- If Automatic control is activated:
- Assign time periods for green and yellow signals.
- If an emergency vehicle is detected, return to step 4.
- End Automatic control.
- If Manual mode is selected, proceed to manual control operations.
- If the rally comes then go to step 8
- Manual control activated
- Assign period for green, and yellow signals according to that particular road
- If the emergency is over then go to step 4.

*Figure 13. Track of intelligent traffic controller system*

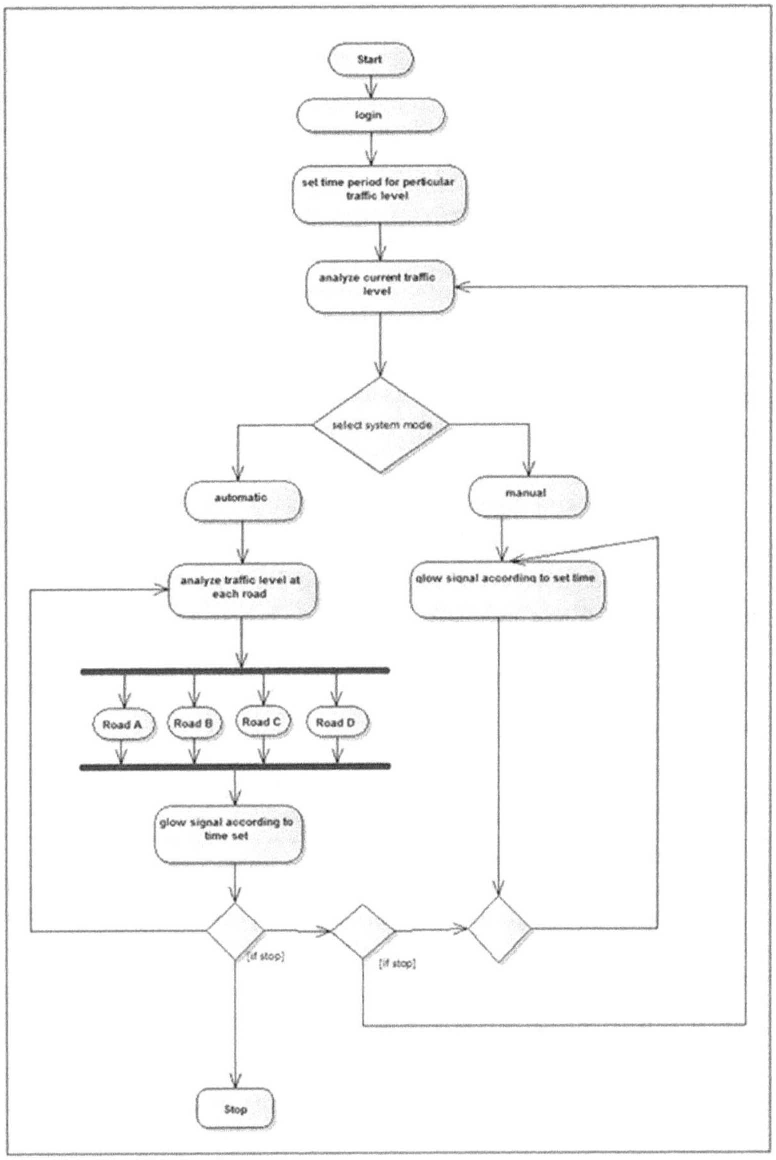


## A. Core of Autonomour Traffic Management

The core of autonomous traffic management is built on the ongoing collection of real-time data. A variety of sensors and cameras are strategically placed at intersections, along roads, and on highways to gather insights about traffic conditions. These include:

**Inductive Loop Sensors:** Installed in the ground, these sensors detect the presence of vehicles at intersections, aiding in the measurement of traffic density and flow.

**Infrared or Ultrasonic Sensors:** These devices monitor the speed, direction, and type of vehicles as they pass through designated areas.

**Cameras:** High-definition cameras, often paired with image processing algorithms, are utilized to identify and track vehicles, oversee traffic flow, and spot incidents such as accidents or congestion.

**Environmental Sensors:** These sensors track weather conditions (like temperature and rainfall) to help adjust traffic control strategies based on external factors that influence traffic flow.

The information collected from these sensors is sent in real-time to a central processing system or local controllers for prompt analysis.

## B. Autonomous Traffic Signal Control

The system uses data analysis and decision-making algorithms to manage traffic signals on its own:

**Dynamic Signal Timing:** It adjusts signal timings in real-time based on traffic density, giving priority to lanes with heavier traffic. For instance, if a lane suddenly sees a surge in vehicles when a red light turns green, the system quickly adapts to this change.

**Adaptive Signal Control:** The signals modify themselves according to environmental conditions, such as weather or accidents. If a sensor picks up on slippery roads or heavy rain, the system might reduce vehicle flow or extend pedestrian crossing times to enhance safety.

**Emergency Vehicle Priority:** When an emergency vehicle is detected, the system gives it precedence by turning the signal green in its direction while ensuring that other traffic is safely halted. It also communicates with traffic lights along the route to create a "green wave," allowing the emergency vehicle to pass through without interruption.

## C. Integration with Traffic Management Center

While the system functions independently, it is frequently connected to a central traffic management center that oversees overall traffic conditions, monitors system performance, and enables remote intervention when necessary.

**Centralized Monitoring:** The traffic management center continuously receives updates from all intersections within the network. Although the system autonomously adjusts signals in real-time, the control center provides operators with the ability to view and analyze data across the entire city or region.

**Remote Intervention:** Even though the system operates on its own, traffic operators can step in remotely if needed, such as during severe weather events or accidents that require immediate manual control. However, such instances are rare since the system is built to manage most situations independently.

**Feedback Loop:** The system is designed to learn and enhance its performance over time. It utilizes feedback from the traffic signals' performance (e.g., decreased congestion, smoother passage for emergency vehicles) to refine its algorithms, making the system increasingly intelligent with each passing day.

## D. Communication Between Traffic Elements

The traffic management system depends on a network of communication technologies to exchange data among traffic signals, sensors, cameras, and the central processing system. This communication takes place over wireless or wired networks like 4G/5G, Wi-Fi, or Ethernet.

**Vehicle-to-Infrastructure (V2I) Communication:** In certain systems, vehicles can communicate directly with the infrastructure. For instance, a vehicle equipped with V2I technology can relay information about its speed and location to traffic signals, allowing those signals to adjust in anticipation of the vehicle's arrival.

**Vehicle-to-Vehicle (V2V) Communication:** If the system supports V2V communication, vehicles can share information with one another to optimize traffic flow, minimize collisions, and enhance safety.

## E. Feedback and Learning

Machine learning is crucial for the ongoing improvement of the system. It utilizes data from sensors, cameras, and user feedback to train models that enhance traffic signal patterns and other decision-making processes.

**Learning from Traffic Data:** The system consistently gathers information on vehicle flow, congestion, emergency vehicle detection, and more. This data is analyzed by machine learning models that identify patterns and predict traffic flows, enabling proactive decision-making.

**Model Training:** As the system accumulates more traffic data, the algorithms become better at making accurate predictions, optimizing traffic signal patterns, and alleviating congestion. It can adjust to changing traffic patterns, ensuring it remains aligned with current trends.

## F. Autonomous System Operation in Various Conditions

The autonomous traffic management system needs to operate effectively under different conditions, such as:

**High Traffic Density:** During peak congestion, the system can dynamically modify signal timings to avoid gridlocks and prioritize lanes based on traffic volume.

**Emergency Situations:** In the event of accidents, the system can automatically change traffic signals to clear the area or facilitate the passage of emergency vehicles.

**Adverse Weather:** The system can modify traffic signal timings in response to environmental factors like rain, fog, or snow to maintain safe driving conditions.

## G. Maintenance and Updates

Although the system operates independently, it still needs regular maintenance and software updates. These updates can be performed remotely via a cloud-based platform, which helps keep the system's algorithms aligned with the latest traffic management techniques and technological innovations.

**Remote Software Updates:** The software that manages the traffic signals and the machine learning models can be updated from a distance to enhance system performance, fix vulnerabilities, or improve the system's decision-making abilities.

**Sensor Calibration:** Sensors are regularly calibrated to maintain accuracy. Fortunately, these calibrations can occur automatically, with the system recognizing when calibration is needed and starting the process on its own.

# 5. DYNAMIC TRAFFIC SIGNAL ADJUSTMENT FOR CONGESTION REDUCTION

## 5.1 Advantages

a. Simplicity, user-friendliness, and easy programmability characterize this system.
b. The system minimizes database server overhead by automatically deleting data every 4 hours.
c. High responsiveness is a hallmark of this system, ensuring rapid adaptation to traffic changes.
d. By adjusting traffic signal lights based on current traffic density, this system effectively reduces waiting times and alleviates traffic congestion.

## 5.2 Increasing the scalability of Intelligent Traffic Management Systems

Scalability is the critical factor that must be addressed when intelligent traffic management systems deploy especially in different city types with different traffic densities, different existing infrastructures or even diverse budgets. There are a number of significant considerations that should be taken into account:

Designed specifically for a city:

System expansion:

It should be constructed in such a manner so that, as cities grow, more sensors, cameras, and networks can ultimately be added in without any issue.

Modular designs in both hardware and software allow simple and rapid upgrade with minimal disruption to what is in place.

Data treatment:

Edge sweetness as the distributed protocol may yet induce some delays that might compel real-time action in high traffic areas.

Interoperability:-

System must be interoperable with a broad range of hardware and different dent communication protocols [MQTT,CoAP] to make it work optimally across various types of environments.

## 5.3 Integration with Smart City Technologies

The integration of intelligent traffic management systems into smart city frameworks ensures the maximum positive impact of intelligent traffic management.

IoT and Sensor Networks

Sensors and cameras are connected with the city-wide IoT networks and provide a more holistic view on urban mobility.

Real-time information is shared between other systems like pollution monitoring and public safety.

Connected and Autonomous Vehicles (CAVs)

The system can interact with CAVs for coordinated movement, optimizing traffic flow and reducing accidents.

Vehicle-to-Infrastructure (V2I) communication allows direct interaction between the system and vehicles.

Public Transportation Coordination:

Traffic signals are synchronized with bus and train schedules to ensure smooth transit and reduce delays for public transportation.

Energy Management:

Smart streetlights powered by renewable energy can integrate with the system, adjusting brightness based on traffic conditions and reducing energy consumption.

## 5.4 Long-Term Implications of Widespread Adoption

Economic Benefits:

Reduced fuel consumption due to smoother traffic flow.

Decreased costs associated with traffic congestion, such as lost productivity and vehicle wear-and-tear.

Social Impact:

Improved emergency response times, potentially saving lives.

Enhanced mobility for non-motorized users, such as cyclists and pedestrians.

Environmental Sustainability:

Lower greenhouse gas emissions from idling vehicles.

Support for electric vehicles (EVs) through smart charging infrastructure integration.

## 5.5 Technical Challenges

Sensor Calibration:

Regular calibration is essential to maintain the accuracy of sensors, particularly in varying environmental conditions (e.g., rain, fog, or extreme temperatures).

Automated calibration algorithms can mitigate human error and reduce maintenance costs.

Network Reliability:

Urban environments with high electromagnetic interference or physical obstructions may face communication disruptions.

Redundant networks and fault-tolerant designs ensure system reliability.

Urban Complexity:

Diverse road layouts, mixed traffic types, and high pedestrian density present unique challenges for system implementation.

Advanced simulations and adaptive algorithms are needed to handle these complexities.

### 5.5.1 Artificial Intelligence and Machine Learning Trends

Deep Learning for Traffic Pattern Analysis:

Convolutional Neural Networks analyze video feeds to determine accurate vehicle classification and traffic density estimation.

Recurrent Neural Networks predict future traffic patterns based on historical data.

Reinforcement Learning for Signal Optimization:

Agents learn optimal signal timings through trial and error, improving over time.

Multi-agent systems may coordinate across intersections for city-wide traffic management.

Federated Learning:

Distributed machine learning models process data locally, preserving privacy while enabling citywide insights.

## 5.5.2 Case Studies and Real-World Examples

### *5.5.2.1 Adaptive Traffic Systems in Singapore:*

Singapore uses AI-driven adaptive traffic systems, cutting travel times by as much as 12%.

The system combines data from cameras, GPS devices, and public transport schedules.

Smart Traffic Infrastructure in Los Angeles:

Los Angeles has deployed the Automated Traffic Surveillance and Control (ATSAC) system, which controls over 4,500 traffic signals using real-time data.

The system has reduced travel times by 16%.

Traffic Management in Delhi:

Delhi's deployment of AI-based traffic systems uses ANPR (Automatic Number Plate Recognition) cameras and radar sensors to monitor and manage congestion effectively.

### *5.5.2.2 Coimbatore – Smart Traffic Signal System*

Background:

Coimbatore is a rapidly growing industrial city in Tamil Nadu. It is characterized by intense traffic congestion caused by rapid urbanization and an increase in vehicle ownership. A smart traffic management system was deployed in the city to mitigate these problems.

Implementation

Automated Traffic Signals

AI-based adaptive signals change the green and red light timings according to real-time traffic density at strategic intersections.

Surveillance Cameras

High-resolution cameras monitor violations like signal jumping and overspeeding, which generate challans automatically.

Emergency Service Integration:

The green corridors for ambulances, fire tenders, and police vehicles have drastically reduced response times.

Effects:

Average travel times decreased by 20%.

Violations of traffic laws decreased by 15% with better adherence to it.

The response time to emergency services was better as there was no break in the green corridor.

Issues

The lack of funds for extension to small-sized intersections

Monsoon seasons affect the camera and sensor maintenance.

### 5.5.2.3 Jaipur – ITMS

Introduction

Jaipur is a tourist and heritage city that suffers from traffic congestion in most places, especially those that have high footfall. ITMS was thus introduced to streamline the traffic flow in the city and to support tourism.

Implementation:

Automated Traffic Surveillance:

The city has CCTV cameras and ANPR systems to enforce speed limits and monitor traffic violations.

Tourist Guidance Integration:

Real-time traffic updates are integrated into tourist apps, guiding visitors to avoid congested routes.

Public Transport Coordination:

ITMS synchronizes traffic signals with public buses, minimizing delays for commuters.

Impact:

Improved tourist satisfaction due to reduced congestion near popular attractions.

25% improvement in public transport efficiency.

Enhanced safety for pedestrians through dedicated crossings monitored by cameras.

### 5.5.2.4 Kolkata – Real-Time Traffic Management with IoT

Background:

Kolkata, one of India's oldest metropolitan cities, implemented a real-time traffic management system to address its complex road network and high population density.

Implementation:

IoT-Enabled Sensors:

Installed at major intersections to detect traffic density and send real-time data to a central command center.

Smart Traffic Signals:

Signals dynamically adjust based on live traffic data, optimizing flow.

Public Alerts:

Mobile apps and roadside LED boards display real-time updates, suggesting alternate routes to avoid congestion.

Impact:

18% decrease in overall congestion during peak hours.

Improved road safety through the reduction of accidents at intersections.

Increased user adoption of mobile apps for traffic updates.

Challenges:

Maintenance of IoT devices in humid and monsoon conditions.

Training personnel to operate and manage the command center efficiently.

### 5.5.2.5 Indore – Traffic Management with AI and ML

Background:

Indore, known for its cleanliness, aimed to complement its urban development efforts by introducing AI-driven traffic management.

Implementation:

AI Algorithms for Traffic Prediction:

Machine learning models analyze historical and real-time data to predict congestion and adjust signals proactively.

Integrated Public Transport:

Signals prioritize buses, ensuring faster transit times for public transport users.

Violation Detection:

High-definition cameras detect offenses such as signal jumping and lane violations, automatically generating challans.

Impact:

Reduction in congestion by 30% during peak hours.

Increased usage of public transport due to reduced delays.

Enhanced compliance with traffic rules, improving overall safety.

Challenges:

High initial investment for AI implementation.

Limited data availability for training machine learning models initially.

Real-World Example: Navi Mumbai – Adaptive Traffic Control System (ATCS)

#### *5.5.2.6 Navi Mumbai - ATCS*

Navi Mumbai implemented ATCS as part of its smart city initiative to manage traffic in its planned urban layout effectively.

Implementation:

Dynamic Signal Control:

Signals adapt to real-time traffic density, using data from vehicle detectors and cameras.

Emergency Vehicle Priority:

Sensors identify emergency vehicles and create uninterrupted green corridors.

Environmental Monitoring:

Sensors measure air quality, integrating environmental data with traffic flow optimization to reduce emissions.

Impact:

22% improvement in traffic flow efficiency.

Reduced carbon emissions through optimal traffic management.

Faster emergency response times due to prioritized corridors.

Challenges:

Ensuring system reliability during network outages.

High costs of maintaining environmental monitoring sensors.

### 5.5.3 Emerging Trends in Data Privacy, Cybersecurity, and Sustainability

Data Privacy:

Anonymization techniques ensure no Personally Identifiable Information (PII) is stored or transmitted.

Data usage policies aligned with global standards like GDPR protect user rights.

Cybersecurity:

Systems are fortified against cyber threats using blockchain technology for secure data transactions and intrusion detection systems (IDS) for real-time threat monitoring.

Sustainable Energy Practices:

Solar-powered sensors and energy-efficient processors reduce environmental impact.

The use of recycled material in system hardware supports circular economy initiatives.

### 5.5.4 Emerging Trends and Lessons Learned

Integration with Smart City Initiatives:

Intelligent traffic systems are increasingly linked with broader smart city projects, incorporating environmental monitoring, public safety, and urban planning.

AI and Machine Learning in Traffic Prediction:

Predictive analytics is being used to anticipate congestion and adjust systems proactively.

Public-Private Partnerships:

Collaboration between government bodies and tech firms helps overcome funding and expertise barriers.

Focus on Data Privacy:

Addressing concerns about surveillance and personal data protection is essential for user trust.

## 6. EXPECTED OUTCOME

The anticipated result of this system is to address congestion issues at junctions autonomously in automatic mode and with human intervention in manual mode. This system facilitates traffic control through both automatic and manual modes, allowing for manual mode activation in scenarios such as rallies. Additionally, in the event of an emergency vehicle detection by sensors, this system ensures the provision of a clear path for these vehicles and adjusts accordingly. traffic system as it is. So, the traffic problem is easily solved by using an Intelligent Traffic Monitoring System.

## 6.1 Security and Concerns

### 6.1.1 System Security Concerns

With intelligent traffic management systems gathering and sharing vast amounts of real-time data, it is crucial to implement strong security measures to safeguard sensitive information and ensure the reliability of the system.

Potential Security Threats

**Data Breaches:** Unauthorized individuals could gain access to traffic data, including vehicle tracking information or surveillance footage.

**System Sabotage:** Malicious individuals might manipulate traffic signals or disable sensors, leading to disorder in urban traffic.

**Device Vulnerabilities:** Weak firmware in sensors and controllers could be targeted for attacks.

Mitigation Strategies

End-to-End Encryption

Ensure that all data sent between sensors, traffic controllers, and central systems is encrypted to block interception by attackers.

Adopt strong encryption standards like AES-256 to protect sensitive information.

Authentication and Access Control

Implement multi-factor authentication (MFA) for system administrators.

Utilize role-based access control (RBAC) to restrict user permissions and prevent unauthorized access.

Regular Security Audits

Perform regular vulnerability assessments and penetration tests to discover and fix weaknesses.

Work with cybersecurity firms to keep the system updated against new threats.

AI-Based Intrusion Detection

### 6.1.2 Scalability Concerns

As cities expand and traffic volumes rise, the traffic management system needs to scale effectively to accommodate the demands of larger and more intricate networks.

Challenges

**Infrastructure Overload:** Current systems may find it difficult to manage the increased number of sensors and data.

**Hardware Limitations:** Older traffic controllers might not be compatible with new devices or protocols.

**Data Bottlenecks:** Centralized systems can face delays when processing large amounts of real-time traffic data.

Strategies for Scalability

Modular System Design

Implement a modular architecture that allows for the easy integration of additional components, such as sensors and controllers.

Ensure that each module functions independently while maintaining effective communication with the overall network.

Cloud-Based Infrastructure

Utilize cloud computing for storage and processing to support large-scale implementations.

Adopt distributed systems to decentralize traffic control, minimizing the risk of bottlenecks.

Edge Computing

Install edge devices for local data processing at intersections, which decreases reliance on central servers and enhances response times.

This method enables the system to manage more devices without necessitating major upgrades to central infrastructure.

Dynamic Resource Allocation

Employ machine learning to forecast traffic volumes and dynamically allocate system resources, ensuring optimal performance under varying conditions.

### 6.1.3. Integration with Existing Traffic Infrastructure

Ensuring that intelligent traffic management systems can work well with current traffic infrastructure is essential for their successful adoption.

Challenges

**Legacy Systems:** Numerous cities continue to depend on outdated traffic controllers and sensors that may not be compatible with modern technologies.

**Heterogeneous Devices:** The differences in sensor types, communication protocols, and data formats across various regions complicate integration efforts.

**Interoperability Issues:** The absence of standardized interfaces and protocols can obstruct the smooth operation of diverse components.

Integration Strategies

Adoption of Open Standards

Implement standards like the National Transportation Communications for Intelligent Transportation System Protocol (NTCIP) to promote interoperability among different devices and systems.

Utilize protocols such as MQTT or CoAP for effective communication between IoT devices.

Middleware for Interfacing

Create middleware solutions to address communication gaps between legacy systems and new components.

Middleware can convert protocols and data formats, facilitating seamless interaction throughout the system.

Pilot Testing and Phased Rollouts

Carry out pilot projects to evaluate integration on a smaller scale before implementing citywide.

Employ phased rollouts to reduce disruptions and collect feedback for ongoing improvements.

## 6.2 Sensor Reliability, Calibration, and Maintenance in Intelligent Traffic Management Systems

### 6.2.1. Importance of Sensor Reliability

Sensors are crucial in intelligent traffic management systems as they gather real-time information on vehicle density, speed, and classification. It's vital to ensure the reliability of these sensors to maintain the accuracy and efficiency of the systems. If sensors are unreliable, it can result in incorrect data collection, leading to poor traffic signal adjustments, increased congestion, and a decline in public trust in the system.

### 6.2.2. Challenges Related to Sensor Reliability

Environmental Factors:

Sensors installed outdoors face tough conditions such as rain, heat, dust, and humidity, which can impair their performance over time.

Electrical Interference:

Being near high-voltage power lines or experiencing electromagnetic interference from nearby devices can distort signals.

Wear and Tear:

Continuous use or vibrations from heavy vehicles can cause physical wear, resulting in sensor malfunctions.

False Positives/Negatives:

Sensors might misinterpret environmental sounds, shadows, or debris on the road as vehicles, leading to inaccuracies in the data.

### 6.2.3. Sensor Calibration:

Ensuring Accuracy Calibration is essential for ensuring that sensors deliver accurate and consistent readings. This process involves comparing the outputs of sensors with standard reference values and making adjustments to minimize errors.

**Steps in Sensor Calibration:** Initial Setup: Calibrate sensors during installation to ensure they are aligned with the system's intended operation.

**Routine Checks:** Conduct periodic calibration, particularly for sensors that are exposed to changing environmental conditions, to maintain consistent accuracy.

**Dynamic Calibration:** Utilize self-calibrating algorithms that automatically adjust sensor parameters in real time based on observed deviations.

**Cross-Validation:** Employ multiple sensors for redundancy. If one sensor fails or provides inconsistent data, others can help validate the results. Examples of Calibration Techniques: For **Cameras:** Adjusting focus, white balance, and alignment to ensure precise image capture. For Loop **Detectors:** Verifying sensitivity settings to accurately detect vehicles without miscounting. For **Piezoelectric Sensors:** Testing output voltage against standard weights or pressures to ensure accurate vehicle weight classification.

### 6.2.4. Sensor Calibration: Ensuring Accuracy

Calibration is crucial for ensuring that sensors deliver accurate and reliable readings. This process involves comparing the outputs of sensors with standard reference values and making adjustments to minimize any errors.

Steps in Sensor Calibration:

Initial Setup:

Calibrate sensors during installation to make sure they are aligned with the system's intended operation.

Routine Checks:

Regular calibration, particularly for sensors that are subject to changing environmental conditions, helps maintain consistent accuracy.

Dynamic Calibration:

Utilize self-calibrating algorithms that automatically adjust sensor parameters in real time based on observed discrepancies.

Cross-Validation:

Employ multiple sensors for redundancy. If one sensor fails or provides inconsistent data, others can help validate the results.

Examples of Calibration Techniques:

**For Cameras:** Adjusting focus, white balance, and alignment to ensure accurate image capture.

**For Loop Detectors:** Verifying sensitivity settings to accurately detect vehicles without miscounting.

**For Piezoelectric Sensors:** Testing output voltage against standard weights or pressures to ensure precise vehicle weight classification.

### 6.2.5. Addressing Maintenance Challenges

Regular maintenance is essential for extending the lifespan of sensors and enhancing system performance. However, it comes with several challenges, especially in large-scale deployments.

Key Maintenance Challenges:

High Costs:

Replacing damaged or outdated sensors in extensive urban networks can be quite costly.

Accessibility:

Sensors that are embedded in roadways or installed at high heights are challenging to reach for repairs or replacements.

Data Downtime:

Maintenance activities can temporarily halt data collection, affecting system functionality.

Skilled Workforce:

Specialized skills are necessary for sensor diagnostics and repairs, leading to a reliance on trained personnel.

Solutions for Effective Maintenance:

Predictive Maintenance:

Utilize machine learning algorithms to forecast sensor failures based on historical performance data, allowing for timely interventions.

Modular Designs:

Incorporate modular sensor components that can be easily swapped out without extensive disassembly.

Remote Monitoring:

Adopt IoT-enabled sensors with real-time diagnostics to detect and resolve issues remotely.

Standardized Protocols:

Create universal maintenance protocols for various sensor types to simplify repairs and replacements.

### 6.2.6 Improving Sensor Reliability

To enhance the reliability of sensors in traffic management systems, it is crucial to tackle both technical and operational factors.

Technical Approaches:

Robust Materials:

Utilize weather-resistant and durable materials to lessen the effects of environmental conditions.

Redundancy Systems:

Install multiple sensors at key locations to ensure backup data in the event of a sensor failure.

Firmware Updates:

Regularly updating sensor firmware can resolve bugs and improve performance.

## 7. FUTURE DIRECTIONS FOR ENHANCING SENSOR RELIABILITY IN TRAFFIC MANAGEMENT SYSTEMS

Over the past decade, there is observed remarkable progress in vehicle classification systems. This progress can be attributed to advancements in sensing, machine learning, and wireless communication technologies, which have significantly enhanced classification accuracy while simultaneously reducing costs.

Despite these advancements, several unresolved questions persist regarding emerging vehicle classification systems. In this section, it is delved into these challenges and explores potential avenues for future research.

*Figure 14. The classification accuracy for different numbers of vehicle types.*

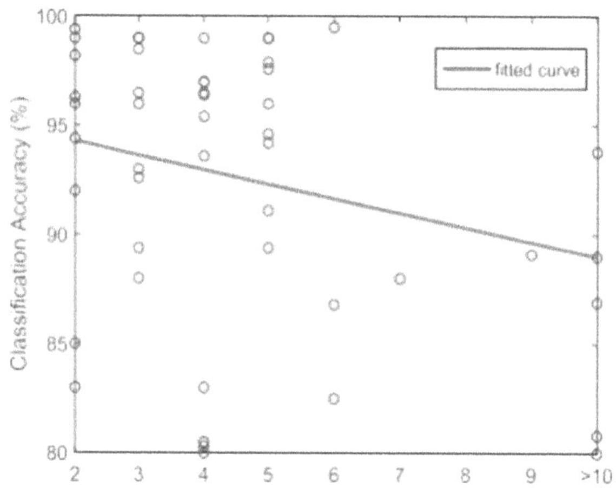


Once implemented, these systems will initiate the training of classification models, enabling them to autonomously and iteratively refine their performance through trial and error.

### 7.1. Advancement of Self-Healing Sensors

Self-healing sensors represent an innovative strategy aimed at improving the durability of sensors while minimizing maintenance expenses. By utilizing sophisticated materials, such as polymers integrated with microcapsules filled with healing agents or nanoparticles, these sensors possess the capability to autonomously mend minor damages, including cracks or abrasions resulting from environmental factors.

Potential Applications:

Sensors embedded in roadways can autonomously repair minor structural damages inflicted by heavy traffic or adverse weather conditions.

Cameras and surface-mounted sensors that are susceptible to dust and debris can restore their protective coatings independently to ensure optimal performance.

## 7.2. AI-Driven Diagnostics for Real-Time Monitoring

AI can be utilized to monitor sensor performance in real-time, detect anomalies, and anticipate failures before they happen. Systems powered by AI can analyze past performance data along with environmental factors to develop predictive maintenance models.

Key Features:

**Anomaly Detection:** Algorithms are capable of identifying unusual patterns in sensor data, such as erratic outputs or delays in communication, which may indicate potential issues.

**Predictive Analytics:** AI can predict failures by examining usage trends, environmental conditions, and historical reliability information.

Example Use Case:

In a smart city, AI systems can issue alerts for road sensors that are approaching failure, allowing for proactive measures and minimizing downtime.

## 7.3. Deployment of Edge Computing for Real-Time Processing

Edge computing focuses on processing data near the source, which minimizes latency and allows for quicker response times. This technology can be seamlessly integrated with traffic management systems to enhance the speed and reliability of decision-making.

Applications in Traffic Management:

Real-time video analysis at traffic cameras for classifying vehicles without depending on central servers.

Prompt detection of anomalies and diagnostics for roadway sensors, facilitating faster responses to sensor malfunctions.

## 7.4. Advanced Sensor Materials with Environmental Resilience

Innovative materials in sensor manufacturing can greatly improve their ability to withstand harsh environmental conditions. For instance:

**Graphene-Based Sensors:** With its remarkable strength and conductivity, graphene enhances both the durability and sensitivity of sensors.

**Nanocoatings:** Applying nanomaterials to sensors helps them resist corrosion, dirt, and water damage, ensuring reliable performance even in tough conditions.

**Flexible Sensors:** Utilizing flexible sensors can help absorb the effects of heavy traffic vibrations, thereby reducing wear and tear.

Example Technology:

Indian startups are beginning to investigate the use of biodegradable materials for creating eco-friendly and durable sensor systems, which are ideal for traffic management in both urban and rural areas.

## 7.5. Integration with 5G and IoT Networks

The combination of sensors with 5G and Internet of Things (IoT) networks has the potential to transform traffic management systems, allowing for real-time communication and control.

Key Features:

**Ultra-Low Latency:** Enables almost instantaneous data transmission from sensors to traffic control systems.

**Massive IoT Connectivity:** Allows for the simultaneous operation of thousands of sensors in urban environments.

**Dynamic Traffic Control:** Improves the flexibility of traffic signals based on real-time data.

## 7.6. Scalability and Standardization for Urban Expansion

As cities expand, traffic management systems need to scale effectively to handle rising vehicle numbers and growing road infrastructures.

Approach to Scalability:

- Create modular sensor networks that can be easily expanded by incorporating additional nodes.
- Implement universal protocols for sensor calibration and maintenance across different cities to guarantee interoperability.

## 7.7. Energy-Efficient and Sustainable Sensor Systems

With the growing focus on sustainability, traffic sensors must embrace energy-efficient designs and utilize renewable energy sources.

Key Innovations:

**Energy Harvesting Sensors:** These sensors harness vibrations from traffic or utilize solar panels for power.

**Low-Power Electronics:** The goal is to create sensors that operate with minimal energy consumption.

**Eco-Friendly Materials:** Sensors should be made from recyclable or biodegradable materials.

Real-World Implementation:

In Bengaluru, the introduction of solar-powered traffic sensors has decreased reliance on grid electricity, supporting the city's sustainability objectives.

## 7.8. Cybersecurity and Data Privacy Measures

As traffic sensors gather extensive data, it is essential to prioritize cybersecurity and safeguard user privacy.

Measures for Improvement:

**Encrypted Communication:** Implement advanced encryption protocols to secure sensor data during transmission.

**Anonymized Data:** Ensure that the data collected does not reveal individual vehicle identities or personal information.

**Regular Audits:** Perform routine security evaluations to detect vulnerabilities within the sensor network.

Emerging Standards:

Partnerships between Indian IT companies and international standards organizations are working to establish comprehensive guidelines for cybersecurity in traffic management systems.

### 7.9. Collaborative research and partnerships between public and private sectors

It can significantly enhance innovation in sensor technologies and traffic management systems.

## 8. RESULT AND CONCLUSION

Aa sensor-based technology for traffic control has been implemented, which is believed to offer a robust solution enhances the existing system with an intelligent traffic light controller.

The two main phases:

The first phase involves adjusting traffic signal lights based on the current traffic level on the road.

The second phase focuses on managing traffic flow when emergency vehicles, such as ambulances or fire trucks, approach. This project aims to contribute to the ongoing research efforts towards automating traffic light systems to alleviate congestion on busy roundabouts. Specifically, an alternative method for efficiently controlling traffic at roundabouts using an I/O Programmable Logic Controller (PLC) and an Ultrasonic IR sensor was successfully demonstrated. The implementation of a timing circuit has enabled us to reduce the number of I/O ports required by the system, thereby enhancing cost-effectiveness and efficiency. Additionally, the robustness of the software programming allows for flexibility and adaptability to various roundabout configurations. The system demonstrates a comprehensive approach to modern traffic management, emphasizing cost-effectiveness, efficiency, and adaptability. By utilizing an I/O Programmable Logic Controller (PLC) and Ultrasonic IR sensors, the system ensures dynamic traffic flow control, particularly at roundabouts. The inclusion of a timing circuit significantly reduces the required number of I/O ports, further optimizing the system's operational costs. The robust software design enhances adaptability, allowing the system to cater to diverse roundabout configurations. Additionally, provisions for emergency vehicle prioritization and real-time traffic density adjustments make the system highly responsive to varying traffic conditions. These features collectively contribute to alleviating congestion and ensuring seamless traffic management.

To further enhance the project, future improvements could include integrating cameras and artificial intelligence for monitoring, detection, and detailed vehicle analysis. These enhancements would facilitate seamless monitoring and management of traffic flow, contributing to even greater efficiency and effectiveness of the system.

Future enhancements aim to integrate advanced technologies such as artificial intelligence (AI) and cameras for real-time monitoring, predictive analysis, and detailed vehicle categorization. The inclusion of AI would enable predictive traffic flow adjustments, reducing delays during peak hours. Moreover, the system's scalability supports integration into larger smart city frameworks, while its energy-efficient design minimizes environmental impact. Cloud integration could facilitate centralized traffic data analysis and long-term improvements, and a public interface could provide commuters with real-time updates to plan their routes effectively. These advancements position the system as a pivotal element in the development of sustainable, intelligent urban infrastructure.

## REFERENCES


Adu-Gyamfi, Y. O., Asare, S. K., Sharma, A., & Titus, T. (2017). Automated vehicle recognition with deep convolutional neural networks. *Transportation Research Record: Journal of the Transportation Research Board*, *2645*(1), 113–122. DOI: 10.3141/2645-13

Ahmed, S.. (2021). IoT-Enabled Traffic Monitoring Systems: Framework and Implementation. *Sensors (Basel)*.

Ali, S.. (2022). *Sustainable Traffic Systems: Energy-Efficient Sensors and Algorithms*. Renewable Energy in Transportation.

Audebert, N., Le Saux, B., & Lefèvre, S. (2017). Segment-before-detect: Vehicle detection and classification through semantic segmentation of aerial images. *Remote Sensing (Basel)*, *9*(4), 368. DOI: 10.3390/rs9040368

Breiman, L. (2001). Random forests. *Machine Learning*, *45*(1), 5–32. DOI: 10.1023/A:1010933404324

Chakravarthy, R. A., & Arun, M. (2020). Multicarrier interference cancellation for channel optimization using artificial neural network. [IJARESM]. *International Journal of All Research Education and Scientific Methods*, *8*(12), 617–623.

Chakravarthy, R. A., & Palaniswami, S. (2014). Recent investigation on cluster-based energy-efficient scheduling scheme for WSN. *International Journal of Applied Engineering Research: IJAER*, *9*(23), 18823–18840.

Chakravarthy, R. A., & Palaniswami, S. (2016). A hybrid butterfly swarm optimization and efficient packet scheduling-based energy-efficient load balancing for WSN. *Journal of Applied Sciences Research*, *12*(9), 37–49.

Chakravarthy, R. A., Palaniswami, S., & Sabitha, R. (2017). Cluster header revolving technique to prolong network lifespan in wireless sensor network. *Journal of Computational and Theoretical Nanoscience*, *14*(12), 5863–5871. DOI: 10.1166/jctn.2017.7028

Chen, Y.. (2020). *Reinforcement Learning for Adaptive Traffic Signal Control*. Machine Learning in Traffic Engineering.

Gupta, N.. (2022). *Predictive Traffic Management Using Machine Learning Models*. Advances in Traffic Control Systems.

Javadi, S., Rameez, M., Dahl, M., & Pettersson, M. I. (2018). Vehicle classification based on multiple fuzzy C-means clustering using dimensions and speed features. *Procedia Computer Science*, *126*, 1344–1350. DOI: 10.1016/j.procs.2018.08.085

Jones, K.. (2023). *Analyzing Driver Behavior for Improved Traffic Management*. Behavioral Science in Transportation.

Khan, A.. (2022). Sensor Fusion for Vehicle Classification in Urban Traffic Monitoring Systems. *IEEE Transactions on Intelligent Transportation Systems*.

Kocer, A.. (2020). Traffic Monitoring Using UAVs: Challenges and Opportunities. *Journal of Transportation Engineering*.

Kouvelas, A.. (2019). Adaptive Traffic Signal Control Using the Webster Method: Real-Time Applications. *Transportation Research Record: Journal of the Transportation Research Board*.

Kumar, R.. (2023). Securing Traffic Data with Blockchain in IoT Ecosystems. *Future Generation Computer Systems*.

Li, F., & Lv, Z. (2017). Reliable vehicle type recognition based on information fusion in multiple sensor networks. *Computer Networks*, *117*, 76–84. DOI: 10.1016/j.comnet.2017.02.013

Li, M., et al. (2022). *Connected Infrastructure in Smart Cities: A Case Study of Intelligent Traffic Systems*. Journal of Smart Cities.

Martinez, P., et al. (2022). *V2I Communication for Autonomous Vehicles in Urban Traffic Systems*. Journal of Intelligent Transportation.

Mitra, R.. (2023). Enhancing Traffic Surveillance Using Deep Learning-Based Video Analytics. *IEEE Transactions on Intelligent Transportation Systems*.

Park, J.. (2021). *Multi-Agent Systems for Autonomous Vehicle Coordination at Intersections*. Transportation Robotics and AI.

Patterson, M., et al. (2021). *Advances in Inductive Loop Technology for Urban Traffic Monitoring*. Journal of Transportation Research.

Ramirez, L.. (2022). *IoT Frameworks for Smart Traffic Management: A Comprehensive Review*. Smart Cities Journal.

Sharma, P.. (2022). IoT and Machine Learning Integration for Dynamic Traffic Signal Control. *IEEE Internet of Things Journal*.

Singh, A.. (2021). *Edge Computing in IoT-Based Traffic Systems: Challenges and Opportunities*. IoT Journal.

Smith, T.. (2022). *LiDAR Applications in Intelligent Traffic Management Systems*. Transportation Science Journal.

Sun, Q.. (2020). *Traffic Prediction Using LSTM Networks: A Comprehensive Review*. Neural Networks and Applications.

Yang, H.. (2023). Hybrid Machine Learning Models for Anomaly Detection in Traffic Patterns. *Neural Computing & Applications*.

Zhang, W., et al. (2023). *5G Network Deployment in Intelligent Traffic Systems: Opportunities and Challenges*. IEEE Access.

Zhang, Y.. (2021). Deep Learning-Based Real-Time Vehicle Classification for Urban Traffic Applications. *Transportation Research Part C, Emerging Technologies*.

# Chapter 3
# Green Future Ideas and Scalable Technologies Essential for Innovators, Scientists, Researchers, and Engineers:
## Cutting-Edge Initiatives and Commercially-Viable Solutions for a Fairer Future

**Cristina Raluca Gh. Popescu**
https://orcid.org/0000-0002-5876-0550
*University of Bucharest, Romania & The Bucharest University of Economic Studies, Romania*

**Rahul Verma**
https://orcid.org/0000-0002-5356-813X
*University of Delhi, India*

## ABSTRACT

*Reducing greenhouse gas emissions and adapting to impacts of climate change are pivotal in developing solutions to secure a greener and fairer future. Building and scaling ideas to support climate tech solutions crucially help society adapt to climate change. Funding cutting-edge ideas and initiatives, while engineering commercially-viable solutions, fosters tailored support in creating sustainable solutions to climate crisis. This research tackles climate and sustainability crisis, addresses studies' outcomes that more people ought to become engineers to provide solutions to climate crisis, and sheds a new light on general believe that a constant supply of electricity without burning fossil fuels is a must for present and future generations. A major accent is placed on circular economy principles, with powerful targets: recycling and reusing metals and plastics as well as recovering and using energy from industrial processes that would otherwise be sadly wasted. Harnessing creativity, innovation, and engineering is paramount for an inclusive economy and sustainable society.*

DOI: 10.4018/979-8-3373-0189-1.ch003

## INTRODUCTION

The book chapter on "Green Future Ideas and Scalable Technologies Essential for Innovators, Scientists, Researchers, and Engineers: Cutting-Edge Initiatives and Commercially-Viable Solutions for a Fairer Future" is dedicated to highlighting the major importance of sustainability and sustainable development in a world that has been far too long driven by acquisitiveness, greediness, materialism, possessiveness, profitability, and the need to address and obtain economic growth at all costs. Individuals' and businesses' eagerness to receive instant satisfaction and success, no matter of the costs and without any consideration towards those affected or in desperate need for survival, has led to health and environment problems with which humanity confronts itself these days (Popescu, 2024a; Popescu, 2024b). On the one hand, there can be encountered the people's need to fulfill their ambitions and dreams, in the context in which everything around suggests that overconsumption is a way of displaying the social statute, power, and unlimited possibilities (Popescu, 2024c; Popescu, 2024d). On the other hand, there can be seen the organizations that have insatiable appetite for money, power, and shaping the future of the business environment in their own advantage and for their own benefit. These behaviors that suggest the thirst for material things rather than for spiritual goods are extremely damaging for the human health as well as for the well-being of the environment: firstly, extreme greed leads to narcissistic and self-centered forms of behavior, since self-indulgence, self-interested, and self-seeking activities generate narrow-minded images regarding one-self (Chawla *et al.*, 2025); secondly, while avidity and money-hunger create businesses that act irrationally and irresponsibly on the marketplace, individuals and communities have come to suffer, while the environment became extremely affected and neglected; and, thirdly, since there are so many economic activities these days that generate great profits to those inclined to bend the law more than others, people have come to believe that hard work, dedication, and responsibility are no longer needed in order to become successful and to be considered a meaningful figure in the society (Popescu & Popescu, 2024a; Popescu & Popescu, 2024b). In other words, people have become more and more concerned with their own immediate satisfaction, being less and less preoccupied by the medium-term and long-term implications of their actions (Popescu & Popescu, 2024c; Popescu & Popescu, 2024d). Likewise, communities, country leaders, and governments have shown in the last decades that they are more concerned with the business environment development and economic growth, rather than displaying care towards people's health and the preservation of the environment (Popescu & Popescu, 2024e). In turn, the values on which the society relied on once may be in some parts of the world long forgotten, while in others faded and are becoming less and less important by comparison to the individuals' general need to prosper and overcome all adversities, and the organizations' desire to flourish and dominate the marketplace (Popescu, 2023a; Popescu, 2023b).

Nevertheless, there are still cases, in which people and communities act responsibly, being centered on preserving their heritage and their natural habitats, but these cases are rare and represent a great sign that everyone should truly worry about the future of the present generations and the ones to come, together with the painful questions that are being raised regarding the environment, nature preservation, biodiversity, and ecosystems (Thomas & Howarth, 2000). In this particular matter, there are numerous questions that the authors of this book chapter have come to ask while reflecting on human nature and human behavior, namely: firstly, an important question that comes to mind is what are the individual values on which people should focus on in order to ensure survival, decent ways of living, and respect for nature, health, and well-being; secondly, another important question that leads to reflection is what should organizations do in order to protect people's health and the environmental preservation, but, in the same time, have successful activities on the marketplace; and, thirdly, what competences and skills are expected from people today, in order to act in the spirit of the new economy, knowledge economy, and green economy, the one that finds the pillars in the values of sustainability, sustainable development, and circular economy (Gailey *et al.*, 2021).

Based on the aforementioned ideas and thoughts, it has been stressed, on far too numerous occasions and in a plethora of international and interdisciplinary studies, that positive and responsible human behavior leads to great results in terms of ensuring better health, supporting well-being, more focused individuals on the personal life and work activities balance, with more strength, and more dedication towards protecting the environment. Besides these, in the last years, researchers have become more and more focused on the principles of the circular economy, especially in the context in which the resources are limited, people's behavior led to unhealthy decisions, and businesses have come to generate tremendous pollution. More and more leaders and managers emphasize the need to reevaluate human and organizational beliefs, while finding, in the same time, those solutions capable to ensure sustainable development and continuity in terms of the transition to responsible forms of economic activities.

Hence, the authors of this book chapter are strongly inclined to support the creation and promotion of green future ideas and scalable technologies essential for innovators, scientists, researchers, and engineers, while centering on cutting-edge initiatives and commercially-viable solutions for a fairer future, addressing, in this way, the following aspects: first of all, research and development activities should be seen, in all countries, as great pillars of the new knowledge economy, based on the fact that creative and innovative thinking will ultimately lead to viable ideas that will be put into practice by specialists, hence ensuring people's health and environmental' preservation (Popescu *et al.*, 2014); second of all, among the most important professions these days, specialists have come to point out that those involved in education programs and long-life-training activities play crucial roles in promoting the principles of circular economy and sustainability, in the context in which individuals and businesses have come to act so irrationally and selfishly (Popescu & Verma, 2025); third of all, engineers are the ones expected to put into practice all those solutions offered through scientific discoveries, since they will be the ones that will have to focus on addressing today's environmental problems with bold and daring solutions; and, fourth of all, the idea behind a fairer future is that the environment should be positioned at the center of all decisions, mainly having in mind the Sustainable Development Goals (SDGs) (Mouloudj & Bouarar, 2025).

The main objective (MO) or the general objective (GO) of this current scientific work is to show, on the one hand, what do green future ideas and scalable technologies represent in terms of ensuring sustainability and sustainable development and, on the other hand, what is the role of innovators, scientists, researchers, and engineers in generating cutting-edge initiatives and promoting commercially-viable solutions for a fairer future. Additionally, there are several secondary objectives (SO) that are derived from the MO or the GO stated above, namely: the first SO is to emphasize the powerful connections that are between sustainability, sustainable development, and circular economy; and, the second SO is to present some of the most relevant reasons why the innovators, scientists, researchers, and engineers are playing such decisive and important parts in today's society in terms of supporting, in the best manner possible, sustainability, sustainable development, and circular economy principles.

The two main research questions (RQ) on which the current book chapter is centered are: (RQ1) what are the green future ideas and measurable technologies that ought to be considered pivotal by innovators, scientists, researchers, and engineers in order to reflect, in the best way possible, sustainability, sustainable development, and circular economy principles; and, (RQ2) how can innovators, scientists, researchers, and engineers ensure and support a fairer future in a world filled with so many controversies, irrational decisions, and irresponsible behavior.

There are several keywords which prove to be essential to this current research, as follows: green future; tech solutions; creativity; research and innovation community; climate innovations; economic development; sustainability; breakthrough technologies; prosperity; and, hard-working people.

The aspects highlighted above, in the introduction section, require reflection from everyone: the individuals ought to think about those moments in their lives in which they took impulsive decisions, without really allocating the time to analyze responsibly the results of one's actions; the communities must profoundly think about the way in which they acted in favor of those big and powerful corporations that showed willingness to open their businesses in their hometowns, although they already had examples of irresponsible economic activities performed by these international companies in other parts of the world, yet they chose to ignore those situations; the organizations must gravely reflect on their business practices and question the manner in which they chose to perform their activities when they decided to bend the law or even ignore the law in the name of money, fortunes, market quotas, unhealthy and unsafe business practices; and, also, leaders, managers, politicians, and governmental officials need to restore the equilibrium most likely forgotten or ignored between doing good and acting according to the principles of good governance. These are times which call not only for profound reflection; these are times that call for immediate analysis of the past actions, in order to rapidly take those right decisions, and ensure the long-term success of the SDGs before the environment will be even more affected than it is at present, and, also, before more children, youth, and adults will have to face the devastating consequences of having their health and environmental problems even more neglected than today. In addition, these are times in which critical thinking is no longer brought into discussion due to the simple requirements of enlarging competences and skills associated with sustainability and sustainable development; these are times in which critical thinking has become a must, due to the general expectations to closely analyze past and present actions in order to ensure that the Global Goals (GG) will generate immense benefits to human beings and environment in an equal and unprecedented manner. That being said, critical thinking ought to be on the agenda of everybody that strives to create and shape a better future for all, since everything around us should be analyzed and questioned accordingly. In this way, no assumptions should be made anymore that all organizations are environmentally-friendly and, also, no assumptions should be made anymore that all individuals are working towards the sustainability principles. On the contrary, by promoting critical thinking, all new ideas and thoughts and technologies should be analyzed, questioned, and evaluated, hence making sure that the interest of human beings will be taken at heart and, also, that organizations will act in the spirit of excellence, but with care, responsibility, and respect towards communities and environment.

Scholars are highly representative figures in any society, which means that their role in academia and research fields should be taken very seriously when reevaluating the principles on which these days' business activities are being built. It is precisely those specialists involved in the educational activities and the life-long training programs that ought to ask the best and more profound questions associated with sustainable development behavior, while being deeply involved in critical thinking processes related to the businesses dynamics, and the leadership and managerial competences and skills.

All in all, the introduction section displayed the reasons why it has become an imperative in the year 2025 to be more eco-friendly. In addition, this section is crucial in tackling the MO or the GO as well as in emphasizing the vital RQs of this current book chapter. Being more eco-friendly in 2025 also comes from willing to bring solutions to the key question: What would a green future look like?

Besides the introduction section, there are other sections part of this book chapter that are believed to be essential, as follows: the conceptual framework section (also acknowledged as the literature review section or the background section) puts an emphasis on the need to work to limit and adapt to climate change by offering those viable and realistic solutions that would lead to the reduction of the demand for carbon-intensive activities in important areas, such as agriculture, construction, and transport; in addition, the same section mentioned above, brings into analysis the way in which infrastructure and public services could become more inclusive, resilient, and sustainable in order to protect biodiversity and support green industries; the materials and methods section accentuates the necessity to find answers and justifications to the MO or the GO as well as in emphasizing the vital RQs of this current book chapter; in like manner, the materials and methods section is extremely powerful and representative in this case, since it presents the way in which establishing specific goals for creating a greener future is made; the next sections are the results section and the discussion and conclusion section which are highly important for this book chapter and which show how those specific and measurable goals allow individuals, communities, companies' leaders, organizations' managers, policymakers, and governments to better understand the impact of their actions in these days' society; in the end, the references section or the bibliography section plays an important part in this current research, since it has the immense power to reflect which are the most representative studies in the field analyzed and which are the most representative publications that come to support and to offer a reasoning behind choosing this current bold and ground-breaking theme.

Seeking answers to the following question represents an imperative today when one is willing to establish specific goals: How can we create a greener future? Yet, there are numerous voices stating that besides the creation of the specific and measurable goals there are other steps and phases to consider, specialists strongly believe that by establish specific goals a lot can be accomplished right from the very begging. On the one hand, the specific and measurable goals established are designed to allow everyone to understand how one's actions impact the environment. Additionally, on the other hand, the specific and measurable goals established are created so that they can help everyone see how their environmental impact can become more sustainable. Nevertheless, interestingly, there are still cases in which some individuals and some companies try to convince the general public that sustainability is not the right way for a better future for all, offering other very tempting alternatives such as, among others: the need to fulfill one's aims, desires, and needs at all costs or the idea that one lives only once, so one has to make the most of that time period or the idea that due to consumerism everyone has to adapt to this trend which is far more than something one can truly manage and overcome. Although such individuals and companies will continue to exist and to promote their unrealistic ideas, the environment requires great care and protection, while individuals and communities need better living conditions, where the accent ought to be positioned on well-being and healthier lifestyles.

## BACKGROUND

This section is dedicated to the conceptual framework section (also acknowledged as the literature review section or the background section) in which the most important concepts related to this theme are displayed and explained as seen by reputed international specialists as well as by the authors of this book chapter. The keywords which prove to be pivotal in this regard are as follows: green future; tech solutions; creativity; research and innovation community; climate innovations; economic development;

sustainability; breakthrough technologies; prosperity; and, hard-working people. In addition, besides the aforementioned ideas, another element needs to be introduced, namely the importance of highlighting in this section why it has become crucial to the environment and to humanity to establish specific goals.

There are several elements that will be highlighted in this particular section of this book chapter. To begin with, one main question that will be addressed and which will receive answers here is: What will a sustainable future look like? In order to have the general background created in this matter, the authors will show that protecting our planet starts with each and every person and, additionally, depends on each and every business, no matter how important that person is and no matter how big that business is. In addition, the authors will argue that a sustainable future has to embrace the principles and rules of a circular economy model in order to be able to offer better and more sustainable solutions in terms of waste minimization. Under these circumstances, it ought to be emphasized that waste is a great concern to us all and waste puts the health of the environment and well-being of people and communities in danger. In continuation, with a circular economy model the resources will be reused, recycled, and restored. Although the cycle of reusing, recycling, and restoring may seem brand new to some, it has been, in fact, used for decades in certain regions, countries, or by certain individuals, based on their policies and beliefs in which they developed and flourished. In other words, the cycle of reusing, recycling, and restoring has been already tested over long periods of time in some countries and by some communities, since it represents an alternative to consumerism and irrational forms of behavior in terms of buying and consuming goods and services. Hence, these days it would be tremendously helpful if products would be designed with longevity and reparability features in mind, since these features would provide great benefits to the environment. In this way products would be used longer by people, they would be restored and reused in additional business cycles and processes, hence implicating that the use of the natural resources would be significantly diminished in time. Having that taken into consideration, the need for constant replacements would be reduced.

Besides the aforementioned question, a new and bold question comes into discussion in order to advance the already started analysis and debate, as follows: How will the healthy world look like, while addressing the future of sustainability? The vision for the healthy world is very complex and is derived from the manner in which people will have the capacity to understand sustainability and put into practice the principles of the SDGs. On the one hand, the future of sustainability depends on finding answers to a key question: What is green growth while having in mind the year 2050? In this matter, an important step is to acknowledge the paramount importance of the Green Growth 2050 Standard which has been carefully and thoroughly developed especially to meet, among others, the needs of tourism and travel businesses which seek solutions these days in the following main areas: helping the Earth to get greener; facilitating the extent of green vegetation in order to have more green spaces today and no less; driving cultural, environmental, economic, and social change; promoting those events, festivals, venues, organizations around the world that have chosen to go green, more sustainable, and centered on reducing environmental impacts. On the other hand, another question needs to be addressed for a better understanding of how the healthy world look will like, while addressing the future of sustainability, as follows: Which are the benefits and challenges of going green? In any situation, in any business, and in any new endeavor, specialists have pointed out that there are benefits and challenges alike, hence all facets of an issue should be closely analyzed and put into balance. Making the world greener means discovering and referring to green tips and solutions for a cleaner and healthier environment, such as: (a) buying local products and encouraging the local economy, since this would reduce the costs with transportation and would reduce the pollution in the area; (b) using e-billing systems rather the traditional systems, since in this way less paper or even no paper will be used, which would greatly benefit the environment and communities; (c) using cold water in those cases in which such an option turns out to be viable is a great example of supporting the environment, since in this way a green future is better addressed and considered; (d) going solar may be considered an optimum way of heating the house or of ensuring electricity for a business, yet there are numerous debates and still unanswered questions regarding the way in which deposing of the solar panels could be done with ought harming the environment even more than other devices performing similar tasks; and, (e) recycling is of essence when it comes to plastics, metals, and other components, taking into account that controversies still exist up to these days when it comes to showing the impact of recycling of some products in certain industries.

In other words, although the capacity to regenerate and to find creative solutions to ensure survival it is embedded in the human nature as well as in the environment, there are so many cases in which the human body as well as the biodiversity and ecosystems were not able to cope any longer with the external damaging factors that have led to the internal deterioration of the human body functions and the plants and animals functions. Under these circumstances, too much pollution, too many sources of stress, and too many negative elements in the environment have led to increased health problems, mortality, and the incapacity of living organisms to cope with the new changes and profound challenges. The two tables below offer substantial answers and solutions to the following vital questions. One of these questions is: In what way can individuals, communities, and organizations become more eco-friendly in the year 2025? The answers to this particular question are displayed in Table no. 1: Ways to Become more Eco-Friendly in the Year 2025. What is more, another highly interesting question is: What is The Green Future Index and why does it represent the guide to sustainable leaders and innovative green policies? The answers to this specific question are displayed in Table no. 2: The Green Future Index – The Guide to Sustainable Leaders and Innovative Green Policies. Furthermore, it should be taken into account that a greened future embodies, among others: (a) firstly, the green future impact analysis, which could be represented by finding green and innovative solutions capable to create and facilitate the use of 100% renewable sources of energy coming from new regional wind or solar facilities, which would, in turn, greatly enhance the lifestyles of individuals and which would substantially ensure businesses' continuity in the areas, hence coping with the ambitious sustainability and carbon reduction goals; (b) secondly, the future of green energy is a hot topic these days, hence the Next Generation Green Technologies (NGGT) are strongly committed to the reduction of the carbon footprint by finding more efficient, inclusive, resilient, and sustainable ways to build, upgrade, and repurpose different categories of instruments, tools, techniques, and technologies, that use, for example, liquid cooling in the Information and Technology (IT) industry, or green energy generation systems using hydrogen; and, (c) thirdly, focusing on the 2030 Plan for a Green Economy which is a very powerful policy framework having as bold purpose the electrification and climate change guidelines that are intended and expected to serve as the governments' roadmaps for at least the next ten years, hence being responsible for helping the countries to meet their greenhouse gas (GHG) emission reduction targets, while focusing on growing, in like manner, their economy (Lekkala *et al.*, 2025); KarimiDermani *et al.*, 2025; Yu *et al.*, 2025).

In the lines below, Table no. 1: Ways to Become more Eco-Friendly in the Year 2025 sheds a new light on the manner in which crafting the path to a greener future represents a must, while using simple guides to sustainability becomes essential for individuals and organizations (see, in this matter, Table no. 1: Ways to Become more Eco-Friendly in the Year 2025).

*Table 1. Ways to Become more Eco-Friendly in the Year 2025*

| What is the green future? | How can individuals and organizations make the world green? |
|---|---|
| • An important goal is reducing greenhouse gas emissions by 50% by 2030; this is a measurable and vital goal, while efforts in this matter need to be made constantly (Erdoğdu *et al.*, 2016).<br>• This is an achievable goal, since it is presented in a specific and measurable way, which implicates that this is an achievable goal rather than a concept (Chiwaridzo & Dzingirai, 2025). | • In this matter, the future of the green industry needs to be seriously and responsibly considered (Tsai *et al.*, 2018).<br>• Based on recent reports, more than 1.5 million new green jobs could be created by 2024, which will lead to the creation of more than 300 unique occupations only by expending the clean energy sector (Tunio *et al.*, 2025).<br>• Interestingly, important steps are taken in countries all over the world, such as, for example, according to a recently approved plan, in Carolina a ban was placed on the sale of new gasoline-powered vehicles by 2030 (Ragazou *et al.*, 2025). |
| • Building a more inclusive workforce is an extremely tempting solution in order to ensure the future of green manufacturing (Management Association, 2019).<br>• The Green Future Index plays a vital role in supporting the future of green manufacturing as well as other industries that require the adaptation and implementation to green practices and policies (Ordóñez de Pablos & Zhang, 2023). | • In this matter, the accent is placed on: (a) assessing each one's capacity to develop low-carbon activities, so that regions and countries would be helped in the process of becoming more sustainable, hence in supporting low-carbon economies; and (b) considering investments in renewable energy as well as in creative, innovative, and environmental policies (Migdadi, 2020). |

Source: The Authors' Own Elaboration, Based on the References Highlighted in the Table and in the Bibliography Section

In the lines below, Table no. 2: The Green Future Index – The Guide to Sustainable Leaders and Innovative Green Policies tackles the implications of climate change, while offering solutions to the heating world, presents the way in which the world will look like in the year 2050, and displays the manner in which helping the environment can be done (see, in this matter, Table no. 2: The Green Future Index – The Guide to Sustainable Leaders and Innovative Green Policies).

*Table 2. The Green Future Index – The Guide to Sustainable Leaders and Innovative Green Policies*

| What will nature look like in 2025 and what is the importance of natural capital? | What are the ways to help the environment? |
|---|---|
| • The natural capital is vital to the health, mental health, and well-being of individuals, given the powerful connections that have always existed between individuals, communities and environment (Giannico *et al.*, 2021).<br>• This relationship is essential to every human being, given its role in the development of each person as well as in the way in which people will be able to define and shape their life values as well as work values (Fields, 2023). | • Individuals and organizations can make simple choices that will lead to a healthier planet. Among these choices, cutting down on what individuals and companies throw away is crucial (Liu *et al.*, 2025).<br>• An important way to help the environment is to guide the life-cycles and business-cycles by the principles of the circular economy which position reduce, reuse, and recycles practices among their top priorities (Li *et al.*, 2025).<br>• There are numerous volunteering programs to which individuals can be part in their communities. A pivotal example is being a volunteer for the cleanups in the community (Smirani *et al.*, 2025). |
| • The implications of a heating world are devastating to the ecosystem and biodiversity, numerous plants and animals being in great danger, while people and communities have their lives and habitats affected (Ponnusamy *et al.*, 2021).<br>• Recent studies have shown that nature will look quite different in 2050, as a result of increased pollution, hence: (a) in the Andes, the glacier loss will reach 70% by 2050; in addition, (b) the summer monsoon in China will fail and, in the same time, the water flows into the great rivers of Asia will be drastically reduced by the loss of more than one-third of the Himalayan ice sheet (Gupta *et al.*, 2025). | • In order to become more sustainable – while focusing on the principles of sustainable development and sustainability, the accent ought to be positioned on: (a) plating trees, in order to have access to oxygen, and be healthy and full of life; (b) making sustainable choices and shopping wisely, which could be done not only when deciding to buy food products, but also cloths and other important devices for the houses or work; (c) conserving water, since water is a precious and vital resource for living, with ought which life cannot even be imagined; (d) using long-lasting light bulbs is of absolute importance today, since pollution reached alarming quotas and finding solutions to use specific appliances for longer periods is crucial; and (e) educating other family or community members, and willing to be better trained in terms the implementation of SDGs and circular economy principles are vital steps that could lead to a sustainable future, with green growth by 2050 (Lee *et al.*, 2025). |

Source: The Authors' Own Elaboration, Based on the References Highlighted in the Table and in the Bibliography Section

This section is immediately followed by the materials and methods section which sheds a new light on the way in which the authors of this book chapter have decided to perform their research on the fight against climate change, which would generate a win-win situation for all countries as well as the planet. Besides these, the materials and methods section is of remarkable importance when it comes to offering a better understating on the motivation of this book chapter. For example, this section will offer significant ways in which the authors have focused in this book chapter in finding the answers to the question: What is the new green theory? Likewise, this section will present those ways in which the authors have centered in this book chapter in finding the answers to the question: Can global warming be reversed and how?

## MATERIALS AND METHODS

Nowadays, researchers' have centered their attention on a plethora of theories that offer great promises that are mainly centered on ensuring better lifestyles for all, more healthier solutions to these days problems, the reduction of poverty, and a better and safer future for all. Among these theories, the new green theory is very strongly imbedded already in the mind of individuals and communities, since it critiques state-centrism and economic growth imperative. On the one hand, reputed specialists have shown that by generating economic growth this will not necessarily reflect the fact that individuals and communities needs have been addressed and, more importantly, it certainly does not mean that their goals and desires have been taken care in a responsible and sustainable manner. On the other hand, renowned scholars have highlighted that the environment deserves and requires equal attention and care, since there are very strong links between the health of individuals and the well-being of the environment. Destroying the natural capital and natural habitats of our planet is not an answer to archiving prosperity and ensuring prosperity on the long-term, but it represents for sure a way to generate more and more health problems, damage the biodiversity and ecosystems, and lead to the lack of balance between the harmonious, positive, and constructive way in which human should live together with nature.

As stated in the introductory part of this book chapter, there are some MO and GO of great essence. The MO or the GO of this current scientific work is to show, on the one hand, what do green future ideas and scalable technologies represent in terms of ensuring sustainability and sustainable development and, on the other hand, what is the role of innovators, scientists, researchers, and engineers in generating cutting-edge initiatives and promoting commercially-viable solutions for a fairer future. Additionally, there are several SO that are derived from the MO or the GO stated above, namely: the first SO is to emphasize the powerful connections that are between sustainability, sustainable development, and circular economy; and, the second SO is to present some of the most relevant reasons why the innovators, scientists, researchers, and engineers are playing such decisive and important parts in today's society in terms of supporting, in the best manner possible, sustainability, sustainable development, and circular economy principles.

Likewise, as displayed in the introductory part of this book chapter, there are two main (RQ) on which the current book chapter is centered are: (RQ1) what are the green future ideas and measurable technologies that ought to be considered pivotal by innovators, scientists, researchers, and engineers in order to reflect, in the best way possible, sustainability, sustainable development, and circular economy principles; and, (RQ2) how can innovators, scientists, researchers, and engineers ensure and support a fairer future in a world filled with so many controversies, irrational decisions, and irresponsible behavior.

There are also other aspects that are interconnected and interrelated with the general structure of the book chapter on "Green Future Ideas and Scalable Technologies Essential for Innovators, Scientists, Researchers, and Engineers: Cutting-Edge Initiatives and Commercially-Viable Solutions for a Fairer Future". Among these aspects, in the lines below some of these ideas have been presented for a better and more in-depth understanding of the current topic, as follows (Yeoh *et al.*, 2020; Yin *et al.*, 2024):

- The fight for climate change should lead to the creation of innovative solutions capable to ensure win-win situations for all participants on the marketplace. Benefits ought to arise from the constant use of sustainable and reusable products, while the health of people should represent a priority for those companies that are responsible with creating these new and innovative products (Petrychenko *et al.*, 2025).
- The green theory supports the ideas according to which: (a) first of all, governance implicates multilevel ways of restructuring the global economy, so that it will focus towards sustainability and sustainable development principles; and, (b) second of all, the non-state actors' role is deeply highlighted since these actors are extremely powerful in shaping the green future expected and have the power with their actions and decisions to reverse global warming (Ziaesaeidi, 2025).
- The global warming implications are a very important aspect these days. By taking action for a healthy planet, global warming can be reversed. There are numerous ways in which global warm-

ing can be reversed and with the aid of this book chapter the solutions will be brought closer to individuals and communities.

This section is followed by the results section or the findings of the study. These results or findings define what the actions for a healthy planet embody, while the center of attention is saving the environment. In this matter, it is of great importance to emphasize, once again, that saving the environment implicates individuals, communities, and organizations constant support in completing the following steps: refuse, reduce, reuse, repurpose, and recycle. These are vital principles that come to support people's responsible behavior and, in the same time, businesses' constructive actions towards the SDGs. Additionally, in this day and age, according to prominent organizations such as the United Nations, it is believed that each of these steps – namely, refuse, reduce, reuse, repurpose, and recycle, have to be followed to the very last detail in order to be able to accomplish the GG and act in the spirit of the circular economy. Moreover, the full potential of these steps – namely, refuse, reduce, reuse, repurpose, and recycle, is considered to have been reached when waste will be managed accordingly, hence more green at homes and at work will be ensured, supported, and sustained on the long-term.

## RESULTS

This section highlights the results section or the findings of the study on "Green Future Ideas and Scalable Technologies Essential for Innovators, Scientists, Researchers, and Engineers: Cutting-Edge Initiatives and Commercially-Viable Solutions for a Fairer Future". This section tackles the findings of the study which make reference to an in-depth analysis of the following key aspects: on the one hand, the role of innovators, scientists, researchers, and engineers is crucial these days, in order to ensure a sustainable future and, on the other hand, becoming more eco-friendly means supporting centering on the preservation of resources, human sustainability, social sustainability, economic sustainability, and environmental sustainability.

In the lines below the Table no. 3: Pillars of Sustainability and Eco-Friendly Behavior focuses on addressing the pivotal part played in these days society by the preservation of resources, human sustainability, social sustainability, economic sustainability, and environmental sustainability (see, in this matter, Table no. 3: Pillars of Sustainability and Eco-Friendly Behavior).

*Table 3. Pillars of Sustainability and Eco-Friendly Behavior*

| The Global Goals and the 2030 Agenda for Sustainable Development | The Organization for Economic Cooperation and Development (OECD) Green Growth Strategy |
|---|---|
| • Key question: What are the pillars of sustainability?<br>• The pillars of sustainability and eco-friendly behavior implicate centering on the following pivotal aspects: preservation of resources, human sustainability, social sustainability, economic sustainability, and environmental sustainability (Queiroz Almeida *et al.*, 2022). | • Key question: What is the Green Growth Strategy?<br>• Aiming to provide concrete recommendations and measurement tools to support sustainability is one of the main objectives of the Green Growth Strategy (Popescu *et al.*, 2015c; Popescu *et al.*, 2015d).<br>• Targeting to create vital indicators to support the countries efforts to sustainability and achieve economic growth and development is another paramount objective of the Green Growth Strategy (Castillo-Vargas *et al.*, 2025). |
| • Key question: In what way is the year 2030 important for sustainability and sustainable development?<br>• Among the vital aims that are part of the GG could be mentioned: (a) ending poverty and hunger, since there are many cases in which individuals and communities face illnesses that they cannot address on their own, live in unbearable conditions, or their food, if any, is not nourishing enough (Popescu, 2017); (b) realizing the human rights for all, taking into consideration that people have rights no matter of their cultural values, ethnicity, religious believes, gender, and so on (Popescu *et al.*, 2017); (c) achieving gender equality in order to offer the empowerment of all girls and all women, hence supporting their rights to being educated, have better living conditions, and raise their families in decent conditions (Popescu *et al.*, 2015a; Popescu *et al.*, 2015b); and, (d) ensuring the long-lasting protection of the natural resources, the natural capital, and the planet (Fournet *et al.*, 2024). | • Key question: What is the Green Growth Strategy in terms of natural capital and the planet?<br>• These days, the natural assets or the natural resources are regarded as immense health creators for individuals and communities (Touya *et al.*, 2025). People rely and have always relied on the environment and their natural habitat in order to ensure the survival. However, due to greed and overconsumption, irrational forms of behavior have been promoted lately, which affected the environment and which severely damaged the planet (Jiang *et al.*, 2021).<br>• Key question: What are the connections between the environment, health, and well-being?<br>• The countries' economic growth and development can only be achieved by ensuring that the natural assets will continue to provide those resources and environmental services on which well-being was build and on which it relies (Cohen & Galperin, 2020). |

Source: The Authors' Own Elaboration, Based on the References Highlighted in the Table and in the Bibliography Section

In this day and age, the authors of this book chapter strongly position themselves among the ones that promote the following ideas: (a) firstly, more and more Green Growth Studies ought to be created and should be diversified and, in like manner, the processes of innovation, and research and development, together with the publication of the results, need to be thoroughly intensified; (b) secondly, the term sustainability should be even more extended, in order to be able to go far beyond the actions, initiatives, and programs that support sustainable development principles and the preservation of some particular resources; and, (c) thirdly, besides green ideas and initiatives, the discussion needs to be extended far more than it is today for connecting topics, such as, among others, eco-friendly behavior, green growth strategies, green finance growing, and so on.

The next section is the discussion and the conclusion section, where the most important ideas derived from this current analysis are drawn. On the one hand, this book chapter aligns with the other studies that have come to support the green growth studies. Yet, there is much more to be said in this matter: (a) to begin with, the aspects regarding the true values of pollution for green industries and technologies, since recent developments in different areas have shown that, in some cases, these industries and these technologies are, in turn, highly polluting and, moreover, they are believed to affect the environment much more than the older, already commonly used industries and technologies – an interesting and valuable example in this area being represented by the new models of solar panels or the new models of car batteries; and, (b) moving further with the analysis, the way in which some industries understand to become "green" and to embody green practices in their activities is still questionable and will, most probably, be questionable for many, many years to come, since by simply adding some words related to sustainable objectives to the businesses' classical ones, does not necessarily mean that those companies are really acting towards sustainable development principles and have accommodated their policies to the new trends in terms of green and sustainable finance, green culture, and the green plan for 2030 or 2050 – examples may be encountered in the highly controversial activities of key industries, such as, the oil and gas industries, which state that they will use less and less petrol for vehicles, but, in turn, have found highly-profitable alternatives in terms of petroleum derivate for products of day-to-day use in heath and cosmetics industries, home appliances, and so on (Akaraci *et al.*, 2020). On the other hand, this book chapter offers a bold, novel, and original perspective when it comes to supporting the sustainability principles and the sustainable development policies. For example, the ideas highlighted in this book chapter come to support the most recent trends in sustainability, while stressing, in the same time, the following pivotal aspects: (a) some countries, such as, for example, Australia, have become greener and are "greener" today than they were decades ago, since they placed a great importance implementing the sustainability principles and on increasing in vegetation, despite the general problems with which the country confronts itself with, namely, the fact that the vegetation increase has not been uniform, recent draughts, land clearing, and urbanization; (b) some areas and some countries, such as, for example, Australia or the countries in the Asia Pacific region, have experienced more and more green financing, since green and sustainable finance is responsible for further growth in those areas, however, there are much more steps to be taken on the long path to sustainability in order to support green and sustainable finance practices on the long-run; and, (c) in essence, climate change has led to disequilibrium in nature, but there is still hope in creating or reacting healthier and greener habitats for all – an eloquent example in this matter is represented by the Sahara, since although the way in which climate will influence the Sahara may not be said with utmost certainty, the desert has shown a greener image in the last 15 years which were generated by the rains (the condensation that rained down onto dry land that facilitated the creation of a greener landscape in the case of Sahara desert came from the stronger evaporation over the sea which was an effect of increased temperatures) (Filippou *et al.*, 2017; Wang *et al.*, 2024).

## DISCUSSION AND CONCLUSION

The discussion and the conclusion section positions the current study among the ones that have chosen to address the causes of people's irresponsible behaviors as well as the devastating effects of such unimaginable and hard to forget behaviors. On the one hand, specialists have shown that it is somehow implemented in the very fabric of some cultures and nations to be more focused towards consumption and sales, given the history of those countries as well as the endless opportunities and unlimited possibilities that those countries have to offer to their inhabitants and the businesses that opened there. The ideas of being part of something big, never seen before, and of living in constant prosperity have defined and will, somehow, one way or another, continue to define some societies no matter how many efforts researchers, leaders, and policymakers will put into demonstrating and showing that human beings do not really need that much to be happy and healthy (Popescu & Popescu, 2019a). Yet, the on-going pressure that some companies place on their consumers and clients that they need more, far more than they have, for better and healthier, and more fulfilled life has led to over-consumerism, questionable decisions in terms of what healthy lifestyles really promote, and the real values on which individuals, communities, and organizations should rely on (Popescu & Popescu, 2019b). On the other hand, there are cases in which individuals may know the dangers of their actions and may start fighting back in order to create safer habitats for themselves and their close family members, but they might be in the situation in which the community in which they live or in which they work has certain expectations from them and, with ought addressing those expectations and with ought supporting those demands, the individuals will face the risks of being excluded from the communities.

There are numerous ways in which people and communities can act sustainable and can learn how to make a different through their way of behaving, their consumption patterns, and the way they address waste. The principles on which the circular economy is based should be embraced not only by these people and communities mentioned above – the ones that truly care about the sustainable development practices; these principles ought to be embraced by all, in order to ensure the healthy future of us all.

Sustainability and sustainable development have changed the way in which people and organizations have to perceive progress. On the one hand, by stating that immense progress was recorded over the last decades in some industries or regions or countries, some might think that progress is synonymous to efficiency and performance, hence making connections with profitability and success. On the other hand, by arguing that great progress was made in certain fields and activities, some could think that the advancements that took place over the years brought benefits to the society and to communities as a whole in terms of leading better, healthier, prosperous lives, filled with joy and well-being. Under these circumstances, sustainability and sustainable development goes far beyond profitability and performance, leading to excellence in environmental protection as well as in supporting healthier lives. Prosperity has been targeted many times by people in the history of mankind and each and every time there are specialists coming to the conclusion that leaving prosperous lives has nothing to do with being wealthy, popular, and with important positions in society. Hence, prosperity comes from within; it may be a feeling, it could be a state of mind, or it could be the manner in which some visualize themselves and their current way of living. That is precisely the reason why the concept of economic growth must be associated with sustainability and sustainable development in order to show that the society and the business environment are concerned not only with the costs, prices, and profit, but also, more importantly, with the standards of living, the happiness indicators, and the indexes that highlight values displaying green initiatives and a farer future for all.

By asking questions and by choosing to be inquisitive, these days' individuals are being challenged to be more creative, innovative, and reflect at all times at thought-provoking problems in order to discover new and powerful solutions for a better future for all. What is more, creative thinking is preferred to any other form of analysis and reflection, since it requires great skills and competences. Furthermore, today, these wonderful skills and competences are associated with green values and green objectives, hence supporting the SDGs. Going even further with the analysis, the center point of these days' preoccupations ought to be discover novel and original instruments and technologies with which lives would be significantly improved by sustainable and resilient human activities. There are many aspects that could lead to being worried about the future, especially in those cases in which people and communities have to face the results of irresponsible use of harmful technologies for themselves and for the environment. Also, there are several questions that one should ask when thinking about the dangers of pollution and the way in which harmful chemicals and technologies have come to shape the environment and destroy, at an extensive rate, the biodiversity, ecosystems, and natural habitats.

The current book chapter has several limitations, among which could be mentioned the following ones: firstly, the hot topic chosen takes into consideration a plethora of facets embodied by what does a green future represent, hence it is impossible to cover the theme to such an extent to cover all areas of interest, offer all the viable solutions possible, to all the existing problems; and, secondly, although the

RQs proposed for analysis and discussion are highly complex and target a multitude of aspects, they limit to certain features that green technologies and green policies stand for these days. Nevertheless, there are vital studies that were recently published that come to support the findings displayed in this book chapter, which highlights the idea that the SDGs represent key objectives based on which all domains should rethink their ideas in order to reconnect with the real values of individuals, communities, and environment (Bastos *et al.*, 2025; Fragoso-Medina *et al.*, 2025; Teixeira *et al.*, 2025; Zareba, 2025).


## Funding (Acknowledgement)

The Authors received no funding for the current research.


## Statement Of Conflict Of Interest

The Authors declare that there are no conflicts of interest. The Authors declare that they have no known competing financial interests or personal relationships that could have appeared to influence the work reported in this manuscript.

## Authors Contributions

Conceptualization, Cristina Raluca Gh. Popescu (C.R.G.P.) and Rahul R. Verma (R.R.V.); methodology, C.R.G.P. and R.R.V.; software, C.R.G.P. and R.R.V.; validation, C.R.G.P. and R.R.V. formal analysis, C.R.G.P. and R.R.V.; investigation, C.R.G.P. and R.R.V.; resources, C.R.G.P. and R.R.V.; data curation, C.R.G.P. and R.R.V.; writing—original draft preparation, C.R.G.P. and R.R.V.; writing—review and editing, C.R.G.P. and R.R.V. All Authors have equally contributed to this manuscript. All Authors have read and agreed to the published version of the manuscript.

## REFERENCES


Akaraci, S., Feng, X., Suesse, T., Jalaludin, B., & Astell-Burt, T. (2020). A Systematic Review and Meta-Analysis of Associations between Green and Blue Spaces and Birth Outcomes. *International Journal of Environmental Research and Public Health, 17*(8), 2949. DOI: 10.3390/ijerph17082949 PMID: 32344732

Bastos, K. V. L. S., de Souza, A. B., Tomé, A. C., & Souza, F. M. (2025). New Strategies for the Extraction of Antioxidants from Fruits and Their By-Products: A Systematic Review. *Plants, 14*(5), 755. DOI: 10.3390/plants14050755 PMID: 40094704

Castillo-Vargas, D. A., Rodríguez-Quesada, L., Ledezma-Espinoza, A., Masís-Meléndez, F., Infante-Alfaro, S., & Starbird-Perez, R. (2025). Biochar-Based Electrochemical Degradation System for Removing Pharmaceutical Pollutants from Aqueous Media as Potential Wastewater Treatment. *Water (Basel), 17*(5), 722. DOI: 10.3390/w17050722

Chawla, M., Sharma, P., Gautam, S., & Popescu, C. R. (2025). Sustainability in Human Capital Management: Shaping the Future With Technology. In Kapoor, T., Singh, A., Sahay, K., Kaur, H., & Verma, R. (Eds.), *Sustainable Management Practices for Employee Retention and Recruitment* (pp. 265–290). IGI Global Scientific Publishing., DOI: 10.4018/979-8-3693-8679-8.ch013

Chiwaridzo, O. T., & Dzingirai, M. (Eds.). (2025). *Strategic Repositioning in Times of Corporate Crisis: Green Management and Technology Adoption*. IGI Global., DOI: 10.4018/979-8-3693-5912-9

Cohen, G., & Galperin, M. (2020). Green's function methods for single molecule junctions. *The Journal of Chemical Physics, 152*(9), 090901. DOI: 10.1063/1.5145210 PMID: 33480741

Erdoğdu, M. M., Arun, T., & Ahmad, I. H. (Eds.). (2016). *Handbook of Research on Green Economic Development Initiatives and Strategies*. IGI Global., DOI: 10.4018/978-1-5225-0440-5

Fields, Z. (Ed.). (2023). *Multidisciplinary Approaches in AI, Creativity, Innovation, and Green Collaboration*. IGI Global., DOI: 10.4018/978-1-6684-6366-6

Filippou, O., Bitas, D., & Samanidou, V. (2017). Green approaches in sample preparation of bioanalytical samples prior to chromatographic analysis. *Journal of Chromatography. B, Analytical Technologies in the Biomedical and Life Sciences, 1043*, 44–62. DOI: 10.1016/j.jchromb.2016.08.040 PMID: 27623110

Fournet, F., Simard, F., & Fontenille, D. (2024). Green cities and vector-borne diseases: emerging concerns and opportunities. *Euro surveillance: bulletin Europeen sur les maladies transmissibles = European communicable disease bulletin, 29*(10), 2300548. DOI: 10.2807/1560-7917.ES.2024.29.10.2300548

Fragoso-Medina, A. J., Hernández-Fernández, J. A., Nicolás-Vázquez, M. I., Martínez, J., Rivera Espejel, A. L., Saavedra-Leos, M. Z., Pérez Flores, F. J., & Miranda Ruvalcaba, R. (2025). Green Chemistry's Contribution to the Kamal Qureshi Protocol: Comparing Various Activating Modes, the Use of Bentonitic Clay as the Catalyst, and the Use of a Green Solvent. *Catalysts, 15*(3), 238. DOI: 10.3390/catal15030238

Gailey, S., McElroy, S., Benmarhnia, T., & Bruckner, T. A. (2021). Green mobility and obesity risk: A longitudinal analysis in California. *Health & Place, 68*, 102503. DOI: 10.1016/j.healthplace.2020.102503 PMID: 33493964

Giannico, V., Spano, G., Elia, M., D'Este, M., Sanesi, G., & Lafortezza, R. (2021). Green spaces, quality of life, and citizen perception in European cities. *Environmental Research*, *196*, 110922. DOI: 10.1016/j.envres.2021.110922 PMID: 33639147

Gupta, S., Maurya, N., Malik, F. A., & Razzak Janjua, L. (Eds.). (2025). *Integrating Blue-Green Infrastructure Into Urban Development*. IGI Global., DOI: 10.4018/979-8-3693-8069-7

Jiang, W., Stickley, A., & Ueda, M. (2021). Green space and suicide mortality in Japan: An ecological study. *Social science & medicine (1982)*, *282*, 114137. .DOI: 10.1016/j.socscimed.2021.114137

KarimiDermani, B., Green, C. T., Tick, G. R., Gholizadeh, H., Wei, W., & Zhang, Y. (2025). Analyzing Multi-Year Nitrate Concentration Evolution in Alabama Aquatic Systems Using a Machine Learning Model. *Environments (Basel, Switzerland)*, *12*(3), 75. DOI: 10.3390/environments12030075

Lee, D. H., Chamberlain, B., & Park, H. Y. (2025). Toward a Construct-Based Definition of Urban Green Space: A Literature Review of the Spatial Dimensions of Measurement, Methods, and Exposure. *Land (Basel)*, *14*(3), 517. DOI: 10.3390/land14030517

Lekkala, V. D. V. V., Muktinutalapati, A. V., Lebaka, V. R., Lomada, D., Korivi, M., Li, W., & Reddy, M. C. (2025). Green Synthesis and Characterization of Silver Nanoparticles from *Tinospora cordifolia* Leaf Extract: Evaluation of Their Antioxidant, Anti-Inflammatory, Antibacterial, and Antibiofilm Efficacies. *Nanomaterials (Basel, Switzerland)*, *15*(5), 381. DOI: 10.3390/nano15050381 PMID: 40072184

Li, Z., Wu, X., Wu, J., & Liu, H. (2025). The Influence of Urban Landscape Ecology on Emotional Well-Being: A Case Study of Downtown Beijing. *Land (Basel)*, *14*(3), 519. DOI: 10.3390/land14030519

Liu, N., Liu, Z., Wang, Y., Zhou, T., Zhang, M., & Yang, H. (2025). Clean and Efficient Thermochemical Conversion Technologies for Biomass in Green Methanol Production. *Biomass*, *5*(1), 13. DOI: 10.3390/biomass5010013

Management Association. I. (Ed.). (2019). *Green Business: Concepts, Methodologies, Tools, and Applications (3 Volumes)*. IGI Global. DOI: 10.4018/978-1-5225-7915-1

Mejías, C., Arenas, M., Martín, J., Santos, J. L., Aparicio, I., & Alonso, E. (2023). Green Assessment of Analytical Procedures for the Determination of Pharmaceuticals in Sewage Sludge and Soil. *Critical Reviews in Analytical Chemistry*, •••, 1–14. Advance online publication. DOI: 10.1080/10408347.2023.2276294 PMID: 37922128

Migdadi, Y. K. (2020). *Airline Green Operations Strategies: Emerging Research and Opportunities*. IGI Global., DOI: 10.4018/978-1-7998-4255-2

Mouloudj, K., & Bouarar, A. (Eds.). (2025). *Digitizing Green Entrepreneurship*. IGI Global., DOI: 10.4018/979-8-3693-7442-9

Ordóñez de Pablos, P., & Zhang, X. (Eds.). (2023). *5G, Artificial Intelligence, and Next Generation Internet of Things: Digital Innovation for Green and Sustainable Economies*. IGI Global., DOI: 10.4018/978-1-6684-8634-4

Petrychenko, O., Levinskyi, M., Goolak, S., & Lukoševičius, V. (2025). Prospects of Solar Energy in the Context of Greening Maritime Transport. *Sustainability (Basel)*, *17*(5), 2141. DOI: 10.3390/su17052141

Ponnusamy, V., Jhanjhi, N. Z., Jung, L. T., & Amin, A. M. (Eds.). (2021). *Role of IoT in Green Energy Systems*. IGI Global., DOI: 10.4018/978-1-7998-6709-8

Popescu, C. R. (2021c). Measuring Progress Towards the Sustainable Development Goals: Creativity, Intellectual Capital, and Innovation. In Popescu, C. (Ed.), *Handbook of Research on Novel Practices and Current Successes in Achieving the Sustainable Development Goals* (pp. 125–136). IGI Global., DOI: 10.4018/978-1-7998-8426-2.ch006

Popescu, C. R. G. (2017). The Role Of Total Quality Management In Developing The Concept Of Social Responsibility To Protect Public Interest In Associations Of Liberal Professions. Amfiteatru Economic. Editura ASE. Volume: 19. pp. 1091-1106. Special Issue: 11. WOS:000413858500012. ISSN: 1582-9146. eISSN: 2247-9104.

Popescu, C. R. G. (2019). Corporate Social Responsibility, Corporate Governance and Business Performance: Limits and Challenges Imposed by the Implementation of Directive 2013/34/EU in Romania. *Sustainability (Basel)*, *11*(19), 5146. DOI: 10.3390/su11195146

Popescu, C. R. G. (2020a). Approaches to Sustainable and Responsible Entrepreneurship: Creativity, Innovation, and Intellectual Capital as Drivers for Organization Performance. In Hernández-Sánchez, B., Sánchez-García, J., & Moreira, A. (Eds.), *Building an Entrepreneurial and Sustainable Society* (pp. 75–95). IGI Global., DOI: 10.4018/978-1-7998-2704-7.ch004

Popescu, C. R. G. (2020b). Developing a Model for Entrepreneurship Competencies: Innovation, Knowledge Management, and Intellectual Capital – Success Competences for Building Inclusive Entrepreneurship and Organizational Performance. In Šebestová, J. (Ed.), *Developing Entrepreneurial Competencies for Start-Ups and Small Business* (pp. 1–22). IGI Global., DOI: 10.4018/978-1-7998-2714-6.ch001

Popescu, C. R. G. (2020c). Analyzing the Impact of Green Marketing Strategies on the Financial and Non-Financial Performance of Organizations: The Intellectual Capital Factor. In Naidoo, V., & Verma, R. (Eds.), *Green Marketing as a Positive Driver Toward Business Sustainability* (pp. 186–218). IGI Global., DOI: 10.4018/978-1-5225-9558-8.ch008

Popescu, C. R. G. (2020d). Sustainability Assessment: Does the OECD/G20 Inclusive Framework for BEPS (Base Erosion and Profit Shifting Project) Put an End to Disputes Over The Recognition and Measurement of Intellectual Capital? *Sustainability (Basel)*, *12*(23), 10004. DOI: 10.3390/su122310004

Popescu, C. R. G. (2021a). Sustainable and Responsible Entrepreneurship for Value-Based Cultures, Economies, and Societies: Increasing Performance Through Intellectual Capital in Challenging Times. In Popescu, C., & Verma, R. (Eds.), *Sustainable and Responsible Entrepreneurship and Key Drivers of Performance* (pp. 33–58). IGI Global., DOI: 10.4018/978-1-7998-7951-0.ch002

Popescu, C. R. G. (2021b). Impact of Innovative Capital on the Global Performance of the European Union: Implications on Sustainability Assessment. In Popescu, C. (Ed.), *Handbook of Research on Novel Practices and Current Successes in Achieving the Sustainable Development Goals* (pp. 90–124). IGI Global., DOI: 10.4018/978-1-7998-8426-2.ch005

Popescu, C. R. G. (Ed.). (2021d). Handbook of Research on Novel Practices and Current Successes in Achieving the Sustainable Development Goals. IGI Global. http://doi:. Indexed in Scopus. WorldCat: 5 editions in 50 libraries. OCLC Number / Unique Identifier: 1260710279.DOI: 10.4018/978-1-7998-8426-2

Popescu, C. R. G. (2022a). Impressive, Inspiring, and Profound Mindfulness Movement in Organizations: Boosting Productivity, Cultivating Joy, and Sharping Awareness. In Popescu, C. (Ed.), *Handbook of Research on Building Inclusive Global Knowledge Societies for Sustainable Development* (pp. 60–96). IGI Global., DOI: 10.4018/978-1-6684-5109-0.ch003

Popescu, C. R. G. (2022b). Mindfulness at Work, a Sound Business Investment: Focusing on the Employee Well-Being While Increasing Creativity and Innovation. In Popescu, C. (Ed.), *Handbook of Research on Changing Dynamics in Responsible and Sustainable Business in the Post-COVID-19 Era* (pp. 1–34). IGI Global., DOI: 10.4018/978-1-6684-2523-7.ch001

Popescu, C. R. G. (2022c). Mindfulness Business Principles: Producing Outstanding Value and Encouraging Community Connections. In Popescu, C. (Ed.), *COVID-19 Pandemic Impact on New Economy Development and Societal Change* (pp. 196–228). IGI Global., DOI: 10.4018/978-1-6684-3374-4.ch010

Popescu, C. R. G. (2022d). Environmental, Social, and Corporate Governance by Avoiding Management Bias and Tax Minimization: Reaching a General Consensus Regarding a Minimum Global Tax Rate. In Popescu, C. (Ed.), *COVID-19 Pandemic Impact on New Economy Development and Societal Change* (pp. 94–132). IGI Global., DOI: 10.4018/978-1-6684-3374-4.ch006

Popescu, C. R. G. (2022e). Fostering Creativity in Business: Empowering Strong Transformational Leaders. In Popescu, C. (Ed.), *Handbook of Research on Changing Dynamics in Responsible and Sustainable Business in the Post-COVID-19 Era* (pp. 349–381). IGI Global., DOI: 10.4018/978-1-6684-2523-7.ch017

Popescu, C. R. G. (2022f). Analyzing the Impact of Green Marketing Strategies on the Financial and Non-Financial Performance of Organizations: The Intellectual Capital Factor. In I. Management Association (Ed.), Research Anthology on Business Continuity and Navigating Times of Crisis (pp. 202-226). IGI Global. https://doi.org/DOI: 10.4018/978-1-6684-4503-7.ch011

Popescu, C. R. G. (2022g). Evaluarea capitalului intelectual i influen a acestuia asupra performan elor economice. Editura Mustang, Bucure ti. ISBN 978-606-652-286-1. Published in Romanian. (Title in English: Intellectual Capital Assessment and Its Influence on Economic Performances); Link editura Mustang: http://www.editura-mustang.ro/carti_stiintifice.php

Popescu, C. R. G. (Ed.). (2022h). COVID-19 Pandemic Impact on New Economy Development and Societal Change. IGI Global. . Indexed in EBSCOhost. WorldCat: 6 editions in 57 libraries. OCLC Number / Unique Identifier: 1277184264.DOI: 10.4018/978-1-6684-3374-4

Popescu, C. R. G. (Ed.). (2022i). Frameworks for Sustainable Development Goals to Manage Economic, Social, and Environmental Shocks and Disasters. IGI Global. . Indexed in EBSCOhost. WorldCat: 3 editions in 34 libraries. OCLC Number / Unique Identifier: 1334007327.DOI: 10.4018/978-1-6684-6750-3

Popescu, C. R. G. (Ed.). (2022j). Handbook of Research on Building Inclusive Global Knowledge Societies for Sustainable Development. IGI Global. . Indexed in EBSCOhost. WorldCat: 4 editions in 46 libraries. OCLC Number / Unique Identifier: 1309072556.DOI: 10.4018/978-1-6684-5109-0

Popescu, C. R. G. (Ed.). (2022k). Handbook of Research on SDGs for Economic Development, Social Development, and Environmental Protection. IGI Global. . WorldCat: 4 editions in 49 libraries. OCLC Number / Unique Identifier: 1323431329.DOI: 10.4018/978-1-6684-5113-7

Popescu, C. R. G. (Ed.). (2022l). Handbook of Research on Changing Dynamics in Responsible and Sustainable Business in the Post-COVID-19 Era. IGI Global. http://doi:. Indexed in EBSCOhost. WorldCat: 4 editions in 49 libraries. OCLC Number / Unique Identifier: 1285370248.DOI: 10.4018/978-1-6684-2523-7

Popescu, C. R. G. (Ed.). (2023a). Positive and Constructive Contributions for Sustainable Development Goals. IGI Global. . WorldCat: 6 editions in 35 libraries. OCLC Number / Unique Identifier: 1344378097. DOI: 10.4018/978-1-6684-7499-0

Popescu, C. R. G. (2023b). Artificial Intelligence and Sustainability in a Game-Changing Post-COVID-19 Era: Key Drivers for Economic Development, Social Development, and Environmental Protection. In Popescu, C. (Ed.), *Positive and Constructive Contributions for Sustainable Development Goals* (pp. 1–20). IGI Global., DOI: 10.4018/978-1-6684-7499-0.ch001

Popescu, C. R. G. (Ed.). (2024a). Building Inclusive Global Knowledge Societies for Sustainable Development. IGI Global. . DOI: . ISBN13: 9798369362983. ISBN13 Softcover: 9798369362990. EISBN13: 9798369363003. https://www.igi-global.com/book/building-inclusive-global-knowledge-societies/343531. (Forthcoming).DOI: 10.4018/979-8-3693-6298-3

Popescu, C. R. G. (2024b). Monitoring Progress towards the Sustainable Development Goals, where Children and Youth Hold the Key to Sustainable Future: Principles and Policy Guidance on Children's Rights to Healthy Environment. Paper presented at the World Children Conference-V. June 07-09, 2024. Hakkari, Turkey. Organizers: Hakkari University, Turkey and IKSAD Institute of Economic Development and Social Research of Turkey, Turkey. Paper due to be published in the Conference Volume Proceedings. https://www.worldchildrenconference.org/

Popescu, C. R. G. (2024c). Intercultural Communication And Social Cohesion At The Heart Of Sustainable Development Goals (SDGS) And Development Policies. International Symposium On Communication, Information And Society. International Symposium on Communication Information and Society. Current Dynamics in Communication. May 09-10 2024. Abstracts Book. Gaziantep University Gaziantep / Türkiye. ISBN: 978-625-367-713-8.

Popescu, C. R. G. (2024d). Envisioning International Trade and Logistics for the Sustainable Development Goals (SDGs): Responsible Plant, Tree, and Livestock Logistics for Greening and Conserving the Environment. Congress Tıtle 7th Internatıonal Antalya Scıentıfıc Research And Innovatıve Studıes Congress Date And Place 11-13 May 2024, Antalya, Turkiye Organızatıon Iksad Instıtute.

Popescu, C. R. G., & Popescu, G. N. (2019a). The Social, Economic, and Environmental Impact of Ecological Beekeeping in Romania. In Popescu, G. (Ed.), *Agrifood Economics and Sustainable Development in Contemporary Society* (pp. 75–96). IGI Global., DOI: 10.4018/978-1-5225-5739-5.ch004

Popescu, C. R. G., & Popescu, G. N. (2019b). An Exploratory Study Based on a Questionnaire Concerning Green and Sustainable Finance, Corporate Social Responsibility, and Performance: Evidence from the Romanian Business Environment. *Journal of Risk and Financial Management*, *12*(4), 162. DOI: 10.3390/jrfm12040162

Popescu, C. R. G., & Popescu, G. N. (2024a). The Power of Data Analysis in Transforming Businesses Performance: Improved Decision-Making, Real-World Applications, and the Sustainable Development Goals. In Popescu C. R. G. (Ed.). Building Inclusive Global Knowledge Societies for Sustainable Development. IGI Global. DOI: 10.4018/979-8-3693-6298-3

Popescu, C. R. G., & Popescu, G. N. (2024b). Socio-Economic Inclusion, Health and Education Nexus: Tackling the European Union (EU) Vital Strategy on the Rights of the Child EU Actions to Withstand Poverty and Boost Inclusive and Child-Friendly Societies, Health and Education Systems.

Popescu, C. R. G., & Popescu, G. N. (2024c). Renewable Energy Industry: Benefits For Economic Growth. International Black Sea Coastline Countries Scientific Assembly by Center for Black Sea Research. Organizer: Center For Black Sea Research, Black Sea Network For Intercultural Communications (BIC). April 7-9, 2024, Samsun, Turkey. Congress website: https://www.blackseacountries.org/congress.

Popescu, C. R. G., & Popescu, G. N. (2024d). Intercultural Communication And Social Cohesion At The Heart Of Sustainable Development Goals (SDGS) And Development Policies. International Symposium On Communication, Information And Society. May 09-10 2024. http://comis.gantep.edu.tr/index.php ?dil=en

Popescu, C. R. G., & Popescu, G. N. (2024e). Envisioning International Trade and Logistics for the Sustainable Development Goals (SDGs): Responsible Plant, Tree, and Livestock Logistics for Greening and Conserving the Environment. Congress Tıtle 7th Internatıonal Antalya Scıentıfıc Research And Innovatıve Studıes Congress Date And Place 11-13 May 2024, Antalya, Turkiye Organızatıon Iksad Instıtute.

Popescu, C. R. G., Popescu, G. N., & Popescu, V. A. (2015a). Corporate Governance in Romania: Theories and Practices. In Boubaker, S., Nguyen, D.K. (Eds.), Corporate Governance And Corporate Social Responsibility: Emerging Markets Focus (pp. 375-401). WORLD SCIENTIFIC PUBL CO PTE LTDPO BOX 128 FARRER RD, SINGAPORE 9128, SINGAPORE. WOS:000349291300016. ISBN: 978-981-4520-37-9. . https://www.worldscientific.com/doi/abs/10.1142/9789814520386_0014DOI: 10.1142/9789814520386_0014

Popescu, C. R. G., Popescu, G. N., & Popescu, V. A. (2017). Assessment Of The State Of Implementation Of Excellence Model Common Assessment Framework (CAF) 2013 By The National Institutes Of Research - Development - Innovation In Romania. Amfiteatru Economic. Editura ASE. Volume: 19. Issue: 44. pp. 41-60. WOS:000395746900004. ISSN: 1582-9146. eISSN: 2247-9104.

Popescu, C. R. G., Popescu, V. A., & Popescu, G. N. (2015b). The Entrepreneur's Role In The Performance Growth Of The Financial Audit Activity In Romania. Amfiteatru Economic. Editura ASE. Volume: 17. Issue: 38. pp. 228-246. WOS:000352213800015. ISSN: 1582-9146. eISSN: 2247-9104.

Popescu, C. R. G., & Verma, R. R. (2025). Quality Education to Meet the Sustainable Development Goals: Tremendous Role of Sustainable Management Practices for Employee Retention and Recruitment. In Kapoor, T., Singh, A., Sahay, K., Kaur, H., & Verma, R. (Eds.), *Sustainable Management Practices for Employee Retention and Recruitment* (pp. 233–242). IGI Global Scientific Publishing., DOI: 10.4018/979-8-3693-8679-8.ch011

Popescu, V. A., Popescu, G. N., & Popescu, C. R. G. (2014). The Economic And Social Dimensions Of Romania's Metallurgical Industry. Metalurgija. CROATIAN METALLURGICAL SOCBERISLAVICEVA 6, ZAGREB, CROATIA. Volume: 53. Issue: 1. pp. 113-115. WOS:000320481400029. ISSN:0543-5846. eISSN:1334-2576.

Popescu, V. A., Popescu, G. N., & Popescu, C. R. G. (2015c). The Relation Productivity - Environment In The Context Of Sustainable Development - Case Study On The Romanian Industry. Metalurgija. CROATIAN METALLURGICAL SOCBERISLAVICEVA 6, ZAGREB, CROATIA. Volume: 54. Issue: 1. pp. 286-288. WOS:000341740000075. ISSN:0543-5846. eISSN:1334-2576.

Popescu, V. A., Popescu, G. N., & Popescu, C. R. G. (2015d). Competitiveness And Sustainability - A Modern Economic Approach To The Industrial Policy. Metalurgija. CROATIAN METALLURGICAL SOCBERISLAVICEVA 6, ZAGREB, CROATIA. Volume: 54. Issue: 2. pp. 426-428. WOS:000343781300031. ISSN:0543-5846. eISSN:1334-2576.

Queiroz Almeida, D., Paciência, I., Moreira, C., Cavaleiro Rufo, J., Moreira, A., Santos, A. C., Barros, H., & Ribeiro, A. I. (2022). Green and blue spaces and lung function in the Generation XXI cohort: A life-course approach. *The European Respiratory Journal*, *60*(6), 2103024. DOI: 10.1183/13993003.03024-2021 PMID: 35896209

Ragazou, K., Garefalakis, A., Papademetriou, C., & Samara, A. (Eds.). (2025). *Sustainability Through Green HRM and Performance Integration*. IGI Global., DOI: 10.4018/979-8-3693-5981-5

Sajid, M., & Płotka-Wasylka, J. (2022). Green analytical chemistry metrics: A review. *Talanta*, *238*(Pt 2), 123046. DOI: 10.1016/j.talanta.2021.123046 PMID: 34801903

Shen, J., Li, M., Wang, Q., Liu, R., Ji, M., & An, R. (2022). The Influence of Green Space on Obesity in China: A Systematic Review. *Obesity Facts*, *15*(4), 463–472. DOI: 10.1159/000524857 PMID: 35545010

Smirani, N., Bouazizi, S., Bettaieb, E., Torkhani, R., & Hamdi, M. (2025). Effect of Environmentally Friendly Betalain Extraction Methods on Antioxidant Compounds of Tunisian *Opuntia stricta* Fruit. *Foods*, *14*(5), 851. DOI: 10.3390/foods14050851 PMID: 40077554

Teixeira, M. S., Mata, T. M., Lourenço, A., Oliveira, F., Oliveira, J., & Martins, A. A. (2025). Life Cycle Assessment of Tinplate Aerosol Cans: Evaluating the Role of Photovoltaic Energy and Green Hydrogen in Environmental Impact Reduction. *Environments (Basel, Switzerland)*, *12*(3), 73. DOI: 10.3390/environments12030073

Thomas, H., & Howarth, C. J. (2000). Five ways to stay green. *Journal of Experimental Botany*, *51*(Spec No, suppl_1), 329–337. DOI: 10.1093/jexbot/51.suppl_1.329 PMID: 10938840

Touya, G., Courtial, A., Kalsron, J., Berli, J., Le Mao, B., & Wenclik, L. (2025). Understanding the Carbon Footprint of Tile Transfer for Web Maps. *ISPRS International Journal of Geo-Information*, *14*(3), 107. DOI: 10.3390/ijgi14030107

Tsai, S., Liu, B., & Li, Y. (Eds.). (2018). *Green Production Strategies for Sustainability*. IGI Global., DOI: 10.4018/978-1-5225-3537-9

Tunio, M. N., Rashid, A., Qureshi, M., Qureshi, J. A., & Rasheed, R. (Eds.). (2025). *Intersecting Entrepreneurship, Internationalization, and Green Innovation*. IGI Global., DOI: 10.4018/979-8-3693-9241-6

Vilcins, D., Sly, P. D., Scarth, P., & Mavoa, S. (2022). Green space in health research: An overview of common indicators of greenness. *Reviews on Environmental Health, 39*(2), 221–231. DOI: 10.1515/reveh-2022-0083 PMID: 36372560

Wang, W., Wen, H., Zhao, C., Ma, X., Liao, J., & Ma, L. (2024). Green space modified the association between air pollutants and hypertension in China. *International Journal of Environmental Health Research, 34*(9), 3232–3244. DOI: 10.1080/09603123.2023.2300047 PMID: 38171020

Yeoh, C. B., Lee, K. J., Coric, V., & Tollinche, L. E. (2020). Simple Green Changes for Anesthesia Practices to Make a Difference. *EC clinical and medical case reports, 3*(12), 1–6.

Yin, L., Yu, L., Guo, Y., Wang, C., Ge, Y., Zheng, X., Zhang, N., You, J., Zhang, Y., & Shi, M. (2024). Green analytical chemistry metrics for evaluating the greenness of analytical procedures. *Journal of Pharmaceutical Analysis, 14*(11), 101013. DOI: 10.1016/j.jpha.2024.101013 PMID: 39759968

Yu, W., Yu, J., & Chen, X. (2025). Research on the Mechanism of the Influence of Farm Scale on the Environmental Efficiency of Apple Production—Tests Based on a Life Cycle Assessment Perspective. *Land (Basel), 14*(3), 516. DOI: 10.3390/land14030516

Zareba, M. (2025). Assessing the Role of Energy Mix in Long-Term Air Pollution Trends: Initial Evidence from Poland. *Energies, 18*(5), 1211. DOI: 10.3390/en18051211

Ziaesaeidi, P. (2025). 'Relax Underneath the Trees and Read a Book': Exploring Social Sustainability in Parks Through the Lens of Young People. *Sustainability (Basel), 17*(5), 2138. DOI: 10.3390/su17052138

## KEY TERMS AND DEFINITIONS

**Cutting-Edge Initiatives and Commercially-Viable Solutions for a Fairer Future:** Today, specialists have come to the conclusion that building a fairer future represents the only viable solution capable to support better and more responsible communities and businesses (Popescu, 2022a). In this matter, policymakers are the ones that should find the solutions to put into practice those ways in which a better future for all could be ensured, having in mind that there are numerous approaches and paths on which individuals, communities, and organizations could take in order to take action and build the Partnerships for the Goals (Popescu, 2022b). Among the general ideas and solutions displayed in this context, this book chapter is dedicated to showing the manner in which cutting-edge initiatives and commercially-viable solutions for a fairer future, while offering a better understanding of the actions that have led to these days health and environmental problems (Popescu, 2022c; Popescu, 2022d). In some cases, it is absolutely vital to state that the health of individuals and the balance of the environment have been severely affected, but, in the same time, it is pivotal to acknowledge that solutions ought to be searched for in this matter so that the damages could be reduced or even reversed, when possible (Popescu, 2022e; Popescu, 2022f; Popescu, 2022g). By cutting-edge initiatives some new and innovative technologies could be implemented so that individuals would have the opportunity to create their personal and work balance, while the environment could little by little restore its balance and the biodiversity and ecosystems could be rebuilt (Popescu, 2022h; Popescu, 2022i; Popescu, 2022j). Likewise, commercially-viable solutions for a fairer future could be represented by new techniques and technologies that could help businesses reduce their pollution, assist new businesses not to generate any more pollution, use less resources, and even discover or create new resources due to be used in the day-to-day life-cycles and economic-cycles as shown by the principles of the circular economy (Institute of Medicine (US) Roundtable on Environmental Health Sciences, Research, and Medicine, 2007).

**Challenges in Implementing Green Culture:** In this day and age, there are several pros and cons when it comes to choosing to go green at home, and, additionally, there are numerous challenges in implementing green culture: on the one hand, a very good solution could be to support green community programs, hence facing challenges in addressing the community's needs, while striving, in the same time, to balance the environmental goals (Popescu, 2022k; Popescu, 2022l); in like manner, on the other hand, among the challenges to implementing green culture could be named addressing cultural and financial barriers, promoting collaboration which should ideally be referring to inter-disciplinarily and international practices, securing funding to support the sustainability path, which may be, in some cases, quite expensive and time consuming, and, also, focusing on creating policy frameworks that would offer a holistic approach, an organic approach to facing the challenges in implementing green culture (Sajid & Płotka-Wasylka, 2022).

**Green Future Ideas and Scalable Technologies Essential for Innovators, Scientists, Researchers, and Engineers:** The importance of the Sustainable Development Goals (SDGs) is vital for the present and future generations, having in mind the well-being of individuals as well as the health of the environment (Popescu, 2021a; Popescu, 2021b). These days, green ideas for a greener and safer future for all will have the power to create the necessary connections leading to innovative and creative solutions capable to ensure continuity in all domains, but having at heart pivotal concepts, such as: responsibility; social responsibility; corporate social responsibility; awareness; respect for nature, biodiversity, and ecosystems; work and environmental ethics; and, profitability and performance, evidenced by dedication towards sustainability and sustainable development (Popescu, 2021c; Popescu, 2021d). What is more, a green future in which the decisions are taken responsibly and with care is not based on ideas such as cutting costs or avoiding legal and moral responsibility (Popescu, 2020a; Popescu, 2020b). Furthermore, a green future implicates the will to change the way in which businesses use the resources so that the individuals, communities, and environment will not be affected as well as the manner in which businesses offer goods and services to their clients (Popescu, 2019). A green future is based on ideas and scalable technologies which are believed to be essential for innovators, scientists, researchers, and engineers, since recent studies highlighted in this book chapter show the importance of innovators, scientists, researchers, and engineers in supporting the Global Goals (GG). Green future ideas are born with the help of creative and dedicated individuals which due to their work are highly inclined to make the world a better and a safer place, while green future scalable technologies are the ones responsible for putting into practice green future ideas and offering solutions when needed (Shen *et al.*, 2022).

**Fellowships and Partnerships for Science and Engineering:** Since it is crucial these days to target the SDGs in all domains and, in the same time, to foster a better future for all, supporting education, research, life-long learning, international fellowships, and international partnerships represents a must and a desiderate not only for the present, but also for the future generations (Popescu, 2020c; Popescu, 2020d). Individual and institutional grants have a major role in helping dedicated specialists to seek viable solutions in science and engineering in order to address today's environmental problems. In addition, these fellowships and partnerships for science and engineering have paramount benefits, namely: firstly, bright and inquisitive scientists and engineers have the opportunity to be part of programs centered on the GG, while having their salaries and benefits paid with the help of Fellow Programs; secondly, these bright and inquisitive scientists and engineers have the chance to further the development of policies in different countries, hence creating the aforementioned green future ideas and scalable technologies; thirdly, extensive orientation programs are essential for these scientists and engineers, based on the fact that these programs will additionally play a crucial role in the advancement of science; and, fourthly, these scientists and engineers will have immense benefits since they will be connected to a broad network of other Fellows having different and diverse backgrounds. The idea of competitiveness may be encountered in this type of environment as well, since these fellowships and partnerships for science and engineering are dedicated to recognizing and supporting those bright researchers and specialists that are willing to work hard and make the best of the outstanding opportunities that such grants are providing them with (Mejías *et al.*, 2023).

**Negatives on Going Green:** Going green may not only have positive effects on human lives and on businesses, going green may also implicate that there is a negative side to such practices, among which could be highlighted that: (a) going green may refer to great time and money commitment, since these patterns of behavior have to be supported on the long-term in order to generate positive and concerted results; (b) there are cases in which going green may be very difficult even for individuals and businesses that can afford high-quality materials, since these right materials may be difficult to get; (c) although green infrastructure is so well promoted and everyone wants to be part of such bold and healthy systems, it may be missing in some regions; (d) going green is very important for us all, yet going green may come with some compatibility issues – namely, some family members or colleagues at work may not support such practices and may generate unpleasant and unhealthy discussions on these topics, some cultures may rely on some long-term practices which implicate, for example, the use of certain ingredients when cooking those traditional meals or when fabricating those specific products and, by not respecting traditions, one may face some problems from the community members; (e) lack of motivation to go green and, additionally, to stay green might exist at all times, mainly due to the fact that these are commitments that people and organizations as well as regions and countries have to take for longer time periods; and, (f) education and life-long training programs have the role of raising awareness to everybody when it comes to sustainability and sustainable development, which means that the lack of awareness and education are negative factors that affect individuals' and companies' activities and decisions in adopting green lifestyles and business styles (Vilcins *et al.*, 2022).

# Chapter 4
# Building a Green Future Through Essential Decision-Making Competencies:
## A Study on the Effects of Green HRM System on Employees in Education Sector

**Deepa Sharma**
https://orcid.org/0000-0003-4374-917X
*Maharishi Markandeshwar University, India*

## ABSTRACT

*This paper focuses on the effects of Green HRM system on employees working in Education sector. Green HRM System lay down guidelines and procedures for integrating and retaining teaching staff and other employees so that the institutions can fulfill the goals and objectives for which they have been established. Due to the emergence of many ecological challenges in the education sector in the last few decades, green human resource management has created like a new idea that has been adopted by many Education sector today. To increase employee awareness, today many Education sector around the world combine traditional corporate social responsibility initiatives with green HR policies. Green HRM System help employees become aware of their duties and many education sector have developed green initiatives to support students and employees in charge of protecting the environment, however, Green HRM system and policies are completely impossible to implement.*

## BACKGROUND

Currently, the idea of Green Human Resource Management (GHRM) is becoming more and more well-liked worldwide. Through the HR requirement process, green HRM practices promote innovative teaching to faculty, staff, and other stakeholders, which in turn improves student productivity, sustainability, environmental friendliness, and structure to deliver positive outcomes. Green HRM practices also drive transferable skills in the areas of waste management, reduction of unnecessary resources, maintaining cleanliness, Green Campus Projects, water management of the campus, CSR projects, yoga, and health. Green HR focuses on the creation, execution, and upkeep of all initiatives meant to

DOI: 10.4018/979-8-3373-0189-1.ch004

foster staff members' support and commitment to sustainable goals. Teaching, learning, and research in higher education institutions can produce generations of new leaders and skilled professionals who will propel social and economic development. Initiatives include HR procedures for hiring, training and development, performance management, and assessment. The innovative concept of sustainable human resource management is being adopted by education sector today. By integrating resource management with traditional corporate social responsibility initiatives, workers may fulfill their environmental responsibilities. Higher education institutions benefit the environment and society. Many educational institutions have launched environmental programs to help instructors, students, and environmental policymakers improve environmental support. However, it is not possible to completely implement the green-man management ideas. This research paper will outline the conventional environmental practices used by universities and assess the extent to which academic institutions implement environmental management strategies. Higher institutions benefit from this as they have an obligation to protect the environment. The processes of hiring, training, compensating, creating policies for employees, and creating retention plans are all part of human resource management. Human resource management includes several pillars such as personnel information systems, pay and benefits, training and continuing education, performance management, personnel data and analysis, and succession arrangements, *etc.*

**History of Green HRM:** The discussion of corporate sustainability, sustainable development, and the United Nations' proposal for sustainable development (SD) are all connected to the history of green human resource management, or GHRM:

a. Sustainable development: This concept, which combines economic growth, environmental preservation, and social inclusion, was put out by the UN.
b. Brundtland Commission: In order to protect natural resources for future generations, the Brundtland Commission in 1987 concentrated on environmental sustainability and sustainable development.
c. Wehrmeyer's concept: In 1996, Wehrmeyer's introduced the phrase "Green HRM" and said that a company's ability to succeed or fail depends on its workforce's environmental consciousness.
d. GHRM as an academic idea: The discussion of business sustainability and sustainable development gave rise to GHRM as an academic term.
e. GHRM as a groundbreaking idea: In both the academic and real-world contexts of human resource management, GHRM is regarded as a groundbreaking idea.
f. GHRM concept: Since 2019, the popularity of GHRM concept has been continuously growing. The discussion of corporate sustainability and sustainable development gave rise to the scholarly idea of green HRM.

**Concept of Green Human Resource Management**: The term green human resources management (GHRM) refers to a collection of procedures, guidelines, and systems that encourage environmentally conscious behavior from workers in order to build a resource-efficient, socially conscious, and ecologically conscious business. Green human resource management employs a number of traditional and eco-friendly techniques in all facets of its operations. Reducing the quantity of printed materials required for performance assessments, pay appraisals, and other processes is one simple green endeavor. GHRM is directly responsible for creating a green workforce that understands, values, and complies with green initiatives as part of the HRM process of recruiting, hiring, training, compensating, developing, and promoting the company's human capital. "Green human resources management" (GHRM) refers to a collection of procedures, guidelines, and systems that encourage environmentally conscious behavior from workers in order to build a resource-efficient, socially conscious, and ecologically conscious business. In other words, the collection of guidelines and processes known as "Green Human Resource Management" (GHRM) encourages employees to adopt environmentally friendly habits. Establishing a sustainable and eco-conscious workplace is the aim of GHRM, which we have discussed in below:

a. **Reduce environmental effect:** Businesses may lessen their environmental impact with the aid of GHRM.
b. **Encourage sustainability:** GHRM may assist companies in accomplishing sustainable goals. Increased employee satisfaction is a possible outcome of GHRM.
c. **Enhance stakeholder interactions:** GHRM can assist in enhancing stakeholder relationships.
d. **Improve staff retention:** GHRM has the potential to improve staff retention.
e. **Enhance social responsibility:** GHRM can assist in enhancing employees' sense of social duty.
f. **Enhance talent acquisition and retention:** GHRM can assist in enhancing the capacity to attract and retain talent.

**Concept of Education Sector:** The term "Educational Sector" describes the system that includes colleges and universities and where assessment studies are carried out to determine the efficacy and efficiency of educational establishments, particularly during periods of restricted budgets and growing demands for responsibility. Both imparting information to others and learning from others are considered forms of education. Education also encompasses the institution of teaching as a whole as well as the information acquired via instruction or schooling. Schools serve as centers for education, learning, and personal growth. They offer an established infrastructure, which includes teachers who are probably knowledge able, and reliable information sources as well as chances for long-term programming through structured curricula. Schools, colleges, and other establishments that offer teaching and training are all part of the educational sector:

a. **What's included:** Schools, colleges, universities, training facilities, and other establishments that offer teaching and training are all included in the educational sector.
b. **Whom it serves:** Students get teaching from the educational sector in a number of locations, such as homes, workplaces, and educational institutions.
c. **How it functions:** It is possible for the educational sector to be publicly owned and run, or privately owned and run for profit or not.
d. **How it's assessed:** Research evaluating the efficacy and efficiency of educational establishments is used to appraise the educational sector.
e. **The analysis method:** The quality of learning, access and coverage, equality and inclusion, and internal and external efficiency are only a few of the variables that are examined in an education sector analysis.

**Employees in education sector:** Employees in the education sector are those who work in establishments including schools, colleges, universities, and teacher training programs that instruct children and youth. These workers consist of principals, support personnel, and certified instructors. The education industry encompasses a wide range of establishments, including as state-run and private colleges and universities, vocational education centers, and public, private, and religious schools. Green human resource management (GHRM) practices can have a positive effect on employees in the education sector in several ways, including:

a. **Employee engagement:** GHRM practices can enhance employee engagement, job satisfaction, and motivation.
b. **Employee green behavior:** GHRM practices can encourage employees to participate in green practices and develop green skills.
c. **Organizational culture:** GHRM practices can create an environmentally friendly organizational culture.
d. **Attracting top talent:** GHRM practices can attract better students, faculty, and staff to educational institutions.
e. **Societal response:** GHRM practices can create a better response from society and policymakers.
f. **Profitability:** GHRM procedures have the potential to increase educational institutions' long-term financial success.

Green HRM practices have been embraced by educational institutions in an effort to further their sustainability objectives. Cost savings, ethical and social responsibility, employee well-being, external reputation, and regulatory compliance are some of the main factors promoting green HRM in the education sector. Educational institutions may lessen their environmental impact, create health-conscious work environments, fulfill social responsibilities, control reputational risks, and comply with sustainability reporting requirements by incorporating environmental concerns into HR procedures. Green HRM activities have a favorable impact on environmental performance, according to studies conducted in the higher education sector. Employee participation in environmental management and training with a sustainability focus improved institutions sustainability outcomes.

## INTRODUCTION

At this time, the idea of Green Human Resource Management (GHRM) is becoming more and more popular around the world. It will be interesting to see the advancements in GHRM and their impact on educational institutions because greenness in an educational setting promotes empathy in both teachers and students, irrespective of their technical proficiency, which contributes to the development of better human resources. If they are involved in service business, the human capital generated from green spaces will be shriveled rather than compelled, but in manufacturing, they will fully understand the customer needs and integrate them through quality work deployment. Green HRM System need to move around the work and expand the accomplish of human resource management practices through the combination of Green HRM System to improve how fundamental human resource management practices are accomplished as organizations currently Shift strategies and priorities towards a more green-oriented agenda. (Aboramadan, M.*et* al., 2022). According to Naser, Abu 2019 human resource management can measure and influence the attitudes, attitudes, awareness, and motivation of employees related to sustainability.

As a result, using green HRM (Bos-Nehles, A.C. *et* al., 2019 and Veenendaal, A.A.R. *et* al., 2019) can effectively create and implement environmentally friendly policies.

A rising quantity of education sector around the world include recently attempted to integrate environmental management and green practices into the services they provide. An increasing number of education sector around the world have recently attempted to integrate environmental management and green practices into the services they provide. Education sector as teaching and research institutions are expected to play an important role in adopting strategies and alternatives to address current environmental concerns (Hameed, Zahid, *et* al., 2020; Khan, Ikram Ullah *et* al., 2021; Islam, Tahir *et* al., 2020; Sheikh, Zaryab *et* al., 2019; Naeem, Rana Muhammad *et* al., 2020). Additionally, they should provide an example for reviving and acknowledging the changing demands and difficulties of environmental management issues (Urvashi, *et* al., 2020). Education sector should adopt a "go green" mindset to promote an eco-friendly work environment (Joshi, M. Trupti *et* al., 2020). (Aboramadan Mohammed *et.al*, 2022) proposed that Green HRM system need to change the objective and develop the reach of Green HRM System through the integration of green management practices so that they understand how to conduct fundamental Green HRM System and enhance employee behaviors, and attitudes, and how to bring sustainability in (Hameed *et al.*,2020) And it serves as an inspiration to the employees as organizations are currently shifting their strategies and priorities towards an eco-friendly agenda. As a result, businesses can effectively create and implement environmentally friendly policies using human resource management. The ever-changing business ecosystem in the modern era, where green HRM is at the forefront of education sector, creates a new trend toward economic, environmental, and social performance on the other hand (Kramar, R. *et al.*, 2014). Organizations today are increasingly concerned about how environmental issues may affect their competitiveness and long-term performance as sustainability becomes a worldwide issue. Elements of sustainable HR management that meet the needs of environmental sustainability are referred to as green human resource management. Green HRM System (Prof. Dr. Muayad Al-Saidi, *et al.*, 2020; Raghad Rae'ed *et al.*, 2020) aim to infuse the workplace with a sense of environmental responsibility. Green HRM system should include developing employees' green competencies, encouraging employee engagement, and providing green opportunities for employees. (Bhatti SH, *et al.*, 2021; Saleem F *et al.*, 2021; Murtaza G *et al.*, 2021; Haq *et al.*, 2021) Employees who take pride in their environmental work may go above and beyond the call of duty to show their dedication to the environment. Intrinsic, self motivated by employees, attached with work and employees emotionally, identity, and involvement in building the relationship with employees at the workplace are some of its definitions. Intrinsic, duty related inspiration, affecting emotions, identity, and involvement in human behaviors are some of its definitions. These dedicated, committed workers who care about the environment deliver outstanding green performance. As a result, organizational green goals can be achieved if workers are committed. The primary objective of the article is to inspect the connection between employee green obligation and Green HRM system at workplace. Green HRM system plays a critical responsibility in harnessing their talent and expertise for improving the ecological environment during recruitment and selection as well as hiring and attracting employees. Green HRM system enables hired personnel to receive coaching and training on their specific concerns and environmental challenges, while not being left to figure out the strategy on their own. Employee motivation is important because, according to study results, it has a stronger correlation than other components. However, the reward system was inadequate and unsatisfactory, as reflected in the confusing promotional structure with delayed benefits to employees and remuneration for meeting green norms. Organizations' ability to balance economic and environmental performance is becoming more and more difficult, especially for those subject to competitive, governmental, and community pressures. In response to increasing pressure for green sustainability, manufacturers must develop new ways to reduce the negative environmental effects of their products and services. Therefore, Green human resource management is a top study priority for academicians. Green concerns are new and growing in every country. The company encourages employee efforts to meet green human resources management that have a significant effect on the competitive sustainability of the business. First, the economic value of an educational institution drove its success; today, however, environmental and social concerns must also be taken into account. To promote employee environmental awareness and the development of management and technical capabilities, it is important to use a number of strategies, including employment selection, recruitment process, and training, rewards, and evaluation system design. Worldwide, environmental management demands a proactive strategy. Rapid industrialization is contributing to the increase in environmental pollutants. In order to reduce the destruction of non-renewable resources, both the government and the business and education sectors implement several policies, laws, and regulations in this direction. The business sector enhances and improves an environmental management system. This new strategic trend is known as green management. Green management is a strategy used by organizations to manage environmental initiatives and protect environmental factors. In sort to maintain environmental sustainability, industrial expansion must be balanced. Consequently, analysts emphasize that a primary goal of educational Education sector should be the implementation of green human resource management system. The concepts of green human resource management are influenced by many theories from the fields of human relations and organization. They should be thoroughly examined in systematically to more in-depth sympathetic of green human resource management. Human resource management can have a good effect by luring skilled, capable, and competent personnel and then rewarding them adequately to increase the level of motivation and productivity. (Arulrajah, A.A, Nawaratne *et al.*, 2015) Additionally, it enhances their effectiveness and efficiency to generate more profits, maximum profits, and better quality. In the current competitive world where every organization is working to improve, find, train, and develop a capable and competent workforce. Therefore, this study sought to offer a model of the effects of Green HRM System on workers green behaviours, namely in-role, extra-role, and green inventive behaviour, in order to advance the literature of Green HRM System in general and in higher education in particular. It was proposed that green work engagement would act as a mediator between the aforementioned linkages. The following are the contributions made by this study: As the association between green human resource management and workers green work-related outcomes is still in its infancy stage ((Zibarras, L.D. *et al*, 2015; Coan, P. *et al.*, 2015). it first contributes to the broader literature of green human resource management. Second, it adds to the scant corpus of human resource management research at education sector (Aboramadan et al., 2020) and green human resource management research (Fawehinmi et al., 2020). Many studies have been done on human resource management strategies. Regarding academic institutions, there is a lack of studies on environmental practices. More research is needed in this area to develop employees' environmental protection skills and to examine their awareness of environmental as green human resource management has the potential to reduce carbon footprints, increase efficiency, and reduce costs, sustainable business. Practices and improved employee engagement.

## LITERATURE REVIEW

In the review literature many studies conducted in the higher education sector. According to Channa (2019) the study analyzed data from education sector to assess the force of Green HRM System on environmental performance using two theoretical lenses. Organizational citizenship behavior and supply-value fit theory to the environment 214 workers were included in this study. The findings found that through employees environmental enthusiasm, Green HRM System significantly boost environmental performance. And this study also shows that the outcome of Green HRM System on environmental enthusiasm is more significant when an employee has a high level of green values than a low one. By linking Green HRM System to environmental performance, the present study adds fresh theoretical insights to the literature on environmental management. According to Abbas Zuhair (2022) the study examined attempts to measure the effects of Green HRM System on sustainability in the context of higher education in a developing nation. This study used a quantitative method to suggest and evaluate a representation based on stability predictions. 190 responses were obtained from personnel including teaching and non-teaching staff working full-time in 40 education sector in Pakistan. Structural and measurement models were calculated using SmartPLS. Green Recruitment and Selection were not supported by sustainability, although top management commitment towards greening workforce had a favorable link with sustainability. It was concluded that GHRM processes encourage employee and overall greenness. According to Dakhan (2019) examined the special effects of Green human resource management on Green Recruitment and Selection (GRS), Green Compensation and Reward, Green Training and Green Training in higher education institutions. How environmental knowledge acts as a mediator between pro-environmental behavior and green training and development. In this test, a total of 320 questionnaires were sent to collect data from women academics and other university staff, of which 240 were returned and the rest were accepted as valid responses. The data analysis techniques used were confirmatory factor analysis partial least squares method and structural equation modeling tools, and the results suggest that Green HRM System can influence pro-environmental behavior. And also has a favorable effect on the employees. In this study, Anwar (2020) examined the role of organizational citizenship behavior towards the environment was investigated in mediating between green human resource management system and environmental performance. A structured questionnaire was sent to academic staff in a Malaysian university. 122 respondents were selected from both campuses using convenience sampling, and the data were analyzed using the partial least squares (PLS) modeling approach. The overall results demonstrated a substantial effect of the three sets of Green HRM System on organizational citizenship behavior towards the environment based on the capability-motivation-opportunity framework. Additionally, there was a substantial relationship between organizational citizenship behavior toward the environment and environmental performance. The findings of the mediation analysis revealed that academic staff members displayed organizational policies, rules and regulations, workforce behavior towards the working environment. According to Farooq (2023) the link between environmental performances through Green HRM system and employee environmental commitment was examined in this study using the moderating effect of green information sharing. An online survey of 155 academic staff members from 25 Pakistani institutions that were highly rated for green campuses. Research showed a strong correlation between university environmental performance, green human resource management system, and employee environmental commitment. Employee environmental commitment acted as a mediator between all three Green HRM System and environmental performance. The results suggest that encouraging the exchange of green information among employees is important for achieving environmental sustainability objectives and improving environmental performance. According to Mose (2019) this study examined how green human resource management strategies affected the organizational effectiveness of Kenyan universities. A semi-structured questionnaire and descriptive research approach were used to collect the primary data.10 universities in Kenya were included in this research. There were 120 respondents included from selected universities. The findings found a positive and substantial correlation between green pay and rewards, green training and development, green training and selection, and green human resource performance management and the organizational success of universities in Kenya. According to Imran (2020) Green Human Resource Management is the forward-thinking of today's society which is one of the most important components of an environment-friendly company. Most academicians are of the opinion that efficiently implementation of green human resource management system at workplace motivated the employees to be empowered self to perform the task effectively. The present study examines how various green human resource management techniques affect environmental performance directly or indirectly through pro-environmental behavior. Green HRM system have significant direct effects on environmental sustainability, while a mediator called pro-environmental behavior mediates the indirect association between green environmental training and a sustainable environment. According to Jabeen (2021), this study suggests a framework that focused on the effects of green human resource management practices. In the research, information was collected from 184 workers in organizations in the United Arab Emirates. According to the findings, the relationship between environmental orientation, development of green competencies, motivation to be green, and organizational business success has a profound effect on employee green behavior. The findings of the study help us understand employee green behavior and its effects on enhancing organizational business performance in emerging nation settings. The originality of this study lies in introducing a comprehensive framework to address the problem that businesses now face in encouraging their employees to adopt green behaviors.

## FUNCTIONS OF GREEN HRM SYSTEM ON EMPLOYEES IN EDUCATION SECTOR

Recruitment, selection, and training are all part of green human resource management (HRM) procedures, which also aim to improve employees environmental awareness, hone their green skills, and equip them to identify environmental problems and put solutions in place. Employees in the education sector can benefit from green human resource management (GHRM) techniques in several ways, such as:

a. **Increasing environmental awareness:** GHRM procedures can teach staff members how to solve environmental problems and increase their awareness of them.
b. **Green skill development:** GHRM procedures can assist staff members in gaining the abilities and information required to be more ecologically aware.
c. **Making the workplace greener:** GHRM practices may contribute to making the workplace greener, which can spur innovation and improve how people view the workplace.
d. **Encouragement of responsible leadership:** GHRM procedures may encourage responsible leadership, which can subsequently make workers feel more accountable.
e. **Offering incentives:** Green awards are one way that GHRM practices may encourage staff members to carry out the company's green goals.

GHRM practices include, for instance:

- Employing workers with expertise and awareness of environmental issues
- Using green performance evaluation standards to deliver green training
- Promoting remote work
- Making use of public transit
- Making the switch to paperless
- Making use of recyclable materials

## NEED FOR GREEN HR

A major problem for Higher Education Institutions (HEIs) is striking a balance between environmental responsibility and organizational competitiveness. HEIs must match their human resource strategies with ecological objectives as more and more businesses embrace Green Human Resource Management (GHRM) techniques to improve sustainability. However, HEIs capacity to successfully incorporate GHRM is hampered by the absence of thorough guidelines and tools designed specifically for them. This problem is resolved at higher education institutions through green HRM awareness and training.

The concern of green HRM method is one that is now in advance recognition. Global Green engagements served as the institution for the conception of Green HRM. The idea of a 'Green HRM system' has gained attractiveness all right through the globe. Each person's explanation of it is exceptional. It makes an endeavor to enhance force preservation or lessen effluence caused by business and everyday actions. The main purpose of human being green is to diminish any probable negative green impacts of force use and effluence. In an ever-evolving world, using green expertise as part of a commercial approach can help business be successful. Organizations will necessarily play a momentous part in the encounter aligned with comprehensive warming. With the support of the supervision and the workers, HRM will maintain the company's assurance to a green organization. It is necessary to clarify the environmental needs of human resources to achieve ecological or organizational environmental goals. Green skills, green attitudes, green behavior and green results are the four categories of environmental job standards. It is important to clarify the demands on the workplace of human resources to meet ecological or organizational goals. Organizations have different work requirements at every workplace. Employees need to have every important information in the work area like many office supplies Reusing, instead of throwing them away, is a strategy to promote environmental consciousness., An employee is not capable of being a green employee without these capabilities and expertise. An empirical study is needed to fill the knowledge gaps in employees' specific environmental competencies. Employees should also adopt their behavior with the proper mindset. The second is to report any damage, potential loss, *etc.* to the authorities.

## ROLE OF GREEN HUMAN RESOURCE MANAGEMENT ON EMPLOYEES AT WORKPLACE

Though it is hard to fully execute the rules for green people management, many educational institutions have developed environmental protection measures to assist students and teachers who are responsible for safeguarding the environment. This research report will assist define environmental best practices used in academic institutions. Determine the green human resource management practice level of research institutions and scientific organizations with various organizations, which is highly important for colleges and various organizations responsible for environmental protection. Toughness is indicated by green. When it comes to workplace human resource management (HRM), the term "green" has at least four meanings. Any element of the earth that was not created by humans or is not under their control is referred to as environmental protection. The environment, which also consists of living things and encompasses land, forests, plants, animals, and other natural phenomena. Please leave it exactly as is to avoid damage, loss, or negative changes. To ensure you can use it, please use it very carefully. Use it as little as possible and preserve it for as long as possible so that future generations can benefit from it.

Regardless of future generations, businesses and the government freely employ natural resources to manufacture a wide range of consumer goods. Environmental problems, including pollution, environmental deterioration, and global warming. Modify people's ways of living and assist them in leading sustainable lives. The implementation of environmentally friendly behaviors, green practices, and green initiatives will support environmental sustainability and have a beneficial effect on the environment. Prevent or reduce global warming. Natural disasters including rain, floods, storms, droughts, and tsunamis brought on by the careless, destructive, and avaricious exploitation of natural resources for production and consumption. Prevent or reduce illnesses brought on by pollution in the environment. Prevent or lessen harm to animals and other living things. Make sure there is a suitable balance in the interactions between people, animals, plants, and their surroundings.

Green initiatives are also started by many educational institutions to make the staff and students accountable for protecting the environment. However GHRM is contributing to the long-term development of educational institutions. If an effective Green HRM system can be implemented, it increases awareness among the management and staff to follow waste management processes, save unnecessary resources and keep the campus clean. Green human resource management is also one of the many methods used by employers, friendly practices, and education institutions using green human management practices, to enhance employee performance and bring sustainability to work, and to achieve the goals of the institutions. (Bohdanowicz, P., Zientara, et *al*., 2011; Novotna, E. *et al*., 2011) Described as actions or behaviors performed by workers that benefit the organization, reduce the negative effects of human activity on the environment, and result in improvements conducive to long-term organization sustainability. To help students and employees to maintain the working environment at the workplace, many educational institutions have developed green human resource management practices. However, it is very difficult for green human resource management to fully comply with the regulations. Green HRM System used in universities play an important role in the smooth development of the organization as well as in the personal development of the employees. It also represents colleges and other organizations in the education sector. Environmentally friendly behavior of employees can be classified into work-related and voluntary green behavior. (Fernández, E., et *al*., 2003; Junquera, B. et *al*., 2003; Ordiz, M. *et al*., 2003) Green behaviors related to work include water conservation, resource efficiency, waste reduction, energy conservation, and recycling. The first thing about environmentally friendly behavior that is carried out within the organizational boundaries and within the limits of the responsibilities assigned to each employee's position within the firm; In other words, it is about duties that are clearly listed and well-known every and each employee's duties and responsibilities.. On the other hand, the definition of intentional worker green behavior is described as green behavior for employee develops of his own volition and goes above and beyond the expectations of the organization. (Haden, S. S. P et *al.*, 2009; Oyler, J. D, et *al.*, 2009; Humphrey, J. H. *et al.*, 2009) Green human resource management academic institutions play a major role in waste generation, resource depletion and environmental damage. Management, faculty, support staff and students of education sector are the human resources that contribute to the development of these institutions. These universities have thousands of students and thousands of faculty. Therefore, it is important to make these resources aware of how their actions affect the ecosystem. Education sector can achieve sustainable development by effectively utilizing their human resources. (Iraldo, F., et *al.*, 2009; Testa, F., et *al.*, 2009; Frey, M. *et al.*, 2009) to prepare their students to be green employees, colleges may also include courses on eco-friendly practices in each area of their curriculum as well as require that all businesses employing students as employees practice green human resources. The following points on the significance of Green HRM in Education sector are described below.

**1. Green (Paperless) Recruiting:** This method uses the internet to perform recruiting processes. This means less impact on the environment and paperless hiring. The HRM team creates hiring processes so that hiring people takes less money, time and effort like online job posting and online application of applications, *etc.* In the conventional recruiting process, a corporation produced all the records of the candidates, including their resumes, diplomas, test results from the interview, *etc.* Newspapers and publications carried the recruiting announcements. Many organizations have reduced their use of paper by switching to an online recruiting approach. A major portion of this resource has been reduced as a result of online exams, web and telephone interviews, and job advertising on the firm website or other online job boards, and the maintenance of online personnel records through HR software. Green goals and responsibilities can be added to the job description to improve it. Green recruitment and selection refers to hiring practices that have the least possible negative impact on the environment and do not use paper. It takes less money, time, and effort to hire applicants thanks to the HRM team's design of the recruiting process. Online job posting and online application submission are two examples of green recruitment methods. The environmental ideals and requirements should be reflected in job advertisements. The sustainability objective should be reflected in the job description and any telephone or video conference interviews. Candidates are asked environment-related questions throughout the selection process.

**2. Green Training and Development:** It's critical to instill in each employee the value of being green. Green awareness training programmes are offered by several organizations. The major goal is to develop the employees' knowledge, abilities, and attitudes towards environmental conservation. Training courses on recycling, carpooling, garbage management and other methods will be helpful. The training sessions can include subjects like water conservation, bio waste, plastic waste segregation, limited paper usage, practical ways to minimize air pollution like carpooling, taking public transport, biking to work, *etc.* Green HR training and development is the term for the training program designed and carried out to educate staff members about their obligations to preserve and protect the environment. It improves workers green attitudes, knowledge, and abilities. After joining, staff members ought to value the company's green policies and practices. Organizations frequently implement green training and development practices, such as discussing environmental issues in the induction program, educating new hires about the company's environmental goals, conducting a need analysis for green training, providing training on eco-friendly practices like carpooling and recycling, and making training materials available online.

A green HR training and development program is one that is designed and executed to educate staff members about their roles in environmental preservation and protection. It improves workers' green attitudes, knowledge, and abilities. Once they join the company, employees should value its green policies and practices. Some examples of green training and development techniques that are often used in businesses are as follows:

a. Environmental problems are discussed in the induction program.
b. The institution's environmental goals should be explained to new hires.
c. An study of the requirement for green training should be done. Employees should get training on eco-friendly behaviors including recycling and carpooling.
d. Online training resources should be available.
e. The institution's environmental goals should be explained to new hires. An analysis of the demand for green training should be done. Employees should get training on eco-friendly behaviors like recycling and carpooling. Training materials should be made available online.

**3. Green Employee Relations:** This entails organizing employee involvement. The HR managers should make sure that staff members are in charge of putting green practices in place at work and that they take part in decision-making alongside management. The relationships between the top management, the employees, and the students will improve as a result of initiatives like campus cleanliness, tree planting, garden maintenance, *etc.* One of the most crucial things to preserve for increased productivity is the relationship between coworkers or between employees and their employers. Workers should be in charge of making decisions on the environment management system. Participation from employees will lead to improved green management. HR managers are in charge of creating an atmosphere at work where workers feel free to share their thoughts.

**4. Green Performance Management and Compensation Management:** HR may establish green objectives, and if they are met, employees may get rewards. For individuals who do not adhere to the green policies and objectives, a disciplinary mechanism may also be put in place. Green practices can be involved in critical occurrences. This will increase the employee's output and dedication to the organization's environmental sustainability. It is possible to reward employees that suggest creative green solutions. These procedures entail establishing environmental goals and targets for the staff members and evaluating their performance in relation to the established objectives. The job description should outline green aims and objectives, and it should be connected to the mechanism for evaluating performance. The purpose of the green reward system, which includes both monetary and non-monetary incentives, is to encourage staff members who meet environmental targets and who have developed innovative ways to preserve the environment while using the fewest resources possible. Rewards based on recognition given to candidates who have achieved the green goals in an exceptionally high manner. Employee productivity, loyalty, job happiness, and motivation will all rise as a result. These procedures entail establishing environmental goals and targets for the staff members and evaluating their performance in relation to the objectives. The job description should outline green aims and objectives and connect them to the performance review system.

5. **Green Exit:** Exit refers to the procedure by which a worker departs a company. The majority of companies are attempting to change their departure policies in order to make them more sustainable. It can therefore be referred to as "green existence". It consists of things like Employees who resign by mail or online portals should also address reaching their green objectives during their exit interview. Criticism directed against

individuals who have failed to meet their green goals, giving out awards to staff members who actively participated in green initiatives while they worked for the company, *etc.* Within enterprises, the green movement revitalizes the culture, inspires workers, boosts production and efficiency, and fosters a feeling of accountability and confidence. The results show that workers in-role green behavior is positively impacted by green HRM methods. Furthermore, the relationship between green HRM practices and employee in-role green behavior is mediated by psychological green atmosphere. In the other words, Exit is the procedure by which a worker departs from a company. The majority of businesses are attempting to change their departure policies about sustainability. It can therefore be referred to as green existence. It consists of:

a. Employees can resign by mail or internet portals.
b. The achievement of his or her green goals should also be discussed during the exit interview.
c. Those who have failed to meet their green goals are subject to criticism.
d. Awarding awards to staff members who shown a high level of engagement in green initiatives while working for the institution.

6. **Green Reward System:** The purpose of the green reward system, which offers both monetary and non-monetary incentives, is to encourage staff members who meet environmental targets and who have developed new ways to the environment while using the fewest resources possible. Rewards based on recognition given to candidates who have achieved the green goals in an exceptionally impressive manner will boost workers' motivation, loyalty, productivity, and job happiness.

## EFFECTS OF GREEN HUMAN RESOURCE MANAGEMENT ON EMPLOYEES IN EDUCATION SECTOR

Green HRM requires a higher institution method, capable domination, and contribution in sustainable progress. HRM is serious to an elevated institution's capacity to manage sustainability with human resources. When energetic a new path of sustainable business, they also have to take into account principled consideration away from profitable routine. The academic institution has a unique function in both the environment and society. Although many educational institutions have developed green initiatives to assist students and staff that are accountable for the situation's protection, it is not feasible to fully adopt green HRM policies. This study will assist in determining the degree of Green HRM practices adopted in the academic institution as well as the standard green practices applied to higher education institutions. The higher education institution, which is in charge of environmental preservation, will benefit from this. HRM can give out as the decent compass of a higher institution. They can proposition a number of actions and measures that assistance of employees. Occasionally such enhancement can seem unfeasible to realize. However, HRM can help top supervision and employees are in touch so that they can jointly extend sustainable work practices.

1. **Initiative take by employees to complete the task at the workplace:** The education sector today is trying to incorporate Green HRM System to carry out their day-to-day operations. Numerous studies have shown that when staff members practice putting green behaviors into practice. And also positively affects the society and employee relations and employee relations. An individual feels responsible for the

environment in addition to contributing to the functional requirements of his/her position. It encourages the expansion of ubiquitous workplace wellness.

**2. Contributes to cost savings for your Institution**: Any organization can expand significantly if it supports green projects. It emphasizes on eco-friendly operations with the potential to reduce environmental carbon footprints. If employees support and follow these programs, they are less likely to get sick. As a result of their increased activity at work, the rate of attendance and absenteeism will decrease. As a result the medical budget of the organization is protected. Green HRM helps cut costs while maintaining its market-specific exclusivity.

**3. Through Green human resource management help beat the competitors easily and can capture the market easily:** Employers, businesses, institutions and manufacturers can improve their brand image and gain influence in society by using green HR practices. Additionally, it raises awareness about the use of natural resources among workers and society at large, promoting more economical and eco-friendly goods. Conducting environmental audits, modernizing workplace culture, managing waste, and helping the community and those affected by pollution are some of the activities that can help build brand awareness about their institutions. Every time an institution introduces a green program at work, it should make a bigger deal out of it to enhance its reputation. Social media marketing that highlights environmental contributions can attract the interest of potential consumers and provide leads.

4. **Can easily increase the number of employees and keep employees in the organization for a long time**: Employer retention rates can be increased by implementing green HR practices. Some employees may feel proud when an institution shows concern for the environment and society. Apart from helping the people to get in better sync with the organizational principles, it gives the impression that the firm appreciates its personnel.

**5. Can easily increase the morale of the employees:** Wellness programs can incorporate environmental and sustainability issues to raise awareness in addition to encouraging physical fitness, good nutrition, and healthy lifestyles among employees and society. Green HRM uses policies to encourage the wise use of resources, which furthers environmental causes and increases employee happiness and morale.

## CHALLENGES IN IMPLEMENTING GREEN HRM AT WORKPLACE

The following are some obstacles to putting Green HRM into practice at work:

a. **Cost:** Using sustainable technology and practices can be costly.
b. **Employee opposition:** Change may encounter resistance from both management and employees.
c. **Impact measurement:** Assessing the effects of green efforts can be challenging.
d. **Goal alignment:** Matching green aims with corporate objectives can be difficult.
e. **Lack of awareness:** Workers might not be aware of environmental issues.
f. Employee education may be challenging for employees of all levels, including international workers, employees of different generations, and employees of different genders.
g. **Advancement and productivity:** Managers may find it challenging to strike a balance between environmental concerns and advancement and productivity.
h. **Changing employee attitudes:** Changing employee attitudes quickly may be challenging.
i. **Absence of organizational support and managerial interest:** This might be the case.

j. **Insufficient documentation:** Documentation guarantees that the company's eco-friendly procedures are followed with diligence. It also aids in maintaining the defined policies and related resources.
k. **Insufficient Funds:** Making the switch to sustainable practices and technology will cost a lot of money. However, budgetary restrictions are a common problem for businesses, making green HRM projects difficult.
l. **Education and Consciousness:** Implementing strong green HRM practices across the enterprise presents additional challenges for the HR department, including employee training and awareness-raising.
m. **Absence of GHRM guidelines:** Organizations do not have established policies or processes for implementing Green HRM practices. The government is putting a greater emphasis on issues pertaining to workplace health and safety, environmental preservation, and other relevant topics. Strict legislation is being drafted to address these concerns. The government does not, however, enforce any clear rules or guidelines on businesses to create sustainable and green workplaces.
n. **Lack of sufficient organizational support:** Another obstacle to the implementation of GHRM practices is the reluctance and lack of collaboration of upper management staff. Almost no one in top management finds green HRM approaches particularly interesting. They believe that the firm may get by just adhering to regulations like corporate citizenship and health and safety protocols. Additionally, top management thinks it would be difficult to create sustainable workplaces.
o. **Change in employee behavior:** It might be challenging to modify an employee's behavior quickly. Not all employees are as interested in the company's adoption of green HRM practices as others are. Therefore, adopting a green HRM lifestyle throughout the whole firm is a difficult and drawn-out process.
p. **Expensive implementation:** Top management considers the implementation of green HR practices to be a long-term investment with little to no return on investment. Since its high cost might reduce the organization's profit margin, they don't seem too interested.

## IMPACT OF GREEN HRM IN THE EDUCATION SECTOR

Green HRM is essential because it incorporates eco-friendly working practices into HR regulations. This strategy improves the company's reputation and draws in talent and clients that value environmental responsibility. Businesses may save a lot of money and increase productivity by supporting green programs like trash reduction and energy conservation. Furthermore, Green HRM engages workers by bringing their personal commitment to sustainability and the company's ideals into alignment, which raises morale and productivity. By using green practices, businesses may lower their risk of fines and maintain compliance with environmental requirements. In the end, Green HRM offers real advantages to the company and its stakeholders while also promoting a sustainable future. In addition to taking into account potential regional variations, a study on the effects of a Green HRM system in education would look at how putting environmentally conscious HRM practices into place within educational institutions affects staff members, their environmental behaviors, and the organization's overall environmental performance. Important things to look into describe below:

a. **Environmental Sustainability:** Promoting environmental sustainability is one of Green HRM's main objectives. Businesses may greatly lower their carbon footprint and improve the health of the world by encouraging eco-friendly activities.

b. **Cost Savings:** Putting Green HRM solutions into practice can result in significant cost savings. Reducing waste, using resources sustainably, and implementing energy-efficient techniques all help to cut operating expenses. By protecting their intellectual capital, GHRM may assist educational institutions in cutting expenses.
c. **Employee Engagement and Morale:** Green HRM methods frequently result in increased staff engagement and morale. Employee loyalty and job satisfaction are increased when they take pleasure in working for an ecologically conscious organization.
d. **Corporate Social Responsibility (CSR):** Green HRM is essential to a business's CSR obligations. It shows that the company is dedicated to sustainable development, which can improve its standing with the public and increase client loyalty.
e. **Competitive Advantage:** Companies may get a competitive edge by implementing green HRM practices. Businesses that exhibit environmental awareness are becoming more and more popular with customers and clients.
f. **Better performance:** By increasing employee motivation, engagement, and work satisfaction, GHRM practices can boost productivity.
g. **Perceptions that are environmentally friendly:** Higher education staff members can cultivate environmentally conscious behavior and understanding.
h. **Conducive workplace:** GHRM is able to establish a welcoming and substantial workplace.

## CURRENT SCENARIO OF GREEN HUMAN RESOURCE MANAGEMENT SYSTEM AT WORKPLACE FOR EMPLOYEES

Green HRM helps in guiding employees and helping workforce to develop their attitude, behaviours, knowledge, abilities, inspiration towards employee dedication at the workplace. Every functional area requires the planning of human resource management customs, rules, regulations, principles and policies that must be tailored to achieve the company's goals (Santos, F. *et al.*, 2008). It also helps foster a workforce that plays a positive role in striving to achieve eco-friendly organizational goals. Today, Green Human Resource Management initiatives can be used as a tool for an organization to monitor and control how its employees work. Specifically, by developing green human resource management personnel who can evaluate and improve environmental concerns in the organization's operations. Green HRM is considered to be one of the biggest strategies to help organizations implement more sustainable programs, according to Bhandari, Raj (2019). Green HRM is recognized as an excellent approach to facilitate institutions to execute the further new programs by recognizing the competencies of green resource management employees who can identify and improve the organizational culture in the organization's to perform the operations smoothly.

Therefore, the execution of Green HRM System in a trade to requires friendly atmosphere by human resource actions to support work culture and also provide the remuneration, privileges, perk to improve the employee's performance, arranged the employees and motivate them to a assign task in team at the workplace. (Schaufeli, W.B.; *et al.*, 2004; Bakker, A.B. *et al.*, 2004) Additionally, training in environmental education will empower employees to consciously engage in environmentally friendly and systematically production process, be further proactive in green human resource management, and promote a organization work culture. As a result of the severe and growing strain of its activities on natural resources, the tourism industry is also facing increasing difficulties, for the most part in relative to the atmosphere of organization, keeping its employees on the frontage of ongoing great effort. On the other hand, with the help of Green HRM System, help to significantly management and employees to reduce the carbon emissions and environmental effects.

Therefore, these actions will represent the environmental thinking of the firms, besides being linked to their environmental strategy and organizational goals of a sustainable nature. (He, J., Zhang, et *al*., 2019; Morrison, A.M. *et al*., 2019) Organizations need to support a good self-image by investing in promoting and solving environmental problems through the adoption of green human resource management practices. Because workers tend to identify with organizations, this is incredibly beneficial to businesses. When an organization has a strong sense of prestige and a favorable public image, employees are more likely to identify with it, which boosts members' self-esteem. Employees inquire about to connect and stay in advanced organizations to establish a good sense of self-worth because such assemblage contribution in satisfying and fosters an intellect of pleasure. The same as a result, through implementing green human resource management practices, the company makes it abundantly clear to its human resources dedicated to the common and basis of going green above and beyond any potential financial gain. Because they are motivated by self-improvement, people are forced to respond favorably to profess the green human resource management coordination. According to Paul. N (2020) when businesses use green human resource management processes, they demonstrate to their workforce that they have a serious commitment to social responsibility. A green HRM system emphasizes implementing environmentally friendly HR methods and approaches that make better efficiency of production activity, reasonable expenditure, and improve commitment and retention. And other facilities and incentives also provided by the institution to their employees i.e. electricity bills paid by the company, petrol for vehicle, and laptop facility and more so on. The service sector and industries rely heavily on green human resource management.

Education sector should create human resource policies and procedures, educate employees about the environment, and enforce environmental protection regulations. Every employer maintains a green HRM system to develop its reputation and be ahead. Additionally, it will promote eco-friendly products and a green HRM system is essential for awareness among the citizens and employees of the society about the need to use natural resources more judiciously.

The benefits of Green HRM system as prescribed by experts are listed below:

- Superior employment satisfaction and career advancement
- Establish a work culture environment in an organization and provide the employees healthy and safety atmosphere for workforce.
- Boost the employees to do work with dedication and retain the employees more and more at workplace and reduce the employee's turnover rate.
- Boost the spirits of staff at the workplace.
- Enhancement in luring superior workers.
- Healthy creation of the company's work culture.
- Boosted performance overall of employees

## RECOMMANDATIONS FOR GHRM PRACTICE IMPLEMENTATION

The following suggestions can be used to help educational institutions adopt green HRM practices:

1. **Environmental knowledge and awareness:** Evaluate how Green HRM initiatives, including as training and awareness campaigns, improve staff member's comprehension of environmental issues. Employee satisfaction and engagement: Assess whether workers are happier and more involved at work when their company actively supports sustainability. Examine how much staff members use eco-friendly procedures at work, such as cutting back on paper use, recycling, and utilizing energy-saving devices. Examine the psychological effects of Green HRM practices on workers pro-environmental sentiments, feeling of purpose, and sense of personal accountability.
2. **Decreased resource usage**: Track the educational institution's decline in waste production, water use, and energy use.
3. **Environmental Outcomes:** Decreased resource consumption: Track the educational institution's decline in waste production, water use, and energy use.
4. **Green innovation:** Assess the degree to which staff members help the company create new sustainable procedures or technological advancements.
5. **Reduction of carbon footprint:** Examine the institution's overall decline in carbon emissions.
6. **Environmental laws:** Examine the potential effects that regional environmental laws and policies may have on the application and efficacy of green human resource management techniques.
7. **Cultural context:** Examine how employee reactions to Green HRM programs may be influenced by cultural norms and attitudes toward sustainability.
8. **Environmental laws:** Examine the potential effects that regional environmental laws and policies may have on the application and efficacy of green human resource management techniques.
9. **Cultural context:** Examine how employee reactions to Green HRM programs may be influenced by cultural norms and attitudes toward sustainability.
10. **Resource accessibility:** Determine whether regional variations in the availability of green technologies or renewable energy have an impact on the viability of specific green human resource management strategies.
11. During the hiring process, management should assess candidates environmental understanding and accept soft copies of papers via email and other online channels.
12. Regular online training sessions that are environmentally friendly should be conducted, and employee performance should be evaluated in light of these sessions.
13. The management should establish green goals and objectives for staff members and provide frequent feedback on how well they are meeting those goals.
14. After achieving their desired green goals, employees ought to earn rewards.
15. When management is developing ways to achieve green goals, employee input should be included.
16. Exams ought to be administered electronically, using exam pads rather than paper.
17. Online techniques should be used by the institutions for attendance, workshops, crucial announcements, assignment submission, *etc.*
18. Create a comprehensive green HRM plan that incorporates top-down and bottom-up methods to win over leadership and encourage employee ownership. Align procedures and regulations vertically with broad environmental objectives while enabling horizontal involvement of employees.
19. Offer training on sustainability and promote creativity, peer learning, involvement, and staff-led green projects.
20. Acknowledge employee green behaviors and integrate green measures into performance management.
21. Use both official and informal green HRM procedures to foster a sustainable culture within the company.

## LIMITATIONS AND IMPLICATIONS FOR FUTURE RESEARCH

The limitations of this study will provide opportunities for supplementary research projects in the future. In the research, managers were asked to assess the environmental practices of their staff members. The data is drawn from employees of higher education institutions, which may restrict the generalizability of the findings. Consequently, future research may consider employing larger samples to replicate the study. Future research could be conducted in service industries other than institutions of education, such as higher education, non-profits, healthcare, and hospitality, to see how green human resource management affects employees in other industries.

## CONCLUSION

The study concluded that Green HRM System have a very favorable and significant effect on the pro-environment behavior of employees working in Education sector. The use of environmental knowledge has a positive effect on the employees. While environmental awareness acts as a mediator to enhance an employee's pro-environmental behavior and positively mediates between hiring and selection practices. Given that Education sector implementation of Green HRM is low, it is important to update their HR practices in line with Green HRM System in the present circumstances. Education sector are an important center for educational institutions. Constraints Staff and Students Face in Education sector when attempting to make the education sector green human resources management practices Education sector staff and students are not responsible for Green human resources management practices activities. Some of them may see it as a distraction from their real priorities. However, it is advised that all universities and other educational institutions implement Green HRM System. Long term, it is beneficial to both the organization and society at large in many ways. Over time, such duties will become easier to perform if you have the right mindset and resources. Therefore, all restrictions will ultimately be insignificant. Maintaining constituent efforts and ensuring that personnel are motivated are both important. The administration of Education sector should be fully aware of the value of sustainable human resource management. By taking the right steps, you can encourage teachers and students to adopt sustainable practices at work. In the last we say that there can be certain challenges while trying to make the education sector "greener". The GHRM activities do not diminish the responsibilities of college staff or students. Some of them could view this as a distraction from their true aims and aspirations. In any case, all universities and other educational institutions should consider presenting Green Human Asset practices. It is possible that this will ultimately benefit not just the organization but also society at large. As time goes on, performing such workouts will become less taxing with the right offices and attitude. As a result, all of the limitations will eventually be negligible. Maintaining constituent endeavors is crucial.

## REFERENCES


Abbas, Z., Sarwar, S., Rehman, M. A., Zámečník, R., & Shoaib, M. (2022). Green HRM promotes higher education sustainability: A mediated-moderated analysis. *International Journal of Manpower*, *43*(3), 827–843. DOI: 10.1108/IJM-04-2020-0171

Aboramadan, M. (2022). The effect of green HRM on employee green behaviors in higher education: The mediating mechanism of green work engagement. *The International Journal of Organizational Analysis*, *30*(1), 7–23. DOI: 10.1108/IJOA-05-2020-2190

Ahmad, F., Hossain, M. B., Mustafa, K., Ejaz, F., Khawaja, K. F., & Dunay, A. (2023). Green HRM System and Knowledge Sharing Improve Environmental Performance by Raising Employee Commitment to the Environment. *Sustainability (Basel)*, *15*(6), 5040. DOI: 10.3390/su15065040

Anwar, N., Nik Mahmood, N. H., Yusliza, M. Y., Ramayah, T., Noor Faezah, J., & Khalid, W. (2020). Green Human Resource Management for organizational citizenship behaviour towards the environment and environmental performance on a university campus. *Journal of Cleaner Production*, *256*, 120401. Advance online publication. DOI: 10.1016/j.jclepro.2020.120401

Arqawi, S., Zaid, A. A., Jaaron, A. A., Al Hila, A. A., Al Shobaki, M. J., & Abu-Naser, S. S. (2019). Green human resource management practices among Palestinian manufacturing firms-an exploratory study.

Arulrajah, A. A., Opatha, H. H. D. N. P., & Nawaratne, N. N. J. (2015). Green human resource management practices: A review. Sri Lankan Journal of human resource management, 5(1).

Bhatti, S. H., Saleem, F., Murtaza, G., & Haq, T. U. (2021). Haq (2021). Exploring the effects of green human resource management on environmental performance: The roles of perceived organizational support and innovative environmental behavior. *International Journal of Manpower*, *43*(3), 742–762. DOI: 10.1108/IJM-05-2020-0215

Bohdanowicz, P., Zientara, P., & Novotna, E. (2011). International hotel chains and environmental protection: An analysis of Hilton's we care! programme (Europe, 2006–2008). *Journal of Sustainable Tourism*, *19*(7), 797–816. DOI: 10.1080/09669582.2010.549566

Bos-Nehles, A. C., & Veenendaal, A. A. R. (2019). Perceptions of HR practices and innovative work behavior: The moderating effect of an innovative climate. *International Journal of Human Resource Management*, *30*(18), 2661–2683. DOI: 10.1080/09585192.2017.1380680

Dakhan, S. A., Sohu, J. M., Jabeen, A., Mirani, M. A., Shaikh, J. A., & Iqbal, S. (2020). Impact of green HRM on employees pro-environmental behavior: Mediating role of women environmental knowledge at higher education institutions. *IJCSNS International Journal of Computer Science and Network Security*, *20*(12), 202–208.

Fernández, E., Junquera, B., & Ordiz, M. (2003). Organizational culture and human resources in the environmental issue: A review of the literature. *International Journal of Human Resource Management*, *14*(4), 634–656. DOI: 10.1080/0958519032000057628

Gilal, F. G., Ashraf, Z., Gilal, N. G., Gilal, R. G., & Channa, N. A. (2019). Promoting environmental performance through green human resource management practices in higher education institutions: A moderated mediation model. *Corporate Social Responsibility and Environmental Management*, *26*(6), 1579–1590.

Gilal, F. G., Ashraf, Z., Gilal, N. G., Gilal, R. G., & Channa, N. A. (2019). Promoting environmental performance through Green HRM practices in higher education institutions: A moderated mediation model.*Corporate Social Responsibility and Environmental Management, John Wiley & Sons*, *26*(6), 1579–1590. DOI: 10.1002/csr.1835

Haden, S. S. P., Oyler, J. D., & Humphrey, J. H. (2009). Historical, practical, and theoretical perspectives on green management. *An Exploratory Analysis Management Decision*, *47*, 1041–1055.

Hameed, Z., Khan, I. U., Islam, T., Sheikh, Z., & Naeem, R. M. (2020). Do Green HRM System influence employees' environmental performance? *International Journal of Manpower*, *41*(7), 1061–1079. DOI: 10.1108/IJM-08-2019-0407

He, J., Zhang, and Morrison, A.M. (. (2019). The effects of corporate social responsibility on organization citizenship behavior and task performance in hospitality: A sequential mediation model. *International Journal of Contemporary Hospitality Management*, *31*(6), 2582–2598. DOI: 10.1108/IJCHM-05-2018-0378

Imran, M. (2020). Effect of Green HRM practices on environmental sustainability. *International Journal of Human Capital in Urban Management*, *5*(2), 153–164. DOI: 10.22034/IJHCUM.2020.02.06

Iraldo, F., Testa, F., & Frey, M. (2009). Is an environmental management system able to influence environmental and competitive performance? The case of the eco-management and audit scheme (EMAS) in the European Union. *Journal of Cleaner Production*, *17*(16), 1444–1452. DOI: 10.1016/j.jclepro.2009.05.013

Jabbour, C. J. C., & Santos, F. (2008). The central role of human resource management in the search for sustainable organizations. *International Journal of Human Resource Management*, *19*(12), 2133–2154. DOI: 10.1080/09585190802479389

Jabeen, F. (2021). The influence of Green HRM practices and employee green behavior on business performance in sustainability-focused organizations. *Journal of Environmental Planning and Management*. Advance online publication. DOI: 10.1080/09640568.2022.2074824

Kramar, R. (2014). Beyond strategic human resource management: Is sustainable human resource management the next approach? *International Journal of Human Resource Management*, *25*(8), 1069–1089. DOI: 10.1080/09585192.2013.816863

Mose, T. (2019). Effect of Green HRM practices on Organizational Effectiveness of Universities in Kenya. *Human Resource and Leadership Journal*, *4*(2). Advance online publication. DOI: 10.47941/hrij.319

Mukherjee, S., Bhattacharjee, S., Paul, N., & Banerjee, U. (2020). Assessing Green HRM practices in Higher Educational Institute (2020). *TEST Engineering & Management*, Volume 82. https://ssrn.com/abstract=3546928

Schaufeli, W. B., & Bakker, A. B. (2004). Job demands, job resources, and their relationship with burn-out and engagement: A multi-sample study. *Journal of Organizational Behavior*, *25*(3), 293–315. DOI: 10.1002/job.248

Zibarras, L. D., & Coan, P. (2015). HRM Practices Used to Promote Pro-Environmental Behavior: A UK Survey. *International Journal of Human Resource Management*, *26*(16), 2121–2142. DOI: 10.1080/09585192.2014.972429

# Chapter 5
# Building Green Competencies in Entrepreneurial Education: A Framework for Sustainable Entrepreneurship and Decision-Making

**Hemlata Parmar**
https://orcid.org/0009-0009-1438-5427
*Manipal University Jaipur, India*

**Utsav Krishan Murari**
https://orcid.org/0009-0007-1606-6775
*Sharda University, India*

## ABSTRACT

*This chapter looks at green competencies in the management of sustainable business by an entrepreneur. This work aims at putting forward a conceptual framework of a structure for teaching entrepreneurial education with sustainability integrated into the curriculum. Innovation priorities include a sustainable decision-making approach for the circular economy, green innovation, and incorporating sustainable developmental and enterprise goals into entrepreneur training. Implications and examples from practices and original research findings are presented to inform the choices of educators, policymakers and those who venture into the world of private enterprise.*

## 1. INTRODUCTION: THE NEED FOR GREEN COMPETENCIES IN ENTREPRENEURSHIP

The development of sustainable practices represents an essential 21st-century risk-plus opportunity landscape for corporations. Entrepreneurial stakeholders must focus on global challenges, including climate change, natural resource depletion, and ecological poverty because they can act as innovative change agents and risk-takers for betterment. Entrepreneurs demonstrate the ability to develop innovative solutions that solve environmental problems by infusing their models with green competencies that advance sustainable development. The old business approach centred on maximising profits is insufficient to satisfy current needs. Today's entrepreneurs must develop complete systems integrating sustainability

DOI: 10.4018/979-8-3373-0189-1.ch005

principles, including environmental protection, social equity, and economic performance (Brundtland, 1987; Geissdoerfer et al., 2017). The full suite of knowledge, skills, and behaviours required for sustainable entrepreneurship, classified as green competencies, empowers businesses to develop and execute circular economy (CE) principles. A circular economy minimises waste and achieves peak resource use by implementing closed-loop production and consumption patterns. Overcoming environmental challenges requires business models that arise from CE expertise, which merge triple bottom-line objectives into sustainable outcomes. According to research that Lüdeke-Freund et al. (2018) conducted, adopting a sustainability-oriented business model innovation remains essential to reaching these objectives. Ecological management practices result in businesses selecting renewable resources alongside reusable designs and emissions-minimizing manufacturing systems. Businesses integrated with eco-entrepreneurship boost their competitive advantages and enhance their resilience as they work toward sustaining global development goals, including the United Nations Sustainable Development Goals (SDGs). SDG 12 aims to foster responsible production alongside responsible consumption practices, and SDG 13 requires immediate climate action through the critical use of green competencies (United Nations, 2015).

Eco-entrepreneurship is a recognised powerful strategy for resolving worldwide environmental and social problems. Modern investigations confirm that eco-entrepreneurs help drive the world's sustainability transition. Gholami et al. (2020) state that entrepreneurial enterprises can produce significant systematic changes through green innovation strategies, fueling technological transformation and sustainable practices industry-wide. Research on renewable energy startup cases illustrates how small-scale launch companies can transform conventional markets through disruption and speed up the adoption of ecologically friendly technologies (Kirkwood & Walton, 2010). The evidence strengthens the understanding that eco-entrepreneurship is a sustainability achievement method and an economic growth force for emerging sectors.

The escalating importance of green competencies demonstrates how attitudes among investors, consumers, and regulators are moving toward environmental preferences. Market research conducted by Nielsen (2018) shows that global consumers comprise 73% of customers who change their purchasing decisions to decrease environmental damage while demonstrating a rising interest in sustainable products and services. Sustainability experts who launch startups can benefit from present market tendencies because they provide novel sustainable solutions that integrate consumer needs and government rules. According to Zahra et al. (2019), sustainable businesses receive increased investor interest from environmentally minded investors who provide essential funding for growing their operations.

Green competency development within entrepreneurs depends heavily on their access to educational instruction. Business schools and professional organisations create sustainability-focused curricula by delivering specialised educational and certification programs and conducting dedicated workshops. The Ellen MacArthur Foundation leads international efforts with academic partners to teach circular economy approaches through educational and research collaboration. The digital learning platforms Coursera and edX make fundamental sustainability and entrepreneurial knowledge available to students worldwide through structured online programs that establish an international community of eco-entrepreneurs. Lans et al. (2014) found that pairing stakeholder engagement and hands-on educational programs creates efficient systems for developing sustainability competencies because entrepreneurs gain practical skills from handling challenging environmental problems.

Sustainable entrepreneurship requires governments and policymakers to establish policies supporting such entrepreneurial environments. By offering tax breaks, renewable project subsidies, and startup grants, governments promote sustainable practices among entrepreneurs. The European Green Deal has established a €1 trillion sustainable investment plan for 2030 as Europeans work to develop eco-entrepreneurship. Developing countries like India benefit from the "Startup India" program's government support, which combines financial resources with technical expertise to boost green startup success (European Commission, 2020).

The growing demand for sustainable practices among entrepreneurs continues to face various impediments that are blocking general acceptance. Among the primary barriers that hinder green entrepreneurship are economic limitations, technical challenges, and organisational reluctance to adapt. Most worldwide commercial operations are in small and medium-sized enterprises since these businesses typically lack the resources and expertise to implement sustainable business models. These challenges require coordinated action by governments with assistance from partnering industries, academic institutions, and civil society organisations. Knowledge-sharing platforms, capacity enhancement initiatives, and collaborative community-building efforts between different sectors overcome these adoption barriers while accelerating the transfer of green practice principles.

Sustainable entrepreneurship benefits from newly emerging digital technologies. Artificial intelligence systems, blockchain, and Internet of Things capabilities provide businesses with new technologies to track performance improvements and operational optimisation of environmental characteristics. Implementing blockchain technology enables better supply chain transparency through material sourcing ethics and waste reduction. Real-time monitoring through IoT sensors enables businesses to discover energy waste areas that they can turn into energy conservation initiatives. A PwC (2021) report demonstrates how connecting digital tools with environmental practices boosts environmentally friendly startup operations' effectiveness and growth potential.

Sustainable entrepreneurship backed by green competencies represents a core response to challenges like climate change, resource scarcity, and ecological damage. The alignment of innovative business models with circular economy principles emerges from entrepreneurs who possess these competencies to design and execute environmental impact reduction and social and economic value creation. Each aspect of educating people in green competencies, with supportive public policies and collaborative joint ventures, is indispensable in making sustainability a key element of business strategy. An accelerating shift toward a sustainable, resilient global economy becomes possible thanks to rising demand for sustainable solutions, technological improvements, and supportive policy structures despite current challenges.

## 1.1. Defining Green Competencies

Green competencies encompass a range of abilities and knowledge areas that enable entrepreneurs to contribute to sustainable development. These competencies include:

- Eco-Friendly Design and Innovation: Companies need to design and develop goods or services regarding the environment. This includes the cost of sourcing Eco-friendly raw materials, controlling for wastage in the production line, and making the manufacturing processes as green as possible. For instance, Tesla has presented brilliant examples of how innovation can lead to time-saving, enhanced environmental preservation and profitability (Schaltegger & Wagner, 2011).
- Resource Efficiency: Resource conservation is another central sustainable management concept of green entrepreneurship. It consists of decreasing the usage of resources and energy and also practising the least waste policies. This is well illustrated by IKEA and other organisations now emphasising recycling and circular economy (Stahel, 2016).

- Sustainability-Driven Decision-Making: Starting-up managers should adopt sustainability into their strategic models to ensure that economic objectives are met with environmental and social factors. This approach is highly relevant in sectors experiencing high environmental pressures, like manufacturing and agriculture (Clarkson et al., 2022).
- Green Financial Literacy: Knowledge of the financial aspects of sustainable investments is crucial to realise green investments and expenditures for implementing environmental measures. In other words, to build resource-sustainable value propositions, mechanisms such as carbon credits, green bonds, or eco-labelling must be managed by entrepreneurs expertly (Geissdoerfer et al., 2017).

These competencies are not standalone skills but are interconnected, requiring an interdisciplinary approach to education and training. They also align with the principles of the triple bottom line—people, planet, and profit—highlighting the interdependence of social, environmental, and economic dimensions in business (Elkington, 1997).

## 1.2. Importance in Entrepreneurial Education

Although the role of sustainability for entrepreneurial organisations has been increasingly recognised, educational programs for future entrepreneurs often provide insufficient training for tackling issues of the green economy. Typically, business curricula have been developed mainly with an economic view of the world by teaching the routine business functional areas like marketing, finance and strategy while paying scant regard to the broader environmental and social aspects (Fayolle & Gailly, 2008). This is a significant gap in that future entrepreneurs will be ill-prepared to deal with the complexities of sustainable development.

Entrepreneurial education plays an important role in forming the perception and competence of future entrepreneurs. The integration of green competencies in schemes of studies within entrepreneurship courses not only avails students of the likely realities of the business world in the future but also cultivates a culture of innovation and resilience within learners. For instance, project-based strategies have been identified to share student interest in real-life sustainable development concerns and afford a means for the subject content knowledge to be applied practically (Wiek et al., 2011). Real-life examples like the case of Patagonia: Their decision about not supplying clothing made in China due to various reasons, their',{'I dream of the day you can buy a nice sweater a shirt or a pair of pants, feel good about the fact that it is not made in China of course not that there is something inherently wrong with China, it is just that fleece my friend is a local industry now'}commitment to sustainable products can

Furthermore, incorporating the component into entrepreneurial education also introduces green competencies, which are among the goals of higher education institutions, such as civil responsibility and global citizenship. Two models of such practices can be identified: the One Planet MBA conducted by the University of Exeter and the Center for Social Innovation of Stanford University. These programs advocate for integrating knowledge across disciplines, interacting with key industry players, and practical problem-solving by incorporating systems approaches (Wiek et al., 2011; University of Exeter, 2020).

Furthermore, there is the potential for the education provided to be entrepreneurial and encourage the change of the entire system within entrepreneurship by impacting the rest of the business systems. Graduates who have developed green competencies can enter an organisation and implement change – positively impacting the environment or creating a company with environmentally friendly and socially responsible goals. Therefore, sustainable education can also be seen as a way of responding to the global sustainability agenda; this makes sustainability-oriented education an ethical and strategic investment of educational institutions.

## 1.3. Objectives

This chapter addresses the critical need for integrating green competencies into entrepreneurial education. Its primary objectives include:

1. Bridging Knowledge Gaps: Based on an analysis of the literature published in the last decade and examples of best practices examined in this chapter, the reader will understand what green competencies mean in the context of entrepreneurship. This paper focuses on the theory of green entrepreneurship and discusses educational and practical implications (Geissdoerfer et al., 2017; Schaltegger & Wagner, 2011).
2. Providing Practical Strategies: Consequently, the chapter presents practical approaches toward the implementation of green competencies into the curricula of entrepreneurs. These use team-based approaches in teaching and learning technology-enhanced simulations and projects for sustainability and teaching experiential learning sweat equity problems pupils face in real life (UNESCO, 2020).
3. Identifying Challenges and Opportunities: Opportunities include the uptake of green competencies in meaningful curriculum education, while threats include resistance to change, restrictive resource access, and lack of proper educator capacity. These are discussed in this chapter, and feasible ways to address these challenges are provided (Tilbury, 2011).
4. Encouraging Policy Alignment: This is due to the important policy frameworks, including the United Nations Sustainable Development Goals 2030 and Environmental, Social, and Governance standards. This chapter explores how entrepreneurial education may be congruent with these frameworks to achieve international applicability and intent (United Nations, 2015).

Through these objectives, this chapter seeks to contribute to developing a new generation of entrepreneurs who are both financially successful and socially and environmentally responsible. It emphasises the importance of fostering a sustainability-first mindset in entrepreneurship, equipping students with the skills and knowledge to drive meaningful change.

*Table 1. Key green competencies and their impacts*

| Green Competency | Key Skills | Impact on Entrepreneurship | Examples |
|---|---|---|---|
| **Eco-Friendly Design** | Sustainable product innovation | Reduces waste and environmental footprint, enhances brand reputation | Tesla's electric vehicles |
| **Resource Efficiency** | Circular economy practices | Optimises resource use lowers operational costs | IKEA's recycling initiatives |
| **Sustainability-Driven Decision-Making** | Ethical decision frameworks | Balances environmental, social, and financial goals | Unilever's sustainable sourcing policies |
| **Green Financial Literacy** | Understanding green investments | Access to green funding opportunities improved financial sustainability | Carbon credits and green bond programs |

## 2. THE CURRENT LANDSCAPE OF ENTREPRENEURIAL EDUCATION

Scientific advancements have forced changes in all aspects of life, and so has entrepreneurial education – a bedrock for the growth of innovation-based businesses that are critical in any economy. However, it has not entirely integrated itself in this way, with sustainability principles as a primary problem. An evaluation of the current market environment supports the argument for the proper integration of change needed to properly equip future business leaders to work with environmental and social issues. The weaknesses of conventional entrepreneurial education are discussed in this section, as the emerging area of focus on green entrepreneurial education prepares and the imperative roles of educators and institutions in closing the gap between conventional entrepreneurship education and sustainable development.

### 2.1. Existing Gaps in Sustainability Integration

Conventional enterprise learning will help students learn the necessary planning, marketing, and accounting skills. However, it ignores environmental and social factors necessary to address modern global sustainable development issues (Fayolle & Gailly, 2008). An interesting challenge that can be named is that few interdisciplinary approaches incorporate ecological, social, and ethical aspects with business ones. Despite recognising entrepreneurial ventures as an effective means for creating new value, conventional entrepreneurship development programs often neglect sustainability as an attribute of successful business management strategies (Hindle, 2010).

Emerging research reveals that few entrepreneurship education programs have elements for modules such as circular economy, green innovation, and ethical leadership (Singh et al., 2021). The conservation of this gap prolongs the gap between entrepreneurial science and the actual implementation of a green economy. According to Henry et al. (2023), only 25% of the Scholars surveyed on entrepreneurship programs in Europe and North America offer mild or no content on sustainability, while the entrepreneurial industry demands green skills. Lack of such competencies means that future entrepreneurs are likely to engage in unsustainable modes of operation.

Thus, systems thinking and the development of sustainability literacy should become significant focuses of educational institutions. These elements should include resource utilisation, ethical decision-making, and assessing programmes and their environmental impact. Partnerships with industry and government can also offer the same understanding to the students and the applications of sustainability (Tilbury, 2011).

### 2.2. Trends in Green Entrepreneurship

Sustainable green entrepreneurship has gained popularity in the global market over the last four decades. This growth is due to growing world concern towards the environment, pressure from lawmakers to comply with laws passed to protect the environment and inhabitants, and a growing market demand for green products. Tesla Motors and Beyond Meat are outstanding examples of how sustainability can create innovation and value (Schaltegger & Wagner, 2011).

### 2.2.1. Drivers of Green Entrepreneurship

Stemming factors contribute to green entrepreneurship: First, new industrial solutions emerged – clean technologies, like renewable energy and carbon capture systems, offer new business opportunities. Second, positive externalities arising from compliance with ESG standards have introduced new, improved business practices that are environmentally sustainable (Elkington, 1997). Third, customer demands for green goods and services have altered markets to possibilities, and potential owners are now embracing new opportunities.

### 2.2.2. Implications for Entrepreneurial Education

These trends emphasised the notion of green entrepreneurship for incorporation into educational programs. Upon this project, educational institutions must be ready to take advantage of the opportunities prevailing in the developing markets, such as renewable energy, sustainable agriculture, and waste management. For example, the case of successful green entrepreneurs such as Elon Musk shows that strategies towards a green economy and sustainability ha installed business models are sustainable both for the business and society in the long run, as testified by evidence (Stahel, 2016).

Moreover, key circular economy concepts are increasingly becoming an essential focus area for green entrepreneurship. These include circular models where organisations involved in circular economies, like IKEA through recycling, confirm that circular economy models are economically sustainable (Ghisellini et al., 2016). These examples demonstrate why, for entrepreneurial curricula, innovation and sustainability should not be treated as mutually exclusive concepts.

## 2.3. Role of Educators and Institutions

Education institutions and faculties have powerful role models to influence the mindset of becoming an entrepreneur. In this way, they can inspire students to achieve sustainable entrepreneurship that deals with multifaceted environmental and social issues. Here, some strategies have been found to work when closing the gap between entrepreneurial education and sustainability.

### 2.3.1. Project-Based Learning

As a result of project-based education, which focuses on authentic activities, the students can practice the concepts explained in the course. For instance, sustainability projects concerned with developing green business models or implementing environmental management procedures enable students to apply specific skills. Kolb's (1984) framework postulates that concrete activity, such as sustainability, is paramount in consolidating knowledge that the organisation requires today or in the future.

### 2.3.2. Collaborations with Industry

Working with partners from the industry allows students to get the best practice samples of sustainability. Working with companies such as Patagonia and Unilever – two players committed to sustainable business – students are being introduced to ethical sourcing and green business innovation. Furthermore, in business and administrative studies, internship interventions were designed in the sustainability-entrepreneurship area, exposing the students to applying green competencies.

### 2.3.3. Institutional Leadership

It is the formation of institution-centred sustainability missions and practices as models for other institutions to emulate. Such institutions as Stanford and the University of Exeter have started developing interdisciplinary curricula between business and environment (Wiek et al., 2011). These institutions also aim for sustainable development through actions like institutional carbon neutrality and green campus construction.

### 2.3.4. Policy Support

Sustainability in entrepreneurial education can only progress through educational policy. Authorities of various states and accreditation organisations can encourage the teaching of sustainability modules by associating state financing with the outcomes of implementing the Sustainable Development Goals. For example, the Horizon 2020 program in the EU provides funding for educational projects promoting sustainability and offering incentives to make institutions prioritise green competencies (European Commission, 2020).

*Table 2. Integration of green competencies in entrepreneurial education*

| Aspect | Traditional Focus | Green Competencies Focus | Examples of Implementation |
|---|---|---|---|
| **Curriculum Content** | Business planning, marketing | Circular economy, resource efficiency | The circular economy module at University X |
| **Teaching Methods** | Lecture-based learning | Project-based, experiential learning | Green innovation projects in MBA programs |
| **Industry Collaboration** | General internships | Sustainability-focused internships | Partnerships with Tesla and Unilever |
| **Institutional Leadership** | Business-as-usual practices | Adoption of green infrastructure | Campus-wide carbon neutrality initiatives |

As it is provided today, entrepreneurial education needs integration of sustainability more than ever. Traditional programs perform very well in building the scholar's fundamental business competencies, but they fail to prepare the learners for issues of the environment and society regarding entrepreneurship. With the increasing nascent nature of green entrepreneurship in global markets, educational institutions need to support green competencies and integrate curricula with sustainability. By integrating cross-disciplinary, project-based, and work-integrated learning strategies, future entrepreneurs can bring positive change to the green economy.

## 3. FRAMEWORK FOR GREEN COMPETENCIES IN ENTREPRENEURIAL EDUCATION

There is no doubt that a clear framework is essential when introducing green competencies as an element of skills preparation in the frame of introducing entrepreneurial education to the future generation of business leaders. This section contains the key content areas of green competencies, their relationship to sustainable norms and standards globally, and key curriculum issues in developing green competencies.

### 3.1 Core Components of Green Competencies

The core components of green competencies serve as the foundation for fostering sustainable entrepreneurship. These include:

- Greening through Product and Service Design Green entrepreneurship covers eco-friendly design and innovation, where the respective product-service systems are designed with the least impact on the environment possible. Business leaders need to know how to make sustainable design practices standard, including life cycle assessment, the use of renewable materials, and energy-efficient processes (Bocken et al., 2016). Organisations like Tesla practice this because they manufacture cars that reduce carbon emissions but are attractive to consumers. However, sustainable innovation enhances market competitiveness, rapidly being defined by environmental standards and Acting Green consumer trends (Hallstedt et al., 2020). They help include sustainability first into entrepreneurship education, which will ensure that the students in entrepreneurship come up with sustainable innovations.
- Circular Economy Practices Circular economy practices enhance resources, minimise waste and contain closed loops. Thus, entrepreneurs should possess competencies such as recycling, remanufacturing, and sustainable supply chain management (Geissdoerfer et al., 2017). For instance, IKEA applies circular strategies through programs that retrieve old furniture and offer easily recycled furniture. Students enrolled in educational programs should be trained in material flow analysis and waste tracking, which allows future business owners to develop effective strategies for applying CE principles to their businesses.
- Green Financial Literacy Green financial literacy involves the capacity to demonstrate capitalistic features of sustainability investments, as well as the possibility of utilising funding opportunities for green businesses (Stahel, 2016). This suggests that sustainability and ecological imperatives can present new revenues and costs or cut costs through unorthodox valuation techniques such as carbon pricing, green bonds, or ESG linkages in investments that may have risks or benefits depending, of course, on the entrepreneur or the company in a particular ecosystem. Such things as finance for sustainability projects and an introduction to impact investing situations prepare the learners with important aspects of profit sustainability (Gianfrate & Peri, 2019).

*Table 3. Core components of green competencies in entrepreneurial education*

| Competency Area | Key Skills | Real-World Example |
|---|---|---|
| Eco-Friendly Design | Lifecycle analysis, renewable material use | Tesla's electric vehicle innovation |
| Circular Economy Practices | Waste reduction, closed-loop systems | IKEA's furniture recycling programs |
| Green Financial Literacy | Carbon pricing, green bonds, ESG investments | Sustain analytics ESG investment analytics |

## 3.2 Alignment with SDGs and ESG Standards

Incorporation of the SDGs and ESG initiatives into the entrepreneurial curriculum makes green competencies culture universal and in harmony with sustainability practices. The UN offered the SDGs plan for achieving effective sustainable development, and ESG guidelines offer companies a way to deal with environmental and social effects and governance matters.

- Significance of Keyword SDGs on Education SDG 12 Entrepreneurial relevance of 'responsible consumption and production'. It stresses sustainable supply chain management, resource productivity, and waste. SDG 12 educates entrepreneurs on the values of sustainable business practices needed to enhance global sustainable development (United Nations, 2015). For example, improving the company's plastic and sustainable materials usage policies meets the aforementioned objectives. It serves as an example of the implementation of SDG into the process of the company's functioning.
- ESG Standards as Business Imperatives ESG standards give frameworks by which investors can judge different businesses' sustainable performance, making some businesses more competitive. ESG education similarly prepares entrepreneurs to navigate opportunities and risks that characterise the modern economy by having the appropriate myriad of intertwined values to fulfil funding expectations and achieve wider stakeholder approval (Clark et al., 2015). ESG reporting and engagement, compliance and stakeholder management are areas that educational programs ought to address to equip their learners to meet these expectations.
- Application in Curricula Various exercises, such as case studies on firms that comply with ESG and preparing sustainability reports, situate the learners on the role of the entrepreneur in integrating the concept of SDGs and ESG in business. Such components have been successfully included in business programs at such universities as Harvard and Oxford; their purpose is stressed to be practical.

## 3.3 Innovative Curriculum Development Strategies for Green Entrepreneurial Education

Developing a robust green entrepreneurial curriculum demands new teaching methods that combine theoretical content with practical skills implementation. The strategies teach students to address practical sustainability issues and develop the green abilities requested to start sustainable business operations.

The framework for training sustainable start-up entrepreneurs encompasses case-based instruction, interdisciplinary study methods, and digital technology and corporate partnership models.

**Case-Based Learning:** Student learning experiences under case-based education focus on studying actual sustainable businesses to grasp tangible solutions and the difficulties of launching green startups. Beyond Meat provides notable insights regarding achieving green business growth against market competition in the food sector and other industries. Students gain better insights into sustainability-profitability balances when they examine how Beyond Meat employs innovation and strategic market strategies to address barriers (Richter et al., 2020). The analysis of Tesla showcases why sustainability requires the adoption of greenhouse technology within businesses that depend fundamentally on fossil fuels.

**Epistemic Integration and Cross-Disciplinary Approaches:** Sustainability research combines multiple disciplines, from environmental science to economics and social policy. Including multiple fields of expertise in the curriculum delivers students a complete comprehension of sustainability complications. According to Wiek et al. (2011), green entrepreneurship education requires epistemic integration through multi-disciplinary collaborations, thus enabling students to understand complex sustainability problems completely. Students who study environmental engineering and business strategy programs learn to utilise practical skills during sustainable venture development. Environmental problem-solving solutions become accessible to students by blending different disciplines' expertise, which connects technical competencies with management skills.

**Digital Technology and Simulation Models:** Productivity advancements in digital systems have transformed educational processes, including green entrepreneurial education. Using digital tools like the En-ROADS climate simulator, students can experience active learning moments that create powerful visuals linking business operational choices to environmental impacts. Through digital tools, students can test different sustainability situations, developing their real-world decision capabilities and problem-solving abilities (Sterman et al., 2015). Through their gameplay, students can enact critical thinking and active involvement, thus producing both effective learning outcomes and engaging sustainability education. Virtual reality tools combined with circular economy practice simulation apps help students better comprehend sustainable ventures within different industry sectors.

**Industry Engagement and Practical Exposure:** Through partnerships with businesses, the academic program remains updated on modern market conditions while students gain expertise that fulfils practical business standards. Students develop green competency applications through engagements with guest speakers, internships, and projects guided by organisations, including the Ellen MacArthur Foundation (Korhonen et al., 2018). Professional interaction programs supply educational institutions with beneficial market data that unite classroom concepts with industry implementation needs. Partnerships with local businesses create opportunities for students to test educational concepts and obtain feedback regarding their sustainable problem-solving methods.

**Emerging Research and Global Trends:** Research recently supports the essential nature of the educational techniques outlined in this paper. According to Dörr et al. (2021), entrepreneurial education must include the framework people need to understand climate adaptation practices and master resource efficiency methods and digital transformation expertise while remaining applicable to today's evolving business world. Their study demonstrates the value of investing in education that prepares students for tomorrow's economy with skills closely linked to sustainable development goals. Students require both life cycle analysis (LCA) tools and sustainability reporting platforms for effective communication regarding environmental venture impact, according to Asif et al. (2023).

**Challenges and Future Directions:** Implementing these strategies have enhanced the quality of green entrepreneurial education at its core, but existing challenges persist in some institutions. Developing an effective curriculum faces challenges because educational resources remain limited, skilled educators are scarce, and institutions demonstrate various degrees of sustainability commitment. For sustainable improvement of educational programs about sustainability, the barriers must be resolved through investments in instructor development and infrastructure enhancement with supportive policies. Academic institutions must collaborate globally with industries to secure access to valuable industry best practices, research findings, and resources that will strengthen their curriculum.

An effective curriculum for green entrepreneurial education needs to use a combination of practical work and theoretical study. Students can develop sustainable skills to address future challenges through teaching that combines case-based learning with epistemic integration and digital tools alongside industry collaborative initiatives. Academic institutions that integrate innovative research alongside global trends prepare upcoming generations to guide sustainable future developments through their startup ventures.

*Table 4. Curriculum development strategies for green competencies*

| Strategy | Key Features | Benefits |
|---|---|---|
| **Case-Based Learning** | Analysing real-world business examples | Fosters critical thinking and application |
| **Interdisciplinary Teaching** | Combining expertise from various disciplines | Provides a holistic view of sustainability |
| **Digital Tools and Simulations** | Gamified learning, climate impact simulators | Enhances engagement and experiential learning |
| **Industry Partnerships** | Internships, guest lectures, collaborative projects | Aligns education with real-world demands |

The recommendations to integrate green competencies into entrepreneurial learning point to the value of sustainable design, sustainable consumption, and sustainable money management. Consequently, these competencies correlate most with SDGs and ESGs to guarantee compliance with globally established benchmarks. This way, educators can design students' intellectual and human developmental curriculum strategies and prepare them to become innovative and responsible leaders in sustainable entrepreneurship. With many institutions now focusing on sustainability, such frameworks will play a crucial role in shaping the relevant future business leadership.

## 4. CASE STUDIES AND REAL-WORLD APPLICATIONS

Real-world applications are invaluable in understanding the practical implementation of green competencies in entrepreneurial education. They provide insights into the transformative potential of these competencies, guiding educators, entrepreneurs, and policymakers in achieving sustainability goals. This section explores notable case studies, evaluates the application of the proposed framework in educational institutions, and discusses lessons learned to refine and improve strategies.

## 4.1 Case Study: Patagonia

As a leader in sustainable entrepreneurship, Patagonia has integrated green competencies into business models, mirroring the path for other organisations to reap the economic and social impact and profitability. Patagonia, founded in 1973, has always prioritised sustainability, developing, promoting, and protecting eco-friendly business practices across its company and supply chains. Product Lifecycle, use of recycled materials, and support for environmental activism (Chouinard, 2016) all prove its commitment to sustainability.

Patagonia's strategy highlights several green competencies:

- Eco-Friendly Product Design: Patagonia's products contain recycled and organic materials that eliminate dependence on virgin resources. For example, it has a Common Threads Partnership that deals with repairability and recycling.
- Sustainable Supply Chain Management: Collaborative with fair trade certified partners, the company also ensures ethical sourcing and transparency in the supply chain.
- Stakeholder Engagement: Patagonia has actively enlisted customers, operations and the community in its mission. Examples include Do not Buy This Jacket for responsible consumption.

### Impact and Insights

Patagonia's success is a business case for green entrepreneurship, showing positive results regarding brand loyalty, operational efficiency and environmental footprint reduction. It models an approach to scaling sustainable practices while keeping the firm profitable for educators and entrepreneurs, integrating green competency into practice (Kiron et al., 2022).

## 4.2 Application of the Framework

Different institutions have implemented the proposed framework for green competencies, reporting important results. Adopting sustainability for educational programs by entrepreneurial institutions is associated with increased student engagement, greater sustainability literacy and improved employability of graduates in green sectors.

### Example 1: The University of Exeter MBA Program

Sustainability is integrated into the MBA curriculum of the University of Exeter. Courses included in these modules are on circular economy, principles of sustainable innovation and green finance. The effectiveness of the curriculum was evidenced by a 30 per cent increase in the number of graduates setting up careers in green entrepreneurship (University of Exeter, 2020).

## Example 2: Stanford Design Impact Program

Sustainability is incorporated into entrepreneurship education at the Design Impact Program at Stanford University. Interdisciplinary projects rooted in real-world challenges, such as plastic waste reduction and energy efficiency, challenge students. Through this approach, theory and practice are aligned to train students in applying green competencies in their ventures (Wiek et al., 2020).

## Example 3: Indian Institute of Management (IIM), Bangalore.

IIM Bangalore's Sustainability and Social Entrepreneurship program specialises in sustainable business models. Students are encouraged to work with NGOs and green startups to exercise, you know, hands-on, you know, in trying to solve some environmental and social issues. Alums of the program tend to have a strong inclination toward sustainability-focused careers (Sharma et al., 2021).

The case studies and institutional examples underline the importance of context-specific approaches, interdisciplinary collaboration, and continuous evaluation in embedding green competencies into entrepreneurial education.

## 1. Context-Specific Approaches

The adoption of green competencies calls for the tailoring of strategies to the location and sector. For example, while Patagonia concentrates on sustainable apparel, educational institutions must focus on what regional priorities they need to align with, particularly if it relates to regional sustainability focused on renewable energy or waste management (Stahel, 2016).

## 2. Interdisciplinary Collaboration Role

The interdisciplinary learning they do bridges business, engineering, environmental science and policy. Some programs combine different fields that give students an overall picture of sustainability, the challenges, and the solutions. For example, Stanford's program shows how collaboration between design and sustainability experts can lead to creativity (Wiek et al., 2020).

## 3. Continuous Evaluation, Continuous Feedback

Refining educational frameworks is crucial if they are using continuous monitoring and feedback loops. To be able to serve the evolving challenges of sustainability, institutions need to adapt to assess student outcomes, industry alignment and curriculum relevance. An example of a tool supporting such evaluations is the Sustainability Tracking, Assessment & Rating System (STARS), which universities use (AASHE, 2021).

*Table 5. Green competencies in practice*

| Institution/Company | Green Competency Focus | Key Outcomes | Real-World Impact |
|---|---|---|---|
| **Patagonia** | Sustainable product design | Increased customer loyalty, reduced environmental footprint | Advocacy for global sustainability initiatives |
| **University of Exeter** | Circular economy, green finance | 30% more graduates in green entrepreneurship | Influence on regional green startup ecosystem |
| **Stanford Design Impact** | Interdisciplinary sustainability | Real-world project outcomes in waste reduction | Enhanced student capacity for addressing challenges |
| **IIM Bangalore** | Social entrepreneurship models | Alum engagement in NGOs and startups | More significant societal impact in local communities |

*Table 6. Green competencies and their application in entrepreneurial education*

| Competency Area | Key Skills | Real-World Application |
|---|---|---|
| **Eco-Friendly Design** | Sustainable product design, resource efficiency | Green startups like *Beyond Meat* and *Tesla* use sustainable design principles. |
| **Circular Economy Practices** | Resource management, waste reduction, product lifecycle | Companies like *IKEA* are implementing circular economy strategies to reduce waste |
| **Green Financial Literacy** | Understanding of sustainable investment, funding strategies for green ventures | *Patagonia* integrates environmental factors into financial decision-making, reducing costs and increasing profit. |
| **Sustainability-driven Decision-Making** | Long-term value creation, stakeholder engagement | *Unilever's* decision to focus on sustainable sourcing of raw materials to improve supply chain sustainability |

The case studies and real-world applications demonstrate how green competencies are transformative in entrepreneurial education. Educational institutions show that a structured framework can foster aspiring entrepreneurs, and organisations like Patagonia show the business viability of sustainability-focused strategies. To integrate green competencies into entrepreneurial education in a context-specific way, the approaches should be tailored, interdisciplinary learning should be fostered, and the integration should be evaluated periodically.

## 5. CHALLENGES AND OPPORTUNITIES IN GREEN COMPETENCIES FOR ENTREPRENEURIAL EDUCATION

### 5.1. Barriers to Implementation

The successful inclusion of green competencies into entrepreneurial education requires overcoming multiple obstacles to achieve widespread adoption of sustainable practice.

**Resistance to Change:** Traditional instructional methods favour traditional business competencies, including financial management and marketing, above sustainability-oriented themes, according to Tilbury (2011). Irrational resistance develops due to a deep commitment toward familiar and straightforward educational material that educators and institutions believe creates better direct business performance results. Stakeholders who measure curricular density tend to treat green competency training as an overloaded requirement in educational institutions that do not recognise sustainability as a primary focus. Severe barriers exist because no established national or international policies require or reward the integration of sustainability education (UNESCO, 2014). Educational personnel encounter resistance to transformation, but so do their students, who neglect to understand how green competencies relate to their entrepreneurial pursuits, thus making sustainable implementation harder to achieve.

**Resource Limitations:** A primary hurdle arises from insufficient resource allocations to develop and maintain green entrepreneurship courses. Educational institutions in developing countries face severe budgetary limitations preventing them from establishing innovative resource-intensive programs since they must address their fundamental operational challenges (Hopwood et al., 2005). The shortages of modern facilities accompanied by limited technological accessibility intensify these obstacles. Sustainability educational initiatives need financing to purchase research equipment while updating educational resources and establishing sustainability-based training sessions. The widespread application of green competencies remains challenging because these underlying resource distribution disparities go unresolved.

**Lack of Expertise among Educators**: Our educational institutions suffer from inadequate numbers of sustainability experts specialising in green entrepreneurship development. The successful implementation of green competencies needs educators who combine subject diversity with hands-on understanding and proven teaching methods since many educational systems currently show these elements are absent (Wiek et al., 2011). Academic recognition of environmental science alongside sustainable development exists, but the connection between these fields and entrepreneurship remains a seldom studied field. Educational institutions must fund professional development opportunities to prepare their educators, but this requirement creates another resource challenge.

**Limited Industry-Academia Collaboration:** Together, academia and industry must build partnerships to connect green entrepreneurship education with practical, real-world experiences. These partnerships frequently struggle to form appropriate connections, which results in educational content that remains disconnected from real-world uses. To become genuinely employable, students need physical learning experiences through internships at green enterprises, case studies, and industry mentorship programs, yet such opportunities remain scarce (Lozano et al., 2015). Institutions fail to keep their curricula updated with industry trends through this disconnect, thus diminishing green competency relevance.

**Inconsistent Policy Support:** The consistent support that government institutions provide to develop educational priorities regarding green entrepreneurship remains difficult to ascertain. Many regions have incorporated innovative sustainability policies into their agenda, although certain areas keep selecting economic growth goals that conflict with environmental sustainability objectives (UNESCO, 2014). Lack of consistency within policy structures creates problems with uniform resource funding and fragmented sustainable entrepreneurial projects that reduce their ability to expand and total impact. Lack of communication with specific targets and funding schemes fosters insufficient institutional drive to establish sustainability education priorities.

## 5.2. Opportunities for Growth

Green competencies embedded in entrepreneurial education demonstrate substantial potential to develop sustainable innovation alongside development opportunities despite existing barriers.

**Economic Growth through Green Entrepreneurship:** Forecasting economic growth through green entrepreneurship generates economic value by establishing new market niches and publishing specialised employment roles in sustainable sectors, including renewable power generation and waste management alongside sustainable agricultural methods. The current market valuation of $13.76 billion indicates that the global green technology and sustainability sector will expand through 2030 with a projected 22.4% compound annual growth rate (Grand View Research, 2022). Future entrepreneurs taught green competencies will become skilled at discovering and monetising such business possibilities, which will help build sustainable economic value and protect natural environments.

**Technological Innovations:** Emerging technological advancements develop modern solutions for urgent sustainability problems, thus allowing green start-up companies to grow successfully. Blockchain technology creates transparent supply chains that enable businesses to monitor environmental impacts, according to Tapscott et al. (2016). Through investing in renewable energy technologies such as solar power and wind energy, green entrepreneurs acquire opportunities to expand their business operations rapidly because of lower costs and widespread availability. Achieving more excellent student proficiency with these technologies requires adding entrepreneurial curriculum content featuring these tools.

**Alignment with Global Sustainability Goals:** Education based on green competencies connects entrepreneur activities to United Nations Sustainable Development Goals (SDGs), specifically emphasis on SDG 12, focusing on responsible consumption and production (United Nations, 2015). Educational institutions help achieve global sustainability goals by fostering sustainable entrepreneurship, practices that prepare graduates to handle environmental and social issues.

**Consumer and Investor Demand for Sustainability:** The mounting public understanding of environmental matters leads consumers and investors to prioritise sustainable products and services. A Deloitte survey from 2022 demonstrates that sustainability now matters to 55% of consumers when they buy products (2022). At the same time, investors have started allocating resources to sustainable business ventures. The marketplace rewards entrepreneurs with green competencies because they successfully address consumers' sustainability requirements.

**Policy Incentives and Funding Opportunities:** International institutions and governmental bodies provide increasing monetary benefits for fostering environmentally friendly startups. Through the European Union's Green Deal Investment Plan, graduates with green competencies can access funding and resources that make sustainable businesses possible (European Commission, 2021). The implemented policy measures demonstrate how sustainability needs to become an essential element of entrepreneurial education.

**Enhanced Employability and Career Opportunities:** Green competencies create professional opportunities for graduates pursuing emerging careers focusing on sustainability consulting, environmental project management and green product design. Industries' growing emphasis on sustainability will increase the demand for professionals with expertise in these areas, resulting in expanded career possibilities for students.

## 5.3. Recommendations for Integrating Green Competencies into Entrepreneurial Education

Successfully implementing green competencies into entrepreneurial education demands a comprehensive, multiple-pronged strategy. Implementing green competencies in entrepreneurial education requires comprehensive changes to curriculum standards and training education programs with industry partnership development, technological innovation and established evaluation guidelines. The recommendations tackle separate business challenges while aligning with sustainability goals and practical implementation needs.

## Curriculum Redesign

Starting sustainable education in entrepreneurship demands complete educational curriculum transformation to embed sustainability skills. Education programs should deliver fundamental knowledge about life cycle assessment alongside renewable energy solutions, circular economy practices, sustainable supply chain management, and green finance as foundational training for entrepreneurs. Student education becomes more sustainable when curricula establish foundational knowledge of efficient resource practices and sustainable technologies, stimulating entrepreneurship toward sustainable ventures (Lozano et al., 2015).

The development of green competencies depends heavily on experiential learning methods. Students gain meaningful insights into sustainability practice through experiential education opportunities such as sustainability hackathons and case studies from realistic settings combined with green company internships. Hack4Climate is an example of an experiential learning method that drives participants to create novel climate action solutions during sustainability hackathons (Reiter & Jentzsch, 2019). Universities should pair up with sustainable startups to deliver complete learning experiences for students, which develop entrepreneurial innovations specifically focused on sustainability principles.

## Capacity Building for Educators

Effective green entrepreneurship education depends on educators, yet most teachers lack the expertise to deliver lessons about green competencies. The training deficiency among educators requires investments in capacity-enhancing initiatives that combine specialised programs and learning activities alongside sustainable content delivery certifications. Results from UNESCO's Education for Sustainable Development (ESD) teacher training program demonstrate how educators gain skills to incorporate sustainability education into their classrooms (UNESCO, 2020).

Research collaborations between academics from multiple fields will help faculty deepen their sustainability knowledge. Participation in collaborative environmental research and entrepreneurship projects with green technology elements enables educators to create advanced educational content from which students can teach (Wiek et al., 2011). Students benefit from strong mentorship programs where experienced sustainability professionals offer delayed professors valuable lessons directly applicable when supporting their students.

## Industry-Academia Collaboration

Academia and industry stakeholders need continuous collaboration to guarantee that their green competencies match the needs and trends experienced by businesses in practice. Business schools that involve their industry partners during curriculum development establish educational programs that effectively mirror sustainable industry needs (Lozano et al., 2015). Through industry-academy partnerships, students gain practical insights into sustainability principles during mentorship sessions and workshops conducted by professionals from the field.

Through collaborative projects, students gain practical experience in resolving sustainability challenges. Universities work with companies to create solutions that prevent waste production, promote renewable power systems, and efficiently utilise resources in manufacturing operations. These educational ventures empower students to solve problems concurrently while enhancing their innovative abilities and preparing them to face the changing sustainability needs of environmentally focused companies. Sustainable entrepreneurship benefits from joint research collaborations between academic institutions and industrial partners who co-create next-generation sustainable technologies and business platforms.

## Policy Advocacy and Support

Implementing green competencies within entrepreneurial education requires active support from policy measures. Implementing sustainability education requires policymakers to design specific policies while offering financial aid mixed with regulatory control. National education policies should require sustainability-focused entrepreneurship curricula to mandate their inclusion in academic programs, according to UNESCO (2014).

Sustainability-focused programs receive increased student participation through financial incentives such as grants and scholarships for those who pursue green entrepreneurship. Public funds go towards institutions to develop and execute green entrepreneurship curricula. Educators and sustainability advocates must stress both economic cost savings and environmental advantages stemming from sustainability-focused education, which should lead policymakers to fund this educational approach.

The United Nations Sustainable Development Goals (SDGs) are essential international foundations guiding policy advocacy practices. SDG goals SDG 4 and SDG 12, along with their education-related targets, enable policymakers to rewrite educational policies to advance sustainable initiatives across learning institutions (United Nations, 2015).

## Leveraging Technology for Learning

Technology's transformative nature enables accessibility improvements and effectiveness enhancement in green entrepreneurship education programs. Modern digital tools offer dynamic educational interactions, including simulations of online and virtual education systems and electronic learning networks. The business simulation platform Capsim enables students to make strategic choices about environmental and social impacts, thus fostering their grasp of sustainable business techniques (Grand View Research, 2022).

AI-learning platforms provide equitable access to green competency learning by letting remote or poor students obtain education about sustainability across vast distances. Students can experience virtual reality and augmented reality spaces to better understand the environmental and social results of business decisions. Educational programs incorporating VR simulations show students how deforestation and climate change affect natural habitats through virtual displays that improve comprehension of sustainable practices.

## Public-Private Partnerships

The combination of public entities and private enterprises through public-private partnerships (PPPs) meets a successful platform to support green entrepreneurship education efforts. Through teamwork between governments, private enterprises, and non-profit organisations, financial support, technical expertise, and human capabilities help sustain sustainability-focused initiatives. PPPs help create green business incubators alongside accelerators, providing aspiring entrepreneurs essential mentorship, funding, and infrastructure (Reiter & Jentzsch, 2019).

PPP organisations demonstrate success through the European Union's Green Deal Investment Plan, which directs financial aid to sustainable startup ventures (European Commission 2021). New green entrepreneurial programs should be established across different areas to build an environment that supports sustainable business development. The support from private industries through scholarship funding and sustainability workshops and competitions attracts increased student interest in green entrepreneurship education.

## Monitoring and Evaluation

Instructional success in green entrepreneurship education demands the implementation of thorough assessment mechanisms that collect data about programming and teaching method effectiveness as well as industry partnership outcomes. Educational systems need established evaluation frameworks to measure how curricular content, educational approaches, and industry-connect programs affect students' achievements. Wiek et al. (2011) note that measuring changes in green sector employment of graduates along with success rates for new green businesses and SDG alignment mechanisms reveal essential educational program effectiveness data.

A thorough understanding of graduates from sustainable entrepreneurship programs emerges from ongoing studies that research their professional development pathways. Student, educator and industry partner feedback helps institutions improve their programs through a continuous effort to maintain both value and impact. Measurements against worldwide benchmarks for sustainability instruction enable institutions to underscore excellence and promote creative breakthroughs in education.

The addition of green competencies into entrepreneurial education demands an elaborate strategy for solving difficulties while making the best of available opportunities. Through new curricular designs, trained educator development, academic-industry partnerships, policy support initiatives, technological implementations and public-private alliance formation, institutions should empower the entrepreneurs of tomorrow by developing their sustainable growth skillsets. Regular tracking through robust evaluation tools leads to continuous enhancement and enhanced alignment with worldwide sustainable objectives with a transformative effect on education and entrepreneurship.

*Table 7. Barriers, opportunities, and recommendations for embedding green competencies*

| **Category** | **Details** |
|---|---|
| **Barriers** | Resistance to change, limited resources, lack of expertise, inadequate collaboration, weak policies |
| **Opportunities** | Economic growth, technological innovations, alignment with SDGs, consumer demand, policy incentives |
| **Recommendations** | Curriculum redesign, educator training, industry partnerships, policy advocacy, tech-enabled learning |

Integrating green competencies into entrepreneurial education is critical for fostering a generation of business leaders capable of addressing global sustainability challenges. While significant barriers exist, the opportunities for economic growth, innovation, and alignment with global goals outweigh these challenges. By implementing the recommended strategies, educational institutions can empower students to drive sustainable change and contribute to a green economy.

## 6. CONCLUSION

Preparing entrepreneurs to navigate an increasingly green, fast-changing world requires green competencies. In fact, given the growing pressure on sustainable matters by the global community, such as climate change, resource depletion, and social inequality, the relevance of green competencies that go into entrepreneurial education grows among such issues (Acs et al., 2020). These competencies aim to give entrepreneurs the knowledge, skills and values necessary to run businesses that create social and environmental value and are economically viable (Acs et al., 2021). By embedding these competencies into curricula, educators can be confident that forthcoming generations of entrepreneurs will not only be able to thrive in a competitive environment but also make measurable contributions to sustained development. A structured approach to embedding green competencies within entrepreneurial education, both theoretically and practically, allows this to occur. The proposed framework offers one way of introducing sustainability ideas into the curricula, including elements of eco-friendly innovation, resource efficiency, circular economy principles and financial literacy in green ventures. According to Reijnders et al. (2021), sustainable entrepreneurship is a field of modern business practice rather than an isolated niche market. So, educational programs must also shift, finding a new generation of entrepreneurs to balance their profitability with social and environmental responsibility.

Research has recently indicated the need to integrate green competencies within entrepreneurship curricula. One of the examples is the work of Dangelico and Vocalelli (2020), which shows the impact of integrating the principles of sustainability in entrepreneurial education not only for increasing the awareness of global challenges for students but also the practical preparation for adoption of innovative business practices based on the Sustainable Development Goals (SDGs). Additionally, educators can use the SDGs to structure curricula focusing on sustainability-driven decision-making and long-term value creation (Giacalone & Thompson, 2020).

Universities and business schools can better prepare students for the complexities of a global market that increasingly demands sustainable solutions if they find appropriate ways to align education strategies with SDGs and Environmental, Social and Governance (ESG) standards. It has been shown that interdisciplinary approaches and experiential learning techniques, including case studies and sustainability simulations, improve students' ability to apply acquired knowledge in real-world scenarios (Wiek et al., 2011). One example is the University of California, Berkeley's Center for Responsible Business. It incorporates sustainability through hands-on projects into its MBA, putting students in front of sustainability challenges businesses face today (UC Berkeley, 2021).

Additionally, the green competencies reflected in the learning bring added value to students and meet the needs of many industries in search of employees versed in sustainability and green innovation. According to a study by Roberts et al. (2021), more and more companies wish for entrepreneurs to be familiar with how to switch economy to green and integrate circular economy principles into business models, reduce carbon footprints, and improve social responsibility. Embedding sustainable entrepreneurship competencies into entrepreneurial education prepares students to meet the challenges implied in sustainable entrepreneurship. It helps achieve environmental sustainability by contributing to the broader societal goals of achieving environmental sustainability. Entrepreneurial education can spur green innovation and, in turn, change businesses and the way the world builds. Those skilled at building profitable businesses and passionate about turning the environmental and social capital of the 21st century are the hands through which the future of entrepreneurial lives is.

## REFERENCES


Acs, Z. J., Autio, E., & Szerb, L. (2020). The Global Entrepreneurship and Development Index 2020. *Entrepreneurship and Regional Development*, *32*(3-4), 187–209.

Acs, Z. J., Szerb, L., & Autio, E. (2021). Green entrepreneurship and the transition to a sustainable economy. *Small Business Economics*, *56*(1), 1–15. DOI: 10.1007/s11187-020-00369-1

Asif, F., Sharif, K., & Malik, A. (2023). Life cycle analysis and sustainability reporting in green entrepreneurship education. *Journal of Cleaner Production*, *367*, 133892. DOI: 10.1016/j.jclepro.2023.133892

Association for the Advancement of Sustainability in Higher Education (AASHE). (2021). *Sustainability Tracking, Assessment & Rating System (STARS)*. Retrieved from https://stars.aashe.org/

Berkeley, U. C. (2021). *Center for Responsible Business*. Retrieved from https://responsiblebusiness .berkeley.edu/

Bocken, N. M., de Pauw, I., Bakker, C., & van der Grinten, B. (2016). Product design and business model strategies for a circular economy. *Journal of Industrial and Production Engineering*, *33*(5), 308–320. DOI: 10.1080/21681015.2016.1172124

Brundtland, G. H. (1987). *Our Common Future: Report of the World Commission on Environment and Development*. Oxford University Press.

Chouinard, Y. (2016). *Let My People Go Surfing: The Education of a Reluctant Businessman*. Penguin.

Clark, G. L., Feiner, A., & Viehs, M. (2015). *From the stockholder to the stakeholder: How sustainability can drive financial outperformance*. Oxford University Press.

Clarkson, P. M., Li, Y., Pinnuck, M., & Richardson, G. D. (2022). The valuation impact of carbon emission disclosures on global markets. *The Accounting Review*, *97*(5), 65–91.

Dangelico, R. M., & Vocalelli, D. (2020). Green innovation and entrepreneurship in the era of sustainable development. *Business Strategy and the Environment*, *29*(4), 1570–1585.

Deloitte. (2022). *2022 Global Sustainability Consumer Report*. Retrieved from https://www.deloitte.com/

Dörr, N., Kappler, B., & Scheuermann, M. (2021). Future-proofing entrepreneurial education: Integrating global trends and sustainability. *Entrepreneurship Research Journal*, *11*(2), 99–112. DOI: 10.1515/erj-2020-0101

Elkington, J. (1997). *Cannibals with Forks: The Triple Bottom Line of 21st Century Business*. Capstone.

European Commission. (2020). *The European Green Deal*. Retrieved from https://ec.europa.eu/clima/policies/eu-climate-action_en

European Commission. (2020). [*A European Framework Programme for Research and Innovation. European Commission.*]. *Horizon*, •••, 2020.

European Commission. (2021). *The European Green Deal Investment Plan*. Retrieved from https://ec .europa.eu/

Fayolle, A., & Gailly, B. (2008). From craft to science: Teaching models and entrepreneurial learning. *Journal of European Industrial Training*, *32*(7), 569–593. DOI: 10.1108/03090590810899838

Geissdoerfer, M., Savaget, P., Bocken, N. M. P., & Hultink, E. J. (2017). The Circular Economy – A New Sustainability Paradigm? *Journal of Cleaner Production*, *143*, 757–768. DOI: 10.1016/j.jclepro.2016.12.048

Ghisellini, P., Cialani, C., & Ulgiati, S. (2016). A review on circular economy: The expected transition to a balanced interplay of environmental and economic systems. *Journal of Cleaner Production*, *114*, 11–32. DOI: 10.1016/j.jclepro.2015.09.007

Gholami, H., Sobhani, A., & Khademi, Z. (2020). Sustainable Entrepreneurship: A Conceptual Framework for Future Research. *Sustainability*, *12*(10), 1–19. DOI: 10.3390/su12104122

Giacalone, R. A., & Thompson, G. R. (2020). Sustainable development goals and entrepreneurial education: A case for a more inclusive curriculum. *Journal of Business Ethics*, *165*(2), 307–323.

Gianfrate, G., & Peri, M. (2019). Sustainable finance and the role of green bonds: A systematic review. *Sustainability*, *11*(23), 6367.

Grand View Research. (2022). *Green Technology and Sustainability Market Size, Share & Trends Analysis Report*. Grand View Research.

Hallstedt, S. I., Thompson, A. W., & Lindahl, P. (2020). Key elements for implementing a strategic sustainability perspective in the product innovation process. *Sustainability*, *12*(4), 1455.

Hemlata, & Rai, M. (2025). An Optimized Demand for Cost and Environment Benefits Towards Smart Residentials Using IOT and Machine Learning. Sustainable Smart Homes and Buildings with Internet of Things, 291-307.

Henry, C., Foss, L., & Ahl, H. (2023). Gender and sustainability in entrepreneurship education: A systematic review. *Entrepreneurship and Regional Development*, *35*(1-2), 1–25.

Hopwood, B., Mellor, M., & O'Brien, G. (2005). Sustainable development: Mapping different approaches. *Sustainable Development (Bradford)*, *13*(1), 38–52. DOI: 10.1002/sd.244

Kirkwood, J., & Walton, S. (2010). What motivates ecopreneurs to start businesses? *International Journal of Entrepreneurial Behaviour & Research*, *16*(3), 204–228. DOI: 10.1108/13552551011042799

Kiron, D., Unruh, G., Reeves, M., & Rubel, H. (2022). Sustainability's Deep Impact on Business. *MIT Sloan Management Review*. Retrieved from https://sloanreview.mit.edu/

Korhonen, J., Honkasalo, A., & Seppälä, J. (2018). Circular economy: The concept and its limitations. *Ecological Economics*, *143*, 37–46. DOI: 10.1016/j.ecolecon.2017.06.041

Lans, T., Blok, V., & Wesselink, R. (2014). Learning apart and together: Towards an integrated competence framework for sustainable entrepreneurship in higher education. *Journal of Cleaner Production*, *62*, 37–47. DOI: 10.1016/j.jclepro.2013.03.036

Lozano, R.. (2015). A review of commitment and implementation of sustainable development in higher education. *International Journal of Sustainability in Higher Education*, *16*(2), 155–172.

Lüdeke-Freund, F., Gold, S., & Bocken, N. M. P. (2018). A Review and Typology of Circular Economy Business Model Patterns. *Journal of Industrial Ecology*, *23*(1), 36–61. DOI: 10.1111/jiec.12763

Nielsen (2018). *The Sustainability Imperative*. Retrieved from https://www.nielsen.com/us/en/insights/report/2018/the-sustainability-imperative/

PwC. (2021). *Tech for Good: Using Technology to Transform Sustainability*. Retrieved from https://www.pwc.com

Reijnders, L., Lukszo, Z., & Albrecht, H. (2021). Sustainability, Green Innovation, and Entrepreneurship: The Green Entrepreneurial Process. *Sustainability*, *13*(4), 2332–2347.

Reiter, S., & Jentzsch, S. (2019). Hack4Climate: A Novel Approach to Foster Climate Change Innovation. *Environmental Innovation and Societal Transitions*.

Richter, F. J., Kleber, L. S., & Müller, S. (2020). Green growth and beyond: The case of Beyond Meat. *Journal of Business Models*, *8*(1), 56–68. DOI: 10.5278/ojs.jbm.v8i1.3665

Roberts, M., Jenkins, M., & Knox, R. (2021). Corporate Sustainability and the Future of Green Entrepreneurship. *Business & Society*, *60*(2), 310–333.

Schaltegger, S., & Wagner, M. (2011). Sustainable entrepreneurship and sustainability innovation: Categories and interactions. *Business Strategy and the Environment*, *20*(4), 222–237. DOI: 10.1002/bse.682

Sharma, A., Kumar, R., & Singh, D. (2021). Emerging Trends in Sustainability Education: A Case Study of IIM Bangalore. *Journal of Sustainability Studies*, *15*(3), 150–172.

Singh, R., Tiwari, K., & Mishra, P. (2021). Sustainability in entrepreneurial education: Challenges and future directions. *International Journal of Management Education*, *19*(2), 100531.

Stahel, W. R. (2016). Circular economy: A new relationship with our goods and materials would save resources and energy and create local jobs. *Nature*, *531*(7595), 435–438. DOI: 10.1038/531435a PMID: 27008952

Stahel, W. R. (2016). The circular economy. *Nature*, *531*(7595), 435–438. DOI: 10.1038/531435a PMID: 27008952

Sterman, J. D., Siegel, L., & Rooney-Varga, J. N. (2015). En-ROADS: A simulation model to engage diverse audiences in climate solutions. *Simulation & Gaming*, *46*(6), 649–668.

Tapscott, D., & Tapscott, A. (2016). *Blockchain Revolution: How the Technology Behind Bitcoin Changes Money, Business, and the World*. Penguin.

Tilbury, D. (2011). *Education for sustainable development: An expert review of processes and learning*. UNESCO.

UNESCO. (2014). *Roadmap for Implementing the Global Action Programme on Education for Sustainable Development*. UNESCO.

UNESCO. (2020). *Education for Sustainable Development: A Crucial Instrument for Achieving the Sustainable Development Goals*. UNESCO.

United Nations. (2015). *Transforming our world: the 2030 Agenda for Sustainable Development*. Retrieved from https://www.un.org/sustainabledevelopment/sustainable-development-goals/

University of Exeter. (2020). *Sustainability in Business Education: Case Studies and Best Practices*. University Reports.

Wiek, A., Withycombe Keeler, L., & Redman, C. L. (2020). Moving Forward: Advancing Key Competencies for Sustainability Education. *Journal of Sustainability Science*, *15*(2), 201–220.

# Chapter 6
# Developing a Model for Sustainable Entrepreneurship Competencies:
## Strategic Decision-Making for a Green Future

**Muhammad Usman Tariq**
https://orcid.org/0000-0002-7605-3040
*Abu Dhabi University, UAE & University College Cork, Ireland*

## ABSTRACT

*The flourishing significance of sustainability in entrepreneurship has led to the requirement for a thorough model that incorporates critical capabilities crucial for making strategic decisions associated with environmental, social, and economic objectives. This chapter develops a model for sustainable entrepreneurship competencies, emphasizing seven core areas: systems thinking, foresight thinking, normative behavior, diversity, interpersonal skills, responsible actions, and strategic management. These competencies enable entrepreneurs to make decisions that balance profitability with sustainability, encouraging long-term business success while addressing global issues. This chapter determines how sustainable competencies drive innovation and evolution in green business practices by investigating real-world case studies and exploring decision-making processes.*

## INTRODUCTION

The global economic and environmental landscape is transforming, driven by the persistent requirement for sustainable development. This shift has placed sustainability in the lead of entrepreneurship, redefining how businesses work and grow. As environmental challenges such as climate change, resource depletion, and biodiversity loss exaggerate, joined with rising social problems like disparity and labor exploitation, it has become imperious for entrepreneurs to adopt strategies that balance economic objectives with environmental and societal responsibilities. This mounting importance of sustainability in entrepreneurship reflects an ethical obligation and a pragmatic response to market dynamics, consumer preferences, and regulatory frameworks. Sustainable entrepreneurship, a theory incorporating environ-

DOI: 10.4018/979-8-3373-0189-1.ch006

mental stewardship, social equity, and economic viability, is critical for long-term success and flexibility (Diepolder et al., 2021). Entrepreneurs are individually positioned to drive sustainability due to their ability to innovate and address complex issues. They are catalysts for change, capable of reimagining business models and creating solutions that address market requirements and broaden sustainability goals. For instance, ventures in renewable energy, sustainable agriculture, and circular economy models demonstrate how entrepreneurial efforts can decrease carbon footprints, support resources, and promote ethical practices. Yet, attaining these conclusions demands more than just advanced ideas; it requires the development of identifiable competencies that allow entrepreneurs to make informed, responsible, and future-oriented decisions. These competencies, collectively called sustainable entrepreneurship competencies, are essential in preparing individuals with the knowledge, skills, and attitudes required to navigate the complex junction of business, society, and the environment.

Sustainable entrepreneurship competencies include a range of attributes that allow entrepreneurs to incorporate sustainability principles into their decision-making procedures. These incorporate systems thinking, which lets entrepreneurs comprehend the interconnection of environmental, social, and economic systems; ethical reasoning, which guides them in making value-driven choices; and foresight, which prepares them to foresee and mitigate long-term risks. These competencies involve innovating sustainably, collaborating across diverse stakeholders, and adapting to dynamic market and ecological conditions. By nurturing these competencies, entrepreneurs can design businesses that generate profits and contribute to sustainable development objectives, such as preventing climate change, lowering inequality, and advocating responsible consumption and production (Tariq, 2025). The impact of sustainable entrepreneurship competencies on long-term decision-making is profound. Traditional entrepreneurship emphasizes short-term returns and instant market prospects. In contrast, sustainable entrepreneurship needs a pronounced perception that considers the long-term effects of business activities on ecosystems, communities, and future generations. For example, an entrepreneur with sustainable competencies is more liable to invest in renewable energy technologies, adopt circular economy principles, or prioritize ethical labor practices, even when these choices may include higher initial costs. Such decisions, guided by sustainability-oriented competencies, improve the endurance and significance of businesses in a swiftly changing world. They permit entrepreneurs to align with shifting consumer demands for eco-friendly and socially responsible products, meet regulatory needs, and decrease exposure to risks allied with untenable practices, such as resource scarcity or reputational damage (Tariq, 2024).

## BACKGROUND

The theoretical foundations of rural social entrepreneurship highlight the relationship between economic activity and social effect. Fundamentally, social entrepreneurship is starting companies that put social change ahead of financial viability and concentrate on developing creative, market-driven solutions to address societal issues. In rural areas, these issues frequently include poverty, lack of access to education and healthcare, and environmental deterioration. Knowledge rural social entrepreneurship requires an understanding of "embeddedness," as these businesses are firmly established in the communities in which they operate, utilizing local networks, resources, and customs to provide sustainable and timely solutions. Defining the key terms that highlight this discourse is necessary to fully appreciate the significance of sustainable entrepreneurship capabilities. Sustainable entrepreneurship identifies, assesses, and exploits prospects contributing to environmental, social, and economic sustainability (Tariq, 2024).

It encompasses creating value for shareholders and stakeholders, involving communities, employees, and the planet. Unlike conventional entrepreneurship, which often prioritizes financial performance, sustainable entrepreneurship focuses on a triple-bottom-line method that balances profit, people, and the planet. Competencies, in this context, refer to the incorporated set of knowledge, skills, attitudes, and behaviors that allow individuals to perform efficiently in complex and dynamic environments. In sustainable entrepreneurship, competencies involve understanding sustainability challenges, innovating responsibly, and involving in ethical decision-making. Finally, green decision-making refers to making business decisions that prioritize environmental sustainability. It involves considering the environmental implications of actions, such as reducing waste, reducing energy consumption, or adopting sustainable supply chain practices, and integrating these considerations into strategic planning and operations (Tariq, 2025; Victor et al., 2024). The interplay of these concepts highlights the potential of sustainable entrepreneurship. As businesses increasingly recognize the risks associated with unsustainable practices and the potential for sustainability, the demand for entrepreneurs who can lead this transition is increasing. It is not just a strategic objective but also a moral responsibility. These competencies enable entrepreneurs to function as individuals of change, capable of driving innovation, fostering inclusivity, and confirming the long-term sustainability of their ventures. They also contribute to broader social objectives, encompassing entrepreneurial attempts with global initiatives such as the United Nations Sustainable Development Goals (SDGs). The requirement for sustainable entrepreneurship competencies reflects businesses' evolving role in addressing global challenges. Integrating sustainability into entrepreneurship is no longer optional but necessary for creating resistant and impactful enterprises. By understanding and developing the competencies necessary for sustainable entrepreneurs, entrepreneurs can make informed decisions that balance economic success with environmental and social stewardship. This paradigm shift enhances businesses' significance and competitiveness and creates a more reasonable and prosperous world. Through the lens of sustainable entrepreneurship, the capability to convert industries, communities, and ecosystems becomes a definite reality, emphasizing the critical role of capabilities in shaping a sustainable future (Atadoga et al., 2024).

## The Core Competencies for Sustainable Entrepreneurship

Sustainable entrepreneurship needs a comprehensive set of skills and attitudes that allow entrepreneurs to address the consistent challenges of environmental, social, and economic sustainability. Developing these skills, often called *core competencies*, forms the backbone of effective, sustainable business practices. This section explores the seven core competencies for sustainable entrepreneurship—systems thinking, foresight thinking, normative behavior, diversity, interpersonal skills, responsible actions, and strategic management. It investigates how these competencies impact decision-making procedures aligned with environmental, social, and governance (ESG) standards and the United Nations Sustainable Development Goals (SDGs). Furthermore, case examples explain how businesses have effectively incorporated these competencies into their sustainability strategies. Systems thinking is understanding and evaluating the interconnectedness and mutuality within complex systems. In sustainable entrepreneurship, this includes identifying the relationships between environmental, social, and economic systems and how entrepreneurial actions affect these dimensions. Entrepreneurs prepared with systems thinking can recognize involuntary consequences and leverage synergies to create solutions that address compound sustainability challenges concurrently. For instance, a systems-thinking entrepreneur in the food industry might realize how unsustainable farming practices worsen soil quality, impact climate change, and threaten food security. By employing regenerative agriculture practices, such entrepreneurs address environmental concerns while upgrading productivity and livelihoods for farmers. Firms like *Patagonia* illustrate this ability by integrating sustainable materials into their supply chains and sponsoring systemic change in the fashion industry. Foresight thinking lets entrepreneurs forecast future trends, challenges, and prospects. It includes imagining prospective scenarios, developing strategies that alleviate risks, and capitalizing on emerging prospects. This competency is necessary for navigating the vagueness inherent in sustainability challenges, such as climate change and resource scarcity (Tariq, 2024).

Entrepreneurs with prevision thinking may, for example, invest in renewable energy technologies in expectation of stricter carbon regulations or modifying consumer preferences toward green energy. Tesla, for instance, has determined foresight thinking by innovative electric vehicles and battery storage solutions well before they became mainstream. This forward-looking method positions firms to stay ahead of controlling changes and market shifts while contributing to global sustainability objectives. Normative behavior reflects the ethical and value-driven dimension of entrepreneurship. It includes a dedication to sustainability principles and an inclination to select long-term societal advantages over short-term profits. Entrepreneurs with normative solid behavior use ethical considerations as a regulatory framework for their decisions, confirming that their actions align with broader societal objectives. A firm that represents normative behavior is *Ben & Jerry's*, which has constantly supported social justice, environmental safety, and ethical sourcing. The firm has promoted a loyal customer base by implanting values such as impartiality and fairness into its business model and contributed to significant social change. Normative behavior improves brand reputation and confirms that businesses remain true to their purpose, nurturing trust among stakeholders (Venesaar et al., 2021). Diversity as a competency involves an admiration for different perspectives, cultures, and ideas. It encompasses promoting inclusive environments where diverse stakeholders can work together to address complex sustainability issues. Entrepreneurs who value diversity are better trained to transform and adapt to contrasting market conditions, as they can draw on an expansive range of perceptions and occurrences. In practice, involving diversity can be exhibited through inclusive hiring practices, cross-cultural collaborations, or designing products that cater to understated groups. For instance, *Unilever* has leveraged diversity by launching products that address local environmental and cultural requirements, such as water-saving hygiene solutions in arid regions. By incorporating diverse perspectives into their strategies, firms can attain commercial accomplishment and social impact. Interpersonal skills are necessary for building connections, advancing collaboration, and connecting stakeholders efficiently. Entrepreneurs must convey their sustainability vision influentially, encourage teams, and work collaboratively with partners, investors, and communities. Strong interpersonal skills also ease conflict resolution and consensus-building, which are critical when navigating challenging interests in sustainability projects (Thelken et al., 2020). For instance, social enterprises such as *Grameen Bank* have relied on interpersonal skills to build trust within underserved communities, enabling microfinance initiatives that empower marginalized populations. Through effective communication and relationship-building, entrepreneurs can mobilize support for their sustainability goals and create networks that amplify their impact. Responsible actions imply translating sustainability principles into tangible business practices. This competency includes taking responsibility for the environmental and social effects of entrepreneurial activities and being determined to decrease adverse outcomes while maximizing positive contributions. Responsible actions need a proactive approach to problems such as carbon emissions, waste management, and ethical labor practices. A prominent example is *IKEA*, which has dedicated to becoming a circular business by 2030. The firm dynamically works to decrease waste via innovative product designs, recycling programs, and sustainable sourcing practices. By taking accountability for their environmental footprint, businesses like IKEA exhibit how responsible actions can drive both sustainability and profitability (Thelken and De Jong, 2020).

Strategic management is the capacity to align sustainability objectives with business purposes and operationalize these goals realistically. This competency implies setting clear priorities, assigning resources effectively, and monitoring progress toward sustainability targets. Entrepreneurs with strong strategic management skills incorporate sustainability into their core business strategies, confirming that it becomes a fundamental part of their organizational culture and long-term vision. Firms such as *Interface*, a global leader in commercial flooring, illustrate strategic management by embedding sustainability into their operations. Through initiatives like its Mission Zero program, Interface has systematically decreased its carbon footprint and implemented circular economy principles, proving that sustainability can drive innovation and market leadership (Tariq, 2024). Incorporating these seven competencies into decision-making procedures allows entrepreneurs to align their actions with ESG standards and SDGs. ESG criteria emphasize evaluating a company's environmental impact, social responsibility, and corporate governance performance. At the same time, the SDGs provide a global framework for addressing sustainability issues. Entrepreneurs who develop these proficiencies are better placed to employ practices that meet ESG expectations, such as lowering greenhouse gas emissions, raising diversity and inclusion, and ensuring transparency in governance (Galvão et al., 2020).

For instance, systems thinking and foresight assist businesses in foreseeing and adjusting to climate-related risks, contributing to SDG 13 (Climate Action). Normative behavior and responsible actions assist in ethical labor practices and fair trade, allied with SDG 8 (Decent Work and Economic Growth). Diversity and interpersonal skills raise inclusivity and partnerships, addressing SDG 10 (Reduced Inequalities) and SDG 17 (Partnerships for the Goals). Strategic management guarantees these efforts are executed cohesively, driving progress across multiple SDGs. Numerous businesses have effectively incorporated these capabilities into their sustainability strategies, indicating their practical significance and influence. For example, *Tesla* demonstrates foresight thinking by driving the transition to renewable energy through electric vehicles and solar technologies. *Unilever* highlights diversity by modifying its sustainability initiatives to local markets while retaining a global commitment to social and environmental objectives. *Patagonia* characterizes systems thinking and normative behavior through its sponsorship of environmental activism and the use of sustainable materials (Ali et al., 2020). Social enterprises like *Grameen Bank* and global brands such as *IKEA* emphasize the significance of interpersonal skills and individual responsible actions in attaining long-term impact. Each of these businesses has leveraged the core competencies of sustainable entrepreneurship to create value for stakeholders while contributing to the global sustainability program. The seven fundamental competencies for sustainable entrepreneurship—systems thinking, foresight thinking, normative behavior, diversity, interpersonal skills, responsible actions, and strategic management—form the base for addressing complex sustainability issues. These competencies enable entrepreneurs to align their strategies with ESG standards and SDGs, driving innovation and long-term impact. The case examples demonstrate how these competencies can be employed in diverse contexts, highlighting their significance and transformative potential. Entrepreneurs can lead toward a more ecological and equitable future by cultivating these competencies (Hussain et al., 2021).

## Systems Thinking and Strategic Integration in Decision-Making

Sustainability in entrepreneurship demands a general approach to identifying and addressing the complex interplay between environmental, social, and economic factors. Systems thinking is at the heart of this approach, a detailed competency that enables entrepreneurs to evaluate and steer complex, interconnected systems. This chapter discovers systems thinking as a foundational tool for sustainable decision-making, presents methods for integrating environmental, social, and economic business domains, and validates how systems thinking improves entrepreneurs' ability to adapt to dynamic business environments. By adopting systems thinking, entrepreneurs can align their strategies with long-term sustainability objectives while ensuring flexibility and adaptability in an ever-changing global landscape. Systems thinking is the procedure of understanding and addressing difficulties by recognizing the associations and interactions between various system components rather than viewing them in isolation. In the context of sustainable entrepreneurship, this means looking beyond the instant limitations of a business to consider its effects on and reliance on broader environmental, social, and economic systems. Systems thinking facilitates entrepreneurs to recognize patterns, causal relationships, and feedback loops that affect their ventures' sustainability (Sousa & Costa, 2022). For instance, consider a manufacturing company aspiring to decrease its carbon footprint. A systems-thinking method would imply investigating the entire lifecycle of its products—from raw material extraction and production to distribution, consumption, and disposal. Such an analysis might reveal prospects to decrease waste, switch to renewable energy sources, or be involved in recycling initiatives. By adopting this broader perspective, entrepreneurs can make decisions that address root causes rather than symptoms, resulting in more sustainable effects (Di Vaio et al., 2022).

As a core competency, systems thinking equips entrepreneurs with several capabilities critical for sustainable decision-making. First, it improves their ability to recognize the interrelation of challenges. Sustainability problems, such as climate change, resource depletion, and social inequality, are deeply correlated and cannot be realistically addressed in isolation. Entrepreneurs with systems thinking can realize how addressing one issue, such as reducing emissions, might positively or negatively affect others, like resource use or community livelihoods. Second, systems thinking fosters a long-term perspective. Entrepreneurs are faced with trade-offs between short-term effectiveness and long-term sustainability. A systems-thinking approach helps them estimate their decisions' broader and longer-term inferences, confirming that immediate actions contribute to primary sustainability aims (Jardim, 2021). Finally, systems thinking supports adaptive decision-making. In dynamic and unpredictable business environments, firm strategies often fail. Systems-thinking entrepreneurs are better equipped to adapt to modifying circumstances by identifying the system's essential dynamics and anticipating how different factors might change over time. To attain long-term sustainability objectives, entrepreneurs must incorporate environmental, social, and economic considerations into their business strategies. This integration needs deliberate procedures and structures that align these domains while retaining business sustainability. The following techniques highlight how systems thinking can facilitate this integration:

The triple bottom line (TBL) framework focuses on assessing three core dimensions: profit (economic), people (social), and planet (environmental). Entrepreneurs using the TBL framework examine the impact of their decisions across these dimensions. For example, a company considering a new product launch might evaluate its prospective economic returns, its effect on community well-being, and its environmental footprint. By doing so, they confirm that their strategies create value across all three domains rather than prioritizing one at the expense of others (Uvarova et al., 2021). Lifecycle assessment is a method that assesses the environmental, social, and economic effects of a product or procedure throughout its lifecycle. Entrepreneurs utilizing LCA can recognize critical areas for improvement, such as reducing energy use during production or minimizing waste during disposal. For instance, firms in the packaging industry often use LCA to design cost-effective and environmentally friendly materials. Effective incorporation of business domains needs input from diverse stakeholders, involving customers, employees, investors, and community members. Entrepreneurs can use stakeholder mapping and dialogue to recognize different perspectives, detect shared objectives, and develop strategies that address collective concerns. For example, renewable energy firms often collaborate with local communities to align their projects with social and environmental priorities, such as job creation and ecosystem protection (Mondal et al., 2023).

Scenario planning includes developing and analyzing potential future scenarios to comprehend how varied factors might interact over time. Entrepreneurs using this method can detect risks and prospects linked with sustainability issues and design strategies that are robust under different conditions. For instance, a food production company might investigate scenarios relevant to climate change impacts on crop yields and adapt its supply chain to mitigate potential disruptions. Circular economy principles underline designing systems that reduce waste and boost resource efficiency by keeping materials in use for as long as possible. Entrepreneurs implementing this method can incorporate environmental and economic objectives by developing closed-loop systems. For example, businesses in the fashion industry are progressively employing recycling programs that repurpose old garments into new products, lowering waste and creating economic value (Del Vecchio et al., 2021). Systems thinking also improves entrepreneurs' ability to assess and adapt to innovative business environments' dynamic, interconnected nature. These environments are categorized by rapid technological improvements, shifting consumer expectations, and complex global challenges such as climate change and geopolitical tensions. Entrepreneurs who relate systems thinking can better steer these complexities by understanding the systemic drivers of change and designing adaptive strategies. One of the critical benefits of systems thinking is its ability to recognize leverage points—strategic areas within a system where slight changes can lead to substantial positive outcomes. For instance, an entrepreneur directing to lower their supply chain's carbon footprint might classify transportation as a critical leverage point and invest in low-emission vehicles or optimize logistics to minimize distances travelled.

Systems thinking also aids entrepreneurs in managing vagueness and uncertainty. The associations between distinct factors are often nonlinear and random in dynamic environments. By focusing on the broader system rather than isolated variables, entrepreneurs can develop robust strategies for sudden changes. For example, during the COVID-19 pandemic, firms that had adopted systems-thinking methods could better pivot their operations by fluctuating to remote work or reconfiguring supply chains, confirming business permanency while supporting employee well-being (Chowdhury et al., 2022). Likewise, systems support cross-sector collaboration, which is vital for addressing sustainability challenges exceeding individual industries. Entrepreneurs can partner with governments, non-profits, and other businesses to develop combined solutions that address shared challenges. For instance, initiatives like public-private partnerships in renewable energy development exhibit how collaboration across sectors can drive systemic change. Several businesses have effectively employed systems to attain sustainability objectives and adapt to dynamic environments. For example, *Patagonia*, an outdoor apparel company, has adopted systems thinking by considering the entire lifecycle of its products. The company invests in sustainable materials, encourages repair and reuse programs, and advocates for environmental activism, indicating how a systemic method can align business success with environmental stewardship (Ikram et al., 2021). Another instance is *Interface*, a global leader in commercial flooring, which adopted a systems-thinking framework to decrease its environmental impact. Through its Mission Zero initiative, Interface identified key leverage points such as material sourcing and energy use, eventually achieving significant carbon emissions and waste reductions. The firm's commitment to circular economic principles focuses on the transformative potential of systems thinking in business strategies.

Tesla demonstrates how systems thinking can drive innovation and market leadership in the renewable energy sector. By detecting the interconnected issues of fossil fuel dependency and climate change, Tesla developed an ecosystem of sustainable products, encompassing electric vehicles, solar panels, and energy storage solutions. This comprehensive approach has made the company a leader in transitioning to a low-carbon economy (Suriyankietkaew et al., 2022). Systems thinking and strategic integration are essential for sustainable decision-making in entrepreneurship. By comprehending the interconnected nature of environmental, social, and economic systems, entrepreneurs can design strategies that address complex issues while attaining long-term sustainability objectives. Methods such as the triple bottom line, lifecycle assessment, stakeholder engagement, scenario planning, and circular economy models provide practical tools for incorporating business domains successfully. Likewise, systems thinking increases entrepreneurs' ability to assess and adapt to dynamic environments, fostering resistance and innovation. Case examples from firms like Patagonia, Interface, and Tesla demonstrate the transformative power of systems thinking in creating sustainable, impactful firms. As global challenges continue to advance, adopting systems-thinking methods will be essential for entrepreneurs striving to build a sustainable and equitable future.

## Recent Advancements in Technology and Policy

It has become evident to the business community that, with the recent advances in technology and policy, sustainable entrepreneurship has developed to a greater extent than ever before, giving the businesses the great tools and frameworks to make their endeavor both profitable and environmentally beneficial. Key technologies underpinning Industry 4.0 technologies like artificial intelligence (AI), blockchain, the Internet of Things (IoT) and big data analytics have changed the way decision making is made in sustainable enterprises. For instance, predictive analytics based on AI can help the business to optimize utilization of resources, getting rid of waste and improving energy efficiency. In this regard, blockchain technology promotes transparency in the supply chains, better ethical sourcing and sustainable production practices. IoT-enabled devices allow the real time monitoring of carbon footprints from the business that helps the adoption of proactive sustainability measures. These technological advancements not only bring in green business models innovations but also equip the entrepreneurs with such data driven sustainability insights for strategic decision making. Apart from technological progress, two policy dimensions, namely, global and national level, have also contributed to the shaping of sustainable entrepreneurship. Examples of policy framework that promote environmental and social responsibility are the European Green Deal, and the United Nations Sustainable Development Goals (SDGs) and the Corporate Sustainability Reporting Directive (CSRD). Investment in low emission technologies makes up a growing part of the budgets of most government agencies worldwide who are now implementing green financing mechanisms such as tax incentives and subsidies for startup of renewable energy businesses. Sustainability is being imposed as best practice by regulatory bodies and is being made a core part of business operations for companies to comply, through ESG (Environmental, Social, and Governance) requirements. In addition to these policy measures that mitigate environmental degradation, this policy also promotes corporate accountability, and it is now a strategic necessity, not an optional initiative.

The ever-changing trend of sustainable entrepreneurship positions itself as a broad field of emerging changes, where the advance of technology and the advancement of the policy frameworks are converging to produce a new paradigm where businesses still strive to achieve long term profitability, yet address global sustainability challenges.

## Foresight Thinking and Innovation in Green Entrepreneurship

Rapid environmental, social, and economic change presents challenges and prospects for progressive entrepreneurs. Addressing these changes involves a clear perception of current sustainability problems and the ability to expect future trends and their consequences. This capacity, known as *foresight thinking*, is an imperative competency for entrepreneurs planning to create sustainable business practices. By predicting long-term effects, entrepreneurs can craft strategies that balance immediate requirements with persistent impacts, eventually driving innovation and fostering flexibility. With creativity and prospect recognition, foresight thinking is a foundation for green entrepreneurship innovation (Stefan et al., 2021). This chapter explores how foresight thinking impacts sustainable decision-making, the role of creativity and innovation in developing green businesses, and case studies indicating its application in circular economies and green start-ups.

Foresight thinking is the ability to predict future developments, identify emerging trends, and assess the long-term consequences of current actions. In green entrepreneurship, this ability aids entrepreneurs to recognize how their decisions impact sustainability and prepare for issues such as resource scarcity, regulatory changes, and shifting consumer demands. Unlike reactive decision-making, which emphasizes addressing immediate issues, foresight thinking supports proactive strategies that align with long-term sustainability objectives. For example, an entrepreneur with foresight might acknowledge the mounting global emphasis on decarbonization and respond by investing in renewable energy solutions. Likewise, foresight thinking can help entrepreneurs detect potential risks, such as supply chain disturbances due to climate change, and take defensive measures to mitigate these risks. By considering the broader context of their decisions, green entrepreneurs can create feasible businesses that are resistant to future doubts (Alkaraan et al., 2023). Foresight thinking reinforces systems-level comprehension by reassuring entrepreneurs to consider how consistent systems advance over time. This perception helps entrepreneurs recognize probable synergies or conflicts between environmental, social, and economic objectives. For instance, an entrepreneur developing electric vehicles (EVs) must expect the technological and market trends in EV adoption and the environmental inferences of battery production and disposal. They can proactively contribute to a sustainable mobility ecosystem by addressing these problems (Seraj et al., 2022). Creativity, prospect recognition, and innovation are closely related to foresight thinking and are vital for fostering sustainable business practices. Creativity allows the generating of novel ideas and methods to address complex sustainability challenges. Opportunity recognition allows entrepreneurs to identify gaps or emerging needs in the market that align with sustainable objectives. Innovation, meanwhile, implies changing creative ideas into actionable solutions, whether through new products, services, or business models. In green entrepreneurship, creativity includes reimagining conventional business models to decrease environmental impact. For instance, the shift from linear "take-make-dispose" models to circular economy models requires entrepreneurs to think creatively about how resources can be reused, recycled, or repurposed.

Opportunity recognition aids entrepreneurs in identifying areas were sustainability traverses with unmet market requirements, such as the growing demand for eco-friendly packaging or renewable energy solutions. Innovation acts as the link between foresight thinking and practical implementation. Entrepreneurs who innovate successfully can translate their vision of the future into tangible products and services. For instance, developing biodegradable materials, carbon capture technologies, and blockchain for supply chain transparency reveals how innovative solutions can address pressing environmental issues while creating competitive benefits. Foresight thinking directly improves the innovation procedure by helping entrepreneurs relate and prioritize prospects that align with future trends. Entrepreneurs predicting changes in consumer preferences, regulatory landscapes, or technological progress are better placed to lead in emerging markets. This ability to "see around the corner" allows green entrepreneurs to act as first movers, acquiring competitive advantages while contributing to sustainable development (Naderi et al., 2022). One way foresight thinking drives innovation is by adopting an approach of experimentation and adaptability. Green entrepreneurs operate in unpredictable markets with rapidly progressing technologies and regulations. By predicting multiple future scenarios, they can test and enhance their ideas to align with current realities and anticipated trends. For instance, the rise of electric mobility has been shaped by entrepreneurs who predicted the merging of dropping battery costs, stricter emissions standards, and increasing environmental awareness. Also, foresight thinking assists collaborative innovation. Sustainability challenges are complex and need solutions that span multiple disciplines and sectors. Entrepreneurs involved in thinking foresight are more likely to seek partnerships and leverage collective expertise to address these issues. For example, renewable energy start-ups collaborate with governments, academic institutions, and non-profits to quicken the adoption of clean energy technologies (Gonçalves et al., 2024).

## CASE STUDIES IN CIRCULAR ECONOMIES AND GREEN START-UPS

The relevance of foresight thinking in green entrepreneurship is apparent in various case studies of businesses operating within circular economies and green start-ups. These examples emphasize how forward-looking strategies have driven innovation and contributed to sustainability.

### Case Study 1: Interface – Pioneering Circularity in Commercial Flooring

Interface, an international leader in modular flooring, exemplifies foresight thinking in the circular economy context. Anticipating the increasing requirement for sustainable business practices, Interface launched its "Mission Zero" initiative in the 1990s, intending to reduce its environmental footprint by 2020. The company embraced circular principles by developing closed-loop manufacturing processes, sourcing recycled materials, and designing products for durability and recyclability. Through continuous innovation, Interface has attained substantial environmental milestones and set industry standards for sustainability, determining the long-term value of foresight thinking (Sahu et al., 2023).

## Case Study 2: Tesla – Redefining Sustainable Mobility

Tesla's projection in the automotive industry proves the power of foresight, thinking, and innovation. Understanding the environmental and economic inferences of fossil fuel dependency, Tesla's leadership projected a future dominated by electric vehicles (EVs) and renewable energy. This vision drove the firm to invest in battery technology, charging foundations, and energy storage solutions long before these markets became mainstream. Tesla's foresight and commitment to innovation have transformed the transportation industry, making sustainable mobility a reality for millions and stimulating widespread adoption of EVs.

## Case Study 3: Loop – Reinventing Consumer Packaging

Loop, a green start-up in the consumer goods sector, leverages foresight thinking to address the global packaging waste crisis. Identifying the unsustainability of single-use packaging, Loop developed a reusable packaging model in partnership with major brands. Customers receive products in durable, reusable containers that are returned, cleaned, and refilled after use. By anticipating regulatory and consumer alterations toward zero-waste solutions, Loop has created an ascendable business model that aligns with circular economy principles while meeting the increasing demand for sustainable packaging (Victar et al., 2024).

## Case Study 4: Beyond Meat – Transforming Food Systems

Beyond Meat, a plant-based protein company, demonstrates how foresight thinking can drive innovation in the food industry. Expecting the environmental and health concerns linked with conventional meat production, Beyond Meat developed plant-based alternatives that simulate the taste and texture of animal products. By leveraging technological advancements and consumer trends toward healthier, more sustainable diets, the company has disrupted conventional food markets and contributed to lowering greenhouse gas emissions and resource consumption in the food system.

## Case Study 5: Unilever's Sustainable Living Plan

Unilever's Sustainable Living Plan exhibits the power of stakeholder involvement in driving sustainability. The company involved suppliers, customers, NGOs, and governments to set ambitious objectives for decreasing its environmental footprint and enhancing social outcomes. By collaborating with farmers, Unilever developed sustainable sourcing practices for key ingredients, such as palm oil and tea. At the same time, partnerships with NGOs helped the company address complicated social problems like gender equality.

## Case Study 6: Patagonia's Activism and Employee Engagement

Patagonia is identified for its commitment to environmental activism and employee involvement. The company authorizes its employees to participate in sustainability initiatives, such as organizing environmental campaigns and volunteering with non-profits. Patagonia's open and transparent communication with customers and environmental groups has also promoted trust and loyalty, making it a leader in sustainable business practices.

### Case Study 7: IKEA's Collaboration for Circularity

IKEA's efforts to transition to a circular economy focus on the significance of cross-sector collaboration. The company partners with suppliers, innovators, and recyclers to develop durable, repairable, and recyclable products. IKEA also involves customers via initiatives like furniture take-back programs, aiding them in participating in circular practices. Interpersonal skills and stakeholder involvement are essential for sustainable entrepreneurship. Entrepreneurs can drive innovative and impactful sustainability initiatives by building strong relationships, fostering collaboration, and leveraging diverse perspectives. Effective communication, empathy, and team-building strategies allow entrepreneurs to align stakeholders around shared objectives. At the same time, real-world instances from firms like Unilever, Patagonia, and IKEA validate the transformative potential of these practices. As sustainability becomes a progressively critical focus for businesses worldwide, mastering interpersonal skills and stakeholder involvement will remain necessary for entrepreneurs seeking to create lasting value for society and the planet (Ahmed et al., 2021).

## CHALLENGES AND OPPORTUNITIES IN APPLYING FORESIGHT THINKING

While foresight thinking proposes significant benefits, it also presents issues. Entrepreneurs may struggle with ambiguity or challenge from stakeholders who prioritize short-term benefits over long-term sustainability. Furthermore, executing foresight-driven innovations needs significant investment in research, development, and infrastructure, which may be unreasonable for small or resource-constrained enterprises (Seikkula-Leino & Salomaa, 2020). Conversely, these challenges also create prospects for differentiation and leadership. Entrepreneurs who effectively incorporate foresight thinking into their strategies can position themselves as pioneers in emerging markets, attracting customers, investors, and partners who share their commitment to sustainability. Also, advances in data analytics, artificial intelligence, and scenario modeling tools make it simpler for entrepreneurs to integrate foresight thinking into their decision-making procedures (Rehman et al., 2023). Foresight thinking is a foundation of green entrepreneurship, allowing entrepreneurs to predict the impacts of their decisions, distinguish prospects for innovation, and develop sustainable business models. By raising creativity and innovation, foresight thinking drives solutions that address complex sustainability issues and align with long-term objectives. Case studies such as Interface, Tesla, Loop, and Beyond Meat demonstrate the transformative power of foresight thinking in diverse sectors, from mobility and manufacturing to food and consumer goods. As the global push for sustainability increases, foresight thinking will remain necessary for entrepreneurs seeking to create meaningful and lasting impact (Mendes et al., 2022).

### Interpersonal Skills and Stakeholder Engagement

Sustainable entrepreneurship succeeds in building strong relationships, fostering collaboration, and retaining diverse stakeholders. The sustainability challenges, such as climate change, resource scarcity, and social inequality, require collective action and cooperative strategies. Therefore, interpersonal skills and stakeholder engagement are critical for driving sustainable business practices. This chapter probes the significance of interpersonal and collaborative skills, discovers how stakeholder engagement augments decision-making procedures, and shapes strategies for encouraging teams and fostering collaboration in sustainability-focused initiatives. Interpersonal skills—communication, empathy, negotiation, and conflict resolution—are foundational for entrepreneurs building sustainable businesses. These skills aid entrepreneurs in connecting with stakeholders, recognizing their perspectives, and inspiring action toward shared sustainability purposes (Khanra et al., 2022).

In the context of sustainable entrepreneurship, effective communication is essential. Entrepreneurs must coherently and influentially present their vision for sustainability to secure buy-in from stakeholders, involving employees, investors, customers, and community participants. For example, an entrepreneur suggesting a shift to renewable energy sources must communicate the long-term environmental and financial gains to stakeholders who may be focused on short-term costs (Pennetta et al., 2024). Empathy is another critical interpersonal skill that lets entrepreneurs comprehend and address their stakeholders' requirements and concerns. Entrepreneurs can build trust and advance stronger relationships by placing themselves in others' shoes. For model, a company launching a new product in a developing market might use empathetic methods to ensure that the product meets the community's cultural, economic, and environmental requirements (Ismail, 2022). Collaboration needs strong interpersonal skills to align diverse teams and stakeholders toward common objectives. Entrepreneurs who can efficiently mediate conflicts, manage expectations, and build consensus are better armed to lead sustainability initiatives. For example, a circular economy project involving suppliers, manufacturers, and consumers needs the entrepreneur to act as a facilitator, confirming that all parties contribute to and benefit from the initiative. Involving diverse stakeholders is essential for making informed, inclusive, and sustainable decisions. Stakeholders bring varied perspectives, expertise, and resources that enhance the entrepreneur's comprehension of sustainability challenges and prospects. By implying stakeholders early and often, entrepreneurs can detect risks, discover innovative solutions, and build support for their initiatives (Venesaar et al., 2021).

Stakeholders, incorporating employees, customers, suppliers, regulators, and non-governmental organizations (NGOs), provide unique insights into a business's impact. For example, employees may highlight operational ineffectiveness that contributes to waste. At the same time, customers may provide feedback on enhancing a product's sustainability. Engaging with regulators and NGOs can help entrepreneurs navigate conformity obligations and align their strategies with broader societal objectives.

Stakeholder engagement builds credibility and trust, which are critical for achieving sustainability initiatives. Translucent communication and authentic alliance signal stakeholders that the entrepreneur values their input and is committed to accountable practices. For example, a company implementing fair trade practices can strengthen relationships with suppliers and consumers by demonstrating its dedication to ethical sourcing. Stakeholder engagement nurtures co-creation, where stakeholders dynamically contribute to designing and executing sustainability solutions. This method generates innovative and effective outcomes and confirms more significant stakeholder commitment. For example, renewable energy projects comprise community stakeholders in planning and decision-making to confirm that the projects address local requirements and concerns. By involving stakeholders, entrepreneurs can detect potential issues and conflicts early in the decision-making procedure, enabling them to address these issues proactively. For instance, a firm planning to launch a new product line might consult with environmental groups to ensure the product complies with sustainability standards, evading reputational risks and regulatory penalties (Luo et al., 2022).

## Strategies for Motivating Teams and Fostering Collaboration

Sustainability-focused initiatives need teams to adopt new mindsets, practices, and objectives. Entrepreneurs must, therefore, be skilled at prompting their teams and raising collaboration to drive profitable outcomes. The following strategies highlight how entrepreneurs can foster cohesive, high-performing teams that are committed to sustainability:

An insistent vision for sustainability serves as a supporting point for teams and stakeholders. Entrepreneurs should be coherent in how their initiatives align with broader environmental, social, and economic objectives and how they contribute to the company's mission. For instance, an entrepreneur leading a zero-waste initiative might communicate the vision of a circular economy that benefits both the planet and the business. Giving team members ownership over specific sustainability initiatives nurtures liability and motivation. Entrepreneurs can appoint responsibilities, foster autonomy, and identify individual contributions to create a sense of purpose and pride. For example, a manufacturing company might encourage its production team to develop waste reduction strategies, incentivizing innovation, and commitment. Sustainability needs cross-functional collaboration, including incorporating environmental, social, and economic considerations into all aspects of the business. Entrepreneurs should create prospects for teams from different departments to collaborate, share insights, and develop holistic solutions. For instance, a product development team might work with the marketing and supply chain groups to design eco-friendly packaging that aligns with customer expectations and operational capabilities.

Sustainability challenges are complex and progressing, requiring teams to learn and adapt continuously. Entrepreneurs can adopt a culture of curiosity and experimentation by promising teams to investigate latest ideas, learn from failures, and celebrate victories. For instance, a start-up developing sustainable materials might create an internal innovation lab where employees can experiment with substitute resources and manufacturing systems (Rosário et al., 2022). Entrepreneurs must provide the necessary training and resources to enable teams to contribute effectively to sustainability initiatives. It involves educating employees on sustainability principles, proposing workshops on green technologies, and investing in tools that aid sustainable practices. For example, a company aspiring to lower its carbon footprint might train employees on energy efficiency practices and provide tools for monitoring and lowering energy use. Identifying and rewarding team members for their contributions to sustainability initiatives supports positive behaviors and supports continued engagement. Entrepreneurs can use formal recognition, such as awards or promotions, and informal gestures, such as verbal praise or team celebrations, to show admiration for employees' efforts. For instance, a company attaining significant waste reduction might celebrate the milestone with a team event and public acknowledgment of employees' contributions.

Diversity improves creativity and problem-solving by bringing individuals with different perspectives and experiences. Entrepreneurs should try to build teams that reflect the diversity of their stakeholders, confirming that sustainability initiatives are inclusive and reasonable. For instance, a social enterprise addressing community health problems might include team members from diverse cultural and professional backgrounds to ensure its solutions are culturally applicable and practical (Jardim, 2021). Digital tools and mediums can improve collaboration by enabling communication, project management, and data sharing. Entrepreneurs can use video conferencing, collaborative documents, and project management software to link teams across locations and ensure alignment on sustainability objectives. For example, a remote team working on renewable energy projects might use online mediums to share real-time updates and coordinate tasks effectively.

## Strategic Management for Sustainable Entrepreneurship

Strategic management is the backbone of sustainable entrepreneurship, providing the framework through which businesses align their goals with sustainability practices. By incorporating environmental, social, and governance (ESG) contemplations and the Sustainable Development Goals (SDGs) into their strategies, entrepreneurs can create businesses that provide value to stakeholders and contribute to long-term global sustainability. This chapter evaluates how strategic management aligns business objectives with sustainability practices, the entrepreneur's role in designing and employing sustainable projects, and practical methods for implanting ESG and SDG principles into strategic planning (Stefan et al., 2021). Sustainable entrepreneurship needs businesses to function in ways that balance economic success with environmental protection and social responsibility. Strategic management is crucial in attaining this balance by embedding sustainability practices into business operations and decision-making procedures. Entrepreneurs must confirm that their strategies align with sustainability objectives while remaining competitive. Strategic management aligns business goals with sustainability by developing a clear mission and vision. A sustainability-focused mission statement defines the company's purpose and enthusiasm for addressing environmental and social challenges. For instance, a renewable energy company might emphasize its role in lowering carbon emissions and promoting energy equity. This mission guides internal decision-making and signals the company's priorities and values to stakeholders (Olurin et al., 2023).

Strategic management also includes setting measurable sustainability goals that complement traditional business objectives. Entrepreneurs can establish key performance indicators (KPIs) to track progress on ESG metrics, such as lowering greenhouse gas emissions, adjusting diversity and inclusion, or enhancing the use of renewable materials. For example, a manufacturing firm might intend to decrease its carbon footprint by 50% within five years while also attaining financial growth targets. By incorporating these goals, businesses can determine that sustainability and profitability are not mutually exclusive. Entrepreneurs play a focal role in strategic management, explicitly designing and employing sustainable projects that meet environmental, economic, and social criteria. Their leadership, vision, and decision-making shape the company's sustainability plan and drive innovation.

Entrepreneurs are the driving force behind the sustainability vision of their businesses. They must predict future trends, detect prospects for impact, and encourage their teams and stakeholders to pursue ambitious objectives. For instance, an entrepreneur in the fashion industry might predict a future where their brand removes waste through circular design and production procedures.

Entrepreneurs design sustainable projects by incorporating ESG principles into every stage of the business cycle. It implies conducting thorough environmental and social impact assessments, collaborating with stakeholders, and recognizing innovative solutions to address sustainability challenges. For example, an entrepreneur launching an urban agriculture initiative might design projects that decrease food miles, increase community resilience, and provide economic prospects for underserved populations. Effective implementation of sustainable projects requires entrepreneurs to align resources, procedures, and teams to achieve their objectives. It involves establishing clear timelines, securing funding, and building stakeholder partnerships. Entrepreneurs must also monitor and assess the progress of their initiatives using established KPIs, adjusting their strategies as required to maximize impact. For instance, a start-up focused on reducing plastic waste might track metrics such as the volume of recycled materials used in its products and customer participation in recycling programs (Yadegaridehkordi et al., 2023).

Strategic planning is necessary for embedding sustainability into business functions and ensuring alignment with ESG and SDG principles. The following methods provide entrepreneurs with practical tools for creating and executing sustainability-focused strategies:

Understanding and engaging with stakeholders is critical for successful strategic planning. Entrepreneurs should recognize key stakeholders, customers, employees, investors, suppliers, and community members—and assess their requirements, prospects, and impact. Engaging stakeholders in the planning procedure ensures that the company's sustainability initiatives address significant concerns and gain broader support. For example, a renewable energy company might be involved with local communities to ensure its projects align with their priorities and provide tangible benefits. A materiality assessment helps entrepreneurs prioritize sustainability problems that are most significant to their business and stakeholders. It includes assessing the environmental, social, and governance factors that affect the company's procedures, reputation, and long-term success. For instance, a food and beverage company might recognize water conservation and ethical sourcing as material issues and focus its strategies on these areas. Life cycle thinking includes assessing a product's or service's environmental and social effects across its entire life cycle—from raw material extraction to end-of-life disposal. Entrepreneurs can use this method to recognize chances for reducing waste, conserving resources, and advancing sustainability performance. For instance, a consumer electronics company might redesign its products to be more durable, repairable, and recyclable.

Scenario planning allows entrepreneurs to prepare for future vagueness by predicting potential outcomes and developing strategies to address them. This approach is precious in sustainability contexts, where climate change, regulatory shifts, and market trends can create significant risks and prospects. For example, an energy company might use scenario planning to assess how different carbon pricing policies could affect its operations and adjust its strategies.

Collaborating with other businesses, non-profits, and governments can augment the effect of sustainability initiatives. Strategic partnerships allow entrepreneurs to pool resources, share expertise, and tackle complex issues that need collective action. For instance, a start-up in the sustainable packaging industry might partner with significant consumer goods brands to develop and scale advanced packaging solutions. The United Nations Sustainable Development Goals (SDGs) provide a universal outline for addressing global sustainability challenges. Entrepreneurs can use the SDGs as a guide to align their business strategies with broader societal objectives. For instance, a healthcare company might focus on SDG 3 (Good Health and Well-Being) by growing affordable, accessible medical technologies for underserved communities. By combining their initiatives with the SDGs, businesses can determine their commitment to global priorities and attract support from stakeholders who share these values.

Integrating ESG metrics into strategic planning confirms that sustainability considerations are rooted in business decision-making. Entrepreneurs can use frameworks like the Global Reporting Initiative (GRI) or the Task Force on Climate-related Financial Disclosures (TCFD) to track and report their ESG performance. For instance, a logistics company might use these frameworks to evaluate its carbon emissions, employee well-being, and governance practices, requiring transparency and accountability to its stakeholders.

Strategic management is integral to sustainable entrepreneurship, allowing businesses to align their aims with sustainability practices while remaining competitive in dynamic markets. Entrepreneurs play a critical role in this procedure, driving visionary leadership, designing impactful projects, and employing strategies that address environmental, social, and economic challenges. Entrepreneurs can create flexible and impactful businesses by implementing practical approaches such as stakeholder engagement, materiality assessments, life cycle thinking, scenario planning, and alignment with ESG and SDG principles. As global sustainability challenges strengthen, the ability to integrate strategic management with sustainability practices will remain a defining factor for the success of future enterprises.

## Methodology for Developing a Sustainable Competency Model

Developing a competency model for sustainable entrepreneurship needs a systematic method that integrates the seven core competencies: systems thinking, foresight thinking, normative behavior, diversity, interpersonal skills, responsible actions, and strategic management. The procedure begins with defining clear goals, such as nurturing entrepreneurial capabilities that align with environmental, social, and economic goals. This foundation confirms that the model reflects the multifaceted demands of sustainability in modern business contexts. A participatory approach involving diverse stakeholders—educators, entrepreneurs, policymakers, and sustainability experts—is needed to create the model. Stakeholder input confirms that the model is practical, context-specific, and aligned with industry requirements. Techniques like surveys, focus groups, and case study analysis can link the behaviors and skills critically to sustainability-focused entrepreneurship. The capabilities can then be organized into a framework highlighting their interconnectivity and relevance across various entrepreneurial scenarios.

Evaluating and estimating competency development needs robust tools like self-assessment surveys, peer reviews, and performance-based assessments. Metrics should emphasize the application of capabilities in real-world sustainability initiatives, tracking progress over time.

Incorporating these capabilities into entrepreneurial education and training programs implies embedding them into curricula through experiential learning, workshops, and simulations. Collaborations with industry leaders and mentorship programs further emphasize practical application, preparing entrepreneurs to address global sustainability challenges efficiently.

## Practical Applications of Successful Sustainable Competencies

Real-world instances of businesses leveraging sustainable competencies provide constructive insights into the practical application of sustainability principles. One leading case is Patagonia, which incorporates systems thinking and normative behavior to produce environmentally responsible outdoor apparel. Patagonia reduces waste by committing to circular economic practices, such as recycling and repair programs, while employing customers in sustainability efforts. Another instance is Tesla, which demonstrates foresight thinking and strategic management by transforming the electric vehicle market. Through relentless innovation and a commitment to renewable energy, Tesla has affiliated economic success with environmental objectives, lowering carbon emissions globally. In the social sphere, Grameen Bank, founded by Muhammad Yunus, showcases interpersonal skills and responsible actions by encouraging underserved communities through microfinance. This model sponsors economic development while addressing social inequality. Key lessons involve aligning business models with core sustainability values, involving stakeholders, and leveraging innovation to address complex challenges. These cases emphasize that sustainable competencies are theoretical construction and transformative tools for creating long-term environmental, social, and economic impacts in entrepreneurship.

## CONCLUSION

Existing entrepreneurial education often lacks highlighting on sustainability, missing key areas like ESG awareness, SDG integration, and sustainable decision-making. To address these gaps, programs must include the seven competencies for sustainable entrepreneurship, highlighting systems thinking, foresight, and responsible action. Strategies involve embedding sustainability into core business courses, proposing specialized workshops, and granting experiential learning prospects, such as green start-up incubators (Liao, 2022). Universities, policymakers, and educators play fundamental roles by restructuring programs, advancing industry partnerships, and progressing interdisciplinary collaboration. Incorporating sustainability-focused case studies and mentorship prepares future entrepreneurs to align productivity with environmental and social impact, preparing them for a green economy.

Developing sustainable competencies in entrepreneurship is vital for building a green future. Businesses can effectively address environmental, social, and economic challenges by equipping entrepreneurs with skills like systems thinking, foresight, and responsible actions. These proficiencies allow entrepreneurs to transform, make informed decisions, and incorporate sustainability into their operations. As education and policy progress to support green entrepreneurship, future leaders will be better prepared to drive positive change. Eventually, these competencies will promote business success and contribute to a more balanced and reasonable global economy.

## REFERENCES


Ahmed, M. F., Mokhtar, M. B., Lim, C. K., Hooi, A. W. K., & Lee, K. E. (2021). Leadership roles for sustainable development: The case of a Malaysian green hotel. *Sustainability (Basel)*, *13*(18), 10260. DOI: 10.3390/su131810260

Akinboade, O. O. A., Taft, T., Weber, J. F., Manoko, O. B., & Molobi, V. S. (2023). How the social entrepreneurship business model designs in South Africa create value: A complex adaptive systems approach. *Journal of Entrepreneurship in Emerging Economies*, *15*(1), 70–95. DOI: 10.1108/JEEE-02-2021-0057

Ali, S., Li, G., Yang, P., Hussain, K., & Latif, Y. (2020). Unpacking the importance of intangible skills in new product development and sustainable business performance; strategies for marketing managers. *PLoS One*, *15*(9), e0238743. DOI: 10.1371/journal.pone.0238743 PMID: 32976509

Alkaraan, F., Elmarzouky, M., Hussainey, K., & Venkatesh, V. G. (2023). Sustainable strategic investment decision-making practices in UK companies: The influence of governance mechanisms on synergy between industry 4.0 and circular economy. *Technological Forecasting and Social Change*, *187*, 122187. DOI: 10.1016/j.techfore.2022.122187

Atadoga, A., Awonuga, K. F., Ibeh, C. V., Ike, C. U., Olu-lawal, K. A., & Usman, F. O. (2024). Harnessing data analytics for sustainable business growth in the us renewable energy sector. *Engineering Science & Technology Journal*, *5*(2), 460–470. DOI: 10.51594/estj.v5i2.806

Chowdhury, S., Dey, P. K., Rodríguez-Espíndola, O., Parkes, G., Tuyet, N. T. A., Long, D. D., & Ha, T. P. (2022). Impact of organisational factors on the circular economy practices and sustainable performance of small and medium-sized enterprises in Vietnam. *Journal of Business Research*, *147*, 362–378. DOI: 10.1016/j.jbusres.2022.03.077

Del Vecchio, P., Secundo, G., Mele, G., & Passiante, G. (2021). Sustainable entrepreneurship education for circular economy: Emerging perspectives in Europe. *International Journal of Entrepreneurial Behaviour & Research*, *27*(8), 2096–2124. DOI: 10.1108/IJEBR-03-2021-0210

Di Vaio, A., Hassan, R., Chhabra, M., Arrigo, E., & Palladino, R. (2022). Sustainable entrepreneurship impact and entrepreneurial venture life cycle: A systematic literature review. *Journal of Cleaner Production*, *378*, 134469. DOI: 10.1016/j.jclepro.2022.134469

Diepolder, C. S., Weitzel, H., & Huwer, J. (2021). Competence frameworks of sustainable entrepreneurship: A systematic review. *Sustainability (Basel)*, *13*(24), 13734. DOI: 10.3390/su132413734

Galvão, A., Marques, C., & Ferreira, J. J. (2020). The role of entrepreneurship education and training programmes in advancing entrepreneurial skills and new ventures. *European Journal of Training and Development*, *44*(6/7), 595–614. DOI: 10.1108/EJTD-10-2019-0174

Gonçalves, H., Magalhães, V. S., Ferreira, L. M., & Arantes, A. (2024). Overcoming barriers to sustainable supply chain management in small and medium-sized enterprises: A multi-criteria decision-making approach. *Sustainability (Basel)*, *16*(2), 506. DOI: 10.3390/su16020506

Hussain, I., Nazir, M., Hashmi, S. B., Shaheen, I., Akram, S., Waseem, M. A., & Arshad, A. (2021). Linking green and sustainable entrepreneurial intentions and social networking sites; the mediating role of self-efficacy and risk propensity. *Sustainability (Basel), 13*(13), 7050. DOI: 10.3390/su13137050

Ikram, M., Sroufe, R., Awan, U., & Abid, N. (2021). Enabling progress in developing economies: A novel hybrid decision-making model for green technology planning. *Sustainability (Basel), 14*(1), 258. DOI: 10.3390/su14010258

Ismail, I. J. (2022). Entrepreneurs' competencies and sustainability of small and medium enterprises in Tanzania. A mediating effect of entrepreneurial innovations. *Cogent Business & Management, 9*(1), 2111036. DOI: 10.1080/23311975.2022.2111036

Jardim, J. (2021). Entrepreneurial skills to be successful in the global and digital world: Proposal for a frame of reference for entrepreneurial education. *Education Sciences, 11*(7), 356. DOI: 10.3390/educsci11070356

Khanra, S., Kaur, P., Joseph, R. P., Malik, A., & Dhir, A. (2022). A resource-based view of green innovation as a strategic firm resource: Present status and future directions. *Business Strategy and the Environment, 31*(4), 1395–1413. DOI: 10.1002/bse.2961

Liao, Y. (2022). Sustainable leadership: A literature review and prospects for future research. *Frontiers in Psychology, 13*, 1045570. DOI: 10.3389/fpsyg.2022.1045570 PMID: 36420377

Luo, L., Guo, M., Huang, J., & Yang, J. (2022). Research on the effect of an entrepreneurial environment on college students' entrepreneurial self-efficacy: The mediating effect of entrepreneurial competence and moderating effect of entrepreneurial education. *Sustainability (Basel), 14*(11), 6744. DOI: 10.3390/su14116744

Mendes, A. C., Ferreira, F. A., Kannan, D., Ferreira, N. C., & Correia, R. J. (2022). A BWM approach to determinants of sustainable entrepreneurship in small and medium-sized enterprises. *Journal of Cleaner Production, 371*, 133300. DOI: 10.1016/j.jclepro.2022.133300

Mondal, S., Singh, S., & Gupta, H. (2023). Assessing enablers of green entrepreneurship in circular economy: An integrated approach. *Journal of Cleaner Production, 388*, 135999. DOI: 10.1016/j.jclepro.2023.135999

Naderi, N., Monavvarifard, F., & Salehi, L. (2022). Fostering sustainability-oriented knowledge-sharing in academic environment: A key strategic process to achieving SDGs through development of students' sustainable entrepreneurship competences. *International Journal of Management Education, 20*(1), 100603. DOI: 10.1016/j.ijme.2022.100603

Olurin, J. O., Gidigba, J. O., Ehiaguina, V. E., Ndiwe, T. C., Ayodeji, S. A., Banso, A. A., & Ojo, G. G. (2023). Engineering Innovations And Sustainable Entrepreneurship: A Comprehensive Literature Review. [MACEM]. *Materials & Corrosion Engineering Management, 4*(2), 62–71. DOI: 10.26480/macem.02.2023.70.79

Pennetta, S., Anglani, F., & Mathews, S. (2024). Navigating through entrepreneurial skills, competencies and capabilities: A systematic literature review and the development of the entrepreneurial ability model. *Journal of Entrepreneurship in Emerging Economies*, *16*(4), 1144–1182. DOI: 10.1108/JEEE-09-2022-0257

Rehman, S. U., Elrehail, H., Nair, K., Bhatti, A., & Taamneh, A. M. (2023). MCS package and entrepreneurial competency influence on business performance: The moderating role of business strategy. *European Journal of Management and Business Economics*, *32*(1), 1–23. DOI: 10.1108/EJMBE-04-2020-0088

Rosário, A. T., Raimundo, R. J., & Cruz, S. P. (2022). Sustainable entrepreneurship: A literature review. *Sustainability (Basel)*, *14*(9), 5556. DOI: 10.3390/su14095556

Sahu, A. K., Sharma, M., Raut, R. D., Sahu, A. K., Sahu, N. K., Antony, J., & Tortorella, G. L. (2023). Decision-making framework for supplier selection using an integrated MCDM approach in a lean-agile-resilient-green environment: Evidence from Indian automotive sector. *The TQM Journal*, *35*(4), 964–1006. DOI: 10.1108/TQM-12-2021-0372

Seikkula-Leino, J., & Salomaa, M. (2020). Entrepreneurial competencies and organisational change—Assessing entrepreneurial staff competencies within higher education institutions. *Sustainability (Basel)*, *12*(18), 7323. DOI: 10.3390/su12187323

Seraj, A. H. A., Fazal, S. A., & Alshebami, A. S. (2022). Entrepreneurial competency, financial literacy, and sustainable performance—Examining the mediating role of entrepreneurial resilience among Saudi entrepreneurs. *Sustainability (Basel)*, *14*(17), 10689. DOI: 10.3390/su141710689

Sousa, M. J., & Costa, J. M. (2022). Discovering entrepreneurship competencies through problem-based learning in higher education students. *Education Sciences*, *12*(3), 185. DOI: 10.3390/educsci12030185

Stefan, D., Vasile, V., Oltean, A., Comes, C. A., Stefan, A. B., Ciucan-Rusu, L., Bunduchi, E., Popa, M.-A., & Timus, M. (2021). Women entrepreneurship and sustainable business development: Key findings from a SWOT–AHP analysis. *Sustainability (Basel)*, *13*(9), 5298. DOI: 10.3390/su13095298

Suriyankietkaew, S., Krittayaruangroj, K., & Iamsawan, N. (2022). Sustainable Leadership practices and competencies of SMEs for sustainability and resilience: A community-based social enterprise study. *Sustainability (Basel)*, *14*(10), 5762. DOI: 10.3390/su14105762

Tariq, M. U. (2024). Integrating ESG Principles Into Corporate Governance for Sustainable Ecosystem Services. In Castanho, R. (Ed.), *ESG and Ecosystem Services for Sustainability* (pp. 89–118). IGI Global., DOI: 10.4018/979-8-3693-3771-4.ch004

Tariq, M. U. (2024). Smart Transportation Systems: Paving the Way for Sustainable Urban Mobility. In Munuhwa, S. (Ed.), *Contemporary Solutions for Sustainable Transportation Practices* (pp. 254–283). IGI Global., DOI: 10.4018/979-8-3693-3755-4.ch010

Tariq, M. U. (2025). Empowering Learning Through Networked and Connected Education: Case Studies in Digital Engagement. In Gierhart, A. (Ed.), *Cases on Enhancing P-16 Student Engagement With Digital Technologies* (pp. 169–198). IGI Global Scientific Publishing., DOI: 10.4018/979-8-3693-5633-3.ch007

Tariq, M. U. (2025). The Belmont Report: Guiding Ethical Principles in Human Research. In Throne, R. (Ed.), *IRB, Human Research Protections, and Data Ethics for Researchers* (pp. 245–268). IGI Global Scientific Publishing., DOI: 10.4018/979-8-3693-3848-3.ch010

Tariq, M. U., & Sergio, R. P. (2025). Ethical Considerations and Social Impact of AI and Computational Intelligence in Society 5.0. In Pandey, R., Srivastava, N., Prasad, R., Prasad, J., & Garcia, M. (Eds.), *Open AI and Computational Intelligence for Society 5.0* (pp. 225–248). IGI Global Scientific Publishing., DOI: 10.4018/979-8-3693-4326-5.ch010

Thelken, H. N., & de Jong, G. (2020). The impact of values and future orientation on intention formation within sustainable entrepreneurship. *Journal of Cleaner Production*, *266*, 122052. DOI: 10.1016/j.jclepro.2020.122052

Uvarova, I., Mavlutova, I., & Atstaja, D. (2021). Development of the green entrepreneurial mindset through modern entrepreneurship education. [). IOP Publishing.]. *IOP Conference Series. Earth and Environmental Science*, *628*(1), 012034. DOI: 10.1088/1755-1315/628/1/012034

Venesaar, U., Malleus, E., Arro, G., & Toding, M. (2021). Entrepreneurship competence model for supporting learners development at all educational levels. *Administrative Sciences*, *12*(1), 2. DOI: 10.3390/admsci12010002

Victar, H. C., Perera, B. A. K. S., Palihakkara, A. D., & Dewagod, K. G. (2024). Roles and competencies of quantity surveyors in achieving a circular built environment: An investigation according to 3R principles. *Smart and Sustainable Built Environment*, *13*(4), 1015–1040. DOI: 10.1108/SASBE-10-2022-0231

Yadegaridehkordi, E., Foroughi, B., Iranmanesh, M., Nilashi, M., & Ghobakhloo, M. (2023). Determinants of environmental, financial, and social sustainable performance of manufacturing SMEs in Malaysia. *Sustainable Production and Consumption*, *35*, 129–140. DOI: 10.1016/j.spc.2022.10.026

## KEY TERMS AND DEFINITIONS

**Sustainability:** The method of sustaining environmental, social, and financial balance for future generations' well-being.

**Entrepreneurship:** The procedure of recognizing prospects, creating ventures, and taking risks to transform and generate value

**Strategic Management:** The planning, implementing, and assessing of business strategies to attain long-term organizational targets and purposes.

**Circular Economies:** A sustainable economic model determined by lowering waste by recycling resources and reprocessing products.

# Chapter 7
# Formulation of Grand Index of Green Growth and Sustainability (GIGGS): A Cross-Country Empirical Study

**Debasish Roy**
https://orcid.org/0000-0002-0706-9743
*Sikkim University, India*

## ABSTRACT

*In the rapidly changing global scenario repleted with escalated levels of pollution, greenhouse effects and global warming, we are currently transitioning through one of the most difficult phases of human civilization. Under these grave circumstances, there is a pressing need for the successful implementation of green economic growth for all the nations of the world regardless of their demographical locations. This research work is aimed at two objectives: first, the conceptualization of IsoEnvironmental Pressure (IEP) Curve – which is my new contribution to the existing literature of Green Economy and Sustainable Development (SD) based on the works of Victor and Sers (2019), and second, formulation of Grand Index of Green Growth and Sustainability (GIGGS) for the time period of 10 years (2012 – 2021) for 5 sample countries in order to analyze the factors that are responsible to influence the green growth and sustainable development of a country from a normative point of view.*

## 1. INTRODUCTION

Since the changes in climate across the globe are adversely affecting (to a great extent) the various types economic agents, there is a pressing need to do and evaluate the businesses in new formats (Voica *et al.*, 2015). The various governments, policymakers and various institutions have joined hands to develop a common goal in the process of transitioning to a low-carbon emission, climate resilient and resource-efficient economy (McCahery and Vermeulen, 2014). The major obstacle in achieving this goal is the *cost* of transition from a high-carbon emission economy to a low-carbon emission one (Popescu, 2014). The main instrument of this economic transition is the promotion of eco-friendly investments or

DOI: 10.4018/979-8-3373-0189-1.ch007

simply known as the Green Investments. Based on the work of Inderst *et al.* (2012), Voica *et al.* (2015) have summarized the major characteristics of green investments as follows:

- Depending on economic and policymaking aspects, there might be many definitions of green investments;
- There are many intersections of definitions of green investment which exist within some sectors like renewable energy, commodities (e.g., carbon or renewable energy credits), services (e.g., waste management), and technologies required to increase energy efficiency;
- Major controversies related to implementation of nuclear or large-scale hydro-electric power projects, changing consensus on biomass, biofuels, shale gas etc., ambiguity in the sectors of Green Information Technology (IT), Green Finance etc., and uncertainties in dealing with conservations of bio-diversities, natural capital etc. have been observed;
- It is easier to define 'green commodities and services', but it is difficult to define 'green technologies and processes'; and
- The metric for "greenness" of technologies and processes is difficult to formulate.

Voica *et al.* (2015, p. 73) have also classified the motivations for realizing the green investment as follows:

a) Financial considerations which include Returns on Investments (ROI), risk; diversification, long-term risk considerations, and internationalization of externalities;
b) Extra-financial considerations that include ecological, scientific, religious, ethical, and political aspects;
c) Reputational factors such as reputation of the investor, reputation of the company, marketing tools, pressure from the media etc.; and
d) Compliance and fiduciary duties that involve domestic law and regulations, international conventions, voluntary industry codes, disclosure codes, good governance codes etc.

Bina (2013) has identified *three* interrelated patterns which may help us to interpret the implications of greening based on Dryzek's (2005) classification of environmental discourse as follows: (a) Scarcity and limits, (b) Means and ends, and (c) Reductionism and unity respectively. By the end of the first decade of 21st century, the combined effect of dwindling economic growth rates and rising inequalities of income and wealth of the developed nations posed a serious threat to the emerging and developing economies as well (Crotty, 2012; The Economist, 2012). Apart from those grave socio-economic issues, another major problem related to global ecosystem started raising its ugly head – which is related to breaching of the planetary 'boundaries'. These planetary boundaries provide safeguards against environmental disasters on the basis of major factors like rate of biodiversity loss, climate change, and human interference with the nitrogen cycle (Rockström *et al.*, 2009). To quote Schoenmaker and Schramade (2019, p. 8): "The zone of uncertainty ranges from 350 to 450 parts per million (ppm) of carbon dioxide. We crossed the planetary boundary of 350 ppm in 1995, with a level of 399 ppm in 2015, and are adding at a rate of around 3 ppm every year."

By breaking those boundaries, the human activities "now rival global geophysical processes" and have given rise to a phenomenon called *Anthropocene* (Steffen *et al.*, 2011). In order to combat the dual crises and adopt Sustainable Development Goals (SDG) as part of Rio+20's agenda, the necessary responses to the crises may be grouped into *three* categories as follows (Refer to Figure 1) (Bernard *et al.*, 2009; ILO/EU/IILS Report, 2011; Bina, 2013):

1. National Stimulus Packages referred to as "Almost Business as Usual" (BAU);
2. Proposals to *green* the economy or "greening"; and
3. Proposals for socio-economic transformation referred to as "All change".

The first category, i.e., *Almost BAU*, refers to the stimulus packages (including 'bail-outs' and recovery programs) provided by the major developed economies to reduce the adverse effects of climate change and often termed as "Green stimulus measures". Keynesian expansionary fiscal policy measures were widely adopted by the OECD and Emerging Economies (Meltzer *et al.*, 2013) characterized by deficit financing.

*Figure 1. A categorization of policy responses to the double crisis*

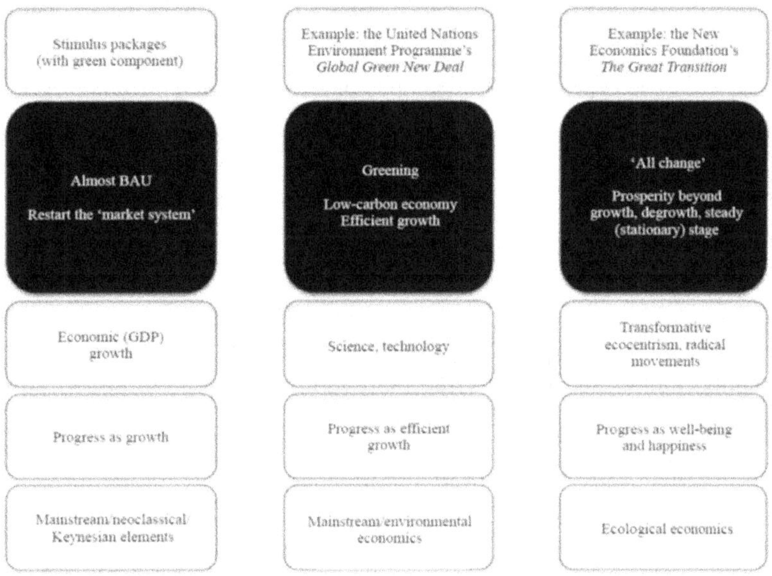


(**Source:***Bina, 2013; p. 1028)*

Schoenmaker and Schramade (2019, p. 181) have identified *six* conditions for investing to encourage Long-term Value Creation (LTVC) as follows: (i) Long investment horizons, (ii) Active management in concentrated portfolios, (iii) Effective engagement with companies, (iv) Performance analysis of value added in the real economy, (v) Long-term alignment of the mandates of asset owners and asset managers; and (vi) Keeping the investment chain short.

GIGGS is computed as the *Geometric Mean (GM)* of two variables, i.e.; Comprehensive Green Growth Index (CGGI) and The Global Sustainable Competitiveness Index ® (GSCI) of SolAbility Sustainable Intelligence respectively.

The first pillar of GIGGS, i.e.; CGGI is enumerated by using 4 major selective variables from the OECD Green Growth Database which encompasses the features of the two out of four groups of *Environmental and Resource Productivity, The Natural Asset Base, Economic Opportunities and Policy Responses*, and *The Environmental Dimension of Quality of Life* respectively (OECD, 2017). The 2 groups from where those 4 variables are chosen are Environmental and Resource Productivity and The Environmental Dimension of Quality of Life respectively. No variable was chosen from the other two groups for two main reasons: first; in order to keep the procedure of formulation and enumeration of CGGI as simple and comprehensive as possible, and second; the variables of the chosen groups address the primary factors that affect the environment, well-being of the individuals and the productivities of the economies. The four chosen variables are *Production-based Carbon Dioxide ($CO_2$) Productivity (PCDO), Non-energy Material Productivity (NEMP), Mean Population Exposure to $PM_{2.5}$ (MPEPM)*, and *Environmentally adjusted Multifactor Productivity (EAMFP) Growth* respectively. In order to fulfil the objective, a time series study of 10 years (2012 – 2021) had been conducted on 5 sample countries, namely; Denmark, Finland, Sweden, Brazil, and South Korea which yielded some interesting results and findings that would pave the way for future research in this extremely significant domain.

By keeping in mind the major objectives of Sustainable Development, LTVC, and Green Economic Growth; this research work is aimed at formulation of Grand Index of Green Growth and Sustainability (GIGGS) which would help to project a country's performance on *dual* fronts of greening of the economy and achieving of the SDGs' respectively in a *normative* manner. The heart of this research lies in the fact that GIGGS would act as a complementary tool in analysis and evaluation of a given country's 'position' in the global perspective in terms of its positive initiatives and efficient implementation of the necessary measures/strategies to encourage green growth, reduce GHG emission, and pave the ways for sustainable development. An increase/decrease in the magnitude of GIGGS would obviously indicate an improvement/deterioration in the country's ranking compared to its counterparts in the global scenario. Moreover, the application of IEP curve in real world scenario would help to determine the equilibrium values of Environmental Intensity (EI) and GDP that would keep the level of Environmental Pressure of an economy unchanged.

## DATA DESCRIPTIONS

The Metadata for the chosen variables to formulate the Grand Index of Green Growth and Sustainability (GIGGS) are given below:

I. Production-based Carbon Dioxide ($CO_2$) Productivity (PCDO), GDP per unit of energy-related $CO_2$ emissions:

"Production-based $CO_2$ productivity is calculated as real GDP generated per unit of $CO_2$ emitted (USD/kg). Included are $CO_2$ emissions from combustion of coal, oil, natural gas and other fuels.

The estimates of $CO_2$ emissions are obtained from the IEA's database of $CO_2$ emissions from fuel combustion.1 Default methods and emission factors are given in the Revised 1996 IPCC Guidelines for National Greenhouse Gas Inventories.

Gross Domestic Product (GDP) is expressed at constant 2015 USD using PPP." [Organisation for Economic Co – Operation and Development (OECD), n. d.];

II. Non-energy Material Productivity (NEMP), GDP per unit of DMC:

"Non-energy material productivity is calculated as GDP generated per unit of materials consumed (USD/kg).

Domestic Material Consumption (DMC) refers to the apparent consumption of materials; it is calculated as the sum of domestic consumption of biomass for food and feed, construction minerals, industrial minerals, metals and wood. Data on DMC are obtained from the Material Resources dataset included in the OECD Environment Database.

Gross Domestic Product (GDP) is expressed at constant 2015 USD using PPP." [Organisation for Economic Co – Operation and Development (OECD), n. d.];

III. Mean Population Exposure to $PM_{2.5}$ (MPEPM):

"Mean population exposure to fine particulate matter is calculated as the mean annual outdoor $PM_{2.5}$ concentration weighted by population living in the area. It is the concentration level, expressed in micrograms per cubic meter ($\mu g/m^3$), to which a typical resident is exposed throughout a year.

Data on exposure to air pollution are obtained from the Exposure to $PM_{2.5}$ – countries and regions dataset from the OECD Environment Database." [Organisation for Economic Co – Operation and Development (OECD), n. d.]; and

IV. Environmentally adjusted Multifactor Productivity Growth (EAMFP):

"EAMFP growth measures the change in productivity at the macroeconomic (country) level encompassing, e.g., technological change, institutional and organisational improvements. EAMFP growth is presented in percentage points of output growth. It is calculated using a growth accounting approach as the residual growth in the joint production of both the desirable and the undesirable outputs that cannot be explained by changes in the consumption of factor inputs (including labour, produced capital and natural capital). Therefore, for a given growth of input use, EAMFP increases when GDP increases or when pollution decreases.

EAMFP data are obtained from the Environmentally adjusted multifactor productivity dataset of OECD Environment Database." [Organisation for Economic Co – Operation and Development (OECD), n. d.]; and

V. The Global Sustainable Competitiveness Index ® (GSCI):

"The Global Sustainable Competitiveness Index (GSCI) measures the TRUE competitiveness of nations. The GSCI is based on 120 purely quantitative indicators, derived from reliable sources (World Bank, UN agencies, the IMF), grouped in the 5 pillars of national competitiveness. The GSCI is calculated based on both the latest available performance data and the development over the past 10 years of the data indicators.

- Grouped into the pillars of development: natural capital, resource efficiency, social capital, intellectual & innovation capital, governance performance
- Based on purely quantitative indicators

- Taking into account 130 indicators derived from recognised global data sources (World Bank, various UN agencies, IMF)
- Evaluating latest available data points and trends over time to better reflect future potential

The integration of all relevant dimensions that form competitiveness is more accurate representation of nation-economies than, for example, the commonly used GDP. The GSCI is the most comprehensive measurement of the competitiveness of nation-states and their future potential." (SolAbility Sustainable Intelligence, n. d.)

## LITERATURE REVIEW

The root cause of global warming is correlated to our current model of economic growth and intensive use of natural resources as the current measures of economic development are overwhelmingly dominated by the measure of GDP. However, the proper evaluation of natural capital should be associated with the solutions and tools to combine economic development with sustainability (Ducoing, 2019; p. 19). The alternative approaches to traditional GDP Accounting are General Savings (GS) and Adjusted Net Savings (ANS). Over the last 25 years or so, GS has emerged as one of the major indicators of Sustainable Development (SD) as it involves wealth accounting in measuring the total capital stocks which include physical, social, natural, human, and institutional capitals (Stiglitz *et al.*, 2009; Ducoing, 2019; p. 21). To quote Ducoing (2019, p. 23): "Current estimates of GS contain gross and net saving/ investment, depreciation of natural capital, education expenditure, total factor productivity (TFP), and pollutants such as CO2 emissions". Larger investments in 'greening' accompanied by an increase in GS help to appreciate the level of Green Saving with Augmented Total Factor Productivity (GSTFP) of an economy (Refer to Table 1).

*Table 1. Genuine Savings (GS) growth rates in selected countries (1990 – 2000)*

| | 1900 – 2000 | | | |
|---|---|---|---|---|
| | **Net Investment %** | **Green %** | **GS %** | **GSTFP %** |
| Britain | 4.6 | 2.8 | 5.5 | 28.6 |
| Alemannia | 9.4 | 8.1 | 11.3 | 49.6 |
| United States | 7.1 | 4.4 | 8.1 | 32.6 |
| Australia | 7.7 | 4.3 | 6.5 | 24.7 |
| France | 8.9 | 8.4 | 11.8 | 29.1 |
| Switzerland | 14.1 | 14.4 | 17.5 | 45.4 |
| Argentina | 3.9 | 3.2 | 3.5 | 5.1 |
| Brazil | 11.1 | 3.9 | 5.5 | 8.4 |
| Chile | 2.1 | -5.6 | -4.1 | -2.3 |
| Colombia | 8.7 | 3.6 | 4.4 | 4.7 |
| Mexico | 8.6 | -1.4 | -0.9 | 2.2 |

*GS- Genuine Savings; GSTFP- Genuine Savings with Total Factor Poructivity Augmented*
[**Source:**Ducoing, 2019; p. 26]

The other major problem related to GDP-based economic growth is that it is unfavorably skewed towards the rich in many of the developing and developed nations which is environmentally destructive. To quote Sachs *et al.* (2019, p. 4): "Given the current trajectory of global fossil-fuel use, the planet's temperature is likely to rise by 4 °C to 6 °C above pre-industrial levels, an increase that would be catastrophic for food production, human health, and biodiversity; indeed, in many parts of the world, it would threaten communities' survival". The major hindrance for long-term investments in green energy projects by shunning the traditional fossil-fuel based technologies requires major investments by the private sector since public sector expenditures are *not* sufficient enough – especially, in case of the developing countries. The reason of private sector's apathy towards long-term investments in green energy projects is the low rate of Return on Investment (ROI) and the associated risks (Yoshino and Taghizadeh-Hesary, 2018; pp. 335 – 357).

Fast developing Asia relies heavily on coal for power generation. According to the statistics of the World Bank's World Development Indicators database (2013), 66% of electricity was generated from coal-fired power plants in the region, compared to 14% in non-Asian developing countries and 32% in Organisation for Economic Cooperation and Development (OECD) countries (Sachs *et al.*, 2019, p. 5). The climate – adjusted estimated infrastructure requirements by sector and region in Developing Asia and Pacific (2016–2030) is shown below (Refer to Figure 2):

*Figure 2. Climate-Adjusted Estimated Infrastructure Investment Needs by Sector and Region in Developing Asia and Pacific (2016 – 2030) (Percentage and $ Billion in 2015 Prices).*

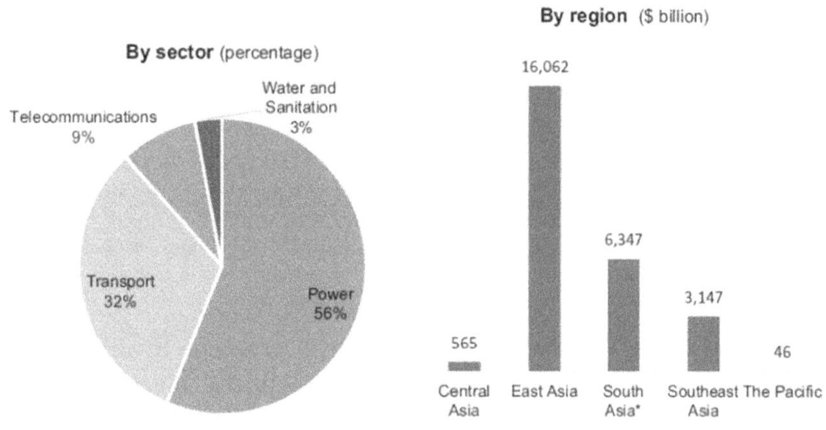


*(Source: Made by authors based on data from ADB (2017).*

*Note: Asia and Pacific stands ADB's 45 developing member countries. * Pakistan and Afghanistan are included in South Asia. Climate change adjusted figures include climate mitigation and climate proofing costs, but do not include other adaptation costs, especially those associated with sea level rise) [***Source:** *Sachs, J. D. et al. (2019), p. 6]*

An important study by Tallis *et al.* (2015, p. 32) has emphasized on "The interactions among emission sources, atmospheric chemistry and local climate influence the nature and transport of atmospheric pollutants. This will subsequently influence the deposition (atmospheric removal rate), re-suspension and transport of the pollutant through the green space, water and soils. These processes need to be understood and quantified in order to establish the most effective greening solution for a particular pollution scenario." In their study aided by computer modelling, Nowak *et al.* (2006) estimated that the urban tree canopy of

55 cities in USA had helped in removing 711,000 tonnes of pollutants annually (PM, $O_3$, $NO_2$, $SO_2$ and CO): an average of 10.8 grams of atmospheric pollution removed annually for each $m^2$ (square meter) of urban tree canopy cover. Removal of pollutants occurs through a combination of processes that are most often separated into dry and wet depositions based upon the procedure of transfer of pollutants to a structure (e.g., vegetation, water, asphalt, brick or concrete surface). The structure, in turn, influences the atmospheric pollutions in *three* ways as follows:

- Short-term removal: It refers to the procedure when the pollutant is re-suspended back to the atmosphere when conditions are appropriate;
- Longer - term removal: Refers to the procedure when the pollutant is incorporated into the structure (*sequestration*); and
- Transfer: The pollution is transferred to a different medium, i.e., washed off the structure to reside in soil and hydrological systems. (Tallis *et al.*, 2015; p. 33)

The deposition of pollutants may be broadly divided into *two* parts: *wet deposition* and *dry deposition*. Wet deposition tends to remove pollutants from a higher level in the atmosphere and it is greater in vegetation compared to built-up environment because the structure of vegetation, particularly trees, is highly efficient in intercepting fogs, mists and aerosols (Freer-Smith *et al.*, 2005). Wet deposition tends to account for a lesser number of pollutants in comparison to dry deposition. Thus, in general, the problem of dry deposition needs to be tackled by encouraging the green infrastructure in order to improve the urban air quality. Dry deposition on the surface occurs through a number of processes; mainly: (i) Through Brownian motion, causing diffusion from the high concentration area in the atmosphere to the low concentration area of the surface, (ii) by settling out of the atmosphere (sedimentation under gravity), and (iii) by direct impaction on a surface and interception by a surface.

The factor which links the rate of pollution related to dry deposition, or Flux (F) with the Concentration of pollution (C) in the atmosphere is a variable called Velocity of Deposition ($V_d$) (Hicks, 1987; Tallis *et al.*, 2015; pp. 34 - 35). The relationship between F, C and $V_d$ may be formally expressed as:

$$F = C \times V_d \tag{1}$$

Since $V_d$ represents the Velocity of Deposition, hence its *inverse* term R would represent the Resistance to pollutant removal from the atmosphere to the surface. Thus, technically;

$$V_d = \frac{1}{R_a + R_b + R_c} = \frac{1}{R} \tag{2}$$

where

$R_a$= The aerodynamic resistance of the pollutant to atmospheric transport;
$R_b$= The resistance to diffusion across the surface boundary layer (a quasi-laminar flow layer immediately surrounding the leaf);
$R_c$= The resistance from the surface itself; and

$R = R_a + R_b + R_c$(Tallis *et al.*, 2015; p. 34 – 35).

Now by substituting the value of R in equation: (2), we have:

$$F = \frac{C}{R} \qquad (3)$$
$$\rightarrow C = F \times R$$

Now by taking total differential of equation: (3), the following results are derived:

$$dC = RdF + FdR$$

$$\Rightarrow R\frac{dF}{dC} + F\frac{dR}{dC} = 1$$

$$\Rightarrow R\left(\frac{1}{\frac{dC}{dF}}\right) + F\left(\frac{1}{\frac{dC}{dR}}\right) = 1$$

$$\Rightarrow \frac{RF}{C}\left(\frac{1}{\frac{F}{C}\cdot\frac{dC}{dF}}\right) + \frac{RF}{C}\left(\frac{1}{\frac{R}{C}\cdot\frac{dC}{dR}}\right) = 1$$

$$\Rightarrow \frac{RF}{C}\left(C_F^{-1} + C_R^{-1}\right) = 1$$

$$\Rightarrow C_F^{-1} + C_R^{-1} = 1 \qquad (4)$$

[Since $C=FR$ as per equation: (3)]

where $C_F^{-1} = \frac{1}{C_F}$= Inverse of Flux elasticity of Concentration ($C_F$);

$C_R^{-1} = \frac{1}{C_R}$= Inverse of Resistance elasticity of Concentration ($C_R$);

$C_F = \frac{\frac{dC}{C}}{\frac{dF}{F}}$= Flux elasticity of Concentration;

$C_R = \frac{\frac{dC}{C}}{\frac{dR}{R}}$ = Resistance elasticity of Concentration.

Equation: (4) helps to establish an important relationship between the elasticities (inverses) of concentration with respect to flux and resistance respectively. It also proves that barring the *singular* case of *unitary elasticity* of either $C_F$ or $C_R$, both of the elasticities should be *greater than 1*; i.e., $C_P C_R > 1$. In other words, the Concentration of pollution (C) is *highly sensitive* to the changes in Flux (F) and Resistance (R) respectively.

Hamilton and Naikal (2014; pp. 28 - 29) have attempted to measure the generation of wealth by keeping the vital factor of sustainable development in mind in line with Fisher (1906), Hamilton and Hartwick (2005) as follows:

$$W_t = \int_{s=t}^{\infty} C(s)\, e^{-r(s-t)}\, ds \qquad (5)$$

where

$W_t$= Current value of wealth composed of man-made, human and natural capital, is in fact equal to the present value of future consumption under the assumption of constant returns to scale;
$C(s)$ = Consumption at time s, as measured under System of National Accounts (SNA); and

r = Discount rate.

Since future consumption is unknown, by applying Ramsey rule, the authors have defined $r=\delta+g$ where $g$= Constant rate of consumption (under the assumption of marginal utility of consumption is 1), $\delta$ = Constant pure rate of time preference, and $C(s) = C(t)e^{g(s-t)}$.

By holding the pure rate of time preference constant at 1.5 percent, wealth could be measured for individual countries (Refer to Figure 3).

*Figure 3. Distribution of the implicit rate of return on total wealth, 2005*

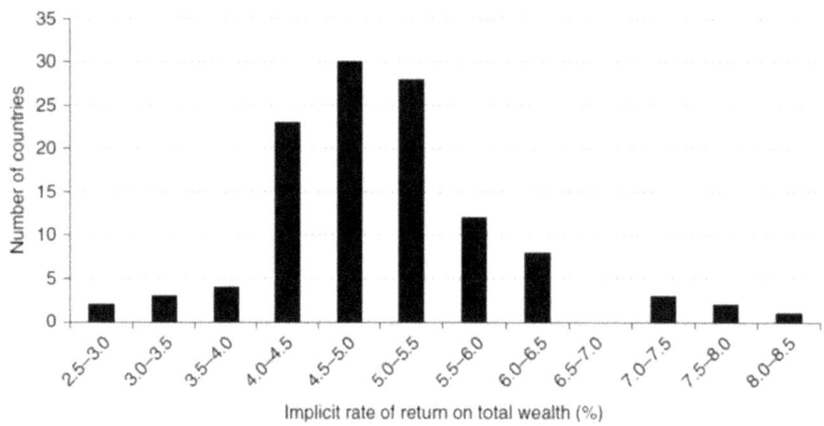


*Source:* World Bank (2011).

(**Source:***Hamilton and Naikal, 2014; p. 29)*

Victor and Sers (2019, p. 30) have raised an extremely pertinent question about the *limits* of green growth by taking a cue from the works of scholars like Hickel and Kallis (2020) that "For economic growth to be green the impacts on the environment of the activities that make up GDP must decline if they are already excessive, or stabilize at levels considered acceptable". They have streamlined the definition of green growth as the economic growth which is 'decoupled' from the material and energy flows and land conversion that are associated with economic activity and broadly classified decoupling into two forms as quoted (*Ibid*., pp. 30 – 31): "Decoupling can take two forms: relative and absolute. Using energy as an example, relative decoupling occurs when energy per unit of economic activity (that is, 'energy intensity') declines. At the level of an entire economy this would mean a decline in energy used per unit of GDP. If the rate of economic growth exceeds the rate of decline in energy used per unit of GDP, then total energy use will rise despite the reduction in energy intensity. Absolute decoupling occurs when total energy use remains constant or declines while GDP continues to grow." In case of economic growth, relative decoupling only requires a fall in $E_t/GDP_t$ ratio where $E_t$ refers to Environmental pressure in time t, $GDP_t$ refers to GDP in time t, and $E_t/GDP_t$ is referred to as Environmental Intensity or simply *Intensity*. Environmental pressure is referred to an environmental flow related to Greenhouse Gas (GHG) emissions per annum. Victor and Sers (2019, pp. 32 - 33) have also broadly classified economic growth and degrowth into 3 categories *each* as follows (Refer to Figure 4):

- Green growth: It is the stage when intensity declines at a faster rate compared to the rate of increase in scale (GDP);
- Brown growth: It is the stage when the rate of increase in scale (GDP) is faster than the rate of decline in intensity;
- Black growth: It refers to the stage when both scale (GDP) and intensity increase;
- Dark green degrowth: It refers to the stage when both scale (GDP) and intensity fall;
- Light green degrowth: It refers to the stage when the rate of increase in intensity is *lesser* than the rate of decline in scale (GDP); and
- Black degrowth: It is the stage when the rate of increase in intensity is *greater* than the rate of decline in scale (GDP).

The researchers have considered Canada's GDP and GHG intensity for classifications of economic growth and degrowth based on color variants by taking the Base Year as 1990. They have developed an isoquant (denoted by the white curve in Figure 4) consisting of combinations of GDP and GHG which would keep the Canadian economy at a *fixed* level of Environmental Pressure (591 MT of Emissions), *ceteris paribus*. Points above and to the right of this line represent increases in GHG emissions and points below and to the left of this line represent decreases in GHG emissions. According to the researchers, although this model was applied for Canada as a sample country, it could be replicated for other countries also.

I have attempted to elaborate the given model based on a quantitative approach under a separate section later in this paper which may be considered as my sole contribution to the Environmental Economic Theory (Refer to the section "Conceptualization of IsoEnvironmental Pressure Curve").

*Figure 4. The colors of growth. Scale and Intensity [Adapted from Victor (2010, 2019).*

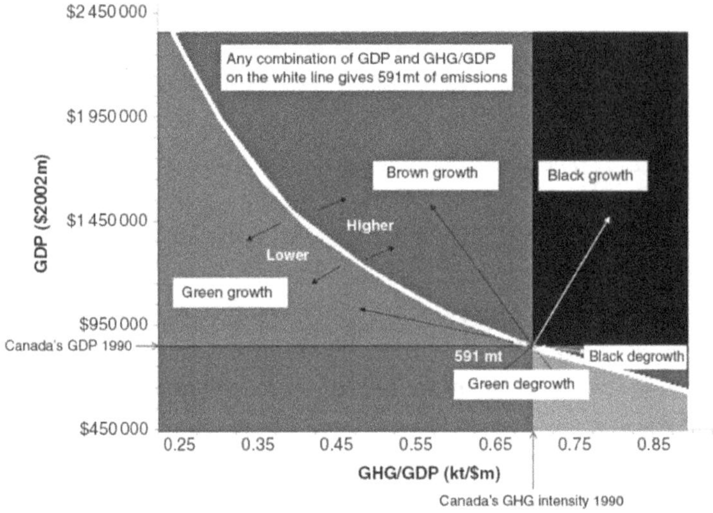


**Source:** *Victor and Sers, 2019; p. 33]*

Dechezleprêtre *et al.* (2019) in their important research work on measuring knowledge spillovers coming from low-carbon and high-carbon patents by using a global dataset of patent citations focusing on two major sectors of transportation and electricity generation proved that knowledge spillovers are much larger for low-carbon technologies as compared to high-carbon technologies (Refer to Figures 5 and 6).

Apart from low-carbon and high-carbon technologies, there are many technologies within high-carbon category that make fossil fuels more efficient. These technologies may be treated as an alternative to clean (zero-carbon) technologies and termed as 'grey' (Dechezleprêtre *et al.*, 2019; p. 226). Dechezleprêtre *et al.* (2019) have also found that spillovers from clean technologies are more economically viable than spillovers from dirty technologies and strongly advocated for greater public support for zero-carbon technologies such as electric and hydrogen cars or renewable energy technologies in comparison to R&D activities in energy-efficient technologies.

*Figure 5. Number of low-carbon and high-carbon innovations 1950 – 2005*

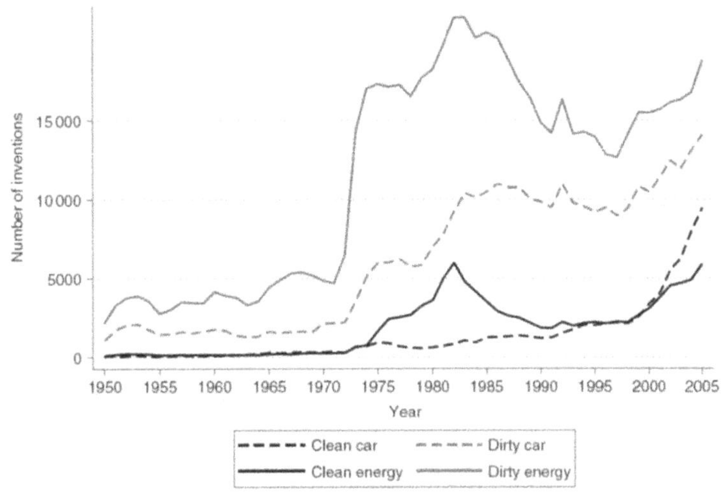


(**Source:** *Dechezleprêtre et al. 2019, p. 225)*

*Figure 6. Visualizing spillovers from clean and dirty technologies*

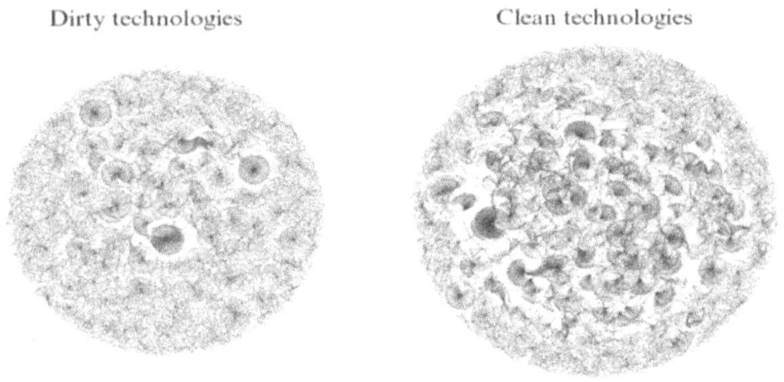


*Notes:* The figure visualises all citations to a sample of 1000 dirty (left panel) and 1000 clean (right panel) innovations. Each node represents an innovation, edges represent citations. The samples were drawn among innovations applying for patent protection in 1995. Interactive versions of these figures can be found online at http://www.eeclab.org.uk/forcedirect_arx.html?tojson_dirlinks0_1995_15_1000_0.json.

(**Source:** *Dechezleprêtre et al. 2019, p. 225)*

In order to reconcile between economic growth and sustainable development, the concept of *circular economy* has come to the fore. Since there are numerous existing definitions of the circular economy, the comprehensive definition is provided by Ellen MacArthur Foundation (EMF) (Kirchherr *et al.*, 2017) as follows:

> An industrial system that is restorative or regenerative by intention and design... It replaces the 'end-of-life' concept with restoration, shifts towards the use of renewable energy, eliminates the use of toxic chemicals, which impair reuse, and aims for the elimination of waste through the superior design of materials, products, systems, and, within this, business models (EMF 2013, p. 7).

EMF has also proposed *three* principles through which there would be value creation for the circular economy as follows:

> "decoupled from the consumption of finite resources… 1) Preserve and enhance natural capital by controlling finite stocks and balancing renewable resource flows; 2) Optimise resource yields by circulating products, components, and materials at the highest utility at all times in both technical and biological cycles; and 3) Foster system effectiveness by revealing and designing out negative externalities (EMF 2015, p. 23)".

In order to operationalize these principles, EMF has developed a 'ReSOLVE' framework of 6 'business actions' for firms to generate circular business strategies and growth initiatives (EMF 2015) as below (Refer to Table 2):

*Table 2. EMF ReSOLVE framework*

| Actions | Description |
|---|---|
| Regenerate | Shifting to renewable energy and materials to reclaim, retain and regenerate ecosystem, heal and return recovered biological resources to the biosphere. |
| Share | Maintaining a low product loop speed and maximizing product utilization by sharing among users (peer-to-peer, business-to-consumer and business-to-business), reusing, maintaining, repairing and designing for durability. |
| Optimize | Increasing the performance and efficiency of products, reduction of waste during production and throughout the supply chain, leveraging big data, automation and remote sensing and steering. |
| Loop | Keeping components and materials in closed loops and prioritizing 'inner loops' through remanufacturing products and components and material recycling as a last resort. |
| Virtualize | Delivering virtual utility through books, music, online shopping, virtual offices and meetings. |
| Exchange | Replacing old materials with advanced non-renewable materials (for example, 3D printing or electric engines). |

(**Sources:**EMF 2015; Lazarevic and Brandão, 2020; p. 16)

The other model – which is both interdisciplinary and transdisciplinary in nature and strongly advocated by many scholars as extremely conducive for preserving Earth's natural diversity is called *The Quintuple Helix Model*. It is the model which explains the ways by which knowledge, innovations, and natural environment are interrelated (Carayannis and Campbell, 2010; Barth, 2011). The diagrammatic representation of The Quintuple Helix Model is illustrated below (Refer to Figure 7):

*Figure 7. The subsystems of The Quintuple Helix Model*

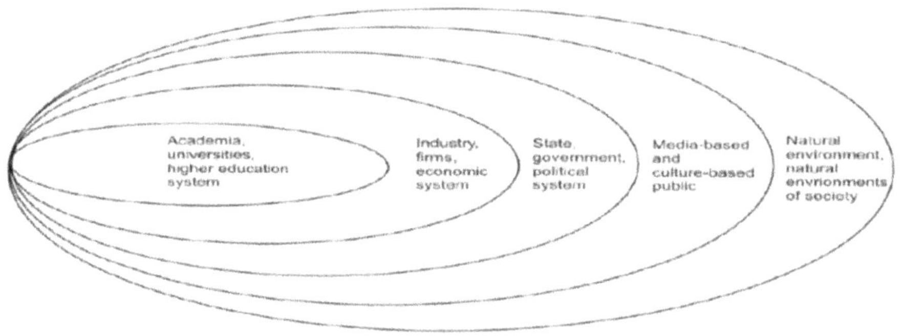


(**Sources:***Carayannis et al. 2012; Etzkowitz and Leydesdorff 2000; Carayannis and Campbell 2009, 2010; Lavrinenko et al. 2019, p. 1116)*

In order to encourage Green Economy, there is an obvious need for Green Finance. To quote Noh (2019, p. 40): "Green finance is a type of future-oriented finance that simultaneously pursues the development of financial industry, improvement of the environment, and economic growth". There are *four* major concepts related to green finance such as Sustainable Finance, Environmental Finance, Carbon Finance, and Climate Finance respectively. Sustainable finance takes into account the investments which not only considers environmental issues, but social and governmental aspects as well. Environmental finance includes investment towards ecological environment. Carbon finance involves investments related to reduction of emissions of Carbon dioxide and other GHGs. Finally, climate finance is related to the investments to achieve a low-carbon economy and implement climate-resilient development. The relationships between the green finance and other related finances may be shown as below (Figure 8).

*Figure 8. Relationships between green finance and other related finances*

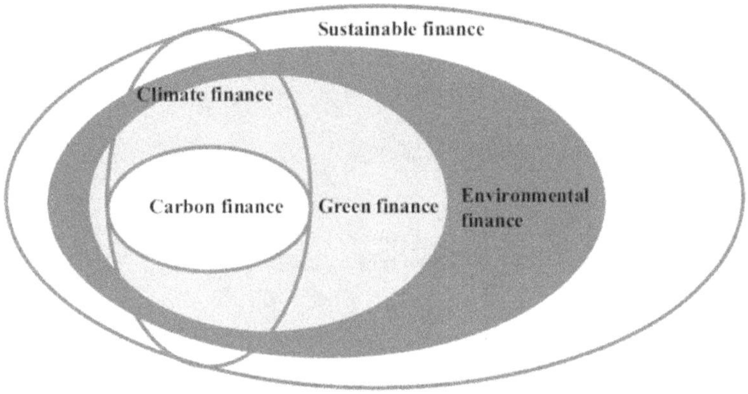


*(**Sources:**Noh, 2018; Noh, 2019; p. 42)*

The expected return from green investments may be derived by the help of traditional Capital Asset Pricing Model (CAPM). The Green Security Market Line (GSML) for Revised CAPM for green investments may be expressed as follows:

$$E(TR_i) = GR_i + E(R_i) = GR_i + \left[R_f + \beta_i\{E(R_m) - R_f\}\right] \tag{6}$$

where

$GR_i$ = Green Return on stock i,
$R_i$ = Economic return on stock i,
$R_f$ = Risk – free rate,
$\beta_i$ = Beta of stock i, and
$R_m$ = Market return on portfolio.

The *optimal* portfolio level is determined by the *tangency* point between the utility indifference surface and the efficient frontier curve (Noh, 2019; pp. 45 – 47) (Refer to Figure 9).

Sertyesilisik and Sertyesilisik (2017) have emphasized on the following aspects in order to promote green economy and green growth as follows:

- Political aspects: The politicians and policymakers can implement different policy instruments like Carbon Taxes, Carbon-motivated Border Tax Adjustments (CBTA), virtual carbon trade etc.;
- Social aspects: The green economy, green growth and Sustainable Development (SD) can be achieved when individuals and the society as a whole will accept and implement the changes towards sustainability. These change agents should be mainly supported through formal and informal education and media; and
- Economic aspects: "Green economy and green growth can be fostered mainly through innovation in green technology; entrepreneurship; EIPs and green supply chains. Green growth and green economy can be achieved through innovations which can result in greening the production processes and products" (Sertyesilisik and Sertyesilisik, 2017; p. 60).

*Figure 9. Determination of optimal green portfolio*

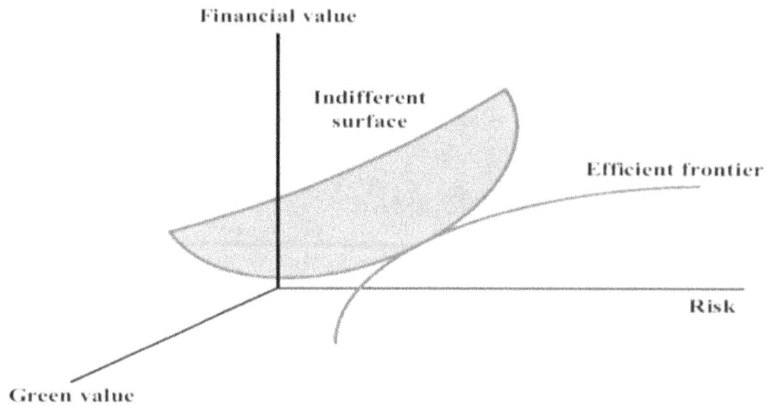


(**Source:***Noh, 2019; p. 47)*

Lee *et al.* (2022, pp. 256 – 263) have endeavored to highlight the importance of supply and demand uncertainties in the context of sustainable entrepreneurship in the form of 2x2 matrix where demand uncertainty is measured on the vertical axis and supply uncertainty on the horizontal axis. They have tried to highlight (p. 256): "… the entrepreneurial opportunities that characterize each quadrant, identify key challenges that entrepreneurs face, and outline the sustainability benefits associated with the successful exploitation of such market opportunities. We use this as a springboard to identify unexplored future research directions for understanding market opportunities as they map across the different quadrants and highlight how the framework as a whole can be used as an organizing framework for the study of sustainable entrepreneurship and market creation and evolution." (Refer to Figure 10)

*Figure 10. Market formation uncertainty and entrepreneurial opportunities and challenges*

*(**Source:**Lee et al. 2022; p. 257)*

Finally, McCollum (2023) has put forward a critical evaluation of the emerging concept of Green New Deal (GND) to foster Sustainable Development (SD) and avoid the 'pitfalls' of capitalism simultaneously. He has raised a warning that although degrowth would impede the capitalist producers to accumulate wealth disproportionately, however, capitalism will not cease to function. To quote McCollum (2023, p. 85): "The GND is exciting, beyond a doubt. However, a poorly conceived GND could threaten the entire enterprise and expend an incredible amount of political capital that may be irrecoverable."

Thus, to sum up, the final goal of productive green growth and SD needs a long and hard way to achieve and requires a concerted effort from all quarters.

## Conceptualization of IsoEnvironmental Pressure Curve

The formulation of IsoEnvironmental Pressure (IEP) curve model is based on the research work of Victor and Sers (2019) and its underpinnings. The IEP curve may be defined as a *locus* of points each representing a combination of Gross Domestic Product (GDP) and Environmental Intensity (EI) that would yield a *constant* Environmental Pressure (EP) for the economy.

**Note:** Environmental Intensity (EI) is defined as the ratio of Greenhouse Gas (GHG) emissions to GDP. Formally, EI = GHG / GDP.

Thus, the equation of the IsoEnvironmental Pressure (IEP) curve in Cobb-Douglas functional form would be:

$$EP = AY^{\alpha}EI^{\beta} = \overline{EP}(Fixed) \quad (A, \alpha, \beta > 0) \tag{7}$$

Let the Environmental Cost (EC) equation be as follows:

$$EC = P_Y Y + P_{EI} EI \tag{8}$$

where

$P_Y$= Price of output (Y),
$P_{EI}$ = Price of Environmental Intensity (EI), i.e., the price paid by the economy for production of different GHGs, and
$Y$= GDP.

Now the objective of the society is to *minimize* the Environmental Cost (EC) subject to the Environmental Pressure (EP) constraint. Hence the required Lagrangian equation would be as follows (Henderson and Quandt, 1980):

$$\mathbb{Z} = P_Y Y + P_{EI} EI + \lambda[E\overline{P} - A Y^{\alpha} EI^{\beta}] \quad (\lambda \geq 0) \tag{9}$$

The required First order conditions are:

$$\frac{\partial \mathbb{Z}}{\partial Y} = P_Y - A\lambda\alpha Y^{\alpha-1} EI^{\beta} = 0 \tag{10}$$

$$\frac{\partial \mathbb{Z}}{\partial EI} = P_{EI} - A\lambda\beta Y^{\alpha} EI^{\beta-1} = 0 \tag{11}$$

$$\frac{\partial \mathbb{Z}}{\partial \lambda} = E\overline{P} - A Y^{\alpha} EI^{\beta} = 0 \tag{12}$$

By using equations: (10) and (11), we have:

$$\frac{EI}{Y} = \frac{P_Y}{P_{EI}} \Rightarrow P_Y Y = P_{EI} EI$$

Finally, by the help of equation: (12), the *equilibrium* values of Y and EI are derived as follows:

$$E\overline{P} = A Y^{\alpha} \left(\frac{P_Y Y}{P_{EI}}\right)^{\beta} = A\,(P_Y/P_{EI})^{\beta}\, Y^{\alpha+\beta}$$

$\Rightarrow Y^{*}$= Equilibrium GDP = $\left(\frac{E\overline{P}}{\kappa_1}\right)^{\frac{1}{\alpha+\beta}}$, and
$EI^{*}$= Equilibrium Environmental Intensity = $\left(\frac{E\overline{P}}{\kappa_2}\right)^{\frac{1}{\alpha+\beta}}$
where $\kappa_1 = A\left(\frac{P_Y}{P_{EI}}\right)^{\beta}$, and $\kappa_2 = A\left(\frac{P_{EI}}{P_Y}\right)^{\alpha}$ are constants.
Finally, by plugging the values of Y* and EI* in equation: (7), we get:

$$E\overline{P} = AY^{*\alpha}EI^{*\beta} = A\left(\frac{591}{K_1}\right)^{\frac{\alpha}{\alpha+\beta}}\left(\frac{591}{K_2}\right)^{\frac{\beta}{\alpha+\beta}} = 591$$
$$\Rightarrow \left(\frac{P_Y}{P_{EI}}\right)^{\frac{\alpha\beta}{\alpha+\beta}}\left(\frac{P_{EI}}{P_Y}\right)^{\frac{\alpha\beta}{\alpha+\beta}} = A \Rightarrow A = 1 \tag{13}$$

Hence the equation of the IEP curve would be:

$$\left(\frac{P_Y}{P_{EI}}\right)^{\beta}\left(\frac{P_{EI}}{P_Y}\right)^{\alpha} = 1 \Rightarrow \left(\frac{P_{EI}}{P_Y}\right)^{\alpha-\beta} = 1 \tag{14}$$

[Since $E\overline{P} = 591MT$(Refer to Figure 4, and Victor and Sers 2019; p. 33)]

The essential condition for satisfaction of equation: (14) requires $\alpha=\beta$ or in other words, the *equality* of the Environmental Intensity (EI) and Income (Y) elasticities of GIGGS.

## METHODOLOGY

The methodology section may be broadly divided into *three* parts as follows:

a) The *first* part consists of estimation of the *missing* observations for the 4 variables, i.e., Production-based Carbon Dioxide ($CO_2$) Productivity (PCDO), Non-energy Material Productivity (NEMP), Mean Population Exposure to $PM_{2.5}$ (MPEPM), and Environmentally adjusted Multifactor Productivity Growth (EAMFP) respectively by using Least Squares method (Das, 2008) for the 5 sample countries to make the time series study of 10 years (2012 – 2021) complete and exhaustive (Refer to Tables 3 – 7);

*Table 3. Estimation of missing observations of Production-based Carbon Dioxide ($CO_2$) Productivity (PCDO), Non-energy Material Productivity (NEMP), Mean Population Exposure to $PM_{2.5}$ (MPEPM), and Environmentally adjusted Multifactor Productivity Growth (EAMFP) respectively (**Country:** Denmark)*

| Year | PCDO (y) | x | x * y | x * x |
|---|---|---|---|---|
| 1995 | 2.87 | -31 | -88.908 | 961 |
| 2000 | 3.62 | -21 | -76.024 | 441 |
| 2005 | 3.68 | -11 | -40.509 | 121 |
| 2010 | 3.69 | -1 | -3.6866 | 1 |
| 2015 | 4.98 | 9 | 44.8421 | 81 |
| 2016 | 5.14 | 11 | 56.5314 | 121 |
| 2017 | 5.30 | 13 | 68.9203 | 169 |
| 2018 | 5.28 | 15 | 79.2582 | 225 |
| | **34.56** | **16** | **40.4246** | **2120** |

**x = 2 * (Year − 2010.5)**

**PCDO (y) = 4.424 + 0.052 (x + 0.5)**

PCDO for the year 2012 = 4.61
PCDO for the year 2013 = 4.71
PCDO for the year 2014 = 4.81
PCDO for the year 2019 = 5.40
PCDO for the year 2020 = 5.41
PCDO for the year 2021 = 5.52

| Year | NEMP (y) | x | x * y | x * x |
|---|---|---|---|---|
| 1995 | 2.07 | -41 | -84.787 | 1681 |
| 2000 | 2.22 | -31 | -68.904 | 961 |
| 2005 | 2.14 | -21 | -44.887 | 441 |
| 2010 | 2.92 | -11 | -32.068 | 121 |
| 2015 | 2.66 | -1 | -2.6556 | 1 |
| 2016 | 2.62 | 1 | 2.61658 | 1 |
| 2017 | 2.61 | 3 | 7.81561 | 9 |
| 2018 | 2.65 | 5 | 14.2541 | 25 |
| 2019 | 2.63 | 7 | 18.3815 | 49 |
| 2020 | 2.59 | 9 | 23.3082 | 81 |
| | **25.09** | **80** | **167.93** | **3370** |

**x = 2 * (Year − 2015.5)**

**NEMP (y) = 2.605 + 0.012 (x + 0.5)**

NEMP for the year 2012 = 2.53
NEMP for the year 2013 = 2.57
NEMP for the year 2014 = 2.6
NEMP for the year 2021 = 2.74

| Year | MEMPM (y) | x | x * y | x * x |
|---|---|---|---|---|
| 1990 | 16.07 | -41 | -658.68 | 1681 |
| 1995 | 14.34 | -31 | -444.51 | 961 |
| 2000 | 14.56 | -21 | -305.71 | 441 |
| 2005 | 13.08 | -11 | -143.92 | 121 |
| 2010 | 13.35 | -1 | -13.351 | 1 |
| 2015 | 10.18 | 9 | 91.661 | 81 |
| 2016 | 9.30 | 11 | 102.323 | 121 |
| 2017 | 10.29 | 13 | 133.746 | 169 |
| 2018 | 9.87 | 15 | 148.091 | 225 |
| 2019 | 9.78 | 17 | 166.344 | 289 |
| | **120.83** | **40** | **924** | **4090** |

**x = 2 * (Year − 2010.5)**

**MEMPM (y) = 11.635 − 0.112 (x + 0.5)**

MEMPM for the year 2012 = 11.24
MEMPM for the year 2013 = 11
MEMPM for the year 2014 = 10.8
MEMPM for the year 2020 = 9.45
MEMPM for the year 2021 = 9.23

| Year | EAMFP (y) | x | x * y | x * x |
|---|---|---|---|---|
| 1995 | 2.01 | -11 | -22.128 | 121 |
| 2000 | 2.61 | -1 | -2.6075 | 1 |
| 2005 | 2.11 | 9 | 19.0265 | 81 |
| 2010 | 2.63 | 19 | 49.9505 | 361 |
| | **9.36** | **16** | **44.241** | **564** |

**x = 2 * (Year − 2000.5)**

**EAMFP (y) = 2.284 + 0.014 (x + 0.5)**

EAMFP for the year 2012 = 2.61
EAMFP for the year 2013 = 2.64
EAMFP for the year 2014 = 2.67
EAMFP for the year 2015 = 2.7
EAMFP for the year 2016 = 2.72
EAMFP for the year 2017 = 2.75
EAMFP for the year 2018 = 2.78
EAMFP for the year 2019 = 2.8
EAMFP for the year 2020 = 2.84
EAMFP for the year 2021 = 2.87

*Table 4. Estimation of missing observations of Production-based Carbon Dioxide ($CO_2$) Productivity (PCDO), Non-energy Material Productivity (NEMP), Mean Population Exposure to $PM_{2.5}$ (MPEPM), and Environmentally adjusted Multifactor Productivity Growth (EAMFP) respectively (**Country:** Finland)*

| Year | PCDO (y) | x | x * y | x * x |
|---|---|---|---|---|
| 1995 | 2.37 | -31 | -73.339 | 961 |
| 2000 | 3.13 | -21 | -65.743 | 441 |
| 2005 | 3.16 | -11 | -34.753 | 121 |
| 2010 | 3.29 | -1 | -3.2885 | 1 |
| 2015 | 4.19 | 9 | 37.695 | 81 |
| 2016 | 4.09 | 11 | 45.023 | 121 |
| 2017 | 4.39 | 13 | 57.052 | 169 |
| 2018 | 4.25 | 15 | 63.74 | 225 |
| | **28.86** | **-16** | **26.386** | **2120** |

**x = 2 * (Year - 2010.5)**

**PCDO (y) = 3.6875 + 0.04 (x + 0.5)**

PCDO for the year 2012 = 3.83
PCDO for the year 2013 = 3.91
PCDO for the year 2014 = 4
PCDO for the year 2019 = 4.39
PCDO for the year 2020 = 4.47
PCDO for the year 2021 = 4.55

| Year | NEMP (y) | x | x * y | x * x |
|---|---|---|---|---|
| 2000 | 1.30 | -16 | -20.85 | 256 |
| 2005 | 1.36 | -11 | -14.936 | 121 |
| 2010 | 1.48 | -6 | -8.9014 | 36 |
| 2015 | 1.58 | -1 | -1.5801 | 1 |
| 2016 | 1.55 | 0 | 0 | 0 |
| 2017 | 1.51 | 1 | 1.51444 | 1 |
| 2018 | 1.49 | 2 | 2.97493 | 4 |
| 2019 | 1.62 | 3 | 4.8674 | 9 |
| 2020 | 1.48 | 4 | 5.92016 | 16 |
| | **13.38** | **-24** | **-30.99** | **444** |

**x = (Year - 2016)**

**NEMP (y) = 1.519 + 0.012x**

NEMP for the year 2012 = 1.47
NEMP for the year 2013 = 1.48
NEMP for the year 2014 = 1.5
NEMP for the year 2021 = 1.6

| Year | MEMPM (y) | x | x * y | x * x |
|---|---|---|---|---|
| 1990 | 8.81 | -41 | -361.04 | 1681 |
| 1995 | 8.08 | -31 | -250.44 | 961 |
| 2000 | 7.65 | -21 | -160.56 | 441 |
| 2005 | 7.21 | -11 | -79.264 | 121 |
| 2010 | 7.35 | -1 | -7.3527 | 1 |
| 2015 | 5.72 | 9 | 51.4726 | 81 |
| 2016 | 5.68 | 11 | 62.4792 | 121 |
| 2017 | 5.33 | 13 | 69.3472 | 169 |
| 2018 | 5.68 | 15 | 85.1253 | 225 |
| 2019 | 5.64 | 17 | 95.8509 | 289 |
| | **67.14** | **-40** | **-494.39** | **4090** |

**x = 2 * (Year - 2010.5)**

**MEMPM (y) = 4.314 - 0.06(x + 0.5)**

MEMPM for the year 2012 = 4.10
MEMPM for the year 2013 = 3.98
MEMPM for the year 2014 = 3.87
MEMPM for the year 2020 = 3.14
MEMPM for the year 2021 = 3.02

| Year | EAMFP (y) | x | x * y | x * x |
|---|---|---|---|---|
| 1995 | 3.24 | -11 | -35.672 | 121 |
| 2000 | 4.60 | -1 | -4.6041 | 1 |
| 2005 | 2.92 | 9 | 26.295 | 81 |
| 2010 | 1.98 | 19 | 37.621 | 361 |
| | **12.75** | **16** | **23.64** | **564** |

**x = 2 * (Year - 2000.5)**

**EAMFP (y) = 3.41 - 0.055 (x + 0.5)**

EAMFP for the year 2012 = 2.12
EAMFP for the year 2013 = 2
EAMFP for the year 2014 = 1.9
EAMFP for the year 2015 = 1.79
EAMFP for the year 2016 = 1.68
EAMFP for the year 2017 = 1.57
EAMFP for the year 2018 = 1.46
EAMFP for the year 2019 = 1.35
EAMFP for the year 2020 = 1.24
EAMFP for the year 2021 = 1.13

*Table 5. Estimation of missing observations of Production-based Carbon Dioxide ($CO_2$) Productivity (PCDO), Non-energy Material Productivity (NEMP), Mean Population Exposure to $PM_{2.5}$ (MPEPM), and Environmentally adjusted Multifactor Productivity Growth (EAMFP) respectively (***Country:** *Sweden)*

| Year | PCDO (y) | x | x * y | x * x |
|---|---|---|---|---|
| 1995 | 3.57 | -31 | -110.68 | 961 |
| 2000 | 4.21 | -21 | -88.315 | 441 |
| 2005 | 4.71 | -11 | -51.862 | 121 |
| 2010 | 5.13 | -1 | -5.127 | 1 |
| 2015 | 6.66 | 9 | 59.9465 | 81 |
| 2016 | 6.75 | 11 | 74.273 | 121 |
| 2017 | 6.82 | 13 | 88.6288 | 169 |
| 2018 | 7.06 | 15 | 105.96 | 225 |
| | **44.91** | **-16** | **72.8218** | **2120** |

**x = 2 * (Year - 2010.5)**

**PCDO (y) = 5.773 + 0.08 (x + 0.5)**

PCDO for the year 2012 = 6.05
PCDO for the year 2013 = 6.21
PCDO for the year 2014 = 6.38
PCDO for the year 2019 = 7.2
PCDO for the year 2020 = 7.33
PCDO for the year 2021 = 7.5

| Year | NEMP (y) | x | x * y | x * x |
|---|---|---|---|---|
| 2000 | 2.20 | -16 | -35.222 | 256 |
| 2005 | 2.19 | -11 | -24.091 | 121 |
| 2010 | 2.33 | -6 | -13.976 | 36 |
| 2015 | 2.35 | -1 | -2.3492 | 1 |
| 2016 | 2.36 | 0 | 0 | 0 |
| 2017 | 2.27 | 1 | 2.27052 | 1 |
| 2018 | 2.26 | 2 | 4.51278 | 4 |
| 2019 | 2.17 | 3 | 6.50295 | 9 |
| 2020 | 2.18 | 4 | 8.737 | 16 |
| | **20.30** | **-24** | **-53.614** | **444** |

**x = (Year - 2016)**

**NEMP (y) = 3.01 + 0.283x**

NEMP for the year 2012 = 1.9
NEMP for the year 2013 = 2.16
NEMP for the year 2014 = 2.44
NEMP for the year 2021 = 4.42

| Year | MEMPM (y) | x | x * y | x * x |
|---|---|---|---|---|
| 1990 | 9.54 | -41 | -391.25 | 1681 |
| 1995 | 8.60 | -31 | -266.61 | 961 |
| 2000 | 8.56 | -21 | -179.84 | 441 |
| 2005 | 7.39 | -11 | -81.333 | 121 |
| 2010 | 7.56 | -1 | -7.5584 | 1 |
| 2015 | 5.97 | 9 | 53.6887 | 81 |
| 2016 | 5.53 | 11 | 60.8414 | 121 |
| 2017 | 5.78 | 13 | 75.1537 | 169 |
| 2018 | 5.77 | 15 | 86.5106 | 225 |
| 2019 | 5.72 | 17 | 97.263 | 289 |
| | **70.43** | **40** | **-553.13** | **4090** |

**x = 2 * (Year - 2010.5)**

**MEMPM (y) = 6.763 - 0.07(x + 0.5)**

MEMPM for the year 2012 = 6.52
MEMPM for the year 2013 = 6.4
MEMPM for the year 2014 = 6.24
MEMPM for the year 2020 = 5.4
MEMPM for the year 2021 = 5.26

| Year | EAMFP (y) | x | x * y | x * x |
|---|---|---|---|---|
| 1995 | 2.43 | -11 | -26.738 | 121 |
| 2000 | 3.29 | -1 | -3.2877 | 1 |
| 2005 | 2.39 | 9 | 21.4836 | 81 |
| 2010 | 2.91 | 19 | 55.2474 | 361 |
| | **11.01** | **16** | **46.7054** | **564** |

**x = 2 * (Year - 2000.5)**

**EAMFP (y) = 2.83 - 0.005 (x + 0.5)**

EAMFP for the year 2012 = 2.71
EAMFP for the year 2013 = 2.7
EAMFP for the year 2014 = 2.69
EAMFP for the year 2015 = 2.68
EAMFP for the year 2016 = 2.67
EAMFP for the year 2017 = 2.66
EAMFP for the year 2018 = 2.65
EAMFP for the year 2019 = 2.64
EAMFP for the year 2020 = 2.63
EAMFP for the year 2021 = 2.62

*Table 6. Estimation of missing observations of Production-based Carbon Dioxide ($CO_2$) Productivity (PCDO), Non-energy Material Productivity (NEMP), Mean Population Exposure to $PM_{2.5}$ (MPEPM), and Environmentally adjusted Multifactor Productivity Growth (EAMFP) respectively (**Country:** Brazil)*

| Year | PCDO (y) | x | x * y | x * x |
|---|---|---|---|---|
| 1995 | 7.04 | -31 | -218.36 | 961 |
| 2000 | 6.24 | -21 | -131.07 | 441 |
| 2005 | 7.21 | -11 | -79.337 | 121 |
| 2010 | 6.14 | -1 | -6.1365 | 1 |
| 2015 | 6.18 | 9 | 55.6455 | 81 |
| 2016 | 6.59 | 11 | 72.4831 | 121 |
| 2017 | 6.38 | 13 | 82.9924 | 169 |
| 2018 | 6.68 | 15 | 100.138 | 225 |
| | **52.47** | **-16** | **-123.64** | **2120** |

**x = 2 * (Year - 2010.5)**

**PCDO (y) = 6.54 - 0.009 (x + 0.5)**

PCDO for the year 2012 = 6.51
PCDO for the year 2013 = 6.49
PCDO for the year 2014 = 6.47
PCDO for the year 2019 = 6.38
PCDO for the year 2020 = 6.36
PCDO for the year 2021 = 6.35

| Year | NEMP (y) | x | x * y | x * x |
|---|---|---|---|---|
| 1995 | 0.87 | -41 | -35.584 | 1681 |
| 2000 | 0.83 | -31 | -25.832 | 961 |
| 2005 | 0.86 | -21 | -18.08 | 441 |
| 2010 | 0.88 | -11 | -9.6494 | 121 |
| 2015 | 0.82 | -1 | -0.8172 | 1 |
| 2016 | 0.74 | 1 | 0.74262 | 1 |
| 2017 | 0.73 | 3 | 2.17739 | 9 |
| 2018 | 0.72 | 5 | 3.59324 | 25 |
| 2019 | 0.72 | 7 | 5.06115 | 49 |
| 2020 | 0.70 | 9 | 6.31389 | 81 |
| | **7.87** | **-80** | **-72.075** | **3370** |

**x = 2 * (Year - 2015.5)**

**NEMP (y) = 0.763 - 0.003 (x + 0.5)**

NEMP for the year 2012 = 0.78
NEMP for the year 2013 = 0.78
NEMP for the year 2014 = 0.77
NEMP for the year 2021 = 0.73

| Year | MEMPM (y) | x | x * y | x * x |
|---|---|---|---|---|
| 1990 | 14.81 | -41 | -607.03 | 1681 |
| 1995 | 14.66 | -31 | -454.32 | 961 |
| 2000 | 14.57 | -21 | -306.03 | 441 |
| 2005 | 14.58 | -11 | -160.39 | 121 |
| 2010 | 14.06 | -1 | -14.057 | 1 |
| 2015 | 11.69 | 9 | 105.19 | 81 |
| 2016 | 11.42 | 11 | 125.621 | 121 |
| 2017 | 11.67 | 13 | 151.695 | 169 |
| 2018 | 11.63 | 15 | 174.51 | 225 |
| 2019 | 11.67 | 17 | 198.314 | 289 |
| | **130.75** | **-40** | **-786.51** | **4090** |

**x = 2 * (Year - 2010.5)**

**MEMPM (y) = 12.807 - 0.067 (x + 0.5)**

MEMPM for the year 2012 = 12.57
MEMPM for the year 2013 = 12.44
MEMPM for the year 2014 = 12.3
MEMPM for the year 2020 = 11.5
MEMPM for the year 2021 = 11.37

| Year | EAMFP (y) | x | x * y | x * x |
|---|---|---|---|---|
| 1995 | 3.17 | -11 | -34.899 | 121 |
| 2000 | 2.73 | -1 | -2.7287 | 1 |
| 2005 | 1.35 | 9 | 12.159 | 81 |
| 2010 | 4.57 | 19 | 86.7401 | 361 |
| | **11.82** | **16** | **61.2714** | **564** |

**x = 2 * (Year - 2000.5)**

**EAMFP (y) = 2.843 + 0.028 (x + 0.5)**

EAMFP for the year 2012 = 3.5
EAMFP for the year 2013 = 3.57
EAMFP for the year 2014 = 3.61
EAMFP for the year 2015 = 3.67
EAMFP for the year 2016 = 3.73
EAMFP for the year 2017 = 3.78
EAMFP for the year 2018 = 3.84
EAMFP for the year 2019 = 3.9
EAMFP for the year 2020 = 3.95
EAMFP for the year 2021 = 4

*Table 7. Estimation of missing observations of Production-based Carbon Dioxide ($CO_2$) Productivity (PCDO), Non-energy Material Productivity (NEMP), Mean Population Exposure to $PM_{2.5}$ (MPEPM), and Environmentally adjusted Multifactor Productivity Growth (EAMFP) respectively (***Country:*** *South Korea)*

| Year | PCDO (y) | x | x * y | x * x |
|---|---|---|---|---|
| 1995 | 1.98 | -31 | -61.46 | 961 |
| 2000 | 2.34 | -21 | -49.118 | 441 |
| 2005 | 2.57 | -11 | -28.226 | 121 |
| 2010 | 2.92 | -1 | -2.9202 | 1 |
| 2015 | 3.49 | 9 | 31.45 | 81 |
| 2016 | 3.55 | 11 | 39.1033 | 121 |
| 2017 | 3.46 | 13 | 44.9845 | 169 |
| 2018 | 3.56 | 15 | 53.3878 | 225 |
| | **23.88** | **-16** | **27.2017** | **2120** |

**x = 2 * (Year - 2010.5)**

**PCDO (y) = 3.057 + 0.036 (x + 0.5)**

PCDO for the year 2012 = 3.18
PCDO for the year 2013 = 3.25
PCDO for the year 2014 = 3.33
PCDO for the year 2019 = 3.69
PCDO for the year 2020 = 3.76
PCDO for the year 2021 = 3.83

| Year | NEMP (y) | x | x * y | x * x |
|---|---|---|---|---|
| 1990 | 1.35 | -41 | -55.542 | 1681 |
| 1995 | 1.37 | -31 | -42.613 | 961 |
| 2000 | 1.90 | -21 | -39.804 | 441 |
| 2005 | 2.42 | -11 | -26.665 | 121 |
| 2010 | 3.09 | -1 | -3.0891 | 1 |
| 2015 | 3.12 | 9 | 28.0831 | 81 |
| 2016 | 3.06 | 11 | 33.614 | 121 |
| 2017 | 3.07 | 13 | 39.9264 | 169 |
| 2018 | 3.19 | 15 | 47.8882 | 225 |
| 2019 | 3.25 | 17 | 55.3183 | 289 |
| | **25.83** | **-40** | **37.1166** | **4090** |

**x = 2 * (Year - 2010.5)**

**NEMP (y) = 2.727 + 0.036 (x + 0.5)**

NEMP for the year 2012 = 2.85
NEMP for the year 2013 = 2.92
NEMP for the year 2014 = 3
NEMP for the year 2020 = 3.43
NEMP for the year 2021 = 3.5

| Year | MEMPM (y) | x | x * y | x * x |
|---|---|---|---|---|
| 1990 | 25.15 | -41 | -1031 | 1681 |
| 1995 | 24.39 | -31 | -756.21 | 961 |
| 2000 | 24.25 | -21 | -509.28 | 441 |
| 2005 | 23.57 | -11 | -259.32 | 121 |
| 2010 | 22.90 | -1 | -22.903 | 1 |
| 2015 | 27.00 | 9 | 243.038 | 81 |
| 2016 | 27.83 | 11 | 306.105 | 121 |
| 2017 | 26.90 | 13 | 349.714 | 169 |
| 2018 | 27.45 | 15 | 411.715 | 225 |
| 2019 | 27.45 | 17 | 466.607 | 289 |
| | **256.90** | **-40** | **-801.49** | **4090** |

**x = 2 * (Year - 2010.5)**

**MEMPM (y) = 25.922 + 0.058 (x + 0.5)**

MEMPM for the year 2012 = 26.12
MEMPM for the year 2013 = 26.24
MEMPM for the year 2014 = 26.36
MEMPM for the year 2020 = 27
MEMPM for the year 2021 = 27.17

| Year | EAMFP (y) | x | x * y | x * x |
|---|---|---|---|---|
| 1995 | 3.84 | -11 | -42.191 | 121 |
| 2000 | 2.61 | -1 | -2.6088 | 1 |
| 2005 | 3.24 | 9 | 29.1445 | 81 |
| 2010 | 3.60 | 19 | 68.3639 | 361 |
| | **13.28** | **16** | **52.7087** | **564** |

**x = 2 * (Year - 2000.5)**

**EAMFP (y) = 3.323 - 0.0008 (x + 0.5)**

EAMFP for the year 2012 = 3.30
EAMFP for the year 2013 = 3.30
EAMFP for the year 2014 = 3.30
EAMFP for the year 2015 = 3.29
EAMFP for the year 2016 = 3.29
EAMFP for the year 2017 = 3.29
EAMFP for the year 2018 = 3.29
EAMFP for the year 2019 = 3.29
EAMFP for the year 2020 = 3.29
EAMFP for the year 2021 = 3.29

b) The *second* part involves standardization of the Comprehensive Green Growth Index (CGGI) function in the Classic Linear Regression Model (CLRM) form as follows (Gujarati, 2003):

$$CGGI = EAMFP^{\alpha} PCDO^{-\beta} NEMP^{-\gamma} MPEPM^{-\delta} \tag{1}$$

where α, β, γ, and δ are the coefficients of EAMFP, PCDO, NEMP, and MPEPM respectively (α, β, γ, δ ≠ 0)

By taking log of both sides of equation: (1), we have:

$$CGGI^{*} = \alpha EAMFP^{*} - \beta PCDO^{*} - \gamma NEMP^{*} - \delta MPEPM^{*} + \varepsilon \tag{2}$$

where $CGGI^*$, $EAMFP^*$, $PCDO^*$, $NEMP^*$, $MEPM^*$ are the logarithmic values of CGGI, EAMFP, PCDO, NEMP, and MPEPM respectively; ε = Residual.

By using equation: (2), the logarithmic values of CGGI are estimated for 5 sample countries for the time period of 10 years (2012 – 2021). The derived values of CGGI* were then converted to CGGI values by applying antilogarithm. Formally, $CGGI = anti\log(VGGI^*)$.

The estimated values of $CGGI^{*}, EAMFP^{*}, PCDO^{*}, NEMP^{*}, MEPM^{*}$ are denoted as CGGI1, EAMFP1, PCDO1, NEMP1, and MPEPM1 while the antilogarithmic values are simply denoted as CGGI, EAMFP, PCDO, NEMP, and MEPM respectively on the Excel sheets (Refer to Tables 8 – 12); and

c) The *third* and final part comprises of the computation of the Grand Index of Green Growth and Sustainability (GIGGS) for 5 sample countries during the time period of 10 years (2012 – 2021). GIGGS is computed as the *Geometric Mean (GM)* of Comprehensive Green Growth Index (CGGI) and The Global Sustainable Competitiveness Index ® (GSCI) respectively. Formally, $GIGGS = \sqrt{CGGI \times GSCI}$

Refer to Tables 13 – 17

*Table 8. Estimation of Comprehensive Green Growth Index (CGGI) (2012 – 2021) [***Country:** *Denmark]*

| Year | PCDO | NEMP | MPEPM | EAMFP | PCDO1 | NEMP1 | MPEPM1 | EAMFP1 | CGGI1 | CGGI |
|---|---|---|---|---|---|---|---|---|---|---|
| 2012 | 4.61 | 2.53 | 11.24 | 2.61 | 1.52823 | 0.92822 | 2.419479 | 0.95935 | -3.9166 | 0.0199 |
| 2013 | 4.71 | 2.57 | 11 | 2.64 | 1.54969 | 0.94391 | 2.397895 | 0.970779 | -3.9207 | 0.0198 |
| 2014 | 4.81 | 2.6 | 10.8 | 2.67 | 1.5707 | 0.95551 | 2.379546 | 0.982078 | -3.9237 | 0.01977 |
| 2015 | 4.98 | 2.66 | 10.18 | 2.7 | 1.60592 | 0.97665 | 2.320873 | 0.993252 | -3.9102 | 0.02004 |
| 2016 | 5.14 | 2.62 | 9.30 | 2.72 | 1.6369 | 0.96187 | 2.230235 | 1.000632 | -3.8284 | 0.02174 |
| 2017 | 5.30 | 2.61 | 10.29 | 2.75 | 1.668 | 0.95751 | 2.330991 | 1.011601 | -3.9449 | 0.01935 |
| 2018 | 5.28 | 2.65 | 9.87 | 2.78 | 1.66466 | 0.9748 | 2.289779 | 1.022451 | -3.9068 | 0.02011 |
| 2019 | 5.30 | 2.63 | 9.78 | 2.8 | 1.66771 | 0.96544 | 2.280843 | 1.029619 | -3.8844 | 0.02056 |
| 2020 | 5.41 | 2.59 | 9.45 | 2.84 | 1.68825 | 0.95158 | 2.246015 | 1.043804 | -3.842 | 0.02145 |
| 2021 | 5.52 | 2.74 | 9.23 | 2.87 | 1.70838 | 1.00796 | 2.222459 | 1.054312 | -3.8845 | 0.02056 |

*Table 9. Estimation of Comprehensive Green Growth Index (CGGI) (2012 – 2021) [***Country:** *Finland]*

| Year | PCDO | NEMP | MPEPM | EAMFP | PCDO1 | NEMP1 | MPEPM1 | EAMFP1 | CGGI1 | CGGI |
|---|---|---|---|---|---|---|---|---|---|---|
| 2012 | 3.83 | 1.47 | 4.1 | 2.12 | 1.34286 | 0.38526 | 1.410987 | 0.75142 | -2.3877 | 0.09184 |
| 2013 | 3.91 | 1.48 | 3.98 | 2 | 1.36354 | 0.39204 | 1.381282 | 0.69315 | -2.4437 | 0.08684 |
| 2014 | 4 | 1.5 | 3.87 | 1.9 | 1.38629 | 0.40547 | 1.353255 | 0.64185 | -2.5032 | 0.08183 |
| 2015 | 4.19 | 1.58 | 5.72 | 1.79 | 1.4323 | 0.45751 | 1.743825 | 0.58222 | -3.0514 | 0.04729 |
| 2016 | 4.09 | 1.55 | 5.68 | 1.68 | 1.40927 | 0.44136 | 1.736939 | 0.51879 | -3.0688 | 0.04648 |
| 2017 | 4.39 | 1.51 | 5.33 | 1.57 | 1.47902 | 0.41505 | 1.674176 | 0.45108 | -3.1172 | 0.04428 |
| 2018 | 4.25 | 1.49 | 5.68 | 1.46 | 1.44677 | 0.39707 | 1.736074 | 0.37844 | -3.2015 | 0.0407 |
| 2019 | 4.39 | 1.62 | 5.64 | 1.35 | 1.47933 | 0.48395 | 1.729581 | 0.3001 | -3.3928 | 0.03362 |
| 2020 | 4.47 | 1.48 | 3.14 | 1.24 | 1.49739 | 0.39207 | 1.144223 | 0.21511 | -2.8186 | 0.05969 |
| 2021 | 4.55 | 1.60 | 3.02 | 1.13 | 1.51513 | 0.47 | 1.105257 | 0.12222 | -2.9682 | 0.0514 |

*Table 10. Estimation of Comprehensive Green Growth Index (CGGI) (2012 – 2021) [***Country:** *Sweden]*

| Year | PCDO | NEMP | MPEPM | EAMFP | PCDO1 | NEMP1 | MPEPM1 | EAMFP1 | CGGI1 | CGGI |
|---|---|---|---|---|---|---|---|---|---|---|
| 2012 | 6.05 | 1.9 | 6.52 | 2.71 | 1.80006 | 0.64185 | 1.874874 | 0.996949 | -3.3198 | 0.03616 |
| 2013 | 6.21 | 2.16 | 6.4 | 2.7 | 1.82616 | 0.77011 | 1.856298 | 0.993252 | -3.4593 | 0.03145 |
| 2014 | 6.38 | 2.44 | 6.24 | 2.69 | 1.85317 | 0.892 | 1.83098 | 0.989541 | -3.5866 | 0.02769 |
| 2015 | 6.66 | 2.35 | 5.97 | 2.68 | 1.89623 | 0.85406 | 1.785978 | 0.985817 | -3.5504 | 0.02871 |
| 2016 | 6.75 | 2.36 | 5.53 | 2.67 | 1.90985 | 0.85708 | 1.710376 | 0.982078 | -3.4952 | 0.03034 |
| 2017 | 6.82 | 2.27 | 5.78 | 2.66 | 1.91951 | 0.82001 | 1.754585 | 0.978326 | -3.5158 | 0.02972 |
| 2018 | 7.06 | 2.26 | 5.77 | 2.65 | 1.95502 | 0.81377 | 1.752216 | 0.97456 | -3.5464 | 0.02883 |
| 2019 | 7.20 | 2.17 | 5.72 | 2.64 | 1.97408 | 0.77364 | 1.744205 | 0.970779 | -3.5212 | 0.02957 |
| 2020 | 7.33 | 2.18 | 5.40 | 2.63 | 1.99198 | 0.78127 | 1.686399 | 0.966984 | -3.4927 | 0.03042 |
| 2021 | 7.50 | 4.42 | 5.26 | 2.62 | 2.0149 | 1.48614 | 1.660131 | 0.963174 | -4.198 | 0.01503 |

*Table 11. Estimation of Comprehensive Green Growth Index (CGGI) (2012 – 2021) [***Country:** *Brazil]*

| Year | PCDO | NEMP | MPEPM | EAMFP | PCDO1 | NEMP1 | MPEPM1 | EAMFP1 | CGGI1 | CGGI |
|---|---|---|---|---|---|---|---|---|---|---|
| 2012 | 6.51 | 0.78 | 12.57 | 3.5 | 1.87334 | -0.2485 | 2.531313 | 1.252763 | -2.9034 | 0.05483 |
| 2013 | 6.49 | 0.78 | 12.44 | 3.57 | 1.87026 | -0.2485 | 2.520917 | 1.272566 | -2.8702 | 0.05669 |
| 2014 | 6.47 | 0.77 | 12.3 | 3.61 | 1.86718 | -0.2614 | 2.509599 | 1.283708 | -2.8317 | 0.05891 |
| 2015 | 6.18 | 0.82 | 11.69 | 3.67 | 1.82178 | -0.2018 | 2.458542 | 1.300192 | -2.7783 | 0.06215 |
| 2016 | 6.59 | 0.74 | 11.42 | 3.73 | 1.88546 | -0.2976 | 2.435372 | 1.316408 | -2.7069 | 0.06675 |
| 2017 | 6.38 | 0.73 | 11.67 | 3.78 | 1.8538 | -0.3205 | 2.456923 | 1.329724 | -2.6605 | 0.06991 |
| 2018 | 6.68 | 0.72 | 11.63 | 3.84 | 1.8985 | -0.3304 | 2.453934 | 1.345472 | -2.6766 | 0.0688 |
| 2019 | 6.38 | 0.72 | 11.67 | 3.90 | 1.85317 | -0.3243 | 2.456637 | 1.360977 | -2.6245 | 0.07248 |
| 2020 | 6.36 | 0.70 | 11.50 | 3.95 | 1.85003 | -0.3545 | 2.442347 | 1.373716 | -2.5642 | 0.07698 |
| 2021 | 6.35 | 0.73 | 11.37 | 4.00 | 1.84845 | -0.3147 | 2.430978 | 1.386294 | -2.5784 | 0.07589 |

*Table 12. Estimation of Comprehensive Green Growth Index (CGGI) (2012 – 2021) [***Country:** *South Korea]*

| Year | PCDO | NEMP | MPEPM | EAMFP | PCDO1 | NEMP1 | MPEPM1 | EAMFP1 | CGGI1 | CGGI |
|---|---|---|---|---|---|---|---|---|---|---|
| 2012 | 3.18 | 2.85 | 26.12 | 3.3 | 1.15688 | 1.04732 | 3.262701 | 1.193922 | -4.273 | 0.01394 |
| 2013 | 3.25 | 2.92 | 26.24 | 3.3 | 1.17865 | 1.07158 | 3.267285 | 1.193922 | -4.3236 | 0.01325 |
| 2014 | 3.33 | 3 | 26.36 | 3.3 | 1.20297 | 1.09861 | 3.271848 | 1.193922 | -4.3795 | 0.01253 |
| 2015 | 3.49 | 3.12 | 27.00 | 3.29 | 1.25117 | 1.13794 | 3.295995 | 1.190888 | -4.4942 | 0.01117 |
| 2016 | 3.55 | 3.06 | 27.83 | 3.29 | 1.26831 | 1.11705 | 3.326034 | 1.190888 | -4.5205 | 0.01088 |
| 2017 | 3.46 | 3.07 | 26.90 | 3.29 | 1.24137 | 1.12209 | 3.292168 | 1.190888 | -4.4647 | 0.01151 |
| 2018 | 3.56 | 3.19 | 27.45 | 3.29 | 1.26953 | 1.16082 | 3.312282 | 1.190888 | -4.5517 | 0.01055 |
| 2019 | 3.69 | 3.25 | 27.45 | 3.29 | 1.30563 | 1.17989 | 3.312275 | 1.190888 | -4.6069 | 0.00998 |
| 2020 | 3.76 | 3.43 | 27.00 | 3.29 | 1.32442 | 1.23256 | 3.295837 | 1.190888 | -4.6619 | 0.00945 |
| 2021 | 3.83 | 3.5 | 27.17 | 3.29 | 1.34286 | 1.25276 | 3.302113 | 1.190888 | -4.7069 | 0.00903 |

*Table 13. Computation of Grand Index of Green Growth and Sustainability (GIGGS) (2012 – 2021) [***Country:** *Denmark]*

| Year | CGGI | GSCI | GIGGS |
|---|---|---|---|
| 2012 | 0.0199 | 58.8 | 1.08172 |
| 2013 | 0.0198 | 62.8 | 1.1151 |
| 2014 | 0.01977 | 51.6 | 1.00997 |
| 2015 | 0.02004 | 52.7 | 1.02758 |
| 2016 | 0.02174 | 56 | 1.1035 |
| 2017 | 0.01935 | 57.2 | 1.05214 |
| 2018 | 0.02011 | 57.2 | 1.07238 |
| 2019 | 0.02056 | 57 | 1.08257 |
| 2020 | 0.02145 | 61 | 1.14387 |
| 2021 | 0.02056 | 60.2 | 1.11248 |

*Table 14. Computation of Grand Index of Green Growth and Sustainability (GIGGS) (2012 – 2021) [**Country:** Finland]*

| Year | CGGI | GSCI | GIGGS |
|---|---|---|---|
| 2012 | 0.09184 | 57.6 | 2.30001 |
| 2013 | 0.08684 | 60.9 | 2.29966 |
| 2014 | 0.08183 | 53.6 | 2.09425 |
| 2015 | 0.04729 | 54.4 | 1.60395 |
| 2016 | 0.04648 | 56.2 | 1.61618 |
| 2017 | 0.04428 | 57.4 | 1.59431 |
| 2018 | 0.0407 | 57.4 | 1.52849 |
| 2019 | 0.03362 | 59.5 | 1.41427 |
| 2020 | 0.05969 | 60.4 | 1.89878 |
| 2021 | 0.0514 | 60.7 | 1.7663 |

*Table 15. Computation of Grand Index of Green Growth and Sustainability (GIGGS) (2012 – 2021) [**Country:** Sweden]*

| Year | CGGI | GSCI | GIGGS |
|---|---|---|---|
| 2012 | 0.03616 | 58.5 | 1.4544 |
| 2013 | 0.03145 | 61.6 | 1.3919 |
| 2014 | 0.02769 | 54.1 | 1.22399 |
| 2015 | 0.02871 | 55.5 | 1.26234 |
| 2016 | 0.03034 | 60.9 | 1.35934 |
| 2017 | 0.02972 | 60.5 | 1.34103 |
| 2018 | 0.02883 | 60.5 | 1.32062 |
| 2019 | 0.02957 | 60.6 | 1.33853 |
| 2020 | 0.03042 | 62.1 | 1.37443 |
| 2021 | 0.01503 | 61.2 | 0.95894 |

*Table 16. Computation of Grand Index of Green Growth and Sustainability (GIGGS) (2012 – 2021) [**Country:** Brazil]*

| Year | CGGI | GSCI | GIGGS |
|---|---|---|---|
| 2012 | 0.05483 | 49.5 | 1.64752 |
| 2013 | 0.05669 | 50.6 | 1.69367 |
| 2014 | 0.05891 | 48.2 | 1.68511 |
| 2015 | 0.06215 | 47.3 | 1.71449 |
| 2016 | 0.06675 | 46.9 | 1.76929 |

continued on following page

*Table 16. Continued*

| Year | CGGI | GSCI | GIGGS |
|---|---|---|---|
| 2017 | 0.06991 | 47.6 | 1.82423 |
| 2018 | 0.0688 | 47.6 | 1.80964 |
| 2019 | 0.07248 | 46.8 | 1.84169 |
| 2020 | 0.07698 | 49.1 | 1.94417 |
| 2021 | 0.07589 | 48.8 | 1.92447 |

*Table 17. Computation of Grand Index of Green Growth and Sustainability (GIGGS) (2012 – 2021) [***Country:** *South Korea]*

| Year | CGGI | GSCI | GIGGS |
|---|---|---|---|
| 2012 | 0.01394 | 47.7 | 0.81544 |
| 2013 | 0.01325 | 50.1 | 0.81482 |
| 2014 | 0.01253 | 47.6 | 0.77233 |
| 2015 | 0.01117 | 45.7 | 0.71458 |
| 2016 | 0.01088 | 46.9 | 0.71445 |
| 2017 | 0.01151 | 53.3 | 0.78317 |
| 2018 | 0.01055 | 53.3 | 0.74983 |
| 2019 | 0.00998 | 50.8 | 0.71212 |
| 2020 | 0.00945 | 51.3 | 0.6962 |
| 2021 | 0.00903 | 53.9 | 0.69777 |

## RESULTS AND FINDINGS

There are some interesting observations regarding the results and findings which are listed below:

- The regression results are summarized with reference to the econometrical results as below (Refer to Table 43). The detailed findings of different statistical tests that were performed for 5 sample countries are documented below (Refer to Table 18 – Table 42):

Model 1: TSLS, using observations 2012-2021 (T = 10)
Dependent variable: GIGGS
Instruments: const PCDO NEMP MPEPM EAMFP GSCI
HAC standard errors, bandwidth 1 (Bartlett kernel)

*Table 18. Regression results of Grand Index of Green Growth and Sustainability (GIGGS) on Production-based Carbon Dioxide ($CO_2$) Productivity (PCDO), Non-energy Material Productivity (NEMP), Mean Population Exposure to $PM_{2.5}$ (MPEPM), Environmentally adjusted Multifactor Productivity Growth (EAMFP), and The Global Sustainable Competitiveness Index ® (GSCI) respectively based on Two-Stage Least Squares (2SLS) method [Country: Denmark]*

| | Coefficient | Std. Error | t-ratio | p-value | |
|---|---|---|---|---|---|
| **const** | 1.60956 | 0.0389651 | 41.31 | <0.0001 | *** |
| **PCDO** | −0.113121 | 0.00255685 | −44.24 | <0.0001 | *** |
| **NEMP** | −0.210877 | 0.0135397 | −15.57 | <0.0001 | *** |
| **MPEPM** | −0.0540889 | 0.000373309 | −144.9 | <0.0001 | *** |
| **EAMFP** | 0.218114 | 0.0125068 | 17.44 | <0.0001 | *** |
| **GSCI** | 0.00957933 | 0.000163189 | 58.70 | <0.0001 | *** |

| | | | |
|---|---|---|---|
| **Mean dependent var** | 1.080133 | **S.D. dependent var** | 0.041384 |
| **Sum squared resid** | 0.000018 | **S.E. of regression** | 0.002140 |
| **R-squared** | 0.998812 | **Adjusted R-squared** | 0.997327 |
| **F(5, 4)** | 672.5888 | **P-value(F)** | 6.17e-06 |
| **Log-likelihood** | 51.86342 | **Akaike criterion** | −91.72684 |
| **Schwarz criterion** | −89.91133 | **Hannan-Quinn** | −93.71845 |
| **rho** | −0.423595 | **Durbin-Watson** | 2.177663 |

*Table 19. Documentation of Correlation Matrix between Grand Index of Green Growth and Sustainability (GIGGS) and Production-based Carbon Dioxide (CO2) Productivity (PCDO), Non-energy Material Productivity (NEMP), Mean Population Exposure to PM2.5 (MPEPM), Environmentally adjusted Multifactor Productivity Growth (EAMFP), and The Global Sustainable Competitiveness Index ® (GSCI) respectively [Country: Denmark]*

| Correlation | | | | | | |
|---|---|---|---|---|---|---|
| | **GIGGS** | **EAMFP** | **MPEPM** | **NEMP** | **PCDO** | **GSCI** |
| GIGGS | 1.000000 | 0.407046 | -0.423211 | -0.013644 | 0.342035 | 0.874990 |
| EAMFP | 0.407046 | 1.000000 | -0.868096 | 0.705570 | 0.972376 | 0.219582 |
| MPEPM | -0.423211 | -0.868096 | 1.000000 | -0.692405 | -0.889279 | -0.068201 |
| NEMP | -0.013644 | 0.705570 | -0.692405 | 1.000000 | 0.692707 | -0.123658 |
| PCDO | 0.342035 | 0.972376 | -0.889279 | 0.692707 | 1.000000 | 0.154688 |
| GSCI | 0.874990 | 0.219582 | -0.068201 | -0.123658 | 0.154688 | 1.000000 |

*Table 20. Documentation of Descriptive Statistics of Grand Index of Green Growth and Sustainability (GIGGS), Production-based Carbon Dioxide ($CO_2$) Productivity (PCDO), Non-energy Material Productivity (NEMP), Mean Population Exposure to $PM_{2.5}$ (MPEPM), Environmentally adjusted Multifactor*

*Productivity Growth (EAMFP), and The Global Sustainable Competitiveness Index ® (GSCI) respectively [**Country:** Denmark]*

Date: 02/12/24 Time: 16:10
Sample: 2012 2021

| | GIGGS | EAMFP | MPEPM | NEMP | PCDO | GSCI |
|---|---|---|---|---|---|---|
| Mean | 1.080133 | 2.738000 | 10.11524 | 2.618370 | 5.106712 | 57.45000 |
| Median | 1.082148 | 2.735000 | 10.02866 | 2.610893 | 5.211551 | 57.20000 |
| Maximum | 1.143869 | 2.870000 | 11.24000 | 2.740000 | 5.520000 | 62.80000 |
| Minimum | 1.009972 | 2.610000 | 9.230000 | 2.530000 | 4.610000 | 51.60000 |
| Std. Dev. | 0.041384 | 0.085609 | 0.715453 | 0.056522 | 0.312364 | 3.493247 |
| Skewness | -0.271972 | 0.048878 | 0.276922 | 0.680826 | -0.362456 | -0.245682 |
| Kurtosis | 2.183047 | 1.870935 | 1.741778 | 3.497149 | 1.751820 | 2.257838 |
| Jarque-Bera | 0.401369 | 0.535144 | 0.787444 | 0.875522 | 0.868105 | 0.330101 |
| Probability | 0.818170 | 0.765235 | 0.674541 | 0.645480 | 0.647878 | 0.847851 |
| Sum | 10.80133 | 27.38000 | 101.1524 | 26.18370 | 51.06712 | 574.5000 |
| Sum Sq. Dev. | 0.015414 | 0.065960 | 4.606851 | 0.028753 | 0.878144 | 109.8250 |
| Observations | 10 | 10 | 10 | 10 | 10 | 10 |

*Table 21. Documentation of pairwise Granger Causality Tests for Grand Index of Green Growth and Sustainability (GIGGS) and Production-based Carbon Dioxide ($CO_2$) Productivity (PCDO), Non-energy Material Productivity (NEMP), Mean Population Exposure to $PM_{2.5}$ (MPEPM), Environmentally ad-*

*justed Multifactor Productivity Growth (EAMFP), and The Global Sustainable Competitiveness Index ® (GSCI) respectively [**Country:** Denmark]*

Pairwise Granger Causality Tests
Date: 02/12/24 Time: 16:21
Sample: 2012 2021
Lags: 1

| Null Hypothesis: | Obs | F-Statistic | Prob. |
|---|---|---|---|
| EAMFP does not Granger Cause GIGGS | 9 | 1.67649 | 0.2430 |
| GIGGS does not Granger Cause EAMFP | | 0.47062 | 0.5183 |
| MPEPM does not Granger Cause GIGGS | 9 | 0.62263 | 0.4601 |
| GIGGS does not Granger Cause MPEPM | | 1.65401 | 0.2458 |
| NEMP does not Granger Cause GIGGS | 9 | 0.23791 | 0.6430 |
| GIGGS does not Granger Cause NEMP | | 0.45160 | 0.5266 |
| PCDO does not Granger Cause GIGGS | 9 | 1.17593 | 0.3198 |
| GIGGS does not Granger Cause PCDO | | 0.00043 | 0.9840 |
| GSCI does not Granger Cause GIGGS | 9 | 0.30327 | 0.6017 |
| GIGGS does not Granger Cause GSCI | | 0.74532 | 0.4211 |
| MPEPM does not Granger Cause EAMFP | 9 | 0.13467 | 0.7262 |
| EAMFP does not Granger Cause MPEPM | | 4.14296 | 0.0880 |
| NEMP does not Granger Cause EAMFP | 9 | 2.64879 | 0.1548 |
| EAMFP does not Granger Cause NEMP | | 4.30704 | 0.0833 |
| PCDO does not Granger Cause EAMFP | 9 | 0.22635 | 0.6511 |
| EAMFP does not Granger Cause PCDO | | 1.02839 | 0.3497 |
| GSCI does not Granger Cause EAMFP | 9 | 0.36783 | 0.5664 |
| EAMFP does not Granger Cause GSCI | | 0.66783 | 0.4450 |
| NEMP does not Granger Cause MPEPM | 9 | 2.42987 | 0.1701 |
| MPEPM does not Granger Cause NEMP | | 1.36240 | 0.2874 |
| PCDO does not Granger Cause MPEPM | 9 | 2.39111 | 0.1730 |
| MPEPM does not Granger Cause PCDO | | 8.45566 | 0.0271 |
| GSCI does not Granger Cause MPEPM | 9 | 0.73597 | 0.4239 |
| MPEPM does not Granger Cause GSCI | | 0.47368 | 0.5170 |
| PCDO does not Granger Cause NEMP | 9 | 3.14650 | 0.1265 |
| NEMP does not Granger Cause PCDO | | 0.47052 | 0.5184 |
| GSCI does not Granger Cause NEMP | 9 | 0.15794 | 0.7048 |
| NEMP does not Granger Cause GSCI | | 0.10661 | 0.7551 |
| GSCI does not Granger Cause PCDO | 9 | 1.13905 | 0.3269 |
| PCDO does not Granger Cause GSCI | | 0.58639 | 0.4729 |

*Table 22. Documentation of normality test (Jarque – Bera) results of residuals [**Country:** Denmark]*

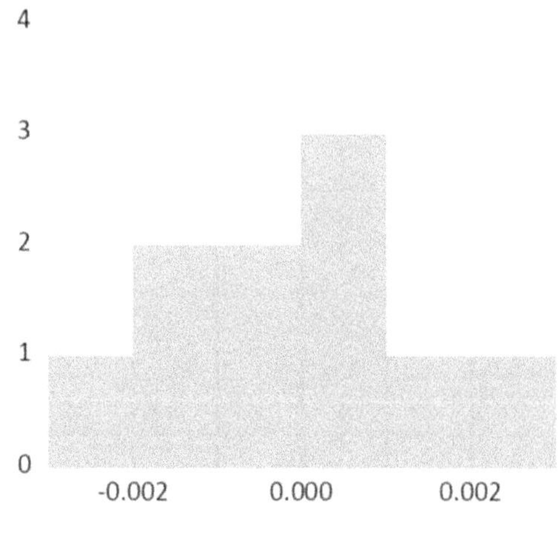


Series: Residuals
Sample 2012 2021
Observations 10

| | |
|---|---|
| Mean | 4.33e-16 |
| Median | 4.69e-05 |
| Maximum | 0.002588 |
| Minimum | -0.002132 |
| Std. Dev. | 0.001426 |
| Skewness | 0.368279 |
| Kurtosis | 2.362311 |
| Jarque-Bera | 0.395485 |
| Probability | 0.820581 |

Model 1: TSLS, using observations 2012-2021 (T = 10)
Dependent variable: GIGGS
Instruments: const PCDO NEMP MPEPM EAMFP GSCI
HAC standard errors, bandwidth 1 (Bartlett kernel)

*Table 23. Regression results of Grand Index of Green Growth and Sustainability (GIGGS) on Production-based Carbon Dioxide ($CO_2$) Productivity (PCDO), Non-energy Material Productivity (NEMP), Mean Population Exposure to $PM_{2.5}$ (MPEPM), Environmentally adjusted Multifactor Productivity Growth (EAMFP), and The Global Sustainable Competitiveness Index ® (GSCI) respectively based on Two-Stage Least Squares (2SLS) method [***Country:*** *Finland]*

| | Coefficient | Std. Error | t-ratio | p-value | |
|---|---|---|---|---|---|
| const | 2.67251 | 0.129279 | 20.67 | <0.0001 | *** |
| PCDO | −0.264836 | 0.0220047 | −12.04 | 0.0003 | *** |
| NEMP | −0.565513 | 0.0446109 | −12.68 | 0.0002 | *** |
| MPEPM | −0.188539 | 0.00207866 | −90.70 | <0.0001 | *** |
| EAMFP | 0.533216 | 0.0153074 | 34.83 | <0.0001 | *** |
| GSCI | 0.0194116 | 0.000781887 | 24.83 | <0.0001 | *** |

| | | | |
|---|---|---|---|
| **Mean dependent var** | 1.811620 | **S.D. dependent var** | 0.321943 |
| **Sum squared resid** | 0.000341 | **S.E. of regression** | 0.009228 |
| **R-squared** | 0.999635 | **Adjusted R-squared** | 0.999178 |
| **F(5, 4)** | 2190.193 | **P-value(F)** | 5.83e-07 |
| **Log-likelihood** | 37.24750 | **Akaike criterion** | −62.49501 |
| **Schwarz criterion** | −60.67950 | **Hannan-Quinn** | −64.48662 |
| **rho** | 0.193910 | **Durbin-Watson** | 1.485614 |

*Table 24. Documentation of Correlation Matrix between Grand Index of Green Growth and Sustainability (GIGGS) and Production-based Carbon Dioxide ($CO_2$) Productivity (PCDO), Non-energy Material Productivity (NEMP), Mean Population Exposure to $PM_{2.5}$ (MPEPM), Environmentally adjusted Multifactor Productivity Growth (EAMFP), and The Global Sustainable Competitiveness Index ® (GSCI) respectively [***Country:*** *Finland]*

Correlation

| | EAMFP | GIGGS | GSCI | MPEPM | NEMP | PCDO |
|---|---|---|---|---|---|---|
| EAMFP | 1.000000 | 0.639024 | -0.462106 | 0.122581 | -0.479621 | -0.959193 |
| GIGGS | 0.639024 | 1.000000 | 0.116069 | -0.665010 | -0.656335 | -0.672775 |
| GSCI | -0.462106 | 0.116069 | 1.000000 | -0.453707 | 0.020425 | 0.381329 |
| MPEPM | 0.122581 | -0.665010 | -0.453707 | 1.000000 | 0.300827 | -0.072673 |
| NEMP | -0.479621 | -0.656335 | 0.020425 | 0.300827 | 1.000000 | 0.511155 |
| PCDO | -0.959193 | -0.672775 | 0.381329 | -0.072673 | 0.511155 | 1.000000 |

*Table 25. Documentation of Descriptive Statistics of Grand Index of Green Growth and Sustainability (GIGGS), Production-based Carbon Dioxide ($CO_2$) Productivity (PCDO), Non-energy Material Productivity (NEMP), Mean Population Exposure to $PM_{2.5}$ (MPEPM), Environmentally adjusted Multifactor Productivity Growth (EAMFP), and The Global Sustainable Competitiveness Index ® (GSCI) respectively [***Country:** *Finland]*

Date: 02/12/24 Time: 17:48
Sample: 2012 2021

| | EAMFP | GIGGS | GSCI | MPEPM | NEMP | PCDO |
|---|---|---|---|---|---|---|
| Mean | 1.624000 | 1.811620 | 57.81000 | 4.615682 | 1.528937 | 4.206929 |
| Median | 1.625000 | 1.691241 | 57.50000 | 4.717200 | 1.507221 | 4.218846 |
| Maximum | 2.120000 | 2.300007 | 60.90000 | 5.719180 | 1.622467 | 4.550000 |
| Minimum | 1.130000 | 1.414267 | 53.60000 | 3.020000 | 1.470000 | 3.830000 |
| Std. Dev. | 0.331770 | 0.321943 | 2.577445 | 1.104773 | 0.055892 | 0.245317 |
| Skewness | -0.004363 | 0.504593 | -0.292409 | -0.252459 | 0.530681 | -0.152979 |
| Kurtosis | 1.780659 | 1.803899 | 1.874868 | 1.421617 | 1.727637 | 1.732350 |
| Jarque-Bera | 0.619528 | 1.020465 | 0.669973 | 1.144264 | 1.143916 | 0.708562 |
| Probability | 0.733620 | 0.600356 | 0.715348 | 0.564321 | 0.564419 | 0.701678 |
| Sum | 16.24000 | 18.11620 | 578.1000 | 46.15682 | 15.28937 | 42.06929 |
| Sum Sq. Dev. | 0.990640 | 0.932824 | 59.78900 | 10.98471 | 0.028115 | 0.541624 |
| Observations | 10 | 10 | 10 | 10 | 10 | 10 |

*Table 26. Documentation of pairwise Granger Causality Tests for Grand Index of Green Growth and Sustainability (GIGGS) and Production-based Carbon Dioxide ($CO_2$) Productivity (PCDO), Non-energy Material Productivity (NEMP), Mean Population Exposure to $PM_{2.5}$ (MPEPM), Environmentally ad-*

*justed Multifactor Productivity Growth (EAMFP), and The Global Sustainable Competitiveness Index ® (GSCI) respectively [***Country:*** *Finland]*

Pairwise Granger Causality Tests
Date: 02/12/24 Time: 17:52
Sample: 2012 2021
Lags: 1

| Null Hypothesis: | Obs | F-Statistic | Prob. |
|---|---|---|---|
| GIGGS does not Granger Cause EAMFP | 9 | 0.06566 | 0.8063 |
| EAMFP does not Granger Cause GIGGS | | 0.00179 | 0.9676 |
| GSCI does not Granger Cause EAMFP | 9 | 0.65811 | 0.4482 |
| EAMFP does not Granger Cause GSCI | | 1.56150 | 0.2580 |
| MPEPM does not Granger Cause EAMFP | 9 | 0.01528 | 0.9057 |
| EAMFP does not Granger Cause MPEPM | | 1.13871 | 0.3270 |
| NEMP does not Granger Cause EAMFP | 9 | 0.00150 | 0.9704 |
| EAMFP does not Granger Cause NEMP | | 2.10262 | 0.1972 |
| PCDO does not Granger Cause EAMFP | 9 | 0.00234 | 0.9630 |
| EAMFP does not Granger Cause PCDO | | 24.1358 | 0.0027 |
| GSCI does not Granger Cause GIGGS | 9 | 2.35690 | 0.1756 |
| GIGGS does not Granger Cause GSCI | | 0.99961 | 0.3560 |
| MPEPM does not Granger Cause GIGGS | 9 | 0.17894 | 0.6870 |
| GIGGS does not Granger Cause MPEPM | | 0.42587 | 0.5382 |
| NEMP does not Granger Cause GIGGS | 9 | 2.52579 | 0.1631 |
| GIGGS does not Granger Cause NEMP | | 2.02000 | 0.2051 |
| PCDO does not Granger Cause GIGGS | 9 | 0.01474 | 0.9073 |
| GIGGS does not Granger Cause PCDO | | 0.13840 | 0.7227 |
| MPEPM does not Granger Cause GSCI | 9 | 0.20743 | 0.6648 |
| GSCI does not Granger Cause MPEPM | | 10.3091 | 0.0183 |
| NEMP does not Granger Cause GSCI | 9 | 0.10509 | 0.7568 |
| GSCI does not Granger Cause NEMP | | 0.65176 | 0.4503 |
| PCDO does not Granger Cause GSCI | 9 | 1.00589 | 0.3546 |
| GSCI does not Granger Cause PCDO | | 0.01209 | 0.9160 |
| NEMP does not Granger Cause MPEPM | 9 | 2.15719 | 0.1923 |
| MPEPM does not Granger Cause NEMP | | 0.01406 | 0.9095 |
| PCDO does not Granger Cause MPEPM | 9 | 0.61162 | 0.4639 |
| MPEPM does not Granger Cause PCDO | | 0.02011 | 0.8919 |
| PCDO does not Granger Cause NEMP | 9 | 1.31337 | 0.2954 |
| NEMP does not Granger Cause PCDO | | 0.00251 | 0.9617 |

*Table 27. Documentation of normality test (Jarque – Bera) results of residuals [***Country:*** *Finland]*

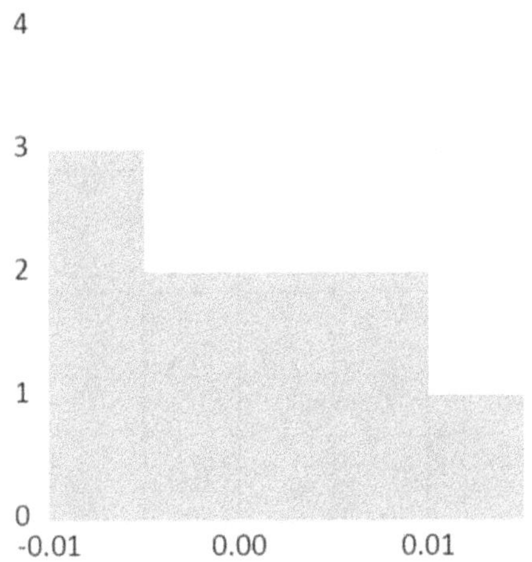


Series: Residuals
Sample 2012 2021
Observations 10

| | |
|---|---|
| Mean | 4.88e-16 |
| Median | 0.000596 |
| Maximum | 0.010121 |
| Minimum | -0.008929 |
| Std. Dev. | 0.006152 |
| Skewness | 0.015536 |
| Kurtosis | 1.988136 |
| Jarque-Bera | 0.427014 |
| Probability | 0.807747 |

Model 1: TSLS, using observations 2012-2021 (T = 10)
Dependent variable: GIGGS
Instruments: const PCDO NEMP MPEPM EAMFP GSCI

HAC standard errors, bandwidth 1 (Bartlett kernel)

*Table 28. Regression results of Grand Index of Green Growth and Sustainability (GIGGS) on Production-based Carbon Dioxide ($CO_2$) Productivity (PCDO), Non-energy Material Productivity (NEMP), Mean Population Exposure to $PM_{2.5}$ (MPEPM), Environmentally adjusted Multifactor Productivity Growth (EAMFP), and The Global Sustainable Competitiveness Index ® (GSCI) respectively based on Two-Stage Least Squares (2SLS) method [***Country:** *Sweden]*

| | Coefficient | Std. Error | t-ratio | p-value | |
|---|---|---|---|---|---|
| const | 2.80675 | 4.07656 | 0.6885 | 0.5290 | |
| PCDO | −0.117540 | 0.0842847 | −1.395 | 0.2356 | |
| NEMP | −0.173172 | 0.00474289 | −36.51 | <0.0001 | *** |
| MPEPM | −0.0525372 | 0.0157537 | −3.335 | 0.0290 | ** |
| EAMFP | −0.348173 | 1.27322 | −0.2735 | 0.7980 | |
| GSCI | 0.0160316 | 0.00171895 | 9.326 | 0.0007 | *** |

| | | | |
|---|---|---|---|
| **Mean dependent var** | 1.302553 | **S.D. dependent var** | 0.136786 |
| **Sum squared resid** | 0.002358 | **S.E. of regression** | 0.024280 |
| **R-squared** | 0.985997 | **Adjusted R-squared** | 0.968493 |
| **F(5, 4)** | 56.33046 | **P-value(F)** | 0.000846 |
| **Log-likelihood** | 27.57321 | **Akaike criterion** | −43.14642 |
| **Schwarz criterion** | −41.33091 | **Hannan-Quinn** | −45.13803 |
| **rho** | −0.143515 | **Durbin-Watson** | 1.712456 |

*Table 29. Documentation of Correlation Matrix between Grand Index of Green Growth and Sustainability (GIGGS) and Production-based Carbon Dioxide ($CO_2$) Productivity (PCDO), Non-energy Material Productivity (NEMP), Mean Population Exposure to $PM_{2.5}$ (MPEPM), Environmentally adjusted Multifactor Productivity Growth (EAMFP), and The Global Sustainable Competitiveness Index ® (GSCI) respectively [***Country:** *Sweden]*

Correlation

| | EAMFP | GIGGS | GSCI | MPEPM | NEMP | PCDO |
|---|---|---|---|---|---|---|
| EAMFP | 1.000000 | 0.516762 | -0.509979 | 0.926980 | -0.547764 | -0.995495 |
| GIGGS | 0.516762 | 1.000000 | 0.120342 | 0.499704 | -0.948749 | -0.525699 |
| GSCI | -0.509979 | 0.120342 | 1.000000 | -0.489408 | 0.130588 | 0.473531 |
| MPEPM | 0.926980 | 0.499704 | -0.489408 | 1.000000 | -0.556116 | -0.935754 |
| NEMP | -0.547764 | -0.948749 | 0.130588 | -0.556116 | 1.000000 | 0.543994 |
| PCDO | -0.995495 | -0.525699 | 0.473531 | -0.935754 | 0.543994 | 1.000000 |

*Table 30. Documentation of Descriptive Statistics of Grand Index of Green Growth and Sustainability (GIGGS), Production-based Carbon Dioxide (CO2) Productivity (PCDO), Non-energy Material Productivity (NEMP), Mean Population Exposure to PM2.5 (MPEPM), Environmentally adjusted Multi-factor Productivity Growth (EAMFP), and The Global Sustainable Competitiveness Index ® (GSCI) respectively [***Country:*** *Sweden]*

Date: 02/12/24 Time: 23:27
Sample: 2012 2021

| | EAMFP | GIGGS | GSCI | MPEPM | NEMP | PCDO |
|---|---|---|---|---|---|---|
| Mean | 2.665000 | 1.302553 | 59.55000 | 5.858622 | 2.450424 | 6.796445 |
| Median | 2.665000 | 1.339778 | 60.55000 | 5.774210 | 2.263453 | 6.784848 |
| Maximum | 2.710000 | 1.454401 | 62.10000 | 6.520000 | 4.420000 | 7.500000 |
| Minimum | 2.620000 | 0.958941 | 54.10000 | 5.260000 | 1.900000 | 6.050000 |
| Std. Dev. | 0.030277 | 0.136786 | 2.694954 | 0.421181 | 0.707625 | 0.484136 |
| Skewness | -1.64E-16 | -1.658508 | -1.163533 | 0.242530 | 2.443603 | -0.110816 |
| Kurtosis | 1.775758 | 5.154962 | 2.869500 | 1.895501 | 7.465202 | 1.835659 |
| Jarque-Bera | 0.624487 | 6.519358 | 2.263446 | 0.606334 | 18.25950 | 0.585338 |
| Probability | 0.731803 | 0.038401 | 0.322477 | 0.738476 | 0.000108 | 0.746269 |
| Sum | 26.65000 | 13.02553 | 595.5000 | 58.58622 | 24.50424 | 67.96445 |
| Sum Sq. Dev. | 0.008250 | 0.168393 | 65.36500 | 1.596544 | 4.506595 | 2.109486 |
| Observations | 10 | 10 | 10 | 10 | 10 | 10 |

*Table 31. Documentation of pairwise Granger Causality Tests for Grand Index of Green Growth and Sustainability (GIGGS) and Production-based Carbon Dioxide (CO2) Productivity (PCDO), Non-energy Material Productivity (NEMP), Mean Population Exposure to PM2.5 (MPEPM), Environmentally adjusted Multifactor Productivity Growth (EAMFP), and The Global Sustainable Competitiveness Index ® (GSCI) respectively [***Country:*** *Sweden]*

Pairwise Granger Causality Tests
Date: 02/12/24 Time: 23:32
Sample: 2012 2021
Lags: 1

| Null Hypothesis: | Obs | F-Statistic | Prob. |
|---|---|---|---|
| GIGGS does not Granger Cause EAMFP | 9 | -1.18848 | 1.0000 |
| EAMFP does not Granger Cause GIGGS | | 1.24157 | 0.3078 |
| GSCI does not Granger Cause EAMFP | 9 | -4.68261 | 1.0000 |
| EAMFP does not Granger Cause GSCI | | 1.85192 | 0.2225 |
| MPEPM does not Granger Cause EAMFP | 9 | -0.97705 | 1.0000 |
| EAMFP does not Granger Cause MPEPM | | 2.56440 | 0.1604 |
| NEMP does not Granger Cause EAMFP | 9 | -4.80280 | 1.0000 |
| EAMFP does not Granger Cause NEMP | | 2.18750 | 0.1896 |
| PCDO does not Granger Cause EAMFP | 9 | -5.86226 | 1.0000 |
| EAMFP does not Granger Cause PCDO | | 6.12824 | 0.0481 |
| GSCI does not Granger Cause GIGGS | 9 | 1.03938 | 0.3473 |
| GIGGS does not Granger Cause GSCI | | 0.10288 | 0.7593 |
| MPEPM does not Granger Cause GIGGS | 9 | 0.96934 | 0.3629 |
| GIGGS does not Granger Cause MPEPM | | 2.03788 | 0.2033 |
| NEMP does not Granger Cause GIGGS | 9 | 0.31962 | 0.5923 |
| GIGGS does not Granger Cause NEMP | | 0.22426 | 0.6526 |
| PCDO does not Granger Cause GIGGS | 9 | 1.01543 | 0.3525 |
| GIGGS does not Granger Cause PCDO | | 0.57612 | 0.4766 |
| MPEPM does not Granger Cause GSCI | 9 | 1.97800 | 0.2092 |
| GSCI does not Granger Cause MPEPM | | 1.69131 | 0.2411 |
| NEMP does not Granger Cause GSCI | 9 | 0.33852 | 0.5819 |
| GSCI does not Granger Cause NEMP | | 0.78088 | 0.4109 |
| PCDO does not Granger Cause GSCI | 9 | 2.11098 | 0.1965 |
| GSCI does not Granger Cause PCDO | | 0.28612 | 0.6119 |
| NEMP does not Granger Cause MPEPM | 9 | 0.12344 | 0.7373 |
| MPEPM does not Granger Cause NEMP | | 2.33017 | 0.1777 |
| PCDO does not Granger Cause MPEPM | 9 | 4.86950 | 0.0695 |
| MPEPM does not Granger Cause PCDO | | 0.68378 | 0.4399 |
| PCDO does not Granger Cause NEMP | 9 | 1.97076 | 0.2100 |
| NEMP does not Granger Cause PCDO | | 0.17194 | 0.6928 |

*Table 32. Documentation of normality test (Jarque – Bera) results of residuals [**Country:** Sweden]*

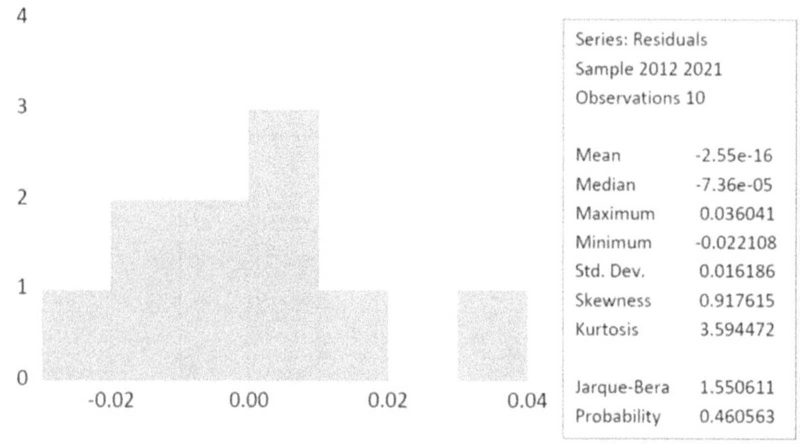


Model 1: TSLS, using observations 2012-2021 (T = 10)
Dependent variable: GIGGS
Instruments: const PCDO NEMP MPEPM EAMFP GSCI
HAC standard errors, bandwidth 1 (Bartlett kernel)

*Table 33. Regression results of Grand Index of Green Growth and Sustainability (GIGGS) on Production-based Carbon Dioxide (CO2) Productivity (PCDO), Non-energy Material Productivity (NEMP), Mean Population Exposure to PM2.5 (MPEPM), Environmentally adjusted Multifactor Productivity Growth (EAMFP), and The Global Sustainable Competitiveness Index ® (GSCI) respectively based on Two-Stage Least Squares (2SLS) method [**Country:** Brazil]*

| | Coefficient | Std. Error | t-ratio | p-value | |
|---|---|---|---|---|---|
| const | 2.69254 | 0.136552 | 19.72 | <0.0001 | *** |
| PCDO | −0.147001 | 0.00672127 | −21.87 | <0.0001 | *** |
| NEMP | −1.19134 | 0.0467473 | −25.48 | <0.0001 | *** |
| MPEPM | −0.0768892 | 0.00294906 | −26.07 | <0.0001 | *** |
| EAMFP | 0.236240 | 0.0123302 | 19.16 | <0.0001 | *** |
| GSCI | 0.0197724 | 0.000823543 | 24.01 | <0.0001 | *** |

| | | | |
|---|---|---|---|
| **Mean dependent var** | 1.785429 | **S.D. dependent var** | 0.101426 |
| **Sum squared resid** | 0.000029 | **S.E. of regression** | 0.002681 |
| **R-squared** | 0.999689 | **Adjusted R-squared** | 0.999301 |
| **F(5, 4)** | 2574.720 | **P-value(F)** | 4.22e-07 |
| **Log-likelihood** | 49.60642 | **Akaike criterion** | −87.21284 |
| **Schwarz criterion** | −85.39733 | **Hannan-Quinn** | −89.20445 |
| **rho** | −0.543888 | **Durbin-Watson** | 2.907737 |

*Table 34. Documentation of Correlation Matrix between Grand Index of Green Growth and Sustainability (GIGGS) and Production-based Carbon Dioxide (CO2) Productivity (PCDO), Non-energy Material Productivity (NEMP), Mean Population Exposure to PM2.5 (MPEPM), Environmentally adjusted Multifactor Productivity Growth (EAMFP), and The Global Sustainable Competitiveness Index ® (GSCI) respectively [***Country:*** *Brazil]*

Correlation

| | EAMFP | GIGGS | GSCI | MPEPM | NEMP | PCDO |
|---|---|---|---|---|---|---|
| EAMFP | 1.000000 | 0.971758 | -0.326934 | -0.853903 | -0.786555 | -0.194962 |
| GIGGS | 0.971758 | 1.000000 | -0.181425 | -0.809749 | -0.823798 | -0.208756 |
| GSCI | -0.326934 | -0.181425 | 1.000000 | 0.604346 | 0.188463 | 0.063766 |
| MPEPM | -0.853903 | -0.809749 | 0.604346 | 1.000000 | 0.578907 | 0.204061 |
| NEMP | -0.786555 | -0.823798 | 0.188463 | 0.578907 | 1.000000 | -0.285913 |
| PCDO | -0.194962 | -0.208756 | 0.063766 | 0.204061 | -0.285913 | 1.000000 |

*Table 35. Documentation of Descriptive Statistics of Grand Index of Green Growth and Sustainability (GIGGS), Production-based Carbon Dioxide (CO2) Productivity (PCDO), Non-energy Material Productivity (NEMP), Mean Population Exposure to PM2.5 (MPEPM), Environmentally adjusted Multifactor Productivity Growth (EAMFP), and The Global Sustainable Competitiveness Index ® (GSCI) respectively [***Country:*** *Brazil]*

Date: 02/12/24 Time: 23:38
Sample: 2012 2021

| | EAMFP | GIGGS | GSCI | MPEPM | NEMP | PCDO |
|---|---|---|---|---|---|---|
| Mean | 3.755000 | 1.785429 | 48.24000 | 11.82562 | 0.748886 | 6.439211 |
| Median | 3.755000 | 1.789468 | 47.90000 | 11.66719 | 0.736312 | 6.427017 |
| Maximum | 4.000000 | 1.944172 | 50.60000 | 12.57000 | 0.817224 | 6.675872 |
| Minimum | 3.500000 | 1.647522 | 46.80000 | 11.37000 | 0.701543 | 6.182832 |
| Std. Dev. | 0.168342 | 0.101426 | 1.237560 | 0.439774 | 0.036218 | 0.138888 |
| Skewness | -0.019444 | 0.243893 | 0.569066 | 0.740422 | 0.538539 | -0.055897 |
| Kurtosis | 1.758293 | 1.843991 | 2.254046 | 1.929209 | 2.195734 | 2.695014 |
| Jarque-Bera | 0.643062 | 0.655955 | 0.771581 | 1.391456 | 0.752893 | 0.043964 |
| Probability | 0.725038 | 0.720379 | 0.679913 | 0.498711 | 0.686296 | 0.978258 |
| Sum | 37.55000 | 17.85429 | 482.4000 | 118.2562 | 7.488856 | 64.39211 |
| Sum Sq. Dev. | 0.255050 | 0.092585 | 13.78400 | 1.740614 | 0.011806 | 0.173608 |
| Observations | 10 | 10 | 10 | 10 | 10 | 10 |

*Table 36. Documentation of pairwise Granger Causality Tests for Grand Index of Green Growth and Sustainability (GIGGS) and Production-based Carbon Dioxide (CO2) Productivity (PCDO), Non-energy Material Productivity (NEMP), Mean Population Exposure to PM2.5 (MPEPM), Environmentally ad-*

*justed Multifactor Productivity Growth (EAMFP), and The Global Sustainable Competitiveness Index ® (GSCI) respectively [**Country:** Brazil]*

Pairwise Granger Causality Tests
Date: 02/12/24 Time: 23:40
Sample: 2012 2021
Lags: 1

| Null Hypothesis: | Obs | F-Statistic | Prob. |
|---|---|---|---|
| GIGGS does not Granger Cause EAMFP | 9 | 0.22079 | 0.6550 |
| EAMFP does not Granger Cause GIGGS | | 9.79549 | 0.0203 |
| GSCI does not Granger Cause EAMFP | 9 | 1.11769 | 0.3311 |
| EAMFP does not Granger Cause GSCI | | 0.00984 | 0.9242 |
| MPEPM does not Granger Cause EAMFP | 9 | 0.03324 | 0.8613 |
| EAMFP does not Granger Cause MPEPM | | 0.45864 | 0.5235 |
| NEMP does not Granger Cause EAMFP | 9 | 0.00883 | 0.9282 |
| EAMFP does not Granger Cause NEMP | | 4.29382 | 0.0836 |
| PCDO does not Granger Cause EAMFP | 9 | 0.00592 | 0.9412 |
| EAMFP does not Granger Cause PCDO | | 0.19924 | 0.6710 |
| GSCI does not Granger Cause GIGGS | 9 | 5.94128 | 0.0506 |
| GIGGS does not Granger Cause GSCI | | 0.02995 | 0.8683 |
| MPEPM does not Granger Cause GIGGS | 9 | 1.37254 | 0.2858 |
| GIGGS does not Granger Cause MPEPM | | 0.07777 | 0.7897 |
| NEMP does not Granger Cause GIGGS | 9 | 0.00352 | 0.9546 |
| GIGGS does not Granger Cause NEMP | | 2.64598 | 0.1549 |
| PCDO does not Granger Cause GIGGS | 9 | 0.01253 | 0.9145 |
| GIGGS does not Granger Cause PCDO | | 0.07018 | 0.7999 |
| MPEPM does not Granger Cause GSCI | 9 | 0.23384 | 0.6458 |
| GSCI does not Granger Cause MPEPM | | 0.44713 | 0.5286 |
| NEMP does not Granger Cause GSCI | 9 | 0.20561 | 0.6662 |
| GSCI does not Granger Cause NEMP | | 2.34598 | 0.1765 |
| PCDO does not Granger Cause GSCI | 9 | 0.01761 | 0.8988 |
| GSCI does not Granger Cause PCDO | | 0.01103 | 0.9198 |
| NEMP does not Granger Cause MPEPM | 9 | 0.17840 | 0.6875 |
| MPEPM does not Granger Cause NEMP | | 6.70284 | 0.0413 |
| PCDO does not Granger Cause MPEPM | 9 | 2.91418 | 0.1387 |
| MPEPM does not Granger Cause PCDO | | 0.00876 | 0.9285 |
| PCDO does not Granger Cause NEMP | 9 | 0.98284 | 0.3598 |
| NEMP does not Granger Cause PCDO | | 0.09386 | 0.7697 |

*Table 37. Documentation of normality test (Jarque – Bera) results of residuals [**Country:** Brazil]*

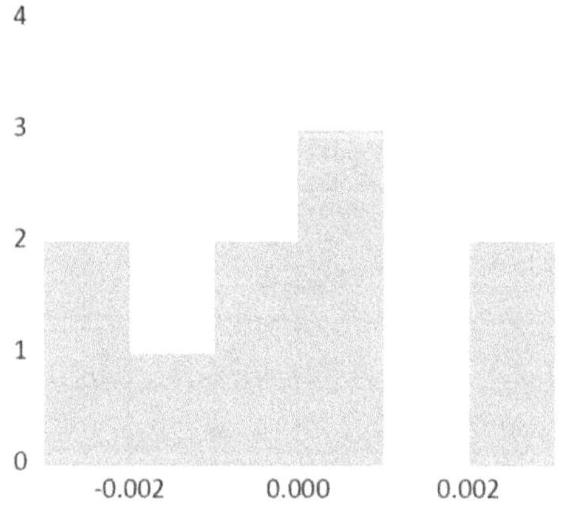


Series: Residuals
Sample 2012 2021
Observations 10

| | |
|---|---|
| Mean | 6.88e-16 |
| Median | 0.000258 |
| Maximum | 0.002590 |
| Minimum | -0.002942 |
| Std. Dev. | 0.001788 |
| Skewness | -0.179348 |
| Kurtosis | 2.001874 |
| Jarque-Bera | 0.468716 |
| Probability | 0.791079 |

Model 1: TSLS, using observations 2012-2021 (T = 10)
Dependent variable: GIGGS
Instruments: const PCDO NEMP MPEPM EAMFP GSCI
HAC standard errors, bandwidth 1 (Bartlett kernel)

*Table 38. Regression results of Grand Index of Green Growth and Sustainability (GIGGS) on Production-based Carbon Dioxide (CO2) Productivity (PCDO), Non-energy Material Productivity (NEMP), Mean Population Exposure to PM2.5 (MPEPM), Environmentally adjusted Multifactor Productivity Growth (EAMFP), and The Global Sustainable Competitiveness Index ® (GSCI) respectively based on Two-Stage Least Squares (2SLS) method [***Country:*** *South Korea]*

| | Coefficient | Std. Error | t-ratio | p-value | |
|---|---|---|---|---|---|
| const | −0.126894 | 0.853171 | −0.1487 | 0.8890 | |
| PCDO | −0.0738249 | 0.00804490 | −9.177 | 0.0008 | *** |
| NEMP | −0.139093 | 0.00957471 | −14.53 | 0.0001 | *** |
| MPEPM | −0.0186789 | 0.00184371 | −10.13 | 0.0005 | *** |
| EAMFP | 0.513528 | 0.246658 | 2.082 | 0.1058 | |
| GSCI | 0.00763500 | 0.000176795 | 43.19 | <0.0001 | *** |

| | | | |
|---|---|---|---|
| **Mean dependent var** | 0.747073 | **S.D. dependent var** | 0.046635 |
| **Sum squared resid** | 0.000023 | **S.E. of regression** | 0.002406 |
| **R-squared** | 0.998817 | **Adjusted R-squared** | 0.997338 |
| **F(5, 4)** | 675.3966 | **P-value(F)** | 6.12e-06 |
| **Log-likelihood** | 50.68964 | **Akaike criterion** | −89.37929 |
| **Schwarz criterion** | −87.56378 | **Hannan-Quinn** | −91.37090 |
| **rho** | −0.005423 | **Durbin-Watson** | 1.702056 |

*Table 39. Documentation of Correlation Matrix between Grand Index of Green Growth and Sustainability (GIGGS) and Production-based Carbon Dioxide (CO2) Productivity (PCDO), Non-energy Material Productivity (NEMP), Mean Population Exposure to PM2.5 (MPEPM), Environmentally adjusted Multifactor Productivity Growth (EAMFP), and The Global Sustainable Competitiveness Index ® (GSCI) respectively [***Country:*** *South Korea]*

Correlation

| | EAMFP | GIGGS | GSCI | MPEPM | NEMP | PCDO |
|---|---|---|---|---|---|---|
| EAMFP | 1.000000 | 0.795980 | -0.372425 | -0.870926 | -0.712825 | -0.829321 |
| GIGGS | 0.795980 | 1.000000 | -0.103593 | -0.765954 | -0.839566 | -0.913024 |
| GSCI | -0.372425 | -0.103593 | 1.000000 | 0.206896 | 0.565998 | 0.493105 |
| MPEPM | -0.870926 | -0.765954 | 0.206896 | 1.000000 | 0.550500 | 0.737772 |
| NEMP | -0.712825 | -0.839566 | 0.565998 | 0.550500 | 1.000000 | 0.963891 |
| PCDO | -0.829321 | -0.913024 | 0.493105 | 0.737772 | 0.963891 | 1.000000 |

*Table 40. Documentation of Descriptive Statistics of Grand Index of Green Growth and Sustainability (GIGGS), Production-based Carbon Dioxide (CO2) Productivity (PCDO), Non-energy Material Productivity (NEMP), Mean Population Exposure to PM2.5 (MPEPM), Environmentally adjusted Multi-*

*factor Productivity Growth (EAMFP), and The Global Sustainable Competitiveness Index ® (GSCI) respectively [**Country:** South Korea]*

Date: 02/12/24 Time: 23:52
Sample: 2012 2021

| | EAMFP | GIGGS | GSCI | MPEPM | NEMP | PCDO |
|---|---|---|---|---|---|---|
| Mean | 3.293000 | 0.747073 | 50.06000 | 26.95183 | 3.139399 | 3.510882 |
| Median | 3.290000 | 0.732206 | 50.45000 | 27.00213 | 3.095799 | 3.524645 |
| Maximum | 3.300000 | 0.815443 | 53.90000 | 27.82776 | 3.500000 | 3.830000 |
| Minimum | 3.290000 | 0.696200 | 45.70000 | 26.12000 | 2.850000 | 3.180000 |
| Std. Dev. | 0.004830 | 0.046635 | 2.952287 | 0.564009 | 0.209167 | 0.214303 |
| Skewness | 0.872872 | 0.381671 | -0.070586 | -0.141855 | 0.443763 | -0.072960 |
| Kurtosis | 1.761905 | 1.601759 | 1.575074 | 1.915438 | 2.192955 | 1.929048 |
| Jarque-Bera | 1.908541 | 1.057403 | 0.854310 | 0.523653 | 0.599592 | 0.486763 |
| Probability | 0.385093 | 0.589370 | 0.652362 | 0.769645 | 0.740969 | 0.783973 |
| Sum | 32.93000 | 7.470725 | 500.6000 | 269.5183 | 31.39399 | 35.10882 |
| Sum Sq. Dev. | 0.000210 | 0.019573 | 78.44400 | 2.862955 | 0.393756 | 0.413330 |
| Observations | 10 | 10 | 10 | 10 | 10 | 10 |

*Table 41. Documentation of pairwise Granger Causality Tests for Grand Index of Green Growth and Sustainability (GIGGS) and Production-based Carbon Dioxide ($CO2$) Productivity (PCDO), Non-energy Material Productivity (NEMP), Mean Population Exposure to PM2.5 (MPEPM), Environmentally adjusted Multifactor Productivity Growth (EAMFP), and The Global Sustainable Competitiveness Index ® (GSCI) respectively [**Country:** South Korea]*

Pairwise Granger Causality Tests
Date: 02/12/24 Time: 23:55
Sample: 2012 2021
Lags: 1

| Null Hypothesis: | Obs | F-Statistic | Prob. |
|---|---|---|---|
| GIGGS does not Granger Cause EAMFP | 9 | 1.42334 | 0.2779 |
| EAMFP does not Granger Cause GIGGS | | 0.00966 | 0.9249 |
| GSCI does not Granger Cause EAMFP | 9 | 0.12334 | 0.7374 |
| EAMFP does not Granger Cause GSCI | | 2.95633 | 0.1363 |
| MPEPM does not Granger Cause EAMFP | 9 | 0.19608 | 0.6734 |
| EAMFP does not Granger Cause MPEPM | | 5.79456 | 0.0528 |
| NEMP does not Granger Cause EAMFP | 9 | 0.52341 | 0.4966 |
| EAMFP does not Granger Cause NEMP | | 0.98913 | 0.3584 |
| PCDO does not Granger Cause EAMFP | 9 | 0.76223 | 0.4162 |
| EAMFP does not Granger Cause PCDO | | 0.61349 | 0.4633 |
| GSCI does not Granger Cause GIGGS | 9 | 1.62823 | 0.2491 |
| GIGGS does not Granger Cause GSCI | | 1.77000 | 0.2317 |
| MPEPM does not Granger Cause GIGGS | 9 | 0.60415 | 0.4665 |
| GIGGS does not Granger Cause MPEPM | | 0.89771 | 0.3800 |
| NEMP does not Granger Cause GIGGS | 9 | 3.78223 | 0.0998 |
| GIGGS does not Granger Cause NEMP | | 2.54812 | 0.1615 |
| PCDO does not Granger Cause GIGGS | 9 | 1.04536 | 0.3460 |
| GIGGS does not Granger Cause PCDO | | 1.32893 | 0.2928 |
| MPEPM does not Granger Cause GSCI | 9 | 2.79864 | 0.1454 |
| GSCI does not Granger Cause MPEPM | | 0.03875 | 0.8504 |
| NEMP does not Granger Cause GSCI | 9 | 0.92694 | 0.3728 |
| GSCI does not Granger Cause NEMP | | 3.15566 | 0.1260 |
| PCDO does not Granger Cause GSCI | 9 | 2.19016 | 0.1894 |
| GSCI does not Granger Cause PCDO | | 2.13217 | 0.1945 |
| NEMP does not Granger Cause MPEPM | 9 | 1.00478 | 0.3549 |
| MPEPM does not Granger Cause NEMP | | 0.32769 | 0.5878 |
| PCDO does not Granger Cause MPEPM | 9 | 0.65260 | 0.4500 |
| MPEPM does not Granger Cause PCDO | | 3.18331 | 0.1247 |
| PCDO does not Granger Cause NEMP | 9 | 0.03605 | 0.8557 |
| NEMP does not Granger Cause PCDO | | 7.66706 | 0.0325 |

*Table 42. Documentation of normality test (Jarque – Bera) results of residuals [**Country:** South Korea]*

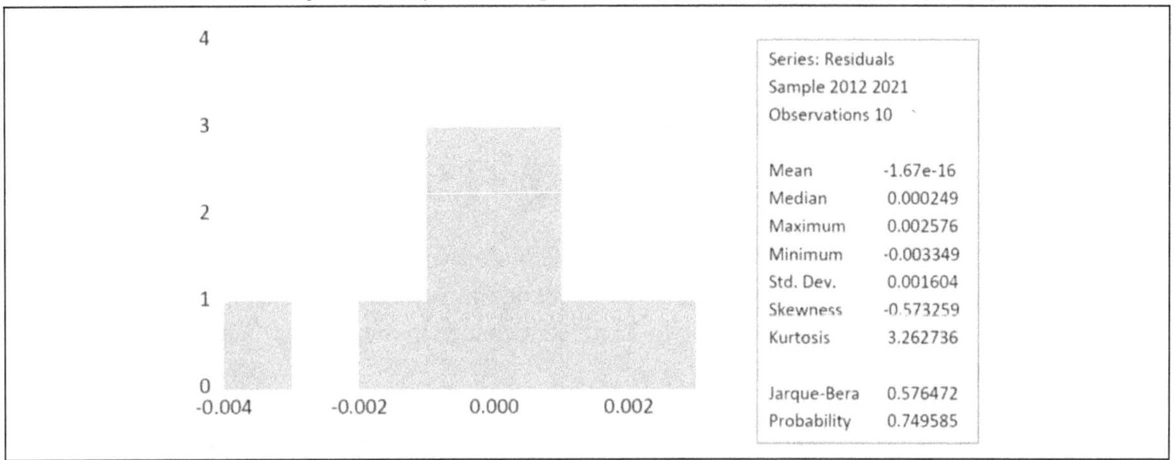


*Table 43. Regression equations of Grand Index of Green Growth and Sustainability (GIGGS) on Production-based Carbon Dioxide ($CO_2$) Productivity (PCDO), Non-energy Material Productivity (NEMP), Mean Population Exposure to $PM_{2.5}$ (MPEPM), Environmentally adjusted Multifactor Productivity Growth (EAMFP), and The Global Sustainable Competitiveness Index ® (GSCI) respectively for 5 sample countries (2012 – 2021)*

| Country | Regression equation | Reference |
|---|---|---|
| Denmark | $GIGGS = 1.61 - 0.11PCDO - 0.21NEMP - 0.05MPEPM + 0.22EAMFP + 0.01GSCI$ | Table 19 |
| Finland | $GIGGS = 4.65 - 0.37PCDO - 0.62NEMP - 0.02MPEPM + 0.39EAMFP$ | Table 24 |
| Sweden | $GIGGS = - 0.17NEMP - 0.05MPEPM + 0.02GSCI$ | Table 29 |
| Brazil | $GIGGS = 2.69 - 0.15PCDO - 1.19NEMP - 0.08MPEPM + 0.24EAMFP + 0.02GSCI$ | Table 34 |
| South Korea | $GIGGS = - 0.07PCDO - 0.14NEMP - 0.02MPEPM + 0.51EAMFP + 0.008GSCI$ | Table 39 |

i) In case of the *first* sample country Denmark, the Cross-NEMP elasticity of PCDO may be expressed as:

$$\text{Cross-NEMP elasticity of PCDO} = \frac{\partial GIGGS}{\partial NEMP} \div \frac{\partial GIGGS}{\partial PCDO} = \frac{-0.21}{-0.11} = 1.9$$

Hence it proves that for Denmark, productivity of $CO_2$ is highly sensitive to changes in MEMP as 1 percent change in NEMP would facilitate 2 percent change in the level of PCDO. Since the sign of the Cross-NEMP elasticity of PCDO is *positive*, NEMP and PCDO would be treated as *substitutes*. In a similar manner, the Cross-NEMP elasticity of MPEPM could be expressed as below:

$$\text{Cross-NEMP elasticity of MPEPM} = \frac{\partial GIGGS}{\partial NEMP} \div \frac{\partial GIGGS}{\partial MPEPM} = \frac{-0.21}{-0.05} = 4.2$$

The high value of Cross-NEMP elasticity of MPEPM proves that for 1 percent change in NEMP there would be 4 percent change in the level of MPEPM for Denmark. Just like PCDO, MPEPM is also a very strong substitute for NEMP. Finally, the Cross-EAMFP elasticity of GSCI for Denmark is defined as follows:

$$\text{Cross-EAMFP elasticity of GSCI} = \frac{\partial GIGGS}{\partial EAMFP} \div \frac{\partial GIGGS}{\partial GSCI} = \frac{0.22}{0.01} = 22$$

The very high value of Cross-EAMFP elasticity of GSCI proves that fact that Environment adjusted Multifactor Production methods have a significant effect on the Sustainable Development for Denmark as 1 percent change in EAMFP would bring in 22 percent change in the level of GSCI and they proved to be extremely strong substitutes;

ii) In case of the *second* sample country Finland, the Cross-NEMP elasticity of PCDO is estimated as 1.68 (approximately), whereas the estimated value of the Cross-NEMP elasticity of MPEPM is 31. Thus, in comparison to Denmark, Finland is much more *susceptible* to the changes in NEMP and Domestic Material Consumption (DMC) as higher DMC refers to high level of $CO_2$ production and extremely high level of $PM_{2.5}$ production as well for the said country;

iii) In case of the *third* sample country Sweden, the estimated Cross-NEMP elasticity of MPEPM is 3.4. It shows that as a country, Sweden is extremely sensitive to changes in NEMP / DMC also as 1 percent change in the level of NEMP would be accompanied by a 3 percent change in the level of MPEPM. Hence NEMP and MPEPM are considered to be strong substitutes for Sweden;

iv) In case of the *fourth* sample country Brazil, the estimated value of Cross-NEMP elasticity of PCDO will be 8 (approximately) and the estimated value of Cross-NEMP elasticity of MPEPM is 15 (approximately). Finally, the estimated value of the Cross-EAMFP elasticity of GCSI will be 12. Hence the comprehensive results state that Brazil is extremely sensitive in terms of changes in NEMP / DMC and EAMFP as well. For Brazil, 1 percent increase in DMC would invite 8 percent increase in $CO_2$ emission and 15 percent increase in $PM_{2.5}$ production respectively. On the other hand, 1 percent increase in Environment adjusted Multifactor production would facilitate 12 percent increase in GCSI score; and

v) Finally, in case of the *fifth* and final sample country South Korea, the estimated values of the Cross-NEMP elasticity of PCDO, Cross-NEMP elasticity of MPEPM, and Cross-EAMFP elasticity of GSCI are 2, 7, and 64 respectively. Like the 4 other sample countries, Brazil is also highly susceptible to the changes in NEMP / DMC and EAMFP respectively.

A perusal of the findings for 5 sample countries spread over 3 different continents (Europe, South America and Asia) provides us a clear idea that Domestic Material Consumption (DMC) plays the most crucial role in appreciation of $CO_2$ emission and $PM_{2.5}$ production of a country regardless of its demographical location. If the *most common* defining factor that needs to be chosen among the 5 sample countries to highlight the impact of Non-energy Material Productivity (NEMP) on environment, it would be definitely Cross-NEMP elasticity of MPEPM. If it is arranged in the *ascending* order for the 5 sample countries, the sequencing would be as follows: Sweden (3.4) < Denmark (4.2) < South Korea (7) < Brazil (15) < Finland (31). Although all the sample countries' environments are highly sensitive to the changes in DMC; South Korea, Brazil, and Finland are most vulnerable to air pollution due to $PM_{2.5}$ concentration. Apart from the Cross-

NEMP elasticity of MPEPM, the other important parameter is of course the Cross-NEMP elasticity of PCDO. Very interestingly, Brazil proved to be highly sensitive to changes in DMC as its environment gets *most* affected by $CO_2$ emission in comparison to Denmark, Finland, and South Korea respectively.

Note: The regression results of GIGGS on Production-based Carbon Dioxide ($CO_2$) Productivity (PCDO), Non-energy Material Productivity (NEMP), Mean Population Exposure to $PM_{2.5}$ (MPEPM), Environmentally adjusted Multifactor Productivity Growth (EAMFP), and The Global Sustainable Competitiveness Index ® (GSCI) respectively were derived by the use of Two-Stage Least Squares (2SLS) method and the results were found to be statistically significant at 5 percent level of significance or better and they successfully passed the Granger and Newbold's (1974)*Thumb rule test of Econometric Regression* by using the software GRETL v.1.9.4. Moreover; the statistical results of the Correlation Matrix, Descriptive Statistics, Pairwise Granger Causality Tests, and Normality Tests (Jarque and Bera, 1987) for Residuals in case of sample countries Denmark (Tables 20 – 23), Finland (Tables 25 – 28), Sweden (Tables 30 – 33), Brazil (Tables 35 – 38), and South Korea (Tables 40 – 43) respectively by the help of software EViews 12 SV have helped to prove the robustness and validity of the regression tests.

## Transition to Green Economy and Its Policy Implications

An appropriate prelude for the topic of transitioning to the Green Economy from the traditional production-based economy would be to venture about the *real* drivers of economic growth. A panel data analysis on 36 sample European countries for the time period Q32018 – Q32021 by Batrancea *et al.* (2022, p. 1) showed that economic growth measured by GDP, Gross Value Added (GVA), Final Household Consumption Expenditure (C), and Gross Fixed Capital Formation respectively has strong causal relationship with Exports (X), Imports (M), Net Foreign Direct Investment, Social Contributions, and Wages. However, as per the need of the hour of transitioning from production-based to green economy substantiated by green growth requires overcoming of strong hurdles. The essence of green growth is characterized by Sustainable Development (SD), more uses of renewable energy sources, and low carbon emission. Nevertheless, the models applied for transitioning to green economy for the Developed Countries may not be applicable for Developing and Emerging Economies as their goals and priorities are different (Batrancea *et al.*, 2021; p. 1). The major initiative for climate financing needs to be borne by the Developed Countries, however, due to complexities of 'The Adaptation Fund' under UN has made it difficult to achieve its final objective in a broad manner (Cadman and Sarker, 2022; p. 391).

In Cadman and Sarker's words (2022, p. 392): "The reality for much of the Earth's population, poor as they are, is that they have little influence over the climate negotiations, are unlikely to benefit from carbon markets, will bear the brunt of climate change impacts and are among those most affected by COVID-19." They further noted that: "...This chapter reinforces previous observations that the many different social and economic sectors currently being affected by the pandemic, and likely to be impacted in the future by climate change, need strong public fiscal management processes to encourage responsible private investment. In both public and private contexts, well-governed institutions are needed to foster resilience in the face of societal shocks. Systemic change is also necessary to tackle the interconnected and complex global challenges of climate change, poverty, inequality and biodiversity loss." (*Ibid.*, p. 393). Moreover, the drastic changes in socio-ecological systems have made the present scenario most challenging for the people dedicated to fight the adverse effects of climate change across the world. To quote Biggs *et al.* (2022, p. 4): "The pressing environmental and social sustainability challenges we face in the 21st century are clearly deeply intertwined. These challenges result from the confluence and interaction of multiple, mutually reinforcing social and ecological processes at multiple scales (Folke *et al.* 2016), where social processes include economic, political, cultural and technological processes, and ecological processes include biotic (e.g. population dynamics, food web interactions) and abiotic (e.g. nutrient flows, climate patterns) processes. The climate emergency and other environmental changes are underlain by a complex, interacting array of social changes, which themselves are shaped by the environment and environmental disruptions. Similarly, problems of poverty and inequality are often linked to and exacerbated by environmental change and disruption." The broad framework of Socio-ecological Systems (SES) includes different areas like adaptive governance, resilience assessment, and transformations toward sustainability. Biggs *et al.* (2022, p. 10) have succinctly illustrated the different core areas of SES approach as follows (Refer to Figure 11):

*Figure 11. The SES is a set of an intertwined, complex adaptive systems embedded in the biosphere*

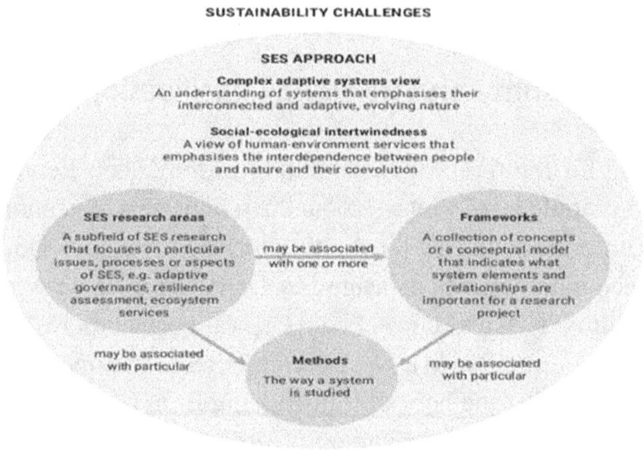


(**Source:***Biggs et al., 2022; p. 10)*

Wu *et al.* (2016, p. 14) have recommended three adaptation measures to fight the adverse effects of human infectious diseases due to climate change as follows: "1) to go beyond empirical observations of the association between climate change and infectious diseases and develop more scientific explanations, 2) to improve the prediction of spatial–temporal process of climate change and the associated shifts in infectious diseases at various spatial and temporal scales, and 3) to establish locally effective early warning systems for the health effects of predicated climate change." The current *linear* model of economy is based on 'Take-Make-Consume-Waste' system which often results in environmental degradation and exacerbates climate change. This model has already reached its limit of effectiveness (Hysa *et al.*, 2020; Nhamo *et al.*, 2024, pp. 2 – 3). On the other hand, the circular economy differs from the linear model by focusing on decoupled economic growth from finite resource consumption (Velenturf and Purnell, 2021) and it is regenerative and restorative by design and "maintains resources, products, and related materials at their highest value at all times" (Jørgensen and Pedersen, 2018; Nhamo *et al.* 2024, p. 3).

The major differences between a linear and a circular economy may be elucidated as follows (Refer to Table 44):

*Table 44. Comparison between a linear and a circular economy*

| Attribute | Linear Economy | Circular Economy |
|---|---|---|
| Business Model | Take-Make-Consume-Waste | Reduce-Reuse-Recycle |
| Efficiency Process | Eco-efficiency | Eco-effectivity |
| Product Time Frame | Short-term, focuses on profits | Long-term, multiple product values |
| Product Life Cycle | Downcycling quickly discards by-products into the environment | Upcycling, allowing products to stay long in use, regenerative and restorative |
| Vision | Focuses on products for profits | Focuses on the sustainability of product services |

(**Source:**Nhamo *et al.*, 2024; p. 4)

Thus, in order to achieve SD in the long run, a concerted effort is immediately solicited to balance efficient use of resources and maintain economic growth. To quote Nhamo *et al.* (2024, p. 5): "… Contemporary grand challenges, including climate change, the emergence of novel infectious diseases, environmental degradation, resource depletion, increasing inequality, and poverty, among other challenges, are interlinked and cut across sectors (Naidoo *et al.*, 2021b). The intricate interlinkages of the challenges and how they trigger crises in all sectors calls for integrated and transformative approaches (nexus planning, circular economy, just transition, one health, horizon scanning, sustainable food systems, and scenario planning) that apply cross-sectoral interventions and seek integrated solutions (Nhamo and Ndlela, 2021; Whitmee *et al.*, 2015)." To sum up, the major policy implications for transition to green economy are as follows: "According to the green technological innovation and CO2 emission average index in the G7 and BRICS countries, the green technology innovation level in the G7 countries is much higher than that in the BRICS countries, and that the CO2 emissions of the G7 countries are controlled. In contrast, CO2 emissions from the BRICS countries are still increasing. Therefore, this study provides some environmental benefits for policymakers. In terms of the G7 countries, they should continue to implement their green international cooperation technology, make full use combined effect of green technology development and green technology diffusion as well as maintain the sustainability of favorable ecological environment. For the BRICS countries, efforts to control CO2 emissions should include measures of promoting in the R&D and green technology development and preventing further environmental degradation through the combined effects of green international cooperation technology and green technology diffusion, aiming to achieve the sustainability." (Tan and Cao, 2023; p. 7).

## Climate Change, Ecosystems, and Environmental Impact Assessment (EIA)

The process of transition to green economy is intricately associated with the environmental, economic, and social benefits that ecosystems provide for Disaster Risk Reduction (DRR) and Climate Change Adaptation (CCA). The major benefits of healthy and well-managed ecosystems are: (1) They serve as a natural infrastructure or buffer to mitigate hazards and their impacts, (2) They help to reduce the exposure of people and assets to hazards, and (3) They reduce vulnerabilities by supporting sustainable and resilient livelihoods (Renauld *et al.*, 2013; Uy *et al.* 2022, p. 249). To quote Uy *et al.* (2022, p. 249): "IUCN (n.d.) provides five reasons for the critical role of ecosystems in DRR: (i) Ecosystems provide multiple livelihood benefits for human well-being, including enhancing resilience to hazards, (ii) Ecosystems act as cost-effective natural buffers against hazards and climate change impacts, (iii) People benefit from having healthy and diverse ecosystems due to their resilience to extreme weather events,

(iv) Ecosystem degradation generates adverse impacts in the ecosystem's reduced ability to sequester carbon and increasing the incidence and impacts of climate variability and change, including extreme weather events, and (v) Ecosystem degradation can result in human conflicts from competition over scarce natural resources, which can cause further ecosystem degradation. As an underlying driver of disaster risk, ecosystem degradation, particularly the loss of forests, wetlands, and coastal areas with mangroves and coral reefs, directly impacts human well-being (UNISDR 2015)." In this connection, the emerging concepts of Nature-based Solutions (NbS), Ecosystem-based Adaptations (EbA), and Blue-Green Infrastructure (BGI) are coming to the fore.

"The International Union for the Conservation of Nature (IUCN 2016, p. 1) defines NbS as "actions that protect, manage, and restore natural capital in ways that address societal challenges effectively and adaptively while simultaneously providing human well-being and biodiversity benefits." The European Commission (n.d.) describes NbS as "solutions that are inspired and supported by nature, which are cost-effective, simultaneously provide environmental, social and economic benefits and help build resilience. Such solutions bring more diverse nature and natural features and processes into cities, landscapes and seascapes, through locally adapted, resource-efficient and systemic interventions." (Uy *et al.*, 2022; p. 250). Whereas, to qualify as an EbA, "FEBA (2017) proposes three elements and five criteria to screen any activity or measure as the following:

> Element A: EbA helps people adapt to climate change
> Criterion 1. Reduces social and environmental vulnerabilities.
> Criterion 2. Generates societal benefits in the context of climate change adaptation.
> Element B: EbA makes active use of biodiversity and ecosystem services
> Criterion 3. Restores, maintains, or improves ecosystem health.
> Element C: EbA is part of an overall adaptation strategy
> Criterion 4. Is supported by policies at multiple levels.
> Criterion 5. Supports equitable governance and enhances capacities." (*Ibid.*, pp. 250 – 251)

Finally, "Nature-based Solutions combined with gray infrastructure form Blue-Green Infrastructure (BGI), hybrid solutions referred to as green infrastructure, bioengineering, or next-generation infrastructure. BGI exploits an ecosystem's natural ability to substitute for or strengthen infrastructure systems by preserving, enhancing, or restoring elements of a natural system to build high-quality, resilient and lower-cost infrastructure. Combining natural systems with technological and engineering systems such as dams, levees, reservoirs, treatment systems, and pipes enhances system performance for a more protected population (Browder et al. 2019). Integrating these natural building materials into infrastructure design increases their (i) strength over time, (ii) flexibility and capability to absorb ground movement and energy from water and wind, (iii) ability to recover from damage (ADB 2020)." (*Ibid.*, p. 251).

Keeping in mind the understanding of climate change is based on the hypothesis of anthropocentric and a 'direct effect of development and capitalism', Nordensvärd and Urban (2023, pp. 458 – 459) have emphasized on the mainstream global political consensus for tackling climate change "by creating a set of global policies and commitments that do not disrupt markets too much and that do not involve too radical changes. Another premise of the international climate policy system has historically been the differentiated responsibilities between developed and developing countries as the former have a historical responsibility for climate change and should therefore carry a larger burden." (*Ibid.*, p. 459). In this context, Gough (2011, p. 53) should be quoted as: "There is a need for integration across environmental, economic and social policy domains. This will require a much more active state than the dominant model under neo-liberalism."

Finally, Fonseca (2022, p. 132) has identified *four* major analyses that directly influence Environmental Impact Assessments (EIA) or can support overall evaluations of impact significance or acceptability as quoted:

- "Cost-benefit Analysis (CBA) and Environmental Cost-benefit Analysis (ECBA): Various methods that attempt to put a monetary value on a proposal's positive and negative impacts, so that they can be expressed in the same units and, therefore, aggregated and compared.
- Economic Impact Analysis (EconIA): Various methods that use input-output models to evaluate a proposal's overall economic impact in a particular area or region.
- Multi-criteria or multi-objective decision analysis (MCDA): A wide range of methods, from simple scoring/weighting checklists to sophisticated software-based decision-making models, that try to systematically evaluate the relative values or impacts, considering one or multiple points of view, as well as one or multiple goals or objectives. Among the many tools under this category are multi-attribute utility analysis, structured decision-making, goal achievement matrix, and rapid impact assessment matrix.
- Deliberative approaches: This category overlaps with the previous categories, as it refers to many types of methods that tend to put people at the forefront of impact judgment. It can be done through qualitative workshops and deliberative roundtables or employing more structured, quantitative processes. Examples of the latter include the Delphi method and game theory-based decision-making approaches."

During the phase of $4^{th}$ Industrial Revolution (4IR), the extensive use of digital and automated technologies including Artificial Intelligence (AI) has yielded mixed results in the domain of EIA. Fonseca (2022, p. 140) has aptly summed up the advantages and disadvantages of using digital and automated technologies to evaluate EIA as follows: "...While the many 4IR technologies can improve the technical and scientific quality of EIAs, one needs to remember that EIA is a multifaceted tool with political and cultural dimensions (Cashmore, 2004; Bond et al., 2020). Technical and scientific information are expected to influence decisions amid public participation and deliberations that are inherently value-laden and context-dependent. Therefore, the actual contributions of new technologies to the methodological soundness of EIA will depend on the quality of the political systems and governance schemes within and around them."

## Land Carbon Cycle Modeling, Life Cycle Sustainability Assessment, and Future Directions of Green Economy

The other major issues pertinent to the Green Economy that call for discussion are Land Carbon Cycle Modeling, and Life Cycle Sustainability Assessment respectively.

The major fundamental framework of Land Carbon Cycle rests upon the concept that "ecosystems converge toward some attractor states after anthropogenic and natural disturbances are removed. This convergence is done by 'Mother Nature' and actually results from the internal processes of the land carbon cycle." (Luo, 2024; pp. 3 – 4).

The *four* fundamental properties that govern the dynamics of land carbon cycle are:

- The Donor pool-dominated carbon transfer;
- Photosynthesis as the primary carbon influx pathway;
- Compartmentalization of carbon processes into plant, litter, and soil; and
- The first-order kinetics of carbon transfer from the donor pool (Luo and Weng, 2011; Luo 2024, p. 5).

Among these four properties, the donor pool-dominated carbon transfer is the most important one in determining the trajectory of the land carbon cycle and this is the reason which may turn Manhattan into a deciduous forest and Liujiazui of Shanghai into a lowland forest if human disturbances are removed (Luo, 2024; p. 5). The certainty of any ecosystem converging to some attractor state after human and natural disturbances reflects the high predictability of the land carbon cycle (Refer to Figure 12; Luo 2024, p. 9).

*Figure 12. Predictability of the terrestrial carbon cycle. Responses of the carbon cycle to a given type of external forcing is highly predictable*

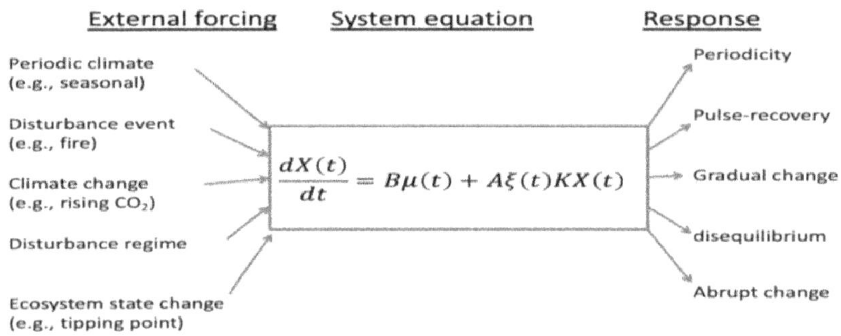


(**Source:***Luo, 2024; p. 9)*

*[**Note:** X(t) = A vector of litter (dead and decomposed parts of plants) pool sizes as a function of time t, B = A vector of partitioning coefficients from carbon input to each of the pools, μ(t) = The carbon input rate, A = A matrix with −1 in the diagonal and transfer coefficients in the off- diagonal to quantify carbon movement along the pathways, ξ(t) = A scalar or a diagonal matrix of environmental modifiers to represent responses of the carbon cycle to changes in temperature, moisture, and oxygen, and K = A diagonal matrix of process rates (mortality for plant pools and decomposition coefficients for litter and soil pools) from donor pools. Refer to Luo, 2024; pp. 6 – 9]*

Thus, the system equation displayed in Figure 12 gives us an overview how land carbon cycle modeling works in the context of external forcings and responds to a given set of stimuli.

Over the last decades, the concept of Life Cycle Thinking (LCT) has emerged as one of the founding pillars to address majority of today's sustainability challenges. In Strothmann and Fava's words (2024, p. 26): "LCT can help to identify opportunities for reducing the environmental impact of a product or service and can also help to optimize the use of resources. Additionally, LCT can help to support decision making and policy development by providing a comprehensive and holistic view of the impacts of a product or service."

*Figure 13. Evolution of the Life Cycle Thinking (LCT), Life Cycle Assessment (LCA), Life Cycle costing (LCC) and Product Environment Footprint (PEF) / Organizational Environment Footprint (OEF) in policies and communication*

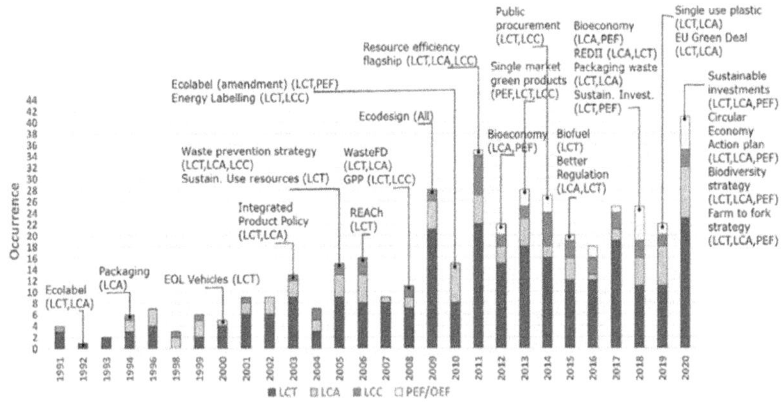


[**Sources:** *Sala et al., 2021; Strothmann and Fava (2024, p. 24)*]

Figure 13 provides us an overview of how "...universities gradually trained their students to take a life cycle perspective, over time the relevance and importance of LCT also made its way to governments and policy makers. Governmental programmes often lead to meaningful changes in how operations are managed and how products are designed, used and managed at their end of life. While many governments around the world have by now adopted various policies and regulations around LCT, the EU has been pushing legislation with LCT in mind for decades." (Strothmann and Fava, 2024; p. 23). Although several approaches and methodologies have been proposed for comprehensive assessment of sustainability of products and services (Sala *et al.* 2013; Schaubroeck and Rugani, 2017); the well-known applied framework is the Life Cycle Sustainability Assessment (LCSA) (UNEP/SETAC Life Cycle Initiative, 2011) which consists of *three* applied methodologies: Life Cycle Assessment (LCA) and Social LCA (S-LCA) – for assessing environmental and social impacts, and Life Cycle Costing (LCC) – for the economic impacts; although these are neither comprehensive nor exhaustive in nature (Cordella *et al.*, 2024; pp. 343 – 344).

In this regard, the assessment of sustainability of products/services and organization goes beyond the environmental issues, and requires addressal of socio-economic impacts also. Hence, the concept of Product Sustainability Footprint (PSF) (Pelletier *et al.*, 2014) may play a comprehensive role in depicting sustainable impacts. The major issue of PSF calls for a brief discussion about the 'Footprint family'. Footprints are the quantitative tools that give us the holistic pictures of the burdens and impacts related to human activities at different scales.

The *Footprint family* is broadly divided in 3 types: Ecological, Water, and Carbon respectively (Čuček *et al.*, 2012; Galli *et al.*, 2013; Vanham *et al.*, 2019; Cordella *et al.* 2024, p. 344). The Ecological Footprint (EF) is a composite indicator "quantifying the theoretical land demanded to sustain six types of human activities: 1) growing crops for food, animal feed, fibre, oil and rubber; 2) grazing of animals for meat, hides, wool and milk; 3) harvesting timber for wood, fibre and fuel; 4) marine and freshwater fishing; 5) accommodating infrastructure for housing, transportation, industrial production and hydro-electric power; and 6) burning fossil fuel (Wackernagel et al., 2002)." (Cordella *et al.* 2024, p. 345).

The Water Footprint (WF) aims to quantify impacts associated with the (mis) use and degradation of water systems related to consumption and scarcity of water as per the standards set by ISO 14046:2014. Finally, "The Carbon Footprint (CF) refers to the sum of greenhouse gas (GHG) emissions and removals, expressed as carbon dioxide equivalents (CO2-eq), occurring in the analysed system. CF is used for quantifying and setting appropriate emission reduction and climate change mitigation targets. At the level of products, international harmonisation has been achieved through the standard ISO 14067:2018." (*Ibid*., p. 345). In order to address the major issues related to socio-economic impacts and footprints family, the LCSA principles should incorporate more practical aspects of LCSA-based PSF that have raised some key challenges and potential concerns related to the followings:

1. "The availability of a robust, widely accepted, and applicable methodology for the sustainability assessment of products.
2. The needs in terms of rules, data, tools, resources and cross-disciplinary expertise necessary to carry out a sound LCSA – especially for the economic and social assessment.
3. Interpretation of results and their clear, responsible, and transparent communication to stakeholders (e.g., consumers, value chain actors, investors, regulators).
4. The comparability of the sustainability performance of products, taking the example set by the Product Environment Footprint Category Rules (PEFCRs), which resemble ISO 14025 and ISO 14027." (Ibid., p. 347)

Based on LCA, the sustainable circular procurement procedures may be implemented in the following ways:

1. "Select procurement criteria based on environmental, economic and social impact indicators (e.g., buying only from suppliers that consider good working conditions of primary collectors upstream of recycling of electronic products),
2. develop a holistic approach considering the processes and needs throughout the organization, and
3. apply an LCA-based methodology to quantify and compare the impacts of goods and services offered by potential suppliers where such an approach facilitates the incorporation of aspects related to supply and value chains." (UNDP, 2015; Peña et al. 2024, p. 372)

The relevant circular procurement criteria necessary for smooth functioning of a Circular Economy (CE) should be based on the concept of material and resource efficiency. There are different ways to improve the products' circularity performances and functions through product design and innovations such as:

- "The increase of the use of recycled materials and renewable resources,
- Constructions that consider recycled materials and dismountable components for extending their lifetime,
- The increase of the repair, maintenance and refurbishment potentials of products,
- The simplification of disassembly of products to facilitate the further use of components as spare parts, and
- The minimization of the content of environmentally hazardous substances and chemicals." (Peña et al., 2024; pp. 373 – 374)

The implementation of the CE strategy involves 3 main basic actions as follows:

(i) Retain Product Ownership (RPO), (ii) Product Life Extension (PLE), and (iii) Design for Recycling (DFR) – combinedly known as *The Circularity Matrix* (Refer to Figure 14).

*Figure 14. Circularity matrix to create circular business models*

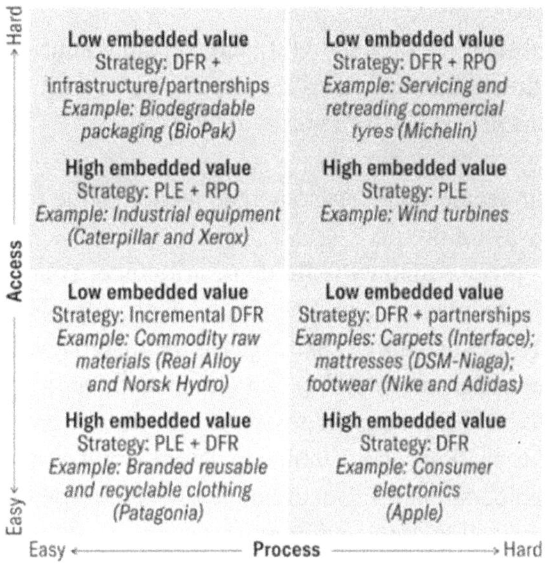


(**Sources:***Atasu et al. 2021; Peña et al. 2024, p. 374)*

The CE quantitative indicators are helpful in evaluating multiple CE strategies and can facilitate decision-making processes for policy makers by applying trade – offs associated with specific product systems. Material circularity and longevity indicators are the examples of broadly used metrices that help in measuring a more circular use of resources by keeping their optimum usages in mind. Figge *et al.* (2018) have proposed the integration of Material Circularity Indicator (MCI) and Longevity Indicator (LI). The equation of the MCI is expressed as below:

$$MCI = 1 - (LFI \times \frac{L}{L_{av}} \times \frac{U}{U_{av}}) \quad (1)$$

where LFI = Linear flow Index = Ratio of the used virgin material and generated waste to the product's total mass and the waste fraction from the upstream and downstream processes,

L = Lifetime of the product,
$L_{av}$ = Mean industry life time,
U = Intensity use of the product's functional unit, and
$U_{av}$ = Mean intensity us of the industry (Moraga *et al.* 2020).

On the other hand, the LI is an indicator used for measuring the time a resource is used and it is expressed as the sum of the time of first use of the material (as in a product), the time of its use when remanufactured, and the time of its use when recycled. It may be expressed as:

$$LI = L^{A} + L^{B} + L^{C} \tag{2}$$

where

$L^A$ = The initial lifetime of a product,
$L^B$ = The increased lifetime if the product returns for remanufacturing, and
$L^C$ = The increased lifetime if the material is recycled in a new format for the same product by the company (Franklin-Johnson *et al.* 2016; Peña *et al.* 2024, p. 375).

Finally, there are *four* clear avenues that have emerged related to the future directions of research in the domain of green economy as follows:

First, since the concept of green economy is fluid and still under continual development, the prioritization of the global climate emergency should be treated as the top policy priority to achieve a low-carbon and sustainable society. Despite all its challenges at the macro level, endeavors should continue towards the fusion of environmental sustainability and global economy;

Second, in the midst of the transitioning process to a 'genuinely' green economy, the problem of greenwashing remains. If the transition is not genuine in nature or not as a long-term commitment from the public and private stakeholders, the result will be clearly counterproductive and ultimately defeat the long-term goal of decarbonization of the environment;

Third, for the conceptual understanding of the green economy, the increased role of inter-sectoral research is highly solicited. For example, the financial sectors have received more attention in comparison to agricultural sector. The broader parts of service industries along with the intersection of services and manufacturing sectors have gained lower attention also.

Future research trends should be directed toward the major issues of digitalization of both public and private sectors, uses of Artificial Intelligence (AI) in better utilization of resources during transition, and how industries are adopting to *Lean production* systems in the IR 4.0; and

Fourth and final, there is an urgent need of the hour to emphasize on multilevel transdisciplinary approaches for the study of firms, industries and regions across the world to evaluate and analyze the impacts of 'greening' of economy as there remain a complexity of issues while transitioning to green economy based on single disciplinary approach. There is an increasing body of policy discourse that calls for concerted collaboration between governments at all scales leading to a greater economic and social cohesion at a global scale. (Jones and Ström, 2024; pp. 299 – 300)

## LIMITATIONS AND CONCLUSION

The major limitations of this research are two-fold: first; the number of sample countries is small which completely excludes the North American continent, and second; the time series study is of 10 years (2012 – 2021) only. The study would have been more robust had the length of the time series been greater or it would have been a panel data.

"Climate change is the result of the greatest market failure the world has ever seen" (Stern, 2007). To quote Henry (2020, p. 25): "Firms producing fossil fuels control proven reserves, the burning of which would generate about 2500–3000 Gt of $CO_2$ emissions – that is, more than four times the amount beyond which the increase in the Earth's mean temperature would exceed 1.5°C (IPCC, 2018)". Undoubtedly, the world is going through the greatest disastrous phase right now – the phase of environmental disaster. Apart from the grave issues of global warming and emission of GHGs, another extremely alarming issue regarding exposure of pathogens that were previously kept away in the depths of the forests is coming to the fore. In the words of Wilcox and Ellis (2006, p. 12): "Today, both deforestation and emerging infectious diseases remain largely associated with tropical regions but have impacts that extend globally". Apart from that, "Climate change will impact the spatial distributions of hosts, vectors, and pathogens, but may just as often lead to declines or shifts rather than expansions. Some habitats or environments may become too hot or too dry or too wet, whereas others that have previously been unsuitable habitats could perhaps shift to facilitate disease transmission (Lafferty and Mordecai 2016). Some pathogens and vectors may be resilient to climate change, and even thrive, and the incidence of these diseases will increase; but other vectors and pathogens may decline or disappear altogether." (Salkeld *et al.*, 2023; p. 218).

In order to fight these adversities, all forms of dominant capitalism and their practices should be resisted and dismantled. To quote Henry (2020, p. 41): "… Nevertheless, on the unsustainable path on which dominant capitalism keeps accelerating, all worthwhile initiatives will be wiped away, as will the rest of us. We cannot survive under such dominant capitalism; it must be dismantled, or it is the planet- and life-support systems that will be dismantled (see the World Economic Forum's Global Risks Report 2020)".

This major objective of this research paper is to formulate a comprehensive index named Grand Index of Green Growth and Sustainability (GIGGS) that would help us to accurately project a county's situation and standing based on two interconnected planks; i.e., green growth and sustainable development. Although, the study was confined to 5 sample countries, the formulation procedure of GIGGS could be replicated for any country for further analysis. However, GIGGS should be used judiciously and in a *normative* manner by the researchers for further advancements in this domain. By keeping this important factor in mind, this paper should be treated as a 'stepping-stone' for advanced research and critical analyses in one of the most pressing and burning issues of the contemporary world and human civilization as well.

## REFERENCES


ADB. (2017). ADB Annual Report 2017. Manila, Philippines: Asian Development Bank. https://www.adb.org/documents/adb-annual-report-2017

ADB. (2020). *Bioengineering for Green Infrastructure*. Manila, Philippines: Asian Development Bank. https://www.adb.org/sites/default/files/publication/577066/bioengineering-green-infrastructure.pdf

Atasu, A., Dumas, C., & Van Wassenhove, L. N. (2021). The circular business model: Pick a strategy that fits your resources and capabilities. *Harvard Business Review*. https://hbr.org/2021/07/the-circular-business-model

Barth, T. D. (2011). The Idea of a Green New Deal in a Quintuple Helix Model of Knowledge, Know-How and Innovation. *International Journal of Social Ecology and Sustainable Development*, *2*(1), 1–14. DOI: 10.4018/jsesd.2011010101

Batrancea, L., Balcı, M. A., Akgüller, Ö., & Gaban, L. (2022). What Drives Economic Growth across European Countries? A Multimodal Approach. *Mathematics*, *10*(3660), 1–20. DOI: 10.3390/math10193660

Batrancea, L., Pop, M. C., Rathnaswamy, M. M., Batrancea, I., & Rus, M.-I. (2021). An Empirical Investigation on the Transition Process toward a Green Economy. *Sustainability (Basel)*, *13*(13151), 1–12. DOI: 10.3390/su132313151

Bernard, S., Asokan, S., Warrell, H., & Lemer, J. (2009, August 17). The greenest bail-out? *Financial Times*. Retrieved from http://ig-legacy.ft.com/content/cc207678-0738-11de-9294-000077b07658#axzz7f2qUQzDG

Biggs, R., Clements, H., de Vos, A., Folke, C., Manyani, A., Maciejewski, K., Martín-López, B., Preiser, R., Selomane, O., & Schlüter, M. (2022). What are social-ecological systems and social-ecological systems research? In Biggs, R., de Vos, A., Preiser, R., Clements, H., Maciejewski, K., & Schlüter, M. (Eds.), *The Routledge Handbook of Research Methods for Social-Ecological Systems* (pp. 3–26). Routledge/ Taylor & Francis., DOI: 10.4324/9781003021339-2

Bina, O. (2013). The green economy and sustainable development: An uneasy balance? *Environment and Planning. C, Government & Policy*, *31*(6), 1023–1047. DOI: 10.1068/c1310j

Bond, A., Pope, J., Fundingsland, M., Morrison-Saunders, A., Retief, F., & Hauptfleisch, M. (2020). Explaining the political nature of environmental impact assessment (EIA): A neo-Gramscian perspective. *Journal of Cleaner Production*, *244*(January), 118694. DOI: 10.1016/j.jclepro.2019.118694

Browder, G., Ozment, S., Rehberger-Bescos, I., Gartner, T., & Lange, G-M. (2019, March 21). Integrating Green and Gray: Creating Next Generation Infrastructure. Washington, D.C.: World Resources Institute (WRI). DOI: DOI: 10.46830/wrirpt.18.00028

Cadman, T., & Sarker, T. (2022). Climate finance for sustainable development. In Cadman, T., & Sarker, T. (Eds.), *De Gruyter Handbook of Sustainable Development and Finance* (pp. 385–395). Walter de Gruyter GmbH., DOI: 10.1515/9783110733488-017

Carayannis, E. G., Barth, T. D., & Campbell, D. F. J. (2012). The Quintuple Helix innovation model: Global warming as a challenge and driver for innovation. *Journal of Innovation and Entrepreneurship, 1*(2), 1–12. DOI: 10.1186/2192-5372-1-1

Carayannis, E. G., & Campbell, D. F. J. (2009). 'Mode 3' and 'Quadruple Helix': Toward a 21st century fractal innovation ecosystem. *International Journal of Technology Management, 46*(3-4), 201–234. DOI: 10.1504/IJTM.2009.023374

Carayannis, E. G., & Campbell, D. F. J. (2010). Triple Helix, Quadruple Helix and Quintuple Helix and how do knowledge, innovation and the environment relate to each other? A proposed framework for a trans-disciplinary analysis of sustainable development and social ecology. [IJSESD]. *International Journal of Social Ecology and Sustainable Development, 1*(1), 1–29. DOI: 10.4018/jsesd.2010010101

Cashmore, M. (2004). The role of science in environmental impact assessment: Process and procedure versus purpose in the development of theory. *Environmental Impact Assessment Review, 24*(4), 403–426. DOI: 10.1016/j.eiar.2003.12.002

Cordella, M., Pihkola, H., Pajula, T., & Zamagni, A. (2024). Towards a future product sustainability footprint. In Valdivia, S., & Sonnemann, G. (Eds.), *Handbook on Life Cycle Sustainability Assessment* (pp. 343–356). Edward Elgar Publishing., DOI: 10.4337/9781800378650.00036

Crotty, J. (2012). The great austerity war: what caused the US deficit crisis and who should pay to fix it? *Cambridge Journal of Economics (January), 36(1)*, 79 – 104. DOI: DOI: 10.1093/cje/ber029

Čuček, L., Klemeš, J., & Kravanja, Z. (2012). A Review of Footprint analysis tools for monitoring impacts on sustainability. *Journal of Cleaner Production, 34*(October), 9–20. DOI: 10.1016/j.jclepro.2012.02.036

Das, N. G. (2008). Statistical Methods: Vol. I & II. *New Delhi: McGraw Hill Education*. Private Limited.

Dechezleprêtre, A., Martin, R., & Bassi, S. (2019). Climate change policy, innovation and growth. In Fouquet, R. (Ed.), *Handbook on Green Growth* (pp. 217–239). Edward Elgar Publishing., DOI: 10.4337/9781788110686.00018

Dryzek, J. S. (2005). *The Politics of the Earth: Environmental Discourses* (2nd ed.). Oxford University Press.

Ducoing, C. (2019). How to handle natural capital within the context of the green economy? In Acar, S., & Yeldan, E. (Eds.), *Handbook of Green Economics* (pp. 19–30). Academic Press / Elsevier., DOI: 10.1016/B978-0-12-816635-2.00002-X

EMF. (2013). *Towards the Circular Economy: Economic and Business Rationale for an Accelerated Transition*. Ellen MacArthur Foundation., DOI: 10.1162/108819806775545321

EMF. (2015). *Growth within: a circular economy vision for a competitive Europe*, Ellen MacArthur Foundation. https://ellenmacarthurfoundation.org/growth-within-a-circular-economy-vision-for-a-competitive-europe

Etzkowitz, H., & Leydesdorff, L. (2000). The dynamics of innovation: From National Systems and "Mode 2" to a Triple Helix of university–industry–government relations. *Research Policy, 29*(2), 109–123. DOI: 10.1016/S0048-7333(99)00055-4

Figge, F., Stevenson Thorpe, A., Givry, P., Canning, L., & Franklin-Johnson, E. (2018). Longevity and Circularity as Indicators of Eco-Efficient Resource Use in the Circular Economy. *Ecological Economics*, *150*(August), 297–306. DOI: 10.1016/j.ecolecon.2018.04.030

Fisher, I. (1906). *The Nature of Capital and Income*. The Macmillan Company Ltd. DOI: 10.1515/9783112351369

Folke, C., Biggs, R., Norström, A. V., Reyers, B., & Norström, J. (2016). Social-ecological resilience and biosphere-based sustainability science. *Ecology and Society*, *21*(3), 41. DOI: 10.5751/ES-08748-210341

Fonseca, A. (2022). The benefits and perils of digital and automated technologies: impact assessment methods in the fourth industrial revolution. In Fonseca, A. (Ed.), *Handbook of Environmental Impact Assessment* (pp. 126–145). Edward Elgar Publishing., DOI: 10.4337/9781800379633.00013

Franklin-Johnson, E., Figge, F., & Canning, L. (2016). Resource duration as a managerial indicator for Circular Economy performance. *Journal of Cleaner Production*, *133*(October), 589–598. DOI: 10.1016/j.jclepro.2016.05.023

Freer-Smith, P. H., Beckett, K. P., & Taylor, G. (2005). Deposition velocities to Sorbus aria, Acer campestre, Populus deltoides × trichocarpa 'Beaupré', Pinus nigra and × Cupressocyparis leylandii for coarse, fine and ultra-fine particles in the urban environment. *Environmental Pollution (January), 133(1)*, 157 – 167. DOI: DOI: 10.1016/j.envpol.2004.03.031

Friends of Ecosystem-based Adaptation (FEBA). (2017). *Making ecosystem-based adaptation effective: A framework for defining qualification criteria and quality standards. FEBA technical paper developed for UNFCCC-SBSTA 46*. Bonn (Germany): GIZ, London (UK): IIED, and Gland (Switzerland): IUCN. https://www.iucn.org/sites/default/files/2022-07/feba_eba_qualification_and_quality_criteria_final_en.pdf (accessed on June 21, 2024)

Galli, A., Weinzettel, J., Cranston, G., & Ercin, E. (2013). A Footprint Family extended MRIO model to support Europe's transition to a One Planet Economy. *The Science of the Total Environment*, *461-462*(September), 813–818. DOI: 10.1016/j.scitotenv.2012.11.071 PMID: 23273807

Gough, I. (2011). *Climate change and public policy futures*. The British Academy., https://www.thebritishacademy.ac.uk/publications/new-paradigms-climate-change-public-policy-futures/

Granger, C. W. J., & Newbold, P. (1974). Spurious regressions in econometrics. *Journal of Econometrics*, *2*(2), 111–120. DOI: 10.1016/0304-4076(74)90034-7

Gujarati, D. N. (2003). *Basic Econometrics* (4th ed.). McGraw – Hill, Inc.

Hamilton, K., & Hartwick, J. M. (2005). Investing exhaustible resource rents and the path of consumption. *The Canadian Journal of Economics. Revue Canadienne d'Economique*, *38*(2), 615–621. DOI: 10.1111/j.0008-4085.2005.00295.x

Hamilton, K., & Naikal, E. (2014). Comprehensive wealth accounting and sustainable development. In Atkinson, G., Dietz, S., Neumayer, E., & Agarwala, M. (Eds.), *Handbook of Sustainable Development* (2nd ed., pp. 25–40). Edward Elgar Publishing., DOI: 10.4337/9781782544708.00010

Henderson, J. M., & Quandt, R. E. (1980). Microeconomic Theory: A Mathematical Approach *(3rd International ed.)*. Singapore: McGraw – Hill Book Company (Originally published by McGraw – Hill Inc., New York, USA).

Henry, C. (2020). Capitalism and the curse of external effects. In Henry, C., Rockström, J., & Stern, N. (Eds.), *Standing up for a Sustainable World: Voices of Change* (pp. 24–46). Edward Elgar Publishing., DOI: 10.4337/9781800371781.00011

Hickel, J., & Kallis, G. (2020). Is green growth possible? *New Political Economy*, *25*(4), 469–486. DOI: 10.1080/13563467.2019.1598964

Hicks, B. B., Baldocchi, D. D., Meyers, T. P., Hosker, R. P.Jr, & Matt, D. R. (1987). A preliminary multiple resistance routine for deriving dry deposition velocities from measured quantities. *Water, Air, and Soil Pollution*, *36*(3-4), 311–330. DOI: 10.1007/BF00229675

Hysa, E., Kruja, A., Rehman, N. U., & Laurenti, R. (2020). Circular Economy Innovation and Environmental Sustainability Impact on Economic Growth: An Integrated Model for Sustainable Development. *Sustainability (Basel)*, *12*(12), 4831. DOI: 10.3390/su12124831

ILO/EU/IILS. (2011). TOWARDS A GREENER ECONOMY: THE SOCIAL DIMENSIONS. *International Institute for Labour Studies (IILS)*, 1 – 103. https://www.ilo.org/wcmsp5/groups/public/---dgreports/---dcomm/---publ/documents/publication/wcms_168163.pdf

Inderst, G., Kaminker, C., & Stewart, F. (2012). Defining and Measuring Green Investments: Implications for Institutional Investors' Asset Allocations. *OECD Working Papers on Finance, Insurance and Private Pensions, No. 24*. Paris, France: OECD Publishing. DOI: DOI: 10.1787/20797117

International Union for the Conservation of Nature (IUCN). (2016). World Conservation Congress 2016 Resolution 069: Defining nature-based solutions. https://portals.iucn.org/ library/ sites/ library/ files/ resrecfiles/ WCC_ 2016_ RES_ 069_ EN .pdf

International Union for the Conservation of Nature (IUCN). (n.d.). *Five reasons why ecosystems are central to disaster risk reduction*. https://www.iucn.org/ theme/ ecosystem -management/ our -work/ environment -and -disasters/ about -ecosystem -based -disaster -risk -reduction -eco -drr/ five -reasons -why-ecosystems -are -central -disaster -risk -reduction

ISO 14025:2006. *Environmental labels and declarations – Type III environmental declarations – Principles and procedures.*

ISO 14046:2014. *Environmental management – Water footprint – Principles, requirements, and guidelines.*

ISO/TS 14027:2017. *Environmental labels and declarations – Development of product category rules.*

Jarque, C. M., & Bera, A. K. (1987). A Test for Normality of Observations and Regression Residuals. *International Statistical Review*, *55*(2), 163–172. DOI: 10.2307/1403192

Jones, A., & Ström, P. (2024). Coda: future directions and challenges for research into the green economy. In Jones, A., & Ström, P. (Eds.), *Research Handbook on the Green Economy* (pp. 299–300). Edward Elgar Publishing., DOI: 10.4337/9781789904833.00029

Jørgensen, S., & Pedersen, L. J. T. (2018). The Circular Rather than the Linear Economy. In *RESTART Sustainable Business Model Innovation* (pp. 103–120). Palgrave Macmillan/ Springer Nature., DOI: 10.1007/978-3-319-91971-3_8

Kirchherr, J., Reike, D., & Hekkert, M. (2017). Conceptualizing the circular economy: An analysis of 114 definitions. *Resources, Conservation and Recycling*, *127*(December), 221–232. DOI: 10.1016/j.resconrec.2017.09.005

Lafferty, K. D., & Mordecai, E. A. (2016, August 19). The rise and fall of infectious disease in a warmer world. *F1000 Research Review 5: 2040*. PMID: 27610227; DOI: https://doi.org/DOI: 10.12688%2Ff1000research.8766.1

Lavrinenko, O., Ignatjeva, S., Ohotina, A., Rybalkin, O., & Lazdans, D. (2019). The Role of Green Economy in Sustainable Development (Case Study: The EU States). *Journal of Entrepreneurship and Sustainability Issues*, *6*(3), 1113–1126. DOI: 10.9770/jesi.2019.6.3(4)

Lazarevic, D., & Brandão, M. (2020). The circular economy: a strategy to reconcile economic and environmental objectives? In Brandão, M., Lazarevic, D., & Finnveden, G. (Eds.), *Handbook of the Circular Economy* (pp. 8–27). Edward Elgar Publishing., DOI: 10.4337/9781788972727.00009

Lee, B. H., Georgallis, P., & Struben, J. (2022). Sustainable entrepreneurship under market uncertainty: opportunities, challenges and impact. In George, G., Haas, M., Joshi, H., Mcgahan, A., & Tracey, P. (Eds.), *Handbook on the Business of Sustainability* (pp. 252–272). Edward Elgar Publishing., DOI: 10.4337/9781839105340.00022

Luo, Y. (2024). Theoretical Foundation of the Land Carbon Cycle and Matrix Approach. In Luo, Y., & Smith, B. (Eds.), *Land Carbon Cycle Modeling: Matrix Approach, Data Assimilation, Ecological Forecasting, and Machine Learning* (2nd ed., pp. 3–10). CRC Press / Taylor & Francis., DOI: 10.1201/9781032711126-2

Luo, Y., & Weng, E. (2011). Dynamic disequilibrium of the terrestrial carbon cycle under global change. *Trends in Ecology & Evolution*, *26*(2), 96–104. DOI: 10.1016/j.tree.2010.11.003 PMID: 21159407

McCahery, J. A., & Vermeulen, E. P. M. (2014). Business Growth and Firm Value Creation: The "Ignored" Third Dimension of Corporate Governance. *Journal of Self-Governance and Management Economics*, *2*(4), 69–76.

McCollum, J. (2023). Avoiding the pitfalls of Capitalism in the Green New Deal. In Tienhaara, K., & Robinson, J. (Eds.), *Routledge Handbook on The Green New Deal* (pp. 73–87). Routledge/ Taylor & Francis., DOI: 10.4324/9781003110880

Meltzer, J., Steven, D., & Langley, C. (2013, February). The United States after the Great Recession: The Challenge of Sustainable Growth. *Global Economy and Development: Brookings Working Paper No. 60*, 1 – 52. https://www.brookings.edu/wp-content/uploads/2016/06/02-us-post-great-recession-meltzer-steven.pdf

Moraga, G., Huysveld, S., de Meester, S., & Dewulf, J. (2020). Towards a circularity indicator to assess products' materials and lifetime: In-use occupation. *Procedia CIRP*, *90*, 10–13. DOI: 10.1016/j.procir.2020.01.085

Naidoo, D., Nhamo, L., Mpandeli, S., Sobratee, N., Senzanje, A., Liphadzi, S., Slotow, R., Jacobson, M., Modi, A. T., & Mabhaudhi, T. (2021). Operationalising the water-energy-food nexus through the theory of change. *Renewable & Sustainable Energy Reviews, 149*(October), 111416. DOI: 10.1016/j.rser.2021.111416 PMID: 37693280

Nhamo, L., Mpandeli, S., Liphadzi, S., & Mabhaudhi, T. (2024). Understanding circularity and transformative approaches and their role in achieving sustainability. In Nhamo, L., Mpandeli, S., Liphadzi, S., & Mabhaudhi, T. (Eds.), *Circular and Transformative Economy: Advances towards Sustainable Socio-economic Transformation* (pp. 1–8). CRC Press/ Taylor & Francis., DOI: 10.1201/9781003327615-1

Nhamo, L., & Ndela, B. (2021). Nexus planning as a pathway towards sustainable environmental and human health post Covid-19. *Environmental Research, 192*(January), 110376. DOI: 10.1016/j.envres.2020.110376 PMID: 33115599

Noh, H. J. (2018, September). Financial Strategy to Accelerate Green Growth. *ADBI Working Paper No. 866*, 1 – 23. Tokyo: Asian Development Bank Institute. https://www.adb.org/publications/financial-strategy-accelerate-green-growth

Noh, H. J. (2019). Financial Strategies to Accelerate Green Growth. In Sachs, J. D., Woo, W. T., Yoshino, N., & Taghizadeh-Hesary, F. (Eds.), *Handbook of Green Finance: Energy Security and Sustainable Development* (pp. 37–61). Springer Nature., DOI: 10.1007/978-981-13-0227-5_16

Nordensvärd, J., & Urban, F. (2023). The role of energy and climate policy in mitigating global climate change. In Urban, F., & Nordensvärd, J. (Eds.), *Handbook on Climate Change and Technology* (pp. 446–463). Edward Elgar Publishing., DOI: 10.4337/9781800882119.00047

Nowak, D. J., Crane, D. E., & Stevens, J. C. (2006). Air pollution removal by urban trees and shrubs in the United States. *Urban Forestry & Urban Greening (April), 4(3-4)*, 115 – 123. DOI: DOI: 10.1016/j.ufug.2006.01.007

OECD. (2017). *Green Growth Indicators 2017*. https://www.oecd.org/env/green-growth-indicators-2017-9789264268586-en.htm

Pelletier, N., Maas, R., Goralczyk, M., & Wolf, M.-A. (2014). Conceptual basis for development of the European Sustainability Footprint. *Environmental Development, 9*(January), 12–23. DOI: 10.1016/j.envdev.2013.12.003

Peña, C., Ryding, S.-O., Židonienė, S., & Saldivar, S. (2024). Life cycle sustainability thinking for measuring and assessing circularity towards sustainable procurement. In Valdivia, S., & Sonnemann, G. (Eds.), *Handbook on Life Cycle Sustainability Assessment* (pp. 370–377). Edward Elgar Publishing., DOI: 10.4337/9781800378650.00039

Popescu, G. H. (2014). Economic aspects influencing the rising costs of health care in the United States. *American Journal of Medical Research (New York, N.Y.), 1*(1), 47. https://link.gale.com/apps/doc/A426766518/AONE?u=googlescholar&sid=bookmark-AONE&xid=66531cd9

Renauld, F. G., Sudmeier-Rieux, K., & Estrella, M. (2013). *The Role of Ecosystems in Disaster Risk Reduction*. United Nations University Press.

Rockström, J., Steffen, W., Noone, K., Persson, Å., Chapin, F. S.III, Lambin, E. F., Lenton, T. M., Scheffer, M., Folke, C., Schellnhuber, H. J., Nykvist, B., de Wit, C. A., Hughes, T., van der Leeuw, S., Rodhe, H., Sörlin, S., Snyder, P. K., Costanza, R., Svedin, U., & Foley, J. A. (2009). A safe operating space for humanity. *Nature*, *461*(7263), 472–475. DOI: 10.1038/461472a PMID: 19779433

Sachs, J. D., Woo, W. T., Yoshino, N., & Taghizadeh-Hesary, F. (2019). Importance of Green Finance for Achieving Sustainable Development Goals and Energy Security. In Sachs, J. D., Woo, W. T., Yoshino, N., & Taghizadeh-Hesary, F. (Eds.), *Handbook of Green Finance: Energy Security and Sustainable Development* (pp. 3–12). Springer Nature., DOI: 10.1007/978-981-13-0227-5_13

Sala, S., Amadei, A. M., Beylot, A., & Ardente, F. (2021). The evolution of life cycle assessment in European policies over three decades. *The International Journal of Life Cycle Assessment*, *26*(12), 2295–2314. DOI: 10.1007/s11367-021-01893-2

Sala, S., Farioli, F., & Zamagni, A. (2013). Life cycle sustainability assessment in the context of sustainability science progress (part 2). *The International Journal of Life Cycle Assessment*, *18*(9), 1686–1697. DOI: 10.1007/s11367-012-0509-5

Schaubroeck, T., & Rugani, B. (2017). A Revision of What Life Cycle Sustainability Assessment Should Entail: Towards Modeling the Net Impact on Human Well-Being. *Journal of Industrial Ecology*, *21*(6), 1464–1477. DOI: 10.1111/jiec.12653

Schoenmaker, D., & Schramade, W. (2019). *Principles of Sustainable Finance*. Oxford University Press.

Selkald, D., Hopkins, S., & Hayman, D. (2023). *Emerging Zoonotic and Wildlife Pathogens: Disease Ecology, Epidemiology, and Conservation*. Oxford University Press., DOI: 10.1093/oso/9780198825920.001.0001

Sertyesilisik, B., & Sertyesilisik, E. (2017). Ways of Fostering Green Economy and Green Growth. In Filho, W. L., Pociovalisteanu, D.-M., & Al-Amin, A. Q. (Eds.), *Sustainable Economic Development: Green Economy and Green Growth* (pp. 49–65). Springer Nature., DOI: 10.1007/978-3-319-45081-0_3

Steffen, W., Persson, Å., Deutsch, L., Zalasiewicz, J., Williams, M., Richardson, K., Crumley, C., Crutzen, P., Folke, C., Gordon, L., Molina, M., Ramanathan, V., Rockström, J., Scheffer, M., Schellnhuber, H. J., & Svedin, U. (2011). The Anthropocene: From Global Change to Planetary Stewardship. *Ambio*, *40*(7), 739–761. DOI: 10.1007/s13280-011-0185-x PMID: 22338713

Stern, N. (2007, November 29 - 30). Climate change, ethics and the economics of the global deal. *Proceedings of The Royal Economic Society Annual Public Lecture*, University of Manchester and Institute of Education, London. Available at https://cepr.org/voxeu/columns/climate-change-ethics-and-economics-global-deal#:~:text=The%20extra%20costs%20developing%20countries,is%20not%20separate%20from%20it

Stiglitz, J. E., Sen, A., & Fitoussi, J.-P. (2009). *Report by the Commission on the Measurement of Economic Performance and Social Progress*, 1 – 291. Paris: France. https://ec.europa.eu/eurostat/documents/8131721/8131772/Stiglitz-Sen-Fitoussi-Commission-report.pdf

Strothmann, P., & Fava, J. (2024). Evolution of life cycle thinking as part of the global sustainable consumption and production agenda. In Valdivia, S., & Sonnemann, G. (Eds.), *Handbook on Life Cycle Sustainability Assessment* (pp. 17–29). Edward Elgar Publishing., DOI: 10.4337/9781800378650.00011

Tallis, M. J., Amorim, J. H., Calfapietra, C., Freer-Smith, P., Grimmond, S., Kotthaus, S., de Oliviera, L., Miranda, A. I., & Toscano, P. (2015). The impacts of green infrastructure on air quality and temperature. In Sinnett, D., Smith, N., & Burgess, S. (Eds.), *Handbook on Green Infrastructure: Planning, Design and Implementation* (pp. 30–49). Edward Elgar Publishing., DOI: 10.4337/9781783474004.00008

Tan, W., & Cao, T. (2023). Can green technology reduce carbon dioxide emissions? Evidence from G7 and BRICS countries. *Heliyon*, *9*(5, e15683), 1–10. DOI: 10.1016/j.heliyon.2023.e15683 PMID: 37305514

The Economist (2012, October 13). *True Progressivism.* Retrieved from https://www.economist.com/leaders/2012/10/13/true-progressivism

UNDP. (2015). *UNDP Procurement Strategy 2015–2017.* New York: NY: United Nations Development Programme. https://www.undp.org/procurement/strategy

UNEP/SETAC Life Cycle Initiative. (2011, February 26). *Towards a life cycle sustainability assessment: making informed choices on products.* https://www.unep.org/resources/report/towards-life-cycle-sustainability-assessment-making-informed-choices-products (accessed on June 21, 2024)

United Nations Office for Disaster Risk Reduction (UNISDR). (2015). *Making development sustainable: The future of disaster risk management. Global Assessment Report on Disaster Risk Reduction.* Geneva, Switzerland: UNISDR. https://www.preventionweb.net/files/43847_01efdrr07oct2015franceandrewmaskrey.pdf?startDownload=true

Uy, N., Tapnio, C., & Dineros, A. (2022). Ecosystem-based risk reduction in policy and practice. In Shaw, R. (Ed.), *Handbook on Climate Change and Disasters* (pp. 249–267). Edward Elgar Publishing., DOI: 10.4337/9781800371613.00031

Vanham, D., Leip, A., Galli, A., Kastner, T., Bruckner, M., Uwizeye, A., van Dijk, K., Ercin, E., Dalin, C., Brandão, M., Bastianoni, S., Fang, K., Leach, A., Chapagain, A., Van der Velde, M., Sala, S., Pant, R., Mancini, L., Monforti-Ferrario, F., & Hoekstra, A. Y. (2019). Environmental footprint family to address local to planetary sustainability and deliver on the SDGs. *The Science of the Total Environment*, *693*(November), 133642. DOI: 10.1016/j.scitotenv.2019.133642 PMID: 31635013

Velenturf, A. P. M., & Purnell, P. (2021). Principles for a sustainable circular economy. *Sustainable Production and Consumption*, *27*(July), 1437–1457. DOI: 10.1016/j.spc.2021.02.018

Victor, P. A. (2010). Ecological economics and economic growth. *Annals of the New York Academy of Sciences*, *1185*(1), 237–245. DOI: 10.1111/j.1749-6632.2009.05284.x PMID: 20146773

Victor, P. A. (2019). *Managing Without Growth: Slower by Design, Not Disaster* (2nd ed.). Edward Elgar Publishing., DOI: 10.4337/9781785367380

Victor, P. A., & Sers, M. (2019). The limits to green growth. In Fouquet, R. (Ed.), *Handbook on Green Growth* (pp. 30–51). Edward Elgar Publishing., DOI: 10.4337/9781788110686.00008

Voica, M. C., Panait, M., & Radulescu, I. (2015). Green Investments – Between Necessity, Fiscal Constraints and Profit. *Procedia Economics and Finance*, *22*, 72–79. DOI: 10.1016/S2212-5671(15)00228-2

Wackernagel, M., Schulz, N. B., Deumling, D., Linares, A. C., Jenkins, M., Kapos, V., Monfreda, C., Loh, J., Myers, N., Norgaard, R., & Randers, J. (2002). Tracking the ecological overshoot of the human economy. *Proceedings of the National Academy of Sciences of the United States of America*, *99*(14), 9266–9271. DOI: 10.1073/pnas.142033699 PMID: 12089326

WEF. (2020). The Global Risks Report 2020. https://www.weforum.org/reports/the-global-risks-report-2020/

Whitmee, S., Haines, A., Beyrer, C., Boltz, F., Capon, A. G., Ferreira de Souza Dias, B., Ezeh, A., & Frumkin, H. (2015). Safeguarding human health in the Anthropocene epoch: Report of The Rockefeller Foundation–Lancet Commission on planetary health. *Lancet*, *386*(10007), 1973–2028. DOI: 10.1016/S0140-6736(15)60901-1 PMID: 26188744

Wilcox, B. A., & Ellis, B. (2006). Forests and emerging infectious diseases of humans. *Unasylva*, *57*, 11–18. https://www.fao.org/3/a0789e/a0789e03.htm

Wu, X., Lu, Y., Zhou, S., Chen, L., & Xu, B. (2016). Impact of climate change on human infectious diseases: Empirical evidence and human adaptation. *Environment International*, *86*, 14–23. DOI: 10.1016/j.envint.2015.09.007 PMID: 26479830

Yoshino, N., & Taghizadeh-Hesary, F. (2018). Alternatives to Private Finance: Role of Fiscal Policy Reforms and Energy Taxation in Development of Renewable Energy Projects. In Anbumozhi, V., Kalirajan, K., & Kimura, F. (Eds.), *Financing for Low-carbon Energy Transition: Unlocking the Potential of Private Capital* (pp. 335–357). Springer Nature., DOI: 10.1007/978-981-10-8582-6_13

## ABBREVIATIONS

**C:** Concentration of pollution
**$C_F$:** Flux elasticity of Concentration
**CGGI:** Comprehensive Green Growth Index
**$C_R$:** Resistance elasticity of Concentration
**DMC:** Domestic Material Consumption
**EAMFP:** Environmentally adjusted Multifactor Productivity Growth
**EC:** Environmental Cost
**EI:** Environmental Intensity
**EP:** Environmental Pressure
**F:** Flux
**GDP:** Gross Domestic Product (In Current US Dollar)
**GHG:** Greenhouse Gas
**GIGGS:** Grand Index of Green Growth and Sustainability
**GSCI:** The Global Sustainable Competitiveness Index ®
**IEP:** IsoEnvironmental Pressure Curve
**MPEPM:** Mean Population Exposure to $PM_{2.5}$ [Expressed in micrograms per cubic meter ($\mu g/m^3$)]
**NEMP:** Non-energy Material Productivity, GDP per unit of DMC [Measured in US Dollar/kg]

**PCDO:** Production-based Carbon Dioxide ($CO_2$) Productivity, GDP per unit of energy-related $CO_2$ emissions [Measured in US Dollar/kg]

**R:** Resistance to pollutant removal from the atmosphere to the surface

**SD:** Sustainable Development

**$V_d$:** Velocity of Deposition

# Chapter 8
# The Violation of Human Rights by the Chevron–Texaco Oil Company in the Ecuadorian Amazon:
## The Lago Agrio Case

**Arturo Luque González**
https://orcid.org/0000-0002-4872-891X
*Universidad Técnica de Manabí, Ecuador*

**Geomayra Lisbeth Castro Cedeño**
*Universidad Técnica de Manabí, Ecuador*

**Maira Yadira Pinargote Mendoza**
*Universidad Técnica de Manabí, Ecuador*

**Cristina Raluca Gh. Popescu**
https://orcid.org/0000-0002-5876-0550
*University of Bucharest, Romania & The Bucharest University of Economic Studies, Romania*

## ABSTRACT

*This research explores a complex lawsuit between Chevron Corporation and the Huaorani community of Lago Agrio, an indigenous group affected by oil pollution in the Ecuadorian Amazon. It focuses on the consequences of this pollution from legal, ethical, and socio-environmental perspectives within the oil fields operated by the international company. The issue has sparked heated debates and litigation both domestically and internationally for years, highlighting the environmental devastation and socio-economic, human, and cultural damages still impacting local communities. This necessitates a normative study of harmful practices leading to complete destruction of rivers, soil, and air, causing serious health issues like respiratory, dermatological diseases, cancer, and numerous deaths, alongside environmental damage affecting both flora and fauna. Chevron's negligence and multiple legal claims have led to significant but unenforced compensations, drawing global attention to this historic conflict marked by international power abuses, particularly by the USA, with several judgments yet*

DOI: 10.4018/979-8-3373-0189-1.ch008

## INTRODUCTION

This research delves into the long-standing impact of the petroleum company Chevron, operated through Texaco, in the Ecuadorian Amazon, and its clear disregard for the environment and human life. It also looks into the corporation's extensive transnational connections and influence. The international oil company Texaco arrived in Ecuador in 1964 and remained there until the 1990s with its main field of extraction in the provinces of Sucumbíos and Orellana (Orellana, 2019). Over nearly three decades, the corporation intentionally released millions of gallons of crude oil and other toxic waste into the environment, drastically affecting one of the world's richest and most diverse ecosystems. This behavior was driven by a clear goal: to maximize economic gains (Ministerio de Relaciones Exteriores y Movilidad Humana, 2013). For the time that its operating license was in effect, it is thought that the U.S. transnational drilled 356 wells and constructed at least 1,000 clandestine pools for the management of polluting waste (Cancilleria del Ecuador- ministerio de Relaciones exteriores y movilidad Humana, 2015).

This study also attempts to uncover how it was possible for Chevron maintain such flagrantly unsustainable operations for so long without significant interventions to stop them (Soto, 2019). The historical analysis dates back to the political changes of 1963 when a military coup in Ecuador, indirectly supported by U.S. policies that aimed at furthering corporate interests, facilitated a favorable environment for Texaco to initiate and expand its destructive activities without adequate ethical or legal controls (Sanchez, Cesar; Becerra & Thais, 2015). According to an interview with Justino Piaguaje (2023), in 1993 the first lawsuit was filed by him and 87 other indigenous people in New York (USA). The action did not prosper because Chevron successfully argued that they were outside the jurisdiction where the case had to be tried, but Piaguaje persisted and took the case to Ecuador. Despite legal rulings, such as that handed down by Ecuador's Constitutional Court in 2011 ordering Chevron to pay compensation of $9.5 billion for the damages caused, the company has maneuvered to evade meeting these responsibilities. Through appeals and proceedings in international tribunals such as the Permanent Court of Arbitration in The Hague, Chevron has challenged the enforcement of the judgment, underscoring the power disparity between multinational corporations and affected indigenous communities (Piaguage, 2023).

There is an urgent need to establish a global justice system that prevents corporate injustices in contexts of intensive exploitation of resources from going unpunished and promote effective reparation for indigenous communities, which would in turn guarantee the protection of human rights and the conservation of the environment (Zubizarreta & Ramiro, 2016). This is the background to the objectives of this study, which are: 1) to analyze the legal and ethical implications of Chevron's operations in the Ecuadorian Amazon, considering both local legislation and international standards of human rights and environmental protection (Percival, 2020); 2) to examine the socio-environmental impact of oil pollution on the Huaorani community of the Lago Agrio canton, assessing how this population has been affected in terms of health, economy and culture (Cely, 2013); 3) to investigate the long-term effects of oil pollution on the biodiversity of the Ecuadorian Amazon, using scientific data and testimonies of environmental experts; 4) to analyze the role of non-governmental organizations and national activists in providing support; 5) to explore the repercussions of the Chevron case for foreign investment policies and exploitation of natural resources in developing countries, considering how the case has influenced the global perception of the risks associated with these activities (Romero & Krauss, 2011).

## 2. THEORETICAL FRAMEWORK

In the past, the Ecuadorian Amazon was considered a marginal area in the country's Far East, but oil discoveries placed it at the center of Ecuador's economy (Dilema, 2019). At the same time, disputes over the appropriation and commodification of its resources began. In the 1960s, the powerful U.S. oil company Texaco (now Chevron) began operations in the Ecuadorian Amazon. It came to occupy five million hectares in the northeastern Amazon, in what are now the provinces of Sucumbíos and Orellana (Presidencia de la Republica del Ecuador, 2024). The environment was contaminated by the use of various pollutants in specially constructed pools[1]. In addition, waste was sometimes incinerated next to the vegetation in a 200-meter radius around the extraction blocks, and polluting gases were released into the atmosphere, subsequently contaminating the waterways, soil, the environment and any living being in the vicinity (Cancilleria Humana del Ecuador- ministerio de Relaciones exteriores y movilidad, 2015). It is well established that oil extraction has a significant impact on the environment, which is compounded when waste is dumped directly into the natural environment and left to affect the air, water, flora and the people who live in it (Universidad de las Americas, 2014). The state oil company, Petroecuador EP, has inherited responsibility for the 1,107 environmental liabilities caused by Chevron-Texaco. These same liabilities caused by petroleum extraction in Ecuador multiply every year without the state or corporations undertaking effective remedial action, which has led to a further 3568 "sources of pollution", as the environmental authority calls them (Cazar Baquero, 2023). Researchers agree that oil exploitation not only changed the way of life of the Amazon peoples, but also generated poverty in the wider community (Narvaez, 2011; Luque, Quishpi & Espín, 2023). The socio-environmental impact suffered by the Huaorani community and other communities in the Lago Agrio canton by the oil company Chevron is of especially significant dimensions in terms of health, economy and culture. As stated by Piaguaje, "It totally changed our lives, which forced us to look for another way to survive because there was no longer any hunting or fishing" (Piaguaje, 2023). Many ethnic groups that historically lived in the area had to abandon their territories (INREDH, 2024).

In addition to all the aforementioned aspects, it ought to be highlighted that one of the most representative figures, strongly focused on the Chevron Texaco Case, belongs to Pablo Fajardo Mendoza, the attorney representing the victims of Ecuadorian Amazon in the trial against Chevron Corporation. In this matter, Pablo Fajardo Mendoza draw particular attention to the fact that the Amazonian communities living in the areas profoundly affected by Texaco (now, Chevron), had their lives forever affected, severely altered and decisively changed, having in mind that, in the very beginning, there was a "peaceful system of human coexistence where the relationship between local communities and their natural surroundings was a harmonious one" and, immediately afterwards, due to the company's need to focus on running a "profitable business", based on cutting costs as much as possible, without even considering the environment or the individuals, "one of the largest contaminations ever recorded and which can be directly traced back to the systematic use of inadequately cheap technology not used in any other country in the world" was caused (Mendoza, 2013). These are indeed aspects of grave nature upon which everyone has to seriously reflect on, in order for such unfortunate situations and wrongdoings never to be repeated in the history of mankind, since specialists strongly believe that sustainability and sustainable development must be the immediate results of sustainable investments, without creating any prejudice to the heath of individuals and the well-being of the powerful relationship that governs and that has always governed nature and people (Popescu, 2021; Popescu, 2022).

Having in mind all the aspects related to the pivotal concept of "sustainability" – among which a major emphasis needs to be placed on environmental sustainability, economic sustainability, natural environment, sustainable cities and communities, responsible consumption and production, sustainable development, clean water and sanitation, efficient waste management, sustainable business growth, and inclusive and equitable quality education, it has to be taken into account that "sustainability" focuses on meeting the needs of the present generations, without making any compromises in being able to ensure the same needs to the future generations to come (Kimerling, 2006; Popescu & Verma, 2024).

In this given context, however, there are numerous reputed specialists that have constantly drawn attention, over the last years, to the fact that there is an on-going problem in the transnational and multinational companies' "aggressive" use of international law and arbitration proceedings, one of the most often cited cases being the one belonging to the complex legal battle over oil pollution in the Amazon (Patel, 2012; Buccina & Chene & Gramlich, 2013; Columbia Law School, 2015). Interestingly, Jeffrey D. Sachs – reputed Columbia University professor and economist, the director of The Earth Institute at Columbia University, stated in 2015 that, in his opinion, the Chevron litigation represents "the most complicated legal case I have ever seen", while adding at a lecture that was organized in 2017 by the Grantham Research Institute on Climate Change and the Environment at the London School of Economics and Political Science the fact that "major polluters and governments" could be held accountable and could be responsible when leading to "losses and damages caused by climate change" (Columbia Law School, 2015; The London School of Economics and Political Science & Grantham Research Institute on Climate Change and the Environment, 2017). In continuation to the elements brought to the attention in the lines above, in a valuable testimony delivered on April 9, 2019 by Professor Jeffrey D. Sachs to the Subcommittee on Environment U.S. House Committee on Oversight and Reform, the following key details were brought to light, namely: (a) to begin with, although in "October 1992, the United States Senate ratified the UN Framework Convention on Climate Change (UNFCCC), with the objective to achieve "stabilization of greenhouse gas concentrations in the atmosphere at a level that would prevent dangerous anthropogenic interference with the climate system"", according to the professor's opinion "the US Congress has failed to adopt any major legislation to implement this treaty", even though several decades have passed from that crucial moment (Sachs, 2019, p. 1); (b) in addition, "since 1992, greenhouse gases have risen relentlessly", while the figures are truly alarming, displaying that carbon dioxide has risen "from 357 parts per million in February 1992 to 411 ppm in February 2019" (Sachs, 2019, p. 1); (c) also, due to not taking serious and rigorous actions as well as concerted and long-term measures in this regard, "climate safety is now nearly out of reach", which is truly worrying and a situation that requires vital reflection upon, although "since 1990, five assessment reports of the Inter-Governmental Panel on Climate Change (IPCC) have confirmed the human role in climate change" (Sachs, 2019, p. 1); and (d) in the end, the attention is positioned to the fact that, according to the professor, the "Congress has so flagrantly failed to pursue the interests of the American people", in the context in which "the evidence is overwhelming", having in mind that "it is widely believed (…) that Congress has neglected the science, the disasters, the risks, and the solutions because it abides by the wishes of the oil and gas industry, an industry that endangers the nation and the world in its reckless pursuit of profits" (Sachs, 2019, pp. 4-5). In the same document, Professor Jeffrey D. Sachs – a highly powerful and influential voice in the USA, points out the following vital ideas: "In addition to the campaign spending, the oil-and-gas industry spends an astonishing sum on lobbying. The sector's lobbying outlays totaled $124.8 million during 2018, which comes to $232,000 per member of Congress. The top five lobbying clients were ExxonMobil, Koch Industries, Chevron, Royal Dutch Shell, and the American Petroleum Institute;

with a combined lobbying spend of $46.7 million. The oil-and-gas industry's total lobbying outlays during 2010-18 summed to a shocking $1.225 billion. (…) The New York State Attorney General is suing ExxonMobil to seek "redress for a longstanding fraudulent scheme by Exxon, one of the world's largest oil and gas companies, to deceive investors and the investment community, including equity research analysts and underwriters of debt securities (together, "investors"), concerning the company's management of the risks posed to its business by climate change regulation"" (Sachs, 2019, p. 4). In other words, although the Sustainable Development Goals (SDGs) are the ones that require immediate action, attention, and consideration, based on the most recent studies, there are other factors less objective and pressing, such as the immediate interests of big, controversial, and highly influential companies, which automatically generates a severe balance between the well-being of communities, the health of individuals, and the outstanding need to preserve the nature, the natural habitats, the biodiversity, and the ecosystems (Farrington, 2024; Popescu & Popescu, 2025).

## 2.1 Local Legislation Such as International Human Rights and Environmental Protection Standards

It is considered that worldwide regulation of environmental remediation issues began in 1989 when the Exxon Valdez oil tanker ran aground in Alaska and the oil it carried affected about 2,000 km of coastline, polluting the soil, water and marine life of that area (Atlas & Hazen, 2011). It was considered one of the worst environmental disasters in the world, and systematic reparation of the resulting damage was mandated through a clean-up operation that ended in 1992 (Kinver, 2010). In 1990, the Oil Pollution Law was enacted (Salassa, Alderete, & Bach, 2015), which included as a fundamental objective, "to improve the legal channels when it comes to preventing, repairing and holding responsible those responsible for the damages caused by oil spills (p. 141)".

Until 1967, the Ecuadorian economy was overwhelmingly agricultural by nature, but from that date, the country was transformed into an oil producing and exporting state and Texaco-Chevron was a key player in this transformation (Cuvi & Bejarano, 2015). Since that time, constant oil spills and mismanagement of waste have wreaked havoc in the Amazon. Although the indigenous people of the area filed a lawsuit in the courts of the United States that successfully pressured the company to invest 40 million in remediation of damages (Fourtané, 2013), multiple Ecuadorian governments, from that of Sixto Durán Ballén through to the presidency of Alfredo Palacio, have dealt with the Chevron case without any significant success in forcing the company to undertake remediation. It was not until 2008, with the new Ecuadorian Constitution promoted by President Rafael Correa Delgado, which the rights of the natural environment were recognized (Serrano, 2013).

Below is Table No. 1, Environmental Legislation, which sets out the evolution of Ecuadorian laws on environmental redress from 1990 to the present (see, in this matter, Table N° 1.- Environmental Legislataion).

*Table 1.* **Environmental legislation**

| Environmental Remediation Laws | Outstanding aspects |
|---|---|
| **Civil Code, 1906** | This did not establish anything specific on environmental remediation issues, but it contemplated general principles on property and civil liability, which laid the foundations for future environmental regulations. |
| **Forests and Conservation of Natural Areas and Wildlife Act, 1981** | This law sought to protect and conserve forests and wildlife. Another point in favor of this legislation was its encouragement of the principles of the conservation of natural areas. |
| **Environmental Pollution Prevention and Control Act, 1982** | This is considered one of the first attempts to address pollution comprehensively by creating standards to prevent and control air, water and land pollution. |
| **Environmental Management Act 1999** | This provides a general framework for environmental management in the country, for which purpose the Environmental Impact Assessment (EIA) was introduced as a requirement for projects that may affect the environment. The fundamental objectives of this regulation are: 1) to create of the National Decentralized Environmental Management System, 2) to introduce the "polluter pays" principle, and 3) to oblige projects to present an environmental management plan. |
| **Constitution of the Republic of Ecuador, 2008** | This marks a historic and most significant change because the rights of nature, also known as the rights of Pachamama [Mother Earth], were recognized, and specific articles were established to this end, such as Art. 14, the right to live in a healthy and ecologically balanced environment, and Art. 66, specific rights of nature, including its restoration. |
| **Organic Environmental Code, 2017** | Here, the provisions of the constitution were consolidated, and with it the environmental legislation in Ecuador updated. This legislation has the following points in its favor: 1) detail on the processes of environmental remediation and ecological restoration; 2) regulation of environmental licenses; 3) a clear definition of environmental responsibilities; 4) strengthening of the environmental impact assessment system; 5) specific regulations for the remediation of contaminated soils. |

Source: Compiled by the author from the relevant legislation.

## 2.2 The Role of Non-Governmental Organizations and National Activists in Supporting Affected Communities

The United Nations (UN) was founded on October 24, 1945 after the ratification of its founding charter by most of the 51 states that it initially comprised. Currently, the UN is composed of 193 member countries, which participate in its main organ, the General Assembly. Over time, the UN has evolved to adapt to a changing geopolitical environment, maintaining its role as the only global forum where countries come together to discuss and solve problems for the benefit of humanity (Naciones Unidas, 2024). On June 26, 1945, the Charter of the United Nations was adopted in San Francisco, and Ecuador was among the founding member states. However, Ecuador did not vote to ratify the Charter on October 24, 1945, since the country's National Congress did not approve the Charter until December 7, 1945, and so its ratification was delayed until December 21 (Montalvo, 2016).

An outstanding achievement of non-governmental organizations (NGOs) as social actors is their identification and promotion of new areas of individual, collective and environmental rights. The revitalization of the democratic system brought with it a wave of social mobilization, which facilitated the creation of a network of social organizations with various objectives. Chief among these objectives was to ensure that social demands were met by the political system. Since the mid-1990s, many NGOs, driven by development processes, have prioritized the integrated management of natural resources, focusing especially on the connection between poverty and the environment and paying special attention to fragile ecosystems. This approach has included supporting the creation of tools for sustainable resource management, promoting dialogue, concerted action and advocacy, as well as facilitating multi-stakeholder dialogue and supporting the new roles of autonomous decentralized governments (Chiriboga, 2014).

NGOs and national activists play a crucial role in defending the rights of affected communities. They act as spokespersons, bringing the concerns of these communities to national and international forums and working to influence the formulation of policies that protect the environment and human rights. These entities often organize and facilitate the participation of communities in public consultations, helping them navigate complex legal and political systems (Keck & Sikkink, 2000). NGOs are vital in defending the rights of vulnerable groups by working against discrimination and abuse. Through awareness campaigns and legal assistance, they defend human rights and fight against social injustice. Pérez identifies "the power of NGOs in support networks" in his comprehensive analysis of the topic, which underlines how these organizations work to ensure equal opportunities and access to basic services for all members of the community (Pérez, 2023). NGOs also foster synergy and cooperation through strategic alliances and collaborative projects. These networks include communities, other NGOs, businesses, and governments all working together to address social issues holistically (San Patricio, 2024).

## 2.3 Repercussions of the Chevron Case for Foreign Investment Policies and Exploitation of Natural Resources in Developing Countries, Taking into Account How the Case Has Influenced the Global Perception of the Risks Associated With These Activities

The Amazon, which covers about half of the surface area of Ecuador, is a crucial source of economic income for the country, mainly through oil exploitation (Durá López, 2016). The Amazon is home to about half of the Planet's biodiversity, and is an important provider of the basic components of ecosystems, making it critical for the climate and the functioning of ecosystems at the local, regional and global levels (UNDP, 2016). According to Pablo Fajardo and María Guadalupe de Heredia, oil companies such as Texaco employed cost-cutting technologies and low-quality materials, which resulted in oil spillages on land and water, and the burning-off of gas. These practices have devastated the natural environment in the Amazon rainforest, and have displaced local communities, eroding their culture and identity as indigenous peoples. In the worst cases, these practices have led to deaths among the inhabitants (Fajardo & De Heredia, 2009).

The Chevron case has had significant repercussions from foreign investment policies and the exploitation of natural resources in developing countries, significantly influencing the global perception of the risks associated with these activities (Chávez Salazar, 1999). There is a widespread theory that investment continues because of Texaco's unfulfilled obligations of environmental remediation for the damage caused by its oil extraction activities. The theory broadly distorts the concept of investment and investor in ways that contradict legal logic. This interpretation challenges the reasons why a state would decide to participate in investment agreements, which are intended to encourage the generation and growth of new investments in the country (Garcia Carrión, 2015).

Joseph Stiglitz, (2017), argues that governments have a fundamental role in the economy, not only in correcting market failures, but also in promoting the knowledge economy. He argues that industrial policies can modify the economic structure to boost knowledge and learning, and these policies can be effective tools to promote equality and environmental responsibility. President Rafael Correa focused part of his political agenda on the petroleum sector, as well as on foreign investment. He promoted the reform of the Hydrocarbons Law and renegotiated oil contracts. Additionally, he established the Commission for the Comprehensive Citizen Audit of the Treaties of Reciprocal Protection of Investments and the International Investment Arbitration System (CAITISA) while withdrawing Ecuador from the Convention with the ICSID arbitration center. He also initiated a lawsuit against Chevron-Texaco for environmental damages. These actions reflect a marked nationalist focus in policy, coupled with a critical stance towards transnational corporations (Castillo Argañarás, 2016). Arbitration tribunals such as ICSID are always at the service of those who make them up, that is, companies with power and governments eager for investment, both of which are complicit in minimizing the processes of redress (Luque & de Pablos, 2016).

The protracted litigation and the results of the Chevron case have prompted many developing countries to review and strengthen their foreign investment policies. These countries are implementing stricter regulatory frameworks to ensure that foreign investments not only bring economic benefits, but also respect the environment and the rights of local communities (Ortiz, 2006). Through their role in activism and civil society in overseeing corporate activities and the fight for environmental justice, NGOs have been empowered to demand more transparency and accountability, both from companies and governments. A clear example of this is the "Amazon for Life" campaign and the Amazon Defense Front, whose main objectives are to unite efforts to promote knowledge of environmental challenges in the Amazon, to identify strategies that contribute to halting the degradation of the region's natural and human environment, and to encourage the involvement of communities in identifying solutions to ecological problems (Latorre Tomás, 2009).

## 3. METHOD

The methodology used a multidisciplinary approach due to the combined social impacts, economic considerations and legal analyses involved, thereby providing a comprehensive view of the problem (Guevara Alban, Verdesoto Arguello, & Castro Molina, 2020). Initially, a document-based study was used to analyze the considerable collection of primary and secondary sources, including reports from state entities (Tancara, 1993). Qualitative research was then applied to the testimonies taken from defense attorney Pablo Estenio Fajardo Mendoza and a key professional within an oil company in the Amazon (Ramos Galarza, 2020). A dynamic environmental and human rights impact analysis was also carried out to evaluate their application and effectiveness in the context of the case and to contextualize corporate practices and the legal and social responses of this case. (Astier Calderón, Masera Cerutti, & Galván Miyoshi, 2008). These methodological approaches allowed the identification of patterns of behavior and the potential legal liabilities and social and environmental impacts arising from Chevron-Texaco's activities in the Amazon region of Ecuador.

For the qualitative analysis, two key individuals were interviewed. The first, on June 29, 2024, was Pablo Fajardo Mendoza, who acts as a defense lawyer for the indigenous groups known collectively as La Unión de Afectados por Texaco [The Union of Victims of Texaco] (UDAPT) in the lawsuit filed against the corporation for the contamination of the Ecuadorian Amazon. This interviewee is identified in the data analysis as E1. The second interviewee, on July 2, 2024, was a civil engineer with 20 years of experience in the oil sector, specialized in quality control, supervision and field management. This interviewee asked to remain anonymous and is identified in the data analysis as E2.

For the interview, a questionnaire was designed with questions classified into four dimensions: environmental, economic, social and legal. The economic dimension includes aspects such as the costs associated with environmental pollution and its impact on the local economy, including the loss of traditional livelihoods such as agriculture and fishing (Sánchez, 2019). The environmental dimension addresses key aspects such as the impact on ecosystems and biodiversity, the contamination of soil and bodies of water with toxic substances, and the consequences for the health of local communities. Additionally, environmental mitigation and restoration measures were evaluated (Vega, 2013). The social dimension addresses aspects pertaining to the indigenous communities, such as the loss of traditional livelihoods, the impact on health due to pollution, and the displacement of people, leading to the rupture of the social and cultural fabric and the struggle for justice and the recognition of rights (Gámez, 2015). Finally, the legal dimension examines aspects such as the legal responsibility of the company for the environmental and human damages caused, including the judicial processes and sentences issued. It also includes the applicable national and international legal framework, the environmental regulations violated, the mechanisms of reparation and compensation to the affected communities, and the strategies used in the tribunals (Guaranda, 2010). The legal dimension questions were only given to E1.

## 4. ANALYSIS AND RESULTS

Below is Table No. 2, Environmental Dimension, which presents of the interviews, conducted with both E1 and E2 (see, in this matter, Table N° 2.- Environmental Dimension):

*Table 2.* **Environmental dimension**

| Questions | Responses |
|---|---|
| **What legal changes do you think are necessary to prevent future environmental disasters like the one at Chevron-Texaco?** | E1: It must be understood, in this context, as continuous harm, not as a specific damage, so much so that that is why the constitution itself declares it to not be subject to the statute of limitations. Therefore, you can see here damages and/or violations of rights to life, nature, environment, culture, economy—a truly multilateral, multi-multidimensional issue created by the oil activity of the Texaco company. All these aspects must be considered in the future. E2: We really have to improve the system of contracting companies since today the quality management manuals are based on copies of foreign models. |
| **Is the project of an Earth Constitution a utopian hypothesis?** | E1 I think that for there to be a substantial change in things, I believe that at least four fundamental elements are needed: Attitude, multidisciplinary education (life, environment, nature), state and laws. E2 As I mentioned before, the main guideline to improve the environment in the region, and especially in the Amazon area, is to see the realities of the peoples, and therefore not idealizations. |

Source: Compiled by the author from interviews conducted with Pablo Fajado and an anonymous field manager at an oil company.

From this environmental dimension, it can be seen that the impacts are not the result of isolated disasters but are cumulative and avoidable, and that the existing systems for environmental quality management must be improved. Indeed, recurrent and serious oil spills are widely documented yet are poorly addressed (Maestripieri and Saqalli, 2016). It is also evident that the damage has multiple consequences; for example, pollution in the Amazon has led to a reduction in plant and community diversity (Arellano et al., 2017). As a result, the interviewees advocate for deeper changes based on a more realistic approach that takes into account the particularities of the affected areas.

Further questions were put to the interviewees to analyze the economic impacts of Texaco-Chevron activities. These are presented in Table No. 3, Economic Dimension (see, in this matter, Table N° 3.- Economic Dimension).

*Table 3.* **Economic dimension**

| Questions | Responses |
|---|---|
| **How do you see the influence of large corporations on legal systems at a global level and the support of different governments since the legal process began; from which government did the local people receive the most support?** | **E1:** Among the historical problems concerning the excessive influence of large corporations, what is most notable is how these companies have grown to be more powerful than many states, enjoying rights without obligations, as well as the inadequacy of self-regulation, such as corporate social responsibility and ISO standards, combined with the lack of binding laws that sanction their abuses. Unlike individuals who must try all domestic avenues of redress before resorting to international justice, transnational corporations evade local laws through international arbitration. Over the course of twelve government administrations in Ecuador since 1993, only the government of Rafael Correa showed a firm stance against Chevron, while the others shared interests with the corporation, facilitating persecutions and trials against environmental defenders. This is how incidents of defamation and persecution are defined, with the hallmarks of corporate authority on them, while former government officials have worked for these companies, perpetuating their influence and protecting their economic interests over human and environmental rights.<br>**E2:** Specifically in the Chevron case, it is noted how large corporations can influence legal systems at a global level, using their economic power to employ delaying tactics in legal proceedings to wear down the opposing party. The ability to take disputes to international arbitration tribunals and the manipulation of these forums adds complexity and reveals the inequality and vulnerability of legal systems in the face of the power of large companies. If we think about the governments in power, it was former President Rafael Correa who showed solidarity and made the human part of the case visible. |
| **What relationship does capitalism have with Ecuador's environmental problems and with the Chevron case?** | **E1:** The environmental disaster in Ecuador is not only due to capitalism, but also to economic, cultural and educational factors. All governments, regardless of their ideology, have followed an extractivist model. The key is in how they distribute resources and enforce their policies. This stresses the importance of promoting a culture and education that fosters sustainability and responsibility towards future generations.<br>**E2:** In part, the capitalist model has been one of the great drivers of environmental problems, but also the governments of the day have only thought about the extraction of the resource and not about remediation, and even less about the ancestral populations of the country. |

Source: compiled by the author based on interviews conducted with Pablo Fajado and the field manager in an oil company.

Within the economic dimension, it can be seen that Ecuador from 2019 to 2023 produced 531, 479, 473, 481, 475 thousand barrels per day in each year, which in economic terms represents an average of 8.45 billion dollars per year, allowing for the variations in oil price (Opecorg, 2008). Both interviewees agree that the governments of the day, whatever their political ideology, have been responsible for the economic problems in the Amazon. While E1 argues that cultural and environmental education must be fostered in future generations, E2 believes that authorities must pay more attention to the economic needs of the indigenous populations in the areas where the exploitation of this resource is located, and redistribute part of the profits to them. When asked about the government from which indigenous people they had the most support, both interviewees agreed that it was Rafael Correa who made their plight more visible. E1 explains that Correa refused to sit down to negotiate individually, but insisted on dialogue with all parties in the case. Chevron did not agree to this and began smear campaigns that led to other problems. E2 states that Rafael Correa tried to bring order to the situation. As a result, it became possible to define quality management in each project, and, although it is true that there was still much left undone, it was the clearest example of support for the indigenous people.

Table No. 4, Social Dimension, sets out the thoughts of the interviewees with regard to social impacts (see, in this matter, Table N° 4.- Social Dimension).

*Table 4.* **Social dimension**

| Questions | Responses |
|---|---|
| **Is the appropriation of natural resources a dynamic for which certain people are willing to kill or die?** | **E1:** Corruption in Ecuador impedes state control of natural resources, especially in the oil and mining sectors. The situation exposes how mafias and public officials, such as mayors and ministers, benefit illicitly while allowing the supply of drinking water to be endangered and resources to be exploited without environmental control. This situation reflects a deep corruption that fosters violence and hinders any attempt at reform. Therefore, it could be considered that one is even willing to kill for individual gain. **E2:** From the interviewee's perspective, people are willing to do anything—as long as they obtain "profits"—even more than international companies, because they do consider that killing or being killed is a language widely used here. |
| **What is the social impact that the Chevron case has had?** | **E1:** Socially, this activity directly affects the life and traditions of the native peoples, the health of the local population, and generates social problems such as the proliferation of brothels. The government's indifference to the Amazon is also clear, which is seen only as a resource, and not as an integral part of Ecuadorian territory, as evidenced by the lack of repair of crucial infrastructure for the local population. **E2:** At the local level, apart from the diseases and changes in culture, I believe that the other social impact is what occurred at the national and international level, which set unique precedents, and made visible the shortcomings of the international corporate system. When developing countries like ours seek justice, multinationals are condemned; the road is not easy, but the indigenous people have been persevering. |
| **Can environmental remediation processes be viable?** | **E1:** Remediation should be distinguished from environmental restoration. Restoration involves returning the environment to its original state before the damage, which is stricter and more expensive. Restoration is viable, but companies prefer less expensive and superficial solutions to maximize their profits. In addition, prevention to avoid environmental damage is essential, but this also increases costs and reduces business profits. **E2:** To be honest, with current legislation, remediation is almost nil, because it could be said that, in order to obtain greater profits, companies merely appear to comply with what the law requires, a law that has shortcomings. |

Source: compiled by the author based on interviews conducted with Pablo Fajado and the field manager in an oil company.

Based on the social dimension, it is evident that the government of Ecuador has allocated oil revenues to promote urbanization, improve health services and education, and in part address the cleanup of oil spills. Despite these measures, oil spills continue to be significant and recurrent (Maestripieri and Saqalli, 2016). Again, the deep corruption in Ecuador facilitates the violent and uncontrolled exploitation of natural resources (Inecgobec). This can be added to the lack of responsibility of complicit companies and governments that claim to be transparent and ethical while doing the opposite of what they publicly state (Luque & Herrero-García, 2019). The interviewees consider that this situation helped Chevron devastate local communities in terms of health, culture and social life. Companies prefer superficial solutions to true environmental restoration in order to maximize their profits, while current legislation is clearly inadequate to guarantee effective remediation. The Chevron case has also exposed the failures of the global corporate system and the struggle of indigenous communities for justice and corporate accountability (Pigrau, 2014).

Table No. 5, Legal Dimension, sets out the interviewees' responses regarding attempts at justice (see, in this matter, Table N° 5.- Legal Dimension).

*Table 5.* **Legal dimension**

| Questions | Responses |
|---|---|
| **What were the biggest challenges you faced at the beginning of the legal process?** | **E1:** Among the legal challenges faced in the Chevron case, we should highlight the disrespect shown for the Ecuadorian judicial system and the regulatory and jurisdictional obstacles. Unfavorable agreements were signed by Ecuadorian governments; for example, that of Sixto Duran and Alberto Dahik, which exempted Chevron from responsibilities while allowing the company to sue the state. There is a lack of global regulation that allows transnational corporations to be sued for human rights violations and we should consider the complexity of the "corporate veil" that Chevron uses to evade responsibility through a network of subsidiaries and tax havens. |
| **What was the main strategy you adopted, and its obstacles, to confronting a corporation as large as Chevron-Texaco?** | **E1:** The main strategy to confront Chevron was based on internal knowledge of the company, since I worked there and experienced the problems first-hand. Likewise, having a multifaceted strategy is important, one that includes legal, social, communicational and political elements. This comprehensive approach involves building a strong social base, articulating effective communication, advocacy, and thinking globally. Knowing your opponent well and planning each action in detail are also crucial aspects of your strategy. |
| **What weaknesses does the prior consultation process in the territories have?** | **E1:** It was non-binding. Although ILO Convention 169 and the Ecuadorian Constitution mention free and informed prior consultation, the regulations are not clear and are often weakened by decrees or regulations. This result in communities being able to voice their opinion, but their responses have no real impact on decisions as authorities go ahead with their plans regardless of local opposition. |
| **Based on your comments, is the ILO Convention 169 on Indigenous and Tribal Peoples, the Escazú International Agreement or the Nagoya Protocol on access to genetic resources worth the paper they are written on? Are international organizations and/or international resolutions a problem rather than a solution?** | **E1:** Supranational bodies such as the UN and the OAS should be criticized, since they are influenced by transnational corporations, which prevent them from effectively protecting human and environmental rights. They are more influenced by business interests than by the needs of states or peoples, as exemplified by the financing of climate summits by the biggest polluters. The resolutions of these bodies and government policies often benefit large corporations to the detriment of the public interest, creating a global system of injustice and lack of control over corporate crimes. Today here in Ecuador, our challenge is to get the Ecuadorian government, whoever is in power, to respect the judicial and constitutional court rulings, which today they want to disrespect. |

Source: compiled by the author based on interviews conducted with Pablo Fajado and the field manager in an oil company.

In the legal dimension, the initial lawsuit was filed in New York, but was transferred to Ecuador after a legal battle (Aguinda v. Chevron-Texaco, 2003). In 2011, the Provincial Court of Sucumbíos ordered Chevron to pay $8,646 million for environmental damages, a figure that doubled when it did not issue a public apology. However, the corporation did not have any assets in Ecuador at the time from which payments could be leveraged (Cely, 2013). Chevron refused to comply and accused the Ecuadorian government of fraud by taking the case to an international arbitration tribunal (BBC World, 2018). In 2014, a U.S. judge found "evidence of fraud" in the Ecuadorian judgment further complicating the judicial process (Chevron Corporation v. Steven Donziger et al., 2011). Interviewee E1 underscores the ongoing and multifaceted struggle for justice in the Chevron case by highlighting the numerous legal and strategic challenges faced by those seeking to hold large corporations accountable for their actions. The lack of binding outcomes in prior consultation and the influence on supranational bodies by corporate interests are significant obstacles in this fight, which reveal an urgent need for reforms to ensure the protection of human and environmental rights at the global level.

## 5. CONCLUSION

The case of Chevron-Texaco in the Ecuadorian Amazon, especially in Lago Agrio, exposes one of the most serious environmental catastrophes of the 20th-21st century. Oil pollution has left an indelible mark on the region, affecting both nature and human communities. The release of millions of gallons of crude oil and other toxic waste has devastated rivers, soils and air, causing serious illnesses as well as generating respiratory and dermatological problems among the local population. The biodiversity of the Amazon has also suffered significant damage, endangering the flora and fauna of the area.

Economically, Chevron-Texaco's presence has radically altered life in the region. Indigenous communities, such as the Huaorani, have seen their traditional livelihoods of agriculture and fishing destroyed due to pollution. This has led to economic dependence on extractive industries, perpetuating cycles of poverty and vulnerability. In addition, the corporation's economic power has influenced legal systems, allowing them to evade responsibility and minimize compensation.

The litigation against Chevron has been an arduous process that has exposed the failures of both the local and international judicial systems. Despite favorable rulings, such as that of Ecuador's Constitutional Court in 2011, the enforcement of these compensations has been elusive. Chevron has used legal and political strategies to evade its responsibilities, underscoring the clear lack of corporate accountability. This case highlights the need for global regulations that allow transnational corporations to be sued effectively for human rights violations and environmental damage.

Non-governmental organizations and national activists have played an important role in defending the rights of affected communities. These organizations have acted as spokespersons for communities, taking their concerns to national and international forums, and have influenced the formulation of policies to protect the environment and human rights. They have organized and facilitated the participation of communities in public consultations, helping them navigate complex legal and political systems.

The Chevron case has also had significant repercussions for foreign investment policies and natural resource exploitation in developing countries. It has prompted many countries to review and strengthen their regulatory frameworks to ensure that foreign investments respect the environment and the rights of local communities. The fight for justice in this case has exposed the flaws of the global corporate system and highlighted the need for deep reforms to ensure corporate accountability and the protection of human rights globally.

This research suggests that it is essential to foster an environmental and educational culture that promotes sustainability and responsibility for future generations. Industrial policies must be effective tools to promote equality and environmental responsibility. There is an urgent need to implement a global justice system that prevents corporate injustices from going unpunished and promotes effective redress for affected communities. The protection of human rights and the conservation of the environment in contexts of intensive exploitation of resources are tasks that must be prioritized in the concession of operating licenses.

The Chevron-Texaco case in the Ecuadorian Amazon is a stark reminder of the devastating impacts that irresponsible exploitation of natural resources can have. It highlights the importance of strengthening environmental laws and justice systems to protect communities and the environment. The struggle for justice and redress continues, and deep reforms are essential to ensure corporate accountability and the protection of human rights globally.

What is more, the current in-depth analysis together with other studies that were closely reviewed in order to be able to highlight the most important issues under consideration, while adapting the debate to the current context and on-going situation, place a new light on the following pivotal elements: (a) firstly, these days, transnational litigations – such as the highly controversial one, currently brought to the attention, have interestingly managed to raise numerous controversies and disputes, especially when thinking about the sensible matters of the judgment enforcement across borders, in the context in which the multinational and the transnational companies are extremely powerful players on the marketplace, having numerous supporters in all important places, hence being able to influence, in some cases more than in others, the way in which some concepts, such as sustainability, sustainable development, corporate social responsibility, and health and well-being, may be acknowledged and interpreted; (b) secondly, in this day and age, seeking more favorable venues, when not being able to penetrate a certain marketplace as desired and as initially anticipated and expected, represents a well-known practice that has come to characterize the big and influential entities all over the world, that are avid seekers of profitability and high market quotas, hence leading to negligence and to the breach of the world trade agreements; (c) and, thirdly, these days the international arbitration strongly relies on the highly interconnected world trade agreements, but there are, also, other factors that require immediate consideration, such as the influence of corruption, legal maneuvering, and different types of relationships that have come to dominate the economic and the financial interests of some governs and some powerful individuals, the idea according to which the clean up pollution processes ought to be dully carried out by companies before transferring the operations to the governments and/or to other companies, and, additionally, the on-going conflicts that somehow tend to occur while centering on the responsibility for the pollution and the contaminated sites.

Furthermore, there is a vital concept that requires a particular attention and emphasis in today's context, namely: the risks that some multinational companies take to deliver their actions and judgment outside the legal systems – hence, hindering the well-being of the communities and the individuals, while severely affecting nature's balance, and, in the same time, to encourage costly legal maneuverings that, unfortunately, have their basis on the new international trade agreements – hence, questioning the mechanisms on which some of these new international trade agreements function on as well as the structures that these new international trade agreements really protect and serve. In this given context, there are some interesting new international trade agreements upon which USA specialists call for analysis and attention, namely: the new international trade agreements containing mechanisms for investor-state dispute settlement (ISDS), like the Trans-Pacific Partnership reached by the U.S. and 11 Pacific rim nations (United Nations Conference on Trade and Development (UNCTAD), 2014; Pucci, 2015; Rimmer, 2016; Ben-Moussa, 2017; Yu, 2018; Organization for Economic Cooperation and Development (OECD), 2020).

## ACKNOWLEDGMENT

This research received no specific grant from any funding agency in the public, commercial, or not-for-profit sectors. Author Contributions: Conceptualization, A.L.G. (Arturo Luque González), G.L.C. (Geomayra Lisbeth Castro), (M.Y.P.) Maira Yadira Pinargote and C.R.P. (Cristina Raluca Gh. Popescu); methodology, A.L.G., G.L.C., M.Y.P. and C.R.P.; software, A.L.G., G.L.C., M.Y.P. and C.R.P.; validation, A.L.G., G.L.C., M.Y.P. and C.R.P.; formal analysis, A.L.G., G.L.C., M.Y.P. and C.R.P.; investigation, A.L.G., G.L.C., M.Y.P. and C.R.P.; resources, A.L.G., G.L.C., M.Y.P. and C.R.P.; data curation, A.L.G., G.L.C., M.Y.P. and C.R.P.; writing—original draft preparation, A.L.G., G.L.C., M.Y.P. and C.R.P.; writing—review and editing, A.L.G., G.L.C., M.Y.P. and C.R.P.; visualization, A.L.G., G.L.C., M.Y.P. and C.R.P.; supervision, A.L.G., G.L.C., M.Y.P. and C.R.P.; project administration, A.L.G., G.L.C., M.Y.P. and C.R.P.; funding acquisition, A.L.G., G.L.C., M.Y.P. and C.R.P. All authors have equally contributed to the manuscript. All authors have read and agreed to the published version of the manuscript.

**CONFLICTS OF INTEREST**

All authors declare that they have no conflicts of interest.

## REFERENCES

Aguinda v. Chevron-Texaco, 0002 (Corte Provincial de Sucumbíos 2003).

Anthropologies. (20 de 04 de 2015). *El impacto de Chevron en la Amazonía ecuatoriana*. Obtenido de https://www.anthropologies.es/el-impacto-de-chevron-en-la-amazonia-ecuatoriana/

Arellano, P., Tansey, K., Balzter, H., & Tellkamp, M. (2017). Plant family-specific impacts of petroleum pollution on biodiversity and leaf chlorophyll content in the Amazon rainforest of Ecuador. *PLoS One*, *12*(1), e0169867. DOI: 10.1371/journal.pone.0169867 PMID: 28103307

Astier Calderón, M., Masera Cerutti, O., & Galván Miyoshi, Y. (2008). Evaluación de sustentabilidad. Un enfoque dinámico y multidimensional Evaluación de sustentabilidad. Un enfoque dinámico y multidimensional. Valencia, España: Sociedad Española de Agricultura Ecológica (SEAE), Centro de Investigaciones en Geografía Ambiental (CIGA-UNAM), El Colegio de la Frontera Sur (ECOSUR), Centro de Investigaciones en Ecosistemas (CIECO-UNAM).

Atlas, R., & Hazen, T. (2011). Oil Biodegradation and Bioremediation: A Tale of the Two Worst Spills in U.S. History. *Environmental Science & Technology, 45*(16), 6709-6715. Obtenido de https://pubs.acs.org/doi/epdf/10.1021/es2013227

Baquero, C. (2023). Fosas, derrames y piscinas abandonadas: las huellas de medio siglo de contaminación petrolera no remediada en Ecuador. Obtenido de https://es.mongabay.com/2023/06/huellas-de-medio-siglo-de-contaminacion-petrolera-no-remediada-en-ecuador/

Ben-Moussa, S. (2017). A Tale Of Two Trade Powers: Balancing Investor-State Dispute Settlement And Environmental Risk Between The Eu And Us In A Changing Political Climate. *Fordham Environmental Law Review, 29*(1), 95–124. https://www.jstor.org/stable/26413295

Buccina, S. & Chene, D. & Gramlich, J. (2013). Accounting for the environmental impacts of Texaco's operations in Ecuador: Chevron's contingent environmental liability disclosures. Accounting forum, Elsevier, vol. 37(2), pages 110-123. DOI: .DOI: 10.1016/j.accfor.2013.04.003

Cancilleria del Ecuador- ministerio de Relaciones exteriores y movilidad Humana. (Abril de 2015). *El caso Chevron / Texaco en Ecuador Una lucha por la justicia ambiental y social.* Obtenido de https://www.cancilleria.gob.ec/wp-content/uploads/2015/06/Expediente-Caso-Chevron-abril-2015.pdf

Castillo Argañarás, L. (2016). *Inversiones Extranjeras y populismo en Argentina, Bolivia y Ecuador entre 2003 y 2015.* Obtenido de https://notablesdelaciencia.conicet.gov.ar/bitstream/handle/11336/78526/CONICET_Digital_Nro.f5d57907-5140-40bb-899c-af1dfba5c0a4_A.pdf?sequence=2&isAllowed=y

Cely, N. (2013). Balancing profit and environmental sustainability in Ecuador: Lessons learned from the Chevron case. *Duke Envtl. L. & Pol'y F.*, *24*, 353.

Chávez Salazar, R. (1999). *Protección ambiental y explotación petrolera en la región amazónica Ecuatoriana.* Quito. Obtenido de https://repositorio.flacsoandes.edu.ec/bitstream/10469/289/3/TFLACSO-1999RLCS.pdf

Chevron Corporation vs. Steven Donziger, et al., 1:11-cv-00691LAK-JCF (Southern Distirct of New York, April 3th, 2014).

Chiriboga, M. (2014). *Las ONG ecuatorianas en los procesos de cambio* (Primera ed.). Quito: Abya-Yala. Obtenido de https://www.ceosc.org/recursos/5_ong_cambio.pdf

Codigo civil. (1906). Ecuador. Obtenido de https://www.epn.edu.ec/wp-content/uploads/2015/06/Codigo-Civil1.pdf

Código Orgánico del Ambiente. (2017). Ecuador. Obtenido de https://www.ambiente.gob.ec/wp-content/uploads/downloads/2018/01/CODIGO_ORGANICO_AMBIENTE.pdf

Columbia Law School. (2015). Chevron, Ecuador, and the Hazards of Transnational Litigation. Retrieved on-line from https://www.law.columbia.edu/news/archive/chevron-ecuador-and-hazards-transnational-litigation. Accessed on the 28th of January 2025.

Comisión Económica para América Latina y el Caribe (CEPAL). (2019). *Recursos naturales,medio ambiente y sostenibilidad 70 años de pensamiento de la CEPAL.* Santiago, Comisión Económica para América Latina y el Caribe (CEPAL): Libros de la CEPAL, N° 158 (LC/PUB.2019/18-P).

Constitución de la República del Ecuador [Const.]. (2008). Ecuador. Obtenido de https://www.defensa.gob.ec/wp-content/uploads/downloads/2021/02/Constitucion-de-la-Republica-del-Ecuador_act_ene-2021.pdf

Cuvi, N., & Bejarano, M. (2015). Los halos de inhibición en la remediación de suelos amazónicos contaminados con petróleo. *História, Ciências, Saúde-Manguinhos, 22*, 1693-1714. Obtenido de https://www.scielo.br/j/hcsm/a/TXyyPdgyLDpHj3n5cPrtV4L/?format=pdf&lang=es

Dilema, R. (2019). El caso Chevrón-Texaco. Problemática actual de la Amazonia ecuatoriana. *Revista Dilema.* Obtenido de https://dilemascontemporaneoseducacionpoliticayvalores.com/index.php/dilemas/article/view/669

Durá López, M. (13 de 06 de 2016). Obtenido de https://www.researchgate.net/publication/303931907_Indigenas_Amazonicos_Ecuatorianos_versus_Chevron_la_lucha_de_la_dignidad_por_la_vida_versus_el_derrame_de_la_selva

Fajardo, P., & De Heredia, M. (2009). *El Caso Texaco: un trabajo por la restitución de derechos colectivos y de la naturaleza.* Quito: ABYA-YALA. Obtenido de https://repositorio.uasb.edu.ec/bitstream/10644/940/1/DDHH-Inf-9-Fajardo-El%20caso%20Texaco.pdf

Farrington, F. (2024). Oil in the Amazon: A Case Study in Corporate Power and the Formation of Transnational Legal Norms. Retrieved on-line from https://www.abdn.ac.uk/law/blog/oil-in-the-amazon-a-case-study-in-corporate-power-and-the-formation-of-transnational-legal-norms/. Accessed on the 28th of January 2025.

Fourtané, N. (2013). Las poblaciones indígenas y campesinas de la Amazonía frente a la petrolera Chevron - Texaco: un juicio histórico. *AFESE 59*, 11-30. Obtenido de https://afese.com/img/revistas/revista59/poblaind.pdf

Gámez, F. (2015). La dimensión social: un proceso sinérgico en la interacción universidad-comunidad a través de la función de extensión. *Investigación y Postgrado, 30*(1), 103-123. Obtenido de https://ve.scielo.org/scielo.php?script=sci_arttext&pid=S1316-00872015000100006

Garcia Carrión, D. (2015). *Caso Chevron - Defensa del Ecuador frente al uso indebido del Arbitraje de inversión.* Quito.

Guaranda, W. (2010). *Acciones jurídicas para establecer responsabilidades por daño ambiental en el Ecuador* . Quito: Fundación Regional de Asesoría en Derechos Humanos, INREDH.

Guevara Alban, G., Verdesoto Arguello, A., & Castro Molina, N. (2020). Metodologías de investigación educativa (descriptivas, experimentales, participativas, y de investigación-acción). *Revista cientifica Mundo de la investigación y el conocimiento RECIMUNDO, 4*(3), 163-173. Obtenido de https://recimundo.com/index.php/es/article/view/860

Inecgobec. Censo de Información Ambiental Económica en Gobiernos Autónomos Descentralizados Provinciales 2014. [Online]. Available from: http://anda.inec.gob.ec/anda/index.php/catalog/509 [Accessed 4 June 2024].

INREDH. (2024). *CASO: Empresa Petrolera CHEVRON TEXACO y su contaminación en la Amazonía ecuatoriana.* Obtenido de https://www.inredh.org/archivos/boletines/resumen_caso_chevron_texaco_contaminacion_amazonia.pdf

Joseph, S. (2012). Protracted lawfare: The tale of Chevron Texaco in the Amazon. *Journal of Human Rights and the Environment*, *3*(1), 70–91. DOI: 10.4337/jhre.2012.01.03

Keck, M., & Sikkink, K. (2000). *Activistas sin fronteras* (Primera Edición ed.). México: Siglo veintiuno.

Kimerling, J. (2006). Transnational Operations, Bi-National Injustice: Chevrontexaco and Indigenous Huaorani and Kichwa in the Amazon Rainforest in Ecuador. *American Indian Law Review*, *31*(2), 445–508. DOI: 10.2307/20070795

Kinver, M. (2010). Derrame del Exxon Valdez sigue en Alaska. *BBC news mundo*. Obtenido de https://www.bbc.com/mundo/ciencia_tecnologia/2010/01/100114_0457_exxon_sigue_desastre_jrg

Latorre Tomás, S. (2009). *El ecologismo popular en el Ecuador pasao y presente*. Obtenido de https://www.iee.org.ec/index.php?option=com_zoo&Itemid=186&element=61bbca97-1c5d-4227-965a-3c4ab91c2a32&format=raw&item_id=86&lang=es&method=download&task=callelement

Ley de Bosques y Conservación de areas Naturales y vida silvestre. (1981). Ecuador. Obtenido de https://www.corteidh.or.cr/tablas/4033.pdf

Ley de Gestión Ambiental. (1999). Ecuador. Obtenido de https://www.acnur.org/fileadmin/Documentos/BDL/2008/6618.pdf

Ley de Prevención y Control de la Contaminación Ambiental. (1982). Ecuador. Obtenido de https://vlex.ec/vid/codificacion-20-ley-prevencion-643461217

Luque, A., & de Pablos, C. (2016). Factores que promocionan la falta de ética en las prácticas de producción y logística de las empresas transnacionales. Lan Harremanak, 34(1), pp 336-370. ISSN: 1575-7048 e-ISSN: 2444-5819. DOI: https://doi.org/DOI: 10.1387/lan-harremanak.16578

Luque, A., & Herrero-García, N. (2019). How corporate social (ir)responsibility in the textile sector is defined, and its impact on ethical sustainability: An analysis of 133 concepts. *Corporate Social Responsibility and Environmental Management*, *26*(6), 1–22. DOI: 10.1002/csr.1747

Luque, A., Quishpi, F. R., & Espín, D. F. (2023). Analysis of Spirituality Processes in Women of the Waorani AMWAE Indigenous Nationality in Ecuador. Özsungur, F. and Bekar, F. (Ed.) Spirituality Management in the Workplace, Emerald Publishing Limited, Leeds, pp. 173-196. . ISBN: 978-1-83753-451-7, eISBN: 978-1-83753-450-0DOI: 10.1108/978-1-83753-450-020231008

Maestripieri, N., & Saqalli, M. (2016). Assessing health risk using regional mappings based on local perceptions: A comparative study of three different hazards. *Human and Ecological Risk Assessment*, *22*(3), 721–735. DOI: 10.1080/10807039.2015.1105099

Mendoza, P. F. (2013). The price of wealth. The Chevron Texaco Case. ICIP International Catalan Institute for Peace. Per la Pau / Peace in Progress. ICIP E-Review. Issue 18. November 2013. Retrieved on-line from https://www.icip.cat/perlapau/old/e-review/issue-18-november-2013/price-wealth-chevron-texaco-case.htm. Accessed on the 28th of January 2025.

Ministerio de Relaciones Exteriores y Movilidad Humana. (2013). *Caso Chevron un ejemplo de lucha soberana contra la arbitrariedad*. Recuperado el 13 de 05 de 2024, de https://www.cancilleria.gob.ec/wp-content/uploads/2013/07/folleto_chevron-web.pdf

Ministerio de Relaciones Exteriores y movilidad Humana. (2013). *Chevron-Texaco pretende que el pueblo ecuatoriano pague lo que ellos contaminaron*. Recuperado el 13 de 05 de 2024, de https://www.cancilleria.gob.ec/wp-content/uploads/2013/04/la-cruda-realidad-del-caso-chevron-texaco-esp.pdf

Montalvo, M. (30 de 09 de 2016). Ecuador en Naciones Unidas: Miembro fundador y algunos referentes. 63. Obtenido de https://www.afese.com/img/revistas/revista64a/ecuadornnuu.pdf

Mundo, B. B. C. (2018, septiembre 8). Caso Chevron-Texaco: qué implica el fallo de La Haya sobre la contaminación en la Amazonía de Ecuador y por qué no lo cambia todo. BBC. https://www.bbc.com/mundo/noticias-america-latina-45454965

Narvaez, H. S. (2011). Luchas politicas y poder economico transnacional:estrategias de comunicacion en el caso Texaco. *Luchas politicas y poder economico transnacional:estrategias de comunicacion en el caso Texaco*. Ecuador. Obtenido de http://hdl.handle.net/10644/2877

Opecorg. OPEC Annual Statistical Bulletin. [Online]. Available from: https://asb.opec.org/ [Accessed 9 Agosto 2024].

Orellana, A. (27 de marzo de 2019). *Chevron vs Ecuador: Arbitraje internacional e impunidad corporativa*. Obtenido de Amazon watch: https://amazonwatch.org/es/news/2019/0327-chevron-vs-ecuador-international-arbitration-and-corporate-impunity#:~:text=Texaco%2C%20que%20fue%20adquirida%20por,provincias%20de%20Sucumb%C3%ADos%20y%20Orellana

Organization for Economic Cooperation and Development (OECD). (2020). OECD Trade and Environment Working Papers 2020/03. Greening regional trade agreements on investment. DOI: 10.1787/18166881

Ortiz, P. (2006). *Petróleo y desarrollo sostenible en el Ecuador*. Rispergraf.

Patel, S. (2012). Delayed Justice: A Case Study of Texaco and the Republic of Ecuador's Operations, Harms, and Possible Redress in the Ecuadorian Amazon. *Tulane Environmental Law Journal*, *26*(1), 71–110. https://www.jstor.org/stable/24673677

Patricio, S. (11 de 03 de 2024). *ONG ecuatorianas que protegen el medio ambiente*. Obtenido de https://blog.sanpatricio.com.ec/ong-ecuatorianas-que-protegen-el-medio-ambiente

Percival, R. V. (2020). Transnational litigation: what can we learn from Chevron–Ecuador? In *Research Handbook on Transnational Environmental Law* (pp. 318–339). Edward Elgar Publishing. DOI: 10.4337/9781788119634.00031

Pérez, D. (28 de 12 de 2023). El poder de las ONG en redes de apoyo: Un análisis completo. Obtenido de https://daniperezmalaga.es/el-poder-de-las-ong-en-redes-de-apoyo-un-analisis-completo/

Piaguage, J. (01 de 05 de 2023). Treinta años de impunidad de la contaminación de Chevron-Texaco en Ecuador: "La Amazonía sigue sangrando". (J. SULÉ, Entrevistador) Obtenido de https://www.publico.es/internacional/treinta-anos-impunidad-contaminacion-chevron-texaco-ecuador-amazonia-sigue-sangrando.html

Pigrau, A. (2014). The Texaco-Chevron case in Ecuador: Law and justice in the age of globalization. Revista catalana de dret ambiental, 5(1).

PNUD. (2016). La Amazonía y la Agenda 2030. Retrieved from https://www.undp.org/es/latin-america/publicaciones/la-amazonia-y-la-agenda-2030

Popescu, C. R. (2021). Sustainable and Responsible Entrepreneurship for Value-Based Cultures, Economies, and Societies: Increasing Performance Through Intellectual Capital in Challenging Times. In Popescu, C., & Verma, R. (Eds.), *Sustainable and Responsible Entrepreneurship and Key Drivers of Performance* (pp. 33–58). IGI Global Scientific Publishing., DOI: 10.4018/978-1-7998-7951-0.ch002

Popescu, C. R. G. (2022). Mindfulness Business Principles: Producing Outstanding Value and Encouraging Community Connections. In Popescu, C. (Ed.), *COVID-19 Pandemic Impact on New Economy Development and Societal Change* (pp. 196–228). IGI Global Scientific Publishing., DOI: 10.4018/978-1-6684-3374-4.ch010

Popescu, C. R. G., & Popescu, G. N. (2025). The Power of Data Analysis in Transforming Businesses Performance: Improved Decision-Making, Real-World Applications, and the Sustainable Development Goals. In Popescu, C. (Ed.), *Building Inclusive Global Knowledge Societies for Sustainable Development* (pp. 169–208). IGI Global Scientific Publishing., DOI: 10.4018/979-8-3693-6298-3.ch008

Popescu, C. R. G., & Verma, R. (2024). Industry 4.0 Entrepreneurship Education and Sustainability in a Game-Changing Post-COVID-19 Era: Innovation, Creativity, Business Integration, Technology Skills, Leadership, and Communication. In Naidoo, V., & Verma, R. (Eds.), *Reshaping Entrepreneurial Education Within an Industry 4.0 Context* (pp. 81–95). IGI Global Scientific Publishing., DOI: 10.4018/979-8-3693-0409-9.ch005

Presidencia de la Republica del Ecuador. (2024). *Texaco (Chevron) se vanagloriaba de su influencia en gobiernos pasados*. Quito. Obtenido de https://www.presidencia.gob.ec/texaco-chevron-se-vanagloriaba-de-su-influencia-en-gobiernos-pasados/

Pucci, M. (2015). The Investor-State Dispute Settlement Provision in the Trans-Pacific Partnership: Not the Death Knell Critics Are Looking For. Vol. 37. Associate Editor. Retrieved on-line from https://www.mjilonline.org/1489-2/. Accessed on the 28th of January 2025.

Ramos Galarza, C. (2020). Los alcances de una investigación. *CienciAmérica: Revista de divulgación científica de la Universidad Tecnológica Indoamérica, 9*(3), 1-6. Obtenido de https://dialnet.unirioja.es/servlet/articulo?codigo=7746475

Rimmer, M. (2016). Greenwashing. The Trans-Pacific Partnership. October 2016. The Senate Foreign Affairs, Defence And Trade References Committee. Proposed Trans-Pacific Partnership (TPP). Agreement Submission 84 - Supplementary Submission 6.

Romero, S., & Krauss, C. (2011). Ecuador judge orders Chevron to pay $9 billion. New York Times, A4.

Sachs, J. D. (2019). Testimony of Professor Jeffrey D. Sachs, University Professor at Columbia University, Subcommittee on Environment U.S. House Committee on Oversight and Reform. April 9, 2019. pp. 1-4.

Salassa, R., Alderete, P., & Bach, J. (2015). *La protección ambiental a travéz del derecho fiscal*. Facultad de Derecho y Ciencias Sociales de la Universidad Nacional de Córdoba.

Sánchez, J. (. (2019). *Recursos naturales, medio ambiente y sostenibilidad: 70 años de pensamiento de la CEPAL.* Santiago, Comisión Económica para América Latina y el Caribe (CEPAL): Libros de la CEPAL, N° 158 (LC/PUB.2019/18-P. Sánchez, César; Becerra, Thais. (20 de 04 de 2015). *El impacto de Chevron en la Amazonía ecuatoriana*. Obtenido de https://www.anthropologies.es/el-impacto-de-chevron-en-la-amazonia-ecuatoriana/

Serrano, H. (2013). *Caso Chevron-Texaco: cuando los pueblos toman la palabra*. diciembre: Universidad Andina Simón Bolívar, Sede Ecuador; Corporación Editora Nacional.

Soto, N. (21 de 05 de 2019). *Chevron: El poder y la impunidad de las grandes corporaciones*. Recuperado el 13 de 05 de 2024, de https://es.greenpeace.org/es/noticias/chevron-el-poder-y-la-impunidad-de-las-grandes-corporaciones/

Stiglitz, J. (2017). *The practice of industrial Policy.*

Tancara, C. (1993). La investigación documental. *Temas Sociales*(17), 91-106. Obtenido de http://www.scielo.org.bo/scielo.php?script=sci_arttext&pid=S0040-29151993000100008

The London School of Economics and Political Science & Grantham Research Institute on Climate Change and the Environment. (2017). Sue major polluters for climate compensation - and ask Exxon to pay for Harvey's damages says Jeffrey Sachs. Retrieved on-line from https://www.lse.ac.uk/granthaminstitute/news/sue-major-polluters-for-climate-compensation-and-ask-exxon-to-pay-for-harveys-damages-says-jeff-sachs/. Accessed on the 28th of January 2025.

Unidas, N. (2024). Obtenido de https://www.un.org/es/about-us

United Nations Conference on Trade and Development (UNCTAD). (2014). Investor-State Dispute Settlement. UNCTAD Series on Issues in International Investment. Agreements II. United Nations. New York and Geneva, 2014.

Universidad de las Americas. (2014). Ejecucion de la sentencia en el caso Chevron Corporation en el ambito internacional. In Garcia, L. V. (Ed.), *Ejecucion de la sentencia en el caso Chevron Corporation en el ambito internacional.*

Vega, L. (2013). Dimensión Ambiental, Desarrollo Sostenible y Sostenibilidad Ambiental del Desarrollo. *Eleventh LACCEI Latin American and Caribbean Conference for Engineering and Technology (LACCEI'2013)*. Obtenido de https://www.laccei.org/LACCEI2013-Cancun/RefereedPapers/RP256.pdf

Yu, P. K., Settlement, I.-S. D., & the Trans-Pacific Partnership. (August 23, 2018). Intellectual Property And The Judiciary, Christophe Geiger, Craig Allen Nard and Xavier Seuba, eds., Edward Elgar Publishing, pp. 463-93, 2018, Texas A&M University School of Law Legal Studies Research Paper No. 18-32, Available at SSRN: https://ssrn.com/abstract=3237541

Zubizarreta, J. H., & Ramiro, P. (2016). *Contra la lex mercatoria*. Ed. Icaria.

## KEY TERMS AND DEFINITIONS

**ECONOMIC GLOBALIZATION:** this is a phenomenon in expansion that causes profound changes on the world stage. It revolves around trade, the flow of investment, financial capital, division of labor and specialization. The concept is not limited only to economic variables since its effects extend to individuals, society to the state. Developing countries are experiencing stagnation in the face of their inability to cope with globalization, which is compounded by poor management of their financial markets, leading to an increase in the income inequality gap. Economic globalization brings with it the mobilization of goods and capital, reduces distance between borders and energizes international trade with some alterations to sovereignty.

**PUBLIC POLICY:** this refers to decisions and actions that a government takes when addressing public or collective issues.

**RESILIENCE:** transformations within a complex system related to the capacity for self-organization while maintaining internal structure, together with the ability to create adaptive responses, generate knowledge, experience, and learning. Resilience and sustainability are directly related to changes within societies, economies, and the human system as a whole. The transformation of systems is inevitable since it allows systems to strengthen.

**SOCIAL ECONOMY:** encompasses a variety of businesses, organizations and different legal entities. They share the objective of systematically putting people first, producing a positive impact on local communities and pursuing a social cause.

**WELFARE STATE:** A system whereby the state and supranational organizations undertakes to protect the health and well-being of its citizens, especially those in financial or social need, by means of grants, pensions, and other benefits.

## ENDNOTES

1 In the process of drilling oil wells, onshore pools are used to contain and recirculate drilling fluids.

Chapter 9
# Rights of Nature in Ecuador

**Arturo Luque González**
https://orcid.org/0000-0002-4872-891X
*Universidad Técnica de Manabí, Ecuador*

**Dolores Alexandra Bravo Bravo**
https://orcid.org/0009-0004-3106-7424
*Universidad Técnica de Manabí, Ecuador*

**Ligia Nevárez Vera**
https://orcid.org/0009-0004-0661-1600
*Universidad Técnica de Manabí, Ecuador*

**Cristina Raluca Gh. Popescu**
https://orcid.org/0000-0002-5876-0550
*University of Bucharest, Romania & The Bucharest University of Economic Studies, Romania*

## ABSTRACT

*In this work we will analyze as an objective the legal approach regarding the rights of nature in Ecuador. For the development of this work, we have proposed to investigate the historical sources, the current Constitution, analyze environmental documentaries, theses, articles, and everything that is reliable regarding the topic in question, therefore, at the same time exposing the novelties found in the research performed. The Constitution of Ecuador of 2008 is the first in the world to explicitly recognize nature as a subject of law, accepting its essential value regardless of its benefit. In this country it was a constant struggle of environmentalists and nature protectors, who after achieving the inclusion of articles with which nature can be protected, feel after their achievement progress for their purpose of caring for the environment. It has been confirmed that these laws have had an effect and although we cannot turn back time to stop the damage caused to our ecosystem, we are doing something so that our descendants can breathe fresh air, through the projects of certain insti*

DOI: 10.4018/979-8-3373-0189-1.ch009

## 1. INTRODUCTION

Nature is the key element from which all life arises. However, from the hegemonic anthropocentric historical vision, nature is a mere object at the service of the interests of humanity to be exploited by the capitalist system. In contrast, from the non-hegemonic worldview of indigenous peoples, nature is a whole of which the human being is nothing more than a constituent part (Rodriguez & Valle, 2023); in this vision, everything is related to everything else (Martínez, 2009, pp, 12-13) and the need for environmental protection, recognition and respect is inherent. It should be remembered that the United Nations General Assembly declared on July 28, 2022, that all people in the world have the right to a healthy environment. Inger Andersen, executive director of UNEP (United Nations Environment Programme) pointed out that "this resolution sends the message that no one can take away nature, clean air or clean water, or deprive us of a stable climate. At least not without fighting for it" (United Nations, 2022).

The industrial revolution was a succession of events that brought about essential technological advances (Palacios, 2004). In turn, the increase in the use of human and natural resources to sustain and feed the emerging production process came with all manner of abuses (Passet, 2013). These technical-industrial, social and economic advances concluded in the final transition from the feudal system to the capitalist system (Hobsbawm, 1971). However, the need for more resources brought on a voracious depredation of ecosystems: in just 200 years, human activities have caused changes in the climate that would naturally have taken millions of years to carry out (Bárcena 2020, p.43). At the end of the twentieth century, climate change and its consequences were largely recognized in what is known as a triple planetary crisis: "the climate change crisis, the crisis of nature and biodiversity loss, and the pollution and waste crisis" (UNEP, 2022).

In 1972, the first international conference of the United Nations was held (1972) whose central axis was the environment, and it resulted in the Report of the United Nations Conference on the Human Environment. This highlighted environmental issues and the link between economic growth and air, water and ocean pollution and on their effects on people's well-being. A generation later came the Our Common Future Report (Brundtland Report) (1987), which introduced for the first time the concept of sustainable development and highlighted the potential of human activities to radically modify the planet and exterminate species, including humans. In 1992, the Rio Declaration on the Environment and Development drew up a series of principles for development and sustainability with respect to the protection of the environment, in addition to dealing with the United Nations Convention on Climate Change and the United Nations Convention on Biological Diversity. In 2015, during the United Nations Climate Change Conference (COP21), one of the most important international treaties on the subject was agreed and, despite its limited impact, the legally binding 2015 Paris Agreement came into force in 2016.

The proposes of the Paris Agreement is mitigate global warming through reducing greenhouse gas emissions by calling for the commitment of nations to adopt measures in accordance with the agreement. It also reaffirms the need for multilateral cooperation, such as the provision of aid by developed countries for developing and more vulnerable countries. At the same time, the adoption of the 2030 Agenda for Sustainable Development sets out a collection of seventeen goals—Sustainable Development Goals (SDGs)—to eradicate poverty, protect the planet and ensure prosperity for all its inhabitants (UN, 2015). Within the context of this research, the following goals stand out: SDG 2, "Zero Hunger"; SDG 6, "Clean water and sanitation"; SDG 7, "Affordable and clean energy"; SDG 11, "Sustainable Cities and Communities"; SDG 12, "Responsible consumption and production"; SDG 13, "Climate Action"; SDG 14, "Life Below Water"; and, SDG 15, Life on Land". However, despite such international efforts and multilateral discussions, the future is increasingly threatened by desertification and land degradation (UN, 2024)

Historically, there has been debate about the recognition of nature and the need for its protection, mainly from the field of ecological philosophy, which posits that the roots of ecological crises are fundamentally philosophical (Crespo, 2013). An example of this debate is the transcendental paper by Professor Christopher Stone (2010) originally published in 1972 in the "Southern California Law Review", entitled "Should trees have standing – toward legal rights for natural objects". The paper points out that under the existing legal structure, nature is stripped of rights, without any legal provision to establish, defend or reinforce them.

At the national level, countries have used environmental law as a means of mitigating the damage done to nature. In a general definition, environmental law can be conceptualized as a set of legal norms that regulate human behavior in relation to environmental systems and living organisms in order to affect the living conditions of ecosystems (Brañes, 2007). In Latin America, at the end of the twentieth century and the beginning of the twenty-first century, the era of New Constitutionalism emerged. This is a conjunction of political-social transformations as a response to hegemony and dependency (Maniglio et al., 2020). The constitutions of Venezuela in 1999 and Bolivia in 2009 stipulate the recognition and protection of collective and social rights to guarantee a social welfare state (Luque & Casado, 2020). They advocate the recognition of indigenous peoples (together with their knowledge and customs) with the addition of a constitutional recognition of the right to the environment.

In Ecuador, earlier constitutions not only established limitations to the access to rights for ethnic, gender, social and economic reasons, but also totally excluded indigenous peoples and certain other social groups (Martínez, 2014), thereby excluding knowledge, customs, philosophy, and ideology different from the dominant anthropocentric ones. Therefore, the Ecuadorian constitution of 1998 marked a new beginning for the rights of nature in the country, albeit as an "object of protection" in the context of the "environment" (Rodriguez & Valle, 2023, p. 19). However, it is the constitution of the Republic of Ecuador (CRE) of 2008 that places this recognition as the subject of constitutional rights, making it a watershed moment in the global approach to nature. Essentially, Ecuador became the first country in which the state and its citizens accepted a new social contract wherein the rights of nature are recognized and subjectivized (Gudynas, 2015). In other words, nature was no longer the object of rights, but became the subject of rights (Rodriguez & Valle, 2023, p. 20), and connected with the vision of vindicating planet Earth as an entity. This move opened the world to a new legal paradigm in which nature can be a subject of law without being human. The 2008 constitution, also known as the Magna Carta of Montecristi, includes articles n°71, 72 and 73, which comprehensively establish legal protection, recognition and respect for nature, and also *per se* establish the right to the restoration of life cycles.

Ecuador therefore began a transformation in progress aimed at the concept of good living [Sumak Kawsay] (Luque, et al., 2024), and, as the first country to constitutionally recognize such rights, blazed the trail for other countries to join the protection of the environment at a global level. That this paradigm shift happened in Ecuador is particularly symbolic since it is one of the mega-biodiverse countries on the planet, ranking among the 17 most biodiverse countries in relation to the density of natural species per square meter. Within the sovereign territory, there are 4,801 species of vertebrates, 833 species of marine fish, 951 species of freshwater fish, 658 species of amphibians, 498 species of reptiles, 1691 species of birds and 465 species of mammals (*PNUD*, 2023). Currently, there are approximately eleven nature reserves, including Galapagos, Cotopaxi, Cayambe, Coca, Yasuní, and others (Gudynas, 2009).

This analysis complements and in some cases expands on other detailed examinations of the political ecology of the constitution of Montecristi, and does so from a non-legal, political ecology perspective (Gudynas, 2009). In response to the criticisms and objections surrounding these constitutional rights—"[...] if law exists because of men, it also exists for men, for the simple and inescapable reason that its language only makes sense to them" (Crespo, 2009, p.1)—it is necessary to examine the efficacy of legal provisions that create a holder of rights that is not human. In view of this, the idea of adding a new branch to the law is appropriate, since "the constitutionalization of the recognition of nature as a subject of law "not only generates a new constitutional principle, but also contributes to the construction of a new legal order that must develop that principle" (Macías, 2010, p.22). However, it should also be born in mind that the principles, constitutional duties, rights, and guarantees represent the legal spectrum of national scope (Morales, 2018).

With the constitutionalization of the rights of nature come formalistic-legal transformations that fall beyond the analysis of the dichotomies of positivization in the 2008 constitution (Rodriguez & Valle, 2023). It also brings the legal juxtaposition of what *should be* (formal) and what *is* (practice), and involves profound changes in ideological and social schemata that require bold approaches (Acosta & Martinez, 2009, p.15). It is necessary to understand the reciprocity that must exist between human beings and the living earth as the source of our sustenance and existence (Boff, 2013), even when the ancestral knowledge grounded in our natural origins has been eroded almost completely over recent generations. Indigenous peoples occupy about 25% of the world's land, but it is land that contains much of the planet's biodiversity and the carbon stored in soil and biomass. Most of this land is covered by forests, which are central to the traditions, cultures and livelihoods of the 70 million indigenous peoples who are therefore responsible for the environmental management of at least 36% of the world's intact forests (UNDP, 2024). Despite increasing external pressures on land, many forests and other ecosystems located in areas managed by indigenous peoples are in a healthier state than those environments outside these areas (Townsend; Moola & Craig, 2020).

Besides all the aforementioned vital ideas that come to crucially emphasize as well as to vitally support the rights of nature at a worldwide level and, in this case, in particular, in Ecuador, it needs to be highlighted that there are far more connections between nature and individuals and communities than anticipated and foreseen at a first glance, namely: first of all, people's health and well-being is indispensably and strongly related to nature's balance and harmony (Bautista-Valarezo *et al.*, 2020); second of all, people's health and illnesses are far better understood and far more acknowledged as a direct resultant of the equitable or inequitable and respectful or disrespectful interrelationships between communities and nature (González *et al.*, 2023; González & Popescu, 2025); and, third of all, the frameworks and pillars responsible for developing inclusive health plans that rely on people's perspectives on nature, biodiversity, ecosystems, and habitats, have proven to be critically important to health and, also, to display the existence of each culture's respect towards traditional values and the constructs of health (Ycaza *et al.*, 2022; Matute-Petroche *et al.*, 2022).

Although there are voices that stand out far more than others and that constantly tend to emphasize that growth and progress are in the benefit of all people and organizations – since growth and progress are strategically portrayed as immediate advantages of modern societies, capable to offer instant success and long-term financial incentives to those willing to get rich or even richer than the present moment, it must be acknowledged that irrational behaviors have been known to create history and to sabotage the initial "good thoughts" and apparently "genuine" credulity if not managed optimally and rationally (Popescu, 2020; Saiz-Alvarez *et al.*, 2021; Šebestová & Popescu, 2022). Interestingly, living good ("Buen

Vivir") through integrated healthcare is the right approach on which specialists' worldwide and, in this particular situation, in Ecuador, ought to start building their projects, since optimizing intercultural connections in all areas implicates continuing the legacy of the ancestors and praising nature for the resources provided and the care given to people and communities for centuries (Popescu & Popescu, 2019; Afanador *et al.*, 2021).

Even though some might regard the topic of the rights of nature at a worldwide level and, in this case, in particular, in Ecuador, a very sensible one and, also, even though others could try to strengthen the wrongly promoted beliefs that human activities are not affecting the environment, ecosystems, human heath, and well-being of natural regions in Ecuador, the environment and the natural resources are vital to life and health (Arteaga *et al.*, 2018; Vera-Arias *et al.*, 2019; Paz *et al.*, 2020; Aguirre *et al.*, 2021; Vargas *et al.*, 2022). What is more, offering a better and more profound understanding of the ecological variables and implementing inclusive, resilient, rigorous, and sustainable public policies that should support the balance between the socio-economic aspects and the environmental ones needs to be a key priority in showing that the rights of nature are properly protected (Ocaña-Mayorga *et al.*, 2018; Mestanza-Ramón *et al.*, 2022). Furthermore, another element that requires immediate attention in order to address and make changes in the spirit of the Sustainable Development Goals and sustainable development is represented by being able to place the accent on the social-environmental impacts of the serious effects that some human activities have on nature – such as, for example, the large-scale (industrial) mining which leads to historical contamination of water sources by dangerous heavy metals, alteration of the surrounding precious and vital aquatic and terrestrial systems, affecting irreversibly human lives and generating unthinkable illnesses (Guijarro-Garvi *et al.*, 2022; González *et al.*, 2023; González & Popescu, 2025). Additionally, disinformation, lack of education, and inequalities are believed to represent some of the major problems today when willing to facilitate people, communities, and organizations the access to the outcomes of their decisions taken in time and which have affected, one way or another, the balance between nature, ecosystems, and health: to begin with, education is crucial in offering individuals the necessary competences and skills that would make them access, from the very beginning, the information that is of real use, process it accordingly, and take the right decisions in the spirit of ethical and responsible behavior (Popescu, 2019; Popescu & Ban a, 2019; Rios Quituizaca *et al.*, 2021; Calvopiña *et al.*, 2022; Vásconez-González *et al.*, 2023; Ozayturk, 2025); in continuation, enabling access to people to valuable lifelong learning programs and trainings offers the right edge as well as the optimum angle that will show them how to adequately transform their knowledge into sources of income that will not generate harm to themselves, their communities, and the environment, but will foster prosperity and well-being in an ethical, responsible, and sustainable way (Cuéllar *et al.*, 2022; Díaz *et al.*, 2023); in the end, inequalities are extremely dangerous in any society, given the fact that they divert individuals and communities attention from medium-term and long-term effects of human activities, businesses, and industries, since due to the pressing financial and social nature of some decisions people may live with the impression that their actions may be pardoned and will not affect the communities or the environment at all or that much as, for instance, bigger corporations might do (Parra-Gaete & Hermosa-Bosano, 2023; Domínguez & Faytong-Haro, 2024; Molina *et al.*, 2024; Ozayturk, 2025).

## 2. METHOD

This research used a positivist methodology, together with a qualitative approach, which provided a framework for explanation, prediction, confirmation of documentation and norms, and control of phenomena (Ramos, 2015). It identified precedent or synchronous causality through the accumulation and critical analysis of documents, together with a literature review. It is based on an organized, unflinching and transcendent examination of different sources of evidence in the form of regulations and academic articles. The procedure used in the research is descriptive analysis and explanation from documented observation (Menger, 1996).

## 3. THE PARADIGMS OF THE LAW OF NATURE IN THE ECUADORIAN CONSTITUTION OF 2008

The evolution of the rights of nature is relatively recent, and it arose from the need to regulate human impacts and effects—predominantly negative—on living systems (Solecki, Roberts & Seto 2024). From the outset, environmental law has had the dual personality of defending nature from man while being conceived and developed for the protection of the environmental rights of human beings (Morales, 2018). Therefore, the new legal conception of nature as a subject of the law made it possible to provide a separate legal institution (Rodríguez-Estévez, 2022), different from environmental law (Jaria-Manzano, 2019).

The protection of nature seen from other approaches—different from the dominant anthropocentric one—involved transcending the environmental ethics of Western culture itself and understanding the indigenous worldview (Gudynas, 2015). This was reflected in the 2008 constitution by incorporating the term *Pacha Mama* (Art. 71, CRE, 2008) in an attempt to equate the nature of the Western cultural heritage (Gudynas, 2015, pp. 71-75) with the indigenous worldview concept of Mother Earth. *Pacha Mama is* a term that had already been universalized, passing from Quechua and Aymara to South American Spanish (Mamami & Clavero, 2010, p.9). However, the constitution also incorporates other approaches that advocate values of respect and protection that are dissimilar to Western instrumentalism. From the ecocentric approach, nature is recognized as a community of living beings that faces tensions because it is subsumed by human judgment and subjectivity about the environment. At the same time, biocentrism aims to place the intrinsic values of life, both human and non-human, within the individual, the species or the ecosystem (Gudynas, 2015, pp. 55-60).

The entry of the knowledge of the Ecuadorian indigenous peoples and their perception of the environment to the 2008 Constitution in turn opened the door to the indigenous vision of Buen Vivir [good living] or *Sumak Kawsay*. This states that the fullness of life is based on the balance and harmony of the universal whole: the family, the community, the people, *Pacha Mama*, the nation, the world. Consequently, the imbalance of one of these elements has a serious impact on collective well-being (Council for the Development of the Nationalities and Peoples of Ecuador, 2011). According to Muyolema (2012), "each term is recorded and defined separately: Sumak means "pleasant, beautiful, kind", while Kawsay means "life, to live". The combination of both concepts, which is possible in everyday communication, does not denote an extraordinary epistemological range as with other concepts such as Pacha (time-space), Pachakutik (profound transformation of the order of things), etc."

This conceptualization puts a certain amount of distance from the dual Western perspective that divides human beings from nature (Gudynas, 2015). Such egalitarian ideology comes with the recognition of diversities, the influence of social movements in some aspects of the constitution, the promotion of material equality, the distribution of wealth and social goods, and the recognition of indigenous knowledge. It is a non-Western utopian proposal, which includes the recognition of both Pacha *Mama* (the rights of nature) and Sumak Kawsay (Ávila Santamaría, 2012), thereby emphasizing the importance of creating a healthy environment for the application of human rights and the right to life itself. This combination establishes the inappropriateness of altering nature in land, air or water and depriving citizens of a stable climate as opposed to fighting for a healthy environment (UN, 2022), one that allows the application of human rights and includes the right to life, health, among others. This approach is in essence the vision of the Ecuadorian Constitution, which recognizes that human well-being and health are intrinsically linked to nature.

In the legal field, the positivization of the rights of nature produces the breakdown of the *status quo*, triggering classic legal positions in three approaches. Firstly, there is the rupture of the traditional conception of human rights, as nature becomes the holder of rights, regardless of the definitions of environment and human being. It is then unhelpful to generalize as "human" rights those that have special protection in the constitution, rather, it is better to talk of "fundamental" or "constitutional" rights. Secondly, the concept of ownership of rights breaks with the conventional legal conception, and brushes aside the hegemonic anthropocentric philosophy of law. Thirdly, there is a break with traditional legal formalism and an overturning of the dominant legal culture (Ávila, 2011).

The subjectivity of nature in the Ecuadorian constitution is established in Chapter VII; Articles 71 to 74, which explain and justify the right of nature to be respected in its entirety simply by virtue of its existence. This respect means that nature's evolutionary vital processes must be guaranteed, or the necessary means of redress must be put in place to mitigate the damage caused in order not to permanently alter the ecosystem in its natural cycles. Nature or *Pacha Mama* is defined as the creator of life, and while any individual, group or community may demand the vindication of the rights of nature (art. 71), the right to redress should not be understood as reparation to the individuals or groups that depend on the affected natural systems, but as mitigation of harmful environmental effects on nature itself, such as those caused by extractive activities of non-renewable natural resources (art. 72). Similarly, the state must apply precautionary measures and restrictions against any activity that threatens species, ecosystems and natural cycles, including the introduction of organisms that impact the national genetic heritage (art. 72). Finally, individuals, communities, peoples and nationalities have the right to benefit from natural resources for their good living [Sumak Kawsay] (art. 74). This last recognition introduces a contradiction that creates a dichotomous dogmatic position within the constitution. On the one hand, it establishes that nature in and of itself has the right to respect and preservation of its natural cycles (art. 71); and on the other hand, it preserves the right of all persons and communities to exploit the natural resources of their environment (art. 74). Thus, despite the efforts to take the indigenous worldview of the value of the inherent value of nature as an entity of life, the utilitarian values of the dominant anthropocentric and capitalist culture persist (Rodriguez & Valle, 2023).

The new legal framework has sparked debates and changes in other constitutions, placing Ecuador as a global benchmark with respect to the rights of nature. However, the practical implementation of these rights has been limited by the tensions of political and economic interest. Certainly, the recognition of the rights to nature in Ecuador has inspired other nations to take its underlying principles into consideration, such as in the Law of the Rights of Mother Earth, which was presented by the World People's

Conference on Climate Change and approved in Bolivia. This was clearly based on the model of the Ecuadorian Law of Rights of Mother Earth of 2010. Nature considered as a subject of law, with intrinsic value, drives the change in attitudes to be able to solve urgent global demands and the manifestations of the right to exist. In other words, it leads change in the culture of individuals and in the values of society that allows us to live in harmony with all lifestyles (Morales, 2018).

## 3.1 The Evolution Of The National Regulatory Framework In Relation To The Constitutional Law Of Nature

The constitution of Ecuador took the lead in recognizing the guaranteed development and promotion of the rights of nature. It emerged as a standard-bearer in the march to improve the planet more consciously and reduce the effects of climate change. It is radically transforming politics by providing the framework to face any environmental crisis. In legal terms, the Ecuadorian constitution proposes a model of transformation in the relationship of individuals with nature in which the deterioration of the planet is arrested. By introducing the rights of nature into the constitution, legal test cases emerged which highlighted these principles. In the Constitutional Court of Ecuador, the resolutions that broadly clarify these rights were issued, providing the legal precedents for future interpretations (Constitutional Court of Ecuador, 2011). These cases frequently include issues of deforestation or exploitation of natural resources, such as in the case of the Sarayaku community, which obtained a ruling in its favor in the Inter-American Court of Human Rights in 2012 (Martínez, 2014). This case was an important precedent for tying together human rights and nature since it accentuated the need to orient environmental processes towards environmental justice to prevent violations. It also highlighted the protection of Yasuni Park as one of the most biodiverse protected areas worldwide. The preservation of Yasuni from petroleum exploitation has been fraught, and at the same time a key battleground in the rights of nature in the Ecuadorian constitution. In 2019, the Constitutional Court declared in favor of keeping the Yasuni free of any extraction activity, reaffirming the need to preserve the ecosystem unspoiled for generations to come (Fundación Pachamama, 2021). In this way, Ecuador intervened energetically in both national and international projects in search of allies to support and strengthen environmental policies for sustainable development.

Ecuador has one of the greatest biodiversities globally, despite its relatively small size. This is reflected in its many natural reserves, which maintain the conservation of the biodiversity under the protection of the rights of nature. These protected areas preserve the native flora and fauna and also function as a conservation model for ecosystems to maintain pure air, clean water and climate regulation. Biological theory shows that human beings are integral parts of ecosystems and that their well-being is intrinsically linked to the health of the natural enviornment. The approach pioneered in Ecuador helps ensure that the activities of individuals are committed to protecting the life of nature, by reaffirming that the degradation of the environment can be halted and reversed, with positive impacts on the quality of life of humans.

However, despite the advances in the understanding and integration in environmental management, there are a number of challenges for the effective execution of these concepts. Chief among these is economic pressure, the lack of resources for conservation and restoration, and the resistance of sectors that do not want to change their environmentally damaging practices. According to Chesnais, (2010, p.30), “the valuation of capital through the production and sale of commodities that correspond to ‘created’ needs not only represents a useless expenditure of labor, it also means a useless expenditure of raw materials, of soil and subsoil resources, as well as increasingly serious damage (harm) … to the biosphere and ecosystems." However, such challenges can be a spur to continue to fight for the protection and restoration of nature. Certainly, there is a growing global awareness of the environmental crisis—albeit with few tools for redress—along with the development of new technologies and management approaches. All of this can facilitate the adoption of more sustainable practices (Sutherland, 2009).

This relationship between society and nature influences the cultural and philosophical approaches that inform how we value the environment. In indigenous culture, mother nature and the environment are not merely resources to be used, they are seen as a living entity with intrinsic rights and values (Luque, Quishpi & Espín, 2023). This holistic vision of nature is fundamental to the concept of "good living" [sumak kawsay] since it emphasizes harmony and balance between individuals and the world around them. By granting legal rights to nature, Ecuador has adopted an approach that recognizes the interdependence of all living beings and the need to protect ecosystems as a whole (Gudynas, 2011). This perspective has legal and political implications, but also promotes cultural change in terms of responsibility and care for the environment. Table N°1 sets out a comparison of the laws of the rights of nature in Ecuador (2013-2023). It highlights the achievements made in the different pieces of legislation, and that, over the past ten years, Ecuador has demonstrated a continuous effort to integrate and strengthen the rights of nature into its legal framework. From the initial formation of the Organic Administrative Code (COA) to the recent reforms, there is evidence of a trend towards the consolidation of environmental laws. The impact of these laws has been significant for the conservation and protection of biodiversity, and the management and creation of protected areas and ecological restoration projects.

*Table 1.* **Legislative advances related to the Rights of Nature**

| Year | Legislation | Description | Impact | Challenges |
|---|---|---|---|---|
| **2013** | Organic Environmental Code (COA)- Bill | The formation of the COA begins with the aim of integrating the rights of bature | First legislative effort to consolidate environmental standards through a single code. | There is a lack of conformity between the economic and environmental sectors. |
| **2014** | Water Resources Act. | Establishes water as a human right and a right of nature. | Strengthens protections of water sources and community management. | Conflicts in agricultural and industrial interests over the greater demands of each. |
| **2015** | Resolution 197-2015 | Regulation of mining and the impact it has on nature. | Restrictions on mining in protected areas and ecologically important areas. | Tensions begin between mining operations and the communities that are benefiting. |
| **2016** | National Climate Change Policy | Integrates the rights of nature into mitigation strategies and climate adaptation. | Protections of vulnerable ecosystems are strengthened and sustainable practices are promoted. | Uneven implementation and lack of adequate funding emerge. |
| **2017** | Organic Environmental Code (COA) - Enactment | Passing of the COA into law, with the rights of nature incorporated into environmental regulations. | Consolidation of various environmental laws within the comprehensive legislative framework | There is a need for adjustments that can be adapted to environmental realities. |
| **2018** | National Forest Restoration Plan | Initiatives for the restoration of degraded ecosystems and reforestation begin. | Support for the recovery of deforested areas and a plan to improve biodiversity. | Difficulties in areas of high deforestation and economic activities. |

continued on following page

*Table 1. Continued*

| Year | Legislation | Description | Impact | Challenges |
|---|---|---|---|---|
| **2019** | Executive Order 752 | Creation of the National System of Protected Areas (SNAP) to improve the management of nature reserves. | Improvement in the management and conservation of protected areas | Local community resistance and land tenure conflicts. |
| **2020** | Organic Law on Biodiversity | Develops the protection of biodiversity and regulation of access to genetic resources. | Promotes species conservation and scientific research | Challenges to effective enforcement and controls on "biopiracy". |
| **2021** | Blue Carbon Initiative | Project for the conservation of marine and coastal ecosystems that store carbon. | Contribution to climate change mitigation and mangrove protection. | Lack of inter-agency coordination and financial resources. |
| **2022** | Executive Order 499 | Declaration of the rights of all in a healthy environment, in line with the UN declaration. | Reinforcement of environmental rights and international standard commitments. | Limits to practical implementation and the compliance of industry sectors. |
| **2023** | Amendments to the COA and the Ecological Transition Act | Updates the COA to include new environmental challenges and transitions to green economies. | Regulations are modernized and clean energy and sustainable practices are promoted. | The opposition of traditional sectors and the lack of adequate infrastructure. |

Source: compiled by the authors

Despite the progress made, there are challenges in the effective implementation of the legislation. There are obstacles to overcome in order to protect nature at a global level, and the application and enforcement of laws is uneven between the different social and economic actors. However, the inclusion of ideas such as ecological restoration, blue carbon and the transition to a green economy is an innovative and proactive approach, and one largely pioneered by Ecuador in the protection of the rights of nature. This legislation places Ecuadorian jurisprudence as an environmental leader worldwide. In 2022 the UN underlined Ecuador's commitment in context to the environmental agenda and the protection of the rights of nature.

## 3.2 The Justiciability of the Law of Nature

The treatment of the law of nature in the legislation is reflected in the legal interpretation made in the highest court of Ecuador; the jurisprudence provided by the Constitutional Court of Ecuador (forthwith, the Court) sets the precedents and the scope of the protection of the rights of nature, which frequently cut across other constitutional precepts. In Table n°2, some rulings of the Court related to the right of nature are set out.

*Table 2.* **Jurisprudence of the Constitutional Court of Ecuador**

| Judgment | Date | Actors | Ruling |
|---|---|---|---|
| **Judgment No. 065-15-SEP-CC** | 11-03-2015 | Jefferson Loor Moreira v. Judgment No. 0145-2012, Provincial Court of Manabí | The Court partially rules in favor of the plaintiff; however, it recognizes the constitutional guarantees aimed at protecting ecosystems. It brings in the rights of the peoples to use their communal territory. |
| **Judgment No. 166-15-SEP-CC** | 20-05-2015 | Ministry of Environment vs. Manuel Meza Macías (Shrimp Fishing Case MARMEZA-Cayapas Reserve) | The Court declares the violation of Article 76 of the CRE, recognizing that the rights of nature were violated by allowing the activities of the shrimp farm within the Cayapas reserve, Esmeraldas. In effect, it annuls the judgment of the Provincial Court of Justice of Esmeraldas and to retrogress the process to the moment when the violation of constitutional rights occurred. |
| **Judgment No. 218-15-SEP-CC** | 9-07-2015 | Riobamba Mining Regulation and Control Agency vs. Mireya Ríos Guijarro and Marcelo Lalama | The Court declares the violation of the rights of nature contained in Article 71 of the constitution and orders the following reparation measures: to annul the judgment of the Provincial Court of Justice of Pastaza, to order the Ministry of Environment to quantify the damages and to compensate the material damages and the restoration of the area to the defendants. |
| **Judgment No. 034-16-SIN-CC** | 27-04-2016 | Totoracocha Agricultural Workers Association Vs. Ministry of Environment | The Court dismisses the claim of unconstitutionality filed by the plaintiff and decides to rule Ministerial Agreement No. 007, of 01-25-2012 of the Ministry of the Environment, constitutionally correct in accordance with Articles 71, 72, 73 and 74, declaring the "Quimsacocha" an area of natural heritage of the state. |
| **Judgment No. 32-17-IN/21** | 9-06-2021 | Public Action of Unconstitutionality of the Environmental Regulation of Mining Activities (RAAM) | The Court declares the unconstitutionality of articles: 86 and 136 of the Environmental Regulation of Mining Activities for failing to observe the following articles of the constitution: 3.7. Protect natural and cultural heritage; 11.1. Principle of enforceability of rights; 10 Nature will be subject to those rights recognized in the constitution; 71 Right of Nature, 73 Right to the preservation of spieces; 424 Constitutional hierarchy |
| **Judgment No. 22-18-IN/21** | 8-09-2021 | Public Action of Unconstitutionality of the Organic Environmental Code (COAM) and its Regulations | The Court rules the partial unconstitutionality of the Organic Code of the Environment and its Regulations, arguing that the phrase, "other productive activities" contained in Article 104.7, violates the legal security of mangrove ecosystems as a title of rights of nature; likewise, it rules the unconstitutionality of Article 121 of the COAM for contravening Article 409 of the constitution. |
| **Judgment No. 1149-19-JP/21** | 10-11-2021 | Review of appeal issued by the Provincial Court of Justice of Imbabura | The Court rules in favor of the action for the protection of the Los Cedros Protected Forest, issued by the Provincial Court of Justice of Imbabura, due to the violations of the rights of nature, the right to a healthy environment, the right to water and the right to environmental consultation stipulated in the constitution. |

continued on following page

*Table 2. Continued*

| Judgment | Date | Actors | Ruling |
|---|---|---|---|
| **Judgment No. 1185-20-JP/21** | 15-12-2021 | Fanny Realpe Herrera et al. v. National Water Secretariat (SENAGUA) | The Court rules in favor of the plaintiffs and recognizes that SENAGUA violated the rights of the Aquepí River, Santo Domingo, to have its structure, operation, flow and preservation respected as a subject of rights. In addition, it recognizes the violation of the rights of the inhabitants of "Julio Moreno Espinosa y Aquepi" for not carrying out the environmental consultation on the design of the "Unión Carchense Irrigation Project" and the "Aquepeí Multipurpose". |
| **Judgment No. 253-20-JH/22** | 27-01-2022 | Filing of *Habeas Corpus on behalf of a* chorongo monkey named "Estrellita" | The Court upholds the ruling of the violation of the rights of nature, mainly due to the events that ended in the death of the monkey, Estrellita, who was confiscated from her "human home" by the Management Center as authorized by the National Environmental Authority. However, the habeas corpus that sought the wildlife license and return of Estrelllita is denied on the grounds that the jurisdictional guarantees must be adapted in an appropriate way and in the context of the case. In addition, it is denied on the grounds that the chorongo monkey had already died. |

Source: Compiled by the authors based on the records of the Constitutional Court of Ecuador

The judgments set out here recognize—in multiple dimensions—the positioning of nature as a subject of constitutional rights, independently of the rights contemplated for human beings, and establish jurisprudential precedents that move away from the classical and dominant legal perceptions inherited from Roman-Germanic law. The legal analysis of these constitutional rulings shows that values approximating to ecocentric and biocentric philosophies permeate, as explained by Eduardo Gudynas (2015) in the book, "Rights of Nature". These values go hand-in-hand with the constitutional mandate provided by the indigenous worldview of the *Sumak Kawsay;* as Silva, (2008, p. 123) argues, "the Sumak Kawsay is a philosophical principle that has a precise meaning and content whose origin is found in indigenous thought".

In Judgment No. 166-15-SEP-CC, 2015, the Court recognized nature as a subject of rights, in addition to considering violations of due process (art. 76.7, Constitution, 2008), by failing to observe nature as the holder of rights. Consequently, state agencies must ensure the protection of nature and ensure its restoration in compliance with the constitutional mandate. Similarly, the Court extended constitutional guarantees by ordering the protection of ecosystems over private property, as expressed in the ruling contained in Judgment No. 065-15-SEP-CC, 2015. Here, it delimited the actions of exploitation of natural resources on the basis of productive activities, but also invoked the right of indigenous peoples to have the use of their ancestral communal territory respected. In line with this, Pope Francis (2020, p.73) points out that "the principle of the subordination of private property to the universal destination of goods and, therefore, the universal right to their use is a 'golden rule' of social behavior and the 'first principle of the entire ethical-social order'. The Christian tradition never recognized the right to private property as absolute or untouchable and highlighted the social function of any form of private property."

Judgment No. 218-15-SEP-CC, 2015 contained a corollary on the integral right of nature, which included respect for the redress of its life cycles and the protection of natural systems over the utilitarian ideology of Western culture. It also established the legal subjectivity of nature arising from the anthropological axis of the original peoples of the affected territory. Likewise, in Judgment No. 1185-20-JP/21, 2021 and Judgment No. 1149-19-JP/21, 2021, the Court ruled in favor of the Aquepí River in Santo Domingo, and the Los Cedros Protective Forest in Cotacachi, Imbabura, considering the violation of their constitutional rights contained in the law of nature. In the first case, the state actions were couched within the framework of the water projects that were developed there; in the second case, they were due to public and judicial non-compliance in granting and ratifying the permits for intervention in this protected natural area and the concessions on the Magdalena River. In this sense, the Court not only recognized the rights of natural entities, it also highlighted the intrinsic value of the natural commodity of water as a social right, the right of species, the biodiversity that flows from the law of nature itself, and the obligation to preserve it beyond any debate. In addition, in both cases, the Court again argued for the imperative of applying prior (environmental) consultation to the indigenous peoples and communities with respect to interventions within ancestral spaces. In Judgment No. 034-16-SIN-CC, 2016, the Court established the interdependence of human beings and nature, and that the exploitation of the latter should not be justified by invoking other rights of a civil-political or economic-social kind. Consequently, it left it up to the state to demand the justiciability of nature through legal norms for its protection outside of the constitution.

In line with the above, the Court also settled the unconstitutionality—total or partial—of regulations or legal acts outside of the constitution. In Judgment No. 32-17-IN/21, 2021, the Court ruled that articles 86 and 136 of the Environmental Regulations for Mining Activities were unconstitutional for contravening not only the rights of nature contained in Chapter VII of the constitution, but also for violating the constitutional mandates for the protection of natural heritage (art. 3.7, CRE, 2008) and the principle of enforceability of constitutional rights (art. 11.1., CRE, 2008) in accordance with Art. 10 that stipulates nature's ownership of constitutional rights. Similarly, the Court ruled the partial unconstitutionality of the Organic Environmental Code (COAM) and its regulations, through Judgment No. 22-18-IN/21, 2021, arguing that the legal security of the Mangrove ecosystems had been violated (basing the rights of these ecosystems on the law of nature).

Finally, in the case of the monkey, "Estrellita", a writ of *habeas corpus* was filed to obtain the custody of a wild animal in response to its confiscation by the environmental authority. The monkey had previously spent 18 years living in a "human home". Although the Court recognized that there are no prohibitive or mandatory rules that determine that the rights of nature (including those of fauna) may not be protected by constitutional guarantees, they do require an evaluation of the object, context and claims of the cause that invokes them. Furthermore, the admissibility of the action for protection requires that its object not be rights that are protected by another jurisdictional guarantee. The writ of *habeas corpus* was therefore denied following this argument, and was also rejected since the Chornogo monkey had died before the time of the ruling. However, the jurisprudential value of this judgment lies in the view that the ownership of the rights of nature does not apply merely to the macro environment (ecosystems, forests, jungles), but also can be transferred, in a specific and particular way, to any of the organisms that coexist within it, that is, animals and other wildlife.

## 4. ANALYSIS

The Ecuadorian constitution recognizes the rights of nature based on a worldview that connects individuals with the natural environment of which they are an integral part. This perspective takes its influence from indigenous traditions, which conceive of the Pacha Mama as a living being of which human beings are a complement. The ground-breaking constitution of 2008, the first to recognize nature as a subject of rights, marks a historic step in environmental jurisprudence after decades of struggle by environmental movements and indigenous communities. These latter groups, especially, fought tirelessly for a new paradigm between human beings and their natural environment. The inclusion of these rights in the Ecuadorian constitution meant a radical change in the traditional conceptions in relation to environmental law, which had previously been responsible only for regulating the use of natural resources; the new perspective recognized the intrinsic value of nature regardless of its use.

There is a latent tension between the protection of nature and the pressure of economic development, especially in a country where the economy depends largely on extractivist activities in both oil and mining. Therefore, national plans needed to be developed to create a model that harmonizes economic growth in relation to respect for natural cycles. The incorporation of the rights of nature also led to changes in the area of procedural law, developing innovative legal figures for the effective representation of nature in judicial processes and it encouraged experimentation in how to validate non-human entities within a legal system. Ecuador's experience has led to reflection on the universality of these rights, which required a reconsideration of business practices despite their widespread irresponsibility (Luque & Herrero-García, 2019).

There is the need to analyze more closely today's patterns of cultural, ethic, economic, and socio-demographic diversity, especially when willing to defy the current universal models of healthy aging and those that rely on living in balance with the environment and with nature (Benítez *et al.*, 2021; Castillo-Nazareno *et al.*, 2021; Santamaria-Garcia *et al.*, 2023; Casagrande & Matherly, 2024). Although, to the untrained eye and to the over-trustful minds, it may seem that science has evolved in such a manner that everything is replaceable, limitless, and large-scale accessible, all of us should acknowledge, before it becomes too late, that the environment and nature are irreplaceable and, additionally, have been always and will always be linked with human lives, their existence, and survival.

Additionally, academics and researchers drawn on the importance of guiding the children and youth on the safe path of sustainability and sustainable development, rather than on immediate and shallow advantages and rewards that modern beliefs and modern irrational forms of human behavior stand for (López-Paredes & Carrillo-Andrade, 2022; Chiliquinga *et al.*, 2023; López-Padrón *et al.*, 2024; Popescu & Popescu, 2024). The reason for displaying so much care and infinite concern these days towards the children and youth comes from distressing findings according to which the most affected groups of pollution are the children and youth when it comes to the dangers of pollution, the effects of damaged soils and water, air pollution from different sources, including biomass, solid-fuel use, and that is just to offer some examples in this particular matter (Harari & Harari, 2006; Rinne *et al.*, 2006; Díaz *et al.*, 2017; Jolly *et al.*, 2021).

Some relevant questions come in this context in order to complete the current analysis and are believed to be extremely representative for this current, novel, and original scientific work. One pivotal question is: What do reducing risks and promoting healthy lives stand for? Interestingly, a possible answer could come by simply making the right choices that an individual or a business close to the needs of the environment and nature would do and that is applying the vital principles of the circular economy, which have been long used but strategically forgotten by some due to the pressure to acquire goods and access services without applying one basic principle of economics, namely, the fact that resources are limited in time and space. Another crucial question is: Are all countries affected by pollution and does pollution create environmental and health challenges everywhere? In general lines, based on studies, since there are different types of pollutants for which there are multiple activities and industries which are could be held responsible, the degree in which the environment and individuals are effected mainly depends on the nature of the agents generating the pollution in a specific area or region. Although, initially, it may seem that pollution will only affect people, communities, and nature in the immediate surroundings of the agents that generate pollution, the reality has shown that, due to the ecosystems and relationships created in nature, the extent of polluting agents may never be truly evaluated and foreseen. The case of "forever chemicals" comes immediately to support the aforementioned ideas, since it is a great example of how some companies may work "against" nature and, willingly, sacrifice biodiversity, ecosystems, and lives, while targeting fortunes and taking advantage of communities that have been, somehow, misled to believe, on the one hand, that health should be taken for granted and someone else has the power do decide, in their place and for them, what is healthy and what is not and, on the other hand, that money, and not decent behavior and reason, have come to make the rules in the world (Ruiz-Urigüen *et al*, 2022; Jaffé *et al*, 2024; Kornher *et al*, 2024; Kornher *et al*, 2025). In continuation, it needs to be emphasized that there are numerous other questions that could naturally follow and that could help shed a new light on the importance of the rights of nature in Ecuador and everywhere else. However, the very essence would be one and the same: it is in people's power to start making changes and to begin by analyzing and questioning their own patterns of behavior so far, in order to be able to decide, first of all, on their own, based on their own reasoning, whether or not they are dedicated to sustainable ways of living and, second of all, by making some comparisons between their way of living and their peers, in order to establish ways to become better, more responsible, and more dedicated to the real meaning of protecting nature and supporting the equality principles for the benefit of the present and future generations.

The terms, nature, ecosystem and environment, have similar denotations, but different conceptualizations in argument and analysis. The environment is all of the biotic and abiotic components that make it up. This concept has been used to externalize each locus of human activity; the ecosystem, however, is a biological nexus where the interconnection of the variety of species incorporated in nature is studied. In the Ecuadorian constitution these terms are expressed as Mother Earth [Pacha Mama], which is the legal entity that has ownership over the rights of nature. It has been a prodigious journey to move nature from the prior conceptualization of nature to one that has become the subject of rights, and consequently vicissitudes still persist around this shift. However, the model created by the 2008 constitution of Ecuador is an example to be followed by other countries, and such idealistic changes that highlight the development-oriented benefits of Mother Earth is one of humanity's greatest challenges.

## 5. CONCLUSIONS

We can conclude that the constitutional changes in Ecuador presented nature as life itself. *Pacha Mama,* as it is recognized in our environment, is part of the origin of life. Citizens deserve clean air along with effective conservation policies for water, flora and fauna. With the phrase, "the nature of rights and the rights of nature," many issues can be understood, such as the struggles that have nature as a backdrop. Socio-economic organization, which traditionally prevails over environmental protection by effectuating its own continuous and systematic submission, is called into question. In Ecuador, some 80% of exports depend on natural resources, leading to impoverishing growth. Change must be immediate, but at the same time consensual: an unsustainable business such as extractivism cannot be eliminated without offering an alternative to the lifestyle that promotes it, which pivots on exacerbated consumerism. In Ecuador, indigenous peoples have an enormous wealth of environmental knowledge and little need for the liquid modernity from the West. They know how to communicate with nature through its flora and fauna, connecting in a natural and harmonious way, and they are a better guide to how to take care of nature since they know how to demonstrate the respect it deserves. They also do not falter in the fight for its rights despite the continual predation of active subjects with vested interests. In reality, environmental corruption has always been a unifying system of cultures from East to West. It is to be hoped that the cultural battle in favor of biodiversity will continue to strengthen since all life depends on it.

## ACKNOWLEDGMENT

This research received no specific grant from any funding agency in the public, commercial, or not-for-profit sectors. Author Contributions: Conceptualization, A.L.G. (Arturo Luque González), D.A.B.B. (Dolores Alexandra Bravo Bravo), L.N.V. (Ligia Nevárez Vera) and C.R.P. (Cristina Raluca Gh. Popescu); methodology, A.L.G., D.A.B.B., L.N.V. and C.R.P.; software, A.L.G., D.A.B.B., L.N.V. and C.R.P.; validation, A.L.G., D.A.B.B., L.N.V. and C.R.P.; formal analysis, A.L.G., D.A.B.B., L.N.V. and C.R.P.; investigation, A.L.G., D.A.B.B., L.N.V. and C.R.P.; resources, A.L.G., D.A.B.B., L.N.V. and C.R.P.; data curation, A.L.G., D.A.B.B., L.N.V. and C.R.P.; writing—original draft preparation, A.L.G., D.A.B.B., L.N.V. and C.R.P.; writing—review and editing, A.L.G., D.A.B.B., L.N.V. and C.R.P.; visualization, A.L.G., D.A.B.B., L.N.V. and C.R.P.; supervision, A.L.G., D.A.B.B., L.N.V. and C.R.P.; project administration, A.L.G., D.A.B.B., L.N.V. and C.R.P.; funding acquisition, A.L.G., D.A.B.B., L.N.V. and C.R.P. All authors have equally contributed to the manuscript. All authors have read and agreed to the published version of the manuscript.

**Conflicts Of Interest**

All authors declare that they have no conflicts of interest.

## REFERENCES

Acosta, A., & Martínez, E. (2009). *Derechos de la naturaleza. El futuro es ahora* [Rights of nature. The future is now]. Abya-Yala.

Afanador, N., Becerra, E. D., & Andrango, J. C. (2021). The Paradoxes Between Business Performance and Organizational Behavior in Colombian and Ecuadorian Companies. In R. Perez-Uribe, D. Ocampo-Guzman, N. Moreno-Monsalve, & W. Fajardo-Moreno (Eds.), *Handbook of Research on Management Techniques and Sustainability Strategies for Handling Disruptive Situations in Corporate Settings* (pp. 396-415). IGI Global Scientific Publishing. DOI: 10.4018/978-1-7998-8185-8.ch019

Agreement, P. (2015, noviembre 12). https://unfccc.int/sites/default/files/spanish_paris_agreement.pdf

Aguirre, W. E., Alvarez-Mieles, G., Anaguano-Yancha, F., Burgos Morán, R., Cucalón, R. V., Escobar-Camacho, D., Jácome-Negrete, I., Jiménez Prado, P., Laaz, E., Miranda-Troya, K., Navarrete-Amaya, R., Nugra Salazar, F., Revelo, W., Rivadeneira, J. F., Valdiviezo Rivera, J., & Zárate Hugo, E. (2021). Conservation threats and future prospects for the freshwater fishes of Ecuador: A hotspot of Neotropical fish diversity. *Journal of Fish Biology*, *99*(4), 1158–1189. DOI: 10.1111/jfb.14844 PMID: 34235726

Arteaga, A., Salazar-Valenzuela, D., Mebert, K., Peñafiel, N., Aguiar, G., Sánchez-Nivicela, J. C., Pyron, R. A., Colston, T. J., Cisneros-Heredia, D. F., Yánez-Muñoz, M. H., Venegas, P. J., Guayasamin, J. M., & Torres-Carvajal, O. (2018). Systematics of South American snail-eating snakes (Serpentes, Dipsadini), with the description of five new species from Ecuador and Peru. *ZooKeys*, *766*, 79–147. DOI: 10.3897/zookeys.766.24523 PMID: 29942172

Ávila Santamaría, R. (2012, septiembre 6). Evolución de los derechos fundamentales en el constitucionalismo ecuatoriano [Evolution of fundamental rights in Ecuadorian constitutionalism]. Congreso Ecuatoriano de Historia 2012 (Montecristi), Ecuador. https://repositorio.uasb.edu.ec/bitstream/10644/3015/1/%C3%81vila%2C%20R-CON-008-Evoluci%C3%B3n.pdf

Bárcena, A. (2020). La emergencia del cambio climático en América Latina y el Caribe [The climate change emergency in Latin America and the Caribbean]. CEPAL. Retrieved from https://www.cepal.org/es/presentaciones/la-emergencia-cambio-climatico-america-latina-caribe-seguimos-esperando-la-catastrofe

Bautista-Valarezo, E., Duque, V., Verdugo Sánchez, A. E., Dávalos-Batallas, V., Michels, N. R. M., Hendrickx, K., & Verhoeven, V. (2020). Towards an indigenous definition of health: An explorative study to understand the indigenous Ecuadorian people's health and illness concepts. *International Journal for Equity in Health*, *19*(1), 101. DOI: 10.1186/s12939-020-1142-8 PMID: 32571404

Benítez Gaibor, M. K., Martínez Mesías, J. P., & Jara Vásquez, E. A. (2021). Challenges for Measuring Value Chain Relation Coordination of SMEs of the Textile and Apparel Industry: The Case of a Small Family Industrial Safety Footwear Firm of Ambato, Ecuador. In I. Management Association (Ed.), *Research Anthology on Small Business Strategies for Success and Survival* (pp. 475-496). IGI Global Scientific Publishing. DOI: 10.4018/978-1-7998-9155-0.ch024

Boff, L. (2013). "Constitucionalismos ecológicos en América Latina" [Ecological constitutionalisms in Latin America]. Visita 15 de mayo de 2013 en: http//leonardoboof.wordpress.com/2013/05/14/constitucionalismo ecologico-en-america-latina/

Brañes, R. (2007). Derecho ambiental mexicano [Mexican Environmental Law]. Volumen 1 de Colección medio ambiente. Universidad de Texas. Retrieved from https://archivos.juridicas.unam.mx/www/bjv/libros/13/6429/13.pdf

Brown, K. (2009). Ecuador 's Constitutional Rights of Nature: Implementation and Implications. *Ecology Law Quarterly*, *36*(3), 797–824.

Calvopiña, M., Vásconez, E., Coral-Almeida, M., Romero-Alvarez, D., Garcia-Bereguiain, M. A., & Orlando, A. (2022). Leptospirosis: Morbidity, mortality, and spatial distribution of hospitalized cases in Ecuador. A nationwide study 2000-2020. *PLoS Neglected Tropical Diseases*, *16*(5), e0010430. DOI: 10.1371/journal.pntd.0010430 PMID: 35551530

Casagrande, D., & Matherly, C. (2024). Lehigh Launch Ecuador: A Case Study for First Semester Experience Abroad. In Stauff, J., & Blondin, J. (Eds.), *Promoting Intercultural Agility and Leadership Development at Home and Abroad for First-Year Students* (pp. 236–257). IGI Global Scientific Publishing., DOI: 10.4018/978-1-6684-8832-4.ch011

Castillo-Nazareno, U. H., Matute-Petroche, J. S., & Alcívar-Avilés, M. (2021). Chamber of Popular Micro-Businesses, Popular Brands, and Multi-Place Fairs: Entrepreneurial Association in Monte Sinai (Guayaquil, Ecuador). In Gamez-Gutierrez, J., & Saiz-Alvarez, J. (Eds.), *Entrepreneurial Innovation for Securing Long-Term Growth in a Short-Term Economy* (pp. 32–47). IGI Global Scientific Publishing., DOI: 10.4018/978-1-7998-3568-4.ch003

Chesnais, F. (2010). *Écologie, luttes sociales et projet révolutionnaire pour le 21e siècle. Gay, Vincent (coord.), Pistes pour un anticapitalisme vert.* Syllepse.

Chiliquinga, V. E., Popescu, C. R., & González, A. L. (2023). The Impact of Cooperative Control Regulations for the Assessment of Environmental and Social Risk: The Case of Credit Placement in Ecuador. In Popescu, C., Yu, P., & Wei, Y. (Eds.), *Achieving the Sustainable Development Goals Through Infrastructure Development* (pp. 198–214). IGI Global Scientific Publishing., DOI: 10.4018/979-8-3693-0794-6.ch008

Consejo de Desarrollo de las Nacionalidades y Pueblos del Ecuador [Council for the Development of the Nationalities and Peoples of Ecuador]. (2011). Sumak Kawsay (Primera). CODENPE y AECID. http://www.pueblosynacionalidades.gob.ec/wp-content/uploads/downloads/2023/03/sumakkawsay.pdf

Constituent Assembly of Montecristi. (2008). Constitution of the Republic of Ecuador. Retrieved from https://www.oas.org/juridico/pdfs/mesicic4_ecu_const.pdf

Constitution of Ecuador. (2008). Retrieved from https://www.oas.org/juridico/pdfs/mesicic4_ecu_const.pdf

Constitutional Court of Ecuador. (2011). Judgment on the Vilcabamba River Case. Retrieved from https://www.derechosdelanaturaleza.org.ec/wp-content/uploads/2018/04/CUMPLIMIENTO-R%C3%8DO-VILCABAMBA.pdf

Crespo, R. (2009). La naturaleza como sujeto de derechos: ¿Símbolo o realidad jurídica? [Nature as a Subject of Rights: Symbol or Legal Reality?], Iuris Dictio: Vol. 8 Núm. 12. Retrieved from https://revistas.usfq.edu.ec/index.php/iurisdictio/article/view/685

Cuéllar, L., Torres, I., Romero-Severson, E., Mahesh, R., Ortega, N., Pungitore, S., Hengartner, N., & Ke, R. (2022). Excess deaths reveal the true spatial, temporal and demographic impact of COVID-19 on mortality in Ecuador. *International Journal of Epidemiology*, *51*(1), 54–62. DOI: 10.1093/ije/dyab163 PMID: 34387670

Daily, G. C., & Matson, P. A. (2008). Ecosystem Services: From Theory to Implementation. *Proceedings of the National Academy of Sciences of the United States of America*, *105*(28), 9455–9456. https://www.pnas.org/doi/pdf/10.1073/pnas.0804960105. DOI: 10.1073/pnas.0804960105 PMID: 18621697

Diario El Comercio. (2007). Ecuador reconoce derechos de la naturaleza en su nueva Constitución [Ecuador recognizes the rights of nature in its new Constitution]. Retrieved from https://www.elcomercio.com/tendencias/ambiente/seis-casos-debate-derechos-naturaleza-ecuador.html

Díaz, A. A., Veliz, P. M., Rivas-Mariño, G., Mafla, C. V., Altamirano, L. M. M., & Jones, C. V. (2017). Etiquetado de alimentos en Ecuador: implementación, resultados y acciones pendientes [Food labeling in Ecuador: implementation, results, and pending actions]. *Revista panamericana de salud publica = Pan. American Journal of Public Health*, *41*, e54. DOI: 10.26633/RPSP.2017.54 PMID: 28614474

Díaz, S. C., Quezada, L. C., Álvarez, L. J., Loján-Córdova, J., & Carrión-Paladines, V. (2023). Indigenous use of fire in the paramo ecosystem of southern Ecuador: A case study using remote sensing methods and ancestral knowledge of the Kichwa Saraguro people. *Fire Ecology*, *19*(1), 5. DOI: 10.1186/s42408-022-00164-1 PMID: 36712840

Domínguez, R., & Faytong-Haro, M. (2024). Impact of early work start on mental health outcomes in older adults: A cross-sectional study from Ecuador. *PLoS One*, *19*(11), e0310448. DOI: 10.1371/journal.pone.0310448 PMID: 39509429

Espinosa, C. (2011). Los derechos de la naturaleza y la naturaleza de sus derechos [The Rights of Nature and the Nature of Your Rights]. Ministerio de Justicia, Derechos de Humanos y Cultos. Retrieved from https://biblio.flacsoandes.edu.ec/libros/146502-opac

Francesco, P. (2020). Laudato Si': Enciclica sulla cura della casa comune. Le vie della Cristianità.

Fundación Ecológica Rumicocha. (2019). Estudios de Biodiversidad en la Reserva Ecológica Cayambe Coca [Biodiversity Studies in the Cayambe Coca Ecological Reserve]. Retrieved from https://www.ambiente.gob.ec/wp-content/uploads/downloads/2012/07/Parque-Nacional-Cayambe-Coca.pdf

González, A. L., Ponce, J. H., & Popescu, C. R. (2023). Best Practice in the Use of the Water Sources of Portoviejo Canton, Ecuador, and Its Parishes. In J. Keengwe & B. Nyatuka (Eds.), *Climate Change Education for Sustainable Development* (pp. 263-287). IGI Global Scientific Publishing. DOI: 10.4018/978-1-6684-9099-0.ch012

González, A. L., & Popescu, C. R. (2025). Analysis of the Absence of Corporate Social Responsibility in the Cooperative Savings and Credit Sector: The Case of Ecuador. In Popescu, C. (Ed.), *Building Inclusive Global Knowledge Societies for Sustainable Development* (pp. 245–274). IGI Global Scientific Publishing., DOI: 10.4018/979-8-3693-6298-3.ch010

Gudynas, E. (2009). Derechos de la naturaleza el futuro es ahora [Rights of Nature: The Future Is Now]. Abya Ayala. Quito, Ecuador. Retrieved from https://gudynas.com/wp-content/uploads/GudynasDerechosNaturalezaLima14r.pdf

Gudynas, E. (2011). Buen Vivir: Today's Tomorrow. Development, 54(4), 441-447. Retrieved from ttps://www.gudynas.com/publicaciones/GudynasBuenVivirTomorrowDevelopment11.pdf

Gudynas, E. (2015). *Derechos de la naturaleza* [Rights of Nature]. Tinta Limón.

Guijarro-Garvi, M., Miranda-Escolar, B., Cedeño-Menéndez, Y. T., & Moyano-Pesquera, P. B. (2022). Education as a dimension of human development: A Provincial-level Education Index for Ecuador. *PLoS One*, *17*(7), e0270932. DOI: 10.1371/journal.pone.0270932 PMID: 35802576

Harari, R., & Harari, H. (2006). Children's environment and health in Latin America: The Ecuadorian case. *Annals of the New York Academy of Sciences*, *1076*(1), 660–677. DOI: 10.1196/annals.1371.082 PMID: 17119244

Herrera, J. (2018). Las prácticas investigativas contemporáneas. Los restos de sus nuevos planteamientos epistemológicos [Contemporary research practices. The remains of his new epistemological approaches]. *Revista Scientific*, *3*(7), 6–15. DOI: 10.29394/Scientific.issn.2542-2987.2018.3.7.0.6-15

Hobbs, R., & Harris, J. (2001). Restoration Ecology: Repairing the Earth's Ecosystems in the New Millenniun. *Restoration Ecology*, *9*(2), 239–246. DOI: 10.1046/j.1526-100x.2001.009002239.x

Hobsbawm, E. (1971). The Birth of the Industrial Revolution. Siglo Veintiuno Ed.

Jaffé, P. R., Huang, S., Park, J., Ruiz-Urigüen, M., Shuai, W., & Sima, M. (2024). Defluorination of PFAS by Acidimicrobium sp. strain A6 and potential applications for remediation. *Methods in Enzymology*, *696*, 287–320. DOI: 10.1016/bs.mie.2024.01.013 PMID: 38658084

Jaria-Manzano, J. (2019). Los principios del derecho ambiental: Concreciones, insuficiencias y reconstrucción [The Principles of Environmental Law: Concreteness, Insufficiencies and Reconstruction]. *Ius et Praxis*, *25*(2), 403–432. DOI: 10.4067/S0718-00122019000200403

Jolly, P. M., Van Hoof, H., Chen, F., Kim, B., Duran, M. E., Navas, A. C., Valle, J. G., & Pérez, G. M. (2021). Quantifying cultural tightness-looseness in Ecuador. *PLoS One*, *16*(1), e0246064. DOI: 10.1371/journal.pone.0246064 PMID: 33513147

Judgment, No. 065-15-SEP-CC, Case N.° 0796-12-EP (Constitutional Court of Ecuador March 11, 2015). https://buscador.corteconstitucional.gob.ec/buscador-externo/principal/fichaSentencia?numero=065-15-SEP-CC

Judgment, No. 166-15-SEP-CC, Case N° 0507-12-EP (Constitutional Court of Ecuador May 20, 2015). https://buscador.corteconstitucional.gob.ec/buscador-externo/principal/fichaSentencia?numero=166-15-SEP-CC

Judgment, No. 218-15-SEP-CC, Case N° 1281-12 (Constitutional Court of Ecuador July 9, 2015). https://buscador.corteconstitucional.gob.ec/buscador-externo/principal/fichaSentencia?numero=218-15-SEP-CC

Judgment, No. 034-16-SIN-CC, Case N° 0011-13-IN (Constitutional Court of Ecuador April 27, 2016). https://buscador.corteconstitucional.gob.ec/buscador-externo/principal/fichaSentencia?numero=034-16-SIN-CC

Judgment, No. 1149-19-JP/21, Case No. 1149-19-JP/20 (Constitutional Court of Ecuador November 10, 2021). https://buscador.corteconstitucional.gob.ec/buscador-externo/principal/fichaSentencia?numero=1149-19-JP%2F21

Judgment, No. 1185-20-JP/21 (Constitutional Court of Ecuador December 15, 2021). https://buscador.corteconstitucional.gob.ec/buscador-externo/principal/fichaSentencia?numero=1185-20-JP%2F21

Judgment, No. 22-18-IN/21 (Constitutional Court of Ecuador September 8, 2021). https://buscador.corteconstitucional.gob.ec/buscador-externo/principal/fichaSentencia?numero=22-18-IN%2F21

Judgment, No. 32-17-IN/21, Case No. 32-17-IN (Constitutional Court of Ecuador June 9, 2021). https://buscador.corteconstitucional.gob.ec/buscador-externo/principal/fichaSentencia?numero=32-17-IN%2F21

Kauffman, C., & Martin, P. (2018). Can Rights of Nature Make Development More Sustainable? Why Some Ecuadorian Lawsuits Succeed and Others Fail. *Development*, *92*, 130–142.

Kornher, K., Gould, C. F., Manzano, J. M., Baines, K., Kayser, G., Tu, X., Suarez-Torres, J., Martinez, D., Peterson, L. A., Huset, C. A., Barr, D. B., & Suarez-Lopez, J. R. (2025). Associations of PFAS and pesticides with lung function changes from adolescence to young adulthood in the ESPINA study. *International Journal of Hygiene and Environmental Health, 265*, 114526. Advance online publication. DOI: 10.1016/j.ijheh.2025.114526 PMID: 39904133

Kornher, K., Gould, C. F., Manzano, J. M., Baines, K., Kayser, G., Tu, X., Suarez-Torres, J., Martinez, D., & Suarez-Lopez, J. R. (2024). Associations of PFASs and Pesticides with Lung Function Changes from Adolescence to Young Adulthood in the ESPINA study. medRxiv*: the preprint server for health sciences*, 2024.10.09.24315189. DOI: 10.1101/2024.10.09.24315189

Larrea, C., & Warnars, L. (2009). Ecuador's Yasuni-ITT Initiative: Avoiding Emissions by Keeping Petroleum Underground. *Energy for Sustainable Development, 13*(3), 219–223. DOI: 10.1016/j.esd.2009.08.003

López-Padrón, A., Roig-Vila, R., & Rico-Gómez, M. L. (2024). Profile of Academic Use of Smartphones by Postgraduate Students in Manabí, Ecuador. In Segarra, J., Mengual-Andres, S., & Cortijo Ocaña, A. (Eds.), *Educational Innovation to Address Complex Societal Challenges* (pp. 186–200). IGI Global Scientific Publishing., DOI: 10.4018/979-8-3693-3073-9.ch013

López-Paredes, M., & Carrillo-Andrade, A. (2022). Legitimation by Digital Discourses: The Case of the Indigenous Protest in Ecuador, October 2019 (pp. 235-250). DOI: 10.4018/978-1-6684-4523-5.ch012

Luque, A. & Casado, F. (2020). Public Strategy and Eco-Social Engagement in Latin American States: An Analysis of Complex Networks Arising from Their Constitutions. MDPI Sustainability, 12(20), 8558, pp. 1-29; DOI: 10.3390/su12208558

Luque, A., Garofalo, C. E., Vinces, S. K., & Popescu, Gh. Cr. (2024). Empleo informal, políticas públicas y buen vivir: El caso de Rocafuerte, Ecuador [Informal Employment, Public Policies and Good Living: The Case of Rocafuerte, Ecuador]. Revista CIRIEC Colombia. Vol. 2(1), octubre. Pp. 43-53. ISSN: 2954-8179. DOI: https://doi.org/DOI: 10.58415/revciriec.v2n1a4

Luque, A., & Herrero-García, N. (2019). How corporate social (ir)responsibility in the textile sector is defined, and its impact on ethical sustainability: An analysis of 133 concepts. *Corporate Social Responsibility and Environmental Management, 26*(6), 1–22. DOI: 10.1002/csr.1747

Luque, A., Quishpi, F. R., & Espín, D. F. (2023). Analysis of Spirituality Processes in Women of the Waorani AMWAE Indigenous Nationality in Ecuador. Özsungur, F. and Bekar, F. (Ed.) Spirituality Management in the Workplace, Emerald Publishing Limited, Leeds, pp. 173-196. . ISBN: 978-1-83753-451-7, eISBN: 978-1-83753-450-0DOI: 10.1108/978-1-83753-450-020231008

Macias, L. (2010). El constitucionalismo ambiental en la nueva Constitución de Ecuador. Un reto a la tradición constitucional [Environmental constitutionalism in the new Constitution of Ecuador. A challenge to constitutional tradition], Iuris Dictio: Vol. 8 Núm. 12.

Mamami, y Clavero. (2010). Derechos de la Naturaleza, globalización y cambio climático 1. Corte Internacional de Derechos Humanos [Rights of Nature, Globalization and Climate Change 1. International Court of Human Rights]. Retrieved from https://www.corteidh.or.cr/tablas/r32323.pdf

Maniglio, F., Casado Gutiérrez, F., & Chávez Vallejo, G. (2020). La justiciabilidad de los derechos sociales. El caso del derecho al hábitat y a la vivienda en Ecuador (2007-2017) [The justiciability of social rights. The Case of the Right to Habitat and Housing in Ecuador (2007-2017)]. *Revista Latinoamericana de Derecho Social, 1*(37), 143. DOI: 10.22201/iij.24487899e.2020.37.14866

Matute-Petroche, J. S., Castillo-Nazareno, U. H., & Pazmiño-Crespo, L. F. (2022). Collaborative Trade Exchange and the COVID-19 Event: Barter in the Andean Subregion of Ecuador. In Hai-Jew, S. (Ed.), *Career Re-Invention in the Post-Pandemic Era* (pp. 140–162). IGI Global Scientific Publishing., DOI: 10.4018/978-1-7998-8626-6.ch007

Menger, C. (1996). *Investigations into the Method of the Social Sciences*. Ludwig von Mises Institute.

Mestanza-Ramón, C., Ordoñez-Alcivar, R., Arguello-Guadalupe, C., Carrera-Silva, K., D'Orio, G., & Straface, S. (2022). History, Socioeconomic Problems and Environmental Impacts of Gold Mining in the Andean Region of Ecuador. *International Journal of Environmental Research and Public Health, 19*(3), 1190. DOI: 10.3390/ijerph19031190 PMID: 35162216

Ministry of the Environment. Water and Ecological Transition of Ecuador. (2020). Plan de Gestión del Parque Nacional Cotopaxi [Cotopaxi National Park Management Plan]. Retrieved from https://www.ambiente.gob.ec/parque-nacional-cotopaxi-mantiene-su-administracion-en-la-provincia-de-cotopaxi/

Ministry of the Environment of Ecuador. (2011). Reservas Naturales y Biodiversidad [Reserves and Biodiversity]. Retrieved from https://www.ambiente.gob.ec/areas-protegidas-3/

Ministry of the Environment of Ecuador. (2015). Resolución 197-2015: Regulación sobre minería y su impacto en la naturaleza [Resolution 197-2015: Regulation on Mining and its Impact on Nature]. Retrieved from https://www.ambiente.gob.ec/wp-content/uploads/downloads/2015/02/REGLAMENTO_AMBIENTAL_DE_ACTIVIDADES_MINERAS_MINISTERIO_AMBIENTE.pdf

Ministry of the Environment of Ecuador. (2016). Política Nacional de Cambio Climático [National Climate Change Policy]. Retrieved from https://www.ambiente.gob.ec/ministerio-del-ambiente-presento-los-resultados-obtenidos-en-materia-de-cambio-climatico-durante-el-periodo-2016-2022/

Ministry of the Environment of Ecuador. (2018). Plan Nacional de Restauración Forestal [National Forest Restoration Plan]. Presidencia de la Republica de Ecuador. (2019). Decreto Ejecutivo 752: Sistema Nacional de Áreas Protegidas (SNAP). Retrieved from https://www.ambiente.gob.ec/wp-content/uploads/downloads/2023/11/PLAN-NACIONAL-DE-RESTAURACION-FORESTAL-2019-2030.pdf

Ministry of the Environment of Ecuador. (2021). Iniciativa de Carbono Azul [Blue Carbon Initiative]. Retrieved from https://www.ambiente.gob.ec/programa-ecuador-carbono-cero/

Molina, M. Y., Rodríguez-Pallas, Á., & Vaque Reyes, G. L. (2024). Informality and Tourist Development on the Ecuadorian Coast. In P. Kumar, S. Gupta, M. Korstanje, P. Rout, & Madhurima (Eds.), *Managing Tourism and Hospitality Sectors for Sustainable Global Transformation* (pp. 62-76). IGI Global Scientific Publishing. DOI: 10.4018/979-8-3693-6260-0.ch005

Mongabay, D. (2021). "Nuevo estudio: en los últimos 26 años Ecuador ha perdido más de 2 millones de hectáreas de bosque" [New study: in the last 26 years Ecuador has lost more than 2 million hectares of forest]. Retrieved from https://es.mongabay.com/2021/01/desafios-ambientales-ecuador-2021-hidroelectricas-mineria-petroleo/

Morales, M. (2018). Derechos de la naturaleza en la Constitución Ecuatoriana [Rights of nature in the Ecuadorian Constitution]. Revista Justicia Ambiental art 05-05. Retrieved from https://www.revistajusticiaambiental.cl/wp-content/uploads/2018/03/art_05_05.pdf

Muyolema, A. (2012). Las poéticas del Sumak Kawsay en un horizonte global [The poetics of Sumak Kawsay in a global horizon]. En: Houtart, François, Daiber, Virgit (comps.), Un paradigma poscapitalista: el Bien Común de la Humanidad, La Habana, Ruth Casa Editorial.

National Assembly of Ecuador. (2013). Anteproyecto del Código Orgánico del Ambiente [Preliminary draft of the Organic Environmental Code]. Retrieved from https://www.asambleanacional.gob.ec/es/search/node/codigo%20del%20ambiente?page=64

National Assembly of Ecuador. (2014). Ley Orgánica de Recursos Hídricos, Usos y Aprovechamiento del Agua [Organic Law on Water Resources, Water Uses and Exploitation]. Registro Oficial Suplemento 305. Retrieved from https://www.asambleanacional.gob.ec/es/multimedios-legislativos/35146-ley-organica-de-recursos-hidricos-usos-y-aprovechamiento-d-1

National Assembly of Ecuador. (2017). Código Orgánico del Ambiente [Environmental Code]. Registro Oficial Suplemento 983. Retrieved from https://www.epmrq.gob.ec/images/servicios2020/CODIGO_ORGANICO_DEL_AMBIENTE_COAM.pdf

National Assembly of Ecuador. (2020). Ley Orgánica de Biodiversidad [Organic Law on Biodiversity]. Registro Oficial Suplemento 115. Retrieved from https://www.ambiente.gob.ec/wp-content/uploads/downloads/2018/01/CODIGO_ORGANICO_AMBIENTE.pdf

National Assembly of Ecuador. (2023). Reformas al Código Orgánico del Ambiente y Ley de Transición Ecológica [Reforms to the Organic Environmental Code and the Ecological Transition Law]. Registro Oficial Suplemento 2023. Retrieved from https://www.ambiente.gob.ec/wp-content/uploads/downloads/2022/02/REGLAMENTO-AL-CODIGO-ORGANICO-DEL-AMBIENTE.pdf

Ocaña-Mayorga, S., Lobos, S. E., Crespo-Pérez, V., Villacís, A. G., Pinto, C. M., & Grijalva, M. J. (2018). Influence of ecological factors on the presence of a triatomine species associated with the arboreal habitat of a host of Trypanosoma cruzi. *Parasites & Vectors*, *11*(1), 567. DOI: 10.1186/s13071-018-3138-4 PMID: 30373640

Our, C. F. R. (Brundtland Report). (1987). United Nations. https://www.un.org/es/ga/president/65/issues/sustdev.shtml

Ozayturk, I. (2025). The Role of IMF on Goods and Services Importing of Argentina, Egypt, and Ecuador. In J. Martínez-Falcó, E. Sánchez-García, B. Marco-Lajara, & R. Fuentes-Fernández (Eds.), *Global Economic Interconnectedness: International Trade and Finance* (pp. 295-320). IGI Global Scientific Publishing. DOI: 10.4018/979-8-3693-5303-5.ch014

Pachamama, F. (2021). Iniciativas de Restauración Ecológica en Ecuador [Ecological Restoration Initiatives in Ecuador]. Retrieved from https://www.pachamama.org.ec/

Palacios, J. C. (2004). Desarrollo tecnológico en la Primera Revolución Industrial [Technological development in the First Industrial Revolution]. 17. Norba. Revista de Historia, ISSN 0213-375X, Vol. 17, 93-109.

Parra-Gaete, C., & Hermosa-Bosano, C. (2023). A pilot exploration of the relationships between optimism, affect, and cardiovascular reactivity. *Frontiers in Psychology*, *14*, 1233900. DOI: 10.3389/fpsyg.2023.1233900 PMID: 37908813

Passet, R. (2013). Las grandes representaciones del mundo y la economía a lo largo de la historia: del universo mágico al torbellino creador [The great representations of the world and the economy throughout history: from the magical universe to the creative whirlwind]. Clave intelectual

Paz, C., Mascialino, G., & Evans, C. (2020). Exploration of the psychometric properties of the Clinical Outcomes in Routine Evaluation-Outcome Measure in Ecuador. *BMC Psychology*, *8*(1), 94. DOI: 10.1186/s40359-020-00443-z PMID: 32873334

PNUD. (2023). Ecuador celebrará todo el mes de mayo a la Biodiversidad [Ecuador celebrará todo el mes de mayo a la Biodiversidad]. https://www.undp.org/es/ecuador/noticias/ecuador-celebrara-todo-el-mes-de-mayo-la-biodiversidad

PNUD. (2024). Los conocimientos indígenas son cruciales para la lucha contra el cambio climático: he aquí el porqué [Indigenous knowledge is crucial to the fight against climate change: here's why]. Retrieved from https://climatepromise.undp.org/es/news-and-stories/los-conocimientos-indigenas-son-cruciales-para-la-lucha-contra-el-cambio-climatico

Popescu, C. R. G. (2019). Corporate Social Responsibility, Corporate Governance and Business Performance: Limits and Challenges Imposed by the Implementation of Directive 2013/34/EU in Romania. *Sustainability (Basel)*, *11*(19), 5146. DOI: 10.3390/su11195146

Popescu, C. R. G. (2020). Sustainability Assessment: Does the OECD/G20 Inclusive Framework for BEPS (Base Erosion and Profit Shifting Project) Put an End to Disputes Over The Recognition and Measurement of Intellectual Capital? *Sustainability (Basel)*, *12*(23), 10004. DOI: 10.3390/su122310004

Popescu, C. R. G., & Ban a, V. C. (2019). Performance Evaluation of the Implementation of the 2013/34/EU Directive in Romania on the Basis of Corporate Social Responsibility Reports. *Sustainability*, *11*(9), 2531. DOI: 10.3390/su11092531

Popescu, C. R. G., & Popescu, G. N. (2019). An Exploratory Study Based on a Questionnaire Concerning Green and Sustainable Finance, Corporate Social Responsibility, and Performance: Evidence from the Romanian Business Environment. *Journal of Risk and Financial Management*, *12*(4), 162. DOI: 10.3390/jrfm12040162

Popescu, C. R. G., & Popescu, G. N. (2024). The Health-Environment Nexus: Tackling Vital Hemp Policies, Addressing Cutting-Edge Research For Sustainable Development, And Managing Decisive Human Rights. International Multidisciplinary Environment And Hemp Congress, May 20-22, 2024

President's office of the Republic of Ecuador. (2022). Executive order 499: Derecho a un ambiente sano [Right to a healthy environment]. Retrieved from https://www.ambiente.gob.ec/wp-content/uploads/downloads/2022/02/REGLAMENTO-AL-CODIGO-ORGANICO-DEL-AMBIENTE.pdf

Ramos, C. A. (2015). Los paradigmas de la investigación científica [The paradigms of scientific research]. Avances en psicología, 23(1), 9-17.

Report of the United Nations Conference on the Human Environment (A/CONF.48/14/Rev.l). (1972). United Nations. https://documents.un.org/doc/undoc/gen/n73/039/07/pdf/n7303907.pdf

Rinne, S. T., Rodas, E. J., Bender, B. S., Rinne, M. L., Simpson, J. M., Galer-Unti, R., & Glickman, L. T. (2006). Relationship of pulmonary function among women and children to indoor air pollution from biomass use in rural Ecuador. *Respiratory Medicine*, *100*(7), 1208–1215. DOI: 10.1016/j.rmed.2005.10.020 PMID: 16318916

Rio Declaration on Environment and Development. (1992, junio 3). United Nations. https://www.un.org/spanish/esa/sustdev/documents/declaracionrio.htm

Rios Quituizaca, P., Gatica-Domínguez, G., Nambiar, D., Ferreira Santos, J. L., Brück, S., Vidaletti Ruas, L., & Barros, A. J. D. (2021). National and subnational coverage and inequalities in reproductive, maternal, newborn, child, and sanitary health interventions in Ecuador: A comparative study between 1994 and 2012. *International Journal for Equity in Health*, *20*(1), 48. DOI: 10.1186/s12939-020-01359-1 PMID: 33509210

Rodriguez, F., & Valle, A. (2023). La Naturaleza como sujeto de derechos: Reconocimiento formal y material en el ordenamiento jurídico ecuatoriano [Nature as a Subject of Rights: Formal and Material Recognition in the Ecuadorian Legal System]. En Derechos de la Naturaleza y territorio en Ecuador. Diálogos desde los saberes, quehaceres jurídicos y antropológicos (Primera). https://dspace.ups.edu.ec/handle/123456789/27775

Rodríguez-Estévez, F. (2022). El medio ambiente en el Tribunal Europeo de Derechos Humanos y la Corte Interamericana de Derechos Humanos [The environment in the European Court of Human Rights and the Inter-American Court of Human Rights] [master's thesis]. https://reunir.unir.net/handle/123456789/15594

Ruiz-Urigüen, M., Shuai, W., Huang, S., & Jaffé, P. R. (2022). Biodegradation of PFOA in microbial electrolysis cells by Acidimicrobiaceae sp. strain A6. *Chemosphere*, *292*, 133506. DOI: 10.1016/j.chemosphere.2021.133506 PMID: 34995627

Saiz-Alvarez, J. M., Castillo-Nazareno, U. H., Matute de León, J. S., & Alcívar-Avilés, M. T. (2021). Post-COVID Indigenous Women Entrepreneurship: A Case of the Kichwa-Puruha in Ecuador. In Baporikar, N. (Ed.), *Handbook of Research on Strategies and Interventions to Mitigate COVID-19 Impact on SMEs* (pp. 430–456). IGI Global Scientific Publishing., DOI: 10.4018/978-1-7998-7436-2.ch021

Santamaria-Garcia, H., Sainz-Ballesteros, A., Hernandez, H., Moguilner, S., Maito, M., Ochoa-Rosales, C., Corley, M., Valcour, V., Miranda, J. J., Lawlor, B., & Ibanez, A. (2023). Factors associated with healthy aging in Latin American populations. *Nature Medicine*, *29*(9), 2248–2258. DOI: 10.1038/s41591-023-02495-1 PMID: 37563242

Šebestová, J. D., & Popescu, C. R. G. (2022). Factors Influencing Investments into Human Resources to Support Company Performance. *Journal of Risk and Financial Management, 15*(1), 19. DOI: 10.3390/jrfm15010019

Silva, C. (2008). Qué es el buen vivir en la Constitución? [What is good living in the Constitution?] In Ávila, R. (Ed.), *La Constitución del 2008 en el contexto andino. Análisis desde la doctrina y el derecho comparado*. Ministerio de Justicia y Derechos Humanos.

Solecki, W., Roberts, D., & Seto, K. C. (2024). Strategies to improve the impact of the IPCC Special Report on Climate Change and Cities. *Nature Climate Change, 14*(7), 685–691. DOI: 10.1038/s41558-024-02060-9

Stone, C. D. (2010). Should trees have standing?: law, morality, and the environment. Oxford University Press. Original text retrieved from https://iseethics.wordpress.com/wp-content/uploads/2013/02/stone-christopher-d-should-trees-have-standing.pdf

Sutherland, W., Adams, W. M., Aronson, R. B., Aveling, R., Blackburn, T. M., Broad, S., Ceballos, G., Côté, I. M., Cowling, R. M., Da Fonseca, G. A. B., Dinerstein, E., Ferraro, P. J., Fleishman, E., Gascon, C., Hunter, M.Jr, Hutton, J., Kareiva, P., Kuria, A., MacDonald, D. W., & Watkinson, A. R. (2009). One Hundred Questions of Importance to the Convervation of Global Biological Diversity. *Conservation Biology, 23*(3), 557–567. DOI: 10.1111/j.1523-1739.2009.01212.x PMID: 19438873

Tanasescu, M. (2020). Nature Advocacy in the Ecuadorian Amazon: The Sarayaku Case. *Journal of Human Rights and the Environment, 11*(1), 36–56.

Townsend, J., Moola, F., & Craig, M. K. (2020). Indigenous Peoples are critical to the success of nature-based solutions to climate change. *Facets, 5*(1), 551–556. DOI: 10.1139/facets-2019-0058

UNEP. (2022). Action on the triple planetary crisis. Retrieved from https://www.unep.org/news-and-stories/speech/action-triple-planetary-crisis

United Nations. (1972). United Nations Conference on the Human Environment. Retrieved from https://docs.un.org/en/A/CONF.48/14/Rev.1

United Nations. (2015). A/RES/70/1: Transformar nuestro mundo: La Agenda 2030 para el Desarrollo Sostenible [Transforming our world: The 2030 Agenda for Sustainable Development]. Retrieved from https://ggim.un.org/documents/A_Res_70_1_s.pdf

United Nations. (2022). Declaración sobre los Derechos a un Medio Ambiente Saludable [Declaration on the Rights to a Healthy Environment]. Retrieved from https://www.ohchr.org/sites/default/files/documents/issues/climatechange/information-materials/r2heinfofinalweb-sp.pdf

United Nations. (2022). The human right to a clean, healthy and sustainable environment. Retrieved from https://digitallibrary.un.org/record/3982508?ln=es&v=pdf

United Nations. (2024). En primera línea contra la desertización [On the front line against desertification]. Retrieved from https://news.un.org/es/story/2024/12/1534941

United Nations General Assembly. (2022). "Resolution A/76/L.75: The human right to a clean, healthy and sustainable Environment. Retrieved from https://digitallibrary.un.org/record/3983329?ln=en&v=pdf

Vargas, A., Herrera, I., Nualart, N., Guézou, A., Gómez-Bellver, C., Freire, E., Jaramillo Díaz, P., & López-Pujol, J. (2022). The Genus *Kalanchoe* (Crassulaceae) in Ecuador: From Gardens to the Wild. *Plants*, *11*(13), 1746. DOI: 10.3390/plants11131746 PMID: 35807700

Vásconez-González, J., Izquierdo-Condoy, J. S., Fernandez-Naranjo, R., Gamez-Rivera, E., Tello-De-la-Torre, A., Guerrero-Castillo, G. S., Ruiz-Sosa, C., & Ortiz-Prado, E. (2023). Severe Chagas disease in Ecuador: A countrywide geodemographic epidemiological analysis from 2011 to 2021. *Frontiers in Public Health*, *11*, 1172955. DOI: 10.3389/fpubh.2023.1172955 PMID: 37143984

Vera-Arias, C. A., Castro, L. E., Gómez-Obando, J., & Sáenz, F. E. (2019). Diverse origin of Plasmodium falciparum in northwest Ecuador. *Malaria Journal*, *18*(1), 251. DOI: 10.1186/s12936-019-2891-y PMID: 31349843

Ycaza, A., Baquerizo, V., Vallejo, J., & Valero, G. (2022). Analysis of the Traditional Gastronomic Offer as an Engine for Local Tourism Development: Guayas, Ecuador. In Pinto Borges, A., Lopes de Almeida, A., Vieira, E., Dias, R., & Rodrigues, P. (Eds.), *Gastronomy, Hospitality, and the Future of the Restaurant Industry: Post-COVID-19 Perspectives* (pp. 48–70). IGI Global Scientific Publishing., DOI: 10.4018/978-1-7998-9148-2.ch003

## KEY TERMS AND DEFINITIONS

**Public Policy:** This refers to decisions and actions that a government takes when addressing public or collective issues.

**Resilience:** Transformations within a complex system related to the capacity for self-organization while maintaining internal structure, together with the ability to create adaptive responses, generate knowledge, experience, and learning. Resilience and sustainability are directly related to changes within societies, economies, and the human system as a whole. The transformation of systems is inevitable since it allows systems to strengthen.

**Social Economy:** Encompasses a variety of businesses, organizations and different legal entities. They share the objective of systematically putting people first, producing a positive impact on local communities and pursuing a social cause.

**Social And Solidarity Economy:** This places human beings as the first and last consideration in economic activities and is an alternative approach to the market economy. It relates to organizations, co-operatives, associations, or companies that aim to produce goods, services, and knowledge for economic purposes while simultaneously focusing on social implications and fostering solidarity.

**Sumak Kawsay:** Describes a way of doing things that is community-centric, ecologically-balanced and culturally-sensitive.

**Traditional Practices:** Actions and knowledge produced by local communities over many generations through which their behavior and autochthonous environment may be better understood.

# Chapter 10
# The Organizational Economics of Knowledge Management: A Comprehensive Analysis

**José G. Vargas-Hernandez**
https://orcid.org/0000-0003-0938-4197
*Financial Literacy Research Center, Universidad Cristóbal Colón, Mexico & Tecnológico Nacional de México, Mexico*

**Francisco Javier J. González**
*Tecnológico Nacional de México, ITS Fresnillo, Mexico*

**Teresea I. Salazar-Echeagaray**
https://orcid.org/0000-0001-8785-6300
*Universidad Autónoma de Sinaloa, Mexico*

**Omar C. Vargas-González**
https://orcid.org/0000-0002-6089-956X
*Tecnológico Nacional de México, Ciudad Guzmán, Mexico*

## ABSTRACT

*This study aims to analyze comprehensively the conceptual theoretical and empirical implications of the organizational economics theory to the knowledge management approach. The analysis departs from the assumption that the principles of organizational economics theory do not rival or contradicts the development of knowledge management approach to organizations, as it has been argued by research. The method employs is the meta-cognitive and meta-analytical description based on the literature review. This research concludes that contrary to what some of the studies contend in a supposed rivalry existent between the principles of knowledge management-based approach and the organizational economics, both theoretical perspectives are complementary and consistent.*

DOI: 10.4018/979-8-3373-0189-1.ch010

## INTRODUCTION

Organizational economics examines how organizations function, make decisions, and manage resources. Organizational economics is the disciplinary support of knowledge management. Knowledge management is a critical aspect of organizational economics, focusing on the creation, sharing, and utilization of knowledge within organizations. Knowledge management (knowledge management) has emerged as a critical organizational capability in the contemporary business landscape. It involves the systematic identification, creation, capture, sharing, and utilization of knowledge to enhance organizational performance.

This study explores the intersection of organizational economics and knowledge management, highlighting the conceptual, theoretical, and empirical frameworks, methodologies, analysis of results, discussions, implications, and conclusions.

Organizational economics of knowledge management (knowledge management) examines how organizations can effectively manage knowledge to enhance economic performance and competitive advantage. In today's rapidly evolving knowledge economy, the ability to acquire, create, disseminate, and utilize knowledge is paramount for organizations seeking to thrive. However, organizational economics has a small contribution in the evolution of knowledge management including its cost of activities.

This essay explores the conceptual, theoretical, and empirical frameworks of knowledge management within organizational economics, highlighting methodologies used in research, analyzing results, discussing implications, and concluding with insights on future directions. The relevance of knowledge management is the potential it has to unify several research fields leading to organizational outcomes (Staples *et al.*, 2001; Holsapple & Wu, 2008).

The specificity of most of the investigations and studies based on organizational economics leave some gaps in the field of knowledge management that emphasize the strategic perspective that influences organizational competitiveness (Hassan *et al.*, 2016). According to Serenko and Dumay (2015) the normative and conceptual studies dominate the knowledge management research and therefore, more empirical analysis are required. Knowledge management as a field of organizational economics is being debated on its associations with organizational knowledge and performance.

Organizational economics research can further the conceptual, theoretical and empirical practice of knowledge management by applying notions of transaction costs, contracting, agency costs, team production, etc., with implications in organizational development and transformation. Knowledge management in the development of studies and practices based on organizational economics and productivity (Drucker, 1968; Polanyi, 1967), attracting organizational management as the source of strategic direction to developing competitive advantages. Transaction cost economics (Williamson 1985, 1996), and property rights insights (Hart, 1995) have been brought to bear on issues related to allocation of rights and design of contracts when investments in human capital are firm-specific, agents may behave in an opportunistic manner, and contracts are incomplete.

Organizational economics provides a valuable lens for understanding how firms manage knowledge, a crucial resource in the modern economy. Knowledge management (knowledge management) involves creating, sharing, and utilizing knowledge within and across organizations to enhance performance (Grant, 1996). In economic terms, knowledge can be seen as an asset that, unlike traditional resources, increases in value with usage. This essay delves into the organizational economics perspective of knowledge management, examining how economic principles can be applied to understand and optimize knowledge-related activities within organizations.

This essay examines the organizational economics of knowledge management, focusing on theories explaining the costs, benefits, and mechanisms involved in the internal and external management of knowledge resources. Organizational economics is a theoretical framework applied to issues of internal organizational dynamics (Coase, 1937; Williamson, 1985) in knowledge management.

Given the broad scope and depth of this topic, the structure of this study includes discussions on how organizational economics intersects with knowledge management, the importance of managing knowledge assets, and empirical research methods in this field. This structured study integrates key economic theories with knowledge management practices, presenting the complex relationship between organizational economics and effective knowledge utilization.

This comprehensive analysis of the organizational economics theory in knowledge management perspective is divided in several sections. It begins with the introduction to follow with the conceptual, theoretical an empirical analysis. A special section on the methodologies employed by most of the research is reviewed. After this review of methodologies, the analysis of results show the main findings of research followed by a discussion. Finally, some conclusions are presented.

## CONCEPTUAL FRAMEWORK

As can be seen in table 1 Knowledge management framed by organizational economics theory began to develop in the 1960s (Lambe, 2011) divided in three cumulative generations (Tzortzaki & Mihiotis, 2014) each one based on a previous one The recent generation is developing addressing the complexities of the knowledge domain leading to new paradigms, metaphors and tools (Serenko, 2013). Organizational economics theory has developed the characteristics of the defined academic structure of several theoretical developments and scientometric studies of knowledge management to encourage research (Serenko *et al.*, 2007; Harman & Koohang, 2005; Nonaka & Peltokorpi, 2006; Serenko *et al.*, 2010; Serenko & Bontis, 2004).

Despite the development of the organizational economics perspective of knowledge management, with significant benefits (Hassan *et al.*, 2016) the field lacks of conceptual robustness leading to future research (Serenko & Dumay, 2015a; Tzortzaki & Mihiotis, 2014).

*Figure 1.*

| Generation | Focus Areas | Conceptual Advancement (Scale) | Years |
|---|---|---|---|
| 1st Generation (1990s) | Explicit Knowledge Sharing | 30 | 1990s |
| 2nd Generation (2000s) | System Integration & Collaboration | 60 | 2000s |
| 3rd Generation (2010s and beyond) | Dynamic, Real-Time Practices | 90 | 2010s and beyond |

The conceptual framework of this study integrates key concepts from organizational economics and knowledge management. Organizational economics perspective on knowledge management supported by scholars and practitioners is seeking to use fundamental concepts (Serenko *et al.*, 2011). Organizational economics provides insights into how firms optimize resource allocation, including knowledge as a strategic asset (Grant, 1996). Organizational economics is the disciplinary foundation and supports the practice of knowledge management by focusing on the incentives and investments on creation, sharing and exploiting knowledge by identifying benefits and costs of integrated knowledge practices and activities.

A conceptual and theoretical framework approach of organizational economics focuses on the co-ordination human coordination of activities and incentive issues that process the creating, sharing and exploiting organizational knowledge giving rise to the governance of such issues. Organizational economics extends from the economic mainstream theory drawing on learning as an updating of multiple subjective possibilities based on new information at the extent of knowledge management-based theories (Kogut & Zander 1996).

An organizational economics approach is a theoretical framework aimed to analyze the nature of coordination within and between organizations, suggesting that team based learning is expensive knowledge creation mechanisms to deal with issues providing protection of property rights and allocations of incentives, among others, investments and action decisions of individual agents. Property rights protection economics is one perspective of organizational economics that constitute a micro-foundation for the knowledge management-based perspective.

Organizations invest in common knowledge creation and sharing present in high task interdependence under low task uncertainty. Organizational economics focus on the coordination and incentive problems caused by the organizational dysfunctionalities due to asymmetric information, problems of performance incentives and measurement, moral hazard, redundant efforts, bargaining difficulties, etc.

Organizational economics perspectives apply to knowledge management, creation, integration and exploitation beyond learning and innovation processes and making the best use of existing knowledge in the organizations. Organizational economics approaches to knowledge management-oriented perspective to organizations appears to have little to offer with respect to learning processes (Kogut & Zander 1992; Madhok, 1996).

Organizational knowledge management is defined as the set of processes of knowledge acquisition, creation, building, conversion, storage, application and protection (Garcia-Perez & Mitra, 2008; Garcia-Perez & Ayres, 2009, 2015). Knowledge management is defined as the management of access, creation, storage, and dissemination of the organizational intellectual resources (Song, Nerur, & Teng, 2007). The concept of knowledge management has an evaluative link with organizational learning and memory. Organizational economics is concerned with knowledge management including learning processes and social relations in the landscape of interests and power positions and relationships since the beginning in the nineteen-seventies (Easterby-Smith, Crossan and Nicolini, 2000). Alchian & Demsetz, 1972).

Stable governance structures combine organizational elements of complementarities such as delegation of rights, payment schemes, supervision methods, etc. (Milgrom & Roberts, 1990, 1995; Thompson, 1967; Williamson, 1996). Organizational economics focuses on motivating and coordinating human practices, activities and tasks in efficient organizational arrangements of the nature of firms. Organizational economics explains and alleviates problems related to organizational arrangements with different kinds of authority, delegation and decision rights, payment schemes, etc.

Knowledge management involves processes and systems that facilitate the creation, sharing, and application of knowledge (Nonaka & Takeuchi, 1995). Knowledge management has emerged as a fundamental process in organizations seeking to maintain competitive advantage. Knowledge management emerged as a theoretical framework and practice of organizational economics including transaction cost economics, team theory, agency theory, property rights theory, etc. Team theory addresses the individual bounded rationality in the design of organizational structures (Marschak & Radner, 1972; Casson, 1994).

Learning is being neglected in organizational economics in exploring the organizational boundaries and examining the consequences in the context of labor changes, incremental and innovation between the basic rights protection framework (Foss, 1998). The literature review of knowledge management distinguishes knowledge creating teams in terms of "communities of practice" as a team of peers learning about the execution of tasks with pre-defined outcomes and learning in "epistemic groups."(Lave & Wenger, 1990; Brown & Duguid, 1991; Brown, 1998).

In the organizational economics framework, rational actors design organizational structures and forms, governance and contracts that maximize joint surplus and split it among them. From an organizational economics perspective, knowledge is both a valuable and complex resource to manage due to its non-rivalries and partially excludable nature (Arrow, 1962).

Knowledge management practices are deeply influenced by economic considerations, including transaction costs, property rights, and agency costs (Williamson, 1985). Knowledge within firms is shared across hierarchical levels, with the organization acting as a "repository" (Nonaka & Takeuchi, 1995), where economic mechanisms can be used to facilitate effective knowledge creation and diffusion. Exploration of the knowledge management supported by organizational knowing in public organizations lead to a comprehensive overview and reflecting on the concepts as the mechanism of generation, production and articulation of new knowledge management (Agrifoglio, Metallo, & di Nauta, 2021).

The theoretical base of the organizational economics literature is concerned with the efficient allocation of resources in organizations aimed to yield the maximum value leading to the value creation as the economic efficiency. The allocation of resources is a matter of organization and governance of resources in efficient perspective that discriminates the economic organization forms in terms of economic efficiency. The literature offers common threads in the study of organizational economics despite the number of diverse theories (Foss, 2000).

Research on pertinent literature review of knowledge management protection is essential in achieving and preserving the organizational sustainable competitive advantage, although is an area that has been underdeveloped and tends to concentrate on the facilitation perspective of knowledge. The intellectual property rights protects the formal and informal knowledge as intangible assets in the organizational management acting as organizational knowledge protection (Ali, Tang, 2023).

An overview of the organizational knowledge protection for the state of practice consider the common factors for measures such as people, social factors, internal social capital, social media knowledge management, culture, leadership, technologies, capabilities, resources, social resources, inter-organizational structural social capital, structure, strategy, organizational characteristics, organizational knowledge, among others. The knowledge management capability is affected by technology, including human resources, resources and capabilities, relationships, information systems, etc.

Some analytical dimensions of knowledge management to take into account are the theoretical perspectives, research domains, methods and models, technological innovation artefacts, and measures to enforce knowledge management protection. Manhart & Thalmann, (2015) investigated on knowledge protection, research methods and theoretical perspectives supported on information technology leading to develop portfolio of measures.

Recent literature in knowledge management suggest creating and enhancing a climate of corporate spirit of reciprocity in mutual care appealing to intrinsic motivation, symbolic rewards and peer recognition. Nevertheless, the literature on knowledge management has neglected organizational economics. Organizational economics is questioned by the neglected in the knowledge management literature operating on the firm level that do not have and explicit individualistic perspective.

The motivational assumptions of organizational economics as any other type of organizational behavior are subject to critical discussion of the cynical assumption driven by organizational economic analysis of human nature. Motivation is related to the transaction costs in organizational economics theories influencing the value created from organization and governance of scarce organizational resources.

Knowledge management encompasses a range of practices aimed at leveraging organizational knowledge assets. It involves identifying, capturing, and sharing tacit and explicit knowledge among employees to improve efficiency and innovation. The knowledge economy is characterized by the predominance of knowledge as a critical asset, where organizations that effectively manage their knowledge resources can achieve superior economic outcomes (OECD, 1996). Organizations have the ability to use, create, share and leverage knowledge management as the process of management of access, creation, storage, and dissemination of organizational intellectual resources (Ginja Antunes, & Gonçalves Pinheiro, 2020)

Key components of knowledge management include:

1) **Business Processes**: Streamlining workflows to facilitate knowledge sharing.
2) **People**: Empowering employees to contribute their expertise.
3) **Information Technology**: Utilizing digital tools to enhance communication and collaboration.

The interplay between these components significantly influences organizational performance metrics such as liquidity, indebtedness, and profitability (Mikulić & Prebežac, 2022).

At its core, organizational economics provides a framework for analyzing how economic incentives, information asymmetries, and transaction costs influence organizational behavior. An organizational economics perspective attends the incentive conflicts related to knowledge management, knowledge creation, integration and exploitation complications leading to induced to making human capital firm specific. That is, organizational economics prone to solve problems related to knowledge management practices beneficial to corporate culture, which is essential to their embodiment (Kreps, 1990). An organizational economics perspective identifies the organizational alternatives and their benefits and costs. In the context of knowledge management, this framework highlights the following key concepts:

Knowledge as a Resource: Knowledge can be viewed as a valuable organizational resource that can be acquired, developed, and deployed.

Knowledge Creation and Sharing: Organizations must foster environments that encourage knowledge creation and facilitate its dissemination among employees. Organizational economics perspectives do not conceptualize organizations as knowledge-based entities per se, but offer theoretical-methodological frameworks of organizational knowledge creation processes, which are uncertain in the distribution of benefits variance difficult to anticipate over time requires of a more complicated analysis.

Knowledge Utilization: Effective knowledge management systems enable organizations to leverage knowledge to improve decision-making, innovation, and problem solving.

Knowledge Protection: Organizations need to safeguard their intellectual property and prevent knowledge leakage.

Knowledge Valuation: Assigning appropriate value to knowledge assets is crucial for strategic decision-making.

## THEORETICAL FRAMEWORK

Organizational economics provides a robust theoretical foundation for understanding knowledge management. The knowledge management-based approach complements and is consistent with the organizational economics by constituting a micro-foundation for knowledge-based perspective. Knowledge-management based theories are formulated in different theoretical languages in terms of organizational economics. It posits that organizations are motivated by economic incentives and that their structures are designed to minimize transaction costs while maximizing efficiency (Williamson, 1981).

Organizational economics brings benefits and costs of alternative and comparative institutional, organizational and contractual structures. The diversity of modern organization economics and a flexible approach required for the analysis leads to find conceptual, theoretical, methodological and empirical support on the organizational economics as the most explicit micro-analytic framework.

Organizational economics may power incentives provided for investment in firm specific knowledge management supported through actions such as promotion rules, access to critical resources and capabilities, etc. Some organizational knowledge capabilities required by organizational knowledge management are environmental management, entrepreneurship culture, market-sensing capability, organizational learning capabilities, etc.

Organizational economics is concerned with incentives and investments for firm specific knowledge in creating and making choices between diverse alternatives in the integration and sharing knowledge. Internal organizational dynamics can be better analyzed by knowledge management -based on the creation of a shared context and avoidance of "blunt incentives" Ghoshal, Moran & Almeida-Costa 1995) without contradicting organizational economics.

The perspective of organizational economics suggests that knowledge management depends of the team creating efforts, tradeoffs of incentives design, rules of exclusion, matching uncertainty. The theoretical framework incorporates key theories from organizational economics that apply to knowledge management. The theoretical framework draws on several theories. The theoretical translation and reconstruction of propositions in the knowledge management-based approach are associated with organizational economics perspectives.

The convergence of organizational economics and knowledge management provides a dynamic framework for organizations to thrive in a rapidly evolving knowledge economy. Organizational economics lays the structural foundation by prioritizing resource optimization and cost efficiency, while knowledge management complements this by enabling the acquisition, storage, and dissemination of knowledge, ensuring its transformation into actionable insights. This alignment allows organizations to enhance decision-making and process efficiency, ultimately fostering a culture of continuous improvement and innovation (Salazar, Cervantes, Aguirre, y Carbache, 2023).

By integrating these two perspectives, organizations can not only adapt to globalization and technological advancements but also achieve sustainable growth. Knowledge sharing and innovation, enabled by structured knowledge management processes, reinforce the resource optimization strategies of organizational economics. This mutual reinforcement creates a pathway for organizations to maintain a competitive edge, addressing complex market dynamics while prioritizing both efficiency and innovation as drivers of long-term success (Salazar, Cervantes, Aguirre, y Carbache, 2023).

Organizational economics theories have an impact on organizational administration by addressing issues, among others, the existence of firms, market boundaries, and internal dynamics of the organization in terms of the perspective of comparative contracting. Among the organizational economics theory perspectives are the transaction costs (Coase, 1937; Williamson, 1985, 1996), the agency theory (Holmström, 1982; Holmström & Milgrom 1991), costs measurement (Barzel, 1989), incomplete contracts (Hart, 1995).

Several economic theories can be applied to understand the organizational economics of knowledge management:

1) **Information Economics.** This theory explores the economic implications of information, including its production, distribution, and consumption. In knowledge management, this theory can be used to analyze the value of information and the costs of acquiring and processing it (Arrow, 1962).
2) **Transaction Cost Economics (TCE):** According to TCE, firms organize internally to minimize the transaction costs associated with creating and sharing knowledge, particularly tacit knowledge that is costly to codify (Williamson, 1985). This theory emphasizes the costs associated with transactions, including search, bargaining, and monitoring costs. Conventional organizational economics approach is linked to the transaction cost theory involved in organizational coordination (Coase, 1937).

Transaction costs give existence to efficient organizations. Organizational economics literature review includes the transaction costs theory to create and develop efficient organizations through different types of transactions within and between organizations. This occurs in response to market failures due to common ownership, incomplete contracts in asset specificity. The price mechanisms driving to the organizational management order are stressed to explain the transaction costs needed to coordinate the organizational activities.

In the context of knowledge management, these costs can arise from knowledge transfer, sharing, and protection. This theory suggests that firms will adopt knowledge management practices to reduce costs associated with information asymmetry and coordination failures. TCE examines the costs of transactions within and between organizations (Williamson, 1985). In knowledge management, TCE helps understand the costs associated with knowledge transfer and sharing.

3) **Resource-Based View (RBV):** RBV posits that competitive advantage is rooted in unique resources, such as knowledge, which are difficult to imitate (Barney, 1991). In knowledge management, this means organizations develop capabilities to protect and leverage unique knowledge assets. RBV emphasizes the importance of leveraging unique resources—such as intellectual capital—as a source of sustained competitive advantage (Barney, 1991). Knowledge management-based analysis of a sustained competitive advantage in terms of organizational economics.

Knowledge assets are viewed as critical resources that can differentiate firms in the marketplace. RBV posits that organizations gain competitive advantage through unique resources, including knowledge (Barney, 1991). Knowledge management practices enhance the value of these resources. The resources based view emphasizes the organizational internal resources and capabilities to formulate strategic choices to compete in the organizational external environment. This theory has the ability to connect organizational resources to the organization sustainable competitive advantage, adding value and innovation to the customer value chain (Madhani, 2009; Poazi, Tamunosiki-Amadi, & Fems, 2017).

Organizational resources have the effect to leverage organizational capabilities and performance by introducing complementary resources and knowledge management as mediators (Liang, You & Liu, 2010).

The traditional organizational resources has an effect on knowledge management capabilities. Organizations should apply industry 4.0 capabilities to leverage the organizational knowledge management capabilities and other organizational resources such as the data-driven decision making culture, transactional and transformational leadership, among others (Microsoft, 2018; Deloitte, 2018). Social factors, organizational knowledge and characteristics and other organizational capabilities, among others, influence organizational knowledge management capabilities.

4) **Agency Theory:** In knowledge management, agency theory addresses the challenges of incentivizing employees to share knowledge, considering the potential for moral hazard and information asymmetry between management and employees (Jensen & Meckling, 1976).This theory focuses on the relationship between principals (e.g., managers) and agents (e.g., employees) and the potential for information asymmetry and moral hazard. In knowledge management, this theory can be applied to understand how to align the incentives of knowledge workers with organizational goals (Jensen & Meckling, 1976).

The agency theory perspective of organizational economics addresses assumptions of asymmetric information and moral hazards on issues of decision rights, payment schemes, managerial commitment, multitasking, etc. (Holmström 1979, 1982; Fama & Jensen 1983; Holmström & Milgrom 1991; Jensen & Meckling 1992; Aghion & Tirole 1997; Baker, Gibbons, & Murphy 1999; etc.

5) **Knowledge-Based View (KBV):** The KBV extends RBV by emphasizing knowledge as a critical, strategic asset. Knowledge flows within firms are structured through formal (e.g., codification) and informal (e.g., mentorship) mechanisms (Grant, 1996). KBV extends RBV by emphasizing knowledge as the most strategically significant resource (Grant, 1996). Effective knowledge management practices are crucial for leveraging this resource. The knowledge-based view (KBV) integrates knowledge through coordination mechanism to be applied to change organizational capabilities (Grant, 1996).
6) **Property Rights Theory**: This theory examines the allocation of property rights to resources, including knowledge assets. In knowledge management, this theory can help to clarify ownership rights and incentivize knowledge creation and sharing (Alchian, 1965). Property rights economics approach identifies the overlapping between the organizational economics and knowledge management-based theories interpreted.

The Figure 2 below provides a comparison of various economic theories applied to knowledge management. It highlights their key focus areas, foundational authors, and specific applications to knowledge management practices.

*Figure 2.*

| Theory | Authors | Focus | Application to Knowledge Management |
|---|---|---|---|
| Information Economics | Arrow (1962) | Economic implications of producing, distributing, and consuming information. | Analyzing the value of information and the costs of acquiring and processing it. |
| Transaction Cost Economics (TCE) | Coase (1937); Williamson (1985) | Minimizing transaction costs in organizational coordination and knowledge transfer. | Reducing costs associated with knowledge transfer, sharing, and protection. |
| Resource-Based View (RBV) | Barney (1991) | Leveraging unique, inimitable resources (e.g., knowledge) for competitive advantage. | Enhancing the value of intellectual capital to sustain competitive advantage. |
| Knowledge-Based View (KBV) | Grant (1996) | Emphasizing knowledge as the most strategically significant resource. | Structuring knowledge flows to coordinate and leverage knowledge assets effectively. |
| Agency Theory | Jensen & Meckling (1976) | Aligning employee incentives with organizational goals, addressing information asymmetry. | Designing incentive systems to encourage knowledge sharing and reduce moral hazards. |
| Property Rights Theory | Alchian (1965) | Clarifying ownership and incentivizing knowledge creation and sharing. | Defining ownership rights to encourage knowledge creation and sharing. |

These theoretical perspectives highlight the effective knowledge management can lead to improved decision-making processes and enhanced organizational agility. The theories of resources-based view and knowledge-based view have effects of the organizational resources and capabilities on sustainable advantage, competitiveness and innovation leveraged by the mediating effect of knowledge management capabilities.

Knowledge management and innovation capabilities are supported and leveraged by innovation in industry 4.0 resources and capabilities, transformational and transactional leadership styles data-driven decision-making culture, among others. Organizational knowledge management uses theories of knowledge-based view and resources based view more than the organizational culture and dynamic capabilities theories.

The organizational economics literature has diverse approaches to the internal dynamics of organizations proving that there is intellectual fertile field, although in general terms, these approaches are lacking descriptive and predictive accuracy. Relying on conceptual and theoretical models among the organizational economics approaches facilitates the practical implementation in organizations. Most of these organizational models are subsumed under the property rights approach. Alternative organizational economics approaches have different costs specifying, determining, exchanging, protecting and enforcing rights.

Critics of organizational economics consider their own work as rivalries or complementary and more pragmatic of this perspective (Kogut & Zander 1992; Madhok 1996; Conner & Prahalad 1996; Teece, Pisano & Shuen 1997; Langlois & Foss, 1997).

## EMPIRICAL REVIEW

The empirical organizational economics is strong in corroborations of predictions of the diverse theoretical frameworks (Shelanski & Klein, 1995; Prendergast, 1999). The empirical literature review determines a research gap on knowledge management in organizational practices related with organizational performance (Inkinen, 2016). Empirical research in organizational economics examines how firms manage knowledge through various practices and incentives, drawing insights from case studies, surveys, and econometric analyses.

**Data Sources:** Studies often utilize internal data on employee performance, knowledge-sharing metrics, and organizational outcomes. Publicly available data, like patents and publications, are also valuable proxies for knowledge management (Foss & Pedersen, 2002).

**Variables:** Commonly measured variables include the frequency and quality of knowledge sharing, financial outcomes (e.g., revenue, cost savings), and employee engagement in knowledge management activities.

**Outcomes:** Typical outcomes of interest include improved innovation, reduced costs, enhanced decision-making, and overall organizational efficiency (Haas & Hansen, 2007). Research on knowledge management and other organizational outcomes positively affected considering the nature of opportunities and complexities in firm innovation, employee and product improvement.

Empirical studies have demonstrated the positive impact of knowledge management on organizational performance. For instance, research indicates that companies with robust knowledge management systems experience increased liquidity and reduced indebtedness (Mikulić & Prebežac, 2022). Knowledge management leadership and organizational arrangements aligned to achieve organizational performance through knowledge management practices, resulting in efficiency and effective knowledge management resources and capabilities.

The convergence of organizational economics and knowledge management offers a unified framework for organizations to achieve both efficiency and innovation. Organizational economics lays the foundation for resource optimization and cost efficiency, while knowledge management enriches these principles by capitalizing on human capital and information systems to foster creativity and adaptability (Ramírez Sáenz de Viteri, 2020). Together, these frameworks empower organizations to navigate complex global markets while maintaining operational stability and strategic foresight.

This integration is further strengthened through the adoption of knowledge management systems that align with economic principles. Such systems transform raw information into actionable insights, enhancing organizational learning and decision-making capabilities. By strategically combining resource distribution with knowledge processes, organizations can create adaptive strategies that respond effectively to changing market dynamics and stakeholder needs, ensuring long-term competitive advantages (Ramírez Sáenz de Viteri, 2020).

Ultimately, the perceived rivalry between these frameworks is debunked, showcasing their symbiotic potential in modern organizational contexts. The use of technology and organizational learning as enablers of knowledge management amplifies the benefits of economic efficiency, creating a robust model for sustainable growth. This complementary approach not only redefines traditional organizational strategies but also establishes a strong foundation for innovation and resilience in the face of rapid technological and market transformations (Ramírez Sáenz de Viteri, 2020).

Additionally, the integration of technology in knowledge management practices has been shown to facilitate better communication and collaboration among employees, leading to higher innovation rates (Davenport & Prusak, 1998).

Empirical studies in organizational economics and knowledge management provide evidence on the effectiveness of knowledge management practices. Organizational economics in knowledge management resources identifies by empirical research to propose recommendations (Nabeel, Rabiah & Gouher, 2019; Heisig2009). Empirical research on the organizational economics of knowledge management has examined various aspects of knowledge management practices, including research often focusing on:

1) **Knowledge Sharing**: Studies examine factors influencing knowledge sharing, such as organizational culture and incentives (Cabrera & Cabrera, 2005; Nahapiet & Ghoshal, 1998).

Knowledge sharing is a cornerstone for fostering collaboration and innovation in modern organizations. By encouraging employees to transform their tacit knowledge into explicit insights, organizations can make this knowledge accessible and actionable across teams. Open communication and mentorship programs further enable the transfer of knowledge across generations, preserving institutional memory and creating a culture of continuous learning. These practices mitigate the risks of knowledge loss while driving creativity and adaptability, particularly in environments where innovation is essential for long-term success (López Aguirre, López Salazar, Falconi Tello, & Pomaquero Yuquilema, 2018; Gairín Sallán, Milton, Peiró Rubio & Piscitelli, 2020).

Technology plays a pivotal role in enabling effective knowledge sharing. Systems such as enterprise resource planning and business intelligence streamline the collection, storage, and dissemination of knowledge, ensuring real-time access to critical information. These tools empower employees to collaborate dynamically and make informed decisions, fostering a culture of transparency and integration. As highlighted by Ramírez Sáenz de Viteri (2020), this alignment of technology with knowledge-sharing processes drives competitive advantages by enhancing innovation and adaptability.

Ultimately, knowledge sharing transcends individual contributions, establishing knowledge as a collective organizational asset. In service-oriented industries, where adaptability and responsiveness are crucial, the ability to exchange and apply knowledge dynamically creates significant competitive advantages. By promoting a culture of collaboration, supported by mentorship programs, structured systems, and technological tools, organizations can navigate the challenges of a rapidly evolving market while ensuring sustainability and growth (Ciro-Atehortúa, Bermúdez-Hernández, & Valencia-Arias, 2023).

2) **Knowledge Creation**: Empirical research explores how organizations foster innovation through knowledge creation processes (Nonaka & Takeuchi, 1995). Researchers have explored the processes of knowledge creation, including individual and collective creativity. Knowledge management literature review recommend the use of interdisciplinary and cross-functional work teams and work groups to foster organizational knowledge creation Brown & Eisenhardt, 1995, Meyer & deTore, 1999, Krogh *et al.*, 2000).

The active creation of knowledge within organizations is fundamental to maintaining relevance and achieving growth in today's complex and uncertain environments. By systematically transforming tacit knowledge into explicit strategies, organizations can develop innovative solutions that address evolving market demands and technological advancements. This process fosters the creation of new products, business models, and processes that align with long-term goals, securing competitive advantages even in volatile markets (Lima, Prada Vargas & Vanegas Alfonso, 2022).

Collaboration and experimentation are critical enablers of knowledge creation. Organizations that cultivate environments encouraging strategic thinking and collective efforts benefit from novel insights that drive transformation. This approach not only supports problem-solving but also positions organizations to capitalize on emerging opportunities. By promoting these practices, organizations enhance their ability to respond to challenges with agility and innovation (Gairín Sallán, Milton, Peiró Rubio, & Piscitelli, 2020).

Additionally, the integration of participatory methodologies, technology, and collective intelligence strengthens the foundations for continuous learning and innovation. These strategies enable organizations to design tailored solutions that ensure adaptability in the face of dynamic challenges. By embedding these practices into their culture, organizations create sustainable systems that prioritize agility and resilience, ensuring long-term success in competitive landscapes (El Homrani et al., 2020).

3) **Knowledge Utilization**: Investigations into how knowledge is applied to improve organizational performance (Zack, 1999). Empirical studies have examined how organizations can effectively utilize knowledge to improve performance (Grant, 1996). From the organizational economics perspective on organizational knowledge management, to induce individual contributions on team performance to avoid some recommendations that mistake the individual rewards as the antithesis to teamwork.

Knowledge management systems are pivotal in ensuring that organizational knowledge is not just stored but strategically utilized. By integrating both explicit and tacit knowledge into decision-making frameworks, organizations can innovate and create value. This strategic alignment transforms stored intellectual capital into actionable insights, enabling companies to enhance productivity and maintain a competitive edge. The use of knowledge management systems thus supports long-term sustainability by fostering operational efficiency in rapidly changing markets (Pulido Reina & Muñoz, 2020).

Additionally, knowledge utilization bridges the gap between stored knowledge and its practical application. Strategies such as reskilling and upskilling illustrate how organizations can empower their workforce to adapt to new challenges and shifts in technology or society. These initiatives not only enhance employee competencies but also ensure that the organization remains aligned with external changes, maintaining competitiveness and fostering innovation (Ereñaga de Jesús, 2023).

Ultimately, the combination of effective knowledge management systems and strategic knowledge utilization creates a foundation for organizational success. These practices ensure that intellectual capital is continuously applied to drive productivity and adaptability, equipping organizations to thrive in dynamic and competitive environments. By investing in both the technological infrastructure of knowledge management systems and the development of their workforce, organizations can align their operational goals with long-term sustainability.

4) **Knowledge Protection**: Research has focused on the strategies that organizations can employ to protect their intellectual property (Teece, 1977).

Safeguarding organizational knowledge is essential for maintaining competitiveness and sustainability in today's dynamic and unpredictable environments. As a strategic resource, knowledge encompasses intellectual property, confidential information, and critical insights that are vital for innovation and competitive intelligence. To protect these assets, organizations must implement robust systems and policies that guard against risks such as internal misuse and external threats, including cyberattacks. This proactive approach ensures the secure management of valuable knowledge, allowing organizations to remain resilient and maintain their edge in competitive global markets (Lima, Prada Vargas, & Vanegas Alfonso, 2022).

In industries where innovation drives success, knowledge protection becomes a cornerstone of long-term viability. By mitigating risks and safeguarding intellectual resources, organizations can strengthen their operational foundations and enhance their capacity to adapt to changing market demands. These efforts not only reduce vulnerabilities but also position organizations to capitalize on emerging opportunities, fostering growth and sustainability. Ultimately, the secure management of knowledge is a critical enabler for achieving strategic objectives and thriving in volatile and complex business environments (Lima, Prada Vargas & Vanegas Alfonso, 2022).

## METHODOLOGIES APPLIED

Knowledge management has emerged in the field of organizational economics as one of the new management methods. This section reviews commonly employed methodologies in the empirical study of knowledge management. Organizational economics provides a methodological instruments and tools for the analysis of behavioral conditions and constraints of shared norms, values, beliefs, conventions, etc., aimed for efficiency enhancing systems of rights in organizations.

Organizational economics is individualistic in nature in the sense that organizational phenomena is explained as the leading result of the choice behavior of individual agents. The individualist focused methodology of organizational economics emphasize the level of the individual agent, rather than the firm. Various methodologies have been employed in researching knowledge management within organizational economics. The methodologies used in studying the organizational economics of knowledge management include:

1) **Qualitative Methods**: Case studies and interviews provide in-depth insights into KNOWLEDGE MANAGEMENT practices and their impact (Yin, 2018).
2) **Quantitative Methods**: Surveys and statistical analyses measure the effectiveness of knowledge management initiatives (Hair *et al.*, 2010). Surveys and statistical analyses are commonly used to measure the correlation between knowledge management practices and economic indicators. Quantitative studies identify the organizational knowledge management resources and capabilities (enablers), matching the already described by Heisig (2009) such as culture, people, structure, leadership, resources, capabilities, technology and strategy.
3) **Mixed Methods**: Combining qualitative and quantitative approaches offers a comprehensive understanding of knowledge management (Creswell & Plano Clark, 2018).
4) **Comparative Studies**: These studies assess differences in knowledge management effectiveness across industries or company sizes.

A variety of research instruments methodologies can be used to study the organizational economics of knowledge management:

1) **Surveys and Interviews:** To capture subjective insights into knowledge management practices and perceptions of knowledge-sharing cultures, researchers conduct surveys and interviews with employees and managers (Cabrera & Cabrera, 2005). Surveys: Surveys can be used to collect quantitative data on a large scale. Surveys can be used to collect quantitative data on a large scale (Malhotra, 2010).
2) **Case Studies:** Case studies allow for an in-depth examination of knowledge management practices within specific organizations, illustrating how economic principles are applied in unique contexts (Yin, 2018). An-depth examinations of specific organizations provide insights into the practical applications of knowledge management strategies. Case Studies: In-depth case studies can provide rich insights into the knowledge management practices of specific organizations (Yin, 2018).
3) **Experiments:** Experiments can be conducted to test hypotheses about the effects of different knowledge management interventions (Shadish, Cook, & Campbell, 2002).
4) **Econometric Analysis:** Econometric methods are used to identify causal relationships between knowledge management practices and economic outcomes. For instance, regression models can quantify the impact of knowledge management initiatives on organizational performance metrics (Haas & Hansen, 2007). Econometric techniques can be used to analyze large datasets and identify causal relationships (Wooldridge, 2010).

Knowledge management is a field of organizational economics academic research using science mapping based co-citations and concurrent keywords, and performance analysis based on series of bibliometric indicators. Research on knowledge management framed by organizational economics has increased significantly, although the advance of science and data in organizational and management areas, change rapidly (Gaviria-Marin, Merigó, & Baier-Fuentes, 2019).

Research in organizational economics centered on knowledge management should complement previous studies using science mapping, performance analysis and bibliometric instruments applied to different units of analysis (Cobo *et al.*, 2011a). Performance analysis use bibliometric indicators. The science mapping analysis uses techniques such as the bibliographic coupling, co-citation analysis (Small, 1973), co-occurrence of keywords analysis (Callon *et al.*, 1983), among others.

## ANALYSIS OF RESULTS

Empirical findings generally indicate that well-managed knowledge resources lead to improved organizational outcomes. Studies consistently show that firms adopting effective knowledge management strategies—such as implementing reward systems for knowledge-sharing or formalizing knowledge repositories—experience significant productivity gains (Foss & Pedersen, 2002). Knowledge management requires individuals sharing experiences and efforts of organizations to create and capture knowledge (Drucker, 1993).

Additionally, organizations that invest in social capital, like trust building among employees, find higher participation in knowledge-sharing activities, positively affecting innovation rates (Nahapiet & Ghoshal, 1998). The findings demonstrate that knowledge management practices drive for organizational innovation.

Organizational economics analysis of the different approaches states and interprets the knowledge management-based propositions, not necessarily in contrast or conflict when analyzing and expressing complementary principles of economic organization from different theoretical perspectives.

The analysis of results from empirical studies reveals several key findings:

**Impact on Performance**: Effective knowledge management practices are positively correlated with organizational performance (Gold, Malhotra, & Segars, 2001).

The implementation of knowledge management systems, particularly Enterprise Resource Planning tools, demonstrates the transformative impact of structured data management and process automation on organizational performance. In the energy sector of Ecuador, the introduction of Enterprise Resource Planning not only enhanced financial oversight through targeted controls but also improved operational efficiency and adaptability, underscoring the critical role of technology in streamlining administrative functions (Ramírez Sáenz de Viteri, 2020). By automating processes and enabling resource optimization, organizations achieve sustainable competitive advantages, particularly in industries where precision and adaptability are essential.

Effective knowledge management practices, supported by intellectual capital and a culture aligned with organizational goals, contribute to measurable improvements in productivity and competitiveness. Structured knowledge management frameworks help organizations adapt to rapid market changes, fostering a collaborative environment that drives financial and operational success (Pulido Reina & Muñoz, 2020). The integration of knowledge management into core business operations not only enhances day-to-day efficiency but also encourages a culture of continuous innovation, which is essential for thriving in dynamic markets.

Innovation is a key outcome of effective knowledge management systems, as they align knowledge processes with strategic goals to create value and maintain agility in competitive industries. Robust technological integration, coupled with a supportive organizational culture, fosters creativity and the development of sustainable business models (Lima, Prada Vargas, & Vanegas Alfonso, 2022). These practices ensure organizations can adapt to uncertain market conditions while building a lasting presence in the global economy. Ultimately, knowledge management acts as a foundation for long-term success by combining innovation, technology, and strategic alignment to achieve operational excellence.

As it can be observed in Figure 1. While knowledge management offers numerous advantages, challenges such as lack of trust, inadequate technology, and cultural resistance persist (Riege, 2005). Conversely, strong leadership, robust IT infrastructure, and supportive culture serve as key enablers (Alavi & Leidner, 2001).

*Figure 3.*

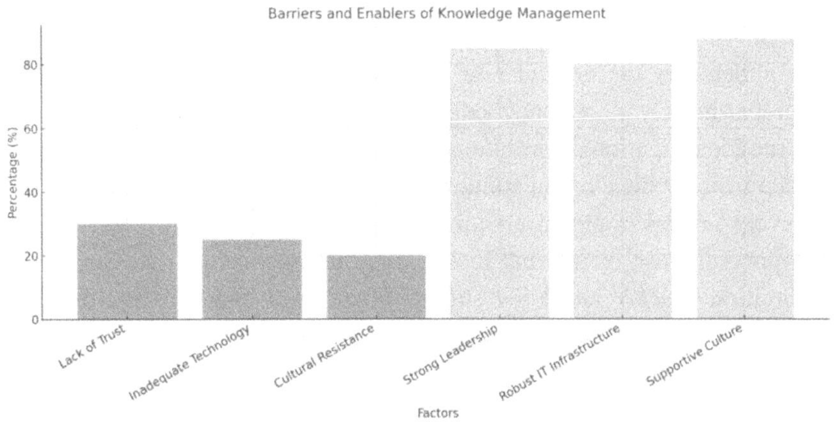


**Barriers to knowledge management**: Common barriers include lack of trust, inadequate technology, and cultural resistance (Riege, 2005).

**Enablers of knowledge management**: Successful knowledge management initiatives often involve strong leadership, supportive culture, and robust IT infrastructure (Alavi & Leidner, 2001). Knowledge management initiatives in public organizations may increase the salient enablers for the generation and development of concepts, tools and practices matching the unique organizational objectives (Loo Geok Pee, 2008).

Knowledge management is a cornerstone of organizational sustainability, addressing barriers such as knowledge loss and inefficiency through structured strategies and supportive cultures. Standards like ISO 30401 ensure systematic knowledge retention and utilization, while training initiatives like reskilling and upskilling empower organizations to stay competitive in an evolving business environment (Villafuerte Valdés & Pérez Hernández, 2023; Ereñaga de Jesús, 2023). By adopting such practices, organizations can bridge skill gaps, enhance adaptability, and align operational goals with employee well-being.

The integration of cultural, technological, and intellectual factors is equally essential for effective knowledge management. A positive organizational culture fosters collaboration and shared knowledge, while technological tools streamline knowledge processes and improve decision-making (Ciro-Atehortúa et al., 2023; López Aguirre, López Salazar, Falconi Tello, & Pomaquero Yuquilema, 2018). Leadership plays a crucial role in setting priorities and creating a knowledge-centric environment. These components, working in harmony, enable organizations to adapt, innovate, and maintain competitive advantages in fast-paced markets.

Additionally, intergenerational knowledge transfer through mentorship programs and structured succession planning ensures continuity and sustainability. These practices preserve institutional knowledge while empowering younger talent to build on established expertise. Participatory processes and supportive strategies, such as collaborative learning and self-evaluation, further enhance the organization's capacity for innovation and strategic growth (Gairín Sallán, Milton, Peiró Rubio, & Piscitelli, 2020). Together, these enablers ensure a resilient, knowledge-driven organization capable of thriving in complex environments.

The analysis of empirical data reveals a consistent trend: organizations that prioritize knowledge management tend to outperform their peers in key economic metrics. For example:

Companies implementing comprehensive knowledge management systems report higher profitability due to improved operational efficiencies.

Organizations that foster a culture of knowledge sharing experience enhanced employee engagement and retention rates.

These findings underscore the critical role of knowledge management in driving economic performance. In the global market place, knowledge management focus in research of firm performance outcomes, despite the identification of problems derived from motivations and incentives, which limit the scope and impact in some developing countries.

The findings reveal several implications for organizational economics. First, transaction cost and agency theories support the use of internal incentive structures to facilitate knowledge management. Secondly, the integration of RBV and KBV suggests that firms can benefit from developing unique, hard-to-replicate knowledge management capabilities that provide a competitive edge. Lastly, firms should consider the costs of under-utilizing tacit knowledge, which can lead to diminished returns if critical knowledge is not adequately shared and applied (Grant, 1996).

The implications of effective knowledge management are profound. By investing in knowledge management systems and fostering a culture that values knowledge sharing, organizations can achieve significant economic benefits. This includes not only improved financial performance but also enhanced innovation capabilities and adaptability in a dynamic market environment. Knowledge management has a positive influence on improvement of product, firm innovation and organizational capabilities in the economic transitions.

However, challenges remain. Many small and medium-sized enterprises (SMEs) struggle to implement effective knowledge management strategies due to resource constraints or lack of awareness about its benefits (Mikulić & Prebežac, 2022)

Therefore, it is essential for policymakers to support SMEs in developing their knowledge management capabilities through targeted initiatives.

The analysis of empirical results often reveals the following insights:

**Organizational Culture:** A strong organizational culture that values knowledge sharing and innovation is essential for effective knowledge management.
**Incentive Systems:** Properly designed incentive systems can motivate employees to create, share, and utilize knowledge.
**Information Technology**: Information technology can facilitate knowledge sharing and collaboration.
**Leadership**: Strong leadership is crucial for driving knowledge management initiatives.

## DISCUSSIONS AND IMPLICATIONS

The knowledge management-based perspective is not in conflict but complementary and consistent with the principles of organizational economics related to the property rights protection.

The discussions highlight the implications of knowledge management for organizational economics:

**Strategic Advantage**: Organizations that effectively manage knowledge can achieve sustainable competitive advantage (Grant, 1996). The analysis of sustained competitive advantage can be interpreted and rephrased in terms of organizational economics.

**Policy Recommendations**: Recommendations for policymakers include promoting knowledge management practices through incentives and support for technology adoption (Davenport & Prusak, 1998).

**Future Research**: Suggestions for future research include exploring the role of emerging technologies in knowledge management and their economic implications (Von Krogh, Nonaka, & Aben, 2001). Organizational economics research on knowledge management derives practical propositions related with value creation and appropriation by involved stakeholders and dealing with the organizational context and boundaries (Foss, 2001a, and b).

The findings from empirical research have important implications for organizations seeking to improve their knowledge management practices. Research on knowledge management may add structure to practices.

Invest in Knowledge Infrastructure: Organizations should invest in the development of knowledge repositories, collaboration tools, and training programs.

Foster a Knowledge-Sharing Culture: Leaders should create a culture that encourages open communication, trust, and respect.

Align Incentives with knowledge management Goals: Incentive systems should be designed to reward knowledge creation, sharing, and utilization.

Measure knowledge management Performance: Organizations should develop metrics to track the impact of knowledge management initiatives on organizational performance. Knowledge management enhances the use of information management, organizational learning and knowledge practices to measure organizational performance (Ahmad, Lodhi, Zaman, *et al.* 2017). The term of knowledge management projects are related to information management projects (Schwier, Campbell, & Kenny, 2004).

The integration of organizational economics and knowledge management has provided a solid foundation for analyzing how organizations optimize knowledge resources. However, there remain several underexplored areas that merit further research to deepen understanding and enhance practical applications. By addressing these gaps, scholars can develop more robust frameworks that guide organizational strategies in dynamic economic landscapes.

First, the role of emerging technologies in knowledge management is an area ripe for investigation. Technologies such as artificial intelligence (AI), blockchain, and the Internet of Things (IoT) have the potential to revolutionize knowledge management practices. Future studies should explore how these tools can streamline knowledge sharing, protect intellectual property, and foster innovation. Specifically, AI-driven analytics could predict organizational knowledge needs, while blockchain can enhance security and transparency in knowledge transactions (Grant, 1996; Serenko & Dumay, 2015).

Another critical area is the sector-specific application of knowledge management within the organizational economics framework. Industries such as healthcare, education, and agriculture present unique challenges and opportunities for knowledge optimization. Research should focus on tailoring knowledge management strategies to these contexts, exploring, for instance, how public health organizations can leverage knowledge sharing to improve patient outcomes or how agricultural businesses can use collaborative knowledge platforms to enhance sustainable practices (Nonaka & Takeuchi, 1995).

The interplay between cultural and behavioral dynamics and knowledge management systems also requires further exploration. Organizational culture significantly impacts knowledge-sharing behaviors, with resistance often stemming from deeply ingrained practices or hierarchical structures. Research could examine how incentive structures, trust-building initiatives, and leadership styles can mitigate these barriers. Additionally, studies could delve into how behavioral economics influences decision-making processes related to knowledge utilization and protection (Nahapiet & Ghoshal, 1998).

Empirical validation of theoretical frameworks is another underexplored domain. While theories like transaction cost economics and the resource-based view provide valuable insights, their application to real-world scenarios often lacks empirical depth. Future research should prioritize longitudinal studies and case analyses that measure the tangible outcomes of implementing knowledge management practices. These investigations could provide clearer correlations between knowledge management investments and organizational performance (Williamson, 1985).

Finally, sustainability and ethical considerations in knowledge management offer an emerging frontier. As organizations increasingly prioritize environmental and social governance goals, there is a growing need to understand how knowledge management can support these objectives. Research should focus on how organizations can leverage knowledge-sharing practices to drive sustainable innovations and address global challenges, such as climate change and inequality (Serenko et al., 2007).

Expanding research into the intersections of technology, sector-specific applications, cultural dynamics, empirical validation, and sustainability within the knowledge management framework can significantly enhance its theoretical and practical impact. These avenues not only promise to address existing gaps but also ensure that knowledge management remains a critical tool for achieving economic efficiency and competitive advantage in an evolving global market (Serenko & Dumay, 2015; Grant, 1996).

While the chapter establishes the complementarity of knowledge management knowledge management and organizational economics, various counterarguments provide a deeper understanding of the complexities involved in integrating these perspectives. These alternative viewpoints question the universal applicability, economic viability, and strategic effectiveness of knowledge management practices, prompting a more nuanced discussion.

One common critique is that knowledge management systems often overemphasize codified knowledge while neglecting the subtleties of tacit knowledge. Tacit knowledge, embedded in individual expertise and interpersonal interactions, is difficult to document and share through formal systems. Critics argue that the pursuit of codification may lead to a mechanistic approach that undermines the dynamic nature of knowledge. This concern highlights the need for organizations to balance codification with practices such as mentorship programs and collaborative platforms to foster tacit knowledge sharing (Nonaka & Takeuchi, 1995).

Another significant challenge relates to the financial and operational costs associated with implementing knowledge management systems. Critics argue that the high cost of advanced technology, training, and maintenance can deter smaller organizations from adopting such systems. While this is a valid concern, proponents counter that these investments often yield long-term benefits in innovation, operational efficiency, and competitive advantage. Tailored solutions for small and medium enterprises (SMEs) can help mitigate these financial barriers (Serenko & Dumay, 2015).

Behavioral and cultural resistance to knowledge sharing also poses significant challenges. In hierarchical organizations, employees may view knowledge as a source of personal power, leading to reluctance in sharing. Additionally, cognitive biases, such as loss aversion, can further impede knowledge dissemination. Addressing these barriers requires fostering a culture of trust and collaboration, supported by leadership initiatives and incentive structures that align individual and organizational goals (Nahapiet & Ghoshal, 1998).

Critics also question the universal applicability of knowledge management across sectors. While knowledge-intensive industries such as technology and finance reap clear benefits, traditional sectors like manufacturing and agriculture may find knowledge management less relevant. However, even in these industries, knowledge management can enhance process efficiencies, resource utilization, and innovation. For example, in agriculture, knowledge-sharing platforms can disseminate sustainable farming practices, illustrating its adaptability across contexts (Grant, 1996).

Finally, the critique of economic rationality in organizational economics frameworks calls for a broader, more human-centered perspective. Critics argue that focusing solely on economic incentives ignores the emotional and social dimensions of organizational behavior. This gap underscores the importance of integrating behavioral economics and social dynamics into knowledge management practices, creating more holistic and adaptive frameworks for knowledge sharing and utilization (Williamson, 1985).

By addressing these counterarguments, the discussion on knowledge management's impact is enriched with insights into its limitations and potential. These critiques not only reveal areas for improvement but also emphasize the need for adaptive, sector-specific, and culturally sensitive strategies to ensure the effective integration of knowledge management within organizational economics frameworks.

## CONCLUSION

The organizational economics of knowledge management provides a valuable framework for understanding and optimizing knowledge-related activities. By applying economic principles to knowledge management, organizations can make informed decisions about resource allocation, incentive design, and knowledge management strategies. Future research should continue to explore the complex interplay between economic factors and knowledge management practices.

The study offers a comprehensive analysis of how organizational economics complements knowledge management, demonstrating their symbiotic relationship in enhancing organizational performance. The integration of these two perspectives challenges the perception of rivalry and instead emphasizes their mutual reinforcement. This study intended to make a comprehensive analysis of the conceptual theoretical and empirical implications of the organizational economics theory to the knowledge management approach, departing from the assumption that the principles of organizational economics theory do not rival or contradicts the development of knowledge management approach to organizations, as it has been argued by research. The study concludes that contrary to what some of the studies contend in a supposed rivalry existent between the principles of knowledge management-based approach and the organizational economics, both theoretical perspectives are complementary and consistent. Some other considerations are given below.

The organizational economics of knowledge management plays a vital role in enhancing economic performance in today's knowledge-driven economy. By understanding the conceptual underpinnings and empirical evidence supporting knowledge management practices, organizations can better position themselves for success.

Future research should continue to explore innovative approaches to knowledge management that leverage emerging technologies while addressing the unique challenges faced by different sectors. Future research on the analysis of effects in industry 4.0 technology resources on knowledge management capabilities expected to boost all organizational processes and capabilities. These areas offer opportunities for advancing both academic and practical understanding of knowledge management.

The organizational economics of knowledge management underscores the importance of knowledge as a strategic asset. By leveraging economic theories, organizations can design knowledge management systems that align with organizational goals and enhance overall performance. Theories like TCE, agency theory, and RBV provide a foundation for understanding how firms navigate the complexities of knowledge as an economic resource, enabling firms to achieve sustainable competitive advantages through robust knowledge management practices. Empirical evidence underscores that organizations adopting knowledge management practices aligned with economic principles enjoy improved performance. These practices streamline workflows, enhance innovation, and optimize decision-making. For example, integrating knowledge-sharing systems fosters collaboration and helps organizations adapt to changing market demands, securing a sustainable competitive edge.

Measuring organizational knowledge management performance in the context of organizational complexity demonstrates that innovation is the outcome of the knowledge management practices and other relevant factors. Knowledge management is a spanning process of access, creation storage, and dissemination of the organizational intellectual resources, able to generate sustainable competitive advantage, which have to be valuable, inimitable, irreplaceable and rare. The integration of emerging technologies, such as artificial intelligence and blockchain, has transformative potential in knowledge management. These tools enhance the efficiency of knowledge processes, ensure data security, and provide predictive insights. Organizations leveraging these technologies can achieve higher innovation rates, mitigate operational risks, and maintain transparency.

Despite its benefits, the implementation of knowledge management faces challenges, including financial constraints, resistance to change, and the complexities of tacit knowledge. Organizational economics offers strategies to address these challenges, such as designing incentive systems, fostering trust-based cultures, and balancing codified and tacit knowledge-sharing mechanisms. Different industries face unique challenges in knowledge management. For instance, healthcare benefits from structured knowledge-sharing systems to improve patient outcomes, while agriculture uses knowledge management to promote sustainable farming practices. Tailored approaches that consider these sectoral nuances are critical for maximizing the impact of knowledge management.

The insights of the knowledge management-based perspective is reformulated in terms of complementary and consistent organizational economics principles, besides offering the lesson that not everything can be reducible to both approaches. Knowledge management is not only an economic tool but also a driver for achieving sustainability goals. By integrating environmental and social governance objectives, organizations can leverage knowledge-sharing practices to address global challenges, such as climate change and inequality. This alignment ensures ethical and sustainable growth.

The study highlights the importance of empirical research in validating theoretical frameworks. Longitudinal studies and sector-specific case analyses are necessary to understand the tangible outcomes of knowledge management. These insights can guide organizations in fine-tuning their strategies for better results.

Knowledge-sharing behaviors are influenced by organizational culture and individual motivations. Organizational economics emphasizes the need for trust-building initiatives and aligned incentives to overcome barriers. This approach fosters an environment where employees willingly contribute to collective knowledge.

Protecting intellectual property remains a cornerstone of effective knowledge management. Organizations must adopt robust systems to safeguard their knowledge assets against misuse and external threats, ensuring long-term sustainability and innovation.

Organizations should invest in knowledge infrastructures, such as digital tools and training programs, to enhance their knowledge capabilities. Aligning these investments with organizational goals ensures that knowledge management becomes a strategic asset rather than an operational cost.

Policymakers can play a vital role in supporting knowledge management by incentivizing technology adoption and fostering industry-specific knowledge-sharing frameworks. This support is particularly crucial for small and medium-sized enterprises, which often lack the resources to implement effective systems. Leadership is critical in creating a knowledge-centric culture. By championing knowledge-sharing initiatives and aligning organizational incentives, leaders can ensure that knowledge management is deeply embedded in the organizational fabric.

In an increasingly globalized economy, the ability to manage knowledge effectively is a competitive necessity. Organizations that prioritize knowledge management are better equipped to navigate complex market dynamics and seize opportunities in emerging markets.

In conclusion, the organizational economics of knowledge management is a vital area of study that offers insights into how organizations can optimize their knowledge resources. Effective knowledge management practices lead to improved performance, innovation, and competitive advantage. Future research should continue to explore the dynamic interplay between organizational economics and knowledge management. The integration of organizational economics and knowledge management offers a powerful framework for achieving sustainable growth. By addressing challenges and exploring emerging opportunities, organizations can harness the full potential of their knowledge assets. This approach not only ensures economic efficiency but also fosters innovation and resilience in the face of rapid technological and market transformations.

The organizational economics of knowledge management provides a valuable framework for understanding and optimizing knowledge-related activities. By applying economic principles to knowledge management, organizations can make informed decisions about resource allocation, incentive design, and knowledge management strategies. Future research should continue to explore the complex interplay between economic factors and knowledge management practices.

## REFERENCES


Aghion, P., & Tirole, J. (1997). Formal and real authority in organization. *Journal of Political Economy*, *105*(1), 1–29. DOI: 10.1086/262063

Agrifoglio, R., Metallo, C., & di Nauta, P. (2021). Understanding Knowledge management in Public Organizations through the Organizational Knowing Perspective: A Systematic Literature Review and Bibliometric Analysis. *Public Organization Review*, *21*(1), 137–156. DOI: 10.1007/s11115-020-00480-7

Ahmad, N., Lodhi, M. S., Zaman, K., & Naseem, I. (2017). Knowledge management: A Gateway for Organizational Performance. *Journal of the Knowledge Economy*, *8*(3), 859–876. DOI: 10.1007/s13132-015-0282-3

Alavi, M., & Leidner, D. E. (2001). Review: Knowledge management and knowledge management systems: Conceptual foundations and research issues. *Management Information Systems Quarterly*, *25*(1), 107–136. DOI: 10.2307/3250961

Alchian, A. A. (1965). Some economics of property rights. *Politico (Pavia, Italy)*, *30*(1), 816–829.

Alchian, A. A., & Demsetz, H. (1972). Production, information costs, and economic organization. In *Armen A. Alchian. (1977). Economic Forces at Work*. Liberty Press.

Ali, S., & Tang, H. (2023). Is Intellectual Property Beneficial to Knowledge management? Literature Review on Organizational Knowledge Protection. *Journal of the Knowledge Economy*, *14*(4), 4100–4118. DOI: 10.1007/s13132-022-00904-3

Arrow, K. J. (1962). Economic welfare and the allocation of resources for invention. In Nelson, R. R. (Ed.), *The rate and direction of inventive activity: Economic and social factors* (pp. 609–626). Princeton University Press. DOI: 10.1515/9781400879762-024

Baker, G., Gibbons, R., & Murphy, K. J. (1999). Informal authority in organizations. *Journal of Law Economics and Organization*, *15*(1), 56–73. DOI: 10.1093/jleo/15.1.56

Barney, J. (1991). Firm resources and sustained competitive advantage. *Journal of Management*, *17*(1), 99–120. DOI: 10.1177/014920639101700108

Barzel, Y. (1989). *Economic Analysis of Property Rights*. Cambridge University Press.

Brown, J. S. (1998). Internet technology in support of the concept of "communities-of-practice": The case of Xerox. *Accounting Management and Information Technologies*, *8*(4), 227–236. DOI: 10.1016/S0959-8022(98)00011-3

Brown, J. S., & Duguid, P. (1991). Organizational Learning and Communities of Practice: Toward a Unified View or Working, Learning, and Innovation. *Organization Science*, *2*(1), 40–57. DOI: 10.1287/orsc.2.1.40

Brown, S., & Eisenhardt, K. (1995). Product development: Past research, recent findings, and future directions. *Academy of Management Review*, *20*(3), 342–283. DOI: 10.2307/258850

Cabrera, Á., & Cabrera, E. F. (2005). Fostering knowledge sharing through people management practices. *International Journal of Human Resource Management, 16*(5), 720–735. DOI: 10.1080/09585190500083020

Callon, M., Courtial, J. P., Turner, W. A., & Bauin, S. (1983). From translations to problematic networks: An introduction to co-word analysis. *Social Sciences Information. Information Sur les Sciences Sociales*, *22*(2), 191–235. DOI: 10.1177/053901883022002003

Casson, M. (1994). Why are firms hierarchical? *International Journal of the Economics of Business*, *1*(1), 47–76. DOI: 10.1080/758540499

Ciro-Atehortúa, J. M., Bermúdez-Hernández, J., & Valencia-Arias, J. (2023). Modelos de gestión del conocimiento como herramientas de eficiencia en procesos organizacionales. Revista Virtual Universidad Católica del Norte, (70), 260-296. https://www.doi.org/10.35575/rvucn.n70a10

Coase, R. H. (1937). The nature of the firm, in Nicolai J. Foss, ed. 2000. *The theory of the firm: Critical perspectives in business and management,* vol II. London: Routledge.

Cobo, A., & Diaz, C. (2011). Clinical application of oocyte vitrification: A systematic review and meta-analysis of randomized controlled trials. *Fertility and Sterility*, *96*(2), 277–285. DOI: 10.1016/j.fertnstert.2011.06.030 PMID: 21718983

Conner, K. R., & Prahalad, C. K. (1996). A resource based theory of the firm: Knowledge versus opportunism. *Organization Science*, *7*(5), 477–501. DOI: 10.1287/orsc.7.5.477

Creswell, J. W., & Plano Clark, V. L. (2018). *Designing and conducting mixed methods research* (3rd ed.). Sage.

Davenport, T. H., & Prusak, L. (1998). *Working knowledge: How organizations manage what they know*. Harvard Business School Press.

Deloitte. (2018). Knowledge management & big data. Retrieved November 12, 2019, from https://www2.deloitte.com/content/dam/Deloitte/in/Documents/technology-media-telecommunications/in-tmt-knowledge-management-and-big-data-noexp.pdf

Drucker, P. (1993). *Post-Capitalist Society*. Butterworth Heinemann.

Drucker, P. F. (1968). *The Age of Discontinuity: Guidelines to Our Changing Society*. Harper and Row, 1968

Easterby-Smith, M., Crossan, M., & Nicolini, D. (2000). Organizational learning: Debates past, present and future. *Journal of Management Studies*, *38*(6), 783–796. DOI: 10.1111/1467-6486.00203

El Homrani, M., Aravena Gaete, M., Báez Zarabanda, D. E., Bernal Lozano, M. F., Luque de la Rosa, A., & Luis Rodríguez, C. (2020). *Capitulo 9. La gestión del conocimiento intergeneracional*. In J. Gairín Sallán, C. I. Suárez, & A. Díaz-Vicario (Eds.), *La nueva gestión del conocimiento* (pp. 351-381).

Ereñaga, N. (2023). La gestión del conocimiento en las organizaciones como medida de adaptación al nuevo entorno laboral. *Lan Harremanak*, *49*(49), 15–36. DOI: 10.1387/lan-harremanak.24830

Fama, E., & Michael, C. J. (1983). Separation of ownership and control. *The Journal of Law & Economics*, *26*(2), 301–325. DOI: 10.1086/467037

Foss, K. (1998). *Technological Interdependencies, Specialization, and Coordination: a Property Rights Perspective on the Firm*, DRUID Working Paper.

Foss, N. J. (2000). The theory of the firm, in idem., ed. 2000. *The Theory of the Firm: Critical Perspectives in Economic Organization* (4 vols.), London: Routledge.

Foss, N. J. (2001a). Hayek vs Coase: Economic organization and the knowledge economy. *International Journal of the Economics of Business*.

Foss, N. J. (2001b). *Selective intervention and internal hybrids*. Manuscript.

Foss, N. J., & Pedersen, T. (2002). Transferring knowledge in MNCs: The role of sources of subsidiary knowledge and organizational context. *Journal of International Management*, *8*(1), 49–67. DOI: 10.1016/S1075-4253(01)00054-0

Gairín Sallán, J., Milton, N., Peiró Rubio, K., & Piscitelli, A. (2020). Capitulo 1. La nueva gestión del conocimiento. In Gairín Sallán, J., Suárez, C. I., & Díaz-Vicario, A. (Eds.), *La nueva gestión del conocimiento* (pp. 39–50). Wolters Kluwer España.

Gairín Sallán, J., Vila Figareda, M., Rodríguez, M., Herrero, E., & Comellas Carbó, M. J. (2020). Capitulo 6. La gestión del conocimiento intergeneracional. In Gairín Sallán, J., Suárez, C. I., & Díaz-Vicario, A. (Eds.), *La nueva gestión del conocimiento* (pp. 231–242). Wolters Kluwer España.

Garcia-Perez, A., & Ayres, R. (2009). Collaborative development of knowledge representations – A novel approach to knowledge elicitation and transfer. *Electronic Journal of Knowledge Management*, *7*(1), 55–62.

Garcia-Perez, A., & Ayres, R. (2015). Wikifailure: The limitations of technology for knowledge sharing. *Leading Issues in Knowledge management. Volume Two*, *2*, 242.

Garcia-Perez, A., & Mitra, A. (2008). *Tacit knowledge elicitation and measurement in research organisations: A methodological approach*.

Gaviria-Marin, M., Merigó, J. M., & Baier-Fuentes, H. (2019). Knowledge management: A global examination based on bibliometric analysis, *Technological Forecasting and Social Change,* 140, 2019, Pages 194-220, https://doi.org/. (https://www.sciencedirect.com/science/article/pii/S0040162517304055DOI: 10.1016/j.techfore.2018.07.006

Ghoshal, S., Moran, P., & Almeida-Costa, L. (1995). The Essence of the Megacorporation: Shared Context, Not Structural Hierarchy. *Journal of Institutional and Theoretical Economics*, *151*, 748–759.

Ginja Antunes, H. J., & Gonçalves Pinheiro, P. (2020). Linking knowledge management, organizational learning and memory. *Journal of Innovation & Knowledge*, *5*(2), 140–149. https://www.sciencedirect.com/science/article/pii/S2444569X19300319. DOI: 10.1016/j.jik.2019.04.002

Gold, A. H., Malhotra, A., & Segars, A. H. (2001). Knowledge management: An organizational capabilities perspective. *Journal of Management Information Systems*, *18*(1), 185–214. DOI: 10.1080/07421222.2001.11045669

Grant, R. M. (1996). Toward a knowledge-based theory of the firm. *Strategic Management Journal, 17*(S2), 109–122. DOI: 10.1002/smj.4250171110

Haas, M. R., & Hansen, M. T. (2007). Different knowledge, different benefits: Toward a productivity perspective on knowledge sharing in organizations. *Strategic Management Journal, 28*(11), 1133–1153. DOI: 10.1002/smj.631

Hair, J. F., Black, W. C., Babin, B. J., & Anderson, R. E. (2010). *Multivariate data analysis* (7th ed.). Pearson.

Harman, K., & Koohang, A. (Eds.). (2007). *Learning objects: Applications, implications, & future directions*. Informing Science.

Hart, O. (1995). *Firms, contracts, and financial structure*. Oxford University Press. DOI: 10.1093/0198288816.001.0001

Hassan, A.. (2016). Effect of knowledge management on growth performance in construction industry. *Management Decision, 54*(3), 735–749. DOI: 10.1108/MD-01-2015-0006

Heisig, P. (2009). Harmonisation of knowledge management - comparing 160 KNOWLEDGE MANAGEMENT frameworks around the globe. *Journal of Knowledge Management, 13*(4), 4–31. DOI: 10.1108/13673270910971798

Heisig, P. (2009). Harmonisation of knowledge management - comparing 160 KM frameworks around the globe. *Journal of Knowledge Management, 13*(4), 4–31. DOI: 10.1108/13673270910971798

Holmström, B. (1979). Moral Hazard and Observability. *The Bell Journal of Economics, 10*(1), 74–91. DOI: 10.2307/3003320

Holmström, B. (1982). Moral Hazard in Teams. *The Bell Journal of Economics, 13*(2), 324–340. DOI: 10.2307/3003457

Holmström, B., & Milgrom, P. (1991). Multitask Principal-Agent Analyses: Incentive Contracts, Asset Ownership, and Job Design. *Journal of Law Economics and Organization, 7*(special_issue), 24–52. DOI: 10.1093/jleo/7.special_issue.24

Holsapple, C. W., & Wu, J. (2011). An elusive antecedent of superior firm performance: The knowledge management factor. *Decision Support Systems, 52*(1), 271–283. DOI: 10.1016/j.dss.2011.08.003

Inkinen, H. (2016). Review of empirical research on knowledge management practices and firm performance. *Journal of Knowledge Management, 20*(2), 230–257. DOI: 10.1108/JKM-09-2015-0336

Jensen, M. C., & Meckling, W. H. (1976). Theory of the firm: Managerial behavior, agency costs and ownership structure. *Journal of Financial Economics, 3*(4), 305–360. DOI: 10.1016/0304-405X(76)90026-X

Jensen, M. C., & Meckling, W. H. (1992). Specific and general knowledge and organizational structure, in Lars Werin og Hans Wijkander, eds. 1992. *Contract Economics*. Oxford: Blackwell.

Kogut, B., & Zander, U. (1992). Knowledge of the firm, combinative capabilities, and the replication of technology. *Organization Science, 3*(3), 383–397. DOI: 10.1287/orsc.3.3.383

Krogh, G., Ochijo, K., & Nonaka, I. (2000). *Enabling knowledge creation*. Oxford University Press. DOI: 10.1093/acprof:oso/9780195126167.001.0001

Lambe, P. (2011). The unacknowledged parentage of knowledge management. *Journal of Knowledge Management*, *15*(2), 175–197. DOI: 10.1108/13673271111119646

Langlois, R. N., & Foss, N. J. (1997). Capabilities and governance: the rebirth of production in the theory of economic organization. DRUID Working Paper No. 97-2

Lave, J., & Wenger, E. (1990). *Situated learning: Legitimate peripheral participation*. Cambridge University Press.

Lima, W. E., Prada Vargas, C., & Vanegas Alfonso, O. L. (2022). Gestión del conocimiento para el proceso de innovación en las organizaciones. CITAS. *Suplemento*, (1). Advance online publication. DOI: 10.15332/22563067.7412

López Aguirre, J. F., López Salazar, J. L., Falconi Tello, L. X., & Pomaquero Yuquilema, J. C. (2018). Gestión del conocimiento en las organizaciones: Fundamentos, metodologías y praxis. Revista Contribuciones a la Economía. https://eumed.net/ce/2018/3/gestion-conocimiento.html

Madhani, P. M. (2009). Resource Based View (RBV) of Competitive Advantages: Importance, Issues and Implications, *Indian Management Research Journal,* 1(2).

Madhok, A. (1996). The Organization of Economic Activity: Transaction Costs, Firm Capabilities, and the Nature of Governance. *Organization Science*, *7*(5), 577–590. DOI: 10.1287/orsc.7.5.577

Malhotra, N. K. (2010). *Marketing research: An applied orientation*. Pearson Education.

Manhart, M. & Thalmann, S. (2015), Protecting organizational knowledge: a structured literature review, *Journal of Knowledge management*, 19 (2), pp. 190-211. https://doi.org/ MANAGEMENT-05-2014-0198DOI: 10.1108/JKNOWLEDGE

Marschak, J., & Radner, R. (1972). *The Theory of Teams*. Yale University Press.

Meyer, M., & DeTore, A. (1999). A. Product development for services. *The Academy of Management Perspectives*, *13*(3), 64–76. DOI: 10.5465/ame.1999.2210315

Microsoft. (2018). Driving effective data governance for improved quality and analytics. Retrieved November 25, 2019, from https://query.prod.cms.rt.microsoft.com/cms/api/am/binary/RWs2bX

Mikulić, J., & Prebežac, D. (2022). The Impact of Knowledge management on the Economic Performance of Companies. *Journal of Economics*, *27*(1), 13–30.

Milgrom, P., & Roberts, J. (1990). The Economics of Modern Manufacturing: Technology, Strategy and Organization. *The American Economic Review*, *80*, 511–528.

Milgrom, P., & Roberts, J. (1995). Complementarities and fit strategy, structure, and organizational change in manufacturing. *Journal of Accounting and Economics*, *19*(2-3), 179–208. DOI: 10.1016/0165-4101(94)00382-F

Nabeel, A. A., Rabiah, A. R., & Gouher, R. (2019). The organizational resources and knowledge management capability: A systematic review. *Business and Economic Horizons*, *15*(5), 636–647.

Nahapiet, J., & Ghoshal, S. (1998). Social capital, intellectual capital, and the organizational advantage. *Academy of Management Review*, *23*(2), 242–266. DOI: 10.2307/259373

Nonaka, I., & Peltokorpi, V. (2006). Objectivity and subjectivity in knowledge management: A review of 20 top articles. *Knowledge and Process Management*, *13*(2), 73–82. DOI: 10.1002/kpm.251

Nonaka, I., & Takeuchi, H. (1995). *The Knowledge-Creating Company: How Japanese Companies Create the Dynamics of Innovation*. Oxford University Press. DOI: 10.1093/oso/9780195092691.001.0001

OECD. (1996). *The Knowledge-Based Economy*. OECD Publishing.

Pee, L. G. (2008). Authors Info & Claims Understanding the drivers, enablers, and performance of knowledge management in public organizations *ICEGOV '08: Proceedings of the 2nd international conference on Theory and practice of electronic governance* Pages 439 – 466 DOI: 10.1145/1509096.1509188

Poazi, F. D. W., Tamunosiki-Amadi, J. O., & Fems, M. (2017). The resource-base view of organization and innovation: Recognition of significant relationship in an organization. *International Journal of Economics and Management Engineering*, *11*(3), 697.

Polanyi, M. (1967). *The Tacit Knowledge Dimension*. Routledge & Kegan Paul.

Prendergast, C. (1999). *The Tenuous Tradeoff of Risk and Incentives*, working paper.

Pulido Reina, J. S., & Muñoz, F. A. (2020). Knowledge management, a critical success factor in organizational performance. *Criterio Libre*, *18*(33), 131–149. DOI: 10.18041/1900-0642/criteriolibre.2020v18n33.7535

Ramírez Sáenz de Viteri, S. (2020). Knowledge management: Applications and organizational practices. FORHUM International Journal of Social Sciences and Humanities, 53-66. .DOI: 10.35766/jf20225

Riege, A. (2005). Three-dozen knowledge-sharing barriers managers must consider. *Journal of Knowledge Management*, *9*(3), 18–35. DOI: 10.1108/13673270510602746

Salazar, T.I., Cervantes, L., Aguirre, J.P. y Carbache, C. (2023). Generación de valor en las organizaciones con la gestión del conocimiento e información. Revista Latinoamericana de Ciencias Sociales – Relacis, 1(2), 3 – 16.

Schwier, R. A., Campbell, K., & Kenny, R. (2004). Instructional designers' observations about identity, communities of practice and change agency.

Serenko, A. (2013). Meta-analysis of scientometric research of knowledge management: Discovering the identity of the discipline. *Journal of Knowledge Management*, *17*(5), 773–812. DOI: 10.1108/JKM-05-2013-0166

Serenko, A., & Bontis, N. (2004). Meta-review of knowledge management and intellectual capital literature: Citation impact and research productivity rankings. *Knowledge and Process Management*, *11*(3), 185–198. DOI: 10.1002/kpm.203

Serenko, A., Bontis, N., Booker, L., Sadeddin, K., & Hardie, T. (2010). A scientometric analysis of knowledge management and intellectual capital academic literature (1994-2008). *Journal of Knowledge Management*, *14*(1), 3–23. DOI: 10.1108/13673271011015534

Serenko, A., Bontis, N., & Hardie, T. (2007). Organizational size and knowledge flow: A proposed theoretical link. *Journal of Intellectual Capital*, *8*(4), 610–627. DOI: 10.1108/14691930710830783

Serenko, A. & Cox, R. A.K. & Bontis, Nick & Booker, Lorne D., (2011). The superstar phenomenon in the knowledge management and intellectual capital academic discipline, *Journal of Informetrics*, Elsevier, vol. 5(3), pages 333-345.

Serenko, A., & Dumay, J. (2015). Citation classics published in knowledge management journals. Part I: Articles and their characteristics. *Journal of Knowledge Management*, *19*(2), 401–431. DOI: 10.1108/JKM-06-2014-0220

Shadish, W. R., Cook, T. D., & Campbell, D. T. (2002). *Experimental and quasi-experimental designs for generalized causal inference*. Houghton Mifflin Harcourt.

Shelanski, H., & Klein, P. G. (1995). Empirical research in transaction cost economics: A review and assessment. *Journal of Law Economics and Organization*, •••, 335–361.

Small, H. (1973). Co-citation in the scientific literature: A new measure of the relationship between two documents. *Journal of the American Society for Information Science*, *24*(4), 265–269. DOI: 10.1002/asi.4630240406

Song, S., Nerur, S., & Teng, J. T. (2007). An exploratory study on the roles of network structure and knowledge processing orientation in work unit knowledge management. *The Data Base for Advances in Information Systems*, *38*(2), 8–26. DOI: 10.1145/1240616.1240620

Staples, D. S., Greenaway, K., & McKeen, J. D. (2001). Opportunities for research about managing the knowledge-based enterprise. *International Journal of Management Reviews*, *3*(1), 1–20. DOI: 10.1111/1468-2370.00051

Teece, D. J. (1977). Technology transfer by multinational firms: The resource cost of transferring technological know-how. *Economic Journal (London)*, *87*(346), 242–261. DOI: 10.2307/2232084

Teece, D. J., Pisano, G. & Shuen, A. (1997). Strategic Management and Resources, Firms, and Strategies: A Reader in the Resource-Based Perspective.

Tzortzaki, A., & Mihiotis, A. (2014). A Review of Knowledge management Theory and Future Directions. *Knowledge and Process Management*, *21*(1), 29–41. DOI: 10.1002/kpm.1429

Von Krogh, G., Nonaka, I., & Aben, M. (2001). Making the most of your company's knowledge: A strategic framework. *Long Range Planning*, *34*(4), 421–439. DOI: 10.1016/S0024-6301(01)00059-0

Williamson, O. E. (1981). *Markets and Hierarchies: Analysis and Antitrust Implications*. Free Press.

Williamson, O. E. (1985). *The economic institutions of capitalism: Firms, markets, relational contracting*. Free Press.

Williamson, O. E. (1996). *The Mechanisms of Governance.* Oxford University Press. DOI: 10.1093/oso/9780195078244.001.0001

Williamson, O. E. (1996). *The Mechanisms of Governance.* Oxford University Press. DOI: 10.1093/oso/9780195078244.001.0001

Wooldridge, J. M. (2010). *Econometric analysis of cross section and panel data.* MIT Press.

Yin, R. K. (2018). *Case Study Research and Applications: Design and Methods.* Sage publications.

Zack, M. H. (1999). Developing a knowledge strategy. *California Management Review, 41*(3), 125 145. DOI: 10.2307/41166000

# Chapter 11
# Green Manufacturing Practices for Sustainable Development:
## Selected Scenarios of Bangladesh

**S. S. M. Sadrul Huda**
*North South University, Bangladesh*

## ABSTRACT

*One of the major concerns of the present-day business environment is to create environmentally friendly business enterprises for sustainable business practices. This paper aims to scan the business environment of Bangladesh to find out the environmentally friendly business operations. This paper considers the secondary method of collecting the necessary information. It found that several business organizations adopted green manufacturing practices in Bangladesh. This paper presents environmentally friendly manufacturing practices of ready-made garments, electronics, and construction and proposes a green manufacturing operations framework. It found that green manufacturing practices ensure emission control and improve workplace conditions and employees' well-being.*

## 1. INTRODUCTION

Industry development has an undeniable significance in the economic growth of a country. Interestingly, it is frequently contested that economic development and environmental quality cannot always be assumed to be linear because a growing economy leads to increased consumption of natural resources, which causes climate change. The Swiss Re Institute warns that a 3.2°C increase in global temperatures could have devastating consequences for the world economy. By 2050, climate change could wipe out as much as 18% of global GDP, with Asia experiencing a loss of roughly 26.5%. However, they also suggested that if specific mitigating efforts are performed, the anticipated percentage may be decreased to 14%, and companies have a significant role to play in addressing such activities (Marchant, 2021). As discussed in the previous chapter, firms may embrace various ideas, such as green human resources,

DOI: 10.4018/979-8-3373-0189-1.ch011

green financing, and green marketing. Moreover, they can benefit from obtaining 'green' alternatives as much as feasible.

The green industry effort is a significant driver of long-term industrial growth worldwide. Additionally, it is a crucial engine for Bangladesh's achievement of the SDGs by 2030. As the globe faces an environmental problem that impacts many aspects, **we cannot ignore the environmental problems when we pursue economic growth.** Moreover, since the world is moving toward a greener economy, companies are implementing regulations that support this aim. Similarly, Bangladesh follows these policies and implements green concepts in several businesses, including the textile, cement, and electronic industries (Reza et al., 2017).

Furthermore, the industries' adherence to specific criteria in promoting sustainability can be a primary method for attaining this aim (Reza et al., 2017). Many corporations have started taking initiatives like green manufacturing, green human resource management, green financing, and green marketing to be kinder to earth. As a result, Bangladesh has no choice but to implement or comply with international environmental and social safety requirements. To appreciate and encourage these initiatives, international organizations, development partners, and financiers such as AFD, ADB, DFID, and others offer technical and development help in the form of loans for green sector growth. Additionally, Bangladesh Bank has refinanced a “Green Transformation Fund” program, which aims to access export-oriented sectors and provide financing for environmentally beneficial activities. Aside from that, national and international private banks and financial institutions have launched a 5–10-year duration loan program with a fixed interest rate to help green enterprises get started (The Financial Express, 2020). **This chapter aims to present the green practices adopted by different industries to address the issue of sustainable development and climate change. Furthermore, it focuses on these industries' impact on social, economic, and environmental factors.**

## 2. METHODOLOGY

Conclusion to this chapter is reached based on secondary data. The project draws on the views of other authors from journal articles and UN reports on the issue. It also examines press stories on how Bangladesh is adopting green practices and how different businesses are applying sustainability principles. This helps to understand how Bangladesh is pursuing green manufacturing.

### 2.1 Archival Method:

The archival method holds significance in the domain of secondary research, providing researchers with a plethora of information and insights. In this approach, scholars explore existing records, documents, and data that have endured the test of time. The primary objective is to extract valuable knowledge from historical artifacts, texts, and various materials. Archives encompass a broad spectrum, including official government documents, organizational records, newspapers, personal letters, manuscripts, photographs, and more. The researcher engages deeply with the historical context, meticulously scrutinizing and interpreting these archival sources.

A significant strength of the archival method is its capacity to offer a vivid and genuine window into historical periods. These archival materials function as tangible remnants of past eras, encapsulating the thoughts, actions, and events of individuals and organizations. This approach grants researcher's entry to an extensive wellspring of information that might not be accessible through alternative methods. The extensive range and depth of archival materials empower scholars to build a thorough comprehension of historical evolutions, shifts in society, and changes in culture.

Conducting archival research is a thorough undertaking that calls for patience, meticulous attention to detail, and a discerning approach. Researchers frequently engage in the meticulous task of examining aged manuscripts covered in dust, sifting through weathered documents, and deciphering handwritten letters. The archival method demands a profound appreciation for historical intricacies and a grasp of the larger social and political frameworks from which these materials emerged.

Beyond its emphasis on history, the archival method holds a pivotal position across diverse academic disciplines such as sociology, anthropology, political science, and others. Scholars may resort to archives to scrutinize patterns and trends, trace the development of ideas, or delve into the origins of societal norms and structures. This method exhibits versatility, enabling researchers to uncover concealed connections, question established narratives, and introduce innovative viewpoints into academic discussions.

Moreover, the archival method extends beyond physical archives. The rise of digital technology has led to the digitization of many archives, rendering historical documents accessible on the internet. This digital transformation has revolutionized the field of archival research, providing researchers with the convenience of remotely accessing a wide range of materials. Nevertheless, it brings forth fresh challenges, including navigating digital interfaces, evaluating the credibility of online sources, and addressing concerns related to data preservation and sustainability.

While the archival method offers notable benefits, it is not devoid of drawbacks. Archives can be incomplete, mirroring the biases of their creators and curators. Certain voices and perspectives may find themselves marginalized or omitted from the historical narrative. It is crucial for researchers to recognize these constraints and engage with archival materials thoughtfully. Additionally, the extensive volume of archival data can be daunting, requiring researchers to carefully select and prioritize sources aligned with their research aims and objectives.

Engaging in archival research introduces ethical considerations, particularly when handling sensitive or private information. Researchers must address concerns related to confidentiality, obtain informed consent, and ensure the responsible utilization of archival materials. Prioritizing the rights and privacy of individuals represented in the archives is of utmost importance, and ethical guidelines significantly influence the conduct of archival research.

This method aslo plays a crucial part in conserving cultural heritage. Archives frequently contain uncommon artifacts, manuscripts, and documents that provide perspectives on the artistic, literary, and linguistic dimensions of societies over different periods. Scholars in disciplines such as art history, linguistics, and literature derive significance from delving into archives to unearth concealed gems that enhance their understanding of cultural development.

Moreover, the archival method acts as a driving force for interdisciplinary research. While exploring a variety of documents, researchers may identify points of convergence among historical events, social structures, and scientific advancements. This interdisciplinary approach empowers scholars to establish connections between seemingly disparate fields, nurturing a comprehensive understanding of intricate phenomena. To illustrate, a historian exploring medical records from a specific era might collaborate with a medical anthropologist to investigate the sociocultural implications of prevailing health practices.

The transformation of archives into digital formats, while increasing accessibility, has also ushered in inventive research methodologies. Utilizing text and data mining techniques on extensive digitized archives empowers researchers to pinpoint patterns, trends, and correlations that could have eluded discovery through conventional manual scrutiny. This data-centric approach supplements traditional qualitative analyses, providing a more encompassing viewpoint on historical and societal phenomena.

As archives achieve global accessibility, the significance of international collaborations in archival research has risen. Researchers now have the opportunity to interact with materials from diverse corners of the world, promoting a more comprehensive and varied comprehension of history and culture. This interconnected methodology facilitates comparative analyses, enabling scholars to juxtapose archival materials from different regions, discerning commonalities, distinctions, and overarching global trends.

The archival method intersects with public history initiatives, extending its impact beyond academic realms. As precious reservoirs of information, archives serve as valuable tools for public historians, educators, and museum curators. They leverage these archives to craft exhibitions, documentaries, and educational programs, aiming to present historical information in a manner that is both accessible and captivating for a wider audience. Through this outreach, public awareness and appreciation for history are heightened.

In archival research, ethical considerations go beyond ensuring confidentiality and obtaining informed consent. Researchers are tasked with addressing issues related to cultural sensitivity, particularly when handling materials of cultural or religious importance. It is imperative to show respect for the cultural context from which archival materials originated. Collaborating with local communities can offer valuable insights into the proper use and interpretation of these materials.

In summary, the archival method serves as a foundational element of secondary research, providing scholars with a valuable means to investigate, assess, and interpret historical materials. Whether immersing themselves in physical archives or navigating the digital domain, researchers utilizing this method contribute to the ongoing discourse on the past, enhancing our comprehension of human experiences and societal development. The archival method is a dynamic and evolving approach that continues to influence the landscape of academic exploration, bridging the present with the wealth of knowledge preserved in historical archives.

## 3. BANGLADESH'S APPROACH TO GREEN INDUSTRIES

One of the key drivers of sustainable growth is the green sector. In the current globalized era Bangladesh has been working to achieve industrial change. As the globe moves toward a greener economy, companies are implementing regulations that support this aim. Bangladesh is also following these policies and implementing green concepts in several businesses, including the textile industry (Reza et al., 2017). The textile industry has a huge environmental impact by releasing carbon dioxide into the air. The CO2 emissions come mainly from the weaving and spinning processes. A research examined the environmental effects of different tailoring methods. It grouped the production data into three types: resource, energy, and waste. These were either used or produced during the process. The industry mostly used materials like cotton fabric, lining and stitching material, plastic, paper and cardboard, and others. The study found that the jackets' material had a big environmental influence. Energy was the next major factor, followed by waste. The flow chart in Figure 1 shows the material and process flow, and the sustainability aspects of garment production (Nayak et al., 2019). Hence, the material used during production should be chosen intensively since the ecological footprint of the garments may vary depending on the material used.

*Figure 1. Flow chart for the material and process flow, and sustainable factors in garment manufacturing*

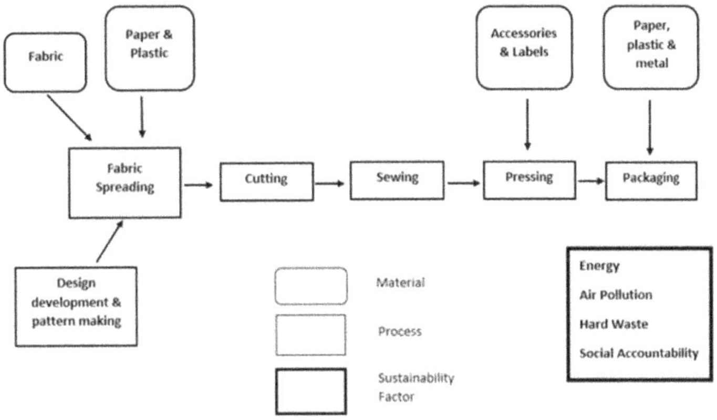


*Compiled by authors*
*Source: (Herva et al., 2008; Nayak et al., 2019)*

Unfortunately, if we let the environment get worse, we may not be able to fix or reduce the damage it causes. Undoubtedly, for Bangladesh's economic growth, this has become one of the government's, policymakers, and environmentalists' primary worries. Thus, there has been a greater emphasis on remedial measures to reduce environmental risks in recent years. **More and more people want products that are good for the environment and production methods that are green and the practice is increasing each day.** These decrease costs, increase resource efficiency, minimize risks, and reduce greenhouse gas emissions (Reza et al., 2017).

Some efforts have been made in Bangladesh to create a green industry, but the main way they are doing this is by building green structures. Bangladesh began its road toward green building implementation in 2011 with the first LEED-certified project, CIPL, located in Savar, Dhaka. Following that, Bangladesh embarked on a dramatic shift in industrial growth, with specific attention paid to environmental concerns and USGBC guidelines (Reza et al., 2017). Furthermore, Bangladesh has made significant progress in **greening RMG industries** and has around 171 LEED-certified green RMG factories. Even though the initial cost of establishing such facilities may be higher, these green factories drastically reduce operating expenses in the long term. According to the BGMEA, green manufacturers may reduce energy use by 40% and water use by more than 30% while emitting less carbon dioxide, ensuring environmental safety. **People in the industry say that Bangladesh's garment sector can become a global leader by dealing with major issues like sustainability, climate change, groundwater loss, efficiency, and others. BGMEA leaders called Bangladesh a great opportunity for investing in the growing garment sector. They said that they want to make a green, energy-saving, and eco-friendly clothing industry and do more recycling, circular economy, and innovation.** (Hossain, 2022).

Moreover, different industry stakeholders are more willing to do business to create an ecologically friendly industry. For instance, buyers from other countries who purchase Ready-Made Garments (RMG) care about the quality of the product and the standards of society, ethics, and environment. (Reza et al., 2017). Since there are several related problems to unsustainable consumption in the twenty-first century, including wasteful consumption in fashion, several countermeasures have emerged during the last decade, notably in recent years. In 2009, the Copenhagen Fashion Summit marked the first notable occurrence of a sustainable fashion event, and then in 2010, Green Fashion Week was held in partnership with the United Nations Framework Convention on Climate Change. Many people have advocated for consumers to support slow fashion in informal attempts to modify norms and social customs (purchasing garments that last longer). Many businesses have also taken the initiative of stocking fewer collections in stores and producing more lasting items (Atasu et al., 2008). This phenomenon has led countries like Bangladesh, India, and Vietnam, who offshore textiles to fashion brands like H&M, Zara, Primark, and Ralph Lauren, to adopt green processes and sustainability in their factories. Thus, RMG factories are taking significant steps to make their factories green, from using environmentally friendly machinery to sustainable raw materials.

## 3.1 'Green' Initiatives by Ready-Made Garments

Bangladesh's economy has grown astonishingly in the previous decade, making it one of the fastest-growing in Asia. The readymade garments (RMG) sector has significantly contributed to this journey. This industry earned almost $34.133 billion in the fiscal year 2018-19 (Woven wear: $17.24, Knitwear: $16.89). These earnings account for 84.21 percent of total export earnings and 11.2% of GDP. Bangladesh has surpassed China to become the world's second-largest RMG exporter (Bhattacherja et al., 2020).

Furthermore, this industry has significantly contributed to improving socioeconomic development, such as female empowerment, poverty reduction, job creation, social life pattern improvement, per-capita income, and economic upgradation. **Although the RMG business has significantly contributed to this socioeconomic elevation, its environmental concern remains debatable**. Factories often need groundwater, hazardous chemicals, and energy for manufacturing and operation. A significant volume of groundwater and toxic chemicals have been employed for dyeing and washing since this nation's commencement of RMG industrialization. Due to a lack of investment and understanding, most firms could not apply water-efficient technologies in production, resulting in water waste. Again, wastewater treatment technologies appeared prohibitively costly for small-scale industries (Bhattacherja et al., 2020). However, Nowadays, when business is not limited to the traditional meaning of earning money, sustainability and environmental concern are popular terms.

The clothing industry already has several environmentally conscious factories and aspires to establish an ecologically inclusive business. These industries, in particular, have been actively engaged in environmental improvements such as operating effluent treatment plants (ETPs), utilizing energy-efficient equipment, installing renewable energy technologies, and generally making the firm more environmentally friendly. A few examples of such RMGs are explained below, which follow the international sustainability standards and steer Bangladesh toward a greener economy.

### 3.1.1 Envoy Group

Envoy Textile Ltd is an environmentally friendly RMG organization in Bangladesh. However, this is not a conventional textile factory, where the management is only concerned with manufacturing and profit. Envoy Textiles is concerned about the environment and offers leisure alternatives in the workplace. The firm has received various quality certificates, earning Bangladesh great honor. In March 2016, the US Green Building Council (USGBC), which is an organization that promotes sustainability in the construction industry, awarded the firm a LEED (Leadership in Energy and Environmental Design) Platinum designation, which is the highest level of certification for green buildings. The firm achieved this remarkable feat by scoring 80 points out of a possible 110 for its environmentally friendly activities in its buildings, operations, and maintenance, according to a study by Uddin (2019). Engineer Kutubuddin Ahmed, the chairman and founder of Envoy Group, had a dream project of Envoy Textiles, where he aimed to establish a comfortable work environment. The founder aimed to establish a factory with recreational amenities and employment. He was also quite concerned about environmental challenges. To address environmental issues, the factory's founder directed the consulting firm to provide the required amenities in the workplace, adding Tk20 crore to the building budget. According to the LEED Platinum designation, Envoy Textiles Ltd is a model of sustainable design and a leader in changing the construction industry. Envoy Textiles Ltd became the top among all textile mills around the world after getting the Platinum LEED certification (Uddin, 2019).

#### *Use of Technologies in Envoy Textiles*

The organization uses a technique called "Rope Dyeing Technology," which involves twisting the yarns into a rope-like shape and then immersing them in indigo baths to create yarn with a better color. The organization claims that it has tried to find the best possible mix of labor and machinery to reach the highest level of productivity. It is also the country's first to introduce robotic technologies. The technique aims to increase yarn output and quality. Some notable advantages of robotic technology include safety, labor cost reductions, decreased cycle time and waste, and enhanced product quality, productivity, and efficiency. The factory's lake is utilized for rainwater gathering, fish aquaculture, and as a fire hydrant. The water that is released from the ETP (Effluent Treatment Plant) after being treated is stored in this place as well. It acts as a reservoir for the discharged water from the ETP. The ETL installed inverters in all loom to increase the factory's energy efficiency. They added fiberglass on the roof to allow light in, and they regenerated energy by reusing heat from generators (Uddin, 2019).

#### *Social Welfare and Corporate Social Responsibility*

More than 50 activities that help the workers and their families are covered by the worker welfare of Envoy group and the Corporate Social Responsibility (CSR) initiatives. These activities include paying for the medical expenses of the workers and their family members. The children of the workers also get help with their education through scholarships and with their marriages through financial assistance. The corporation gives free lodging and meals to its employees. Profit-sharing advantages are available to all employees in the organization. The management has done something unusual by giving 12 yearly rewards to encourage staff to achieve the annual profit goal. The business has established a pediatric intensive care unit (ICU) for burn victims at Dhaka Medical College Hospital. The ETL pays the salary of the unit's four employees. The factory employs 15 physically challenged people, according to the company's general manager for human resources. The management also has rules to keep a worker's salary if he becomes physically incapacitated due to an accident or other reasons while on the job (Uddin, 2019).

### 3.1.2 Fatullah Apparels

Fatullah Apparel is a knitwear production factory with 600 employees that got the US Green Building Council's LEED Platinum Certification in September 2007. It received 97 out of 110 points, tying it for first place in the world with Remi Holdings, another textile and apparel business in Bangladesh. Among the knitwear factories that have USGBC certification, it also has a unique record score. The picturesque view of the factory is a resort on 2.7 acres of land with orchards flourishing in abundance The site is made more attractive by the lavender water hyacinth. In an interview with a local newspaper, CEO and Founder Fazlee Shamim Ehsan stated that this accomplishment is not only for the factory itself but also for Bangladesh's whole garment sector since it can be asserted with great pride that this industry is as safe as the others. Besides Fatullah, Sharaf Apparels Washing and Dyeing Industries and Debonair and Orbitex Knitwear also got LEED Platinum Certification. Based on information provided by the Bangladesh Garment Manufacturers and Exporters Association (BGMEA), the nation currently boasts 171 clothing manufacturers with green certifications, setting a noteworthy record in comparison to other countries. According to the BGMEA, up to 500 more factories also seek accreditation. Following the collapse of Rana Plaza, the whole Bangladesh garment sector suffered a huge turn, and industry revenues began to drop. Buyers and civic society began to exert pressure on workers' safety. Although Bangladesh had LEED-certified facilities before the disaster, several firms intended to convert to green ones following the disaster at Rana Plaza. Fatullah apparels intended to build a green plant soon after the collapse and began operations in January 2019. To the owner's amazement, the firm only had to spend 10% more money when compared to non-green factories. The factory is located in a two-story building, one for manufacturing and the other for administration. Both structures are powered by renewable energy and a national grid line. Workers at Fatullah Apparels asserted that the firm followed all rules of conduct and had several advantages over other factories, such as higher earnings. In the face of the government's directive to shutter all companies in response to the Covid-19 outbreak, employees were granted full compensation, a notable deviation from the authorities' stipulation that employers were only required to disburse 65 percent of their wages (Tuhin, 2022). Despite the mandated reduction, the comprehensive compensation provided to workers demonstrated a commitment to safeguarding their financial well-being during the challenging circumstances imposed by the pandemic.

### 3.1.3 AKH Group

AKH Group is one of Bangladesh's most integrated garment manufacturing and exporting firms, supplying retailers such as M&S, Gap Inc, H&M, Primark, PVH, and Debenhams. Every month, the AKH group employs around 14,000 people. It produces approximately 2.4 million pieces of knitting and knitted fleece clothing in its vertical knit division and approximately 1.2 million pieces of shirts in its woven division. It has established a new green plant, AKH Eco Apparel Ltd, and has invested Tk150 crore (US$25 million) in its establishment. The recently established facility has been awarded LEED certification by the US Green Building Council (USGBC) in recognition of its eco-friendly attributes. Additionally, the recently constructed facility has achieved LEED (Leadership in Energy and Environmental Design) gold certification, which is the second-highest LEED rating, following platinum (AKH Group, n.d.).

The AKH Group intends to generate US$80 million in yearly exports from the facility, labeled as "the new future of Bangladesh" by Marcia Bernicat, the US ambassador to Bangladesh. According to AKH, the new factory's sustainability features will lower energy use by 1,295 megawatt-hours per year, fuel oil consumption by 325 tonnes, and water consumption by 30%. Solar power will provide around 25% of the factory's electrical requirement. According to the corporation, the plant lies on 13 acres of land and features a rainwater collecting system, with rainwater repurposed to minimize groundwater demand (AKH Groupl, n.d.).

According to Siddiqur Rahman, president of the BGMEA, green factories, and buyer assistance are required if the clothing sector intends to export textile products. According to Eco-textile News, Bangladesh's textile sector significantly contributes to the country's water scarcity and pollution problems. Most textile mills in Dhaka depend on non-metered and non-priced self-supply of groundwater from boreholes. Hence, green factories in the RMG sector are highly required and appreciated (AKH Groupl, n.d.).

### 3.1.4 AKH Group

SM Sourcing, located in Gazipur, has garnered official acclaim as the preeminent environmentally conscious garment factory worldwide. This recognition stems from its outstanding score of 106 out of 110 in the globally recognized Leadership in Energy and Environmental Design (LEED) Green Factory ranking, firmly establishing its status as the foremost eco-friendly facility on a global scale.

In the pursuit of this achievement, SM Sourcing surpassed Green Textile of Mymensingh, another notable factory from Bangladesh. Green Textile had maintained its leading position until then, holding a commendable score of 104.

The official certification was bestowed upon the Gazipur factory by the US Green Building Council (USGBC) on a Tuesday. This certification acknowledges the factory's location on a four-bigha plot at Konabari. Notably, it outshone both local and international counterparts in earning this prestigious distinction.

According to disclosures by the Bangladesh Garment Manufacturers and Exporters Association (BGMEA), Bangladesh currently hosts nine out of the top ten environmentally friendly factories worldwide. This reflects a commendable trend in the country's commitment to sustainability.

Among the recognized factories, in addition to SM Sourcing and Green Textile, are Knit Asia, Integra Dresses, Remi Holdings, Fatullah Apparels, Lida Textiles and Dyeing, Liz Fashion Industries, and Tarasima Apparels. This collective recognition further establishes Bangladesh's prominence in fostering environmentally responsible manufacturing practices.

The proprietor of SM Sourcing, Mirza Shams Mahmud, expressed deep satisfaction in contributing to the elevation of Bangladesh's standing on the global platform. His pride in the factory's accomplishments mirrors the collective efforts of the nation's garment industry in championing sustainable initiatives.

When unveiling the environmentally friendly features of the factory, Mahmud highlighted the innovative rainwater storage system beneath the garden within the premises. He emphasized the diverse applications of this system within the facility, showcasing a commitment to resource efficiency. Additionally, a solar power system has been seamlessly integrated onto the roof, further underlining the factory's dedication to clean energy practices.

Faruque Hassan, President of BGMEA, extended heartfelt commendation for this significant achievement. He underscored the unparalleled recognition that SM Sourcing now enjoys, holding the highest score among eco-friendly factories globally. This accomplishment not only speaks to the factory's excellence but also reflects positively on Bangladesh's commitment to sustainable and responsible manufacturing practices. (13 December, 2023, Prothom Alo)

## 3.2 'Green' Practices of Electronic Industry

Bangladesh has also achieved significant progress in the electronics sector. Interestingly, while it helps the economy, some light should be put on its role in climate change. The environmental effect of the communication technology sector, from cellphones to smart automobiles, is significant yet mostly unseen. Nonetheless, it is expected to skyrocket over the next decade, with scientists estimating that it would account for up to 14% of carbon emissions by 2040 (Green Journal, 2020). As a result, electronic industries are urged to follow green practices to mitigate the environmental issues present in recent times. One of the prominent examples of electronic companies adopting sustainable practices is Singer Bangladesh. The company's initiatives in addressing climate change issues are explained below.

### 3.2.1 Singer Bangladesh

Singer, a global corporation known for its expertise in electronics and home appliances, plans to initiate activities at its recently constructed environmentally-friendly facilities, with an estimated worth of $78 million (around Tk800 crore), by the end of 2023. The emphasis lies in capitalizing on the swiftly growing domestic market and investigating potential export avenues. Singer is committed to introducing sophisticated and sustainable in-house production techniques, guaranteeing the creation of high-quality products through the establishment of this new manufacturing unit. Furthermore, Singer Bangladesh is launching cutting-edge energy-saving devices and household appliances, which will be expedited in the coming days. The factory's initial capacity on the 1.35 lakh square meter industrial property would be to produce 15 lakh units of refrigerators, TVs, washing machines, air conditioners, and other vital appliances yearly, strengthening Singer's market position. Singer Bangladesh's CEO and MD stated that the company's new state-of-the-art production facility would be designed following the gold requirements of LEED. The global acknowledgment of this green building certification is noteworthy. Additionally, Singer plans to share its knowledge in energy-efficient products and manufacturing technology with Bangladesh, contributing to the country's shift towards a low-carbon economy (The Business Standard, 2022).

The construction of the facility will prioritize harnessing natural daylight by incorporating skylight roof surfaces, promoting sustainable energy management and resulting in potential energy savings of up to 50% and a reduction of up to 60% in carbon emissions. Additionally, rainwater will be harvested and stored for both plumbing use and garden irrigation. Power monitoring will be employed to achieve quality and sustainability goals. During construction, local and repurposed building materials will be utilized. This will have a long-term effect on Bangladesh's electronics sector by encouraging the adoption and development of environmentally friendly goods while maintaining quality standards (The Business Standard, 2022).

## 3.3 'Green' Practices in Construction

It is no surprise that construction has a substantial effect on the environment. It involves brick manufacturing, the use of cement, deforestation, and many more. However, these can also be mitigated if the stakeholders are mindful of using sustainable raw materials and green practices in construction sites and factories. One of the significant materials used in construction is the cement which generates roughly 5% of global CO2 emissions. According to estimates, cement mills will emit 5 billion tonnes of CO2 worldwide by 2050. Because of the intrinsic chemical processes integral to cement manufacturing, the carbon dioxide ($CO_2$) emissions originating from the cement industry have a notable effect on contributing to climate change. Research published in 2014 by the United Nations Industrial Development Organization highlights that the main component of cement, clinker, significantly contributes to both $CO_2$ emissions and energy consumption. This is due to the process of creating clinker through the sintering of limestone and clay. According to studies, alternative raw materials and fuels, alternative techniques in crushing and grinding raw materials, energy-efficient manufacturing technologies, and increased use of blends to reduce the amount of clinker are vital areas that can promote green manufacturing in this segment while reducing energy consumption and waste (Saxena & Srivastava, 2022). Few cement and brick factories in Bangladesh have contributed remarkably to mitigating the climate change issues involved with construction. Such practices adopted by the companies are presented in the next section.

### 3.3.1 Green Block

The green block is a firm that makes environmentally friendly concrete blocks and tiles out of stone, sand, and cement, focusing on sustainability. Green blocks are being utilized in various building projects, including LGED, PWD, Payra Seaport, and companies at Bangabandhu Sheikh Mujib Industrial City. According to experts involved in the creation of eco-friendly blocks, using blocks in large projects like these can save costs by 20%-30%. Officials claim that no soil is required to produce these blocks since they are only made using stone, cement, sand, and chemicals. Using German technology, the Green Block plant manufactures hollow concrete blocks, universal paving blocks, erosion control blocks, edging blocks, curb stones, parking pavement, and roof tiles. According to the Housing and Building Research Institute (HBRI), the government has released guidelines for utilizing eco-friendly blocks instead of burnt bricks, the manufacture of which is harmful to the environment. The Ministry of Environment has also instructed that all government projects should employ blocks as an alternative to bricks. Remarkably, the government offers several forms of aid to those interested in investing in the concrete block building business, including a VAT rebate facility. This will encourage many manufacturers to lean more toward sustainability, as it lowers production costs and adds value to the brand's image (Chowdhury, 2022).

### 3.3.2 Crown Cement-GPH Ispat

In 2017, Crown Cement, Building Research Institute (HBRI), and Prothom Alo addressed the social and environmental difficulties the world is facing and committed to utilizing environmentally friendly raw materials, such as cement-made blocks, instead of burning bricks, considering brick manufacture pollutes the environment. According to AKM Abul Kalam, who serves as the president of the Bangladesh Institute of Planners, he emphasized the importance of ensuring the environmental friendliness of the surroundings of buildings, rather than solely relying on the choice of construction materials. He believes that rural areas, where more buildings are being constructed, along with metropolitan areas, should be prioritized (The Daily Star, 2017). Crown Cement further announced a Memorandum of Understanding (MoU) with GPH Ispat and HBRI to develop environmentally friendly construction materials. Crown Cement and GPH Ispat will get technical and scientific assistance from the Housing and Building Research Institute in order to develop and enhance environmentally friendly building materials like as cement, steel, and concrete (bdnews24, 2017). Since the brick-burning business has a devastating influence on the environment, these activities are essential for Bangladesh in combating climate change.

However, specific contentious concerns are associated with the manufacture of eco-friendly bricks, such as ecological harm caused by 'sustainable' brick production, dredging, and erosion.

The operations and procedures employed in manufacturing processes and systems, which convert input materials and energy into marketable goods, play a role in shaping sustainability. Wastes and emissions, which are often categorized as outputs, are, in turn, inputs to other industrial and natural systems, where their influence is felt socially, ecologically, and economically (Paul et al., 2014). The diagram below depicts the sustainable manufacturing process in a closed loop.

*Figure 2. The role of the manufacturing industry in a sustainable system*

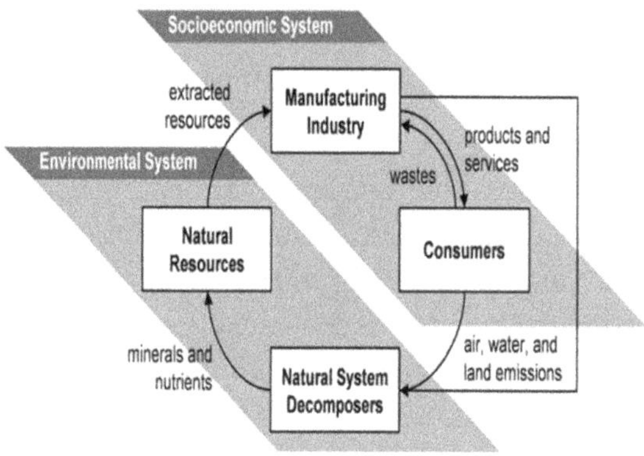


*Source: (Paul et al., 2014)*

The initiatives taken by the companies mentioned above significantly contribute to ameliorating the environmental issues involved with each particular industry. However, these initiatives also play immense roles in benefitting the nation's social, economic, and environmental factors.

## 4. COLLABORATION BETWEEN BUYERS AND SUPPLIERS

In the quest to steer manufacturers towards sustainable practices and inspire their initiatives, the onus lies on both buyers and brands. They share the responsibility of not just offering improved prices but also elevating the regularity of work orders. Khondaker Golam Moazzem, the research director at the Centre for Policy Dialogue, underscores the significant investments made by manufacturers in embracing eco-friendly measures to diminish their environmental impact. Acknowledging the financial commitment involved in this green transition, Moazzem emphasizes the pivotal role of buyers. It is essential for buyers to embrace purchasing norms that guarantee fair pricing for goods, recognizing the manufacturers' strides in championing sustainability. This collaborative approach is vital for fostering a harmonious and mutually beneficial relationship between manufacturers and buyers in the pursuit of environmentally conscious business practices.

Preserving the Earth via sustainable and eco-friendly manufacturing is a collective obligation, necessitating collaboration between buyers and manufacturers. Simultaneously, the economist emphasizes that the government plays a crucial role by offering not only financial assistance but also policy support. This entails the establishment of additional green factories, ensuring a more robust and comprehensive approach to environmental protection. In this collaborative endeavor, buyers and manufacturers contribute to the broader initiative, while governmental support becomes integral in shaping a landscape where sustainable practices thrive and flourish.

Expressing its commitment to an ambitious sustainability agenda, H&M Group, recognized as the largest purchaser from Bangladesh, extends a warm embrace to initiatives aimed at steering the industry towards a circular, equitable, and just textile landscape. Ziaur Rahman, the Country Manager for Bangladesh, underscores the company's steadfast dedication. H&M Group actively embraces and endorses initiatives geared towards advancing fairness, equality, and circular practices. The overarching objective is for H&M Group to assume a pivotal role in steering the textile industry in Bangladesh towards greater responsibility and environmental consciousness through its active support and engagement in such initiatives.

"We don't require our suppliers to endorse a specific environmental certification; what is important to us is that they share our ambition to shift towards circular production processes, GHG emissions reductions and taking climate action."

Emphasizing H&M Group's commitment to instigating positive transformations in the textile sector, Ziaur Rahman, the Country Manager for Bangladesh, underscores the company's steadfast dedication. H&M Group actively embraces and endorses initiatives geared towards advancing fairness, equality, and circular practices. The overarching objective is for H&M Group to assume a pivotal role in steering the textile industry in Bangladesh towards greater responsibility and environmental consciousness through its active support and engagement in such initiatives.

## 5. COST AND BENEFIT ANALYSIS

Establishing a green factory comes with a price tag that is 25-30% higher compared to the setup cost of a conventional factory. The increased expenditure is attributed not only to the initial infrastructure investment but also to the elevated costs associated with machinery and technology. This is primarily due to the incorporation of energy-efficient features that contribute to higher power consumption efficiency. Despite the higher upfront expenses, it's important to note that embracing green practices entails long-term benefits. The initial higher costs are an investment that yields return over time, making green factories economically advantageous in the grand scheme of sustainable and eco-friendly manufacturing.

Khaled highlighted that the return on investment becomes achievable over a specific timeframe. This is attributed to the factory's efficient utilization of resources, notably its reduced water consumption and electricity usage. By implementing innovative strategies like rainwater harvesting, the factory not only preserves water but also actively participates in the recycling process. This comprehensive approach serves to highlight not just the economic feasibility of the investment but also underscores the factory's dedication to sustainable methodologies. In doing so, the factory plays a role in resource conservation and assumes responsibility for environmental stewardship.

Consider, for instance, the comparative costs of lighting options where an LED light, priced at around 1,000 takas ($9), contrasts with a conventional tube light, available at a more economical 100 takas ($0.90). While the initial investment in LED lights might seem higher, their energy efficiency becomes apparent in the long run due to significantly lower electricity consumption. This translates into a tangible return on investment over a specific duration. Moreover, the incorporation of solar panels in the energy mix represents a strategic step towards harnessing renewable energy sources, aligning the factory with sustainable practices and promoting the utilization of environmentally friendly technologies.

It's noteworthy that green-certified factories are not the sole participants in this initiative. Compliant factories, which diligently implement safety measures encompassing fire safety, electrical safety, and structural safety, and undergo audits by buyers, have also embraced various measures. In collaboration with BGMEA, these compliant factories are proactively working to curtail the consumption of natural resources, thereby mitigating their environmental footprint. This collective effort underscores the industry's commitment to sustainability, where both green-certified and compliant factories contribute to positive environmental outcomes through conscientious practices and resource conservation.

Several apparel manufacturers in Bangladesh have embraced the Partnership for a Cleaner Textile (PaCT) initiative, a collaborative effort involving the International Finance Corporation, BGMEA, and the Netherlands embassy. This initiative is geared towards fostering sustainable water resources management and instigating positive environmental transformations specifically within textile wet processing. It signifies a proactive move by Bangladeshi manufacturers to engage in environmentally responsible practices and underscores their commitment to effecting positive change in the textile industry. Additionally, it's crucial to recognize that the commitment to sustainability extends beyond green-certified factories; compliant factories, which adhere to safety precautions and buyer audits, are actively involved in diverse measures facilitated by BGMEA to curtail natural resource usage and mitigate environmental impacts. This collaborative approach amplifies the collective impact of both green-certified and compliant factories in advancing sustainable practices and environmental stewardship in the apparel manufacturing sector.

They also initiated Zero Discharge of Hazardous Chemicals to stop pollution.

“Undoubtedly, Bangladesh RMG sector is a leader in sustainability and environment protection as we turned the sector safeties and compliance from the disastrous incident,” BGMEA president Faruque Hassan said.

“Compared to our closest competitors — Vietnam, Turkey, Pakistan and India — and the number-one exporter of fashion goods, we housed the highest green factory in the world,” said Hassan.

Our aspiration is to emerge as a frontrunner in carbon reduction and attaining a state of zero environmental impacts. However, achieving this goal hinges significantly on the active participation of buyers and stakeholders in the overall process. The business leader emphasizes that ethical buying practices are imperative in this endeavor. It underscores the necessity for buyers and stakeholders to conscientiously engage in ethical purchasing practices as a crucial element in the larger mission of minimizing carbon footprint and fostering sustainability. This underscores the interconnected responsibility shared by all involved parties in collectively working towards a future with minimal environmental impact.

## 6. RECOMMENDATION

- The initiation of a robust green financing policy is paramount for achieving effectiveness and efficiency. A significant obstacle hindering the establishment of green industries in Bangladesh is the comparatively elevated interest rate for bank loans, currently peaking at 9% (as opposed to the conventional bank rate of 5% plus the highest additional 4%). To catalyze the expansion of green factories, there is an urgent need for a substantial reduction in interest rates for bank loans. This underscores the critical importance of swiftly addressing this issue to create a conducive financial environment that encourages and supports the development of environmentally sustainable industries.

- The expense associated with incorporating green initiatives in Bangladesh poses a significant challenge. To address this, there is a potential avenue for the government to explore. This involves considering the initiation of duty-free import policies for a diverse range of machinery and equipment specifically intended for establishing export-oriented green factories. Such a measure could prove instrumental in facilitating the effective adoption of green practices, particularly for medium and small industries. Additionally, another viable strategy is to provide tax abatement facilities for entrepreneurs involved in the green industry. By implementing these measures, the government can actively contribute to fostering a more financially viable and supportive environment for the development of sustainable and environmentally conscious initiatives.
- The potential for an increased number of green factories throughout the country, coupled with the establishment of an eco-industrial park, could be significantly enhanced if the government takes the initiative to allocate lands and utility services through economic zones or eco-friendly industrial zones. This proactive step would not only contribute to the growth of green initiatives but also lay the groundwork for a comprehensive eco-industrial park, aligning with sustainable practices and promoting environmental responsibility on a broader scale.
- The focus on environmental safety necessitates a more extensive development of central effluent treatment plants within factories, particularly within special economic zones. This strategic approach would contribute significantly to ensuring environmental sustainability and fostering a safer industrial landscape. By prioritizing the establishment and enhancement of central effluent treatment plants in special economic zones, there is a tangible opportunity to fortify environmental safety measures and align industrial practices with a broader commitment to ecological responsibility.
- To effectively carry out and advance green initiatives in Bangladesh, both the government and the financial sector need to work together. By offering incentives and creating a balance in the strictness of rules and regulations, they can motivate the growth of sustainable practices. This cooperative approach makes sure that there is a favorable environment that not only supports the adoption of green initiatives but also keeps a balance between the regulatory actions and the flexibility required for their effective implementation.
- The establishment of a comprehensive policy-based framework is essential for the formulation of a unified standard for the green industry. This structured approach is crucial to ensure that the industry experiences widespread growth on a national scale, guided by overarching national guidelines. By adopting a policy-oriented structure, there is an opportunity to create a framework that not only sets standards for the green industry but also fosters its flourishing development in alignment with a unified national vision.

## 7. BENEFITS AND JUSTIFICATION OF GREEN FACTORY IN BANGLADESH

While Bangladesh has already accepted certain green concepts, natural resources must be utilized ecologically and sustainably. Moreover, besides building a better brand image, green practices assist in achieving some advantageous factors outlined in this section (Reza et al., 2017).

1) **Social**: A green sector is especially welcoming regarding social issues since it helps alleviate poverty through economic growth and employment creation. In Bangladesh, for example, the plastic industry offers substantial employment opportunities through recycling, even though it is categorized as an informal sector. Formalizing this business in a green industry would create money, better working conditions, and more productivity.

In Bangladesh, there has been a rise in the adoption of solar installations in areas lacking conventional power sources, leading to positive social developments in low-income households. Furthermore, for rural communities, having access to renewable energy would imply reliance on oneself to care for one's family while being financially sound. This has a good influence on health; for example, greener cooking methods do not generate hazardous gases.

2) **Economic**: The economic benefits of a green industry stem from a company's enhanced business performance resulting from the adoption of environmentally friendly practices. This is because consumer requirements are put in the green business in such a way that it delivers a good view, a healthy ecology, and supports a sustainable future. Adopting a greener market creates more jobs, as evidenced by the energy business. Renewable energy consumption has created 3.5 million new employments in the market, compared to 2.5 million new jobs created by the oil and gas business.
3) **Environmental**: A more environmentally conscious industry has the potential to minimize resource consumption by optimizing the utilization of natural capital. This proves particularly advantageous as it helps offset any inefficiencies in the system and eliminates waste. Enhanced resource efficiency, i.e., more efficient energy, materials, and water use, allows for resource conservation. Impacts related to extraction and harvesting are reduced by lowering the demand for raw materials and using them more efficiently. For example, recycling waste materials into industrial production minimizes the need for virgin natural resource extraction and processing (Reza et al., 2017).

Even though many firms practice green businesses and sustainable management, the world is experiencing several climate change difficulties and setting worrying new records each year. This suggests that the firm should involve more of its departments in the greening process to make the notion viable. In that context, human resource management may also be used to achieve long-term sustainability. Appropriate greening of HRM systems may assist many firms in reducing their usage of environmentally unfriendly materials and adopting more sustainable ways of operating. Furthermore, various organizations' human resource management (HRM) may be essential in motivating employees to participate in climate change mitigation procedures and activities to make beneficial societal changes.

## 8. CONCLUSION

Climate change has severely influenced every country's economy, decreased GDP and dramatically raised health hazards for citizens. However, bearing the difficulties in mind, the policymakers and environmentalists collaboratively started focusing on mitigating carbon footprints in the environment. Bangladesh has achieved remarkable progress in 'greening' several industries, including RMGs, electronics, and cement. Furthermore, they concentrated on greening the manufacturing grounds and procuring sustainable raw materials and machinery. Surprisingly, these approaches will raise stakeholder awareness and lead to more sustainable practices across various enterprises, including green finance, green marketing, green supply chain, and green human resource management.

## ACKNOWLEDGEMENT

This article was written as a part of the "Green HRM as a tool to address Climate Change: Organizational Perspectives" project, which was funded by the Conference Travel and Research Grants Committee (CTRGC) of North South University, Dhaka, Bangladesh.

## CONFLICT OF INTEREST STATEMENT

- The author has no conflict of interest relevant to this article.

## DATA AVAILABILITY

Data sharing not applicable to this article as no datasets were generated or analysed during the current study

## REFERENCES


Ahmed, M. F., & Islam, M. S. (2014). Urbanization and environmental problem: An empirical study in Sylhet City, Bangladesh. *Research on Humanities and Social Sciences*, *4*(3), 161–172.

*AKH Group sets up new green factory in Bangladesh* |. (n.d.). YnFx. https://www.yarnsandfibers.com/news/textile-news/akh-group-sets-up-new-green-factory-in-bangladesh/amp/ application of the Ecological Footprint as environmental indicator in the textile sector.

Atasu, A., Sarvary, M., & Van Wassenhove, L. N. (2008). Remanufacturing as a Marketing Strategy. *Management Science*, *54*(10), 1731–1746. DOI: 10.1287/mnsc.1080.0893

bdnews24. (2017, May 8). Crown Cement, GPH Ispat sign deals on eco-friendly construction. *Bdnews24. Com*. https://bdnews24.com/business/crown-cement-gph-ispat-sign-deals-on-eco-friendly-construction

Bhattacherja, P., Islam, S., & Xeenia, F. T. (2020). *Green industry development in Bangladesh: Challenges and Prospects*. Tech Monitor.

Business, N. E. W. A. G. E. (2022, May 23). Grameenphone employees observe Green Week 2022. *New Age | the Most Popular Outspoken English Daily in Bangladesh*. https://www.newagebd.net/article/171318/grameenphone-employees-observe-green-week-2022

Chowdhury, S. H. (2022, March 13). Green Block: A journey towards eco-friendly construction. *The Business Standard*. https://www.tbsnews.net/economy/green-block-journey-towards-eco-friendly-construction-383986

Hossain, S. (2022, September 12). Bangladesh boasts 171 Leed-certified green RMG factories now. *Dhaka Tribune*. https://www.dhakatribune.com/business/2022/09/12/bangladesh-boasts-171-leed-certified-green-rmg-factories-now DOI: 10.1016/j.jhazmat.2007.12.077

Hühne, F. (2021, November 12). Why electronics cause climate change? *Syllucid B.V.*https://syllucid.com/blogs/news/this-is-a-recommended-blog-2

Marchant, N. (2021, June 28). This is How Climate Change Could Impact The Global Economy. *World Economic Forum*. https://www.weforum.org/agenda/2021/06/impact-climate-change-global-gdp/

Nayak, R., Singh, A., Panwar, T., & Padhye, R. (2019). A Review of Recent Trends in Sustainable Fashion and Textile Production. *Current Trends in Fashion Technology & Textile Engineering*, *4*(5). Advance online publication. DOI: 10.19080/CTFTTE.2019.04.555648

Paul, I., Bhole, G., & Chaudhari, J. (2014). A Review on Green Manufacturing: It's Important, Methodology and its Application. *Procedia Materials Science*, *6*, 1644–1649. DOI: 10.1016/j.mspro.2014.07.149

Reza, A. K., Islam, M. S., & Shimu, A. A. (2017). Green Industry in Bangladesh: An Overview. *Environmental Management and Sustainable Development*, *6*(2), 124. DOI: 10.5296/emsd.v6i2.11027

Saxena, A., & Srivastava, A. (2022). Industry Application of Green Manufacturing: A Critical Review. *Ournal of Sustainability and Environmental Management*, *1*(1), 32–45.

The Business Standard. (2022, August 2). Standard Chartered Bangladesh embraces sustainability as a way of life. *The Business Standard*. https://www.tbsnews.net/economy/corporates/standard-chartered-bangladesh-embraces-sustainability-way-life-469986?amp

The Business Standard. (2022, October 10). Singer's $78m green factory aims at growing local electronics market. *The Business Standard*. https://www.tbsnews.net/economy/industry/singers-78m-green-factory-aims-growing-local-electronics-market-511374

The Daily Star. (2017, February 13). Use eco-friendly materials in construction work. *The Daily Star*. https://www.thedailystar.net/city/eco-friendly-materials-construction-work-stressed-1360285

The Financial Express. (2020, April 15). BB introduces €200m green transformation fund. *The Financial Express*. https://thefinancialexpress.com.bd/trade/bb-introduces-200m-green-transformation-fund-1586956071

Tuhin, A. R. (2022, September 12). Fatullah Apparels turns into an iconic green factory. *The Business Post*. https://businesspostbd.com/back/fatullah-apparels-turns-into-an-iconic-green-factory-2022-09-13

Uddin, J. (2019, August 27). Envoy of green textiles. *The Business Standard*. https://www.tbsnews.net/economy/envoy-green-textiles

# Chapter 12
# Talent Management as a Pillar of Sustainable HRM in the V4 Region

**Helena Markova**
https://orcid.org/0009-0003-9235-530X
*School of Business Administration in Karviná, Silesian University in Opava, Czech Republic*

**Sampras Femi Robert**
https://orcid.org/0009-0002-7272-7543
*School of Business Administration in Karviná, Silesian University in Opava, Czech Republic*

## ABSTRACT

*Talent management is a key element of sustainable HRM, crucial for long-term organizational success. In the Visegrád Four (V4) region—Czech Republic, Slovakia, Poland, and Hungary—talent management remains underutilized, often overshadowed by short-term HR functions. This study explores its role in fostering economic, social, and environmental sustainability. Findings highlight low investment in training, challenges in talent retention, and a lack of structured development programs. Organizations risk higher turnover, reduced innovation, and weaker resilience. Integrating talent management with sustainability goals can enhance workforce stability, diversity, and green HRM practices. Recommendations include increasing awareness, investing in training, leveraging data-driven HR strategies, and fostering cross-sector collaboration. Strengthening talent management in the V4 region is essential for competitive, sustainable growth in a dynamic global market.*

## INTRODUCTION

Talent management, which is essential for discovering, developing, and maintaining talented workers who boost corporate performance and success, is the foundation of HRM. The strategic approach links human resources to an organization's goals. This boosts productivity, innovation, and firm competitiveness. Talent management includes HR duties like recruitment, training, development, and succession

DOI: 10.4018/979-8-3373-0189-1.ch012

planning. This feature is increasingly important to an organization's performance, as it affects everyday operations and strategic goals.

Human resource management (HRM) relies on talent management to identify and develop skills needed for growth and competitive advantage. Enhancing employee engagement helps retain key people and boost corporate success. Samuel and Isa (2024) show that talent management improves employee engagement and organizational success.

Effective personnel management is essential for leadership development. Selective recruitment, ongoing training, and strong retention can help organizations develop future leaders. People management techniques that include diversity, inclusion, and innovative technologies attract top people and create a more dynamic, open-minded workplace. 2024 (Nurmala, Hermina). This complete approach helps companies react to market conditions and stay competitive.

Succession planning, which prepares internal candidates for key leadership roles, is integral to talent management. This proactive approach reduces leadership transition risks and aligns talent plans with long-term sustainability goals. Prioritizing succession planning ensures well-trained internal candidates are appointed to leadership jobs. This prevents problems and maintains strategy. (2024, Samuel and Isa).

Global talent management identifies important positions and develops highly potential candidates. Global corporations get a sustainable competitive advantage. Global talent management is essential for foreign companies to compete globally. 2024 (Collings and Conroy). A deep understanding of varied commercial and cultural traditions and the capacity to implement global strategies are necessary.

Despite the importance of personnel management for organizational performance, finding and keeping good hires in a competitive labor market is difficult. These difficulties require organizations to adapt their talent management methods to market conditions and optimize human resources. Talent management strategies must adapt to market changes to sustain development and success. (2024) Raut and Collings and Conroy.

Digital change and economic globalization create major challenges and opportunities for talent management in the Visegrád Four (V4) region, which includes the Czech Republic, Hungary, Poland, and Slovakia. Technology is advancing rapidly in this region. Human capital management must be strategic to preserve competitiveness and innovation. V4's changing environment presents talent management problems and an opportunity to boost organizational success.

Digital technology accelerates the V4 skills gap. Continuous learning and development are needed to close this gap and adapt to technology advances (Fortunisa et al., 2024; Sinulingga, 2024). People often oppose new technologies and methods, making talent management difficult (Fortunisa et al., 2024.02). The region's strict labor laws and complex legal frameworks may also restrict flexible workforce management, especially in industries like automotive that must adapt to demand changes (Polekar & Lodha, 2024).

Talent management has several potentials in the digital age. Sinulingga et al. (2024) suggest using AI-driven employment tools and data analytics to find and schedule eligible individuals. To increase talent pool and worker flexibility, remote work and virtual collaboration solutions are increasing popularity (Палярс́ук, 2024). This can boost employee happiness and retention.

IT companies in Romania demonstrate the importance of talent management for long-term success. Strategic talent management offers many employment and innovation prospects in this company. Tamas (2024).

The V4 region has corporate and social issues. Youth unemployment affects the quest for competent workers. Many young people are eager to relocate for work, making it difficult to retain talented people in the area (Kulakova et al., 2021). The rapid evolution of Industry 4.0 requires people to learn advanced digital capabilities. This requires talent management that emphasizes constant learning and technological adaptation. (2024, Firdaus and Ambar Wati).

Talent management helps HRM become more sustainable by aligning economic aims with social and environmental goals. Businesses create a culture of environmental stewardship that boosts viability and competitiveness by hiring, retaining, and developing sustainable employees. This link is essential for turning HR tasks into economic and environmental benefits.

Green HRM practices, which include sustainability in recruiting and training, are essential for fostering ecologically responsible behavior. Sustainable talent management can boost an organization's environmental reputation and commitment to sustainability by attracting eco-conscious employees. (2024 Pilania).

Green HRM goals are met by using AI tools to reduce waste and optimize energy use in HR processes. Data-driven decisions are made easier with AI-driven talent management. This makes sustainable HR operations more efficient and effective, helping organizations meet their sustainability goals more precisely (John & Pramila, 2024).

Talent management is essential for sustainable performance by ensuring the right people manage creation and productivity. When combined with Total Quality Management (TQM), effective people management can improve sustainability in medium-sized businesses. This shows how integrated strategies can boost company synergies. (Yücel, 2024).

Leadership continuity and organizational stability are necessary for success; hence succession planning is critical in people management. Integrating people management with succession planning ensures smooth transfer and long-term success, preparing firms for future issues and maintaining their competitive edge. (2024, Samuel and Isa).

Sustainable human resource management requires a careful balance of short-term costs and long-term rewards due to the lack of a clear procedure. Including sustainability goals in human management boosts a company's performance and longevity.

Integrating HR operations with sustainability goals improves recruiting, training, and retention, leading in more engaged and productive employees. When integrated with sustainability goals, sustainable talent management improves financial performance. Singh and Bhatnagar (2023; Breez and Jaradat, 2024).

Talent management and sustainability must be integrated to create a workforce that can adapt to technological advances and meet oil and gas industry expectations. This harmony helps businesses navigate today's difficult business climate. (Indrawati et al., 2024)

Sustainable HRM methods, especially in recruitment, can cut costs and improve personnel management. Technology and information systems improve these processes, reducing environmental, social, and economic consequences (Koman et al., 202).

Integrating people management with sustainability raises various issues. The long-term benefits, such as improved financial and operational performance, often outweigh these short-term hurdles, making this alignment essential for innovative organizations.

## 1. THE CRITICAL ROLE OF TALENT MANAGEMENT IN SUSTAINABLE HRM

Sustainable Human Resource Management (HRM) is a developing idea that impacts modern corporate practices by incorporating economic, environmental, and social aspects into workforce management. This integration seeks to improve organizational efficiency and sustainability performance while ensuring that the workforce favorably impacts broader environmental and societal results. This section examines the fundamental elements of sustainable HRM, its importance in modern business, and the obstacles businesses encounter in its execution.

Sustainable HRM involves integrating sustainability ideas into conventional HR operations, including recruitment, training, performance management, and employee engagement. This strategy guarantees that HR practices align with and actively promote the organization's sustainability objectives. By integrating eco-friendly factors into recruitment and training processes, firms promote environmental stewardship among employees (Sagandykova et al., 2024). Likewise, the triple bottom line approach in sustainable HRM prioritizes economic returns alongside environmental conservation and social equality, promoting a comprehensive strategy for company sustainability (Kutaula et al., 2024).

The implementation of sustainable HRM practices provides several advantages for firms aiming to maneuver through the complexity of the global market. These strategies augment organizational resilience by cultivating a culture firmly rooted in sustainable principles, hence enhancing employee motivation and overall organizational performance (Sagandykova et al., 2024). Moreover, sustainable HRM assists organizations in achieving their environmental goals via Green HRM practices, which diminish the ecological imprint of the firm and enhance overarching sustainability objectives (Zournatzidou et al., 2024). Furthermore, by prioritizing social responsibility and stakeholder involvement, sustainable HRM improves an organization's reputation and builds trust, essential for enduring success (Ahmad et al., 2024).

Notwithstanding its advantages, the implementation of sustainable HRM presents certain problems. Organizations frequently face resource limitations and cultural opposition, which can impede the successful incorporation of sustainable practices within HR responsibilities. Addressing these obstacles necessitates a strategic commitment from leadership and a unified effort to synchronize HR initiatives with the organization's long-term sustainability objectives (Shahrulnizam et al., 2024). Moreover, a frequent conflict exists between fulfilling short-term financial targets and long-term sustainability objectives, requiring a balanced strategy in planning and implementation (Ahmad et al., 2024).

Sustainable HRM has several advantages, although it also entails challenges in its execution. Organizations must address issues such as resource constraints and cultural opposition to fully actualize the potential of sustainable HRM practices. The dynamic nature of sustainability necessitates ongoing adaptation and innovation in HR strategies to meet developing environmental and social expectations, allowing firms to utilize sustainable HRM to improve their resilience and flexibility in the contemporary corporate climate.

## 1.1 Role of Talent Management in Sustainable HRM

Talent management is essential to Sustainable Human Resource Management (HRM) by aligning human capital strategies with overarching sustainability objectives. This strategic alignment improves an organization's capacities in innovation, adaptability, and competitive advantage, which are essential for attaining sustainable business results. Efficient personnel management strategies, including talent attraction, retention, and development, are essential for building a workforce capable of maneuvering through the complexities of modern business. This section explores the foundational role of talent management in sustainable HRM and emphasizes its influence on organizational success.

Talent management is crucial for maintaining human capital by aligning the interests of the firm and its employees, hence promoting mutual value creation. Through the adoption of inclusive people management techniques, firms can reduce performance pressure and improve workplace equity, thereby significantly contributing to the sustainability of human capital in the long term (Yerlitas & Bučiūnienė, 2024).

Talent management is a strategic necessity for improving organizational performance and sustainability, especially in private companies. It is essential for succession planning by recognizing and developing internal talent for leadership roles, hence assuring organizational continuity and stability (Samuel & Isa, 2024).

Incorporating sustainability into human resources strategies, particularly talent management, is essential for realizing a triple bottom line: economic performance, environmental stewardship, and social accountability. Sustainable HR strategies improve employee engagement, promote environmental conservation, increase cost efficiency, hence encouraging long-term competitiveness (J. et al., 2024).

Moreover, personnel management significantly impacts sustainable performance, with process innovation serving as a moderator to amplify this link. In industries such as automotive, personnel management methods have demonstrated an enhancement in sustainable performance, underscoring the significance of innovation in talent strategies (Tunio, 2024).

Although talent management is vital for connecting human capital strategies with sustainability objectives, it is important to acknowledge possible problems, including excessive performance pressure and workplace inequalities. Organizations should pursue inclusive talent management approaches that align organizational goals with employee well-being to guarantee sustainable human capital growth (Yerlitas & Bučiūnienė, 2024).

Talent management methods are essential for attaining sustainability objectives in firms by connecting human capital strategies with long-term goals. These approaches emphasize the attraction, retention, and development of talent, which are crucial for promoting innovation, guaranteeing continuity, and strengthening organizational resilience. Integrating personnel management with sustainability objectives enables firms to cultivate a workforce that is both proficient and dedicated to sustainable practices, hence enhancing the organization's success and sustainability in modern business.

## 1.2 Talent Management Practices in the V4 Region

The economic and social contexts of the Visegrad Four (V4) nations—Czech Republic, Slovakia, Poland, and Hungary—substantially influence human resource practices. These factors arise from the distinct economic environments, labor market characteristics, and technological progress of each country. This section examines how these elements combined influence HR activities, frequently redirecting attention towards short-term HR practices rather than strategic long-term personnel management. The discourse will elucidate the problems and opportunities inherent in these environments, highlighting the necessity for customized personnel management techniques.

The V4 nations, recognized for their modest innovation performance, display differing levels of economic integration and technological proficiency. The Czech Republic excels in innovation, closely succeeded by Slovakia and Poland, with Hungary lagging marginally behind. This ranking greatly affects their capacity to respond to swift changes and sustain competitiveness in the global market (Hanáčková & Takáč, 2024). Economic inequalities, exemplified by Slovakia's alignment with the Eurozone, distinctly influence regional economic integration, hence significantly impacting HR practices and labor market dynamics (Aliu et al., 2023).

The labor market in the V4 nations is defined by SMEs that prioritize diverse HR practices to maintain viability and competitiveness. Czech enterprises emphasize enhancing staff credentials, Slovak firms prioritize incentive structures, while Polish SMEs focus on human capital and performance assessments. Conversely, Hungarian SMEs exhibit no substantial influence from HRM determinants on their market activities, suggesting varied priorities and tactics throughout the region (Belás et al., 2024). Moreover, corporate ethics, influenced more by the individual traits of firm proprietors than by industry-specific elements, indicate a consistent ethical framework across diverse sectors, uniformly impacting HR practices throughout the V4 (Belás et al., 2024).

Although acknowledging the significance of innovation and human capital, a discernible tendency exists in the V4 countries towards the inadequate utilization of comprehensive people management techniques. The underutilization is apparent in the focus on immediate HR activities like performance assessments and incentive systems, frequently to the detriment of long-term talent development plans (Belás et al., 2024; Hanáčková & Takáč, 2024). This inclination towards immediate benefits rather than long-term talent strategy highlights a considerable obstacle in promoting sustainable growth and innovation in the region.

The economic expansion in the V4, propelled by higher education, is pivotal in influencing HR practices by guaranteeing a supply of trained workers that aligns with the requirements of technological advancements (Gruševá & Blašková, 2022). The swift incorporation of digital technologies, including AI and cloud systems, compels the modification of HR processes to improve efficiency and employee engagement (Hamidi et al., 2024; Reddy, 2024).

Innovations in human resources and strategic investments in sophisticated HR technologies are crucial for enhancing organizational performance, underscoring the necessity for agile workforce management and future-oriented leadership (Reddy, 2024). The execution of age-specific and inclusive human resource practices, shaped by national institutional and cultural frameworks, can either promote or obstruct these practices, creating an intricate setting for HR management in the V4 region (Napathorn, 2022). Even before the Covid 19 pandemic, and subsequently since, the need for quality workers has increased significantly. Given the right framework and conditions, talented employees/prospective leaders can move up the career ladder and turn their potential into individual and organizational success (Potháczky 2022). The available literature clearly supports this. Other research confirms that the global epidemic of Covid and its consequences have had a significant impact on talent management and its various methods (Vaiman et al., 2021).

Although the V4 countries exhibit certain similarities, including an emphasis on short-term HR practices and moderate innovation performance, their distinct economic and social environments result in divergent HR strategies. These variations highlight the need for region-specific strategies in talent management that can accommodate the unique economic and technical environments of each country. The amalgamation of strategic HR modifications with an awareness of local circumstances will be essential for improving the efficacy of talent management processes throughout the V4 region, hence supporting sustained organizational growth and competitiveness.

## 1.3 Comparative Analysis V4 Region to Other EU Regions in Talent management

The Visegrád Four (V4) region—Czech Republic, Slovakia, Poland, and Hungary—differs significantly from other EU regions in terms of talent management priorities, workforce structure, and labor market trends. Compared to Western Europe (e.g., Germany, France, Netherlands), where talent management is deeply integrated into corporate strategy, V4 countries still focus heavily on operational HRM activities rather than long-term workforce planning (Eurofound, 2021).

### 1.3.1 Key Differences in Talent Management Across EU Regions

Western Europe generally offers higher salaries, stronger benefits, and more comprehensive talent retention programs, while the V4 region experiences significant brain drain, with skilled professionals relocating to Western EU countries for better opportunities (OECD, 2022).

Nordic and Western European countries emphasize lifelong learning and continuous upskilling, whereas in V4 countries, investment in employee training remains inconsistent, especially among SMEs (European Commission, 2023).

There are specifics of talent demand by industry. The V4 region is heavily dependent on manufacturing, automotive, and industrial sectors, which require strong vocational training and technical expertise (Collings et al., 2022). In contrast, Western and Northern Europe have a greater emphasis on IT, finance, and high-tech industries, leading to a demand for digital and knowledge-based skillsets (OECD, 2023). Southern European nations (Spain, Italy, Greece) experience higher unemployment rates, particularly among younger workers, making talent retention a key challenge (Eurostat, 2022). These differences highlight the need for V4 countries to adopt more strategic talent management approaches, particularly in high-tech and service-oriented industries, to remain competitive within the EU labor market.

These differences highlight the need for V4 countries to adopt more strategic talent management approaches, particularly in high-tech and service-oriented industries, to remain competitive within the EU labor market.

## 1.4 Industry-Specific Talent Management Trends in the V4 Region

Talent management strategies vary significantly across industries in the V4 region.

- Manufacturing & Automotive: Due to the region's strong industrial base, there is a growing need for technically skilled workers. However, talent shortages and automation trends are forcing companies to invest in vocational education, AI-driven workforce planning, and employee upskilling programs (Šipikal et al., 2022).
- Information Technology & Digital Economy: The IT sector in the V4 region is expanding, particularly in Poland and the Czech Republic, which serve as outsourcing hubs for global tech companies. However, retaining skilled software developers remains a challenge due to higher salary offers in Western Europe (Pereira & Patel, 2022).
- Healthcare & Life Sciences: The public healthcare system faces severe staffing shortages, with a high rate of migration among doctors and nurses moving to countries with better pay and working conditions (World Bank, 2023).

- Financial Services: HR practices in finance are evolving toward hybrid work models and AI-driven HR analytics, especially in banking and fintech sectors in Warsaw and Prague (KPMG, 2022).
- Green Energy & Sustainability: As EU sustainability goals drive demand for green jobs, talent management strategies must integrate new competencies in environmental science, renewable energy, and circular economy principles (Jabbour et al., 2023).

Companies across industries must align talent strategies with digital transformation, sustainability initiatives, and employee well-being programs to remain resilient and competitive.

## 1.5 Labor Regulations and Government Incentives Affecting HRM in the V4 Region

Labor laws and government policies play a crucial role in shaping HRM and talent management strategies in the V4 region.

V4 countries have less rigid labor laws than Western Europe, allowing for easier hiring and firing processes. However, temporary contracts and gig economy jobs are increasing, creating challenges in job security and employee benefits (European Labour Authority, 2023).

V4 countries have **lower wages** than Western Europe, but governments are gradually raising minimum wages to reduce income disparities and retain skilled workers (Eurostat, 2022).

**Labor flexibility** varies in V4 countries: Poland and Hungary have relatively longer working hours, whereas the Czech Republic and Slovakia enforce stricter overtime regulations (OECD, 2023).

National programs in Poland and the Czech Republic offer **funding for digital skills training, vocational education, and technical apprenticeships** (European Commission, 2023).

Companies that invest in employee training and professional development receive **tax reductions** in Slovakia and Hungary (World Bank, 2023).

EU-Funded HR Initiatives are used but not equaly in sectors. V4 countries benefit from EU structural funds for workforce development, particularly in tech and sustainable industries (Jabbour et al., 2023).

Despite these policies, bureaucratic challenges and inconsistent implementation hinder the effectiveness of government-backed HRM initiatives, requiring more streamlined support systems for businesses investing in talent development.

## 1.6 Impact of Crises on Workforce Mobility & HRM Flexibility

The COVID-19 pandemic, geopolitical instability, and economic uncertainty have had a profound impact on HRM and talent management in the V4 region.

COVID-19 helped workforce adaptation and remote work acceleration. The pandemic forced a rapid shift to digital work environments, particularly in IT and financial services (Deloitte, 2022).

Because hospitals struggled to retain staff, leading to an increased demand for international recruitment and telemedicine solutions (World Bank, 2023).

Upskilling & Digital Training: Companies increased investment in virtual learning platforms to adapt to the new work environment (KPMG, 2022).

V4 the same as the other countries of Europe met with the impact of geopolitical instability caused by Russia agression in Ukraine. The V4 region has experienced significant refugee inflows, with many Ukrainian workers joining local labor markets, particularly in Poland and the Czech Republic (European Labour Authority, 2023). Rising energy costs have affected manufacturing jobs, leading companies to restructure HR policies for cost efficiency (OECD, 2023).

According to above mentioned critical moments businesses had to do changes in HRM strategies diversifying recruitment channels and expanding cross-border hiring strategies to mitigate labor shortages (Collings et al., 2022).

These crises have reinforced the importance of adaptable HRM practices, urging companies in the V4 region to build workforce resilience through talent agility, digital transformation, and crisis-preparedness strategies.

## 1.7 Challenges and Opportunities for Sustainable HRM in the V4

The shift to sustainable Human Resource Management (HRM) practices in the Visegrád Four (V4) nations involves a complicated interaction of difficulties and opportunities. The incorporation of sustainable practices into Human Resource Management is essential for improving corporate sustainability and environmental accountability. Organizations encounter numerous challenges, such as resource limitations, cultural opposition, and the necessity for strategic coherence. This section examines these difficulties comprehensively and delineates prospects for enhancement via novel HRM practices and technical progress.

### 1.7.1 Challenges in Adopting Sustainable HRM

**Resource Limitations:** Numerous companies, particularly in industries with low profit margins like agriculture, face financial constraints that hinder their capacity to invest in sustainable human resource management techniques. These limitations are especially evident in sectors where financial resources for sustainable initiatives are limited, hindering the prioritization of long-term sustainability over short-term financial gains ("Sustainable HRM practices in the agriculture industry: Challenges and Opportunities," 2023).

**Cultural Resistance:** Opposition to change is a common obstacle in multiple areas, including education and agriculture. Deep entrenched procedures and conventional mindsets can substantially hinder the implementation of innovative, sustainable HRM strategies. This cultural resistance frequently arises from insufficient awareness or comprehension of the advantages linked to sustainable behaviors (Abhisha & Melvin, 2024).

**Leadership Commitment:** The successful implementation of Green HRM (GHRM) practices necessitates strong commitment from leadership. In the absence of active engagement from senior management and alignment with business goals, sustainable HRM efforts may fail. Leaders are essential in advocating sustainability efforts and embedding them inside the business culture (Shahrulnizam et al., 2024).

**Measurement Challenges:** A notable obstacle is quantifying the effects of green projects. Organizations frequently encounter difficulties in developing standardized measures to assess the efficacy of GHRM activities, which can impede the optimization and validation of these programs (Abhisha & Melvin, 2024).

**Workforce Mobility and Retention Issues:** One of the most pressing HRM challenges in the V4 region is the increasing outflow of skilled labor to Western European countries. The brain drain phenomenon, particularly in sectors such as healthcare, IT, and engineering, has created severe workforce shortages (OECD, 2023). While Western European countries provide higher salaries and better working conditions, many V4 companies struggle to retain top talent due to limited career advancement opportunities and lower wages (Eurostat, 2022).

**Limited Integration of Strategic Talent Management:** Despite the growing awareness of strategic HRM, many businesses in the V4 region still focus on short-term, reactive HR practices rather than proactive, sustainability-driven talent management (European Commission, 2023). SMEs, in particular, lack the financial resources and HR expertise to develop long-term workforce planning strategies, leading to high employee turnover and skill shortages.

**Rigid Labor Regulations and Bureaucracy:** While V4 countries have more flexible labor laws compared to Western Europe, bureaucratic inefficiencies and inconsistent policy implementation create obstacles for HRM innovation (European Labour Authority, 2023). Employment protection laws in some industries limit workforce adaptability, while temporary contracts and gig economy employment trends raise concerns about job security and sustainability.

**The Impact of Crises on HRM Resilience:** The COVID-19 pandemic and geopolitical tensions, such as the Russia-Ukraine war, have significantly disrupted workforce mobility, hiring practices, and employee well-being in the V4 region.

The shift to remote and hybrid work models has challenged traditional HR policies, particularly in manufacturing and service industries (Deloitte, 2022).

The influx of Ukrainian refugees has added complexity to labor markets, creating both opportunities for talent integration and challenges in workplace adaptation (European Labour Authority, 2023).

The energy crisis and inflation have forced many organizations to restructure workforce strategies, leading to layoffs and hiring freezes (OECD, 2023).

### 1.7.2 Opportunities for Improvement

**Technological Advancements:** The emergence of digital transformation offers new possibilities for innovative HR solutions, including remote monitoring and data-driven decision-making. These technologies can enhance sustainable HRM practices by enhancing efficiency and facilitating more accurate management of human resources ("Sustainable HRM practices in the agriculture industry: Challenges and Opportunities," 2023).

**Green recruiting and Training:** The implementation of green recruiting and training initiatives can attract environmentally aware people and cultivate a culture of sustainability inside enterprises. These actions boost the organization's environmental impact and increase its appeal to potential employees who prioritize sustainability (Abhisha & Melvin, 2024).

**Rising Demand for Ethical Practices:** There is a rising consumer demand for ethically manufactured goods and services, which offers a financial incentive for firms to implement sustainable HRM practices. This trend moves firms to synchronize their operations with overarching environmental and social objectives, potentially resulting in enhanced profitability and market share ("Sustainable HRM practices in the agriculture industry: Challenges and Opportunities," 2023).

The shift to sustainable HRM practices in the V4 countries encounters considerable obstacles, however the potential advantages and prospects for enhancement are considerable. Organizations can utilize technical improvements and match their plans with sustainability objectives to overcome these challenges. Highlighting leadership dedication and cultivating a culture receptive to change are crucial for establishing an environment that supports sustainable HRM practices. By addressing these issues and utilizing the available opportunities, firms can improve their resilience and adaptability in a progressively competitive and environmentally aware business environment.

### 1.7.3 Future Implications for HRM in the V4 Region

To fully capitalize on sustainable HRM opportunities, companies and policymakers in the V4 region must:

- Strengthen workforce planning by integrating predictive HR analytics and AI-driven talent management solutions.
- Enhance training and upskilling programs in key areas such as digital skills, sustainability, and leadership development.
- Encourage policy reforms to reduce bureaucratic inefficiencies and enhance labor market flexibility.
- Promote diversity and inclusion in HRM strategies to integrate migrant workers and build more resilient talent pipelines.
- Support innovation in HR technology by incentivizing businesses to adopt AI-driven HRM systems, virtual learning platforms, and digital talent acquisition tools.

By addressing these challenges and leveraging opportunities for strategic workforce development, organizations in the V4 region can build a more resilient, adaptable, and competitive labor market aligned with global sustainability goals.

## 1.8 Aspects of Talent Management for Sustainability

Talent management is essential for maintaining organizational sustainability and improving employee retention. By connecting strategic practices with long-term objectives, businesses ensure the successful development and retention of essential personnel while also facilitating critical activities such as succession planning and the establishment of a sustainable work environment. This section examines how different aspects of talent management enhance organizational sustainability and strengthen employee loyalty and retention rates.

### 1.8.1 Sustainability and Talent Retention

Succession planning is an essential component of strategic people management, crucial for ensuring continuity and stability within the business. By methodically identifying and cultivating internal candidates for prospective leadership positions, organizations reduce risks linked to leadership transitions.

This promotes organizational sustainability and guarantees that leadership competencies develop in accordance with the organization's long-term objectives (Samuel & Isa, 2024).

An inclusive people management strategy aligns company and employee interests, establishing a culture of mutual value development. This technique reduces performance pressure and promotes workplace equity, essential for employee well-being and long-term retention (Yerlitas & Bučiūnienė, 2024). By emphasizing inclusiveness, firms can create a welcoming workplace that appreciates and effectively utilizes varied skills.

Sustainable recruitment strategies are essential for incorporating sustainability into human resource management. These approaches utilize information systems to enhance recruitment procedures, therefore minimizing the environmental and cost repercussions linked to conventional recruitment methods. Effective people management via sustainable recruitment is crucial for reducing expenses and maintaining long-term staff retention (Koman et al., 2024).

Efforts to improve social sustainability in the workplace substantially influence employee retention by strengthening social capital among personnel. These programs cultivate a supporting network within the organization, enhancing loyalty and improving overall retention rates. A socially sustainable workplace environment is essential for favorable organizational outcomes (Siddiqui et al., 2024).

The Ability, Motivation, Opportunity (AMO) theory provides a significant foundation for incorporating personnel management into comprehensive organizational sustainability initiatives. Organizations can enhance sustainable performance and increase retention by augmenting employees' skills, offering incentive, and facilitating growth opportunities. This comprehensive approach guarantees that personnel management practices significantly advance the organization's sustainability goals (Tunio et al., 2023).

Talent management is vital for promoting sustainability and improving retention; yet it is important to balance exclusive and inclusive strategies to prevent excessive pressure on high achievers. Organizations must pursue comprehensive policies that prioritize the welfare of all employees and ensure equitable possibilities. By adopting these approaches, firms may guarantee that talent management aligns with organizational objectives while also benefiting individuals' aspirations, thus minimizing turnover costs and strengthening organizational stability.

Efficient retention techniques are essential for reducing the expenses linked to the continual recruitment and training of new personnel. By concentrating on enhancing work satisfaction and organizational commitment, firms can markedly decrease turnover rates. This reduces recruitment and training costs but also sustains productivity and service quality across several sectors. Establishing a constructive organizational culture and enhancing employee motivation through suitable recognition and support systems are crucial for cultivating a stable and dedicated team.

### 1.8.2 Diversity and Inclusion

Leadership commitment is vital in promoting diversity, equality, and inclusion (DEI) efforts inside a business. When senior management focuses and endorses DEI, it establishes a standard that promotes a culture in which diversity is esteemed, and inclusion is standard practice. This entails offering cultural competency training to all employees, which is crucial for cultivating an environment where varied perspectives are recognized and appreciated, hence promoting effective collaboration throughout the organization (Samuel et al., 2024).

Diversity and inclusion initiatives are fundamentally connected to employee engagement. Organizations that actively endorse these principles are likely to recruit and retain top-tier talent, hence improving overall workplace engagement. Employee Resource Groups (ERGs) play a crucial role by offering a platform for employees to share their experiences, connect through common backgrounds, and advocate for their needs, thus enhancing their sense of belonging and commitment to the organization (Samuel et al., 2024).

In globalization, the management of talent on a worldwide scale is becoming progressively essential. Effective global talent management involves acquiring, developing, and retaining different talent pools essential for maintaining a competitive advantage in the international market. Diverse and inclusive management strategies promote resource sharing and collaborative innovation, resulting in substantial enhancements in organizational performance (Baporikar, 2024; Xu, 2024).

Notwithstanding the evident advantages, advancing diversity and inclusion through talent management encounters enduring obstacles, including underrepresentation and institutional discrimination. These concerns require ongoing evaluation and enhancement of solutions to guarantee they successfully mitigate such inequities. Integrating diversity and inclusion into the fundamental principles of an organization, as exemplified by companies is crucial for attaining sustained success and harmonizing with corporate values (Howell, 2024).

An inclusive and diverse workplace advances societal objectives like equality and cultural competence and markedly enhances business culture. This encourages innovation, augments problem-solving abilities, and supports employee engagement and retention. These elements are essential for organizational adaptation and coherence, guaranteeing sustained performance (Xu, 2024; Arvind & S, 2024).

The incorporation of diversity and inclusion in talent management poses several problems, although the opportunities and advantages it provides are significant. Organizations that proficiently manage this integration experience improved competitiveness and are more adept at responding to global market needs. Consequently, prioritizing inclusive personnel management techniques is essential for organizational success, sustainability, and cultivating a culture that reflects contemporary social ideals.

### 1.8.3 Skill Development for Sustainability

Skill development is widely acknowledged as a vital element of people management, particularly relevant in connecting staff competencies with business sustainability objectives. In the context of the post-pandemic period, firms are promptly restructuring their human resources to address skill deficiencies, improve employability, and conform to sustainable development goals (SDGs). These initiatives are crucial for firms aiming to prosper in the face of swift technical advancements and worldwide issues.

Skill development programs are essential for overcoming the gaps in organizational talent pools, particularly in areas experiencing rapid technological changes. In India, corporate social responsibility (CSR) initiatives have been vital in bridging these gaps by concentrating on the enhancement of both technical and interpersonal skills, thus augmenting the adaptability and versatility of the workforce ("Enabling Skill Development for a Sustainable Future", 2023).

The continual necessity for reskilling, upskilling, and even deskilling is essential for ensuring corporate survival and enhancing employability in sectors confronting technology obsolescence. Skill development programs are essential for preparing the workforce with the requisite abilities to address global challenges efficiently, particularly in the logistics and transport industries, which are at the forefront of technology integration and operational difficulties (Mathur, 2022).

Green Human Resource Management (GHRM) methods prioritize skill development as a fundamental element of sustainability strategies. These approaches underscore the necessity for tailored training and knowledge dissemination to ensure personnel are adequately equipped to advance the organization's sustainability goals. Moreover, skill development is intrinsically connected to the establishment of work positions that reduce environmental effect and promote ecosystem conservation, hence building a sustainable future (A.V, 2024; Mathur, 2022).

Notwithstanding its significance, skill development encounters considerable obstacles, including insufficient infrastructure and unsustainable public funding schemes, especially in emerging areas. These constraints highlight the necessity for innovative funding strategies and resilient infrastructure to facilitate the ongoing growth of a skilled workforce ("Sustainability of Public Financing of Skill Development Programs in India", 2023).

Skill development is essential for enabling employees to actively participate in sustainability-focused projects and adjust to new business models that emphasize resource efficiency, environmental stewardship, and creativity.

Crucial competencies for executing circular business models encompass innovation, operations management, and systems thinking. A comprehensive skill taxonomy highlights the necessity for a combination of general and specialized competences aligned with circular economic requirements (Hartley et al., 2023).

In domains like electric vehicle (EV) battery recycling, talent development improves resource efficiency and mitigates environmental damage. Education for Sustainable Development (ESD) is essential for providing the workforce with the requisite skills for efficient recycling and resource management (Chigbu, 2024).

Customized training programs and customized development activities under GHRM are essential for aligning employee competencies with sustainability objectives, enabling the incorporation of sustainable practices into daily operations (A.V, 2024).

The incorporation of skill development into talent management strategies poses several problems; nonetheless, the potential benefits for improving sustainability and employability are significant. Organizations must address these problems by cultivating a culture of continual learning and adaptation, ensuring their workforce remains competitive and equipped to fulfill the requirements of a sustainable future. The strategic integration of skill development with sustainability objectives strengthens organizational resilience and establishes organizations as leaders in sustainable business practices.

## 2 TALENT MANAGEMENT IN THE V4 COUNTRIES

The background of HR processes in Human Resource Management has a significant role in the life of organizations. In recent you the role of HRM has evolved from a tactical function to the role of a strategic partner. HR professionals are the part of top management with the crucial influence on setting the business goals an workforce strategy (Torrington et al., 2014, Carnet, 2023). Data and data analysis help HR professionals better understand employee behavior, expectations and performance and optimize HR strategies accordingly (Poor at al., 2024). Meanwhile, talent management and retention have become a key competitiveness priority: HR professionals need to find and retain talent and develop employees' professional and personal skills. HR professionals need to pay increasing attention to workplace culture and well-being, as employee satisfaction and well-being have a direct impact on performance and the success of the company, making strategic and conscious HR operations an expectation in the 21st century (Morley et al., 2021).

The members of the Visegrad Cooperation (V4) – the Czech Republic, Hungary, Poland and Slovakia – have a long historical and cultural heritage, which has many common characteristics (Brixiova, Li & Yousef, 2009; Astrov, 2019). The V4 countries are in a similar economic situation and have all experienced the challenges of the post-socialist transition. Their cooperation can help to promote economic development and increase competitiveness in the region. At the same time, they face several common challenges, such as demographic change, labor market challenges and improving economic competitiveness. Cooperation offers an opportunity to address and overcome these challenges in a coordinated way.

Cooperation of V4 countries in the field of HRM research has many forms. Sharing experiences and results from one country can help other countries to address HR challenges more effectively. Joint research enables the V4 countries to collect and analyze more data, which will provide a better overall understanding of HR phenomena. In addition, data from several countries can provide a more representative picture of HR trends and issues in the region. Through joint research and cooperation, the V4 countries can foster development and competitiveness in the field of HR in the Central European region, which can contribute to the economic growth and stability of the region (Poor et al., 2017).

## 2.1 Socioeconomic Situation in V4 countries

After the fall of the communist regime in 1989, the Visegrád Group countries (Czech Republic, Slovakia, Poland, and Hungary) underwent a significant political and economic transformation. The transition from a centrally planned economy to a market-oriented system was accompanied by structural reforms, market liberalization, privatization of state-owned enterprises, and integration into the global economy.

During the 1990s, the V4 countries faced economic turbulence, including high inflation, unemployment, and social disparities, but gradually managed to stabilize their economies. Their accession to the European Union in 2004 brought a substantial influx of foreign investments, improved infrastructure, and an overall rise in living standards. However, these nations continued to face challenges such as regional inequalities, demographic shifts, and political polarization.

Today, the V4 countries are dynamic economies with advanced industries, strong export orientation, and a growing service sector. However, they also confront new challenges, including digitalization, ecological transformation, and geopolitical instability.

### Selected socio-economic indicators

Table 1 shows the socio-economic indicators in the V4 countries and the EU

*Table 1. Socio-economic indicators*

| indicator | rok | CZ | HU | PL | SK | EU |
|---|---|---|---|---|---|---|
| **inhibitants** | **2023** | 10,9 | 9,8 | 19,2 | 5,45 | |
| **GDP (in %)** | **2022** | 0,03 | 0,08 | 0,07 | 0,04 | |
| | **2023** | 0,00 | -0,01 | 0,00 | 0,01 | |
| **unemployment (in %)** | **2023** | 0,04 | 0,05 | 0,04 | 0,02 | 0,06 |
| **minimum wage (EUR)** | **2023** | 710 | 578 | 746 | 700 | 1102 |
| **average wage (v EUR)** | **2023** | 1700 | 1300 | 1500 | 1400 | 2452 |

Source: Eurostat

## 2.2 Comparison of V4 Countries

### Wages and Employment Trends

- V4 countries have lower minimum and average wages compared to the EU average.
- Wages have grown significantly in the past five years due to economic expansion, inflation, and union pressure.
- The COVID-19 pandemic slowed wage growth temporarily, but post-pandemic recovery led to rapid increases, exceeding 10% in some cases.
- Despite wage growth, labor costs remain lower than in Western Europe, attracting foreign investments.

### Low Unemployment:

- The V4 region has consistently low unemployment, particularly in the Czech Republic (around 3%).
- Poland and Slovakia have slightly higher rates, but regional disparities exist, with rural areas experiencing higher unemployment.
- A major challenge remains the shortage of qualified workers in technical, IT, and industrial fields.

### Industrial Dependency:

- The V4 countries rely heavily on the manufacturing sector, particularly automotive and engineering industries.
- While providing economic stability and jobs, this dependency makes economies vulnerable to global market shifts.

### Foreign Investments and Outsourcing:

- V4 countries attract substantial foreign investments due to lower labor costs and a skilled workforce.

- Shared service centers, IT outsourcing, and logistics hubs are common, particularly in Poland and Hungary.
- A key challenge is the outflow of profits to foreign headquarters rather than reinvesting locally.

Labor Migration and Demographic Challenges:

- Many skilled workers have migrated to Western Europe, creating labor shortages in healthcare, engineering, and IT.
- Recently, rising wages and improved conditions have encouraged some workers to return.
- Immigration from Ukraine, Belarus, and Asia (Bangladesh, Mongolia, the Philippines) helps fill labor gaps.
- Aging populations and low birth rates pose long-term labor supply concerns.

## 2.3 Past, present and future challenges of HR practice in the V4 region

Human resources are becoming an activating factor for the development of companies. If we examine the genesis of the development of opinions on the position of people in the work process, we state that the philosophy of human resource management has changed when theory and practice have been formed in economics and management. More than thirty years have passed since the beginning of the process of transformation of the economies of the Eastern Bloc countries. According to some experts, it ends when the regulatory mechanism of the market economy can generate sustainable growth and when structural distortions attributable to the previous economic system are removed. The above-mentioned developments and changes led us to try to get to know the level of human resources management in companies in the V4 countries. Despite the many similarities, there are significant differences between countries in almost all indicators. From the HRM point of view, it is interesting to see what processes companies devote their time and effort to. These facts are the focus of this research project. The initial phase was already implemented in 2022 and it run until April 2024.

The research team involved scholars of Matej Bel University in Banská Bystrica, Silesian University in Opava, University of Szczecin and of Hungarian University of Agriculture and Life Sciences.

The project included workshops, collection of primary data, preparation of written materials and publication of results in business, professional and scientific periodicals.

The aim of the project was to compare HR processes that are implemented in companies in the V4 countries. The output of the project are recommendations for increasing the competitiveness of companies in the region on the labor market and for achieving optimal economic results.

For the purposes of the goal and outputs, the project was based on the collection of primary data. A questionnaire survey was carried out in companies that employed at least 1 employee in the V4 countries. A representative number of valid questionnaires was achieved in all countries. The questionnaire consisted of closed questions that mapped the approach to challenges within individual HR processes, strategic HR management, investments in HR, but also threats arising from economic and social developments. The questionnaire mapped in detail the implementation of individual HR processes in companies and the challenges that HR managers must face.

Within the primary data collection, answers were provided by 500 respondents from Poland, 832 from the Czech Republic, 384 from Slovakia and Hungary. Refer figure 1 for a country wise response overview followed by the Table 1 which shows the size of the companies included based on employees in the company.

*Figure 1. Number of respondents*

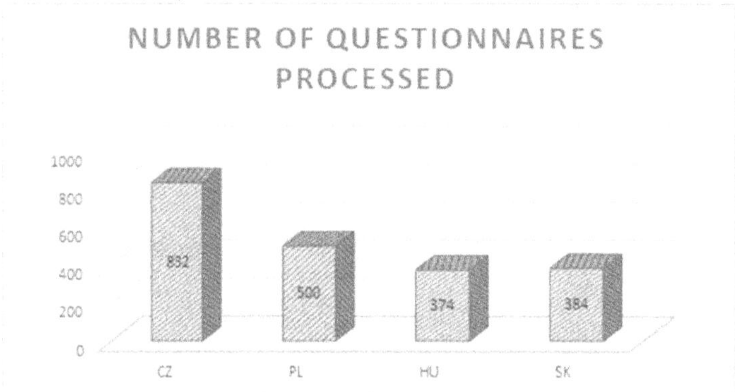


*Table 2. Size of the company*

| less than 10 employees | 10 to 49 employees | 50 to 249 employees | more than 250 empoloyees |
|---|---|---|---|
| 37,98% | 24,70% | 18,25% | 19,06% |

*Figure 2. Size of the company*

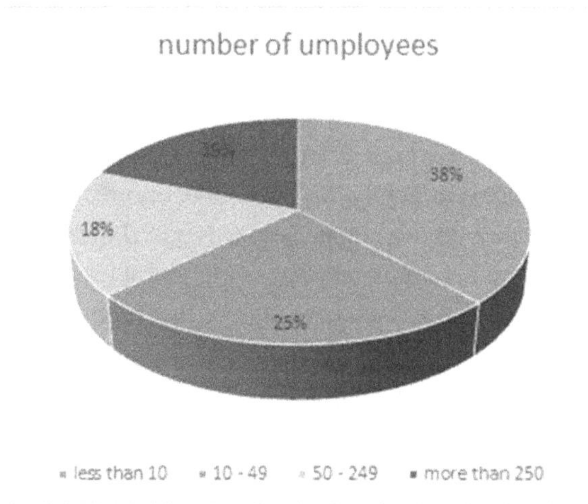

The pie chart shows the breakdown of company sizes among the survey respondents. The chart segments represent companies with fewer than 10 employees (18%), 10-49 employees (19%), 50-249 employees (25%), and more than 250 employees (38%). Figure 2 shows the distribution of company sizes among the survey respondents, segmented by the number of employees. The data showed that 48.3% of companies use HR strategies in management. The biggest challenges are activities such as recruitment and hiring caused by a lack of workforce, and in this context also activities aimed at retaining employees. The covid pandemic has affected the perception of priorities in terms of greater emphasis on the health aspects of employment.

After processing the data from the primary research, a panel discussion with practitioners took place on 15.12.2023.

The part of the panel discussion was focused on talent management in practice of the participants.

## 2.4 HR Challenges and Opportunities in the Visegrád Four: Balancing Short-Term Needs with Long-Term Growth

The economic and social contexts of the Visegrád Four (V4) nations—Czech Republic, Slovakia, Poland, and Hungary—substantially influence human resource practices. These factors arise from the distinct economic environments, labor market characteristics, and technological progress of each country. This section examines how these elements combined influence HR activities, frequently redirecting attention towards short-term HR practices rather than strategic long-term personnel management. The discourse will elucidate the problems and opportunities inherent in these environments, highlighting the necessity for customized personnel management techniques.

The V4 nations, recognized for their modest innovation performance, display differing levels of economic integration and technological proficiency. The Czech Republic excels in innovation, closely succeeded by Slovakia and Poland, with Hungary lagging marginally behind. This ranking greatly affects their capacity to respond to swift changes and sustain competitiveness in the global market (Hanáčková & Takáč, 2024). Economic inequalities, exemplified by Slovakia's alignment with the Eurozone, distinctly influence regional economic integration, hence significantly impacting HR practices and labor market dynamics (Aliu et al., 2023).

The labor market in the V4 nations is defined by SMEs that prioritize diverse HR practices to maintain viability and competitiveness. Czech enterprises emphasize enhancing staff credentials, Slovak firms prioritize incentive structures, while Polish SMEs focus on human capital and performance assessments. Conversely, Hungarian SMEs exhibit no substantial influence from HRM determinants on their market activities, suggesting varied priorities and tactics throughout the region (Belás et al., 2024). Moreover, corporate ethics, influenced more by the individual traits of firm proprietors than by industry-specific elements, indicate a consistent ethical framework across diverse sectors, uniformly impacting HR practices throughout the V4 (Belás et al., 2024).

Although acknowledging the significance of innovation and human capital, a discernible tendency exists in the V4 countries towards the inadequate utilization of comprehensive people management techniques. The underutilization is apparent in the focus on immediate HR activities like performance assessments and incentive systems, frequently to the detriment of long-term talent development plans (Belás et al., 2024; Hanáčková & Takáč, 2024). This inclination towards immediate benefits rather than long-term talent strategy highlights a considerable obstacle in promoting sustainable growth and innovation in the region.

The economic expansion in the V4, propelled by higher education, is pivotal in influencing HR practices by guaranteeing a supply of trained workers that aligns with the requirements of technological advancements (Gruševá & Blašková, 2022). The swift incorporation of digital technologies, including AI and cloud systems, compels the modification of HR processes to improve efficiency and employee engagement (Hamidi et al., 2024; Reddy, 2024).

Innovations in human resources and strategic investments in sophisticated HR technologies are crucial for enhancing organizational performance, underscoring the necessity for agile workforce management and future-oriented leadership (Reddy, 2024). The execution of age-specific and inclusive human resource practices, shaped by national institutional and cultural frameworks, can either promote or obstruct these practices, creating an intricate setting for HR management in the V4 region (Napathorn, 2022).

Although the V4 countries exhibit certain similarities, including an emphasis on short-term HR practices and moderate innovation performance, their distinct economic and social environments result in divergent HR strategies. These variations highlight the need for region-specific strategies in talent management that can accommodate the unique economic and technical environments of each country. The amalgamation of strategic HR modifications with an awareness of local circumstances will be essential for improving the efficacy of talent management processes throughout the V4 region, hence supporting sustained organizational growth and competitiveness

## 3 Findings

### What is Talent?

The research showed that 21.35% of companies in the V4 countries do not distinguish talented employees. This is an important signal that the majority of companies are aware of the importance of talent management activities, even in view of the increasing demand on employee maturity.

The highest response rate (41.39%) was obtained for the item “creativity”.

Hungary leads in this respect (70.56%), followed by Poland (45.00%), then the Czech Republic (28.37%) and Slovakia (21.61%).

Employee creativity is vital for economic growth as it fosters innovation and unique ideas, which are essential for organizational success. Creativity training programs enhance employees' working styles and habits, motivating them to perform at their best. By cultivating a creative environment, organizations can leverage employees' innovative capabilities, leading to improved problem-solving and adaptability in a competitive business landscape. Ultimately, this contributes to the long-term success and sustainability of the company (Lamichhane, 2024). Employee creativity is crucial for economic growth as it enables organizations to tap into the unique expertise and innovative potential of their workforce (Leible et al., 2024) and essential for companies to remain competitive (Salsabila & Mansyur, 2024).

The second most important aspect in terms of talent management was 'long-term stability' (38.03%), with Hungary also leading the way (62.60%), followed by Poland (36.00%), Slovakia (30.21%) and the Czech Republic (36.00%).The Czech Republic (23.32%). Long-term stability in the V4 countries has its roots in traditional management practices, where long-standing employees who stayed with one employer for their entire career were considered the most valued employees. This trend has changed significantly in recent decades. Lifelong learning opportunities allow employees to change career focus and achieve personal career goals in different areas through individual development, without being tied to one employer as in the past.

In third place, "long-term high performance" (35.56%) was highlighted under "long-term high performance". Hungary's privileged position was confirmed by the respondents' answers: 45.09% of respondents in Hungary emphasized the importance of "long-term high performance". In the Czech Republic, the Republic ranked second (36.66%), followed by Slovakia (34.90%) and Poland (25.60%). Long-term high performance is a product and an ideal goal that employees should achieve. Long-term high performance in organisations is intricately linked to effective talent management strategies. Talent management serves as a critical component in fostering environments where high performance can be sustained over time. This relationship is underscored by the need for strategic human resource practices, high-performance work systems, and succession planning to attract, develop, and retain talent. These elements collectively contribute to building a robust organizational framework that supports continuous improvement and competitive advantage.

## Talent Management Performance and Importance Across the V4 Region

Czechia exhibits the highest involvement in Talent Management (TM) practices, with 31.15% of firms participating and an average importance rating of 2.11 on a scale of 1 to 10, where 1 signifies the utmost priority. This indicates a deliberate focus of talent management within firms.

Hungary and Poland exhibit modest engagement, with TM performance rates of 10.02% and 12.76%, respectively. The average importance ratings are 3.81 for Hungary and 4.85 for Poland, suggesting a balanced albeit less concentrated approach relative to Czechia.

Slovakia has the lowest talent management performance and significance, with merely 10.26% of firms actively overseeing talent and an average importance grade of 4.53, indicating varying organizational priorities or maturity levels in talent management techniques. The disparities in TM performance and importance across the V4 are depicted in Figure 3.

*Figure 3. TM performance and importance*

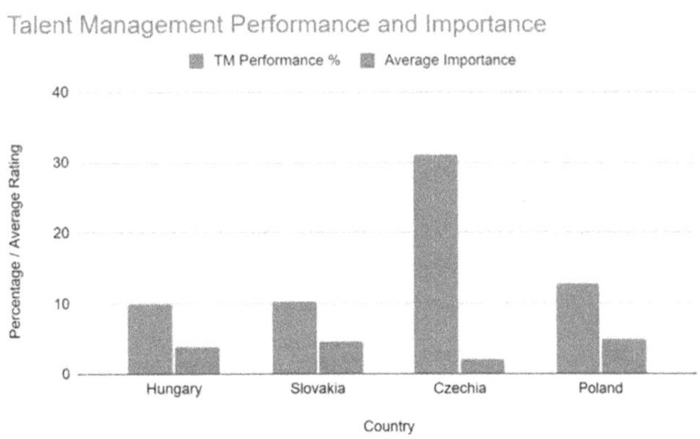

## Talent Management by Company Size

Small enterprises (fewer than 50 employees) exhibit diminished participation in talent management methods, with merely 23.7% using talent management initiatives. This may result from resource limitations or an emphasis on pressing operational issues. Figure 4 shows the variation in talent management adoption rates by company size, providing a visual representation of strategic engagement across different business scales

Medium-sized enterprises (50 to 249 people) demonstrate a TM adoption rate of 28.4%, and large enterprises (250 or more employees) display the highest involvement at 45.1%. This pattern indicates that as firms expand, the necessity and systematic methodology for personnel management become increasingly vital. These findings are also supported by the study of Savov et al (2020) focused on the implementation of talent management in Slovakia. The authors state that the size of the company significantly influences talent management processes. Larger enterprises tend to focus more on talent identification and development, use structured human resource plans and have greater resources to nurture talent. Conversely, small companies excel at talent retention because employees in these environments often exhibit higher loyalty and longer retention. This suggests that while larger companies can attract and develop talent more effectively, smaller companies are more successful at retaining talented employees.

*Figure 4. TM by company size*

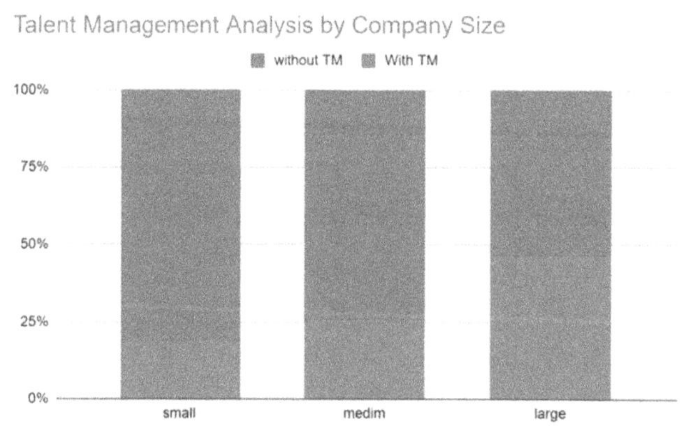


Studies around the world also work with similar conclusions, highlighting the specificities of small and medium-sized firms (Koppa et al, 2024). Business size has a significant impact on talent management, especially in small and medium-sized enterprises (SMEs). SMEs often face resource constraints and talent acquisition challenges, which can hinder their ability to attract and retain skilled workers. However, their smaller scale allows for a more individual approach to workforce development, which fosters a strong organizational culture. Despite these challenges, SMEs can leverage innovations in technology and strategic collaboration to increase their competitiveness and effectively manage talent.

Koppa et al. (2024), Talent management in small family business (2022), Atieno et al. (2023) point out the role of corporate culture, The relationship between talent management and corporate culture is multifaceted, with both elements playing a vital role in enhancing organizational performance and climate. Talent management involves acquisition, development and retention of skilled employees, while corporate culture encompasses the values, beliefs and behaviors that shape the organizational environment. Together, they create a synergistic effect that can significantly impact an organization's success. Thus, the strong influence of organizational culture can help small, especially family-owned, resource-constrained companies to create a favorable environment for talent management, acquisition and development.

## Influence of Market Presence on Talent Management

Analyzing the implementation of talent management (TM) across varying firm maturities in the Visegrad Four (V4) region reveals diverse patterns indicative of the developmental phases of these organizations. Established enterprises, defined as those with over 15 years in the market, exhibit a moderate commitment to talent management strategies, with around 25.77% actively engaging in talent management. This indicates a well-integrated approach to TM, likely due to long-standing HR frameworks and a deeper understanding of its strategic value over time. Figure 5 illustrates how TM adoption rates differ among companies based on their years active in the market.

*Figure 5. TM by years active in market*

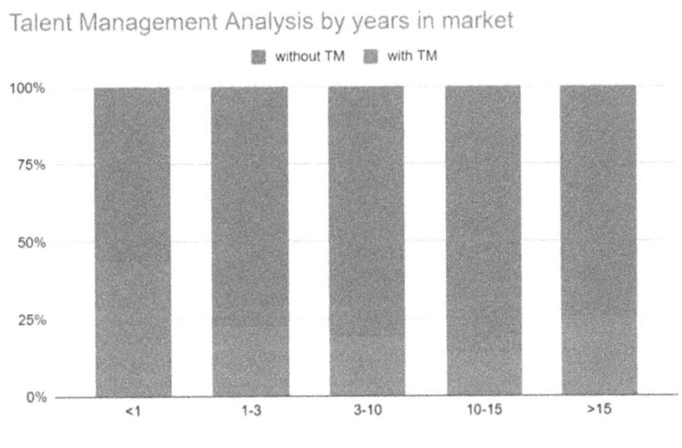


In contrast, the most recent enterprises in the market, established for less than one year, exhibit the greatest percentage of TM adoption at 44.00% as shown in figure 5. This could indicate that new firms are emphasizing personnel management as a core component of their company strategy from the outset, potentially motivated by the necessity to swiftly gain competitive advantages and react to market demands.

Nonetheless, for organizations aged 1 to 10 years, there is a discernible decrease in TM engagement. Firms aged 1-3 years demonstrate a 22.86% active TM rate, whereas those aged 3-10 years exhibit a reduced rate of 19.42%. This trend may indicate the transitional difficulties encountered by expanding enterprises as they scale operations and resources, potentially resulting in a temporary deprioritization of systematic talent management initiatives.

A similar pattern was found in Iscandarov (2018), Poltoratska (2021) and Köse (2018) studies, that working with talent has a significant impact on the market presence of the companies. Like the research on HRM in V4 countries, it was found that talent work is most practiced by companies that are just finding their place in the market, as they perceive the importance of the unique contribution of talented employees. Similarly, companies that have been in the market for more than 15 years and have defended their existence are more committed to talent work, which is also a significant factor in their sustainability.

## Impact of Ownership on Talent Management

The relationship between private or public ownership of companies and talent management is multifaceted, involving differences in strategic objectives, resource allocation, and organizational culture. Talent management is crucial for both private and public sectors, but the approach and impact can vary significantly depending on the ownership structure.

As shown in figure 6, private entities encompassing non-profit organizations, exhibit greater involvement in TM practices (37.6% active engagement) than public entities (21.4%). The adaptability and competitive demands of the private sector undoubtedly necessitate a heightened emphasis on talent as a critical resource. Figure 6 compares TM engagement between private and public entities, underscoring the strategic differences in their approaches.

Bureaucratic and regulatory constraints commonly linked to the public sector may hinder the implementation of flexible and proactive talent management techniques.

*Figure 6. TM by ownership*

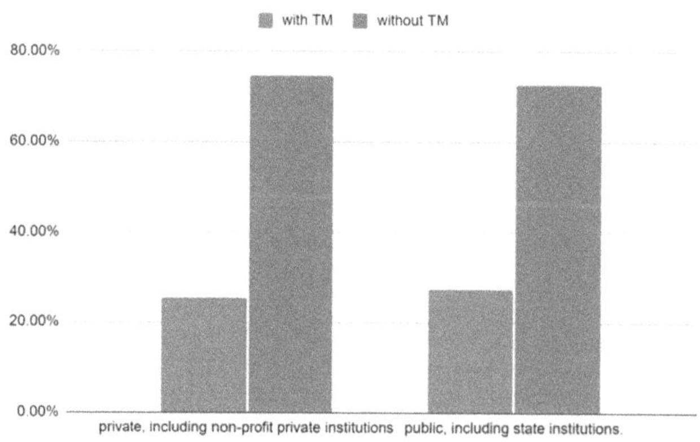


After 1989, a change in the social paradigm took place in all 4 countries, which brought with it significant changes in business ownership. Returns to the original owners and privatization have set a similar course over the last 35 years. Digitalization and automation then play a significant role in this area as well, with the state and public sector lagging the private sector in all countries. The one area where talent management is working well, albeit more out of necessity, is the healthcare sector. For the reasons mentioned above, the bulk of the health service delivery sector is provided within the public sector. Therefore, given the significant legislative regulation regarding continuing education, it is also good to work with staff development to maintain their skills in a rapidly evolving environment.

## Sector-Specific Importance of Talent Management

High-priority sectors such as Healthcare and Social Welfare demonstrate a significant average importance rating of 10.27, emphasizing the essential requirement for proficient workers to oversee complex and sensitive medical facilities. The sector's focus on personnel management is essential for upholding superior patient care and operational efficiency.

The High-Tech and Knowledge Intensive sector, encompassing industries like IT and Telecommunications, registers an average significance of 8.14. This signifies a substantial acknowledgment of talent management, particularly considering the swift technological progress and the necessity for ongoing innovation and a proficient staff in these domains.

Conversely, more traditional industries like Infrastructure & Construction, encompassing Transportation, possess a diminished average importance rating of 7.737. This indicates a diminished emphasis on talent management, perhaps attributable to the operational characteristics of the work, which may not necessitate continuous innovation as seen in high-tech settings.

The Education and Culture, and Tourism and Leisure sectors exhibit a significant valuation of talent management, with ratings of 8.435 and 9.455 respectively, underscoring the critical role of talented individuals in promoting educational advancement and enriching tourism experiences. Figure 7 provides a breakdown of talent management valuation by sector, highlighting areas of high and low strategic focus.

*Figure 7. TM by sector*

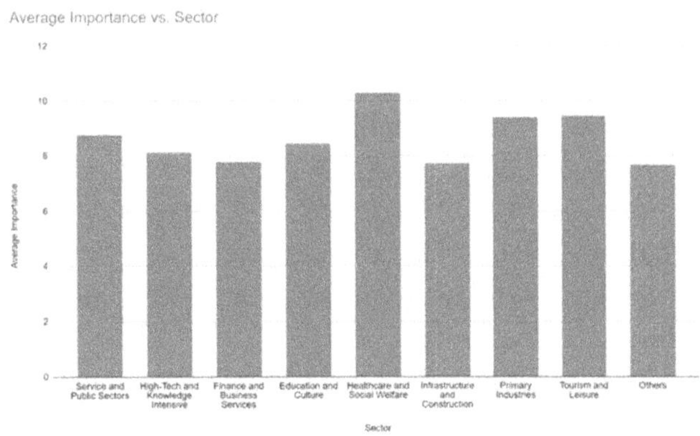

## 4 RECOMMENDATIONS FOR STRENGTHENING TALENT MANAGEMENT IN THE V4 REGION

Small and medium-sized enterprises frequently encounter resource limitations absent in larger firms. Creating scalable, tailored talent management solutions can enable SMEs to improve their human management practices effectively. Establishing a strong business culture that reflects key values may attract and retain people, aiding SMEs in addressing the challenge of constrained resources.

Industries such as IT, Engineering, and Healthcare, which prioritize talent management due to the essential role of qualified people, could gain from tailored training and development initiatives. Furthermore, sectors where TM is presently undervalued, including Trade and Post Services, ought to be incentivized by industry groups and chambers of commerce to use TM practices that can enhance innovation and efficiency.

Firms operating for less than a decade exhibit diverse levels of TM adoption. Raising awareness and offering startup-specific TM resources could assist these companies in implementing strong TM practices early in their development, which may be vital for their long-term success and stability.

The public sector and non-profit organizations exhibit diminished involvement in talent management methods. Governments and funding entities could provide incentives, including grants, awards, and recognition programs, to encourage the implementation of TM practices inside these organizations.

The incorporation of Talent Management (TM) into corporate strategy is more common among organizations with over 15 years in the market, indicating that such integration may be advantageous. Emerging organizations can adopt these techniques by including talent management strategies into their business development goals from the outset.

In all industries and scales, the application of technology in talent management—such as AI-powered HR tools, digital training platforms, and performance management systems—can improve the efficiency and efficacy of talent management procedures. This is especially crucial for enterprises in technologically sophisticated industries such as Telecommunications and IT.

Facilitate cross-sector collaboration via workshops, seminars, and roundtables, enabling enterprises to exchange best practices and gain insights from the talent management strategies of prominent firms in diverse industries. This may be especially beneficial in areas where specific sectors are deficient in TM practices.

Governmental support through policies that promote talent management techniques, especially in sectors vital to national growth, can establish a framework for enterprises to innovate and enhance their people management capabilities.

These guidelines seek to offer pragmatic ways that can assist V4 countries and their enterprises in enhancing their TM practices while also promoting general business success and economic advancement in the region.

## CONCLUSION

Talent management is a critical pillar of sustainable human resource management (HRM) in the Visegrád Four (V4) region, yet its implementation remains inconsistent across industries and company sizes. Despite growing recognition of its strategic importance, findings from the study indicate that many organizations still prioritize short-term HR activities such as recruitment and performance evaluation over long-term talent development. The lack of structured talent management programs leads to missed opportunities in employee retention, succession planning, and workforce sustainability.

## Potential Barriers to Implementation

Several barriers hinder the effective implementation of talent management in the V4 region:

**Financial and Resource Constraints** – Small and medium-sized enterprises (SMEs) often lack the necessary financial resources to invest in long-term talent development programs. This is especially evident in Hungary and Slovakia, where many businesses operate with limited HRM budgets.
**Limited Awareness and Strategic Integration** – Many companies, particularly in Poland and Slovakia, perceive talent management as a secondary HR function rather than an essential driver of business sustainability.
**Workforce Mobility and Labor Migration** – The study revealed significant talent outflows from the V4 region, particularly among highly skilled professionals in IT, healthcare, and engineering, contributing to labor shortages and increased recruitment costs.
**Demographic and Structural Challenges** – Aging populations, evolving workforce expectations, and the shift toward remote work demand new HR strategies that many organizations have yet to fully integrate.
**Digital Transformation and Technological Adaptation** – While digital transformation presents opportunities, it also creates resistance to change, as organizations struggle to upskill employees to meet evolving industry demands.

## Implementation Significance

Findings from the study underline that companies with strong talent management strategies outperform those that neglect them in key areas such as employee retention, innovation, and workforce stability. The Czech Republic demonstrated the highest engagement in talent management among the V4 countries, with 31,15% of firms actively implementing TM strategies. Larger enterprises tend to have more structured talent management programs, whereas SMEs, due to resource limitations, often focus on operational HR tasks.

Industry-wise, the healthcare and high-tech sectors reported the greatest emphasis on talent management due to their reliance on skilled professionals. Conversely, traditional industries such as manufacturing, trade, and logistics showed lower engagement in structured talent development initiatives, highlighting a potential risk to long-term workforce sustainability in these sectors.

The public sector lags behind the private sector in adopting proactive talent management strategies, which impacts workforce stability in education, healthcare, and public administration. Addressing this gap requires policy-level interventions to modernize HR practices in state-run institutions.

## Comparative Regional Perspective

Compared to Western Europe, V4 countries invest less in lifelong learning and upskilling, leading to limited workforce adaptability.

Nordic countries emphasize sustainability-driven HRM, integrating green HRM practices into talent development, while V4 organizations still struggle to align HRM with broader sustainability objectives.

The Southern European labor market faces youth unemployment issues, whereas the V4 region's challenge lies in skill shortages due to outmigration.

## Future Implications

As organizations in the V4 region navigate global economic shifts, the future of talent management will be shaped by key trends: AI-Driven HRM, Green HRM practise ana Life Long Learning. All of these aspects are connected with need of developement, eco-learning and eco-approach to the company strategy and environmental responsibility. Life Long Learning and Continuous learning must solve the skill gap, particularly in digital and technological competencies.

Remote and Hybrid Work Model are required for talent retention.

For future is very important the cooperation of governments, educational institutions, and businesses. They must collaborate to develop talent pipelines that align with industry needs and national economic priorities.

For sustainable talent management to thrive in the V4 region, companies must move beyond short-term HR practices and invest in long-term workforce strategies. Based on the study's finding should be prioritized the following recommendations: develop targeted talent retention initiatives, especially for industries facing skill shortages, training and upskilling programs, particularly in digital skills, AI, and sustainability, improving workforce planning by integrating predictive HR analytics and AI-driven talent management solutions.

Strengthen succession planning in both private and public sector organizations i salso important for leadership continuity.

Encourage policy interventions that support HRM reforms in the public sector, including improved workforce planning, professional development, and employee incentives.

By adopting these strategies, organizations in the V4 region can mitigate workforce risks, enhance competitiveness, and ensure long-term sustainability. As economic and technological landscapes continue to evolve, the ability to attract, develop, and retain top talent will define the future success of businesses in the region. Strategic talent management is not just an HR function—it is a necessity for long-term organizational resilience and economic stability.

## REFERENCES


Abhisha, N., & Melvin, C. L. J. (2024). *Green human resource management practices for sustainability: a comprehensive review*., DOI: 10.58532/V3BHMA24CH1

Adisa, O., Ajadi, T. H., & Keshtiban, A. (2024). Navigating Human-Technology Nexus for Environmental and Organizational Sustainability in Industry 5.0. *Practice, Progress, and Proficiency in Sustainability*, •••, 222–246. DOI: 10.4018/979-8-3693-7322-4.ch011

Ahmad, B., Salam, M., Ullah, W., Iqbal, S., & Shahid, M. (2024). Let the Employees Strengthen for a Sustainable Future: A Systematic Literature Review of Sustainable HRM. *Journal of Policy Research*. https://doi.org/DOI: 10.61506/02.00357

Aliu, F., Asero, V., Asllani, A., & Kučera, J. (2023). Spillover effects and transmission of shocks in Visegrad equity markets. *Studies in Economics and Finance*. Advance online publication. DOI: 10.1108/SEF-07-2023-0395

Ambarawati, N. G. M. A., & Wijoyo, R. P. (2023). *The Implementation of Talent Management Implementation at Regional Employee Agency Wonogiri Regency Central Java*. Jurnal MSDA., DOI: 10.33701/jmsda.v11i2.3764

Anand, J., Hemasundari, M., Selvaranee, J. K., & Mariadhas, J. M. (2024). *Integrating SDGs into Human Resource Management: Pathways to Sustainable Workforce Development*. https://doi.org/DOI: 10.47172/2965-730X.SDGsReview.v4.n04.pe03556

Anshima, A., Bhardwaj, B., Sharma, D., & Dhiman, M. C. (2024). Ensuring sustainability through green HRM practices: a review, synthesis and research avenues. *Journal of Organizational Effectiveness*. https://doi.org/DOI: 10.1108/JOEPP-10-2023-0493

Anusuya, M., & Soundarapandian, M. (2024). Exploring human capital management practices: A comprehensive review. *World Journal of Advanced Research and Reviews*, *21*(3), 2343–2348.

Arvind, D., & Priya, B. (2024). *Workplace Culture: Creating A Positive and Inclusive Environment*. Shanlax International Journal of Management., DOI: 10.34293/management.v11iS1-Mar.8082

A.V. (2024). The impact of green hrm on employee skill development for sustainability initiatives. *International Journal of Trendy Rresearch in Engineering and Technology*, *08*(06), 77–82. DOI: 10.54473/IJTRET.2024.8610

Barakat, S., Alneyadi, R., Alderei, M., Malek, S., Alahbabi, F., & Jasim, M. (2024). The impact of sustainable hrm practices on job performance in uae organizations. *International Journal of Management Trends: Key Concepts and Research*, *3*(1), 29–38. DOI: 10.58898/ijmt.v3i1.29-38

Belás, J., Machova, R., Oláh, J., & Metzker, Z. (2024). The impact of selected HRM factors on company's survival of SMEs: Empirical research in V4 countries. *Journal of International Students*, *17*(1), 108–123. Advance online publication. DOI: 10.14254/2071-8330.2024/17-1/7

Breaz, T. O., & Jaradat, M. (2024). Strategic Human Resource Management: Aligning HR Practices with Organizational Goals. https://doi.org/DOI: 10.24818/IMC/2023/04.01

*Building Skills for Sustainable Development – A Key for Business Excellence* (pp. 147–159). (2022). Routledge eBooks. https://doi.org/DOI: 10.4324/9781003173311-15

Chaker, B., & Damak, C. (2024). Developing a Strategic Framework for Aligning Human Resource Management Practices With Sustainability Goals. *Practice, Progress, and Proficiency in Sustainability*, •••, 127–148. DOI: 10.4018/979-8-3693-2699-2.ch007

Chakib, S. (2024). The Historical Development of Employee Retention Theories. *The Pinnacle*, *2*(2). Advance online publication. DOI: 10.61643/c23515

Chigbu, B. I. (2024). Advancing sustainable development through circular economy and skill development in EV lithium-ion battery recycling: A comprehensive review. *Frontiers in Sustainability*, *5*, 1409498. Advance online publication. DOI: 10.3389/frsus.2024.1409498

Collings, D. G., & Conroy, K. M. (2024). Global talent management. https://doi.org/DOI: 10.4337/9781800884045.ch40

Collings, D. G., McDonnell, A., & Scullion, H. (2022). *Global talent management: Principles and practices*. Oxford University Press.

Cooke, G. B., Chowhan, J., Mac Donald, K., & Mann, S. L. (2021). Talent management: Four "buying versus making" talent development approaches. *Personnel Review*. Advance online publication. DOI: 10.1108/PR-08-2020-0621

Čulková, K., Hrehová, D., & Janošková, M. (2021). *Global problems of the employment in V4 region. 92*, 07014. https://doi.org/DOI: 10.1051/shsconf/20219207014

Czeglédi, C., Marosné Kuna, Z., & Hajós, L. (2013). *Current challenges of talent management in the V4 countries with special respect to Hungary*. https://dspace5.zcu.cz/bitstream/11025/16264/1/Czegledi.pdf

Deloitte. (2022). *The future of work in Central Europe: Trends and challenges in post-pandemic talent management*. Deloitte Insights.

Dhandayudam, P., & Raajarajeswari, M. A. (2024). *Exploring Sustainable Green HRM Practices: An Investigation of Employee Perspectives and Organizational Challenges*. Springer International Publishing., DOI: 10.1007/978-981-99-7798-7_25

Dip, H. S. (2024). *Circular Economy Initiatives in Food Manufacturing Industry*. https://doi.org/DOI: 10.21203/rs.3.rs-4996705/v1

*Diversity in the Workplace: Providing Equal Opportunities and Effective Management*. (2023). https://doi.org/DOI: 10.53819/81018102t30129

Ejibe, I., Okoye, C. C., Nwankwo, E. E., Nwankwo, T. C., & Scholastica, U. C. (2024). *Eco-sustainable practices through strategic HRM: A review and framework for SMEs in the creative industries*. World Journal Of Advanced Research and Reviews., DOI: 10.30574/wjarr.2024.21.3.0658

Elshaer, I. A., Azazz, A. M. S., Kooli, C., Alqasa, K., Afaneh, J. A. A., Fathy, E. A., Fouad, A. M., & Fayyad, S. (2024). Resilience for Sustainability: The Synergistic Role of Green Human Resources Management, Circular Economy, and Green Organizational Culture in the Hotel Industry. *Administrative Sciences*, *14*(11), 297. DOI: 10.3390/admsci14110297

Enabling Skill Development for a Sustainable Future. (2023). *Advances in Human Resources Management and Organizational Development Book Series*, 1–13. https://doi.org/DOI: 10.4018/978-1-6684-6990-3.ch001

Endrawati, Y., Putra, I. S., & Ningsih, R. (2024). Building a Sustainable Workforce: Cross-Posting and Secondment Strategies in Indonesia's Oil and Gas Operations. https://doi.org/DOI: 10.2118/223255-MS

Eurofound. (2021). *Labor market trends in Central and Eastern Europe: The role of HRM in workforce stability*.

European Commission. (2023). *Skills and lifelong learning in the EU labor market*. Publications Office of the European Union.

European Labour Authority. (2023). *Labor market dynamics and regulatory frameworks in Central and Eastern Europe*.

Eurostat. (2022). *Employment and labor market statistics in the EU*.

Firdaus, F., & Ambarwati, R. (2024). Challenges and Opportunities Management Human Resources in Industry 4.0 Focuses on Digital Skills. *International Journal of Economics*. https://doi.org/DOI: 10.55299/ijec.v3i1.812

Fortunisa, A., Djamaris, A., Hanathasia, M., Nurmadewi, D., Suyuthy, M. S., Permadi, C. A., & Hidayati, F. (2024). Talent Management in the Era of Digital Transformation: Challenges and Prospects. *Global International Journal of Innovative Research*. https://doi.org/DOI: 10.59613/global.v2i10.330

Gilster, S. D., Langhout, K. J., & Dalessandro, J. L. (2021). Staff Stability Through Service: Promoting a Person-Centered Culture for Work and Care in Long-Term Services and Supports Environments. *Journal of Gerontological Nursing*, *47*(11), 6–10. DOI: 10.3928/00989134-20211012-01 PMID: 34704868

Goichuk, V., & Lyubomudrova, N. (2024). The impact of strategic human capital management on the competitiveness of an enterprise. *Three Seas Economic Journal*, *5*(2), 1–6. DOI: 10.30525/2661-5150/2024-2-1

Gruševá, E., & Blašková, V. (2022). Education as a factor influencing the economic growth of the V4 countries. *Review of Applied Socio-Economic Research*, *24*(2). Advance online publication. DOI: 10.54609/reaser.v24i2.139

Hamidi, D. Z., Hakiki, R., & Pandiangan, H. (2024). AI and Human Collaboration: The Future of HR in the Fourth Industrial Revolution. *Escalate*, *2*(01), 17–25. DOI: 10.61536/escalate.v2i01.49

Hanáčková, D., & Takáč, I. (2024). Innovation performance of V4 countries. *Entrepreneurship and Sustainability Issues*, *11*(4), 293–310. DOI: 10.9770/jesi.2024.11.4(18)

Hartley, K., Gupta, H., van Vuuren, D., & Kirchherr, J. (2023). Employee skills for circular business model implementation: A taxonomy. *Journal of Cleaner Production*, *410*, 137027. DOI: 10.1016/j.jclepro.2023.137027

Howell, B. (2024). Developing a Diversity and Inclusion Performance Management Strategy. *Advances in Logistics, Operations, and Management Science Book Series*, 97–116. https://doi.org/DOI: 10.4018/979-8-3693-7327-9.ch006

Imtiaz, Q., & Iqbal, S. (2024). Impact of HR Practices on Eco-Friendly Behaviour in Higher Education Institutions: Mediating Mechanism of Organizational Culture & Sustainable Work Environment. *Bulletin of Multidisciplinary Studies*, *1*(3), 105–113.

Indrajaya, A. N., Setiawan, D. L., Marshella, I., Tarigan, J., & Oktaviana, N. (2024). Creating Sustainability Through Talent Management Improvement: PT USAHA DAGANG INDONESIA. [JSCD]. *Journal of Sustainable Community Development*, *6*(1), 22–32. DOI: 10.32924/jscd.v6i1.113

Jabbour, C. J. C., Seuring, S., & de Sousa Jabbour, A. B. L. (2023). *Sustainable human resource management: Strategies and practices for a resilient workforce*. Springer.

Jejeniwa, T. O., Mhlongo, N. Z., & Jejeniwa, T. O. (2024). Diversity and inclusion in the workplace: A conceptual framework comparing the USA and Nigeria. *International Journal of Management & Entrepreneurship Research*, *6*(5), 1368–1394. DOI: 10.51594/ijmer.v6i5.1090

John, J. E., & Pramila, S. (2024). Integrating AI Tools into HRM to Promote Green HRM Practices. https://doi.org/DOI: 10.1007/978-981-99-9489-2_22

Khawaja, A., & Janjua, K. N. (2024). The Effect of Sustainable HRM Practices on Organizational Sustainability in Textile Industry of Pakistan. *Bulletin of Business and Economics*. https://doi.org/DOI: 10.61506/01.00515

Koman, G., Boršoš, P., & Kubina, M. (2024). Sustainable Human Resource Management with a Focus on Corporate Employee Recruitment. *Sustainability (Basel)*, *16*(14), 6059. DOI: 10.3390/su16146059

Kurniawan, A., & Wijoyo, S. (2024). Leveraging Talent for a Sustainable Future: A Multidisciplinary Examination of Public Sector Talent Management Strategies. *Research Synergy Foundation Conference Proceeding Series*. https://doi.org/DOI: 10.31098/bmss.v4i1.857

Kutaula, S., Chowdhury, S., Gillani, A., Budhwar, P. S., & Dey, P. (2024). Linking HRM with Sustainability Performance Through Sustainability Practices: Unlocking the Black Box. *British Journal of Management*. Advance online publication. DOI: 10.1111/1467-8551.12861

Lumbanraja, P. (2023). Evaluation of talent management at pt. pertamina gas niaga medan, north sumatera. *International Journal of Educational Review, Law And. Social Sciences*, *3*(5), 1590–1599. Advance online publication. DOI: 10.54443/ijerlas.v3i5.1051

Malyarchuk, N. (2024). Current challenges and opportunities of personnel management. *Ekonomìčnì gorizonti*. https://doi.org/DOI: 10.31499/2616-5236.3(28).2024.312411

Matei, M.-C., Abrudan, L. C., & Abrudan, M.-M. (2024). Financial Perspectives on Human Capital: Building Sustainable HR Strategies. *Sustainability (Basel), 16*(4), 1441. Advance online publication. DOI: 10.3390/su16041441

Mathur, V. (2022). *Skilling for Sustainability* (pp. 66–68). Routledge eBooks. https://doi.org/DOI: 10.4324/9781003311157-11

Napathorn, C. (2022). Meso-level factors fostering or hindering the implementation of age-related HR practices in firms. *The International Journal of Organizational Analysis*. Advance online publication. DOI: 10.1108/IJOA-04-2022-3241

Noor, K. A. B. M., & Ahmad, M. (2024). *Circular Economy: Rethinking Security Sustainability Through Ransom Project*. https://doi.org/DOI: 10.2118/223015-MS

Nson, Y. D. (2024). Sustainability of the society through green human resources management practices: A proposed model. *Annals of Human Resource Management Research, 4*(1), 43–59. DOI: 10.35912/ahrmr.v4i1.2161

Nurmala, N., & Hermina, N. (2024). Talent management: Preparing future leaders. *International journal of business, economics and management*. https://doi.org/DOI: 10.21744/ijbem.v7n3.2314

Pereira, V., & Patel, C. (2022). *Talent management in digital industries: A global perspective*. Palgrave Macmillan.

Pilania, A. (2024). *Green HRM Practices*. Indian Scientific Journal Of Research In Engineering And Management., DOI: 10.55041/IJSREM33488

Polekar, J. S., & Lodha, K. (2024). *Challenges in Manpower Management: Discuss the Challenges Faced by the Automotive Industry in Managing Manpower Due to Rigid Labor Laws and Complex Legal Systems, Especially Concerning Temporary Increases in Workforce to Meet Demand Fluctuations*. International Journal For Multidisciplinary Research., DOI: 10.36948/ijfmr.2024.v06i03.20233

Potháczky, R.I. (2022) Talent management characteristics of small and medium-sized enterprises and the effects of Covid19, (In Hungarian) Acta Periodica XXVI. kötet, 2022/december, pp 45-59, DOI https://doi.org/DOI: 10.47273/AP.2022.26.45-59

Prasanna, J. H., Hemalatha, S., Deepa, N., & Rani, S. (2022). A Study on Relationship between Employee Turnover Intention and Perceived Organisational Support. *Asian Journal of Agricultural Extension. Economia e Sociologia, 251–255*, 251–255. Advance online publication. DOI: 10.9734/ajaees/2022/v40i1031070

Rajpurohit, S. (2024). Study on Turnover and Retention Strategies Identifying Causes and Implementing Solutions. *Indian Scientific Journal Of Research In Engineering And Management, 08*(06), 1–5. DOI: 10.55041/IJSREM35815

Ramachandaran, S. D. (2024). Challenges in Implementing Quality Education at INTI International University: An Examination of Human Resource Management Practices. *Journal of Ecohumanism, 3*(8). Advance online publication. DOI: 10.62754/joe.v3i8.4727

Rambe, M. T. (2024). Building an Inclusive Work Environment: Challenges and Opportunities in HR Management. *Jurnal EMT KITA*, *8*(4), 1557–1568. DOI: 10.35870/emt.v8i4.3281

Raut, V. N. (2024). Driving success: The strategic role of talent management in HR's promotion of employee engagement. *International Journal of Research Publication and Reviews*. https://doi.org/DOI: 10.55248/gengpi.5.0524.1296

Reddy, S. (2024). Dr.K V Subba Reddy School of Business Management. *Indian Scientific Journal Of Research In Engineering And Management*, *08*(06), 1–5. DOI: 10.55041/IJSREM36129

Sagandykova, L. S., Tayauova, G., & Ketengi, N. (2024). The role of sustainable human resources management in the organizational effectiveness of the company. *Tu ran Universitetìnìn Habarsysy*, *3*(3), 258–270. DOI: 10.46914/1562-2959-2024-1-3-258-270

Saha, A., & Md, S. N. (2021)... *Factors Influencing Employee Retention.*, *14*(01), 20–38. DOI: 10.36481/diujbe.v014i1.460k4723

Samuel, I. A., & Isa, M. Y. B. M. (2024). The mediating role of talent management in succession planning and private organization sustainability: A conceptual article. *Journal of Current Social and Political Issues*. https://doi.org/DOI: 10.15575/jcspi.v2i1.703

Sarjito, A. (2023). *Unlocking The Potential: Transforming Defense Through Human Capital Management*. https://doi.org/DOI: 10.58812/wsis.v1i11.333

Shahrulnizam, N. A. A., Hassan, M. A., Mohamad Azizie, N. A. M., Rashid, A. H. A., & Wahab, S. R. A. (2024). Roles of Ghrm in Sustainable Organization Practices: A Systematic Literature Review. *International Journal of Academic Research in Business & Social Sciences*, *14*(10). Advance online publication. DOI: 10.6007/IJARBSS/v14-i10/23110

Siddiqui, S. M. F., Zafar, H., & Gilani, S. A. (2024). *Sustainable HR Practices and Employee Retention: The Impact of Social Capital in Pakistan's Banking Sector*. https://doi.org/DOI: 10.56976/jsom.v3i4.133

Singh, M., & Bhatnagar, M. (2023). *Sustainability's Symphony*. Advances in Finance, Accounting, and Economics Book Series., DOI: 10.4018/979-8-3693-1388-6.ch002

Sinulingga, G., Gunawan, A., Wibowo, U. D. A., Rina, R., & Damayanti, H. A. (2024). Talent Management in the Age of Digital Disruption: Challenges and Opportunities. *Global International Journal of Innovative Research*. https://doi.org/DOI: 10.59613/global.v2i9.311

Šipikal, M., Rehák, Š., & Grenčík, J. (2022). Vocational education and workforce planning in the automotive sector: Challenges and future trends. *Journal of Economic Development*, *47*(2), 89–110.

Sitarska-Piwko, A., & Rogozińska-Pawełczyk, A. (2024). Perceptions of sustainable human resource management (SHRM) and personal risk: Findings from the Pilot Study. *Edukacja Ekonomistów i Menedżerów*, *69*(3). Advance online publication. DOI: 10.33119/EEIM.2024.69.2

Surianto, S., Badaruddin, B., & Firman, A. (2024). Human Resource Management Strategies to Increase Adaptability in the Digital Age. *Human Resource Management Strategies to Increase Adaptability in the Digital Age.*, *2*(1), 1–15. DOI: 10.37476/presed.v2i1.56

(2023, August 28). Talent management. (2023). *Human Resource Management International Digest, 31*(6), 3–4. Advance online publication. DOI: 10.1108/HRMID-05-2023-0109

Tamaş, I. (2024). Strategic Development in IT Sector.

Tunio, M. (2024). *Impact Of Talent Management On Organizational Sustainable Performance: A Moderating Role Of Process Innovation*. https://doi.org/DOI: 10.53555/kuey.v30i5.3458

Tunio, M., Abdul Hamid, A. B., Abdul Latiff, A. S., & Hafeez, M. (2023). Unlocking Organizational Sustainability: The Role of Talent Management through the Lens of the AMO Theory. *Pakistan Journal of Humanities and Social Sciences*. https://doi.org/DOI: 10.52131/pjhss.2023.1103.0634

Vaiman, V., Cascio, W. F., Collings, D. G., & Swider, B. W. (2021). The shifting boundaries of talent management. *Human Resource Management*, *60*(2), 253–257. DOI: 10.1002/hrm.22050

Whysall, Z., Owtram, M., & Brittain, S. (2019). The new talent management challenges of Industry 4.0. *Journal of Management Development*, *38*(2), 118–129. DOI: 10.1108/JMD-06-2018-0181

World Bank. (2023). *Global talent migration and healthcare workforce sustainability: Trends and policy recommendations*.

Yerlitas, T., & Bučiūnienė, I. (2024). Sustaining Human Capital in an Organization: The Role of Talent Management. *Edukacja Ekonomistów i Menedżerów*, *71*(1). Advance online publication. DOI: 10.33119/EEIM.2024.71.3

Yoo, D. Y. (2024). Eco-Leadership in Action: Integrating Green HRM and the New Ecological Paradigm to Foster Organizational Commitment and Environmental Citizenship in the Hospitality Industry. *Sustainability (Basel)*, *16*(20), 9044. DOI: 10.3390/su16209044

Yücel, D. (2024). *Enhancing Organizational Sustainability: The Role of Total Quality Management in Fostering Talent Management Practices*. Sosyal Mucit Academic Review., DOI: 10.54733/smar.1438949

Zournatzidou, G., Ragazou, K., Sklavos, G., & Sariannidis, N. (2024). Linking HRM With Sustainability. *Advances in Human Resources Management and Organizational Development Book Series*, 281–304. https://doi.org/DOI: 10.4018/979-8-3693-5981-5.ch012

Zubair, S. (2021). *Talent abuse: challenges turning talent management into talent abuse. 5*(2).

# Chapter 13
# Taxonomy and Standardization of Information for and About Sustainable Entrepreneurship in the EU

**Radka MacGregor Pelikánová**
https://orcid.org/0000-0001-9628-7146
*University of New York in Prague, Czech Republic*

## ABSTRACT

*Current global society is marked by aggressive competition and an abundance of information with dramatically different levels of relevancy. The lack of the publication of relevant information undermines the sustainability commitment of all and destroys sustainable entrepreneurship. Building a green future is a common endeavor which is feasible only if proper information is shared, i.e. decision-making competencies rely on relevant, reliable, readable and freely accessible information about sustainability. The EU policies and law have been heralding this idea and led to the taxonomy and standardization of information for and about sustainable entrepreneurship. This chapter explores their roots and current setting by comparatively and critically mapping the pertinent EU norms, visualizing them via tables and analyzing what, how, why and where is taxonomized and standardized and by providing an assessment glossing. The pathway towards relevant information for sustainable entrepreneurship is not smooth and easy, it is rather a dynamically advancing crusade upon which the EU has embarked.*

## 1. DETERMINATION AND HISTORICAL DEVELOPMENT OF THE CONCEPT OF SUSTAINABILITY AND ITS IMPORTANCE FOR ENTREPRENEURSHIP AND INFORMING

The concept of sustainability has millennial roots within the continental law tradition and Biblical and Roman Law features (MacGregor Pelikánová, 2017). The first Industrial Revolution along with the emerging *mondialisation* progressively turning into the growing interdependence of both international law subjects and national law subjects, globalization, led to the modern stage of the concept of sustainability. The key role was played the United Nations ("UN"), which launched in 1948 the Universal Declaration of

DOI: 10.4018/979-8-3373-0189-1.ch013

Human Rights ("UDHRs") and emphasized, in 1987, by the Brundtland Report mutual interdependence and the need to fight against poverty ("Brundtland Report"). Since the Brundtland Report linked together three problems which (allegedly) cannot be addressed separately – poverty, environmental degradation and population growth, it laid down the foundation for the three pillars structure - economic, environmental and social (Balcerzak *et al.,* 2023). It is visualized by the famous diagram with three overlapping circles (Purvis *et al.,* 2019) and expects the involvement of all stakeholders (Van Tulder & Van Mil, E. (2023). Interestingly enough, during the 1980's the priority was the environment pillar, in the 1990s the social pillar and, since 2000, the idea of mutual balancing prevails. Consequently, businesses are expected to be sustainably effective, efficient and legitimate regarding all three pillars and vis-à-vis the entire society (MacGregor Pelikánová *et al.,* 2024a), i.e. to accept their Corporate Social Responsibility ("CSR") (Bali Swain & Yang-Wallentin, 2019) and perhaps to even move to its higher stage, aka the creation of shared values ("CSV") (MacGregor Pelikánová & Sani, 2024). CSR is visualized via Carroll's pyramid with required economic, required legal, expected ethical and desired philanthropic responsibilities (Carroll, 2016) while these four layers are overlapping and mutually penetrating and this further emphasizes the organic move to CSV as a demonstration of the capacity of a business, which is both socially responsible and pragmatic, to create economic value by creating societal value (Porter & Kramer, 2011).

Such information needs to be communicated not only to consumers, but as well business partners and investors, via both regularly issued reports and permanent types documents such as Codes of Ethics (MacGregor Pelikánová *et al.,* 2021). Such a plethora of data and platforms inherently lead to disorganized heterogeneity. Consequently, in 2004 a group of 20 financial institutions endorsed a report facilitated by the UN Global Compact Who Cares Wins: Connecting Financial Markets to a Changing World ("Who Cares Wins") integrating Environmental, Social, and (good) Governance ("ESG") value drivers into financial market research, analysis and investment. One year later, in 2005, the UN Global Compact, Federal Department of Foreign Affairs Switzerland, and International Finance Corporation organized events which led to Conference Report Investing for Long-Term Value Integrating ESG value drivers in asset management and financial research. Firstly investors, but then even customers, partners and other stakeholders are to be made aware about ESG aspects before making their purchase and/or co-operation and/or investment decision. The firm determination of the UN to advance the modern three pillars concept of sustainability while taking advantage of CSR of business and its assessment by ESG criteria led, in 2015, to the two latest international milestones in this arena, which in addition were prepared in co-operation with the EU and keeps being endorsed by the EU - UN Climate Change Conference (COP21) with the Paris Climate Accords under the UN Framework Convention on Climate Change ("Paris Agreement") and the Agenda for Sustainable Development – People, Planet, Prosperity, Peace, and Partnership ("Agenda 2030") with 17 Sustainable Development Goals ("SDGs"), 169 associated targets and 244 indicators (Balcerzak & MacGregor Pelikánová, 2020).

In Antiquity, the leadership often had individualistic despotic features, but that did not mean the lack of accountability. Linguistically, "to account for something" means to recognize and describe something, while "to be accountable" means to explain what one has done with entrusted resources (Stolowy & Ding, 2017, p. 10). Naturally, these leaders were accountable often only to Gods or to their conscience, but still this led to a duty to answer for their own actions and omissions (MacGregor Pelikánová, 2023, pp. 238-257). Hence *accountability* has an individual dimension, focuses on results and is about informing what one has achieved, while *responsibility* has a collective dimension and is about answering for what was caused to an authority and this authority evaluates it and sets damages (Schüz, 2012). If a legal framework is provided for such a responsibility and the authority is the judge, then this responsibility turns into a *liability* (MacGregor Pelikánová & MacGregor, 2020).

Business is about changing and exchanging, in particular about transforming resources and commercializing them (Stolowy & Ding, 2017, p. 2). Business decisions involve which, how and by whom these resources will be obtained, processed, and transformed into semi- and final products and how and for how much the resulting goods or services will be sold so as to ultimately receive more resources from sales than what was spent on creating them (Stolowy & Ding, 2017, p. 3). Such decisions require not only proper data, competencies to reflect it and act accordingly it, but as well the recording and publication (MacGregor Pelikánová, 2023, pp. 238-257). The business cycle is not a one-way linear equation, instead it is rather an ongoing reciprocal and mutual communication and re-adjustment process which is studied by and within social science (MacGregor Pelikánová, 2023, pp. 258-275). Each transaction inside the transformation process needs to be recorded in a standardized and readable manner and be published so the business itself as well as all stakeholders can examine it and make appropriate decisions (Pakšiová & Oriskoová, 2020). This recording is done via a system of acknowledging the socially defined parameters describing the economic life of an enterprise, i.e. accounting (Stolowy & Ding, 2017, p. 10). Managerial accounting assists with the value creation by supporting resource acquisition, allocation, and decision-making (Stolowy & Ding, 2017, p. 10), while the financial accounting informs stakeholders about the amount of value created during a given period (Stolowy & Ding, 2017, p. 10).

Informing about a business and business contact means reporting the flow of information allowing for controlling the business and the agent by the principal, in particular, the information about what the agent did with the resources from the principal (Stolowy & Ding, 2017, p. 5). A report with such information is a basis for an analysis for decision-making (Stolowy & Ding, 2017, p. 10). A report shows either the effort (internal and specific reporting about value creation called managerial accounting), or the result (standardized general reporting about created value for third parties called financial reporting) or both (Stolowy & Ding, 2017, p. 5).

Traditionally, reporting focused on providing financial information and until now, the shareholder theory and normative theory of business ethics of Milton Friedman are presented in an (over)simplified version, i.e. as the applicable command "the (only social) responsibility of business is to increase its profits" (Friedman, 2007). However, this does not mean the rejection of the concept of sustainability, instead the it is about the deference of the decision about sustainability to stockholders, i.e. businesses should generate (as much as possible) financial funds and stockholders should spend these funds based on their free (and hopefully pro-sustainable) will. Perhaps Milton Friedman should be perceived rather as pragmatically pro-CSR than sarcastically against-CSR and his pragmatism is testified by his another heavily cited quote "One of the great mistakes is to judge policies and programs by their intentions rather than their results" (Bali Swain & Yang-Wallentin, 2019).

Interestingly, the independent and autonomous will and the protection of private property are the fundamental values to which refer both the shareholder theory of Milton Friedman (since 1970) as well as the stakeholder theory of R. Edward Freeman (since 1984), which requires a business considers not only the interests of its owners and investors (generate financial funds), but all stakeholders, while ideally creating value with them and for them (Hühn, 2023). They both should be appreciated from various perspectives, including the famous logic of Howard R. Bowen (since 1953) - "who impacts has the responsibility for it" (Bowen, 1953).

Since 2015, the concept of sustainability with its international public law features and the CSR/ CSV with its national features clearly overlap and demand that entrepreneurs and businesses have to focus and be responsible for all three dimensions aka pillars of sustainability, genuinely consider the long the long-term survival of the business and be persistent (Caliendo et al., 2019). As a result, the current entrepreneurship must be economically, socially and environmentally sustainable and to achieve such a sustainable balance, perhaps at least partially reflecting SDGs (Galindo-Martín *et al.,* 2020) as witnessed by empiric studies within EU jurisdictions (D'Adamo & Gastaldi, 2023). There are many challenges to do so (Thelken & de Jong, 2020), both extrinsic, such as the inappropriate political and legal framework or the lack of government, and intrinsic, such as the insufficiency of cash flow to launch and maintain sustainable entrepreneurship. A common denominator of these challenges is the content, format, availability and capacity to process and share the information. To put it differently, sustainable entrepreneurship requires ashared commitment based on the information.

Indeed, the modern concept of sustainability with the emergence of CSR and CSV inevitably leads to the increased need of shared information, both financial and non-financial, which needs to be communicated to all, and especially the key finance providers – investors and consumers (Hála *et al.*, 2024). Even more importantly, sustainability issues and double materiality turn non-financial reporting into sustainability reporting and make it massively significant not only for customers, but as well business partners and investors, which are carefully considering ESG aspects and criteria of the business before making their purchase and/or co-operation and/or investment decision. Considering the webs of supply chains, inquisitive nature of customers, etc., the information about sustainable entrepreneurship influences the choices made not only by stockholders but as well other stakeholders and ultimately bounce back and impact the business itself. As a result, the information about the sustainable entrepreneurship stimulates pro-sustainable behavour and should increase the effectiveness and efficiency of the economic system, both in the macro-perspective as well as the micro-perspective (Borseková et al., 2021). However, this is feasible only if relevant information is provided to a right person in an ongoing and reflexing manner (Atrill & McLaney, 2017, p. 2). Informed, educated and pro-sustainability decision making occurs neither in a vacuum nor in the case of lack of information or of overwhelming and hardly (if at all) understandable data or not shared information. And naturally even the best information loses its usefulness if not provided to somebody who is able to process it in a proper manner.

Starting with the first element of this triad relevant information - competent decision maker – sustainability responsiveness, it cannot be overemphasized that relevant and shared information is sine qua non and that being relevant means not only to have a proper content but also to have a proper format and on a proper platform, i.e. understandable content is freely communicated in a recipient friendly manner (Weygandt et al., 2013, p. 4).

The Agenda 2030 as the global to-do list for sustainable development, expressed by 17 SDGs, in order to eradicate poverty, establish socioeconomic inclusion and protect the environment (Bali Swain & Yang-Wallentin, 2019) appears to be hardly achieved and perhaps too ambitious, excessively expansive and inherently contradictory (Spaiser *et al.,* 2016). However, there are no doubts that Agenda 2030 demands informed interaction by „devoting ourselves collectively to the pursuit of global development and of "win-win" cooperation" and implies proper mutual informing. And exactly this was the starting point of the EU policy and legal framework. Regarding EU policies, this occurred in 2010 with the famous Strategy Europe 2020 for smart, sustainable and inclusive growth and since the term "sustainable development" is their central point (Zavřelová & MacGregor Pelikánová, 2024). Regarding the EU law, this evolution towards relevancy of information for and about sustainable information to be properly communicated via reporting by a growing number of businesses (MacGregor Pelikánová, 2021) started in 2014. Over time this general duty has become more specific, more enforceable, and entailing a growing number of subjects. The general EU legislation on business information reporting became paralleled by the EU taxonomy, sectorial and consumer protection legislation.

At the same time, the provided information was often hardly understandable and comparable, sometimes even overwhelming and misleading, occasionally even manipulating and disinforming. Greenwashing and cherry-picking practices have emerged and the concept of sustainability got abused and misused and even abused to serve as a cover for entrepreneurial activities entirely incompatible with each and every pillar of sustainability. Based on the firm belief that each and every European should be informed and involved in building a sustainable green future, the EU decided to fight against such repugnant practices by several strategies while taking the advantage of the multistakeholder model and approach (Van Tulder et *al.,* 2016; Van Tulder & Keen, 2018). These strategies include the command to a growing pool of businesses to provide taxonomic and standardized information about sustainability matters based on the double materiality principle, i.e. about external impact of the (sustainability in the) society on the business and how the business affects the (sustainability in) society. Such sustainability/CSR/ESG reports under the auspices of the non-financial reporting are to be disclosed and published, typically by a dedicated section of management report or even separately, while including measurable and comparable standardized information. This progressively more standardized and enforceable legal duty to do sustainability reporting via a dedicated section or separately is further supported by other legal duty to provide information, see e.g. labelling in the context of the consumer protection law, the market to be more innovative and digitalized and within the economy to be more circular than linear (Shpak et al. 2021).

Well, the pendulum has swung from the exclusive position of the national state as the decision-maker regarding sustainability to the involvement of the society at large in the building of a green future. This move got even magnified during recent crises (Cowling & Dvouletý, 2023) confirming that crises emphasize pre-existing trends, pursuant to Einstein bring progress (D´Adamo & Lupi, 2021) and that we should "Never waste a good crisis" (Van Tulder & Van Miller, xxxi-xxxiii).

Consequently, businesses need to master decision-making competencies to be able to generate taxonomic and standardized information about their sustainability (about sustainable entrepreneurship) as well as to analyze information and data generated by other stakeholders and act accordingly (for sustainable entrepreneurship) in the general setting for a better information to build a green future. In order to understand and appreciate this pro-information framework, after this determination and historical development of the concept of sustainability and its importance for entrepreneurship and informing in the EU (1.), the applicable EU law needs to be mapped and interpreted in a teleological manner (2). Therafter, the focus should move to two current most important instrument to boost the quality and accessibility of provided information for and about sustainable entrepreneurship – taxonomic terminology (3.) and sustainability standardization (4.). Their critical and comparative mapping, analyzing and glossing reveals that the pathway towards relevant information for and about sustainable entrepreneurship is not smooth and easy, it is rather a crusade on which the EU embarks (5.).

## 2. MAPPING THE EU LAW ON INFORMATION FOR AND ABOUT SUSTAINABLE ENTREPRENEURSHIP

The concept of sustainability is an integral and inherent part of EU primary law, secondary law and even supplementary law. Regarding the EU primary law, it needs to be emphasized that the sustainability and sustainable development are core principles of the Treaty on European Union (Art. 3), at least since 97 C 340/01 Treaty of Amsterdam, and that the EU fully endorses both the last international milestone legal treaties - Agenda 2030 and the Paris Agreement. Regarding the supplementary law, the Court of Justice of EU ("CJ EU") has already made a long line of influential decisions with a quasi-precedential nature about sustainability issues and for example one of the regular subject categories to search the case law of CJ EU is "environment." Without undermining the importance of EU primary law norms and of the EU supplementary law as expressed by the case law of CJ EU, the most developed part of the EU law regarding the concept of sustainability is obviously the secondary law, in particular the secondary law directly reflecting the key EU strategies and policies. The European Commission of José Manuel Barroso brought a new vision of sustainable development strategies, see Europe 2020 for smart, sustainable and inclusive growth (Balcerzak, & Pietrzak, 2017) which was continued by the European Commission of Jean-Claude Juncker. The previous Commission of Ursula von der Leyen as well as her current Commission of the EU appear rather consistent and committed to advance sustainability and sustainable development, see Political Guidelines 2019-2024: A Union that strives for more. My agenda for Europe, and Political Guidelines 2024-2029: Europe's Choice. A new plan for Europe's sustainable prosperity and competitiveness. Consequently, the European Commission keeps issuing such policies and preparing proposals of such a secondary EU law. To put it differently, Ursula von der Leyen and her team are the driving force for policies as well green papers to stimulate discussion about sustainability matters and following white papers containing proposals of matching EU secondary law, typically Regulations and Directives to be approved by the EU parliament and the Council of EU (ministers).

Within the EU secondary law, there are Regulations and Directives specifically designed to address only one of the sustainability pillars and/or in one industry, such as Regulation (EU) 2021/1119 establishing the framework for achieving climate neutrality ("European Climate Law") and/or addressing individual aspects such as proposals to boost environmental sustainability by taxes and incentives (Kot & Ojinji, 2023) or to achieve sustainable agriculture (Polcyn *et al.,* 2023) or fashion industry (MacGregor Pelikánová *et al.,* 2024b). However, a more typical approach is to address more than one sustainability pillar via Regulations and Directive, which deal not only with sustainability. This more holistic approach in the EU secondary law can be observed within a myriad of fields and arenas of EU legislation, such as consumer protection law, sectorial regulation, unified taxonomy regulation and generally applicable reporting.

Regarding the EU consumer protection law, both fundamental Directives from the 1990s are still valid and fully applicable - Directive 93/13/EEC on unfair terms in consumer contracts ("Unfair Contract Terms Directive") and Directive 98/6/EC on consumer protection in the indication of the prices of products offered to consumers ("Price Indication Directive"). One decade later, two additional Directives came to boost the scope and enforceability of the EU consumer protection law - Directive 2005/29/EC concerning unfair business-to-consumer (B2C) commercial practices in the internal market ("Unfair Commercial Practices Directive" or "UCPD") and Directive 2006/114/EC concerning misleading and comparative advertising ("Advertising Directive"). Finally, the classic quintuplet was completed by Directive 2011/83/EU on consumer rights ("Consumer Rights Directive"). The

UCPD was adopted to "contribute to the proper functioning of the internal single market and achieve a high level of consumer protection by approximating laws" (Art.1 UCPD) via a full harmonization (Art.4 UCPD). A thorough analysis of UCPD reveals a number of provisions indirectly targeting the concept of sustainability and directly addressing the misuse and abuse of the concept of sustainability via information, see misleading actions (Art. 6 UCPD), misleading omissions (Art. 7 UCPD), Black list (Annex I UCPD), etc. However the combined effect of Agenda 2030, Europe 2020 and both European Commissions of Ursula von der Leyen led to four proposals marked by the multi-stakeholder drive for sustainability in the internal single market in 2022 and 2023. Three of these four proposals were smoothly adopted in 2024, while one "got stuck" in the ordinary legislative procedure, namely in the first reading in the Parliament:

- Regulation (EU) 2024/1781 establishing a framework for the setting of ecodesign requirements for sustainable products aka digital product passport ("Ecodesign Regulation");
- Directive (EU) 2024/825 amending the UCPD and Consumer Rights Directive for empowering consumers for the green transition through better protection against unfair practices and through better information ("Green Empowerment Directive"),
- Directive (EU) 2024/1799 on common rules promoting the repair of goods ("Repair Goods Directive" aka "Right to Repair Directive" aka "R2R Directive");
- Proposal 2023/0085(COD) for a Directive on substantiation and communication of explicit environmental claims ("Proposal for Green Claims Directive").

Regarding EU sectorial regulation, a perfect example is Regulation (EU) 2019/2088 on sustainability-related disclosures in the financial services sector ("SFDR"). SFDR was adopted as part of the legislative framework for sustainable finance to harmonised transparency rules for financial market participants and financial advisers on how they integrate ESG factors into their investment decisions and financial advice. Namely, SFDR which requires financial market participants and advisers to classify their funds depending on their level of sustainability and to report about it (MacGregor Pelikánová & Rubáček, 2022). The underlying reason for SFDR was the fight against greenwashing and similar practices attempting to falsely or misleadingly present financial products as sustainable and/or green. Specifically, SFDR regulates the mandatory disclosure by financial institutions and/or about financial products and so enhance the provided information and contributes to sustainable investment decisions by investors (addresses of the SFDR disclosure) and to sustainable strategic decisions by financial institutions (authors of the SFDR disclosure). SFDR lays down the foundation of the double materiality principle by distinguishing between outside-in sustainability risk (external ESG events with negative impact on the value of investment) and adverse impacts on sustainability factors (internal ESG conditions impacting the society). SFDR defines sustainable investment as an investment that contributes to an environmental or social objective provided it does not significantly harm any other sustainability objectives (Art.2 al. 17 SFDR). Further, SFDR defines sustainability risk as an ESG event or condition that could cause an actual or a potential material negative impact on the value of the investment (Art. 2 al. 22 SFDR). Finally, SFDR defines five categories of sustainability factors: environmental, social and employee matters, respect for human rights, anti-corruption and anti-bribery matters (Art. 2 al. 24 SFDR). Considering the importance of the principle of do no significant harm for the determination of sustainability, the European Supervisory Authorities ("ESAs") shall develop draft regulatory technical standards to specify this principle. ESAs include three special EU institutions entrusted with the development, standardization and monitoring of sustainability-related disclosures based on SFDR: European Banking Authority ("EBA"), European Insurance and Occupational Pensions Authority ("EIOPA") and European Securities and Markets Authority ("ESMA") (Rubáček *et al.,* 2023). Despite this rather robust setting of SFDR and involvement of ESAs, shortly after the begin of its application, it has been suggested that the endorsement of SFDR by EU institutions varies, that morality appears to be underplayed and that the interpretation litigates against an artificial disassociation of concepts linked to sustainability, CSR, and shared values (Balcerzak *et al.,* 2023). Delegated Regulation (EU) 2022/1288 supplemented SFDR with regard to regulatory technical standards, specifying the content, methodologies and presentation of the information relating to sustainability indicators and adverse sustainability impacts, the principle of "do no significant harm" and the promotion of environmental or social characteristics and sustainable investment objectives.

However, this highly detailed-oriented and meticulously standardized regulation regarding the information for and about sustainable entrepreneurship applies only to financial services sector. The EU was fully aware about it and moved via two pathways to massive extension of harmonized, if not unified, rules about sustainable entrepreneurship to be revealed and openly shared by almost all, if not all, businesses. These pathways were the brand new technical terminological unification aka unified taxonomy regulation and the radical extension of the already one decade developing harmonization of sustainability reporting.

Regarding the unified taxonomy regulation, a critically important measures was adopted to inform (not only) investors about the environmental sustainability of economic activity and the entrepreuneurship in general - Regulation (EU) 2020/852 on the establishment of a framework to facilitate sustainable investment and amending SFDR ("Taxonomy Regulation"). As much the financial sector oriented SFDR was the legislative product created by the European Commission of Jean-Claude Juncker, so much the more reaching and terminology unifying Taxonomy Regulation was the legislative product created by the European Commission of Ursula von der Leyen going for a "more green Europe". Undoubtedly, the Taxonomy Regulation is designed to support the transformation of the EU economy to meet its European Green Deal objectives and which should serve as both a classification tool to bring clarity as well as a screening tool to support investment flows into environmentally sustainable economic activities (MacGregor Pelikánová & Rubáček, 2022). Consequently, the Taxonomy Regulation is perceived as an integral part of the (allegedly) weakly pragmatic and competitive and partially controversial EU sustainability-environmentally oriented policy (Czyżewski et al., 2020).

Plainly, Taxonomy Regulation establishes specific environmental criteria related to economic activities for investment purposes (including the principle of do no significant harm) and forms part of the enhanced disclosure obligations required by SFDR. Since the Taxonomy Regulation defines criteria to assess the environmental sustainability, it increases the transparency and quality of information as well as it supports the reorientation of capital flows and the management of financial risks linked to sustainability issues. Perhaps the most important point of the Taxonomy Regulation is the setting of six environmental objectives and the amendment of SFDR by adding the specification of the principle of do no significant harm (new Art.2a SFDR). Consequently, at least one of these six objectives must be observed and none of them significantly harmed plus technical criteria must be observed, otherwise the investment is not sustainable. Technical screening criteria for each of these six environmental objectives are set by four delegated Acts: the Climate Delegated Regulation (EU) 2021/2393, the Disclosures Delegated Regulation (EU) 2021/2178, the Complementary Climate Delegated Regulation (EU) 2022/1214 and the Environmental Delegated Regulation (EU) 2023/2486. The Taxonomy Regulation applies since 2020 and is closely related to the line of Directives about the harmonization of sustainability reporting as well as various Communications from the European Commission, see COM(2021) 390 Strategy for Financing the Transition to a Sustainable Economy, COM(2018) 97 Action Plan: Financing Sustainable Growth, OJ C 209 (2019) Guidelines on non-financial reporting: Supplement on reporting climate-related information, COM(2019) 640 The European Green Deal ("European Green Deal"), etc.

After Taxonomy Regulation came another Regulation amending SFDR, i.e. Regulation (EU) 2023/2869 certain Regulations as regards the establishment and functioning of the European single access point ("Single Access Point Regulation"). It is enlightening to compare the original wording of SFDR and the amended wording, see Table 1.

*Table 1. SFDR original and after amendments*

| SFDR original, not amended, still valid | SFDR as amended by Taxonomy Regulation and Single Access Point Regulation |
|---|---|
| Art. 2(17)<br>*'sustainable investment' means an investment in an economic activity that contributes to an environmental objective, as measured, for example, by key resource efficiency indicators on the use of energy, renewable energy, raw materials, water and land, on the production of waste, and greenhouse gas emissions, or on its impact on biodiversity and the circular economy, or an investment in an economic activity that contributes to a social objective, in particular an investment that contributes to tackling inequality or that fosters social cohesion, social integration and labour relations, or an investment in human capital or economically or socially disadvantaged communities, provided that such investments do not significantly harm any of those objectives and that the investee companies follow good governance practices, in particular with respect to sound management structures, employee relations, remuneration of staff and tax compliance;* | Art. 2a<br>Principle of do no significant harm<br>*1. The European Supervisory Authorities ... develop draft regulatory technical standards to specify the details of the content and presentation of the information in relation to the principle of 'do no significant harm' referred to in point (17) of Article 2 of this Regulation consistent with the content, methodologies, and presentation in respect of the sustainability indicators in relation to the adverse impacts referred to in paragraphs 6 and 7 of Article 4 of this Regulation.*<br>*2. ....*<br>*3. Power is delegated to the Commission to supplement this Regulation by adopting the regulatory technical standards referred to in paragraph 1 of this Article ...* |
| Art. 2(22) *'sustainability risk' means an environmental, social or governance event or condition that, if it occurs, could cause an actual or a potential material negative impact on the value of the investment;* | Article 18a<br>Accessibility of information on the European single access point<br>*1. From 10 January 2028, when making public any information ..., financial market participants and financial advisers shall submit that information at the same time to the relevant collection body referred to in paragraph 3 of this Article for the purpose of making it accessible on the European single access point (ESAP) established under Regulation (EU) 2023/2859 of the European Parliament and of the Council ...* |
| Art. 2(24)<br>*'sustainability factors' mean environmental, social and employee matters, respect for human rights, anti-corruption and anti-bribery matters.* | |

Source: Prepared by the Author based on Eur-Lex.

Regarding the harmonization of sustainability reporting, the evolution towards relevancy of information f, or and about sustainable information to be properly communicated via reporting by a growing number of businesses (MacGregor Pelikánová, 2021) goes back even to times before the switch to IFRS, i.e. already two decades ago the EU wanted to achieve the accounting harmonization and was forced to realize that country effects were considerably greater than sector effects (McLeay & Jaafar, 2007). In 2014, this was one of the motivations leading to the amendment of the Directive 2013/34/EU on the annual financial statements, consolidated financial statements and related reports of certain types of undertakings, ("Accounting Directive") by the famous Directive as regards the disclosure of non-financial and diversity information by certain large undertakings and groups ("Non-Financial Reporting Directive" or "NFRD"). NFRD added to Chapter 5 Management Report of Accounting Directive the famous Art. 19a Non-financial statement. The Rubicon was crossed and along various prior Regulations and Directives dealing with individual sustainability aspects in particular disciplines and field emerged a general legal norm asking large undertakings which were public-interest entities exceeding on their balance sheet dates the criterion of the average number of 500 employees to include in their management report at least a basic sustainability information, i.e. a report a non-financial statement about the undertaking's development, performance, position and impact of its activity, relating to, as a minimum, environmental, social and employee matters, respect for human rights, anti-corruption and bribery matters. In addition, based on the Directive 2017/1132 relating to certain aspects of company law ("Company Law Directive"), EU member states shall change their national law to ensure compulsory disclosures by companies of the accounting documents for each financial year which are required to be published in accordance with Accounting Directive (Art.14 Company Law Directive). In addition, e-version of these documents must be made publicly available trough the system of interconnection of registers (Art.18 Company Law Directive). Pursuant to the Commission Implementing Regulation (EU) 2021/1042 laying down rules for the application of Company Law Directive as regards technical specifications and procedures for the system of interconnection of registers ("BRIS Implementing Regulation"), this system of interconnection of registers is the electronic 'Business Registers Interconnection System ("BRIS")'using the ejustice platform and Hypertext Transfer Protocol Secure ("HTTPS"). As mentioned above, the Single Access Point Regulation bring the collection body regarding information from the financial sector.

Over time the general non-financial statement duty has become more specific, more enforceable, and entailing a growing number of subjects, see further amendments of the Accounting Directive, in particular by Directive (EU) 2022/2464 as regards corporate sustainability reporting ("CSRD") which updated Art. 19a by moving from the Non-financial Statement to Sustainability reporting and added Chapter 6a Sustainability Reporting Standards (Art. 29b et foll.). CSRD assigned a new role to European Financial Reporting Advisory Group ("EFRAG"), which is a private association established in 2001 and which focusses on both financial reporting pillar and sustainability reporting pillar while cooperating with national setters and authorities (Pittroff, 2021). Namely EFRAG provides Technical Advice to the European Commission regarding (re)drafting and amending standards and should do it while advancing the European public interest in both financial and sustainability reporting by developing and promoting European views in the field of corporate reporting. The rather softer induction of voluntary transition to CSR commitment by NFRD was progressively reinforced by and adding mandatory taxonomy, see SFDR and Taxonomy Regulation, and by expanding the pool of duty carriers by CSRD. Hence it is relevant to appreciate the wording development of the Accounting Directive by NFRD and CSRD, see Table 2.

*Table 2. Accounting Directive as amended by NFRD and CSRD*

| Accounting Directive as amended by NFRD | Accounting Directive as amended by CSRD |
|---|---|
| | Art. 2(17)<br>*'sustainability matters' means environmental, social and human rights, and governance factors, including sustainability factors defined in point (24) of Article 2 of Regulation (EU) 2019/2088;* |
| | Art. 2(18)<br>*'sustainability reporting' means reporting information related to sustainability matters in accordance with Articles 19a, 29a...* |
| Art. 19a Non-financial statement<br>*1. Large undertakings which are public-interest entities exceeding on their balance sheet dates the criterion of the average number of 500 employees during the financial year shall include in the management report a non-financial statement containing information to the extent necessary for an understanding of the undertaking's development, performance, position and impact of its activity, relating to, as a minimum, environmental, social and employee matters, respect for human rights, anti-corruption and bribery matters, including:* | Art. 19a Sustainability reporting<br>*1. Large undertakings, and small and medium-sized undertakings, except micro undertakings, which are public-interest entities as defined in point (a) of point (1) of Article 2 shall include in the management report information necessary to understand the undertaking's impacts on sustainability matters, and information necessary to understand how sustainability matters affect the undertaking's development, performance and position.*<br>*The information referred to in the first subparagraph shall be clearly identifiable within the management report, through a dedicated section of the management report.* |
| | Art. 29b Sustainability reporting standards<br>*1. The Commission shall adopt delegated acts in accordance with Article 49 supplementing this Directive to provide for sustainability reporting standards. Those sustainability reporting standards shall specify the information that undertakings are to report in accordance with Articles 19a and 29a and, where relevant, shall specify the structure to be used to present that information....which shall at least include the information that financial market participants subject to the disclosure obligations of Regulation (EU) 2019/2088 need in order to comply with those obligations.* |

Source: Prepared by the Author based on Eur-Lex.

And this was not all. One year later, the first set of the requested European Sustainability Reporting Standards ("ESRS") was prepared based on technical advice provided by EFRAG and adopted by the Commission Delegated Regulation (EU) 2023/2772 supplementing the Accounting Directive as regards sustainability reporting standards ("Sustainability Reporting Standards Regulation" or "SRSR") and is to be used by subjects to CSRD. ESRS cover all three pillars of sustainability as projected in ESG in the large sense, i.e. including climate change, biodiversity and human rights. ESRS should be compatible with the International Sustainability Standards Board ("ISSB") and the Global Reporting Initiative ("GRI") in order to ensure a very high degree of interoperability between EU and global standards and to prevent unnecessary double reporting by companies.

Well, the harmonization of sustainability reporting and the unification of taxonomy and standards to be used appear the be accomplished and proper information is to be shared, i.e. decision-making competencies relying on relevant, reliable, readable and freely accessible information about sustainability should be boosted. However is this the reality? Is the greenwashing and cherry-picking season over? Before engaging in any empiric studies and ergonometric and other assessment, it is critically important to pause and have a comparative and critical look on the so far resulting legislative measures regarding taxonomy and standardization to be used, i.e. Taxonomy Regulation and CSRD with Sustainability Reporting Standards Regulation are to be analyzed to achieve a deeper understanding about what, how, why and where is taxonomized and standardized.

## 3. UNIVERSALITY AND TAXONOMY OF INFORMATION FOR AND ABOUT SUSTAINABLE ENTREPRENEURSHIP – SOCIALLY GREEN TERMINOLOGY

As stated above, the CSRD amended the Accounting Directive and added to it the duty for a growing pool of businesses to include in their management report a dedicated section with the double materiality sustainability information, i.e. information necessary to understand the business's impacts on sustainability matters, and information necessary to understand how sustainability matters affect the business's development, performance and position (Art.19a Accounting Directive as amended by CSRD). Further, it has specified that such a dedicated section of the management report, Sustainability Report, must comply with standards, which are to be issued by the European Commission, and at least include the information to be disclosed by the financial market participants based on SFDR as amended by the Taxonomy Regulation (Art.29b Accounting Directive). These two provisions became a bridge putting together the so far in the parallel developing general legislative harmonization line regarding reporting around the continuously updated Accounting Directive, see NFRD and CSRD, and to the highly specific and mono-sector oriented regulation, see SFDR amended by the Taxonomy Regulation.

As a result, currently, SFDR, Taxonomy Regulation and Sustainability Reporting Standards Regulation with ESRS provide a universal framework for disclosing and publishing the information for and about sustainable entrepreneurship. This is about the information not only for investors, but for all stakeholders, and even retro-projecting to the business itself. Namely, this is about information about sustainable entrepreneurship based on the double materiality principle and going potentially above and beyond the ESG stricto sensu. In sum, the universality and taxonomy of such an information is clearly set by the EU law and the tool par excellence for it is the Taxonomy Regulation.

As stated above, the Taxonomy Regulation has a hybrid nature. On one hand, it sets general criteria to be applied across all industries and sectors, and on another hand it amends the highly specific and mono-sector oriented SFDR. This prima facia dichotomy is supported by the structure of the Taxonomy Regulation (Chapter I and Chapter II about general criteria v Chapter III about SFDR), but a closer examination reveals that after all the general criteria are not so much general and the amendments regarding SFDR are not so specific. As a matter of fact, Taxonomy Regulation offers neither standardization nor specific financial regulations to inform investors. Instead, it provides a particular approach to the perception of a green future based on the principle with a partially misleading name "do not significantly harm". This "socially green" universality and general applicability is cemented by CSRD.

The Preamble of the Taxonomy Regulation is very clear and explicit about the exhaustive list (!) for environment sustainability with six environmental objectives (Preamble 23) and the need regarding their specification in the context of the "do not significantly harm" principle (Preamble 34), but rather ambiguous regarding the combining of environmental and social aspects (Preamble 35), see Table 3.

*Table 3. Taxonomy Regulation Preamble*

| Taxonomy Regulation Preamble wording | Comments |
|---|---|
| *(23) For the purpose of determining the environmental sustainability of a given economic activity, an exhaustive list of environmental objectives should be laid down. The six environmental objectives that this Regulation should cover are: climate change mitigation; climate change adaptation; the sustainable use and protection of water and marine resources; the transition to a circular economy; pollution prevention and control; and the protection and restoration of biodiversity and ecosystems.* | Environment sustainable:<br>E1 climate mitigation<br>E2 climate adaption<br>E3 water<br>E4 circular economy<br>E5 pollution prevent<br>E6 biodiversity |
| (34) *For each environmental objective, uniform criteria for determining whether economic activities contribute substantially to that objective should be laid down. One element of the uniform criteria should be to avoid significant harm to any of the environmental objectives set out in this Regulation. …* | Not hurting any of E1-E6 |
| *(35) Recalling the joint commitment of the European Parliament, the Council and the Commission to pursuing the principles enshrined in the European Pillar of Social Rights in support of sustainable and inclusive growth, and recognising the relevance of international minimum human and labour rights and standards, compliance with minimum safeguards should be a condition for economic activities to qualify as environmentally sustainable. For that reason, economic activities should only qualify as environmentally sustainable where they are carried out in alignment with the OECD Guidelines for Multinational Enterprises and UN Guiding Principles on Business and Human Rights, including the declaration on Fundamental Principles and Rights at Work of the International Labour Organisation (ILO), the eight fundamental conventions of the ILO and the International Bill of Human Rights. The fundamental conventions of the ILO define human and labour rights that undertakings should respect. Several of those international standards are enshrined the Charter of Fundamental Rights of the European Union, in particular the prohibition of slavery and forced labour and the principle of non-discrimination.* | E1-E6 only if ILO observed<br>x slavery<br>x forced labour<br>x discrimination |

Source: Prepared by the Author based on Eur-Lex.

The Chapter I and Chapter II follow the vision of the for environment sustainability with six environmental objectives (Art. 3), but instead of explicitly speaking about its exhaustive nature, it engages in the setting of four criteria (Art. 3). Consequently, the substantial contribution to E1-E6 and "do not significantly harm" principle is complemented by the compliance with technical standards regarding E1-E6 and rather weakly defined OECD, UN and ILO principles (Art. 18) and this perhaps confuses further the (alleged) overlap of the environment and social pillars, perhaps even mix Social and Governance from the ESG, see Table 4.

*Table 4. Taxonomy Regulation – Chapter I and Chapter II*

| **Chapter I (Art. 1 – Art. 2) and Chapter II (Art. 3 – Art. 24)** | **Comments** |
|---|---|
| *Article 1 Subject matter and scope*<br>*1. This Regulation establishes the criteria for determining whether an economic activity qualifies as environmentally sustainable for the purposes of establishing the degree to which an investment is environmentally sustainable.*<br>*2. This Regulation applies to:*<br>*(a) measures adopted by Member States or by the Union that set out requirements for financial market participants or issuers in respect of financial products or corporate bonds that are made available as environmentally sustainable;*<br>*(b) financial market participants that make available financial products;*<br>*(c) undertakings which are subject to the obligation to publish a non-financial statement or a consolidated non-financial statement pursuant to Article 19a or Article 29a of Directive 2013/34/EU of the European Parliament and of the Council (68), respectively.* | Taxonomy establishes<br>- Only criteria about environmental sustainability (neither economic sustainability, nor social sustainability);<br>- Applies to financial markets participants and businesses in the reach of CSRD. |
| *Article 2 Definitions*<br>*For the purposes of this Regulation, the following definitions apply:*<br>*(1) 'environmentally sustainable investment' means an investment in one or several economic activities that qualify as environmentally sustainable under this Regulation;.* | Environment sustainable investment is set by this Regulation |
| *Article 3 Criteria for environmentally sustainable economic activities*<br>*For the purposes of establishing the degree to which an investment is environmentally sustainable, an economic activity shall qualify as environmentally sustainable where that economic activity:*<br>*(a) contributes substantially to one or more of the environmental objectives set out in Article 9 in accordance with Articles 10 to 16;*<br>*(b) does not significantly harm any of the environmental objectives set out in Article 9 in accordance with Article 17;*<br>*(c) is carried out in compliance with the minimum safeguards laid down in Article 18; and*<br>*(d) complies with technical screening criteria that have been established by the Commission in accordance with Article 10(3), 11(3), 12(2), 13(2), 14(2) or 15(2).* | 4 criteria for environment sustainability<br>- Substantially contribute to E1-E6<br>- do not significantly harm E1-E6;<br>- compliance of minimum (social) safeguards;<br>- compliance with technical screening for E1-E6 |
| *Article 9 Environmental objectives*<br>*For the purposes of this Regulation, the following shall be environmental objectives:*<br>*(a) climate change mitigation;*<br>*(b) climate change adaptation;*<br>*(c) the sustainable use and protection of water and marine resources;*<br>*(d) the transition to a circular economy;*<br>*(e) pollution prevention and control;*<br>*(f) the protection and restoration of biodiversity and ecosystems.* | E1 – E6 substantially contribute to<br>Art. 10 climate change mitigation<br>Art. 11 climate change adaptation<br>Art. 12 sustainable use and protection of water and marine resources<br>Art. 13 transition to a circular economy<br>Art. 14 pollution prevention and control<br>Art. 15 protection and restoration of biodiversity and ecosystems |
| *Article 18 Minimum safeguards*<br>*1. The minimum safeguards referred to in point (c) of Article 3 shall be procedures implemented by an undertaking that is carrying out an economic activity to ensure the alignment with the OECD Guidelines for Multinational Enterprises and the UN Guiding Principles on Business and Human Rights, including the principles and rights set out in the eight fundamental conventions identified in the Declaration of the International Labour Organisation on Fundamental Principles and Rights at Work and the International Bill of Human Rights.*<br>*2. When implementing the procedures referred to in paragraph 1 of this Article, undertakings shall adhere to the principle of 'do no significant harm' referred to in point (17) of Article 2 of Regulation (EU) 2019/2088.* | OECD Guidelines:<br>- Disclosure;<br>- Human Rights;<br>- Employment;<br>- Environment;<br>- Combating Bribery;<br>- Consumer Interest;<br>- Science, Technology;<br>- Competition;<br>- Taxation.<br>UN Guiding Principles.<br>- Human Rights;<br>Declaration of ILO:<br>- Collective bargaining;<br>- No discrimination;<br>- No slavery … |

Source: Prepared by the Author based one Eur-Lex.

Unlike the rather universally applicable Chapter I and Chapter II, Chapter III focuses only on the financial sector and amends SFDR by adding that ESAs will prepare draft regulatory technical standards for *"do not significantly harm"* principle to be adopted by the Commission (Art. 25), i.e. the *"do not significant harm"* is turning to be more technical and objective, see Table 5.

*Table 5. Taxonomy Regulation – Chapter III (Art. 25 – Art. 27)*

| **Chapter III of Taxonomy Regulation (Art. 25) adding Art. 2a to SFDR** | |
|---|---|
| *Article 25 Amendments to Regulation (EU) 2019/2088*<br>*Regulation (EU) 2019/2088 is amended as follows:*<br>*(1) the following Article is inserted:*<br>*"Article 2a Principle of do no significant harm*<br>*1. The European Supervisory Authorities established by Regulations (EU) No 1093/2010, (EU) No 1094/2010 and (EU) No 1095/2010 of the European Parliament and of the Council (collectively, the 'ESAs') shall, through the Joint Committee, develop draft regulatory technical standards to specify the details of the content and presentation of the information in relation to the principle of 'do no significant harm' referred to in point (17) of Article 2 of this Regulation consistent with the content, methodologies, and presentation in respect of the sustainability indicators in relation to the adverse impacts referred to in paragraphs 6 and 7 of Article 4 of this Regulation.*<br>*2. The ESAs shall submit the draft regulatory technical standards referred to in paragraph 1 to the Commission by 30 December 2020.*<br>*3. Power is delegated to the Commission to supplement this Regulation by adopting the regulatory technical standards referred to in paragraph 1 of this Article ....";* | ESAs prepare the technical standards regarding the principle of "do not significant harm" |

Source: Prepared by the Author based one Eur-Lex.

However considering the bridging effect of the Taxonomy Regulation, this addition to SFDR has definitely a reach exceeding the financial sector, indeed pursuant to this Art. 25 Taxonomy Regulation adding Art.2a to SFDR, already in 2023 European Commission adopted ESRS by Sustainability Reporting Standards Regulation reshaping E1-E6 of the Environmental part of ESG into ESRS E1-E5 and genuinely engaging in an independent manner with Social and Governance parts of ESG, i.e. the umbilical cord was cut and ESRS S1-S4 and ESRS G1 emerge along with two general ESRS 1 and ESRS 2.

## 4. STANDARDIZATION OF INFORMATION FOR AND ABOUT SUSTAINABLE ENTREPRENEURSHIP -SOCIALLY GREEN MEASURABILITY

Using the same terms does not mean to get the same meaning. For over one decade, businesses all over the word use, often heavily, terms such as sustainability, social responsibility, green, circular, etc. Abbreviations such as CSR, CSV and ESG are omnipresent. However, both experts and the society at large complain that sustainability reporting is misleading and ESG accounting is a mess (Eccles & Mirchandi, 2022). Sustainable entrepreneurship terminology needs both universal taxonomy and standardization, i.e. taxonomically set terms needs to have a measurable dimension. To put it differently, it is not only about providing the taxonomic data about the indicated phenomenon, but as well in comparable manner (Frintrup *et al.,* 2022).

In 2004, NFRD, made the first step towards the measurability of provided information by bringing five categories for information to be included in the non-financial statement, i.e. in the management report. These five included: environmental matters, social matters, employee matters, Human Rights and anti-corruption with bribery matters. Since the prevailing focus of European policies had prioritizing environment aspects, the ESG focus of the SFDR from 2019 was the strongest regarding the environmental aspect and the Taxonomy Regulation from 2020 cemented it by predominantly dealing with the environmental aspect and related methodology reflecting the European Green Deal. Nevertheless the ESG pendulum kept moving from E to S and perhaps even G and so the green focus turned to be rather socially green focus. The era of the almost exclusivity of green sustainability came to the end with Sustainability Standard Regulation with ESRS in 2023 and the transitions to pragmatic versions of the European Green Deal, see Clean Industrial Deal. It is educative to visualize the re-categorization and enlargement of the reach since NFRD, see Table 6.

*Table 6. Sustainability categories – NFDR, SFDR,v Taxonomy Regulation, SRSR with ESRS*

<table>
<tr><th>ESG</th><th>Art. 19a NFRD<br>Art.2 SFDR</th><th>Art. 9 Taxonomy Regulation</th><th>SRSR – ESRS</th></tr>
<tr><td>E</td><td>- environmental</td><td>- climate change mitigation<br>- climate change adaptation;<br>- the sustainable use and protection of water and marine resources;<br>- circular economy;<br>- pollution prevention and control;<br>- biodiversity</td><td>ESRS E1 Climate Change<br>ESRS E2 Pollution<br>ESRS E3 Water and marine resources<br>ESRS E4 Biodiversity and ecosystems<br>ESRS E5 Resource use and circular economy</td></tr>
<tr><td>S</td><td>- social,<br>- employees, Human Rights</td><td rowspan="2">OECD Guidelines:<br>- Disclosure;<br>- Human Rights;<br>- Employment;<br>- Environment;<br>- Combating Bribery;<br>- Consumer Interest;<br>- Science, Technology;<br>- Competition;<br>- Taxation.<br>UN Guiding Principles.<br>- Human Rights;<br>Declaration of ILO:<br>- Collective bargaining;<br>- No discrimination;<br>No slavery …</td><td>ESRS S1 Own workforce<br>ESRS S2 Workers in the value chain<br>ESRS S3 Affected communities<br>ESRS S4 Consumers and end-users</td></tr>
<tr><td>G</td><td>- anti-corruption,<br>- anti-bribery</td><td>ESRS G1 Business conduct</td></tr>
</table>

Source: Prepared by the Author based on Eur-Lex.

Interestingly, a similar transition occurred regarding three pillars of sustainability. Namely, the era of the purely economic focus with hard macro-economic indicators in the context of the Cold War (Tulloch, 2013), was ended around 1970 by the modern environmental movement in the West (Dunlap and Mertig, 1991), which played the prime until 1987, when the Brundtland Report proclaimed the crusade against poverty as the biggest evil and make social concerns at least as import as environment protection concerns. The depart from the trichotomy competition between sustainability pillars was completed by the Agenda 2030 with 17 SDGs.

Although Sustainability Reporting has not probably achieved such a multispectral maturity, the adoption of ESRS and their imposition via CSRD to a growing pool of businesses is clearly a move from the exclusively green approach. Plainly, the first colour of ESRS is green, but by no means this neither the only colour nor the automatically most important colour. The social dilution of the green dominance by the Taxonomy Regulation is already visible prima facia from the structure of the Sustainability Reporting Standards Regulation, see Table 7.

*Table 7. Sustainability Reporting Standards Regulation - Structure*

| **Sustainability Reporting Standards Regulation – wording** | **Comments** |
|---|---|
| *Art. 1 Subject Matter*<br>*The sustainability reporting standards that undertakings are to use for carrying out their sustainability reporting in accordance with Articles 19a and 29a of Directive 2013/34/EU following the timetable set out in Article 5(2) of Directive (EU) 2022/2464 are set out in Annexes I and II of this Regulation.* | ESRS for sustainability reporting by all from CSRD |
| *Art. 2 Entry into force and application*<br>*This Regulation shall enter into force on the third day following that of its publication in the Official Journal of the European Union.*<br>*It shall apply from 1 January 2024 for financial years beginning on or after 1 January 2024.*<br>*This Regulation shall be binding in its entirety and directly applicable in all Member States.* | ESRS are valid and directly applicable |
| *ANNEX I European sustainability reporting standards (ESRS)* | |
| *ANNEX II ACRONYMS AND GLOSSARY OF TERMS*<br>*This Annex presents all the acronyms found in the ESRS (Table 1) as well as all terms defined in the ESRS (Table 2).* | |

Source: Prepared by the Authors based one Eur-Lex.

Already a cursory overview of ESRS as indicated in Annex I of Sustainability Reporting Standards Regulation reveals that the common denominator is the famous double materiality principle and that there are various categories of ESRS.

Regarding the double materiality principle, it needs to be emphasized that ESRS demand qualitative characteristics of information for the sustainability statement to be prepared\ (Annex I Sustainability Reporting Standards – ESRS 1, chapter 2 and Appendix B). This means that the information presented in the sustainability statement meet the following requirements: relevance, faithful representation, comparability, verifiability and understandability. Starting with the relevance, a proper information for the sustainability statement, i.e. sustainability information must be relevant and this means "*it may make a difference in the decisions of users under a double materiality approach*" (Annex I Sustainability Reporting Standards – ESRS 1, chapter 3.3 and Appendix B, QC 1.). This means that the double materiality approach is really more an approach than a principle, it is about the potential and consequently the double materiality approach is satisfied "*even if some users choose no to take advantage of it or are already aware of it from other sources*" Annex I Sustainability Reporting Standards – ESRS 1, Appendix B, QC 2.). In sum, "*materiality is an entity-specific aspect of relevance based on the nature or magnitude or both*" Annex I Sustainability Reporting Standards – ESRS 1, Appendix B, QC 3.) which may (does not need to) assist in decision making of any user of the sustainability statement. This materiality has two dimensions: impact materiality and financial materiality and their assessment is inter-related" (Annex I Sustainability Reporting Standards – ESRS 1, chapter 3.3, 37 & 38). The impact materiality means the business´ "*material actual or potential, positive or negative impacts on people or environment over the short-, medium- or long term*" (Annex I Sustainability Reporting Standards – ESRS 1, chapter 3.4, 43). Financial materiality means information "*material for primary users of general-purpose financial reports in making decisions relating to providing resources to the entity*" ((Annex I Sustainability Reporting Standards – ESRS 1, chapter 3.5, 48).

Regarding categories, 1.1 ESRS (point 4) states that there are three categories of ESRS: cross-cutting standards, topical standards (E, S and G standards) and sector-specific standards, while cross-cutting standards and topical standards are sector-agnostic, i.e. apply to all businesses, see Table 8.

*Table 8. Sustainability Reporting Standards Regulation – Annex I*

| *ANNEX I European sustainability reporting standards (ESRS)* | **Selected points** |
|---|---|
| *ESRS 1 General requirements* | 3.3 double materiality (impact materiality and financial materiality) as the bases for sustainable disclosure.<br>3.4. impact materiality = material impact of undertaking on people or environment<br>3.5 financial materiality = material financial effect on the undertaking |
| *ESRS 2 General disclosures* | ESRS 2 GOV-1 The role of the administrative, management and supervisory bodies<br>ESRS 2 GOV-2 Information provided to these bodies<br>ESRS 2 GOV-3 Integration of sustainability-related performance in incentive schemes<br>ESRS 2 GOV-4 Statement on due diligence<br>ESRS 2 GOV-5 Risk management and internal controls over sustainability reporting<br>ESRS 2 SBM-1 Strategy, business model and value chain<br>ESRS 2 SBM-2 Interest and views of stakeholders<br>ESRS 2 SBM-3 Material impact, risks and opportunities and their interaction with strategy and business model<br>ESRS 2 IRO-1 Identify risk and opportunities<br>ESRS 2 IRO-2 Requirements complied<br>ESRS 2 MDR-P Minimal disclosure policies – policies adopted to manage material sustainable matters ..... |
| *ESRS E1 Climate Change* | Limiting the increase in the global average temperature 1.5 Celsius above pre-industrial levels in the line with Paris Agreement<br>Covers both Climate change mitigation and climate change adoption |
| *ESRS E2 Pollution* | How the undertaking affects pollution of air, water and soil, in terms of material positive and negative actual or potential impacts; |
| *ESRS E3 Water and marine resources* | Marine resources, blue economy, water consumption |
| *ESRS E4 Biodiversity and ecosystems* | How the undertaking affects biodiversity and ecosystems, in terms of material positive and negative, actual and potential impacts, including the extent to which it contributes to the drivers of biodiversity and ecosystem loss and degradation; |
| *ESRS E5 Resource use and circular economy* | !!! Minimising waste !!! preserving resources, increasing efficiency, avoiding depletion |
| *ESRS S1 Own workforce* | secure employment; working time;adequate wages;social dialogue;<br>freedom of association, the existence of works councils and the information, consultation and participation rights of workers;collective bargaining, including the rate of the undertaking's workforce covered by collective agreements; work-life balance; health and safety;equal treatment and opportunities |
| *ESRS S2 Workers in the value chain* | - working conditions (for example, secure employment, working time, adequate wage, social dialogue, freedom of association, including the existence of work councils, collective bargaining, work-life balance and health and safety);<br>- equal treatment and opportunities for all (for example, gender equality and equal pay for work of equal value, training and skills development, the employment and inclusion of persons with disabilities, measures against violence and harassment in the workplace, and diversity);<br>- other work-related rights (for example, child labour, forced labour, adequate housing, water and sanitation and privacy). |

continued on following page

*Table 8. Continued*

| *ANNEX I European sustainability reporting standards (ESRS)* | **Selected points** |
|---|---|
| *ESRS S3 Affected communities* | - communities' economic, social and cultural rights (for example, adequate housing, adequate food, water and sanitation, land-related and security-related impacts);<br>- communities' civil and political rights (for example, freedom of expression, freedom of assembly, impacts on human rights defenders); and<br>- particular rights of indigenous peoples (for example, free, prior and informed consent, self-determination, cultural rights). |
| ESRS S4 Consumers and end-users | how the undertaking affects the consumers and/or end-users of its products and/or services (referred to in this Standard as "consumers and end-users"), in terms of material positive and negative actual or potential impacts;....<br>the financial effects on the undertaking over the short-, medium- and long-term of material risks and opportunities arising from the undertaking's impacts and dependencies on consumers and/or end-users. |
| *ESRS G1 Business conduct* | = to understand the undertaking's strategy and approach, processes and procedures: business ethics and corporate culture, including anti-corruption and anti-bribery, the protection of whistleblowers, and animal welfare; the management of relationships with suppliers, including payment practices, especially with regard to late payment to small and medium-sized undertakings;activities and commitments of the undertaking related to exerting its political influence, including its lobbying activities.. |

Source: Prepared by the Author based one Eur-Lex.

Table 8 shows that there are two cross-cutting standards, i.e. applying to all business and to all their aspects: ESRS 1 general requirements and ESRS 2 general disclosure, and 10 specific requirements – five for E, four for S and one for G. This Annex I is followed by Annex II which includes the list of used acronyms and glossary of terms, i.e. the list of used abbreviation and definitions of ESRS terms, including terms such as double materiality.

## 5. CONCLUSION

Taxonomy and standardization of information for and about sustainable entrepreneurship in the EU policies and law has undergonme a rather radical, perhaps even aggressive, development during the last decade. This development was progressively linear with a clear drive to move from a rather passive and facultative offering of certain non-financial data in whatsoever format into an active and mandatory providing of sustainable information taxonomically unified and measurably standardized by an exponential pool of businesses.

This development had a set of milestones, represented firstly by policies, then by Directives and recently more and more by Regulations priorly Directives, while the CJ EU has not had so far a sufficient chance and time to develop a matching case law. Nevertheless, the general message is clear – information regarding sustainable entrepreneurship has become integral information needed by investors, consumers, business partners and the entire society in order to make educated decision about the particular business as well as information needed by the business itself to reassess and readjust its vision, missions, priorities and strategies, including regular day-to-day conduct.

The EU framework for taxonomy and standardization of such information has definitely created the potential for more transparency, understanding and measurable comparisons of critical and highly relevant information about business and business conduct which do not fit in conventional financial statements documents.

In addition to these rather conventional propositions and conclusions, the performed contextual, comparative and teleological exploration of the dynamic pathway towards relevant information for sustainable entrepreneurship and its milestones, in particular the most recent ones, leads to four sets of new suggestions.

Firstly, the double materiality is not a principle regarding two separated phenomena, instead it is rather an approach to two inter-related set of information and concerns. This approach is employed not from a perspective of an expert, but any user. Plainly, if the information might be relevant in decision making process of any user about any external effects on the business and/or any impact of the business on the society, then it is along with the double materiality approach. In addition, this is not only about relevancy (about almost anything influencing decision-making), this is as well about understanding, etc.

Secondly, regarding E, the entire environment encompassing approach is obvious and expected along with the reference to Paris Agreement, but it should be emphasized the recognition of the virtue of waste avoidance. Thirdly, regarding S, a clear community and even global spill-over is manifest with a rather controversial gender issues and with a well expected rediscovery of the importance of the consumer view. Fourthly, regarding G, it is worthy to note the direct reference to ethics blurring further the difference between the enforceable law and only morally binding sphere of ethics.

Finally, it needs to be pointed out the Annex II to SRSR further reinforcing the given taxonomy and thus bridging towards the standardized taxonomy sui generis.

Well, the taxonomy and standardization saga witnesses a rather progressive development during current turbulent era and the performed study offers just a current snapshot having inherent limitations and shortcomings. Manifestly, longitudinal studies as well as the consideration of the case law, once established, along with empirical observations and national and supranational industries and segment case studies will be necessary to achieve a deeper understanding. However, once this done, the policy and legislative changes might occur and modify the current setting of taxonomy and standardization. After all, each analysis and study of taxonomy and standardization is rather about the fast evaporating past. Indeed, right now, we are witnessing the move from the Green Deal to the more pragmatic Clean Industrial Deal as well as many external events with global dimensions which can lead to both evolutionary and revolutionary changes. This is a chase after train which left and this chase is not to be given up. "*Tempora mutantur, nos et mutamur in illis*" - Times keep changing and we change with them, we change them and they change us, so after all, the double materiality approach and the omnipresent and omnireaching ESG are not so foreign to us humans.

## REFERENCES


Atrill, P., & McLaney, E. (2017). *Accounting and Finance for Non-Specialists* (10th ed.). Pearson.

Balcerzak, A., MacGregor, R. K., MacGregor Pelikánová, R., Rogalska, E., & Szostek, D. (2023). The EU regulation of sustainable investment: The end of sustainability trade-offs? *Entrepreneurial Business and Economics Review*, *11*(1), 199–212. DOI: 10.15678/EBER.2023.110111

Balcerzak, A., & MacGregor Pelikánová, R. (2020). Projection of SDGs in Codes of Ethics – Case study about Lost in Translation? *Administrative Sciences, 10*(4): 1-18. Paper 95. .DOI: 10.3390/admsci10040095

Balcerzak, A. P., & Pietrzak, M. B. (2017). Sustainable Development in the European Union in the Years 2004–2013. In Bilgin, M., Danis, H., Demir, E., & Can, U. (Eds.), *Regional Studies on Economic Growth, Financial Economics and Management. Eurasian Studies in Business and Economics* (Vol. 7). Springer. DOI: 10.1007/978-3-319-54112-9_12

Bali Swain, R., & Yang-Wallentin, F. (2019). Achieving sustainable development goals: Predicaments and strategies. *International Journal of Sustainable Development and World Ecology*, *27*(2), 96–106. DOI: 10.1080/13504509.2019.1692316

Borseková, K., Vaňová, A., Šúrová, J., Kráľ, P., Turečková, K., Nevima, J., & Martinát, S. (2021). The Nexus between Creative Actors and Regional Development. *Land (Basel)*, *10*(3), 276. DOI: 10.3390/land10030276

Bowen, H. R. (1953). *Social responsibility of the Businessman*. Harper & Row.

Caliendo, M., Goethner, M., & Weißenberger, M. (2019). Entrepreneurial persistence beyond survival: Measurement and determinants. *Journal of Small Business Management*, *58*(3), 617–647. DOI: 10.1080/00472778.2019.1666532

Carroll, A. B. (2016). Carroll's pyramid of CSR: Taking another look. *International Journal of Corporate Social Responsibility*, *1*(1), 3. DOI: 10.1186/s40991-016-0004-6

Cowling, M., & Dvouletý, O. (2023). Who is brave enough to start a new business during the Covid-19 pandemic? *Baltic Journal of Management*, *18*(3), 402–419. DOI: 10.1108/BJM-11-2022-0414

Czyżewski, B., Matuszczak, A., Polcyn, J., Katarzyna Smędzik-Ambroży, K., & Staniszewski, J. (2020). Deadweight loss in environmental policy: The case of the European Union member states. *Journal of Cleaner Production*, *260*, 121064. Advance online publication. DOI: 10.1016/j.jclepro.2020.121064

D'Adamo, I., & Gastaldi, M. (2023). Monitoring the Performance of Sustainable Development Goals in the Italian Regions. *Sustainability (Basel)*, *15*(19), 14094. DOI: 10.3390/su151914094

D'Adamo, I., & Lupi, G. (2021). Sustainability and Resilience after COVID-19: A Circular Premium in the Fashion Industry. *Sustainability (Basel)*, *13*(4), 1861. DOI: 10.3390/su13041861

Dunlap, R. E., & Mertig, A. G. (1991). The evolution of the US environmental movement from 1970 to 1990: An overview. *Society & Natural Resources*, *4*(3), 209–218. DOI: 10.1080/08941929109380755

Eccles, R. G., & Mirchandi, B. (2022, 15th February). We Need Universal ESG Accounting Standards. *Harvard Business Review*. https://hbr.org/2022/02/we-need-universal-esg-accounting-standards

Friedman, M. (2007). The social responsibility of business is to increase its profits. In Zimmerli, W. Ch., Richter, K., & Holzinger, M. (Eds.), *Corporate Ethics and Corporate Governance* (pp. 173–178). Springer. DOI: 10.1007/978-3-540-70818-6_14

Frintrup, M., Schmidthuber, L., & Hilgers, D. (2022). Towards accounting harmonization in Europe: A multinational survey among budget experts. *International Review of Administrative Sciences*, *88*(2), 390–410. DOI: 10.1177/0020852320915640

Galindo-Martín, M.-A., Castaño-Martínez, M.-S., & Méndez-Picazo, M.-T. (2020). The Relationship between Green Innovation, *Social Entrepreneurship, and Sustainable Development. Sustainability (Basel)*, *12*(11), 4467. DOI: 10.3390/su12114467

Hála, M., MacGregor Pelikánová, R., & Rubáček, F. (2024). Negative Determinants of CSR Support by Generation Z in Central Europe - Infodemic's Gender-Sensitive Impacts in a 'COVID-19' Era. *Central European Business Review*, *13*(2), 1–26. DOI: 10.18267/j.cebr.344

Hühn, M. P. (2023). Business ethics: Between Friedman and Freeman? A response to A Puzzle about Business Ethics. *Business Ethics, the Environment & Responsibility*, *32*(2), 868–876. DOI: 10.1111/beer.12523

Kot, S., & Ojinji, S. (2023). Environmental Sustainability and Freight Transport Performance in the EU – An Autoregressive Conditional Heteroscedasticity (ARCH) Model Analysis. *Promet - Traffic&Transportation, 35*(5), 621–634. DOI: 10.7307/ptt.v35i5.293

MacGregor Pelikánová, R. (2017). Constatine's Christianity for the (Dis)integrated EU. Déjà vu of Constantine's Roman governance reflecting of the mistrial of Jesus for EU? *Dialogo*, *4*(1), 81–98. DOI: 10.18638/dialogo.2017.4.1

MacGregor Pelikánová, R. (2021). Internal Website Presentation of Czech Luxury Fashion Businesses in the Covid-19 Era. *Marketing and Management of Innovations*, *3*(3), 211–222. DOI: 10.21272/mmi.2021.3-18

MacGregor Pelikánová, R. (2023). Accounting Science's Historical Development and Its Role in Social Science. In: Knihová, Ladislava (Ed.) *Applying Interdisciplinarity to Globalization, Management, Marketing, and Accountancy Science*. IGI Global, pp. 238-257 of 333. DOI: . ISBN 9781799886693. Available from https://www.igi-global.com/book/applying-interdisciplinarity-globalization-management-marketing/272220#descriptionDOI: 10.4018/978-1-7998-8669-3.ch009

MacGregor Pelikánová, R. (2023). Accounting Theories and Their Application in Accounting Sciences. In: Knihová, Ladislava (Ed.) *Applying Interdisciplinarity to Globalization, Management, Marketing, and Accountancy Science*. IGI Global, pp. 258-275 of 333. . ISBN 9781799886693. Available from https://www.igi-global.com/book/applying-interdisciplinarity-globalization-management-marketing/272220#descriptionDOI: 10.4018/978-1-7998-8669-3.ch010

MacGregor Pelikánová, R. (2024). EU legislative proposals to involve customers in the greening of the economy proposals. *The Lawyer Quarterly, 2*, 218-235. https://tlq.ilaw.cas.cz/index.php/tlq/article/view/597

MacGregor Pelikánová, R., & MacGregor, R. K. (2020). The EU puzzling CSR regime and the confused perception by ambassadors of luxury fashion businesses: A case study from Pařížská. *Central European Business Review*, *9*(3), 74–108. DOI: 10.18267/j.cebr.240

MacGregor Pelikánová, R., MacGregor, R. K., & Černek, M. (2021). New trends in codes of ethics: Czech business ethics preferences by the dawn of COVID-19. *Oeconomia Copernicana*, *12*(4), 973–1009. DOI: 10.24136/oc.2021.032

MacGregor Pelikánová, R., Nesbitt, T., Balcerzak, A. P., & Oulehla, J. (2024). (In)Effective Communication about Social Responsibility? Examining Large European Businesses in the Czech Republic. *Business. Management and Economics Engineering*, *22*(2), 214–239. DOI: 10.3846/bmee.2024.21414

MacGregor Pelikánová, R., & Rubáček, F. (2022). Taxonomy for transparency in non-financial statements – clear duty with unclear sanction. *Danube*, *13*(3), 173–195. DOI: 10.2478/danb-2022-0011

MacGregor Pelikánová, R., & Sani, M. (2023). Luxury, Slow and Fast Fashion – A Case study on the (Un)sustainable Creating of Shared Values. *Equilibrium.Quarterly Journal of Economics and Economic Policy*, *18*(3), 813–851.

MacGregor Pelikánová, R., Sani, M., & Rubáček, F. (2024). Sustainable And Responsible Creation Of Shared Values In The Fast Fashion Industry – I Will Believe It When I See It. *Visions for Sustainability, 21*, 8873, 1-29. DOI: 10.13135/2384-8677/8873

McLeay, S., & Jaafar, A. (2007). Accounting Harmonization in Europe: Country Effects and Sector Effects. *Abacus – a Journal of Accounting. Finance and Business Studies*, *43*(2), 156–189. DOI: 10.1111/j.1467-6281.2007.00224.x

Pakšiová, R., & Oriskóová, D. (2020). Capital Maintenance Evolution Using Outputs From Accounting System. *Scientific Annals of Economics and Business. - Iasi: University of Iasi. 67*(3),311-331.

Pittroff, E. (2021). The legitimacy of global accounting rules: A note on the challenges from path-dependence theory. *The Journal of Management and Governance*, *25*(2), 379–396. DOI: 10.1007/s10997-020-09546-6

Polcyn, J., Stratan, A., & Lopotenco, V. (2023). Sustainable Agriculture's Contribution to Quality of Life. *Sustainability (Basel)*, *15*(23), 16415. DOI: 10.3390/su152316415

Porter, M. E., & Kramer, M. R. (2011). Creating Shared Value. *Harvard Business Review*, *89*(1-2), 62–77. https://hbr.org/2011/01/the-big-idea-creating-shared-value

Purvis, B., Mao, Y., & Robinson, D. (2019). Three pillars of sustainability: In search of conceptual origins. *Sustainability Science*, *14*(3), 681–695. DOI: 10.1007/s11625-018-0627-5

Rubáček, F., MacGregor Pelikánová, R. and MacGregor R.K. (2023). The sustainability of ESAs triumvirate for sustainability-related disclosures in the financial sector – all for one and one for all. *Acta Universitatis Lodziensis. Folia Iuridica, 105*, 123-143. OI: DOI: 10.18778/0208-6069.105.08

Schüz, M. (2012). Sustainable Corporate Responsibility – The Foundation of successful Business in the New Millennium. *Central European Business Review*, *1*(2), 7–15. DOI: 10.18267/j.cebr.12

Shpak, N., Melnyk, O., Horbal, N., Ruda, M., & Sroka, W. (2021). Assessing the Implementation of the Circular Economy in the EU Countries. *Forum Scientiae Oeconomia*, *9*(1). Advance online publication. DOI: 10.23762/FSO_VOL9_NO1_2

Spaiser, V., Ranganathan, S., Swain, R. B., & Sumpter, D. J. T. (2016). The sustainable development oxymoron: Quantifying and modelling the incompatibility of sustainable development goals. *International Journal of Sustainable Development and World Ecology*, *24*(6), 457–470. DOI: 10.1080/13504509.2016.1235624

Stolowy, H., & Ding, Y. (2017). *Financial accounting and reporting: a global perspective* (5th ed.). Cengage Learning.

Thelken, H. N., & de Jong, G. (2020). The impact of values and future orientation on intention formation within sustainable entrepreneurship. *Journal of Cleaner Production*, *266*, 122052. DOI: 10.1016/j.jclepro.2020.122052

Tulloch, L. (2013). On science, ecology and environmentalism. *Policy Futures in Education*, *11*(1), 100–114. DOI: 10.2304/pfie.2013.11.1.100

Van Tulder, R., & Keen, N. (2018). Capturing Collaborative Challenges: Designing Complexity-Sensitive Theories of Change for Cross-Sector Partnerships. *Journal of Business Ethics*, *150*(2), 315–332. DOI: 10.1007/s10551-018-3857-7 PMID: 30996500

Van Tulder, R., Seitanidi, M. M., Crane, A., & Brammer, S. (2016). Enhancing the Impact of Cross-Sector Partnerships. Four Impact Loops for Channeling Partnership Studies. *Journal of Business Ethics*, *135*(1), 1–17. DOI: 10.1007/s10551-015-2756-4

Van Tulder, R., & Van Mil, E. (2023). *Principles of Sustainable Business – Frameworks for Corporate Action on the SDGs*. Routledge.

Weygandt, J. J., Kimmel, P. D., & Kieso, D. E. (2013). *Financial Accounting*. IFRS Edition (2nd Ed.). John Willey & Sons, Inc.

Zavřelová, V., & MacGregor Pelikánová, R. (2024). The ephemeral term "sustainable development" in current EU policies. *Folia Oeconomica Stetinensia*, *24*(2), 389–418. DOI: 10.2478/foli-2024-0031

# Chapter 14
# Building Competencies for Sustainability Decision-Making Among Management Students

**Renata Paksiova**
https://orcid.org/0000-0002-3833-9339
*University of Economics in Bratislava, Slovakia*

**Petra Pribilova**
https://orcid.org/0000-0003-4707-2135
*Newton University, Czech Republic*

**Roman Brauner**
https://orcid.org/0000-0002-9246-3154
*Newton University, Czech Republic*

## ABSTRACT

*This study analyzes the integration of sustainability principles and circular economy concepts into the higher management education curriculum at a specific university (Newton University). The aim is to assess students' awareness, knowledge, and readiness to apply these principles in future managerial roles. A quantitative questionnaire was administered to 115 final-year management students. Findings reveal that although 56% of respondents were aware of the term "circular economy," only 10% could accurately define it. Moreover, while all students recognized "sustainability," 70% were unable to provide an accurate definition within the environmental and social context of business. Nearly 90% consider these topics essential for their future practice. These results underscore the need for deeper curricular integration and innovative pedagogical approaches to enhance practical readiness for sustainable management.*

DOI: 10.4018/979-8-3373-0189-1.ch014

## INTRODUCTION

In today's business environment, sustainability and the principles of a circular economy are becoming key factors for organisations' long-term success. Integrating these principles into business strategies enables companies to minimise environmental risks while gaining a competitive advantage through innovation and resource efficiency.

The development of students' competencies in sustainability and green management is a current topic created by society-wide demand on the labour market. The competencies of green managers and their development at universities represent a critical area of study, especially in sustainable development and environmental care. As the global community becomes increasingly aware of the problem of tackling climate change and ecological degradation, the role of educational institutions in cultivating the necessary competencies for future sustainability leaders is becoming crucial. The baseline literature review of this chapter synthesises various studies that examine the competencies needed for managers, the integration of sustainability into financial education and university initiatives to promote these competencies, the pedagogical approaches used in higher education, and the implications for curriculum development, which supports the importance of ongoing research in the core theme of our chapter, which is building the competencies of managers in higher education institutions in the field of sustainability.

Despite the growing importance of these topics, there is a gap in management education between theoretical knowledge and its practical application. Many curricula have not yet integrated sustainability and circular economy, which may lead to future managers' lack of preparedness to face environmental and social challenges.

This research aims to analyse the current state of students' knowledge of sustainability and circular economy in management education at a Czech university, which will represent a starting point for further research direction and complement the existing research in management education. We will focus on identifying students' awareness and knowledge of these concepts and assessing their readiness to implement them in future practice. The results of this study can contribute to the design of effective learning strategies that ensure that future managers are equipped with the necessary skills and knowledge to address current and future sustainability challenges.

In the following subchapters, we will first focus on an overview of the literature related to sustainability and the circular economy in the context of management education. Subsequently, we will describe our research methodology, including the data collection and analysis methods used. In the chapter Results, we will present the main findings of our survey. In the discussion, we will compare these results with existing studies and discuss their implications for educational programs. Finally, we will summarise the key findings and propose recommendations for future research and practice.

## LITERATURE REVIEW

Green managers are expected to have unique competencies that combine environmental knowledge with financial acumen. According to Zhelev et al. promoting the green transition through higher education highlights the need for competencies that align with green standards, which are essential for effective governance in the context of sustainability (Zhelev et al., 2023). This is also confirmed by Abtahi, who discusses initiatives at the Technical University of Isfahan aimed at creating a green campus, emphasising the need for managers to understand both the environmental and financial implications of their decisions (Abtahi, 2021). In addition, Fuchs et al. suggest that a balanced approach to the scorecard can help integrate sustainability into strategic management, thereby strengthening the competencies of green managers in financial contexts (Fuchs et al., 2020). The concept of competence encompasses a range of skills, knowledge, and attitudes necessary for effective sustainability management. According to Priyanka and Bansal, the concept of a "green campus" is an integral part of promoting these competencies, as it includes smart resource sharing, green building development, and reducing the carbon footprint within the university environment (Priyanka & Bansal, 2019). Students need to see examples of sustainability management in their college. This basic understanding is crucial for developing curricula that prepare students to address sustainability challenges effectively. Cebrián et al. highlight the importance of integrating sustainability competencies into educational frameworks and the need for a comprehensive approach that includes action research, project-based learning, and validation of assessment tools to link sustainability competencies to employability (Cebrián et al., 2021; Cebrián et al., 2020). This perspective is confirmed by Galleli et al., who argue that the development of competencies related to the Sustainable Development Goals (SDGs) is crucial for business administration education and advocate for a systematic review of the literature to identify the key competencies needed to achieve these goals (Galleli et al., 2022).

Lambrechts et al. emphasise the importance of professional development in developing sustainability competencies and suggest that educational institutions must empower students through targeted training and organisational change processes (Mohammed et al., 2023; Lambrechts et al., 2017). This is consistent with the findings of Valle et al., who highlight the role of green people management in developing organisational competencies for sustainability. They suggest that educational programs should provide knowledge and cultivate practical skills that students can apply in real-world scenarios (Valle et al., 2024).

Developing green governance competencies is increasingly recognised as essential to promote sustainability in higher education. The role of organisational culture in promoting knowledge management and green innovation is crucial, as stated in a study on private universities ("The role of organisational culture in knowledge management and green innovation in private universities", 2024). This suggests that universities need to cultivate an environment that fosters the development of green competencies among their staff and students. The implementation of green university concepts, Abakumov says, illustrates how universities can create a sustainable image while strengthening the competencies of their management teams (Abakumov, 2023). Universities are implementing various strategies to improve their sustainability practices. A case study by King Abdul Aziz University illustrates how comprehensive infrastructure and energy management initiatives can serve as a model for other institutions aimed at achieving sustainability (Farooq et al., 2023). Similarly, a study on waste management strategies at the University of Mahasarakham highlights the importance of establishing guidelines that align with the evaluation criteria of green universities, thereby increasing the competencies of those involved in sustainability management (Phrophayak et al., 2024). These practical examples highlight the need for universities to adopt a holistic approach to sustainability that includes both financial and environmental considerations.

In addition, the role of green technology transfer in improving sustainability practices in universities is gaining attention. Research by Silva et al. suggests that effective technology transfer mechanisms are essential to promote green practices within higher education institutions (Silva et al., 2023). This is especially important for green managers, who need to navigate the complexities of integrating new technologies into existing systems while ensuring financial viability. The emphasis on collaboration and knowledge-sharing between universities can facilitate this process, as highlighted by the findings of the bibliometric analysis of green management (Oduncu & Cengiz, 2022).

The challenges faced by universities in implementing green initiatives are multifaceted. The Tshivhase study highlights the need for comprehensive education and outreach programs to equip university staff with the necessary skills to manage sustainability effectively (Tshivhase, 2024). This is consistent with the findings of Alqudah and Yusof, which suggest that academic citizenship behavior can mediate the relationship between green performance management and environmental outcomes (Alqudah & Yusof, 2024). By promoting a culture of sustainability and encouraging the active participation of all stakeholders, universities can strengthen the competencies of their green managers and promote meaningful change.

The role of engaging students in improving corporate image and sustainability initiatives cannot be overlooked. Al-Dmour emphasises that engaged students make a significant contribution to the success of green initiatives on campus, which in turn fosters a culture of sustainability that green managers can leverage (Al-Dmour, 2023). This is consistent with the findings of Cheng et al., who argue that collaborative efforts between universities can increase the effectiveness of sustainability initiatives and thus improve the competencies of those who manage these programs (Cheng et al., 2018). The importance of student involvement in sustainability efforts is further supported by research on campus greening initiatives in Romania, which suggests that student participation is critical to successfully implementing sustainable practices (Sima et al., 2019).

The development of green competencies is not limited to managerial roles but extends to all stakeholders within the university ecosystem. The Green Human Resource Management (GHRM) concept is crucial in this context, encompassing practices promoting environmental awareness and employee behaviour. Studies have shown that GHRM practices significantly influence the environmental behaviour of employees, which is essential for achieving sustainability goals in universities (Miah et al., 2024). This is especially important in the context of educational programs aimed at strengthening the competencies of green managers, as highlighted by the need for continuous education and awareness-raising initiatives (Saleh, 2023).

Integrating sustainability into financial education is another critical aspect of developing green competencies. As universities seek to align their financial practices with sustainability goals, the role of green managers is becoming increasingly complex. Research conducted by Xuemin et al. highlights the relationship between green management, organisational culture, and green behaviour, suggesting that financial education must incorporate sustainability principles to effectively prepare future leaders (Xuemin et al., 2024). This is supported by the findings of Miah et al., which suggest that understanding the financial implications of sustainability initiatives is crucial for green managers (Miah et al., 2024).

Pedagogical methodologies used in higher education play an important role in shaping these competencies. Martín-Peña et al. discuss the effectiveness of the flipped classroom methodology in promoting a holistic understanding of sustainability principles among students, equipping them with skills to promote sustainable practices (Martín-Peña et al., 2023). This innovative approach complements Khoiriyah et al.'s exploration of sustainable Islamic education that emphasises the importance of contextual learning in achieving the SDGs (Khoiriyah et al., 2023). Such methodologies improve students' understanding and prepare them for real-world challenges in sustainability management.

Integrating sustainability into curricula is essential for preparing future green managers, which highlights the need for educational institutions to adapt their programs to include sustainability-focused content (Vesperi et al., 2024). In addition to pedagogical strategies, integrating sustainability competencies into curricula is essential to promote a culture of sustainability in educational institutions. Mirčetić et al. discuss the impact of green competencies on an organisation's performance and suggest that colleges should integrate these competencies into their curricula to increase the employability of graduates in sustainable industries (Mirčetić et al., 2022). This view is supported by Kalinowski et al., who identify specific competencies needed for environmentally responsible managers, including strategic thinking and the ability to implement sustainable practices within supply chains (Kalinowski et al., 2018). Lambrechts et al.. provide a comprehensive analysis of how different management bachelor's programs have incorporated sustainability competencies, noting that many universities have made significant progress in incorporating sustainability into their educational offerings (Lambrechts et al.., 2013). This integration is further supported by the development of sustainability competency maps, as demonstrated by Gil-Domenech ct al., which serve as valuable tools to guide curriculum design in the disciplines of business administration and management (Gil-Domenech et al., 2021). The integration of green competencies into higher education curricula is further supported by the findings of Tetteh et al., which explore how green logistics practices can impact supply chain performance, highlighting the need for students to understand the broader implications of their role in sustainability (Tetteh et al., 2024). Similarly, Naharuddinova et al.'s systematic analysis of the literature highlights the need for educational programs that address the skills and abilities needed for effective environmental management, suggesting that a comprehensive approach to curriculum design is essential (Naharuddin et al., 2024).

In terms of practical implementation, Shaov et al.'s research on green talent management strategies emphasises the importance of aligning learning outcomes with industry needs and advocates for curricula that teach theoretical concepts and include hands-on experience with green management practices (Shao et al., 2024). This is crucial to ensure that graduates are well-equipped to meet the demands of the evolving labour market, especially in sustainability-focused sectors.

The role of experiential learning in developing green management competencies cannot be overstated. Wawer emphasises the importance of internships in shaping students' competencies for sustainable development and suggests that hands-on experience is essential for bridging the gap between theoretical knowledge and real-world application (Wawer, 2023). This sentiment is reinforced by the findings of Venn et al., who identify key competencies for sustainability professionals and highlight the need for hands-on learning and opportunities for experiential learning in higher education (Venn et al., 2022).

Chanveasna et al. also highlight the role of green human resource management practices (GHRM; Green Human Resource Management) in promoting green competencies, which explores how GHRM can increase organisational innovation and employee creativity in the context of small and medium-sized enterprises (SMEs) (Chanveasna et al., 2024). Higher education institutions should also focus on developing GHRM competencies among students and preparing them for tasks that require environmental awareness and human resource management skills.

Yafi et al. underline the importance of green training as a mechanism for improving environmental performance. They show that green training can significantly improve employee competencies and motivation, leading to better organisational outcomes (Yafi et al., 2021). This finding suggests that universities should incorporate green training modules into their programs to better prepare students for the challenges they will face in the workforce.

The concept of a green psychological contract, as Sulich and Kozar say, emphasises the need to align employee and management commitments to environmental standards and values (Sulich & Kozar, 2024). This alignment is crucial for fostering a culture of sustainability in organisations, and educational institutions must play a key role in instilling these values in their students.

In addition, Bombiak's findings suggest that the growing interest in sustainable business practices requires a shift in how managerial competencies are defined and taught in higher education (Bombiak, 2019). This shift should focus on the ethical implications of business decisions and the importance of corporate social responsibility in promoting sustainable practices.

Also, the evolving environment of sustainability education requires a focus on interdisciplinary approaches encompassing different knowledge areas. Moradi's research on sustainable entrepreneurship in agricultural higher education illustrates the need to integrate different competencies, such as systems thinking and foresight thinking, to prepare students for the complexities of sustainable development (Moradi, 2021). This interdisciplinary approach is also confirmed by Khare and MacNeil, who advocate for the adoption of sustainability competencies in management education to address the multifaceted challenges posed by the SDGs (Khare & MacNeil, 2024).

Sustainability competency assessment is another critical aspect of developing effective green managers. Cebrián and Junyent examine students' views on sustainability competencies and highlight the need for robust assessment tools to assess the effectiveness of educational programmes in promoting these competencies (Cebrián & Junyent, 2015). Similarly, López-Alcarria et al. highlight the importance of agile methodologies in education to strengthen sustainability competencies, advocating for the continuous evaluation and adaptation of teaching practices (López-Alcarria et al., 2019).

Integrating green competencies into higher education curricula is not without its challenges. As Wielewska et al. note that ongoing research is needed to identify effective pedagogical approaches that can improve the teaching of green management principles (Wielewska et al., 2023). This includes exploring innovative teaching methods that engage students and encourage critical thinking about sustainability issues.

In this context, the development of competencies for green managers in higher education is a multifaceted endeavour that requires a comprehensive approach to curriculum design, pedagogical methodologies and evaluation strategies. Educational institutions must provide not only theoretical knowledge but also practical experience that prepares students for the complexities of sustainability in the workplace. By incorporating green competencies into their curricula, universities can play a key role in shaping the next generation of environmentally responsible leaders. Therefore, it is necessary to focus on the topic of building competencies for decision-making in the field of sustainability among management students, which requires research and deepening of knowledge in this area, which is developed in this chapter from the point of view of a case study on the topic of circular economy as one of the fundamental pillars of sustainability.

## QUESTIONNAIRE SURVEY ON A SAMPLE OF ANSWERS FROM BUSINESS AND MANAGEMENT STUDENTS: PERCEPTIONS OF THE CIRCULAR ECONOMY AND SUSTAINABILITY AMONG UNIVERSITY STUDENTS

This study focused on analysing the knowledge and attitudes of management students towards the concepts of circular economy and sustainability. Methodologically, a quantitative survey was used in the form of a questionnaire, which was filled in by 115 management students at a university in the Czech Republic. The research was conducted among fifth-year Modern Business and Corporate Financial Management students at a university focused on economics and management studies. These students are in their final year of study before obtaining their engineering degree and have participated in research as part of compulsory coursework.

### Research Questions And Their Intention

The questionnaire was designed to examine not only the level of declared knowledge but also the personal attitude of students to the importance of these topics. The questions focused on several key aspects:

1. Basic understanding of concepts (Questions 1 and 3),
2. Ability to define them (questions 2 and 4),
3. Subjective perception of their importance (question 5),
4. Arguing why these areas are relevant for future managerial practice (question 6).

The research aimed to find out to what extent students really understand the terms "circular economy" and "sustainability", whether they are aware of their importance for managerial practice, and how they are able to apply these concepts in a professional context. A preliminary analysis of the responses indicated that although most students are familiar with these concepts and consider them important, their knowledge is often superficial or incomplete. These findings led to an effort to systematically integrate the concepts of circular economy and sustainability issues into courses, which was reflected by the opening of a specialised course: *Circular Economy and Sustainability*.

## DATA COLLECTION AND ANALYSIS

The data was collected through an online questionnaire created in Google Forms. During the first lecture/seminar of the semester, a QR code was projected to make the questionnaire available to students. The questionnaire contained six questions that assessed the level of awareness of the circular economy and sustainability and their importance for managerial practice.

In particular, the following questions were asked:

1. Have you ever heard the term "circular economy"?
2. What do you mean by the term "circular economy"?
3. Have you ever heard the term "sustainability"?
4. What do you mean by "sustainability"?
5. Do you think these topics are important to you as a (future) manager?
6. Why do you think so?

The students' answers were analysed manually based on the categorisation of answers according to qualitative criteria in open questions and then quantified into a sample of data for the resulting quantitative analysis. To ensure objectivity, the answers to open questions were analysed using the DELPHI method, which allows expert evaluation of ambiguous answers. The categorisation of answers took place on four levels:

- Correct definition – answers that fully corresponded to the scientific concept of concepts.

- Partial understanding – answers containing relevant elements but incomplete or not entirely accurate.
- Wrong answer – answers that were factually wrong or did not reflect the essence of the concepts.
- No answer – students did not answer or they wrote that they did not know the term.

Independent evaluators evaluated the responses and classified them into categories based on predetermined qualitative criteria and keywords. This allowed for the identification of not only the level of knowledge but also frequent conceptual errors that may be important for future teaching adaptation.

The wordcloud technique was used to visualise the keywords in the answers, which made it possible to identify the most frequently used expressions/words in the students' answers and their semantic connections.

## EVALUATION OF THE RESEARCH RESULTS

The questionnaire survey examined the level of knowledge and students' attitudes toward the concepts of circular economy and sustainability. The responses were categorised based on predefined criteria, which allowed for their quantitative processing and identification of key patterns in the perception of these concepts. Table 1 provides a summary overview of the frequency of responses and represents a starting point for a more detailed analysis of each question.

*Table 1. Absolute values of the number of individual responses (n=115)*

| | YES | | NO | |
|---|---|---|---|---|
| **Have you ever heard the term "circular economy"?** | **64** | | **51** | |
| **Have you ever heard the term "sustainability"?** | **115** | | **0** | |
| | **YES** | **Rather YES** | **Probably NOT** | **NO** |
| Do you think these topics are important to you as a (future) manager? | 72 | 32 | 4 | 7 |
| | **Correct Definition** | **Partial Understanding** | **Incorrect Answer** | **No Answer** |
| What do you understand under the term 'circular economy'? | 11 | 25 | 67 | 12 |
| What do you understand under the term 'sustainability'? | 5 | 19 | 85 | 6 |

Source: Analysis by the authors.

The first question of the questionnaire focused on finding out whether students had ever heard the term "circular economy". The results showed that 56% (64 students) of respondents answered positively. This result suggests that more than half of the students have already encountered the term, whether in their studies, the media or the work environment. However, upon closer analysis, it became clear that knowledge of the concept existence alone does not mean a deeper understanding of it. However, a more detailed analysis of the answers to the following question revealed that only 10% (11 students) of respondents were able to define this term adequately. In comparison, more than 58% (67 students) gave an incorrect definition (Figure 1). This result indicates a significant discrepancy between awareness of the concept and its actual understanding.

*Figure 1. What do you understand under the term 'circular economy'? (%, n= 115)*

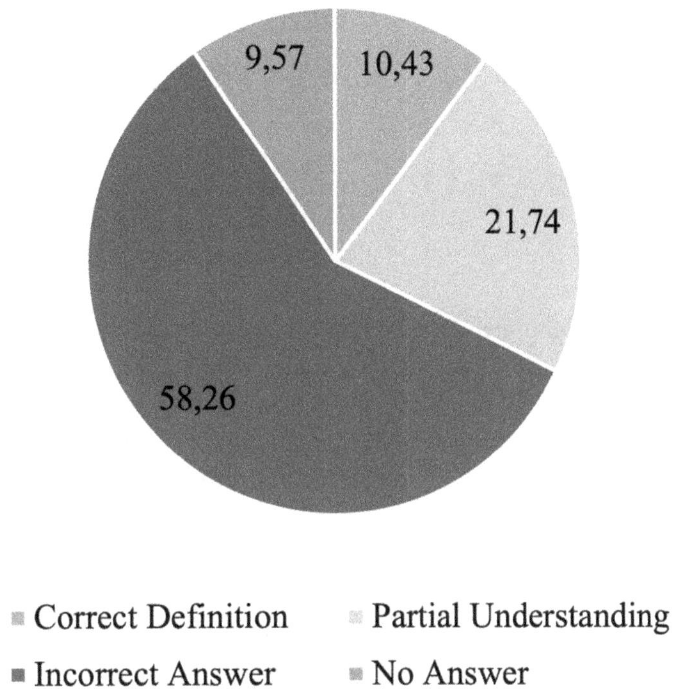


*Source: Analysis by the authors.*

The students' text answers to the question of what they mean by the term "circular economy" were analysed using the wordcloud method. The results show (Figure 2) that students most often associated the term with words such as sustainable, economy, waste, resources, development, and circular economy.

Naturally, the words "circular" and "economy" often appeared in the students' answers, which can be attributed to the question's wording. When defining the term, the students probably relied on the term "circular economy" word composition and tried to derive its meaning directly from the assignment. This phenomenon is common in open-ended questions, where respondents attempt to semantically reconstruct meaning on the basis of familiar linguistic elements without necessarily having a more profound knowledge of the concept.

*Figure 2. Wordcloud of the most common words in answers to a question about understanding the term circular economy*

*Source: Analysis by the authors.*

The results suggest that students are aware of the connection between the circular economy and sustainability and efficient resource use. However, their understanding of the concept is limited to essential environmental aspects. For example, the dominant presence of the word waste suggests that students often associate the circular economy only with waste reduction and recycling. In contrast, broader principles such as the circular economy, eco-design, regenerative production models, or long-term economic strategy are not as strongly represented in their answers.

This trend may be due to the way sustainability and circular economy topics are presented in the media and mainstream discourse. Public communication about the circular economy often focuses on recycling and reuse of materials, which are key components of the concept, but do not capture its more complex economic and systemic aspects. Thus, students may have fragmentary knowledge that is not sufficiently connected to the economic and managerial context.

These findings suggest the need to deepen education in the field of the circular economy, especially in relation to business strategies, innovative business models and broader impacts on the global economy. Curricula should place greater emphasis not only on the ecological dimension of the circular economy but also on its potential as a competitive advantage for businesses and its role in a long-term sustainable economy.

A similar trend has been observed for the concept of "sustainability." When asked if they had ever heard the term, the students all answered in the affirmative. However, a deeper analysis has shown that their knowledge is often not sufficiently sophisticated or professionally based. More than 70% (85 students) of respondents were unable to accurately define sustainability in the context of a business's environmental, social, and economic impacts (see Figure 3).

*Figure 3. "What do you understand under the term 'sustainability'?" (%, n= 115)*

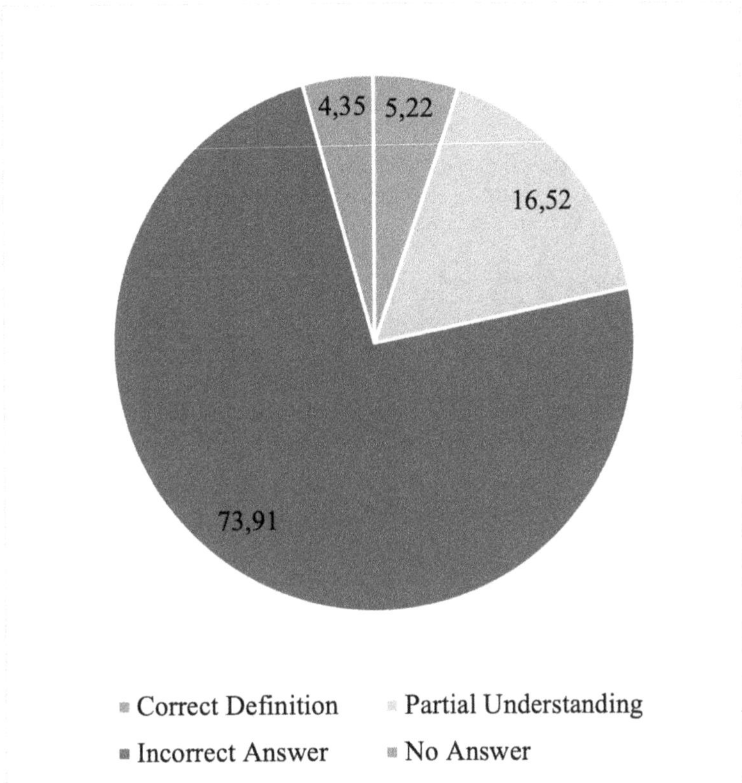


*Source: Analysis by the authors.*

This result confirms that although the concept of sustainability is widespread, students' interpretations of it remain very diverse. Many responses referred only to the environmental aspect of sustainability, while the broader concept, which includes social responsibility, economic stability, and long-term strategic planning, was mentioned less often. Higher education should provide students with a more comprehensive framework for understanding this concept, not just at its basic environmental level.

As in the case of the circular economy, the answers to the question "What do you mean by sustainability?" were analysed using the wordcloud method. The resulting Figure 4 shows that students associated the concept of sustainability mainly with expressions such as resources, environment, future, long-term, planet, use, and generations.

Unlike the definitions of the circular economy, the answers here reflect the broader concept of sustainability. An important element is the time dimension, which students express in terms such as long-term and future. This indicates that they understand sustainability as a concept focused on the long-term conservation of resources and their availability for future generations. This view is in line with the standard definition of sustainable development, which emphasises the balance between environmental, economic, and social aspects.

Nevertheless, even here, we can observe limitations in the perception of this concept. Dominant terms such as resources and environment show that students primarily associate sustainability with environmental issues, while social and economic aspects remain less represented. Terms such as responsibility, equity or policy, which suggest a deeper understanding of sustainability in the context of social responsibility and regulation, are absent from the answers.

*Figure 4. Wordcloud of the most common words in answers to a question about understanding the term sustainability*

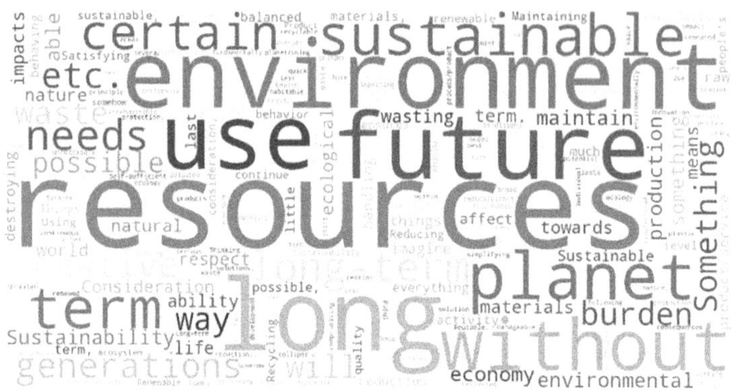


*Source: Analysis by the authors.*

By comparing the two wordclouds (Figure 2 and 4), several key differences can be identified:

1. The circular economy is seen as a process linked to recycling and material flows, while sustainability is associated with the long-term conservation of resources.
2. The definitions of sustainability have a more substantial time perspective (words such as future, long-term, and generations). At the same time, students focused more on specific mechanisms and principles of recycling and reusing materials in the circular economy.
3. The economic aspect of sustainability is less emphasised, while it appears in the definitions of the circular economy, at least in the form of the word economy. This suggests that students understand sustainability in an environmental context rather than as part of economic strategies.

Table 2 provides representative examples of responses across each rating category to illustrate the differences in how students defined the concepts of circular economy and sustainability. These examples reflect the most common formulations and conceptual frameworks in the answers and provide a deeper insight into how students perceive these concepts.

*Table 2. Examples of respondents' verbal answers*

| | *Correct Definition* | *Partial Understanding* | *Incorrect Answer* |
|---|---|---|---|
| **What do you understand under the term 'circular economy'?** | It is an economy that uses resources that are a product/residue/remnant of previous outputs of the economy, e.g. in construction - recycled concrete blocks that are made from the remains of damaged/demolished buildings | It is an economy that deals with more sustainable ways and the environment | An economy that can be replicated |
| | Economy that minimizes waste and loss, e.g. designing products so that they can be reused, recycled or repaired | Keeping products or services on the market for as long as possible. | Something that takes place continuously in the economy, repeats itself (processes, activities, etc.) |
| | An economy in which resources are wasted minimally or limited, and resources that can be reused are reused | Economy of sustainability. Economic growth in harmony with the environment and efficient use of resources. | The circulation of things in the money and labour market |
| **What do you understand under the term 'sustainability'?** | It is a way to manage and develop society in a way that does not damage the environment and natural resources. | So that the next generation can live here sensibly | For me, sustainability means doing something that doesn't endanger the environment so much that nature becomes polluted. |
| | Sustainability is a principle of balanced development that provides for the needs of the present without compromising the ability of future generations to meet their own needs. | Considerate behaviour towards nature and natural resources so that they are here for future generations | Reusable, recyclable, sustainable product is made from leftovers from other products |
| | Sustainability means the use of natural and economic resources that enables the long-term development of society without depleting them or harming the environment. | The ability to maintain or maintain a particular state, activity, or ecosystem so that it is able to exist and function for a long time without depleting or damaging the available resources and environment. | If I'm doing something sustainable, it should be "self-functioning". |

Source: Analysis by the authors.

Another important aspect was the perception of the importance of these topics for future managerial practice. Almost 90% (104 students) of respondents answered "Yes" or "Somewhat Yes", confirming the high level of awareness of the relevance of these topics. This result is a positive signal that students are aware of the importance of the circular economy and sustainability for their future careers (see Figure 5). Although students perceive the topics as crucial, their lack of expertise may mean they may have a problem with their practical application in practice. This mismatch between the perception of importance and the level of knowledge poses a significant challenge for educational institutions. Suppose future managers are to be able to integrate sustainability principles into strategic decision-making processes. In that case, they need to be provided with theoretical knowledge and practical tools for implementing these concepts in companies.

*Figure 5. Do you think these topics are important for you as a (future) manager? (n=115)*

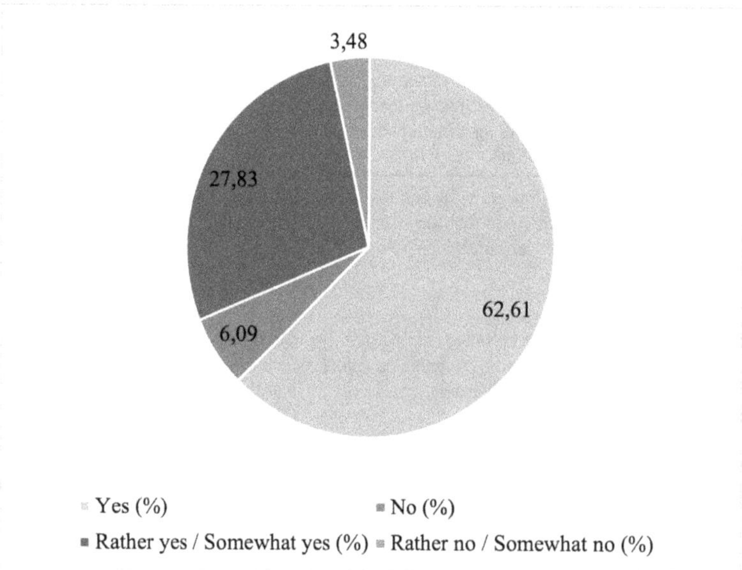


*Source: Analysis by the authors.*

An analysis of students' responses to why they consider sustainability topics important revealed several key areas of interest. Students often mentioned sustainability as an essential aspect, emphasising the importance of environmental protection and long-term ecological balance (18 mentions). The second most frequently emerging topic was governance and management (10 mentions), suggesting that students perceive sustainability as a key element of corporate governance and corporate governance.

Another important motive was social responsibility, which was mentioned 5 times and pointed to students' awareness of the business's ethical and social impacts. In addition, students often reflected on trends and current topics related to sustainability (11 mentions), indicating that they are aware of the growing importance of this concept in the current business and regulatory environment.

The results show that students consider sustainability a key topic that significantly affects both economic and business processes as well as the environmental and social spheres. Frequent mentions of trends and regulations show that students are aware of how sustainability is becoming an increasingly important part of strategic decision-making in companies. These findings highlight the need to integrate sustainability education into management education to prepare future leaders for responsible and environmentally friendly decision-making.

These results point to the need for better integration of these concepts into educational curricula, especially in higher education, in order to prepare future leaders in the field of sustainable management.

The results can, therefore, be interpreted in the context of the literature as confirmation of the need for systematic building of green competencies within higher education. As professional teaching practice shows, although sustainability is perceived as an important topic, students often lack sufficient knowledge and skills to implement it effectively.

## COMPARISON OF ANSWERS BETWEEN FULL-TIME AND PART-TIME STUDENTS

A chi-square test was performed to verify whether there are differences in answers between full-time and part-time students. Part-time students tend to be older, have more extended work experience, and can be exposed to sustainability and circular economy issues in a real business environment. Their view of these concepts may be influenced by practical experience, while full-time students are introduced to these topics primarily in an academic context. This difference in experience could lead to different understandings and attitudes towards the importance of sustainability in managerial practice.

However, statistical analysis showed that no significant difference was found between the responses of the two groups of students. The p-value was in the range of 0.5–0.8, which is well above the threshold of statistical significance ($\alpha = 0.05$). This result suggests that neither the combined students' age nor the work experience significantly impacted their level of knowledge or attitudes towards the topic of circular economy and sustainability. The ratio of respondents in the full-time and combined form of study was approximately 2:1, corresponding to the usual distribution of students within the study program. From the point of view of sample size, it can be stated that both groups were sufficiently represented for a reliable statistical comparison.

These findings confirm that students' perceptions of these topics are not primarily tied to their work experience but are probably related to their overall education, awareness, and approach to the topics studied. This is a key in terms of curriculum design, as it suggests that efforts to develop sustainability competencies should be targeted at all students, regardless of their form of study. Factors such as length of experience do not automatically guarantee a deeper understanding of these topics—instead, structured education and effective practical pedagogical approaches seem to play a decisive role.

This conclusion supports the need to create educational modules that not only inform about the principles of the circular economy but also enable their practical grasp through case studies and applied projects. The surprising absence of differences between student groups suggests that even contact with the business environment does not automatically lead to a better understanding of these concepts.

At the same time, these findings raise further questions about how sustainability knowledge can best be developed in different educational contexts. It would be helpful to conduct a more detailed analysis of the factors that affect the understanding of the circular economy – for example, whether there are differences between students of different study programs or between students of different levels of management education. Further research could also focus on the longitudinal tracking of changes in perceptions of these topics after completing sustainability training courses to better understand the long-term impact of environmental education on graduates' career decisions.

## INTRODUCTION OF THE SUBJECT OF CIRCULAR ECONOMY AND SUSTAINABILITY INTO THE STUDY CURRICULUM: PRACTICAL EXAMPLE

Based on the research results, a new compulsory-elective course, "Circular Economy and Sustainability," was introduced. This course is intended for fifth-year students and aims to provide future managers with theoretical knowledge and practical tools for effective decision-making in sustainability.

The course focuses on the significant environmental challenges of today and their connection to managerial decisions. Students learn about methods for assessing the environmental impact of products, such as water footprint, carbon footprint or life cycle analysis (LCA), and how to use these tools in practice to evaluate business processes and strategies. An important part of the course is also a critical analysis of greenwashing, i.e. misleading claims about the sustainability of products and companies that can manipulate consumer behaviour and investment decisions. The course provides a comprehensive view of current ESG reporting legislation, which allows students to navigate regulations at the Czech and European levels and understand the requirements for responsible corporate governance.

The course structure combines theoretical lectures with practical seminars, where students work on a semester project focused on applying the principles of circular economy in practice. In this task, they analyse the environmental impacts of selected products or processes using quantitative and qualitative evaluation methods. This approach allows theoretical knowledge to be combined with real-world sustainability challenges, providing students with a deeper understanding of the topic and practical skills that can be used in their future careers. During the course, fundamental corporate strategies in the field of sustainability are also discussed, allowing students to link academic knowledge with current corporate trends directly.

The effectiveness of the introduction of the subject "Circular Economy and Sustainability" was evaluated at the end of the semester through students' performance in obtaining a graded credit and on the basis of student evaluation. Part of the credit was a practical verification of knowledge, during which students had to demonstrate the ability to apply the acquired knowledge to specific managerial situations and critically evaluate companies' environmental strategies. The results showed that more than 85% of students were able to correctly define and contextualise key concepts such as carbon footprint, water footprint, ESG or circular economy while applying them to real-world sustainable business scenarios.

The course was also evaluated through standard student evaluation, which is part of all courses taught at the school. The evaluation focused on the quality of teaching, the comprehensibility of lectures, the connection with practice and the possibilities of applying knowledge during seminars. Over 90% of students completed the questionnaire, with more than 85% of them evaluating the subject positively, i.e. answering with the categories "agree" or "somewhat agree". This result confirms that students perceive the subject as practically beneficial, innovative and relevant for their future professional career.

The high success rate of students in the graded credit program, together with the positive evaluation of the course, indicates that the course not only fulfils its educational goal but also contributes to the development of managerial competencies in the field of sustainability. These results confirm that targeted education focused on sustainability can significantly affect students' ability to understand environmental challenges and apply sustainable strategies in business practice. By combining theoretical knowledge with practical skills, this course has proven to be an effective model for developing the professional competence of future managers in the field of circular economy and sustainable development.

## DISCUSSION

The results of this study provide important insights into the perception of sustainability and the circular economy among management students and confirm the need for the systematic development of environmental competencies in higher education. As Montanari (2023) points out, distinguishing between "green skills" and "sustainability competencies" is essential for effectively preparing future managers (Montanari, 2023). Our results show that while students consider the concepts of circular economy and sustainability to be important, their understanding of these concepts is often fragmentary. This is in line with the findings of Salovaara and Soini (2021), who emphasise that sustainable education should include knowledge and the development of practical skills and attitudes to apply these principles in practice effectively (Salovaara & Soini, 2021).

Our study's results revealed the gap between the perception of the importance of these concepts and students' actual level of knowledge. Cebrián and Junyent (2015) and Fuchs et al. (2020) confirmed that a similar trend has been identified in other studies focused on higher education. Only 10% of students (11 students) correctly defined the circular economy, while more than 70% of students (85 students) could not accurately describe the concept of sustainability. This confirms the arguments of Khare and MacNeil (2024) about the lack of integration of environmental and social aspects into management education.

However, a positive finding is that almost 90% of students (104 students) consider sustainability and the circular economy to be key to their future managerial practice. This interest can be seen as an opportunity to develop more effective teaching methods to allow students to apply the acquired knowledge in practice (Galleli et al., 2022). Research suggests that innovative pedagogical approaches such as flipped classrooms, simulations, and project-based learning can significantly contribute to the development of managerial competencies in the field of sustainability (Martín-Peña et al., 2023; López-Alcarria et al., 2019).

In line with this trend, a new course, "Circular Economy and Sustainability", has been introduced at our institution, which combines theoretical concepts with practical experience and reflects modern teaching strategies, as Cebrián and Junyent (2015) recommended. Pedagogical approaches that combine theoretical concepts with case studies and practical projects allow students to acquire skills relevant to future management practice. As Corres et al. (2020) report, one of the biggest challenges in implementing environmental competencies in management education is the lack of practical assessment tools, which is consistent with our finding that while students perceive the importance of these concepts, their practical application is problematic.

From a pedagogical perspective, higher education institutions need to rethink current teaching approaches and implement more effective models that include a multidisciplinary approach and the use of technological tools to support interactive learning (Cebrián et al., 2021). As Tetteh et al. (2024) emphasise that the effective integration of the circular economy into education requires closer cooperation between the academic and business sectors. Companies should play a more active role in educating future managers by providing them with opportunities to apply the concepts of the circular economy and sustainability in practice.

The relationship between the development of environmental competencies and the competitiveness of enterprises is also important. As Lichtenthaler (2023) states, sustainable management requires linking environmental and managerial skills that enable companies to achieve long-term strategic advantage. Our results suggest that students are only limitedly aware of this aspect, which is confirmed by a study by Dzhengize and Niesten (2019). According to this study, companies' ability to effectively absorb new knowledge in the field of sustainability is crucial for business innovation and growth.

Furthermore, our findings confirm the conclusions of Hallinger and Chatpinyakoop (2019) on the importance of reflective and anticipatory competences in the field of sustainable management. Although students perceive the circular economy and sustainability as important topics, their ability to connect them to specific management decisions is limited. This points to the need to expand the educational content to include practical applications and strategic planning. Wesselink et al. (2015) emphasise the importance of action competence, i.e. the ability to transform knowledge into practical decisions, a dimension that was not sufficiently developed in our research.

As Hassan (2020) states, the successful implementation of sustainability in managerial decision-making requires targeted competence development, including traditional teaching methods and the practical involvement of students in real projects and case studies.

Based on these findings of the discussion of the existing research, it is necessary to consider:

1. Expand cooperation between universities and companies so that students can apply the acquired knowledge in a real corporate environment.
2. Implementing innovative pedagogical approaches such as simulations, gamification, and the Lego Serious Play methodology that promote active learning and a deeper understanding of environmental issues.
3. Increasing the emphasis on practical competency assessment through applied projects and case studies.
4. Systematic integration of technological tools for monitoring environmental impacts, such as ESG reporting and LCA analysis, into management education.

## SUMMARY OF KEY FINDINGS AND RECOMMENDATIONS FOR FUTURE RESEARCH AND PRACTICE

This research was carried out on a sample of students from one Czech university, representing a specific limitation regarding the generalisation of results. While it can be assumed that similar trends could occur at other regional universities, the results may not fully represent all higher education institutions. To verify and disseminate these findings, conducting further studies at different universities and in different geographical areas would be appropriate.

The results of our research point to a lack of knowledge of the principles of sustainability and circular economy among current students of the university's management education programs. Although students show interest in these topics, their more profound understanding and ability to apply them in practice are limited.

Following the findings, the following recommendations for future research and practice can be formulated:

1. Revise and update curricula: Educational institutions should rethink their curricula to include current topics related to sustainability and the circular economy, focusing on linking theory and practice.
2. Implementing interactive teaching methods: Case studies, simulations, and project-based learning can help students better understand and apply these concepts in real-world situations.

3. Collaboration with practice: Partnerships between universities and businesses can provide students with opportunities to gain hands-on experience and an understanding of implementing sustainable practices in various sectors.

Research on effective teaching methods of sustainability and identifying obstacles to implementing these principles in business practice should be promoted and carried out. Extending this research to different areas, territories, levels of education, and categories of respondents will create the basis for appropriate teaching processes, methods, and techniques for efficient and practical education in sustainability topics in an interdisciplinary context.

Teachers are a priority part of quality education. Investing in the education and training of educators in sustainability will ensure that they can effectively impart this knowledge and skills to students.

By implementing these recommendations, educational institutions can better prepare future managers for sustainability challenges and the circular economy, contributing to creating more responsible and environmentally conscious leaders.

Future research should focus on identifying the most effective methods and tools for developing the necessary competencies and assessing their impact on graduates' readiness to implement sustainable practices. At the same time, it is necessary to examine how different cultural and institutional contexts influence the success of these educational initiatives.

Overall, educational institutions, businesses, and policymakers must collaborate to create an environment that fosters the development of competencies for sustainable decision-making. This will ensure that future managers have the knowledge and skills to lead organisations toward a sustainable future.

## CHALLENGES OF EDUCATING MANAGERS' COMPETENCIES IN THE FUTURE

As current trends show, growing regulatory requirements, technological innovations, and changes in the business environment require managers to have theoretical knowledge in the field of sustainability and practical skills to implement environmental strategies effectively in corporate practice. The results of our study confirm that while students perceive sustainability as an important topic, their knowledge is often superficial and incomplete, which highlights the need for systematic development of these competencies.

One of the main challenges is integrating environmental topics into existing academic programmes. As Viphanova et al. (2021) emphasise, effective sustainability education requires systematically linking environmental and legal aspects with managerial decision-making. Today, these concepts are often seen as a complement to traditional economics and strategy courses, lacking full integration into the core curriculum. This deficiency can lead to a situation where students theoretically understand the importance of sustainability but are not ready to apply it in practice in the corporate environment (Viphanova et al., 2021).

Moreover, as Sudar et al.'s (2024) research shows, managers must understand the general principles of sustainability and their legislative anchoring in the context of European integration. This includes navigating ESG reporting legal frameworks, regulations limiting the carbon footprint, and other policies supporting the circular economy (Sudar et al., 2024).

Another major challenge is the adoption of innovative pedagogical approaches that will enable more effective development of environmental competencies. Campbell et al. (2024) reported that peer-to-peer learning can significantly improve environmental management education by encouraging active student engagement and knowledge sharing within a group. This approach is efficient in the context of sustainability, which requires interdisciplinary collaboration and critical thinking skills (Campbell et al., 2024).

In this context, the practical aspects of teaching need to be strengthened, for example, through simulations, case studies and project-based learning. These methods not only improve students' understanding but also prepare them for the real-world challenges they will encounter in their professional lives. The results of our study suggest that students appreciate the practical component of the subject "Circular Economy and Sustainability", which corresponds to the findings of Rahmaningtyas et al. (2023), who emphasise the positive relationship between environmental literacy and the development of managerial "green skills" (Rahmaningtyas et al., 2023).

Another key area for future management education is using modern technologies and innovations to solve environmental problems. Mazhitov et al. (2019) reported that technological development and innovation in environmental management can significantly contribute to achieving sustainability. This trend is also reflected in business practice, where companies increasingly implement digital tools for tracking carbon footprints, optimising material flows, and reporting environmental impacts (Mazhitov et al., 2019).

Educational institutions should, therefore, integrate new technologies into the classroom, such as analytical software for sustainability assessment, artificial intelligence in environmental management, or blockchain solutions for supply chain traceability. These skills will be crucial for future managers, who will have to combine environmental strategy with technological innovation.

Overall, future generations of managers will face increasingly complex environmental challenges, which is why training programs must provide a robust and flexible framework for their preparation. Sudar et al. (2024) state that a key success factor will be the connection between theory and practice, with an emphasis on the strategic management of environmental challenges in the business sphere (Sudar et al., 2024).

An important question remains on how to evaluate environmental competencies and ensure that students not only gain theoretical knowledge but also effectively apply these concepts in the corporate environment. This requires further research and innovation in educational approaches, with increased cooperation between universities and businesses.

As sustainability regulations become increasingly stringent and companies focus on environmental, social, and governance (ESG) factors, managers must be adequately prepared not only for current requirements but also for future developments in this area. As the literature shows (Mazhitov et al., 2019; Viphanova et al., 2021; Campbell et al., 2024), the ability to adapt to new trends and flexibility in decision-making processes will be key elements of success.

## CONCLUSION

Building competencies in sustainability decision-making among management students is essential for preparing future leaders capable of facing environmental and social challenges. Integrating sustainability into management education programs supports the development of critical thinking, ethical decision-making, and strategic planning that considers long-term impacts on society and the environment.

Innovative pedagogical approaches, such as interactive teaching methods, project-based learning, and collaboration with practice, must be implemented to achieve these goals. Interdisciplinary education, which allows students to understand the complexity of sustainable solutions and apply them in different contexts, must also be promoted.

Developing green managers' competencies in higher education is a prerequisite for effective sustainability management in corporate and financial practice. The analysis's results point to the growing need to integrate the concepts of circular economy and sustainability into educational programs so that future managers acquire not only theoretical knowledge but also practical skills applicable in a real business environment.

Although students are aware of the importance of sustainability, their more profound understanding and ability to implement these principles in managerial practice remain limited. The questionnaire survey results showed that 56% of respondents (64 students) had heard the term "circular economy," but only 10% (11 students) could define this concept correctly. Similarly, while all respondents were familiar with the term "sustainability," 95% (110 students) could not provide an accurate definition in the context of the environmental and social aspects of business.

A positive finding is that almost 90% of students (104 students) perceive the circular economy and sustainability topics as important for their future managerial practice. The most frequently mentioned reasons included environmental protection, long-term ecological balance (18 mentions), the importance of sustainability for management and business management (10 mentions) and social responsibility (5 mentions).

These results point to the need for the systematic development of competencies in the field of sustainability and circular economy in higher education. The introduction of a specific curriculum focused on the development of green management competencies, complemented by the involvement of business practice and academic research, will enable students to prepare for new challenges and demands of the labour market. Educational institutions play a key role in preparing future leaders to address environmental, social and economic challenges. At the same time, the effective implementation of sustainability competencies will contribute to the long-term strategic sustainability of organisations and society as a whole.

There is currently a significant demand for green managers on the labor market. Green managers' competencies in sustainable finance and their development in universities represent a critical intersection of environmental supervision and financial management in higher education. As universities increasingly adopt sustainable practices, the role of green managers is becoming crucial in guiding these institutions toward achieving their sustainability goals. Joint efforts between universities, students, and stakeholders will play an important role in a sustainability culture and increase sustainability managers' competencies.

This research was prepared as an output of the VEGA project no. 1/0377/25 titled "*Innovative Methods of Enterprise Risk Management and Their Application in Risk Management and Modeling*"

## REFERENCES


Abakumov, E., & Beresten, S.Petersburg State University. (2023). Green campus as a part of environmental management of St. Petersburg State University. *Sustainability (Basel)*, *15*(16), 12515. DOI: 10.3390/su151612515

Abtahi, S. (2021). Isfahan University of Technology (IUT): Towards a green campus energy, climate and sustainable development initiatives at IUT. *Journal of Sustainability Perspectives*, 1. DOI: 10.14710/jsp.2021.12035

Al-Dmour, H. (2023). Green-smart university campuses: The mediating role of student engagement in enhancing corporate image. *SAGE Open*, *13*(4), 21582440231219591. Advance online publication. DOI: 10.1177/21582440231219591

Alqudah, M. K., & Yusof, Y. S. (2024). Academic citizenship behaviour mediates between green performance management, green training and development, and organization environmental performance in the Jordanian government universities. *International Journal of Academic Research in Business & Social Sciences*, *14*(2). Advance online publication. DOI: 10.6007/IJARBSS/v14-i2/20981

Bansal, I. (2019). Green Management: A study of best green practices in Haryana Private Universities. *Think India Journal*, *22*(4), 4539–4548.

Bombiak, E. (2019). Green human resource management – The latest trend or strategic necessity? *Journal of Entrepreneurship and Sustainability Issues*, *6*(4), 1647–1662. DOI: 10.9770/jesi.2019.6.4(7)

Campbell, J., Shaul, K., Slagle, K., & Sović, D. (2024). Sustainable community development through peer-to-peer learning in the online and in-person classroom. *International Journal of Sustainability in Higher Education*, *25*(8), 1803–1819. DOI: 10.1108/IJSHE-07-2023-0321

Cebrián, G., & Junyent, M. (2015). Competencies in education for sustainable development: Exploring the student teachers' views. *Sustainability (Basel)*, *7*(3), 2768–2786. DOI: 10.3390/su7032768

Cebrián, G., Junyent, M., & Mulà, I. (2020). Competencies in education for sustainable development: Emerging teaching and research developments. *Sustainability (Basel)*, *12*(2), 579. DOI: 10.3390/su12020579

Cebrián, G., Junyent, M., & Mulà, I. (2021). Current practices and future pathways towards competencies in education for sustainable development. *Sustainability (Basel)*, *13*(16), 8733. DOI: 10.3390/su13168733

Chanveasna, U., Veasna, S., & Sovannara, K. (2024). The antecedents of career development competency in SMEs, Cambodia. *Open Journal of Business and Management*, *12*(03), 1347–1376. DOI: 10.4236/ojbm.2024.123072

Cheng, T., Chang, H., Yen, C., & Chen, M. (2018). Creating a low-carbon campus in Chaoyang University of Technology (CYUT). *E3s Web of Conferences*, 48, 03001. DOI: 10.1051/e3sconf/20184803001

Corres, A., Rieckmann, M., Espasa, A., & Ruíz-Mallén, I. (2020). Educator competences in sustainability education: A systematic review of frameworks. *Sustainability (Basel)*, *12*(23), 9858. DOI: 10.3390/su12239858

Dzhengiz, T., & Niesten, E. (2019). Competences for environmental sustainability: A systematic review on the impact of absorptive capacity and capabilities. *Journal of Business Ethics*, *162*(4), 881–906. DOI: 10.1007/s10551-019-04360-z

Farooq, M., Bakhsh, A., & Watto, W. A. (2023). A quality approach to smart sustainable universities in digital natives era: The case of King Abdul Aziz University. 25 September 2023, PREPRINT (Version 1), DOI: 10.21203/rs.3.rs-3341500/v1

Fuchs, P., Raulino, C., Conceição, D., Neiva, S., Amorim, W., Soares, T., & Guerra, J. (2020). Promoting sustainable development in higher education institutions: The use of the balanced scorecard as a strategic management system in support of green marketing. *International Journal of Sustainability in Higher Education*, *21*(7), 1477–1505. DOI: 10.1108/IJSHE-02-2020-0079

Galleli, B., Onevetch, R., Santos, J., & Lopes, G. (2022). Competences for sustainable development goals: The challenge in business administration education. *Journal of Teacher Education for Sustainability*, *24*(1), 73–86. DOI: 10.2478/jtes-2022-0006

Gil-Doménech, D., Magomedova, N., Sánchez-Alcázar, E., & Lechuga, M. (2021). Integrating sustainability in the business administration and management curriculum: A sustainability competencies map. *Sustainability (Basel)*, *13*(16), 9458. DOI: 10.3390/su13169458

Gkogkidis, V., & Dacre, N. (2021). Exploratory Learning Environments for Responsible Management Education Using Lego Serious Play. *arXiv preprint arXiv:2104.12539*. https://arxiv.org/abs/2104.12539 DOI: 10.31235/osf.io/ek7th

Hallinger, P., & Chatpinyakoop, C. (2019). A bibliometric review of research on higher education for sustainable development, 1998–2018. *Sustainability (Basel)*, *11*(8), 2401. DOI: 10.3390/su11082401

Hassan, A. (2020). Managerial competencies required to achieve sustainable development projects: A proposed model for managers. *Environmental Management and Sustainable Development*, *9*(3), 68. DOI: 10.5296/emsd.v9i3.17603

Kalinowski, T., Rudnicka, A., Wieteska, G., Wronka, A., Diglio, A., Piccolo, C., & Genovese, A. (2018). Competences required for environmentally responsible managers - a European perspective. *Proceedings of the 36th International Academic Conference*, London, DOI: 10.20472/IAC.2018.036.022

Khare, A., & MacNeil, P. (2024). Adopting sustainability competencies in management education - a scoping review of progress. Preprint. DOI: 10.20944/preprints202410.0652.v1

Khoiriyah, S., Asror, M., Ruzakki, H., & Hilmy, M. (2023). Sustainable Islamic education: Literature study towards achieving the vision of sustainable development goals (SDGs). *Jurnal Pendidikan Islam Indonesia*, *8*(1), 12–28. DOI: 10.35316/jpii.v8i1.492

Lambrechts, W., Mulà, I., Ceulemans, K., Molderez, I., & Gaeremynck, V. (2013). The integration of competences for sustainable development in higher education: An analysis of bachelor programs in management. *Journal of Cleaner Production*, *48*, 65–73. DOI: 10.1016/j.jclepro.2011.12.034

Lambrechts, W., Verhulst, E., & Rymenams, S. (2017). Professional development of sustainability competences in higher education. *International Journal of Sustainability in Higher Education, 18*(5), 697–714. DOI: 10.1108/IJSHE-02-2016-0028

Lichtenthaler, U. (2023). Sustainability skills and sustainable natives: Key competencies and maturity model for sustainability management. *Journal of Innovation Management, 11*(3). Advance online publication. DOI: 10.24840/2183-0606_011.003_0005

López-Alcarria, A., Olivares-Vicente, A., & Vilches, F. (2019). A systematic review of the use of agile methodologies in education to foster sustainability competencies. *Sustainability (Basel), 11*(10), 2915. DOI: 10.3390/su11102915

Martín-Peña, M., Diaz-Garrido, E., Sanchez-Lopez, J. M., & Garcia-Magro, C. (2023). Flipped classroom as a methodology for acquiring skills in sustainability in the subject production management: An assessment of the students. *Journal of Management and Business Education, 6*(Special), 529–546. DOI: 10.35564/jmbe.2023.00028

Mazhitov, D., Ermilova, M., Алтухова, E., Maksimova, T., & Zhdanova, O. (2019). Development of technologies and processes in environmental management. *E3s Web of Conferences*, 135, 04045. DOI: 10.1051/e3sconf/201913504045

Miah, M., Rahman, S. M. M., Biswas, S., Szabó-Szentgróti, G., & Walter, V. (2024). Effects of green human resource management practices on employee green behavior: The role of employee's environmental knowledge management and green self-efficacy for greening workplace. *The International Journal of Organizational Analysis*. Advance online publication. DOI: 10.1108/IJOA-04-2024-4462

Mirčetić, V., Ivanović, T., Knežević, S., Arsić, V., Obradović, T., Karabašević, D., Vukotić, S., Brzaković, T., Adamović, M., Milojević, S., Milašinović, M., Mitrović, A., & Špiler, M. (2022). The innovative human resource management framework: Impact of green competencies on organisational performance. *Sustainability (Basel), 14*(5), 2713. DOI: 10.3390/su14052713

Mohammed Ali Saleh, N., Mahmoud Eldeep, N., & Mohammed Soliman, S. (2023). Effect of Green Management Training Program on Nursing Managers' Perception of Occupational Safety and Green Management Practices. *Egyptian Journal of Health Care, 14*(3), 381–395. DOI: 10.21608/ejhc.2023.317241

Montanari, S., Agostini, E., & Francesconi, D. (2023). Are we talking about green skills or sustainability competences? A scoping review using scientometric analysis of two apparently similar topics in the field of sustainability. *Sustainability (Basel), 15*(19), 14142. DOI: 10.3390/su151914142

Moradi, E. (2021). Investigating the competencies required for sustainable entrepreneurship development in agricultural higher education. *International Journal of Sustainable Entrepreneurship and Corporate Social Responsibility, 6*(2), 1–14. DOI: 10.4018/IJSECSR.2021070101

Naharuddin, N. S., Abdul Rahim, R., & Ngah, R. (2024). Determinants Impacting the Triple Bottom Line Sustainability Performance in SMEs: A Systematic Literature Analysis and Future Research Agenda. *Advances in Social Sciences Research Journal, 11*(2.2), 66–77. DOI: 10.14738/assrj.112.2.16401

Oduncu, F., & Cengíz, E. K. (2022). Bibliometric analysis of international studies on green management. *Iedsr Association, 7*(20), 80–108. DOI: 10.46872/pj.566

Phrophayak, J., Techarungruengsakul, R., Khotdee, M., Thuangchon, S., Ngamsert, R., Prasanchum, H., Sivanpheng, O., & Kangrang, A. (2024). Enhancing Green University Practices through Effective Waste Management Strategies. *Sustainability (Basel)*, *16*(8), 3346. DOI: 10.3390/su16083346

Rahmaningtyas, W., Joyoatmojo, S., Kristiani, K., & Murwaningsih, T. (2023). Building a sustainable future: Unraveling the link between environmental awareness and the cultivation of employability and green skills-a literature review. *IOP Conference Series. Earth and Environmental Science*, *1248*(1), 012021. DOI: 10.1088/1755-1315/1248/1/012021

Salovaara, J., & Soini, K. (2021). Educated professionals of sustainability and the dimensions of practices. *International Journal of Sustainability in Higher Education*, *22*(8), 69–87. DOI: 10.1108/IJSHE-09-2020-0327

Shao, J., Ahmad, H., Butt, A. H., Shao, H., Liu, Y. D., & Alam, F. (2024). Optimizing Sustainable Performance Green Talent Management Strategies Focused on Core Competencies. [JGIM]. *Journal of Global Information Management*, *32*(1), 1–24. DOI: 10.4018/JGIM.352495

Silva, L., Caten, C., & Gaia, S. (2023). Tool for assessment of the green technology transfer structure in Brazilian public universities. *Administratie Si Management Public*, *40*, 156–170. DOI: 10.24818/amp/2023.40-10

Sima, M., Grigorescu, I., & Bălteanu, D. (2019). An overview of campus greening initiatives at universities in Romania. *International Journal of Sustainability in Higher Education*, *20*(3), 410–422. DOI: 10.1108/IJSHE-01-2019-0036

Sudar, S., Cvetković, V., & Ivanov, A. (2024). Harmonization of soft power and institutional skills: montenegro's path to accession to the european union in the environmental sector. DOI: 10.20944/preprints202404.1034.v1

Sulich, A., & Kozar, L. (2024). Green competences: A review and future research in the context of green human resource management. *Theoretical and Methodological Problems, EiS, 89*(2), 713. DOI: 10.34659/eis.2024.89.2.713

Tetteh, F. K., Mensah, J., & Owusu Kwateng, K. (2024). Understanding what, how and when green logistics practices influence carbon-neutral supply chain performance. *International Journal of Productivity and Performance Management*. Advance online publication. DOI: 10.1108/IJPPM-08-2024-0517

Tshivhase, M., & Bisschoff, C. A. (2024). Investigating green initiatives at South African public universities. *Nurture*, *18*(2), 245–263. DOI: 10.55951/nurture.v18i2.599

Valle, C., Alves Pacheco de Campos, S., Klein, L. L., Rizzetti, D. M., & da Silva Sotero, N. (2024). The contributions of green people management to the development of organizational competencies for sustainability. *Social Responsibility Journal*, *20*(9), 1724–1746. DOI: 10.1108/SRJ-09-2023-0496

Venn, R., Perez, P., & Vandenbussche, V. (2022). Competencies of sustainability professionals: An empirical study on key competencies for sustainability. *Sustainability (Basel)*, *14*(9), 4916. DOI: 10.3390/su14094916

Vesperi, W., Gagnidze, I., & Soboleva, T. (2024). Understanding the impact of the ecological transaction on the human capital of university students: A cross-country analysis. Conference: 8th FEB International Scientific Conference: Challenges in the Turbulent Economic Environment and Organizations' Sustainable Development At: Maribor University, Maribor, Slovenia. DOI: 10.18690/um.epf.5.2024.37

Viphanova, G., Voronina, N., & Vedysheva, N. (2021). Training of sustainable development specialists within the environmental education system. *E3s Web of Conferences*, 295, 05013. DOI: 10.1051/e3sconf/202129505013

Wawer, M. (2023). Shaping sustainable development competencies through student internships. *Scientific Papers of Silesian University of Technology Organization and Management Series*, *2023*(170), 595–628. DOI: 10.29119/1641-3466.2023.170.37

Wesselink, R., Blok, V., Leur, S., Lans, T., & Dentoni, D. (2015). Individual competencies for managers engaged in corporate sustainable management practices. *Journal of Cleaner Production*, *106*, 497–506. DOI: 10.1016/j.jclepro.2014.10.093

Wielewska, I., Kacprzak, M., Król, A., Czech, A., Zuzek, D., Gralak, K., . . . Marks-Bielska, R. (2023). Green human resource management. *Ekonomia I Środowisko - Economics and Environment, 83*(4), 276-302. DOI: 10.34659/eis.2022.83.4.496

Xuemin, M., Widerman, B., & Kelana, B. Y. (2024). The relationship between green management of organizational culture, green behavior and green campus in private universities: A conceptual paper. *International Journal of Academic Research in Business & Social Sciences*, *14*(6). Advance online publication. DOI: 10.6007/IJARBSS/v14-i6/21813

Yafi, E., Tehseen, S., & Haider, S. (2021). Impact of green training on environmental performance through mediating role of competencies and motivation. *Sustainability (Basel)*, *13*(10), 5624. DOI: 10.3390/su13105624

Zhelev, Y., Monova-Zheleva, M., & Sabotinova, D. (2023). Workshop "Promoting the green transition through university education on green standards". *Digital Presentation and Preservation of Cultural and Scientific Heritage*, *13*, 353–358. DOI: 10.55630/dipp.2023.13.37

# Chapter 15
# Challenges and Innovations in Applying SDG and ESG Frameworks

**Akshat Jain**
*Christ University, India*

**Deeksha Gupta Ganguly**
https://orcid.org/0000-0002-5502-8276
*Christ University, India*

## ABSTRACT

*Entrepreneurial skills have evolved significantly since initiatives like the "Green Paper on Entrepreneurship" (EU Commission, 2003) and the "Small Business Act" (European Commission, 2008), which emphasized knowledge, competencies, and sustainability. Entrepreneurs today prioritize long-term sustainability over short-term profits (Elkington, 2018), leveraging frameworks like the Sustainable Development Goals (SDGs) and Environmental, Social, and Governance (ESG) standards to integrate ethical practices with financial performance.Despite these obstacles, ESG and SDG frameworks present opportunities for innovation through systems thinking, foresight, and interdisciplinary collaboration (Senge, 1990). By adopting "green thinking," entrepreneurs mitigate external threats, foster innovation, and drive sustainability. This chapter explores the role of networking, strategic thinking, and ethics in sustainable practices, offering insights into aligning business strategies with global sustainability goals for long-term success.*

## INTRODUCTION

Sustainability has become a key element in the corporate world of today for the long-term success of the businesses. Not merely the Sustainable Development Goals (SDGs) set forth by UN in 2015 but also the Environmental, Social, and Governance (ESG) standards are there for the businesses to force inside the sustainability in a firm's very core strategy. According to García-Sánchez et al. (2020) and Hörisch et al. (2014), the emphasis is shifted toward a corporate operational framework which ends up

DOI: 10.4018/979-8-3373-0189-1.ch015

resulting in an approach to harmonizing between social responsibility, environmental preservation, and economic growth.

SDG-ESG is very much a challenge in itself for any business, for such concepts are to be introduced into existing business strategies. Others are insufficient government subsidies and lack of access to useful and reliable data sources (George et al., 2020; Schneider et al., 2017). These barriers often stand in the way of an entrepreneur's ability to merge sustainability with strategic decisions, giving rise to situations contrary to objectives of short-term financial gain versus long-term sustainability.

Yet, it is innovation that allows a business to overcome these hurdles and open up avenues for impacts from sustainability. Entrepreneurs with skills such as creativity, systems thinking, and ethical leadership are more likely to provide necessary nudges toward sustainable practices and to foresee greater repercussions from their decisions. In addition, technological advances such as blockchain, AI and data analytics have ushered in powerful instruments to create transparency, track progress and achieve SDG and ESG goals.

The innovations and difficulties pertaining to SDG and ESG frameworks are examined in this chapter. By examining the connection between entrepreneurship and sustainability, it shows how business owners may use both frameworks to obtain a competitive edge and support global sustainable goals.

## Overview of the SDG and ESG Frameworks in the Context of Business

In 2015, the United Nations unveiled the Sustainable Development Goals, which offered a comprehensive roadmap for tackling issues ranging from environmental preservation to social justice and poverty elimination. The UN Sustainable Development Goals (SDGs) provide the framework that businesses need to align their strategic goals with global goals in order to guarantee a sustainable growth dimension that benefits society. Businesses can significantly contribute to accomplishing these goals by integrating sustainable practices into their value chains and core operations through creative tactics (Pedersen, 2018).

ESG frameworks complement the SDGs by establishing robust criteria for assessing business performance in the area of sustainability. They have provided metrics through which organizations can assess and report on their environmental and social impact in conjunction with sound governance systems that guarantee ethical decision-making and accountability. Investors, policymakers, and consumers are becoming increasingly cognizant of this in the wake of proving that excellent ESG practices are correlated to long-term performance in finance.

The Sustainable Development Goals (SDGs) and Environmental, Social, and Governance (ESG) frameworks thus, collectively articulate a foundation for a life in sustainable business practice. The SDGs advance social objectives, which appear to be causally general for businesses and are further steered by ESG indicators that inform of progress achieved toward realizing those objectives (Adams, 2017). Businesses would integrate such a schema to help promote innovations for enduring profits amidst a rapidly evolving global economy and in light of global calamities.

## The Significance of Sustainability in Contemporary Business

In essence, sustainability is now a cornerstone of modern business, as companies appreciate the interrelatedness of many issues involving environment, society, and economy. This issue has moved from being a detractant to organizational resilience and competitiveness to a strategic consideration in a rapidly transforming world economy. If firms integrate sustainability into their core business processes, they will then be in a better capacity to manage risks emanating from resource shortages, legal changes, and shifts in consumer preference.

To add to these benefits, the companies are encouraged to innovate on their products, services, and methods so that they satisfy the changing consumer demand, with a reduced negative environmental effect. For example, the circular economy encourages efficiency in resources and a reduction of waste, benefiting both the environment and finances (Geissdoerfer et al., 2017). As consumers increasingly demand more from socially and ecologically conscious companies, companies with higher sustainability practices are reaping notoriety and customer loyalty.

There are analogous economic consequences of sustainability. To date, investors are adopting ESG criteria to their investing criteria because those companies that are sustainability focused usually outperform the others over the period. At the same time, it is also because of certain legal pressure on businesses to adopt sustainability practices to comply with several international agreements such as the Paris Climate Agreement and gain competitive advantage over time for profitability.

As such, sustainability is not some fad to be lost in the whirlwind of a few years; rather, it is transformation-the reconfiguration of the way the company works, evolves, and most importantly creates value for all its stakeholders. This enhances the global thrust for sustainability by providing business incentives to gain a competitive edge while at the same time building trust with the stakeholders (Lozano, 2015).

## LITERATURE REVIEW

### Knowing the ESG and SDG Frameworks

Since the introduction of the SDGs along with the ESG framework, most firms are intending now to align themselves with global sustainability outcomes. The framework of ESG serves as a guide for ethical decision making, focusing on a company's performance in matters of corporate governance, social responsibility, and environmental sustainability. ESG standards also include diversity, labour rights, and ethical corporate governance which form part of their commitment to environmental concerns.

17 global objectives were recently announced together as the Sustainable Development Goals by the United Nations which were to ensure that by 2030 poverty is totally eradicated, the environment may be preserved, and everyone may prosper (United Nations, 2015). All these goals deal with health, education, economic injustice, and climate change-and provide a common path that would push businesses toward making their business plans more sustainable.

ESG works with SDGs, hence adding a scope to these goals. For example, Goal 8 talks about the social components of ESG; Goal 13 is the direct reference for Climate action. Businesses will be able to boost their resilience, attract socially conscious investors, and manage regulatory demands through the integration of these frameworks to their structures (Clark et al. 2015)

Because of compliance with the ESG and SDG frameworks, companies can mitigate reputational risks alongside other innovative avenues to secure success in sustainable markets. Through the use of renewable energy or the endorsement of gender equality, companies achieve the dual impact of contributing to the world's goals while establishing their positions as pioneers in the quick-changing space of sustainability.

In order for companies to involve sustainability as a true and impactful centrepiece of their business strategy, they must be able to understand the intricacies that surround the ESG and SDG framework.

## The Definition and Essential Components of the Sustainable Development Goals (SDGs) of the United Nations

The 17 global goals that comprise the Sustainable Development Goals (SDGs), taken on by the UN in 2015 in the framework of the 2030 Agenda for Sustainable Development, are aimed at addressing some of the most pressing issues facing the world - issues like poverty, inequality, environmental degradation, and peace and justice. SDGs provide a universal framework for action and demand revolutionary transformations across all sectors to guarantee that no one is left behind (UNDP, 2016).

Interdependence being one of the underlying tenets for sustainability becomes highly important, as in the case where economic, social, and environmental considerations are included in any of the SDGs. For example, Goal 1 presents the idea to end extreme poverty, while Goal 13 makes a case for climate action to mitigate that impact of climate change. In a similar vein, the World Bank (2017) states that objectives like Goal 4 on Quality Education and Goal 5 on Gender Equality are meant to lessen major social problems by encouraging equality and inclusivity for all.

This is also a vital aspect of the SDGs: its universality. These SDGs are not for some countries but for every country, rich or otherwise; sustainable development knows no border (Hák et al., 2016). This universality is needed for fostering international cooperation to respond to really common global issues.

This means that the SDGs are interconnected; thus, the progress from one area mostly has an effect on others. For instance, it was possible to enhance the benefit of high-quality education (Goal 4) to grow economies (Goal 8) and reduce inequality (Goal 10). Governments, the private sector, and civil society organizations need to cut across sectors to put this integrated approach to action-find comprehensive solutions for global challenges (Jones et al., 2019).

Socially-driven companies have a unique opportunity to achieve competitive advantages and sustainable long-term growth by integrating the SDGs into their business plans. These SDGs provide both a framework for sustainable development and one in which to evaluate how far we've come in the journey of making this planet a better, more equitable, just, and sustainable space to inhabit by the year 2030.

## A Description of the Environmental, Social, and Governance (ESG) Standards for Companies

Environmental, social, and governance, or ESG, is currently the most important criterion that a business must meet in order to gauge its moral and long-term effects. Friede et al. (2015) state that the criteria help investors, stakeholders, and companies themselves assess how well companies are managing the risks and opportunities related to environmental sustainability, social responsibility, and corporate governance.

1. **Environmental (E):** This element focuses on how a business affects the environment, including how it consumes resources, manages waste, controls pollution, and mitigates the effects of climate change. It covers topics including conservation initiatives, sustainable sourcing, energy efficiency, and carbon footprint reduction. Key measures of environmental performance include a company's dedication to using renewable energy sources, cutting emissions, and limiting its environmental impact (Kotsantonis et al., 2016). Businesses that follow environmental standards are required to assist environmental conservation by implementing innovative strategies in addition to meeting regulatory criteria.

2. **Social (S):** The social aspect encompasses the relationships of a business with its employees, customers, vendors, and the public at large. It deals with consumer protection, diversity and inclusion, human rights, labor practices, and community involvement. For instance, companies are evaluated based on their treatment of employees, commitment to safe working conditions, fair labor standards, and contribution to social justice. This involves adhering to ethical corporate norms, such as ensuring fair opportunities and maintaining customer confidentiality (Harrison et al., 2016). Businesses that comply with such principles form great relationships with stakeholders and enhance the well-being of society.
3. **Governance (G):** Governance refers to the corporate governance structure and practices governing the decisions of an organization. It encompasses shareholder rights, composition of the board, the pay of the CEO, as well as transparency. Some very important elements of governance are accountability, ethical leadership, and transparent and balanced financial disclosure. High governance companies should be the bedrock for encouraging honesty, countering corruption, and ensuring decisions are made keeping the long-run interest of workers, shareholders, and society as a whole (Laise, 2017). Good governance procedures are an important prerequisite in making businesses run honestly and accountable.

While critically essential for risk management, integration of ESG considerations in business operations offers organizations the possibility of enhancing long-term value and thus attracting socially conscious investors (Bouri et al., 2020). With priority given to ESG criteria, a business can help improve its brand, attract investments, reduce costs of operation, and foster resilience in a more sustainability-oriented marketplace.

## These Frameworks' Function in Encouraging Sustainable Business

What the Environmental, Social, and Governance (ESG) and Sustainable Development Goals (SDG) frameworks do is ensure that businesses are provided with rules for coordinating their plans in relation to long-term goals on the environmental and social levels. It helps organizations control sustainability risks and seek opportunities that promote economic growth and societal well-being by enticing them to adopt a holistic approach to their operations.

1. **Environmental Stewardship**: Both the ESG and SDG frameworks promote environmental sustainability by encouraging businesses to reduce their ecological footprint. SDG Goal 13 (Climate Action) and ESG criteria related to emissions, waste reduction, and resource consumption encourage companies to adopt green practices such as energy efficiency, renewable energy usage, and recycling of waste (Lehmann et al., 2016). Businesses help realize the global collective action to battle resource depletion and climate change as they integrate the standards into their business practices.
2. **Social Responsibility:** The social aspect of these frameworks motivates businesses to focus on diversity, human rights, and community welfare. For example, SDG Goal 5, that of Gender Equality, alongside ESG standards for labor practices and community engagement, pressurizes the businesses to make their workplaces more inclusive and treat employees and customers without bias. Companies that adopt social responsibility will most likely have trust bonds with their stakeholders, hence enhancing their reputation and fostering repeat business (Kitzmueller & Shimshack, 2012).

3. **Good Governance:** Corporate governance norms under both the ESG and SDG frameworks guide companies to implement business processes that are ethical, accountable, and transparent. Effective corporate governance is the bedrock for establishing confidence with stakeholders, investors, and consumers over the long-term performance of companies. By promoting moral leadership, anti-corruption initiatives, and strong internal controls, SDG Goal 16 (Peace, Justice, and Strong Institutions) aligns with ESG principles. In linking their objectives to universal values of justice and transparency, organizations that practice exemplary governance can ensure long-term success (Guerard, 2014).
4. **Innovation:** Through inspiring businesses to make sustainable goods and services, these frameworks also serve as innovation accelerators. The SDGs and ESG standards also open up new avenues for growth through pushing businesses towards more sustainable ways of doing things and beyond the ordinary business models. Businesses that embrace such frameworks are more likely to fulfill the evolving needs of customers and regulations by innovating in areas like clean technologies, sustainable agriculture, and social impact initiatives (Bocken et al., 2014).

In short, these frameworks are all-encompassing tools that help businesses mitigate risks and comply with regulations while promoting a more ethical, equitable, and environmentally conscious business practice. The better the integration of ESG and SDG ideas into the business's core strategies, the more able it is to generate long-term profit, build stakeholder trust, and create a sustainable future.

## Instances of Businesses Effectively Combining the SDG and ESG Frameworks

A variety of organizations, worldwide have succeeded in merging SDG and ESG in a business strategy proving that profit goes hand-in-hand with sustainability. Such businesses help illustrate the reality that business performance in support of international sustainability goals facilitates long-term enterprise success for people as well. A few excellent examples follow

1. Unilever

Unilever has been at the forefront of utilizing the SDG and ESG frameworks. The company has strived to reduce environmental impacts through sustainable sourcing, reducing greenhouse gas emissions, and waste reduction through coordinating their operations with the SDGs, particularly Goal 12 (Responsible Consumption and Production) and Goal 13 (Climate Action). The Sustainable Living Plan of Unilever, which describes its commitment to sustainability, incorporates ESG concepts by emphasizing responsibility, openness, and moral business conduct (Unilever, 2020). The strategy of Unilever places it as a leader in corporate sustainability because it shows how sustainability can be included into stakeholder involvement, operational procedures, and product innovation.

2. Patagonia

An example to further demonstrate the ways companies may successfully integrate SDG and ESG ideas into their practices can be found with the outdoor apparel company Patagonia. According to the ESG standards for governance and social responsibility, this company is aggressively committed to supply chain processes and environmental sustainability based on SDG Goal 13: Climate Action. Besides supporting recycling and product repair, Patagonia has embraced the circular economy and gives a share of its profits to environmental charities. Besides enhancing Patagonia's brand image, this commitment to SDG and ESG principles has fortified its customers (Murray, 2018). The company demonstrates an integrated approach to corporate sustainability through its application of ESG indicators to measure its social and environmental impact.

3. Tesla

Tesla has successfully applied both ESG and SDG frameworks by coordinating its activities with SDG Goals 7 (Affordable and Clean Energy) and 13 (Climate Action). Tesla's development of solar energy and electric vehicle technologies helps support global efforts to reduce carbon emissions. The company's ESG strategies include strong governance procedures, open reporting, and dedication to sustainable technology innovation. Tesla's business strategy is an example of how embracing sustainability can increase global environmental goals and make profits (Zengler, 2021). An example of how Tesla balances environmental care with financial performance is the company's integration of ESG criteria into its operations.

4. IKEA

IKEA is the best evidence that the frameworks SDG and ESG actually work, specifically with regard to environmental accountability and responsible sourcing as the 12th SDG: Responsible Consumption and Production. By using recyclable and renewable material in their products and environmentally friendlier modes of production, the company should make its goods more sustainable. Robust corporate governance, moral business conduct, and open supply chain management of IKEA reflect the commitment of the company towards ESG standards (IKEA, 2020). With the help of combining SDG and ESG measures, IKEA has developed its business, enhanced its brand, reduced its costs, and achieved the goals of global sustainability.

5. Microsoft

Microsoft's efforts to address social fairness, reduce its carbon footprint, and maintain good governance show the company's commitment to SDG and ESG standards. In keeping with SDG Goal 13 (Climate Action), the company has pledged to become carbon negative by 2030 and to power its data centers and operations entirely on renewable energy. Moreover, the governance architecture of Microsoft is based on accountability and transparency, which further enhances its ESG credentials (Smith, 2020). Microsoft is a good example of how integrating SDG and ESG frameworks may lead to innovation, operational efficiency, and positive environmental and social impact through the integration of sustainability into its operations.

## DIFFICULTIES IN IMPLEMENTING ESG AND SDG FRAMEWORKS

There are a lot of challenges facing businesses when it comes to putting the ESG and SDG frameworks into action. These could range from lack of resources to the complexities involved in matching tactics to changing sustainability goals. The main challenges that businesses face when they put these concepts into action include:

1. Lack of knowledge and understanding:

The lack of knowledge and understanding about the fundamental aspects of the SDG and ESG frameworks poses a major barrier for enterprises to adopt them. Quite many business organizations face a problem in totally comprehending how sustainability measures may be introduced successfully into day-to-day working. This gap in information might be creating a hindrance in the proper implementation of ESG criteria as well as alignment with the criteria of SDGs (Barton et al., 2019). Poor training and limited availability of professional assistance can further aggravate the task of developing a comprehensive sustainability strategy.

2. Regulatory and Policy Barriers:

Governments often do not have the laws and regulations in place to assist companies with their sustainability efforts. While some laws have been enacted to promote sustainability, they often are ambiguous, outdated, or contradictory. The absence of robust ESG reporting regulations in some countries makes it challenging for companies to align their strategies with global sustainability goals. Furthermore, changes in government law may cause companies trying to adopt long-term sustainability programs to face uncertainty (Sullivan & Mackenzie, 2019).

3. Cost and Resource Restraints:

Financial and resource limitations are one of the challenges most organizations face, especially small and medium-sized firms (SMEs). There is often a need to incur costs in advance, such as investment in new technology, training programs, and adjustments in operations to implement ESG and SDG frameworks. For small enterprises, these costs are unaffordable, making it difficult to pursue sustainable business without external support (Bocken et al., 2014). Balancing financial realities with sustainability initiatives can be a challenging task for companies that are not yet totally committed to sustainable practices.

4. Complexity of Integration:

Another challenge that companies face in implementing SDG and ESG frameworks is the difficulty of integrating them into existing business models. Many businesses' structures, processes, and legacy systems are not designed to accommodate sustainability-oriented strategies. It can be challenging to integrate ESG considerations into supply chain management, product development, and decision-making processes, especially when they conflict with short-term financial objectives (Mackenzie et al., 2018). Furthermore, it could be necessary to make major organizational and cultural adjustments in order to match the SDG ambitions with a company's operational goals.

5. Difficulties with Evaluation and Reporting:

One of the significant challenges to applying SDG and ESG frameworks is the inability to measure and report success. It may require a lot of time and effort for companies to establish systems for tracking sustainability KPIs. In addition, many companies are challenged by various reporting standards and transparency, and standardizing ESG and SDG reporting remains in progress (KPMG, 2020). It is quite hard for organizations to report about their sustainability objectives and accurately quantify their impact if there are no standardized indicators accepted at the world level.

## Lack of Knowledge and Understanding: Having Trouble Locating Trustworthy Facts and Deciphering Frameworks

A key challenge is a lack of awareness and understanding about the frameworks for SDGs and ESGs. Generally, many firms are challenged when seeking trustworthy information regarding these frameworks, their nature, and application. It will be hard to pinpoint dependable, standard, and truthful sources of data due to how relatively new SDG and ESG reporting guidelines are. Those organizations that are new to incorporating such frameworks or sectors where sustainability practices are not strong are most adversely affected by this knowledge gap (Hoffman, 2018).

Deciphering the complex rules and norms of sustainability is another area where there is a lack of understanding. Many firms are struggling to interpret the ESG criteria and apply it to their specific operations. Businesses may face a problem in creating an effective sustainability plan if there is no proper roadmap that may impact them while trying to compete with other businesses in a market that is fast becoming increasingly sustainable. This problem is worsened by the lack of adequate training materials or educational programs focused on improving business understanding of SDG and ESG frameworks.

In addition, the lack of standard definitions and metrics for ESG and SDG reporting makes it more challenging for businesses to identify what data is credible, which complicates tracking progress and setting clear sustainability targets (Clark et al., 2015).

## Policy and Regulatory Obstacles: Government Support and Legislation That Are Inconsistent or Inadequate

Probably, it is one of the significant challenges faced by companies in implementing the SDG and ESG frameworks: the lack of proper, reliable government support. Regional differences in sustainability regulatory frameworks are very prevalent. There, governments treat companies, which try to implement these standards, with decidedly different types of incentives, sanctions, and directives. This difference may cause confusion in the minds of organizations and make it challenging for them to successfully integrate these frameworks into their business plans.

Even so, some governments have enacted legislation in support of sustainability. However, the laws are often obsolete or inadequate, and companies are therefore left operating in a regulatory vacuum. For instance, many countries still do not have laws demanding disclosures in full scale on the ESG front or SDG-aligned engagements for private organizations. Absence of law justifies why businesses may think that they are not obliged to make investments in sustainability in the long-term (Kolk et al., 2017). Further, in some regions, governments would still be more interested in spurting immediate economic growth, and this would inhibit the laying down of legislation to support businesses in their SDG and ESG initiatives.

Many multinational firms that must adhere to several sets of rules experience issues due to variations in regulatory support amongst nations, making strategy execution far more difficult (Sullivan & Mackenzie, 2020)

## Resource and Cost Limitations: Keeping Financial Realities and Sustainability Initiatives in Balance

Resource and financial limitations pose significant barriers to businesses wishing to implement ESG and SDG frameworks. Many sustainability initiatives involve high initial outlays in terms of technology, infrastructure, and knowledge, though they may later provide benefits in the form of enhanced brand reputation and reduced operating costs (Porter & Kramer, 2011). The cost of implementing the sustainable practices in many small and medium-sized businesses would be too prohibitive, where there is not even a chance of getting quick returns on investment; hence, no business can undertake sustainable practices to ensure that the money invested will always be profitable and bring returns.

These also require regular funds for monitoring, reporting, and continuous improvement as far as integrating ESG practices into business models is concerned. Most companies find it hard to even out the short-term costs of sustainable initiatives against their long-term benefits. For example, the transition or investment in the use of energy-efficient technologies or of renewable supply chains incurs a huge short-term cost, even though such upfront costs would be compensated over time by lower operating costs and improved regulatory compliance (Sarkis et al., 2011). Long-term financial reasons will keep most companies from seriously adhering to SDG and ESG criteria as long as they are outweighed by other reasons.

It is also harder for firms in developing countries to meet international sustainability objectives because they often encounter more significant resource limitations, including limited access to sustainable technologies and financing options (Kolk et al., 2014).

## Integration Complexity: Matching Corporate Objectives with Changing SDG and ESG Standards

Because sustainability standards are always evolving and businesses need to align their goals with these dynamic frameworks, it is often challenging to include SDG and ESG frameworks in corporate plans. Businesses striving to maintain compliance while making huge contributions to sustainability face significant hurdles because of the frequent updates and changes in both SDG targets and ESG reporting standards (Serafeim, 2020). As global sustainability agendas change, organizations need to constantly adapt their operations and strategies to conform to new legislation or targets. This can create a gap between the current goals of an organization and new sustainability frameworks.

Moreover, due to the complexity that accompanies it, industries sometimes are unable to balance short-term financial targets and long-term sustainability. For example, companies often find it difficult to prioritize and implement inter-related goals in an effective and consistent manner with the overall business strategy, even while the sustainable development goals may promote social inclusion, economic growth, and environmental sustainability (Müller et al., 2020). This complexity is further enhanced by the need for cross-functional collaboration within the company and a myriad of stakeholders, each with their own interests and expectations.

Furthermore, against the backdrop of ESG metrics, companies often have to adapt their supply chains, business models, and product lines; this involves tremendous organizational transformation and flexibility. Balancing such change can be tricky since these changes to maintain changing sustainability expectations can be costly and time-consuming to other pressing business objectives (Adams & Frost, 2008).

### Evaluation and Reporting Difficulties: Difficulties in Monitoring and Reporting Sustainable Progress

It is indeed a significant challenge for businesses to track and report sustainable progress in line with SDG and ESG frameworks. Such obstacles are often caused by the lack of standardized reporting guidelines, irregular data collection techniques, and challenges in quantifying long-term sustainability impacts (Sullivan & Mackenzie, 2017). Companies are supposed to track thousands of SDG indicators and ESG metrics, which creates inconsistent reporting and makes it difficult to measure progress accurately. This is particularly true in sectors that significantly rely on resource extraction or supply chain management, where the effects of sustainability are more complicated.

Further, it is hard for companies to integrate sustainability data into their conventional reporting frameworks, and this affects the credibility of the sustainability reports. The overall effectiveness of their sustainability reports is undermined because most companies struggle to ensure that data collection methods are reliable and uniform across all aspects of their operations. The problem is compounded by the fact that internationally recognized standards of sustainability reporting do not exist; therefore, various organizations might have different approaches to sustainability reporting, making it difficult to compare and assess their performance (Ioannou & Serafeim, 2015).

Moreover, it can be particularly difficult to measure and quantify the qualitative aspects of sustainability, such as social and governance-related factors. These measurement issues make it harder for businesses to give stakeholders a complete and accurate picture of their sustainable development, which in turn makes it harder for them to assess how well sustainability programs are working.

## OPPORTUNITIES AND INNOVATIONS IN THE APPLICATION OF SDG AND ESG

There are chances for innovation within corporate practices from the use of the SDG and ESG frameworks. Businesses could increase their chances of competitiveness based on the degree to which such frameworks are employed in their businesses, goods, and services by integrating them and sustainability becoming a serious issue. By leveraging the use of cutting-edge technologies, reviewing business plans, and fostering a sustainable culture that works to the benefit of the company and society, entrepreneurs can spur sustainable innovation. Such opportunities will help businesses come up with new value propositions for clients, investors, and other stakeholders in addition to aligning with global sustainability goals.

One important possibility is the utilization of digital technologies and data analytics that can enhance decision-making and assist companies in maximizing their sustainability initiatives as concluded by Choi and Lee in 2021. Artificial intelligence (AI) and machine learning have increasingly been used to improve environmental performance by maximizing resource use, reducing emissions, and improving the efficiency of the supply chain. Furthermore, the blockchain technology would provide transparency to the recording of ESG-related data, hence improving stakeholder trust and supporting companies in their ESG reporting obligations (Tapscott & Tapscott, 2016).

It is worth taking into account other fields where the entrepreneurial spirit pushes for innovation: the so-called adoption of circularity concepts in favor of SDG 12 (Responsible Consumption and Production) and ESG targets. This transition enables companies to improve resource efficiency and minimize waste while creating new income from the waste and by-products generated through their operations (Lacy & Rutqvist, 2015). Companies adopting sustainability in their corporate branding and core business strategies stand to attract talent, retain customers, and increase revenues. This becomes unarguably one of the rare win-win situations between a business and the environment.

## Capabilities of Entrepreneurs for Sustainability: Foresight, Innovation, Creativity, and Systems Thinking

Through their skills, especially in foresight, invention, creativity, and systems thinking, entrepreneurs play a critical role in advancing sustainability. Entrepreneurs with these competencies are better equipped to handle challenging sustainability issues and put SDG and ESG framework-aligned solutions into action. For instance, entrepreneurs need foresight to be able to predict future possibilities and problems pertaining to social and environmental trends in order to make strategic decisions that guarantee long-term economic success. This enables entrepreneurs to proactively modify their business strategies to lessen vulnerabilities such as resource shortages and climate change.

Innovation and creativity are basic for entrepreneurs looking to incorporate sustainability into their business practices. Entrepreneurs embracing innovative solutions can develop new products and services that meet the needs of customers and society while reducing environmental impact (Dangelico & Pujari, 2010). The ability to think creatively also enables entrepreneurs to find new ways to repurpose existing resources, reduce waste, and create value from what would otherwise be discarded, fostering a more sustainable business approach.

The other critical ability that entrepreneurs, when seeking to leverage SDG and ESG frameworks, require is systems thinking. It is the understanding of how various corporate processes, environmental factors, and societal issues interlink. A systems-thinking entrepreneur can more easily identify the leverage points within their organization's processes where slight changes can create large impacts. Companies will then be able to maximize the operational effectiveness while minimizing the adverse social and environmental impacts and attain sustainability objectives.

## Technological Advancements: Using Data Analytics, Blockchain, and Artificial Intelligence to Promote Sustainability

Technological innovations, such as the use of data analytics, blockchain, and artificial intelligence, would be very significant in driving sustainable development in companies' operations. For example, data analytics gives companies the opportunity to collect and analyze enormous quantities of social and environmental data in order to take better decisions concerning resource allocation, waste reduction, and energy control. Companies can use predictive analytics to forecast trends and reduce the possible environmental concerns and thereby enhance operational efficiency and sustainability (Gartner, 2019).

Blockchain technology advances traceability and transparency in the supply chain and is yet another revolutionary tool. With blockchain technology, businesses can trace a product's entire lifecycle from the sourcing of raw ingredients through delivery to consumers, ensuring each stage adheres to social and environmental regulations. The increased transparency helps businesses meet the standards of ESG, builds accountability, and fosters trust among stakeholders and customers. Blockchain can also facilitate the secure and real-time submission of ESG data, which minimizes the risk of fraud or misreporting and ensures accuracy (Saberi et al., 2019).

Artificial intelligence greatly strengthens sustainability initiatives by promoting energy efficiency, improving resource usage, and automating procedures. Businesses can reduce waste and minimize their carbon footprint by using AI-powered systems that can monitor and control energy usage in real-time. Other ways AI can be applied include creating smart infrastructure solutions, improving supply chain management, and designing sustainable products-all that help a business achieve its long-term sustainability objectives (García-Melón et al., 2020). Technical tools provide business and entrepreneurs the opportunity to adapt innovative solutions that are not only financially successful but also socially and environmentally conscious.

## EXAMPLES OF CASES:

Many companies have integrated the ESG and SDG frameworks into a comprehensive framework with substantial sustainability initiatives. These are some of the examples of creative ways in which various businesses overcame obstacles to implement sustainability concepts.

1. The Patagonia

Patagonia, an outdoors apparel company for many years has been a leader on environmentally friendly operations of the corporates. By using recycled sources, reducing their carbon footprint as well as ethically producing so that environmental sustainability is included in its business strategy, SDGs, notably Goal 12, Responsible consumption and production dovetail with its commitment to Patagonia of openness, accountability, and taking care of environment (Schmidt-Bleek, 2019). The corporation also engages in corporate activism by supporting environmental causes, arguing for laws that preserve the environment, and funding climate change projects. Patagonia, for instance, supports both ESG and SDG goals by adopting a circular economy model, in which products are made to be repaired and reused.

2. Unilever

The international consumer goods firm Unilever is another company that has clearly shown how it includes sustainability in its core business activities. In 2010, the company started working on its Sustainable Living Plan for improving livelihoods, better health and wellbeing, and lesser environmental impact. The reduction of greenhouse gas emissions, renewable sources of energy, and sustainable products are some examples of how the company has demonstrated a commitment to sustainability (Unilever, 2020). More, the operations are aligned by the business in its operations along SDGs (6) and Goal 13-Climate action. The embedding of ESG consideration into its corporate strategy gives Unilever an edge position on sustainable business, which consequently improves its brand value as established by Kenton in 2020.

3. Tesla

For instance, electric automobile manufacturer Tesla is an example of how innovation is intimately related with the SDGs. Goal 7 (Affordable and Clean Energy) and Goal 13 (Climate Action) directly relate to Tesla's work of revolutionizing the automotive and energy industries through the advancement in the development and uptake of electric automobiles and renewable energy products. Tesla is assisting in reducing carbon emissions worldwide and promoting sustainable energy use through its electric vehicles, solar energy products, and energy storage solutions. Additionally, Tesla's commitment to transparency in reporting its ESG performance has increased its reputation as an environmentally responsible company (Tesla, 2020).

4. Interface

Interface, a leader in modular flooring across the globe, has adopted sustainability through its Climate Take Back initiative, which strives to reverse global warming and becomes a climate-positive company. The company has made a commitment towards using only recycled or bio-based components in their products and will completely eliminate carbon footprint. Interface supports several SDGs, including Goal 13: Climate Action and Goal 9: Industry, Innovation, and Infrastructure. Interface has revealed how companies may utilize sustainability for competitive advantage whilst achieving considerable improvements toward ESG objectives by deploying state-of-art sustainable technologies including carbon-negative carpet tiles and recycling waste.

## Examples of Actual Companies Using Creative Approaches to Overcome SDG and ESG Difficulties

Several businesses have taken innovative approaches to the challenges that the SDG and ESG frameworks pose, which demonstrates how these can be used to overcome challenges and turn sustainability goals into competitive advantages. Some examples of how businesses have creatively addressed SDG and ESG issues include:

1. **IKEA:** It has been known for its commitment to sustainability, integrating SDG and ESG frameworks into its operations. One of the creative approaches IKEA has taken is its commitment to using circular economy principles, such as designing products for reuse, recycling, and repair. The company aims to become climate positive by 2030 by reducing carbon emissions across its entire value chain. To address the challenge of the unavailability of sustainable materials, IKEA has collaborated with suppliers to create new materials, such as using sustainable cotton and recycled polyester in their products. IKEA also confronts regulatory hurdles in resource utilization and has resolved them by making investments in renewable sources of energy, such as wind and solar, and has managed to make a strong stride toward SDG 7 (Affordable and Clean Energy) and SDG 12 (Responsible Consumption and Production) (IKEA, 2020).
2. **Nestle**: It has creatively solved a series of ESG issues by focusing on waste reduction, water conservation, and sustainable sourcing. The company buys essential ingredients such as cocoa, coffee, and palm oil from certified sustainable sources to fulfill SDG 2 (Zero Hunger) and SDG 12 (Responsible Consumption and Production) (Nestlé, 2020). It has also faced challenges with water use, especially in areas where the supply of water is limited. In its effort to achieve SDG 6 (Clean Water and Sanitation), it has overcome this by implementing cutting-edge water-saving technologies in its

factories and collaborating with local communities to enhance water access and quality. Moreover, the moves by Nestlé to foster a circular economy, and also investing in recyclable packaging to curb plastic waste, support both ESG and SDG goals.

3. **Microsoft:** It has approached the ESG challenges creatively by using technology in a bid to drive sustainability efforts. The company has vowed to become carbon-negative by 2030, and to achieve this, it is not only focusing on reducing its carbon emissions but also on removing historical carbon emissions from the environment. Microsoft creatively uses data analytics, artificial intelligence, and cloud computing to monitor and reduce its carbon footprint, which enables it to measure and mitigate its environmental impact effectively (Microsoft, 2020). The company also addresses the challenges of data privacy and governance by enforcing strict cybersecurity policies and transparency in reporting, addressing critical components of the ESG framework. It has used these innovations to align with the operations towards SDG 13, which is Climate Action, and also towards SDG 16, which is Peace, Justice, and Strong Institutions, to develop best practices within the tech industry.
4. **Danone:** It is another company that applies innovation to ESG challenges. The company has made a commitment to be net-zero by 2050 and to reduce its carbon footprint by 50% by 2030. Danone is trying to use recycled plastic in its packaging and innovatively used bioplastics to change the packaging issue of being non-environmental friendly (Danone, 2020). The company has also faced challenges in addressing social injustice in the supply chain and ensuring sustainable farming practices. Danone has reacted by initiating programs to support smallholder farmers and improve working conditions, which is in line with SDGs 8 (Decent Work and Economic Growth) and 12 (Responsible Consumption and Production). The company's innovative approach to ESG challenges shows commitment to using innovation to address both environmental and social impacts.
5. **Starbucks**: It has adopted various innovative strategies in addressing ESG and SDG issues, particularly those on ethical sourcing and environmental sustainability. By investing in sustainable agriculture and renewable energy and changing to more eco-friendly packaging alternatives, the corporation has promised to reduce its carbon footprint (Starbucks, 2020). Starbuck cooperated with farmers in ensuring that the labor is ethical and the environment is conserved to mitigate the challenge of sustainable sourcing of coffee beans in adherence to SDG 2: Zero Hunger and SDG 13: Climate Action. Additionally, Starbucks has invested in social responsibility projects on diversity, equity, and inclusion, which falls in line with SDG 10: Reduced Inequality and ESG. Starbucks' initiatives show how businesses can overcome obstacles by incorporating cutting-edge environmental principles into their business plans.

## Examination of both Successful and Unsuccessful Attempts to Use SDG and ESG Frameworks

The SDG and ESG frameworks have been integrated in the operations of many firms. However, several others have faced problems which have limited them from further integration. Exploring both successful and unsuccessful attempts in introducing these frameworks may provide interesting and valuable information that guides business leaders on how to face the sustainability issues.

## Successful Attempts

1. **Patagonia** One of the best examples of a firm that successfully integrates SDG and ESG principles into its operations is Patagonia. Patagonia has shown its commitment to environmental sustainability through the use of recycled materials, reduction of its carbon footprint, and ethical labor practices. Patagonia supports SDG 12, Responsible Consumption and Production, by encouraging consumers to buy less, repair more, and reuse items. The company also made a commitment to become carbon neutral by 2025, and it also donated a big part of its profit to the environment-related foundations. Patagonia is an example of how companies can successfully apply SDG and ESG because of the strong commitment toward sustainability, open reporting, and for supporting environmental issues.
2. **Unilever** Another company that has successfully implemented the SDG and ESG guidelines within its organization is Unilever. Since 2010, the Sustainable Living Plan of the company identifies areas that need improvement in enhancing social impact, reducing the environmental impact, and health and well-being. So far, carbon emissions in operations are reduced to zero waste to landfills along with sourcing all its raw materials for agriculture responsibly (Unilever, 2020). The firm has shown to have a holistic approach towards sustainability through environmental, social, and governance factors by aligning its projects with SDGs 2 (Zero Hunger), 12 (Responsible Consumption and Production), and 13 (Climate Action).

## Unsuccessful Attempts

1. **Volkswagen** (the scandal of Dieselgate) Volkswagen is one of the most high-profile and unsuccessful attempts at following ESG principles. The company's commitment to environmental sustainability was compromised in 2015 when it was revealed that it had installed software to cheat on emissions tests for diesel automobiles. This betrayal caused the company's reputation to suffer greatly, and it had serious operational, financial, and legal repercussions. The controversy highlighted the dangers of not incorporating ethical principles into the business model as well as the significance of accountability and transparency in ESG operations. This is an example that businesses trying to incorporate sustainability frameworks but failing to match their operations with the fundamentals of ESG and SDG should take note of.
2. **British Petroleum (BP)** BP's sustainability strategy was severely dented by the devastating environmental and social impacts of the 2010 Deepwater Horizon oil spill. Although BP had previously announced publicly its intention to reduce its carbon footprint and embrace more sustainable ways of operation, the disaster laid bare fundamental flaws in its governance and risk management structures. BP faced severe regulatory and public censure, and the disaster severely impacted its ESG rating. The company has since worked to improve its sustainability efforts, but the incident serves as an example of how lapses in governance and environmental stewardship can undermine ESG and SDG initiatives. BP's failure to fully integrate safety and environmental considerations into its operations directly contradicts SDG 13 (Climate Action) and SDG 6 (Clean Water and Sanitation), showcasing the intricacies and risks that accompany the applicability of sustainability frameworks in huge corporations.

## PROSPECTS FOR FUTURE RESEARCH

The continuous evolution of the use of SDG and ESG frameworks in corporate and entrepreneurial environments opens up future study opportunities. Further research in these fields can provide deeper insights into how to overcome obstacles and take advantage of sustainability-related possibilities.

1. Enhancing Regulatory and Policy Support

Future research can explore policy frameworks that are likely to ease the integration of SDG and ESG within companies. Of course, the process of homogenizing regulations across borders also requires an understanding of how government and international structures work. Innovative policy instruments like grants for sustainable technology, green tax breaks, or increased penalties on non-compliance with ESG principles can be further explored (Dalal-Clayton & Bass, 2021; Steffen et al., 2018).

2. Technological Advancements for Sustainability

More research is needed to understand how technologies such as blockchain, AI, and big data may transform ESG reporting for SDG alignment. Scholars may focus on how such technologies support sustainability programs that are plagued by a lack of accountability, traceability, and transparency (Elkington, 2018). For example, real-time tracking of supply chain emissions through blockchain may significantly enhance ESG compliance.

3. Sustainability's behavioural aspect

There is a lot to learn about the behavioural barriers to SDG and ESG frameworks. Future studies should analyze how leadership philosophies, organizational culture, and cognitive biases impact the integration of sustainable practices. This study could focus on developing curricula for employee and business owner training that promotes sustainable views.

4. Sector-specific use of ESG and SDG

Although much research has been devoted to major firms, it is also important to find out how start-ups and small and medium-sized businesses may implement these frameworks effectively. Research works that center on a particular industry may unveil specific opportunities and issues, hence offering sector-specific suggestions for implementation like in the sectors of manufacturing, technology, and agriculture.

5. Assessing Long-Term Effects

Another significant area of research is the development of methods to measure the long-term impact of SDG and ESG integration on corporate success and social well-being. This includes considering metrics that include social and environmental benefits along with financial performance (KPMG, 2020).

6. Regional and Cross-Cultural Studies

Future studies can identify how regional and cultural differences influence the adoption of SDG and ESG frameworks. Elements facilitating or hindering adoption in other geographic and economic contexts can be highlighted through a comparative study by Hofstede, 2011.

## New Research Directions to Enhance Implementations of the SDG and ESG Frameworks

There are many opportunities to enhance and develop the practical application of SDG and ESG frameworks in the future due to the changing context. Investigating new ideas and solving existing issues can help businesses better align with sustainability goals.

1. Next Generation Measures for SDG and ESG Analysis

There is a need for more sophisticated and internationally standardized metrics to measure the success of SDG and ESG. Improving reporting practices to enhance comparability and industry transparency is part of this. For a detailed analysis of sustainability effects, research can focus on the integration of qualitative and quantitative metrics (Adams, 2017).

2. Sector-specific ESG Strategies

Sector-specific requirements demand tailored approaches to implementing the SDG and ESG frameworks. With a focus on sectoral innovation, future research can delve into the strategic ways in which sectors like energy, technology, and agriculture may overcome the unique challenges they face.

3. Behavioral perspectives on the adoption of ESG

A proper understanding of leadership philosophies and organizational behavior designed to foster a sustainable culture is highly important. SDG and ESG integration is significantly affected by decision-makers' attitudes, motives, and values (Dyllick & Muff, 2016).

4. Sustainable Innovation in Technology

New technologies, such as blockchain, artificial intelligence, and the Internet of Things, can potentially facilitate easier tracking, implementation, and growth of SDG and ESG initiatives. Future research could focus on the effects of these technologies on stakeholder engagement, costs, and data accuracy (Chen et al., 2021).

5. Cross-Cultural and Regional Dynamics

Comparing cultural and geographical variations in implementing SDG and ESG models may highlight the ability of such frameworks to adapt around the globe. In this regard, comparative studies concentrating on developed and emerging economies can shed light on best practices and context-specific difficulties.

6. Governance and Policy Improvement

It is critical to research the connection between public policies and corporate actions. Through tax rebates, subsidies, or fines for non-compliance, governments can encourage companies to embrace sustainable goals (Dalal-Clayton & Bass, 2021; KPMG, 2020).

## Examining the Shortcomings of Present Government Regulations and Entrepreneurial Practices

The loopholes in current legal and business procedures often limit opportunities for SDG and ESG frameworks. Systemic constraints and inefficiencies need to be critically analyzed in a bid to address these weaknesses.

1. Disjoined Regulatory Guidelines

Inconsistent or disjointed government policy hinders the wide implementation of SDG and ESG principles. Regulations often do not provide clear instructions to firms, which causes uncertainty in implementation and compliance. For example, regional differences in sustainability reporting requirements make it harder for multinational firms to operate across borders.

2. Lack of Adequate Sustainability Incentives

Most governments offer limited incentives to attract companies to embrace SDG and ESG practices. The lack of tax rewards, grants, or subsidies for the adoption of sustainable practices reduces entrepreneurial motivation to achieve long-term sustainability goals (Dalal-Clayton).

3. Inadequate Enforcement Systems

Their lack of strict implementation often undermines the effectiveness of existing sustainability legislation. The companies may pay less attention to their SDG and ESG responsibilities if severe penalties are not in place for non-compliance.

4. Weaknesses in Entrepreneurial Know-how and Tools

Entrepreneurs often do not know or understand how to include SDG and ESG principles in their business operations. This knowledge gap has led to the superficial adoption of these frameworks, where the focus is more on fulfilling minimum compliance requirements than on driving change (Dyllick & Muff, 2016; Morioka & Carvalho, 2016).

5. Business Models Short Term Focused

Much entrepreneurship is short-sighted and aimed at quick short-term returns over long-term survival. The SDG and ESG frameworks require an integrated and strategic approach, contrary to the former short-term mindset (Elkington, 2018).

## Possibility of Creative Approaches to Sustainable Business Plans

Organizations can bring profitability in line with long-term environmental and social goals by developing innovative methods to sustainable business planning. Such strategies often use cutting-edge business models, stakeholder cooperation, and breakthrough technologies.

1. Models of the Circular Economy

These principles of the circular economy can significantly reduce waste and resources while creating a new avenue of economic opportunities. Companies can design sustainable value chains by implementing such strategies as product-as-a-service, recycling, and remanufacturing. (Stahel, 2016; Ellen MacArthur Foundation, 2015).

2. Technologies

Advanced technologies such as blockchain, IoT, and artificial intelligence provide tools for tracking sustainability indicators, ensuring transparency, and optimizing resource use. These innovations enhance operational efficiency and decision-making (Ghadge et al., 2020; Stock et al., 2018).

3. Cooperation Alliances

Alliances with governmental bodies, non-governmental organizations, and other companies can boost the impact of sustainability programs. In order to address global problems, collaboration makes resource sharing possible, co-innovation, and group problem-solving.

4. Triple Bottom Line Framework

Creative approaches often adopt the Triple Bottom Line (TBL) framework, which incorporates environmental, social, and economic performance. Such an approach would help businesses in achieving comprehensive and balanced sustainability goals.

5. Innovative Financing Models

The use of green bonds, impact investing, and sustainability-linked loans enables businesses to raise capital while pledging measurable sustainability outcomes (Flammer, 2021; Chen et al., 2019).

## CONCLUSION

The application of SDG and ESG frameworks in modern corporate environments has brought both major challenges and ground-breaking advancements. Entrepreneurs who try to incorporate these frameworks face problems like inconsistent regulations, lack of resources, and problems in assessing and disclosing sustainable progress. Despite such challenges, the frameworks act as stimulants to support long-term sustainability, improve corporate resilience, and stimulate innovation.

In order to overcome these barriers, entrepreneurial skills such as systems thinking, foresight, and interdisciplinary collaboration are required.

Entrepreneurs can handle complexity better, encourage innovative solutions to global problems, and align sustainability goals with strategic objectives by using these skills. Adopting cutting-edge technologies, creative business strategies, and cooperative alliances enhances their ability to successfully apply these frameworks.

The sustainable entrepreneurship will potentially have a massive impact on future global issues related to resource depletion, inequality, and climate change. Companies integrating sustainability into their core plans will ensure their survival and contribute to achieving the SDGs. Future research should focus on developing entrepreneurial competencies, regulatory frameworks, and novel approaches in order to maximize the impact of SDG and ESG frameworks. This would mean that with our combined effort, a more inclusive and sustainable global economy will be possible.

## REFERENCES


Amel-Zadeh, A., & Serafeim, G. (2018). Why and How Investors Use ESG Information: Evidence from a Global Survey. *Financial Analysts Journal*, *74*(3), 87–103. DOI: 10.2469/faj.v74.n3.2

Barton, D., Koller, G., & Wiseman, M. (2019). *Capitalism for the Long Term: A Guide for Investors*. Harvard Business Review Press.

Benn, S., Edwards, M., & Williams, T. (2018). *Organizational Change for Corporate Sustainability*. Routledge. DOI: 10.4324/9781315619620

Benn, S., Edwards, M., & Williams, T. (2018). *Organizational Change for Corporate Sustainability*. Routledge. DOI: 10.4324/9781315619620

Bocken, N. M., Short, S. W., Rana, P., & Evans, S. (2019). A literature and practice review to develop sustainable business model archetypes. *Journal of Cleaner Production*, *65*, 42–56. DOI: 10.1016/j.jclepro.2013.11.039

Bouri, A., Mertens, F., & Perrini, F. (2020). Understanding Corporate Sustainability and Its Implications for Business Performance. *Journal of Business Research*, *111*, 1–10. DOI: 10.1016/j.jbusres.2019.05.004

Bromfield, E. (2020). Microsoft's Approach to Sustainability: Leveraging Technology for Environmental Impact. *Tech for Good Journal*, *8*(2), 41–55.

Chen, X., Chong, D., & Kang, M. (2021). Blockchain Technology in Sustainable Supply Chains: A Literature Review. *Sustainability*, *13*(3), 1239.

Chen, Y., Hung, M., & Wang, Y. (2019). The Effect of Mandatory CSR Disclosure on Firm Profitability and Social Externalities: Evidence from China. *Journal of Accounting and Economics*, *68*(1), 101–122.

Choi, S., & Lee, H. (2021). How Data Analytics Can Foster Sustainability in the Era of Digital Transformation. *Sustainability*, *13*(10), 5639. DOI: 10.3390/su13105639

Dalal-Clayton, B., & Bass, S. (2021). *Sustainable Development Strategies: A Resource Book*. Earthscan Publications.

Danone. (2020). *Danone 2020 Sustainability Report*. Retrieved from https://www.danone.com

Eccles, R. G., Ioannou, I., & Serafeim, G. (2019). The Impact of Corporate Sustainability on Organizational Processes and Performance. *Management Science*, *60*(11), 2843–2857. DOI: 10.1287/mnsc.2014.1940

Eccles, R. G., & Krzus, M. P. (2018). *The Integrated Reporting Movement: Meaning, Momentum, Motives, and Materiality*. John Wiley & Sons.

Elkington, J. (2018). *Cannibals with Forks: The Triple Bottom Line of 21st Century Business*. New Society Publishers.

Fatemi, A., Glaum, M., & Kaiser, S. (2018). ESG Performance and Firm Value: The Moderating Role of Disclosure. *Global Finance Journal*, *38*, 45–64. DOI: 10.1016/j.gfj.2017.03.001

García-Melón, M., Gómez-Pérez, L., & Cabello, R. (2020). Artificial Intelligence for Sustainability: Challenges and Applications. *Springer Handbook of Computational Intelligence*, 303-322. https://doi.org/DOI: 10.1007/978-3-030-45143-4_22

García-Sánchez, I. M., Hussain, N., & Martínez-Ferrero, J. (2020). Sustainability reporting and assurance: The role of institutional investors. *Corporate Social Responsibility and Environmental Management*, *27*(6), 2951–2967. DOI: 10.1002/csr.1973

Gartner. (2019). *Predicts 2020: Data and Analytics*. Gartner. Retrieved from https://www.gartner.com

Garton, E. (2019). Tesla's Green Energy Revolution: The Role of Electric Vehicles in Achieving SDGs. *Energy Economics Review*, *6*(1), 34–48.

Geissdoerfer, M., Savaget, P., Bocken, N. M. P., & Hultink, E. J. (2017). The Circular Economy – A New Sustainability Paradigm? *Journal of Cleaner Production*, *143*, 757–768. DOI: 10.1016/j.jclepro.2016.12.048

George, G., Schillebeeckx, S. J. D., & Liak, T. L. (2020). The Management of Natural Resources: An Overview and Research Agenda. *Academy of Management Journal*, *63*(3), 731–738. DOI: 10.5465/amj.2019.4004

Gillan, S. L., Koch, A., & Starks, L. T. (2021). Firms and Social Responsibility: A Review of ESG and CSR Research in Corporate Finance. *Journal of Corporate Finance*, *66*, 101889. DOI: 10.1016/j.jcorpfin.2021.101889

Gough, K. (2020). Circular Economy Strategies: IKEA's Commitment to Sustainability. *Sustainability Innovations Review*, *10*(4), 16–28.

Hawken, P. (2017). *Drawdown: The Most Comprehensive Plan Ever Proposed to Reverse Global Warming*. Penguin.

Hawken, P. (2019). Patagonia's Sustainable Business Model: A Case Study. *Green Business Review*, *12*(1), 55–67.

Hawn, O., Chatterji, A. K., & Mitchell, W. (2018). A New Approach to Combating Climate Change: Businesses and Government Cooperation. *Business and Society Review*, *123*(3), 375–413. DOI: 10.1111/basr.12127

Hoffman, A. J. (2018). *The Business Guide to Circular Water and Climate Action*. Oxford University Press.

Hoffman, A. J. (2018). *Climate Change: What's Your Business Strategy?* Harvard Business Press.

IKEA. (2020).. . *Sustainability Report*, *2020*, •••. https://www.ikea.com/sustainability

IKEA. (2020). *IKEA Sustainability Strategy: A Circular Economy Approach*. Retrieved from https://www.ikea.com

Jones, P., Comfort, D., & Hillier, D. (2019). Sustainable Development Goals and Corporate Sustainability: The Role of Business in Achieving the SDGs. *Journal of Business Research*, *103*, 280–286. DOI: 10.1016/j.jbusres.2019.01.032

Kahn, M. (2019). Nestlé's Journey to Sustainability: Overcoming Environmental and Social Challenges. *Business & Sustainability Journal*, *14*(3), 52–63.

Kenton, W. (2020). Unilever: A Leader in Sustainable Business Practices. *Investopedia*. Retrieved from https://www.investopedia.com

Kolk, A., van Tulder, R., & Welters, C. (2017). *Business and Sustainability: A Global Perspective*. Springer.

KPMG. (2020). *The Time Has Come: The KPMG Survey of Sustainability Reporting 2020*.

KPMG. (2020). *The KPMG Survey of Sustainability Reporting 2020*. KPMG International. https://home.kpmg/xx/en/home/insights/2020/11/survey-of-sustainability-reporting-2020.html

KPMG. (2020). *The Time Has Come: The KPMG Survey of Sustainability Reporting 2020*.

KPMG. (2020). *The Time Has Come: The KPMG Survey of Sustainability Reporting 2020*.

Laise, D. (2017). *Corporate Governance and Corporate Social Responsibility: A Global Perspective*. Palgrave Macmillan.

Lozano, R. (2018). Sustainable Business Models: A Holistic Approach to Sustainability. *Business Strategy and the Environment*, *27*(7), 1312–1325. DOI: 10.1002/bse.2156

Mackenzie, C., Gifford, R., & Reser, J. (2018). Implementing Corporate Sustainability through ESG Metrics: Challenges and Opportunities. *Business Strategy and the Environment*, *27*(8), 1278–1288. DOI: 10.1002/bse.2162

Meyer, C., Sanyal, S., & Rangarajan, S. (2019). Navigating Regulatory Hurdles for Sustainable Business Practices: A Global Perspective. *Business Strategy and the Environment*, *28*(5), 708–724. DOI: 10.1002/bse.2225

Microsoft. (2020). *Microsoft's Sustainability Efforts: Carbon-Negative by 2030*. Retrieved from https://www.microsoft.com

Miller, D., & O'Leary, J. (2018). Achieving the Sustainable Development Goals: The Role of Education and the Economy. *The Journal of Development Studies*, *54*(9), 1530–1545. DOI: 10.1080/00220388.2018.1481486

Moneva, J. M., Archel, P., & Correa, C. (2019). Government Regulations, Corporate Social Responsibility, and Sustainability Reporting: An Empirical Analysis. *Corporate Social Responsibility and Environmental Management*, *26*(6), 1264–1274. DOI: 10.1002/csr.1751

Morioka, S. N., & Carvalho, M. M. (2016). Measuring Sustainability in Practice: Exploring the Inclusion of Sustainability into Corporate Performance Systems in Brazilian Case Studies. *Journal of Cleaner Production*, *136*, 123–133. DOI: 10.1016/j.jclepro.2016.01.103

Müller, F., Rieder, R., & Sihvonen, S. (2020). Corporate Sustainability and the SDGs: How Business and Strategy Align with the Global Agenda. *Journal of Business Ethics*, *164*(1), 1–12. DOI: 10.1007/s10551-020-04435-z

Murray, A. (2018). Patagonia's Environmental Commitment: The Power of Purpose-Driven Business. *Journal of Business Ethics*, *147*(3), 655–667. DOI: 10.1007/s10551-016-3169-0

Nestlé. (2020). *Nestlé Creating Shared Value Report*. Retrieved from https://www.nestle.com

Nwachukwu, S. L., & Nwachukwu, C. S. (2020). The Role of Businesses in Climate Change Mitigation and the Sustainable Development Goals. *International Journal of Environmental Science and Technology*, *17*(7), 3633–3645. DOI: 10.1007/s13762-020-02788-5

O'Neill, L., Raghubir, P., & Pham, M. T. (2020). Implementing ESG Metrics in Corporate Sustainability: Challenges and Best Practices. *Journal of Business Research*, *106*, 167–176. DOI: 10.1016/j.jbusres.2019.08.031

Pedersen, C. S. (2018). The UN Sustainable Development Goals (SDGs) are a Great Gift to Business! *Procedia CIRP*, *69*, 21–24. DOI: 10.1016/j.procir.2018.01.003

Rockström, J., Steffen, W., Noone, K., Persson, Å., Chapin, F. S.III, Lambin, E. F., Lenton, T. M., Scheffer, M., Folke, C., Schellnhuber, H. J., Nykvist, B., de Wit, C. A., Hughes, T., van der Leeuw, S., Rodhe, H., Sörlin, S., Snyder, P. K., Costanza, R., Svedin, U., & Foley, J. A. (2017). A Safe Operating Space for Humanity. *Nature*, *461*(7263), 472–475. DOI: 10.1038/461472a PMID: 19779433

Saberi, S., Kouhizadeh, M., & Sarkis, J. (2019). Blockchain Technology in Supply Chain Management: A Review of the Literature and Applications. *International Journal of Production Research*, *57*(7), 2117–2135. DOI: 10.1080/00207543.2018.1533261

Schmidt, M. A., Klein, J. M., & Breitenbach, M. (2020). The Role of Government Policy in Promoting Corporate Sustainability. *Journal of Cleaner Production*, *275*, 123132. DOI: 10.1016/j.jclepro.2020.123132

Schmidt-Bleek, F. (2019). *The Factor 10 Debate: Why Business Needs to Engage with the SDGs*. Earthscan.

Schramade, W. (2017). Investing in the UN Sustainable Development Goals: Opportunities for Companies and Investors. *The Bank of America Journal of Applied Corporate Finance*, *29*(2), 87–99. DOI: 10.1111/jacf.12236

Serafeim, G. (2020). How to Build Enduring Business Models in a Changing World. *Harvard Business Review*. https://hbr.org/2020/12/how-to-build-enduring-business-models-in-a-changing-world

Smith, A. (2020). Microsoft's Commitment to Sustainability: Leading the Digital Transformation. *Journal of Corporate Responsibility*, *9*(2), 85–98.

Starbucks. (2020). *Starbucks Global Environmental and Social Impact Report*. Retrieved from https://www.starbucks.com

Steffen, W., Richardson, K., Rockström, J., Cornell, S. E., Fetzer, I., Bennett, E. M., & Sörlin, S. (2018). Sustainability and Planetary Boundaries. *Science*, *347*(6223), 736–746. PMID: 25592418

Sullivan, R., & Mackenzie, C. (2019). *The Global Business Environment: Meeting the Challenges of International Business*. Routledge.

Telesca, D. (2018). BP and the Deepwater Horizon Oil Spill: Analyzing ESG Failures. *Business Ethics Quarterly*, *28*(3), 399–420.

Tesla. (2020). *Environmental Impact Report*. Retrieved from https://www.tesla.com

Unilever. (2020). *Sustainable Living Plan: Annual Report*. Retrieved from https://www.unilever.com

Unilever. (2020). *Sustainable Living Plan: Progress Report*. Retrieved from https://www.unilever.com

Unilever. (2020). *Unilever Sustainable Living Plan Progress Report*. https://www.unilever.com/sustainable-living/

United Nations. (2015). *Transforming Our World: The 2030 Agenda for Sustainable Development*. Retrieved from https://sdgs.un.org/2030agenda

United Nations. (2015). Transforming Our World: The 2030 Agenda for Sustainable Development.

World Bank. (2017). *World Development Report 2017: Governance and the Law*. World Bank.

Wurtmann, H., & Seuring, S. (2020). Managing Climate Change Risks in Global Supply Chains: A Review and Research Agenda. *International Journal of Production Research*, *58*(1), 44–64. DOI: 10.1080/00207543.2019.1629670

Zengler, T. (2021). The Impact of Innovation on Tesla's ESG Performance. *Technology and Innovation*, *24*(4), 255–267.

Zhou, Y., Yang, J., & Zheng, Z. (2018). Smart Grids and AI: Towards Sustainable Energy. *IEEE Access : Practical Innovations, Open Solutions*, *6*, 25217–25228. DOI: 10.1109/ACCESS.2018.2839026

# Chapter 16
# Analysis of Factors Influencing Brownfield Redevelopment in the Context of Regional Development

**Jaroslav Škrabal**
https://orcid.org/0000-0002-4685-9836
*Moravian Business College, Olomouc, Czech Republic*

**Martin Vybiral**
https://orcid.org/0009-0001-8314-2578
*Moravian Business College, Olomouc, Czech Republic*

## ABSTRACT

*This chapter examines key factors influencing brownfield regeneration in the Czech Republic within regional development. The aim is to identify and evaluate determinants of successful revitalization by developing a systematic framework for assessing redevelopment potential. Using factor analysis and comparative methods, the study analyzes economic, environmental, and social factors based on CzechInvest (2024) data. Key determinants include land ownership, prior land use, contamination levels, and investment potential. The findings show that clear ownership, economic incentives, and infrastructure investments enhance regeneration, while regulatory complexity and remediation costs hinder it. The study contributes to data-driven policy recommendations to optimize land-use planning and investment incentives for sustainable brownfield redevelopment.*

## INTRODUCTION

The revitalization of brownfields-unused, often contaminated sites-is a critical challenge in regional development. As urban areas face increasing land scarcity, environmental degradation, and stricter regulations, brownfield regeneration offers a sustainable alternative to urban expansion. It reduces

DOI: 10.4018/979-8-3373-0189-1.ch016

environmental hazards, enhances land efficiency, and supports economic revitalization (Li et al. 2019; Ahmad et al. 2021).

Scholarly definitions of brownfields vary. Alker et al. (2000) describe them as previously developed sites that require intervention before reuse, while Thomas (2003) highlights the financial and social burdens of their redevelopment. These sites emerge primarily from industrial decline, urban restructuring, and economic shifts (Ferber et al. 2006; Frantal et al. 2013). In post-socialist countries, brownfield revitalization only gained traction after 2010, significantly later than in Western Europe (Hurnikova, 2009).

The European Union emphasizes brownfield redevelopment as a key component of sustainable urban policy, promoting it within the European Green Deal and Circular Economy Action Plan (European Commission, 2020). Brownfield revitalization not only prevents urban sprawl but also supports climate resilience and sustainable infrastructure integration (Pizzol et al. 2016; Tendero and Bazart, 2023).

A structured classification system is essential for assessing redevelopment potential. The CABERNET model categorizes brownfields based on economic feasibility and public-sector dependency (Concerted Action on Brownfield and Economic Regeneration Network, 2014). Other classifications consider previous land use, contamination levels, and ownership structure, which significantly influence investment potential (Zamarsky, Tylcer and Strelec, 2011).

Despite the economic and environmental benefits of brownfield regeneration, significant barriers remain. These include high remediation costs, fragmented ownership, and complex legal frameworks (Frantal et al. 2015). Investor decision-making is also influenced by location factors-urban brownfields near city centers attract greater interest, whereas rural sites often struggle to secure funding (Hagget, 2001).

The aim is to identify and evaluate determinants of successful revitalization by developing a systematic framework for assessing redevelopment potential. By applying factor analysis to CzechInvest data (2024), this research develops a systematic framework for assessing redevelopment potential. The findings will provide policy recommendations for optimizing land-use strategies and investment incentives, ultimately supporting sustainable regional development.

## BACKGROUND

Brownfield redevelopment has become a critical component of urban sustainability strategies, attracting increasing attention from policymakers and scholars. The term "brownfield" refers to previously developed sites that are now abandoned, underutilized, or contaminated, requiring remediation before they can be repurposed for productive use (Alker et al. 2000). These sites are a legacy of industrial decline, urban expansion, and economic transitions, often posing both environmental risks and opportunities for sustainable urban development (Frantal et al. 2013). As cities seek to balance economic growth with environmental preservation, brownfields present a compelling alternative to greenfield development, reducing urban sprawl and promoting the efficient use of existing land resources (BenDor et al. 2011).

Spatial characteristics play a key role in determining the feasibility of brownfield redevelopment. Skrabal (2020), analyzing data from the National Brownfield Database, found that most abandoned sites in the Czech Republic are located on the periphery of settlements, making them less attractive to investors. This aligns with the broader trend observed in post-industrial regions, where peripheral brownfields face challenges related to infrastructure accessibility, market demand, and investment risk (Osman et al. 2015). At the same time, urban core brownfields tend to attract more interest due to their proximity to existing economic and social infrastructure, though they often require more complex remediation efforts due to a history of intensive land use (Frantal et al. 2015).

A growing body of research underscores the role of brownfield sites in sustainable urban development. For instance, Laprise et al. (2018) argue that integrating brownfields into urban sustainability frameworks requires continuous monitoring of environmental, social, and economic indicators to ensure holistic redevelopment. Similarly, Li et al. (2019) advocate for multi-criteria sustainability assessment models that quantify the long-term benefits of brownfield regeneration, facilitating better decision-making for municipalities and investors. Brownfield redevelopment is not merely about land reuse; it is increasingly seen as a tool for achieving climate resilience. Studies have demonstrated that successful brownfield transformations can contribute to decarbonization efforts, with Ahmad et al. (2021) emphasizing the role of brownfields in mitigating greenhouse gas emissions through urban infill strategies and energy-efficient land use planning.

The economic viability of brownfield redevelopment remains a subject of debate. While regenerating these sites can lead to increased property values, expanded tax bases, and job creation (Wang et al. 2011), financial challenges persist. High remediation costs, regulatory compliance, and investment risks often deter private sector engagement (Hammond et al. 2024). In response, many cities have introduced financial incentives, public-private partnerships, and adaptive reuse models to enhance project feasibility (Frantal et al. 2015). Skrabal et al. (2021) highlight the crucial role of municipalities in financing brownfield regeneration, often leveraging public budgets, European grants, and external subsidies to support redevelopment efforts. This underscores the importance of well-defined institutional frameworks and financial mechanisms that align with broader urban sustainability goals.

Recent research also points to innovative redevelopment approaches, particularly in post-industrial and emerging urban contexts. Song et al. (2022) demonstrate how multi-source spatial data can improve brownfield identification and prioritization, enabling data-driven regeneration policies. In Europe, creative and cultural regeneration models have gained traction, with Popa et al. (2025) showing that abandoned industrial sites can be transformed into cultural and artistic hubs, attracting creative industries and fostering economic renewal. Similar trends are observed in the United Kingdom, where brownfields have been repurposed for recreational green spaces, improving urban biodiversity and public health outcomes (Li et al. 2019).

A specialized focus on contaminated brownfields is particularly relevant given the environmental and public health risks they pose. Hagmanna et al. (2020) conducted a forensic analysis of soil contamination at a brownfield site in the U.S., identifying persistent pollutants that require advanced remediation strategies. Similarly, Tendero and Bazart (2024) emphasize the need for stricter regulatory frameworks to ensure that soil remediation efforts align with broader sustainability goals. Addressing contamination challenges is especially critical in countries with weaker regulatory enforcement, where brownfields remain significant sources of urban pollution (Kovalicka and Montgomery, 2014).

Brownfield redevelopment is a complex yet essential element of urban sustainability. The reviewed literature highlights the interplay of environmental, economic, social, and governance factors in shaping the success of regeneration efforts. Key determinants include regulatory frameworks, land ownership structures, contamination levels, and stakeholder engagement, all of which influence the feasibility and long-term viability of redevelopment projects. Moving forward, policymakers must integrate advanced analytical tools-such as multi-criteria decision-making and sustainability modelling-to enhance the strategic planning of brownfield regeneration (Pizzol et al. 2016). This chapter employs descriptive and factor analysis techniques to evaluate Czech brownfields, providing insights into how these sites can be leveraged for sustainable urban development and investment optimization.

## FACTORS INFLUENCING THE REGENERATION OF BROWNFIELDS IN THE CZECH REPUBLIC

In the initial phase, this study employed desk research (i.e., secondary analysis) to establish a theoretical framework and define fundamental concepts related to brownfields, their classification, and standard regeneration approaches. This theoretical groundwork was followed by an empirical analysis based on data from the National Brownfield Database (2024), maintained by CzechInvest. The database provides comprehensive information on abandoned or contaminated sites requiring remediation or revitalization. The dataset (n = 642) includes key variables such as land size, location, ownership structure, contamination levels, and previous land use, all of which are crucial for understanding brownfield regeneration dynamics. The data were analyzed at both the national and regional levels (NUTS III classification) to capture spatial variations.

For an initial overview of the dataset, descriptive statistical methods were applied to explore the distribution of key indicators, including the prevalence of various brownfield types, contamination frequency, and land size characteristics. This was followed by comparative analysis across different regions and brownfield categories to identify potential spatial and functional patterns. The theoretical insights from the literature guided the deductive approach employed in the study.

To uncover latent relationships among the selected variables, Principal Component Analysis (PCA) was applied. This method allows for the extraction of a smaller number of principal components that explain the highest variance within the dataset, reducing complexity while preserving critical information. Unlike regression analysis, which focuses on direct relationships between dependent and independent variables, PCA identifies underlying latent factors shaping brownfield redevelopment dynamics. This approach provides a more holistic perspective on interdependencies among economic, environmental, and ownership-related factors.

All data were processed and analyzed using R software (version 2024.12.0+467), a widely used open-source statistical platform. Data preprocessing included error detection, removal of inconsistent records, and imputation of missing values. Multiple imputation (predictive mean matching for numerical variables and mode imputation for categorical variables) was applied to minimize bias. Exploratory Data Analysis (EDA) was used to visualize initial data trends before applying more advanced statistical techniques.

The selection of key variables was based on prior studies and available empirical data, with an emphasis on economic, environmental, and social factors known to influence brownfield regeneration. The definition of successful regeneration was operationalized as sites that have been either fully repurposed (residential, commercial, or mixed-use development) or have undergone significant environmental remediation with an active redevelopment plan. The classification was based on municipal reports, investment records, and planning documents.

Previous research has identified several critical factors influencing brownfield regeneration. One of the most significant is land size, as larger brownfields often exhibit complex ownership structures, higher investment requirements, and increased environmental burdens, which can delay redevelopment (Frantal et al. 2013; Pizzol et al. 2016). Conversely, smaller brownfields-particularly those in attractive locations-tend to be revitalized more quickly and offer greater flexibility in their repurposing (Skrabal, 2020).

The next crucial variable is ownership structure, as brownfields with clear legal ownership exhibit a significantly higher likelihood of successful redevelopment compared to sites with uncertain or disputed ownership (Osman et al. 2015; Dolezelova et al. 2014). This issue is particularly pronounced in post-socialist countries, where unresolved land claims continue to complicate regeneration efforts (Frantal et al. 2015).

Below, Figure 1 illustrates the regional distribution of brownfields at the NUTS III level in the Czech Republic. The capital city, Prague, was excluded from the analysis due to its unique spatial and economic characteristics.

*Figure 1. Regional Distribution of NUTS III Territories within the Czech Republic*

*Source: ČÚZK, own processing*

Figure 1 provides a spatial overview of the regional distribution of brownfields across NUTS III regions in the Czech Republic. To complement this visualization, Table 1 presents the total land area (in hectares) for each region, highlighting regional disparities in land availability and potential redevelopment capacity.

*Table 1. Area of NUTS III Regions in the Czech Republic (ha)*

| NUTS III Region | Area (ha) |
|---|---|
| Central Bohemia Region | 1,092,900 |
| South Bohemia Region | 1,005,700 |
| Plzen Region | 756,100 |
| Karlovy Vary Region | 331,400 |
| Ustí nad Labem Region | 533,500 |
| Liberec Region | 316,300 |
| Hradec Kralove Region | 475,800 |
| Pardubice Region | 451,900 |
| Vysocina Region | 679,600 |
| South Moravian Region | 718,800 |
| Olomouc Region | 526,700 |

continued on following page

*Table 1. Continued*

| NUTS III Region | Area (ha) |
|---|---|
| Zlin Region | 396,400 |
| Moravian-Silesian Region | 542,700 |

Source: ČÚZK, own processing

To enhance regional identification, this study classifies NUTS III regions based on their respective codes. The Nomenclature of Territorial Units for Statistics (NUTS) is an official geocode standard used for statistical and administrative purposes in the Czech Republic. Table 2 presents the corresponding NUTS III codes alongside their respective region names, ensuring consistency in territorial classification.

*Table 2. NUTS III Codes and Corresponding Regions in the Czech Republic*

| CZ NUTS III | Region Name |
|---|---|
| CZ041 | Karlovy Vary Region |
| CZ042 | Usti nad Labem Region |
| CZ063 | Vysocina Region |
| CZ053 | Pardubice Region |
| CZ051 | Liberec Region |
| CZ071 | Olomouc Region |
| CZ064 | South Moravian Region |
| CZ032 | Plzen Region |
| CZ031 | South Bohemian Region |
| CZ020 | Central Bohemian Region |
| CZ052 | Hradec Kralove Region |
| CZ080 | Moravian-Silesian Region |
| CZ072 | Zlin Region |

*Source:* ČÚZK, own processing

Brownfield regeneration is a key issue in regional development and urban planning, offering significant environmental, economic, and social benefits (Teo et al. 2021; Sessa et al. 2022). However, challenges such as ownership disputes, high remediation costs, and market demand limitations hinder redevelopment efforts. In the Czech Republic, brownfield regeneration is particularly relevant due to its industrial history and ongoing economic restructuring. Unlike in Western European countries, where many brownfields have already undergone transformation, the Czech Republic still faces significant legal and economic barriers stemming from its post-socialist land ownership structure (Frantal et al. 2015).

Brownfields are defined as sites previously used for industrial, commercial, or other purposes that now require intervention due to contamination or urban neglect (Longo and Campbell, 2017). Their successful revitalization can lead to new industrial zones, commercial centers, public spaces, or residential developments, supporting economic growth while mitigating urban sprawl (Rizzo et al. 2018). This approach aligns with sustainable development and circular economy principles, emphasizing efficient land use and resource optimization (Gibbs and Deutz, 2007). However, in the Czech Republic, brownfield redevelopment is heavily dependent on external funding, particularly from EU structural funds and national subsidy programs (Bez et al. 2024).

Among the primary factors influencing brownfield regeneration, geographic location plays a critical role. Brownfields near major cities are more likely to be redeveloped due to better infrastructure access and stronger economic viability (Osman et al. 2015). Within the Czech Republic, brownfield revitalization is concentrated in urbanized regions with high population density and active real estate markets. Ownership structure also significantly impacts regeneration speed, as privately owned sites tend to be redeveloped more rapidly than publicly owned ones, which often face bureaucratic delays and funding constraints (Longo and Campbell, 2017). Furthermore, restitution claims and complex legal ownership histories often prevent the timely redevelopment of brownfields, especially those under mixed ownership (Frantal et al. 2015).

A major barrier to brownfield redevelopment is soil contamination, which increases remediation costs and legal complexity. Sorvari and Seppälä (2010) emphasize that unclear liability for contamination further complicates legal disputes and extends project timelines. From a policy perspective, brownfield regeneration aligns with sustainable development goals, as highlighted by the European Commission (2020), which promotes brownfield revitalization through targeted funding programs, environmental regulations, and incentives for low-carbon redevelopment. In the Czech Republic, these mechanisms are reflected in EU cohesion funds, the Green Deal strategy, and municipal sustainability policies.

Economically, successful brownfield redevelopment is defined as projects that lead to measurable increases in property values, job creation, and private sector investment, contributing to long-term regional economic stability (Wang, Fang and Hipel, 2011). The most effective projects integrate commercial and residential uses, promoting economic diversification and regional competitiveness. However, regional disparities persist, with some areas facing greater regeneration challenges due to lower investment attractiveness and weaker real estate markets (Bez et al. 2024).

Another determinant of regeneration success is community engagement in the decision-making process. Hackworth (2014) notes that collaborative approaches involving public authorities, investors, and local residents enhance project legitimacy and acceptance. This is particularly important in urban renewal initiatives, where stakeholder involvement can accelerate planning and implementation. In post-socialist countries like the Czech Republic, municipal involvement remains essential due to the complexity of land ownership and the reliance on state-led remediation programs (Frantal et al. 2015).

The table below (Table 3) illustrates the ownership of non-regenerated brownfields at the national level within the Czech Republic.

*Table 3. Ownership of Unregistered Brownfields*

| Ownership | Percentage | Frequency |
|---|---|---|
| Public | 37.4 | 240 |
| Private | 55.9 | 359 |
| Combined | 6.7 | 43 |
| Total | 100.0 | 642 |

Source: own processing, National Brownfield Database, 2024

Ownership structure is a significant determinant of brownfield redevelopment, influencing the speed and complexity of revitalization efforts. In the Czech Republic, private ownership dominates, accounting for approximately 56% of all brownfield sites. Publicly owned brownfields constitute 37%, primarily managed by national or local government authorities, while 7% fall under mixed ownership, involving both public and private entities. This distribution is consistent with findings by Longo and Campbell (2017), who emphasize that privately owned brownfields are more likely to be redeveloped due to streamlined decision-making processes and direct investment incentives. However, in some cases, private entities engage in land banking, holding brownfield sites for speculative purposes rather than immediate redevelopment, which further delays regeneration efforts (Bartke et al. 2013).

While public ownership provides access to state and EU subsidies, bureaucratic constraints and budgetary limitations often hinder regeneration efforts, resulting in prolonged redevelopment timelines (Skrabal, 2020). Brownfields under mixed ownership present unique challenges, requiring complex negotiations among multiple stakeholders, which can delay investment decisions and complicate project coordination (Bartke et al. 2013). According to Osman et al. (2015), public institutions frequently stabilize brownfields first—through land acquisition, planning, or environmental assessment-before transferring them to private investors. Conversely, privately owned sites may remain inactive if owners lack financial resources or incentives for redevelopment (Thomas, 2003).

Given the high prevalence of private ownership, successful brownfield regeneration in the Czech Republic depends on effective public-private partnerships, particularly in cases where administrative barriers or financial constraints hinder investment. One example of successful public-private collaboration in brownfield regeneration is the revitalization of the former Škoda Plzeň industrial complex. This project combined municipal planning, EU funding, and private investment to transform an underutilized industrial zone into a mixed-use area, demonstrating the potential of coordinated redevelopment strategies (Bez et al. 2024).

Targeted policy instruments, such as tax incentives, regulatory simplification, and public co-financing mechanisms, could facilitate a more efficient transformation of brownfields into productive urban spaces (Bez et al. 2024). In the Czech Republic, funding programs under the Ministry of Regional Development and EU cohesion funds have played a crucial role in supporting brownfield revitalization efforts. The descriptive statistical analysis of ownership structures suggests that brownfields with clearly defined property rights, whether fully private or fully public, exhibit a higher likelihood of redevelopment, whereas sites with fragmented or contested ownership face prolonged stagnation. These findings align with broader research on brownfield revitalization, which underscores the importance of ownership clarity, regulatory frameworks, and financial incentives in overcoming redevelopment barriers (Dixon, Raco and Catney, 2007; Adams, De Sousa and Tiesdell, 2010).

The following table (Table 4) focuses on the previous use of sites from the National Brownfield Database at the national level within the context of the Czech Republic.

*Table 4. Previous Use of Unregenerated Brownfields*

| Previous Use | Percentage | Frequency |
|---|---|---|
| Industry | 36.0 | 231 |
| Civic | 27.9 | 179 |
| Agriculture | 17.0 | 109 |
| Military | 7.5 | 48 |
| Other | 7.2 | 46 |
| Transport | 2.3 | 15 |
| Mining | 2.2 | 14 |
| Total | 100.0 | 642 |

Source: own processing, National Brownfield Database, 2024

Brownfields in the Czech Republic exhibit diverse land-use histories. Industrial sites (36%), including former manufacturing plants and warehouses, are primarily located in urban centers, benefiting from existing infrastructure for redevelopment (Frantal et al. 2015). Civic brownfields (28%), such as former schools and hospitals, often occupy central locations but face redevelopment constraints due to preservation regulations (Davis and Sherman, 2010). While industrial sites are often attractive for commercial redevelopment, civic brownfields are subject to legal and architectural constraints that can limit their reuse potential.

Agricultural brownfields (17%) are typically in rural areas, where limited infrastructure reduces investment appeal (Osman et al. 2015). Military brownfields (7.5%) present challenges due to contamination risks and land-use restrictions (Hackworth, 2014). Mixed-use brownfields (7.2%), such as logistics centers and administrative buildings, offer flexible redevelopment potential, whereas transport-related sites (2.3%), primarily railway infrastructure, face high regulatory barriers (Frantal et al. 2013). Mining brownfields (2.2%) require extensive remediation due to severe environmental burdens, such as heavy metal contamination and groundwater pollution, which substantially increase regeneration costs (Sorvari and Seppälä, 2010; Li et al. 2019).

Given their higher redevelopment feasibility, industrial and civic brownfields should be prioritized in policy efforts. However, military and mining sites demand targeted interventions, including public-private partnerships and financial incentives, to support their regeneration (Laprise et al. 2018). In particular, military brownfields often require specialized remediation efforts, including soil decontamination and structural stabilization, making their redevelopment complex and resource-intensive.

At the national level, 24% of brownfields are confirmed as contaminated, while 59% remain non-contaminated or unconfirmed. An additional 17% fall into the "Unknown" category, reflecting gaps in environmental records (Osman et al. 2015; Sorvari and Seppälä, 2010). The 'N/A' contamination category often results from gaps in historical land-use records, the absence of environmental monitoring, or the lack of mandated soil testing prior to listing in the National Brownfield Database. These uncertainties complicate investment planning, as potential developers must conduct independent environmental assessments, increasing upfront costs and extending project timelines (Hackworth, 2014).

Investors frequently conduct independent environmental assessments, which increase transaction costs and slow down the regeneration process (Thomas, 2003). Research suggests that contaminated brownfields, particularly in post-industrial regions, pose a significant financial burden, as high decontamination costs hinder land redevelopment efforts (Frantal et al. 2015). To improve the attractiveness of contaminated brownfields for redevelopment, targeted policy measures-such as state-funded preliminary environmental assessments or tax incentives for remediation-could help reduce investment risks and accelerate land reuse. Similar strategies have been successfully implemented in Germany and the Netherlands, where early-stage contamination mapping has facilitated brownfield revitalization (Laprise et al. 2018).

*Table 5. Contamination of Unregenerated Brownfields*

| Contamination Status | Percentage | Frequency |
|---|---|---|
| Yes | 24.0 | 154 |
| No | 59.2 | 380 |
| N/A | 16.8 | 108 |
| Total | 100.0 | 642 |

Source: own processing, National Brownfield Database, 2024

The ownership structure of brownfields is a key determinant of their regeneration potential and redevelopment speed. The results indicate (Figure 2) that private ownership prevails in many regions (e.g., CZ020, CZ041), whereas in others, such as CZ051 and CZ053, public ownership has a more significant share. This regional variation suggests that ownership type directly influences redevelopment strategies and investment dynamics.

Research by Longo and Campbell (2017) indicates that privately owned brownfields are more likely to undergo faster regeneration, as private owners are motivated to maximize land value and reduce holding costs. Conversely, publicly owned brownfields often require long-term planning and strategic decision-making at the municipal level, which can slow down redevelopment due to bureaucratic constraints and multi-level governance processes. In addition, these sites are frequently subject to stricter land-use regulations and political considerations, which can deter private investment (Skrabal, 2020).

The complexity of mixed ownership structures presents an additional barrier to regeneration. Bartke et al. (2013) emphasize that coordination among multiple stakeholders often results in delays and negotiation difficulties, particularly when property rights are disputed or unclear. This can discourage private investors, as prolonged legal proceedings and administrative approvals increase uncertainty and financial risks associated with redevelopment. As a result, brownfields under mixed ownership frequently face stagnation due to protracted negotiations between public and private entities.

Further empirical analysis is needed to determine whether such sites indeed experience prolonged regeneration processes and to identify potential policy interventions that could facilitate their redevelopment. Possible solutions include state-funded land consolidation programs for mixed-ownership brownfields and legislative simplifications to accelerate public-sector regeneration efforts. Policymakers could also explore financial incentives for investors willing to engage in public-private partnerships aimed at resolving ownership disputes and streamlining redevelopment procedures.

*Figure 2. Ownership Structure of Unregenerated Brownfields in NUTS III Regions of the Czech Republic*

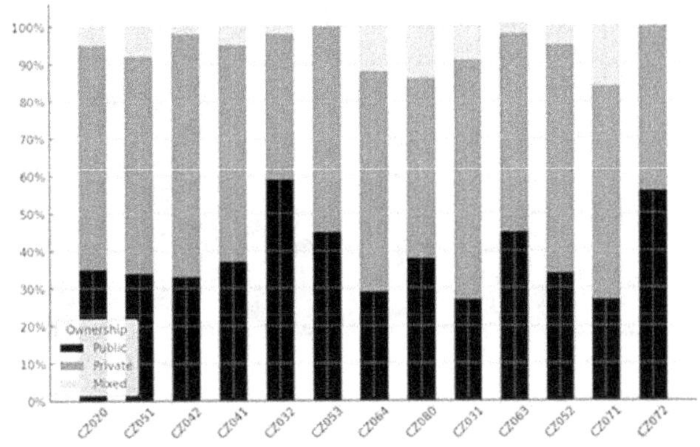


*Source: own processing, National Brownfield Database, 2024, RStudio (R version 2024.12.0+467)*

The distribution of different brownfield types (Figure 3) reflects both historical land use and future redevelopment potential. Industrial and agricultural brownfields are the most prevalent categories, aligning with Frantal et al. (2013), who confirm that industrial brownfields dominate in Central European countries, largely due to the legacy of socialist economic planning.

In CZ053 and CZ072, industrial brownfields significantly prevail, whereas CZ031 and CZ080 have a higher concentration of agricultural brownfields. This variation likely stems from regional economic specialization-highly industrialized areas tend to have more former factory sites, while rural regions are more prone to abandoned agricultural estates. Industrial brownfields are generally more attractive for redevelopment due to their proximity to existing transport and energy infrastructure, as well as their historical integration into regional economic networks (Frantal et al. 2013). In contrast, agricultural brownfields, while abundant, often lack basic infrastructure and market connectivity, making their regeneration more challenging and less appealing to private investors.

Urbanization plays a key role in brownfield regeneration prospects. Luck and Wu (2002) highlight that urban brownfields are more attractive to investors, leading to a higher likelihood of redevelopment. In contrast, rural brownfields often face lower demand, resulting in longer stagnation periods. This challenge is particularly evident in military brownfields, where high adaptation costs make redevelopment more complex (Skrabal, 2020). Military brownfields present unique redevelopment challenges due to high adaptation costs, stringent environmental regulations, and contamination risks associated with former military activities. Many sites require extensive soil remediation and compliance with national security and land-use policies, which can prolong redevelopment timelines and reduce investment appeal.

*Figure 3. Previous Land Use of Unregenerated Brownfields in NUTS III Regions of the Czech Republic*

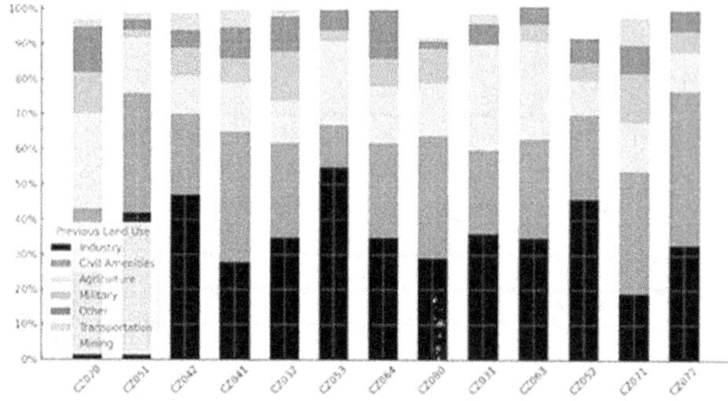


*Source: own processing, National Brownfield Database, 2024, RStudio (R version 2024.12.0+467)*

The analysis of regional disparities in brownfield contamination reveals significant variation across different areas (Figure 4). The highest contamination rate is observed in CZ072, where nearly 94% of brownfields are classified as contaminated, representing a notable outlier compared to other regions. This can be attributed to the historical concentration of heavy industry, including metallurgy, chemical manufacturing, and coal processing, which have contributed to extensive soil and groundwater contamination. These industrial activities typically generate persistent pollutants such as heavy metals and hydrocarbons, requiring complex and costly remediation efforts. Longo and Campbell (2017) identify former industrial sites as the most challenging to regenerate, primarily due to high environmental risks and remediation costs.

Conversely, CZ071 and CZ032 exhibit the lowest contamination rates, with less than 20% of sites classified as contaminated. This can be attributed to their historically lower concentration of heavy industry and a greater prevalence of agricultural and administrative land uses, which generally pose lower environmental risks. Additionally, these regions may have benefited from earlier or more effective state-led remediation programs, reducing the residual contamination burden. Sorvari and Seppälä (2010) emphasize that decontamination costs represent a major barrier to brownfield redevelopment, with highly contaminated regions often experiencing slower regeneration due to financial and legislative constraints.

The effectiveness of brownfield regeneration is closely tied to remediation technologies. Rizzo et al. (2018) highlight that advanced decontamination methods significantly enhance redevelopment potential. Techniques such as bioremediation, chemical soil stabilization, and in-situ filtration of pollutants can accelerate site recovery and reduce long-term environmental risks, making contaminated brownfields more attractive for investors. In regions with a high proportion of brownfields without confirmed contamination, it is likely that successful remediation efforts have been applied, improving the prospects for site redevelopment.

*Figure 4. Contamination Status of Unregenerated Brownfields in NUTS III Regions of the Czech Republic*

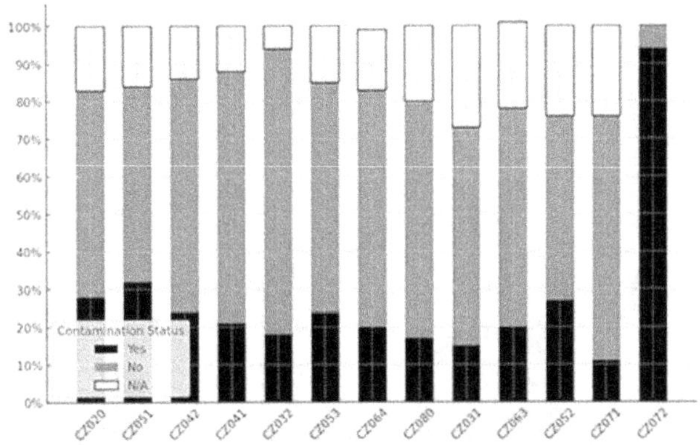


*Source: own processing, National Brownfield Database, 2024, RStudio (R version 2024.12.0+467)*

The size of brownfields is a key factor influencing regeneration potential, though its impact varies significantly. The results (Figure 5) indicate that certain regions (e.g., CZ072, CZ053) contain significantly larger brownfields, which aligns with Pizzol et al. (2016), who found that large brownfields are commonly associated with former industrial complexes or military sites, while smaller sites typically originate from commercial or residential sectors.

Longo and Campbell (2017) argue that smaller brownfields have a higher likelihood of regeneration, as they require lower financial investments, involve fewer regulatory hurdles, and allow for more flexible redevelopment options, making them particularly attractive to private investors. In contrast, large brownfields may only attract investors if a clear redevelopment strategy exists and strong public sector support is provided. These sites often face additional challenges, including fragmented ownership structures, higher costs for infrastructure rehabilitation, and prolonged permitting and approval processes, which can delay investment decisions (Pizzol et al. 2016). One example of successful large-scale brownfield redevelopment is the transformation of Ostrava's Karolina Park, where coordinated public investment and strategic planning facilitated the conversion of a former industrial site into a vibrant commercial and residential hub (Skrabal, 2020).

Due to insufficient statistical homogeneity, brownfield size was excluded from the factor analysis (PCA). This decision is supported by Rizzo et al. (2018), who emphasize that brownfield regeneration is influenced not only by size but by a combination of economic, environmental, and legal factors. Descriptive analysis confirmed that brownfield size alone does not adequately predict regeneration potential, as its impact is highly dependent on other characteristics, such as brownfield type, location, and contamination level. This approach aligns with the conclusions of Longo and Campbell (2017) and Skrabal (2020), who stress that regeneration feasibility is determined by a complex interplay of factors rather than size alone.

*Figure 5. Total Area of Unregenerated Brownfields in NUTS III Regions of the Czech Republic (ha)*

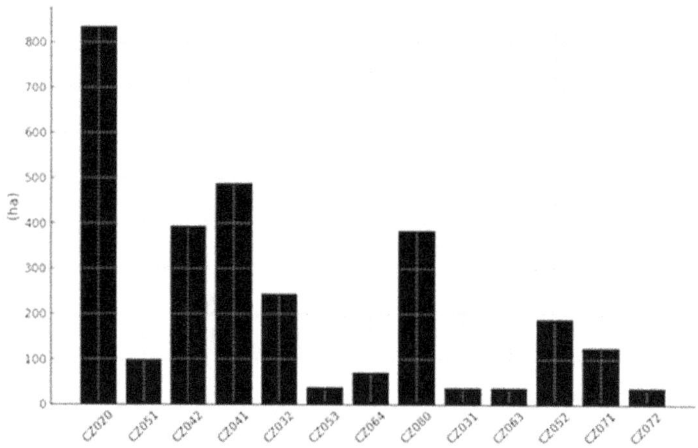


*Source: own processing, National Brownfield Database, 2024, RStudio (R version 2024.12.0+467)*

The results of the principal component analysis (PCA) reveal key factors influencing brownfield regeneration in the Czech Republic. The first principal component (PC1), explaining 39.9% of the variance, represents economic activity and investment attractiveness. Regions with high PC1 values, such as CZ042, are characterized by strong private ownership, an industrial legacy, and well-developed transportation infrastructure, which facilitates faster regeneration. These findings align with the work of Green and Jones (2020), who emphasize the importance of economic maturity and business networks in brownfield redevelopment.

Conversely, regions with low PC1 values, such as CZ063, are associated with military or agricultural land use, which hinders regeneration due to administrative and environmental constraints. Military brownfields often require costly decontamination processes due to hazardous residues, while agricultural brownfields may be subject to strict zoning regulations that limit redevelopment potential (Sorvari and Seppälä, 2010).

The second principal component (PC2), accounting for 19.6% of the variance, reflects the complexity of ownership structures and regulatory constraints. Regions with high PC2 values, such as the Moravian-Silesian and Ústí nad Labem regions, exhibit complicated ownership structures, including mixed ownership and historically ambiguous property rights. These issues often lead to prolonged legal disputes, higher transaction costs, and increased financial uncertainty for potential investors (Bartke et al. 2013; Kovarik et al. 2019).

The PCA biplot (Figure 6) illustrates that PC1 differentiates economically strong regions with developed infrastructure and industrial heritage from those dominated by public ownership and military or agricultural land use. The direction of the arrows for Industry and Transport indicates their strong influence on investment attractiveness. Conversely, PC2 captures the complexity of ownership structures and environmental factors. Regions with high PC2 values exhibit a greater share of brownfields with uncertain property rights, a phenomenon particularly evident in former mining areas, where regeneration is often hindered by historical legal disputes (Frantal et al. 2015). For example, Usti nad Labem Region (CZ042) exhibits high PC2 values due to its history of state-owned industrial enterprises and subsequent privatization challenges, which have led to long-standing legal uncertainties. In contrast, Central Bohemian Region

(CZ020) has high PC1 values, benefiting from its proximity to Prague, strong transport networks, and high levels of private investment (Frantal et al. 2015).

The analysis confirms that brownfields with clear private ownership and well-developed infrastructure have a higher likelihood of regeneration, whereas regions with a military or agricultural background face more significant redevelopment challenges. These findings align with the conclusions of De Sousa (2003) and Raco and Henderson (2009), who highlight the pivotal role of economic activity and infrastructure quality in brownfield redevelopment.

*Figure 6. Principal Component Analysis (PCA) of Unregenerated Brownfields in NUTS III Regions of the Czech Republic*

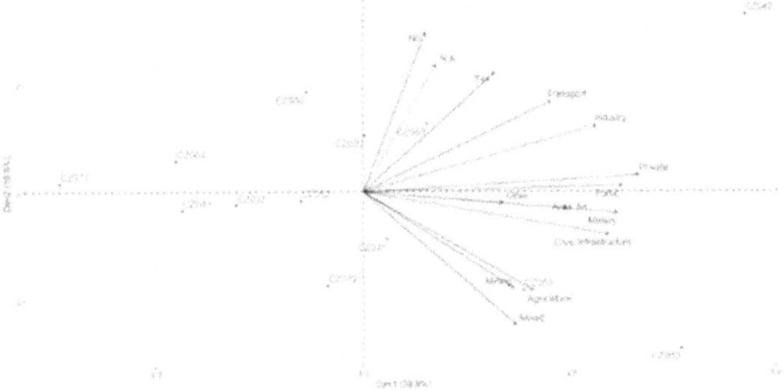


*Source: own processing, RStudio (R version 2024.12.0+467)*

Principal Component Analysis (PCA) is a valuable tool for identifying key factors influencing regional disparities in brownfield regeneration (Figure 7). The biplot visualizes the relationship between regions and variables characterizing their economic and infrastructural structure. The first principal component (PC1) explains the largest share of variance and differentiates regions based on industrial activity and private ownership. Regions with a high proportion of industrial and transport infrastructure, such as Ústí nad Labem Region (CZ042), are positioned on the right, indicating greater economic activity and a higher likelihood of successful brownfield regeneration. For instance, the Central Bohemian Region (CZ020) has benefited from its proximity to Prague, attracting significant private investment and infrastructure development, which has accelerated the transformation of former industrial brownfields into commercial and residential projects (Frantal et al. 2015).

Conversely, regions on the left, such as Olomouc Region (CZ071), exhibit lower industrialization levels and a stronger reliance on the public sector, which may slow down redevelopment. Public-sector-led regeneration projects often face longer approval processes, limited funding availability, and regulatory complexities, making them less responsive to market-driven redevelopment opportunities (Levin et al. 2017).

The second principal component (PC2) captures environmental and land-use factors, particularly contamination levels and previous land utilization. Regions at the top of the graph, such as Moravian-Silesian Region (CZ080) and Liberec Region (CZ051), are associated with contamination-related variables, indicating potential regulatory constraints. Brownfields with high contamination levels require costly remediation efforts, complex environmental assessments, and extensive regulatory approvals, all of which can delay redevelopment and reduce investor interest (De Sousa, 2003). In contrast, regions at the bottom, such as Vysočina Region (CZ063), show links to Mixed, Agriculture, and Military, suggesting land previously used for agricultural or military purposes. These areas may require distinct regeneration strategies compared to industrial brownfields.

Research on brownfield regeneration emphasizes that industrial regions with high economic activity and robust transport infrastructure tend to experience faster revitalization, especially when supported by private investment (De Sousa, 2003; Raco and Henderson, 2009). In contrast, regions historically reliant on public-sector involvement and with limited economic diversification often face prolonged challenges in redeveloping brownfields (Levin et al. 2017). Identifying critical factors that facilitate regeneration is essential for fostering sustainable development and optimizing land use policies.

*Figure 7. PCA Biplot of Unregenerated Brownfields in NUTS III Regions of the Czech Republic (Regions vs. Variables)*

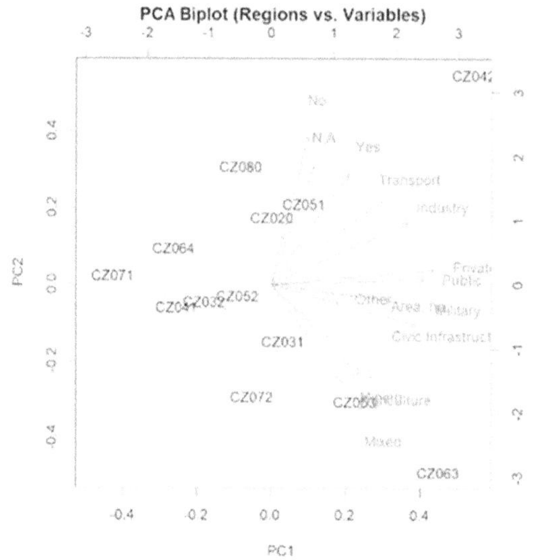


*Source: own processing, RStudio (R version 2024.12.0+467)*

The PCA biplot (Figure 8) provides a structured classification of brownfield sites based on two principal components. PC1 (Development Potential) explains 64.7% of variance and differentiates regions by economic activity, infrastructure, and private investment. Higher PC1 values indicate greater regeneration potential, as seen in Ústí nad Labem Region (CZ042), which benefits from strong industrial infrastructure and private capital. In contrast, regions such as Olomouc Region (CZ071) show lower PC1 values, reflecting weaker economic conditions and limited investor interest (Green and Jones, 2020; De Sousa, 2003).

PC2 (Ownership Complexity) accounts for 24.7% of variance, highlighting the challenges posed by fragmented or historically unclear property structures. Regions with high PC2 values, such as Plzeň Region (CZ032), face administrative barriers that slow down redevelopment due to complex land ownership and regulatory constraints. Conversely, areas like Olomouc Region (CZ071) exhibit low PC2 values, indicating simpler ownership structures that facilitate investment, consistent with findings on legal constraints affecting brownfield redevelopment (Bartke et al. 2013; Kovarik et al. 2019).

The biplot categorizes regions into four quadrants with distinct characteristics. The lower-right quadrant contains regions such as Moravian-Silesian Region (CZ080), which exhibit both high development potential and clear ownership, making them particularly attractive for private investment. In contrast, the upper-left quadrant, including Zlín Region (CZ072), represents sites with limited investment appeal and ownership complications, posing the greatest regeneration challenges. The lower-left quadrant consists of regions with low PC1 and low PC2 values, where redevelopment may be slow but ownership structures are relatively straightforward. Meanwhile, the upper-right quadrant includes economically attractive areas with complex ownership arrangements, requiring legal resolution before substantial investment can take place.

These results emphasize the importance of targeted interventions tailored to regional conditions. High-PC1 regions may benefit from investment incentives, such as tax reliefs, infrastructure support, or regulatory facilitation, to further accelerate brownfield redevelopment. On the other hand, areas with low PC1 and high PC2 values require legal and regulatory reforms to clarify ownership structures, resolve disputes, and enhance overall market appeal. Previous studies suggest that combining public-private partnerships with regulatory adjustments can significantly improve the feasibility of brownfield revitalization, aligning with successful redevelopment strategies in Germany and the United Kingdom (Pizzol et al. 2016; Hackworth, 2014).

This analysis reinforces the need for region-specific brownfield redevelopment policies that consider economic potential, ownership complexity, and legal barriers to transformation. Policymakers and investors should focus on areas with strong economic fundamentals and clear ownership first, while simultaneously implementing long-term reforms to address the structural barriers in more challenging regions.

*Figure 8. PCA Analysis of Brownfield Regions*

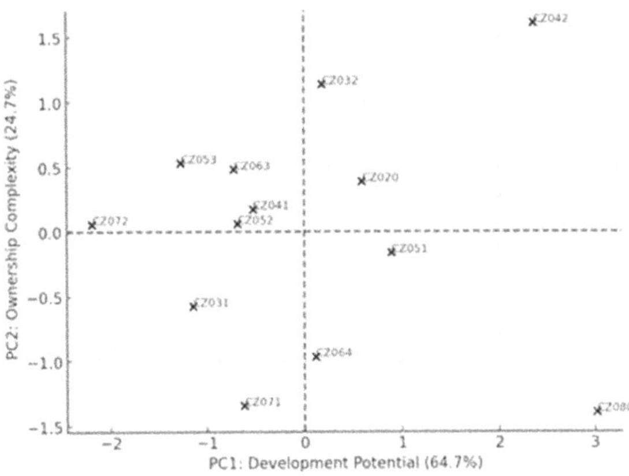


*Source: own processing, RStudio (R version 2024.12.0+467)*

As illustrated in Figure 9, the PCA biplot provides a classification of brownfield sites based on two primary dimensions: development potential (PC1) and ownership complexity (PC2). PC1, which explains 64.7% of the variance, measures the extent to which a given site presents attractive opportunities for investment and redevelopment. Higher PC1 values typically indicate privately owned, formerly industrial properties located in strategic urban areas with strong infrastructure and fewer administrative barriers. In contrast, lower PC1 values correspond to sites burdened by environmental contamination, inadequate infrastructure, or unresolved planning regulations, making them less attractive for redevelopment (Dixon, Raco, and Catney, 2007; Adams, Disberry, and Hutchison, 2010).

PC2, accounting for 24.7% of the variance, reflects the legal and administrative complexity of brownfield ownership. Higher PC2 values are associated with multiple or overlapping ownership structures, often involving former state-owned enterprises, military zones, or properties entangled in legal disputes. These factors extend redevelopment timelines, increase transaction costs, and require more substantial regulatory intervention (De Sousa, 2003; Raco and Henderson, 2009).

From a regional perspective, areas with high PC1 and low PC2 values, such as the Central Bohemian Region (CZ020) and South Moravian Region (CZ064), demonstrate strong market potential and relatively straightforward ownership structures, making them attractive for private investment. Conversely, regions such as the Zlín Region (CZ072), which exhibit low PC1 and high PC2 values, present significant redevelopment challenges due to weak market appeal and complex ownership arrangements. Sites in this category often require direct public-sector intervention, including financial subsidies, regulatory simplifications, and long-term urban planning, to facilitate their transformation.

Figure 9 also highlights the distinction between publicly owned, privately owned, and mixed-ownership brownfields, which are categorized using different symbols in the biplot. Privately owned brownfields, typically linked to former industrial and transport infrastructure, tend to have a higher development potential due to clearer ownership structures and the involvement of market-driven investment. Publicly owned brownfields, on the other hand, often face bureaucratic delays and budgetary constraints, slowing the regeneration process. Mixed-ownership sites, represented in the biplot, exhibit the greatest complexity, as they often require lengthy negotiations among multiple stakeholders before redevelopment can proceed.

Overall, Figure 9 underscores the finding that privately owned brownfields with an industrial legacy are more likely to regenerate through market forces, while public or mixed-ownership sites rely more heavily on governmental assistance and regulatory intervention. These results align with prior research emphasizing the importance of policy reforms, financial incentives, and institutional coordination in facilitating brownfield revitalization (Dixon, Raco, and Catney, 2007; Adams, De Sousa, and Tiesdell, 2010). Policymakers should prioritize sites with strong investment potential and minimal ownership complications while simultaneously developing long-term strategies—such as tax incentives, regulatory streamlining, and targeted public investment-to address more structurally challenging properties.

*Figure 9. PCA Analysis of Brownfield Regions by Ownership*

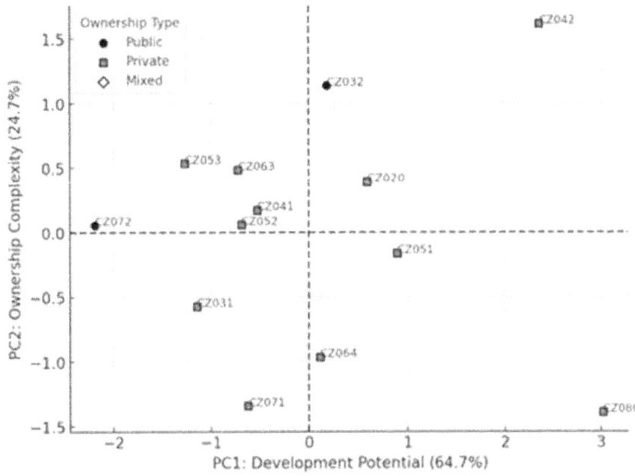


*Source: own processing, RStudio (R version 2024.12.0+467)*

Figure 10 presents the results of a PCA analysis that classifies brownfield regions according to their previous land uses and identifies two primary dimensions: development potential (PC1) and ownership complexity (PC2).

PC1, which explains 44.5% of the total variance, reflects development potential, distinguishing brownfields with strong economic viability from those with structural redevelopment challenges. Brownfields with higher PC1 values, such as those formerly used for industry or transportation, typically possess well-established infrastructure, favorable locations within economically active regions, and a track record of attracting private investment. These sites are more likely to undergo market-driven regeneration due to clear ownership structures and high demand for redevelopment. In contrast, lower PC1 values often characterize agricultural and some military sites, where insufficient infrastructure, contamination risks, or peripheral locations significantly hinder redevelopment prospects.

PC2, accounting for 19.3% of the variance, indicates ownership complexity, reflecting the extent to which land tenure issues affect redevelopment feasibility. Higher PC2 values typically point to intricate property relations, particularly in mining or military brownfields, where mixed ownership, unresolved legal disputes, or overlapping entitlements require longer-term planning, negotiation, and regulatory intervention. In contrast, lower PC2 values indicate simpler ownership structures, either entirely private or public, which generally facilitate revitalization efforts and accelerate investment processes.

From a regional perspective, Moravian-Silesian Region (CZ080) and Ústí nad Labem Region (CZ042) exhibit high PC1 values, confirming their strong redevelopment potential due to industrial heritage and robust infrastructure networks. Conversely, regions such as Zlín (CZ072) and South Bohemian Region (CZ031) have low PC1 scores, reflecting limited investment appeal and weaker economic integration. Mining and military brownfields, such as those in Pardubice Region (CZ053) and Liberec Region (CZ051), tend to have higher PC2 values, signaling more complex ownership patterns that slow down regeneration efforts.

The results indicate that industrial and transportation brownfields generally exhibit strong market-driven regeneration potential, as they combine high development appeal with relatively manageable ownership structures. By contrast, sites with high PC2 scores-such as many mining brownfields—face persistent barriers to revitalization, requiring targeted legislative and financial interventions to address legal and regulatory complexities (De Sousa, 2003; Dixon, Raco, and Catney, 2007).

Overall, this analysis underscores the importance of considering not only economic factors in brownfield redevelopment but also the legal and infrastructural frameworks that influence investment feasibility and project timelines. Policymakers should prioritize sites with high PC1 scores for immediate regeneration efforts, while developing long-term strategies to resolve ownership disputes and facilitate reinvestment in more legally complex brownfields.

*Figure 10. PCA Analysis of Brownfield Regions by Previous Use*

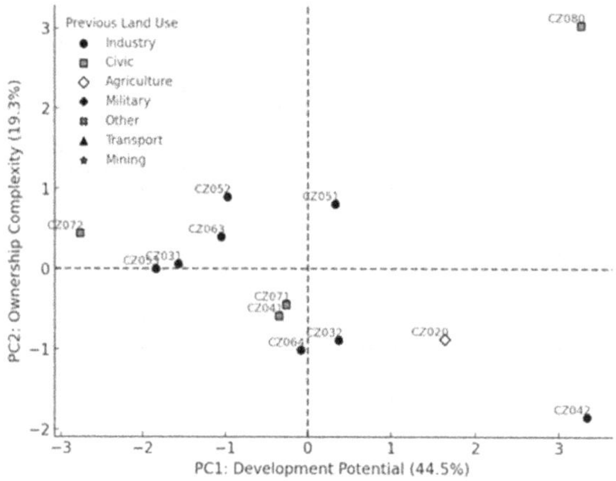


*Source: own processing, RStudio (R version 2024.12.0+467)*

Figure 11 presents a Principal Component Analysis (PCA) of brownfield sites classified by their contamination status, offering valuable insights into the relationship between environmental burdens, ownership complexity, and investment potential.

The first principal component (PC1), which explains 63.3% of the total variance, reflects development potential, incorporating factors such as infrastructure availability, economic conditions in the surrounding area, and the ease with which sites can be repurposed. Higher PC1 values generally indicate stronger redevelopment prospects, often due to favorable geographic positioning, existing infrastructure, and reduced environmental constraints. These sites are typically more attractive to investors and require fewer regulatory interventions to facilitate their transformation. In contrast, lower PC1 values correspond to brownfields with limited transport accessibility, weak market demand, or significant environmental liabilities, all of which complicate regeneration efforts and prolong investment timelines (De Sousa, 2003).

The second principal component (PC2), accounting for 27.0% of the variance, reflects ownership complexity, including the presence of overlapping claims, mixed public–private arrangements, or historically contested property rights. Sites with higher PC2 scores tend to have fragmented or unclear ownership structures, often requiring prolonged legal approvals, extended stakeholder negotiations, or governmental intervention before redevelopment can proceed (Raco and Henderson, 2009). Conversely, lower PC2 scores indicate simpler ownership conditions, such as fully public or fully private land tenure, which facilitates more efficient remediation efforts and accelerates investment decision-making.

The contamination status of brownfields plays a crucial role in their redevelopment feasibility. Contaminated sites ("Yes") cluster predominantly toward the lower end of PC1, indicating heightened environmental challenges and weaker overall development conditions. These brownfields typically require extensive decontamination efforts, often necessitating public-sector funding, specialized remediation technologies, and stringent regulatory oversight. This finding aligns with Dixon, Raco, and Catney (2007), who emphasize that legacy pollution significantly increases project costs and reduces investment appeal.

In contrast, non-contaminated sites ("No") are concentrated toward the right side of the plot, suggesting higher development potential, reduced regulatory burdens, and greater likelihood of attracting private sector interest. These brownfields benefit from lower cleanup costs and fewer environmental restrictions, making them more competitive alternatives to greenfield investments.

The "N/A" category, which represents sites with insufficient contamination data, is scattered throughout the graph. This suggests that uncertainty regarding ecological risks may further complicate investment decisions for both private developers and public authorities. The lack of comprehensive environmental assessments may result in delayed project planning, increased due diligence costs, or heightened risk perceptions among potential investors.

Overall, Figure 11 underscores that contamination is not only an environmental issue but also a significant economic and institutional factor. The extent of pollution influences project feasibility, regulatory requirements, and the potential for private sector engagement. Policymakers should therefore prioritize brownfields with low contamination risks for immediate redevelopment efforts, while simultaneously developing targeted financial mechanisms-such as state-backed remediation funds or public-private partnerships-to facilitate the regeneration of highly contaminated sites.

*Figure 11. PCA Analysis of Brownfield Regions by Contamination Status*

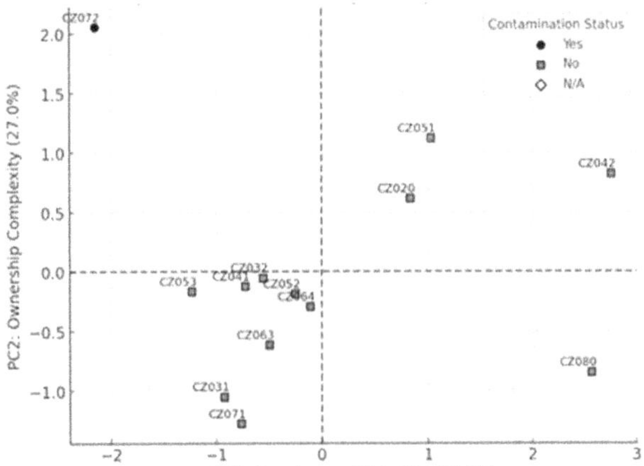


*Source: own processing, RStudio (R version 2024.12.0+467)*

Figure 12 illustrates the outcomes of a factor analysis of brownfield sites across 13 NUTS III regions in the Czech Republic, identifying three primary dimensions that shape the brownfield regeneration process: development potential, ownership complexity, and sector-specific challenges. These factors were derived through Principal Component Analysis (PCA), which extracted the most influential patterns in the data, allowing for a structured classification of brownfield sites. To improve interpretability, a Varimax rotation was applied, clarifying the relationship between individual factors and regional conditions.

The first factor, development potential, captures the economic attractiveness of brownfield sites and their ability to attract investors and redevelopment efforts. This dimension incorporates indicators such as infrastructure quality, regional economic growth, and financial resource availability. Regions with high scores in this factor, such as Central Bohemian Region (CZ020) and Moravian-Silesian Region (CZ080), exhibit favorable geographic positioning, strong economic activity, and well-developed transport networks, making them prime candidates for market-driven revitalization (Greenstein and Sendorf, 2004). In contrast, Karlovy Vary Region (CZ041) shows lower development potential, indicating limited infrastructure and weaker investment incentives, which can slow down the regeneration process.

The second factor, ownership complexity, represents administrative and legal challenges associated with multi-layered property rights, unresolved historical disputes, or mixed public–private ownership structures. Regions with high scores in this category, including Ústí nad Labem Region (CZ042) and Pardubice Region (CZ053), face prolonged negotiation processes and legal obstacles, making brownfield redevelopment more complex and time-consuming. These findings align with Adams, De Sousa, and Tiesdell (2010), who emphasize the importance of clear land ownership structures in accelerating brownfield revitalization. Conversely, Olomouc Region (CZ071) exhibits lower ownership complexity, suggesting simpler legal conditions that promote more efficient redevelopment and investment attraction.

The third factor, sector-specific challenges, reflects the extent to which brownfields are linked to environmentally intensive industries, mining activities, or former military operations. Regions with high scores in this dimension, such as Moravian-Silesian Region (CZ080) and South Moravian Region (CZ064), require extensive remediation efforts or customized redevelopment strategies due to historical pollution or industrial legacy. These areas often necessitate specialized interventions, including soil decontamination, groundwater monitoring, or targeted financial support. In contrast, Vysočina Region (CZ063) has a lower score in this category, indicating that its brownfield sites present fewer technical barriers and are therefore more likely to be revitalized in a cost-effective manner (Alberini, Longo, and Tonin, 2005).

The findings from this factor analysis emphasize that brownfield regeneration is shaped by a combination of economic viability, legal complexity, and historical land use patterns. Regions with strong development potential and clear ownership structures are best positioned for market-driven renewal, whereas those burdened by legal uncertainty or industrial contamination require strategic public intervention. To maximize regeneration outcomes, policymakers should incorporate tailored financial incentives, legislative reforms that simplify property transfers, and urban planning policies that align with sustainability goals. These targeted strategies can facilitate more effective land repurposing, attract investment, and support long-term regional development.

*Figure 12. Factor Scores for 13 Regions of the Czech Republic*

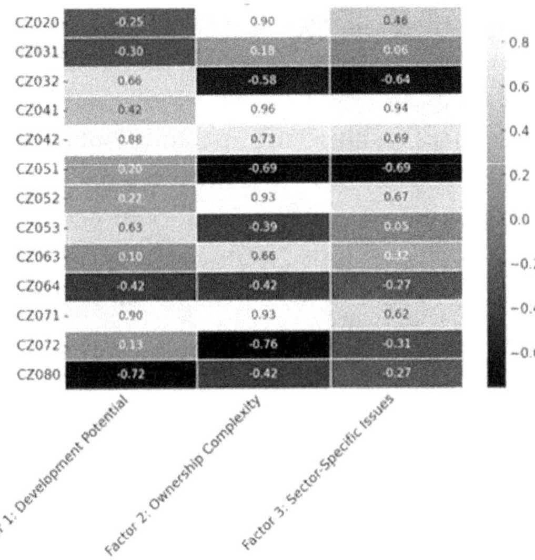


*Source: own processing, RStudio (R version 2024.12.0+467)*

Brownfield regeneration in the Czech Republic is a complex process influenced by economic, environmental, and legal factors. This study analyzes 642 brownfield sites based on data from the National Brownfield Database (2024) to identify key determinants of successful redevelopment. Ownership structure plays a crucial role, as sites with clear ownership tend to be revitalized more efficiently, while those with mixed or unclear ownership face prolonged stagnation. Geographic location is another significant factor—brownfields in urban centers are more attractive to investors compared to those in rural areas. Contamination levels present a major barrier, with highly polluted sites requiring costly and time-consuming remediation efforts. Site size also affects redevelopment feasibility, as larger brownfields often face ownership complexities and environmental burdens. Principal Component Analysis (PCA) revealed that economic factors, such as infrastructure availability and investment incentives, drive regeneration. To enhance brownfield redevelopment, legislative simplifications, financial incentives for investors, targeted public investments, and public-private partnerships (PPP) are recommended. A strategic approach to prioritizing brownfield sites can lead to more efficient land use, fostering sustainable urban and regional development.

## SOLUTIONS AND RECOMMENDATIONS

A sustainable approach to brownfield regeneration in the Czech Republic requires an integrated strategy that addresses economic, legal, and environmental aspects while aligning with EU sustainability objectives and national urban development policies. The findings of this study, particularly the Principal Component Analysis (PCA), highlight the complexity of brownfield revitalization and identify key factors influencing successful redevelopment.

From an economic perspective, brownfields in regions with low investment attractiveness (low Development Potential in PCA) require targeted financial mechanisms to mitigate market failures and stimulate redevelopment. Public subsidies, preferential tax regimes, and improved access to financing have been recognized as key incentives for attracting investment into underutilized sites (Greenstein and Sendorf, 2004; Rizzo et al. 2018). In line with the European Commission's Circular Economy Action Plan (2020), funding for brownfield redevelopment should prioritize projects that integrate climate resilience, energy efficiency, and sustainable urban infrastructure. Additionally, smart land-use planning tools, such as GIS-based monitoring systems, can help municipalities identify strategic investment zones and optimize public spending (Song et al. 2022).

On the legal and administrative front, ownership complexity (high Ownership Complexity in PCA) represents a significant barrier to effective brownfield regeneration. Studies confirm that fragmented or unclear property rights extend decision-making processes and increase transaction costs (Adams, De Sousa, and Tiesdell, 2010). Streamlining property transfers, digitizing land registries, and aligning brownfield redevelopment regulations with EU land-use frameworks could significantly reduce administrative delays (Osman et al. 2015). Additionally, the adoption of standardized brownfield assessment methodologies-such as the Conceptual Site Model approach used in the UK (Laprise et al. 2018)-could improve regulatory consistency and facilitate compliance with environmental standards.

From an environmental standpoint, brownfields with extensive contamination (high Sector-Specific Challenges in PCA) require tailored remediation strategies based on their specific pollution profile. Recent research highlights the effectiveness of nature-based solutions, such as phytoremediation, in lowering cleanup costs while ensuring long-term ecological restoration (Li et al., 2019). Green remediation techniques, including bioremediation and managed natural attenuation, have been successfully implemented in Northwest England, offering cost-effective methods for restoring heavily polluted sites (Sustainable Ecological Restoration of Brownfield Sites, 2012). Furthermore, public-private partnerships (PPPs) focused on remediation financing, as suggested by Tendero and Bazart (2024), can distribute financial risks and accelerate the decontamination process.

A comprehensive brownfield redevelopment strategy must also involve active participation from public authorities, investors, and local communities. Creative interim use strategies, such as temporary cultural spaces or eco-recreation areas, can revitalize brownfields before full-scale redevelopment while enhancing community engagement (Creative Intervention in a Dynamic City, 2023). Moreover, aligning brownfield revitalization efforts with Smart Growth policies and Net Zero carbon targets can ensure that redevelopment contributes to long-term sustainability goals (European Commission, 2020).

Ultimately, integrating brownfield regeneration into a national sustainable land-use strategy is essential for balancing economic revitalization with climate resilience, social inclusion, and biodiversity preservation. Policymakers should focus on designing adaptive financial mechanisms, implementing regulatory reforms, and promoting nature-based remediation approaches to maximize the long-term benefits of brownfield transformation. By ensuring that redevelopment efforts are economically viable, legally streamlined, and environmentally sustainable, the Czech Republic can transform underutilized brownfields into catalysts for regional development and urban sustainability.

## FUTURE RESEARCH DIRECTIONS

Brownfield revitalization remains a complex challenge that requires an interdisciplinary approach, integrating economic, legal, and environmental perspectives. Future research should prioritize the development of integrative assessment models that can more effectively capture the interactions between these factors. Previous studies (Pottse and Cloete, 2012; Alker et al. 2000) have highlighted the necessity of remediation before redevelopment, while others (Thomas, 2003; Davis and Sherman, 2010) emphasize the financial and social burdens associated with brownfield sites. Emerging methodologies, including multi-criteria decision analysis (MCDA) and real-time monitoring tools (Rey et al. 2022), offer promising pathways to enhancing predictive capabilities in brownfield redevelopment planning. These approaches should be further integrated with sustainable construction practices (Green, 2018) and adaptive reuse strategies, which contribute to reducing urban sprawl and aligning redevelopment with broader green policy objectives.

A crucial area for future research is the evaluation of regional disparities in investment attractiveness. Skrabal (2020), based on an analysis of the National Brownfield Database, demonstrated that peripheral brownfields attract significantly less investment than those located in or near urban centers. This suggests a need for regionally specific financial incentives and tailored public-private partnerships (PPP) to promote balanced investment distribution. Further studies should explore the effectiveness of different funding mechanisms, such as urban regeneration bonds, tax credits, and risk-sharing financial instruments, in stimulating private-sector engagement in brownfield redevelopment (Skrabal, 2021).

From a legal and governance standpoint, the efficiency of property transfer and land-use planning regulations warrants further investigation. Research by Adams, De Sousa, and Tiesdell (2010) emphasizes that streamlined administrative processes are crucial for accelerating redevelopment, particularly in post-socialist countries where fragmented ownership structures and unclear property rights persist (Frantal et al. 2013). A comparative study of land banking models, centralized urban redevelopment agencies, and simplified zoning procedures could help identify best practices for expediting brownfield transformations.

The environmental dimension of brownfield redevelopment also requires deeper exploration, particularly in terms of cost-effective remediation techniques. Recent studies (Li et al. 2019; Sorvari and Seppälä, 2010) highlight phytoremediation, bioremediation, and managed natural attenuation as viable alternatives to traditional decontamination methods, offering lower-cost and ecologically sustainable solutions. Future research should examine how these technologies can be integrated with climate adaptation strategies, such as green infrastructure, flood resilience measures, and low-carbon redevelopment approaches (Bleicher and Gross, 2010; McCarthy, 2002).

Another promising research direction is the role of participatory planning and community engagement in brownfield transformation. As Meer and Lyons (2000) and Rizzo et al. (2015) argue, inclusive governance models enhance legitimacy and foster long-term project success. Future studies should investigate co-governance mechanisms, in which municipal authorities, investors, and local communities jointly develop brownfield revitalization strategies. Understanding how participatory frameworks influence decision-making, land-use prioritization, and social acceptance of redevelopment projects could significantly improve policy efficiency and accelerate urban regeneration.

Although this study provides a comprehensive analytical framework for brownfield redevelopment assessment, several methodological limitations must be acknowledged. The reliance on secondary data from the National Brownfield Database introduces potential biases, as data collection inconsistencies and reporting gaps may affect analytical outcomes. Future research should incorporate primary data collection methods, such as expert interviews, stakeholder surveys, and field observations, to validate findings and enhance empirical robustness.

Moreover, the Principal Component Analysis (PCA) approach, while effective for identifying key factors in brownfield redevelopment, does not fully capture the causal relationships between economic, legal, and environmental variables. To address this, future studies should consider structural equation modeling (SEM) or spatial econometric techniques, which can provide deeper insights into how various determinants interact over time.

Another limitation is that this study focuses solely on the Czech Republic, which has a unique socio-economic and legislative context. While some findings may be generalizable to other post-socialist countries, further comparative studies are needed to assess whether similar trends apply in different regulatory and economic environments. Examining case studies from Western Europe, North America, and emerging economies could offer valuable insights into the transferability of best practices and the adaptation of policy instruments across diverse urban settings.

Future research should build upon the findings of this study by refining predictive analytical models, exploring alternative financing mechanisms, and evaluating policy innovations that enhance brownfield redevelopment efficiency. By integrating sustainability principles, technological advancements, and legal reforms, scholars and practitioners can contribute to the creation of resilient urban spaces that not only mitigate environmental degradation but also foster inclusive and long-term economic growth.

## CONCLUSION

This study has systematically examined the factors influencing brownfield regeneration in the Czech Republic, offering an empirical framework for assessing the redevelopment potential of abandoned and contaminated sites. By applying a rigorous factor analysis, three primary dimensions-economic potential, ownership complexity, and sector-specific challenges-were identified as critical determinants of successful regeneration. These findings expand on the theoretical foundation established by Pottse and Cloete (2012) and Alker et al. (2000) while building on the empirical insights of Thomas (2003) and Davis and Sherman (2010), who emphasize the multifaceted social, economic, and environmental challenges associated with brownfield redevelopment.

The results confirm that regions with robust economic fundamentals, such as Central Bohemia, Plzeň, and Moravian-Silesian, exhibit higher regeneration rates due to superior infrastructure, increased economic activity, and greater investor appeal (Greenstein and Sendorf, 2004). In contrast, Karlovy Vary and Zlín face significant obstacles, including weak market demand, contamination issues, and administrative barriers. Additionally, the study corroborates that complex ownership structures, prevalent in Ústí nad Labem and Pardubice, lengthen the regeneration process due to extensive legal procedures and fragmented property relations (Adams, De Sousa and Tiesdell, 2010). These findings underscore the importance of transparent property rights and streamlined legal mechanisms for efficient redevelopment.

Environmental contamination remains one of the most significant barriers to successful regeneration. As confirmed by Alberini, Longo, and Tonin (2005), alongside Davis and Sherman (2010), highly contaminated sites-particularly in post-industrial regions such as Moravian-Silesian and Ústí nad Labem-require substantial public-sector intervention due to the high costs and prolonged timelines associated with remediation. Innovative decontamination technologies, such as phytoremediation and managed natural attenuation, could improve the long-term sustainability of brownfield redevelopment, as suggested by Laprise et al. (2022) and Rizzo et al. (2018). Furthermore, historical land use—whether industrial, military, or mining—significantly influences redevelopment potential, as previously highlighted by Adeleja et al. (2010), Ferber et al. (2006), and Frantal et al. (2013). Typological frameworks, such as the A–B–C model (CABERNET, 2014; Dolezelova et al., 2014; Jackson, 2004), further validate these conclusions by categorizing brownfields based on economic feasibility and the extent of required intervention.

In a broader context, these findings align with European sustainability policies and urban regeneration frameworks. Recent contributions from Green (2018) and Pizzola et al. (2016) affirm the critical role of brownfield regeneration in sustainable urban development, preventing urban sprawl and advancing circular economy principles through the reuse of underutilized land (Laprise et al. 2022). Moreover, the integration of spatial modeling techniques and Geographic Information Systems (GIS) has been increasingly recognized as a valuable tool for enhancing regional competitiveness and supporting data-driven policymaking (Hackworth, 2014; Osman et al. 2015; Lange and McNeil, 2004; Skala et al. 2013). This corresponds with the evolving European agenda for ecological resilience and sustainable land use, as emphasized by Skrabal (2020, 2021).

The study aimed to identify and evaluate determinants of successful revitalization by developing a systematic framework for assessing redevelopment potential. This objective was successfully achieved through factor analysis, which quantified the key barriers and opportunities for regeneration while integrating environmental, legal, and economic perspectives. The resulting framework provides an empirically grounded tool for policymakers, urban planners, and private investors, enabling evidence-based decision-making in brownfield redevelopment.

However, certain limitations must be acknowledged. The availability and reliability of regional data remain a constraint, particularly in areas with inconsistent historical records of contamination and ownership disputes. Additionally, while this study offers a static assessment of brownfield redevelopment potential, future research should include longitudinal studies to capture the evolving nature of regeneration processes over time. Further comparative studies examining brownfield regeneration across various European contextsespecially in post-socialist regions—could improve the adaptability of the proposed framework to different institutional environments.

This study advances both theoretical and applied perspectives on brownfield regeneration. By integrating economic incentives, legal reforms, and targeted environmental remediation, it provides a comprehensive strategy for sustainable urban redevelopment that is relevant not only to the Czech Republic but also to broader European planning initiatives. Collaboration between public and private stakeholders, supported by robust analytical tools, will be crucial in transforming brownfields from liabilities into assets that contribute to regional economic growth, sustainability, and the broader green policy objectives of the European Union.

A practical implication of this research is the need for targeted policies that enhance brownfield redevelopment efficiency. Municipalities and state authorities should focus on simplifying legal processes related to land ownership disputes, improving access to financial incentives for high-risk brownfield sites, and fostering public-private partnerships (PPP) to distribute the financial burden of remediation. For private investors, the availability of structured redevelopment incentives, such as tax reductions or grants for environmental remediation, could improve investment predictability. Additionally, regional development strategies should integrate brownfield redevelopment into broader urban planning frameworks, ensuring that these sites contribute to economic revitalization, sustainable infrastructure, and climate resilience. By implementing these targeted measures, policymakers can facilitate the transformation of brownfields into functional urban and industrial spaces, strengthening regional competitiveness and long-term sustainability.

## ACKNOWLEDGMENT

This chapter was created with the financial support of an Internal Grant agency of The Moravian Business College Olomouc "Utilization of Brownfields for Entrepreneurial Purposes and Their Impact on Regional Economic Growth" [2_2024/2025].

## REFERENCES

Adams, D., De Sousa, C., & Tiesdell, S. (2010). Brownfield development: A comparison of North American and British approaches. *Urban Studies (Edinburgh, Scotland), 47*(1), 75–104. DOI: 10.1177/0042098009346868

Adams, D., Disberry, A., Hutchison, N., & Munjoma, T. (2000). Taxes, subsidies and the behaviour of brownfield owners. *Land Use Policy, 17*(2), 135–145. DOI: 10.1016/S0264-8377(00)00003-X

Adelaja, S., Shaw, J., Beyea, W., & McKeown, J. C. (2010). Renewable energy potential on brownfield sites: A case study of Michigan. *Energy Policy, 38*(11), 7021–7030. DOI: 10.1016/j.enpol.2010.07.021

Ahmad, N., Zhu, Y., Ullah, Z., Iqbal, M., Hussain, K., & Ahmed, R. I. (2021). Sustainable solutions to facilitate brownfield redevelopment projects in emerging countries – Pakistani scenario. *Land Use Policy, 109*, 105727. DOI: 10.1016/j.landusepol.2021.105727

Alberini, A., Longo, A., Tonin, S., Trombetta, F., & Turvani, M. (2005). The role of liability, regulation and economic incentives in brownfield remediation and redevelopment: Evidence from surveys of developers. *Regional Science and Urban Economics, 35*(4), 327–351. DOI: 10.1016/j.regsciurbeco.2004.05.004

Alker, S., Joy, V., Roberts, P., & Smith, N. (2000). The definition of brownfield. *Journal of Environmental Planning and Management, 43*(1), 49–69. DOI: 10.1080/09640560010766

Bartke, S., Rizzo, E., Giubilato, E., Pizzol, L., Critto, A., & Marcomini, A. (2013). Improvement of brownfield regeneration in Europe through tailored information platform, communication, prioritisation and assessment. In Skowronek, J. (Ed.), *Innowacyjne rozwiązania rewitalizacji terenów zdegradowanych* (pp. 135–143). IETU & Centrum Badań.

BenDor, T. K., Metcalf, S. S., & Paich, M. (2011). The dynamics of brownfield redevelopment. *Sustainability (Basel), 3*(6), 914–936. DOI: 10.3390/su3060914

Bez, C. S., Ash, M., & Boyce, J. K. (2023b). Environmental inequality in industrial brownfields: Evidence from French municipalities. *Ecological Economics, 217*, 108018. DOI: 10.1016/j.ecolecon.2023.108018

Bleicher, A., & Gross, M. (2010). Sustainability assessment and the revitalization of contaminated sites: Operationalizing sustainable development for local problems. *International Journal of Sustainable Development and World Ecology, 17*(1), 57–66. DOI: 10.1080/13504500903488263

CABERNET. (2014). Brownfield definition [online]. EU: Projects. Retrieved January 20, 2020, from http://www.cabernet.org.uk/index.asp?c=1134

CLARINET. (2002). Brownfields and redevelopment of urban areas. Austria: Federal Environment Agency. Retrieved August 2002, from [online source]

Czech Office for Surveying. Mapping and Cadastre (ČÚZK). (2024, December 20). *INSPIRE datasets - Administrative Units*. Retrieved from https://geoportal.cuzk.cz/

CzechInvest. (2024). Brownfield database. CzechInvest Brownfields Portal. Retrieved December 20, 2024, from https://brownfieldy-dotace.czechinvest.org/Aplikace/bf-public-x.nsf/bfs.xsp

CzechInvest. (2024). National Brownfield Database. *CzechInvest*.https://brownfieldy-dotace.czechinvest .org/Aplikace/bf-public-x.nsf/bfs.xsp

Davis, T. S., & Sherman, S. A. (2010). *Brownfields: A comprehensive guide to redeveloping contaminated property* (3rd ed.). American Bar Association.

De Sousa, C. A. (2002). Brownfield redevelopment in Toronto: An examination of past trends and future prospects. *Land Use Policy*, *19*(4), 297–309. DOI: 10.1016/S0264-8377(02)00024-8

Dixon, T., Raco, M., Catney, P., & Lerner, D. N. (Eds.). (2007). *Sustainable brownfield regeneration: Liveable places from problem spaces*. Blackwell Publishing., DOI: 10.1002/9780470692110

Dolezelova, L. (2015). Regenerace brownfieldů: vývoj politik a příklady realizací. Praha: IREAS, Institut pro strukturální politiku. ISBN 978-80-86684-96-3

Dolezelova, L., Hadlac, M., Kadlecova, M., & Polednik, S. (2014). Redevelopment potential of brownfields: A-B-C classification and its practical application. *E+M. Ekonomie a Management*, *XVII*(2), 34–44. DOI: 10.15240/tul/001/2014-2-003

Ferber, U., Grimski, D., Millar, K., & Nathanail, P. (2006). *Sustainable brownfield regeneration: CABERNET Network Report* (1st ed.). University of Nottingham.

Frantál, B., Greer-Wootten, B., Klusáček, P., Krejčí, T., Kunc, J., & Martinát, S. (2015). Exploring spatial patterns of urban brownfields regeneration: The case of Brno, Czech Republic. *Cities (London, England)*, *44*, 9–18. DOI: 10.1016/j.cities.2014.12.007

Frantál, B., Kunc, J., Klusáček, P., & Martinát, S. (2013). Assessing success factors of brownfields regeneration: International and inter-stakeholder perspective. *Transylvanian Review of Administrative Sciences*, *44*, 91–107.

Gibbs, D., & Deutz, P. (2007). Reflections on implementing industrial ecology through eco-industrial park development. *Journal of Cleaner Production*, *15*(17), 1683–1695. DOI: 10.1016/j.jclepro.2007.02.003

Green, T. (2018). Evaluating predictors for brownfield redevelopment. *Land Use Policy*, *73*, 299–319. DOI: 10.1016/j.landusepol.2018.01.008

Hackworth, J. (2014). The limits to market-based strategies for addressing land abandonment in shrinking American cities. *Progress in Planning*, *90*, 1–37. DOI: 10.1016/j.progress.2013.03.004

Hagget, P. (2001). *Geography: A global synthesis*. Prentice Hall.

Hagmann, D. F., Kruge, M. A., Goodey, N. M., & Krumins, J. A. (2019). Characterization of coal particles in the soil of a former rail yard and urban brownfield: Liberty State Park, Jersey City (NJ), USA. *International Journal of Coal Geology*, *217*, 103328. DOI: 10.1016/j.coal.2019.103328

Hammond, E. B., Coulon, F., Hallett, S. H., Thomas, R., Dick, A., Hardy, D., Dickens, M., Washbourn, E., & Beriro, D. J. (2023). The development of a novel decision support system for regional land use planning for brownfield land. *Journal of Environmental Management*, *349*, 119466. DOI: 10.1016/j.jenvman.2023.119466 PMID: 37952377

Hurníková, J. (2009). Brownfieldy a územní rozvoj. Urbanismus a územní rozvoj, 12(6), 3-5. Retrieved January 7, 2019, from http://www.uur.cz/images/publikace/uur/2009/2009-06/01_brownfieldy%20rozvoj.pdf

Jackson, B. J. (2004). Brownfields snadno a lehce: Příručka zejména pro pracovníky a zastupitele obcí [online]. Institut pro udržitelný rozvoj sídel o.s. Dostupné z: http://rrajm.data.quonia.cz/brownfieldy/publikace/Brownfields1.pdf

Kovalick, W. W., Jr., & Montgomery, R. H. (2014). Developing a program for contaminated site management in low and middle income countries [online]. The World Bank. Retrieved 2014, from https://openknowledge.worldbank.org/bitstream/handle/10986/18631/880700WP0Conta00Box385209B00PUBLIC0.pdf?sequence=1&isAllowed=y

Lange, D., & McNeil, S. (2004). Clean it and they will come? Defining successful brownfield development. *Journal of Urban Planning and Development, 130*(2), 101–108. https://doi.org/(101DOI: 10.1061/(asce)0733-9488(2004)130:2

Laprise, M., Lufkin, S., & Rey, E. (2018). An operational monitoring tool facilitating the transformation of urban brownfields into sustainable neighborhoods. *Building and Environment*, *142*, 221–233. DOI: 10.1016/j.buildenv.2018.06.005

Levin, M. E., Haeger, J., Pierce, B., & Cruz, R. A. (2017b). Evaluating an adjunctive mobile app to enhance psychological flexibility in acceptance and commitment therapy. *Behavior Modification*, *41*(6), 846–867. DOI: 10.1177/0145445517719661 PMID: 28689449

Li, X., Bardos, P., Cundy, A. B., Harder, M. K., Doick, K. J., Norrman, J., Williams, S., & Chen, W. (2018). Using a conceptual site model for assessing the sustainability of brownfield regeneration for a soft reuse: A case study of Port Sunlight River Park (U.K.). *The Science of the Total Environment*, *652*, 810–821. DOI: 10.1016/j.scitotenv.2018.10.278 PMID: 30380488

Longo, A., & Campbell, D. (2016b). The determinants of brownfields redevelopment in England. *Environmental and Resource Economics*, *67*(2), 261–283. DOI: 10.1007/s10640-015-9985-y PMID: 32025099

Luck, M., & Wu, J. G. (2002). A gradient analysis of urban landscape pattern: A case study from the Phoenix metropolitan region, Arizona, USA. *Landscape Ecology*, *17*(4), 327–339. DOI: 10.1023/A:1020512723753

McCarthy, J. J. (2002). *A thematic guide to Optimality Theory*. Cambridge University Press.

Meer, P. B., & Lyons, T. S. (2000). Lessons from private sector brownfield redevelopers. *Journal of the American Planning Association*, *66*(1), 46–57. DOI: 10.1080/01944360008976083

Osman, R., Frantál, B., Klusáček, P., Kunc, J., & Martinát, S. (2015). Factors affecting brownfield regeneration in post-socialist space: The case of the Czech Republic. *Land Use Policy*, *48*, 309–316. DOI: 10.1016/j.landusepol.2015.06.003

Pizzol, L., Zabeo, A., Klusáček, P., Giubilato, E., Critto, A., Frantál, B., Martinát, S., Kunc, J., Osman, R., & Bartke, S. (2015). Timbre Brownfield Prioritization Tool to support effective brownfield regeneration. *Journal of Environmental Management*, *166*, 178–192. DOI: 10.1016/j.jenvman.2015.09.030 PMID: 26496848

Popa, N., Pop, A., & Marian-Potra, A. (2025). Culture-led urban regeneration in post-socialist cities: From decadent spaces towards creative initiatives. *Cities (London, England)*, *158*, 105707. DOI: 10.1016/j.cities.2025.105707

Potts, L., & Cloete, C. E. (2012). Developing guidelines for brownfield development in South Africa. *WIT Transactions on Ecology and the Environment*, *1*, 389–399. DOI: 10.2495/EID120341

R Core Team. (2024). *R: A language and environment for statistical computing* (Version 2024.12.0+467) [Computer software]. R Foundation for Statistical Computing. https://www.R-project.org/

Raco, M., & Henderson, S. (2009). Sustainable urban planning and the brownfield development process in the United Kingdom: Lessons from the Thames Gateway. *Local Environment*, *11*(5), 499–509. DOI: 10.1080/13549830600853098

Rey, E., Laprise, M., & Lufkin, S. (2021). Sustainability issues at the neighbourhood scale. In *The urban book series* (pp. 77–93). https://doi.org/DOI: 10.1007/978-3-030-82208-8_5

Rizzo, E., Pesce, M., Pizzol, L., Alexandrescu, F. M., Giubilato, E., Critto, A., Marcomini, A., & Bartke, S. (2015). Brownfield regeneration in Europe: Identifying stakeholder perceptions, concerns, attitudes and information needs. *Land Use Policy*, *48*, 437–453. DOI: 10.1016/j.landusepol.2015.06.012

Sessa, M. R., Russo, A., & Sica, F. (2022). Opinion paper on green deal for the urban regeneration of industrial brownfield land in Europe. *Land Use Policy*, *119*, 106198. DOI: 10.1016/j.landusepol.2022.106198

Skála, J., Čechmánková, J., Vácha, R., & Horváthová, V. (2013). Various aspects in the genesis and perspectives on agricultural brownfields in the Czech Republic. *Moravian Geographical Reports*, *21*(2), 46–55. DOI: 10.2478/mgr-2013-0010

Skrabal, J. (2020). What can we learn from brownfield databases? Exploring specifics of the location of brownfields in the Czech Republic. *Geography Teacher*, *15*(2), 191–201. DOI: 10.21163/GT_2020.152.18

Skrabal, J., Chmielova, P., Tureckova, K., & Nevima, J. (2021). Applicability of tools for brownfield regeneration in the Czech Republic: A regional perspective. *Geography Teacher*, *16*(2), 132–148. DOI: 10.21163/GT_2021.162.11

Song, Y., Lyu, Y., Qian, S., Zhang, X., Lin, H., & Wang, S. (2022). Identifying urban candidate brownfield sites using multi-source data: The case of Changchun City, China. *Land Use Policy*, *117*, 106084. DOI: 10.1016/j.landusepol.2022.106084

Sorvari, J., & Seppälä, J. (2010). A decision support tool to prioritize risk management options for contaminated sites. *The Science of the Total Environment*, *408*(8), 1786–1799. DOI: 10.1016/j.scitotenv.2009.12.026 PMID: 20138649

Tendero, M., & Bazart, C. (2023). "I can't get no satisfaction": Soil contaminated brownfield redevelopment in France. *Cities (London, England)*, *145*, 104719. DOI: 10.1016/j.cities.2023.104719

Teo, H. C., Zeng, Y., Sarira, T. V., Fung, T. K., Zheng, Q., Song, X. P., Chong, K. Y., & Koh, L. P. (2021). Global urban reforestation can be an important natural climate solution. *Environmental Research Letters*, *16*(3), 034059. DOI: 10.1088/1748-9326/abe783

Thomas, M. R. (2003). Brownfield redevelopment: Information issues and the affected public. *Environmental Practice*, *5*(1), 62–68. DOI: 10.1017/S1466046603030175

Wang, L., Fang, L., & Hipel, K. W. (2009). Negotiation over Costs and Benefits in Brownfield Redevelopment. *Group Decision and Negotiation*, *20*(4), 509–524. DOI: 10.1007/s10726-009-9179-5

Yacovone, K. (2011). Brownfields and the poor: Is clean-up a hazardous waste of time? An analysis of the United States' efforts at remediation and their applicability to Brazil. *Fordham International Law Journal, 35(1)*, 201-247. ISSN 0747-9395.

Zamarský, V., Tylčer, J., & Střelec, T. (2011b). *Regeneration of Industrial Areas*. VŠB–TU Ostrava.

## KEY TERMS AND DEFINITIONS

**Brownfield:** Previously developed land that has been abandoned or remains underutilized due to contamination, structural decay, or economic constraints, requiring intervention for redevelopment.

**Brownfield Redevelopment:** The process of revitalizing contaminated, vacant, or underutilized land parcels through environmental remediation, infrastructural investment, and land-use planning to enable sustainable reuse.

**Circular Economy in Brownfield Redevelopment:** A sustainability-oriented approach that promotes resource efficiency, waste reduction, and material reuse in land reclamation and redevelopment efforts.

**Economic Feasibility:** The financial viability of brownfield redevelopment, assessed through cost-benefit analysis, investment potential, and expected economic returns.

**Environmental Remediation:** A set of strategies and technologies used to remove or mitigate pollutants in soil and water to ensure compliance with environmental regulations and facilitate site reuse.

**Factor Analysis:** A statistical method applied to identify and interpret key determinants influencing the success of brownfield redevelopment, improving decision-making in land-use planning.

**Infrastructure Availability:** The extent to which essential services, including transportation networks, energy supply, and utilities, support the redevelopment potential of brownfield sites.

**Market Demand:** The level of investor interest and economic attractiveness of brownfield sites, shaped by location, financial incentives, and regulatory frameworks.

**Regeneration Barriers:** Challenges hindering brownfield redevelopment, such as financial constraints, legal disputes, contamination issues, and complex administrative processes.

**Sustainable Development:** An integrative framework for brownfield redevelopment that balances economic, social, and environmental objectives to ensure long-term land-use viability and resilience.

# Chapter 17
# Green Decision-Making Competencies in Sustainable Development:
## A Systematic Review

**Mouhcine Rhouiri**
https://orcid.org/0009-0007-7115-871X
*Sidi Mohamed Ben Abdellah University, Morocco*

**Mehdi Bensouda**
https://orcid.org/0000-0002-7320-3795
*Sidi Mohamed Ben Abdellah University, Morocco*

**Mohamed-Habiboullah Meyabe**
https://orcid.org/0009-0005-0935-7211
*Nouakchott Business School, Mauritania*

## ABSTRACT

*The chapter identifies and discusses various challenges affecting adoption with the emergence of green decision-making into sustainable development. The study finds major barriers in traditional practice ICT, finance, resistance to change, and lack of digital skills especially in SMEs. This research highlights the potential role of emerging technologies, such as artificial intelligence (AI), Internet of Things (IoT), and blockchain, in improving sustainable decisions based on systematic reviewing 277 articles and textual analysis with IRaMuTeQ. This research indicates that overcoming such challenges and ensuring a resilient transition would call for an integrated strategy comprising financial incentives, training, and sound regulatory frameworks. The study encourages the development of a culture of sustainability and technological innovation to maintain values through time.*

DOI: 10.4018/979-8-3373-0189-1.ch017

## 1. INTRODUCTION

It is becoming more and more important to incorporate green decision-making techniques in light of the expanding environmental issues and the demands of sustainable development. The ability of people and organizations to concurrently take economic, social, and environmental factors into account while making decisions is essential for the adoption of green decision-making skills. This idea fits into a global framework that is characterized by significant technical advancements, economic volatility, and climate crises, all of which call for creative and adaptable solutions (Duan, Edwards & Dwivedi, 2019).

Blockchain, the Internet of Things, and artificial intelligence (AI) are examples of emerging technologies that present fresh chances to improve green decision-making abilities. According to Boukherroub et al. (2024), these techniques facilitate better supply chain sustainability, enhanced risk anticipating, and optimum resource management. However, because of behavioral, technical, and budgetary obstacles, their adoption is still restricted despite these benefits. The primary barriers to their integration, especially at SMEs, are high implementation costs, a lack of digital skills, and aversion to change (Kamble, Gunasekaran & Gawankar, 2020).

Concurrently, the COVID-19 pandemic exposed supply networks' weaknesses and emphasized the necessity of enhancing organizational resilience via more sustainable and knowledgeable decision-making (Camur et al., 2023). Certain technologies were adopted more quickly as a result of this crisis, which also brought attention to inequalities in their usability and accessibility.

Even though green decision-making abilities are essential to the shift to sustainable development, a variety of factors, including behavioral, technological, and economic ones, affect how they are developed and integrated. Therefore, the following is a formulation of the study's main question: What elements influence the development and uptake of green decision-making abilities?

Therefore, the purpose of this study is to examine green decision-making abilities and the factors that facilitate their successful implementation. This chapter looks for ways to improve organizational green decision-making capacities using a textual factor analysis using IRaMuTeQ and a comprehensive literature assessment. The goal is to create specific suggestions for getting beyond these challenges and promoting a smooth transition to more resilient and sustainable practices.

## BACKGROUND

In combating environmental degradation, social inequality and economic instability, sustainable development has consequently become a major global priority. Green decision-making skills refer to the structured process by which individuals and organizations develop and execute strategies with regard to environmental, social and economic considerations into their decision-making process to achieve the objectives of development. Demand for these skills is surging as they are acknowledged as a potent instrument in managing multilayered challenges spawned by the global disruptions of climate change, economic crises and pandemics.

According to Duan, Edwards and Dwivedi (2019), sustainable decision-making skills come together when emerging technologies are mastered and adaptation to environmental and economic changes becomes manageable. Integration of AI and advanced analytical tools helps, meanwhile, to reduce the uncertainties involved in risk estimation stemming from climatic and economic disruptions. This skill also includes leveraging emerging technologies, such as AI and IoT, to optimize processes and reduce ecological footprints.

Emerging green technologies must therefore remain at the forefront of their nature and scope in proper decision-making skills. AI and digital twins can model complex scenarios to identify strategies to reduce carbon emissions. These technologies improve visibility and flexibility across the supply chain, which allows for adapting and effectively responding to disruptions caused by sudden changes in demand (Boukherroub et al, 2024). In addition, IoT allows real-time monitoring of natural resources for better environmental asset management.

However, financial and technical barriers often impede the adoption of such technologies. High initial cost and shortage of digital skills are some of the limiting factors for the integration of emerging technologies, particularly in small and medium-sized enterprises (SMEs) (Kamble, Gunasekaran and Gawankar, 2020). Also behavioral, such as resistance to change and negative predispositions with regards to new technologies, make their adoption more awkward and rather exhausting (Duan, Edwards & Dwivedi, 2019).

The COVID-19 pandemic has highlighted the importance of resilience and sustainability in supply chains. Camur et al (2023) insist that companies must rethink their strategic approaches to be more in tune with resilience and sustainability and implement more extended systems to help their companies deal with crises through using Industry 4.0 technologies. Blockchain will thus improve transparency and traceability in the supply chain, which reduces the risk connected with opaque supply networks.

Therefore, green decision-making skills will play a significant role in regenerating resilient and sustainable systems capable of withstanding any type of global disruption. Although emerging technologies afford a major opportunity for deepening these skills, their adoption has largely suffered the great squeeze of financial, technical, and behavioral challenges. This chapter examines these topics in detail and provides an exhaustive literature review and possible avenues to overcoming the identified challenges.

## 2. LITERATURE REVIEW

Green decision-making has become central to sustainable development strategy, particularly within a context of economic, environmental and social disruption. This section untangles the skillset required to integrate sustainable practices within decision-making mechanisms, focusing on the challenges and opportunities brought by implementing emerging technology and managing supply chains.

### 1. Context and Definition of Green Decision-Making Skills

Ecological decision-making depends on the skills of individuals or groups to bring about the consideration of environmental, social, and economic aspects in their decision-making procedures. From Stead and Stead (2000), these skills imply an in-depth understanding of the environmental impacts of each decision and an ability to foresee and manage both economic and climatic risks. It also includes the skill to employ technology tools like AI and IoT to ensure efficiency, and to lower the ecological footprint.

## 2. Role of Emerging Technologies in Green Decision-Making

Emerging technologies are key enabling factors for bolstered green decision-making. AI and digital twins allow modeling of complex scenarios to investigate mitigation strategies for emissions. Boukherroub et al (2024) expresses that such technologies allow more visibility and flexibility in supply chains, which is integral to immediate response to disruptions and demand changes. Like-wise, IoT enables the real-time monitoring of natural resources which enables more sustainable management of the environmental assets.

Nevertheless, the deployment of those technologies is usually slowed down by financial and technological barriers. Kamble, Gunasekaran and Gawankar (2020) imply that the high initial cost addition and lack of digital skills has limited the integration of emerging technologies among small and medium-sized enterprises (SMEs).

## 3. Economic Disruption and Supply Chain Resilience

Various economic disruptions, the most recent of which being the COVID-19 pandemic, have pointed towards the need to strengthen supply chain resilience through sustainable practices. Such changes should be part of the revised strategies in the companies, made resilient and sustainable through the adaption of Industry 4.0 technologies in managing crisis moments (Camur et al 2023). In addition, they may increase product transparency and traceability, thus lowering disruption risks attributed to opaque supply chains.

## 4. Behavioral and Financial Challenges

Though the impetus of green decision-making initiatives is beset by challenges: both attitudinal and financial-incompatibility. On the one hand, resistance to change and lack of digital skills keep organizations from integrating novel technologies. Perceptions that are in opposition to emerging technologies such as AI may influence their adoption, especially when traditional human interactions are preferred, according to Duan, Edwards, and Dwivedi (2019).

Moreover, there are financial constraints like extremely high upfront cost and uncertainty about return on investment which stand as major hurdles. McKinsey and Company, 2022, points out that the lack of convincing economic data has often impeded investment in sustainable technologies.

## 5. Prospects for Sustainable Adoption

These methodologies will be very useful in solving the problem under consideration. First and foremost, for the reaffirmation of digital skills and against the resistance to change, training and capacity development programs, as well as awareness campaigns, are also essential. Secondly, public policies and subsidies might play an important role in overcoming financial constraints for small and medium enterprises. Finally, establishing clear regulatory frameworks would encourage responsible use of new technologies and stakeholders' concerns.

To summarize, the existing literature demonstrates the importance of "green decision-making skills" in boosting supply chains' resilience and responsiveness toward economic and environmental disruptions. Cutting-edge technologies like AI, IoT, and blockchain hugely contribute to strengthening the sustainability of decision-making. However, their adoption frequently has a bottleneck due to the behavioral and financial constraints, requiring integrated approaches to tackle the issues. This literature review lays a good foundation for the identification of the necessary skills for effective and sustainable green decisions.

## 3. METHODOLOGICAL APPROACH AND TOOLS USED

The methodology used in this study consists of a systematic review of literature, supported by textual factor analysis, run with the aid of IRaMuTeQ. This will help to further evaluate the skills necessary for green decision-making in the context of sustainable development and environmental management. The study will focus on finding emerging trends and stubbornly persistent gaps in the scientific literature. The goal is to structure and organize existing knowledge in order to reflect upon skills critical to making effective sustainable decisions.

### Query string 1 Green decision-making and sustainable development skills

TITLE-ABS-KEY ((green OR environmental OR "Sustainable Development") AND ("Decision Making") AND (competencie* OR skill*)) AND (LIMIT-TO (SUBJAREA, "SOCI") OR LIMIT-TO (SUBJAREA, "BUSI") OR LIMIT-TO (SUBJAREA, "ENVI") OR LIMIT-TO (SUBJAREA, "ENER")) AND (LIMIT-TO (DOCTYPE, "ar")) AND (LIMIT-TO (LANGUAGE, "English")) AND (LIMIT-TO (EXACTKEYWORD, "Decision Making"))

In fact, the methodology consists of three different but interdependent phases: (1) selection of articles relevant to the subject; (2) textual factor analysis to discern themes; (3) interpretation of the results obtained to reach meaningful conclusions.

### 1.1. Product selection

The first task was to choose appropriate articles for the study. A systematic search of SCOPUS-the largest academic database-was conducted. The SCOPUS database was chosen for the quality of scientific material, the international selection, and a broad representation of various opinions on the topic. We employed the PRISMA guideline to ensure our selection was well-founded and adequately transparent.

#### 1.1.1. Inclusion and exclusion criteria

Specific criteria were defined to ensure that the articles analyzed dealt with sustainable development decision-making and the skills and aptitudes required in the sectors studied.

#### 1.1.2. Inclusion criteria

The articles that were selected would be subject to the next criteria:

1- Theme: Articles were to reflect sustainable development decision-making along with skills associated with it.
2- Language criteria: Publications were to be written in English for this study.

3- Year constraint: Only articles that have been published between 2016 and 2023 were taken into account. The choice of this timeframe reflects advances in AI during the last decade and its impact in the studied sector.
4- Databases: Articles were extracted from the SCOPUS academic database, renowned for its wealth of high-quality scientific publications.
5- Number of articles: A total of 277 articles were selected for analysis.

### 1.1.3. Exclusion criteria

Articles that did not meet the following criteria were excluded from the analysis:

1- Sector relevance: publications dealing exclusively with the concept of "green decision" in the following publication fields: Environmental Science, Social Sciences, Energy, Business, Management and Accounting.
2- Languages: Publications in languages other than English were not considered.
3- Conference proceedings and reports: Conference proceedings and reports: Conference proceedings and reports are excluded. These are often not just as rigorously peer-reviewed as articles published in academic journals, which may thus affect the reliability and scientific rigor of the information they contain.

## 1.2. Selection result

Figure 1 shows that 277 relevant articles were identified for this study, covering the period from 2016 to 2023. 186 articles were excluded, as they all met the defined selection criteria. These articles are written in English and come from a variety of fields, including Environmental Science, Social Sciences, Energy, Business, Management and Accounting.

All keywords mostly found in the chosen articles were sustainable development, decision-making, skills, environmental skills, and decision-making skills. These terms occur most frequently in the corpus itself, showing their relevance during this study.

It is to be noted in this context that all the publications included in this research according to their selection criteria were from the period 2016 to 2023, showing evidence for the recency of the theme discussed.

*Figure 1. Adapted PRISMA flow chart*

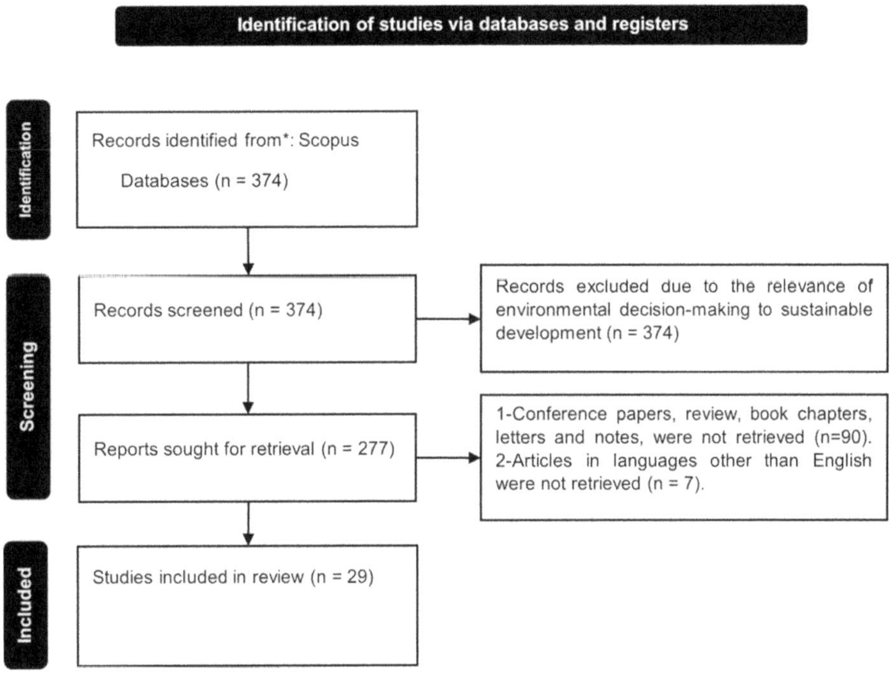


## 1.3. Textual factor analysis with IRaMuTeQ

Once the articles had been selected, the textual corpus comprising the abstracts of the publications was analyzed using IRaMuTeQ software. This software, based on advanced textual statistics, is particularly well suited to extracting recurring themes and conceptual relationships from a voluminous corpus.

### 1.3.1. Corpus construction

The abstracts of the 277 articles were grouped together to form a unified corpus. This corpus was then imported into IRaMuTeQ to perform a hierarchical top-down classification (DHC), grouping the text segments into distinct thematic classes.

### 1.3.2. Descending hierarchical classification (DHC)

HCD is a statistical method that divides the corpus into homogeneous text segments, grouped into classes according to their lexical content. Each class represents a recurring theme or sub-theme in the articles analyzed. This approach is particularly useful for identifying hidden patterns and complex conceptual structures.

*Figure 2. Distribution of descending hierarchical classes (DHC) in our study*

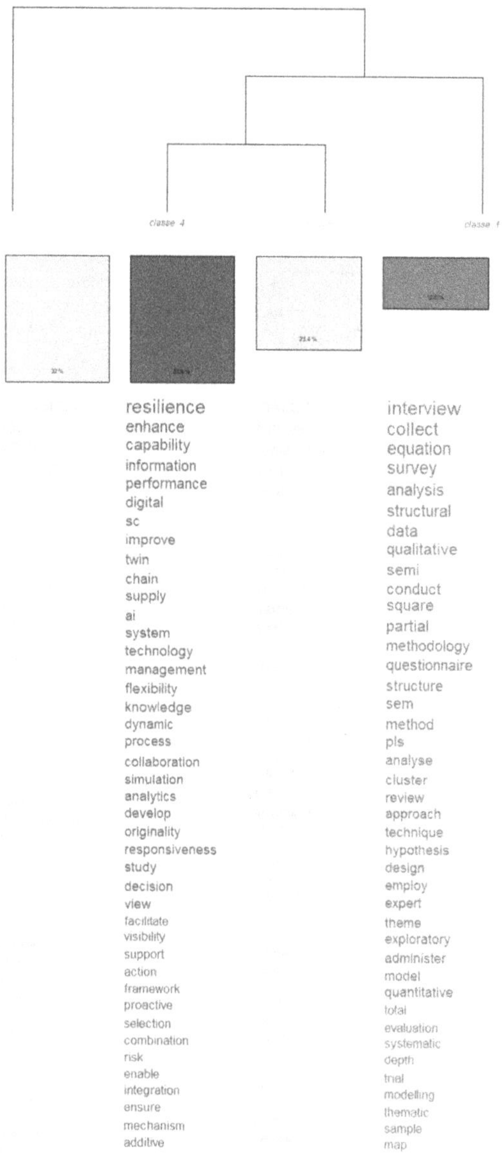


In this study, congenital heart disease was used to identify four main classes:

1. Class 3 focused on economic disruption and the consequences of pandemic Covid-19
2. Class 4 focuses on building resilience through digital technologies
3. Class 2 on research, innovation and digital solutions
4. Class 1 focuses on research methodologies and analytical approaches in resilience studies.

Analysis of the four word classes reveals a crucial interplay between economic disruption, the importance of digital technologies, research challenges and analytical methodologies. The abstracts show that the pandemic has been a catalyst for innovation in supply chains, driving companies to adopt digital solutions and refine their analytical approaches to strengthen their resilience and performance in the face of future crises.

### 1.3.3. Validation of results

To guarantee the robustness of the results, rigorous validation was carried out. In this study, over 80% of text segments were retained in the analyses, a threshold considered robust in similar studies. This high retention ensures that the conclusions drawn from the textual data are representative of the corpus as a whole. These results were then used to classify the texts into clusters (or broad classes) in order to identify the key themes addressed in the articles dealing with skills related to sustainable development, more specifically the environment and associated decision-making.

### 1.3.4. Triangulation of results

The results obtained via IRaMuTeQ were triangulated with the results of the original studies included in the corpus. This step confirmed the consistency between the themes identified in the textual analysis and the observations made in the literature.

## 4. RESULTS OF TEXTUAL ANALYSIS

It has become even more important to adopt analternative hybrid blend of decision-making skills towards meeting modern sustainable development challenges, given a backdrop of heightened socio-economic and ecological disturbances. Notwithstanding these, several obstacles, including those of the agitations, such as a typical crisis around the globe, the limitations of new technologies, and social as well as financial constraints, hinder the actual implementation. This systematic review, conducted using IRaMuTeQ software, explores these issues through in-depth textual analysis. The results focus on three main areas: the impact of disruption on green decision-making skills, the role of digital technologies and research methodologies in building decision-making resilience, and the innovations and challenges associated with sustainable crisis and disruption management.

### 4.1. Impact of Disruptions on Green Decision Skills in Sustainable Development

The first group consists only of class 3 in light blue representing 32% of shapes for the 80.84% of classified segments. This class highlights the impact of economic disruptions induced by the COVID-19 pandemic on green decision-making skills and sustainable development strategies. The primary concern of the class tackled how the risks posed by global crises, such as the pandemic, have underscored the vulnerability of supply chains to material shortages and economic disruption and the recognition for sustainable management skills to be adapted to respond effectively to these challenges.

The pandemic unveiled the fragility of global supply chains, and thus impinged giant economic disturbances prompting tiny and middle enterprises to reinvent how they operate in order to survive. The need for sustainable business models enhanced further by the use of digital technologies to enhance visibility and flexibility in supply chains has gained wide acceptance. One clear impact noted involves AI and data analytics, which have enabled some companies to forecast risks better and make more informed sustainability decisions.

However, even with advancements in technology, challenges persevered. In particular, the SMEs found themselves face-to-face with financial and technical constraints that limited their options of absorbing immense amounts of new practices. Some of these technologies come with high initial costs, while the unacquainted adoption of these kinds of methods on behalf of management with limited levels of digital competency are other key impediments holding the process back from the full integration of sustainable development strategies. Another obstacle is the resistance to change, which would imply the use of traditional tools.

Among this group is one rated at balancing such opportunities provided by sustainability technologies and practices to strengthen corporate resilience in light of crises presented as challenges to overcome to enact those measures widely and effectively. This ultimately means that companies will invest in innovation and train employees on ways to manage the inevitable disruptions in the future sustainably.

The COVID-19 pandemic, therefore, has acted as a wake-up call towards rethinking sustainable development strategies in building more efficiently green decision-making skills. However, for these practices to be well adopted, there is need to transcend financial, technical, and behavioral challenges for these changes to be uniformly integrated.

## 4.2. Digital Technologies, Research Methodologies and Resilience for Sustainable Decisions

This cluster relates classes 2 and 4 in percentages of 31.9% and 23.4%, respectively among the 80.84% of classified segments, noting the interaction of digital technology adoption with advanced research methodologies to promote supply chain resilience and sustainable decision-making. This cluster represents 55.3% of the analyzed data and underlines the need for developing processes on integration of Industry 4.0 technologies and research methodologies to reinforce decision-making in disrupted contexts.

First, the integration of Industry 4.0 technologies upon artificial intelligence, digital twins, and the Internet of Things is primary for enhancing supply chain resilience. These technologies provide utmost visibility, flexibility, and collaboration within supply chains, which are crucial for interruption anticipation and timely response. More specifically, digital twins allow disruptions within simulated scenarios, which can be done in real-time for testing response strategies while at the same time enabling AI-based predictive analytics of risks and catching them before they become an issue (Boukherroub et al., 2024).

Further, intelligent AI-based recommendation systems can help bolster more informed decision-making by companies for unexpected disruptions; the COVID-19 pandemic is a case in point. Such systems allow for a fast response to demand change and the optimization of resource availability (Hu, 2024).

the mix of research designs, quantitative and qualitative analyses allow for the proper creation of theoretical frameworks to promote improved sustainable decision-making as well. Such approaches, such as PLS-SEM and thematic analyses, provide the basis for complex hypotheses testing and identifying key factors influencing supply chain resilience. For example, LCA is an often-used methodology to assess the environmental impact of decisions, thus leading to more sustainable practices. This approach enables companies to consider their decisions' implications over the long-term and to identify opportunities for minimizing their environmental footprint (Camur et al., 2023).

Furthermore, the literature suggests the need to adopt digital technologies to bolster the resilience of supply chains, with one recent study reporting that integrating AI and digital twins enhances the ability of companies to anticipate and react to disruptions, allowing for increased flexibility and collaboration within supply chains (Boukherroub et al., 2024). In the context of an emergency, these technologies will allow the companies to respond promptly and optimize their resources.

An equally important application of robust research methodologies would allow for the study and improvement of the sustainable decision-making arsenal within a business. Life Cycle Assessment approaches provide frameworks for assessing the environmental impact of decisions, hence enhancing sustainable practices (Camur et al., 2023). In addition, the use of simulation models such as system dynamics would allow for complex scenarios to be tested, identifying effective strategies for enhanced resilience.

The ongoing challenges notwithstanding, there are distinct advantages of the digital technologies and advanced research methodologies in use in this instance. It must be noted that adoption of these technologies requires a sizeable investment of financial and human resources, which can be withering on small and medium enterprises (SMEs). The complexity of the research methodologies also somewhat hinders utilization by practitioners, particularly under scarce resource settings.

Thus, the cluster accentuates the need for the digital technologies and research methodologies to be integrated into supply chain resilience to facilitate sustainable decision-making. However, in order for these practices to be adopted on a sustainable basis, it is necessary to knock out the different financial, technical, and operational obstacles that constrain their large-scale application.

## 4.3. Innovations and Challenges for Sustainable Disturbance Management

The latest cluster consists of Class 1, which is 12.8% of the total number of 226 papers. It considers technological innovations and the challenges related to managing sustainable disruptions, with particular reference to solutions such as IoT and blockchain. it has accentuated the significance of innovations in combating technological and operational hurdles, particularly with respect to food supply chains and other important sectors.

First and foremost, Industry 4.0 technologies are considered key facilitators in enhancing supply chain resiliency, such as IoT and blockchain. Indeed, IoT allows the real-time monitoring of production, storage, and transportation conditions from a position that is very important in food supply chains where safety and traceability matters are concerned. IoT sensors, for instance, are used in monitoring the temperature and humidity of perishable products, hence the expected reduction in spoilage and waste (Boukherroub et al., 2024).

Blockchain, on the other hand, provides for better visibility and immutable tracking of transactions that guarantee the integrity of supply chains. This allows products to be traced from the origin to the final consumer, thus increasing stakeholder confidence and lowering fraud and contamination risk (Camur et al., 2023).

Though they are advantageous, adoption of such technologies presents great challenges to companies. Integrating technology itself is complicated and requires an investment in capital, infrastructure, and training. High initial costs, particularly for small and medium enterprises, are major stumbling blocks for their adoption. Besides, specific skills and sophisticated IT infrastructure are required to handle the generated data, restricting their usage in contexts where resources are limited (Boukherroub et al., 2024).

Another challenge entails the resistance to change posed by traditional players, who would not like to adopt new technologies, seeing this as complex or disruptive to the regular processes of working. In the context of food supply chains, some actors may stick to traditional methods of inventory management and tracking, even when these prove less efficient and transparent Camur et al., 2023).

Moreover, the literature furthers that such technological innovations in supply chains have direct positive implications for risk management, including reactive and preventive measures. Indeed, recent studies found that IoT and blockchain allow companies to improve their capabilities for anticipating and responding to disruptions with improvement in product visibility and traceability (Boukherroub et al., 2024). However, they require a strategic plan to mitigate the odds of implementation barriers regarding cost, skills, and technology integration.

Furthermore, integrated approaches, like those that combine system dynamics and discrete event simulation, enable realistic modeling of intricate scenarios, thus surfacing resilient solutions. Such methodologies are valuable to response contexts afflicted by disruption-like conditions; for instance, the effects triggered by the COVID-19 pandemic, in which demand is normally not stationary and often volatile (Camur et al., 2023).

Easing of financial, technical, and operational constraints would be crucial for their sustainable adoption. Governments and institutions can be utilized to support technological innovation initiatives using subsidies, training programs, and public-private partnerships. Concerning the addition of other efforts, increasing awareness of the positive aspects of these technologies and demonstrating their added value may obviate their difficulty at changing.

In conclusion, this class portrays how technological innovations are critical by potentially enhancing supply chain resilience and enabling more sustainable disruption management. To reap maximum benefits, these innovations need users to adopt strategic approaches concerning the cost-to-benefit ratio, the technology of integration, and resistance to change.

## 5. DISCUSSION OF RESULTS

Based on the results obtained from this systematic study, analyzed using IRaMuTeQ software, we have identified several significant clusters, each grouping specific themes related to technology adoption in the context of economic and supply chain disruption. These clusters reflect distinct dynamics in terms of technological obstacles and opportunities. An analysis of the results by group is given below:

### 5.1. Discussion of Group Analysis Results

#### Group 1: Impact of Disruptions on Green Decision-Making Skills in Sustainable Development

The wideness of their affects provides evidence of some issues arising as a result of the economic disruption of these green decision-making capabilities and sustainable development strategies, such as the COVID-19 pandemic. These quite substantiate the works of Alami et al. (2021), citing that global crises have matched the call for a much-needed integration of sustainable practices into decision-making procedures to quicken the resilience of supply chains. Nevertheless, full-blown adoption will be without efforts hampered by economic and technical barriers among small and medium-sized enterprises (SMEs) through lack of capacity to invest in modern technology. Such observations go ahead to bar the process of researching the need to formulate financial support programs and training initiatives to promote large scale adoption of sustainable practices.

#### Group 2: Digital Technologies and Research Methodologies for Resilience

The said group emphasizes the role of digital technologies, such as artificial intelligence (AI), digital twins, and the Internet of Things (IoT), in improving the supply chain resilience. The findings are in line with the content of Boukherroub et al. (2024), who demonstrate that these technologies create more visibility, flexibility, and collaboration within supply chains. Nevertheless, its adoption continues to face technical and financial challenges, especially in lower economic region countries with bad technological infrastructure. Their findings support the idea that strategic investments in the infrastructures and training of professionals are imperative to overcoming these barriers and reducing the global divide in technology.

#### Group 3: Technological Innovations and Challenges in Sustainable Disturbance Management

The conclusions of this group draw attention to how technological innovations such as the IoT (Internet of Things) and blockchain can positively influence the management of disruptions sustainably, especially in food supply chains. The findings affirm those expressed by Camur et al (2023) citing the potential of those technologies in improving traceability and transparency of supply chains. In all, there are several challenges to traverse, especially regarding integration costs and resistance to change by traditional players. These observations imply the necessity for setting up regulative measures and financial incentives to induce the adoption of such technologies, safeguarding the sanctity of existing processes.

#### Group 4: Research Methodologies for Sustainable Decisions

This group brings up potential directions to make more sustainable decisions, such as advanced research methodologies like structural equation modeling (PLS-SEM) and life cycle assessment (LCA). These results are in parallel with Hu's work in 2024, who argued that these methods can test complex hypotheses and find efficient resilience strategies. In opposition, the complexity of the methodologies maybe even limit their usage by practitioners, especially those working in resource-scarce contexts. The conclusion arrives at the exponential need for simple tools and training programs while maintaining the aforementioned methodology.

In summary, the findings of the study show how digital technologies and research methodologies can be used to enhance supply chain resilience and sustainable decision-making, yet they are beset by challenges in costs, technical complexity, and lack of enthusiasm for change. Integrated strategies must be developed to unify investment in infrastructure, training, and continuous regulatory adjustment to address these weaknesses. Such an approach would not only maximize the benefits of innovative technologies but also convince a greater and fairer implementation of such practices globally.

## 5.2. Theoretical and practical implications

### Theoretical implications

This study thus contributes to the already existing literature by theorizing the interplay of emerging technologies, culture and economics along with the exposition of behavioral and financial barriers likely to sustain their adoption. With these findings, one would attain an amount of insight concerning the underlying mechanisms constraining the integration of technologies in such an environment of high interactivity, such as the production and supply chain management and sustainable decision-making.

A more recent study conducted by Duan, Edwards and Dwivedi (2019) that deals specifically with the way human perceptions work on technology adoption is taken as a frame of reference to create conceptual frameworks for building the links between the economic and cultural dimensions. This study further investigates, among other things, the operating mechanisms by which the perception of perceived risks regarding emerging technologies such as AI and Blockchain influence their uptake, particularly in scenarios where more traditional human interactions seem to take precedence in the decision-making process.

In addition, this study adds to the literature on supply chain resilience by showing how Industry 4.0 technologies, IoT and digital twins, can improve companies' capability of anticipating and responding to disruptions. These findings are in line with Boukherroub et al. (2024) discussing how digital technologies help provide supply chains enhanced flexibility and collaboration.

### Practical implications

With regard to implementation, the results of this study provide a concrete basis for promoting inclusion and lessening technological inequities. They stress the need to invest in adequate infrastructures and create incentive programs to combat behavioral resistance and financial constraints. The results show that high up-front costs and lack of adequate infrastructure represent the biggest hurdles to adopting digital technologies. Therefore, there is a need for both public and private investments in deployment infrastructure such as IoT networks and cloud platforms to scale up adoption in less privileged areas.

Technology adoption can be made easy by creating awareness campaigns and training programs. This can create a change in the negative perception of emerging technologies while improving employees' digital skills, particularly for SME workers. For example, the workshops could train the workforce on the application of AI and Blockchain and demonstrate their added value in supply chain management.

More generally, the results indicate that financial incentives such as subsidies and tax breaks could be effective in fostering the overall acceptance of technologies among stakeholders. Such measures, as suggested by Kamble, Gunasekaran and Gawankar, will ease the burden of upfront costs and promote investment among all actors towards innovative technologies. A sound regulatory framework needs to be established for answering this question, as this will help solve uncertainties regarding privacy, employment, and various other ethical ramifications of AI technologies. Stakeholder confidence will be duly empowered through this process, which should ease the adoption process into a smoother and more accepted social framework.

### 5.3. Limitations and avenues for future research

However, certain limitations may influence the analysis of barriers to the integration of digital technologies, particularly AI, in the management of supply chains and economic disruption. Firstly, the exclusive use of the Scopus database, although recognized for the quality and breadth of its publications, may restrict the coverage of certain scientific contributions available in other databases, such as Web of Science. This may limit the diversity of perspectives and results analyzed.

In addition, the lack of publications before 2019 reflects the emerging nature of the theme of integrating AI and digital technologies in supply chain management. This novelty limits understanding of behavioral barriers, such as resistance to change and distrust of automation, as well as financial barriers, including high implementation costs and uncertainties related to return on investment.

## ISSUES, CONTROVERSIES AND PROBLEMS

This chapter highlights several issues and controversies related to the adoption of green decision-making skills in sustainable development. One of the main challenges is the financial and technical barriers to integrating emerging technologies such as AI, IoT and blockchain into decision-making processes. Kamble, Gunasekaran and Gawankar (2020) point to high upfront costs and a lack of digital skills, particularly in SMEs, as major obstacles. This problem is exacerbated by behavioral resistance to change, as many organizations and individuals are reluctant to adopt new technologies due to fear of disruption or lack of confidence in their effectiveness (Duan, Edwards & Dwivedi, 2019).

Another major issue is the uncertainty surrounding the return on investment (ROI) of sustainable technologies. Many companies are reluctant to invest in green technologies due to the lack of clear economic data demonstrating their long-term benefits (McKinsey & Company, 2022). This is particularly problematic in industries where short-term profitability is prioritized over long-term sustainability.

The COVID-19 pandemic has also exposed the vulnerabilities of global supply chains, highlighting the need for more resilient and sustainable practices. However, the transition to sustainable supply chains is often hampered by regulatory and infrastructural challenges. for example, although blockchain technology offers significant potential for improving transparency and traceability, its adoption is limited by the lack of standardized regulations and the high costs associated with its implementation (Camur et al., 2023).

In contrast to these challenges, some organizations have successfully integrated green decision-making skills into their operations. Notably, companies that have adopted AI and IoT technologies have reported improved efficiency, reduced environmental impact and more resilient supply chains (Boukherroub et al., 2024). However, these successes often remain the exception rather than the rule, highlighting the need for wider adoption of sustainable practices.

This chapter argues that overcoming these challenges requires a multifaceted approach including financial incentives, regulatory support and educational initiatives. By addressing these issues, organizations can unlock the full potential of green decision-making skills and contribute to a more sustainable future.

## SOLUTIONS AND RECOMMENDATIONS

To effectively overcome the challenges and controversies surrounding the adoption of green decision-making competencies in sustainable development, a multifaceted approach is required. This approach must involve collaborative efforts between policymakers, business leaders, researchers, and employees to design and implement effective strategies.

A key solution is the establishment of financial incentives and support mechanisms to encourage investment in sustainable technologies. Governments and international organizations should provide grants, tax credits, and subsidies to assist companies—especially SMEs—in adopting eco-friendly technologies such as AI, IoT, and blockchain. Public-private partnerships can also help mitigate financial burdens by fostering knowledge transfer and technological innovation.

Additionally, capacity building and specialized training programs must be implemented to bridge the digital skills gap. Organizations should invest in upskilling employees in emerging technologies and sustainable management practices. Universities and research institutions should collaborate with industry leaders to develop curricula focused on green decision-making, ensuring that future professionals are equipped with the necessary competencies.

Clear regulatory frameworks and standardized guidelines are also essential to facilitate the adoption of sustainable practices. Governments should establish transparent policies to encourage compliance and provide incentives for sustainable business models. Standardized sustainability certifications can enhance corporate reputation and promote market competitiveness.

Furthermore, leveraging technological innovation is crucial for integrating sustainability into decision-making processes. Pilot projects and scalable technological solutions can provide proof of concept, demonstrating the feasibility and effectiveness of green innovations. The integration of AI and IoT can optimize resource utilization, minimize waste, and improve supply chain resilience through predictive analytics.

Behavioral and cultural shifts within organizations must also be addressed. Leadership commitment is vital in fostering a sustainability-driven corporate culture. Employee engagement initiatives, such as gamification and participatory decision-making processes, can encourage proactive contributions to sustainability efforts. Organizations should implement reward-based programs to recognize and incentivize sustainable behaviors.

Investment in research and development is another critical factor for advancing sustainable practices. Governments and private sector entities should allocate funding to collaborative research initiatives that focus on innovative green technologies and long-term environmental impact assessments.

Finally, transparency and accountability mechanisms must be strengthened to ensure corporate responsibility. Companies should publish sustainability reports, undergo third-party audits, and engage stakeholders in continuous dialogue to build trust and credibility.

By adopting these strategic solutions, organizations can enhance their ability to implement green decision-making competencies effectively, ensuring long-term sustainability and resilience. This holistic and integrative approach aligns economic growth with environmental responsibility, paving the way for a more sustainable and equitable future.

The adoption of green decision-making skills is essential to achieving sustainable development goals, but requires a concerted effort to overcome financial, technical, behavioral and regulatory barriers. By implementing the solutions and recommendations outlined above, organizations can unlock the full potential of emerging technologies and sustainable practices. Governments, businesses and individuals all have a role to play in this transformation. Through collaboration, innovation and a commitment to sustainability, we can build a more resilient and equitable future for all.

## CONCLUSION

This study examined the importance of green decision-making skills in the context of sustainable development, highlighting the opportunities and challenges associated with the adoption of emerging technologies. Three main areas emerged from this analysis.

Firstly, the integration of technologies such as artificial intelligence (AI), the Internet of Things (IoT) and blockchain is playing a key role in optimizing decision-making processes and making supply chains more resilient. These tools enable us to better anticipate risks and reduce our ecological footprint. However, their adoption remains hampered by financial barriers, notably high implementation costs, and by a lack of digital skills. It is therefore crucial to strengthen training and economic incentives to encourage their integration.

Secondly, sustainable disruption management, exacerbated by crises such as the COVID-19 pandemic, has revealed the need for greater flexibility and transparency in decision-making. Companies need to rethink their strategies and adopt more adaptive models in order to respond effectively to environmental and economic challenges. However, resistance to change and the lack of a harmonized regulatory framework are slowing down this transition.

Finally, this study highlights the importance of a holistic approach that combines technological innovation, financial support and appropriate public policies. The establishment of clear regulatory frameworks and the development of advanced research methodologies are essential levers for ensuring the sustainable adoption of green decision-making skills.

On a theoretical level, this study contributes to a better understanding of the barriers and facilitators to the transition to sustainable decision-making. Unlike research that focuses on technological benefits, our systematic approach allows us to identify specific behavioral and financial barriers. Nevertheless, certain limitations need to be considered, including the exclusion of databases other than Scopus and the lack of in-depth empirical studies.

## FUTURE RESEARCH DIRECTIONS

The future of green decision-making skills in sustainable development is closely linked to the ongoing evolution of emerging technologies and the development of new frameworks for their implementation. Firstly, a promising area of research is the integration of AI and IoT into sustainable supply chain management. Future studies could explore how these technologies can be used to create more resilient and adaptive supply chains, capable of responding to disruptions in real time.

In addition, another important direction for future research is the development of standardized frameworks for the adoption of blockchain technology in supply chains. Although blockchain has the potential to improve transparency and traceability, its adoption is currently limited by a lack of regulatory clarity and high implementation costs. Future research could focus on developing cost-effective, scalable blockchain solutions that are easily adopted by SMEs.

In addition, more research is needed into the behavioral aspects of green decision-making. Understanding the psychological and cultural factors that influence the adoption of sustainable practices can help organizations design more effective training and awareness programs. Future studies could also explore the role of gamification and other innovative approaches in promoting sustainable behaviors.

Meanwhile, another emerging trend is the circular economy, which aims to minimize waste and maximize resource use through the reuse, recycling and regeneration of materials. Future research could explore how green decision-making skills can be applied to promote circular economy practices in various sectors.

In addition, the inclusion of other databases, such as Web of Science, could enable future research to broaden the coverage of available publications, offering a more comprehensive perspective on the challenges associated with the adoption of digital technologies.

Finally, more longitudinal studies are needed to track the impact of green decision-making skills on organizational performance over time. Such studies could provide valuable information on the long-term benefits of sustainable practices, and help organizations make more informed decisions about their investments in green technologies.

In conclusion, the future of green decision-making skills lies in the ongoing development and integration of emerging technologies, the creation of standardized frameworks for their adoption, and a deeper understanding of the behavioral factors that influence sustainable practices. By addressing these areas, researchers and practitioners can contribute to a more sustainable and resilient future.

## REFERENCES


Alami, S., Rhouiri, M., & Marghich, A. (2021). Active resilience, the cornerstone of firm competitiveness in the post-COVID-19 era: Industrial sector companies in Morocco. *Revue Management Innovation*, *4*(2), 135–155. DOI: 10.3917/rmi.204.0135

Boukherroub, T., Ruiz, A., & Pellerin, R. (2024). Exploration de la contribution des technologies de l'industrie 4.0 à la résilience des chaînes d'approvisionnement. *Journal of Decision Systems*.

Camur, M. C., Tseng, C.-Y., Thanos, A. E., White, C. C., Yund, W., & Iakovou, E. (2023). *An Integrated System Dynamics and Discrete Event Supply Chain Simulation Framework for Supply Chain Resilience with Non-Stationary Pandemic Demand*. arXiv preprint arXiv:2305.00086. DOI: 10.1109/WSC60868.2023.10407779

Duan, Y., Edwards, J. S. et Dwivedi, Y. K. (2019). L'intelligence artificielle au service de la prise de décision à l'ère du Big Data: évolution, défis et programme de recherche. *Revue internationale de gestion de l'information, 48*, 63-71.

Duan, Y., Edwards, J. S., & Dwivedi, Y. K. (2019). Artificial intelligence for decision making in the era of Big Data. *International Journal of Information Management*, *48*, 63–71. DOI: 10.1016/j.ijinfomgt.2019.01.021

Dwivedi, Y. K., Hughes, D. L., Ismagilova, E., et al. (2021). Intelligence artificielle (IA): Perspectives multidisciplinaires sur les défis, les opportunités et les programmes émergents en matière de recherche, de pratique et de politique. *Revue internationale de gestion de l'information*, 57, 101994. https://doi.org/ DOI: 10.1016/j.ijinfomgt.2019.08.002

Kamble, S. S., Gunasekaran, A., & Gawankar, S. A. (2020). Achieving sustainable performance in a data-driven agriculture supply chain: A review for research and applications. *International Journal of Production Economics*, *219*, 179–194. DOI: 10.1016/j.ijpe.2019.05.022

McKinsey & Company. (2022). L'état de l'IA en 2022 et une demi-décennie en revue. Extrait de https://www.mckinsey.com

McKinsey and Company. (2022). The future of work after [McKinsey Global Institute.]. *COVID*, •••, 19.

Stead, J. G., & Stead, W. E. (2000). Eco-Enterprise Strategy: Standing for Sustainability. *Journal of Business Ethics*, *24*(4), 313–329. DOI: 10.1023/A:1006188725928


## KEY TERMS AND DEFINITIONS

**Green decision-making:** is the practice of integrating environmental, social, and economic determinants into decision-making, aiming to achieve sustainable development. It helps in keeping strategic decisionsaligned with the long-terms ecological and social wellbeing with a balancing act between progress and responsibility.

**Sustainable Development:** A progressive development model that meets current needs without compromising future generations' ability to meet their own. It is anchored on environmental preservation, social equity, and economic growth-all of which are integrated for a healthy planet.

**Artificial Intelligence, AI:** A subset of computer science which deals with the creation of systems that can learn, reason, or solve problems, and which emulates human-like intelligence. Ai plays a prominent role in sustainability by optimizing resources management, predictive analysis, or implementing automatic decision-making.

**The Internet of Things:** A set of technology that links information processing capacities between connected devices to collect, process and transfer real-time data. It would improve operational efficiency and would enable intelligent resource management through actionable insight.

**Digital Twins:** Virtual replicas of physical systems that, by simulating, analyzing, and optimizing real-world processes, can support better decision-making and predictive maintenance, mainly in supply chain and infrastructure management.

**Supply Chain Resilience:** This is the ability of a supply chain to predict, adapt, and recover from disruption while allowing for continuity of operations. Resilient supply chains possess flexibility, are technology-savvy, and employ risk reduction measures to remain solid against various challenges.

**Blockchain Technology:** A decentralized digital ledger that ensures transactions regarding transparency, security, and traceability. For sustainability measures, blockchain is used for tracking supply chains, certifying carbon credits, and ethical sourcing, thereby building trust and accountability.

**Industry 4.0:** All the ongoing digital transformations of manufacturing and supply chains via innovations such as AI, IoT, robotics, and automation. This revolution aims to enhance productivity, sustainability, and operational efficiency while paving the way for smarter and greener industries.

**Behavioral Barriers:** These are the psychological and cultural barriers that prevent the adoption of newer technologies and sustainable practices. Common factors include a fear of change, the growing menace of ignorance, and job security concerns. This would be countered by education, upper-level communication, and relaxing stakeholder engagement for trust-building and advancement.

**Circular Economy:** It is an economic model aimed to limit waste and make the most of resources through recycling, reuse, and regenerative design. This would create less impact on the environment while creating sustainability that lasts well into the distant future by keeping resources in use to the maximum extent possible.

# Chapter 18
# Does ESG-Oriented Leadership Pay Off in Startups?
## A Theoretical Perspective

**Burak Özdoğan**
https://orcid.org/0000-0002-8504-5085
*Manisa Celal Bayar University, Turkey*

**Deniz Dirik**
https://orcid.org/0000-0002-7652-5079
*Manisa Celal Bayar University, Turkey*

## ABSTRACT

*This chapter addresses the role of ESG-oriented leadership in startups, exploring whether integrating ESG principles contributes to long-term success or come with additional challenges. While sustainability has become a strategic imperative for businesses worldwide, its adoption among startups remains complex mostly because of financial constraints. Despite this, emerging trends suggest that investors are gradually recognizing ESG as a competitive advantage. While entrepreneurship is becoming more challenging due to financial and market uncertainties, an increasing number of early-stage entrepreneurs prioritize their social and environmental impact over pure profitability. Yet, the lack of standardized ESG metrics continues to be a significant barrier, creating an "acronym soup". While the financial benefits of ESG leadership in startups may not be immediately apparent, the long-term advantages such as stronger talent retention and investor interest make sustainability a strategic asset rather than a cost.*

## 1. INTRODUCTION

Startups exist to shake things up. They thrive on breaking old molds, rewriting industry rules, and scaling at breakneck speed, often moving so fast that regulation scrambles to catch up. They are the wild cards of the business world, celebrated for their ingenuity and agility. But behind the scenes, the pressure is relentless. Founders are expected to be everything at once: visionaries, risk-takers, and execution machines, balancing on a knife's edge between securing funding and running out of runway. And now? They're also expected to be ESG-conscious leaders. Investors, consumers, and regulators

DOI: 10.4018/979-8-3373-0189-1.ch018

increasingly demand that even the youngest companies embed environmental, social, and governance (ESG) principles into their DNA. It sounds reasonable. After all, why shouldn't the businesses shaping the future do so responsibly? But here's the catch: most startups barely have enough capital to survive their next funding round, let alone invest in sustainability initiatives. They operate in a world where every dollar is a lifeline, and every decision is a trade-off between idealism and survival. This raises an uncomfortable question: Can startups afford to take ESG seriously, or is sustainability just a privilege of well-established corporations with the luxury of long-term planning?

The growing number of studies, regulatory efforts, and investor expectations make it clear sustainability is now a fundamental part of long-term corporate strategy. While large corporations face mounting pressure to embed ESG into their operations, startups exist in a paradox. In theory, agility and disruptive potential of startups should position them as frontrunners in the race for sustainable innovation. However, most of them struggle to integrate ESG principles, mostly as a result of resource constraints, investor expectations, and the relentless urgency of scaling fast.

At this intersection, ESG leadership has the potential to make a difference. A startup with a strong ESG leadership and commitment doesn't consider sustainability a separate function or a concern for the future nor treats as a policy, report, or a way of checking boxes for compliance. Rather, it embeds ESG into its strategy, incorporating it into everything from product design to hiring practices and investor relations, and making ESG central to every decision at every stage of its growth. This startup prefers seeing ESG not as a costly obligation, but as a competitive edge, one that attracts impact-driven investors, aligns with shifting consumer preferences, and builds long-term resilience in a VUCA (volatile-uncertain-complex-ambiguous) world.

Corporate giants have long been under the microscope for their sustainability commitments. Today, startups are no longer flying under the radar. Investors, regulators, and even consumers are increasingly demanding more than just groundbreaking products or disruptive business models. They are asking for businesses that are responsible from day one, demonstrating environmental commitment, social impact, and ethical governance from the outset. The Global Entrepreneurship Monitor (2023) notes a growing trend with new entrepreneurs who are increasingly prioritizing sustainability over short-term financial gains. Yet, paradoxically, ESG-oriented startups do not necessarily attract more funding or outperform their peers in measurable ways (World Economic Forum, 2022). This disconnect between ambition and investor behavior raises a critical question: *Does ESG leadership provide a tangible competitive advantage for startups, or does it create more hurdles in an already challenging environment?* Faced with competing priorities, startups have to deal with short-term funding pressures, and the challenge of quantifying ESG impact in ways that resonate with venture capitalists. While many investors claim to value ESG, in practice financial returns often take precedence. Global Entrepreneurship Monitor 2024/2025 report (GEM, 2025) has just announced financial imperatives, in the form of either a desire to make money or to stop losing it, as the leading reason for starting or exiting a business across many economies. This leaves startups in a conundrum: Should they sacrifice sustainability for the sake of survival? Or is there a way to build businesses where profit and ESG goals could coexist and reinforce each other?

To answer this question, we should be prepared to rethink what ESG leadership means at the startup level. This chapter invites the audience to do that by exploring how founders, investors, and the broader startup ecosystem can bridge the gap between ambition and execution. Specifically, we seek to address some pressing questions by exploring the relationship between startup leadership and ESG orientation, along with their broader implications for startup performance. Rather than viewing sustainability as a privilege reserved for well-established corporations, we argue that ESG should be recognized as a strategic imperative, one that enhances resilience, fosters innovation, and serves as a key differentiator in an increasingly competitive and values-driven world. Beyond theoretical discussions, this chapter also offers practical insights for startup ecosystem, shedding light on how ESG principles can be effectively integrated to navigate both current and emerging challenges while driving sustainable growth.

## 2. ESG AND STARTUP LEADERSHIP NEXUS

The starting goal of the report created by the United Nations with the joint efforts of 20 financial institutions that managed over 6 trillion dollars in 2004 was to create an awareness for financial markets and stakeholders about environmental, social, and governance (ESG) oriented business models that are more sustainable and to start a positive impact on future. At this stage, ESG has accomplished creating the impact of awareness and went beyond expectations by becoming a priority for different stakeholder groups (Global Compact, 2004). The arguments of ESG to reveal sustainable development without sacrificing growth and even to increase the stakeholder value of the corporations were the main arguments of the ESG practices, government regulations, and, as a whole, sustainable business model proponent.

The UN report expected corporations to lead ESG and policy implementations. This was because the main duty was to enhance transparency, accountability, and eventually corporate governance in the organization to sustain an ESG-oriented transformation. The return of this goal was expected to be achieved by aligning other market players with the same perspective of the business model. The following years showed a structure that partly parallel with the expectations of outcomes yet is still under development. One of the most notable of the different stakeholder groups supporting the efforts is the latest definition of the purpose of a corporation, updated in 2019 by the "Business Roundtable" organization, which was published with the signatures of the CEOs of 181 American companies, including the world's largest companies. The organization included the creation of value for customers, investment in employees, fair and ethical supplier relations, support for communities and protection of the environment, and long-term value creation for shareholders in its redefined purpose of a corporation (Business Roundtable, 2019). Later, at the 2020 meeting of the World Economic Forum, the subject was comprehensively addressed within the framework of the concept of "stakeholder capitalism" and the transformation of long-term value creation into a common purpose of companies was emphasized (Schwab, 2021).

Environmental, social, and governance performance as a strategic challenge for businesses has created a strong and competitive environment in both financial and leadership terms. According to Google Trends' keyword trend analysis, the term ESG has received significant attention and the search volume for the term "ESG" has increased by more than threefold since 2019. According to a Stanford University study including 2470 investors, Millennials and Generation Z make much different and more sensitive investment decisions to environmental, social, and governance factors than do Baby Boomers and Generation X (Haber et al., 2022). Nations and regulatory bodies are striving to use the resources available to them efficiently to implement corporate governance and sustainability initiatives in a focused and systematic way. Furthermore, due to the endeavors of civil society organizations and activists, we observe that investors as key stakeholders within the business ecosystem are increasingly prioritizing ESG-oriented objectives in their agendas and including them as essential criteria.

To elaborate on ESG, while sustainability is the primary focus, its structure also prioritizes financial success, distinguishing it from impact investing, green investing, and other sustainability initiatives (Hornberger, 2023). Alongside the above-mentioned shift in the definition of the business's purpose, ESG's E, or environmental governance, explains how companies are working to manage their relationships with their effects on the environment and develop a sustainable model, while S, or social governance, focuses on how companies are working to comprehend, manage, and communicate both their positive and negative effects on the social environment in which they operate, from suppliers to employees. Lastly, G, or corporate governance, deals with how to build, oversee, and communicate accountability, transparency, and ethical decision-making in business management. When taken as a whole, an ESG emphasis gives companies the chance to examine their business models from many angles, identify possibilities and risks, build trusting relationships with stakeholders, and use sustainable components to boost financial success.

Meanwhile, sustainable entrepreneurship is one of the key areas for researchers with both micro and meso-level focuses (Sreenivasan & Suresh, 2023). While there are different definitions and approaches to the term sustainable entrepreneurship, approaching an environmentally, ecology-friendly, responsible, and competitive way to business model when compared with traditional entrepreneurial motivations is at the core of those enterprises (Schaltegger & Wagner, 2011). This is because entrepreneurship is seen as a reliable way with its innovation orientation and disruptive structure for challenging goals including environmental, societal, and governance linked with sustainability (Dean & McMullen, 2007; Huang, Li, Bu & Zhao, 2023).

On the other hand, today the world presents startups with much more dynamic and variable conditions than in the past 20 years. Moreover, this variability eliminates the concept of a safe country for startups and creates global effects. In the last 10 years, issues such as the COVID-19 pandemic, regional conflicts, and conflicts between countries have created new conditions for all startups, regardless of the country they are located in. Therefore, when constructing the perspective on ESG, it is necessary not to evaluate the ideal in question solely within the framework of ESG, but to evaluate it by considering other perspectives that can provide startups with the structure they need to be resilient to the changes. According to the Global Entrepreneurship Monitor 2023/2024 Report (GEM), entrepreneurs are increasingly focusing on their businesses' environmental, social, and governance impacts. This motivation is higher for new entrepreneurs than for entrepreneurs with existing ventures. The report indicates that new entrepreneurs prioritize good environmental or sustainability practices above economic performance (GEM, 2023).

It is considered one of the important advantages that startups, especially those led by technology initiatives, have started to directly design their business models as ESG-oriented. Startups with an ESG-oriented business model may face a variety of managerial and financial challenges while aiming to adopt high corporate governance principles on the one hand, and to operate with sustainable resource management and impact measurement models on the other. Entrepreneurs are valued by society and encouraged to design and run business models with a focus on impact on society including corporate governance, sustainability, and environmental effects. However, one of the primary concerns that has to be addressed is whether the same support and encouragement are also evident in the interactions that entrepreneurs have with investors and their ability to secure funding.

Today, it is seen that different venture capitals (VC) want to invest in more sustainable startups, can measure their environmental and governance impacts, and build their business models from this perspective, directly through ESG-focused investment funds. But the question is, are those funding initiatives to enhance the ESG priority of startups and their founders motivating enough? Is the ESG-oriented leadership for startups paying off as a less challenging funding process?

We attempt to address these questions via the lens of leadership and entrepreneurship theory while examining the literature to comprehend the fundamental motives from both entrepreneurial leadership and venture capital perspectives.

## 3. A HISTORICAL ACCOUNT OF THE ESG FRAMEWORK

There were certainly earlier attempts before the UN report to approach the sustainable business matter from a different perspective. Elkington's "Triple Bottom Line" concept is at the forefront of these. At the time, Elkington argued, inspired by the values report of the oil giant Shell, that the path to a sustainable business model would be opened by measuring and reporting the actions companies took or did not take against the economic, environmental, and social bottom lines (Elkington, 1998). Also, the intersecting goals and objectives of different initiatives can be encountered on the journey to sustainable institutions and business models. The United Nations Sustainable Development Goals represent one of these intersections. Although SDG and ESG ultimately have the same ultimate aim, they represent separate goals: a significant intersection and a distinction. The Sustainable Development Goals (SDG) advocate for social transformation through a comprehensive approach that involves diverse stakeholders, including the public, institutions, and individuals. In contrast, Environmental, Social, and Governance (ESG) criteria have gained prominence among investors in recent years, emphasizing corporate performance rather than broader social change.

The significance of investors made sustainability a top goal for many early ventures and startups, which are essential for generating outside funding to support innovation and growth. Access to funding is one of the most vital elements of an endeavor; in a competitive ecosystem, securing funding as soon as possible and in greater amounts is essential. While some research indicates that sustainable entrepreneurs face financial obstacles (Hoogendoorn, Van der Zwan & Thurik, 2019), other research suggests that the opposite is true, with investment increasing as sustainability becomes more paramount (Mansouri & Momtaz, 2022). On the other hand, the research on the performance and focus of those ESG-oriented funds brings some critical arguments. According to a study by the National Bureau of Economic Research (NBER), U.S. investors' willingness for ESG-oriented funding is fluctuating year by year from 2019 to 2023, while European investors have more solid interest and focus on ESG-oriented funding (Baker, Egan & Sarkar, 2022). Another study argues that the ESG fund's financial performance is relatively low compared to other funds (Raghunandan & Rajgopal, 2022).

Numerous studies throughout the years have highlighted that the primary motive for sustaining firms and driving success pertains to a value that transcends mere profitability or stock value (Cohen, Smith & Mitchell, 2008). This value delineates the company's societal position and imposes a significant mission on its founders. The personal perspectives of the founders have a greater impact on the vision, purpose of existence, and ultimate objectives of the enterprise, particularly during the initial stages (Taneja & Chenault, 2019). Strong leadership is one of the critical factors for businesses to fully achieve ESG focus. We can see this most simply in the International Standards Organization's (ISO) IWA 48 standard, which includes application principles regarding ESG (ISO, 2024; IWA 48:7.5). The standard also reveals the importance of leadership in terms of ESG.

When integrated into the corporate culture and business practices as a whole, ESG represents a very powerful vision. When it is ingrained in the company's DNA, it can become an even more powerful instrument. This is because the process of growth is extremely unpleasant and can occasionally disclose crucial decision-making processes where entrepreneurs may decide to take shortcuts rather than the proper routes. Therefore, embedding ESG focus on the foundations of a startup has the potential to significantly impact the direction of the decisions it will make in the future (Singh & Tarkar, 2024).

Accurately reporting and communicating these practices will ensure that the aforementioned vision becomes tangible for all parties involved, particularly VCs and investor groups. Even if it is believed that relatively new businesses have far smaller social and environmental effects than those that are older and that governance challenges have not yet surfaced, the ESG culture ingrained in the business's core will likely pay off in the long run. The findings of a master's thesis conducted on 47 Dutch startups indicate that venture capitalists' investment decisions are influenced by a startup's capacity to effectively manage ESG risks. According to the study, firm valuation and ESG risk are negatively correlated (Bos, 2023). Previous literature has varying answers to the question of ESG and firm value. The research of Mervelskemper & Streit (2017) posits that enterprises with superior ESG performance and reporting are valued more favorably by the market. Another study looking for an answer to the value of the firm and its efforts in ESG from Fatemi, Glaum & Kaiser (2018) argues that this superiority of companies with strong ESG aspects is also reflected in company valuations. However, when it comes to ESG communication, i.e., disclosures, the results appear to be more complicated, which brings us to a double-edged sword. The relationship between ESG and financial success is multifaceted with varying conclusions drawn from different studies. While Buallay's (2020) research concluded that ESG has opposite effects on manufacturing and banking sectors, Khan's (2022) meta-analysis of ESG research revealed a substantial positive correlation between the sustainability performance of firms and their financial performance.

Singh & Tarkar (2024) suggest a three-phase framework for implementing ESG practices as a whole, where the first phase is to set the basis for ESG in the organization, while the second phase is taking solid actions on ESG components and using KPIs. In the third phase, it is expected to be communicated via reporting and evaluation of the practices. When it comes to startups, the aforementioned role of the founders in creating the culture and ensuring the vision of the endeavor is shared by the organization becomes crucial. The founders' close relationship and impact on the organization reveal diverse perspectives on ESG adaptation, such as organizational resilience, which links the process with strategic management (Wang, Jiao & Ma, 2024). Because, especially during the establishment phase, startups pivot from the business model to the product/service many times. To put it another way, startups ought to be more equipped and ahead of larger firms regarding organizational resilience. In support of this, Leoni (2024) asserts in her research that ESG influences the institution's organizational resilience components. Consequently, the claim that organizational resilience is strengthened by ESG compliance arises (Leoni, 2024).

The efforts of creating a sustainable business have attracted the broad attention of scholars, which eventually turned into a research field called "Sustainable Entrepreneurship" (SE) (Dean & McMullen, 2007; Cohen, Smith & Mitchell, 2008). Dean & McMullen (2007) defines sustainable entrepreneurship as *"the process of discovering, evaluating, and exploiting economic opportunities that are present in market failures which detract from sustainability, including those that are environmentally relevant."* This definition essentially coincides with the desired endpoint to be achieved with ESG. Yet, the impact of the ESG focus and sustainable entrepreneurship approach, which are founded on developing and overseeing a sustainable business model without deviating from the drive to generate economic value, on the financial performance of businesses generates distinct debates. In their research, Mansouri & Momtaz (2022) concluded that ESG has a positive impact on the financial performance of enterprises in the short term but may have negative effects on long-term economic performance.

## 4. VENTURE CAPITAL, STARTUPS, AND ESG-ORIENTATION TRIANGLE

The preceding section briefly addressed the varying perspectives in the literature regarding the financial outcomes that enterprises employing an ESG-focused model attain in exchange for their efforts. The primary anticipated outcome, though, is that business's attempts to meet their financial objectives sustainably by taking governance, social, and environmental concerns into account would be recognized. One of these benefits can be explained by investors prioritizing ESG in their portfolio strategy. Investors are a fairly diverse group when it comes to their investment preferences. The choices made by the fund managers who oversee the process directly have a significant impact on final investment selections, even while financial institutions have general regulations governing investing processes, portfolio preferences, and management procedures. Haber and colleagues (2022) found that individual investors' decision to invest in ESG-focused funds shows different patterns related to demographic factors. From a different perspective, the 2024 Annual Report of the Principles for Responsible Investment (PRI) program states that over 5,000 investment firms have signed on to the effort and that these firms worldwide account for more than half of all institutional assets (PRI, 2024). The initiative's participants agree to uphold six principles that give ESG considerations top priority while making investment decisions and beyond.

Investment is a prerequisite for growth and a sustainable business model, especially for startups. From this standpoint, entrepreneurs will concentrate on any strategy that streamlines investment processes or raises investment rounds to significantly higher valuations. Startup founders spend the most time on this obligation throughout the growth process, beginning with the seed phase. Entrepreneurs have been promoted to run businesses with an ESG-based vision and corporate culture to benefit from the growing number and volume of sustainability-focused investment funds in recent years, as well as the ESG-oriented investment policies of venture capitalists.

The outcomes of these investments have two crucial implications for the market as a whole. The viewpoint of investors is the first of these. Investors keep a careful eye on their ESG-focused portfolios and accept their return as a performance measure. An increase in venture capitalists and funds that value sustainability—also known as impact-focused—will be made possible by the performance of ESG portfolios. It is undeniable that a growing number of investors are establishing ESG and/or sustainability-focused funds and investors' interest in those funds.

*Table 1. Global sustainable net fund flows*

| Quarter | Net Fund Flow (US $bn) |
|---|---|
| 1Q20 | 46 |
| 2Q20 | 71 |
| 3Q20 | 81 |
| 4Q20 | 152 |

continued on following page

*Table 1. Continued*

| Quarter | Net Fund Flow (US $bn) |
|---|---|
| 1Q21 | 185 |
| 2Q21 | 159 |
| 3Q21 | 134 |
| 4Q21 | 142 |
| 1Q22 | 69 |
| 2Q22 | 33 |
| 3Q22 | 23 |
| 4Q22 | 37 |
| 1Q23 | 31 |
| 2Q23 | 18 |
| 3Q23 | 14 |
| 4Q23 | -0.1 |
| 1Q24 | 1 |

Source: Institute for Energy Economics and Financial Analysis (2024) https://ieefa.org/articles/esg-funds-continue-thrive-and-outperform-traditional-funds-across-equity-and-fixed-income

Nonetheless, prior literature indicates different findings on performance outcomes. Abate and colleageus (2021) conducted a study that revealed that European funds with high ESG performance exhibited superior financial efficiency. Additionally, investors who selected ESG-oriented equity funds experienced substantially better performance than those who chose conventional funds. However, Milonas and colleageus (2022) analyzed European and US funds to identify any performance disparities between ESG investing and conventional funds. They did not find any. Also noteworthy is the study by Petridis et al. (2023), which used a sizable sample of 17,961 mutual funds globally to analyze the performance of funds related to their ESG controversies. They discovered that funds with higher scores—that is, fewer controversies—performed noticeably better than funds with lower scores. It is possible to increase the number of studies that reach positive conclusions (El Ghoul & Karoui, 2022; Wang, 2024) and negative conclusions (El Ghoul et al., 2023; Kuzmina et al., 2023) regarding the performance of ESG funds.

On the other hand, the entrepreneurs' viewpoint is the second. Entrepreneurs will also want to see that having an ESG-focused business model, measuring the enterprise's environmental, social, and governance impacts, setting goals, and reporting the results to stakeholders will result in easier access to financing, higher valuation rounds, and positive effects on the enterprise's financial performance. There are differing opinions in the literature regarding the degree to which all of these expectations are fulfilled. Friede, Busch & Bassen's (2015) review study demonstrates a significant positive finding on the ESG and financial performance of corporations. The study by Mansouri & Momtaz (2022) examines the initial coin offerings of startups and argues that an ESG orientation increases the investment amount by 28%. On the other side of the medallion, Calascione's (2023) study of 120 startups discovered that while investors do take into account a startup's ESG scores, they do so only after giving the startup's financial data priority. If the startup has a strong financial foundation, the author contends that ESG influences the investment choice. There is no doubt that it would be erroneous to attribute the ESG focus of startups solely to the pursuit of financial benefits, as this contradicts the essence of entrepreneurship. Entrepreneurs may have much more compelling reasons for wanting to disrupt established norms, alter the status quo, and build superior companies (Dirik & Özdoğan, 2025). Ultimately, nevertheless, regardless of the final goal or vision, entrepreneurs in the current market competition climate must have a strong enough financial performance to sustain this goal or vision. The vision of having an ESG-focused enterprise is not independent of these facts.

At this point, it is necessary to emphasize once again the importance of venture capital companies in the success and proliferation of ESG-focused initiatives. Startups operate on a much smaller scale than publicly traded companies and, therefore, within a much narrower financing window. In this limited framework, the objective of ESG-focused entrepreneurship, which is formed by the founders' vision, and the endeavor to survive in competitive market conditions must coexist. At this point, one of the most important intermediaries that will support founders for an ESG-focused vision and initiative is venture capital. According to Crunchbase data, venture capitalists globally invested $314 billion in startups in 2024, while $32 billion was for seed funding and $118,4 billion of it was early-stage funding (Crunchbase, 2025).

Venture capital companies' investment decisions are based on the startup's business model, product/market fit, team quality, innovation, competitive power, and several traditional financial indicators. Additionally, some funds within venture capital companies focus on startups of different sizes and/or sectors. Venture capital following an investment preference strategy that prioritizes ESG will enable ESG-focused initiatives to access a much more vibrant financing ecosystem (Zhang, 2022). The available literature is limited regarding the performance comparison between ESG-focused VCs and traditional ones, as well as their methods for incorporating ESG orientation into their investment decision-making processes.

A European Investment Fund Working Paper found that 7 in 10 VCs incorporate ESG criteria into their investment decision process (Botsari & Lang, 2020) however, Lange & Banadaki's (2024) research with 11 VCs located in Germany found that VCs are following the developments and practices in ESG but are facing difficulties when it comes to the implementation of the ESG focus into the investment decision process. The results of another study that sheds light on Chinese VCs argue that VCs contribute significantly to the ESG focus of the companies they invest in (Wang, Ke & Shen, 2023).

Another important aspect of focusing on ESG for VCs is the effects on fund creation. On this aspect, Meles (2021) asserts that VCs concentrating on ESG can simplify their fund creation process. This is an important aspect of VCs focusing on ESG when investing in startups. To provide further detail, venture capital firms typically establish funds using capital from various groups of investors and make investments in startups via these funds. The groups of investors, comprising individual investors, family offices, and various other institutional investors, are referred to as limited partners (LP). Hence, the main focus of VCs is to persuade LPs to put their money into the funds they will establish, which eventually causes LPs to have a strong influence on the investment decisions of VCs (Abdou & Gupta, 2024). The growing awareness of sustainability in the business context over recent years, along with various countries' regulations and/or incentive structures related to sustainability and ESG, can prompt LPs to direct investments toward ESG-oriented targets. According to the survey of Bain & Company with 100 LP organizations, the top three reasons for LPs to incorporate ESG are (Lino et al., 2022);

- To offer clear ESG communications to stakeholders,
- Seeing ESG as an additive to investment performance and,
- Want investments to make a positive contribution.

This mechanism of indirect effect can also result in VCs adhering to investment policies centered around ESG. According to the research of Xiong et al. (2024), VC funds invested by more social-impact-oriented LPs invest more in sustainability-focused startups. Another consideration is the possibility that the long-term relationships VCs build with the startups they invest in could foster the emergence and maintenance of an ESG-focused business model (Lin, 2022). It is a natural process for founders to prioritize internal investors when it comes to the financing needs of the venture in future investment rounds and, consequently, to consider the priorities of current investors. Because of the nature of their investments, VCs have been involved in the venture for a long time and maintain a long-term partnership with the founders for many reasons beyond funding, and this will support the integration of ESG focus into corporate culture (Bian et al., 2023).

## 5. CRITICAL PERSPECTIVES AND CHALLENGES FOR VCS AND FOUNDERS REGARDING ESG

Startups are structures that differ from traditional enterprises and corporate companies in terms of their working methods, motivations, and business models. Within this structure, continuous intense competition, rapid growth pressure, a corporate culture that is shaped and spread around the founders, an innovation-first business model, and continuous investment needs are realities specific to the nature of the startup. Being able to create sustainability-first initiatives by operating with ESG-focused business models represents an important vision for startups, but founders and startups cannot achieve this vision alone. One of the biggest challenges for startups in terms of the applicability of the ESG vision, which starts with institutional investors, will be their expectation of reporting and communication similar to that of corporate companies. One of the biggest concerns based on this argument should be the startups that cannot meet this great expectation are likely to move away from this field. Regulations are therefore crucial at this stage and can help startups by easing the route of communication by setting some unified principles and roadmaps especially designed for startups.

Another challenge ahead of ESG-oriented startup vision is the lack of solid VC support on impact investments. Unlike publicly listed companies, startups are not businesses that can draw in substantial institutional funding. Thus, the number of ESG funds aimed at equity investment or the size of their portfolios holds no significance for startups. The founders' vision is crucial—whether it is focused on impact, and whether sustainability genuinely aids financial performance. The lack of sufficient funding options that recognize the founders' efforts and give priority to ESG will impede growth, even though founders with a clear vision for developing and delivering sustainable business models have the determination and drive to launch an ESG-focused startup in the first place.

However, two significant issues that reinforce one another now emerge. The first of them is the dearth of venture capitalists who prioritize ESG. This situation will inevitably have a significant impact on the decisions founders make and their plans. For early-stage startups in particular, founders cannot afford to take risks regarding timely fulfillment of funding needs and the emergence of valuations that will facilitate their growth processes. As a result of these concerns, the ESG focus may not be concretized to the expected extent.

Another crucial problem is the absence of a clear roadmap for VCs regarding the incorporation of ESG into their investment processes and the criteria to assess, just as there is no such roadmap for startups on implementing and reporting ESG (Lange & Banadaki, 2024). These two problems also carry the potential to influence the solutions of one another. Concrete progress in this area is not evident due to the limited number of ESG-focused VCs and funds. Furthermore, the lack of evaluation criteria, standards, and reporting principles—essential components of the aforementioned progress—leaves new VCs entering this field uncertain.

Governments can effectively eliminate the aforementioned disadvantages for ESG-focused startups and VCs through regulations and constructive interventions (Lin, 2022). While international organizations like the United Nations and the European Union invest considerable efforts and regulation in sustainability and ESG, countries must bolster these initiatives. Additionally, local incentive mechanisms geared towards impact-oriented, ESG-focused business models should be developed.

Lastly, we believe that the lists released by ESG rating firms are one of the important subjects. The process of the institutions that create these lists and the impact of the lists on investors and enterprises have long been the subject of criticism (Berg et al., 2023). Although it was not the starting point of the criticisms of ESG scores, Elon Musk made a significant contribution to bringing them to the agenda. His statements after his company, Tesla, received low ESG scores ignited some fundamental discussions about the creation of these scores (Jones, 2022). Berg et al. (2023) reveal in their study that the scores of ESG rating agencies show a low correlation. At this point, criticisms about the inconsistency of the measurements made on ESG and questions about the possible consequences of this inconsistency arise.

Aware of these criticisms and trying to establish the rating issue on more objective grounds, the European Union aimed to make ESG rating activities more consistent, transparent, and comparable with a new regulation in 2024. With the new regulation, ESG rating companies established in EU member countries are required to operate subject to the license of the European Securities and Markets Authority (EU Council, 2024). While this is undoubtedly an important step for the quality of measurements within the EU, when evaluated on a global scale, it is waiting its turn on the ESG agenda as one of the areas where other countries need to regulate globally with similar steps and perhaps with a collective effort.

## 6. DISCUSSION AND IMPLICATIONS

Sustainability has moved beyond a corporate trend to become a global business imperative. Frameworks like the Global Reporting Initiative (GRI) Standards and the United Nations' Sustainable Development Goals (SDGs) have pushed organizations toward a triple-bottom-line approach, balancing economic, social, and environmental priorities. In response, companies across industries have integrated sustainability into their core strategies, not just as a compliance requirement but as a foundation for long-term resilience and competitive advantage. However, ESG adoption remains uneven across industries and regions, shaped by factors such as company size, resource availability, and industry-specific pressures. Some firms have deeply embedded ESG into their DNA, while others struggle to move beyond superficial commitments and fragmented initiatives (Lemus-Aguilar et al., 2019).

### 6.1 The Leadership Imperative in ESG Adoption

The complexity of ESG implementation places leadership at the heart of sustainability efforts. An ESG-oriented leader does not merely react to regulatory demands but actively embeds ESG principles into strategic decision-making. Such leaders act as connectors between stakeholders, ensuring alignment between employees, investors, policymakers, media, and consumers to build a sustainability strategy that is both impactful and enduring. Without strong leadership, ESG efforts risk becoming fragmented, performative, or reactive rather than transformational (Fonseca, 2021).

The role of leadership in ESG adoption extends beyond policymaking and compliance, and it is shaped by personal motivations, strategic vision, and values, particularly those of founders. As architects of organizational culture, founders set the strategic and ethical foundation upon which ESG initiatives are built. Research has linked founder characteristics, including age, gender, political affiliation, personality, and cultural background to ESG commitment and accomplishments (Al-Shammari et al., 2019; Borghesi et al., 2014; Yuan et al., 2019; Zhang et al., 2021). Businesses driven by intrinsic sustainability values rather than external pressures develop more authentic and long-term ESG strategies (Bansal & Roth, 2000). Additionally, entrepreneurial orientation, which is a combination of innovation, proactiveness, and risk-taking is a strong predictor of ESG engagement (Lumpkin & Dess, 1996). Founders with high entrepreneurial orientation are more inclined to adopt sustainability technologies, experiment with circular economy models, and address social challenges through business innovation.

Furthermore, the time horizon of a founder's strategic decision-making significantly influences ESG adoption. Long-term-oriented founders are more likely to invest in sustainability initiatives that may take decades to materialize, rather than prioritizing short-term financial gains (Slawinski & Bansal, 2015). Another crucial factor is gender diversity in leadership. Research indicates that female founders and gender-diverse leadership teams tend to prioritize social responsibility, employee well-being, and ethical governance, which correlates with higher ESG engagement (Glass et al., 2016; Cook & Glass, 2018). Additionally, studies show that corporate board diversity enhances sustainability performance on an international scale (Elsheikh et al., 2024). So, an emphasis on S of ESG has the potential to self-reinforce ESG initiatives, and contribute to improved implementation and effectiveness.

## 6.2 The Search for Meaningfulness and ESG Integration

An emerging perspective in sustainability research suggests that the pursuit of meaningfulness in work is a key driver of ESG engagement. As organizations move beyond profit maximization as their sole purpose, the search for meaning in business decision-making has gained increasing attention (Martela, & Pessi, 2018). For many entrepreneurs, ESG integration goes beyond business strategy, and aligns with their personal values and aspirations. The idea that work should be meaningful, socially beneficial, and incorporate a greater purpose has been widely explored in organizational psychology, with research suggesting that employees and founders alike experience higher job satisfaction and long-term commitment when they see their work as contributing to a broader societal good (Rosso et al., 2010). Founders who genuinely connect with ESG principles on a personal level are more likely to integrate sustainability into their companies not just for reputational reasons, but as an extension of their own search for meaning and purpose (Shepherd, & Patzelt, 2011). From the venture capitalists' perspective, some evidence suggests that the rise of impact investing and ESG-focused funds is partially driven by a desire among certain investors to align their financial decisions with their personal values (Agrawal & Hockerts, 2021). Institutional investors, family offices, and high-net-worth individuals with strong personal convictions about sustainability are increasingly directing capital toward ESG-aligned startups. This aligns with the broader "finance for good" movement, which seeks to redefine the role of capital in society beyond wealth accumulation (Eccles & Klimenko, 2019). Given startups' dependence on venture capitalists' funding, promoting, encouraging, and regulating their decisions towards ESG-oriented investments is likely to incentivize a more socially responsible startup ecosystem.

## 6.3 Barriers to ESG Implementation in Startups

Despite its strategic importance, embedding ESG into leadership and startup culture is far from straightforward. Achieving meaningful ESG integration requires more than good intentions; it demands a structured, multi-layered approach that aligns founder characteristics, digital capabilities, and institutional frameworks. Several challenges hinder this process, particularly for startups operating with resource constraints and high-risk environments.

a. **The ESG Data Dilemma: Overcoming "Acronym Soup":** One of the biggest obstacles to ESG adoption is data management. According to the World Business Council for Sustainable Development (WBCSD, 2022), data gaps, limited awareness, and risk assessment difficulties are among the top barriers to effective ESG execution. Companies struggle to track and report ESG performance due to the overwhelming number of frameworks, rankings, and indicators, often referred to as the "acronym soup" or "metrics madness" of sustainability reporting. With competing standards such as GRI, SASB, TCFD, CDP, IFRS, and SFDR, the lack of standardization creates inefficiencies that make it difficult to compare ESG performance across industries, complicate investor decision-making, and slow down sustainability progress. Without a unified approach to ESG data collection and reporting, many companies risk engaging in performative ESG exercises rather than implementing strategies that drive real impact.
b. **The Social Pillar: The Overlooked Component of ESG:** If sustainability research over the last few decades has taught us anything, it is that business sustainability is not just about carbon footprints or energy efficiency—it's also about people. Yet, while companies readily highlight their environmental efforts and economic sustainability, the social pillar of ESG is often neglected (Lemus-Aguilar et al., 2019). Issues such as employee well-being, diversity, equity, and inclusion (DEI) frequently receive less attention in corporate sustainability strategies. This imbalance raises ethical concerns, invites public skepticism, and contributes to workforce disengagement.

Employees, consumers, and investors are increasingly demanding corporate accountability on social issues such as fair labor practices, workplace diversity, and mental health initiatives. Organizations that fail to integrate the human element of ESG risk being perceived as performative or insincere, which is a growing concern amid criticisms of greenwashing and social washing in ESG reporting. A study published in Nature (Cai et al., 2024) reinforces this argument, showing that companies with strong ESG-driven HR strategies gain a competitive edge not only in ethical performance but also in market positioning. Incorporating sustainability into HR strategies isn't just about compliance—it's about fundamentally rethinking how companies engage, develop, and retain talent in the long run.

c. **The ESG-Financing Gap: Investment Trade-Offs for Startups:** Another major challenge is the disconnect between ESG aspirations and financial realities. While businesses acknowledge the long-term value of ESG-aligned investment, financial constraints and market norms often push them toward short-term, profit-driven funding sources. Zhang (2024) highlights this dilemma, showing that while founders recognize the reputational and strategic benefits of ESG-oriented investors, concerns over financial trade-offs make them hesitant. The KfW Capital and Boston Consulting Group report (2021) further underscores this issue, revealing that while two-thirds of venture capital firms claim to incorporate ESG into investment decisions, 60% of startups report that ESG topics are never even discussed with their investors. This misalignment suggests that many investors still prioritize traditional financial indicators over ESG performance, making it difficult for startups to justify sustainability investments in the short term.

d. **Digital Transformation as a Catalyst for ESG Success:** Amid these challenges, digital transformation is emerging as a crucial enabler of ESG effectiveness. Research by Niu et al. (2022) indicates that companies with strong digital capabilities are better equipped to manage ESG initiatives and drive innovation. Digital tools provide real-time data collection, predictive analytics, and automated reporting, enhancing decision-making, transparency, and compliance with regulatory standards. AI-powered analytics can identify ESG risks and opportunities, blockchain can enhance supply chain traceability, and IoT-based monitoring systems can track carbon footprints and workplace safety in real time. However, leaders must develop digital fluency to leverage these tools effectively, ensuring that technology-driven sustainability strategies translate into tangible business benefits.

## 7. CONCLUSION: THE FUTURE OF ESG-ORIENTED LEADERSHIP IN STARTUPS

For ESG to be more than a corporate buzzword, startups must integrate sustainability from the ground up. However, achieving this requires strong leadership, strategic investment in digital transformation, and more aligned investor incentives. ESG is not a solo effort; it thrives when startups, investors, and regulatory bodies collaborate to create an ecosystem where sustainability is not just a compliance requirement, but a true business driver. To overcome the persistent challenges in ESG adoption, leaders must take a proactive, strategic approach that moves beyond compliance and toward meaningful integration. ESG-oriented leadership should focus on the following:

1) Standardizing ESG Metrics: The fragmented ESG reporting landscape remains one of the biggest obstacles to effective sustainability implementation. Without standardized, universally accepted metrics, firms struggle to compare ESG performance, track progress, and communicate value to stakeholders. Policymakers, regulatory bodies, and industry leaders must harmonize reporting frameworks to create clearer, more comparable benchmarks that reduce confusion and enable informed decision-making (Cort & Esty, 2020)
2) Leveraging Digital Transformation for ESG Impact: Given the correlation between digital capabilities and ESG effectiveness, leaders must prioritize investments in technology-driven sustainability solutions. Big data analytics, AI-driven ESG insights, blockchain for supply chain transparency, and IoT-based monitoring systems can significantly enhance reporting accuracy, regulatory compliance, and risk assessment. Firms that fail to integrate digital tools into their ESG strategies risk inefficiencies, blind spots, and missed opportunities (Ding et al, 2024; Jiang, 2025).
3) Balancing ESG Dimensions: Too often, companies emphasize the economic and environmental pillars of ESG while neglecting the social dimension. To build a holistic and credible ESG strategy, firms must strengthen diversity, equity, and inclusion policies, invest in employee well-being, and foster authentic community engagement. Organizations that fail to integrate social sustainability risk workforce disengagement, reputational damage, and growing scrutiny from stakeholders (Sierdovski et al., 2022)

4) Supporting ESG in Startups: Startups operate under different constraints than established firms, yet current ESG evaluation metrics are often designed for large corporations. Investors and policymakers must develop startup-friendly ESG assessment frameworks that recognize early-stage resource limitations, industry-specific challenges, and long-term impact potential. Without context-sensitive ESG benchmarks, sustainability risks becoming an unattainable ideal for young ventures rather than an integrated business advantage (Bernow et al., 2017).
5) Developing ESG Leadership Competencies: Strong ESG outcomes depend on leaders who are equipped to navigate complex regulatory landscapes, engage stakeholders, and drive sustainability initiatives with clarity and conviction. Leadership development programs should incorporate cross-functional ESG training, digital fluency, ethical decision-making frameworks, and stakeholder management strategies (Pless at al., 2012).

ESG-oriented leadership is essential for navigating the evolving sustainability landscape despite existing and potential future challenges. While companies face data-related problems, inconsistent reporting standards, and imbalances in ESG focus, the strategic use of digital technologies, stakeholder engagement, and harmonized reporting frameworks can significantly enhance ESG adoption for both established corporations and start-up ventures.

We want to close this chapter on a hopeful note because despite the challenges, the future of sustainable entrepreneurship is full of possibility. As we worked on this chapter, the Global Entrepreneurship Report 2024/2025 was released, offering fresh insights from 56 economies worldwide (GEM, 2025). The findings are a stark reminder of the economic pressures shaping entrepreneurship today. According to global findings, more individuals are reporting declining household incomes, making both necessity and opportunity entrepreneurship increasingly critical for achieving UN's sustainable development goals such as reducing poverty, promoting decent work, and eliminating inequalities. Yet, starting and sustaining a business is becoming more difficult than ever. The report highlights a rising fear of failure, which has become a major barrier to entrepreneurial activity, deterring many from taking the leap. Even for those who do, the reality is sobering as business survival rates are declining. In addition, it is no longer enough to simply help entrepreneurs get started as the real challenge lies in helping them endure and scale. Financial barriers remain the number one reason entrepreneurs enter and exit the market, a finding that emphasizes the urgent need for more resilient, supportive, and inclusive startup ecosystems. And yet, there is hope. In 40 out of the 51 surveyed economies, more than half of early-stage entrepreneurs prioritize their social and environmental footprint over sheer profitability or growth. This shift is particularly pronounced in high-income economies and among women entrepreneurs, signaling a growing recognition that profit alone is not the ultimate measure of success. Startups are learning that when they prioritize social and environmental responsibility, they gain a competitive edge in attracting and retaining talent, especially among employees who seek workplaces aligned with their personal values. Sustainability is no longer just a moral or legal imperative. And in this realization lies the true promise of a better world: one where entrepreneurship is not only about innovation and economic gains, but also about creating lasting, positive change for people and the planet.

## 7.1 Our Response to the Initial Question: Does ESG-leadership Pay Off?

The title of a Harvard Business Review article from 2022 reads, "yes, investing in ESG pays off" (Polman, & Winston, 2022). We would like to echo the authors' claim, with only a slight twist that "maybe not on a large scale today, but it'll very soon". There are some mental hiccups that come in the way of sustainability investments for both major and smaller companies, but the way to building responsible business models is a matter of mindset, not just a matter of financial costs. Only when we are ready to collaborate for solving large-scale problems that are affecting our societies (such as climate change, inequality, clean tech economics, AI and etc.), will we be able to see the real payoffs from ESG initiatives. Until then, the answer to our question is not a simple yes or no, but rather a nuanced exploration of trade-offs, for in the short run, startups face financial and operational challenges but in the long run startups that incorporate ESG into their practices will develop greater resilience, stronger brand reputation, and better access to talent. The ESG-leadership itself is context- dependent with regional and industry-level variations but the future will hopefully belong to businesses that will position ESG at the forefront of their business model, operations, and strategic orientation. And that will be a world in which values-driven business models will be the new normal.

## REFERENCES


Abate, G., Basile, I., & Ferrari, P. (2021). The level of sustainability and mutual fund performance in Europe: An empirical analysis using ESG ratings. *Corporate Social Responsibility and Environmental Management*, *28*(5), 1446–1455. DOI: 10.1002/csr.2175

Abdou, K., & Gupta, P. (2024). Limited partners' contribution to venture capital fund returns: Newbies versus experienced. *Managerial Finance*, *50*(7), 1387–1406. DOI: 10.1108/MF-10-2023-0606

Agrawal, A., & Hockerts, K. (2021). Impact Investing: Review and Research Agenda. *Journal of Small Business and Entrepreneurship*, *33*(2), 153–181. DOI: 10.1080/08276331.2018.1551457

Al-Shammari, M., Rasheed, A., & Al-Shammari, H. A. (2019). CEO narcissism and corporate social responsibility: Does CEO narcissism affect CSR focus? *Journal of Business Research*, *104*(C), 106–117. DOI: 10.1016/j.jbusres.2019.07.005

Bain (2022). ESG, Not A Solo Game. Report prepared in collaboration with Türkiye Investment Office. Available at https://www.invest.gov.tr/en/library/publications/lists/investpublications/esg-not-a-solo-game .pdf. Accessed on February 1st, 2025.

Baker, M., Egan, M. L., & Sarkar, S. K. (2022). How do investors value ESG? (No. w30708). National Bureau of Economic Research. BCG and KfW Capital (2021).Growing the Seeds of ESG: Venture Capital, Start-ups and the Need for Sustainability. Available at: https://www.kfw-capital.de/Dokumente/ESG-Report-ESG-säen-Nachhaltigkeit-ernten-(Nov.-2021).pdf. Accessed on February 8th, 2025.

Berg, F., Jay, J., Kölbel, J., & Rigobon, R. (2023). The Signal In The Noise. *EconPol Forum.*, *1*(24), 23–27.

Bernow, S., Klempner, B., & Magnin, C. (2017). From 'why' to 'why not': Sustainable investing as the new normal. McKinsey & Company. Available at https://www.mckinsey.com/~/media/McKinsey/Industries/Private%20Equity%20and%20Principal%20Investors/Our%20Insights/From%20why%20to%20why%20not%20Sustainable%20investing%20as%20the%20new%20normal/From-why-to-why-not-Sustainable-investing-as-the-new-normal.pdf. Accessed on February 1st, 2025.

Bian, Y., Gao, H., Wang, R., & Xiong, X. (2023). Sustainable development for private equity: Integrating environment, social, and governance factors into partnership valuation. *Business Strategy and the Environment*, *32*(6), 3359–3370. DOI: 10.1002/bse.3304

Borghesi, R., Houston, J., & Naranjo, A. (2014). Corporate Socially Responsible Investments: CEO Altruism, Reputation, and Shareholder Interests. *Journal of Corporate Finance*, *26*, 164–181. DOI: 10.1016/j.jcorpfin.2014.03.008

Bos, T. (2023). The impact of ESG characteristics on startup valuation: An empirical study in the Venture Capital setting, Master thesis Delft University of Technology.

Botsari, A., & Lang, F. (2020). ESG considerations in venture capital and business angel investment decisions: Evidence from two pan-European surveys (No. 2020/63). EIF Working Paper.

Buallay, A. (2020). Sustainability reporting and firm's performance: Comparative study between manufacturing and banking sectors. *International Journal of Productivity and Performance Management, 69*(3), 431–445. DOI: 10.1108/IJPPM-10-2018-0371

Cai, X., Xiang, H., Neskorodieva, I., & Durmanov, A. (2024). Interrelation between human capital management and ESG engagement: Evidence from S&P 500 firms. *Humanities & Social Sciences Communications, 11*(1), 1654. DOI: 10.1057/s41599-024-04189-6

Calascione, V. (2023). Is Sustainability a Competitive Advantage? Unveiling the Relationship Between ESG Scores and Corporate Financial Performance in IT Startups., Università Ca' Foscari Venezia, https://unive.unitesi.cineca.it/handle/20.500.14247/17830

Cohen, B., Smith, B., & Mitchell, R. (2008). Toward a sustainable conceptualization of dependent variables in entrepreneurship research. *Business Strategy and the Environment, 17*(2), 107–119. DOI: 10.1002/bse.505

Cook, A., & Glass, C. (2018). Women on corporate boards: Do they advance corporate social responsibility? *Human Relations, 71*(7), 897–924. DOI: 10.1177/0018726717729207

Cort, T., & Esty, D. (2020). ESG standards: Looming challenges and pathways forward. *Organization & Environment, 33*(4), 491–510. DOI: 10.1177/1086026620945342

Council, E. U. (2024). Environmental, social and governance (ESG) ratings: Council greenlights new regulation. Press Release, https://www.consilium.europa.eu/en/press/press-releases/2024/11/19/environmental-social-and-governance-esg-ratings-council-greenlights-new-regulation/

Crunchbase (2025). Startup Funding Regained Its Footing In 2024 As AI Became The Star Of The Show, https://news.crunchbase.com/venture/global-funding-data-analysis-ai-eoy-2024/#:~:text=Overall%20startup%20funding%20in%202024,billion%20and%20%24350%20billion%2C%20respectively

Dean, T. J., & McMullen, J. S. (2007). Toward a theory of sustainable entrepreneurship: Reducing environmental degradation through entrepreneurial action. *Journal of Business Venturing, 22*(1), 50–76. DOI: 10.1016/j.jbusvent.2005.09.003

Dean, T. J., & McMullen, J. S. (2007). Toward a theory of sustainable entrepreneurship: Reducing environmental degradation through entrepreneurial action. *Journal of Business Venturing, 22*(1), 50–76. DOI: 10.1016/j.jbusvent.2005.09.003

Ding, X., Sheng, Z., Appolloni, A., Shahzad, M., & Han, S. (2024). Digital transformation, ESG practice, and total factor productivity. *Business Strategy and the Environment, 33*(5), 4547–4561. DOI: 10.1002/bse.3718

Dirik, D., & Özdoğan, B. (2025). To start or not to start? An exploratory study of work meaningfulness among start-up co-founders. *Frontiers in Psychology, 15*, 1500036. DOI: 10.3389/fpsyg.2024.1500036 PMID: 39949976

Eccles, G. R., & Klimenko, S. (2019). The Investor Revolution. *Harvard Business Review, 97*, 106–116.

El Ghoul, S., & Karoui, A. (2022). Fund performance and social responsibility: New evidence using social active share and social tracking error. *Journal of Banking & Finance*, *143*, 106598. DOI: 10.1016/j.jbankfin.2022.106598

El Ghoul, S., Karoui, A., Patel, S., & Ramani, S. (2023). The green and brown performances of mutual fund portfolios. *Journal of Cleaner Production*, *384*, 135267. DOI: 10.1016/j.jclepro.2022.135267

Elkington, J. (1998). Accounting for the triple bottom line. *Measuring Business Excellence*, *2*(3), 18–22. DOI: 10.1108/eb025539

Elsheikh, T., Almaqtari, F. A., Al-Hattami, H. M., Al-Bukhrani, M. A., & Ettish, A. A. (2024). The moderating effect of women in boardrooms on the relationship between control of corruption and corporate sustainability performance. *Discover Sustainability*, *5*(1), 502. DOI: 10.1007/s43621-024-00490-1

Fatemi, A., Glaum, M., & Kaiser, S. (2018). ESG performance and firm value: The moderating role of disclosure. *Global Finance Journal*, *38*, 45–64. DOI: 10.1016/j.gfj.2017.03.001

Fonseca, A., Abreu, I., & Silvestre, W. J. (2021). Investigating context factors in the strategic management of corporate sustainability integration. *Journal of Cleaner Production*, *314*, 128002. DOI: 10.1016/j.jclepro.2021.128002

Friede, G., Busch, T., & Bassen, A. (2015). ESG and financial performance: Aggregated evidence from more than 2000 empirical studies. *Journal of Sustainable Finance & Investment*, *5*(4), 210–233. DOI: 10.1080/20430795.2015.1118917

GEM (Global Entrepreneurship Monitor). (2023). *Global Entrepreneurship Monitor 2023/2024 Global Report: 25 Years and Growing*. GEM.

GEM (Global Entrepreneurship Monitor). (2025). GEM 2024/2025 Global report: Entrepreneurship reality check. Available at https://gemconsortium.org/report/gem-20242025-global-report-entrepreneurship-reality-check-4. Accessed on February 19th, 2025.

Glass, C., Cook, A., & Ingersoll, A. R. (2016). Do women leaders promote sustainability? Analyzing the effect of corporate governance composition on environmental performance. *Business Strategy and the Environment*, *25*(7), 495–511. DOI: 10.1002/bse.1879

Haber, S., Kepler, J. D., Larcker, D. F., Seru, A., & Tayan, B. (2022). ESG Investing: What Shareholders Do Fund Managers Represent? Rock Center for Corporate Governance at Stanford University Working Paper Forthcoming, Stanford University Graduate School of Business Research Paper, (4267270).

Hemingway, C. A., & Maclagan, P. W. (2004). Managers' Personal Values as Drivers of Corporate Social Responsibility. *Journal of Business Ethics*, *50*(1), 33–44. DOI: 10.1023/B:BUSI.0000020964.80208.c9

Hoogendoorn, B., Van der Zwan, P., & Thurik, R. (2019). Sustainable entrepreneurship: The role of perceived barriers and risk. *Journal of Business Ethics*, *157*(4), 1133–1154. DOI: 10.1007/s10551-017-3646-8

Hornberger, K. (2023). The difference between ESG and impact investing and why it matters. In *Scaling Impact: Finance and Investment for a Better World* (pp. 93–112). Springer International Publishing. DOI: 10.1007/978-3-031-22614-4_8

Huang, Y., Li, P., Bu, Y., & Zhao, G. (2023). What entrepreneurial ecosystem elements promote sustainable entrepreneurship? *Journal of Cleaner Production*, *422*, 138459. DOI: 10.1016/j.jclepro.2023.138459

ISO. (2024). IWA 48 Framework for Implementing Environmental, Social and Governance (ESG) Principles. https://www.iso.org/obp/ui/en/#iso:std:iso:iwa:48:ed-1:v1:en

Jiang, F. (2025). Digital transformation and green innovation: The mediating role of green management disclosure and the moderating role of institutional pressure. *Journal of General Management*, *0*(0), 03063070241308100. Advance online publication. DOI: 10.1177/03063070241308100

Jones, J. (2022). How Elon Musk is adding fuel to growing criticism about ESG ratings. Globe & Mail (Toronto, Canada), B1. Gale Academic OneFile, link.gale.com/apps/doc/A704659964/AONE?u=anon~919cbd94&sid=googleScholar&xid=8ae5dbfe

Khan, M. A. (2022). ESG disclosure and firm performance: A bibliometric and meta analysis. *Research in International Business and Finance*, *61*, 101668. DOI: 10.1016/j.ribaf.2022.101668

Kuzmina, J., Atstaja, D., Purvins, M., Baakashvili, G., & Chkareuli, V. (2023). In search of sustainability and financial returns: The case of ESG energy funds. Sustainability, 15, 3, 2716.

Lange, E. M., & Banadaki, N. G. (2024). ESG consideration in venture capital: Drivers, strategies and barriers. *Studies in Economics and Finance*, *41*(3), 724–739. DOI: 10.1108/SEF-06-2023-0380

Lemus-Aguilar, I., Morales-Alonso, G., Ramirez-Portilla, A., & Hidalgo, A. (2019). Sustainable Business Models through the Lens of Organizational Design: A Systematic Literature Review. Sustainability, 11, 19, 5379. https://doi.org/DOI: 10.3390/su11195379

Leoni, L. (2024). Integrating ESG and organizational resilience through system theory: the ESGOR matrix. Management Decision. Vol. ahead-of-print No. ahead-of-print. https://doi.org/DOI: 10.1108/MD-10-2023-1924

Lin, L. (2022). Venture capital in the rise of sustainable investment. *European Business Organization Law Review*, *23*(1), 187–216. DOI: 10.1007/s40804-021-00238-8

Lino, M., Connolly, L., Hoverman, D., McCoy, D., Schey, M., & Anders, S. (2022). *Limited partners and private equity firms embrace ESG*. Bain & Company.

Lumpkin, G. T., & Dess, G. G. (1996). Clarifying the entrepreneurial orientation construct and linking it to performance. *Academy of Management Review*, *21*(1), 135–172. DOI: 10.2307/258632

Mansouri, S., & Momtaz, P. P. (2022). Financing sustainable entrepreneurship: ESG measurement, valuation, and performance. Journal of Business Venturing, 37, 6, 106258.

Martela, F., & Pessi, A. B. (2018). Significant work is about self-realization and broader purpose: Defining the key dimensions of meaningful work. *Frontiers in Psychology*, *9*, 363. Advance online publication. DOI: 10.3389/fpsyg.2018.00363 PMID: 29632502

Meles, A. (2021). Venture Capital and Responsible Investing: Progress, Problems and Perspectives. In: The Evolution of Sustainable Investments and Finance. Palgrave Macmillan, Cham. https://doi.org/DOI: 10.1007/978-3-030-70350-9_5

Mervelskemper, L., & Streit, D. (2017). Enhancing market valuation of ESG performance: Is integrated reporting keeping its promise? *Business Strategy and the Environment*, *26*(4), 536–549. DOI: 10.1002/bse.1935

Milonas, N., Rompotis, G., & Moutzouris, C. (2022). The performance of ESG funds vis-à-vis non-ESG funds. *The Journal of Impact and ESG Investing*, *2*(4), 96–115. DOI: 10.3905/jesg.2022.1.041

Niu, S., Park, B. I., & Jung, J. S. (2022). The effects of digital leadership and ESG management on organizational innovation and sustainability. Sustainability, 14, 23, 15639. https://doi.org/DOI: 10.3390/su142315639

Petridis, K., Kiosses, N., Tampakoudis, I., & Ben Abdelaziz, F. (2023). Measuring the efficiency of mutual funds: Does ESG controversies score affect the mutual fund performance during the COVID-19 pandemic? Operational research, 23, 3, 54.

Pless, N. M., Maak, T., & Stahl, G. K. (2012). Promoting corporate social responsibility and sustainable development through management development: What can be learned from international service-learning programs? *Human Resource Management*, *51*(6), 873–903. DOI: 10.1002/hrm.21506

Polman, P., & Winston, A. (2022). Yes, investing in ESG pays off. Harvard Business Review. Available at: https://hbr.org/2022/04/yes-investing-in-esg-pays-off. Accessed on January 10th, 2025.

PRI. U. (2024). Principles for responsible investment—Annual report 2024. https://www.unpri.org/about-us/about-the-pri/annual-report

Raghunandan, A., & Rajgopal, S. (2022). Do ESG funds make stakeholder-friendly investments? *Review of Accounting Studies*, *27*(3), 822–863. DOI: 10.1007/s11142-022-09693-1

Rosso, B. D., Dekas, K. H., & Wrzesniewski, A. (2010). On the Meaning of Work: A Theoretical Integration and Review. *Research in Organizational Behavior*, *30*, 91–127. DOI: 10.1016/j.riob.2010.09.001

Schaltegger, S., & Wagner, M. (2011). Sustainable entrepreneurship and sustainability innovation: Categories and interactions. *Business Strategy and the Environment*, *20*(4), 222–237. DOI: 10.1002/bse.682

Shepherd, D. A., & Patzelt, H. (2011). The New Field of Sustainable Entrepreneurship: Studying Entrepreneurial Action Linking "What is to be Sustained" with "What is to be Developed". *Entrepreneurship Theory and Practice*, *35*(1), 137–163. DOI: 10.1111/j.1540-6520.2010.00426.x

Sierdovski, M., Pilatti, L. A., & Rubbo, P. (2022). Organizational competencies in the development of environmental, social, and governance (ESG) criteria in the industrial sector. Sustainability, 14, 20, 13463. https://doi.org/DOI: 10.3390/su142013463

Singh, R., & Tarkar, P. (2024). An empirical analysis on sustainable start-up: Embedding Environmental, Social and Governance (ESG) into high growth business strategy. *Brazilian Journal of Operations & Production Management*, *21*(3), 1810–1810. DOI: 10.14488/BJOPM.1810.2024

Slawinski, N., & Bansal, P. (2015). Short on Time: Intertemporal Tensions in Business Sustainability. *Organization Science*, *26*(2), 531–549. DOI: 10.1287/orsc.2014.0960

Sreenivasan, A., & Suresh, M. (2023). Exploring the contribution of sustainable entrepreneurship towards sustainable development goals: A bibliometric analysis. Green Technologies and Sustainability, 100038.

Taneja, H., & Chenault, K. (2019). Building a startup that will last. *Harvard Business Review*, *7*, 23–27.

Wang, H. (2024). ESG investment preference and fund vulnerability. *International Review of Financial Analysis*, *91*, 103002. DOI: 10.1016/j.irfa.2023.103002

Wang, H., Jiao, S., & Ma, C. (2024). The impact of ESG responsibility performance on corporate resilience. *International Review of Economics & Finance*, *93*, 1115–1129. DOI: 10.1016/j.iref.2024.05.033

Wang, J., Ke, Y., & Shen, Y. (2023). Venture Capital and ESG Performance: Hindrance or Help? *Economic Computation and Economic Cybernetics Studies and Research*, *57*(4/2023), 4. DOI: 10.24818/18423264/57.4.23.16

WBCSD. (2022). Roadmap to ESG leadership. Available at https://www.wbcsd.org/wp-content/uploads/2023/10/Roadmap-to-ESG-Leadership-English.pdf. Accessed on February 12th, 2025.

World Economic Forum. (2022). ESG Pulse Check: Getting the Basics Right for Start-ups and Venture Capital Firms. Insight Report. Available at https://www3.weforum.org/docs/WEF_ESG_Pulse_Check_2022.pdf. Accessed on February, 10th, 2025.

Xiong, Q., Fosfuri, A., Misani, N., & Cheng, Y. (2024). Greening the Portfolio: LP Preferences for Social Impact and Sustainability Orientation of VC Funds. In Academy of Management Proceedings (Vol. 2024, No. 1, p. 16245). Valhalla, NY 10595: Academy of Management.

Yuan, Y., Tian, G., Lu, L., & Yu, Y. (2019). CEO Ability and Corporate Social Responsibility. *Journal of Business Ethics*, *157*(2), 391–411. DOI: 10.1007/s10551-017-3622-3

Zhang, Ye. (2022). Startups' Strategies for ESG Funding Adoption. Available at *SSRN*: https://ssrn.com/abstract=4239239 or http://dx.doi.org/DOI: 10.2139/ssrn.4239239

Zhang, Z., Wang, X., & Jia, M. (2021). Echoes of CEO Entrepreneurial Orientation: How and When CEO Entrepreneurial Orientation Influences Dual CSR Activities. *Journal of Business Ethics*, *169*(4), 609–629. DOI: 10.1007/s10551-020-04553-x

# Chapter 19
# From Theory to Practice:
## Developing Green Skills Through Social Economy and Higher Education

**Amanda Aliende Da Matta**
https://orcid.org/0000-0003-0972-0242
*University of Barcelona, Spain*

**Mihaela Vancea**
https://orcid.org/0000-0002-7970-1322
*University of Barcelona, Spain*

**Lukas Valek**
https://orcid.org/0000-0003-4267-6538
*Prague University of Economics and Business, Czech Republic*

**Olga Valkova Tarasova**
*Prague University of Economics and Busines, Czech Republic*

## ABSTRACT

*This chapter presents lessons from the SDG Labs project, a transnational initiative fostering green skills by integrating social economy entities and higher education. Through socially driven green Labs, the project explored innovative educational methods, including Living Labs, simulation-based learning, and participatory co-creation. Findings highlight gaps between theoretical environmental knowledge and practical sustainability skills. While social economy entities grasp basic concepts like the circular economy, advanced green competencies—such as environmental impact assessment—are less integrated. Effective interventions involve hands-on learning through green business simulations and multi-stakeholder collaboration Institutional barriers, including limited policy support and regulatory challenges, often hinder scaling sustainable projects. Addressing these requires strengthening institutional frameworks and enhancing environmental literacy. The project underscores the need to align education with social economy demands, setting a benchmark for knowledge-driven green economies*

DOI: 10.4018/979-8-3373-0189-1.ch019

# 1. INTRODUCTION

The visible consequences of climate change have brought about increasing pressure toward a paradigm shift that accounts for the complex consequences of environmental and social crises. This shift emphasises the need for a more inclusive and ecological transition, driven by the Social Economy sector. Social economy entities (SEEs) such as social enterprises, cooperatives, mutual societies, and non-profit associations, play a crucial role in this green transformation. They introduce and develop innovative solutions and operate in an inclusive-ecological-transition-drive role in areas such as the circular economy, renewable energy, sustainable agriculture, and social housing.

The presence of SEEs is also significant at the level of intersectoral cooperation, involving collaborations with enterprises and citizens. In this context, the role of education emerges as paramount. Higher education institutions (HEIs) have a particular responsibility to build students' green knowledge, skills, and competencies. By doing so, they harness the opportunity to contribute to the full potential of SEEs towards a green transition. However, there are notable deficiencies in how HEIs align their curricula and syllabi with the requirements of environmental sustainability and the increasing demand for green skills in SEEs. Innovation in education, through specific training programs and innovative teaching methodologies such as simulation-based learning, is key to addressing these deficiencies and aligning with the paradigm shift towards a green transition.

In this sense, the SDG Labs project was created to explore these aspects in-depth and provide a comprehensive analysis of the role of SEEs in the green transition, the importance of green skills, and the critical role of education in developing these skills. The project introduces the concept of Socially Driven Green Labs (SDG Labs) as a framework for fostering green skills and promoting sustainable practices within universities and beyond.

## 1.1. Green Transition and Green Growth

Climate change and economic crises since the early 2000s have drawn attention to the need for a sustainable future, prompting transnational organisations and local governments to implement green transition and green growth frameworks. According to the Global Green Growth Institute (2016, p 6-8), green growth is structured around four fundamental dimensions and encompasses ten key priorities.

The four fundamental dimensions of green growth are:

- Efficient and sustainable use of resources, including energy, water, land, and materials.
- Protection of natural capital and recognition of the limits of Earth system processes.
- Green economic opportunities for investment, trade, employment, and innovation.
- Inclusive growth which ensures access to basic services and resources, health and safety, social equality, and social protection.

The ten key priorities are:

- Shifting away from and replacing the conventional, resource-intensive model of economic growth with green growth.
- Implementation of appropriate green growth strategies, policies, and plans.
- Ensuring the green transformation is just, fair, and inclusive.

- Achieving zero-emissions targets.
- Embracing sustainable energy and scaling back the use of fossil fuels or replacing them altogether.
- Reversing land degradation and the decline of ecosystem and biodiversity.
- Smarter, cleaner, and more efficient and productive ways of managing water resources.
- Green transformation in cities.
- Greening infrastructure and construction in cities.
- Green technology disruptions and smart solutions.

This transformation is intrinsically linked to the green economy, which encompasses low-carbon, circular, and blue economies. A low-carbon economy focuses on reducing greenhouse gas emissions, promoting renewable energy, and enhancing energy efficiency. A circular economy shifts from a linear production-consumption model to one prioritising sharing, leasing, reusing, repairing, refurbishing, and recycling. The blue economy includes economic activities linked to oceans, seas, and coastal regions.

A successful green transition implies systemic efforts from governments, enterprises, and non-governmental organisations, each complementing the other's role in sustainability initiatives. This chapter further explores the contributions of social enterprises and green entrepreneurship in this transformative process.

## 1.2. Social and Green Entrepreneurship

Social entrepreneurship involves the provision of goods and services that neither the market nor the public sector is willing or able to supply. It contributes to skill development, employment generation, workspace management, and enhanced civic engagement (Smallbone et al., 2001). Essentially, social enterprises employ business strategies to tackle social or environmental challenges (Rhoden, 2014).

According to Nyssens (2006), social entrepreneurship gained prominence in the 1970s and 1980s and garnered significant attention from governments and academia by the 1990s. The 2000s witnessed the rise of notable social entrepreneurs, including Muhammad Yunus, founder of the Grameen Bank for Microfinance and recipient of the 2006 Nobel Prize, and Jeffrey Skoll, founder of the Skoll Foundation and one of Time Magazine's 100 People of the Year 2006.

During this period, international frameworks addressing climate change and economic crises further emphasised the necessity of a green transition. Some of those documents are United Nation Environment's "green stimulus packages", the UN Department of Economic and Social Affairs' 2012 Guidebook to the Green Economy, and European Union's "Europe 2020" in which smart, sustainable and inclusive growth is promoted. In this favourable context, social enterprises have become the fastest-growing category of organisations (Jain, 2019).

The success and growth of social enterprises are aligned with their potential: due to their small-scale and low-cost solutions, they adapt to their local contexts and can help the public sector be innovative and more cost-effective. At their essence lies the *Triple Bottom Line*: associating the generation of profit (standard bottom line) with positive social and environmental impact, with the objective of generating more social wealth than economic wealth. These organisations strategically respond to the frailties of the public and philanthropic sectors (Kong, 2010), contributing to creating social capital to promote more advanced social interactions and learning processes in diverse societies (Hasan, 2005).

Among social enterprises, green entrepreneurship strives to neutralise practices that damage the environment. This means promoting more meaningful and responsible choices and letting go of easy ones, such as bicycling instead of driving a car. Strategies are, for example, launching new products and creating new markets for environmentally friendly solutions. Green enterprises integrate the change they promote in their day-to-day practice, not only advocating a different perspective but modelling one. In doing so, they can trigger a "cascade of mutually reinforcing changes that create and sustain transformed social environments" (Alvord et al., 2004, p. 262). With their ethos and structures, they empower their members and beneficiaries to act according to the aims, virtues and practices of a green economy.

## 1.3. Green Skills

To conduct the paradigm transformation necessary for social and environmental changes, there need to be changes in regulation, financial instruments, planning and management, educational activities, etc. SEEs may promote these changes but implementing them requires new green skills.

Green skills, also known as skills for sustainability, are defined as the technical skills, knowledge, values and attitudes needed in the workforce to develop and support sustainable social, economic and environmental outcomes in business, industry and the community (COAG, 2009). Their core is that they allow for bringing profits without jeopardising natural ecosystems and ensuring sustainable economic growth and development.

According to the OECD (2010), working skills can be classified as into three categories: basic skills (including generic skills such as numeracy and literacy and routine skills such as making copies or packing in a factory), advanced/knowledge-intensive skills (technical, management, social and communication or multi-language and cultural skills), and converging skills (entrepreneurial and green skills).

Entrepreneurial skills are specific skills for creating and running new business ventures and innovative projects in existing firms. These include risk assessment and warranting, strategic thinking, self-confidence, the ability to leverage personal networks, motivating others to achieve common goals, co-operation for success, and the ability to deal with various challenges and requirements faced by entrepreneurs. Green skills, on the other hand, are specific skills needed to modify products, services or operations due to climate change adjustments, requirements or regulations. Examples include water purification and site remediation planning/engineering in mining, solar panels installation, wind turbines design, green management, and carbon capture and storage techniques (OECD, 2010, p. 164).

Every job has the potential to become more environmentally friendly. The first step is incorporating sustainable development and environmental awareness into education and training at all levels, beginning with early childhood education. This approach helps shift consumer behaviour and stimulate market forces to advance the green agenda. Employers who invest in new technologies need access to workers with the appropriate skills. Additionally, workers and communities affected by job losses in traditional industries need opportunities to acquire new skills and find employment (Strietska-Illina et al., 2011).

A green transition requires a whole system transformation. Existing jobs need to incorporate ethics and sustainability, relying on varying degrees of new expertise and new technical skills. Existing industries also need to create new jobs that arise, for example, from climate change adaptation initiatives, and which require a new mix of technical skills and ethics. Additionally, new and expanded industries require a combination of existing and new technical skills and ethics. Furthermore, new and expanded industries create new professions within existing industries and activity sectors, for which technical skills and ethics are yet to be developed.

Therefore, there are at least three ways greening economies affect skills needs: green expanded skills occupations (GESOs), green new and emerging occupations (GNEOs), and green increased demand occupations (GIDOs) (CEDEFOP, 2012). GESOs refer to the greening of existing occupations, adapting current jobs and professional profiles, which also requires training. GNEOs refer to the development of new occupations: entirely new economic activities that require appropriate training and the adaptation of qualification and training systems. GIDOs refer to the shifts between industries that workers will experience, requiring them to move from sectors and occupations in decline to those that are growing (Figure 1).

*Figure 1. Reasons for the need for green skills in the transition to a green economy*

*Source: Own elaboration, adapted from Kowalska et al., 2021, p. 10*

All skills will need to become greener or to adapt to a green economy, and any area of knowledge will require skills creation and transformation. Design, leadership, management, city and landscape planning, energy, financial, procurement, waste management, and communications will all require new ways of working that integrate new materials and exclude old ones, operate new tools and machinery, and minimise negative outcomes such as energy consumption.

In each phase of the green transition (from brown to low carbon, to circular, to green economy), the specificities of the needed green skills will be different. The green economy also requires adaptability and transferability, systems and risk analysis, entrepreneurship, innovation, marketing, consulting, networking, information technology (IT), and language skills (Strietska-Ilina et al., 2011).

## 1.4. The Role of Education in Developing Green Skills

Education, particularly higher education, has the potential to teach and promote green skills along with the knowledge, values, and attitudes necessary for a green transition. Attributes such as empathy, moral obligation, social entrepreneurship ideals, and self-efficacy can motivate students toward meaningful change.

Higher education institutions (HEIs) play a crucial role in embedding sustainability into curricula. Education involves not only the transmission of abstract knowledge (such as definitions, frameworks and theories) but also the cultivation of spirit, predisposition, mindset, passion, skills, and readiness to engage. Learning is both a cognitive and a social process (Gherardi et al., 1998) that requires collective and independent actions. According to Bandura (1971) and other social learning theorists, people learn through observing, imitating, and modelling behaviours. Hockerts (2018) emphasises that students must acquire knowledge, then enact certain practices, and finally reflect on them and the learning process.

In this context, several practices and methodologies are key for social enterprise and green learning. One effective approach is combining problem or project-based learning with the creation of communities of practice. Problem or project-based learning helps students actively engage in real-world and meaningful projects or problems, fostering critical thinking, collaboration, and practical application of knowledge. Communities of practice, on the other hand, are informal, self-organising social systems that benefit from deliberate cultivation, leadership, and sponsorship to thrive and gain legitimacy (Wenger 2008). By integrating these communities with problem or project-based learning, students are divided into small working groups and receive tasks to complete. After completion, they return to the whole group to exchange ideas, ask questions, critique, discuss, and develop consensus. Through this process, students take an active role and participate in the co-creation of the learning experience.

Another effective methodology is the use of laboratory spaces for social entrepreneurship. In these spaces, students engage in real-world situations, observing and reflecting on them, interacting with social enterprise managers, and getting involved in solving real social problems. This practice not only develops social entrepreneurship skills and values but also promotes easier integration of students within the social economy.

Based on this theoretical framework, the SDG Labs project was developed as a transnational initiative to foster green skills development by integrating SEEs and HEIs.

## 2. DIAGNOSING DEFICIENCIES AND OPPORTUNITIES

For the development of the SDG Labs Educational Programme, Kowalska et al. (2022) diagnosed the green skills within the social economy sector and higher education institutions, as well as the cooperation opportunities between these sectors. The study explored three key questions: the extent to which social economy entities (SEE) possess and develop green skills, the gaps in collaboration between SEEs and HEIs, and the effectiveness of higher education in fostering sustainability competencies. Data was collected from 80 social enterprises, 25 university teachers, and 50 students from four partner countries (Belgium, Czechia, Greece, and Poland) through surveys, in-depth interviews, and case studies.

The first research question—"To what extent do social economy entities (SEEs) possess and develop green skills adequately to market needs?"—was addressed through the verification of the research hypotheses H1, which proposed that SEEs, despite their engagement in green initiatives, lack significant competencies in green skills relevant to the market. The findings confirmed this hypothesis, revealing that while many SEEs incorporate sustainability-oriented activities, they struggle with key skill gaps. Although 65,4% of SEEs were familiar with the term green skills, the possibility of acquiring these skills in the workplace was assessed as average and mostly related to soft skills (such as adaptability to future challenges, creativity, and resilience awareness), which does not indicate a green business mindset. Additionally, few circular behaviours were adopted.

The second research question—"Are there any cooperation gaps between social economy entities (SEEs) and educational institutions in the field?"—was analysed through the verification of the research hypothesis H2, which suggested that deficiencies in green skills within SEEs create barriers to cross-sectoral cooperation and hinder the acquisition of circular business projects. This hypothesis was partially rejected. The study identified that external or technical barriers, such as bureaucracy (54,35), institutional constraints (41,9%), and lack of appropriate legal frameworks (39,55), are the main factors hindering SEEs from fully integrating green practices into their operations. These barriers are more significant than the lack of environmental knowledge among members (28,4%) or a lack of organisational skills (16%). Additionally, 74% of SEE representatives declared that they were not able to generate revenue through their green economy activities.

The third research question—"Does the higher education system provide real support for the acquisition and development of green skills?"—was examined through the verification of the research hypothesis H3, which proposed that existing educational programmes require modifications to effectively support green skills development and drive the green transformation. The research findings validated this hypothesis, demonstrating that while universities play a crucial role in sustainability education, their current curricula are insufficient in equipping students with the necessary green skills. Most students were not familiar with the term "green skills" (40% didn't know it and 26% weren't sure), and 58.9% didn't report seeing it in study programmes. The number of teachers unfamiliar with the term "green skills" was lower, though still high: 39,4% didn't know it and 12,1% weren't sure. Both students and teachers related green skills mostly to production, transport and storage, implying a technical rather than a holistic understanding. Only 15,1% of teachers evaluated the green skills acquired in their courses. A high percentage of teachers (over 30%) and students (49,6%) assessed that programmes remain overly theoretical, with limited emphasis on practical applications. Teachers pointed to the need for more practice (27,2%) and group work, while students (34,04%) claimed they do not work on enough case studies.

The research identified significant deficiencies in green skills education, a disconnect between academia and market needs, and barriers such as bureaucracy and institutional constraints that hinder green innovation in SEEs. The findings emphasise the necessity of curriculum reform, experiential learning approaches (such as Living Labs and simulation-based education), and stronger university-industry partnerships to effectively support sustainability-driven entrepreneurship. This research serves as the conceptual groundwork for SDG Labs, informing its pedagogical strategies and operational framework to drive systemic change in higher education and the social economy sector.

## 3. THE SDG LABS EDUCATIONAL PROGRAMME FRAMEWORK

The SDG Labs Educational Programme, developed by Kowalska et al. (2022), was designed to address the diagnosed needs, presented in the previous section. By incorporating methodologies such as Living Labs and simulation-based learning, the SDG Labs initiative sets a benchmark for future projects that aim to integrate social entrepreneurship with environmental stewardship, ensuring that sustainability becomes a core element of higher education and economic transition strategies. An innovative approach was used during the summer school activity with the use of non-formal learning participative methods (Brown et al., 2020; Klockner, 2009; Tarasova et al., 2020) and co-creation with students (Glumac, 2018) to analyse the needs of students in green and social economy education. More about the summer school in part 3.3.

### 3.1. The Conceptual Model for Sustainability

The basis for the SDG Labs is a conceptual model of evolution towards sustainable entrepreneurship, which emphasises green competencies. According to this framework, citizens first enter an awareness field, then a competencies field, and finally enter an active responsibility field. The dynamism of the process involves green transformation through evolving green competencies alongside social participation and civil responsibility (Figure 2).

*Figure 2. Framework for the evolution towards sustainable entrepreneurship*

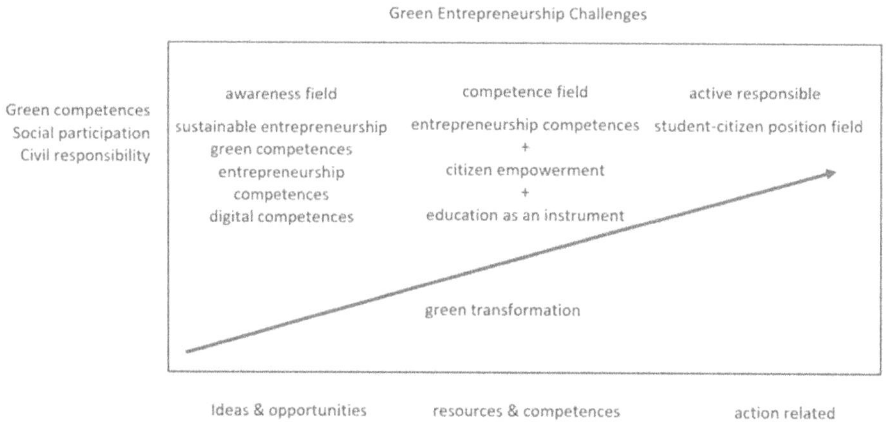


*Source: Own elaboration, adapted from Mets et al., 2021, p. 15.*

In the first level, the awareness field, people identify the need for environmental action as crucial for fighting global climate change. The core of this level consists of ideas and opportunities. According to Flynn et al. (2021, p. 9), a person's educational background is identified as "the most profound socio-demographic driver" for demanding climate action. Citizens in this field acquire digital, entrepreneurial, and finally sustainable entrepreneurship competencies.

In the competencies field, education serves as an instrument of citizen empowerment through entrepreneurship competencies. At the core of this field are resources and competences, and people move from demanding change to actively participating in it and understanding the potential influence of their contributions. Students in this field can work through case studies, field visits, inquiries, interactions, and cooperation with practitioners, designing self-reliant organisations with a leadership orientation to create new eco-friendly goods and practices.

Finally, in the active responsibility field, knowledge acquisition becomes a social experience, one that is shared rather than appropriated or owned. Learners are expected to share responsibility for the learning of others, to resonate with other students, support others in expanding their self-awareness, participate more deeply in interdependent communities, and expand the boundaries of empathy. Skills developed in this field include accepting criticism, empathy, and a motivational displacement towards helping others.

## 3.2. The Living Laboratories Methodology

The living laboratories are open, community designed ecosystems that promote the escalation of social innovation and business through simulation-based learning, where students experience co-creation, rapid prototyping, and validation. The core objectives pf applying the living labs methodology are the integration of HEI and SEE communities with society, the promotion of a greater matching of green skills, and the establishment of a common "language" among the target groups.

The methodology is based on a three-element framework: exploration, experimentation, and evaluation (Malberg et al., 2017), applied to issues such as renewable energy, sustainable housing, sustainable food systems, or the circular economy. The educational programme is multi-disciplinary and challenge-driven, promoting green competencies. It is based on multiple approaches: user-cantered methodologies, participatory research, co-design, user engagement, and the participation of all stakeholders (students, teachers, and social economy entities).

At the beginning of its implementation, various tools and strategies are applied. First, a digital repository is made available with case studies, co-creation activities, resources, and lecture plans. Then, teachers are trained, for example, through MOOCs about the Social Economy for a green transition. The educational community experiences simulation-based learning, working with green business models. Finally, they go through an academic programme, such as a summer school, which incorporates theoretical and practical elements of green skills literacy.

The living labs then unfold in four phases. First, at the defining stage, an introductory lecture is presented on sustainability issues and green business areas. Second, at the ideation stage, students implement the SDG business canvas to design socially driven green business solutions. Third, at the experimenting stage, SEE partners accompany students in testing their ideas using business simulation models. Finally, at the validation stage, participants identify areas for further improvement.

### 3.3. The SDG Labs Educational Programme

The SDG Labs Educational Programme incorporates blended learning, flexible training, and multi stakeholder cooperation to design an innovative and holistic educational programme that offers HEI teachers and students in SE-related fields all the necessary skills, methodologies, and knowledge to foster the next generation of green social entrepreneurs. It aims to (i) respond to the current and future green skills shortages in SEEs, (ii) provide an online repository supporting social and green entrepreneurial competence development, (iii) equip HEI teachers with the necessary training to incorporate environmental-related issues into SE curricula, and (iv) train students with the knowledge and skills that required in the green labour market.

The programme features four innovative outputs, addressed at HEI students and teachers. First, the SDG Labs Digital Gallery, an online depository of interactive teaching materials on environmental studies, aimed at the entire educational community. Then, for teachers, a capacity-building programme that includes a MOOC and training workshops. For students, business simulations and online and on-campus learning programme are provided

The SDG Labs Digital Gallery is an interactive online repository designed to support higher education teachers and students in developing green skills and fostering sustainability-driven social entrepreneurship. It serves as a one-stop shop for teaching materials on environmental studies, providing open educational resources (OERs), case studies, articles, videos, and co-creation activities that enhance learning and engagement. The gallery follows clear pedagogical principles, ensuring that the materials are accessible, interactive, and aligned with current environmental and climate change debates. Additionally, it includes a digital package of lecture plans to facilitate the integration of social and green entrepreneurial competencies into SE curricula.

The SDG Labs Capacity-Building Programme for HE Teachers is a comprehensive training initiative aimed at equipping higher education instructors with the necessary skills and methodologies to integrate environmental sustainability into Social Economy curricula. A key component of this programme is the MOOC "Social Economy for a Green Transition", which provides flexible, online training on crucial topics such as renewable energy, the circular economy, sustainable housing, and food systems. Additionally, the programme includes a teachers' handbook, offering structured guidance on how to implement and facilitate the SDG Labs educational framework, covering phases such as defining, ideating, experimenting, and validating green business ideas. To ensure practical application, face-to-face training workshops, webinars, coaching sessions, and mentoring activities are conducted, allowing educators to engage in hands-on, simulation-based learning experiences and peer collaboration. Through this blended approach, the capacity-building programme fosters innovation in teaching practices, enhances green literacy among faculty members, and ultimately strengthens the green social economy education ecosystem within universities.

Finally, the SDG Labs educational programme offers two key initiatives for students: business simulations and a blended learning programme combining online and on-campus experiences. The SDG Labs business simulation models provide students with over 20 interactive learning environments, acting as mind tools that allow them to design, test, and refine their own environmentally sustainable business models. These simulations create a risk-free space where students can explore the real-world consequences of business decisions, fostering critical thinking and entrepreneurial skills in the green economy. Complementing this, the SDG Labs students' upskilling programme incorporates both theoretical and practical elements through a mix of online pocket courses and an on-campus summer school. The online pocket courses guide students through the four phases of the SDG Labs framework—define, ideate, experiment, and validate—while engaging them in interactive learning experiences. These pocket courses were finally integrated in curricula by e-learning platforms that respective universities use (mostly Moodle).

As a final step a summer school was organised. The on-campus summer school serves as a testbed for the overall programme, bringing students together with social economy enterprises (SEEs) and academic mentors to co-create and refine sustainable business solutions, such as projects in sustainable farming or renewable energy. Session plans – teaching notes were created three months in advance and feedbacked meticulously. The summer school took part at the Prague University of Economics and Business for six days and Czech, Polish and Greek students took part in it. Greek students were only present online due to natural disasters happening in Greece at that time. This forced organisers to switch to a hybrid form, which complicated the non-formal part, and Greek students participated mostly only in lectures or discussions. To add a variety of opinions and knowledge base and provide networking, at some points, Prague students of the international social entrepreneurship course joined. The programme started with more formal lectures about social and green economy and systems thinking to bring everyone on the same level. During the non-formal part that followed, students developed their own ideas for green businesses. Finally, the co-creation part was to empower students to come up with ideas for teaching content on the topic of social and green economy. Topics they would like to learn and enjoy. This needs analysis was not as focused as we hoped for because it did not bring really specific topics to be integrated into education, yet it helped us to design future projects that would refine this concept of bottom-up co-creation of educational content. Ones where teachers and students would work as partners to bring education to the rhythm of ever-changing world.

By integrating simulation-based learning with hands-on, collaborative experiences, these initiatives empower students with the skills, knowledge, and confidence needed to drive green innovation within the social economy sector.

## 4. LESSONS LEARNED

The SDG Labs project provides several key lessons that help us understand the role of social economy entities (SEEs) in the green transition and the importance of developing green skills in higher education. One of the primary lessons is the significant role that SEEs play in providing innovative, small-scale, and low-cost solutions that are adapted to the local contexts and are more inclusive. Their activities span various areas such as the circular economy, renewable energy, sustainable agriculture, and social housing, highlighting their integral role in the green transition.

Another important lesson is the critical need for developing green skills to address global environmental challenges. These skills are necessary across various sectors and include technical, managerial, and soft skills. The SDG Labs project emphasises that higher educational institutions must align their curricula with the demands of a green economy to equip graduates with the necessary skills. This alignment is essential for fostering a workforce capable of driving sustainable development and addressing the environmental challenges we face. Targeted educational reforms focusing on experiential learning, simulations, interdisciplinary collaboration, and institutional support can significantly boost students' environmental literacy and their capacity to contribute to sustainable economic models.

The project also highlights the importance of bridging the gap between theory and practice. By engaging students in real-world projects and problems, they can apply theoretical knowledge in practical settings, enhancing their learning experience and preparing them for future challenges. Moreover, interdisciplinary approaches foster comprehensive understandings of sustainability issues. By integrating diverse fields such as education, social economy, environmental science, and business management, a holistic learning environment is created that equips students with the skills needed to address complex environmental challenges.

Co-creation and co-participation play an important role by engaging students, teachers, and social economy entities in the co-creation process and fostering a sense of ownership and collaboration. This participatory approach ensures that the educational content is relevant and tailored to the needs of all stakeholders, leading to more effective and impactful learning outcomes. Teachers are often afraid that they will lose their respect as educators if they work on an equal plane with students, but experience shows that innovative educational methods, such as problem-based learning, project-based learning, and the creation of communities of practice, become instrumental in engaging students and enhancing their learning experience. These methods encourage active participation, critical thinking, and practical application of knowledge, making the learning process more dynamic and impactful, and they work both ways as teachers learn naturally about learners´ needs.

Community engagement is also a key component. By involving local communities and social economy entities in the educational process, we foster a strong connection between students and the communities they serve. This engagement not only enriches the learning experience but also ensures that the skills and knowledge acquired are directly applicable to real-world contexts. However, policy support is needed to sustain and scale up educational initiatives focused on green skills. Supportive policies can facilitate

## REFERENCES


Allen, C., & Clouth, S. (2012). *A guidebook to the Green Economy Issue 1: Green Economy, Green Growth, and Low-Carbon Development – history, definitions and a guide to recent publications*. UN Division for Sustainable Development. https://sdgs.un.org/publications/guidebook-green-economy-issue-1-green-economy-green-growth-and-low-carbon-development

Alvord, S. H., Brown, L. D., & Letts, C. W. (2004). Social Entrepreneurship and Societal Transformation: An Exploratory Study. *The Journal of Applied Behavioral Science*, *40*(3), 260–282. DOI: 10.1177/0021886304266847

Bandura, A. (1971). *Social learning theory*. Prentice-Hall.

Brown, E. J., Dunlop, L., & Scally, J. (2020). 'It's about not achieving the outcomes that you necessarily expected': Non-formal learning in higher education. *Teaching in Higher Education*, *25*(1), 52–67. DOI: 10.1080/13562517.2018.1541880

European Commission. (2010). *EUROPE 2020: A strategy for smart, sustainable and inclusive growth*. https://op.europa.eu/s/z19L

Flynn, C., Yamasumi, E., Fisher, E., Snow, D., Grant, Z., Kirby, M., Browning, P., Rommerskirchen, M., & Russell, I. (2021). *Peoples' Climate Vote*. UNDP, University of Oxford, https://www.undp.org/publications/peoplesclimate-vote

Gherardi, S., Nicolini, D., & Odella, F. (1998). Toward a social understanding of how people learn in organizations: The notion of situated curriculum. *Management Learning*, *9*(3), 234–256. DOI: 10.1177/1350507698293002

Global Green Growth Institute – GGGI. (2016, october). *Achieving Global Green Transformation: Report Summary*.

Glumac, O. (2018). *Lab of Collaborative Youth: shaping a learning framework in an active citizenship. Universidade do Porto*. FBAUP.

Hasan, S. (2005). Social capital and social entrepreneurship in Asia: Analyzing the link. *Asia Pacific Journal of Public Administration*, *27*(1), 1–17. DOI: 10.1080/23276665.2005.10779296

Hockerts, K. (2018). The Effects of Experimental Social Entrepreneurship Education on Intention Formation in Students. *Journal of Social Entrepreneurship*, *9*(3), 234–256. DOI: 10.1080/19420676.2018.1498377

Howorth, C., Smith, S. M., & Parkinson, C. (2012). Social Learning and Social Entrepreneurship Education. *Academy of Management Learning & Education*, *11*(3), 371–389. http://. DOI: 10.5465/amle.2011.0022

Jain, T. K. (2019). Towards the Theory of Green Entrepreneurship, *NOLEGEIN-Journal of Entrepreneurship Planning*. *SSRN*, *2*(1), 1–5. DOI: 10.2139/ssrn.3284935

Klockner, S. (2009). *Manual for facilitators in non-formal education*. Council of Europe.

Kong, E. (2010). Innovation Processes in Social Enterprises: An IC Perspective. *Journal of Intellectual Capital*, *11*(2), 158–178. DOI: 10.1108/14691931011039660

Kowalska, K., Szczygiel, E., Szyja, P., & Sliwa, R. (2022). *SDG Labs Research Report. Green skills in the field of Social Economy. The theoretical model of Socially Driven Green Labs programme.*https://sdglabs.uom.edu.gr/sdg-labs-research-report/

Malberg, K., Vaittinen, I., Evans, P., Schuurman, D., Ståhlbröst, A., & Vervoort, K. (2017). *Living Lab Methodology Handbook*, U4IoT Consortium.

Mets, T., Holbrook, J., & Läänelaid, S. (2021). Entrepreneurship Education Challenges for Green Transformation. *Administrative Sciences*, *11*(1), 15. DOI: 10.3390/admsci11010015

Nyssens, M. (Ed.). (2006). *Social Enterprise. At the Crossroads of Market, Public Policies and Civil Society*. Routledge.

OECD (2010). *SMEs, entrepreneurship and innovation.*

Rhoden, L. (2014). The Capacity of NGOs to Become Sustainable by Creating Social Enterprises. *Journal of Small Business and Entrepreneurship Development*, *2*(2), 1–36. https://jsbed.thebrpi.org/journals/jsbed/Vol_2_No_2_June_2014/1.pdf

Smallbone, D., Evans, M., Ekanem, I., & Butters, S. (2001). *Researching Social Enterprise, Centre for Enterprise and Economic Development Research*. Middlesex University Business School.

Strietska-Ilina, O., Hofmann, C., Durán Haro, M., & Jeon, S. *Skills for green jobs: a global view: synthesis report based on 21 country studies*. International Labour Office, Skills and Employability Department, Job Creation and Enterprise Development Department. - Geneva: ILO, 2011.

Tarasova, O. V., Stindl, P., Yom, J., Chardymova, N., Imre, S.-B., & Valek, L. (2020). Integration of Non-Formal Learning Approaches into the Formal Education by Peer Learning of Teachers and Youth Workers. Revista Romaneasca pentru Educatie Multidimensionala, 12, 345-365. https://doi.org/https://doi.org/10.18662/rrem/12.1sup1/239

United Nations Environment Programme. (2020). *Greening Fiscal Stimulus and Finance Packages to Achieve the SDGs - UNEP Factsheet.*https://wedocs.unep.org/20.500.11822/32280

Wenger, E. (1998). Community of practice: A brief introduction. *Learning in Doing*, *15*(4), 1–7.

# Chapter 20
# Sustainable Decision-Making for SME Resilience:
## The Role of Governance and Leadership in Ghana

**Isaac Nketsiah**
https://orcid.org/0000-0003-1336-2468
*University of KwaZulu-Natal, South Africa*

**Thea Van der Westhuizen**
https://orcid.org/0000-0001-8795-4023
*University of KwaZulu-Natal, South Africa*

## ABSTRACT

*Small and medium enterprises (SMEs) are vital to Ghana's economy, contributing 70% of GDP and providing key employment. However, business volatility, intensified by crises like COVID-19, exposes SMEs to significant risks. Sustainable decision-making through governance and leadership is crucial for resilience. This chapter explores governance frameworks and leadership practices that enhance SME resilience, focusing on sustainability-driven decision-making. A systematic literature review synthesises research on governance structures, leadership strategies, and environmental uncertainties. Findings highlight the importance of board diversity, risk management, transformational leadership, and stakeholder engagement in strengthening resilience. The chapter offers recommendations for policymakers, business leaders, and researchers to develop sustainable governance and leadership frameworks for SMEs in an increasingly uncertain, environmentally conscious global economy.*

## INTRODUCTION

Small and medium enterprises (SMEs) form the backbone of the economy of Ghana, contributing approximately 70% of the country's GDP and employing a significant portion of the workforce (Doagbodzi, 2024). Despite their critical role, SMEs remain highly vulnerable to external shocks such as financial downturns, regulatory shifts, and environmental uncertainties (Nketsiah & van der Westhuizen, 2024). The COVID-19 pandemic, for instance, exposed significant gaps in SMEs' ability to withstand and

DOI: 10.4018/979-8-3373-0189-1.ch020

adapt to crises, leading to widespread business closures, supply chain disruptions, and reduced consumer demand (Korankye, 2020). These challenges have raised pertinent questions about the effectiveness of governance and leadership structures in fostering resilience and sustainability within SMEs.

Governance frameworks provide the strategic foundation for decision-making, ensuring accountability, transparency, and risk mitigation. Effective governance structures, such as diverse boards and robust risk management systems, are essential for navigating the complexities of the modern business environment (Nketsiah & van der Westhuizen, 2024; Amoako et al., 2021). In Ghana, however, many SMEs operate with informal governance structures, which often lack the rigor needed to address systemic risks and align with global sustainability standards (Asante, 2023). This gap underscores the need for governance reforms that promote sustainable decision-making and long-term resilience.

Leadership, on the other hand, plays a crucial role in guiding SMEs through uncertainty, fostering innovation, and embedding resilience within organisational culture. Transformational leadership, characterised by visionary thinking and the ability to inspire collective action, has been identified as a key driver of SME resilience in volatile environments (Marfo, et al. 2024). Leaders who prioritise sustainability and stakeholder engagement are better positioned to navigate environmental uncertainties and align their businesses with global sustainability goals, such as the United Nations Sustainable Development Goals (SDGs) (Ogunyemi, 2022). In Ghana, where SMEs often operate within resource-constrained environments, leadership practices that emphasise adaptability and sustainability are critical for survival and growth.

The interplay between governance and leadership is particularly significant in sustainability-driven decision-making. Sustainable decision-making involves balancing economic, social, and environmental considerations to ensure long-term viability (Amaglo, 2019). For SMEs, this requires integrating sustainability into core business strategies, fostering stakeholder collaboration, and adopting innovative practices that reduce environmental impact (Adomako et al., 2021). However, achieving this balance is often challenging due to limited resources, lack of awareness, and competing priorities.

Despite the growing recognition of the role of governance and leadership in enhancing SME resilience, significant research gaps persist. Existing studies have largely focused on general SME challenges, such as financial constraints and market access (Saad et al., 2021), but there is limited empirical research on how governance structures and leadership styles influence sustainability-driven decision-making in SMEs in Ghana. Additionally, while risk management and stakeholder engagement are acknowledged as critical to resilience (Yahya, 2023), there is a paucity of research on how SMEs operationalise these frameworks amidst environmental uncertainties. Furthermore, most studies on SME resilience in Africa have been conducted in broader contexts without a specific focus on Ghana's unique institutional and policy landscape (Kato, 2024; Okeke, 2024). The intersection between board diversity, transformational leadership, and long-term SME sustainability remains underexplored, necessitating further investigation into governance models that enhance adaptability and innovation in SMEs in Ghana. Addressing these gaps is essential for developing actionable strategies that enhance SME resilience in an increasingly uncertain and sustainability-driven global economy.

Hence, this chapter explores how governance and leadership contribute to sustainable decision-making, ultimately enabling SMEs to withstand disruptions and align with global sustainability goals. By synthesising existing research on governance structures, leadership styles, and environmental uncertainties, the chapter highlights the critical role of board diversity, risk management frameworks, transformational leadership and stakeholder engagement in strengthening SME resilience. The findings provide valuable insights for policymakers, business leaders and academic researchers seeking to develop sustainable governance and leadership frameworks that enable SMEs to thrive in an increasingly uncertain and environmentally conscious global economy.

Three major research questions guide our study synthesis, focusing on sustainable decision-making, governance, leadership, and SME resilience in Ghana.

1. How do governance structures influence the resilience of SMEs in Ghana's volatile business environment?
2. What leadership practices contribute to effective and sustainable decision-making among SMEs in Ghana?
3. What governance and leadership strategies can policymakers and business leaders implement to enhance SME resilience in Ghana?

## METHODOLOGY

### Methodological Choice Made

This study employs a systematic literature review (SLR) approach to examine the existing body of knowledge on SME resilience, governance, and leadership in Ghana. The SLR methodology was chosen for its ability to provide a comprehensive, transparent, and replicable synthesis of existing research, ensuring that the findings are grounded in a robust evidence base (Agrawal, et al., 2024; Tranfield et al., 2003). By adhering to the Preferred Reporting Items for Systematic Reviews and Meta-Analyses (PRISMA) guidelines, this study ensures methodological rigour, minimizes bias and enhances the credibility of the findings (Linares-Espinós et al., 2018). The PRISMA framework was particularly useful for structuring the search, selection, and analysis processes, ensuring that all relevant studies were systematically identified and evaluated.

### Research Sample and Scope

The research sample consists of peer-reviewed journal articles, government reports, and industry publications published between 2016 and 2024. This timeframe was selected to capture the most recent and relevant developments in SME resilience, governance, and leadership, particularly in the context of emerging challenges such as the COVID-19 pandemic and the growing emphasis on sustainability. The scope of the study is limited to SMEs in Ghana, with a focus on how governance and leadership practices influence their resilience and sustainability outcomes.

### Search Strategy

A comprehensive search strategy was developed to identify relevant literature across multiple academic and industry databases, including Scopus, Web of Science and Google Scholar. Additionally, government reports and industry publications were sourced from reputable platforms such as the World Bank, Ghana Statistical Service and the Ghana Enterprises Agency. The search terms used included combinations of keywords such as “SME resilience,” “corporate governance,” “leadership,” “sustainability,” “Ghana,” and “decision-making.” Boolean operators (AND, OR) were employed to refine the search and ensure that the results were both comprehensive and relevant. The search was conducted iteratively, with adjustments made to the search terms and databases based on preliminary findings to ensure no key studies were overlooked.

## Article Selection Criteria

The selection of articles was guided by predefined inclusion and exclusion criteria to ensure the relevance and quality of the studies reviewed. Inclusion criteria included: (1) studies published between 2016 and 2024, (2) studies focusing on SMEs in Ghana (3) studies addressing governance, leadership, resilience, or sustainability, and (4) studies published in English.

Exclusion criteria included: (1) studies outside the specified timeframe, (2) studies not directly related to SMEs or the Ghanaian context, (3) opinion pieces or non-peer-reviewed articles, and (4) studies lacking empirical or theoretical rigor. The initial search yielded a large number of articles, which were screened based on their titles and abstracts. Full-text reviews were conducted for articles that met the inclusion criteria, and those that did not align with the study's objectives were excluded.

## Sample Size

Our systematic search yielded 856 articles; of these, 47 were included in the systematic review since they provided sufficient data for our analysis and discussion. This sample size was deemed sufficient to provide a comprehensive overview of the existing literature while maintaining a manageable scope for analysis. The distribution of studies across different sources ensured a balanced representation of academic, policy, and industry perspectives, enriching the depth and applicability of the findings.

## Method of Data Extraction and Analysis

Data extraction was conducted using a standardised template to ensure consistency and comparability across studies. Key information extracted included the study's objectives, methodology, key findings, and relevance to the research questions. Thematic analysis was employed to categorize the studies into key themes, including governance structures, leadership styles, environmental uncertainty, and sustainability in SME decision-making. This approach allowed for the identification of patterns, trends and gaps in the literature, providing a holistic understanding of the interplay between governance, leadership and SME resilience. The analysis also involved a critical evaluation of the methodologies used in the selected studies, highlighting strengths and limitations to contextualize the findings.

## Limitations

While the SLR approach provides a robust framework for synthesizing existing research, it is not without limitations. First, the reliance on published literature may introduce publication bias, as studies with significant or positive findings are more likely to be published than those with null or negative results. Second, the focus on English-language publications may exclude relevant studies published in other languages, particularly in local Ghanaian contexts. Third, the inclusion of government reports and industry publications, while valuable, may introduce variability in the quality and rigor of the data. Finally, the dynamic nature of the SME landscape in Ghana means that some findings may quickly become outdated, particularly in light of ongoing economic and environmental changes. Despite these limitations, the study's adherence to PRISMA guidelines and its comprehensive search strategy mitigate potential biases and ensure the reliability of the findings.

Figure 1 illustrates the graphical representation of the Methodology section in the form of a flowchart. It follows the systematic literature review (SLR) approach, highlighting the key steps, including identification, database search, screening, thematic coding, synthesis, and conclusion.

*Figure 1. Methodology flowchart*

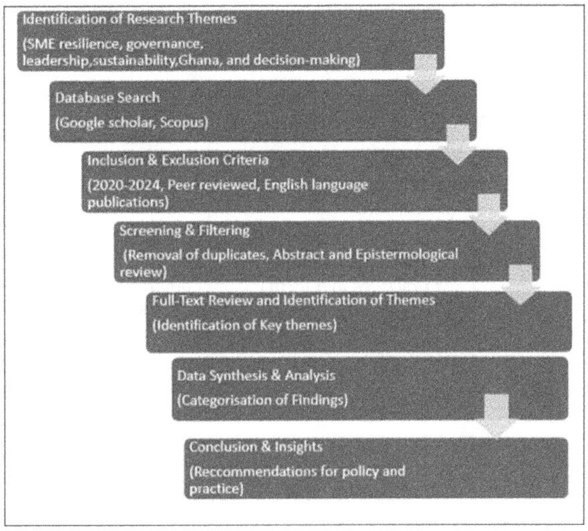


## GOVERNANCE AND SME RESILIENCE

Governance frameworks provide SMEs with the structural support necessary to navigate crises effectively. In the context of Ghana, where SMEs contribute significantly to economic growth and employment, the role of governance in fostering resilience has become increasingly critical, particularly in the face of external shocks such as the COVID-19 pandemic, economic downturns, and environmental disruptions. This section synthesises the literature on governance and SME resilience, focusing on four key elements: formalised governance structures, board diversity, risk management and accountability, and stakeholder engagement.

### Formalised Governance Structures

Formalised governance structures are foundational to SME resilience, providing clarity in decision-making, ownership, and compliance. Studies have shown that SMEs with well-defined governance frameworks are better equipped to respond to crises, as these structures facilitate efficient resource allocation and strategic planning (Damoah & Peprah, 2021; Doagbodzi, 2024). In Ghana, however, many SMEs operate with informal governance structures, often lacking the rigour to address systemic risks.

For instance, Nketsiah and van der Westhuizen (2024) report that SMEs with formalised governance mechanisms, such as documented decision-making hierarchies and compliance protocols, were more likely to survive the economic disruptions caused by the COVID-19 pandemic. These structures enhance operational efficiency and improve access to external funding, as investors and financial institutions are more likely to support businesses with transparent and accountable governance practices (Amaglo, 2019).

Table 1 provides an at-a-glance comparison of how each study frames and investigates the role of formalised governance structures within Ghanaian SMEs. The synthesis highlights the varying epistemological positions—from realist and positivist to pragmatic and interpretivist—illustrating that while approaches differ, there is a converging recognition of the critical role of structured governance in enhancing SME sustainability and resilience.

*Table 1. Epistemological table for key studies on formalised governance structures within SMEs in Ghana*

| Author(s) & Year | Research Focus | Epistemological Assumptions | Methodological Approach | Key Contributions/Findings |
|---|---|---|---|---|
| **Amaglo (2019)** | Strategies for the sustainability of SMEs in Ghana | Adopts a realist stance, assuming sustainable practices and formal governance have objective, measurable impacts on SME success. | Qualitative analysis is drawn from a doctoral dissertation examining sustainability strategies within formalised governance frameworks. | Emphasizes the necessity of formal governance structures for long-term SME sustainability; provides strategic recommendations to enhance governance mechanisms. |
| **Damoah & Peprah (2021)** | Synthesis of SME research in Ghana | Operates from a positivist/ objectivist perspective, treating empirical findings as a basis for generalizable conclusions about governance and SME performance. | Systematic literature review synthesizing prior empirical studies on SMEs, highlighting governance dimensions. | Offers an integrated overview of the challenges and opportunities facing Ghanaian SMEs; identifies gaps in the literature regarding the role of formalised governance in SME resilience. |
| **Doagbodzi (2024)** | Ghanaian SMEs' readiness for AfCFTA implementation | Embraces a pragmatic approach, recognizing that practical socio-economic realities inform the effectiveness of governance structures in preparing SMEs for trade integration. | Mixed-method approach combining surveys and interviews with SME stakeholders to assess governance readiness. | Demonstrates that robust formalised governance practices are pivotal for enhancing SME readiness for the AfCFTA, linking governance to trade competitiveness and sustainability. |
| **Nketsiah & Van der Westhuizen (2024)** | Governance and leadership in enhancing SME resilience in Ghana | Leans toward an interpretivist orientation, emphasizing the construction of meaning through qualitative insights into governance and leadership practices. | Systematic literature review (SLR) that collates and interprets findings from multiple studies on governance, leadership, and SME resilience. | Identifies critical governance and leadership practices—including formalised structures—as central to bolstering SME resilience; underscores the interplay between formal governance and effective leadership in managing environmental uncertainties. |

## Board Diversity

Board diversity has emerged as a critical factor in enhancing SME resilience, particularly in dynamic and uncertain environments (Akomea-Frimpong, Asogwa and Tenakwah, 2022). Diverse boards, incorporating different genders, professional backgrounds, and expertise, bring various perspectives to strategic decision-making, enabling SMEs to identify and respond to risks more effectively (Damoah et al. 2021). In Ghana, where SMEs often operate in resource-constrained environments, including diverse voices on boards can drive innovation and improve crisis responsiveness. For example, Adomako et al. (2021) highlighted the role of gender diversity in fostering sustainable decision-making, with female board members often advocating for long-term environmental and social considerations. Similarly, Ledi et al., (2024) emphasised the importance of professional diversity, noting that boards with members from varied industries and disciplines are better equipped to navigate complex challenges. Despite these benefits, board diversity remains underutilised in many Ghanaian SMEs, highlighting the need for targeted interventions to promote inclusive governance practices.

Table 2 illustrates how different epistemological perspectives—positivist, interpretivist, and pragmatist—influence how scholars approach board diversity in SME governance. While some emphasize empirical, measurable impacts (e.g., Adomako et al., 2021), others focus on conceptual frameworks (e.g., Akomea-Frimpong et al., 2022) or practical applications (e.g., Ledi et al., 2024).

*Table 2. Epistemological table for key studies on board diversity within SMEs in Ghana*

| Author(s) & Year | Research Focus | Epistemological Assumptions | Methodological Approach | Key Contributions/Findings |
|---|---|---|---|---|
| **Adomako et al. (2021)** | CEO sustainability orientation and firm environmental performance | Positivist stance—assumes an objective relationship between CEO leadership, board diversity, and environmental performance. | Quantitative study using structural equation modeling (SEM) to analyze CEO networking, board resource contingencies, and environmental impact. | Finds that board diversity enhances sustainability outcomes when coupled with CEO networking capabilities; diverse boards contribute to improved firm environmental performance. |
| **Akomea-Frimpong et al. (2022)** | Sustainable corporate governance in SMEs | Interpretivist approach—focuses on conceptualizing governance structures, including board diversity, through existing literature. | Systematic literature review (SLR) exploring corporate governance theories and their application to SMEs. | Identifies board diversity as a key driver of sustainable decision-making, proposing governance models that integrate gender and expertise diversity for SME resilience. |
| **Damoah & Peprah (2021)** | Synthesis of SME research in Ghana | Positivist and pragmatic approach—aims to generalize SME governance challenges and opportunities, including board composition. | Systematic review analyzing prior empirical studies on SME governance. | Highlights the lack of gender diversity and professional diversity in SME boards as a governance weakness in Ghana; calls for policy interventions to encourage inclusivity. |
| **Ledi et al. (2024)** | The role of strategic thinking and gender diversity in crisis management | Pragmatist stance—acknowledges that governance practices, including board diversity, are shaped by complex socio-economic realities. | Mixed-method study using surveys and case analyses to assess how diverse boards influence crisis response in SMEs. | Demonstrates that gender-diverse boards improve crisis management capabilities, fostering adaptability and innovation in uncertain business environments. |

## Risk Management and Accountability

Effective risk management and accountability mechanisms are essential for SME resilience, particularly in volatile business environments. SMEs with formalised risk mitigation strategies, such as contingency planning and financial transparency, are more likely to withstand disruptions and sustain long-term growth (Korankye, 2020). In Ghana, where SMEs face significant environmental and regulatory uncertainties, adopting robust risk management frameworks is critical for survival. For instance, Akpamah and Matkó (2023) posit that SMEs with proactive risk management practices were better positioned to adapt to the economic challenges posed by the COVID-19 pandemic. These practices include regular financial audits, compliance with regulatory requirements, and establishing internal controls to prevent fraud and mismanagement. Additionally, Neequaye (2020) argues that accountability measures, such as transparent reporting and stakeholder engagement, enhance trust and credibility, enabling SMEs to secure funding and build strong relationships with investors and customers.

Table 3 illustrates how different epistemological perspectives shape the understanding of risk management and accountability in SMEs. While some focus on empirical, measurable impacts (e.g., Akpamah & Matkó, 2023), others examine governance challenges through case studies (e.g., Neequaye, 2020) or analyse real-world crises like COVID-19 (e.g., Korankye, 2020).

*Table 3. Epistemological table for key studies on risk management and accountability within SMEs in Ghana*

| Author(s) & Year | Research Focus | Epistemological Assumptions | Methodological Approach | Key Contributions/Findings |
|---|---|---|---|---|
| **Akpamah & Matkó (2023)** | Impact of SME leadership styles on business development and job creation | Positivist stance—assumes that leadership styles have a direct, measurable impact on risk management and accountability. | Quantitative study using surveys and statistical analysis to assess leadership influence on SME performance. | Finds that transformational leadership enhances risk mitigation strategies and accountability, while autocratic styles hinder sustainable growth. |
| **Korankye (2020)** | Impact of COVID-19 on SMEs in Ghana | Pragmatist stance—acknowledges that unpredictable external factors like the pandemic shape risk management. | A mixed-method study combining surveys and interviews with SME owners to assess the pandemic's effects. | Highlights that poor risk management frameworks left SMEs vulnerable during COVID-19, emphasizing the need for better financial accountability and crisis preparedness. |
| **Neequaye (2020)** | Corporate governance practices among SMEs in Ghana | Interpretivist stance—explores governance and accountability from a social constructivist perspective, recognizing varied SME experiences. | The case study approach analyses selected SMEs in Accra through interviews and document analysis. | This reveals that many SMEs lack formalized governance structures and accountability measures, making them prone to financial mismanagement and operational inefficiencies. |

## Stakeholder Engagement

Stakeholder engagement is a cornerstone of SME resilience, enabling businesses to build strong relationships with financial institutions, regulatory bodies, and community networks (Owusu, Tauringana & Asare, 2024; Eyiah-Botwe, Aigbavboa & Thwala, 2016). In Ghana, where SMEs often rely on informal networks for support, fostering collaborative relationships with stakeholders is critical for survival during crises. Studies have shown that SMEs with strong stakeholder engagement practices are more likely to access funding, navigate regulatory challenges, and gain community support (Rumasukun & Noch, 2023; Adomako et al., 2021; Ansong, 2017). For example, (Kuada, (2023) reports that during the COVID-19 pandemic, SMEs that maintained open communication with financial institutions could secure loans and grants to sustain their operations. Similarly, Atanga (2019) argues that engagement with regulatory bodies ensures compliance with legal requirements, reducing the risk of penalties and disruptions. On the other hand, community networks provide SMEs with access to local resources, markets, and support systems, enhancing their ability to withstand external shocks (Atiase et al., 2023). Despite these benefits, many Ghanaian SMEs cannot engage effectively with stakeholders, highlighting the need for capacity-building initiatives to strengthen these relationships.

Table 4 highlights the interplay between stakeholder engagement, financial resilience, and sustainability, illustrating different research perspectives from constructivist, positivist, pragmatist, and interpretivist paradigms.

*Table 4. Epistemological table on stakeholder engagement in business sustainability within SMEs in Ghana*

| Author(s) & Year | Research Focus | Epistemological Assumptions | Methodological Approach | Key Contributions/Findings |
|---|---|---|---|---|
| **Adomako et al. (2021)** | Relationship between CEO sustainability orientation and environmental performance | Constructivist stance—assumes that leadership mindset shapes corporate sustainability practices. | Empirical study using survey data from firms in emerging markets. | Finds that CEOs with strong sustainability orientations enhance environmental performance, particularly when leveraging stakeholder networks. |
| **Ansong (2017)** | The impact of corporate social responsibility (CSR) on SME access to finance through stakeholder engagement | Pragmatist stance—recognizes the dual role of CSR in fostering social good and financial access. | Quantitative study using regression analysis on SME financial data. | Demonstrates that SMEs engaging in CSR gain better access to finance, as stakeholders view them as lower-risk investments. |
| **Atiase et al. (2023)** | Financial resilience and survival of SMEs in Africa through stakeholder collaboration | Interpretivist stance—views financial resilience as an outcome of interactive stakeholder relationships. | Case study approach examining SME financial strategies. | Highlights that strong stakeholder relationships improve financial resilience, especially in economic downturns. |
| **Eyiah-Botwe, Aigbavboa, & Thwala (2016)** | The role of stakeholder engagement in SME growth | Positivist stance—assumes direct correlation between stakeholder collaboration and business sustainability. | Survey-based research focusing on SME owners' perspectives on stakeholder relations. | Finds that proactive stakeholder engagement is critical for long-term SME growth, fostering trust and resource access. |
| **Kuada (2023)** | Role of financial stakeholders in rural enterprise growth | Interpretivist stance—views financial stakeholder involvement as a dynamic process shaping rural business sustainability. | Qualitative study analyzing financial practices in rural enterprises. | Suggests that inclusive financial stakeholder policies contribute to rural business growth, particularly in underserved areas. |
| **Owusu, Tauringana, & Asare (2024)** | SME sustainability reporting and stakeholder engagement | Pragmatist stance—examines how sustainability reporting influences stakeholder perception. | Survey and interview-based research on SMEs in Ghana. | Finds that transparent sustainability reporting strengthens SME credibility, leading to better stakeholder relations and market opportunities. |

## LEADERSHIP IN ENHANCING SME RESILIENCE

Leadership is fundamental in determining how SMEs respond to external shocks and maintain long-term sustainability. In Ghana, where SMEs are a cornerstone of the economy, effective leadership has been identified as a critical factor in navigating crises such as the COVID-19 pandemic, economic instability, and environmental challenges. This section synthesises the literature on leadership and SME resilience, focusing on four key leadership styles and practices: transformational leadership, servant leadership, entrepreneurial leadership, and strategic financial management.

### Transformational Leadership

Transformational leadership has emerged as a powerful driver of SME resilience, particularly in volatile and uncertain environments (Sabbah, 2024; Dankwa, 2020). Transformational leaders inspire vision, innovation, and agility, enabling SMEs to adapt to changing circumstances and seize new opportunities. Studies have shown that SMEs led by transformational leaders are more likely to exhibit resilience during crises, as these leaders foster a culture of adaptability and continuous improvement (Adadevoh, et al., 2024). In Ghana, where SMEs often face resource constraints and market uncertainties, transformational leadership has been instrumental in driving innovation and strategic pivots. For example, Sabbah (2024) found that SMEs led by transformational leaders were better equipped to navigate the disruptions caused by the COVID-19 pandemic, as these leaders encouraged creative problem-solving and proactive risk management. By fostering a shared vision and empowering employees, transformational leaders enhance organizational agility and long-term sustainability.

Table 5 illustrates how transformational leadership is a key driver of SME sustainability, business continuity, and global competitiveness, reinforcing its role in sustainable decision-making and organisational resilience.

*Table 5. Epistemological table on transformational leadership in business sustainability*

| Author(s) & Year | Research Focus | Epistemological Assumptions | Methodological Approach | Key Contributions/Findings |
|---|---|---|---|---|
| **Adadevoh et al. (2024)** | Role of transformational leadership in succession planning and sustainability of SMEs | Constructivist stance—assumes leadership behaviours shape organisational sustainability and career development. | Empirical study using surveys and structural equation modelling (SEM). | Finds that transformational leadership positively influences SME sustainability, particularly when integrated with succession planning and career development programs. |
| **Dankwa (2020)** | Ghanaian businesses' global competitiveness and leadership impact | Pragmatist stance—views leadership as an adaptive mechanism in global economic participation. | Qualitative case study analysing Ghanaian firms' leadership strategies. | Highlights that businesses led by transformational leaders are better positioned for global competitiveness as they foster innovation and strategic adaptability. |
| **Owusu (2023)** | Effectiveness of leadership approaches in manufacturing industries in Accra | Positivist stance—assumes a direct relationship between leadership styles and business performance. | Mixed-method study combining surveys and interviews with manufacturing industry leaders. | Transformational leadership is the most effective leadership style in manufacturing, enhancing productivity, employee engagement, and long-term business success. |
| **Sabbah (2024)** | A systematic review of transformational leadership and business continuity | Interpretivist stance—views leadership as a dynamic force shaping organisational resilience. | Systematic literature review analysing global empirical studies on leadership resilience. | Transformational leadership fosters agility, innovation, and crisis management, making businesses more adaptable to disruptions. |

## Servant Leadership

Servant leadership, which emphasises community and employee well-being, has also been identified as a key factor in enhancing SME resilience (Nketsiah & van der Westhuizen, 2024). Abukari et al., (2024) report that servant leaders prioritise the needs of their employees and stakeholders, creating supportive networks that strengthen the capacity of SMEs to recover from disruptions. This leadership style is particularly effective in fostering trust, collaboration, and loyalty, which are critical for sustaining operations during crises (Adomako, Danso & Boateng, 2023). In Ghana, where SMEs often rely on close-knit community networks, servant leadership has been shown to enhance resilience by building strong relationships with employees, customers, and local communities. For instance, Ametefe et al., (2025) highlighted the role of servant leadership in promoting employee well-being and reducing turnover during the COVID-19 pandemic. By prioritising the welfare of their teams, servant leaders create a resilient organisational culture that can withstand external shocks and maintain productivity.

Table 6 shows the role of servant leadership in SME sustainability, resilience, and stakeholder trust, positioning it as a strategic model for responsible business growth in Ghana and beyond.

*Table 6. Epistemological table: servant leadership and SME performance*

| Author(s) & Year | Research Focus | Epistemological Assumptions | Methodological Approach | Key Contributions/Findings |
|---|---|---|---|---|
| **Abukari et al. (2024)** | Role of servant leadership in linking entrepreneurial bricolage to competitive advantage and sustainability performance | Constructivist stance—assumes leadership influences entrepreneurial innovation and sustainable outcomes. | An empirical study using structural equation modelling (SEM) on SMEs in emerging markets. | Servant leadership enhances SME sustainability by fostering creativity, ethical decision-making, and stakeholder trust. |
| **Adomako et al. (2023)** | Relationship between responsible leadership and corporate sustainability in Africa | Interpretivist stance—views leadership as a moral and strategic driver of sustainability. | Edited volume compiling multiple case studies and empirical research on African businesses. | Demonstrates that servant leadership strengthens corporate responsibility, long-term performance, and ethical business practices in African enterprises. |
| **Ametefe et al. (2025)** | Systematic review of leadership's impact on SME performance | Positivist stance—assumes leadership styles have measurable effects on business outcomes. | Systematic literature review synthesising leadership research in SME contexts. | Servant leadership is key to employee engagement, trust-building, and sustainable business growth. |
| **Nketsiah & Van der Westhuizen (2024)** | Governance and leadership strategies for SME sustainability | Pragmatist stance—focuses on actionable leadership models for resilience. | Systematic literature review on governance and leadership frameworks in SMEs. | Servant leadership is essential for fostering collaboration, adaptability, and resilience in SMEs. |

## Entrepreneurial Leadership

Entrepreneurial leadership, characterised by risk-taking, continuous learning, and digital transformation, is another critical factor in promoting SME resilience. Entrepreneurial leaders embrace innovation and experimentation, enabling SMEs to identify new opportunities and adapt to changing market conditions. This leadership style is particularly relevant in digital transformation, where SMEs must leverage technology to remain competitive and resilient (Conduah & Essiaw, 2022). In Ghana, entrepreneurial leadership has been instrumental in driving the adoption of digital tools and platforms, particularly during the COVID-19 pandemic. For example, Nketsiah and van der Westhuizen (2024) report that SMEs led by entrepreneurial leaders were more likely to adopt e-commerce solutions and remote work practices, enabling them to sustain operations during lockdowns. By fostering a culture of continuous learning and innovation, entrepreneurial leaders enhance SMEs' capacity to navigate disruptions and achieve long-term sustainability.

## Strategic Financial Management

Strategic financial management is a critical component of leadership in enhancing SME resilience. Leaders who proactively engage with financial institutions, leverage financial literacy training, and implement sound financial practices improve SMEs' access to funding and their ability to withstand economic shocks (Atiase et al., 2023). In Ghana, where SMEs often face challenges in accessing formal credit, strategic financial management has been identified as a key factor in promoting resilience (World Bank, 2021). For instance, Kuada (2023) found that SMEs with financially literate leaders were more likely to secure loans and grants during the COVID-19 pandemic, as these leaders were better equipped to navigate the complexities of financial systems. Additionally, strategic financial management involves the implementation of robust budgeting, cash flow management, and risk mitigation practices, which are essential for sustaining operations during crises. Leaders enhance SMEs' financial resilience and long-term viability by prioritising financial literacy and engagement with financial institutions (Eyiah-Botwe, Aigbavboa & Thwala, 2016).

## OPPORTUNITIES FOR SUSTAINABLE SME RESILIENCE IN GHANA

Small and medium-sized enterprises (SMEs) are pivotal to Ghana's economic development, contributing significantly to employment and GDP. Enhancing their resilience is essential for sustainable growth, especially in global uncertainties. This discussion explores three strategic avenues to bolster SME resilience in Ghana: entrepreneurship education programs, systems thinking approaches, and digital transformation.

### Entrepreneurship Education Programs

Entrepreneurship education equips SME leaders with essential strategic planning, risk management, and innovation skills, enabling them to navigate uncertainties effectively. In Ghana, initiatives like the National Entrepreneurship and Innovation Programme (NEIP) have been instrumental. NEIP's "Skills For Jobs" project aims to train 100,000 individuals, creating 120,000 jobs by enhancing entrepreneurial competencies (Okoro, et al., 2022)

The Ghana Enterprises Agency (GEA) also plays a crucial role through its "Business in a Box (Biz-Box)" project, designed in partnership with the Mastercard Foundation. This four-year initiative focuses on youth entrepreneurship and employment, providing training and resources to young entrepreneurs (Assibey-Yeboah, 2019).

Empirical studies underscore the impact of such programs. For instance, research indicates that entrepreneurial capability, bolstered by targeted education, significantly enhances SME performance in dynamic markets (Mensah-Williams & Derera, 2024; Tumaku, 2024). These programs impart technical skills and foster a proactive mindset, enabling entrepreneurs to identify and exploit new opportunities.

Table 7 illustrates the different epistemological perspectives shaping entrepreneurship education research in Ghana. While some studies focus on policy and funding constraints (e.g., Assibey-Yeboah, 2019), others examine psychological and behavioural factors (e.g., Tumaku, 2024) or curriculum limitations (e.g., Mensah-Williams & Derera, 2024).

*Table 7. Epistemological table for key studies on entrepreneurship education programs within SMEs in Ghana*

| Author(s) & Year | Research Focus | Epistemological Assumptions | Methodological Approach | Key Contributions/Findings |
|---|---|---|---|---|
| **Mensah-Williams & Derera (2024)** | Entrepreneurship education in Ghanaian universities and its impact on SME development | Constructivist stance—views education as a transformative tool for shaping entrepreneurial mindset and competencies. | A qualitative study analysing selected universities' curriculum structures, teaching methods, and student perspectives. | Finds that entrepreneurship education lacks practical application in Ghanaian universities, with recommendations for experiential learning and industry collaboration. |
| **Assibey-Yeboah (2019)** | Government budget allocations for entrepreneurship education and SME support programs | Positivist stance—assumes a direct relationship between government funding and SME development. | Policy analysis of Ghana's 2020 budget for the Ministry of Business Development. | Highlights insufficient government funding for entrepreneurship training programs, limiting SME capacity-building efforts. |
| **Okoro et al. (2022)** | The role of entrepreneurship education in addressing youth unemployment in Ghana | Pragmatist stance—acknowledges both structural and behavioural factors in SME education and employment outcomes. | A mixed-method study combining surveys and policy review to assess the effectiveness of entrepreneurship education in reducing unemployment. | Finds that entrepreneurship education is critical for youth employability, but curriculum gaps, lack of mentorship, and limited access to finance hinder impact. |
| **Tumaku (2024)** | The link between regulatory focus, entrepreneurial resilience, and SME innovation | Interpretivist stance—explores how psychological and behavioural factors influence SME growth through education. | An empirical study using structural equation modelling (SEM) to analyse SME innovation and education factors. | Demonstrates that entrepreneurial resilience, mindset, and learning orientation mediate the relationship between education and SME success. |

## Adoption of Systems Thinking Approaches

Integrating systems thinking can facilitate a culture of continuous learning and adaptability within Ghanaian SMEs, which is vital for navigating the uncertainties posed by external shocks such as economic downturns or pandemics. By fostering an environment where feedback loops are valued, these enterprises can better identify weaknesses in their operations and swiftly implement corrective measures. For instance, research indicates that SMEs with robust monitoring and evaluation frameworks enhance their resilience and significantly improve their growth trajectories through informed decision-making (Agyapong et al 2024).

Furthermore, embracing digital tools and technologies as part of a systems-oriented approach allows SMEs to streamline processes and engage more effectively with stakeholders, ultimately leading to sustainable business practices (Bamfo, 2024). This holistic perspective empowers businesses to leverage interconnectedness in their strategies, making them more resilient against both anticipated and unforeseen challenges. By fostering a continuous improvement and adaptability culture, these enterprises position themselves to thrive in an ever-evolving market landscape, ensuring long-term success and competitiveness. Investing in employee training and development becomes crucial, as a skilled workforce is better equipped to navigate changes and implement innovative solutions that drive growth.

Table 8 illustrates how pragmatist and interpretive perspectives shape research on systems thinking within SMEs in Ghana. While Agyapong et al. (2024) focus on practical applications of M&E systems, Bamfo et al. (2023) provide a theoretical model for understanding SME ecosystems holistically.

*Table 8. Epistemological table for key studies on systems thinking approaches in SMEs in Ghana*

| Author(s) & Year | Research Focus | Epistemological Assumptions | Methodological Approach | Key Contributions/Findings |
|---|---|---|---|---|
| **Agyapong, Agyapong, & Agyei-Poku (2024)** | The role of monitoring and evaluation (M&E) systems in SME performance in Ghana | Pragmatist stance—assumes that M&E systems provide actionable insights for improving SME decision-making. | Empirical study using surveys and case studies to assess M&E adoption in selected Ghanaian SMEs. | Finds that integrating M&E systems enhances SME efficiency, accountability, and resilience by enabling data-driven decision-making and continuous improvement. |
| **Bamfo, Asiedu-Appiah, & Ameza-Xemalordzo (2023)** | Entrepreneurship ecosystem development in developing countries through institutional theory | Interpretivist stance—views entrepreneurship ecosystems as complex, adaptive systems shaped by institutional dynamics. | Conceptual study developing a framework for entrepreneurship ecosystems using institutional theory. | Proposes a systems-thinking approach to SME development, emphasizing policy, finance, culture, and networks as interdependent factors influencing SME growth and sustainability. |

## Digital Transformation

Moreover, the integration of digital transformation within Ghanaian SMEs extends beyond mere financial services; it encompasses a holistic approach that includes enhancing operational efficiency through technology adoption. For instance, implementing cloud-based solutions can streamline supply chain management and improve communication channels, facilitating quicker decision-making processes in times of crisis (Nketsiah & Westhuizen, 2024). Furthermore, fostering a culture of innovation among employees encourages adaptability to new technologies, which is crucial for resilience during unpredictable market shifts (Sagala & Őri, 2024)

The role of leadership is pivotal here, as transformational leaders who emphasise continuous learning and skill development can significantly influence their organisations' capacity to embrace digital tools effectively (Achieng & Malatji, 2022).

Collaboration with tech startups or local universities can also provide SMEs access to cutting-edge innovations and research, further strengthening their competitive edge in an increasingly digital marketplace. Thus, by prioritising these multifaceted strategies, Ghanaian SMEs can survive and thrive amidst challenges, securing their position as vital contributors to economic growth.

Table 9 illustrates the different epistemological perspectives shaping digital transformation research within SMEs in Ghana. While some studies explore contextual barriers and opportunities (e.g., Achieng & Malatji, 2022), others focus on governance and leadership (e.g., Nketsiah & Van der Westhuizen, 2024) or quantifiable digital strategies (e.g., Sagala & Őri, 2024).

*Table 9. Epistemological table for key studies on digital transformation in SMEs within SMEs in Ghana*

| Author(s) & Year | Research Focus | Epistemological Assumptions | Methodological Approach | Key Contributions/Findings |
|---|---|---|---|---|
| **Achieng & Malatji (2022)** | Digital transformation of SMEs in Sub-Saharan Africa | Pragmatist stance—acknowledges that digital transformation is context-dependent and shaped by socio-economic realities. | Scoping review analysing trends, challenges, and opportunities in SME digitalisation. | Finds that infrastructure gaps, digital literacy, and financial constraints hinder SME digital adoption, but government support and policy interventions can drive progress. |
| **Nketsiah & Van der Westhuizen (2024)** | Governance and leadership in SME resilience in Ghana, with a focus on digitalisation | Interpretive approach—explores digital transformation as a governance and leadership issue shaped by institutional dynamics. | Systematic literature review (SLR) synthesising research on SME governance, leadership, and digital adoption. | Highlights that strong governance structures enhance SME digital transformation, and leaders with digital skills drive technology adoption and innovation. |
| **Sagala & Őri (2024)** | Digital transformation strategy for SME resilience and antifragility | Positivist stance—assumes digitalisation has objective, measurable effects on SME resilience. | Systematic literature review analysing empirical studies on digital transformation strategies. | Demonstrates that data-driven decision-making, AI integration, and cloud technologies improve SME resilience, with digitalisation as a key antifragility strategy. |

## CHALLENGES FOR SUSTAINABLE SME RESILIENCE IN GHANA

Despite the potential benefits of governance and leadership in fostering SME resilience, several challenges persist in the entrepreneurial landscape in Ghana. These challenges hinder the ability of SMEs to withstand external shocks, adapt to changing environments, and achieve long-term sustainability. This section synthesises the literature on the key challenges facing SMEs in Ghana, focusing on three critical areas: limited access to finance, poor infrastructure and policy support, and a lack of entrepreneurship education.

### Limited Access to Finance

Access to finance remains one of the most significant challenges for SMEs in Ghana, limiting their ability to invest in growth, innovation, and resilience-building measures. Studies have consistently highlighted the difficulties SMEs face in securing credit, particularly from formal financial institutions. A key barrier is the lack of formal governance structures and financial record-keeping, which makes it difficult for SMEs to meet the stringent requirements of banks and other lenders (Nketsiah, 2018). For instance, Turkson, Amissah and Gyeke-Dako (2022) found that only 20% of SMEs in Ghana have access to formal credit, with the majority relying on informal sources such as family, friends, and personal savings. This reliance on informal financing limits the scale and sustainability of SMEs, as these sources often provide insufficient funds and lack the stability of formal credit.

The COVID-19 pandemic exacerbated these challenges, as many SMEs faced cash flow shortages and reduced revenue, making it even harder to secure loans (Ofori-Atta, 2020). Additionally, high interest rates and collateral requirements further restrict access to finance, particularly for small and micro-enterprises. Aidoo (2022) emphasised the need for innovative financing solutions, such as digital lending platforms and microfinance institutions, to bridge the gap and provide SMEs with the capital they need to thrive. However, the adoption of these solutions remains limited, highlighting the need for policy interventions to improve financial inclusion and support SME resilience.

Table 10 illustrates how SME financial constraints stem from poor financial management, external shocks, and reliance on informal lending, highlighting the need for policy interventions to improve access to formal credit in Ghana in order to strengthen SME resilience in Ghana.

*Table 10. Epistemological table: limited access to finance and SME resilience*

| Author(s) & Year | Research Focus | Epistemological Assumptions | Methodological Approach | Key Contributions/Findings |
|---|---|---|---|---|
| **Aidoo (2022)** | Impact of COVID-19 on SME growth and financial access in Ghana | Pragmatist stance—acknowledges that external shocks influence SME financing and survival strategies. | Empirical study using surveys and financial performance analysis of SMEs. | Finds that SMEs struggled to access formal financing during COVID-19, leading many to rely on alternative financial strategies such as digital finance and informal lending. |
| **Nketsiah (2018)** | Financial record-keeping practices among small business operators | Positivist stance—assumes a direct link between financial management practices and SME financing access. | Quantitative study using survey data from SME owners in Sekondi-Takoradi. | Highlights that poor financial record-keeping limits SME access to credit, as many businesses fail to meet formal banking requirements. |
| **Turkson, Amissah, & Gyeke-Dako (2022)** | Role of formal and informal finance in the informal sector in Ghana | Constructivist stance—views SME financing as a social and institutional process shaped by trust, accessibility, and regulatory constraints. | Mixed-method study analyzing survey data and case studies of SME financing sources. | Demonstrates that informal financial institutions (e.g., susu collectors, family loans) play a crucial role in SME survival, especially for businesses excluded from formal banking systems. |

## Poor Infrastructure and Policy Support

Weak infrastructure and inadequate policy support are significant barriers to SME growth and resilience in Ghana. Poor physical infrastructure, such as unreliable electricity, inadequate transportation networks, and limited access to technology, increases operational costs and reduces the competitiveness of SMEs (Oduro, 2020). For example, frequent power outages disrupt production processes and increase reliance on expensive alternative energy sources, such as generators. Similarly, poor road networks and transportation systems hinder the distribution of goods and services, particularly in rural areas where many SMEs operate.

In addition to physical infrastructure, weak institutional frameworks and policy support further constrain SME development. Many SMEs lack access to capacity-building initiatives, such as training programs, mentorship, and technical assistance, essential for improving governance, leadership, and operational efficiency (Kuada, 2023). Moreover, regulatory burdens, such as complex tax systems and bureaucratic procedures, create additional challenges for SMEs, particularly those with limited resources and expertise. Kato (2024) highlighted the need for streamlined policies and targeted support programs to address these challenges and create an enabling environment for SME growth. Without adequate infrastructure and policy support, SMEs in Ghana will continue to struggle to achieve resilience and sustainability. Table 11 illustrates the different epistemological perspectives on poor infrastructure and policy support for SMEs in Ghana

*Table 11. Epistemological table: poor infrastructure and policy support for SMEs in Ghana*

| Author(s) & Year | Research Focus | Epistemological Assumptions | Methodological Approach | Key Contributions/Findings |
|---|---|---|---|---|
| **Kuada (2023)** | Role of financial infrastructure in supporting rural SME growth | Constructivist stance—views SME financing as a dynamic interaction between policy frameworks, financial institutions, and local economic conditions. | Qualitative study using interviews with SME owners and financial experts in rural Ghana. | Finds that poor financial infrastructure, weak regulatory enforcement, and limited rural banking services hinder SME growth, making financial inclusion difficult for rural entrepreneurs. |
| **Oduro (2020)** | Barriers to open innovation adoption among SMEs in Ghana | Pragmatist stance—acknowledges both structural barriers (e.g., policy inefficiencies) and organizational factors (e.g., lack of resources) in shaping SME innovation. | Mixed-method approach using surveys and interviews with SME owners and policymakers. | Identifies inadequate government policy support, unreliable infrastructure (e.g., electricity, internet), and lack of collaboration between SMEs and research institutions as major barriers to innovation. |

## Lack of Entrepreneurship Education

A lack of entrepreneurship education is another critical challenge for SMEs in Ghana, limiting owner-managers' ability to make informed decisions and implement effective governance and leadership practices (Asante, 2020). Many SME owner-managers lack formal training in key areas such as financial management, strategic planning, and risk management, essential for navigating the complexities of the modern business environment (Biney, 2023). This knowledge gap often results in poor decision-making, inefficient operations, and a lack of long-term planning, undermining the resilience and sustainability of SMEs. Agyapong and Attram (2019) report that the absence of entrepreneurship education is particularly pronounced in rural areas, where access to training programs and educational resources is limited. They argue that this disparity highlights the need for targeted interventions to improve access to entrepreneurship education and equip SME owner-managers with the skills and knowledge they need to succeed. Additionally, integrating entrepreneurship education into formal school curricula and vocational training programs could help build a culture of innovation and resilience among future entrepreneurs (Van der Westhuizen, 2023, 2024). Table 12 illustrates the different epistemological perspectives on lack of entrepreneurship education in Ghana

*Table 12. Epistemological table: lack of entrepreneurship education in Ghana*

| Author(s) & Year | Research Focus | Epistemological Assumptions | Methodological Approach | Key Contributions/Findings |
|---|---|---|---|---|
| **Agyapong & Attram (2019)** | Impact of financial literacy on SME performance in Cape Coast | Positivist stance—assumes that financial literacy directly influences business success, independent of socio-cultural factors. | Quantitative study using surveys of SME owner-managers. | Finds that a lack of financial literacy negatively affects SMEs' profitability, decision-making, and access to funding, highlighting the need for structured entrepreneurship education. |
| **Asante (2023)** | Business sustainability among women entrepreneurs in Ghana | Constructivist stance—views entrepreneurial education as a tool for empowering women entrepreneurs and addressing gender-specific challenges. | Qualitative case study using interviews with women entrepreneurs. | Identifies limited entrepreneurship education and mentorship programs as key barriers to women-owned SME sustainability, emphasizing the need for targeted training and policy interventions. |
| **Biney (2023)** | Role of adult education in fostering entrepreneurship | Pragmatist stance—acknowledges the interplay between formal education, practical skills, and entrepreneurial outcomes. | Mixed-method approach, combining surveys and focus groups with young adults. | Highlights that young adults lack exposure to entrepreneurship education in formal schooling, making it difficult for them to transition into self-employment. Recommends integrating entrepreneurship training into adult education programs. |

## SYNTHESIS AND IMPLICATIONS OF THE THREE THEMATIC AREAS

### Governance and SME Resilience

The synthesis of the thematic area (Governance and SME Resilience) underscores the critical role of governance in fostering SME resilience in Ghana. Formalised governance structures provide the foundation for effective decision-making (Damoah & Peprah, 2021; Doagbodzi, 2024) and resource allocation, while board diversity enhances strategic thinking and innovation (Adomako et al., 2021; Ledi et al., 2024). Risk management compliance (Akpamah & Matkó, 2023) and accountability mechanisms (Neequaye, 2020) ensure financial stability, while stakeholder engagement builds trust and support (Owusu, Tauringana & Asare, 2024; Eyiah-Botwe, Aigbavboa & Thwala, 2016). These elements enable SMEs to navigate crises, adapt to changing environments, and align with global sustainability goals.

### Leadership in Enhancing SME Resilience

The synthesis of the thematic area (Leadership in Enhancing SME Resilience) underscores the critical role of leadership in fostering SME resilience in Ghana. Transformational leadership drives innovation and adaptability, enabling SMEs to pivot during crises (Sabbah, 2024; Dankwa, 2020). Servant leadership prioritises employee and community well-being, creating supportive networks that enhance recovery and sustainability (Abukari et al., 2024). Entrepreneurial leadership embraces risk-taking and digital transformation, positioning SMEs to seize new opportunities and navigate disruptions (Conduah & Essiaw, 2022). Strategic financial management improves access to funding and financial stability, ensuring SMEs can withstand economic shocks (Atiase et al., 2023). Together, these leadership practices enable SMEs to navigate crises, adapt to changing environments, and achieve long-term sustainability.

### Opportunities and Challenges for Sustainable SME Resilience in Ghana

The synthesis of the thematic area (Opportunities and Challenges for Sustainable SME Resilience in Ghana) underscores the significant challenges facing SMEs in Ghana as they strive to achieve resilience and sustainability. Limited access to finance restricts SMEs' ability to invest in growth and innovation, while poor infrastructure and policy support create operational barriers and reduce competitiveness (Nketsiah, 2018). A lack of entrepreneurship education further compounds these challenges, limiting the capacity of SME owner-managers to make informed decisions and implement effective governance and leadership practices (Asante, 2020). Addressing these challenges requires a multi-faceted approach, including policy reforms, capacity-building initiatives, and targeted support programs. By improving access to finance, enhancing infrastructure, and promoting entrepreneurship education, stakeholders can create an enabling environment for SME growth and resilience, ultimately contributing to Ghana's economic development and sustainability goals.

## CONCLUSION

This systematic review critically examined the interplay between governance, leadership, and sustainable decision-making in enhancing the resilience of small and medium enterprises in Ghana. Addressing the first research question, the findings reveal that formalised governance structures, such as diverse boards and robust risk management systems, are pivotal in enabling SMEs to navigate volatile environments. These structures foster accountability, transparency, and strategic adaptability, which are essential for crisis response and long-term sustainability.

In response to the second question, the review highlights the significance of transformational and servant leadership practices. Leaders who inspire innovation, prioritise employee well-being and engage stakeholders effectively drive sustainable decision-making. Such practices enhance organisational agility and build supportive networks that strengthen resilience during disruptions.

Finally, the review identifies actionable strategies for policymakers and business leaders to strengthen SME resilience. These include promoting financial literacy, fostering stakeholder collaboration, and integrating sustainability into core business strategies. Additionally, targeted capacity-building programs and policy reforms are needed to address systemic challenges such as limited access to finance and inadequate infrastructure.

In conclusion, integrating effective governance and leadership practices is critical for fostering sustainable decision-making and resilience in SMEs in Ghana. By addressing these issues, stakeholders can create an enabling environment for SMEs to thrive amidst uncertainties and contribute to broader economic and sustainability goals.

## RECOMMENDATIONS

To develop sustainable decision-making for SME resilience in Ghana:

a. Policymakers should promote formalised governance frameworks, including board diversity and risk management systems, to enhance SME resilience. Providing training and resources for SMEs to adopt transparent and accountable practices will improve their ability to navigate volatile environments.
b. Business leaders should adopt transformational and servant leadership styles to inspire innovation, prioritise employee well-being, and build stakeholder networks. Leadership training programs can equip SME owners with skills to drive sustainable decision-making and adaptability.
c. Governments and financial institutions should develop targeted policies and innovative financing solutions, such as digital lending platforms, to address SMEs' funding challenges. Additionally, integrating entrepreneurship education into national curricula will empower SME leaders with the knowledge to implement effective governance and leadership strategies.

## REFERENCES


Abukari, A. J., Wenyuan, L., Abubakari, M. S., Pomegbe, W. W. K., & Sulemana, I. (2024). Extending the consequences of entrepreneurial bricolage to competitive advantage and sustainability performance: The role of servant leadership. *Leadership and Organization Development Journal*, *45*(3), 499–511. DOI: 10.1108/LODJ-06-2023-0330

Achieng, M., & Malatji, M. (2022). Digital transformation of small and medium enterprises in sub-Saharan Africa: A scoping review. *The Journal for Transdisciplinary Research in Southern Africa*, *18*(1). Advance online publication. DOI: 10.4102/td.v18i1.1257

Adadevoh, L., Marfo, M., Carlo, A., Ofei, E. F., & Asante, C. R. (2024). Succession Planning and Sustainability of Small and Medium Enterprises: The Moderating and Mediating Role of Transformational Leadership and Career Development. *International Journal (Toronto, Ont.)*, *5*(10), 2576–2597.

Adomako, S., Amankwah-Amoah, J., Danso, A., & Dankwah, G. O. (2021). Chief executive officers' sustainability orientation and firm environmental performance: Networking and resource contingencies. *Business Strategy and the Environment*, *30*(4), 2184–2193. DOI: 10.1002/bse.2742

Adomako, S., Danso, A., & Boateng, A. (Eds.). (2023). *Corporate Sustainability in Africa: Responsible Leadership*. Opportunities, and Challenges. DOI: 10.1007/978-3-031-29273-6

Agrawal, S., Oza, P., Kakkar, R., Tanwar, S., Jetani, V., Undhad, J., & Singh, A. (2024). Analysis and recommendation system-based on PRISMA checklist to write systematic review. *Assessing Writing*, *61*, 100866. DOI: 10.1016/j.asw.2024.100866

Agyapong, D., Agyapong, G., & Agyei-Poku, B. (2024). Implications of monitoring and evaluation systems for SMEs in some selected metropolis in Ghana. [JOBED]. *Journal of Business and Enterprise Development*, *12*(1). Advance online publication. DOI: 10.47963/jobed.v12i.1529

Agyapong, D., & Attram, A. B. (2019). Effect of owner-manager's financial literacy on the performance of SMEs in the Cape Coast Metropolis in Ghana. *Journal of Global Entrepreneurship Research*, *9*(1), 67. DOI: 10.1186/s40497-019-0191-1

Aidoo, S. (2022). The growth of SMEs amid the COVID-19 pandemic in Ghana. *Journal of Sustainable Tourism and Entrepreneurship*, *3*(3), 175–192.

Akomea-Frimpong, I., Asogwa, I. E., & Tenakwah, E. J. (2022). Systematic review of sustainable corporate governance of SMEs: Conceptualisation and propositions. *Corporate Ownership & Control*, *19*(3), 74–91. DOI: 10.22495/cocv19i3art5

Akpamah, P., & Matkó, A. (2023). Assessing SMES Leadership Styles Impact on Business Development and Job Creation: Evidence from Ghana. *Problems and Perspectives in Management*, *21*(1), 448–458. DOI: 10.21511/ppm.21(1).2023.38

Amaglo, J. K. (2019). Strategies for Sustainability of Small and Medium-Sized Enterprises in Ghana. *Walden Dissertations and Doctoral Studies*. 6963. https://scholarworks.waldenu.edu/dissertations/6963

Ametefe, M. D., Adamu, A. G., Umaru, F. A., & Ametefe, F. G. (2025). Leadership's impact on SME performance: A systematic review of its role in enterprise. *Journal of the International Council for Small Business*, 1-32.

Ansong, A. (2017). Corporate social responsibility and access to finance among Ghanaian SMEs: The role of stakeholder engagement. *Cogent Business & Management*, *4*(1), 1385165. DOI: 10.1080/23311975.2017.1385165

Araba, S. O. (2023). *Impact of Entrepreneurship Education on micro, small and medium enterprises (MSME) growth in north Central and South-West Nigeria*.

Asante, G. Y. (2023). *Business Sustainability Among Women Entrepreneurs in Ghana* (Doctoral dissertation, Walden University).

Assibey-Yeboah, M. D. (2019). Report of the Finance Committee on the programme based budget estimates for he Ministry of Business Development for the 2020 financial year.

Atanga, J. W. A. (2019). *Sustainable Business Growth: An Exploration of Ghanaian Small Business Survival*. Walden University.

Atiase, V., Agbanyo, S., Ganza, P., Ameh, J., & Sambian, R. (2023). Understanding SME financial resilience and survivability in Africa. In *Entrepreneurial Financial Resilience and Financial Innovation in a Turbulent Era* (pp. 106–133). Edward Elgar Publishing. DOI: 10.4337/9781802203929.00014

Bamfo, B. A., Asiedu-Appiah, F., & Ameza-Xemalordzo, E. (2023). Developing a framework for entrepreneurship ecosystem for developing countries: The application of institutional theory. *Cogent Business & Management*, *10*(2), 2195967. DOI: 10.1080/23311975.2023.2195967

Biney, I. K. (2023). Adult education and entrepreneurship: Getting young adults involved. *Journal of Innovation and Entrepreneurship*, *12*(1), 13. DOI: 10.1186/s13731-023-00277-0 PMID: 36919092

Conduah, A. K., & Essiaw, M. N. (2022). Resilience and entrepreneurship: A systematic review. *F1000 Research*, *11*, 348. DOI: 10.12688/f1000research.75473.1

Damoah, O. B. O., Lamptey, Y. A., Anlesinya, A., & Tetteh, B. N. A. (2021). Gendering Corporate Boards and Conditional Effectiveness of Board Processes: Insights from a Sub-Saharan African Country. *Global Business Review*, •••, 09721509211036271. DOI: 10.1177/09721509211036271

Damoah, O. B. O., & Peprah, A. A. (2021). Synthesis of small and medium enterprise research in Ghana. *Journal of Global Entrepreneurship Research*, *11*(1), 451–468. DOI: 10.1007/s40497-021-00286-x

Dankwa, S. M. E. (2020). *The Efficacy of Ghana's Business Interest in the Global Economy* (Doctoral dissertation, Walden University).

Eyiah-Botwe, E., Aigbavboa, C., & Thwala, W. D. (2016). Sustaining small and medium-size enterprises growth through stakeholder engagement.

Kato, A. I. (2024). Building resilience and sustainability in small businesses enterprises through sustainable venture capital investment in sub-Saharan Africa. *Cogent Economics & Finance*, *12*(1), 2399760. DOI: 10.1080/23322039.2024.2399760

Korankye, B. (2020). The Impact of Global Covid-19 Pandemic on Small and Medium Enterprises in Ghana. *International Journal of Management, Accounting & Economics, 7*(6).

Kuada, J. (2023). Changing role of finance in rural small enterprise growth in Ghana. *Journal of Entrepreneurship in Emerging Economies*, *15*(6), 1438–1458. DOI: 10.1108/JEEE-07-2021-0269

Ledi, K. K., Adu Asare Obeng, I., Ameza-Xemalordzo, E., & Dumeda, R. B. (2024). All hands on the pump: The role of strategic thinking and gender diversity on crisis management. *Current Issues in Tourism*, *27*(17), 1–17. DOI: 10.1080/13683500.2024.2320428

Linares-Espinós, E., Hernández, V., Domínguez-Escrig, J. L., Fernández-Pello, S., Hevia, V., Mayor, J., Padilla-Fernández, B., & Ribal, M. J. (2018). Methodology of a systematic review. *Actas Urológicas Españolas (English Ed.)*, *42*(8), 499–506. DOI: 10.1016/j.acuroe.2018.07.002 PMID: 29731270

Marfo, M., Armah, A. A., Ofei, E. F., Adadevoh, L., & Reindoph, C. A. (2024). Do Government Interventions and Transformational Leadership Matter? A Moderation-Mediation Analysis of SME Performance During COVID-19 in Ghana. *International Journal of Organizational Leadership*, *13*(1), 59–78. DOI: 10.33844/ijol.2024.60399

Mensah-Williams, E., & Derera, E. (2024). Entrepreneurship education landscape in selected universities in Ghana. In *Entrepreneurship and Enterprise Development in Africa* (pp. 159–175). Edward Elgar Publishing. DOI: 10.4337/9781803925417.00023

Neequaye, K. J. A. (2020). *Examining Corporate Governance Practices among SMEs in Ghana: A Case Study of Some Selected SMEs in Accra* (Doctoral dissertation, University Of Ghana).

Nketsiah, I. (2018). Financial record keeping practices of small business operators in the Sekondi-Takoradi metropolitan area of Ghana. *Asian Journal of Economics. Business and Accounting*, *6*(3), 1–9.

Nketsiah, I., & Van der Westhuizen, T. (2024, November). Governance and Leadership in Enhancing SME Resilience in Ghana: A Systematic Literature Review. In *European Conference on Management, Leadership & Governance* (pp. 417-424). Academic Conferences International Limited. https://doi.org/ DOI: 10.34190/ecmlg.20.1.3138

Oduro, S. (2020). Exploring the barriers to SMEs' open innovation adoption in Ghana: A mixed research approach. *International Journal of Innovation Science*, *12*(1), 21–51. DOI: 10.1108/IJIS-11-2018-0119

Ofori-Atta, K. (2020). Economic impact of the covid-19 pandemic on the economy of Ghana, Republic of Ghana. Retrieved from https://www.food-security.net/wp-content/uploads/2020/04/Ghana-Economic-Impact-of-COVID-on-Ghanas-Economy.pdf

Ogunyemi, K. (2022). Leadership for Sustainable Development in Africa: Roles and Responsibilities. In *Management and Leadership for a Sustainable Africa, Volume 2: Roles, Responsibilities, and Prospects* (pp. 1-17). Cham: Springer International Publishing.

Okoro, J. P., Nassè, T. B., Ngmendoma, A. B., Carbonell, N., & Nanema, M. (2022). Entrepreneurship education and youth unemployment challenges in Africa: Ghana in perspective. *International Journal of management & entrepreneurship Research, 4*(5), 213-231.

Owusu, A., Tauringana, V., & Asare, N. (2024). Sustainability performance reporting in Ghana: The views of SMEs. *Small Enterprise Research, 31*(1), 56–75. DOI: 10.1080/13215906.2024.2304847

Owusu, K. (2023). *Examining the Effectiveness of Leadership Approaches in Manufacturing Industries in Accra*. Walden University.

Rumasukun, M. R., & Noch, M. Y. (2023). The Role of Community Engagement in SME Management: A Qualitative Synthesis. *Golden Ratio of Community Services and Dedication, 3*(1), 40–48. DOI: 10.52970/grcsd.v3i1.605

Sabbah, M. (2024). Transformational Leadership and Business Continuity: A systematic review of empirical studies. *Management Research Quarterly, 1*(2), 4–24. DOI: 10.63029/kyzckn37

Sagala, G. H., & Őri, D. (2024). Exploring digital transformation strategy to achieve SMEs resilience and antifragility: A systematic literature review. *Journal of Small Business and Entrepreneurship*, •••, 1–30. DOI: 10.1080/08276331.2024.2392080

Tranfield, D., Denyer, D., & Smart, P. (2003). Towards a methodology for developing evidence-informed management knowledge by means of systematic review. *British Journal of Management, 14*(3), 207–222. DOI: 10.1111/1467-8551.00375

Tumaku, J. (2024). The relationship between regulatory focus and innovative performance of SMEs in Ghana: The role of entrepreneurial resilience, orientation and learning. *Management Science Letters, 14*(2), 127–138. DOI: 10.5267/j.msl.2023.9.001

Turkson, F. E., Amissah, E., & Gyeke-Dako, A. (2022). The role of formal and informal finance in the informal sector in Ghana. *Journal of Small Business and Entrepreneurship, 34*(3), 333–356. DOI: 10.1080/08276331.2020.1724002

Van der Westhuizen, T. (2023). *Youth Entrepreneurship: An Ecosystem Theory for Young Entrepreneurs in South Africa and Beyond*. Springer Nature. DOI: 10.1007/978-3-031-44339-8

Van der Westhuizen, T. (2024). *Practical Tools for Youth Entrepreneurs: An Applied Approach for South Africa and Beyond*. Springer Nature. DOI: 10.1007/978-3-031-44362-6

## KEY TERMS AND DEFINITIONS

**Sustainability-driven decision-making:** This refers to business choices that prioritise long-term environmental, social, and economic benefits. In SMEs, it involves adopting eco-friendly practices, ethical governance, and strategies that ensure growth while minimizing negative impacts on future generations.

**SME resilience:** This is the ability of small and medium enterprises to recover from disruptions, adapt to changing business environments, and sustain growth despite economic, social, or environmental challenges. It often depends on governance, leadership, and financial stability.

**Governance framework:** This refers to the set of rules, policies, and structures that guide business decision-making, accountability, and transparency. A strong governance framework helps SMEs establish ethical leadership, stakeholder trust, and regulatory compliance.

**Leadership:** Leadership in SMEs involves guiding, motivating, and managing teams to achieve business goals. Effective leadership styles, such as transformational or servant leadership, play a crucial role in decision-making, resilience, and long-term success.

**Risk mitigation strategies:** These are proactive measures taken by SMEs to identify, assess, and reduce potential threats to their operations. Examples include financial planning, diversification, insurance, and adopting crisis response frameworks to withstand market uncertainties.

**Crisis management approaches:** These are structured strategies used by businesses to respond effectively to unexpected disruptions, such as economic downturns, pandemics, or supply chain failures. Effective crisis management involves risk assessment, contingency planning, and rapid decision-making.

**Innovation-driven enterprises:** These are businesses that prioritise creativity, technology, and new ideas to improve products, services, and processes. Such enterprises often leverage digital transformation, research, and development to stay competitive in dynamic markets.

# Compilation of References


A.V. (2024). The impact of green hrm on employee skill development for sustainability initiatives. *International Journal of Trendy Rresearch in Engineering and Technology*, *08*(06), 77–82. DOI: 10.54473/IJTRET.2024.8610

Abakumov, E., & Beresten, S.Petersburg State University. (2023). Green campus as a part of environmental management of St. Petersburg State University. *Sustainability (Basel)*, *15*(16), 12515. DOI: 10.3390/su151612515

Abate, G., Basile, I., & Ferrari, P. (2021). The level of sustainability and mutual fund performance in Europe: An empirical analysis using ESG ratings. *Corporate Social Responsibility and Environmental Management*, *28*(5), 1446–1455. DOI: 10.1002/csr.2175

Abbas, Z., Sarwar, S., Rehman, M. A., Zámečník, R., & Shoaib, M. (2022). Green HRM promotes higher education sustainability: A mediated-moderated analysis. *International Journal of Manpower*, *43*(3), 827–843. DOI: 10.1108/IJM-04-2020-0171

Abdou, K., & Gupta, P. (2024). Limited partners' contribution to venture capital fund returns: Newbies versus experienced. *Managerial Finance*, *50*(7), 1387–1406. DOI: 10.1108/MF-10-2023-0606

Abhisha, N., & Melvin, C. L. J. (2024). *Green human resource management practices for sustainability: a comprehensive review*., DOI: 10.58532/V3BHMA24CH1

Aboramadan, M. (2022). The effect of green HRM on employee green behaviors in higher education: The mediating mechanism of green work engagement. *The International Journal of Organizational Analysis*, *30*(1), 7–23. DOI: 10.1108/IJOA-05-2020-2190

Abtahi, S. (2021). Isfahan University of Technology (IUT): Towards a green campus energy, climate and sustainable development initiatives at IUT. *Journal of Sustainability Perspectives*, 1. DOI: 10.14710/jsp.2021.12035

Abukari, A. J., Wenyuan, L., Abubakari, M. S., Pomegbe, W. W. K., & Sulemana, I. (2024). Extending the consequences of entrepreneurial bricolage to competitive advantage and sustainability performance: The role of servant leadership. *Leadership and Organization Development Journal*, *45*(3), 499–511. DOI: 10.1108/LODJ-06-2023-0330

Achieng, M., & Malatji, M. (2022). Digital transformation of small and medium enterprises in sub-Saharan Africa: A scoping review. *The Journal for Transdisciplinary Research in Southern Africa*, *18*(1). Advance online publication. DOI: 10.4102/td.v18i1.1257

Acosta, A., & Martínez, E. (2009). *Derechos de la naturaleza. El futuro es ahora* [Rights of nature. The future is now]. Abya-Yala.

Acs, Z. J., Autio, E., & Szerb, L. (2020). The Global Entrepreneurship and Development Index 2020. *Entrepreneurship and Regional Development*, *32*(3-4), 187–209.

Acs, Z. J., Szerb, L., & Autio, E. (2021). Green entrepreneurship and the transition to a sustainable economy. *Small Business Economics*, *56*(1), 1–15. DOI: 10.1007/s11187-020-00369-1

Adadevoh, L., Marfo, M., Carlo, A., Ofei, E. F., & Asante, C. R. (2024). Succession Planning and Sustainability of Small and Medium Enterprises: The Moderating and Mediating Role of Transformational Leadership and Career Development. *International Journal (Toronto, Ont.)*, *5*(10), 2576–2597.

Adams, D., De Sousa, C., & Tiesdell, S. (2010). Brownfield development: A comparison of North American and British approaches. *Urban Studies (Edinburgh, Scotland)*, *47*(1), 75–104. DOI: 10.1177/0042098009346868

Adams, D., Disberry, A., Hutchison, N., & Munjoma, T. (2000). Taxes, subsidies and the behaviour of brownfield owners. *Land Use Policy*, *17*(2), 135–145. DOI: 10.1016/S0264-8377(00)00003-X

ADB. (2017). ADB Annual Report 2017. Manila, Philippines: Asian Development Bank. https://www.adb.org/documents/adb-annual-report-2017

ADB. (2020). *Bioengineering for Green Infrastructure*. Manila, Philippines: Asian Development Bank. https://www.adb.org/sites/default/files/publication/577066/bioengineering-green-infrastructure.pdf

Adelaja, S., Shaw, J., Beyea, W., & McKeown, J. C. (2010). Renewable energy potential on brownfield sites: A case study of Michigan. *Energy Policy*, *38*(11), 7021–7030. DOI: 10.1016/j.enpol.2010.07.021

Adisa, O., Ajadi, T. H., & Keshtiban, A. (2024). Navigating Human-Technology Nexus for Environmental and Organizational Sustainability in Industry 5.0. *Practice, Progress, and Proficiency in Sustainability*, •••, 222–246. DOI: 10.4018/979-8-3693-7322-4.ch011

Adomako, S., Amankwah-Amoah, J., Danso, A., & Dankwah, G. O. (2021). Chief executive officers' sustainability orientation and firm environmental performance: Networking and resource contingencies. *Business Strategy and the Environment*, *30*(4), 2184–2193. DOI: 10.1002/bse.2742

Adomako, S., Danso, A., & Boateng, A. (Eds.). (2023). *Corporate Sustainability in Africa: Responsible Leadership*. Opportunities, and Challenges. DOI: 10.1007/978-3-031-29273-6

Adu-Gyamfi, Y. O., Asare, S. K., Sharma, A., & Titus, T. (2017). Automated vehicle recognition with deep convolutional neural networks. *Transportation Research Record: Journal of the Transportation Research Board*, *2645*(1), 113–122. DOI: 10.3141/2645-13

Afanador, N., Becerra, E. D., & Andrango, J. C. (2021). The Paradoxes Between Business Performance and Organizational Behavior in Colombian and Ecuadorian Companies. In R. Perez-Uribe, D. Ocampo-Guzman, N. Moreno-Monsalve, & W. Fajardo-Moreno (Eds.), *Handbook of Research on Management Techniques and Sustainability Strategies for Handling Disruptive Situations in Corporate Settings* (pp. 396-415). IGI Global Scientific Publishing. DOI: 10.4018/978-1-7998-8185-8.ch019

Aghion, P., & Tirole, J. (1997). Formal and real authority in organization. *Journal of Political Economy*, *105*(1), 1–29. DOI: 10.1086/262063

Agrawal, A., & Hockerts, K. (2021). Impact Investing: Review and Research Agenda. *Journal of Small Business and Entrepreneurship*, *33*(2), 153–181. DOI: 10.1080/08276331.2018.1551457

Agrawal, S., Oza, P., Kakkar, R., Tanwar, S., Jetani, V., Undhad, J., & Singh, A. (2024). Analysis and recommendation system-based on PRISMA checklist to write systematic review. *Assessing Writing*, *61*, 100866. DOI: 10.1016/j.asw.2024.100866

Agreement, P. (2015, noviembre 12). https://unfccc.int/sites/default/files/spanish_paris_agreement.pdf

Agrifoglio, R., Metallo, C., & di Nauta, P. (2021). Understanding Knowledge management in Public Organizations through the Organizational Knowing Perspective: A Systematic Literature Review and Bibliometric Analysis. *Public Organization Review*, *21*(1), 137–156. DOI: 10.1007/s11115-020-00480-7

Aguinda v. Chevron-Texaco, 0002 (Corte Provincial de Sucumbíos 2003).

Aguirre, W. E., Alvarez-Mieles, G., Anaguano-Yancha, F., Burgos Morán, R., Cucalón, R. V., Escobar-Camacho, D., Jácome-Negrete, I., Jiménez Prado, P., Laaz, E., Miranda-Troya, K., Navarrete-Amaya, R., Nugra Salazar, F., Revelo, W., Rivadeneira, J. F., Valdiviezo Rivera, J., & Zárate Hugo, E. (2021). Conservation threats and future prospects for the freshwater fishes of Ecuador: A hotspot of Neotropical fish diversity. *Journal of Fish Biology*, *99*(4), 1158–1189. DOI: 10.1111/jfb.14844 PMID: 34235726

Agyapong, D., Agyapong, G., & Agyei-Poku, B. (2024). Implications of monitoring and evaluation systems for SMEs in some selected metropolis in Ghana. [JOBED]. *Journal of Business and Enterprise Development*, *12*(1). Advance online publication. DOI: 10.47963/jobed.v12i.1529

Agyapong, D., & Attram, A. B. (2019). Effect of owner-manager's financial literacy on the performance of SMEs in the Cape Coast Metropolis in Ghana. *Journal of Global Entrepreneurship Research*, *9*(1), 67. DOI: 10.1186/s40497-019-0191-1

Ahmad, B., Salam, M., Ullah, W., Iqbal, S., & Shahid, M. (2024). Let the Employees Strengthen for a Sustainable Future: A Systematic Literature Review of Sustainable HRM. *Journal of Policy Research*. https://doi.org/DOI: 10.61506/02.00357

Ahmad, F., Hossain, M. B., Mustafa, K., Ejaz, F., Khawaja, K. F., & Dunay, A. (2023). Green HRM System and Knowledge Sharing Improve Environmental Performance by Raising Employee Commitment to the Environment. *Sustainability (Basel)*, *15*(6), 5040. DOI: 10.3390/su15065040

Ahmad, N., Lodhi, M. S., Zaman, K., & Naseem, I. (2017). Knowledge management: A Gateway for Organizational Performance. *Journal of the Knowledge Economy*, *8*(3), 859–876. DOI: 10.1007/s13132-015-0282-3

Ahmad, N., Zhu, Y., Ullah, Z., Iqbal, M., Hussain, K., & Ahmed, R. I. (2021). Sustainable solutions to facilitate brownfield redevelopment projects in emerging countries – Pakistani scenario. *Land Use Policy*, *109*, 105727. DOI: 10.1016/j.landusepol.2021.105727

Ahmed, M. F., & Islam, M. S. (2014). Urbanization and environmental problem: An empirical study in Sylhet City, Bangladesh. *Research on Humanities and Social Sciences*, *4*(3), 161–172.

Ahmed, M. F., Mokhtar, M. B., Lim, C. K., Hooi, A. W. K., & Lee, K. E. (2021). Leadership roles for sustainable development: The case of a Malaysian green hotel. *Sustainability (Basel)*, *13*(18), 10260. DOI: 10.3390/su131810260

Ahmed, S.. (2021). IoT-Enabled Traffic Monitoring Systems: Framework and Implementation. *Sensors (Basel)*.

Aidoo, S. (2022). The growth of SMEs amid the COVID-19 pandemic in Ghana. *Journal of Sustainable Tourism and Entrepreneurship*, *3*(3), 175–192.

Akaraci, S., Feng, X., Suesse, T., Jalaludin, B., & Astell-Burt, T. (2020). A Systematic Review and Meta-Analysis of Associations between Green and Blue Spaces and Birth Outcomes. *International Journal of Environmental Research and Public Health*, *17*(8), 2949. DOI: 10.3390/ijerph17082949 PMID: 32344732

*AKH Group sets up new green factory in Bangladesh* |. (n.d.). YnFx. https://www.yarnsandfibers.com/news/textile-news/akh-group-sets-up-new-green-factory-in-bangladesh/amp/ application of the Ecological Footprint as environmental indicator in the textile sector.

Akinboade, O. O. A., Taft, T., Weber, J. F., Manoko, O. B., & Molobi, V. S. (2023). How the social entrepreneurship business model designs in South Africa create value: A complex adaptive systems approach. *Journal of Entrepreneurship in Emerging Economies*, *15*(1), 70–95. DOI: 10.1108/JEEE-02-2021-0057

Akomea-Frimpong, I., Asogwa, I. E., & Tenakwah, E. J. (2022). Systematic review of sustainable corporate governance of SMEs: Conceptualisation and propositions. *Corporate Ownership & Control*, *19*(3), 74–91. DOI: 10.22495/cocv19i3art5

Akpamah, P., & Matkó, A. (2023). Assessing SMES Leadership Styles Impact on Business Development and Job Creation: Evidence from Ghana. *Problems and Perspectives in Management*, *21*(1), 448–458. DOI: 10.21511/ppm.21(1).2023.38

Alami, S., Rhouiri, M., & Marghich, A. (2021). Active resilience, the cornerstone of firm competitiveness in the post-COVID-19 era: Industrial sector companies in Morocco. *Revue Management Innovation*, *4*(2), 135–155. DOI: 10.3917/rmi.204.0135

Alavi, M., & Leidner, D. E. (2001). Review: Knowledge management and knowledge management systems: Conceptual foundations and research issues. *Management Information Systems Quarterly*, *25*(1), 107–136. DOI: 10.2307/3250961

Alberini, A., Longo, A., Tonin, S., Trombetta, F., & Turvani, M. (2005). The role of liability, regulation and economic incentives in brownfield remediation and redevelopment: Evidence from surveys of developers. *Regional Science and Urban Economics*, *35*(4), 327–351. DOI: 10.1016/j.regsciurbeco.2004.05.004

Alchian, A. A. (1965). Some economics of property rights. *Politico (Pavia, Italy)*, *30*(1), 816–829.

Alchian, A. A., & Demsetz, H. (1972). Production, information costs, and economic organization. In *Armen A. Alchian. (1977). Economic Forces at Work*. Liberty Press.

Al-Dmour, H. (2023). Green-smart university campuses: The mediating role of student engagement in enhancing corporate image. *SAGE Open*, *13*(4), 21582440231219591. Advance online publication. DOI: 10.1177/21582440231219591

Aldosemani, T., Lytras, M. D., & Ordóñez de Pablos, P. (Eds.). (2025). *Innovative Educational Frameworks for Future Skills and Competencies*. IGI Global., DOI: 10.4018/979-8-3693-7555-6

AlHashmi, M. H., Khan, M. M., & Ajmal, M. M. (2021). Implementing Sustainable Procurement Strategy in the Oil and Gas Sector: Analytic Hierarchy Process Approach. [IJSSMET]. *International Journal of Service Science, Management, Engineering, and Technology*, *12*(2), 59–77. DOI: 10.4018/IJSSMET.2021030104

Ali, S.. (2022). *Sustainable Traffic Systems: Energy-Efficient Sensors and Algorithms*. Renewable Energy in Transportation.

Ali, S., Li, G., Yang, P., Hussain, K., & Latif, Y. (2020). Unpacking the importance of intangible skills in new product development and sustainable business performance; strategies for marketing managers. *PLoS One*, *15*(9), e0238743. DOI: 10.1371/journal.pone.0238743 PMID: 32976509

Ali, S., & Tang, H. (2023). Is Intellectual Property Beneficial to Knowledge management? Literature Review on Organizational Knowledge Protection. *Journal of the Knowledge Economy*, *14*(4), 4100–4118. DOI: 10.1007/s13132-022-00904-3

Aliu, F., Asero, V., Asllani, A., & Kučera, J. (2023). Spillover effects and transmission of shocks in Visegrad equity markets. *Studies in Economics and Finance*. Advance online publication. DOI: 10.1108/SEF-07-2023-0395

Alkaraan, F., Elmarzouky, M., Hussainey, K., & Venkatesh, V. G. (2023). Sustainable strategic investment decision-making practices in UK companies: The influence of governance mechanisms on synergy between industry 4.0 and circular economy. *Technological Forecasting and Social Change*, *187*, 122187. DOI: 10.1016/j.techfore.2022.122187

Alker, S., Joy, V., Roberts, P., & Smith, N. (2000). The definition of brownfield. *Journal of Environmental Planning and Management*, *43*(1), 49–69. DOI: 10.1080/09640560010766

Allen, C., & Clouth, S. (2012). *A guidebook to the Green Economy Issue 1: Green Economy, Green Growth, and Low-Carbon Development – history, definitions and a guide to recent publications*. UN Division for Sustainable Development. https://sdgs.un.org/publications/guidebook-green-economy-issue-1-green-economy-green-growth-and-low-carbon-development

Alqudah, M. K., & Yusof, Y. S. (2024). Academic citizenship behaviour mediates between green performance management, green training and development, and organization environmental performance in the Jordanian government universities. *International Journal of Academic Research in Business & Social Sciences*, *14*(2). Advance online publication. DOI: 10.6007/IJARBSS/v14-i2/20981

Al-Shammari, M., Rasheed, A., & Al-Shammari, H. A. (2019). CEO narcissism and corporate social responsibility: Does CEO narcissism affect CSR focus? *Journal of Business Research*, *104*(C), 106–117. DOI: 10.1016/j.jbusres.2019.07.005

Alvord, S. H., Brown, L. D., & Letts, C. W. (2004). Social Entrepreneurship and Societal Transformation: An Exploratory Study. *The Journal of Applied Behavioral Science*, *40*(3), 260–282. DOI: 10.1177/0021886304266847

Amaglo, J. K. (2019). Strategies for Sustainability of Small and Medium-Sized Enterprises in Ghana. *Walden Dissertations and Doctoral Studies*. 6963. https://scholarworks.waldenu.edu/dissertations/6963

Ambarawati, N. G. M. A., & Wijoyo, R. P. (2023). *The Implementation of Talent Management Implementation at Regional Employee Agency Wonogiri Regency Central Java*. Jurnal MSDA., DOI: 10.33701/jmsda.v11i2.3764

Amel-Zadeh, A., & Serafeim, G. (2018). Why and How Investors Use ESG Information: Evidence from a Global Survey. *Financial Analysts Journal*, *74*(3), 87–103. DOI: 10.2469/faj.v74.n3.2

Ametefe, M. D., Adamu, A. G., Umaru, F. A., & Ametefe, F. G. (2025). Leadership's impact on SME performance: A systematic review of its role in enterprise. *Journal of the International Council for Small Business*, 1-32.

Anand, J., Hemasundari, M., Selvaranee, J. K., & Mariadhas, J. M. (2024). *Integrating SDGs into Human Resource Management: Pathways to Sustainable Workforce Development*. https://doi.org/DOI: 10.47172/2965-730X.SDGsReview.v4.n04.pe03556

Anshima, A., Bhardwaj, B., Sharma, D., & Dhiman, M. C. (2024). Ensuring sustainability through green HRM practices: a review, synthesis and research avenues. *Journal of Organizational Effectiveness*. https://doi.org/DOI: 10.1108/JOEPP-10-2023-0493

Ansong, A. (2017). Corporate social responsibility and access to finance among Ghanaian SMEs: The role of stakeholder engagement. *Cogent Business & Management*, *4*(1), 1385165. DOI: 10.1080/23311975.2017.1385165

Anthropologies. (20 de 04 de 2015). *El impacto de Chevron en la Amazonía ecuatoriana*. Obtenido de https://www.anthropologies.es/el-impacto-de-chevron-en-la-amazonia-ecuatoriana/

Anusuya, M., & Soundarapandian, M. (2024). Exploring human capital management practices: A comprehensive review. *World Journal of Advanced Research and Reviews*, *21*(3), 2343–2348.

Anwar, N., Nik Mahmood, N. H., Yusliza, M. Y., Ramayah, T., Noor Faezah, J., & Khalid, W. (2020). Green Human Resource Management for organizational citizenship behaviour towards the environment and environmental performance on a university campus. *Journal of Cleaner Production*, *256*, 120401. Advance online publication. DOI: 10.1016/j.jclepro.2020.120401

Araba, S. O. (2023). *Impact of Entrepreneurship Education on micro, small and medium enterprises (MSME) growth in north Central and South-West Nigeria*.

Arellano, P., Tansey, K., Balzter, H., & Tellkamp, M. (2017). Plant family-specific impacts of petroleum pollution on biodiversity and leaf chlorophyll content in the Amazon rainforest of Ecuador. *PLoS One*, *12*(1), e0169867. DOI: 10.1371/journal.pone.0169867 PMID: 28103307

Armacanqui, J. S., Nash, S. S., Eyzaguirre Gormendia, L., & Moghanloo, R. (Eds.). (2024). *Sustainability Applied to Unconventional Oil and Gas Field Exploration and Development*. IGI Global., DOI: 10.4018/979-8-3693-0740-3

Arqawi, S., Zaid, A. A., Jaaron, A. A., Al Hila, A. A., Al Shobaki, M. J., & Abu-Naser, S. S. (2019). Green human resource management practices among Palestinian manufacturing firms-an exploratory study.

Arrow, K. J. (1962). Economic welfare and the allocation of resources for invention. In Nelson, R. R. (Ed.), *The rate and direction of inventive activity: Economic and social factors* (pp. 609–626). Princeton University Press. DOI: 10.1515/9781400879762-024

Arteaga, A., Salazar-Valenzuela, D., Mebert, K., Peñafiel, N., Aguiar, G., Sánchez-Nivicela, J. C., Pyron, R. A., Colston, T. J., Cisneros-Heredia, D. F., Yánez-Muñoz, M. H., Venegas, P. J., Guayasamin, J. M., & Torres-Carvajal, O. (2018). Systematics of South American snail-eating snakes (Serpentes, Dipsadini), with the description of five new species from Ecuador and Peru. *ZooKeys*, *766*, 79–147. DOI: 10.3897/zookeys.766.24523 PMID: 29942172

Arulrajah, A. A., Opatha, H. H. D. N. P., & Nawaratne, N. N. J. (2015). Green human resource management practices: A review. Sri Lankan Journal of human resource management, 5(1).

Arvind, D., & Priya, B. (2024). *Workplace Culture: Creating A Positive and Inclusive Environment*. Shanlax International Journal of Management., DOI: 10.34293/management.v11iS1-Mar.8082

Asante, G. Y. (2023). *Business Sustainability Among Women Entrepreneurs in Ghana* (Doctoral dissertation, Walden University).

Asif, F., Sharif, K., & Malik, A. (2023). Life cycle analysis and sustainability reporting in green entrepreneurship education. *Journal of Cleaner Production*, *367*, 133892. DOI: 10.1016/j.jclepro.2023.133892

Asrin, F., Saide, S., & Ratna, S. (2021). Data to Knowledge-Based Transformation: The Association Rules With Rapid Miner Approach and Predictive Analysis in Evergreen IT-Business Routines of PT Chevron Pacific Indonesia. [IJSKD]. *International Journal of Sociotechnology and Knowledge Development*, *13*(4), 141–152. DOI: 10.4018/IJSKD.2021100109

Assibey-Yeboah, M. D. (2019). Report of the Finance Committee on the programme based budget estimates for he Ministry of Business Development for the 2020 financial year.

Association for the Advancement of Sustainability in Higher Education (AASHE). (2021). *Sustainability Tracking, Assessment & Rating System (STARS)*. Retrieved from https://stars.aashe.org/

Assyne, N. (2022). Towards a Security Competence of Software Developers: A Literature Review. In I. Management Association (Ed.), *Research Anthology on Agile Software, Software Development, and Testing* (pp. 2050-2064). IGI Global Scientific Publishing. DOI: 10.4018/978-1-6684-3702-5.ch098

Astier Calderón, M., Masera Cerutti, O., & Galván Miyoshi, Y. (2008). Evaluación de sustentabilidad. Un enfoque dinámico y multidimensional Evaluación de sustentabilidad. Un enfoque dinámico y multidimensional. Valencia, España: Sociedad Española de Agricultura Ecológica (SEAE), Centro de Investigaciones en Geografía Ambiental (CIGA-UNAM), El Colegio de la Frontera Sur (ECOSUR), Centro de Investigaciones en Ecosistemas (CIECO-UNAM).

Atadoga, A., Awonuga, K. F., Ibeh, C. V., Ike, C. U., Olu-lawal, K. A., & Usman, F. O. (2024). Harnessing data analytics for sustainable business growth in the us renewable energy sector. *Engineering Science & Technology Journal*, *5*(2), 460–470. DOI: 10.51594/estj.v5i2.806

Atanga, J. W. A. (2019). *Sustainable Business Growth: An Exploration of Ghanaian Small Business Survival*. Walden University.

Atasu, A., Dumas, C., & Van Wassenhove, L. N. (2021). The circular business model: Pick a strategy that fits your resources and capabilities. *Harvard Business Review*. https://hbr.org/2021/07/the-circular-business-model

Atasu, A., Sarvary, M., & Van Wassenhove, L. N. (2008). Remanufacturing as a Marketing Strategy. *Management Science*, *54*(10), 1731–1746. DOI: 10.1287/mnsc.1080.0893

Atiase, V., Agbanyo, S., Ganza, P., Ameh, J., & Sambian, R. (2023). Understanding SME financial resilience and survivability in Africa. In *Entrepreneurial Financial Resilience and Financial Innovation in a Turbulent Era* (pp. 106–133). Edward Elgar Publishing. DOI: 10.4337/9781802203929.00014

Atlas, R., & Hazen, T. (2011). Oil Biodegradation and Bioremediation: A Tale of the Two Worst Spills in U.S. History. *Environmental Science & Technology, 45*(16), 6709-6715. Obtenido de https://pubs.acs.org/doi/epdf/10.1021/es2013227

Atrill, P., & McLaney, E. (2017). *Accounting and Finance for Non-Specialists* (10th ed.). Pearson.

Audebert, N., Le Saux, B., & Lefèvre, S. (2017). Segment-before-detect: Vehicle detection and classification through semantic segmentation of aerial images. *Remote Sensing (Basel)*, *9*(4), 368. DOI: 10.3390/rs9040368

Ávila Santamaría, R. (2012, septiembre 6). Evolución de los derechos fundamentales en el constitucionalismo ecuatoriano [Evolution of fundamental rights in Ecuadorian constitutionalism]. Congreso Ecuatoriano de Historia 2012 (Montecristi), Ecuador. https://repositorio.uasb.edu.ec/bitstream/10644/3015/1/%C3%81vila%2C%20R-CON-008-Evoluci%C3%B3n.pdf

Bacigalupo M, Kampylis P, Punie Y and Van Den Brande L. (2016) EntreComp: The Entrepreneurship Competence Framework. EUR 27939 EN. Luxembourg (Luxembourg): Publications Office of the European Union. JRC101581.

Bahl, A. S. (2021). Topical Use of Plant Extract-Based Oil Blend in Relieving the Symptoms of Primary Dysmenorrhea: An Independent Clinical Study. [IJHSTM]. *International Journal of Health Systems and Translational Medicine*, *1*(1), 47–61. DOI: 10.4018/IJHSTM.2021010102

Bain (2022). ESG, Not A Solo Game. Report prepared in collaboration with Türkiye Investment Office. Available at https://www.invest.gov.tr/en/library/publications/lists/investpublications/esg-not-a-solo-game.pdf. Accessed on February 1st, 2025.

Baker, M., Egan, M. L., & Sarkar, S. K. (2022). How do investors value ESG? (No. w30708). National Bureau of Economic Research. BCG and KfW Capital (2021).Growing the Seeds of ESG: Venture Capital, Start-ups and the Need for Sustainability. Available at: https://www.kfw-capital.de/Dokumente/ESG-Report-ESG-säen-Nachhaltigkeit-ernten-(Nov.-2021).pdf. Accessed on February 8th, 2025.

Baker, G., Gibbons, R., & Murphy, K. J. (1999). Informal authority in organizations. *Journal of Law Economics and Organization*, *15*(1), 56–73. DOI: 10.1093/jleo/15.1.56

Balcerzak, A., & MacGregor Pelikánová, R. (2020). Projection of SDGs in Codes of Ethics – Case study about Lost in Translation? *Administrative Sciences, 10*(4): 1-18. Paper 95. .DOI: 10.3390/admsci10040095

Balcerzak, A. P., & Pietrzak, M. B. (2017). Sustainable Development in the European Union in the Years 2004–2013. In Bilgin, M., Danis, H., Demir, E., & Can, U. (Eds.), *Regional Studies on Economic Growth, Financial Economics and Management. Eurasian Studies in Business and Economics* (Vol. 7). Springer. DOI: 10.1007/978-3-319-54112-9_12

Balcerzak, A., MacGregor, R. K., MacGregor Pelikánová, R., Rogalska, E., & Szostek, D. (2023). The EU regulation of sustainable investment: The end of sustainability trade-offs? *Entrepreneurial Business and Economics Review*, *11*(1), 199–212. DOI: 10.15678/EBER.2023.110111

Bali Swain, R., & Yang-Wallentin, F. (2019). Achieving sustainable development goals: Predicaments and strategies. *International Journal of Sustainable Development and World Ecology*, *27*(2), 96–106. DOI: 10.1080/13504509.2019.1692316

Bamfo, B. A., Asiedu-Appiah, F., & Ameza-Xemalordzo, E. (2023). Developing a framework for entrepreneurship ecosystem for developing countries: The application of institutional theory. *Cogent Business & Management*, *10*(2), 2195967. DOI: 10.1080/23311975.2023.2195967

Bandura, A. (1971). *Social learning theory*. Prentice-Hall.

Bansal, I. (2019). Green Management: A study of best green practices in Haryana Private Universities. *Think India Journal*, *22*(4), 4539–4548.

Baquero, C. (2023). Fosas, derrames y piscinas abandonadas: las huellas de medio siglo de contaminación petrolera no remediada en Ecuador. Obtenido de https://es.mongabay.com/2023/06/huellas-de-medio-siglo-de-contaminacion-petrolera-no-remediada-en-ecuador/

Barakat, S., Alneyadi, R., Alderei, M., Malek, S., Alahbabi, F., & Jasim, M. (2024). The impact of sustainable hrm practices on job performance in uae organizations. *International Journal of Management Trends: Key Concepts and Research*, *3*(1), 29–38. DOI: 10.58898/ijmt.v3i1.29-38

Bárcena, A. (2020). La emergencia del cambio climático en América Latina y el Caribe [The climate change emergency in Latin America and the Caribbean]. CEPAL. Retrieved from https://www.cepal.org/es/presentaciones/la-emergencia-cambio-climatico-america-latina-caribe-seguimos-esperando-la-catastrofe

Barney, J. (1991). Firm resources and sustained competitive advantage. *Journal of Management*, *17*(1), 99–120. DOI: 10.1177/014920639101700108

Barth, T. D. (2011). The Idea of a Green New Deal in a Quintuple Helix Model of Knowledge, Know-How and Innovation. *International Journal of Social Ecology and Sustainable Development*, *2*(1), 1–14. DOI: 10.4018/jsesd.2011010101

Bartke, S., Rizzo, E., Giubilato, E., Pizzol, L., Critto, A., & Marcomini, A. (2013). Improvement of brownfield regeneration in Europe through tailored information platform, communication, prioritisation and assessment. In Skowronek, J. (Ed.), *Innowacyjne rozwiązania rewitalizacji terenów zdegradowanych* (pp. 135–143). IETU & Centrum Badań.

Barton, D., Koller, G., & Wiseman, M. (2019). *Capitalism for the Long Term: A Guide for Investors*. Harvard Business Review Press.

Barzel, Y. (1989). *Economic Analysis of Property Rights*. Cambridge University Press.

Bastos, K. V. L. S., de Souza, A. B., Tomé, A. C., & Souza, F. M. (2025). New Strategies for the Extraction of Antioxidants from Fruits and Their By-Products: A Systematic Review. *Plants*, *14*(5), 755. DOI: 10.3390/plants14050755 PMID: 40094704

Batrancea, L., Balcı, M. A., Akgüller, Ö., & Gaban, L. (2022). What Drives Economic Growth across European Countries? A Multimodal Approach. *Mathematics*, *10*(3660), 1–20. DOI: 10.3390/math10193660

Batrancea, L., Pop, M. C., Rathnaswamy, M. M., Batrancea, I., & Rus, M.-I. (2021). An Empirical Investigation on the Transition Process toward a Green Economy. *Sustainability (Basel)*, *13*(13151), 1–12. DOI: 10.3390/su132313151

Bautista-Valarezo, E., Duque, V., Verdugo Sánchez, A. E., Dávalos-Batallas, V., Michels, N. R. M., Hendrickx, K., & Verhoeven, V. (2020). Towards an indigenous definition of health: An explorative study to understand the indigenous Ecuadorian people's health and illness concepts. *International Journal for Equity in Health*, *19*(1), 101. DOI: 10.1186/s12939-020-1142-8 PMID: 32571404

Bayliss, C., Ouelhadj, D., Dadashzadeh, N., & Fletcher, G. (2025). Mobility-as-a-Service Personalised Multi-Modal Multi-Objective Journey Planning with Machine-Learning-Guided Shortest-Path Algorithms. *Applied Sciences (Basel, Switzerland)*, *15*(4), 2052. DOI: 10.3390/app15042052

bdnews24. (2017, May 8). Crown Cement, GPH Ispat sign deals on eco-friendly construction. *Bdnews24. Com*. https://bdnews24.com/business/crown-cement-gph-ispat-sign-deals-on-eco-friendly-construction

Belás, J., Machova, R., Oláh, J., & Metzker, Z. (2024). The impact of selected HRM factors on company's survival of SMEs: Empirical research in V4 countries. *Journal of International Students*, *17*(1), 108–123. Advance online publication. DOI: 10.14254/2071-8330.2024/17-1/7

BenDor, T. K., Metcalf, S. S., & Paich, M. (2011). The dynamics of brownfield redevelopment. *Sustainability (Basel)*, *3*(6), 914–936. DOI: 10.3390/su3060914

Benítez Gaibor, M. K., Martínez Mesías, J. P., & Jara Vásquez, E. A. (2021). Challenges for Measuring Value Chain Relation Coordination of SMEs of the Textile and Apparel Industry: The Case of a Small Family Industrial Safety Footwear Firm of Ambato, Ecuador. In I. Management Association (Ed.), *Research Anthology on Small Business Strategies for Success and Survival* (pp. 475-496). IGI Global Scientific Publishing. DOI: 10.4018/978-1-7998-9155-0.ch024

Ben-Moussa, S. (2017). A Tale Of Two Trade Powers: Balancing Investor-State Dispute Settlement And Environmental Risk Between The Eu And Us In A Changing Political Climate. *Fordham Environmental Law Review*, *29*(1), 95–124. https://www.jstor.org/stable/26413295

Benn, S., Edwards, M., & Williams, T. (2018). *Organizational Change for Corporate Sustainability*. Routledge. DOI: 10.4324/9781315619620

Berg, F., Jay, J., Kölbel, J., & Rigobon, R. (2023). The Signal In The Noise. *EconPol Forum.*, *1*(24), 23–27.

Berggren, E., & Worth, A. (2023). Towards a future regulatory framework for chemicals in the European Union – Chemicals 2.0, REGULATORY TOXICOLOGY AND PHARMACOLOGY, ISSN 0273-2300, 142, p. 105431, JRC132966.

Berkeley, U. C. (2021). *Center for Responsible Business*. Retrieved from https://responsiblebusiness.berkeley.edu/

Bernard, S., Asokan, S., Warrell, H., & Lemer, J. (2009, August 17). The greenest bail-out? *Financial Times*. Retrieved from http://ig-legacy.ft.com/content/cc207678-0738-11de-9294-000077b07658#axzz7f2qUQzDG

Bernow, S., Klempner, B., & Magnin, C. (2017). From 'why' to 'why not': Sustainable investing as the new normal. McKinsey & Company. Available at https://www.mckinsey.com/~/media/McKinsey/Industries/Private%20Equity%20and%20Principal%20Investors/Our%20Insights/From%20why%20to%20why%20not%20Sustainable%20investing%20as%20the%20new%20normal/From-why-to-why-not-Sustainable-investing-as-the-new-normal.pdf. Accessed on February 1st, 2025.

Bez, C. S., Ash, M., & Boyce, J. K. (2023b). Environmental inequality in industrial brownfields: Evidence from French municipalities. *Ecological Economics*, *217*, 108018. DOI: 10.1016/j.ecolecon.2023.108018

Bhattacherja, P., Islam, S., & Xeenia, F. T. (2020). *Green industry development in Bangladesh: Challenges and Prospects*. Tech Monitor.

Bhatti, S. H., Saleem, F., Murtaza, G., & Haq, T. U. (2021). Haq (2021). Exploring the effects of green human resource management on environmental performance: The roles of perceived organizational support and innovative environmental behavior. *International Journal of Manpower*, *43*(3), 742–762. DOI: 10.1108/IJM-05-2020-0215

Bianchi, G., Pisiotis, U., & Cabrera Giraldez, M. GreenComp The European sustainability competence framework, Punie, Y. and Bacigalupo, M. editor(s). (2022). EUR 30955 EN, Publications Office of the European Union, Luxembourg, ISBN 978-92-76-46485-3, , JRC128040.DOI: 10.2760/13286

Bian, Y., Gao, H., Wang, R., & Xiong, X. (2023). Sustainable development for private equity: Integrating environment, social, and governance factors into partnership valuation. *Business Strategy and the Environment*, *32*(6), 3359–3370. DOI: 10.1002/bse.3304

Biggs, R., Clements, H., de Vos, A., Folke, C., Manyani, A., Maciejewski, K., Martín-López, B., Preiser, R., Selomane, O., & Schlüter, M. (2022). What are social-ecological systems and social-ecological systems research? In Biggs, R., de Vos, A., Preiser, R., Clements, H., Maciejewski, K., & Schlüter, M. (Eds.), *The Routledge Handbook of Research Methods for Social-Ecological Systems* (pp. 3–26). Routledge/ Taylor & Francis., DOI: 10.4324/9781003021339-2

Bina, O. (2013). The green economy and sustainable development: An uneasy balance? *Environment and Planning. C, Government & Policy*, *31*(6), 1023–1047. DOI: 10.1068/c1310j

Biney, I. K. (2023). Adult education and entrepreneurship: Getting young adults involved. *Journal of Innovation and Entrepreneurship*, *12*(1), 13. DOI: 10.1186/s13731-023-00277-0 PMID: 36919092

Bleicher, A., & Gross, M. (2010). Sustainability assessment and the revitalization of contaminated sites: Operationalizing sustainable development for local problems. *International Journal of Sustainable Development and World Ecology*, *17*(1), 57–66. DOI: 10.1080/13504500903488263

Bocken, N. M., de Pauw, I., Bakker, C., & van der Grinten, B. (2016). Product design and business model strategies for a circular economy. *Journal of Industrial and Production Engineering*, *33*(5), 308–320. DOI: 10.1080/21681015.2016.1172124

Bocken, N. M., Short, S. W., Rana, P., & Evans, S. (2019). A literature and practice review to develop sustainable business model archetypes. *Journal of Cleaner Production*, *65*, 42–56. DOI: 10.1016/j.jclepro.2013.11.039

Boff, L. (2013). "Constitucionalismos ecológicos en América Latina" [Ecological constitutionalisms in Latin America]. Visita 15 de mayo de 2013 en: http//leonardoboof.wordpress.com/2013/05/14/constitucionalismo ecologico-en-america-latina/

Boguslawski, R., Van Gansen, K., Valayer, C., Borzacchiello, M., & Pignatelli, F. (2017). European Union Location Framework Blueprint, EUR 28931 EN, Publications Office of the European Union, Luxembourg, ISBN 978-92-79-77060-9 (online),978-92-79-86359-2 (ePub), (online), (ePub), JRC108216. DOI: 10.2760/975822

Bohdanowicz, P., Zientara, P., & Novotna, E. (2011). International hotel chains and environmental protection: An analysis of Hilton's we care! programme (Europe, 2006–2008). *Journal of Sustainable Tourism*, *19*(7), 797–816. DOI: 10.1080/09669582.2010.549566

Bombiak, E. (2019). Green human resource management – The latest trend or strategic necessity? *Journal of Entrepreneurship and Sustainability Issues*, *6*(4), 1647–1662. DOI: 10.9770/jesi.2019.6.4(7)

Bond, A., Pope, J., Fundingsland, M., Morrison-Saunders, A., Retief, F., & Hauptfleisch, M. (2020). Explaining the political nature of environmental impact assessment (EIA): A neo-Gramscian perspective. *Journal of Cleaner Production*, *244*(January), 118694. DOI: 10.1016/j.jclepro.2019.118694

Borghesi, R., Houston, J., & Naranjo, A. (2014). Corporate Socially Responsible Investments: CEO Altruism, Reputation, and Shareholder Interests. *Journal of Corporate Finance*, *26*, 164–181. DOI: 10.1016/j.jcorpfin.2014.03.008

Borja A, Elliott M, Carstensensen J, Heiskanen A, Van De Bund W. (2010). Marine Management - Towards an Integrated Implementation of the European Marine Strategy Framework and the Water Framework Directives. MARINE POLLUTION BULLETIN 60 (12). p. 2175-2186. JRC60639.

Borseková, K., Vaňová, A., Šúrová, J., Kráľ, P., Turečková, K., Nevima, J., & Martinát, S. (2021). The Nexus between Creative Actors and Regional Development. *Land (Basel)*, *10*(3), 276. DOI: 10.3390/land10030276

Bos, T. (2023). The impact of ESG characteristics on startup valuation: An empirical study in the Venture Capital setting, Master thesis Delft University of Technology.

Bos-Nehles, A. C., & Veenendaal, A. A. R. (2019). Perceptions of HR practices and innovative work behavior: The moderating effect of an innovative climate. *International Journal of Human Resource Management*, *30*(18), 2661–2683. DOI: 10.1080/09585192.2017.1380680

Bostancı, S. H., & Yıldırım, S. (2021). Sustainable Communities vs. Climate Refugees: Two Opposite Results of Climate Change. In Popescu, C. (Ed.), *Handbook of Research on Novel Practices and Current Successes in Achieving the Sustainable Development Goals* (pp. 298–319). IGI Global Scientific Publishing., DOI: 10.4018/978-1-7998-8426-2.ch015

Bostancı, S. H., & Yıldırım, S. (2022). The Role of Municipalities in Achieving Water Security: The Case of Turkey. In Castanho, R. (Ed.), *Handbook of Research on Sustainable Development Goals, Climate Change, and Digitalization* (pp. 268–286). IGI Global Scientific Publishing., DOI: 10.4018/978-1-7998-8482-8.ch017

Botsari, A., & Lang, F. (2020). ESG considerations in venture capital and business angel investment decisions: Evidence from two pan-European surveys (No. 2020/63). EIF Working Paper.

Boukherroub, T., Ruiz, A., & Pellerin, R. (2024). Exploration de la contribution des technologies de l'industrie 4.0 à la résilience des chaînes d'approvisionnement. *Journal of Decision Systems*.

Bouri, A., Mertens, F., & Perrini, F. (2020). Understanding Corporate Sustainability and Its Implications for Business Performance. *Journal of Business Research*, *111*, 1–10. DOI: 10.1016/j.jbusres.2019.05.004

Bowen, H. R. (1953). *Social responsibility of the Businessman*. Harper & Row.

Brañes, R. (2007). Derecho ambiental mexicano [Mexican Environmental Law]. Volumen 1 de Colección medio ambiente. Universidad de Texas. Retrieved from https://archivos.juridicas.unam.mx/www/bjv/libros/13/6429/13.pdf

Breaz, T. O., & Jaradat, M. (2024). Strategic Human Resource Management: Aligning HR Practices with Organizational Goals. https://doi.org/DOI: 10.24818/IMC/2023/04.01

Breiman, L. (2001). Random forests. *Machine Learning*, *45*(1), 5–32. DOI: 10.1023/A:1010933404324

Bromfield, E. (2020). Microsoft's Approach to Sustainability: Leveraging Technology for Environmental Impact. *Tech for Good Journal*, *8*(2), 41–55.

Browder, G., Ozment, S., Rehberger-Bescos, I., Gartner, T., & Lange, G-M. (2019, March 21). Integrating Green and Gray: Creating Next Generation Infrastructure. Washington, D.C.: World Resources Institute (WRI). DOI: DOI: 10.46830/wrirpt.18.00028

Brown, E. J., Dunlop, L., & Scally, J. (2020). 'It's about not achieving the outcomes that you necessarily expected': Non-formal learning in higher education. *Teaching in Higher Education*, *25*(1), 52–67. DOI: 10.1080/13562517.2018.1541880

Brown, J. S. (1998). Internet technology in support of the concept of "communities-of-practice": The case of Xerox. *Accounting Management and Information Technologies*, *8*(4), 227–236. DOI: 10.1016/S0959-8022(98)00011-3

Brown, J. S., & Duguid, P. (1991). Organizational Learning and Communities of Practice: Toward a Unified View or Working, Learning, and Innovation. *Organization Science*, *2*(1), 40–57. DOI: 10.1287/orsc.2.1.40

Brown, K. (2009). Ecuador 's Constitutional Rights of Nature: Implementation and Implications. *Ecology Law Quarterly*, *36*(3), 797–824.

Brown, S., & Eisenhardt, K. (1995). Product development: Past research, recent findings, and future directions. *Academy of Management Review*, *20*(3), 342–283. DOI: 10.2307/258850

Brundtland, G. H. (1987). *Our Common Future: Report of the World Commission on Environment and Development*. Oxford University Press.

Buallay, A. (2020). Sustainability reporting and firm's performance: Comparative study between manufacturing and banking sectors. *International Journal of Productivity and Performance Management*, *69*(3), 431–445. DOI: 10.1108/IJPPM-10-2018-0371

Bubevski, V. (2025). *Oil and Gas Risk Assessment and Management: Emerging Research and Opportunities*. IGI Global., DOI: 10.4018/979-8-3373-0959-0

Buccina, S. & Chene, D. & Gramlich, J. (2013). Accounting for the environmental impacts of Texaco's operations in Ecuador: Chevron's contingent environmental liability disclosures. Accounting forum, Elsevier, vol. 37(2), pages 110-123. DOI: .DOI: 10.1016/j.accfor.2013.04.003

*Building Skills for Sustainable Development – A Key for Business Excellence* (pp. 147–159). (2022). Routledge eBooks. https://doi.org/DOI: 10.4324/9781003173311-15

Business, N. E. W. A. G. E. (2022, May 23). Grameenphone employees observe Green Week 2022. *New Age | the Most Popular Outspoken English Daily in Bangladesh*. https://www.newagebd.net/article/171318/grameenphone-employees-observe-green-week-2022

CABERNET. (2014). Brownfield definition [online]. EU: Projects. Retrieved January 20, 2020, from http://www.cabernet.org.uk/index.asp?c=1134

Cabrera, Á., & Cabrera, E. F. (2005). Fostering knowledge sharing through people management practices. *International Journal of Human Resource Management*, *16*(5), 720–735. DOI: 10.1080/09585190500083020

Cacciamani, S., & Fujita, N. (2023). Promoting Life Competences in the Knowledge Society: The Contribution of Knowledge Building Model for Educational Systems. [S]. *Interaction Design & Architecture*, (57), 27–46. DOI: 10.55612/s-5002-057-002

Cadman, T., & Sarker, T. (2022). Climate finance for sustainable development. In Cadman, T., & Sarker, T. (Eds.), *De Gruyter Handbook of Sustainable Development and Finance* (pp. 385–395). Walter de Gruyter GmbH., DOI: 10.1515/9783110733488-017

Caena, F., & Redecker, C. (2019). Aligning teacher competence frameworks to 21st century challenges: The case for the European Digital Competence Framework for Educators (DIGCOMPEDU), EUROPEAN JOURNAL OF EDUCATION, ISSN 0141-8211, 54 (3), p. 356-369, JRC117352.

Cai, X., Xiang, H., Neskorodieva, I., & Durmanov, A. (2024). Interrelation between human capital management and ESG engagement: Evidence from S&P 500 firms. *Humanities & Social Sciences Communications*, *11*(1), 1654. DOI: 10.1057/s41599-024-04189-6

Calascione, V. (2023). Is Sustainability a Competitive Advantage? Unveiling the Relationship Between ESG Scores and Corporate Financial Performance in IT Startups., Università Ca' Foscari Venezia, https://unive.unitesi.cineca.it/handle/20.500.14247/17830

Caliendo, M., Goethner, M., & Weißenberger, M. (2019). Entrepreneurial persistence beyond survival: Measurement and determinants. *Journal of Small Business Management*, *58*(3), 617–647. DOI: 10.1080/00472778.2019.1666532

Callon, M., Courtial, J. P., Turner, W. A., & Bauin, S. (1983). From translations to problematic networks: An introduction to co-word analysis. *Social Sciences Information. Information Sur les Sciences Sociales*, *22*(2), 191–235. DOI: 10.1177/053901883022002003

Calvopiña, M., Vásconez, E., Coral-Almeida, M., Romero-Alvarez, D., Garcia-Bereguiain, M. A., & Orlando, A. (2022). Leptospirosis: Morbidity, mortality, and spatial distribution of hospitalized cases in Ecuador. A nationwide study 2000-2020. *PLoS Neglected Tropical Diseases*, *16*(5), e0010430. DOI: 10.1371/journal.pntd.0010430 PMID: 35551530

Campbell, J., Shaul, K., Slagle, K., & Sović, D. (2024). Sustainable community development through peer-to-peer learning in the online and in-person classroom. *International Journal of Sustainability in Higher Education*, *25*(8), 1803–1819. DOI: 10.1108/IJSHE-07-2023-0321

Camur, M. C., Tseng, C.-Y., Thanos, A. E., White, C. C., Yund, W., & Iakovou, E. (2023). *An Integrated System Dynamics and Discrete Event Supply Chain Simulation Framework for Supply Chain Resilience with Non-Stationary Pandemic Demand.* arXiv preprint arXiv:2305.00086. DOI: 10.1109/WSC60868.2023.10407779

Cancilleria del Ecuador- ministerio de Relaciones exteriores y movilidad Humana. (Abril de 2015). *El caso Chevron / Texaco en Ecuador Una lucha por la justicia ambiental y social.* Obtenido de https://www.cancilleria.gob.ec/wp-content/uploads/2015/06/Expediente-Caso-Chevron-abril-2015.pdf

Carayannis, E. G., Barth, T. D., & Campbell, D. F. J. (2012). The Quintuple Helix innovation model: Global warming as a challenge and driver for innovation. *Journal of Innovation and Entrepreneurship*, *1*(2), 1–12. DOI: 10.1186/2192-5372-1-1

Carayannis, E. G., & Campbell, D. F. J. (2009). 'Mode 3' and 'Quadruple Helix': Toward a 21st century fractal innovation ecosystem. *International Journal of Technology Management*, *46*(3-4), 201–234. DOI: 10.1504/IJTM.2009.023374

Carayannis, E. G., & Campbell, D. F. J. (2010). Triple Helix, Quadruple Helix and Quintuple Helix and how do knowledge, innovation and the environment relate to each other? A proposed framework for a trans-disciplinary analysis of sustainable development and social ecology. [IJSESD]. *International Journal of Social Ecology and Sustainable Development*, *1*(1), 1–29. DOI: 10.4018/jsesd.2010010101

Carretero Gomez, S., Vuorikari, R., & Punie, Y. (2017). DigComp 2.1: The Digital Competence Framework for Citizens with eight proficiency levels and examples of use, EUR 28558 EN, Publications Office of the European Union, Luxembourg. ISBN 978-92-79-68006-9 (pdf),978-92-79-68005-2 (print),978-92-79-74173-9 (ePub), (online), (print), (ePub), JRC106281.DOI: 10.2760/38842

Carroll, A. B. (2016). Carroll's pyramid of CSR: Taking another look. *International Journal of Corporate Social Responsibility*, *1*(1), 3. DOI: 10.1186/s40991-016-0004-6

Cartelli, A. (Ed.). (2012). *Current Trends and Future Practices for Digital Literacy and Competence*. IGI Global., DOI: 10.4018/978-1-4666-0903-7

Casagrande, D., & Matherly, C. (2024). Lehigh Launch Ecuador: A Case Study for First Semester Experience Abroad. In Stauff, J., & Blondin, J. (Eds.), *Promoting Intercultural Agility and Leadership Development at Home and Abroad for First-Year Students* (pp. 236–257). IGI Global Scientific Publishing., DOI: 10.4018/978-1-6684-8832-4.ch011

CASEL. (2020). CASEL'S SEL Framework. https://casel.org/casel-sel-framework-11-2020/

Cashmore, M. (2004). The role of science in environmental impact assessment: Process and procedure versus purpose in the development of theory. *Environmental Impact Assessment Review*, *24*(4), 403–426. DOI: 10.1016/j.eiar.2003.12.002

Casson, M. (1994). Why are firms hierarchical? *International Journal of the Economics of Business*, *1*(1), 47–76. DOI: 10.1080/758540499

Castillo Argañarás, L. (2016). *Inversiones Extranjeras y populismo en Argentina, Bolivia y Ecuador entre 2003 y 2015*. Obtenido de https://notablesdelaciencia.conicet.gov.ar/bitstream/handle/11336/78526/CONICET_Digital_Nro.f5d57907-5140-40bb-899c-af1dfba5c0a4_A.pdf?sequence=2&isAllowed=y

Castillo-Nazareno, U. H., Matute-Petroche, J. S., & Alcívar-Avilés, M. (2021). Chamber of Popular Micro-Businesses, Popular Brands, and Multi-Place Fairs: Entrepreneurial Association in Monte Sinai (Guayaquil, Ecuador). In Gamez-Gutierrez, J., & Saiz-Alvarez, J. (Eds.), *Entrepreneurial Innovation for Securing Long-Term Growth in a Short-Term Economy* (pp. 32–47). IGI Global Scientific Publishing., DOI: 10.4018/978-1-7998-3568-4.ch003

Castillo-Vargas, D. A., Rodríguez-Quesada, L., Ledezma-Espinoza, A., Masís-Meléndez, F., Infante-Alfaro, S., & Starbird-Perez, R. (2025). Biochar-Based Electrochemical Degradation System for Removing Pharmaceutical Pollutants from Aqueous Media as Potential Wastewater Treatment. *Water (Basel)*, *17*(5), 722. DOI: 10.3390/w17050722

Cebrián, G., & Junyent, M. (2015). Competencies in education for sustainable development: Exploring the student teachers' views. *Sustainability (Basel)*, *7*(3), 2768–2786. DOI: 10.3390/su7032768

Cebrián, G., Junyent, M., & Mulà, I. (2020). Competencies in education for sustainable development: Emerging teaching and research developments. *Sustainability (Basel)*, *12*(2), 579. DOI: 10.3390/su12020579

Cebrián, G., Junyent, M., & Mulà, I. (2021). Current practices and future pathways towards competencies in education for sustainable development. *Sustainability (Basel)*, *13*(16), 8733. DOI: 10.3390/su13168733

Cely, N. (2013). Balancing profit and environmental sustainability in Ecuador: Lessons learned from the Chevron case. *Duke Envtl. L. & Pol'y F.*, *24*, 353.

Chaker, B., & Damak, C. (2024). Developing a Strategic Framework for Aligning Human Resource Management Practices With Sustainability Goals. *Practice, Progress, and Proficiency in Sustainability*, •••, 127–148. DOI: 10.4018/979-8-3693-2699-2.ch007

Chakib, S. (2024). The Historical Development of Employee Retention Theories. *The Pinnacle*, *2*(2). Advance online publication. DOI: 10.61643/c23515

Chakravarthy, R. A., & Arun, M. (2020). Multicarrier interference cancellation for channel optimization using artificial neural network. [IJARESM]. *International Journal of All Research Education and Scientific Methods*, *8*(12), 617–623.

Chakravarthy, R. A., & Palaniswami, S. (2014). Recent investigation on cluster-based energy-efficient scheduling scheme for WSN. *International Journal of Applied Engineering Research: IJAER*, *9*(23), 18823–18840.

Chakravarthy, R. A., & Palaniswami, S. (2016). A hybrid butterfly swarm optimization and efficient packet scheduling-based energy-efficient load balancing for WSN. *Journal of Applied Sciences Research*, *12*(9), 37–49.

Chakravarthy, R. A., Palaniswami, S., & Sabitha, R. (2017). Cluster header revolving technique to prolong network lifespan in wireless sensor network. *Journal of Computational and Theoretical Nanoscience*, *14*(12), 5863–5871. DOI: 10.1166/jctn.2017.7028

Chanveasna, U., Veasna, S., & Sovannara, K. (2024). The antecedents of career development competency in SMEs, Cambodia. *Open Journal of Business and Management*, *12*(03), 1347–1376. DOI: 10.4236/ojbm.2024.123072

Chávez Salazar, R. (1999). *Protección ambiental y explotación petrolera en la región amazónica Ecuatoriana.* Quito. Obtenido de https://repositorio.flacsoandes.edu.ec/bitstream/10469/289/3/TFLACSO-1999RLCS.pdf

Chawla, M., Sharma, P., Gautam, S., & Popescu, C. R. (2025). Sustainability in Human Capital Management: Shaping the Future With Technology. In Kapoor, T., Singh, A., Sahay, K., Kaur, H., & Verma, R. (Eds.), *Sustainable Management Practices for Employee Retention and Recruitment* (pp. 265–290). IGI Global Scientific Publishing., DOI: 10.4018/979-8-3693-8679-8.ch013

Chenchouni, L., Kheder, M. K., & Chenchouni, H. (2022). When the Blessed Resource "Oil" Curses: Environmental Degradation Related to Oil Exploration Fueling Socio-Political Conflicts. [IJSESD]. *International Journal of Social Ecology and Sustainable Development*, *13*(1), 1–17. DOI: 10.4018/IJSESD.292076

Cheng, T., Chang, H., Yen, C., & Chen, M. (2018). Creating a low-carbon campus in Chaoyang University of Technology (CYUT). *E3s Web of Conferences*, 48, 03001. DOI: 10.1051/e3sconf/20184803001

Chen, X., Chong, D., & Kang, M. (2021). Blockchain Technology in Sustainable Supply Chains: A Literature Review. *Sustainability*, *13*(3), 1239.

Chen, Y.. (2020). *Reinforcement Learning for Adaptive Traffic Signal Control.* Machine Learning in Traffic Engineering.

Chen, Y., Hung, M., & Wang, Y. (2019). The Effect of Mandatory CSR Disclosure on Firm Profitability and Social Externalities: Evidence from China. *Journal of Accounting and Economics*, *68*(1), 101–122.

Chen, Y., Zhang, J., Wang, F., Zhang, J., Wu, W., & Li, H. (2025). Study on Carbon Emission Reduction Strategy of CCUS Technology in Natural Gas Supply Chain Considering Government Subsidies. *Processes (Basel, Switzerland)*, *13*(2), 550. DOI: 10.3390/pr13020550

Chesnais, F. (2010). *Écologie, luttes sociales et projet révolutionnaire pour le 21e siècle. Gay, Vincent (coord.), Pistes pour un anticapitalisme vert*. Syllepse.

Chevron Corporation vs. Steven Donziger, et al., 1:11-cv-00691LAK-JCF (Southern Distirct of New York, April 3th, 2014).

Chigbu, B. I. (2024). Advancing sustainable development through circular economy and skill development in EV lithium-ion battery recycling: A comprehensive review. *Frontiers in Sustainability*, *5*, 1409498. Advance online publication. DOI: 10.3389/frsus.2024.1409498

Chiliquinga, V. E., Popescu, C. R., & González, A. L. (2023). The Impact of Cooperative Control Regulations for the Assessment of Environmental and Social Risk: The Case of Credit Placement in Ecuador. In Popescu, C., Yu, P., & Wei, Y. (Eds.), *Achieving the Sustainable Development Goals Through Infrastructure Development* (pp. 198–214). IGI Global Scientific Publishing., DOI: 10.4018/979-8-3693-0794-6.ch008

Chiriboga, M. (2014). *Las ONG ecuatorianas en los procesos de cambio* (Primera ed.). Quito: Abya-Yala. Obtenido de https://www.ceosc.org/recursos/5_ong_cambio.pdf

Chiwaridzo, O. T., & Dzingirai, M. (Eds.). (2025). *Strategic Repositioning in Times of Corporate Crisis: Green Management and Technology Adoption*. IGI Global., DOI: 10.4018/979-8-3693-5912-9

Choi, S., & Lee, H. (2021). How Data Analytics Can Foster Sustainability in the Era of Digital Transformation. *Sustainability*, *13*(10), 5639. DOI: 10.3390/su13105639

Chouinard, Y. (2016). *Let My People Go Surfing: The Education of a Reluctant Businessman*. Penguin.

Chowdhury, S. H. (2022, March 13). Green Block: A journey towards eco-friendly construction. *The Business Standard*. https://www.tbsnews.net/economy/green-block-journey-towards-eco-friendly-construction-383986

Chowdhury, S., Dey, P. K., Rodríguez-Espíndola, O., Parkes, G., Tuyet, N. T. A., Long, D. D., & Ha, T. P. (2022). Impact of organisational factors on the circular economy practices and sustainable performance of small and medium-sized enterprises in Vietnam. *Journal of Business Research*, *147*, 362–378. DOI: 10.1016/j.jbusres.2022.03.077

Ciro-Atehortúa, J. M., Bermúdez-Hernández, J., & Valencia-Arias, J. (2023). Modelos de gestión del conocimiento como herramientas de eficiencia en procesos organizacionales. Revista Virtual Universidad Católica del Norte, (70), 260-296. https://www.doi.org/10.35575/rvucn.n70a10

CLARINET. (2002). Brownfields and redevelopment of urban areas. Austria: Federal Environment Agency. Retrieved August 2002, from [online source]

Clark, G. L., Feiner, A., & Viehs, M. (2015). *From the stockholder to the stakeholder: How sustainability can drive financial outperformance*. Oxford University Press.

Clarkson, P. M., Li, Y., Pinnuck, M., & Richardson, G. D. (2022). The valuation impact of carbon emission disclosures on global markets. *The Accounting Review*, *97*(5), 65–91.

Cleveland, S., & Hinojosa, C. (2019). Complexity Framework for the Project Management Curriculum. [IJITPM]. *International Journal of Information Technology Project Management*, *10*(1), 34–54. DOI: 10.4018/IJITPM.2019010103

Coase, R. H. (1937). The nature of the firm, in Nicolai J. Foss, ed. 2000. *The theory of the firm: Critical perspectives in business and management,* vol II. London: Routledge.

Cobo, A., & Diaz, C. (2011). Clinical application of oocyte vitrification: A systematic review and meta-analysis of randomized controlled trials. *Fertility and Sterility*, *96*(2), 277–285. DOI: 10.1016/j.fertnstert.2011.06.030 PMID: 21718983

Codigo civil. (1906). Ecuador. Obtenido de https://www.epn.edu.ec/wp-content/uploads/2015/06/Codigo-Civil1.pdf

Código Orgánico del Ambiente. (2017). Ecuador. Obtenido de https://www.ambiente.gob.ec/wp-content/uploads/downloads/2018/01/CODIGO_ORGANICO_AMBIENTE.pdf

Cohen, B., Smith, B., & Mitchell, R. (2008). Toward a sustainable conceptualization of dependent variables in entrepreneurship research. *Business Strategy and the Environment*, *17*(2), 107–119. DOI: 10.1002/bse.505

Cohen, G., & Galperin, M. (2020). Green's function methods for single molecule junctions. *The Journal of Chemical Physics*, *152*(9), 090901. DOI: 10.1063/1.5145210 PMID: 33480741

Collings, D. G., & Conroy, K. M. (2024). Global talent management. https://doi.org/DOI: 10.4337/9781800884045.ch40

Collings, D. G., McDonnell, A., & Scullion, H. (2022). *Global talent management: Principles and practices*. Oxford University Press.

Columbia Law School. (2015). Chevron, Ecuador, and the Hazards of Transnational Litigation. Retrieved on-line from https://www.law.columbia.edu/news/archive/chevron-ecuador-and-hazards-transnational-litigation. Accessed on the 28th of January 2025.

Comisión Económica para América Latina y el Caribe (CEPAL). (2019). *Recursos naturales,medio ambiente y sostenibilidad 70 años de pensamiento de la CEPAL.* Santiago, Comisión Económica para América Latina y el Caribe (CEPAL): Libros de la CEPAL, N° 158 (LC/PUB.2019/18-P).

Conduah, A. K., & Essiaw, M. N. (2022). Resilience and entrepreneurship: A systematic review. *F1000 Research*, *11*, 348. DOI: 10.12688/f1000research.75473.1

Conner, K. R., & Prahalad, C. K. (1996). A resource based theory of the firm: Knowledge versus opportunism. *Organization Science*, *7*(5), 477–501. DOI: 10.1287/orsc.7.5.477

Consejo de Desarrollo de las Nacionalidades y Pueblos del Ecuador [Council for the Development of the Nationalities and Peoples of Ecuador]. (2011). Sumak Kawsay (Primera). CODENPE y AECID. http://www.pueblosynacionalidades.gob.ec/wp-content/uploads/downloads/2023/03/sumakkawsay.pdf

Constitución de la República del Ecuador [Const.]. (2008). Ecuador. Obtenido de https://www.defensa.gob.ec/wp-content/uploads/downloads/2021/02/Constitucion-de-la-Republica-del-Ecuador_act_ene-2021.pdf

Constituent Assembly of Montecristi. (2008). Constitution of the Republic of Ecuador. Retrieved from https://www.oas.org/juridico/pdfs/mesicic4_ecu_const.pdf

Constitution of Ecuador. (2008). Retrieved from https://www.oas.org/juridico/pdfs/mesicic4_ecu_const.pdf

Constitutional Court of Ecuador. (2011). Judgment on the Vilcabamba River Case. Retrieved from https://www.derechosdelanaturaleza.org.ec/wp-content/uploads/2018/04/CUMPLIMIENTO-R%C3%8DO-VILCABAMBA.pdf

Cook, A., & Glass, C. (2018). Women on corporate boards: Do they advance corporate social responsibility? *Human Relations*, *71*(7), 897–924. DOI: 10.1177/0018726717729207

Cooke, G. B., Chowhan, J., Mac Donald, K., & Mann, S. L. (2021). Talent management: Four "buying versus making" talent development approaches. *Personnel Review*. Advance online publication. DOI: 10.1108/PR-08-2020-0621

Cordella, M., Pihkola, H., Pajula, T., & Zamagni, A. (2024). Towards a future product sustainability footprint. In Valdivia, S., & Sonnemann, G. (Eds.), *Handbook on Life Cycle Sustainability Assessment* (pp. 343–356). Edward Elgar Publishing., DOI: 10.4337/9781800378650.00036

Corres, A., Rieckmann, M., Espasa, A., & Ruíz-Mallén, I. (2020). Educator competences in sustainability education: A systematic review of frameworks. *Sustainability (Basel)*, *12*(23), 9858. DOI: 10.3390/su12239858

Cort, T., & Esty, D. (2020). ESG standards: Looming challenges and pathways forward. *Organization & Environment*, *33*(4), 491–510. DOI: 10.1177/1086026620945342

Council, E. U. (2024). Environmental, social and governance (ESG) ratings: Council greenlights new regulation. Press Release, https://www.consilium.europa.eu/en/press/press-releases/2024/11/19/environmental-social-and-governance-esg-ratings-council-greenlights-new-regulation/

Cowling, M., & Dvouletý, O. (2023). Who is brave enough to start a new business during the Covid-19 pandemic? *Baltic Journal of Management*, *18*(3), 402–419. DOI: 10.1108/BJM-11-2022-0414

Crespo, R. (2009). La naturaleza como sujeto de derechos: ¿Símbolo o realidad jurídica? [Nature as a Subject of Rights: Symbol or Legal Reality?], Iuris Dictio: Vol. 8 Núm. 12. Retrieved from https://revistas.usfq.edu.ec/index.php/iurisdictio/article/view/685

Creswell, J. W., & Plano Clark, V. L. (2018). *Designing and conducting mixed methods research* (3rd ed.). Sage.

Crotty, J. (2012). The great austerity war: what caused the US deficit crisis and who should pay to fix it? *Cambridge Journal of Economics (January), 36(1)*, 79 – 104. DOI: DOI: 10.1093/cje/ber029

Crunchbase (2025). Startup Funding Regained Its Footing In 2024 As AI Became The Star Of The Show, https://news.crunchbase.com/venture/global-funding-data-analysis-ai-eoy-2024/#:~:text=Overall%20 startup%20funding%20in%202024,billion%20and%20%24350%20billion%2C%20respectively

Čuček, L., Klemeš, J., & Kravanja, Z. (2012). A Review of Footprint analysis tools for monitoring impacts on sustainability. *Journal of Cleaner Production*, *34*(October), 9–20. DOI: 10.1016/j.jclepro.2012.02.036

Cuéllar, L., Torres, I., Romero-Severson, E., Mahesh, R., Ortega, N., Pungitore, S., Hengartner, N., & Ke, R. (2022). Excess deaths reveal the true spatial, temporal and demographic impact of COVID-19 on mortality in Ecuador. *International Journal of Epidemiology*, *51*(1), 54–62. DOI: 10.1093/ije/dyab163 PMID: 34387670

Čulková, K., Hrehová, D., & Janošková, M. (2021). *Global problems of the employment in V4 region. 92*, 07014. https://doi.org/DOI: 10.1051/shsconf/20219207014

Cuvi, N., & Bejarano, M. (2015). Los halos de inhibición en la remediación de suelos amazónicos contaminados con petróleo. *História, Ciências, Saúde-Manguinhos, 22*, 1693-1714. Obtenido de https://www.scielo.br/j/hcsm/a/TXyyPdgyLDpHj3n5cPrtV4L/?format=pdf&lang=es

Czech Office for Surveying. Mapping and Cadastre (ČÚZK). (2024, December 20). *INSPIRE datasets - Administrative Units*. Retrieved from https://geoportal.cuzk.cz/

CzechInvest. (2024). Brownfield database. CzechInvest Brownfields Portal. Retrieved December 20, 2024, from https://brownfieldy-dotace.czechinvest.org/Aplikace/bf-public-x.nsf/bfs.xsp

CzechInvest. (2024). National Brownfield Database. *CzechInvest.* https://brownfieldy-dotace.czechinvest .org/Aplikace/bf-public-x.nsf/bfs.xsp

Czeglédi, C., Marosné Kuna, Z., & Hajós, L. (2013). *Current challenges of talent management in the V4 countries with special respect to Hungary*. https://dspace5.zcu.cz/bitstream/11025/16264/1/Czegledi.pdf

Czyżewski, B., Matuszczak, A., Polcyn, J., Katarzyna Smędzik-Ambroży, K., & Staniszewski, J. (2020). Deadweight loss in environmental policy: The case of the European Union member states. *Journal of Cleaner Production*, *260*, 121064. Advance online publication. DOI: 10.1016/j.jclepro.2020.121064

D'Adamo, I., & Gastaldi, M. (2023). Monitoring the Performance of Sustainable Development Goals in the Italian Regions. *Sustainability (Basel)*, *15*(19), 14094. DOI: 10.3390/su151914094

D'Adamo, I., & Lupi, G. (2021). Sustainability and Resilience after COVID-19: A Circular Premium in the Fashion Industry. *Sustainability (Basel)*, *13*(4), 1861. DOI: 10.3390/su13041861

Daily, G. C., & Matson, P. A. (2008). Ecosystem Services: From Theory to Implementation. *Proceedings of the National Academy of Sciences of the United States of America*, *105*(28), 9455–9456. https://www.pnas.org/doi/pdf/10.1073/pnas.0804960105. DOI: 10.1073/pnas.0804960105 PMID: 18621697

Dakhan, S. A., Sohu, J. M., Jabeen, A., Mirani, M. A., Shaikh, J. A., & Iqbal, S. (2020). Impact of green HRM on employees pro-environmental behavior: Mediating role of women environmental knowledge at higher education institutions. *IJCSNS International Journal of Computer Science and Network Security, 20*(12), 202–208.

Dalal-Clayton, B., & Bass, S. (2021). *Sustainable Development Strategies: A Resource Book*. Earthscan Publications.

Damoah, O. B. O., Lamptey, Y. A., Anlesinya, A., & Tetteh, B. N. A. (2021). Gendering Corporate Boards and Conditional Effectiveness of Board Processes: Insights from a Sub-Saharan African Country. *Global Business Review*, •••, 09721509211036271. DOI: 10.1177/09721509211036271

Damoah, O. B. O., & Peprah, A. A. (2021). Synthesis of small and medium enterprise research in Ghana. *Journal of Global Entrepreneurship Research, 11*(1), 451–468. DOI: 10.1007/s40497-021-00286-x

Danailova, I. (2024). The implementation of DigComp (European Digital Skills Framework) for digital competence assessment and evaluation. *Nauchni trudove*, (1), 87-125.

Dangelico, R. M., & Vocalelli, D. (2020). Green innovation and entrepreneurship in the era of sustainable development. *Business Strategy and the Environment, 29*(4), 1570–1585.

Dankwa, S. M. E. (2020). *The Efficacy of Ghana's Business Interest in the Global Economy* (Doctoral dissertation, Walden University).

Danone. (2020). *Danone 2020 Sustainability Report*. Retrieved from https://www.danone.com

Das, N. G. (2008). Statistical Methods: Vol. I & II. *New Delhi: McGraw Hill Education*. Private Limited.

Davenport, T. H., & Prusak, L. (1998). *Working knowledge: How organizations manage what they know*. Harvard Business School Press.

David, K. G., Wu, Y., & Pei, C. (2022). Openness to Innovation as a Driver of Knowledge Integration in High-Tech SMEs: The Roles of Social Capital and Network Competence. [IJKM]. *International Journal of Knowledge Management, 18*(1), 1–21. DOI: 10.4018/IJKM.291102

Davis, T. S., & Sherman, S. A. (2010). *Brownfields: A comprehensive guide to redeveloping contaminated property* (3rd ed.). American Bar Association.

De Sousa, C. A. (2002). Brownfield redevelopment in Toronto: An examination of past trends and future prospects. *Land Use Policy, 19*(4), 297–309. DOI: 10.1016/S0264-8377(02)00024-8

Dean, T. J., & McMullen, J. S. (2007). Toward a theory of sustainable entrepreneurship: Reducing environmental degradation through entrepreneurial action. *Journal of Business Venturing, 22*(1), 50–76. DOI: 10.1016/j.jbusvent.2005.09.003

Dechezleprêtre, A., Martin, R., & Bassi, S. (2019). Climate change policy, innovation and growth. In Fouquet, R. (Ed.), *Handbook on Green Growth* (pp. 217–239). Edward Elgar Publishing., DOI: 10.4337/9781788110686.00018

Del Vecchio, P., Secundo, G., Mele, G., & Passiante, G. (2021). Sustainable entrepreneurship education for circular economy: Emerging perspectives in Europe. *International Journal of Entrepreneurial Behaviour & Research*, *27*(8), 2096–2124. DOI: 10.1108/IJEBR-03-2021-0210

Deloitte. (2018). Knowledge management & big data. Retrieved November 12, 2019, from https://www2.deloitte.com/content/dam/Deloitte/in/Documents/technology-media-telecommunications/in-tmt-knowledge-management-and-big-data-noexp.pdf

Deloitte. (2022). *2022 Global Sustainability Consumer Report*. Retrieved from https://www.deloitte.com/

Deloitte. (2022). *The future of work in Central Europe: Trends and challenges in post-pandemic talent management*. Deloitte Insights.

Dhandayudam, P., & Raajarajeswari, M. A. (2024). *Exploring Sustainable Green HRM Practices: An Investigation of Employee Perspectives and Organizational Challenges*. Springer International Publishing., DOI: 10.1007/978-981-99-7798-7_25

Di Vaio, A., Hassan, R., Chhabra, M., Arrigo, E., & Palladino, R. (2022). Sustainable entrepreneurship impact and entrepreneurial venture life cycle: A systematic literature review. *Journal of Cleaner Production*, *378*, 134469. DOI: 10.1016/j.jclepro.2022.134469

Diario El Comercio. (2007). Ecuador reconoce derechos de la naturaleza en su nueva Constitución [Ecuador recognizes the rights of nature in its new Constitution]. Retrieved from https://www.elcomercio.com/tendencias/ambiente/seis-casos-debate-derechos-naturaleza-ecuador.html

Díaz, A. A., Veliz, P. M., Rivas-Mariño, G., Mafla, C. V., Altamirano, L. M. M., & Jones, C. V. (2017). Etiquetado de alimentos en Ecuador: implementación, resultados y acciones pendientes [Food labeling in Ecuador: implementation, results, and pending actions]. *Revista panamericana de salud publica = Pan. American Journal of Public Health*, *41*, e54. DOI: 10.26633/RPSP.2017.54 PMID: 28614474

Díaz, S. C., Quezada, L. C., Álvarez, L. J., Loján-Córdova, J., & Carrión-Paladines, V. (2023). Indigenous use of fire in the paramo ecosystem of southern Ecuador: A case study using remote sensing methods and ancestral knowledge of the Kichwa Saraguro people. *Fire Ecology*, *19*(1), 5. DOI: 10.1186/s42408-022-00164-1 PMID: 36712840

Diepolder, C. S., Weitzel, H., & Huwer, J. (2021). Competence frameworks of sustainable entrepreneurship: A systematic review. *Sustainability (Basel)*, *13*(24), 13734. DOI: 10.3390/su132413734

Dilema, R. (2019). El caso Chevrón-Texaco. Problemática actual de la Amazonia ecuatoriana. *Revista Dilema*. Obtenido de https://dilemascontemporaneoseducacionpoliticayvalores.com/index.php/dilemas/article/view/669

Ding, X., Sheng, Z., Appolloni, A., Shahzad, M., & Han, S. (2024). Digital transformation, ESG practice, and total factor productivity. *Business Strategy and the Environment*, *33*(5), 4547–4561. DOI: 10.1002/bse.3718

Dip, H. S. (2024). *Circular Economy Initiatives in Food Manufacturing Industry*. https://doi.org/DOI: 10.21203/rs.3.rs-4996705/v1

Dirik, D., & Özdoğan, B. (2025). To start or not to start? An exploratory study of work meaningfulness among start-up co-founders. *Frontiers in Psychology, 15*, 1500036. DOI: 10.3389/fpsyg.2024.1500036 PMID: 39949976

*Diversity in the Workplace: Providing Equal Opportunities and Effective Management.* (2023). https://doi.org/DOI: 10.53819/81018102t30129

Dixon, T., Raco, M., Catney, P., & Lerner, D. N. (Eds.). (2007). *Sustainable brownfield regeneration: Liveable places from problem spaces.* Blackwell Publishing., DOI: 10.1002/9780470692110

Dolezelova, L. (2015). Regenerace brownfieldů: vývoj politik a příklady realizací. Praha: IREAS, Institut pro strukturální politiku. ISBN 978-80-86684-96-3

Dolezelova, L., Hadlac, M., Kadlecova, M., & Polednik, S. (2014). Redevelopment potential of brownfields: A-B-C classification and its practical application. *E+M. Ekonomie a Management, XVII*(2), 34–44. DOI: 10.15240/tul/001/2014-2-003

Domínguez, R., & Faytong-Haro, M. (2024). Impact of early work start on mental health outcomes in older adults: A cross-sectional study from Ecuador. *PLoS One, 19*(11), e0310448. DOI: 10.1371/journal.pone.0310448 PMID: 39509429

Dörr, N., Kappler, B., & Scheuermann, M. (2021). Future-proofing entrepreneurial education: Integrating global trends and sustainability. *Entrepreneurship Research Journal, 11*(2), 99–112. DOI: 10.1515/erj-2020-0101

Drucker, P. F. (1968). *The Age of Discontinuity: Guidelines to Our Changing Society*. Harper and Row, 1968

Drucker, P. (1993). *Post-Capitalist Society*. Butterworth Heinemann.

Dryzek, J. S. (2005). *The Politics of the Earth: Environmental Discourses* (2nd ed.). Oxford University Press.

Duan, Y., Edwards, J. S. et Dwivedi, Y. K. (2019). L'intelligence artificielle au service de la prise de décision à l'ère du Big Data: évolution, défis et programme de recherche. *Revue internationale de gestion de l'information, 48*, 63-71.

Duan, Y., Edwards, J. S., & Dwivedi, Y. K. (2019). Artificial intelligence for decision making in the era of Big Data. *International Journal of Information Management, 48*, 63–71. DOI: 10.1016/j.ijinfomgt.2019.01.021

Ducoing, C. (2019). How to handle natural capital within the context of the green economy? In Acar, S., & Yeldan, E. (Eds.), *Handbook of Green Economics* (pp. 19–30). Academic Press / Elsevier., DOI: 10.1016/B978-0-12-816635-2.00002-X

Dunlap, R. E., & Mertig, A. G. (1991). The evolution of the US environmental movement from 1970 to 1990: An overview. *Society & Natural Resources, 4*(3), 209–218. DOI: 10.1080/08941929109380755

Durá López, M. (13 de 06 de 2016). Obtenido de https://www.researchgate.net/publication/303931907_Indigenas_Amazonicos_Ecuatorianos_versus_Chevron_la_lucha_de_la_dignidad_por_la_vida_versus_el_derrame_de_la_selva

Dwivedi, Y. K., Hughes, D. L., Ismagilova, E., et al. (2021). Intelligence artificielle (IA): Perspectives multidisciplinaires sur les défis, les opportunités et les programmes émergents en matière de recherche, de pratique et de politique. *Revue internationale de gestion de l'information*, 57, 101994. https://doi.org/ DOI: 10.1016/j.ijinfomgt.2019.08.002

Dzhengiz, T., & Niesten, E. (2019). Competences for environmental sustainability: A systematic review on the impact of absorptive capacity and capabilities. *Journal of Business Ethics*, *162*(4), 881–906. DOI: 10.1007/s10551-019-04360-z

Earth Charter. (2000). The Earth Charter. https://earthcharter.org/read-the-earth-charter/preamble/

Easterby-Smith, M., Crossan, M., & Nicolini, D. (2000). Organizational learning: Debates past, present and future. *Journal of Management Studies*, *38*(6), 783–796. DOI: 10.1111/1467-6486.00203

Eberz, S., Lang, S., Breitenmoser, P., & Niebert, K. (2023). Taking the Lead into Sustainability: Decision Makers' Competencies for a Greener Future. *Sustainability (Basel)*, *15*(6), 4986. DOI: 10.3390/su15064986

Eccles, R. G., & Mirchandi, B. (2022, 15th February). We Need Universal ESG Accounting Standards. *Harvard Business Review*. https://hbr.org/2022/02/we-need-universal-esg-accounting-standards

Eccles, G. R., & Klimenko, S. (2019). The Investor Revolution. *Harvard Business Review*, *97*, 106–116.

Eccles, R. G., Ioannou, I., & Serafeim, G. (2019). The Impact of Corporate Sustainability on Organizational Processes and Performance. *Management Science*, *60*(11), 2843–2857. DOI: 10.1287/mnsc.2014.1940

Eccles, R. G., & Krzus, M. P. (2018). *The Integrated Reporting Movement: Meaning, Momentum, Motives, and Materiality*. John Wiley & Sons.

Eimler, S. C., & Straßmann, C. (2023). Future Proof: Hackathons as Occasions to Experience Entrepreneurial Thinking. *Progress in Entrepreneurship Education and Training: New Methods, Tools, and Lessons Learned from Practice*, 417-429.

Ejibe, I., Okoye, C. C., Nwankwo, E. E., Nwankwo, T. C., & Scholastica, U. C. (2024). *Eco-sustainable practices through strategic HRM: A review and framework for SMEs in the creative industries*. World Journal Of Advanced Research and Reviews., DOI: 10.30574/wjarr.2024.21.3.0658

Eklund, L. G., Sibilia, A., Salvi, A., Antofie, T., Rodomonti, D., Salari, S., Poljansek, K., Marzi, S., Gyenes, Z., & Corban, C. (2023). Towards a European wide vulnerability framework. *Publications Office of the European Union, Luxembourg, JRC118850*. Advance online publication. DOI: 10.2760/353889

El Ghoul, S., & Karoui, A. (2022). Fund performance and social responsibility: New evidence using social active share and social tracking error. *Journal of Banking & Finance*, *143*, 106598. DOI: 10.1016/j.jbankfin.2022.106598

El Ghoul, S., Karoui, A., Patel, S., & Ramani, S. (2023). The green and brown performances of mutual fund portfolios. *Journal of Cleaner Production*, *384*, 135267. DOI: 10.1016/j.jclepro.2022.135267

El Homrani, M., Aravena Gaete, M., Báez Zarabanda, D. E., Bernal Lozano, M. F., Luque de la Rosa, A., & Luis Rodríguez, C. (2020). *Capitulo 9. La gestión del conocimiento intergeneracional*. In J. Gairín Sallán, C. I. Suárez, & A. Díaz-Vicario (Eds.), *La nueva gestión del conocimiento* (pp. 351-381).

ELI. (2007). Entrepreneurial Learning Initiative. https://elimindset.com/about/history/

Elkington, J. (1997). *Cannibals with Forks: The Triple Bottom Line of 21st Century Business*. Capstone.

Elkington, J. (1998). Accounting for the triple bottom line. *Measuring Business Excellence*, *2*(3), 18–22. DOI: 10.1108/eb025539

Elshaer, I. A., Azazz, A. M. S., Kooli, C., Alqasa, K., Afaneh, J. A. A., Fathy, E. A., Fouad, A. M., & Fayyad, S. (2024). Resilience for Sustainability: The Synergistic Role of Green Human Resources Management, Circular Economy, and Green Organizational Culture in the Hotel Industry. *Administrative Sciences*, *14*(11), 297. DOI: 10.3390/admsci14110297

Elsheikh, T., Almaqtari, F. A., Al-Hattami, H. M., Al-Bukhrani, M. A., & Ettish, A. A. (2024). The moderating effect of women in boardrooms on the relationship between control of corruption and corporate sustainability performance. *Discover Sustainability*, *5*(1), 502. DOI: 10.1007/s43621-024-00490-1

EMF. (2013). *Towards the Circular Economy: Economic and Business Rationale for an Accelerated Transition*. Ellen MacArthur Foundation., DOI: 10.1162/108819806775545321

EMF. (2015). *Growth within: a circular economy vision for a competitive Europe*, Ellen MacArthur Foundation. https://ellenmacarthurfoundation.org/growth-within-a-circular-economy-vision-for-a-competitive-europe

Enabling Skill Development for a Sustainable Future. (2023). *Advances in Human Resources Management and Organizational Development Book Series*, 1–13. https://doi.org/DOI: 10.4018/978-1-6684-6990-3.ch001

Endrawati, Y., Putra, I. S., & Ningsih, R. (2024). Building a Sustainable Workforce: Cross-Posting and Secondment Strategies in Indonesia's Oil and Gas Operations. https://doi.org/DOI: 10.2118/223255-MS

Erdoğdu, M. M., Arun, T., & Ahmad, I. H. (Eds.). (2016). *Handbook of Research on Green Economic Development Initiatives and Strategies*. IGI Global., DOI: 10.4018/978-1-5225-0440-5

Ereñaga, N. (2023). La gestión del conocimiento en las organizaciones como medida de adaptación al nuevo entorno laboral. *Lan Harremanak*, *49*(49), 15–36. DOI: 10.1387/lan-harremanak.24830

Espinosa, C. (2011). Los derechos de la naturaleza y la naturaleza de sus derechos [The Rights of Nature and the Nature of Your Rights]. Ministerio de Justicia, Derechos de Humanos y Cultos. Retrieved from https://biblio.flacsoandes.edu.ec/libros/146502-opac

Etzkowitz, H., & Leydesdorff, L. (2000). The dynamics of innovation: From National Systems and "Mode 2" to a Triple Helix of university–industry–government relations. *Research Policy*, *29*(2), 109–123. DOI: 10.1016/S0048-7333(99)00055-4

Eurofound. (2021). *Labor market trends in Central and Eastern Europe: The role of HRM in workforce stability.*

European Commission. (2010). *EUROPE 2020: A strategy for smart, sustainable and inclusive growth.* https://op.europa.eu/s/z19L

European Commission. (2020). [*A European Framework Programme for Research and Innovation.* European Commission.]. *Horizon*, •••, 2020.

European Commission. (2020). *The European Green Deal.* Retrieved from https://ec.europa.eu/clima/policies/eu-climate-action_en

European Commission. (2021). *The European Green Deal Investment Plan.* Retrieved from https://ec.europa.eu/

European Commission. (2023). *Skills and lifelong learning in the EU labor market.* Publications Office of the European Union.

European Labour Authority. (2023). *Labor market dynamics and regulatory frameworks in Central and Eastern Europe.*

Eurostat. (2022). *Employment and labor market statistics in the EU.*

Eyiah-Botwe, E., Aigbavboa, C., & Thwala, W. D. (2016). Sustaining small and medium-size enterprises growth through stakeholder engagement.

Fajardo, P., & De Heredia, M. (2009). *El Caso Texaco: un trabajo por la restitución de derechos colectivos y de la naturaleza.* Quito: ABYA-YALA. Obtenido de https://repositorio.uasb.edu.ec/bitstream/10644/940/1/DDHH-Inf-9-Fajardo-El%20caso%20Texaco.pdf

Faller, R. J. (2024). From Working Groups on Facebook to Online Shopping by WhatsApp: Mobilizations From Communication to Development. [IJDLDC]. *International Journal of Digital Literacy and Digital Competence*, *15*(1), 1–17. DOI: 10.4018/IJDLDC.359338

Fama, E., & Michael, C. J. (1983). Separation of ownership and control. *The Journal of Law & Economics*, *26*(2), 301–325. DOI: 10.1086/467037

Farooq, M., Bakhsh, A., & Watto, W. A. (2023). A quality approach to smart sustainable universities in digital natives era: The case of King Abdul Aziz University. 25 September 2023, PREPRINT (Version 1), DOI: 10.21203/rs.3.rs-3341500/v1

Farrington, F. (2024). Oil in the Amazon: A Case Study in Corporate Power and the Formation of Transnational Legal Norms. Retrieved on-line from https://www.abdn.ac.uk/law/blog/oil-in-the-amazon-a-case-study-in-corporate-power-and-the-formation-of-transnational-legal-norms/. Accessed on the 28th of January 2025.

Fatemi, A., Glaum, M., & Kaiser, S. (2018). ESG Performance and Firm Value: The Moderating Role of Disclosure. *Global Finance Journal*, *38*, 45–64. DOI: 10.1016/j.gfj.2017.03.001

Fayolle, A., & Gailly, B. (2008). From craft to science: Teaching models and entrepreneurial learning. *Journal of European Industrial Training*, *32*(7), 569–593. DOI: 10.1108/03090590810899838

Feng, Y., Feng, Y., & Liu, Z. (2025). Normative Influences on Carbon Offset Behavior: Insights from Organic Farming Practices. *Sustainability (Basel)*, *17*(4), 1638. DOI: 10.3390/su17041638

Ferber, U., Grimski, D., Millar, K., & Nathanail, P. (2006). *Sustainable brownfield regeneration: CABERNET Network Report* (1st ed.). University of Nottingham.

Fernández, E., Junquera, B., & Ordiz, M. (2003). Organizational culture and human resources in the environmental issue: A review of the literature. *International Journal of Human Resource Management*, *14*(4), 634–656. DOI: 10.1080/0958519032000057628

Fields, Z. (Ed.). (2023). *Multidisciplinary Approaches in AI, Creativity, Innovation, and Green Collaboration*. IGI Global., DOI: 10.4018/978-1-6684-6366-6

Figge, F., Stevenson Thorpe, A., Givry, P., Canning, L., & Franklin-Johnson, E. (2018). Longevity and Circularity as Indicators of Eco-Efficient Resource Use in the Circular Economy. *Ecological Economics*, *150*(August), 297–306. DOI: 10.1016/j.ecolecon.2018.04.030

Filippou, O., Bitas, D., & Samanidou, V. (2017). Green approaches in sample preparation of bioanalytical samples prior to chromatographic analysis. *Journal of Chromatography. B, Analytical Technologies in the Biomedical and Life Sciences*, *1043*, 44–62. DOI: 10.1016/j.jchromb.2016.08.040 PMID: 27623110

Finkelstein, A., Budd, M. A., Gray, B. E., Mirsky, J., Tirosh, A., & Polak, R. (2025). Personalized Culinary Medicine: Qualitative Analyses of Perceptions from Participants in Action and Contemplation Stages of Change Through a One-Year Bi-Center Randomized Controlled Trial. *Nutrients*, *17*(4), 704. DOI: 10.3390/nu17040704 PMID: 40005034

Firdaus, F., & Ambarwati, R. (2024). Challenges and Opportunities Management Human Resources in Industry 4.0 Focuses on Digital Skills. *International Journal of Economics*. https://doi.org/DOI: 10.55299/ijec.v3i1.812

Fisher, I. (1906). *The Nature of Capital and Income*. The Macmillan Company Ltd. DOI: 10.1515/9783112351369

Flynn, C., Yamasumi, E., Fisher, E., Snow, D., Grant, Z., Kirby, M., Browning, P., Rommerskirchen, M., & Russell, I. (2021). *Peoples' Climate Vote*. UNDP, University of Oxford, https://www.undp.org/publications/peoplesclimate-vote

Folke, C., Biggs, R., Norström, A. V., Reyers, B., & Norström, J. (2016). Social-ecological resilience and biosphere-based sustainability science. *Ecology and Society*, *21*(3), 41. DOI: 10.5751/ES-08748-210341

Fonseca, A. (2022). The benefits and perils of digital and automated technologies: impact assessment methods in the fourth industrial revolution. In Fonseca, A. (Ed.), *Handbook of Environmental Impact Assessment* (pp. 126–145). Edward Elgar Publishing., DOI: 10.4337/9781800379633.00013

Fonseca, A., Abreu, I., & Silvestre, W. J. (2021). Investigating context factors in the strategic management of corporate sustainability integration. *Journal of Cleaner Production*, *314*, 128002. DOI: 10.1016/j.jclepro.2021.128002

Fortunisa, A., Djamaris, A., Hanathasia, M., Nurmadewi, D., Suyuthy, M. S., Permadi, C. A., & Hidayati, F. (2024). Talent Management in the Era of Digital Transformation: Challenges and Prospects. *Global International Journal of Innovative Research.* https://doi.org/DOI: 10.59613/global.v2i10.330

Foss, K. (1998). *Technological Interdependencies, Specialization, and Coordination: a Property Rights Perspective on the Firm*, DRUID Working Paper.

Foss, N. J. (2000). The theory of the firm, in idem., ed. 2000. *The Theory of the Firm: Critical Perspectives in Economic Organization* (4 vols.), London: Routledge.

Foss, N. J. (2001a). Hayek vs Coase: Economic organization and the knowledge economy. *International Journal of the Economics of Business.*

Foss, N. J. (2001b). *Selective intervention and internal hybrids.* Manuscript.

Foss, N. J., & Pedersen, T. (2002). Transferring knowledge in MNCs: The role of sources of subsidiary knowledge and organizational context. *Journal of International Management, 8*(1), 49–67. DOI: 10.1016/S1075-4253(01)00054-0

Fournet, F., Simard, F., & Fontenille, D. (2024). Green cities and vector-borne diseases: emerging concerns and opportunities. *Euro surveillance: bulletin Europeen sur les maladies transmissibles = European communicable disease bulletin, 29*(10), 2300548. DOI: 10.2807/1560-7917.ES.2024.29.10.2300548

Fourtané, N. (2013). Las poblaciones indígenas y campesinas de la Amazonía frente a la petrolera Chevron - Texaco: un juicio histórico. *AFESE 59*, 11-30. Obtenido de https://afese.com/img/revistas/revista59/poblaind.pdf

Fragoso-Medina, A. J., Hernández-Fernández, J. A., Nicolás-Vázquez, M. I., Martínez, J., Rivera Espejel, A. L., Saavedra-Leos, M. Z., Pérez Flores, F. J., & Miranda Ruvalcaba, R. (2025). Green Chemistry's Contribution to the Kamal Qureshi Protocol: Comparing Various Activating Modes, the Use of Bentonitic Clay as the Catalyst, and the Use of a Green Solvent. *Catalysts, 15*(3), 238. DOI: 10.3390/catal15030238

Francesco, P. (2020). Laudato Si': Enciclica sulla cura della casa comune. Le vie della Cristianità.

Franklin-Johnson, E., Figge, F., & Canning, L. (2016). Resource duration as a managerial indicator for Circular Economy performance. *Journal of Cleaner Production, 133*(October), 589–598. DOI: 10.1016/j.jclepro.2016.05.023

Frantál, B., Greer-Wootten, B., Klusáček, P., Krejčí, T., Kunc, J., & Martinát, S. (2015). Exploring spatial patterns of urban brownfields regeneration: The case of Brno, Czech Republic. *Cities (London, England), 44*, 9–18. DOI: 10.1016/j.cities.2014.12.007

Frantál, B., Kunc, J., Klusáček, P., & Martinát, S. (2013). Assessing success factors of brownfields regeneration: International and inter-stakeholder perspective. *Transylvanian Review of Administrative Sciences, 44*, 91–107.

Freer-Smith, P. H., Beckett, K. P., & Taylor, G. (2005). Deposition velocities to Sorbus aria, Acer campestre, Populus deltoides × trichocarpa 'Beaupré', Pinus nigra and × Cupressocyparis leylandii for coarse, fine and ultra-fine particles in the urban environment. *Environmental Pollution (January), 133(1)*, 157 – 167. DOI: DOI: 10.1016/j.envpol.2004.03.031

Friede, G., Busch, T., & Bassen, A. (2015). ESG and financial performance: Aggregated evidence from more than 2000 empirical studies. *Journal of Sustainable Finance & Investment*, *5*(4), 210–233. DOI: 10.1080/20430795.2015.1118917

Friedman, M. (2007). The social responsibility of business is to increase its profits. In Zimmerli, W. Ch., Richter, K., & Holzinger, M. (Eds.), *Corporate Ethics and Corporate Governance* (pp. 173–178). Springer. DOI: 10.1007/978-3-540-70818-6_14

Friends of Ecosystem-based Adaptation (FEBA). (2017). *Making ecosystem-based adaptation effective: A framework for defining qualification criteria and quality standards. FEBA technical paper developed for UNFCCC-SBSTA 46*. Bonn (Germany): GIZ, London (UK): IIED, and Gland (Switzerland): IUCN. https://www.iucn.org/sites/default/files/2022-07/feba_eba_qualification_and_quality_criteria_final_en.pdf (accessed on June 21, 2024)

Frintrup, M., Schmidthuber, L., & Hilgers, D. (2022). Towards accounting harmonization in Europe: A multinational survey among budget experts. *International Review of Administrative Sciences*, *88*(2), 390–410. DOI: 10.1177/0020852320915640

Frolovičeva, V. (2023). Multidimensionality of Digital Research in Educational Science. [IJDLDC]. *International Journal of Digital Literacy and Digital Competence*, *14*(1), 1–17. DOI: 10.4018/IJDLDC.335853

Fuady, M., Buraida, , Kevin, M. A., Farrel, M. R., & Triaputri, A. (1632). Buraida, Kevin, M. A., Farrel, M. R., & Triaputri, A. (2025). Enhancing Urban Resilience: Opportunities and Challenges in Adapting to Natural Disasters in Indonesian Cities. *Sustainability (Basel)*, *17*(4), 1632. Advance online publication. DOI: 10.3390/su17041632

Fuchs, P., Raulino, C., Conceição, D., Neiva, S., Amorim, W., Soares, T., & Guerra, J. (2020). Promoting sustainable development in higher education institutions: The use of the balanced scorecard as a strategic management system in support of green marketing. *International Journal of Sustainability in Higher Education*, *21*(7), 1477–1505. DOI: 10.1108/IJSHE-02-2020-0079

Fundación Ecológica Rumicocha. (2019). Estudios de Biodiversidad en la Reserva Ecológica Cayambe Coca [Biodiversity Studies in the Cayambe Coca Ecological Reserve]. Retrieved from https://www.ambiente.gob.ec/wp-content/uploads/downloads/2012/07/Parque-Nacional-Cayambe-Coca.pdf

Gailey, S., McElroy, S., Benmarhnia, T., & Bruckner, T. A. (2021). Green mobility and obesity risk: A longitudinal analysis in California. *Health & Place*, *68*, 102503. DOI: 10.1016/j.healthplace.2020.102503 PMID: 33493964

Gairín Sallán, J., Milton, N., Peiró Rubio, K., & Piscitelli, A. (2020). Capitulo 1. La nueva gestión del conocimiento. In Gairín Sallán, J., Suárez, C. I., & Díaz-Vicario, A. (Eds.), *La nueva gestión del conocimiento* (pp. 39–50). Wolters Kluwer España.

Galindo-Martín, M.-A., Castaño-Martínez, M.-S., & Méndez-Picazo, M.-T. (2020). The Relationship between Green Innovation, *Social Entrepreneurship, and Sustainable Development.Sustainability (Basel)*, *12*(11), 4467. DOI: 10.3390/su12114467

Galleli, B., Onevetch, R., Santos, J., & Lopes, G. (2022). Competences for sustainable development goals: The challenge in business administration education. *Journal of Teacher Education for Sustainability, 24*(1), 73–86. DOI: 10.2478/jtes-2022-0006

Galli, A., Weinzettel, J., Cranston, G., & Ercin, E. (2013). A Footprint Family extended MRIO model to support Europe's transition to a One Planet Economy. *The Science of the Total Environment, 461-462*(September), 813–818. DOI: 10.1016/j.scitotenv.2012.11.071 PMID: 23273807

Galvão, A., Marques, C., & Ferreira, J. J. (2020). The role of entrepreneurship education and training programmes in advancing entrepreneurial skills and new ventures. *European Journal of Training and Development, 44*(6/7), 595–614. DOI: 10.1108/EJTD-10-2019-0174

Gámez, F. (2015). La dimensión social: un proceso sinérgico en la interacción universidad-comunidad a través de la función de extensión. *Investigación y Postgrado, 30*(1), 103-123. Obtenido de https://ve .scielo.org/scielo.php?script=sci_arttext&pid=S1316-00872015000100006

Garavaglia, A., Petti, L., & Triacca, S. (2021, October). Integration of LifeComp and DigComp 2.2 as a Theoretical Framework for Media Education. In *ATEE Spring Conference* (pp. 59-70). Cham: Springer International Publishing.

Garcia Carrión, D. (2015). *Caso Chevron - Defensa del Ecuador frente al uso indebido del Arbitraje de inversión.* Quito.

García-Melón, M., Gómez-Pérez, L., & Cabello, R. (2020). Artificial Intelligence for Sustainability: Challenges and Applications. *Springer Handbook of Computational Intelligence*, 303-322. https://doi .org/DOI: 10.1007/978-3-030-45143-4_22

Garcia-Perez, A., & Mitra, A. (2008). *Tacit knowledge elicitation and measurement in research organisations: A methodological approach.*

Garcia-Perez, A., & Ayres, R. (2009). Collaborative development of knowledge representations – A novel approach to knowledge elicitation and transfer. *Electronic Journal of Knowledge Management, 7*(1), 55–62.

Garcia-Perez, A., & Ayres, R. (2015). Wikifailure: The limitations of technology for knowledge sharing. *Leading Issues in Knowledge management. Volume Two*, 2, 242.

García-Sánchez, I. M., Hussain, N., & Martínez-Ferrero, J. (2020). Sustainability reporting and assurance: The role of institutional investors. *Corporate Social Responsibility and Environmental Management, 27*(6), 2951–2967. DOI: 10.1002/csr.1973

Gartner. (2019). *Predicts 2020: Data and Analytics*. Gartner. Retrieved from https://www.gartner.com

Garton, E. (2019). Tesla's Green Energy Revolution: The Role of Electric Vehicles in Achieving SDGs. *Energy Economics Review, 6*(1), 34–48.

Gaviria-Marin, M., Merigó, J. M., & Baier-Fuentes, H. (2019). Knowledge management: A global examination based on bibliometric analysis, *Technological Forecasting and Social Change,* 140, 2019, Pages 194-220, https://doi.org/. (https://www.sciencedirect.com/science/article/pii/S0040162517304055DOI: 10.1016/j.techfore.2018.07.006

Geissdoerfer, M., Savaget, P., Bocken, N. M. P., & Hultink, E. J. (2017). The Circular Economy – A New Sustainability Paradigm? *Journal of Cleaner Production*, *143*, 757–768. DOI: 10.1016/j.jclepro.2016.12.048

GEM (Global Entrepreneurship Monitor). (2023). *Global Entrepreneurship Monitor 2023/2024 Global Report: 25 Years and Growing*. GEM.

GEM (Global Entrepreneurship Monitor). (2025). GEM 2024/2025 Global report: Entrepreneurship reality check. Available at https://gemconsortium.org/report/gem-20242025-global-report-entrepreneurship-reality-check-4. Accessed on February 19th, 2025.

George, G., Schillebeeckx, S. J. D., & Liak, T. L. (2020). The Management of Natural Resources: An Overview and Research Agenda. *Academy of Management Journal*, *63*(3), 731–738. DOI: 10.5465/amj.2019.4004

Gherardi, S., Nicolini, D., & Odella, F. (1998). Toward a social understanding of how people learn in organizations: The notion of situated curriculum. *Management Learning*, *9*(3), 234–256. DOI: 10.1177/1350507698293002

Ghisellini, P., Cialani, C., & Ulgiati, S. (2016). A review on circular economy: The expected transition to a balanced interplay of environmental and economic systems. *Journal of Cleaner Production*, *114*, 11–32. DOI: 10.1016/j.jclepro.2015.09.007

Gholami, H., Sobhani, A., & Khademi, Z. (2020). Sustainable Entrepreneurship: A Conceptual Framework for Future Research. *Sustainability*, *12*(10), 1–19. DOI: 10.3390/su12104122

Ghoshal, S., Moran, P., & Almeida-Costa, L. (1995). The Essence of the Megacorporation: Shared Context, Not Structural Hierarchy. *Journal of Institutional and Theoretical Economics*, *151*, 748–759.

Giacalone, R. A., & Thompson, G. R. (2020). Sustainable development goals and entrepreneurial education: A case for a more inclusive curriculum. *Journal of Business Ethics*, *165*(2), 307–323.

Gianfrate, G., & Peri, M. (2019). Sustainable finance and the role of green bonds: A systematic review. *Sustainability*, *11*(23), 6367.

Giannico, V., Spano, G., Elia, M., D'Este, M., Sanesi, G., & Lafortezza, R. (2021). Green spaces, quality of life, and citizen perception in European cities. *Environmental Research*, *196*, 110922. DOI: 10.1016/j.envres.2021.110922 PMID: 33639147

Gibbs, D., & Deutz, P. (2007). Reflections on implementing industrial ecology through eco-industrial park development. *Journal of Cleaner Production*, *15*(17), 1683–1695. DOI: 10.1016/j.jclepro.2007.02.003

Gilal, F. G., Ashraf, Z., Gilal, N. G., Gilal, R. G., & Channa, N. A. (2019). Promoting environmental performance through Green HRM practices in higher education institutions: A moderated mediation model.*Corporate Social Responsibility and Environmental Management, John Wiley & Sons*, *26*(6), 1579–1590. DOI: 10.1002/csr.1835

Gilal, F. G., Ashraf, Z., Gilal, N. G., Gilal, R. G., & Channa, N. A. (2019). Promoting environmental performance through green human resource management practices in higher education institutions: A moderated mediation model. *Corporate Social Responsibility and Environmental Management*, *26*(6), 1579–1590.

Gil-Doménech, D., Magomedova, N., Sánchez-Alcázar, E., & Lechuga, M. (2021). Integrating sustainability in the business administration and management curriculum: A sustainability competencies map. *Sustainability (Basel)*, *13*(16), 9458. DOI: 10.3390/su13169458

Gillan, S. L., Koch, A., & Starks, L. T. (2021). Firms and Social Responsibility: A Review of ESG and CSR Research in Corporate Finance. *Journal of Corporate Finance*, *66*, 101889. DOI: 10.1016/j.jcorpfin.2021.101889

Gilster, S. D., Langhout, K. J., & Dalessandro, J. L. (2021). Staff Stability Through Service: Promoting a Person-Centered Culture for Work and Care in Long-Term Services and Supports Environments. *Journal of Gerontological Nursing*, *47*(11), 6–10. DOI: 10.3928/00989134-20211012-01 PMID: 34704868

Ginja Antunes, H. J., & Gonçalves Pinheiro, P. (2020). Linking knowledge management, organizational learning and memory. *Journal of Innovation & Knowledge*, *5*(2), 140–149. https://www.sciencedirect.com/science/article/pii/S2444569X19300319. DOI: 10.1016/j.jik.2019.04.002

Gkogkidis, V., & Dacre, N. (2021). Exploratory Learning Environments for Responsible Management Education Using Lego Serious Play. *arXiv preprint arXiv:2104.12539*. https://arxiv.org/abs/2104.12539 DOI: 10.31235/osf.io/ek7th

Glass, C., Cook, A., & Ingersoll, A. R. (2016). Do women leaders promote sustainability? Analyzing the effect of corporate governance composition on environmental performance. *Business Strategy and the Environment*, *25*(7), 495–511. DOI: 10.1002/bse.1879

Global Green Growth Institute – GGGI. (2016, october). *Achieving Global Green Transformation: Report Summary*.

Glumac, O. (2018). *Lab of Collaborative Youth: shaping a learning framework in an active citizenship. Universidade do Porto*. FBAUP.

Goichuk, V., & Lyubomudrova, N. (2024). The impact of strategic human capital management on the competitiveness of an enterprise. *Three Seas Economic Journal*, *5*(2), 1–6. DOI: 10.30525/2661-5150/2024-2-1

Gold, A. H., Malhotra, A., & Segars, A. H. (2001). Knowledge management: An organizational capabilities perspective. *Journal of Management Information Systems*, *18*(1), 185–214. DOI: 10.1080/07421222.2001.11045669

Gonçalves, H., Magalhães, V. S., Ferreira, L. M., & Arantes, A. (2024). Overcoming barriers to sustainable supply chain management in small and medium-sized enterprises: A multi-criteria decision-making approach. *Sustainability (Basel)*, *16*(2), 506. DOI: 10.3390/su16020506

González, A. L., Ponce, J. H., & Popescu, C. R. (2023). Best Practice in the Use of the Water Sources of Portoviejo Canton, Ecuador, and Its Parishes. In J. Keengwe & B. Nyatuka (Eds.), *Climate Change Education for Sustainable Development* (pp. 263-287). IGI Global Scientific Publishing. DOI: 10.4018/978-1-6684-9099-0.ch012

Gough, I. (2011). *Climate change and public policy futures*. The British Academy., https://www.thebritishacademy.ac.uk/publications/new-paradigms-climate-change-public-policy-futures/

Gough, K. (2020). Circular Economy Strategies: IKEA's Commitment to Sustainability. *Sustainability Innovations Review*, *10*(4), 16–28.

Grand View Research. (2022). *Green Technology and Sustainability Market Size, Share & Trends Analysis Report*. Grand View Research.

Granger, C. W. J., & Newbold, P. (1974). Spurious regressions in econometrics. *Journal of Econometrics*, *2*(2), 111–120. DOI: 10.1016/0304-4076(74)90034-7

Grant, R. M. (1996). Toward a knowledge-based theory of the firm. *Strategic Management Journal*, *17*(S2), 109–122. DOI: 10.1002/smj.4250171110

Green, T. (2018). Evaluating predictors for brownfield redevelopment. *Land Use Policy*, *73*, 299–319. DOI: 10.1016/j.landusepol.2018.01.008

Gruševá, E., & Blašková, V. (2022). Education as a factor influencing the economic growth of the V4 countries. *Review of Applied Socio-Economic Research*, *24*(2). Advance online publication. DOI: 10.54609/reaser.v24i2.139

Guaranda, W. (2010). *Acciones jurídicas para establecer responsabilidades por daño ambiental en el Ecuador* . Quito: Fundación Regional de Asesoría en Derechos Humanos, INREDH.

Gudynas, E. (2009). Derechos de la naturaleza el futuro es ahora [Rights of Nature: The Future Is Now]. Abya Ayala. Quito, Ecuador. Retrieved from https://gudynas.com/wp-content/uploads/GudynasDerechosNaturalezaLima14r.pdf

Gudynas, E. (2011). Buen Vivir: Today's Tomorrow. Development, 54(4), 441-447. Retrieved from ttps://www.gudynas.com/publicaciones/GudynasBuenVivirTomorrowDevelopment11.pdf

Gudynas, E. (2015). *Derechos de la naturaleza* [Rights of Nature]. Tinta Limón.

Guevara Alban, G., Verdesoto Arguello, A., & Castro Molina, N. (2020). Metodologías de investigación educativa (descriptivas, experimentales, participativas, y de investigación-acción). *Revista cientifica Mundo de la investigación y el conocimiento RECIMUNDO, 4*(3), 163-173. Obtenido de https://recimundo.com/index.php/es/article/view/860

Guijarro-Garvi, M., Miranda-Escolar, B., Cedeño-Menéndez, Y. T., & Moyano-Pesquera, P. B. (2022). Education as a dimension of human development: A Provincial-level Education Index for Ecuador. *PLoS One*, *17*(7), e0270932. DOI: 10.1371/journal.pone.0270932 PMID: 35802576

Gujarati, D. N. (2003). *Basic Econometrics* (4th ed.). McGraw – Hill, Inc.

Gupta, N.. (2022). *Predictive Traffic Management Using Machine Learning Models.* Advances in Traffic Control Systems.

Gupta, S., Maurya, N., Malik, F. A., & Razzak Janjua, L. (Eds.). (2025). *Integrating Blue-Green Infrastructure Into Urban Development.* IGI Global., DOI: 10.4018/979-8-3693-8069-7

Haas, M. R., & Hansen, M. T. (2007). Different knowledge, different benefits: Toward a productivity perspective on knowledge sharing in organizations. *Strategic Management Journal, 28*(11), 1133–1153. DOI: 10.1002/smj.631

Haber, S., Kepler, J. D., Larcker, D. F., Seru, A., & Tayan, B. (2022). ESG Investing: What Shareholders Do Fund Managers Represent? Rock Center for Corporate Governance at Stanford University Working Paper Forthcoming, Stanford University Graduate School of Business Research Paper, (4267270).

Hackworth, J. (2014). The limits to market-based strategies for addressing land abandonment in shrinking American cities. *Progress in Planning, 90*, 1–37. DOI: 10.1016/j.progress.2013.03.004

Haden, S. S. P., Oyler, J. D., & Humphrey, J. H. (2009). Historical, practical, and theoretical perspectives on green management. *An Exploratory Analysis Management Decision, 47*, 1041–1055.

Hagget, P. (2001). *Geography: A global synthesis.* Prentice Hall.

Hagmann, D. F., Kruge, M. A., Goodey, N. M., & Krumins, J. A. (2019). Characterization of coal particles in the soil of a former rail yard and urban brownfield: Liberty State Park, Jersey City (NJ), USA. *International Journal of Coal Geology, 217*, 103328. DOI: 10.1016/j.coal.2019.103328

Hair, J. F., Black, W. C., Babin, B. J., & Anderson, R. E. (2010). *Multivariate data analysis* (7th ed.). Pearson.

Hála, M., MacGregor Pelikánová, R., & Rubáček, F. (2024). Negative Determinants of CSR Support by Generation Z in Central Europe - Infodemic's Gender-Sensitive Impacts in a 'COVID-19' Era. *Central European Business Review, 13*(2), 1–26. DOI: 10.18267/j.cebr.344

Hallinger, P., & Chatpinyakoop, C. (2019). A bibliometric review of research on higher education for sustainable development, 1998–2018. *Sustainability (Basel), 11*(8), 2401. DOI: 10.3390/su11082401

Hallstedt, S. I., Thompson, A. W., & Lindahl, P. (2020). Key elements for implementing a strategic sustainability perspective in the product innovation process. *Sustainability, 12*(4), 1455.

Hameed, Z., Khan, I. U., Islam, T., Sheikh, Z., & Naeem, R. M. (2020). Do Green HRM System influence employees' environmental performance? *International Journal of Manpower, 41*(7), 1061–1079. DOI: 10.1108/IJM-08-2019-0407

Hamidi, D. Z., Hakiki, R., & Pandiangan, H. (2024). AI and Human Collaboration: The Future of HR in the Fourth Industrial Revolution. *Escalate, 2*(01), 17–25. DOI: 10.61536/escalate.v2i01.49

Hamilton, K., & Hartwick, J. M. (2005). Investing exhaustible resource rents and the path of consumption. *The Canadian Journal of Economics. Revue Canadienne d'Economique, 38*(2), 615–621. DOI: 10.1111/j.0008-4085.2005.00295.x

Hamilton, K., & Naikal, E. (2014). Comprehensive wealth accounting and sustainable development. In Atkinson, G., Dietz, S., Neumayer, E., & Agarwala, M. (Eds.), *Handbook of Sustainable Development* (2nd ed., pp. 25–40). Edward Elgar Publishing., DOI: 10.4337/9781782544708.00010

Hammoda, B. (2022). Mapping Digital Technologies Used in Entrepreneurship Education against the Competences They Develop Using Entrecomp Framework as a Reference: A Systematic Literature Review. *INTED2022 Proceedings*, 5489-5498.

Hammond, E. B., Coulon, F., Hallett, S. H., Thomas, R., Dick, A., Hardy, D., Dickens, M., Washbourn, E., & Beriro, D. J. (2023). The development of a novel decision support system for regional land use planning for brownfield land. *Journal of Environmental Management*, *349*, 119466. DOI: 10.1016/j.jenvman.2023.119466 PMID: 37952377

Hanáčková, D., & Takáč, I. (2024). Innovation performance of V4 countries. *Entrepreneurship and Sustainability Issues*, *11*(4), 293–310. DOI: 10.9770/jesi.2024.11.4(18)

Harari, R., & Harari, H. (2006). Children's environment and health in Latin America: The Ecuadorian case. *Annals of the New York Academy of Sciences*, *1076*(1), 660–677. DOI: 10.1196/annals.1371.082 PMID: 17119244

Hardy Bednar, D., & Godkin, L. (2009). An Exploratory, Longitudinal Study of Factors Influencing Development of a Networked Company. [IRMJ]. *Information Resources Management Journal*, *22*(3), 59–72. DOI: 10.4018/irmj.2009070104

Harman, K., & Koohang, A. (Eds.). (2007). *Learning objects: Applications, implications, & future directions*. Informing Science.

Hartley, K., Gupta, H., van Vuuren, D., & Kirchherr, J. (2023). Employee skills for circular business model implementation: A taxonomy. *Journal of Cleaner Production*, *410*, 137027. DOI: 10.1016/j.jclepro.2023.137027

Hart, O. (1995). *Firms, contracts, and financial structure*. Oxford University Press. DOI: 10.1093/0198288816.001.0001

Hasan, S. (2005). Social capital and social entrepreneurship in Asia: Analyzing the link. *Asia Pacific Journal of Public Administration*, *27*(1), 1–17. DOI: 10.1080/23276665.2005.10779296

Hassan, A. (2020). Managerial competencies required to achieve sustainable development projects: A proposed model for managers. *Environmental Management and Sustainable Development*, *9*(3), 68. DOI: 10.5296/emsd.v9i3.17603

Hassan, A.. (2016). Effect of knowledge management on growth performance in construction industry. *Management Decision*, *54*(3), 735–749. DOI: 10.1108/MD-01-2015-0006

Hawken, P. (2017). *Drawdown: The Most Comprehensive Plan Ever Proposed to Reverse Global Warming*. Penguin.

Hawken, P. (2019). Patagonia's Sustainable Business Model: A Case Study. *Green Business Review*, *12*(1), 55–67.

Hawn, O., Chatterji, A. K., & Mitchell, W. (2018). A New Approach to Combating Climate Change: Businesses and Government Cooperation. *Business and Society Review*, *123*(3), 375–413. DOI: 10.1111/basr.12127

Heisig, P. (2009). Harmonisation of knowledge management - comparing 160 KNOWLEDGE MANAGEMENT frameworks around the globe. *Journal of Knowledge Management*, *13*(4), 4–31. DOI: 10.1108/13673270910971798

He, J., Zhang, and Morrison, A.M. (. (2019). The effects of corporate social responsibility on organization citizenship behavior and task performance in hospitality: A sequential mediation model. *International Journal of Contemporary Hospitality Management*, *31*(6), 2582–2598. DOI: 10.1108/IJCHM-05-2018-0378

Heller-Schuh B, Barber M, Henriques L, Paier M, Pontikakis D, Scherngell T, Veltri G, Weber M. (2011). Analysis of Networks in European Framework Programmes (1984-2006). EUR 24759 EN. Luxembourg (Luxembourg): Publications Office of the European Union. JRC63467.

Hemingway, C. A., & Maclagan, P. W. (2004). Managers' Personal Values as Drivers of Corporate Social Responsibility. *Journal of Business Ethics*, *50*(1), 33–44. DOI: 10.1023/B:BUSI.0000020964.80208.c9

Hemlata, & Rai, M. (2025). An Optimized Demand for Cost and Environment Benefits Towards Smart Residentials Using IOT and Machine Learning. Sustainable Smart Homes and Buildings with Internet of Things, 291-307.

Henderson, J. M., & Quandt, R. E. (1980). Microeconomic Theory: A Mathematical Approach *(3rd International ed.)*. Singapore: McGraw – Hill Book Company (Originally published by McGraw – Hill Inc., New York, USA).

Henry, C. (2020). Capitalism and the curse of external effects. In Henry, C., Rockström, J., & Stern, N. (Eds.), *Standing up for a Sustainable World: Voices of Change* (pp. 24–46). Edward Elgar Publishing., DOI: 10.4337/9781800371781.00011

Henry, C., Foss, L., & Ahl, H. (2023). Gender and sustainability in entrepreneurship education: A systematic review. *Entrepreneurship and Regional Development*, *35*(1-2), 1–25.

Herrera, J. (2018). Las prácticas investigativas contemporáneas. Los restos de sus nuevos planteamientos epistemológicos [Contemporary research practices. The remains of his new epistemological approaches]. *Revista Scientific*, *3*(7), 6–15. DOI: 10.29394/Scientific.issn.2542-2987.2018.3.7.0.6-15

Hickel, J., & Kallis, G. (2020). Is green growth possible? *New Political Economy*, *25*(4), 469–486. DOI: 10.1080/13563467.2019.1598964

Hicks, B. B., Baldocchi, D. D., Meyers, T. P., Hosker, R. P.Jr, & Matt, D. R. (1987). A preliminary multiple resistance routine for deriving dry deposition velocities from measured quantities. *Water, Air, and Soil Pollution*, *36*(3-4), 311–330. DOI: 10.1007/BF00229675

Hobbs, R., & Harris, J. (2001). Restoration Ecology: Repairing the Earth's Ecosystems in the New Millenniun. *Restoration Ecology*, *9*(2), 239–246. DOI: 10.1046/j.1526-100x.2001.009002239.x

Hobsbawm, E. (1971). The Birth of the Industrial Revolution. Siglo Veintiuno Ed.

Hockerts, K. (2018). The Effects of Experimental Social Entrepreneurship Education on Intention Formation in Students. *Journal of Social Entrepreneurship*, *9*(3), 234–256. DOI: 10.1080/19420676.2018.1498377

Hoffman, A. J. (2018). *Climate Change: What's Your Business Strategy?* Harvard Business Press.

Hoffman, A. J. (2018). *The Business Guide to Circular Water and Climate Action*. Oxford University Press.

Holmström, B. (1979). Moral Hazard and Observability. *The Bell Journal of Economics*, *10*(1), 74–91. DOI: 10.2307/3003320

Holmström, B. (1982). Moral Hazard in Teams. *The Bell Journal of Economics*, *13*(2), 324–340. DOI: 10.2307/3003457

Holmström, B., & Milgrom, P. (1991). Multitask Principal-Agent Analyses: Incentive Contracts, Asset Ownership, and Job Design. *Journal of Law Economics and Organization*, *7*(special_issue), 24–52. DOI: 10.1093/jleo/7.special_issue.24

Holsapple, C. W., & Wu, J. (2011). An elusive antecedent of superior firm performance: The knowledge management factor. *Decision Support Systems*, *52*(1), 271–283. DOI: 10.1016/j.dss.2011.08.003

Hoogendoorn, B., Van der Zwan, P., & Thurik, R. (2019). Sustainable entrepreneurship: The role of perceived barriers and risk. *Journal of Business Ethics*, *157*(4), 1133–1154. DOI: 10.1007/s10551-017-3646-8

Hopwood, B., Mellor, M., & O'Brien, G. (2005). Sustainable development: Mapping different approaches. *Sustainable Development (Bradford)*, *13*(1), 38–52. DOI: 10.1002/sd.244

Hornberger, K. (2023). The difference between ESG and impact investing and why it matters. In *Scaling Impact: Finance and Investment for a Better World* (pp. 93–112). Springer International Publishing. DOI: 10.1007/978-3-031-22614-4_8

Hossain, S. (2022, September 12). Bangladesh boasts 171 Leed-certified green RMG factories now. *Dhaka Tribune*. https://www.dhakatribune.com/business/2022/09/12/bangladesh-boasts-171-leed-certified-green-rmg-factories-now DOI: 10.1016/j.jhazmat.2007.12.077

Howell, B. (2024). Developing a Diversity and Inclusion Performance Management Strategy. *Advances in Logistics, Operations, and Management Science Book Series*, 97–116. https://doi.org/DOI: 10.4018/979-8-3693-7327-9.ch006

Howorth, C., Smith, S. M., & Parkinson, C. (2012). Social Learning and Social Entrepreneurship Education. *Academy of Management Learning & Education*, *11*(3), 371–389. http://. DOI: 10.5465/amle.2011.0022

Huang, Y., Li, P., Bu, Y., & Zhao, G. (2023). What entrepreneurial ecosystem elements promote sustainable entrepreneurship? *Journal of Cleaner Production*, *422*, 138459. DOI: 10.1016/j.jclepro.2023.138459

Hühne, F. (2021, November 12). Why electronics cause climate change? *Syllucid B.V.*https://syllucid.com/blogs/news/this-is-a-recommended-blog-2

Hühn, M. P. (2023). Business ethics: Between Friedman and Freeman? A response to A Puzzle about Business Ethics. *Business Ethics, the Environment & Responsibility*, *32*(2), 868–876. DOI: 10.1111/beer.12523

Hurníková, J. (2009). Brownfieldy a územní rozvoj. Urbanismus a územní rozvoj, 12(6), 3-5. Retrieved January 7, 2019, from http://www.uur.cz/images/publikace/uur/2009/2009-06/01_brownfieldy%20 rozvoj.pdf

Hussain, I., Nazir, M., Hashmi, S. B., Shaheen, I., Akram, S., Waseem, M. A., & Arshad, A. (2021). Linking green and sustainable entrepreneurial intentions and social networking sites; the mediating role of self-efficacy and risk propensity. *Sustainability (Basel)*, *13*(13), 7050. DOI: 10.3390/su13137050

Hu, Z., & Wang, S. (2025). Multi-Scenario Simulation of Ecosystem Service Value in Beijing's Green Belts Based on PLUS Model. *Land (Basel)*, *14*(2), 408. DOI: 10.3390/land14020408

Hysa, E., Kruja, A., Rehman, N. U., & Laurenti, R. (2020). Circular Economy Innovation and Environmental Sustainability Impact on Economic Growth: An Integrated Model for Sustainable Development. *Sustainability (Basel)*, *12*(12), 4831. DOI: 10.3390/su12124831

IKEA. (2020). *IKEA Sustainability Strategy: A Circular Economy Approach.* Retrieved from https://www.ikea.com

IKEA. (2020).. . *Sustainability Report*, *2020*, •••. https://www.ikea.com/sustainability

Ikram, M., Sroufe, R., Awan, U., & Abid, N. (2021). Enabling progress in developing economies: A novel hybrid decision-making model for green technology planning. *Sustainability (Basel)*, *14*(1), 258. DOI: 10.3390/su14010258

ILO/EU/IILS. (2011). TOWARDS A GREENER ECONOMY: THE SOCIAL DIMENSIONS. *International Institute for Labour Studies (IILS)*, 1 – 103. https://www.ilo.org/wcmsp5/groups/public/---dgreports/---dcomm/---publ/documents/publication/wcms_168163.pdf

Imran, M. (2020). Effect of Green HRM practices on environmental sustainability. *International Journal of Human Capital in Urban Management*, *5*(2), 153–164. DOI: 10.22034/IJHCUM.2020.02.06

Imtiaz, Q., & Iqbal, S. (2024). Impact of HR Practices on Eco-Friendly Behaviour in Higher Education Institutions: Mediating Mechanism of Organizational Culture & Sustainable Work Environment. *Bulletin of Multidisciplinary Studies*, *1*(3), 105–113.

Inderst, G., Kaminker, C., & Stewart, F. (2012). Defining and Measuring Green Investments: Implications for Institutional Investors' Asset Allocations. *OECD Working Papers on Finance, Insurance and Private Pensions, No. 24.* Paris, France: OECD Publishing. DOI: DOI: 10.1787/20797117

Indrajaya, A. N., Setiawan, D. L., Marshella, I., Tarigan, J., & Oktaviana, N. (2024). Creating Sustainability Through Talent Management Improvement: PT USAHA DAGANG INDONESIA. [JSCD]. *Journal of Sustainable Community Development*, *6*(1), 22–32. DOI: 10.32924/jscd.v6i1.113

Inecgobec. Censo de Información Ambiental Económica en Gobiernos Autónomos Descentralizados Provinciales 2014. [Online]. Available from: http://anda.inec.gob.ec/anda/index.php/catalog/509 [Accessed 4 June 2024].

Inkinen, H. (2016). Review of empirical research on knowledge management practices and firm performance. *Journal of Knowledge Management*, *20*(2), 230–257. DOI: 10.1108/JKM-09-2015-0336

INREDH. (2024). *CASO: Empresa Petrolera CHEVRON TEXACO y su contaminación en la Amazonía ecuatoriana.* Obtenido de https://www.inredh.org/archivos/boletines/resumen_caso_chevron_texaco_contaminacion_amazonia.pdf

International Union for the Conservation of Nature (IUCN). (2016). World Conservation Congress 2016 Resolution 069: Defining nature-based solutions. https://portals.iucn.org/ library/ sites/ library/ files/ resrecfiles/ WCC_ 2016_ RES_ 069_ EN .pdf

International Union for the Conservation of Nature (IUCN). (n.d.). *Five reasons why ecosystems are central to disaster risk reduction.* https://www.iucn.org/ theme/ ecosystem -management/ our -work/ environment -and -disasters/ about -ecosystem -based -disaster -risk -reduction -eco -drr/ five -reasons -why-ecosystems -are -central -disaster -risk -reduction

Iraldo, F., Testa, F., & Frey, M. (2009). Is an environmental management system able to influence environmental and competitive performance? The case of the eco-management and audit scheme (EMAS) in the European Union. *Journal of Cleaner Production, 17*(16), 1444–1452. DOI: 10.1016/j.jclepro.2009.05.013

Ismail, I. J. (2022). Entrepreneurs' competencies and sustainability of small and medium enterprises in Tanzania. A mediating effect of entrepreneurial innovations. *Cogent Business & Management, 9*(1), 2111036. DOI: 10.1080/23311975.2022.2111036

ISO 14025:2006. *Environmental labels and declarations – Type III environmental declarations – Principles and procedures.*

ISO 14046:2014. *Environmental management – Water footprint – Principles, requirements, and guidelines.*

ISO. (2024). IWA 48 Framework for Implementing Environmental, Social and Governance (ESG) Principles. https://www.iso.org/obp/ui/en/#iso:std:iso:iwa:48:ed-1:v1:en

ISO/TS 14027:2017. *Environmental labels and declarations – Development of product category rules.*

ISTE. (2024). ISTE Standards. https://cms-live-media.iste.org/ISTE*STANDARDS*2024.pdf

Jabbour, C. J. C., & Santos, F. (2008). The central role of human resource management in the search for sustainable organizations. *International Journal of Human Resource Management, 19*(12), 2133–2154. DOI: 10.1080/09585190802479389

Jabbour, C. J. C., Seuring, S., & de Sousa Jabbour, A. B. L. (2023). *Sustainable human resource management: Strategies and practices for a resilient workforce.* Springer.

Jabeen, F. (2021). The influence of Green HRM practices and employee green behavior on business performance in sustainability-focused organizations. *Journal of Environmental Planning and Management.* Advance online publication. DOI: 10.1080/09640568.2022.2074824

Jackson, B. J. (2004). Brownfields snadno a lehce: Příručka zejména pro pracovníky a zastupitele obcí [online]. Institut pro udržitelný rozvoj sídel o.s. Dostupné z: http://rrajm.data.quonia.cz/brownfieldy/publikace/Brownfields1.pdf

Jaffé, P. R., Huang, S., Park, J., Ruiz-Urigüen, M., Shuai, W., & Sima, M. (2024). Defluorination of PFAS by Acidimicrobium sp. strain A6 and potential applications for remediation. *Methods in Enzymology*, *696*, 287–320. DOI: 10.1016/bs.mie.2024.01.013 PMID: 38658084

Jain, T. K. (2019). Towards the Theory of Green Entrepreneurship, *NOLEGEIN-Journal of Entrepreneurship Planning*. *SSRN*, *2*(1), 1–5. DOI: 10.2139/ssrn.3284935

Jardim, J. (2021). Entrepreneurial skills to be successful in the global and digital world: Proposal for a frame of reference for entrepreneurial education. *Education Sciences*, *11*(7), 356. DOI: 10.3390/educsci11070356

Jaria-Manzano, J. (2019). Los principios del derecho ambiental: Concreciones, insuficiencias y reconstrucción [The Principles of Environmental Law: Concreteness, Insufficiencies and Reconstruction]. *Ius et Praxis*, *25*(2), 403–432. DOI: 10.4067/S0718-00122019000200403

Jarque, C. M., & Bera, A. K. (1987). A Test for Normality of Observations and Regression Residuals. *International Statistical Review*, *55*(2), 163–172. DOI: 10.2307/1403192

Javadi, S., Rameez, M., Dahl, M., & Pettersson, M. I. (2018). Vehicle classification based on multiple fuzzy C-means clustering using dimensions and speed features. *Procedia Computer Science*, *126*, 1344–1350. DOI: 10.1016/j.procs.2018.08.085

Jejeniwa, T. O., Mhlongo, N. Z., & Jejeniwa, T. O. (2024). Diversity and inclusion in the workplace: A conceptual framework comparing the USA and Nigeria. *International Journal of Management & Entrepreneurship Research*, *6*(5), 1368–1394. DOI: 10.51594/ijmer.v6i5.1090

Jensen, M. C., & Meckling, W. H. (1992). Specific and general knowledge and organizational structure, in Lars Werin og Hans Wijkander, eds. 1992. *Contract Economics*. Oxford: Blackwell.

Jensen, M. C., & Meckling, W. H. (1976). Theory of the firm: Managerial behavior, agency costs and ownership structure. *Journal of Financial Economics*, *3*(4), 305–360. DOI: 10.1016/0304-405X(76)90026-X

Jiang, W., Stickley, A., & Ueda, M. (2021). Green space and suicide mortality in Japan: An ecological study. *Social science & medicine (1982)*, *282*, 114137. .DOI: 10.1016/j.socscimed.2021.114137

Jiang, F. (2025). Digital transformation and green innovation: The mediating role of green management disclosure and the moderating role of institutional pressure. *Journal of General Management*, *0*(0), 03063070241308100. Advance online publication. DOI: 10.1177/03063070241308100

Joensuu-Salo, S., Viljamaa, A., & Varamäki, E. (2022). Testing the EntreComp framework and its relation to start-up behaviour in seven European countries. *Journal of Small Business and Enterprise Development*, *29*(6), 920–939. DOI: 10.1108/JSBED-04-2021-0156

John, J. E., & Pramila, S. (2024). Integrating AI Tools into HRM to Promote Green HRM Practices. https://doi.org/DOI: 10.1007/978-981-99-9489-2_22

Jolly, P. M., Van Hoof, H., Chen, F., Kim, B., Duran, M. E., Navas, A. C., Valle, J. G., & Pérez, G. M. (2021). Quantifying cultural tightness-looseness in Ecuador. *PLoS One*, *16*(1), e0246064. DOI: 10.1371/journal.pone.0246064 PMID: 33513147

Jones, J. (2022). How Elon Musk is adding fuel to growing criticism about ESG ratings. Globe & Mail (Toronto, Canada), B1. Gale Academic OneFile, link.gale.com/apps/doc/A704659964/AONE?u=anon~919cbd94&sid=googleScholar&xid=8ae5dbfe

Jones, A., & Ström, P. (2024). Coda: future directions and challenges for research into the green economy. In Jones, A., & Ström, P. (Eds.), *Research Handbook on the Green Economy* (pp. 299–300). Edward Elgar Publishing., DOI: 10.4337/9781789904833.00029

Jones, K.. (2023). *Analyzing Driver Behavior for Improved Traffic Management.* Behavioral Science in Transportation.

Jones, P., Comfort, D., & Hillier, D. (2019). Sustainable Development Goals and Corporate Sustainability: The Role of Business in Achieving the SDGs. *Journal of Business Research*, *103*, 280–286. DOI: 10.1016/j.jbusres.2019.01.032

Jørgensen, S., & Pedersen, L. J. T. (2018). The Circular Rather than the Linear Economy. In *RESTART Sustainable Business Model Innovation* (pp. 103–120). Palgrave Macmillan/ Springer Nature., DOI: 10.1007/978-3-319-91971-3_8

Joseph, S. (2012). Protracted lawfare: The tale of Chevron Texaco in the Amazon. *Journal of Human Rights and the Environment*, *3*(1), 70–91. DOI: 10.4337/jhre.2012.01.03

Judgment, No. 034-16-SIN-CC, Case N° 0011-13-IN (Constitutional Court of Ecuador April 27, 2016). https://buscador.corteconstitucional.gob.ec/buscador-externo/principal/fichaSentencia?numero=034-16-SIN-CC

Judgment, No. 065-15-SEP-CC, Case N.° 0796-12-EP (Constitutional Court of Ecuador March 11, 2015). https://buscador.corteconstitucional.gob.ec/buscador-externo/principal/fichaSentencia?numero=065-15-SEP-CC

Judgment, No. 1149-19-JP/21, Case No. 1149-19-JP/20 (Constitutional Court of Ecuador November 10, 2021). https://buscador.corteconstitucional.gob.ec/buscador-externo/principal/fichaSentencia?numero=1149-19-JP%2F21

Judgment, No. 1185-20-JP/21 (Constitutional Court of Ecuador December 15, 2021). https://buscador.corteconstitucional.gob.ec/buscador-externo/principal/fichaSentencia?numero=1185-20-JP%2F21

Judgment, No. 166-15-SEP-CC, Case N° 0507-12-EP (Constitutional Court of Ecuador May 20, 2015). https://buscador.corteconstitucional.gob.ec/buscador-externo/principal/fichaSentencia?numero=166-15-SEP-CC

Judgment, No. 218-15-SEP-CC, Case N° 1281-12 (Constitutional Court of Ecuador July 9, 2015). https://buscador.corteconstitucional.gob.ec/buscador-externo/principal/fichaSentencia?numero=218-15-SEP-CC

Judgment, No. 22-18-IN/21 (Constitutional Court of Ecuador September 8, 2021). https://buscador.corteconstitucional.gob.ec/buscador-externo/principal/fichaSentencia?numero=22-18-IN%2F21

Judgment, No. 32-17-IN/21, Case No. 32-17-IN (Constitutional Court of Ecuador June 9, 2021). https://buscador.corteconstitucional.gob.ec/buscador-externo/principal/fichaSentencia?numero=32-17-IN%2F21

Kahn, M. (2019). Nestlé's Journey to Sustainability: Overcoming Environmental and Social Challenges. *Business & Sustainability Journal*, *14*(3), 52–63.

Kalinowski, T., Rudnicka, A., Wieteska, G., Wronka, A., Diglio, A., Piccolo, C., & Genovese, A. (2018). Competences required for environmentally responsible managers - a European perspective. *Proceedings of the 36th International Academic Conference*, London, DOI: 10.20472/IAC.2018.036.022

Kamble, S. S., Gunasekaran, A., & Gawankar, S. A. (2020). Achieving sustainable performance in a data-driven agriculture supply chain: A review for research and applications. *International Journal of Production Economics*, *219*, 179–194. DOI: 10.1016/j.ijpe.2019.05.022

KarimiDermani, B., Green, C. T., Tick, G. R., Gholizadeh, H., Wei, W., & Zhang, Y. (2025). Analyzing Multi-Year Nitrate Concentration Evolution in Alabama Aquatic Systems Using a Machine Learning Model. *Environments (Basel, Switzerland)*, *12*(3), 75. DOI: 10.3390/environments12030075

Kato, A. I. (2024). Building resilience and sustainability in small businesses enterprises through sustainable venture capital investment in sub-Saharan Africa. *Cogent Economics & Finance*, *12*(1), 2399760. DOI: 10.1080/23322039.2024.2399760

Kauffman, C., & Martin, P. (2018). Can Rights of Nature Make Development More Sustainable? Why Some Ecuadorian Lawsuits Succeed and Others Fail. *Development*, *92*, 130–142.

Keck, M., & Sikkink, K. (2000). *Activistas sin fronteras* (Primera Edición ed.). México: Siglo veintiuno.

Kenton, W. (2020). Unilever: A Leader in Sustainable Business Practices. *Investopedia*. Retrieved from https://www.investopedia.com

Khan, A.. (2022). Sensor Fusion for Vehicle Classification in Urban Traffic Monitoring Systems. *IEEE Transactions on Intelligent Transportation Systems*.

Khan, F., & Vuopala, E. (2019). Digital Competence Assessment Across Generations: A Finnish Sample Using the Digcomp Framework. [IJDLDC]. *International Journal of Digital Literacy and Digital Competence*, *10*(2), 15–28. DOI: 10.4018/IJDLDC.2019040102

Khan, M. A. (2022). ESG disclosure and firm performance: A bibliometric and meta analysis. *Research in International Business and Finance*, *61*, 101668. DOI: 10.1016/j.ribaf.2022.101668

Khanra, S., Kaur, P., Joseph, R. P., Malik, A., & Dhir, A. (2022). A resource-based view of green innovation as a strategic firm resource: Present status and future directions. *Business Strategy and the Environment*, *31*(4), 1395–1413. DOI: 10.1002/bse.2961

Khare, A., & MacNeil, P. (2024). Adopting sustainability competencies in management education - a scoping review of progress. Preprint. DOI: 10.20944/preprints202410.0652.v1

Khawaja, A., & Janjua, K. N. (2024). The Effect of Sustainable HRM Practices on Organizational Sustainability in Textile Industry of Pakistan. *Bulletin of Business and Economics*. https://doi.org/DOI: 10.61506/01.00515

Khoiriyah, S., Asror, M., Ruzakki, H., & Hilmy, M. (2023). Sustainable Islamic education: Literature study towards achieving the vision of sustainable development goals (SDGs). *Jurnal Pendidikan Islam Indonesia*, *8*(1), 12–28. DOI: 10.35316/jpii.v8i1.492

Kimerling, J. (2006). Transnational Operations, Bi-National Injustice: Chevrontexaco and Indigenous Huaorani and Kichwa in the Amazon Rainforest in Ecuador. *American Indian Law Review*, *31*(2), 445–508. DOI: 10.2307/20070795

Kinver, M. (2010). Derrame del Exxon Valdez sigue en Alaska. *BBC news mundo*. Obtenido de https://www.bbc.com/mundo/ciencia_tecnologia/2010/01/100114_0457_exxon_sigue_desastre_jrg

Kirchherr, J., Reike, D., & Hekkert, M. (2017). Conceptualizing the circular economy: An analysis of 114 definitions. *Resources, Conservation and Recycling*, *127*(December), 221–232. DOI: 10.1016/j.resconrec.2017.09.005

Kirkwood, J., & Walton, S. (2010). What motivates ecopreneurs to start businesses? *International Journal of Entrepreneurial Behaviour & Research*, *16*(3), 204–228. DOI: 10.1108/13552551011042799

Kiron, D., Unruh, G., Reeves, M., & Rubel, H. (2022). Sustainability's Deep Impact on Business. *MIT Sloan Management Review*. Retrieved from https://sloanreview.mit.edu/

Klockner, S. (2009). *Manual for facilitators in non-formal education*. Council of Europe.

Kocer, A.. (2020). Traffic Monitoring Using UAVs: Challenges and Opportunities. *Journal of Transportation Engineering*.

Kogut, B., & Zander, U. (1992). Knowledge of the firm, combinative capabilities, and the replication of technology. *Organization Science*, *3*(3), 383–397. DOI: 10.1287/orsc.3.3.383

Kolk, A., van Tulder, R., & Welters, C. (2017). *Business and Sustainability: A Global Perspective*. Springer.

Koman, G., Boršoš, P., & Kubina, M. (2024). Sustainable Human Resource Management with a Focus on Corporate Employee Recruitment. *Sustainability (Basel)*, *16*(14), 6059. DOI: 10.3390/su16146059

Kong, E. (2010). Innovation Processes in Social Enterprises: An IC Perspective. *Journal of Intellectual Capital*, *11*(2), 158–178. DOI: 10.1108/14691931011039660

Korankye, B. (2020). The Impact of Global Covid-19 Pandemic on Small and Medium Enterprises in Ghana. *International Journal of Management, Accounting & Economics, 7*(6).

Korhonen, J., Honkasalo, A., & Seppälä, J. (2018). Circular economy: The concept and its limitations. *Ecological Economics*, *143*, 37–46. DOI: 10.1016/j.ecolecon.2017.06.041

Kornher, K., Gould, C. F., Manzano, J. M., Baines, K., Kayser, G., Tu, X., Suarez-Torres, J., Martinez, D., & Suarez-Lopez, J. R. (2024). Associations of PFASs and Pesticides with Lung Function Changes from Adolescence to Young Adulthood in the ESPINA study. medRxiv*: the preprint server for health sciences*, 2024.10.09.24315189. DOI: 10.1101/2024.10.09.24315189

Kornher, K., Gould, C. F., Manzano, J. M., Baines, K., Kayser, G., Tu, X., Suarez-Torres, J., Martinez, D., Peterson, L. A., Huset, C. A., Barr, D. B., & Suarez-Lopez, J. R. (2025). Associations of PFAS and pesticides with lung function changes from adolescence to young adulthood in the ESPINA study. *International Journal of Hygiene and Environmental Health, 265*, 114526. Advance online publication. DOI: 10.1016/j.ijheh.2025.114526 PMID: 39904133

Kot, S., & Ojinji, S. (2023). Environmental Sustainability and Freight Transport Performance in the EU – An Autoregressive Conditional Heteroscedasticity (ARCH) Model Analysis. *Promet - Traffic&Transportation, 35*(5), 621–634. DOI: 10.7307/ptt.v35i5.293

Kouvelas, A.. (2019). Adaptive Traffic Signal Control Using the Webster Method: Real-Time Applications. *Transportation Research Record: Journal of the Transportation Research Board.*

Kovalick, W. W., Jr., & Montgomery, R. H. (2014). Developing a program for contaminated site management in low and middle income countries [online]. The World Bank. Retrieved 2014, from https://openknowledge.worldbank.org/bitstream/handle/10986/18631/880700WP0Conta00Box385209B00PUBLIC0.pdf?sequence=1&isAllowed=y

Kowalska, K., Szczygiel, E., Szyja, P., & Sliwa, R. (2022). *SDG Labs Research Report. Green skills in the field of Social Economy. The theoretical model of Socially Driven Green Labs programme.*https://sdglabs.uom.edu.gr/sdg-labs-research-report/

KPMG. (2020). *The KPMG Survey of Sustainability Reporting 2020*. KPMG International. https://home.kpmg/xx/en/home/insights/2020/11/survey-of-sustainability-reporting-2020.html

KPMG. (2020). *The Time Has Come: The KPMG Survey of Sustainability Reporting 2020*.

Kramar, R. (2014). Beyond strategic human resource management: Is sustainable human resource management the next approach? *International Journal of Human Resource Management, 25*(8), 1069–1089. DOI: 10.1080/09585192.2013.816863

Krogh, G., Ochijo, K., & Nonaka, I. (2000). *Enabling knowledge creation*. Oxford University Press. DOI: 10.1093/acprof:oso/9780195126167.001.0001

Kuada, J. (2023). Changing role of finance in rural small enterprise growth in Ghana. *Journal of Entrepreneurship in Emerging Economies, 15*(6), 1438–1458. DOI: 10.1108/JEEE-07-2021-0269

Kumar, R.. (2023). Securing Traffic Data with Blockchain in IoT Ecosystems. *Future Generation Computer Systems.*

Kumpiw, W., Damrongsak, D., Jaitiang, T., Wongsapai, W., Sangkakorn, K., Daroon, S., Khiaolek, K., Srichai, P., Auttarat, S., Krajangchom, S., & Chinachan, T. (2025). Performance Tracking of Sustainable Tourism Goal (STG) Criteria for Achieving Thailand's Greenhouse Gas Mitigation Targets in the Service Sector: A Case Study of Large Thai Hotels. *Sustainability (Basel), 17*(4), 1635. DOI: 10.3390/su17041635

Kuo, C.-C., Lin, G.-F., Farooqui, A., Huang, S.-H., & Tseng, S.-F. (2025). Development of a Next-Generation Cooling Channel Technology with High Cooling Efficiency by Roughing Cooling Channels Using a Combination of Laser Machining and Embossing Techniques. *Micromachines, 16*(2), 225. DOI: 10.3390/mi16020225 PMID: 40047667

Kurniawan, A., & Wijoyo, S. (2024). Leveraging Talent for a Sustainable Future: A Multidisciplinary Examination of Public Sector Talent Management Strategies. *Research Synergy Foundation Conference Proceeding Series*. https://doi.org/DOI: 10.31098/bmss.v4i1.857

Kutaula, S., Chowdhury, S., Gillani, A., Budhwar, P. S., & Dey, P. (2024). Linking HRM with Sustainability Performance Through Sustainability Practices: Unlocking the Black Box. *British Journal of Management*. Advance online publication. DOI: 10.1111/1467-8551.12861

Kuzmina, J., Atstaja, D., Purvins, M., Baakashvili, G., & Chkareuli, V. (2023). In search of sustainability and financial returns: The case of ESG energy funds. Sustainability, 15, 3, 2716.

Lafferty, K. D., & Mordecai, E. A. (2016, August 19). The rise and fall of infectious disease in a warmer world. *F1000 Research Review 5: 2040*. PMID: 27610227; DOI: https://doi.org/DOI: 10.12688%2Ff1000research.8766.1

Laise, D. (2017). *Corporate Governance and Corporate Social Responsibility: A Global Perspective*. Palgrave Macmillan.

Lambe, P. (2011). The unacknowledged parentage of knowledge management. *Journal of Knowledge Management*, *15*(2), 175–197. DOI: 10.1108/13673271111119646

Lambrechts, W., Mulà, I., Ceulemans, K., Molderez, I., & Gaeremynck, V. (2013). The integration of competences for sustainable development in higher education: An analysis of bachelor programs in management. *Journal of Cleaner Production*, *48*, 65–73. DOI: 10.1016/j.jclepro.2011.12.034

Lambrechts, W., Verhulst, E., & Rymenams, S. (2017). Professional development of sustainability competences in higher education. *International Journal of Sustainability in Higher Education*, *18*(5), 697–714. DOI: 10.1108/IJSHE-02-2016-0028

Lange, D., & McNeil, S. (2004). Clean it and they will come? Defining successful brownfield development. *Journal of Urban Planning and Development*, *130*(2), 101–108. https://doi.org/(101DOI: 10.1061/(asce)0733-9488(2004)130:2

Lange, E. M., & Banadaki, N. G. (2024). ESG consideration in venture capital: Drivers, strategies and barriers. *Studies in Economics and Finance*, *41*(3), 724–739. DOI: 10.1108/SEF-06-2023-0380

Langlois, R. N., & Foss, N. J. (1997). Capabilities and governance: the rebirth of production in the theory of economic organization. DRUID Working Paper No. 97-2

Lans, T., Blok, V., & Wesselink, R. (2014). Learning apart and together: Towards an integrated competence framework for sustainable entrepreneurship in higher education. *Journal of Cleaner Production*, *62*, 37–47. DOI: 10.1016/j.jclepro.2013.03.036

Laprise, M., Lufkin, S., & Rey, E. (2018). An operational monitoring tool facilitating the transformation of urban brownfields into sustainable neighborhoods. *Building and Environment*, *142*, 221–233. DOI: 10.1016/j.buildenv.2018.06.005

Larrea, C., & Warnars, L. (2009). Ecuador's Yasuni-ITT Initiative: Avoiding Emissions by Keeping Petroleum Underground. *Energy for Sustainable Development*, *13*(3), 219–223. DOI: 10.1016/j.esd.2009.08.003

Latorre Tomás, S. (2009). *El ecologismo popular en el Ecuador pasao y presente.* Obtenido de https://www.iee.org.ec/index.php?option=com_zoo&Itemid=186&element=61bbca97-1c5d-4227-965a-3c4ab91c2a32&format=raw&item_id=86&lang=es&method=download&task=callelement

Lave, J., & Wenger, E. (1990). *Situated learning: Legitimate peripheral participation.* Cambridge University Press.

Lavrinenko, O., Ignatjeva, S., Ohotina, A., Rybalkin, O., & Lazdans, D. (2019). The Role of Green Economy in Sustainable Development (Case Study: The EU States). *Journal of Entrepreneurship and Sustainability Issues*, *6*(3), 1113–1126. DOI: 10.9770/jesi.2019.6.3(4)

Lazarevic, D., & Brandão, M. (2020). The circular economy: a strategy to reconcile economic and environmental objectives? In Brandão, M., Lazarevic, D., & Finnveden, G. (Eds.), *Handbook of the Circular Economy* (pp. 8–27). Edward Elgar Publishing., DOI: 10.4337/9781788972727.00009

Ledi, K. K., Adu Asare Obeng, I., Ameza-Xemalordzo, E., & Dumeda, R. B. (2024). All hands on the pump: The role of strategic thinking and gender diversity on crisis management. *Current Issues in Tourism*, *27*(17), 1–17. DOI: 10.1080/13683500.2024.2320428

Lee, H., Oliveira Martins, J., & van der Mensbrugghe, D. (1994). "The OECD Green Model: An Updated Overview", *OECD Development Centre Working Papers*, No. 97, OECD Publishing, Paris, https://doi.org/DOI: 10.1787/18151949

Lee, B. H., Georgallis, P., & Struben, J. (2022). Sustainable entrepreneurship under market uncertainty: opportunities, challenges and impact. In George, G., Haas, M., Joshi, H., Mcgahan, A., & Tracey, P. (Eds.), *Handbook on the Business of Sustainability* (pp. 252–272). Edward Elgar Publishing., DOI: 10.4337/9781839105340.00022

Lee, D. H., Chamberlain, B., & Park, H. Y. (2025). Toward a Construct-Based Definition of Urban Green Space: A Literature Review of the Spatial Dimensions of Measurement, Methods, and Exposure. *Land (Basel)*, *14*(3), 517. DOI: 10.3390/land14030517

Lee, S. (2020). Pedagogical Foci of Teaching Cantonese as a Second Language: From Linguistic Competence to Pragmatic Use. [IJCDLM]. *International Journal of Curriculum Development and Learning Measurement*, *1*(1), 1–10. DOI: 10.4018/IJCDLM.2020010101

Leger, M., Valverde, R., & Gagnon, S. (2019). An Innovative Framework to Integrate CIO Competencies Within the Business Technology Management Body of Knowledge. [IJOCI]. *International Journal of Organizational and Collective Intelligence*, *9*(3), 1–18. DOI: 10.4018/IJOCI.2019070101

Lekkala, V. D. V. V., Muktinutalapati, A. V., Lebaka, V. R., Lomada, D., Korivi, M., Li, W., & Reddy, M. C. (2025). Green Synthesis and Characterization of Silver Nanoparticles from *Tinospora cordifolia* Leaf Extract: Evaluation of Their Antioxidant, Anti-Inflammatory, Antibacterial, and Antibiofilm Efficacies. *Nanomaterials (Basel, Switzerland)*, *15*(5), 381. DOI: 10.3390/nano15050381 PMID: 40072184

Lemus-Aguilar, I., Morales-Alonso, G., Ramirez-Portilla, A., & Hidalgo, A. (2019). Sustainable Business Models through the Lens of Organizational Design: A Systematic Literature Review. Sustainability, 11, 19, 5379. https://doi.org/DOI: 10.3390/su11195379

Leoni, L. (2024). Integrating ESG and organizational resilience through system theory: the ESGOR matrix. Management Decision. Vol. ahead-of-print No. ahead-of-print. https://doi.org/DOI: 10.1108/MD-10-2023-1924

Levin, M. E., Haeger, J., Pierce, B., & Cruz, R. A. (2017b). Evaluating an adjunctive mobile app to enhance psychological flexibility in acceptance and commitment therapy. *Behavior Modification*, *41*(6), 846–867. DOI: 10.1177/0145445517719661 PMID: 28689449

Ley de Bosques y Conservación de areas Naturales y vida silvestre. (1981). Ecuador. Obtenido de https://www.corteidh.or.cr/tablas/4033.pdf

Ley de Gestión Ambiental. (1999). Ecuador. Obtenido de https://www.acnur.org/fileadmin/Documentos/BDL/2008/6618.pdf

Ley de Prevención y Control de la Contaminación Ambiental. (1982). Ecuador. Obtenido de https://vlex.ec/vid/codificacion-20-ley-prevencion-643461217

Li, M., et al. (2022). *Connected Infrastructure in Smart Cities: A Case Study of Intelligent Traffic Systems*. Journal of Smart Cities.

Liao, Y. (2022). Sustainable leadership: A literature review and prospects for future research. *Frontiers in Psychology*, *13*, 1045570. DOI: 10.3389/fpsyg.2022.1045570 PMID: 36420377

Lichtenthaler, U. (2023). Sustainability skills and sustainable natives: Key competencies and maturity model for sustainability management. *Journal of Innovation Management*, *11*(3). Advance online publication. DOI: 10.24840/2183-0606_011.003_0005

Li, F., & Lv, Z. (2017). Reliable vehicle type recognition based on information fusion in multiple sensor networks. *Computer Networks*, *117*, 76–84. DOI: 10.1016/j.comnet.2017.02.013

Lima, W. E., Prada Vargas, C., & Vanegas Alfonso, O. L. (2022). Gestión del conocimiento para el proceso de innovación en las organizaciones. CITAS. *Suplemento*, (1). Advance online publication. DOI: 10.15332/22563067.7412

Linares-Espinós, E., Hernández, V., Domínguez-Escrig, J. L., Fernández-Pello, S., Hevia, V., Mayor, J., Padilla-Fernández, B., & Ribal, M. J. (2018). Methodology of a systematic review. *Actas Urológicas Españolas (English Ed.)*, *42*(8), 499–506. DOI: 10.1016/j.acuroe.2018.07.002 PMID: 29731270

Lin, L. (2022). Venture capital in the rise of sustainable investment. *European Business Organization Law Review*, *23*(1), 187–216. DOI: 10.1007/s40804-021-00238-8

Lino, M., Connolly, L., Hoverman, D., McCoy, D., Schey, M., & Anders, S. (2022). *Limited partners and private equity firms embrace ESG*. Bain & Company.

Lin, S., Zhu, H., Liu, J., Li, F., & Zheng, C. (2025). Why Do Tourists Visit the Food Market? A Host–Guest Sharing Model Based on the Theory of Self-Regulation. *Land (Basel)*, *14*(2), 407. DOI: 10.3390/land14020407

Liu, N., Liu, Z., Wang, Y., Zhou, T., Zhang, M., & Yang, H. (2025). Clean and Efficient Thermochemical Conversion Technologies for Biomass in Green Methanol Production. *Biomass*, *5*(1), 13. DOI: 10.3390/biomass5010013

Liu, Y., Zhang, M., Zhao, Y., Wei, J., Zhou, S., & Shi, X. (2025). Effect of Environmental Factors on Grassland Biodiversity and Biomass in the Zhangye Region. *Agronomy (Basel)*, *15*(2), 476. DOI: 10.3390/agronomy15020476

Li, X., Bardos, P., Cundy, A. B., Harder, M. K., Doick, K. J., Norrman, J., Williams, S., & Chen, W. (2018). Using a conceptual site model for assessing the sustainability of brownfield regeneration for a soft reuse: A case study of Port Sunlight River Park (U.K.). *The Science of the Total Environment*, *652*, 810–821. DOI: 10.1016/j.scitotenv.2018.10.278 PMID: 30380488

Li, Z., Wu, X., Wu, J., & Liu, H. (2025). The Influence of Urban Landscape Ecology on Emotional Well-Being: A Case Study of Downtown Beijing. *Land (Basel)*, *14*(3), 519. DOI: 10.3390/land14030519

Longo, A., & Campbell, D. (2016b). The determinants of brownfields redevelopment in England. *Environmental and Resource Economics*, *67*(2), 261–283. DOI: 10.1007/s10640-015-9985-y PMID: 32025099

López Aguirre, J. F., López Salazar, J. L., Falconi Tello, L. X., & Pomaquero Yuquilema, J. C. (2018). Gestión del conocimiento en las organizaciones: Fundamentos, metodologías y praxis. Revista Contribuciones a la Economía. https://eumed.net/ce/2018/3/gestion-conocimiento.html

López-Alcarria, A., Olivares-Vicente, A., & Vilches, F. (2019). A systematic review of the use of agile methodologies in education to foster sustainability competencies. *Sustainability (Basel)*, *11*(10), 2915. DOI: 10.3390/su11102915

López-Núñez, M. I., Rubio-Valdehita, S., Armuña, C., & Pérez-Urria, E. (2022). EntreComp questionnaire: A self-assessment tool for entrepreneurship competencies. *Sustainability (Basel)*, *14*(5), 2983. DOI: 10.3390/su14052983

López-Padrón, A., Roig-Vila, R., & Rico-Gómez, M. L. (2024). Profile of Academic Use of Smartphones by Postgraduate Students in Manabí, Ecuador. In Segarra, J., Mengual-Andres, S., & Cortijo Ocaña, A. (Eds.), *Educational Innovation to Address Complex Societal Challenges* (pp. 186–200). IGI Global Scientific Publishing., DOI: 10.4018/979-8-3693-3073-9.ch013

López-Paredes, M., & Carrillo-Andrade, A. (2022). Legitimation by Digital Discourses: The Case of the Indigenous Protest in Ecuador, October 2019 (pp. 235-250). DOI: 10.4018/978-1-6684-4523-5.ch012

Lozano, R. (2018). Sustainable Business Models: A Holistic Approach to Sustainability. *Business Strategy and the Environment*, *27*(7), 1312–1325. DOI: 10.1002/bse.2156

Lozano, R.. (2015). A review of commitment and implementation of sustainable development in higher education. *International Journal of Sustainability in Higher Education*, *16*(2), 155–172.

Luck, M., & Wu, J. G. (2002). A gradient analysis of urban landscape pattern: A case study from the Phoenix metropolitan region, Arizona, USA. *Landscape Ecology*, *17*(4), 327–339. DOI: 10.1023/A:1020512723753

Lüdeke-Freund, F., Gold, S., & Bocken, N. M. P. (2018). A Review and Typology of Circular Economy Business Model Patterns. *Journal of Industrial Ecology*, *23*(1), 36–61. DOI: 10.1111/jiec.12763

Lumbanraja, P. (2023). Evaluation of talent management at pt. pertamina gas niaga medan, north sumatera. *International Journal of Educational Review, Law And. Social Sciences*, *3*(5), 1590–1599. Advance online publication. DOI: 10.54443/ijerlas.v3i5.1051

Lumpkin, G. T., & Dess, G. G. (1996). Clarifying the entrepreneurial orientation construct and linking it to performance. *Academy of Management Review*, *21*(1), 135–172. DOI: 10.2307/258632

Luo, L., Guo, M., Huang, J., & Yang, J. (2022). Research on the effect of an entrepreneurial environment on college students' entrepreneurial self-efficacy: The mediating effect of entrepreneurial competence and moderating effect of entrepreneurial education. *Sustainability (Basel)*, *14*(11), 6744. DOI: 10.3390/su14116744

Luo, Y. (2024). Theoretical Foundation of the Land Carbon Cycle and Matrix Approach. In Luo, Y., & Smith, B. (Eds.), *Land Carbon Cycle Modeling: Matrix Approach, Data Assimilation, Ecological Forecasting, and Machine Learning* (2nd ed., pp. 3–10). CRC Press / Taylor & Francis., DOI: 10.1201/9781032711126-2

Luo, Y., & Weng, E. (2011). Dynamic disequilibrium of the terrestrial carbon cycle under global change. *Trends in Ecology & Evolution*, *26*(2), 96–104. DOI: 10.1016/j.tree.2010.11.003 PMID: 21159407

Luque, A. & Casado, F. (2020). Public Strategy and Eco-Social Engagement in Latin American States: An Analysis of Complex Networks Arising from Their Constitutions. MDPI Sustainability, 12(20), 8558, pp. 1-29; DOI: 10.3390/su12208558

Luque, A., & de Pablos, C. (2016). Factores que promocionan la falta de ética en las prácticas de producción y logística de las empresas transnacionales. Lan Harremanak, 34(1), pp 336-370. ISSN: 1575-7048 e-ISSN: 2444-5819. DOI: https://doi.org/DOI: 10.1387/lan-harremanak.16578

Luque, A., Garofalo, C. E., Vinces, S. K., & Popescu, Gh. Cr. (2024). Empleo informal, políticas públicas y buen vivir: El caso de Rocafuerte, Ecuador [Informal Employment, Public Policies and Good Living: The Case of Rocafuerte, Ecuador]. Revista CIRIEC Colombia. Vol. 2(1), octubre. Pp. 43-53. ISSN: 2954-8179. DOI: https://doi.org/DOI: 10.58415/revciriec.v2n1a4

Luque, A., Quishpi, F. R., & Espín, D. F. (2023). Analysis of Spirituality Processes in Women of the Waorani AMWAE Indigenous Nationality in Ecuador. Özsungur, F. and Bekar, F. (Ed.) Spirituality Management in the Workplace, Emerald Publishing Limited, Leeds, pp. 173-196. . ISBN: 978-1-83753-451-7, eISBN: 978-1-83753-450-0DOI: 10.1108/978-1-83753-450-020231008

Luque, A., & Herrero-García, N. (2019). How corporate social (ir)responsibility in the textile sector is defined, and its impact on ethical sustainability: An analysis of 133 concepts. *Corporate Social Responsibility and Environmental Management*, *26*(6), 1–22. DOI: 10.1002/csr.1747

MacGregor Pelikánová, R. (2023). Accounting Science's Historical Development and Its Role in Social Science. In: Knihová, Ladislava (Ed.) *Applying Interdisciplinarity to Globalization, Management, Marketing, and Accountancy Science*. IGI Global, pp. 238-257 of 333. DOI: . ISBN 9781799886693. Available from https://www.igi-global.com/book/applying-interdisciplinarity-globalization-management-marketing/272220#descriptionDOI: 10.4018/978-1-7998-8669-3.ch009

MacGregor Pelikánová, R. (2023). Accounting Theories and Their Application in Accounting Sciences. In: Knihová, Ladislava (Ed.) *Applying Interdisciplinarity to Globalization, Management, Marketing, and Accountancy Science*. IGI Global, pp. 258-275 of 333. . ISBN 9781799886693. Available from https://www.igi-global.com/book/applying-interdisciplinarity-globalization-management-marketing/272220#descriptionDOI: 10.4018/978-1-7998-8669-3.ch010

MacGregor Pelikánová, R. (2024). EU legislative proposals to involve customers in the greening of the economy proposals. *The Lawyer Quarterly, 2*, 218-235. https://tlq.ilaw.cas.cz/index.php/tlq/article/view/597

MacGregor Pelikánová, R. (2017). Constatine's Christianity for the (Dis)integrated EU. Déjà vu of Constantine's Roman governance reflecting of the mistrial of Jesus for EU? *Dialogo*, *4*(1), 81–98. DOI: 10.18638/dialogo.2017.4.1

MacGregor Pelikánová, R. (2021). Internal Website Presentation of Czech Luxury Fashion Businesses in the Covid-19 Era. *Marketing and Management of Innovations*, *3*(3), 211–222. DOI: 10.21272/mmi.2021.3-18

MacGregor Pelikánová, R., & MacGregor, R. K. (2020). The EU puzzling CSR regime and the confused perception by ambassadors of luxury fashion businesses: A case study from Pařížská. *Central European Business Review*, *9*(3), 74–108. DOI: 10.18267/j.cebr.240

MacGregor Pelikánová, R., MacGregor, R. K., & Černek, M. (2021). New trends in codes of ethics: Czech business ethics preferences by the dawn of COVID-19. *Oeconomia Copernicana*, *12*(4), 973–1009. DOI: 10.24136/oc.2021.032

MacGregor Pelikánová, R., Nesbitt, T., Balcerzak, A. P., & Oulehla, J. (2024). (In)Effective Communication about Social Responsibility? Examining Large European Businesses in the Czech Republic. *Business. Management and Economics Engineering*, *22*(2), 214–239. DOI: 10.3846/bmee.2024.21414

MacGregor Pelikánová, R., & Rubáček, F. (2022). Taxonomy for transparency in non-financial statements – clear duty with unclear sanction. *Danube*, *13*(3), 173–195. DOI: 10.2478/danb-2022-0011

MacGregor Pelikánová, R., & Sani, M. (2023). Luxury, Slow and Fast Fashion – A Case study on the (Un)sustainable Creating of Shared Values. *Equilibrium. Quarterly Journal of Economics and Economic Policy*, *18*(3), 813–851.

MacGregor Pelikánová, R., Sani, M., & Rubáček, F. (2024). Sustainable And Responsible Creation Of Shared Values In The Fast Fashion Industry – I Will Believe It When I See It. *Visions for Sustainability, 21*, 8873, 1-29. DOI: 10.13135/2384-8677/8873

Macias, L. (2010). El constitucionalismo ambiental en la nueva Constitución de Ecuador. Un reto a la tradición constitucional [Environmental constitutionalism in the new Constitution of Ecuador. A challenge to constitutional tradition], Iuris Dictio: Vol. 8 Núm. 12.

Mackenzie, C., Gifford, R., & Reser, J. (2018). Implementing Corporate Sustainability through ESG Metrics: Challenges and Opportunities. *Business Strategy and the Environment*, *27*(8), 1278–1288. DOI: 10.1002/bse.2162

Madhani, P. M. (2009). Resource Based View (RBV) of Competitive Advantages: Importance, Issues and Implications, *Indian Management Research Journal,* 1(2).

Madhok, A. (1996). The Organization of Economic Activity: Transaction Costs, Firm Capabilities, and the Nature of Governance. *Organization Science*, *7*(5), 577–590. DOI: 10.1287/orsc.7.5.577

Maestripieri, N., & Saqalli, M. (2016). Assessing health risk using regional mappings based on local perceptions: A comparative study of three different hazards. *Human and Ecological Risk Assessment*, *22*(3), 721–735. DOI: 10.1080/10807039.2015.1105099

Malberg, K., Vaittinen, I., Evans, P., Schuurman, D., Ståhlbröst, A., & Vervoort, K. (2017). *Living Lab Methodology Handbook*, U4IoT Consortium.

Malhotra, N. K. (2010). *Marketing research: An applied orientation*. Pearson Education.

Malyarchuk, N. (2024). Current challenges and opportunities of personnel management. *Ekonomìčnì gorizonti*. https://doi.org/DOI: 10.31499/2616-5236.3(28).2024.312411

Mamami, y Clavero. (2010). Derechos de la Naturaleza, globalización y cambio climático 1. Corte Internacional de Derechos Humanos [Rights of Nature, Globalization and Climate Change 1. International Court of Human Rights]. Retrieved from https://www.corteidh.or.cr/tablas/r32323.pdf

Management Association. I. (Ed.). (2019). *Green Business: Concepts, Methodologies, Tools, and Applications (3 Volumes)*. IGI Global. DOI: 10.4018/978-1-5225-7915-1

Manhart, M. & Thalmann, S. (2015), Protecting organizational knowledge: a structured literature review, *Journal of Knowledge management*, 19 (2), pp. 190-211. https://doi.org/ MANAGEMENT-05-2014-0198DOI: 10.1108/JKNOWLEDGE

Maniglio, F., Casado Gutiérrez, F., & Chávez Vallejo, G. (2020). La justiciabilidad de los derechos sociales. El caso del derecho al hábitat y a la vivienda en Ecuador (2007-2017) [The justiciability of social rights. The Case of the Right to Habitat and Housing in Ecuador (2007-2017)]. *Revista Latinoamericana de Derecho Social*, *1*(37), 143. DOI: 10.22201/iij.24487899e.2020.37.14866

Mansouri, S., & Momtaz, P. P. (2022). Financing sustainable entrepreneurship: ESG measurement, valuation, and performance. Journal of Business Venturing, 37, 6, 106258.

Marchant, N. (2021, June 28). This is How Climate Change Could Impact The Global Economy. *World Economic Forum*. https://www.weforum.org/agenda/2021/06/impact-climate-change-global-gdp/

Marfo, M., Armah, A. A., Ofei, E. F., Adadevoh, L., & Reindoph, C. A. (2024). Do Government Interventions and Transformational Leadership Matter? A Moderation-Mediation Analysis of SME Performance During COVID-19 in Ghana. *International Journal of Organizational Leadership*, *13*(1), 59–78. DOI: 10.33844/ijol.2024.60399

Marschak, J., & Radner, R. (1972). *The Theory of Teams*. Yale University Press.

Martela, F., & Pessi, A. B. (2018). Significant work is about self-realization and broader purpose: Defining the key dimensions of meaningful work. *Frontiers in Psychology*, *9*, 363. Advance online publication. DOI: 10.3389/fpsyg.2018.00363 PMID: 29632502

Martinez, P., et al. (2022). *V2I Communication for Autonomous Vehicles in Urban Traffic Systems*. Journal of Intelligent Transportation.

Martín-Peña, M., Diaz-Garrido, E., Sanchez-Lopez, J. M., & Garcia-Magro, C. (2023). Flipped classroom as a methodology for acquiring skills in sustainability in the subject production management: An assessment of the students. *Journal of Management and Business Education*, *6*(Special), 529–546. DOI: 10.35564/jmbe.2023.00028

Martzog, P., Hoyer, S., & Kuttner, S. (2021). Student Teachers' Uncertainty Competence and Its Measurement. [IJTEPD]. *International Journal of Teacher Education and Professional Development*, *4*(2), 50–65. DOI: 10.4018/IJTEPD.2021070104

Matei, M.-C., Abrudan, L. C., & Abrudan, M.-M. (2024). Financial Perspectives on Human Capital: Building Sustainable HR Strategies. *Sustainability (Basel)*, *16*(4), 1441. Advance online publication. DOI: 10.3390/su16041441

Mathur, V. (2022). *Skilling for Sustainability* (pp. 66–68). Routledge eBooks. https://doi.org/DOI: 10.4324/9781003311157-11

Mattar, J., Ramos, D. K., & Lucas, M. R. (2022). DigComp-based digital competence assessment tools: Literature review and instrument analysis. *Education and Information Technologies*, *27*(8), 10843–10867. DOI: 10.1007/s10639-022-11034-3

Matute-Petroche, J. S., Castillo-Nazareno, U. H., & Pazmiño-Crespo, L. F. (2022). Collaborative Trade Exchange and the COVID-19 Event: Barter in the Andean Subregion of Ecuador. In Hai-Jew, S. (Ed.), *Career Re-Invention in the Post-Pandemic Era* (pp. 140–162). IGI Global Scientific Publishing., DOI: 10.4018/978-1-7998-8626-6.ch007

Mazhitov, D., Ermilova, M., Алтухова, E., Maksimova, T., & Zhdanova, O. (2019). Development of technologies and processes in environmental management. *E3s Web of Conferences*, 135, 04045. DOI: 10.1051/e3sconf/201913504045

McCahery, J. A., & Vermeulen, E. P. M. (2014). Business Growth and Firm Value Creation: The "Ignored" Third Dimension of Corporate Governance. *Journal of Self-Governance and Management Economics*, *2*(4), 69–76.

McCallum, E., Weicht, R., McMullan, L., & Price, A. (2018). EntreComp into Action: get inspired, make it happen (M. Bacigalupo & W. O'Keeffe Eds.), EUR 29105 EN, Publications Office of the European Union, Luxembourg. , JRC109128DOI: 10.2760/574864

McCarthy, J. J. (2002). *A thematic guide to Optimality Theory*. Cambridge University Press.

McCollum, J. (2023). Avoiding the pitfalls of Capitalism in the Green New Deal. In Tienhaara, K., & Robinson, J. (Eds.), *Routledge Handbook on The Green New Deal* (pp. 73–87). Routledge/ Taylor & Francis., DOI: 10.4324/9781003110880

McKinsey & Company. (2022). L'état de l'IA en 2022 et une demi-décennie en revue. Extrait de https://www.mckinsey.com

McKinsey and Company. (2022). The future of work after [McKinsey Global Institute.]. *COVID*, •••, 19.

McLeay, S., & Jaafar, A. (2007). Accounting Harmonization in Europe: Country Effects and Sector Effects. *Abacus – a Journal of Accounting. Finance and Business Studies*, *43*(2), 156–189. DOI: 10.1111/j.1467-6281.2007.00224.x

Meer, P. B., & Lyons, T. S. (2000). Lessons from private sector brownfield redevelopers. *Journal of the American Planning Association*, *66*(1), 46–57. DOI: 10.1080/01944360008976083

Mejías, C., Arenas, M., Martín, J., Santos, J. L., Aparicio, I., & Alonso, E. (2023). Green Assessment of Analytical Procedures for the Determination of Pharmaceuticals in Sewage Sludge and Soil. *Critical Reviews in Analytical Chemistry*, •••, 1–14. Advance online publication. DOI: 10.1080/10408347.2023.2276294 PMID: 37922128

Meles, A. (2021). Venture Capital and Responsible Investing: Progress, Problems and Perspectives. In: The Evolution of Sustainable Investments and Finance. Palgrave Macmillan, Cham. https://doi.org/DOI: 10.1007/978-3-030-70350-9_5

Meltzer, J., Steven, D., & Langley, C. (2013, February). The United States after the Great Recession: The Challenge of Sustainable Growth. *Global Economy and Development: Brookings Working Paper No. 60*, 1 – 52. https://www.brookings.edu/wp-content/uploads/2016/06/02-us-post-great-recession-meltzer-steven.pdf

Mendes, A. C., Ferreira, F. A., Kannan, D., Ferreira, N. C., & Correia, R. J. (2022). A BWM approach to determinants of sustainable entrepreneurship in small and medium-sized enterprises. *Journal of Cleaner Production*, *371*, 133300. DOI: 10.1016/j.jclepro.2022.133300

Mendoza, P. F. (2013). The price of wealth. The Chevron Texaco Case. ICIP International Catalan Institute for Peace. Per la Pau / Peace in Progress. ICIP E-Review. Issue 18. November 2013. Retrieved on-line from https://www.icip.cat/perlapau/old/e-review/issue-18-november-2013/price-wealth-chevron-texaco-case.htm. Accessed on the 28th of January 2025.

Menger, C. (1996). *Investigations into the Method of the Social Sciences*. Ludwig von Mises Institute.

Mensah-Williams, E., & Derera, E. (2024). Entrepreneurship education landscape in selected universities in Ghana. In *Entrepreneurship and Enterprise Development in Africa* (pp. 159–175). Edward Elgar Publishing. DOI: 10.4337/9781803925417.00023

Mertens, A., Eppinga, M. B., Arens, P., de Scisciolo, T., John, N., Sultan, S., Buys, N., & Mijts, E. N. (2025). The GreenComp Evaluation Roadmap: a roadmap for in-depth holistic evaluation of the integration of the GreenComp framework in higher-education curricula. International Journal of Sustainability in Higher Education, Vol. ahead-of-print No. ahead-of-print. DOI: 10.1108/IJSHE-02-2024-0119

Mervelskemper, L., & Streit, D. (2017). Enhancing market valuation of ESG performance: Is integrated reporting keeping its promise? *Business Strategy and the Environment*, *26*(4), 536–549. DOI: 10.1002/bse.1935

Mestanza-Ramón, C., Ordoñez-Alcivar, R., Arguello-Guadalupe, C., Carrera-Silva, K., D'Orio, G., & Straface, S. (2022). History, Socioeconomic Problems and Environmental Impacts of Gold Mining in the Andean Region of Ecuador. *International Journal of Environmental Research and Public Health*, *19*(3), 1190. DOI: 10.3390/ijerph19031190 PMID: 35162216

Mets, T., Holbrook, J., & Läänelaid, S. (2021). Entrepreneurship Education Challenges for Green Transformation. *Administrative Sciences, 11*(1), 15. DOI: 10.3390/admsci11010015

Meyer, C., Sanyal, S., & Rangarajan, S. (2019). Navigating Regulatory Hurdles for Sustainable Business Practices: A Global Perspective. *Business Strategy and the Environment, 28*(5), 708–724. DOI: 10.1002/bse.2225

Meyer, M., & DeTore, A. (1999). A. Product development for services. *The Academy of Management Perspectives, 13*(3), 64–76. DOI: 10.5465/ame.1999.2210315

Miah, M., Rahman, S. M. M., Biswas, S., Szabó-Szentgróti, G., & Walter, V. (2024). Effects of green human resource management practices on employee green behavior: The role of employee's environmental knowledge management and green self-efficacy for greening workplace. *The International Journal of Organizational Analysis*. Advance online publication. DOI: 10.1108/IJOA-04-2024-4462

Microsoft. (2018). Driving effective data governance for improved quality and analytics. Retrieved November 25, 2019, from https://query.prod.cms.rt.microsoft.com/cms/api/am/binary/RWs2bX

Microsoft. (2020). *Microsoft's Sustainability Efforts: Carbon-Negative by 2030*. Retrieved from https://www.microsoft.com

Migdadi, Y. K. (2020). *Airline Green Operations Strategies: Emerging Research and Opportunities*. IGI Global., DOI: 10.4018/978-1-7998-4255-2

Mikulić, J., & Prebežac, D. (2022). The Impact of Knowledge management on the Economic Performance of Companies. *Journal of Economics, 27*(1), 13–30.

Miles-Novelo, A., & Anderson, C. A. (2023). Avoiding a grim future: The climate crisis and its effects on human aggression and violence. *Advances in Environmental and Engineering Research, vol. 4*, issue 2. https://www.mendeley.com/catalogue/b2614e57-4a7c-310a-bae1-2a894491697f/ OR Link.

Milgrom, P., & Roberts, J. (1990). The Economics of Modern Manufacturing: Technology, Strategy and Organization. *The American Economic Review, 80*, 511–528.

Milgrom, P., & Roberts, J. (1995). Complementarities and fit strategy, structure, and organizational change in manufacturing. *Journal of Accounting and Economics, 19*(2-3), 179–208. DOI: 10.1016/0165-4101(94)00382-F

Miller, D., & O'Leary, J. (2018). Achieving the Sustainable Development Goals: The Role of Education and the Economy. *The Journal of Development Studies, 54*(9), 1530–1545. DOI: 10.1080/00220388.2018.1481486

Milonas, N., Rompotis, G., & Moutzouris, C. (2022). The performance of ESG funds vis-à-vis non-ESG funds. *The Journal of Impact and ESG Investing, 2*(4), 96–115. DOI: 10.3905/jesg.2022.1.041

Ministerio de Relaciones Exteriores y Movilidad Humana. (2013). *Caso Chevron un ejemplo de lucha soberana contra la arbitrariedad*. Recuperado el 13 de 05 de 2024, de https://www.cancilleria.gob.ec/wp-content/uploads/2013/07/folleto_chevron-web.pdf

Ministerio de Relaciones Exteriores y movilidad Humana. (2013). *Chevron-Texaco pretende que el pueblo ecuatoriano pague lo que ellos contaminaron.* Recuperado el 13 de 05 de 2024, de https://www.cancilleria.gob.ec/wp-content/uploads/2013/04/la-cruda-realidad-del-caso-chevron-texaco-esp.pdf

Ministry of the Environment of Ecuador. (2011). Reservas Naturales y Biodiversidad [Reserves and Biodiversity]. Retrieved from https://www.ambiente.gob.ec/areas-protegidas-3/

Ministry of the Environment of Ecuador. (2015). Resolución 197-2015: Regulación sobre minería y su impacto en la naturaleza [Resolution 197-2015: Regulation on Mining and its Impact on Nature]. Retrieved from https://www.ambiente.gob.ec/wp-content/uploads/downloads/2015/02/REGLAMENTO_AMBIENTAL_DE_ACTIVIDADES_MINERAS_MINISTERIO_AMBIENTE.pdf

Ministry of the Environment of Ecuador. (2016). Política Nacional de Cambio Climático [National Climate Change Policy]. Retrieved from https://www.ambiente.gob.ec/ministerio-del-ambiente-presento-los-resultados-obtenidos-en-materia-de-cambio-climatico-durante-el-periodo-2016-2022/

Ministry of the Environment of Ecuador. (2018). Plan Nacional de Restauración Forestal [National Forest Restoration Plan]. Presidencia de la Republica de Ecuador. (2019). Decreto Ejecutivo 752: Sistema Nacional de Áreas Protegidas (SNAP). Retrieved from https://www.ambiente.gob.ec/wp-content/uploads/downloads/2023/11/PLAN-NACIONAL-DE-RESTAURACION-FORESTAL-2019-2030.pdf

Ministry of the Environment of Ecuador. (2021). Iniciativa de Carbono Azul [Blue Carbon Initiative]. Retrieved from https://www.ambiente.gob.ec/programa-ecuador-carbono-cero/

Ministry of the Environment. Water and Ecological Transition of Ecuador. (2020). Plan de Gestión del Parque Nacional Cotopaxi [Cotopaxi National Park Management Plan]. Retrieved from https://www.ambiente.gob.ec/parque-nacional-cotopaxi-mantiene-su-administracion-en-la-provincia-de-cotopaxi/

Mirčetić, V., Ivanović, T., Knežević, S., Arsić, V., Obradović, T., Karabašević, D., Vukotić, S., Brzaković, T., Adamović, M., Milojević, S., Milašinović, M., Mitrović, A., & Špiler, M. (2022). The innovative human resource management framework: Impact of green competencies on organisational performance. *Sustainability (Basel)*, *14*(5), 2713. DOI: 10.3390/su14052713

Mitra, R.. (2023). Enhancing Traffic Surveillance Using Deep Learning-Based Video Analytics. *IEEE Transactions on Intelligent Transportation Systems*.

Mohammed Ali Saleh, N., Mahmoud Eldeep, N., & Mohammed Soliman, S. (2023). Effect of Green Management Training Program on Nursing Managers' Perception of Occupational Safety and Green Management Practices. *Egyptian Journal of Health Care*, *14*(3), 381–395. DOI: 10.21608/ejhc.2023.317241

Molina, M. Y., Rodríguez-Pallas, Á., & Vaque Reyes, G. L. (2024). Informality and Tourist Development on the Ecuadorian Coast. In P. Kumar, S. Gupta, M. Korstanje, P. Rout, & Madhurima (Eds.), *Managing Tourism and Hospitality Sectors for Sustainable Global Transformation* (pp. 62-76). IGI Global Scientific Publishing. DOI: 10.4018/979-8-3693-6260-0.ch005

Molina, G. J., Onyejizu, E. F., Morrison, J. L., & Soloiu, V. (2020). Surface Effects on Engine Materials of Mineral Oil Dilution With Methyl Esters and Biodiesels. [IJSEIMS]. *International Journal of Surface Engineering and Interdisciplinary Materials Science*, *8*(2), 1–18. DOI: 10.4018/IJSEIMS.2020070101

Mondal, S., Singh, S., & Gupta, H. (2023). Assessing enablers of green entrepreneurship in circular economy: An integrated approach. *Journal of Cleaner Production*, *388*, 135999. DOI: 10.1016/j.jclepro.2023.135999

Moneva, J. M., Archel, P., & Correa, C. (2019). Government Regulations, Corporate Social Responsibility, and Sustainability Reporting: An Empirical Analysis. *Corporate Social Responsibility and Environmental Management*, *26*(6), 1264–1274. DOI: 10.1002/csr.1751

Mongabay, D. (2021). "Nuevo estudio: en los últimos 26 años Ecuador ha perdido más de 2 millones de hectáreas de bosque" [New study: in the last 26 years Ecuador has lost more than 2 million hectares of forest]. Retrieved from https://es.mongabay.com/2021/01/desafios-ambientales-ecuador-2021-hidroelectricas-mineria-petroleo/

Montalvo, M. (30 de 09 de 2016). Ecuador en Naciones Unidas: Miembro fundador y algunos referentes. 63. Obtenido de https://www.afese.com/img/revistas/revista64a/ecuadornnuu.pdf

Montanari, S., Agostini, E., & Francesconi, D. (2023). Are we talking about green skills or sustainability competences? A scoping review using scientometric analysis of two apparently similar topics in the field of sustainability. *Sustainability (Basel)*, *15*(19), 14142. DOI: 10.3390/su151914142

Moradi, E. (2021). Investigating the competencies required for sustainable entrepreneurship development in agricultural higher education. *International Journal of Sustainable Entrepreneurship and Corporate Social Responsibility*, *6*(2), 1–14. DOI: 10.4018/IJSECSR.2021070101

Moraga, G., Huysveld, S., de Meester, S., & Dewulf, J. (2020). Towards a circularity indicator to assess products' materials and lifetime: In-use occupation. *Procedia CIRP*, *90*, 10–13. DOI: 10.1016/j.procir.2020.01.085

Morales, M. (2018). Derechos de la naturaleza en la Constitución Ecuatoriana [Rights of nature in the Ecuadorian Constitution]. Revista Justicia Ambiental art 05-05. Retrieved from https://www.revistajusticiaambiental.cl/wp-content/uploads/2018/03/art_05_05.pdf

Morioka, S. N., & Carvalho, M. M. (2016). Measuring Sustainability in Practice: Exploring the Inclusion of Sustainability into Corporate Performance Systems in Brazilian Case Studies. *Journal of Cleaner Production*, *136*, 123–133. DOI: 10.1016/j.jclepro.2016.01.103

Mose, T. (2019). Effect of Green HRM practices on Organizational Effectiveness of Universities in Kenya. *Human Resource and Leadership Journal*, *4*(2). Advance online publication. DOI: 10.47941/hrlj.319

Mouloudj, K., & Bouarar, A. (Eds.). (2025). *Digitizing Green Entrepreneurship*. IGI Global., DOI: 10.4018/979-8-3693-7442-9

Mukherjee, S., Bhattacharjee, S., Paul, N., & Banerjee, U. (2020). Assessing Green HRM practices in Higher Educational Institute (2020). *TEST Engineering & Management*, Volume 82. https://ssrn.com/abstract=3546928

Müller, F., Rieder, R., & Sihvonen, S. (2020). Corporate Sustainability and the SDGs: How Business and Strategy Align with the Global Agenda. *Journal of Business Ethics*, *164*(1), 1–12. DOI: 10.1007/s10551-020-04435-z

Mundo, B. B. C. (2018, septiembre 8). Caso Chevron-Texaco: qué implica el fallo de La Haya sobre la contaminación en la Amazonía de Ecuador y por qué no lo cambia todo. BBC. https://www.bbc.com/mundo/noticias-america-latina-45454965

Murray, A. (2018). Patagonia's Environmental Commitment: The Power of Purpose-Driven Business. *Journal of Business Ethics*, *147*(3), 655–667. DOI: 10.1007/s10551-016-3169-0

Muyolema, A. (2012). Las poéticas del Sumak Kawsay en un horizonte global [The poetics of Sumak Kawsay in a global horizon]. En: Houtart, François, Daiber, Virgit (comps.), Un paradigma poscapitalista: el Bien Común de la Humanidad, La Habana, Ruth Casa Editorial.

Nabeel, A. A., Rabiah, A. R., & Gouher, R. (2019). The organizational resources and knowledge management capability: A systematic review. *Business and Economic Horizons*, *15*(5), 636–647.

Naderi, N., Monavvarifard, F., & Salehi, L. (2022). Fostering sustainability-oriented knowledge-sharing in academic environment: A key strategic process to achieving SDGs through development of students' sustainable entrepreneurship competences. *International Journal of Management Education*, *20*(1), 100603. DOI: 10.1016/j.ijme.2022.100603

Nahapiet, J., & Ghoshal, S. (1998). Social capital, intellectual capital, and the organizational advantage. *Academy of Management Review*, *23*(2), 242–266. DOI: 10.2307/259373

Naharuddin, N. S., Abdul Rahim, R., & Ngah, R. (2024). Determinants Impacting the Triple Bottom Line Sustainability Performance in SMEs: A Systematic Literature Analysis and Future Research Agenda. *Advances in Social Sciences Research Journal, 11*(2.2), 66–77. DOI: 10.14738/assrj.112.2.16401

Naidoo, D., Nhamo, L., Mpandeli, S., Sobratee, N., Senzanje, A., Liphadzi, S., Slotow, R., Jacobson, M., Modi, A. T., & Mabhaudhi, T. (2021). Operationalising the water-energy-food nexus through the theory of change. *Renewable & Sustainable Energy Reviews*, *149*(October), 111416. DOI: 10.1016/j.rser.2021.111416 PMID: 37693280

Napathorn, C. (2022). Meso-level factors fostering or hindering the implementation of age-related HR practices in firms. *The International Journal of Organizational Analysis*. Advance online publication. DOI: 10.1108/IJOA-04-2022-3241

Narvaez, H. S. (2011). Luchas politicas y poder economico transnacional:estrategias de comunicacion en el caso Texaco. *Luchas politicas y poder economico transnacional:estrategias de comunicacion en el caso Texaco*. Ecuador. Obtenido de http://hdl.handle.net/10644/2877

National Assembly of Ecuador. (2013). Anteproyecto del Código Orgánico del Ambiente [Preliminary draft of the Organic Environmental Code]. Retrieved from https://www.asambleanacional.gob.ec/es/search/node/codigo%20del%20ambiente?page=64

National Assembly of Ecuador. (2014). Ley Orgánica de Recursos Hídricos, Usos y Aprovechamiento del Agua [Organic Law on Water Resources, Water Uses and Exploitation]. Registro Oficial Suplemento 305. Retrieved from https://www.asambleanacional.gob.ec/es/multimedios-legislativos/35146-ley-organica-de-recursos-hidricos-usos-y-aprovechamiento-d-1

National Assembly of Ecuador. (2017). Código Orgánico del Ambiente [Environmental Code]. Registro Oficial Suplemento 983. Retrieved from https://www.epmrq.gob.ec/images/servicios2020/CODIGO_ORGANICO_DEL_AMBIENTE_COAM.pdf

National Assembly of Ecuador. (2020). Ley Orgánica de Biodiversidad [Organic Law on Biodiversity]. Registro Oficial Suplemento 115. Retrieved from https://www.ambiente.gob.ec/wp-content/uploads/downloads/2018/01/CODIGO_ORGANICO_AMBIENTE.pdf

National Assembly of Ecuador. (2023). Reformas al Código Orgánico del Ambiente y Ley de Transición Ecológica [Reforms to the Organic Environmental Code and the Ecological Transition Law]. Registro Oficial Suplemento 2023. Retrieved from https://www.ambiente.gob.ec/wp-content/uploads/downloads/2022/02/REGLAMENTO-AL-CODIGO-ORGANICO-DEL-AMBIENTE.pdf

Nayak, R., Singh, A., Panwar, T., & Padhye, R. (2019). A Review of Recent Trends in Sustainable Fashion and Textile Production. *Current Trends in Fashion Technology & Textile Engineering*, *4*(5). Advance online publication. DOI: 10.19080/CTFTTE.2019.04.555648

Neal, J., & Neal, B. L. (2019). *Workforce Education at Oil and Gas Companies in the Permian Basin: Emerging Research and Opportunities*. IGI Global., DOI: 10.4018/978-1-5225-8464-3

Neequaye, K. J. A. (2020). *Examining Corporate Governance Practices among SMEs in Ghana: A Case Study of Some Selected SMEs in Accra* (Doctoral dissertation, University Of Ghana).

Nestlé. (2020). *Nestlé Creating Shared Value Report*. Retrieved from https://www.nestle.com

Ngai, P. B. (2021). Discourse Analysis for Intercultural Competence Development. [IJBIDE]. *International Journal of Bias, Identity and Diversities in Education*, *6*(1), 17–30. DOI: 10.4018/IJBIDE.2021010102

Nhamo, L., Mpandeli, S., Liphadzi, S., & Mabhaudhi, T. (2024). Understanding circularity and transformative approaches and their role in achieving sustainability. In Nhamo, L., Mpandeli, S., Liphadzi, S., & Mabhaudhi, T. (Eds.), *Circular and Transformative Economy: Advances towards Sustainable Socio-economic Transformation* (pp. 1–8). CRC Press/ Taylor & Francis., DOI: 10.1201/9781003327615-1

Nhamo, L., & Ndela, B. (2021). Nexus planning as a pathway towards sustainable environmental and human health post Covid-19. *Environmental Research*, *192*(January), 110376. DOI: 10.1016/j.envres.2020.110376 PMID: 33115599

Nielsen (2018). *The Sustainability Imperative*. Retrieved from https://www.nielsen.com/us/en/insights/report/2018/the-sustainability-imperative/

Niu, S., Park, B. I., & Jung, J. S. (2022). The effects of digital leadership and ESG management on organizational innovation and sustainability. Sustainability, 14, 23, 15639. https://doi.org/DOI: 10.3390/su142315639

Nketsiah, I., & Van der Westhuizen, T. (2024, November). Governance and Leadership in Enhancing SME Resilience in Ghana: A Systematic Literature Review. In *European Conference on Management, Leadership & Governance* (pp. 417-424). Academic Conferences International Limited. https://doi.org/DOI: 10.34190/ecmlg.20.1.3138

Nketsiah, I. (2018). Financial record keeping practices of small business operators in the Sekondi-Takoradi metropolitan area of Ghana. *Asian Journal of Economics. Business and Accounting*, *6*(3), 1–9.

Noh, H. J. (2018, September). Financial Strategy to Accelerate Green Growth. *ADBI Working Paper No. 866*, 1 – 23. Tokyo: Asian Development Bank Institute. https://www.adb.org/publications/financial-strategy-accelerate-green-growth

Noh, H. J. (2019). Financial Strategies to Accelerate Green Growth. In Sachs, J. D., Woo, W. T., Yoshino, N., & Taghizadeh-Hesary, F. (Eds.), *Handbook of Green Finance: Energy Security and Sustainable Development* (pp. 37–61). Springer Nature., DOI: 10.1007/978-981-13-0227-5_16

Nonaka, I., & Peltokorpi, V. (2006). Objectivity and subjectivity in knowledge management: A review of 20 top articles. *Knowledge and Process Management*, *13*(2), 73–82. DOI: 10.1002/kpm.251

Nonaka, I., & Takeuchi, H. (1995). *The Knowledge-Creating Company: How Japanese Companies Create the Dynamics of Innovation*. Oxford University Press. DOI: 10.1093/oso/9780195092691.001.0001

Noor, K. A. B. M., & Ahmad, M. (2024). *Circular Economy: Rethinking Security Sustainability Through Ransom Project*. https://doi.org/DOI: 10.2118/223015-MS

Nordensvärd, J., & Urban, F. (2023). The role of energy and climate policy in mitigating global climate change. In Urban, F., & Nordensvärd, J. (Eds.), *Handbook on Climate Change and Technology* (pp. 446–463). Edward Elgar Publishing., DOI: 10.4337/9781800882119.00047

Nowak, D. J., Crane, D. E., & Stevens, J. C. (2006). Air pollution removal by urban trees and shrubs in the United States. *Urban Forestry & Urban Greening (April), 4(3-4)*, 115 – 123. DOI: DOI: 10.1016/j.ufug.2006.01.007

Nson, Y. D. (2024). Sustainability of the society through green human resources management practices: A proposed model. *Annals of Human Resource Management Research*, *4*(1), 43–59. DOI: 10.35912/ahrmr.v4i1.2161

Nurmala, N., & Hermina, N. (2024). Talent management: Preparing future leaders. *International journal of business, economics and management*. https://doi.org/DOI: 10.21744/ijbem.v7n3.2314

Nwachukwu, S. L., & Nwachukwu, C. S. (2020). The Role of Businesses in Climate Change Mitigation and the Sustainable Development Goals. *International Journal of Environmental Science and Technology*, *17*(7), 3633–3645. DOI: 10.1007/s13762-020-02788-5

Nyssens, M. (Ed.). (2006). *Social Enterprise. At the Crossroads of Market, Public Policies and Civil Society*. Routledge.

O'Neill, L., Raghubir, P., & Pham, M. T. (2020). Implementing ESG Metrics in Corporate Sustainability: Challenges and Best Practices. *Journal of Business Research*, *106*, 167–176. DOI: 10.1016/j.jbusres.2019.08.031

Ocaña-Mayorga, S., Lobos, S. E., Crespo-Pérez, V., Villacís, A. G., Pinto, C. M., & Grijalva, M. J. (2018). Influence of ecological factors on the presence of a triatomine species associated with the arboreal habitat of a host of Trypanosoma cruzi. *Parasites & Vectors*, *11*(1), 567. DOI: 10.1186/s13071-018-3138-4 PMID: 30373640

Oduncu, F., & Cengîz, E. K. (2022). Bibliometric analysis of international studies on green management. *Iedsr Association*, *7*(20), 80–108. DOI: 10.46872/pj.566

Oduro, S. (2020). Exploring the barriers to SMEs' open innovation adoption in Ghana: A mixed research approach. *International Journal of Innovation Science*, *12*(1), 21–51. DOI: 10.1108/IJIS-11-2018-0119

OECD (2010). *SMEs, entrepreneurship and innovation.*

OECD. (1996). *The Knowledge-Based Economy*. OECD Publishing.

OECD. (2017). *Green Growth Indicators 2017*. https://www.oecd.org/env/green-growth-indicators-2017-9789264268586-en.htm

OECD. (2024). Entrepreneurship 360. https://www.oecd.org/en/about/programmes/skills-for-smes-and-entrepreneurs/entrepreneurship-360.html

OECD. (2024a). Training Supply for the Green and AI Transitions: Equipping Workers with the Right Skills, Getting Skills Right, OECD Publishing, Paris, https://doi.org/DOI: 10.1787/7600d16d-en

OECD. (2024b). Policies for a plastic pollution-free future by 2040. Green Talks LIVE. Retrieved online from https://www.oecd.org/en/events/2024/10/policy-scenarios-for-eliminating-plastic-pollution-by-2040.html. Accessed on the 16th of February 2025.

OECD. (2025). *Empowered Citizens, Informed Consumers and Skilled Workers: Designing Education and Skills Policies for a Sustainable Future*. OECD Publishing., DOI: 10.1787/311cdbeb-

Ofori-Atta, K. (2020). Economic impact of the covid-19 pandemic on the economy of Ghana, Republic of Ghana. Retrieved from https://www.food-security.net/wp-content/uploads/2020/04/Ghana-Economic-Impact-of-COVID-on-Ghanas-Economy.pdf

Ogunyemi, K. (2022). Leadership for Sustainable Development in Africa: Roles and Responsibilities. In *Management and Leadership for a Sustainable Africa, Volume 2: Roles, Responsibilities, and Prospects* (pp. 1-17). Cham: Springer International Publishing.

Okoro, J. P., Nassè, T. B., Ngmendoma, A. B., Carbonell, N., & Nanema, M. (2022). Entrepreneurship education and youth unemployment challenges in Africa: Ghana in perspective. *International Journal of management & entrepreneurship Research, 4*(5), 213-231.

Olesika, A., Lama, G., & Rubene, Z. (2021). Conceptualization of Digital Competence: Perspectives From Higher Education. [IJSEUS]. *International Journal of Smart Education and Urban Society*, *12*(2), 46–59. DOI: 10.4018/IJSEUS.2021040105

Olszewski, S. (2024). *Reaching Professional Competence*. IGI Global., DOI: 10.4018/978-1-6684-8607-8.ch004

Olurin, J. O., Gidigba, J. O., Ehiaguina, V. E., Ndiwe, T. C., Ayodeji, S. A., Banso, A. A., & Ojo, G. G. (2023). Engineering Innovations And Sustainable Entrepreneurship: A Comprehensive Literature Review. [MACEM]. *Materials & Corrosion Engineering Management*, *4*(2), 62–71. DOI: 10.26480/macem.02.2023.70.79

Opecorg. OPEC Annual Statistical Bulletin. [Online]. Available from: https://asb.opec.org/ [Accessed 9 Agosto 2024].

Ordóñez de Pablos, P., & Zhang, X. (Eds.). (2023). *5G, Artificial Intelligence, and Next Generation Internet of Things: Digital Innovation for Green and Sustainable Economies*. IGI Global., DOI: 10.4018/978-1-6684-8634-4

Orellana, A. (27 de marzo de 2019). *Chevron vs Ecuador: Arbitraje internacional e impunidad corporativa*. Obtenido de Amazon watch: https://amazonwatch.org/es/news/2019/0327-chevron-vs-ecuador-international-arbitration-and-corporate-impunity#:~:text=Texaco%2C%20que%20fue%20adquirida%20por,provincias%20de%20Sucumb%C3%ADos%20y%20Orellana

Organization for Economic Cooperation and Development (OECD). (2020). OECD Trade and Environment Working Papers 2020/03. Greening regional trade agreements on investment. DOI: 10.1787/18166881

Ortiz, P. (2006). *Petróleo y desarrollo sostenible en el Ecuador*. Rispergraf.

Osman, R., Frantál, B., Klusáček, P., Kunc, J., & Martinát, S. (2015). Factors affecting brownfield regeneration in post-socialist space: The case of the Czech Republic. *Land Use Policy*, *48*, 309–316. DOI: 10.1016/j.landusepol.2015.06.003

Our, C. F. R. (Brundtland Report). (1987). United Nations. https://www.un.org/es/ga/president/65/issues/sustdev.shtml

Owusu, A., Tauringana, V., & Asare, N. (2024). Sustainability performance reporting in Ghana: The views of SMEs. *Small Enterprise Research*, *31*(1), 56–75. DOI: 10.1080/13215906.2024.2304847

Owusu, K. (2023). *Examining the Effectiveness of Leadership Approaches in Manufacturing Industries in Accra*. Walden University.

Ozayturk, I. (2025). The Role of IMF on Goods and Services Importing of Argentina, Egypt, and Ecuador. In J. Martínez-Falcó, E. Sánchez-García, B. Marco-Lajara, & R. Fuentes-Fernández (Eds.), *Global Economic Interconnectedness: International Trade and Finance* (pp. 295-320). IGI Global Scientific Publishing. DOI: 10.4018/979-8-3693-5303-5.ch014

Özsungur, F. (Ed.). (2021). *Handbook of Research on Policies, Protocols, and Practices for Social Work in the Digital World*. IGI Global., DOI: 10.4018/978-1-7998-7772-1

Özsungur, F. (Ed.). (2024). *Empowering Entrepreneurial Mindsets With AI*. IGI Global., DOI: 10.4018/979-8-3693-7658-4

Özsungur, F. (Ed.). (2025a). *Navigating Organizational Behavior in the Digital Age With AI*. IGI Global., DOI: 10.4018/979-8-3693-8442-8

Özsungur, F. (Ed.). (2025b). *Nexus of AI, Climatology, and Urbanism for Smart Cities*. IGI Global., DOI: 10.4018/979-8-3693-5918-1

Pachamama, F. (2021). Iniciativas de Restauración Ecológica en Ecuador [Ecological Restoration Initiatives in Ecuador]. Retrieved from https://www.pachamama.org.ec/

Pakšiová, R., & Oriskóová, D. (2020). Capital Maintenance Evolution Using Outputs From Accounting System. *Scientific Annals of Economics and Business. - Iasi: University of Iasi. 67*(3),311-331.

Palacios, J. C. (2004). Desarrollo tecnológico en la Primera Revolución Industrial [Technological development in the First Industrial Revolution]. 17. Norba. Revista de Historia, ISSN 0213-375X, Vol. 17, 93-109.

Park, J.. (2021). *Multi-Agent Systems for Autonomous Vehicle Coordination at Intersections*. Transportation Robotics and AI.

Parra-Gaete, C., & Hermosa-Bosano, C. (2023). A pilot exploration of the relationships between optimism, affect, and cardiovascular reactivity. *Frontiers in Psychology, 14*, 1233900. DOI: 10.3389/fpsyg.2023.1233900 PMID: 37908813

Passet, R. (2013). Las grandes representaciones del mundo y la economía a lo largo de la historia: del universo mágico al torbellino creador [The great representations of the world and the economy throughout history: from the magical universe to the creative whirlwind]. Clave intelectual

Patel, S. (2012). Delayed Justice: A Case Study of Texaco and the Republic of Ecuador's Operations, Harms, and Possible Redress in the Ecuadorian Amazon. *Tulane Environmental Law Journal, 26*(1), 71–110. https://www.jstor.org/stable/24673677

Patricio, S. (11 de 03 de 2024). *ONG ecuatorianas que protegen el medio ambiente*. Obtenido de https://blog.sanpatricio.com.ec/ong-ecuatorianas-que-protegen-el-medio-ambiente

Patterson, M., et al. (2021). *Advances in Inductive Loop Technology for Urban Traffic Monitoring*. Journal of Transportation Research.

Paul, I., Bhole, G., & Chaudhari, J. (2014). A Review on Green Manufacturing: It's Important, Methodology and its Application. *Procedia Materials Science, 6*, 1644–1649. DOI: 10.1016/j.mspro.2014.07.149

Paz, C., Mascialino, G., & Evans, C. (2020). Exploration of the psychometric properties of the Clinical Outcomes in Routine Evaluation-Outcome Measure in Ecuador. *BMC Psychology, 8*(1), 94. DOI: 10.1186/s40359-020-00443-z PMID: 32873334

Pedersen, C. S. (2018). The UN Sustainable Development Goals (SDGs) are a Great Gift to Business! *Procedia CIRP, 69*, 21–24. DOI: 10.1016/j.procir.2018.01.003

Pee, L. G. (2008). Authors Info & Claims Understanding the drivers, enablers, and performance of knowledge management in public organizations *ICEGOV '08: Proceedings of the 2nd international conference on Theory and practice of electronic governance* Pages 439 – 466 DOI: 10.1145/1509096.1509188

Pelletier, N., Maas, R., Goralczyk, M., & Wolf, M.-A. (2014). Conceptual basis for development of the European Sustainability Footprint. *Environmental Development, 9*(January), 12–23. DOI: 10.1016/j.envdev.2013.12.003

Pennetta, S., Anglani, F., & Mathews, S. (2024). Navigating through entrepreneurial skills, competencies and capabilities: A systematic literature review and the development of the entrepreneurial ability model. *Journal of Entrepreneurship in Emerging Economies, 16*(4), 1144–1182. DOI: 10.1108/JEEE-09-2022-0257

Peraza, A. V., & Furumura, Y. (2022). Project-Based Learning to Develop Intercultural Communicative Competence in Virtual Exchange Contexts. [IJCALLT]. *International Journal of Computer-Assisted Language Learning and Teaching*, *12*(3), 1–17. DOI: 10.4018/IJCALLT.307059

Percival, R. V. (2020). Transnational litigation: what can we learn from Chevron–Ecuador? In *Research Handbook on Transnational Environmental Law* (pp. 318–339). Edward Elgar Publishing. DOI: 10.4337/9781788119634.00031

Pereira, V., & Patel, C. (2022). *Talent management in digital industries: A global perspective*. Palgrave Macmillan.

Pérez, D. (28 de 12 de 2023). El poder de las ONG en redes de apoyo: Un análisis completo. Obtenido de https://daniperezmalaga.es/el-poder-de-las-ong-en-redes-de-apoyo-un-analisis-completo/

Petridis, K., Kiosses, N., Tampakoudis, I., & Ben Abdelaziz, F. (2023). Measuring the efficiency of mutual funds: Does ESG controversies score affect the mutual fund performance during the COVID-19 pandemic? Operational research, 23, 3, 54.

Petrychenko, O., Levinskyi, M., Goolak, S., & Lukoševičius, V. (2025). Prospects of Solar Energy in the Context of Greening Maritime Transport. *Sustainability (Basel)*, *17*(5), 2141. DOI: 10.3390/su17052141

Phan, T. C., Le, P. A., Phan, T. M., Hoang, L. P., Le, H. T., Ngo, T. T., Nguyen, D. T., & Van Tran, H. (2021). Identifying and Applying the Information Technology Competence Framework in an Online Teaching Environment. In Dhir, H. (Ed.), *Handbook of Research on Barriers for Teaching 21st-Century Competencies and the Impact of Digitalization* (pp. 356–382). IGI Global Scientific Publishing., DOI: 10.4018/978-1-7998-6967-2.ch019

Phrophayak, J., Techarungruengsakul, R., Khotdee, M., Thuangchon, S., Ngamsert, R., Prasanchum, H., Sivanpheng, O., & Kangrang, A. (2024). Enhancing Green University Practices through Effective Waste Management Strategies. *Sustainability (Basel)*, *16*(8), 3346. DOI: 10.3390/su16083346

Piaguage, J. (01 de 05 de 2023). Treinta años de impunidad de la contaminación de Chevron-Texaco en Ecuador: "La Amazonía sigue sangrando". (J. SULÉ, Entrevistador) Obtenido de https://www.publico.es/internacional/treinta-anos-impunidad-contaminacion-chevron-texaco-ecuador-amazonia-sigue-sangrando.html

Pigrau, A. (2014). The Texaco-Chevron case in Ecuador: Law and justice in the age of globalization. Revista catalana de dret ambiental, 5(1).

Pilania, A. (2024). *Green HRM Practices*. Indian Scientific Journal Of Research In Engineering And Management., DOI: 10.55041/IJSREM33488

Pittroff, E. (2021). The legitimacy of global accounting rules: A note on the challenges from path-dependence theory. *The Journal of Management and Governance*, *25*(2), 379–396. DOI: 10.1007/s10997-020-09546-6

Pizzol, L., Zabeo, A., Klusáček, P., Giubilato, E., Critto, A., Frantál, B., Martinát, S., Kunc, J., Osman, R., & Bartke, S. (2015). Timbre Brownfield Prioritization Tool to support effective brownfield regeneration. *Journal of Environmental Management*, *166*, 178–192. DOI: 10.1016/j.jenvman.2015.09.030 PMID: 26496848

Pless, N. M., Maak, T., & Stahl, G. K. (2012). Promoting corporate social responsibility and sustainable development through management development: What can be learned from international service-learning programs? *Human Resource Management*, *51*(6), 873–903. DOI: 10.1002/hrm.21506

PNUD. (2016). La Amazonía y la Agenda 2030. Retrieved from https://www.undp.org/es/latin-america/publicaciones/la-amazonia-y-la-agenda-2030

PNUD. (2023). Ecuador celebrará todo el mes de mayo a la Biodiversidad [Ecuador celebrará todo el mes de mayo a la Biodiversidad]. https://www.undp.org/es/ecuador/noticias/ecuador-celebrara-todo-el-mes-de-mayo-la-biodiversidad

PNUD. (2024). Los conocimientos indígenas son cruciales para la lucha contra el cambio climático: he aquí el porqué [Indigenous knowledge is crucial to the fight against climate change: here's why]. Retrieved from https://climatepromise.undp.org/es/news-and-stories/los-conocimientos-indigenas-son-cruciales-para-la-lucha-contra-el-cambio-climatico

Poazi, F. D. W., Tamunosiki-Amadi, J. O., & Fems, M. (2017). The resource-base view of organization and innovation: Recognition of significant relationship in an organization. *International Journal of Economics and Management Engineering*, *11*(3), 697.

Polanyi, M. (1967). *The Tacit Knowledge Dimension*. Routledge & Kegan Paul.

Polcyn, J., Stratan, A., & Lopotenco, V. (2023). Sustainable Agriculture's Contribution to Quality of Life. *Sustainability (Basel)*, *15*(23), 16415. DOI: 10.3390/su152316415

Polekar, J. S., & Lodha, K. (2024). *Challenges in Manpower Management: Discuss the Challenges Faced by the Automotive Industry in Managing Manpower Due to Rigid Labor Laws and Complex Legal Systems, Especially Concerning Temporary Increases in Workforce to Meet Demand Fluctuations*. International Journal For Multidisciplinary Research., DOI: 10.36948/ijfmr.2024.v06i03.20233

Polman, P., & Winston, A. (2022). Yes, investing in ESG pays off. Harvard Business Review. Available at: https://hbr.org/2022/04/yes-investing-in-esg-pays-off. Accessed on January 10th, 2025.

Ponnusamy, V., Jhanjhi, N. Z., Jung, L. T., & Amin, A. M. (Eds.). (2021). *Role of IoT in Green Energy Systems*. IGI Global., DOI: 10.4018/978-1-7998-6709-8

Popa, N., Pop, A., & Marian-Potra, A. (2025). Culture-led urban regeneration in post-socialist cities: From decadent spaces towards creative initiatives. *Cities (London, England)*, *158*, 105707. DOI: 10.1016/j.cities.2025.105707

Popescu, C. R. G. (2017). The Role Of Total Quality Management In Developing The Concept Of Social Responsibility To Protect Public Interest In Associations Of Liberal Professions. Amfiteatru Economic. Editura ASE. Volume: 19. pp. 1091-1106. Special Issue: 11. WOS:000413858500012. ISSN: 1582-9146. eISSN: 2247-9104.

Popescu, C. R. G. (2022f). Analyzing the Impact of Green Marketing Strategies on the Financial and Non-Financial Performance of Organizations: The Intellectual Capital Factor. In I. Management Association (Ed.), Research Anthology on Business Continuity and Navigating Times of Crisis (pp. 202-226). IGI Global. https://doi.org/DOI: 10.4018/978-1-6684-4503-7.ch011

Popescu, C. R. G. (2022g). Evaluarea capitalului intelectual i influen a acestuia asupra performan elor economice. Editura Mustang, Bucure ti. ISBN 978-606-652-286-1. Published in Romanian. (Title in English: Intellectual Capital Assessment and Its Influence on Economic Performances); Link editura Mustang: http://www.editura-mustang.ro/carti_stiintifice.php

Popescu, C. R. G. (2024b). Monitoring Progress towards the Sustainable Development Goals, where Children and Youth Hold the Key to Sustainable Future: Principles and Policy Guidance on Children's Rights to Healthy Environment. Paper presented at the World Children Conference-V. June 07-09, 2024. Hakkari, Turkey. Organizers: Hakkari University, Turkey and IKSAD Institute of Economic Development and Social Research of Turkey, Turkey. Paper due to be published in the Conference Volume Proceedings. https://www.worldchildrenconference.org/

Popescu, C. R. G. (2024c). Intercultural Communication And Social Cohesion At The Heart Of Sustainable Development Goals (SDGS) And Development Policies. International Symposium On Communication, Information And Society. International Symposium on Communication Information and Society. Current Dynamics in Communication. May 09-10 2024. Abstracts Book. Gaziantep University Gaziantep / Türkiye. ISBN: 978-625-367-713-8.

Popescu, C. R. G. (2024d). Envisioning International Trade and Logistics for the Sustainable Development Goals (SDGs): Responsible Plant, Tree, and Livestock Logistics for Greening and Conserving the Environment. Congress Tıtle 7th Internatıonal Antalya Scıentıfıc Research And Innovatıve Studıes Congress Date And Place 11-13 May 2024, Antalya, Turkiye Organızatıon Iksad Instıtute.

Popescu, C. R. G. (Ed.). (2021d). Handbook of Research on Novel Practices and Current Successes in Achieving the Sustainable Development Goals. IGI Global. http://doi:. Indexed in Scopus. WorldCat: 5 editions in 50 libraries. OCLC Number / Unique Identifier: 1260710279.DOI: 10.4018/978-1-7998-8426-2

Popescu, C. R. G. (Ed.). (2022h). COVID-19 Pandemic Impact on New Economy Development and Societal Change. IGI Global. . Indexed in EBSCOhost. WorldCat: 6 editions in 57 libraries. OCLC Number / Unique Identifier: 1277184264.DOI: 10.4018/978-1-6684-3374-4

Popescu, C. R. G. (Ed.). (2022i). Frameworks for Sustainable Development Goals to Manage Economic, Social, and Environmental Shocks and Disasters. IGI Global. . Indexed in EBSCOhost. WorldCat: 3 editions in 34 libraries. OCLC Number / Unique Identifier: 1334007327.DOI: 10.4018/978-1-6684-6750-3

Popescu, C. R. G. (Ed.). (2022j). Handbook of Research on Building Inclusive Global Knowledge Societies for Sustainable Development. IGI Global. . Indexed in EBSCOhost. WorldCat: 4 editions in 46 libraries. OCLC Number / Unique Identifier: 1309072556.DOI: 10.4018/978-1-6684-5109-0

Popescu, C. R. G. (Ed.). (2022k). Handbook of Research on SDGs for Economic Development, Social Development, and Environmental Protection. IGI Global. . WorldCat: 4 editions in 49 libraries. OCLC Number / Unique Identifier: 1323431329.DOI: 10.4018/978-1-6684-5113-7

Popescu, C. R. G. (Ed.). (2022l). Handbook of Research on Changing Dynamics in Responsible and Sustainable Business in the Post-COVID-19 Era. IGI Global. http://doi:. Indexed in EBSCOhost. WorldCat: 4 editions in 49 libraries. OCLC Number / Unique Identifier: 1285370248.DOI: 10.4018/978-1-6684-2523-7

Popescu, C. R. G. (Ed.). (2023a). Positive and Constructive Contributions for Sustainable Development Goals. IGI Global. . WorldCat: 6 editions in 35 libraries. OCLC Number / Unique Identifier: 1344378097. DOI: 10.4018/978-1-6684-7499-0

Popescu, C. R. G. (Ed.). (2024a). Building Inclusive Global Knowledge Societies for Sustainable Development. IGI Global. . DOI: . ISBN13: 9798369362983. ISBN13 Softcover: 9798369362990. EISBN13: 9798369363003. https://www.igi-global.com/book/building-inclusive-global-knowledge-societies/343531. (Forthcoming).DOI: 10.4018/979-8-3693-6298-3

Popescu, C. R. G., & Popescu, G. N. (2024). The Health-Environment Nexus: Tackling Vital Hemp Policies, Addressing Cutting-Edge Research For Sustainable Development, And Managing Decisive Human Rights. International Multidisciplinary Environment And Hemp Congress, May 20-22, 2024

Popescu, C. R. G., & Popescu, G. N. (2024b). Socio-Economic Inclusion, Health and Education Nexus: Tackling the European Union (EU) Vital Strategy on the Rights of the Child EU Actions to Withstand Poverty and Boost Inclusive and Child-Friendly Societies, Health and Education Systems.

Popescu, C. R. G., & Popescu, G. N. (2024c). Renewable Energy Industry: Benefits For Economic Growth. International Black Sea Coastline Countries Scientific Assembly by Center for Black Sea Research. Organizer: Center For Black Sea Research, Black Sea Network For Intercultural Communications (BIC). April 7-9, 2024, Samsun, Turkey. Congress website: https://www.blackseacountries.org/congress.

Popescu, C. R. G., & Popescu, G. N. (2024d). Intercultural Communication And Social Cohesion At The Heart Of Sustainable Development Goals (SDGS) And Development Policies. International Symposium On Communication, Information And Society. May 09-10 2024. http://comis.gantep.edu.tr/index.php?dil=en

Popescu, C. R. G., & Popescu, G. N. (2024e). Envisioning International Trade and Logistics for the Sustainable Development Goals (SDGs): Responsible Plant, Tree, and Livestock Logistics for Greening and Conserving the Environment. Congress Tıtle 7th Internatıonal Antalya Scıentıfıc Research And Innovatıve Studıes Congress Date And Place 11-13 May 2024, Antalya, Turkiye Organızatıon Iksad Instıtute.

Popescu, C. R. G., Popescu, G. N., & Popescu, V. A. (2015a). Corporate Governance in Romania: Theories and Practices. In Boubaker, S., Nguyen, D.K. (Eds.), Corporate Governance And Corporate Social Responsibility: Emerging Markets Focus (pp. 375-401). WORLD SCIENTIFIC PUBL CO PTE LTDPO BOX 128 FARRER RD, SINGAPORE 9128, SINGAPORE. WOS:000349291300016. ISBN: 978-981-4520-37-9. . https://www.worldscientific.com/doi/abs/10.1142/9789814520386_0014DOI: 10.1142/9789814520386_0014

Popescu, C. R. G., Popescu, G. N., & Popescu, V. A. (2017). Assessment Of The State Of Implementation Of Excellence Model Common Assessment Framework (CAF) 2013 By The National Institutes Of Research - Development - Innovation In Romania. Amfiteatru Economic. Editura ASE. Volume: 19. Issue: 44. pp. 41-60. WOS:000395746900004. ISSN: 1582-9146. eISSN: 2247-9104.

Popescu, C. R. G., Popescu, V. A., & Popescu, G. N. (2015b). The Entrepreneur's Role In The Performance Growth Of The Financial Audit Activity In Romania. Amfiteatru Economic. Editura ASE. Volume: 17. Issue: 38. pp. 228-246. WOS:000352213800015. ISSN: 1582-9146. eISSN: 2247-9104.

Popescu, V. A., Popescu, G. N., & Popescu, C. R. G. (2014). The Economic And Social Dimensions Of Romania's Metallurgical Industry. Metalurgija. CROATIAN METALLURGICAL SOCBERISLAVICEVA 6, ZAGREB, CROATIA. Volume: 53. Issue: 1. pp. 113-115. WOS:000320481400029. ISSN:0543-5846. eISSN:1334-2576.

Popescu, V. A., Popescu, G. N., & Popescu, C. R. G. (2015c). The Relation Productivity - Environment In The Context Of Sustainable Development - Case Study On The Romanian Industry. Metalurgija. CROATIAN METALLURGICAL SOCBERISLAVICEVA 6, ZAGREB, CROATIA. Volume: 54. Issue: 1. pp. 286-288. WOS:000341740000075. ISSN:0543-5846. eISSN:1334-2576.

Popescu, V. A., Popescu, G. N., & Popescu, C. R. G. (2015d). Competitiveness And Sustainability - A Modern Economic Approach To The Industrial Policy. Metalurgija. CROATIAN METALLURGICAL SOCBERISLAVICEVA 6, ZAGREB, CROATIA. Volume: 54. Issue: 2. pp. 426-428. WOS:000343781300031. ISSN:0543-5846. eISSN:1334-2576.

Popescu, C. R. G. (2019). Corporate Social Responsibility, Corporate Governance and Business Performance: Limits and Challenges Imposed by the Implementation of Directive 2013/34/EU in Romania. *Sustainability (Basel), 11*(19), 5146. DOI: 10.3390/su11195146

Popescu, C. R. G. (2020a). Approaches to Sustainable and Responsible Entrepreneurship: Creativity, Innovation, and Intellectual Capital as Drivers for Organization Performance. In Hernández-Sánchez, B., Sánchez-García, J., & Moreira, A. (Eds.), *Building an Entrepreneurial and Sustainable Society* (pp. 75–95). IGI Global., DOI: 10.4018/978-1-7998-2704-7.ch004

Popescu, C. R. G. (2020b). Developing a Model for Entrepreneurship Competencies: Innovation, Knowledge Management, and Intellectual Capital – Success Competences for Building Inclusive Entrepreneurship and Organizational Performance. In Šebestová, J. (Ed.), *Developing Entrepreneurial Competencies for Start-Ups and Small Business* (pp. 1–22). IGI Global., DOI: 10.4018/978-1-7998-2714-6.ch001

Popescu, C. R. G. (2020c). Analyzing the Impact of Green Marketing Strategies on the Financial and Non-Financial Performance of Organizations: The Intellectual Capital Factor. In Naidoo, V., & Verma, R. (Eds.), *Green Marketing as a Positive Driver Toward Business Sustainability* (pp. 186–218). IGI Global., DOI: 10.4018/978-1-5225-9558-8.ch008

Popescu, C. R. G. (2020d). Sustainability Assessment: Does the OECD/G20 Inclusive Framework for BEPS (Base Erosion and Profit Shifting Project) Put an End to Disputes Over The Recognition and Measurement of Intellectual Capital? *Sustainability (Basel), 12*(23), 10004. DOI: 10.3390/su122310004

Popescu, C. R. G. (2021a). Sustainable and Responsible Entrepreneurship for Value-Based Cultures, Economies, and Societies: Increasing Performance Through Intellectual Capital in Challenging Times. In Popescu, C., & Verma, R. (Eds.), *Sustainable and Responsible Entrepreneurship and Key Drivers of Performance* (pp. 33–58). IGI Global., DOI: 10.4018/978-1-7998-7951-0.ch002

Popescu, C. R. G. (2022a). Impressive, Inspiring, and Profound Mindfulness Movement in Organizations: Boosting Productivity, Cultivating Joy, and Sharping Awareness. In Popescu, C. (Ed.), *Handbook of Research on Building Inclusive Global Knowledge Societies for Sustainable Development* (pp. 60–96). IGI Global., DOI: 10.4018/978-1-6684-5109-0.ch003

Popescu, C. R. G. (2022b). Mindfulness at Work, a Sound Business Investment: Focusing on the Employee Well-Being While Increasing Creativity and Innovation. In Popescu, C. (Ed.), *Handbook of Research on Changing Dynamics in Responsible and Sustainable Business in the Post-COVID-19 Era* (pp. 1–34). IGI Global., DOI: 10.4018/978-1-6684-2523-7.ch001

Popescu, C. R. G. (2022c). Mindfulness Business Principles: Producing Outstanding Value and Encouraging Community Connections. In Popescu, C. (Ed.), *COVID-19 Pandemic Impact on New Economy Development and Societal Change* (pp. 196–228). IGI Global., DOI: 10.4018/978-1-6684-3374-4.ch010

Popescu, C. R. G. (2023b). Artificial Intelligence and Sustainability in a Game-Changing Post-COVID-19 Era: Key Drivers for Economic Development, Social Development, and Environmental Protection. In Popescu, C. (Ed.), *Positive and Constructive Contributions for Sustainable Development Goals* (pp. 1–20). IGI Global., DOI: 10.4018/978-1-6684-7499-0.ch001

Popescu, C. R. G., & Ban a, V. C. (2019). Performance Evaluation of the Implementation of the 2013/34/EU Directive in Romania on the Basis of Corporate Social Responsibility Reports. *Sustainability*, *11*(9), 2531. DOI: 10.3390/su11092531

Popescu, C. R. G., & Popescu, G. N. (2019a). The Social, Economic, and Environmental Impact of Ecological Beekeeping in Romania. In Popescu, G. (Ed.), *Agrifood Economics and Sustainable Development in Contemporary Society* (pp. 75–96). IGI Global., DOI: 10.4018/978-1-5225-5739-5.ch004

Popescu, C. R. G., & Popescu, G. N. (2019b). An Exploratory Study Based on a Questionnaire Concerning Green and Sustainable Finance, Corporate Social Responsibility, and Performance: Evidence from the Romanian Business Environment. *Journal of Risk and Financial Management*, *12*(4), 162. DOI: 10.3390/jrfm12040162

Popescu, C. R. G., & Popescu, G. N. (2025). The Power of Data Analysis in Transforming Businesses Performance: Improved Decision-Making, Real-World Applications, and the Sustainable Development Goals. In Popescu, C. (Ed.), *Building Inclusive Global Knowledge Societies for Sustainable Development* (pp. 169–208). IGI Global Scientific Publishing., DOI: 10.4018/979-8-3693-6298-3.ch008

Popescu, C. R. G., & Verma, R. (2024). Industry 4.0 Entrepreneurship Education and Sustainability in a Game-Changing Post-COVID-19 Era: Innovation, Creativity, Business Integration, Technology Skills, Leadership, and Communication. In Naidoo, V., & Verma, R. (Eds.), *Reshaping Entrepreneurial Education Within an Industry 4.0 Context* (pp. 81–95). IGI Global Scientific Publishing., DOI: 10.4018/979-8-3693-0409-9.ch005

Popescu, G. H. (2014). Economic aspects influencing the rising costs of health care in the United States. *American Journal of Medical Research (New York, N.Y.)*, *1*(1), 47. https://link.gale.com/apps/doc/A426766518/AONE?u=googlescholar&sid=bookmark-AONE&xid=66531cd9

Porter, M. E., & Kramer, M. R. (2011). Creating Shared Value. *Harvard Business Review*, *89*(1-2), 62–77. https://hbr.org/2011/01/the-big-idea-creating-shared-value

Potháczky, R.I. (2022) Talent management characteristics of small and medium-sized enterprises and the effects of Covid19, (In Hungarian) Acta Periodica XXVI. kötet, 2022/december, pp 45-59, DOI https://doi.org/DOI: 10.47273/AP.2022.26.45-59

Potts, L., & Cloete, C. E. (2012). Developing guidelines for brownfield development in South Africa. *WIT Transactions on Ecology and the Environment*, *1*, 389–399. DOI: 10.2495/EID120341

Prasanna, J. H., Hemalatha, S., Deepa, N., & Rani, S. (2022). A Study on Relationship between Employee Turnover Intention and Perceived Organisational Support. *Asian Journal of Agricultural Extension. Economia e Sociologia*, *251–255*, 251–255. Advance online publication. DOI: 10.9734/ajaees/2022/v40i1031070

Prendergast, C. (1999). *The Tenuous Tradeoff of Risk and Incentives*, working paper.

Presidencia de la Republica del Ecuador. (2024). *Texaco (Chevron) se vanagloriaba de su influencia en gobiernos pasados*. Quito. Obtenido de https://www.presidencia.gob.ec/texaco-chevron-se-vanagloriaba-de-su-influencia-en-gobiernos-pasados/

President's office of the Republic of Ecuador. (2022). Executive order 499: Derecho a un ambiente sano [Right to a healthy environment]. Retrieved from https://www.ambiente.gob.ec/wp-content/uploads/downloads/2022/02/REGLAMENTO-AL-CODIGO-ORGANICO-DEL-AMBIENTE.pdf

PRI. U. (2024). Principles for responsible investment—Annual report 2024. https://www.unpri.org/about-us/about-the-pri/annual-report

Pucci, M. (2015). The Investor-State Dispute Settlement Provision in the Trans-Pacific Partnership: Not the Death Knell Critics Are Looking For. Vol. 37. Associate Editor. Retrieved on-line from https://www.mjilonline.org/1489-2/. Accessed on the 28th of January 2025.

Pulido Reina, J. S., & Muñoz, F. A. (2020). Knowledge management, a critical success factor in organizational performance. *Criterio Libre*, *18*(33), 131–149. DOI: 10.18041/1900-0642/criteriolibre.2020v18n33.7535

Punie, Y., & Redecker, C. (Eds.). (s). (2017). European Framework for the Digital Competence of Educators: DigCompEdu, EUR 28775 EN, Publications Office of the European Union, Luxembourg. ISBN 978-92-79-73718-3 (print),978-92-79-73494-6 (pdf), (print), (online), JRC107466.DOI: 10.2760/178382

Purvis, B., Mao, Y., & Robinson, D. (2019). Three pillars of sustainability: In search of conceptual origins. *Sustainability Science*, *14*(3), 681–695. DOI: 10.1007/s11625-018-0627-5

PwC. (2021). *Tech for Good: Using Technology to Transform Sustainability*. Retrieved from https://www.pwc.com

Queiroz Almeida, D., Paciência, I., Moreira, C., Cavaleiro Rufo, J., Moreira, A., Santos, A. C., Barros, H., & Ribeiro, A. I. (2022). Green and blue spaces and lung function in the Generation XXI cohort: A life-course approach. *The European Respiratory Journal*, *60*(6), 2103024. DOI: 10.1183/13993003.03024-2021 PMID: 35896209

R Core Team. (2024). *R: A language and environment for statistical computing* (Version 2024.12.0+467) [Computer software]. R Foundation for Statistical Computing. https://www.R-project.org/

Raco, M., & Henderson, S. (2009). Sustainable urban planning and the brownfield development process in the United Kingdom: Lessons from the Thames Gateway. *Local Environment*, *11*(5), 499–509. DOI: 10.1080/13549830600853098

Ragazou, K., Garefalakis, A., Papademetriou, C., & Samara, A. (Eds.). (2025). *Sustainability Through Green HRM and Performance Integration*. IGI Global., DOI: 10.4018/979-8-3693-5981-5

Raghunandan, A., & Rajgopal, S. (2022). Do ESG funds make stakeholder-friendly investments? *Review of Accounting Studies*, *27*(3), 822–863. DOI: 10.1007/s11142-022-09693-1

Rahmaningtyas, W., Joyoatmojo, S., Kristiani, K., & Murwaningsih, T. (2023). Building a sustainable future: Unraveling the link between environmental awareness and the cultivation of employability and green skills-a literature review. *IOP Conference Series. Earth and Environmental Science*, *1248*(1), 012021. DOI: 10.1088/1755-1315/1248/1/012021

Rajpurohit, S. (2024). Study on Turnover and Retention Strategies Identifying Causes and Implementing Solutions. *Indian Scientific Journal Of Research In Engineering And Management*, *08*(06), 1–5. DOI: 10.55041/IJSREM35815

Ramachandaran, S. D. (2024). Challenges in Implementing Quality Education at INTI International University: An Examination of Human Resource Management Practices. *Journal of Ecohumanism*, *3*(8). Advance online publication. DOI: 10.62754/joe.v3i8.4727

Rambe, M. T. (2024). Building an Inclusive Work Environment: Challenges and Opportunities in HR Management. *Jurnal EMT KITA*, *8*(4), 1557–1568. DOI: 10.35870/emt.v8i4.3281

Ramírez Sáenz de Viteri, S. (2020). Knowledge management: Applications and organizational practices. FORHUM International Journal of Social Sciences and Humanities, 53-66. .DOI: 10.35766/jf20225

Ramirez, L.. (2022). *IoT Frameworks for Smart Traffic Management: A Comprehensive Review*. Smart Cities Journal.

Ramos Galarza, C. (2020). Los alcances de una investigación. *CienciAmérica: Revista de divulgación científica de la Universidad Tecnológica Indoamérica, 9*(3), 1-6. Obtenido de https://dialnet.unirioja.es/servlet/articulo?codigo=7746475

Ramos, C. A. (2015). Los paradigmas de la investigación científica [The paradigms of scientific research]. Avances en psicología, 23(1), 9-17.

Raut, V. N. (2024). Driving success: The strategic role of talent management in HR's promotion of employee engagement. *International Journal of Research Publication and Reviews*. https://doi.org/DOI: 10.55248/gengpi.5.0524.1296

Reddy, S. (2024). Dr.K V Subba Reddy School of Business Management. *Indian Scientific Journal Of Research In Engineering And Management*, *08*(06), 1–5. DOI: 10.55041/IJSREM36129

Rehman, S. U., Elrehail, H., Nair, K., Bhatti, A., & Taamneh, A. M. (2023). MCS package and entrepreneurial competency influence on business performance: The moderating role of business strategy. *European Journal of Management and Business Economics*, *32*(1), 1–23. DOI: 10.1108/EJMBE-04-2020-0088

Reijnders, L., Lukszo, Z., & Albrecht, H. (2021). Sustainability, Green Innovation, and Entrepreneurship: The Green Entrepreneurial Process. *Sustainability*, *13*(4), 2332–2347.

Reiter, S., & Jentzsch, S. (2019). Hack4Climate: A Novel Approach to Foster Climate Change Innovation. *Environmental Innovation and Societal Transitions*.

Renauld, F. G., Sudmeier-Rieux, K., & Estrella, M. (2013). *The Role of Ecosystems in Disaster Risk Reduction*. United Nations University Press.

Report of the United Nations Conference on the Human Environment (A/CONF.48/14/Rev.l). (1972). United Nations. https://documents.un.org/doc/undoc/gen/n73/039/07/pdf/n7303907.pdf

Rey, E., Laprise, M., & Lufkin, S. (2021). Sustainability issues at the neighbourhood scale. In *The urban book series* (pp. 77–93). https://doi.org/DOI: 10.1007/978-3-030-82208-8_5

Reza, A. K., Islam, M. S., & Shimu, A. A. (2017). Green Industry in Bangladesh: An Overview. *Environmental Management and Sustainable Development*, *6*(2), 124. DOI: 10.5296/emsd.v6i2.11027

Rhoden, L. (2014). The Capacity of NGOs to Become Sustainable by Creating Social Enterprises. *Journal of Small Business and Entrepreneurship Development*, *2*(2), 1–36. https://jsbed.thebrpi.org/journals/jsbed/Vol_2_No_2_June_2014/1.pdf

Richter, F. J., Kleber, L. S., & Müller, S. (2020). Green growth and beyond: The case of Beyond Meat. *Journal of Business Models*, *8*(1), 56–68. DOI: 10.5278/ojs.jbm.v8i1.3665

Riege, A. (2005). Three-dozen knowledge-sharing barriers managers must consider. *Journal of Knowledge Management*, *9*(3), 18–35. DOI: 10.1108/13673270510602746

Rimmer, M. (2016). Greenwashing. The Trans-Pacific Partnership. October 2016. The Senate Foreign Affairs, Defence And Trade References Committee. Proposed Trans-Pacific Partnership (TPP). Agreement Submission 84 - Supplementary Submission 6.

Rinne, S. T., Rodas, E. J., Bender, B. S., Rinne, M. L., Simpson, J. M., Galer-Unti, R., & Glickman, L. T. (2006). Relationship of pulmonary function among women and children to indoor air pollution from biomass use in rural Ecuador. *Respiratory Medicine*, *100*(7), 1208–1215. DOI: 10.1016/j.rmed.2005.10.020 PMID: 16318916

Rio Declaration on Environment and Development. (1992, junio 3). United Nations. https://www.un.org/spanish/esa/sustdev/documents/declaracionrio.htm

Rios Quituizaca, P., Gatica-Domínguez, G., Nambiar, D., Ferreira Santos, J. L., Brück, S., Vidaletti Ruas, L., & Barros, A. J. D. (2021). National and subnational coverage and inequalities in reproductive, maternal, newborn, child, and sanitary health interventions in Ecuador: A comparative study between 1994 and 2012. *International Journal for Equity in Health*, *20*(1), 48. DOI: 10.1186/s12939-020-01359-1 PMID: 33509210

Rizzo, E., Pesce, M., Pizzol, L., Alexandrescu, F. M., Giubilato, E., Critto, A., Marcomini, A., & Bartke, S. (2015). Brownfield regeneration in Europe: Identifying stakeholder perceptions, concerns, attitudes and information needs. *Land Use Policy*, *48*, 437–453. DOI: 10.1016/j.landusepol.2015.06.012

Roberts, M., Jenkins, M., & Knox, R. (2021). Corporate Sustainability and the Future of Green Entrepreneurship. *Business & Society*, *60*(2), 310–333.

Rockström, J., Steffen, W., Noone, K., Persson, Å., Chapin, F. S.III, Lambin, E. F., Lenton, T. M., Scheffer, M., Folke, C., Schellnhuber, H. J., Nykvist, B., de Wit, C. A., Hughes, T., van der Leeuw, S., Rodhe, H., Sörlin, S., Snyder, P. K., Costanza, R., Svedin, U., & Foley, J. A. (2009). A safe operating space for humanity. *Nature*, *461*(7263), 472–475. DOI: 10.1038/461472a PMID: 19779433

Rodriguez, F., & Valle, A. (2023). La Naturaleza como sujeto de derechos: Reconocimiento formal y material en el ordenamiento jurídico ecuatoriano [Nature as a Subject of Rights: Formal and Material Recognition in the Ecuadorian Legal System]. En Derechos de la Naturaleza y territorio en Ecuador. Diálogos desde los saberes, quehaceres jurídicos y antropológicos (Primera). https://dspace.ups.edu.ec/handle/123456789/27775

Rodríguez-Estévez, F. (2022). El medio ambiente en el Tribunal Europeo de Derechos Humanos y la Corte Interamericana de Derechos Humanos [The environment in the European Court of Human Rights and the Inter-American Court of Human Rights] [master's thesis]. https://reunir.unir.net/handle/123456789/15594

Romero, S., & Krauss, C. (2011). Ecuador judge orders Chevron to pay $9 billion. New York Times, A4.

Rondon, B. (2021). Experimental Characterization of Admittance Meter With Crude Oil Emulsions. [IJECME]. *International Journal of Electronics, Communications, and Measurement Engineering*, *10*(2), 51–59. DOI: 10.4018/IJECME.2021070104

Rosário, A. T., Raimundo, R. J., & Cruz, S. P. (2022). Sustainable entrepreneurship: A literature review. *Sustainability (Basel)*, *14*(9), 5556. DOI: 10.3390/su14095556

Rosso, B. D., Dekas, K. H., & Wrzesniewski, A. (2010). On the Meaning of Work: A Theoretical Integration and Review. *Research in Organizational Behavior*, *30*, 91–127. DOI: 10.1016/j.riob.2010.09.001

Rubáček, F., MacGregor Pelikánová, R. and MacGregor R.K. (2023). The sustainability of ESAs triumvirate for sustainability-related disclosures in the financial sector – all for one and one for all. *Acta Universitatis Lodziensis. Folia Iuridica, 105*, 123-143. OI: DOI: 10.18778/0208-6069.105.08

Ruiz-Urigüen, M., Shuai, W., Huang, S., & Jaffé, P. R. (2022). Biodegradation of PFOA in microbial electrolysis cells by Acidimicrobiaceae sp. strain A6. *Chemosphere*, *292*, 133506. DOI: 10.1016/j.chemosphere.2021.133506 PMID: 34995627

Rumasukun, M. R., & Noch, M. Y. (2023). The Role of Community Engagement in SME Management: A Qualitative Synthesis. *Golden Ratio of Community Services and Dedication*, *3*(1), 40–48. DOI: 10.52970/grcsd.v3i1.605

Sabbah, M. (2024). Transformational Leadership and Business Continuity: A systematic review of empirical studies. *Management Research Quarterly*, *1*(2), 4–24. DOI: 10.63029/kyzckn37

Saberi, S., Kouhizadeh, M., & Sarkis, J. (2019). Blockchain Technology in Supply Chain Management: A Review of the Literature and Applications. *International Journal of Production Research*, *57*(7), 2117–2135. DOI: 10.1080/00207543.2018.1533261

Sachs, J. D. (2019). Testimony of Professor Jeffrey D. Sachs, University Professor at Columbia University, Subcommittee on Environment U.S. House Committee on Oversight and Reform. April 9, 2019. pp. 1-4.

Sagala, G. H., & Őri, D. (2024). Exploring digital transformation strategy to achieve SMEs resilience and antifragility: A systematic literature review. *Journal of Small Business and Entrepreneurship*, •••, 1–30. DOI: 10.1080/08276331.2024.2392080

Sagandykova, L. S., Tayauova, G., & Ketengi, N. (2024). The role of sustainable human resources management in the organizational effectiveness of the company. *Tu ran Universitetinin Habarsysy*, *3*(3), 258–270. DOI: 10.46914/1562-2959-2024-1-3-258-270

Saha, A., & Md, S. N. (2021)... *Factors Influencing Employee Retention.*, *14*(01), 20–38. DOI: 10.36481/diujbe.v014i1.460k4723

Sahu, A. K., Sharma, M., Raut, R. D., Sahu, A. K., Sahu, N. K., Antony, J., & Tortorella, G. L. (2023). Decision-making framework for supplier selection using an integrated MCDM approach in a lean-agile-resilient-green environment: Evidence from Indian automotive sector. *The TQM Journal*, *35*(4), 964–1006. DOI: 10.1108/TQM-12-2021-0372

Saiz-Alvarez, J. M., Castillo-Nazareno, U. H., Matute de León, J. S., & Alcívar-Avilés, M. T. (2021). Post-COVID Indigenous Women Entrepreneurship: A Case of the Kichwa-Puruha in Ecuador. In Baporikar, N. (Ed.), *Handbook of Research on Strategies and Interventions to Mitigate COVID-19 Impact on SMEs* (pp. 430–456). IGI Global Scientific Publishing., DOI: 10.4018/978-1-7998-7436-2.ch021

Sajid, M., & Płotka-Wasylka, J. (2022). Green analytical chemistry metrics: A review. *Talanta*, *238*(Pt 2), 123046. DOI: 10.1016/j.talanta.2021.123046 PMID: 34801903

Sala, A., & Herrero Ramila, C. (2022). LifeComp into Action: Teaching life skills in the classroom and beyond, EUR 31141 EN, Publications Office of the European Union, Luxembourg, ISBN 978-92-76-54524-8, , JRC130003.DOI: 10.2760/22023

Sala, A., Punie, Y., Garkov, V., & Cabrera Giraldez, M. (2020). LifeComp: The European Framework for Personal, Social and Learning to Learn Key Competence, EUR 30246 EN, Publications Office of the European Union, Luxembourg, ISBN 978-92-76-19417-0, , JRC120911.DOI: 10.2760/922681

Sala, S., Amadei, A. M., Beylot, A., & Ardente, F. (2021). The evolution of life cycle assessment in European policies over three decades. *The International Journal of Life Cycle Assessment*, *26*(12), 2295–2314. DOI: 10.1007/s11367-021-01893-2

Sala, S., Farioli, F., & Zamagni, A. (2013). Life cycle sustainability assessment in the context of sustainability science progress (part 2). *The International Journal of Life Cycle Assessment*, *18*(9), 1686–1697. DOI: 10.1007/s11367-012-0509-5

Salassa, R., Alderete, P., & Bach, J. (2015). *La protección ambiental a travéz del derecho fiscal*. Facultad de Derecho y Ciencias Sociales de la Universidad Nacional de Córdoba.

Salazar, T.I., Cervantes, L., Aguirre, J.P. y Carbache, C. (2023). Generación de valor en las organizaciones con la gestión del conocimiento e información. Revista Latinoamericana de Ciencias Sociales – Relacis, 1(2), 3 – 16.

Salovaara, J., & Soini, K. (2021). Educated professionals of sustainability and the dimensions of practices. *International Journal of Sustainability in Higher Education*, *22*(8), 69–87. DOI: 10.1108/IJSHE-09-2020-0327

Samuel, I. A., & Isa, M. Y. B. M. (2024). The mediating role of talent management in succession planning and private organization sustainability: A conceptual article. *Journal of Current Social and Political Issues*. https://doi.org/DOI: 10.15575/jcspi.v2i1.703

Sánchez, J. (. (2019). *Recursos naturales, medio ambiente y sostenibilidad: 70 años de pensamiento de la CEPAL*. Santiago, Comisión Económica para América Latina y el Caribe (CEPAL): Libros de la CEPAL, N° 158 (LC/PUB.2019/18-P. Sánchez, César; Becerra, Thais. (20 de 04 de 2015). *El impacto de Chevron en la Amazonía ecuatoriana*. Obtenido de https://www.anthropologies.es/el-impacto-de-chevron-en-la-amazonia-ecuatoriana/

Santamaria-Garcia, H., Sainz-Ballesteros, A., Hernandez, H., Moguilner, S., Maito, M., Ochoa-Rosales, C., Corley, M., Valcour, V., Miranda, J. J., Lawlor, B., & Ibanez, A. (2023). Factors associated with healthy aging in Latin American populations. *Nature Medicine*, *29*(9), 2248–2258. DOI: 10.1038/s41591-023-02495-1 PMID: 37563242

Sarjito, A. (2023). *Unlocking The Potential: Transforming Defense Through Human Capital Management*. https://doi.org/DOI: 10.58812/wsis.v1i11.333

Saxena, A., & Srivastava, A. (2022). Industry Application of Green Manufacturing: A Critical Review. *Ournal of Sustainability and Environmental Management*, *1*(1), 32–45.

Scalabrino, C. (2022). European sustainability competence framework background document, Publications Office of the European Union, Luxembourg. ISBN 978-92-76-57357-9, , JRC130849.DOI: 10.2760/378627

Schaltegger, S., & Wagner, M. (2011). Sustainable entrepreneurship and sustainability innovation: Categories and interactions. *Business Strategy and the Environment*, *20*(4), 222–237. DOI: 10.1002/bse.682

Schaubroeck, T., & Rugani, B. (2017). A Revision of What Life Cycle Sustainability Assessment Should Entail: Towards Modeling the Net Impact on Human Well-Being. *Journal of Industrial Ecology*, *21*(6), 1464–1477. DOI: 10.1111/jiec.12653

Schaufeli, W. B., & Bakker, A. B. (2004). Job demands, job resources, and their relationship with burnout and engagement: A multi-sample study. *Journal of Organizational Behavior*, *25*(3), 293–315. DOI: 10.1002/job.248

Schmidt-Bleek, F. (2019). *The Factor 10 Debate: Why Business Needs to Engage with the SDGs*. Earthscan.

Schmidt, M. A., Klein, J. M., & Breitenbach, M. (2020). The Role of Government Policy in Promoting Corporate Sustainability. *Journal of Cleaner Production*, *275*, 123132. DOI: 10.1016/j.jclepro.2020.123132

Schoenmaker, D., & Schramade, W. (2019). *Principles of Sustainable Finance*. Oxford University Press.

Schramade, W. (2017). Investing in the UN Sustainable Development Goals: Opportunities for Companies and Investors. *The Bank of America Journal of Applied Corporate Finance*, *29*(2), 87–99. DOI: 10.1111/jacf.12236

Schüz, M. (2012). Sustainable Corporate Responsibility – The Foundation of successful Business in the New Millennium. *Central European Business Review*, *1*(2), 7–15. DOI: 10.18267/j.cebr.12

Schwier, R. A., Campbell, K., & Kenny, R. (2004). Instructional designers' observations about identity, communities of practice and change agency.

Šebestová, J. D., & Popescu, C. R. G. (2022). Factors Influencing Investments into Human Resources to Support Company Performance. *Journal of Risk and Financial Management*, *15*(1), 19. DOI: 10.3390/jrfm15010019

Seiber, M. (2018). Systems Thinking and How It Can Help Build a Sustainable World: A Beginning Conversation. https://thesolutionsjournal.com/systems-thinking-can-help-build-sustainable-world-beginning-conversation/

Seikkula-Leino, J., & Salomaa, M. (2020). Entrepreneurial competencies and organisational change—Assessing entrepreneurial staff competencies within higher education institutions. *Sustainability (Basel)*, *12*(18), 7323. DOI: 10.3390/su12187323

Selkald, D., Hopkins, S., & Hayman, D. (2023). *Emerging Zoonotic and Wildlife Pathogens: Disease Ecology, Epidemiology, and Conservation*. Oxford University Press., DOI: 10.1093/oso/9780198825920.001.0001

Serafeim, G. (2020). How to Build Enduring Business Models in a Changing World. *Harvard Business Review*. https://hbr.org/2020/12/how-to-build-enduring-business-models-in-a-changing-world

Seraj, A. H. A., Fazal, S. A., & Alshebami, A. S. (2022). Entrepreneurial competency, financial literacy, and sustainable performance—Examining the mediating role of entrepreneurial resilience among Saudi entrepreneurs. *Sustainability (Basel)*, *14*(17), 10689. DOI: 10.3390/su141710689

Serenko, A. & Cox, R. A.K. & Bontis, Nick & Booker, Lorne D., (2011). The superstar phenomenon in the knowledge management and intellectual capital academic discipline, *Journal of Informetrics*, Elsevier, vol. 5(3), pages 333-345.

Serenko, A. (2013). Meta-analysis of scientometric research of knowledge management: Discovering the identity of the discipline. *Journal of Knowledge Management*, *17*(5), 773–812. DOI: 10.1108/JKM-05-2013-0166

Serenko, A., & Bontis, N. (2004). Meta-review of knowledge management and intellectual capital literature: Citation impact and research productivity rankings. *Knowledge and Process Management*, *11*(3), 185–198. DOI: 10.1002/kpm.203

Serenko, A., Bontis, N., Booker, L., Sadeddin, K., & Hardie, T. (2010). A scientometric analysis of knowledge management and intellectual capital academic literature (1994-2008). *Journal of Knowledge Management*, *14*(1), 3–23. DOI: 10.1108/13673271011015534

Serenko, A., Bontis, N., & Hardie, T. (2007). Organizational size and knowledge flow: A proposed theoretical link. *Journal of Intellectual Capital*, *8*(4), 610–627. DOI: 10.1108/14691930710830783

Serenko, A., & Dumay, J. (2015). Citation classics published in knowledge management journals. Part I: Articles and their characteristics. *Journal of Knowledge Management*, *19*(2), 401–431. DOI: 10.1108/JKM-06-2014-0220

Serrano, H. (2013). *Caso Chevron-Texaco: cuando los pueblos toman la palabra.* diciembre: Universidad Andina Simón Bolívar, Sede Ecuador; Corporación Editora Nacional.

Sertyesilisik, B., & Sertyesilisik, E. (2017). Ways of Fostering Green Economy and Green Growth. In Filho, W. L., Pociovalisteanu, D.-M., & Al-Amin, A. Q. (Eds.), *Sustainable Economic Development: Green Economy and Green Growth* (pp. 49–65). Springer Nature., DOI: 10.1007/978-3-319-45081-0_3

Sessa, M. R., Russo, A., & Sica, F. (2022). Opinion paper on green deal for the urban regeneration of industrial brownfield land in Europe. *Land Use Policy*, *119*, 106198. DOI: 10.1016/j.landusepol.2022.106198

Shadish, W. R., Cook, T. D., & Campbell, D. T. (2002). *Experimental and quasi-experimental designs for generalized causal inference*. Houghton Mifflin Harcourt.

Shahrulnizam, N. A. A., Hassan, M. A., Mohamad Azizie, N. A. M., Rashid, A. H. A., & Wahab, S. R. A. (2024). Roles of Ghrm in Sustainable Organization Practices: A Systematic Literature Review. *International Journal of Academic Research in Business & Social Sciences*, *14*(10). Advance online publication. DOI: 10.6007/IJARBSS/v14-i10/23110

Shao, J., Ahmad, H., Butt, A. H., Shao, H., Liu, Y. D., & Alam, F. (2024). Optimizing Sustainable Performance Green Talent Management Strategies Focused on Core Competencies. [JGIM]. *Journal of Global Information Management*, *32*(1), 1–24. DOI: 10.4018/JGIM.352495

Sharma, A., Kumar, R., & Singh, D. (2021). Emerging Trends in Sustainability Education: A Case Study of IIM Bangalore. *Journal of Sustainability Studies*, *15*(3), 150–172.

Sharma, P.. (2022). IoT and Machine Learning Integration for Dynamic Traffic Signal Control. *IEEE Internet of Things Journal.*

Shelanski, H., & Klein, P. G. (1995). Empirical research in transaction cost economics: A review and assessment. *Journal of Law Economics and Organization*, •••, 335–361.

Shen, J., Li, M., Wang, Q., Liu, R., Ji, M., & An, R. (2022). The Influence of Green Space on Obesity in China: A Systematic Review. *Obesity Facts*, *15*(4), 463–472. DOI: 10.1159/000524857 PMID: 35545010

Shepherd, D. A., & Patzelt, H. (2011). The New Field of Sustainable Entrepreneurship: Studying Entrepreneurial Action Linking "What is to be Sustained" with "What is to be Developed". *Entrepreneurship Theory and Practice*, *35*(1), 137–163. DOI: 10.1111/j.1540-6520.2010.00426.x

Shpak, N., Melnyk, O., Horbal, N., Ruda, M., & Sroka, W. (2021). Assessing the Implementation of the Circular Economy in the EU Countries. *Forum Scientiae Oeconomia*, *9*(1). Advance online publication. DOI: 10.23762/FSO_VOL9_NO1_2

Siddiqui, S. M. F., Zafar, H., & Gilani, S. A. (2024). *Sustainable HR Practices and Employee Retention: The Impact of Social Capital in Pakistan's Banking Sector*. https://doi.org/DOI: 10.56976/jsom.v3i4.133

Sierdovski, M., Pilatti, L. A., & Rubbo, P. (2022). Organizational competencies in the development of environmental, social, and governance (ESG) criteria in the industrial sector. Sustainability, 14, 20, 13463. https://doi.org/DOI: 10.3390/su142013463

Silva, C. (2008). Qué es el buen vivir en la Constitución? [What is good living in the Constitution?] In Ávila, R. (Ed.), *La Constitución del 2008 en el contexto andino. Análisis desde la doctrina y el derecho comparado.* Ministerio de Justicia y Derechos Humanos.

Silva, L., Caten, C., & Gaia, S. (2023). Tool for assessment of the green technology transfer structure in Brazilian public universities. *Administratie Si Management Public*, *40*, 156–170. DOI: 10.24818/amp/2023.40-10

Sima, M., Grigorescu, I., & Bălteanu, D. (2019). An overview of campus greening initiatives at universities in Romania. *International Journal of Sustainability in Higher Education*, *20*(3), 410–422. DOI: 10.1108/IJSHE-01-2019-0036

Singh, A.. (2021). *Edge Computing in IoT-Based Traffic Systems: Challenges and Opportunities.* IoT Journal.

Singh, M., & Bhatnagar, M. (2023). *Sustainability's Symphony.* Advances in Finance, Accounting, and Economics Book Series., DOI: 10.4018/979-8-3693-1388-6.ch002

Singh, R., & Tarkar, P. (2024). An empirical analysis on sustainable start-up: Embedding Environmental, Social and Governance (ESG) into high growth business strategy. *Brazilian Journal of Operations & Production Management*, *21*(3), 1810–1810. DOI: 10.14488/BJOPM.1810.2024

Singh, R., Tiwari, K., & Mishra, P. (2021). Sustainability in entrepreneurial education: Challenges and future directions. *International Journal of Management Education*, *19*(2), 100531.

Sinulingga, G., Gunawan, A., Wibowo, U. D. A., Rina, R., & Damayanti, H. A. (2024). Talent Management in the Age of Digital Disruption: Challenges and Opportunities. *Global International Journal of Innovative Research.* https://doi.org/DOI: 10.59613/global.v2i9.311

Šipikal, M., Rehák, Š., & Grenčík, J. (2022). Vocational education and workforce planning in the automotive sector: Challenges and future trends. *Journal of Economic Development*, *47*(2), 89–110.

Sitarska-Piwko, A., & Rogozińska-Pawełczyk, A. (2024). Perceptions of sustainable human resource management (SHRM) and personal risk: Findings from the Pilot Study. *Edukacja Ekonomistów i Menedżerów*, *69*(3). Advance online publication. DOI: 10.33119/EEIM.2024.69.2

Skála, J., Čechmánková, J., Vácha, R., & Horváthová, V. (2013). Various aspects in the genesis and perspectives on agricultural brownfields in the Czech Republic. *Moravian Geographical Reports*, *21*(2), 46–55. DOI: 10.2478/mgr-2013-0010

Skrabal, J. (2020). What can we learn from brownfield databases? Exploring specifics of the location of brownfields in the Czech Republic. *Geography Teacher*, *15*(2), 191–201. DOI: 10.21163/GT_2020.152.18

Skrabal, J., Chmielova, P., Tureckova, K., & Nevima, J. (2021). Applicability of tools for brownfield regeneration in the Czech Republic: A regional perspective. *Geography Teacher*, *16*(2), 132–148. DOI: 10.21163/GT_2021.162.11

Slawinski, N., & Bansal, P. (2015). Short on Time: Intertemporal Tensions in Business Sustainability. *Organization Science, 26*(2), 531–549. DOI: 10.1287/orsc.2014.0960

Smallbone, D., Evans, M., Ekanem, I., & Butters, S. (2001). *Researching Social Enterprise, Centre for Enterprise and Economic Development Research.* Middlesex University Business School.

Small, H. (1973). Co-citation in the scientific literature: A new measure of the relationship between two documents. *Journal of the American Society for Information Science, 24*(4), 265–269. DOI: 10.1002/asi.4630240406

Smirani, N., Bouazizi, S., Bettaieb, E., Torkhani, R., & Hamdi, M. (2025). Effect of Environmentally Friendly Betalain Extraction Methods on Antioxidant Compounds of Tunisian *Opuntia stricta* Fruit. *Foods, 14*(5), 851. DOI: 10.3390/foods14050851 PMID: 40077554

Smith, A. (2020). Microsoft's Commitment to Sustainability: Leading the Digital Transformation. *Journal of Corporate Responsibility, 9*(2), 85–98.

Smith, E. C. (2019). Developing Cultural Competence: Challenges and Best Practices in Higher Education. [IJMSE]. *International Journal of Marketing and Sales Education, 2*(2), 1–17. DOI: 10.4018/IJMSE.2019070101

Smith, T.. (2022). *LiDAR Applications in Intelligent Traffic Management Systems.* Transportation Science Journal.

Solecki, W., Roberts, D., & Seto, K. C. (2024). Strategies to improve the impact of the IPCC Special Report on Climate Change and Cities. *Nature Climate Change, 14*(7), 685–691. DOI: 10.1038/s41558-024-02060-9

Soler, K. M., Baltasar, L. B., Díaz, C. K., & González, M. L. (2021). Happiness: An Approach to Labor Competence. In R. Perez-Uribe, D. Ocampo-Guzman, N. Moreno-Monsalve, & W. Fajardo-Moreno (Eds.), *Handbook of Research on Management Techniques and Sustainability Strategies for Handling Disruptive Situations in Corporate Settings* (pp. 342-354). IGI Global Scientific Publishing. DOI: 10.4018/978-1-7998-8185-8.ch016

Song, S., Nerur, S., & Teng, J. T. (2007). An exploratory study on the roles of network structure and knowledge processing orientation in work unit knowledge management. *The Data Base for Advances in Information Systems, 38*(2), 8–26. DOI: 10.1145/1240616.1240620

Song, Y., Lyu, Y., Qian, S., Zhang, X., Lin, H., & Wang, S. (2022). Identifying urban candidate brownfield sites using multi-source data: The case of Changchun City, China. *Land Use Policy, 117*, 106084. DOI: 10.1016/j.landusepol.2022.106084

Sorvari, J., & Seppälä, J. (2010). A decision support tool to prioritize risk management options for contaminated sites. *The Science of the Total Environment, 408*(8), 1786–1799. DOI: 10.1016/j.scitotenv.2009.12.026 PMID: 20138649

Soto, N. (21 de 05 de 2019). *Chevron: El poder y la impunidad de las grandes corporaciones.* Recuperado el 13 de 05 de 2024, de https://es.greenpeace.org/es/noticias/chevron-el-poder-y-la-impunidad-de-las-grandes-corporaciones/

Sousa, M. J., & Costa, J. M. (2022). Discovering entrepreneurship competencies through problem-based learning in higher education students. *Education Sciences*, *12*(3), 185. DOI: 10.3390/educsci12030185

Spaiser, V., Ranganathan, S., Swain, R. B., & Sumpter, D. J. T. (2016). The sustainable development oxymoron: Quantifying and modelling the incompatibility of sustainable development goals. *International Journal of Sustainable Development and World Ecology*, *24*(6), 457–470. DOI: 10.1080/13504509.2016.1235624

Sreenivasan, A., & Suresh, M. (2023). Exploring the contribution of sustainable entrepreneurship towards sustainable development goals: A bibliometric analysis. Green Technologies and Sustainability, 100038.

Stahel, W. R. (2016). Circular economy: A new relationship with our goods and materials would save resources and energy and create local jobs. *Nature*, *531*(7595), 435–438. DOI: 10.1038/531435a PMID: 27008952

Stahl, D. (2021). LifeComp: Competences for life and learning in times of transition. https://epale.ec.europa.eu/en/blog/lifecomp-competences-life-and-learning-times-transition

Staples, D. S., Greenaway, K., & McKeen, J. D. (2001). Opportunities for research about managing the knowledge-based enterprise. *International Journal of Management Reviews*, *3*(1), 1–20. DOI: 10.1111/1468-2370.00051

Starbucks. (2020). *Starbucks Global Environmental and Social Impact Report*. Retrieved from https://www.starbucks.com

Stead, J. G., & Stead, W. E. (2000). Eco-Enterprise Strategy: Standing for Sustainability. *Journal of Business Ethics*, *24*(4), 313–329. DOI: 10.1023/A:1006188725928

Stefan, D., Vasile, V., Oltean, A., Comes, C. A., Stefan, A. B., Ciucan-Rusu, L., Bunduchi, E., Popa, M.-A., & Timus, M. (2021). Women entrepreneurship and sustainable business development: Key findings from a SWOT–AHP analysis. *Sustainability (Basel)*, *13*(9), 5298. DOI: 10.3390/su13095298

Steffen, W., Persson, Å., Deutsch, L., Zalasiewicz, J., Williams, M., Richardson, K., Crumley, C., Crutzen, P., Folke, C., Gordon, L., Molina, M., Ramanathan, V., Rockström, J., Scheffer, M., Schellnhuber, H. J., & Svedin, U. (2011). The Anthropocene: From Global Change to Planetary Stewardship. *Ambio*, *40*(7), 739–761. DOI: 10.1007/s13280-011-0185-x PMID: 22338713

Steffen, W., Richardson, K., Rockström, J., Cornell, S. E., Fetzer, I., Bennett, E. M., & Sörlin, S. (2018). Sustainability and Planetary Boundaries. *Science*, *347*(6223), 736–746. PMID: 25592418

Steponavičius, M., Gress-Wright, C., & Linzarini, A. (2023). Social and emotional skills: Latest evidence on teachability and impact on life outcomes. OECD Education Working Papers, No. 304, OECD Publishing, Paris. DOI: 10.1787/19939019

Sterman, J. D., Siegel, L., & Rooney-Varga, J. N. (2015). En-ROADS: A simulation model to engage diverse audiences in climate solutions. *Simulation & Gaming*, *46*(6), 649–668.

Stern, N. (2007, November 29 - 30). Climate change, ethics and the economics of the global deal. *Proceedings of The Royal Economic Society Annual Public Lecture*, University of Manchester and Institute of Education, London. Available at https://cepr.org/voxeu/columns/climate-change-ethics-and-economics-global-deal#:~:text=The%20extra%20costs%20developing%20countries,is%20not%20separate%20from%20it

Stiglitz, J. (2017). *The practice of industrial Policy.*

Stiglitz, J. E., Sen, A., & Fitoussi, J.-P. (2009). *Report by the Commission on the Measurement of Economic Performance and Social Progress*, 1 – 291. Paris: France. https://ec.europa.eu/eurostat/documents/8131721/8131772/Stiglitz-Sen-Fitoussi-Commission-report.pdf

Stolowy, H., & Ding, Y. (2017). *Financial accounting and reporting: a global perspective* (5th ed.). Cengage Learning.

Stone, C. D. (2010). Should trees have standing?: law, morality, and the environment. Oxford University Press. Original text retrieved from https://iseethics.wordpress.com/wp-content/uploads/2013/02/stone-christopher-d-should-trees-have-standing.pdf

Strietska-Ilina, O., Hofmann, C., Durán Haro, M., & Jeon, S. *Skills for green jobs: a global view: synthesis report based on 21 country studies*. International Labour Office, Skills and Employability Department, Job Creation and Enterprise Development Department. - Geneva: ILO, 2011.

Sudar, S., Cvetković, V., & Ivanov, A. (2024). Harmonization of soft power and institutional skills: montenegro's path to accession to the european union in the environmental sector. DOI: 10.20944/preprints202404.1034.v1

Sulaiman, M. A. B. A. (2025). Green Product Innovation as a Mediator Between Green Market Orientation and Sustainable Performance of SMEs. *Sustainability (Basel)*, *17*(4), 1628. DOI: 10.3390/su17041628

Sulich, A., & Kozar, L. (2024). Green competences: A review and future research in the context of green human resource management. *Theoretical and Methodological Problems, EiS, 89*(2), 713. DOI: 10.34659/eis.2024.89.2.713

Sullivan, R., & Mackenzie, C. (2019). *The Global Business Environment: Meeting the Challenges of International Business*. Routledge.

Sun, Q.. (2020). *Traffic Prediction Using LSTM Networks: A Comprehensive Review*. Neural Networks and Applications.

Surianto, S., Badaruddin, B., & Firman, A. (2024). Human Resource Management Strategies to Increase Adaptability in the Digital Age. *Human Resource Management Strategies to Increase Adaptability in the Digital Age.*, *2*(1), 1–15. DOI: 10.37476/presed.v2i1.56

Suriyankietkaew, S., Krittayaruangroj, K., & Iamsawan, N. (2022). Sustainable Leadership practices and competencies of SMEs for sustainability and resilience: A community-based social enterprise study. *Sustainability (Basel)*, *14*(10), 5762. DOI: 10.3390/su14105762

Sutherland, W., Adams, W. M., Aronson, R. B., Aveling, R., Blackburn, T. M., Broad, S., Ceballos, G., Côté, I. M., Cowling, R. M., Da Fonseca, G. A. B., Dinerstein, E., Ferraro, P. J., Fleishman, E., Gascon, C., Hunter, M.Jr, Hutton, J., Kareiva, P., Kuria, A., MacDonald, D. W., & Watkinson, A. R. (2009). One Hundred Questions of Importance to the Convervation of Global Biological Diversity. *Conservation Biology*, *23*(3), 557–567. DOI: 10.1111/j.1523-1739.2009.01212.x PMID: 19438873

Swim, J. K., Stern, P. C., Doherty, T. J., Clayton, S., Reser, J. P., Weber, E. U., Gifford, R., & Howard, G. S. (2011). Psychology's contributions to understanding and addressing global climate change. *The American Psychologist*, *66*(4), 241–250. DOI: 10.1037/a0023220 PMID: 21553950

Tallis, M. J., Amorim, J. H., Calfapietra, C., Freer-Smith, P., Grimmond, S., Kotthaus, S., de Oliviera, L., Miranda, A. I., & Toscano, P. (2015). The impacts of green infrastructure on air quality and temperature. In Sinnett, D., Smith, N., & Burgess, S. (Eds.), *Handbook on Green Infrastructure: Planning, Design and Implementation* (pp. 30–49). Edward Elgar Publishing., DOI: 10.4337/9781783474004.00008

Tamaş, I. (2024). Strategic Development in IT Sector.

Tanasescu, M. (2020). Nature Advocacy in the Ecuadorian Amazon: The Sarayaku Case. *Journal of Human Rights and the Environment*, *11*(1), 36–56.

Tancara, C. (1993). La investigación documental. *Temas Sociales*(17), 91-106. Obtenido de http://www.scielo.org.bo/scielo.php?script=sci_arttext&pid=S0040-29151993000100008

Taneja, H., & Chenault, K. (2019). Building a startup that will last. *Harvard Business Review*, *7*, 23–27.

Tan, S. C., Chan, C., Bielaczyc, K., Ma, L., Scardamalia, M., & Bereiter, C. (2021). Knowledge building: Aligning education with needs for knowledge creation in the digital age. *Educational Technology Research and Development*, *69*(4), 2243–2266. DOI: 10.1007/s11423-020-09914-x

Tan, W., & Cao, T. (2023). Can green technology reduce carbon dioxide emissions? Evidence from G7 and BRICS countries. *Heliyon*, *9*(5, e15683), 1–10. DOI: 10.1016/j.heliyon.2023.e15683 PMID: 37305514

Tapscott, D., & Tapscott, A. (2016). *Blockchain Revolution: How the Technology Behind Bitcoin Changes Money, Business, and the World.* Penguin.

Tarasova, O. V., Stindl, P., Yom, J., Chardymova, N., Imre, S.-B., & Valek, L. (2020). Integration of Non-Formal Learning Approaches into the Formal Education by Peer Learning of Teachers and Youth Workers. Revista Romaneasca pentru Educatie Multidimensionala, 12, 345-365. https://doi.org/https://doi.org/10.18662/rrem/12.1sup1/239

Tariq, M. U. (2024). Integrating ESG Principles Into Corporate Governance for Sustainable Ecosystem Services. In Castanho, R. (Ed.), *ESG and Ecosystem Services for Sustainability* (pp. 89–118). IGI Global., DOI: 10.4018/979-8-3693-3771-4.ch004

Tariq, M. U. (2024). Smart Transportation Systems: Paving the Way for Sustainable Urban Mobility. In Munuhwa, S. (Ed.), *Contemporary Solutions for Sustainable Transportation Practices* (pp. 254–283). IGI Global., DOI: 10.4018/979-8-3693-3755-4.ch010

Tariq, M. U. (2025). Empowering Learning Through Networked and Connected Education: Case Studies in Digital Engagement. In Gierhart, A. (Ed.), *Cases on Enhancing P-16 Student Engagement With Digital Technologies* (pp. 169–198). IGI Global Scientific Publishing., DOI: 10.4018/979-8-3693-5633-3.ch007

Tariq, M. U. (2025). The Belmont Report: Guiding Ethical Principles in Human Research. In Throne, R. (Ed.), *IRB, Human Research Protections, and Data Ethics for Researchers* (pp. 245–268). IGI Global Scientific Publishing., DOI: 10.4018/979-8-3693-3848-3.ch010

Tariq, M. U., & Sergio, R. P. (2025). Ethical Considerations and Social Impact of AI and Computational Intelligence in Society 5.0. In Pandey, R., Srivastava, N., Prasad, R., Prasad, J., & Garcia, M. (Eds.), *Open AI and Computational Intelligence for Society 5.0* (pp. 225–248). IGI Global Scientific Publishing., DOI: 10.4018/979-8-3693-4326-5.ch010

Tasioulas, S., Watson, J., Kasampalis, D. S., & Tsouvaltzis, P. (2025). Integration of Color Analysis, Firmness Testing, and visNIR Spectroscopy for Comprehensive Tomato Quality Assessment and Shelf-Life Prediction. *Agronomy (Basel)*, *15*(2), 478. DOI: 10.3390/agronomy15020478

Teece, D. J., Pisano, G. & Shuen, A. (1997). Strategic Management and Resources, Firms, and Strategies: A Reader in the Resource-Based Perspective.

Teece, D. J. (1977). Technology transfer by multinational firms: The resource cost of transferring technological know-how. *Economic Journal (London)*, *87*(346), 242–261. DOI: 10.2307/2232084

Teixeira, M. S., Mata, T. M., Lourenço, A., Oliveira, F., Oliveira, J., & Martins, A. A. (2025). Life Cycle Assessment of Tinplate Aerosol Cans: Evaluating the Role of Photovoltaic Energy and Green Hydrogen in Environmental Impact Reduction. *Environments (Basel, Switzerland)*, *12*(3), 73. DOI: 10.3390/environments12030073

Telesca, D. (2018). BP and the Deepwater Horizon Oil Spill: Analyzing ESG Failures. *Business Ethics Quarterly*, *28*(3), 399–420.

Tendero, M., & Bazart, C. (2023). "I can't get no satisfaction": Soil contaminated brownfield redevelopment in France. *Cities (London, England)*, *145*, 104719. DOI: 10.1016/j.cities.2023.104719

Teo, H. C., Zeng, Y., Sarira, T. V., Fung, T. K., Zheng, Q., Song, X. P., Chong, K. Y., & Koh, L. P. (2021). Global urban reforestation can be an important natural climate solution. *Environmental Research Letters*, *16*(3), 034059. DOI: 10.1088/1748-9326/abe783

Tesla. (2020). *Environmental Impact Report.* Retrieved from https://www.tesla.com

Tetteh, F. K., Mensah, J., & Owusu Kwateng, K. (2024). Understanding what, how and when green logistics practices influence carbon-neutral supply chain performance. *International Journal of Productivity and Performance Management.* Advance online publication. DOI: 10.1108/IJPPM-08-2024-0517

The Business Standard. (2022, August 2). Standard Chartered Bangladesh embraces sustainability as a way of life. *The Business Standard.* https://www.tbsnews.net/economy/corporates/standard-chartered-bangladesh-embraces-sustainability-way-life-469986?amp

The Business Standard. (2022, October 10). Singer's $78m green factory aims at growing local electronics market. *The Business Standard.* https://www.tbsnews.net/economy/industry/singers-78m-green-factory-aims-growing-local-electronics-market-511374

The Daily Star. (2017, February 13). Use eco-friendly materials in construction work. *The Daily Star.* https://www.thedailystar.net/city/eco-friendly-materials-construction-work-stressed-1360285

The Economist (2012, October 13). *True Progressivism.* Retrieved from https://www.economist.com/leaders/2012/10/13/true-progressivism

The Financial Express. (2020, April 15). BB introduces €200m green transformation fund. *The Financial Express.* https://thefinancialexpress.com.bd/trade/bb-introduces-200m-green-transformation-fund-1586956071

The London School of Economics and Political Science & Grantham Research Institute on Climate Change and the Environment. (2017). Sue major polluters for climate compensation - and ask Exxon to pay for Harvey's damages says Jeffrey Sachs. Retrieved on-line from https://www.lse.ac.uk/granthaminstitute/news/sue-major-polluters-for-climate-compensation-and-ask-exxon-to-pay-for-harveys-damages-says-jeff-sachs/. Accessed on the 28th of January 2025.

Thelken, H. N., & de Jong, G. (2020). The impact of values and future orientation on intention formation within sustainable entrepreneurship. *Journal of Cleaner Production*, *266*, 122052. DOI: 10.1016/j.jclepro.2020.122052

Thomas, H., & Howarth, C. J. (2000). Five ways to stay green. *Journal of Experimental Botany*, *51*(Spec No, suppl_1), 329–337. DOI: 10.1093/jexbot/51.suppl_1.329 PMID: 10938840

Thomas, M. R. (2003). Brownfield redevelopment: Information issues and the affected public. *Environmental Practice*, *5*(1), 62–68. DOI: 10.1017/S1466046603030175

Tilbury, D. (2011). *Education for sustainable development: An expert review of processes and learning.* UNESCO.

Todino, M. D., Campitiello, L., & Di Tore, S. (2023). Simplexity to Improve Human-Machine Interaction in 3D Virtual Reality. [IJDLDC]. *International Journal of Digital Literacy and Digital Competence*, *14*(1), 1–8. DOI: 10.4018/IJDLDC.330423

Touya, G., Courtial, A., Kalsron, J., Berli, J., Le Mao, B., & Wenclik, L. (2025). Understanding the Carbon Footprint of Tile Transfer for Web Maps. *ISPRS International Journal of Geo-Information*, *14*(3), 107. DOI: 10.3390/ijgi14030107

Townsend, J., Moola, F., & Craig, M. K. (2020). Indigenous Peoples are critical to the success of nature-based solutions to climate change. *Facets*, *5*(1), 551–556. DOI: 10.1139/facets-2019-0058

Tranfield, D., Denyer, D., & Smart, P. (2003). Towards a methodology for developing evidence-informed management knowledge by means of systematic review. *British Journal of Management*, *14*(3), 207–222. DOI: 10.1111/1467-8551.00375

Tsai, S., Liu, B., & Li, Y. (Eds.). (2018). *Green Production Strategies for Sustainability.* IGI Global., DOI: 10.4018/978-1-5225-3537-9

Tshivhase, M., & Bisschoff, C. A. (2024). Investigating green initiatives at South African public universities. *Nurture*, *18*(2), 245–263. DOI: 10.55951/nurture.v18i2.599

Tsionis G. (2015). European building inventory framework. EUR 27603. Luxembourg (Luxembourg): Publications Office of the European Union. JRC98981.

Tuhin, A. R. (2022, September 12). Fatullah Apparels turns into an iconic green factory. *The Business Post*. https://businesspostbd.com/back/fatullah-apparels-turns-into-an-iconic-green-factory-2022-09-13

Tulloch, L. (2013). On science, ecology and environmentalism. *Policy Futures in Education*, *11*(1), 100–114. DOI: 10.2304/pfie.2013.11.1.100

Tumaku, J. (2024). The relationship between regulatory focus and innovative performance of SMEs in Ghana: The role of entrepreneurial resilience, orientation and learning. *Management Science Letters*, *14*(2), 127–138. DOI: 10.5267/j.msl.2023.9.001

Tunio, M. (2024). *Impact Of Talent Management On Organizational Sustainable Performance: A Moderating Role Of Process Innovation*. https://doi.org/DOI: 10.53555/kuey.v30i5.3458

Tunio, M., Abdul Hamid, A. B., Abdul Latiff, A. S., & Hafeez, M. (2023). Unlocking Organizational Sustainability: The Role of Talent Management through the Lens of the AMO Theory. *Pakistan Journal of Humanities and Social Sciences*. https://doi.org/DOI: 10.52131/pjhss.2023.1103.0634

Tunio, M. N., Rashid, A., Qureshi, M., Qureshi, J. A., & Rasheed, R. (Eds.). (2025). *Intersecting Entrepreneurship, Internationalization, and Green Innovation*. IGI Global., DOI: 10.4018/979-8-3693-9241-6

Turkson, F. E., Amissah, E., & Gyeke-Dako, A. (2022). The role of formal and informal finance in the informal sector in Ghana. *Journal of Small Business and Entrepreneurship*, *34*(3), 333–356. DOI: 10.1080/08276331.2020.1724002

Tzortzaki, A., & Mihiotis, A. (2014). A Review of Knowledge management Theory and Future Directions. *Knowledge and Process Management*, *21*(1), 29–41. DOI: 10.1002/kpm.1429

Uddin, J. (2019, August 27). Envoy of green textiles. *The Business Standard*. https://www.tbsnews.net/economy/envoy-green-textiles

UNDP. (2015). *UNDP Procurement Strategy 2015–2017*. New York: NY: United Nations Development Programme. https://www.undp.org/procurement/strategy

UNEP. (2022). Action on the triple planetary crisis. Retrieved from https://www.unep.org/news-and-stories/speech/action-triple-planetary-crisis

UNEP/SETAC Life Cycle Initiative. (2011, February 26). *Towards a life cycle sustainability assessment: making informed choices on products*. https://www.unep.org/resources/report/towards-life-cycle-sustainability-assessment-making-informed-choices-products (accessed on June 21, 2024)

UNESCO. (2014). *Roadmap for Implementing the Global Action Programme on Education for Sustainable Development*. UNESCO.

UNESCO. (2018). UNESCO's ICT Competency Framework for Teachers. https://www.unesco.org/en/digital-competencies-skills/ict-cft

UNESCO. (2020). *Education for Sustainable Development: A Crucial Instrument for Achieving the Sustainable Development Goals*. UNESCO.

UNESCO. (2024). UNESCO's Education for Sustainable Development (ESD). https://www.unesco.org/en/sustainable-development/education

Unidas, N. (2024). Obtenido de https://www.un.org/es/about-us

Unilever. (2020). *Sustainable Living Plan: Annual Report*. Retrieved from https://www.unilever.com

Unilever. (2020). *Sustainable Living Plan: Progress Report*. Retrieved from https://www.unilever.com

Unilever. (2020). *Unilever Sustainable Living Plan Progress Report*. https://www.unilever.com/sustainable-living/

United Nations Conference on Trade and Development (UNCTAD). (2014). Investor-State Dispute Settlement. UNCTAD Series on Issues in International Investment. Agreements II. United Nations. New York and Geneva, 2014.

United Nations Environment Programme. (2020). *Greening Fiscal Stimulus and Finance Packages to Achieve the SDGs - UNEP Factsheet.*https://wedocs.unep.org/20.500.11822/32280

United Nations General Assembly. (2022). "Resolution A/76/L.75: The human right to a clean, healthy and sustainable Environment. Retrieved from https://digitallibrary.un.org/record/3983329?ln=en&v=pdf

United Nations Office for Disaster Risk Reduction (UNISDR). (2015). *Making development sustainable: The future of disaster risk management. Global Assessment Report on Disaster Risk Reduction.* Geneva, Switzerland: UNISDR. https://www.preventionweb.net/files/43847_01efdrr07oct2015franceandrewmaskrey.pdf?startDownload=true

United Nations. (1972). United Nations Conference on the Human Environment. Retrieved from https://docs.un.org/en/A/CONF.48/14/Rev.1

United Nations. (2015). A/RES/70/1: Transformar nuestro mundo: La Agenda 2030 para el Desarrollo Sostenible [Transforming our world: The 2030 Agenda for Sustainable Development]. Retrieved from https://ggim.un.org/documents/A_Res_70_1_s.pdf

United Nations. (2015). Transforming Our World: The 2030 Agenda for Sustainable Development.

United Nations. (2015). *Transforming Our World: The 2030 Agenda for Sustainable Development*. Retrieved from https://sdgs.un.org/2030agenda

United Nations. (2015). *Transforming our world: the 2030 Agenda for Sustainable Development*. Retrieved from https://www.un.org/sustainabledevelopment/sustainable-development-goals/

United Nations. (2022). Declaración sobre los Derechos a un Medio Ambiente Saludable [Declaration on the Rights to a Healthy Environment]. Retrieved from https://www.ohchr.org/sites/default/files/documents/issues/climatechange/information-materials/r2heinfofinalweb-sp.pdf

United Nations. (2022). The human right to a clean, healthy and sustainable environment. Retrieved from https://digitallibrary.un.org/record/3982508?ln=es&v=pdf

United Nations. (2024). En primera línea contra la desertización [On the front line against desertification]. Retrieved from https://news.un.org/es/story/2024/12/1534941

Universidad de las Americas. (2014). Ejecucion de la sentencia en el caso Chevron Corporation en el ambito internacional. In Garcia, L. V. (Ed.), *Ejecucion de la sentencia en el caso Chevron Corporation en el ambito internacional.*

University of Exeter. (2020). *Sustainability in Business Education: Case Studies and Best Practices.* University Reports.

Uvarova, I., Mavlutova, I., & Atstaja, D. (2021). Development of the green entrepreneurial mindset through modern entrepreneurship education. []. IOP Publishing.]. *IOP Conference Series. Earth and Environmental Science*, *628*(1), 012034. DOI: 10.1088/1755-1315/628/1/012034

Uy, N., Tapnio, C., & Dineros, A. (2022). Ecosystem-based risk reduction in policy and practice. In Shaw, R. (Ed.), *Handbook on Climate Change and Disasters* (pp. 249–267). Edward Elgar Publishing., DOI: 10.4337/9781800371613.00031

Vaiman, V., Cascio, W. F., Collings, D. G., & Swider, B. W. (2021). The shifting boundaries of talent management. *Human Resource Management*, *60*(2), 253–257. DOI: 10.1002/hrm.22050

Valle, C., Alves Pacheco de Campos, S., Klein, L. L., Rizzetti, D. M., & da Silva Sotero, N. (2024). The contributions of green people management to the development of organizational competencies for sustainability. *Social Responsibility Journal*, *20*(9), 1724–1746. DOI: 10.1108/SRJ-09-2023-0496

Van der Westhuizen, T. (2023). *Youth Entrepreneurship: An Ecosystem Theory for Young Entrepreneurs in South Africa and Beyond.* Springer Nature. DOI: 10.1007/978-3-031-44339-8

Van der Westhuizen, T. (2024). *Practical Tools for Youth Entrepreneurs: An Applied Approach for South Africa and Beyond.* Springer Nature. DOI: 10.1007/978-3-031-44362-6

Van Tulder, R., & Keen, N. (2018). Capturing Collaborative Challenges: Designing Complexity-Sensitive Theories of Change for Cross-Sector Partnerships. *Journal of Business Ethics*, *150*(2), 315–332. DOI: 10.1007/s10551-018-3857-7 PMID: 30996500

Van Tulder, R., Seitanidi, M. M., Crane, A., & Brammer, S. (2016). Enhancing the Impact of Cross-Sector Partnerships. Four Impact Loops for Channeling Partnership Studies. *Journal of Business Ethics*, *135*(1), 1–17. DOI: 10.1007/s10551-015-2756-4

Van Tulder, R., & Van Mil, E. (2023). *Principles of Sustainable Business – Frameworks for Corporate Action on the SDGs.* Routledge.

Vanham, D., Leip, A., Galli, A., Kastner, T., Bruckner, M., Uwizeye, A., van Dijk, K., Ercin, E., Dalin, C., Brandão, M., Bastianoni, S., Fang, K., Leach, A., Chapagain, A., Van der Velde, M., Sala, S., Pant, R., Mancini, L., Monforti-Ferrario, F., & Hoekstra, A. Y. (2019). Environmental footprint family to address local to planetary sustainability and deliver on the SDGs. *The Science of the Total Environment*, *693*(November), 133642. DOI: 10.1016/j.scitotenv.2019.133642 PMID: 31635013

Vargas, A., Herrera, I., Nualart, N., Guézou, A., Gómez-Bellver, C., Freire, E., Jaramillo Díaz, P., & López-Pujol, J. (2022). The Genus *Kalanchoe* (Crassulaceae) in Ecuador: From Gardens to the Wild. *Plants*, *11*(13), 1746. DOI: 10.3390/plants11131746 PMID: 35807700

Vásconez-González, J., Izquierdo-Condoy, J. S., Fernandez-Naranjo, R., Gamez-Rivera, E., Tello-De-la-Torre, A., Guerrero-Castillo, G. S., Ruiz-Sosa, C., & Ortiz-Prado, E. (2023). Severe Chagas disease in Ecuador: A countrywide geodemographic epidemiological analysis from 2011 to 2021. *Frontiers in Public Health*, *11*, 1172955. DOI: 10.3389/fpubh.2023.1172955 PMID: 37143984

Vega, L. (2013). Dimensión Ambiental, Desarrollo Sostenible y Sostenibilidad Ambiental del Desarrollo. *Eleventh LACCEI Latin American and Caribbean Conference for Engineering and Technology (LACCEI'2013)*. Obtenido de https://www.laccei.org/LACCEI2013-Cancun/RefereedPapers/RP256.pdf

Velenturf, A. P. M., & Purnell, P. (2021). Principles for a sustainable circular economy. *Sustainable Production and Consumption*, *27*(July), 1437–1457. DOI: 10.1016/j.spc.2021.02.018

Venesaar, U., Malleus, E., Arro, G., & Toding, M. (2021). Entrepreneurship competence model for supporting learners development at all educational levels. *Administrative Sciences*, *12*(1), 2. DOI: 10.3390/admsci12010002

Venn, R., Perez, P., & Vandenbussche, V. (2022). Competencies of sustainability professionals: An empirical study on key competencies for sustainability. *Sustainability (Basel)*, *14*(9), 4916. DOI: 10.3390/su14094916

Vera-Arias, C. A., Castro, L. E., Gómez-Obando, J., & Sáenz, F. E. (2019). Diverse origin of Plasmodium falciparum in northwest Ecuador. *Malaria Journal*, *18*(1), 251. DOI: 10.1186/s12936-019-2891-y PMID: 31349843

Vesperi, W., Gagnidze, I., & Soboleva, T. (2024). Understanding the impact of the ecological transaction on the human capital of university students: A cross-country analysis. Conference: 8th FEB International Scientific Conference: Challenges in the Turbulent Economic Environment and Organizations' Sustainable Development At: Maribor University, Maribor, Slovenia. DOI: 10.18690/um.epf.5.2024.37

Victar, H. C., Perera, B. A. K. S., Palihakkara, A. D., & Dewagod, K. G. (2024). Roles and competencies of quantity surveyors in achieving a circular built environment: An investigation according to 3R principles. *Smart and Sustainable Built Environment*, *13*(4), 1015–1040. DOI: 10.1108/SASBE-10-2022-0231

Victor, P. A. (2010). Ecological economics and economic growth. *Annals of the New York Academy of Sciences*, *1185*(1), 237–245. DOI: 10.1111/j.1749-6632.2009.05284.x PMID: 20146773

Victor, P. A. (2019). *Managing Without Growth: Slower by Design, Not Disaster* (2nd ed.). Edward Elgar Publishing., DOI: 10.4337/9781785367380

Vilcins, D., Sly, P. D., Scarth, P., & Mavoa, S. (2022). Green space in health research: An overview of common indicators of greenness. *Reviews on Environmental Health*, *39*(2), 221–231. DOI: 10.1515/reveh-2022-0083 PMID: 36372560

Viphanova, G., Voronina, N., & Vedysheva, N. (2021). Training of sustainable development specialists within the environmental education system. *E3s Web of Conferences*, 295, 05013. DOI: 10.1051/e3sconf/202129505013

Voica, M. C., Panait, M., & Radulescu, I. (2015). Green Investments – Between Necessity, Fiscal Constraints and Profit. *Procedia Economics and Finance*, *22*, 72–79. DOI: 10.1016/S2212-5671(15)00228-2

Von Krogh, G., Nonaka, I., & Aben, M. (2001). Making the most of your company's knowledge: A strategic framework. *Long Range Planning*, *34*(4), 421–439. DOI: 10.1016/S0024-6301(01)00059-0

Vuorikari, R., Kluzer, S., & Punie, Y. (2022). DigComp 2.2: The Digital Competence Framework for Citizens - With new examples of knowledge, skills and attitudes, EUR 31006 EN, Publications Office of the European Union, Luxembourg. ISBN 978-92-76-48883-5, , JRC128415.DOI: 10.2760/490274

Wackernagel, M., Schulz, N. B., Deumling, D., Linares, A. C., Jenkins, M., Kapos, V., Monfreda, C., Loh, J., Myers, N., Norgaard, R., & Randers, J. (2002). Tracking the ecological overshoot of the human economy. *Proceedings of the National Academy of Sciences of the United States of America*, *99*(14), 9266–9271. DOI: 10.1073/pnas.142033699 PMID: 12089326

Wang, H. (2024). ESG investment preference and fund vulnerability. *International Review of Financial Analysis*, *91*, 103002. DOI: 10.1016/j.irfa.2023.103002

Wang, H., Jiao, S., & Ma, C. (2024). The impact of ESG responsibility performance on corporate resilience. *International Review of Economics & Finance*, *93*, 1115–1129. DOI: 10.1016/j.iref.2024.05.033

Wang, J., Ke, Y., & Shen, Y. (2023). Venture Capital and ESG Performance: Hindrance or Help? *Economic Computation and Economic Cybernetics Studies and Research*, *57*(4/2023), 4. DOI: 10.24818/18423264/57.4.23.16

Wang, L., Fang, L., & Hipel, K. W. (2009). Negotiation over Costs and Benefits in Brownfield Redevelopment. *Group Decision and Negotiation*, *20*(4), 509–524. DOI: 10.1007/s10726-009-9179-5

Wang, W., Wen, H., Zhao, C., Ma, X., Liao, J., & Ma, L. (2024). Green space modified the association between air pollutants and hypertension in China. *International Journal of Environmental Health Research*, *34*(9), 3232–3244. DOI: 10.1080/09603123.2023.2300047 PMID: 38171020

Wang, X., Quirke, M., & McGuckin, C. (2022). The Importance of Social Competence for 21st Century Citizens: The Use of Mixed Reality for Social Competence Learning in Mainstream Education. In Correia, A., & Viegas, V. (Eds.), *Methodologies and Use Cases on Extended Reality for Training and Education* (pp. 242–268). IGI Global Scientific Publishing., DOI: 10.4018/978-1-6684-3398-0.ch010

Wawer, M. (2023). Shaping sustainable development competencies through student internships. *Scientific Papers of Silesian University of Technology Organization and Management Series*, *2023*(170), 595–628. DOI: 10.29119/1641-3466.2023.170.37

WBCSD. (2022). Roadmap to ESG leadership. Available at https://www.wbcsd.org/wp-content/uploads/2023/10/Roadmap-to-ESG-Leadership-English.pdf. Accessed on February 12th, 2025.

WEF. (2020). The Global Risks Report 2020. https://www.weforum.org/reports/the-global-risks-report-2020/

Wenger, E. (1998). Community of practice: A brief introduction. *Learning in Doing*, *15*(4), 1–7.

Wesselink, R., Blok, V., Leur, S., Lans, T., & Dentoni, D. (2015). Individual competencies for managers engaged in corporate sustainable management practices. *Journal of Cleaner Production*, *106*, 497–506. DOI: 10.1016/j.jclepro.2014.10.093

Weygandt, J. J., Kimmel, P. D., & Kieso, D. E. (2013). *Financial Accounting*. IFRS Edition (2nd Ed.). John Willey & Sons, Inc.

Whitebell. (2022). Sustainability is all about systems-thinking—here's why. https://www.rit.edu/sustainabilityinstitute/blog/sustainability-all-about-systems-thinking-heres-why

Whitmee, S., Haines, A., Beyrer, C., Boltz, F., Capon, A. G., Ferreira de Souza Dias, B., Ezeh, A., & Frumkin, H. (2015). Safeguarding human health in the Anthropocene epoch: Report of The Rockefeller Foundation–Lancet Commission on planetary health. *Lancet*, *386*(10007), 1973–2028. DOI: 10.1016/S0140-6736(15)60901-1 PMID: 26188744

Whysall, Z., Owtram, M., & Brittain, S. (2019). The new talent management challenges of Industry 4.0. *Journal of Management Development*, *38*(2), 118–129. DOI: 10.1108/JMD-06-2018-0181

Wiek, A., Withycombe Keeler, L., & Redman, C. L. (2020). Moving Forward: Advancing Key Competencies for Sustainability Education. *Journal of Sustainability Science*, *15*(2), 201–220.

Wielewska, I., Kacprzak, M., Król, A., Czech, A., Zuzek, D., Gralak, K., . . . Marks-Bielska, R. (2023). Green human resource management. *Ekonomia I Środowisko - Economics and Environment, 83*(4), 276-302. DOI: 10.34659/eis.2022.83.4.496

Wilcox, B. A., & Ellis, B. (2006). Forests and emerging infectious diseases of humans. *Unasylva*, *57*, 11–18. https://www.fao.org/3/a0789e/a0789e03.htm

Williamson, O. E. (1981). *Markets and Hierarchies: Analysis and Antitrust Implications*. Free Press.

Williamson, O. E. (1985). *The economic institutions of capitalism: Firms, markets, relational contracting*. Free Press.

Williamson, O. E. (1996). *The Mechanisms of Governance*. Oxford University Press. DOI: 10.1093/oso/9780195078244.001.0001

Wooldridge, J. M. (2010). *Econometric analysis of cross section and panel data*. MIT Press.

World Bank. (2017). *World Development Report 2017: Governance and the Law*. World Bank.

World Bank. (2023). *Global talent migration and healthcare workforce sustainability: Trends and policy recommendations*.

World Economic Forum. (2022). ESG Pulse Check: Getting the Basics Right for Start-ups and Venture Capital Firms. Insight Report. Available at https://www3.weforum.org/docs/WEF_ESG_Pulse_Check_2022.pdf. Accessed on February, 10th, 2025.

Wurtmann, H., & Seuring, S. (2020). Managing Climate Change Risks in Global Supply Chains: A Review and Research Agenda. *International Journal of Production Research, 58*(1), 44–64. DOI: 10.1080/00207543.2019.1629670

Wu, X., Lu, Y., Zhou, S., Chen, L., & Xu, B. (2016). Impact of climate change on human infectious diseases: Empirical evidence and human adaptation. *Environment International, 86*, 14–23. DOI: 10.1016/j.envint.2015.09.007 PMID: 26479830

Xin, X., Li, P., Tang, L., & Xu, A. (2025). Entrepreneurship and Education: An Analysis of the Impact of Compulsory Education Policies in Counties in China. *Sustainability (Basel), 17*(4), 1639. DOI: 10.3390/su17041639

Xiong, Q., Fosfuri, A., Misani, N., & Cheng, Y. (2024). Greening the Portfolio: LP Preferences for Social Impact and Sustainability Orientation of VC Funds. In Academy of Management Proceedings (Vol. 2024, No. 1, p. 16245). Valhalla, NY 10595: Academy of Management.

Xuemin, M., Widerman, B., & Kelana, B. Y. (2024). The relationship between green management of organizational culture, green behavior and green campus in private universities: A conceptual paper. *International Journal of Academic Research in Business & Social Sciences, 14*(6). Advance online publication. DOI: 10.6007/IJARBSS/v14-i6/21813

Yacovone, K. (2011). Brownfields and the poor: Is clean-up a hazardous waste of time? An analysis of the United States' efforts at remediation and their applicability to Brazil. *Fordham International Law Journal, 35(1)*, 201-247. ISSN 0747-9395.

Yadegaridehkordi, E., Foroughi, B., Iranmanesh, M., Nilashi, M., & Ghobakhloo, M. (2023). Determinants of environmental, financial, and social sustainable performance of manufacturing SMEs in Malaysia. *Sustainable Production and Consumption, 35*, 129–140. DOI: 10.1016/j.spc.2022.10.026

Yafi, E., Tehseen, S., & Haider, S. (2021). Impact of green training on environmental performance through mediating role of competencies and motivation. *Sustainability (Basel), 13*(10), 5624. DOI: 10.3390/su13105624

Yang, H.. (2023). Hybrid Machine Learning Models for Anomaly Detection in Traffic Patterns. *Neural Computing & Applications.*

Ycaza, A., Baquerizo, V., Vallejo, J., & Valero, G. (2022). Analysis of the Traditional Gastronomic Offer as an Engine for Local Tourism Development: Guayas, Ecuador. In Pinto Borges, A., Lopes de Almeida, A., Vieira, E., Dias, R., & Rodrigues, P. (Eds.), *Gastronomy, Hospitality, and the Future of the Restaurant Industry: Post-COVID-19 Perspectives* (pp. 48–70). IGI Global Scientific Publishing., DOI: 10.4018/978-1-7998-9148-2.ch003

Yeoh, C. B., Lee, K. J., Coric, V., & Tollinche, L. E. (2020). Simple Green Changes for Anesthesia Practices to Make a Difference. *EC clinical and medical case reports, 3*(12), 1–6.

Yerlitas, T., & Bučiūnienė, I. (2024). Sustaining Human Capital in an Organization: The Role of Talent Management. *Edukacja Ekonomistów i Menedżerów, 71*(1). Advance online publication. DOI: 10.33119/EEIM.2024.71.3

Yildirim, S. (2022). The Consumer Role for Sustainable Development: How Consumers Contribute Sustainable Development Goals. In I. Management Association (Ed.), *Research Anthology on Measuring and Achieving Sustainable Development Goals* (pp. 872-888). IGI Global Scientific Publishing. https://doi.org/DOI: 10.4018/978-1-6684-3885-5.ch047

Yildirim, S., & Bostanci, S. H. (2022). Digital Transformation in Public Services: A Review of Turkey During the COVID-19 Pandemic. In Marchisio, E. (Ed.), *Handbook of Research on Applying Emerging Technologies Across Multiple Disciplines* (pp. 30–54). IGI Global Scientific Publishing., DOI: 10.4018/978-1-7998-8476-7.ch003

Yin, L., Yu, L., Guo, Y., Wang, C., Ge, Y., Zheng, X., Zhang, N., You, J., Zhang, Y., & Shi, M. (2024). Green analytical chemistry metrics for evaluating the greenness of analytical procedures. *Journal of Pharmaceutical Analysis*, *14*(11), 101013. DOI: 10.1016/j.jpha.2024.101013 PMID: 39759968

Yin, R. K. (2018). *Case Study Research and Applications: Design and Methods*. Sage publications.

Yoo, D. Y. (2024). Eco-Leadership in Action: Integrating Green HRM and the New Ecological Paradigm to Foster Organizational Commitment and Environmental Citizenship in the Hospitality Industry. *Sustainability (Basel)*, *16*(20), 9044. DOI: 10.3390/su16209044

Yoshino, N., & Taghizadeh-Hesary, F. (2018). Alternatives to Private Finance: Role of Fiscal Policy Reforms and Energy Taxation in Development of Renewable Energy Projects. In Anbumozhi, V., Kalirajan, K., & Kimura, F. (Eds.), *Financing for Low-carbon Energy Transition: Unlocking the Potential of Private Capital* (pp. 335–357). Springer Nature., DOI: 10.1007/978-981-10-8582-6_13

Yu, P. K., Settlement, I.-S. D., & the Trans-Pacific Partnership. (August 23, 2018). Intellectual Property And The Judiciary, Christophe Geiger, Craig Allen Nard and Xavier Seuba, eds., Edward Elgar Publishing, pp. 463-93, 2018, Texas A&M University School of Law Legal Studies Research Paper No. 18-32, Available at SSRN: https://ssrn.com/abstract=3237541

Yuan, Y., Tian, G., Lu, L., & Yu, Y. (2019). CEO Ability and Corporate Social Responsibility. *Journal of Business Ethics*, *157*(2), 391–411. DOI: 10.1007/s10551-017-3622-3

Yücel, D. (2024). *Enhancing Organizational Sustainability: The Role of Total Quality Management in Fostering Talent Management Practices*. Sosyal Mucit Academic Review., DOI: 10.54733/smar.1438949

Yu, W., Yu, J., & Chen, X. (2025). Research on the Mechanism of the Influence of Farm Scale on the Environmental Efficiency of Apple Production—Tests Based on a Life Cycle Assessment Perspective. *Land (Basel)*, *14*(3), 516. DOI: 10.3390/land14030516

Zack, M. H. (1999). Developing a knowledge strategy. *California Management Review*, *41*(3), 125–145. DOI: 10.2307/41166000

Zamarský, V., Tylčer, J., & Střelec, T. (2011b). *Regeneration of Industrial Areas*. VŠB–TU Ostrava.

Zareba, M. (2025). Assessing the Role of Energy Mix in Long-Term Air Pollution Trends: Initial Evidence from Poland. *Energies*, *18*(5), 1211. DOI: 10.3390/en18051211

Zavřelová, V., & MacGregor Pelikánová, R. (2024). The ephemeral term "sustainable development" in current EU policies. *Folia Oeconomica Stetinensia*, *24*(2), 389–418. DOI: 10.2478/foli-2024-0031

Zengler, T. (2021). The Impact of Innovation on Tesla's ESG Performance. *Technology and Innovation*, *24*(4), 255–267.

Zhang, W., et al. (2023). *5G Network Deployment in Intelligent Traffic Systems: Opportunities and Challenges*. IEEE Access.

Zhang, Y.. (2021). Deep Learning-Based Real-Time Vehicle Classification for Urban Traffic Applications. *Transportation Research Part C, Emerging Technologies*.

Zhang, Ye. (2022). Startups' Strategies for ESG Funding Adoption. Available at *SSRN*: https://ssrn.com/abstract=4239239 or http://dx.doi.org/DOI: 10.2139/ssrn.4239239

Zhang, Z., Wang, X., & Jia, M. (2021). Echoes of CEO Entrepreneurial Orientation: How and When CEO Entrepreneurial Orientation Influences Dual CSR Activities. *Journal of Business Ethics*, *169*(4), 609–629. DOI: 10.1007/s10551-020-04553-x

Zhelev, Y., Monova-Zheleva, M., & Sabotinova, D. (2023). Workshop "Promoting the green transition through university education on green standards". *Digital Presentation and Preservation of Cultural and Scientific Heritage*, *13*, 353–358. DOI: 10.55630/dipp.2023.13.37

Zhou, Y., Yang, J., & Zheng, Z. (2018). Smart Grids and AI: Towards Sustainable Energy. *IEEE Access : Practical Innovations, Open Solutions*, *6*, 25217–25228. DOI: 10.1109/ACCESS.2018.2839026

Ziaesaeidi, P. (2025). 'Relax Underneath the Trees and Read a Book': Exploring Social Sustainability in Parks Through the Lens of Young People. *Sustainability (Basel)*, *17*(5), 2138. DOI: 10.3390/su17052138

Zibarras, L. D., & Coan, P. (2015). HRM Practices Used to Promote Pro-Environmental Behavior: A UK Survey. *International Journal of Human Resource Management*, *26*(16), 2121–2142. DOI: 10.1080/09585192.2014.972429

Zournatzidou, G., Ragazou, K., Sklavos, G., & Sariannidis, N. (2024). Linking HRM With Sustainability. *Advances in Human Resources Management and Organizational Development Book Series*, 281–304. https://doi.org/DOI: 10.4018/979-8-3693-5981-5.ch012

Zubair, S. (2021). *Talent abuse: challenges turning talent management into talent abuse. 5*(2).

Zubizarreta, J. H., & Ramiro, P. (2016). *Contra la lex mercatoria*. Ed. Icaria.

# About the Contributors

**Jarmila Duháček Šebestová** is Associate Professor at Silesian University in Opava, School of Business Administration in Karviná, Czechia. She is an experienced researcher focusing on not only on small businesses, non-profit organizations and social enterprises. She has participated in a number of international projects, including IPREG (Innovative Policy Research for Economic Growth) and the E-WORLD project (International Entrepreneurs Network), COST project, named Transnational Collaboration on Bullying, Migration and Integration at School Level (CA18115). She is Vice President of the European Council of Small Businesses for the Czech Republic promoting research activities within that area. Research interests: Small business performance, start-ups, non-profits evaluation, and social enterprises, in more detail: Entrepreneurship:Start up, Lean Canvas model, Discussion about business idea, Idea development. Non-profit organization management: Non-profit sector, how to deal with public money support, how to apply for project, volunteerism, donations Business Economics: Planning business activities, cost and revenues, budgeting, production time planning, cost calculation, stock planning. She has an experience with IGI chapters contribution, also reviewing chapters and finally editing one book.

**Cristina Raluca Gh. Popescu** is Full-Professor Habil. at the University of Bucharest, Bucharest, Romania, PhD. Supervisor and Doctoral School Member at The Bucharest University of Economic Studies, Bucharest, Romania, and an Award-Winning Scientific Researcher. Having more than 23 years of experience, focuses on helping students learn and apply the subjects more effectively, and centers on improving scientific research excellence. Values a special environment where her in-depth knowledge of creative thinking and academic writing can help deliver accurate research results. She is focused on becoming an outstanding researcher, centered on interdisciplinary topics, in a multicultural environment, constantly driven by passion in promoting the Sustainable Development Goals (SDGs). Showing a positive attitude in exploring the endless possibilities of the transformative power of individuals deeply concerned with health and well-being, education, innovation, and responsible production and consumption may be found among the top priorities on her agenda. Her most important skills are: analytical ability and foresight, attention to detail, collaborative spirit, communication skills, creativity, critical thinking, flexibility, intellectual courage, objectivity, persistence, time management, and thirst for knowledge. She is deeply centered on adopting a healthy and balanced lifestyle, thus improving efficiency and productivity in order to be a good and valuable researcher. She is skilled in Business Administration, Economics, Management, Accounting, and Audit. Collaborations: The National Institute for Research and Development in Environmental Protection (I.N.C.D.P.M.), Romania; National Research and Development Institute for Gas Turbines COMOTI, Romania; University of Craiova, Romania; Ministry of Research and Innovation, Romania. She is Member of Chamber of Financial Auditors of Romania (CAFR), Romania as Financial Auditor, and Member of Authority for the Public Oversight of the Statutory Audit Activity (ASPAAS), Ministry of Public Finance, Romania as Financial Auditor. Single author and coauthor of more than 400 scientific works, with national and international publishers, having national and international coauthors: books, book chapters, articles, congress, conference, and symposium papers. She has more than 3000 citations in national and international publications. Single author and coauthor of numerous scientific works indexed in WorldCat – the world's largest library catalog. Editor and Editorial Advisory Board (EAB) Member, IGI Global – Publishing House (Hershey, Pennsylvania, USA). Guest Editor (GE) and Academic Editor (AE), Multidisciplinary Digital Publishing Institute (MDPI, Basel, Switzerland): Mathematics; Sustainability; Journal of Risk and Financial Management (JRFM); Businesses. Guest Editor (GE) and Academic Editor (AE), Emerald Group Publishing (Journal of Management Development), EnPress Publisher, USA (Journal of Infrastructure, Policy and Development (JIPD)). Topic Editor, Multidisciplinary Digital Publishing Institute (MDPI, Basel, Switzerland): Mathematics, Businesses. Editorial Board Member (EBM), Multidisciplinary Digital Publishing Institute (MDPI, Basel, Switzerland): Sustainability. Scientific Committee (SC) Member: International Congress of Management, Economy and Policy (ICOMEP), Turkey, 2022, 2023; Symposium on Migration and Asylum in Turkey, 2022, 2023; International Congress "Multidimensional Sustainability: Transitions and Convergences", Polytechnic Higher Institute of Gaya (ISPGAYA), Portugal, 2022, 2023; 6th International Academic and Professional Congress on Happiness, "Happiness Management. A Social Well-Being Multiplier. Social Marketing and Organizational Communication", University Network of Happiness, University of Salamanca, 2022; 7th International Academic and Professional Congress on Happiness, "The Triple Helix of Social Well-being: Organizational Communication, Social Marketing and Happiness Management", University Network of Happiness, University of Seville, 2023; 2nd International Congress on Teaching Innovation, Education and Knowledge Transfer (CIINECO), 2023; "The 2nd International Symposium on Marketing", Faculty of Economics and Administrative Sciences, Tekirdağ Namık Kemal University, Tekirdağ, Turkey, 2023; "1st International Symposium on Political Science and Public Administration", Faculty of Economics and Administrative Sciences, Tekirdağ Namık Kemal University, Turkey, 2023. Editorial Board (EB) Member: International Journal of Internet Marketing and Advertising (IJIMA), 2022, 2023; Journal of Emerging Economies and Policy (JOEEP), DergiPark, Turkey, 2022, 2023; Journal of Recycling Economy & Sustainability Policy (RESP), Turkey, 2022, 2023. Keynote Speaker/ Invited Speaker: "International Congress of Recycling Economy & Sustainability Policy", Baku Eurasian University, Baku, Azerbaijan, 2023; "13th International Congress on Agriculture, Animal Sciences and Rural Development", Usak University, Turkey, IKSAD Institute of Economic Development and Social Research of Turkey, 2023; "The 2nd International Symposium on Marketing", Faculty of Economics and Administrative Sciences, Tekirdağ Namık Kemal University, Tekirdağ, Turkey, 2023; "1st International Symposium on Political Science and Public Administration", Faculty of Economics and Administrative Sciences, Tekirdağ Namık Kemal University, Turkey, 2023; "6th CIRIEC Colombia Colloquium: Challenges of the Solidarity Economy and its Links with the Popular and Community Economy", Colombia, 2023; "5th CIRIEC Colombia Colloquium, "Local Pacts on Work, Formalization and Consolidation of Circuits in the Social and Solidarity Economy", Medellín, Colombia, 2022; First Ibero-American Conference of Social Economy and Socio-Ecological Innovation, "Ethics, Social Responsibility and Sustainability in Social and Solidarity Economy Companies", Cali, Colombia, 2022; On-line International Congress of Management, Economy and Policy (ICOMEP'22), Ankara Social Sciences University, Düzce University, Trakya University, Bursa Uludağ University, Giresun University, Bandırma Onyedi Eylul University, Istanbul, Turkey, 2022. Reviews for national and international publications: more than 300 reviews. Review Board Member (RBM): IBIMA Conferences and IBIMA Publishing, USA (Journal of E-Government Studies and Best Practices, The MENA Journal of Business Case Studies);

International Conference on Decision making for Small and Medium-Sized Enterprises (DEMSME 2021, 2023); IGI Global – Publishing House (Hershey, Pennsylvania, USA) (Journal of E Business Research (IJEBR)); University of Bucharest (International Journal of Health Economics (IJHE)); The International Academy of Organizational Behavior Management (IAOBM) (International Journal of the Academy of Organizational Behavior Management (IJAOBM)); Multidisciplinary Digital Publishing Institute (MDPI, Basel, Switzerland) (Energies, Economies, Sustainability, Mathematics, Journal of Risk and Financial Management, Businesses, Foods, Microorganisms, Forests, Computation, Agriculture, Water, International Journal of Environmental Research and Public Health, Urban Science, Journal of Open Innovation: Technology, Market, and Complexity, Risks, Agronomy, Symmetry, Administrative Sciences, World, Informatics). Invited Reviewer: Management Decision (MD), Sustainable Development (SD), Corporate Social Responsibility & Environmental Management (CSREM), Journal of Business Economics and Management (JBEM), Engineering Economics (Inzinerine Ekonomika), International Journal of Sustainable Development and Planning (IJSDP), Transformations in Business & Economics (TIBE), Open Research Europe (ORE), Coffee Science (CS), Journal of Management and Economics Research (JMER); Journal of Infrastructure, Policy and Development (JIPD).

***

**Sureshkumar C** received his Master of Engineering in Computer science and engineering from Annamalai University, Chidambaram. He is presently working as an assistant professor in the department of Information Technology, KGiSL Institute of Technology, Coimbatore. He has 13 years of industry, research and teaching experience. He has published papers in International conferences (Paper indexed in IEEE Xplore digital library) and Scopus indexed journal. His research interests includes |Distributed systems |Data Science and Big data.

**Arun Chakravarthy R** has received his Ph.D. in Information and Communication Engineering under Anna University. His research interest includes RF photonics, Intrusion Detection Systems, Meta-Heuristic Optimization, UAV, Micro-Nano Device Modeling and Simulation

**Deniz Dirik** is an Associate Professor of Management at Manisa Celal Bayar University's Faculty of Economics and Administrative Sciences. She completed her PhD in Organizational Behavior. Her research interests cover topics such as effective leadership, power in organizations, gender at the workplace, psychological ownership, and perceived organizational politics among others. She has been teaching Organizational Behavior, Contemporary Management, Global Business and Human Resource Management at undergraduate and graduate levels.

**Arturo Luque** is full professor at the Technical University of Manabí, Ecuador, and member of Euro-Mediterranean Observatory on Public Policies and Democratic Quality at the University King Juan Carlos (Spain) and visiting Professor at the University of Rosario, Colombia. He holds a Ph.D. in Social Sciences and Law and a Master of two years about Labor Relations. He supervises several doctoral theses (Ph.D.) in Córdoba (Spain) and in the Basque Country (GEZKI Institute) like a director and co-director. It has 96 indexed articles and his latest publications includes topics about digitalization (Practicality, support or premeditated calculation in the digital age: the case of Ecuador), Globalization (Analysis of the concept of informal economy through 102 definitions: legality or necessity), corporate social (Ir) responsibility (How corporate social (ir)responsibility in the textile sector is defined, and its impact on ethical sustainability: An analysis of 133 concepts), transnational companies (The transnational textile companies relationship with environment: a Delphi analysis approach) and their relations with ethics (Corruption in the transnational textile industry: an exception or the rule?), social economy and cooperative system like economic alternative (Socially responsible public management: case spinning development in Ecuador), media analysis and social conflicts (Analysis of the indigenous uprising of Ecuador, 2019: between a measured legal response and lawfare, 2019) and sustainability (Public Strategy and Eco-Social Engagement in Latin American States: An Analysis of Complex Networks Arising from Their Constitutions). Arturo Luque, Technical University of Manabí, Portoviejo, (Ecuador) and Euro-Mediterranean Observatory on Public Policies and Democratic Quality, Rey Juan Carlos University (Spain). Email: arturo.luque@utm.edu.ec

**Sampras Femi Robert** I am currently pursuing a PhD in Remote Work Management at Silesian University in Opava, Czech Republic, where I explore a variety of management dynamics to enhance productivity and employee engagement. My academic journey includes a Master's in Business Economics and Management and a Bachelor's in Mathematics, providing me with a solid analytical foundation for my research and writing.

**Deeksha Gupta Ganguly** is an Assistant Professor, School of Business & Management. She is a Post-graduate in Commerce & Management (Human Resource Management & Marketing). She has also cleared UGC NET in Management. Prof. Ganguly has a rich academic & industry experience of 15 plus years and worked for various Educational institutions & universities in Delhi NCR and Chennai. She is very much involved in academic research and has extensively published research papers in various Scopus-indexed academic journals.

**SSM Sadrul Huda** is an Associate Professor at the Department of Management in the school of Business and Economics, North South University. His current research interest includes, climate change effect, sustainability, business development and entrepreneurship, etc.,

**Arun M** has received his M.Tech in Wireless Sensor Networks from Amrita Vishwa Vidyapeetham, Amrita University, Coimbatore and Ph.D in Electronics and Communication Engineering from Karpagam Academy of Higher Education, Coimbatore. He has about 13 years of teaching experience and his areas of interest include Wireless Sensor Networks, Remote Sensing, Computer Networks, GIS and Basic Electronics.

**Radka MacGregor Pelikánová**, Ph.D., LL.M., MBA (ORCID 0000-0001-9628-7146) is a senior lecturer at Metropolitan University Prague (MUP) and a research lead at the University of New York in Prague (UNYP) with an expertise in law, economics, management, business and intellectual property. She completed the study of law at Charles University School of Law in Prague (Mgr., Ph.D., JUDr.), Université Paris XIII – Villetaneuse in Paris (licence) and Wayne State University in Detroit (LL.M.). In addition, she completed the study of accounting at Washtenaw Community College (Accounting certificate - CTACC) and of economics at the National American University in cooperation with the UNYP (MBA). For over two decades, she has been a member of the Czech Bar Association and the Michigan Bar Association. She has a strong and long-lasting experience providing clients with advice regarding intellectual property, economics and law. During the last fifteen years she has been focusing on academic and publication activities, especially regarding Intellectual Property (IP), EU law, Competition law, Business law, Strategic Management and Knowledge Management. In addition, she is a legal and strategic management advisor at the Ministry of Agriculture of the Czech Republic. She has published over twenty high quality multidisciplinary articles about sustainability, corporate social responsibility (CSR) and creating shared values (CSV) while focusing on the evolution of the interaction of their economic and law aspects in Europe.

**Isaac Nketsiah** is a PhD (Management) candidate at the College of Law & Management Studies, University of Kwazulu-Natal, South Africa. His core research areas include small enterprise management, intellectual property management and research integrity and ethics.

**Burak Özdoğan** is an Associate Professor of Accounting at Manisa Celal Bayar University's Faculty of Economics and Administrative Sciences. He completed his PhD in Accounting. His research interests cover topics such as accounting theory, entrepreneurship, blockchain technology and digital accounting among others. He has been teaching Auditing, Entrepreneurship, Blockchain and Digital Assets at undergraduate and graduate levels.

**Renáta Pakšiová**, PhD, is a full professor at the Department of Accounting and Auditing at the Faculty of Economic Informatics, University of Economics in Bratislava, and Newton University in Prague. She is a co-guarantor of study programmes in accounting at all three levels of higher education within the field of economics and management at the University of Economics in Bratislava. Her scientific and research activities are primarily focused on the theory of accounting, ESG (Environmental, Social, and Governance), non-financial information, and sustainability, which are currently key topics in accounting and corporate reporting. She specialises in the reporting of relevant financial and non-financial information, with an emphasis on corporate social responsibility (CSR) and sustainability. As part of her research, she has participated in several international projects, including *"CSR – Reporting in Central and Eastern Europe"* (2014–2017) and *"Exploring the Efficacy of the EU Law concerning Reports on Payments to Governments in country-specific contexts across the EU"* (2018–2020). These projects examined the implementation and effectiveness of non-financial reporting and its impact on companies across various European countries. A significant part of her research also includes participation in domestic grant projects, focusing on the analysis and application of international standards and legislative changes in accounting. In the project *"Preservation and Growth of the Asset Base as a Relevant Tool for Sustainable Business Development"* (2016–2018), she addressed sustainability issues and their integration into corporate accounting. She has an extensive publication record that includes monographs, university textbooks, and scientific articles published in both national and international journals. Among her key publications is her co-authorship of the university textbook *"Theory of Accounting in the Context of Global Development"* (2012). She has also published several articles in peer-reviewed journals and presented papers at international scientific conferences. Her work is widely cited in academic and professional fields.

**Ranjani Shree R S**, a student of III year Information Technology of KGiSL Institute of Technology. Her current research includes data analytics and IoT

**Debasish Roy** is currently a PhD Research Scholar in Marketing Management at Sikkim University, Gangtok, India with backgrounds in Postgraduate Diploma in Transportation and Logistics Management from Indian Institute of Social Welfare and Business Management (IISWBM) - India's one of the premier Business Schools, and Bachelor of Science (Honors) in Economics from University of Calcutta. His works in the fields of Business and Economics had been published in different international journals and reference books.

**Deepa Sharma** has done Ph.D., MBA in Human Resource Management, currently working as Assistant Professor at MMIM, Maharishi Markandeshwar (Deemed to be University), NAAC Accredited Grade 'A++' University, Mullana, Ambala (Haryana). She has more than 9 years of experience in academics. She has written 61+ research papers for various Scopus and UGC listed referred National & International Journals and 13 papers appear on SCOPUS Preview.

**Jaroslav Škrabal** is an academic researcher at Moravian Business College Olomouc. His specialization lies in economics and management, with a particular focus on the utilization of brownfields in business and regional development. Throughout his academic career, he has published numerous scholarly articles in prestigious journals and conference proceedings. He has extensive experience in analyzing the economic impacts of brownfields and their regeneration in both Czech and European contexts. His research also covers investment strategies, innovation, and strategic business management. In addition to his academic work, he actively engages in applied research and collaborates with institutions involved in regional development. Currently, he is closely working with BSc. Martin Vybíral on projects related to the development of the business environment and the sustainable use of brownfields. His work bridges theoretical insights with practical applications in economic growth and regional policy. He has significant experience in leading research projects and contributes to the development of new approaches in economic analysis and planning.

**Muhammad Usman Tariq** has more than 16+ year's experience in industry and academia. He has authored more than 200+ research articles, 110+ case studies, 120+ book chapters and several books other than 4 patents. He is founder and CEO of The Case HQ, a unique repository for courses, narrative and video case studies. He has been working as a consultant and trainer for industries representing six sigma, quality, health and safety, environmental systems, project management, and information security standards. His work has encompassed sectors in aviation, manufacturing, food, hospitality, education, finance, research, software and transportation. He has diverse and significant experience working with accreditation agencies of ABET, ACBSP, AACSB, WASC, CAA, EFQM and NCEAC. Additionally, Dr. Tariq has operational experience in incubators, research labs, government research projects, private sector startups, program creation and management at various industrial and academic levels. He is Certified Higher Education Teacher from Harvard University, USA, Certified Online Educator from HMBSU, Certified Six Sigma Master Black Belt and has been awarded PFHEA, SFSEDA, SMIEEE, and CMBE.

**Thea van der Westhuizen** is an award-winning academic leader, renowned for driving entrepreneurship in academia through innovative teaching and transformative research. She founded SHAPE, earning international recognition at The Innovative Youth Incubator Awards. As the former International Director of Paddle for the Planet, she advocates for global environmental sustainability and enabling youth. With over two decades of international experience in corporate and academic sectors, her impactful collaborations span across high-impact leaders, municipality managers, CEOs of multinational companies and helping youth entrepreneurs. Her remarkable career showcases her entrepreneurial spirit and commitment to excellence. She currently serves as an academic leader at the University of KwaZulu-Natal, School of Management, Information Technology, and Governance.

**Mihaela Vancea** (mihaela.vancea@ub.edu) is a Lecturer Professor in the Department of Research Methods and Diagnostic in Education at the Faculty of Education, Universitat de Barcelona (Spain). She holds bachelor's degrees in Mathematics and Sociology, and master's degrees in Sociology and Sociology of Law. She earned her Ph.D. in Political and Social Sciences from Pompeu Fabra University in 2009. Dr. Vancea has worked at various esteemed institutions, including the University of Lund, Universitat Pompeu Fabra and Universidad de la Frontera. Her research focuses on youth studies, interculturalism, and sustainability. She has published extensively in highly indexed journals.

**Omar Vargas-González** Professor, research assistant and former Head of Computer Systems Department at Tecnológico Nacional de México Campus Ciudad Guzmán, professor at Telematic Engineering at Centro Universitario del Sur Universidad de Guadalajara with a master degree in Computer Systems. Has been trained in Innovation and Multidisciplinary Entrepreneurship at Arizona State University (2018) and a Generation of Ecosystems of Innovation, Entrepreneurship and Sustainability for Jalisco course by Harvard University T.H. Chan School of Health. At present conduct research on diverse fields such as Entrepreneurship, Economy, Statistics, Mathematics and Information and Computer Sciences. Has collaborated in the publication of many scientific articles and conducted diverse Innovation and Technological Development projects.

**Rahul R. Verma** is an accomplished academician and researcher in the field of Commerce, with extensive experience spanning over 15 years at the University of Delhi, India. Holding a Ph.D. in Commerce, Dr. Verma has cultivated expertise in areas including Marketing, International Business, and Finance. A prolific contributor to academia, he has participated in over 150 research engagements - encompassing papers, chapters, and presentations at both national and international levels. He has also edited more than 30 books with esteemed publishers such as IGI Global and Apple Academic Press. In addition, Dr. Verma actively contributes to the academic community as a member of editorial boards for several peer - reviewed journals.

**Martin Vybíral** is a first-year student of the master's degree program at Moravian Business College Olomouc, specializing in Economics and Management. His research and publication activities focus on the regeneration of brownfields in the Czech Republic, in collaboration with MSc., Dr. Jaroslav Škrabal. Together, they have co-authored the scholarly article "Regeneration of Brownfields for Business Purposes in the Context of Regional Development," which analyzes the potential for revitalizing unused industrial sites to support the local economy. In his master's thesis, he aims to examine the factors influencing the successful revitalization of brownfields and their impact on regional and national development. He actively participates in research projects and contributes to the advancement of both theoretical and practical approaches in the field of economic planning.

# Index

# H



# I



# K



# L



# M



# N



# O



# R



# S

## T



## V



## W

www.ingramcontent.com/pod-product-compliance
Lightning Source LLC
LaVergne TN
LVHW080617300926
849162LV00005B/1191